A Companion to World History

WILEY-BLACKWELL COMPANIONS TO HISTORY

This series provides sophisticated and authoritative overviews of the scholarship that has shaped our current understanding of the past. Defined by theme, period and/or region, each volume comprises between twenty-five and forty concise essays written by individual scholars within their area of specialization. The aim of each contribution is to synthesize the current state of scholarship from a variety of historical perspectives and to provide a statement on where the field is heading. The essays are written in a clear, provocative, and lively manner, designed for an international audience of scholars, students, and general readers.

For further information on these and other titles in the series please visit our website at

www.wiley.com

A COMPANION TO WORLD HISTORY

Edited by

Douglas Northrop

WILEY-BLACKWELL

A John Wiley & Sons, Ltd., Publication

This edition first published 2012
© 2012 Blackwell Publishing Ltd

Blackwell Publishing was acquired by John Wiley & Sons in February 2007. Blackwell's publishing program has been merged with Wiley's global Scientific, Technical, and Medical business to form Wiley-Blackwell.

Registered Office
John Wiley & Sons, Ltd, The Atrium, Southern Gate, Chichester, West Sussex, PO19 8SQ, UK

Editorial Offices
350 Main Street, Malden, MA 02148-5020, USA
9600 Garsington Road, Oxford, OX4 2DQ, UK
The Atrium, Southern Gate, Chichester, West Sussex, PO19 8SQ, UK

For details of our global editorial offices, for customer services, and for information about how to apply for permission to reuse the copyright material in this book please see our website at www.wiley.com/wiley-blackwell.

The right of Douglas Northrop to be identified as the author of the editorial material in this work has been asserted in accordance with the UK Copyright, Designs and Patents Act 1988.

Library of Congress Cataloging-in-Publication Data

A companion to world history / edited by Douglas Northrop.
    p.   cm
  Includes bibliographical references and index.
  ISBN 978-1-4443-3418-0 (hardback)
1. History–Methodology.   2. History–Study and teaching.   3. Historiography.
  I. Northrop, Douglas Taylor.
  D13.C628 2012
  907.2–dc23

                                                        2012009799

A catalogue record for this book is available from the British Library.

Cover image: Painting of the Battle of Adwa, 2 March 1896, by unknown Ethiopian artist, c. 1940–1949. Courtesy of the Trustees of the British Museum, London.

Cover design by Richard Boxall Design Associates

Set in 10/12pt Galliard by SPi Publisher Services, Pondicherry, India
Printed in Malaysia by Ho Printing (M) Sdn Bhd

1   2012

For Sawyer and Jeremy, every day a new world

Contents

Maps, Figures, and Tables

Maps

Figures

Table

Notes on Contributors

Michael Adas is the Abraham E. Voorhees Professor and Board of Governors' Chair at Rutgers University. His teaching and research have centered on the comparative study of the impact of Western science and technology on European and American colonialism in Asia and Africa. His recent books include *Machines as the Measure of Men: Science, Technology, and Ideologies of Western Dominance* and *Dominance by Design: Technological Imperatives and America's Civilizing Mission*. Adas has also co-authored six editions of *World Civilizations: The Global Experience*. He is currently working on a comparison of the combat experience in World War I and Vietnam.

Robert B. Bain is Associate Professor of Education and History, and chair of the secondary teacher education program, at the University of Michigan. Bain earned his PhD in American social history at Case Western Reserve University. After working for years as a high-school social-studies teacher, he joined the faculty at Michigan, where his research and clinical work focuses on the translation of historical "habits of mind" into K-12 classrooms: how teachers and students can acquire the methods, approaches, and assumptions of disciplinary historians in teaching and learning. A former World History Association council member, most recently he is a co-designer and researcher in the Big History Project.

Charles Bright is Arthur J. Thurnau Professor and Professor of History at the University of Michigan, Residential College. In addition to his collaborative work with Michael Geyer over two decades on global history, he has worked on prison history, publishing *The Powers That Punish: Prisons and Politics in the Era of the "Big House,"* 1920–1955, and on the history of Detroit, doing oral histories and creative projects with theater groups in the city. The current essay is part of a book project (with Geyer), *The Global Condition in the Long-Twentieth Century*.

Antoinette Burton is Professor of History at the University of Illinois, Urbana-Champaign, where she is also Bastian Professor of Global and Transnational Studies. A historian of Victorian Britain, modern empire, Indian women, feminism and postcoloniality, she is the author most recently of *A Primer for Teaching World History: Ten Design Principles* (2012).

Christopher Chase-Dunn is a Distinguished Professor of Sociology and Director of the Institute for Research on World-Systems at the University of California, Riverside. He is the author of *Rise and Demise: Comparing World-Systems* (with Thomas D. Hall), *The Wintu and Their Neighbors* (with Kelly Mann), and *The Spiral of Capitalism and Socialism* (with Terry Boswell). He is founder and former editor of the *Journal of World-Systems Research*. Chase-Dunn is currently doing research on global party formation and anti-systemic social movements. He also studies the rise and fall of settlements and polities since the Stone Age and global state formation.

Luke Clossey is Associate Professor in the Department of History of Simon Fraser University. His dissertation research won prizes from the World History Association and the Canadian Historical Association, and was published as *Salvation and Globalization in the Early Jesuit Missions* (2008). Now that he has finished fighting over punctuation with the co-authors of the essay included here, he can return to fieldwork preparatory to writing a history of the early modern global cult of Yeshua ben Miriam, a first-century Jewish messiah.

Eduardo Devés-Valdés (PhD, University of Leuven (Lovain), and a second PhD in Latin American Studies from the University of Paris III), a specialist in Latin American thought and thought in peripheral regions, is Professor of American Studies and coordinator of the Postdoctoral Studies Program at the University of Santiago, Chile. He has published more than 150 works, including *El pensamiento africano sud-sahariano en sus conexiones y paralelos con el latinoamericano y el asiático*, and has taught and researched at various locations across Latin America, Asia, Africa, Europe, and the United States.

Felipe Fernández-Armesto teaches at the University of Notre Dame. His books on global history include *The World* (2010), *1492* (2010), *Pathfinders* (2007), *Civilizations* (2000), and *Millennium* (1999).

Anne Gerritsen (PhD, Harvard) is Associate Professor of Chinese History at the University of Warwick. She works on topics that are local in scope, such as the history of the Jiangxi prefecture of Ji'an and ceramics manufacture in the Jiangxi town of Jingdezhen, as well as topics that are global, such as the worldwide trade in porcelain, and global perceptions and knowledge of Chinese material culture and technology. She is currently the director of the Global History and Culture Centre, based in the Department of History at the University of Warwick.

Trevor Getz is a Professor of African History at San Francisco State University. He is the author or co-author of seven books, the latest of which is the graphic history *Abina and the Important Men*. He is currently working on a digital world history textbook with Jonathan Brooke and is editing the Oxford University Press series African World Histories.

Michael Geyer is Samuel N. Harper Professor of German and European History at the University of Chicago and faculty director of the Human Rights Program. His main academic interests are war and violence, the history and theory of Human Rights, and global history in the nineteenth and twentieth centuries. Among his recent publications is *Beyond Totalitarianism: Stalinism and Nazism Compared*, edited with Sheila Fitzpatrick (2009). The current essay is part of a book project (with Charles Bright), *The Global Condition in the Long-Twentieth Century*.

Thomas D. Hall is Professor Emeritus in the Department of Sociology and Anthropology, DePauw University, Greencastle, Indiana. He holds an MA in Anthropology, University of Michigan, and a PhD in Sociology, University of Washington. His interests include indigenous peoples, ethnicity, and comparative frontiers. Recent publications include "World-systems analysis and archaeology: Continuing the dialogue," with P. Nick Kardulias and Christopher Chase-Dunn, *Journal of Archaeological Research* 19 (3) (2011): 233–279; "Resilience and community in the age of world-system collapse," with Glen D. Kuecker, *Nature and Culture* 6 (1) (2011): 18–40; *Indigenous Peoples and Globalization: Resistance and Revitalization*, with James V. Fenelon (2009).

Huri Islamoğlu is Professor of Economic History, Boğazici University, Istanbul; and since 2008, Visiting Professor of History, University of California, Berkeley. Her publications include (with Peter Perdue) *Shared Histories of Modernity in China, India and the Ottoman Empire* (2009); *Constituting Modernity: Private Property in the East and West* (2004); *Ottoman Empire and the World Economy* (1987); and *State and Peasant in the Ottoman Empire* (1994). She has written and lectured in the fields of comparative economic history and political economy, legal history, agricultural history and agriculture and current globalization trends, and global governance.

Paul A. Kramer is an Associate Professor of History at Vanderbilt University, with research and teaching interests in US imperial, transnational and global histories since the mid-nineteenth century. He is the author of *The Blood of Government: Race, Empire, the United States and the Philippines* (2006). He co-edits the Cornell University Press series The United States in the World, and is currently at work on a book-length project on the nexus between empire and US immigration policy across the twentieth century.

Scott C. Levi (PhD, University of Wisconsin-Madison, 2000) is Associate Professor of Central Asian history at Ohio State University. In addition to his articles and book chapters, Levi has authored *The Indian Diaspora in Central Asia and its Trade, 1550–1900* (2002), edited *India and Central Asia: Commerce and Culture, 1500–1800* (2007), and co-edited (with Ron Sela) *Islamic Central Asia: An Anthology of Sources* (2010).

Jie-Hyun Lim is Professor of Comparative History and the director of the Research Institute of Comparative History and Culture at Hanyang University in Seoul. He has held visiting appointments in Krakow, Cardiff, Kyoto, Berlin and Cambridge, Mass. He has written numerous books and articles on the comparative histories of nationalist movements, colonialism, issues of memory, and the sociocultural history of Marxism in East Asia and Eastern Europe. He now edits a Palgrave series on mass dictatorship in the twentieth century. His most recent project is a transnational history of "victimhood nationalism," covering post–World War II Korea, Japan, Poland, Israel, and Germany.

Xinru Liu (PhD, University of Pennsylvania) teaches world history and the history of South Asia and Central Asia at the College of New Jersey in Ewing and is associated with the Institute of History and the Institute of World History, Chinese Academy of Sciences. Among her many publications are *Ancient India and Ancient China* (1988); *Silk and Religion: An Exploration of Material Life and the Thought of People in AD 600–1200* (1996); *Connections across Eurasia: Transportation, Communications, and Cultural Exchange on the Silk Roads*, with Lynda Norene Shaffer (2007); and *The Silk Road in World History* (2010).

Adam McKeown is Associate Professor of History at Columbia University, where he offers courses on the histories of globalization, world migration and drugs, and is the co-coordinator of the PhD track in International and Global History. He wrote *Melancholy Order: Asian Migration and the Globalization of Borders* (2008), and *Chinese Migrant Networks and Cultural Change: Peru, Chicago, Hawaii, 1900–1936* (2001). He is now working on the history of globalization since 1760.

Stephen Morillo, DPhil Oxford, Professor of History and Chair of Division III (Social Sciences) at Wabash College, specializes in premodern comparative world and military history. He is President of De Re Militari, the Society for Medieval Military History. He has written *Structures and Systems: Conceptual Frameworks of World History*, a forthcoming world history textbook, and is working on a cultural history of warrior elites in world history. His numerous other books, articles, and chapters include *What Is Military History?* and *War in World History: Society, Technology and War from Ancient Times to the Present*, a military world history textbook.

Katja Naumann is a researcher at the Center for the History and Culture of East Central Europe at the University of Leipzig, where she coordinates a handbook on the transnational history of the region. She lectures at the Global and European Studies Institute in Leipzig and coordinates the headquarters of the European Network in Universal and Global History. Further, she works on the editorial boards of the geschichte.transnational forum and *Comparativ: A Journal for Global History and Comparative Studies*. In her dissertation she analyzed the development of world history teaching in the United States (1918–1968).

Douglas Northrop is Associate Professor of History and Near Eastern Studies at the University of Michigan, where he teaches modern Central Asian studies and helped create a program in world and global history. His books include *Veiled Empire: Gender and Power in Stalinist Central Asia* and *An Imperial World: Empires and Colonies Since 1750* (forthcoming). His current research brings together environmental, colonial, cultural, and urban history in telling the story of Central Asia through natural disaster – specifically, a series of major earthquakes that struck the region during the last two centuries.

Martin S. Pernick, Professor of History at the University of Michigan, received a PhD in history from Columbia University, and has taught at the Harvard School of Public Health, and the Pennsylvania State University Hershey Medical Center. He authored *A Calculus of Suffering* (1985), on professional and cultural attitudes towards pain treatment in nineteenth-century America, and *The Black Stork* (1996), on eugenics and euthanasia in American medicine and film; plus numerous articles on epidemics, defining death, disability, eugenics, public health films, medical professionalism, informed consent, and the relation between history and bioethics, in US and comparative history.

Kenneth Pomeranz is University Professor of History at the University of Chicago. He previously taught at the University of California, Irvine, and was Founding Director of the University of California's Multi-Campus Research Program in World History. His publications include *The Great Divergence: China, Europe, and the Making of the Modern World Economy* and *The Making of a Hinterland: State, Society and Economy in Inland North China, 1853–1937*. He is a Fellow of the American Academy of Arts and Sciences, and has received fellowships from the Guggenheim Foundation, American Philosophical Society, ACLS, Institute for Advanced Studies, and NEH, among others.

Sebastian R. Prange is Assistant Professor of History at the University of British Columbia. His research centers on the organization of Muslim trade networks in the medieval and early modern Indian Ocean, with a regional focus on South India.

Dominic Sachsenmaier taught transcultural and Chinese history at Duke University before his recent move to become a Professor of Modern Asian History at Jacobs University in Germany. His main current research interests are Chinese and Western approaches to global history as well as the impact of World War I on political and intellectual cultures in China and other parts of the world. He has also published in fields such as seventeenth-century Sino-Western cultural relations, overseas Chinese communities in Southeast Asia, and multiple modernities. His most recent book is *Global Perspectives on Global History: Theories and Approaches in a Connected World* (2011).

Damon Ieremia Salesa is Associate Professor of Pacific Studies at the Centre of Pacific Studies at the University of Auckland, New Zealand. He is the author of *Racial Crossings: Race, Intermarriage and the Victorian British Empire* (2011), one of the contributing authors to *The New Oxford History of New Zealand* (2009), editor (with Kolokesa Māhina and Sean Mallon) of *Tangata o le Moana Nui: The Peoples of the Pacific and New Zealand* (2012), and author of many other articles on race, Pacific, indigenous and imperial history. He is currently completing a book project, *Empire Trouble and Troublesome Half-Castes: Samoans and the Greatest Powers in the World*.

Daniel A. Segal is the Director of the Munroe Center of Social Inquiry and Jean M. Pitzer Professor of Anthropology and History at Pitzer College. He is a past Fellow of the Center for Advanced Study in the Behavioral Sciences and a recipient of the American Historical Association's William Gilbert Award. He has published on race and nationalism in Trinidad, incest in Jane Austen, and on the history of undergraduate history textbooks. He contributes to the Slow Blog movement at http://daniel-segal.blogspot.com/.

Ian Simmons ended his book-writing days with a triad of books on environmental history, each written at a specific spatial scale but all covering the last 10,000 years. The last, *Global Environmental History* (2008), tried to encompass both the scientific outlook in which he was schooled and the broader contributions of the social sciences and humanities. He lives in Durham, UK, and is preparing a website on medieval environmental change in east Lincolnshire, a little-known area to which he was a wartime evacuee. His happy memories also include being a post-doc at Berkeley in the 1960s.

David Simo is Professor of German Literature, Comparative Literature, and Cultural Studies at the University of Yaoundé 1 in Cameroon, and a visiting professor at various German, French, and American universities. Born in Baham, Cameroon, in 1951, he studied German language and literature, comparative literature, and political science in Abidjan, Saarbrücken and Metz, earning a PhD in comparative literature in Metz (France), 1979, and a postdoctoral qualification (*Habilitation*) in Hanover, 1991, on intercultural experiences. He has published articles on German and African literature, postcolonial theory and criticism, and cultural studies. He received the Humboldt Foundation's Reimar Lüst Prize, and serves as Director of the Center for German African Scientific Research Cooperation in Yaoundé.

Mrinalini Sinha is the Alice Freeman Palmer Professor of History at the University of Michigan, Ann Arbor. She is the author of *Colonial Masculinity: The "Manly Englishman"* *and the "Effeminate Bengali" in the Late Nineteenth Century* (1995) and of *Specters of Mother India: The Global Restructuring of an Empire* (2006). She is currently working on the implications of the 1929 nationalist resolution for the complete political independence of India from the British Empire.

Fred Spier is Senior Lecturer in Big History at the University of Amsterdam. Spier has a MSc in biochemistry and both an MA and a PhD in cultural anthropology and social history. He executed a 10-year research project on religion, politics and ecology in Andean Peru. In his book *Big History and the Future of Humanity* (2010), Spier presents an explanatory model for all of history. Translations exist or are forthcoming in Spanish, Chinese and Arabic. Spier currently serves as the first Vice President of the International Big History Association (IBHA).

Heather Streets-Salter received her PhD at Duke University in 1998. She is Associate Professor at Northeastern University, where she directs the graduate program in World History. Previously she directed the graduate program in World History at Washington State University from 2003 to 2011. Recent works include *Martial Races: The Military, Martial Races, and Masculinity in British Imperial Culture, 1857–1914* (2004), *Traditions and Encounters: A Brief Global History* (2006) with Jerry Bentley and Herb Ziegler, and *Modern Imperialism and Colonialism: A Global Perspective* (2010) with Trevor Getz. Her current monograph is called *Empire Crossings: Connections across Imperial Borders in Southeast Asia*.

Karin Vélez is Assistant Professor of History at Macalester College. A doctoral graduate of Princeton University, she has also worked at Northeastern University, Duke University as a Thompson Writing Program Fellow (2008), and Williams College as a Gaius Charles Bolin Fellow (2005). She has recently published on the transatlantic gifts of the Huron of Lorette (*French Colonial History Journal* 12 (2011)) and on early modern missions to the Americas (in Mary Laven et al., eds, *Ashgate Research Companion to the Counter-Reformation* (2012)). She is currently finalizing a book manuscript, "Catholic landings in the early modern world: Jesuits, converts and the collective miracle of Loreto."

Kerry Ward is Associate Professor of World History and Director of African Studies at Rice University. She is the author of *Networks of Empire: Forced Migration in the Dutch East India Company* (2009). Ward has published in the fields of slavery and forced migration, Indian Ocean history, South African and Indonesian colonial history, and historical memory and public history. She is currently Secretary of the World History Association.

Barbara Weinstein is the Silver Professor of History at New York University. Her research has focused primarily on postcolonial Brazil, and includes two monographs, *The Amazon Rubber Boom, 1850–1920* (1983) and *For Social Peace in Brazil: Industrialists and the Remaking of the Working Class in São Paulo, 1920–1964* (1996). She is co-editor of *The Making of the Middle Class: Toward a Transnational History* (2012), and is currently completing *The Color of Modernity*, a study of race, regional inequalities, and national identities in Brazil.

Leslie Witz is a Professor in the Department of History at the University of the Western Cape, in Cape Town, South Africa. His major research centers around how different histories are created and represented in the public domain through memorials, museums, festivals, and tourism. His book *Apartheid's Festival: Contesting South Africa's National*

Pasts was published in 2003. He has also written two books for popular audiences: *Write Your Own History* (1988) and *How to Write Essays* (1990). Witz is the chair of the board of Lwandle Migrant Labour Museum.

Norman Yoffee's research oscillates between the fields of Assyriology (Mesopotamian studies) and Anthropology. These fields come together in *Myths of the Archaic State: Evolution of the Earliest Cities, States, and Civilizations* (2005). After retiring from the Departments of Near Eastern Studies and Anthropology at the University of Michigan, he is now Adjunct Professor in the Departments of Anthropology, University of Nevada, Las Vegas, and University of New Mexico, and is Senior Fellow, Institute for the Study of the Ancient World, New York University. His home page is sitemaker.umich.edu/ nyoffee.

Weiwei Zhang is Associate Professor of History at Nankai University, China. He has taught at Nankai since 1975, offering courses in modern global history and world-systems study and working to develop a noncentric and holistic approach which emphasizes global disequilibrium and social physics. A member of the executive board of the Network of Global and World History Organizations (NOGWHISTO), and of the board of directors of the Asian Association of World Historians, Zhang earned his PhD in 1998 at Nankai, served as visiting scholar at the Institute of Historical Research, University of London (1987–1988, 1999–2000), at Seoul National University, Korea (1997), and the University of Louisville (2002), and received a Teaching Model Award of Higher Education, Tianjin (1996).

Editor's Acknowledgments

No book is an island – and no author stands alone. Every writer's voice appears, and takes on full meaning, in conversation with others: with those who wrote earlier, and those located around the globe. This idea should be particularly obvious to anyone interested in world history, given the field's focus on core themes like interaction, encounter, and mutual influence. It should be just as plain in a large-scale collective book like this one – with its almost three dozen chapters, each of which sets out to map a terrain of scholarship produced by scores of authors. The scale of such an undertaking produces obvious logistical challenges (and the requisite jokes about cat-herding), but the effort also shows at every step the interlocking, iterative character of historical work. As this book now heads out to its own world of readers, I am humbled and grateful for the unstinting contributions of the many who brought it into existence.

This list starts with Tessa Harvey, publisher for History at Wiley-Blackwell, who first proposed the idea of such a book, and framed it as part of the *Companions* series. Tessa encouraged me to take the plunge as editor, helped sharpen my initial ideas as they grew into the volume's overall architecture, and brainstormed details and assisted with the recruitment of an extraordinary slate of authors – who now fill its pages. Gillian Kane likewise helped as the volume took shape, and provided steady encouragement as the months passed. Later in the production process I had the good fortune to work with Isobel Bainton and Sue Leigh, the very best of project editors and managers, who kept track of myriad balls in the air and without whom the book could never have appeared, and with Ann Bone, Glynis Baguley, and Zeb Korycinska, the most vigilant (and patient) of copyeditors, proofreaders, and indexers.

In plotting the table of contents I consulted with, and twisted the arms of, dozens of colleagues. Many, happily, agreed to participate by writing a chapter. Some went above and beyond in thinking about the volume as a whole, and helped me make connections among its various components – here I am particularly grateful to Michael Adas. Among those whose names do not appear in the chapter listing, but who nevertheless played an important role in shaping my ideas about what this book could and should do, I thank Kären Wigen and Martin Lewis.

The essays that follow engage questions of scholarship alongside pedagogy, and confront issues of institution as much as intellect. These practicalities that enable (and channel) intellectual work can be invisible to readers and students, yet are nonetheless critical. Given world history's oft-marginal status in the disciplinary arenas of History, I am astonishingly fortunate to have worked at three institutions that not only allowed, but even encouraged, such exploration. I first taught world history at Pitzer College, where Daniel Segal brought me into his fascinating pedagogical projects and showed me what was at stake in the effort; later I helped design world-oriented graduate and undergraduate programs at the University of Georgia, and then, since 2004, at the University of Michigan. My thinking has been shaped by hundreds of students along the way, first-year undergraduates through PhDs in global history, and by colleagues at every step.

I am particularly mindful of the remarkable support provided by the University of Michigan, an unusually encouraging place for serious efforts to build world/global history. Gratitude is due especially to Geoff Eley, the extraordinary department chair of History, and Kathleen Canning, the dedicated former director of the Eisenberg Institute for Historical Studies (EIHS). In spring 2009 more than two dozen Michigan faculty and PhD students signed up for an EIHS boot camp, which I co-taught with Robert Bain, on "Thinking and Teaching in Global Dimensions." Since then curricula, faculty hires, visiting speakers, and student admissions have all changed – interweaving "the global" (in all its flavors and meanings) throughout institutional life. Unlike most academics, with at most a handful of people working on the margins of a department, I am now privileged to have no fewer than 31 (!!) History faculty self-declared as members of a "globalist" faculty group. (In Michigan's language of acronyms, this status formally means belonging to the "GWITECC" faculty caucus – dedicated to "global, world, international, trans-regional, edges, connective, and comparative history.") A few current members are represented in the pages that follow (Bain, Bright, Pernick, Sinha); others who contribute to the vibrant presence of world history at Michigan, and who have shaped my thinking about it, include Howard Brick, Gabrielle Hecht, Nancy Hunt, Valerie Kivelson, Ian Moyer, Hitomi Tonomura, and Penny Von Eschen.

By authorial convention I save for last the most fundamental and heartfelt of debts. My family has heard much about the challenges of this book, and has seen firsthand the logistical complications of shepherding 33 chapters to completion. My wife, Michelle McClellan, dealt as much as I did with the sharp end of those challenges, and she deserves as much credit for finding their solutions. My sons, Jeremy and Sawyer, saw me working on this book for a long time – but as perhaps the only preadolescents in Michigan simultaneously learning Uyghur alphabets, studying aeronautical engineering, and reading voraciously about world politics, they also served as inspiration for its completion. To me they are emblematic of what it means to let minds range freely, all around the globe, crossing borders wherever and whenever one's interests may go.

The Challenge of World History

Douglas Northrop

What do historians see – and what do they miss? It depends, of course, on how any particular historian chooses to look. She or he must first decide on a time and place to investigate, identify sources to serve as evidence, and pose questions to ask about them. Each choice is shaped by a scholar's training – the way they learned the craft of "history." Usually this happens at an academic institution, through formal education in one or more clearly defined "fields": French history, African history, early modern history, the history of science, and so on. Experienced scholars convey their expertise to students, carefully preparing the next generation of historians, honing linguistic skills and imparting deep knowledge of particular archives, libraries, and publications. New historians thus emerge well versed in their area's theoretical, methodological, and historiographical debates – at least as these are understood at their academic institution, located in its own geographic and cultural context, and at a certain point in time. But what happens if these institutional and intellectual pathways are disrupted – if historical questions are asked in new ways, stretching across the boundaries of the existing fields? Can time and space be stretched, as in Map I.1, and historians take a new, broader, perspective?

This is precisely what practitioners of world and global history aim to do. They represent a young "field," at least by the standards of professional history, one that by most measures has only come into its own over the past quarter-century. World history is still in some ways embattled, harshly criticized by self-styled disciplinary gatekeepers, including some specialists in nationally defined fields – Japanese history, Russian history, American history, etc. World history may represent a practical threat (as a new claimant to limited institutional resources) but is more likely to be attacked in intellectual terms, as a marginal, even doomed approach, too general, impossibly broad, obviously too superficial to permit serious scholarship. Yet world history – as a professional arena – is populated by a diverse and rapidly growing group of scholars and teachers who have worked hard to show the contrary. They have developed all the trappings and infrastructure of a legitimate institutional domain: professional organizations (especially the World History Association, thewha.org), journals (notably the Anglophone *Journal*

A Companion to World History, First Edition. Edited by Douglas Northrop.
© 2012 Blackwell Publishing Ltd. Published 2012 by Blackwell Publishing Ltd.

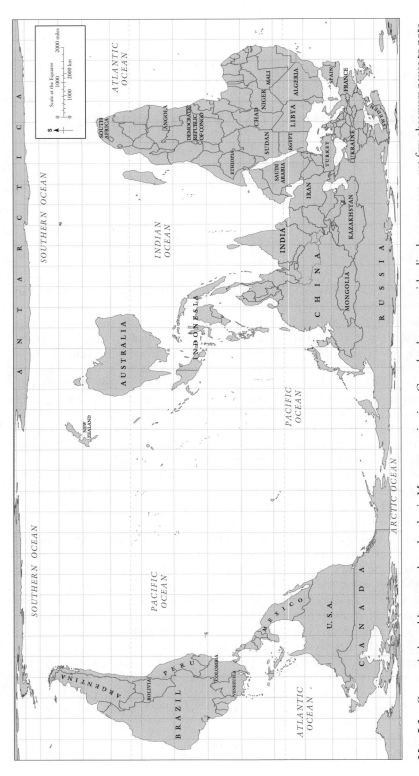

Map I.1 On a typical world map, such as the classic Mercator projection, Greenland appears misleadingly enormous – yet few observers pause to note the inaccuracies. Mapmakers rarely question other basic assumptions, such as drawing north at the top. But if the Earth resembles a ball spinning through space, are "up" and "down" so self-evident? Better maps can provide fresh perspective, and make viewers aware of unspoken assumptions. The Hobo-Dyer projection shows accurately the relative size of different land areas, while preserving north/south and east/west lines of bearing. It also gives the Southern Hemisphere visual prominence, imagining a globe that has been recentered Down Under.

Source: Hobo-Dyer Equal Area Projection. © 2007, ODTmaps. Adapted with permission from www.ODTmaps.com.

of World History and *Journal of Global History*), book prizes, teaching prizes, PhD programs, undergraduate courses, elementary- and secondary-school curricula, textbooks at all levels, handbooks for teachers, scholarly monographs, popular publications, Advanced Placement tests, museum exhibits, television shows – the list goes on.[1] World historians thus stand on much stronger ground now to argue with skeptics than they did a generation ago. The field is sufficiently rooted and broad-based to have moved beyond self-justification; it includes a panoply of internal conversations and arguments about what world-historical work can and should do. World historians take deeply divergent approaches, sometimes evincing little consensus about the field's wider parameters or its common standards. World history is a professional arena visibly in flux, still taking shape, open for dispute. This volume sketches the resulting arguments, and traces the field's principal trajectories. But world historians as a group share the impulse to see the human past differently – more expansively – by reaching beyond the boxes in which history is conventionally taught.

William McNeill, perhaps the best-known world historian of the last century, once memorably defended the field through metaphor. What might a world historian see, he asked, that a national, regional, or period-specific historian would miss? "A tree is a tree," he pointed out. It is also a collection of millions of cells, or trillions of atoms; at the same time, it is also a vanishingly tiny piece of the forest ecosystems that stretch far beyond its trunk. Biologists may analyze how the tree's cells work, parse the chemical processing of chlorophyll, and zoom down to the molecular level of DNA – all valuable endeavors – but that does not make it inaccurate to talk about "the tree." No one needs to understand every individual cell to know what a tree is. Ecologists, likewise, need not start at the atomic level – nor the level of an individual tree – to discuss the "forest": to analyze its seasonal variations, its diseases, or its interactions with other species (such as humans). Put simply, different entities, issues, and patterns emerge at each level of perspective (atom-cell-tree-forest). None are *right* or *wrong* in an absolute sense, merely more or less appropriate to the questions being asked. Every phenomenon is best seen at its own scale; each is also inescapably comprised of smaller units, while interlocking with others to shape larger levels. "Precision and truthfulness," McNeill concluded, "do not necessarily increase as the scale becomes smaller."[2]

McNeill expanded the point – and the concomitant value of adopting a bird's-eye perspective – by describing a walk he had taken long before, when he was a graduate student in New York City. One day in Morningside Park he looked out and saw a major highway, the Hudson Parkway, stretched out beneath him. From his elevated point of view, he suddenly realized, "the stop-and-go traffic on the Parkway constituted a longitudinal wave, with nodes and anti-nodes spaced at regular intervals, moving along the Parkway at a pace considerably faster than any single vehicle could make its way along the crowded roadway." Each individual car was part of this wave, although it far exceeded any one vehicle in both size and speed. The wave, McNeill declared, was "most certainly there – clear and unambiguous," notwithstanding the fact that few if any drivers on the road – in fact, probably no one but McNeill himself, watching from the overlook – could be aware of its existence. Recognizing it required three things: a perceptive observer (McNeill), a proper spot from which to look (Morningside Park), and a concept through which to "see" and understand what was happening (the idea of a longitudinal wave).

This *Companion to World History* provides readers with dozens of such spots from which to look, and key concepts with which to make sense of what they see. World history's defenders often use such conceits, frequently invoking ideas of a "lens" or viewpoint to make the case for adopting a world/global-level perspective. Metaphors of visibility and perspective abound, and contributors to this book are no exception – they use many different lenses (zoom, wide-angle, moving back and forth, and so on). The volume aims to orient readers to world history by showing the globe from as many of these points of view as possible. It sketches the development of world history as a professional field, especially over the past generation of scholarship; identifies principal areas of continuing contention, disagreement and divergence; and suggests fruitful directions for further discussion and research. It also considers issues of scholarship (research) and pedagogy (teaching) – each of which yields fresh insights but also poses particular challenges when approached at transnational, interregional, or world/global scales.

"World history," or various approaches grouped under that label, has exploded recently into prominence in the United States – in university, college, and high-school, middle-school, and elementary-school (K-12) classrooms – and to varying degrees in other countries as well, but it is nevertheless still criticized as disjointed in practice and sometimes dismissed by academic historians as mere "popular" history, lacking scholarly respectability and disciplinary solidity. Such critiques are belied by the steady flow of excellent world-historical research in journals, books, and graduate programs, but "national" or regional historians do not commonly read this work. How has serious scholarship developed in an arena without a readily visible fieldsite or manageable body of languages, and with a proclivity to incorporate methods and sources from disciplines as varied as literature and astrophysics? How can teachers and students educated along national, regional, or chronological lines make sense of a vastly broader sweep of the human past to highlight worldwide patterns, global developments and comparisons, and cross-regional or world-systemic interactions?

More than 30 chapters follow to address these questions. Each chapter provides not so much a neatly packaged description of a canonical topic as a sketch of starting points for further exploration. Each offers an overview of the practices operating within a particular subfield or approach. The chapters collectively suggest that world history is best seen as a field in action, not one clearly defined or even easily summarized. The book adopts a "warts and all" approach that equally celebrates the achievements and breadth of a field that has come of age, explores its fundamental problems, and highlights challenges for the future. Contributors ask forthright questions about core problems: how can practitioners establish distinctive and defensible research methods for world and global history; how should readers think about connections (or the lack thereof) between world-scaled scholarship and teaching; and how does world history appear to the non-Anglophone world?

This final question may seem obvious, but is too often overlooked in practice: how would the world's past change if it were written by all its people? This issue runs throughout the book, but is addressed directly in the concluding group of essays in Part III, "Many Globes: Who Writes the World?" These chapters extend recent efforts to broaden the geographic, linguistic, institutional, and epistemological bases of world history by considering how the field could change were it not so dominated by modern Western (especially American) scholars and their concerns. These scholars are of course situated culturally and historically, with predispositions and theoretical frameworks shaped by positions in a modern, especially Anglophone and capitalist, West. Radical critics, especially those adopting perspectives from postcolonial studies, argue that the character of actually-existing world history – its practitioners' predominant physical locations, shared languages, and core problematics – amounts only to the latest version of the West's assertion of intellectual hegemony. From this point of view, world history studies a "globe" that has been conceived through Euro-American categories and approached with Euro-American historicist epistemologies (for example, assuming professional practices of empirical documentation). It is therefore neither objective nor value-neutral – and far from truly global.[3] Some world historians, speaking with the zeal of partisans and converts, have disagreed forcefully with this characterization, calling it unfair, political/ideological, and a failure of imagination (Bentley 2005; O'Brien 2006). Yet their and others' actions have also conceded that "worlding" the field is indeed a crucially important task, one that has only just begun.[4]

When histories begin at different starting points, as the chapters in Part III show, other questions inevitably arise. Historical subjects will shift, and new frameworks emerge. What, then, are the limits of Anglophone world-historical scholarship? How will categories, emphases, and chronologies shift if the world's past is considered from other points of view? What other possible centers and peripheries come into focus – or does the center/periphery model even apply? Are concepts like "nation," "empire," or "bureaucracy" (to take just a few examples) still as important, and do they mean the same thing? How do the "turning points" of global or interregional history change? What evidence – and what methods – do scholars working in different institutional, linguistic, and disciplinary terrains find most productive? How do their theories, narratives, and epistemologies of a "world" differ? How, most basically, do they think about the past? A concluding chapter leaves history altogether, considering global approaches in other disciplinary terrains – nonhistorical fields in the humanities and social sciences, from art to economics, that are likewise wrestling with theories and practices of world-scaled study.

The bulk of the book before this point is divided into two broad headings. The chapters in Part I discuss the making of world history as a field, on the one hand, and of world historians to populate it, on the other. These chapters sketch the *techniques and methods* through which historians are currently trained to think about the globe – from practicalities of program and course design, to research methods and fieldwork, to the intellectual questions of how to define basic categories and conceive an audience for teaching and scholarship. This section orients readers new to the field by providing a historical backdrop – the emergence of world and global history as a professional domain, the politics and institutional stakes of undertaking world-historic study, and even a personal story of the odyssey of becoming a world historian. As many have found, it is not an easy field to enter, so the professional trajectories that unfold are complicated. Several pieces deal thoughtfully with the critical voices of historians who have questioned the intellectual value, methodological practicalities, and epistemological implications of world history. These critics, like those already mentioned, make important points; it is unfair to brush them off as misinformed or narrow-minded pedants. Rather than taking a straightforwardly evangelical approach or simply lauding the value of global perspectives (as important as such perspectives may be), these chapters reflect on the trade-offs that come with *any* choice of method, concept, approach, or theory – world history included. One topic regrettably almost absent, with only an occasional glancing discussion, relates to the field's own economics, especially with regard to textbooks – the pressures of markets on authors and publishing houses, editorial perceptions of books that will "sell" and are thus worth publishing, shifting practices of remuneration for authors, and how such factors shape (and constrain) the architectures of "the world" that will reach wide audiences.

Part II then delves in detail into the chief concepts, categories, and approaches that are employed today by world and global historians. What makes an essay (or book, or course syllabus, or museum exhibit) "world-historical" or "globally minded"? What are the benefits (and costs) of taking such a perspective? How has world and global history drawn upon – and questioned, challenged, destabilized – the categories of "traditional" history? Several chapters consider various *frameworks* in space and time – ranging from the universe as a whole down to localities and microhistory. World history, perhaps counterintuitively, does not only mean looking at "the globe," as a whole, all at once; any number of other scales are also approachable in ways that are consonant with the field's guiding concerns. Other chapters then consider *comparative* approaches, in which particular themes are taken up and seen afresh in global context. Finally, several chapters cover key aspects of *connective* world history – tracing how historians follow objects, people, and ideas around the globe, and what they can learn by doing so. Each of these general approaches – framing, comparing, connecting – suggests principal modes that world historians have adopted, and how they might answer critics who say the field lacks firm sources, clear methods, recognizable fieldsites, defined historiographies, and/or coherent theoretical frameworks.

Of course, many other topics could have been included: sports and leisure, technology, etc. Yet just as world historians do not purport to offer encyclopedic coverage of everything that ever happened, this *Companion* does not set out to survey the field exhaustively – merely to sketch its major approaches. A planned chapter on "identity" did not material-ize, to take one example, so readers do not hear separately about identity categories such as race, gender, and class. The existing chapters nevertheless provide tools to reflect on these, and many other, themes. Race, class, and gender are key concepts historians use to think about the past, and they have been used productively in many time periods and cultural contexts; but strikingly, they have not yet played a prominent role in the writing of world and global history. This may be changing: some scholars have proposed rewriting world history through a lens of gender, for example, such as Strasser and Tinsman (2010) or Wiesner-Hanks (2007). The potential promise is clear. Identity categories have both an abstract analytic power – offering a powerful way for scholars to interpret the world – and their own independent historical presence – as important ideas that appeared at particular times and places in the actually existing world, and served to organize social groups and movements. They grew, migrated, and had manifold effects; therefore they can be treated as historical subjects in their own right, producing their own discrete, globally dispersed, world histories. One could, for example, write a world history of apartheid and racial ideologies that interlocked South Africa, India, and Haiti; or of women's suffrage, both globally and in specific places such as Japan, Turkey, and Brazil.

Clearly there are many kinds of world and global history, and the details will emerge as the chapters unfold. Just a few more words at the outset suffice to set the stage, and to point out a few additional questions readers may wish to keep in mind. What holds this enterprise together? How do world historians define what they do (apart from McNeill's metaphors of lenses and traffic and trees)? Definitions obviously vary, but most efforts to synthesize the field include at least two key ideas. First is the importance of *scale*, especially the interconnecting of different scales. World historians, plainly, are best known for thinking big. They emphasize the bird's-eye perspective, and are renowned for looking at (comparatively) vast distances and grand issues. They therefore ask questions, use methods, and seek sources that stretch across particular places or individual countries to encompass wider regions, and sometimes the whole globe. (Occasionally, as one chapter below shows, they even move beyond the Earth!) In temporal terms world historians likewise look across larger-than-customary stretches of time to find longer-term developments, comparisons, patterns, and connections. But this stretching – the overall expansion of time and space – is by itself not enough to define world or global history: the big picture is a necessary, but not sufficient, component. Most world historians would agree that it also requires a second key idea: *mobility*. The past is seen less as a collection of discrete stories (of particular places or peoples) than one fundamentally shaped by, and concerned with, the movements, relationships, and connections among them. Individual stories – whether of a single person, a town, a region, a country, even a continent – are therefore not seen in standalone terms. World history instead brings multiple stories together, comparing and/or connecting individuals and communities that are separated in space or time. From this point of view, *any* particular group can be seen in both *relative* (relational, comparative) and *interactive* (mutually constitutive, connective) terms. Any single story emerges and makes sense most fully only in wider contexts, both seen through ongoing processes of exchange, encounter, and relationship with people far away, and as part of systems much larger than any locality.

Institutionally and intellectually, therefore, world history at its heart denies the presumptively foundational character of the nation-state. This modern social form has frequently been assumed to be – or at least it has been unwittingly treated as – a self-evident, naturally fundamental framework for conceptualizing the human past. (Recall those disciplinary fields for historians, generally structured along national lines: American history, French history, Chinese history, and so on.) Area studies scholarship, based on the notion of coherent, separable world "regions," has also, for the last half-century or so, played a related role in this "boxing" of historical knowledge. To be fair, scholarship focused on area and nation has created critical underpinnings for world history today, generating detailed knowledge of peoples and cultures all around the globe, including many not previously well studied by the powerful institutions of Euro-American academia. Yet both the area-studies enterprise and national historiographies start by reifying a unit for study, generally treating it as a more or less self-contained, sometimes almost hermetic box. World history, at its core, posits instead the need to put areal – or national – literatures into connection with one another, to resist institutionally instantiated assertions of specialized "turf" and "expertise" that are built into professional academic discourse. World historians start by adopting very different scalar approaches in space and time. National and regional stories are present, certainly, but are not always presumed to drive the whole.[5]

For this reason, world historians do not see the simple expansion of scale – including to the globe as a whole – as the only story worth telling. Instead, cross-regional, cross-temporal, and global points of view are essential, often overlooked, perspectives; but they are only one (or two) of the levels of analysis to be included. Grand perspectives give new meaning to national (and local) developments, and cross-regional or global developments shape local-to-national stories; but wider narratives also arise from smaller-scaled histories. The basic idea is that none of these histories, at whatever level, exists in isolation. All have been shaped by different scalar layers and by distant places, actors, ideas, and histories. Many world historians are interested in how these scales *interact* – how trajectories, patterns, actors, and contingencies are inescapably part of a vast interlocking interscalar system of space and time. All the levels work together, and each lends structure and composition to others. The relative weight of any particular spatial or temporal scale will shift depending on the questions being asked, but world history requires constant mobility: regularly shifting the lens to move viewers ever upward and ever downward. A world-historical approach thus means always asking what is happening on different levels, and how these levels are shaping one another – tracing interscalar loops of connection and causation. Some world historians, more controversially, then go beyond these scalar interactions to *compare* layers of scale. This happens most visibly in the subfield of Big History, which identifies commensurable patterns across vastly disparate spatial scales, ranging from subatomic particles to intergalactic space. Such a view – drawing its evidence from physics, biology, and other nonhistorical fields via concepts of complexity and energy utilization – is not universally held by world historians, but it suggests the breadth of new perspectives that can be brought out by expanding notions of scale.

World history thus holds that the customary, basic units of disciplinary history are too rigid. As a field it aims to overcome the mutually reinforcing, too often invisible, institutional and intellectual boundaries that constrain historical work. Many of these boundaries are likewise effects of modern states and their politico-cultural projections; they include complicated feedback loops of educational systems (in which national "fields" define the reading lists history students must master, and impel the creation of yet more nationally framed dissertations and books), professional training and advancement (job searches, tenure evaluations, and monographic publication are similarly aligned to certify standing in these fields), institutional locations and financial resources (research is often pursued in national archives, published in nationally or regionally framed journals, and taught in curricula that specialize along national/regional lines). Even language skills – scholars' foundational tool, crucial for access to history's raw materials – are framed by modern national states and their definitions of vernacular/ political culture. (Consider the relative paucity of work on, say, modern Kurdish or Uyghur history.) Historians can be as blind as anyone else to the unspoken, mutually reinforcing elements that predefine a professional world. Taken as a whole, though, these elements make it harder to pursue, even to see, cross-cutting issues and boundary-transgressing questions, much less to investigate histories of, say, humanity as a whole. World history is therefore more radical, in an institutional-intellectual sense, than it may first appear. It asks: What would change if students started not by mastering a national field (or two), but by looking across borders – to topics being investigated in other archives and parts of the world, and asking how they compare, how they could be connected, how they may be similar or divergent responses to shared conditions? If *Homo sapiens sapiens* is a discrete subspecies – if modern humans are an identifiable entity in Earth's biosphere – must not humanity also have a meaningfully collective history?

How could one study such a history? What role could individual women or men possibly play in it – would it not wind up vast and faceless, reduced to statistics and abstract structures, full of general "trends" such as demographics, urbanization, or technology? How can one identify meaningful turning points at global scale, divide time into "periods," or preserve a role for human culture or individual agency? When historians reach into different disciplines (if, for example, they use evolutionary biology to place humans alongside primates as part of a deeper history of life, as in Morris 2010), is it possible to avoid biological determinism and retain a sense of historical contingency? Or is world history hopelessly presentist, impelled by issues such as global warming and the internet, inclined to see all prior eras in the light of – as inexorably leading up to – present-day "globalization"? Is it anachronistic to rethink ancient pasts through modern paradigms such as globalization and "connectivity," as some archaeologists (LaBianca and Scham 2006) have started to do? And in practical terms, how could one possibly know enough about developments everywhere in the world – during any period – to speak broadly about a "globe"? Can primary documents ever really underpin such work, or must it always be a synthesis of others' scholarship – and thus is it inevitably to be deemed less serious, or superficial, by self-respecting professional historians? Or, on the other hand, do world historians need to work collaboratively, writing in teams? If so, how can such practices fit into scholarly arenas predicated on single-author, monographic scholarship as the chief currency for promotion and status? Or into pedagogical realms where team teaching may not fit, if every faculty member must teach a certain number of courses, or meet with students for a fixed number of "contact hours"?

On a theoretical level, at least some of these questions are answerable. Scholars of subaltern studies have long since shown that historians *can* read state-produced, nationally framed records in ways that go "against the grain" of what they seem to discuss. Years ago, too, the *Annales* school treated history in vast time depths and stretched far across national borders. And how, after all, could any historian of seventeenth-century Russia, or Meiji Japan, or modern South Asia – after long years of training, even a lifetime of scholarship – possibly know every province, each individual village, much less every family or person living in his or her area of specialty? Is such encyclopedic preparation really necessary before a historian hazards to speak about "Russian" (or "Japanese," or "South Asian") social history? Professional norms do not – cannot – require such exhaustion. Historians are expected to abstract general, defensible conclusions from particular shreds of evidence, and to speak judiciously and knowledgeably about them. These practices customarily happen at scales ranging up to the national/regional; such conclusions are seen, by professional consensus, as perfectly plausible. It makes sense to talk about "Brazilian" history, notwithstanding the vast differences between Rio's urban *favelas* and the "uncontacted tribes" of the Amazon's far-western Vale do Javari. In temporal terms, too, a historian of France is unlikely to know equally well the diplomatic story of the Maastricht Treaty of 1993 *and* the details of Charlemagne's eighth-century interactions with Rome. Given the limits of any individual's knowledge, interest, and training, she or he would read and rely on secondary scholarship – without going back to check every primary document – if called upon to write a class lecture, compose a textbook, or speak with a local reporter who calls asking for a historical perspective.

Research or teaching at a global scale involves processes that are, in principle, the same. Yet practically speaking, especially given the way most historians are trained, this particular scalar expansion – to a global level – produces qualitatively new challenges. Where does one go to investigate "humanity," or to ask world-level historical questions? What archives should a scholar use, what questions would she or he ask? Must world history dissertations require PhD students to use texts in many *different* languages, held in different archival repositories, and must they be treated independently of existing historiographical questions? If so, how can students possibly be trained? How many cases must they include in a world-historical study – and whatever the number, why not more? In the face of practical limits on any one person's time and mental capacity, is it permissible to rely at least sometimes on secondary literature for evidence, rather than insisting that all scholarship be based on a personally generated foundation of primary documents? How can one design survey classes, or thematic seminars, that will teach students (whether at an elementary, secondary, university, or graduate level) about a "world"? What about the inevitable counterexamples, which multiply endlessly in the face of any general global assertion? (As if one could not find counterexamples to generalizations about Meiji Japan, or Muscovite Russia.)

Moreover, if world history concentrates on particular themes and approaches – as the following chapters show, world historians emphasize ideas such as nodes, systems, interconnections and "thick" networks – what about people or areas not visible or present in these framings? Who gains, and who disappears, when history is reconceived globally? What about groups living far from demographic, political, economic, or cultural "centers" – such as people scattered across millions of square miles of Pacific Oceania, or nomads who appear in written sources only when they invade settled areas? Do they not matter? Or those with poorly known histories – consider the lack of written sources in precolonial North America, or the few non-epigraphical texts that survived the tropics of Southeast Asia before ca. 1400 CE. Such places are already relegated to the margins of existing historical fields. Panama is ignored by most Latin Americanists; Uzbekistan was long judged obscure by Moscow-focused Soviet historians. Such places tend to generate only small, specialized historiographies. But without much secondary scholarship, are they consigned again to be forgotten by world historians, left out of globally scaled metanarratives? Will tomorrow's world historians even be aware of the holes produced by uneven preexisting historiographical developments? Is it up to specialized scholars to show that global metanarratives are inevitably flawed through such exclusions? Is it intellectually defensible to leave such problems to the fullness of time, hoping that the vagaries of field coverage will somehow, someday, self-correct?

These are just some of the daunting questions asked by skeptics and objections lodged by critics. Readers should keep all the hurdles in mind while reading the essays that follow. They chronicle various methods, concepts, and theories world historians have used; they navigate contending schools of thought, point to different bodies of sources, and sketch some of the answers given to critics. Inevitably, some approaches will appeal more than others; every reader will reach his or her individual conclusions.

Throughout the journey, too, consider one last issue: falsifiability. This concern is less often vocalized, but it nonetheless needs attention. How, in short, do we know good world history when we see it – and concomitantly, what does *bad* world history look like? Specialists, after all, must be able to tell the difference, and in broad terms to agree which is which; and students must learn to do so. For good reasons, few chapters in this book frontally address this question. Each essay sets out to show the methods, reach, and potential of a particular approach, not to show how it itself can be called into question; and given strict word limits, there was little space to offer examples of bad work. Few authors wished to do so, in any case, and such an endeavor can quickly prove tiresome. But falsifiability is nevertheless a key question readers need to ask. Ask it of any book these chapters cite, or any article in, say, the *Journal of World History*. Perhaps especially in large-scalar approaches – given the vast distance between individuals (who feature in many historical documents) and interregional analysis – how would one query or contradict the results? National and regional historians debate this question too: arguing about when particular evidence that runs contrary can be discounted as "noise," isolated flotsam not undercutting an interpretation, or when it is a substantive counterexample that necessitates more sweeping reconsideration. At global scale, is it possible to imagine generalizable norms of evidence that have sufficient power to serve as disconfirmation, or that cast serious doubts on an interpretation? Without it, world histories will simply proliferate, with few visible means of demonstrating quality, rigor, or depth.

The challenges of world history, then, run inward as well as outward. As the field comes into its own, enjoying unprecedented scholarly visibility and increased public interest, with new resources and rapid growth fueled by the contexts of twenty-first century globalization, it nevertheless faces old pitfalls and continuing conundrums.

Some problems are methodological or theoretical, others institutional and practical. Taken together, the problems explain why some world historians express pessimism about the field's chances of achieving full disciplinary standing (Manning 2003; 2008). Yet given the same rapid expansion, alongside the sweeping intellectual claims that connect with many powerful constituencies, other voices express more optimism about world history's future (Bentley 2007). Indeed the field's coming of age and surge into prominence is enabled by its posing of such challenges – theoretical and practical – to the existing frameworks of disciplinary history. The possible payoffs, as well as the deep pitfalls, are clear.

By pursuing more flexible and wider perspectives – stressing cross-regional and cross-border approaches, big-picture views, and global-to-local analysis of systems, structures, and interactions – world history sets out to map a globe, many globes, both past and present. It avoids relying on static units, whether "nations" or "civilizations," as a foundational way to approach the human past – not ignoring them, but incorporating them with an eye to their historicity. Beyond that, in globalizing *itself* as a field, and incorporating a newly expanded range of views about what history can be, world history promises no less than to offer fresh insights into the human condition. World history thus stakes a very grand claim of its own: to illumine humanity's history. That is what its converts proclaim. Its critics are not convinced this is possible. The stakes are high, the field yet in formation, and the challenges clear and daunting. How to address them, and where world history goes from here, is what readers will see in the pages that follow.

Notes

1 Overviews include Manning (2003); Bentley (1996; 2006); Dunn (2000); Stearns (2011).
2 Quotations in these two paragraphs are from McNeill (1982: 82–84). Scholars in other disciplines use similar metaphors to defend big-picture, macro perspectives. David Damrosch (2003: 4) justifies the study of world literature, for instance, by noting that no one denies entomologists a category of "insects," even though millions of species exist: so many that it would be impossible to be bitten by even a tiny fraction of them.
3 The principal voices are Lal (2003; 2005), Nandy (1998), and Dirlik (2002; 2003); others who have intervened include Feierman (1993) and Prazniak (2000). For a fuller discussion of these critiques and debates, see Sutherland (2007).
4 See Manning (2008), or the Network of Global and World History Organizations (NOGWHISTO), at www.uni-leipzig.de/~gwhisto (accessed Mar. 2012). Antoinette Burton has noted the dominance of North American-based theory, but also the limits of this critique. Many prominent scholarly voices, she points out, such as Edward Said, Gayatri Spivak, or Homi Bhabha, have "at best an angular relationship to American politics and culture" (2003: 12–13).
5 Environmental historians – who also define subjects that spill beyond, or are irrelevant to, human political units – have much in common, as do some kinds of transnational and comparative history. Comparative approaches, though, may still presuppose national units as the basis for comparison; and international history – as in diplomatic histories – can easily slip into a framework of state-level actors and their interactions. Even some "transnational" approaches ironically place national states at a foundational level, as discussed by Bayly *et al.* (2006). Hence there have been calls for a different approach, such as Dirlik's (2005) pursuit of "translocal" (rather than transnational) history.

References

Bayly, C.A, S. Beckert, M. Connelly, I. Hofmeyr, W. Kozol, and P. Seed. 2006. AHR conversation: On transnational history. *American Historical Review* 111 (5): 1441–1464.

Bentley, J. 1996. *Shapes of World History in Twentieth-Century Scholarship*. Washington DC: American Historical Association.

Bentley, J. 2005. Myths, wagers, and some moral implications of world history. *Journal of World History* 16 (1): 51–82.

Bentley, J. 2006. New world history. In L. Kramer and S. Maza, eds, *A Companion to Western Historical Thought*, pp. 393–416. Oxford: Wiley-Blackwell.

Bentley, J. 2007. Why study world history? *World History Connected* 5 (1), at www.historycoop-erative.org/journals/whc/5.1/bentley.html (accessed Feb. 2012).

Burton, A., ed. 2003. *After the Imperial Turn: Thinking with and through the Nation*. Durham: Duke University Press.

Damrosch, D. 2003. *What Is World Literature?* Princeton: Princeton University Press.

Dirlik, A. 2002. History without a center? Reflections on Eurocentrism. In E. Fuchs and B. Stuchtey, eds, *Across Cultural Borders: Historiography in Global Perspective*, pp. 247–284. Lanham: Rowman & Littlefield.

Dirlik, A. 2003. Confounding metaphors, inventions of the world: What is world history for? In B. Stuchtey and E. Fuch, eds, *Writing World History 1800–2000*, pp. 91–133. Oxford: Oxford University Press.

Dirlik, A. 2005. Performing the world: Reality and representation in the making of world histor(ies). *Journal of World History* 16 (4): 391–410.

Dunn, R.E., ed. 2000. *The New World History: A Teacher's Companion*. Boston: Bedford/St. Martin's.

Feierman, S. 1993. African histories and the dissolution of world history. In R.H. Bates, V.Y. Mudimbe, and J. O'Barr, eds, *Africa and the Disciplines: The Contributions of Research in Africa to the Social Sciences and Humanities*, pp. 167–212. Chicago: University of Chicago Press.

LaBianca, Ø.S., and S.A. Scham, eds. 2006. *Connectivity in Antiquity: Globalization as a Long-Term Historical Process*. London: Equinox.

Lal, V. 2003. Provincializing the West: World history from the perspective of Indian history. In B Stuchtey and E. Fuchs, eds, *Writing World History 1800–2000*, pp. 271–89. Oxford: Oxford University Press.

Lal, V. 2005. Much ado about something: The new malaise of world history. *Radical History Review* 91: 124–130.

Manning, P. 2003. *Navigating World History: Historians Create a Global Past*. New York: Palgrave Macmillan.

Manning, P., ed. 2008. *Global Practice in World History: Advances Worldwide*. Princeton: Markus Weiner.

McNeill, W.H. 1982. A defence of world history: The Prothero Lecture. *Transactions of the Royal Historical Society*, Fifth Series 32: 75–89.

Morris, I. 2010. *Why The West Rules – For Now: The Patterns of History, and What They Reveal about the Future*. New York: Farrar, Straus, & Giroux.

Nandy, A. 1998. History's forgotten doubles. In P. Pomper, R. Elphick, and R.T. Vann, eds, *World History: Ideologies, Structures, and Identities*, pp. 159–178. Oxford: Blackwell.

O'Brien, P. 2006. Historiographical traditions and modern imperatives for the restoration of global history. *Journal of Global History* 1: 3–39.

Prazniak, R. 2000. Is world history possible? An inquiry. In A. Dirlik, V. Bahl, and P. Gran, eds, *History after the Three Worlds: Post-Eurocentric Historiographies*, pp. 221–240. Lanham: Rowman & Littlefield.

Stearns, P. 2011. *World History: The Basics*. New York: Routledge.

Strasser, U., and H. Tinsman. 2010. It's a man's world: Bringing masculinity to world history, in Latin American studies for example. *Journal of World History* 21 (1): 75–96.

Sutherland, H. 2007. The problematic authority of (world) history. *Journal of World History* 18 (4): 491–522.

Wiesner-Hanks, M. 2007. World history and the history of women, gender, and sexuality. *Journal of World History* 18 (1): 53–67.

PART I

Trajectories and Practices

CHAPTER ONE

World History
Departures and Variations

KENNETH POMERANZ AND DANIEL A. SEGAL

"World history" exists today as both an established undergraduate-level teaching field in US higher education and a recognizable – though arguably still fledgling – research field that operates transnationally. In both manifestations, world history has gained a significant foothold only since the early 1980s. That earlier efforts failed to establish world history as either a teaching or research field, and that world history faces continued skepticism from many academic historians, indicates significant tensions between history as an institutionalized discipline and the project of world history. The ongoing work of producing both world history courses and scholarship has thus required that historians depart from some of the received practices of their discipline, even while building on others.

The need for two such departures has been particularly visible to the pioneers of world history. The first and most obvious of these involves acquiring knowledge about areas of the world and their inhabitants that had previously been little studied by historians. The second involves studying phenomena on a scale larger than the national and state units that have been the usual units of historical inquiry and legitimate expertise. During the early emergence of world history this shift upward in geographic scale most often took the form of treating supranational "civilizations" as distinct wholes, in close parallel with the established treatment of nations and states; increasingly, however, the shift upward in scale has involved recognizing and thinking in terms of connections and the ways connections shape the places they connect.

In addition, as historians have pursued comprehensive world history projects – world history survey courses, for example – they have also pursued a third departure, involving working on much larger time-scales than is common for historians. Put simply, just as the inclusive ideal of world history has motivated a concern with neglected spatial regions, it has also motivated increased attention to the large segment of early human time that had previously been left to archaeology and paleoanthropology.

Without question, these departures – particularly the first two – have produced important new knowledge. They have, for instance, led to a much fuller recognition of

A Companion to World History, First Edition. Edited by Douglas Northrop.
© 2012 Blackwell Publishing Ltd. Published 2012 by Blackwell Publishing Ltd.

the extra-European dimensions of historical phenomena that had been understood – prior to recent world history scholarship – as purely European stories. Yet these achievements have not resolved the considerable challenges of extending the spatial and temporal coverage of history to be inclusive of all of humanity.

From Disciplinary Exclusion to Limited Acceptance, circa Late 1800s to 1990

As history was institutionalized as an academic discipline in Europe and the United States in the 1800s, its leading figures produced historical scholarship that served nationalist movements and/or states to which they had allegiance, whether by fostering collective memory and patriotic pride, offering lessons from "past politics" for statesmen, or both.[1] Yet, the mutual recognition of these works as "history" – while other scholarship also on the human past, specifically social evolutionary studies of non-European peoples, was not so recognized – meant that "history" as a discipline was identified with the aggregate of the states and nations these "historians" wrote about. This aggregate was, in turn, a distinct subset of the globe and humanity: it is what we have come to know as "the West." Thus, even though most works of "history" were written about a single state or nation, and even though these texts were written in a voice that identified with their respective national or state subject, the discipline as a whole interpolated an overarching civilizational identity. At its onset, then, disciplinary history at once conjoined, and was shaped by, two projects: the making of nation-states and the making of the Western Self.

Moreover, this double identification of the discipline – with individual states and nations on the one hand and the West on the other – was further supported by the denigration of works of "general history" (as works with some attempt at global coverage were called) as amateurish and popular. The effect, not surprisingly, was that in the wake of the discipline's institutionalization, works of this genre came to be produced only by persons outside of or at the margins of the profession.[2]

Within the discipline, the earliest significant production of supranational and suprastate history appeared in the context of US undergraduate teaching following World War I, when the Western Civ survey course was introduced. This shift upward in geographic scale to the discipline's civilizational Self reflected concerns about the discontents of nationalism, as evidenced by the war and the upsurge of both nativism and isolationism in the United States after the war. Though the Western Civ course is now rightly remembered as "Eurocentric," this label – if no more is said – risks obscuring important aspects of the course's relationship to world history. First, along with its supranational and suprastate geographic scope, the Western Civ survey recognized and narrativized the full span of human time, starting with the emergence of hominids. Indeed, in the years surrounding the Scopes Trial, Western Civ was a significant vector in the United States of the secular chronology of human existence. Second, in a nontrivial sense, Western Civ provided a story about humanity *in toto*. It did this by inscribing a "first-the-West-then-the-rest" grand narrative. Within this schema, the West's trajectory foretold the shared – or if not the shared, then the defining – experiences of all humanity; the West's history was thus humanity's history (Segal 2000).

With the continued success of the Western Civ survey and emergence of area studies programs after World War II, survey courses about other "world areas" entered the undergraduate curriculum in US higher education. These courses were typically organized chronologically, even when they were housed in area studies programs. (See Kramer, this volume.) The most common of these new surveys were devoted to East Asia or East-plus-Southeast Asia.[3] That it was East Asia or a larger Asian area that was the primary addition is a pattern we will see repeated many times in tracing efforts to redress history's institutionalized tie to "the West" – with this being an indication that non-Western areas other than Asia, particularly sub-Saharan Africa and Oceania, were seen as even further behind in (or even more thoroughly lacking) history. Yet even though the broadening of the curriculum was circumscribed by this gradient sense of the historicalness of different peoples and places, by representing the histories of other areas as complex and distinctive, the new area survey courses troubled the social evolutionary notion that the Rest merely followed the West. These courses thus disturbed the conflation of the West's history with human history and thereby suggested that the task of representing human history required a significant broadening of the discipline's geographic scope.

This disturbance was, however, far from sufficient to support the emergence of world history in the 1950s. True, some "world history" surveys did appear, but these were located primarily at institutions of lower prestige (state colleges with teacher training programs, for instance), and the textbooks that served these courses were minimally adapted Western Civ texts, with Asia – and usually East Asia – getting the bulk of the additional coverage. At Northwestern University, Leften Stavrianos made a rare attempt to establish a more robust world history survey at this time – and at an institution of some prestige, no less. Yet, Stavrianos was firmly rebuffed by his own department.[4]

In the postwar period, many journals, conferences, and American Historical Association (AHA) book prizes also came to be organized on areal rather than national or state lines. Here, again, the region that was most prominent was East Asia. Furthermore, most research in this and other new areal fields was conducted on national or state units within the delimited area, and what research there was that focused on a larger region almost always deployed notions of a distinct areal essence or character. Connections were not what this work foregrounded.

A small number of important books of the middle decades of the century escaped or at least pushed at these constraints. Braudel's *Civilization and Capitalism, 15th–18th Century* had significant global coverage and gave considerable attention to connections.[5] The same author's *The Mediterranean and the Mediterranean World in the Age of Philip II* – though narrower in geographic scope – was also an important forerunner of world history, particularly because it demonstrated that, despite what area studies boundaries suggested, North Africa and Southern Europe belonged together as a historical unit of analysis.[6] Indeed, one of Braudel's most profound legacies for world history is the injunction in this text to "imagine a hundred frontiers, not one, some political, some economic, and some cultural": historians should, in short, resist treating any unit of analysis as a discrete, functional whole (1972: 170).

William McNeill's *Rise of the West: A History of the Human Community* (1963) and *Plagues and Peoples* (1976) also operated on a global scale and were nonetheless widely respected by professional historians. But while Braudel's and McNeill's books were admired in the profession, their works were seen neither as models for younger historians to imitate nor as harbingers of an emerging field of world history. Indeed, McNeill tried and failed to persuade his own department (at the University of Chicago) to create a world history program at the graduate level.

Only from the end of the 1970s did world history begin to attract more attention in many departments – in the first instance, as an undergraduate survey course. Departments that had added colleagues who worked on areas outside of the West often sought ways to integrate those colleagues into lower-division teaching. One attempted solution was to have those colleagues participate in Western Civ surveys, on the grounds that this was material every historian had to know. This was never very satisfactory, in no small part because it limited how much the non-Western specialists could teach in their own areas of expertise. A second response was the introduction of various lower-division surveys on other geographic areas: Africa, Latin America, South Asia, and so on. This second response was supported by critiques of Eurocentrism in both the curriculum and scholarship, which had also played a part in creating faculty lines in these areas.[7] So too, this second response was supported by both a decline in the number of schools that required students to take Western Civ and new competition for enrollments from other programs that aimed to bring "diversity" into the curriculum, notably women's studies and ethnic studies. Yet there were important institutional – and intellectual – limits to this second response. Multiplying survey courses had diminishing returns in enrollments, since most students only took one of them, and yet these courses had to be offered regularly in order for students to be able to use them to meet requirements. Consequently, additional survey courses consumed a big chunk of the total courses that could be offered in the new areal fields, which often had just one or two faculty members. This outcome was good neither for these colleagues nor for a department that wanted varied upper-division tracks for its majors and grad students. Offering a world history survey, by contrast, addressed these several problems at once.

Changes in secondary education in the 1980s provided a further incentive for departments to offer a world history survey. A number of US states, also in response to critiques of the curriculum, were shifting from the teaching of the history of Europe or the West to the teaching of world history. (See Bain, this volume.) For many public universities and less elite private ones, aspiring high school teachers comprised a significant fraction of history majors; it thus made sense for those departments to offer students undergraduate training more closely aligned with the curriculum they would be expected to teach.

As world history as a teaching field grew in this context, an important moment of its institutionalization occurred in 1982, when the American Historical Association co-sponsored a conference with an academic institution that many historians, in the post-Vietnam era, would otherwise have avoided: the US Air Force Academy. Yet the Academy was one of the few institutions of higher education with an established world history survey course. This was so, we suspect, because the Academy's mission – like the US military's mission more generally – was inescapably global, while the number of technical and military courses required of students meant that there was no opportunity for them to take a sequence of area surveys. And whether coincidentally or not, the AHA's president-elect in 1982 was Philip Curtin, an early advocate of world history. Whatever the exact reasons for this unusual collaborative venture, the conference drew more people than expected and was judged a major success by its organizers and many participants. Following a post-conference planning meeting, the World History Association (WHA) was founded in 1983, as an affiliated society of the AHA.

Yet while world history surveys were introduced on more and more US campuses in the 1980s, the most prestigious universities and elite colleges remained resistant. Prestigious research departments could afford to have many colleagues who never taught lower-division courses, and historians in these departments, as well as those at elite liberal arts colleges, had the least to gain and the most to lose by championing a new field that was easily dismissed as too broad to meet the discipline's standards of meticulous archival and contextual work.

All of this was reflected at the Air Force Academy conference in 1982. Though some well-known historians (most notably, William McNeill) attended, the prevailing view at the conference was that the focus of world history would be on teaching, not research (Lockard n.d.). So too, most of the members of the first steering committee were from less prestigious institutions, with the best-known of these schools being the Academy, the University of Houston, and Tufts; and finally, throughout the 1980s, about 50 percent of WHA members were high school teachers.[8]

In this context, world history graduate tracks appealed primarily to departments that placed many of their PhD students at the kinds of schools that, by the mid to late 1990s, expected faculty to teach world history to undergraduates. (See Streets-Salter, this volume.) Minnesota, Rutgers, University of California at Irvine, at Santa Cruz, and at Riverside, and the University of Hawai'i were among the pioneers in establishing these graduate programs. Moreover, after some two decades of weak academic job markets, many departments outside the top reputational cluster had faculty who, as individuals, could compete for excellent graduate students, but who were hobbled by having relatively few colleagues in their own geographic area. Because world history allowed these colleagues to collaborate across area fields, this situation also made world history a compelling venture. The 1999 grant application that launched the University of California's Multi-Campus Research Unit in World History, for instance, emphasized that graduate-level world history represented an opportunity for the university's system because (1) many top-ranked departments were ignoring it, and (2) it made use of collaboration among talented faculty whose separate fields and departments lacked critical mass. Tellingly, while the Irvine, Riverside, Santa Cruz, and Davis faculty have been the mainstays of this multi-campus project, UC Berkeley faculty have barely participated.[9]

Influences, Resources, and Canon Formation, circa Late 1980s to 2011

An important step in world history becoming recognized as a research field was the founding in 1990 of the *Journal of World History*, which was sponsored by the WHA and edited by Jerry Bentley at the University of Hawai'i. (Winning a prize as the year's best new scholarly journal made this founding still more emblematic of the field's arrival.) Yet in the decade or so before this moment of institutionalization of world history as a research field, we find a rich panoply of scholarship that did not call itself "world history," but which in retrospect can be seen as pointing to and providing a rich base of knowledge and innovation for world history. Many of these works represented efforts to make older subfields more attentive to non-Europeans, often drawing on other disciplines to do so. (See chapters by Weinstein and by Northrop, this volume.)

An important example is Christopher Bayly's *Imperial Meridian*, which Bayly framed as an effort to revive "imperial history" by both "broadening" its concerns to include "the history of the colonised" and contesting its pro-empire bias (1989: xiv). As this suggests, Bayly was strongly influenced by the many scholars, including subaltern studies scholars, who had produced histories of the colonized. The subalternists had, in turn, extended into new geographic areas the efforts of European and American social historians to study the everyday lives of ordinary – often nonliterate – people, and, like the social historians before them, had often drawn on works from other disciplines, particularly anthropology.

Interestingly, within a strictly South Asian studies context, Bayly's work has often been seen as central to a "Cambridge School" that represents a polar opposite to subalternist approaches: he pays more attention to collaborating indigenous elites than to insurgent impoverished masses, and he is more inclined than the subalternists to see at least some positive legacies of British imperialism. But through a retrospective lens informed by the emergence of world history, areas of commonality between Bayly and the subaltern school seem striking. There is, for instance, Bayly's insistence that the agency of both colonized and colonizers be taken seriously and, along with this, his recognition that colonizing shaped the colonizers – and not just vice versa. (See Sinha, this volume.)

Perhaps even more important for world history, and building on this last point, Bayly demonstrated that one can fruitfully frame the most canonical of "European" events – the French Revolution, the Napoleonic wars and early nationalism, and the reshuffling of class and ethnic alignments leading to both British electoral reform and the "rise of the middle class" – within a world historical context. It was this last element that John Wills highlighted in a review essay in the *American Historical Review* as likely to create "a profoundly de-centering experience for many historians" (1993: 89) and which has led to an ongoing discussion about the pros and cons of reframing the Atlantic "Age of Revolutions" as part of a larger "Global Crisis" (see Armitage and Subrahmanyam 2010).

Meanwhile environmental history – which became prominent through works by William Cronon (1983), Richard White (1991), and others – made a number of important contributions that world history later drew upon. First, environmental history made a compelling case for doing historical work that was not tied to national or state units, since environmental phenomena were so obviously not contained within such units. In addition, through its analyses of ecological webs, food chains, and nutrient cycles (analyses that were taken from the natural sciences), environmental history demonstrated the possibility and payoffs of focusing on connections and flows. Finally, environmental history powerfully challenged the identification of historical scholarship with the study of "documents." (See Simmons, this volume.)

Also crucial for the subsequent emergence of world history was the accelerated growth of historical literatures on geographic areas other than Europe and the United States. The roster of important works in African history produced from the mid-1970s through the early 1990s is particularly impressive, including as it does Alpers (1975), Miller (1976), Cooper (1980), Ehret and Posnansky (1982), Harms (1981), Hiskett (1984), Nurse and Spear (1985), Hall (1987), Pouwels (1987), Feierman (1990), Vansina (1990), and Vaughan (1991). In the aggregate, these and other works established that one could in fact write professionally irreproachable history of times and places that had previously been dismissed as, at once, outside of history and refractory to historical investigation.

The dearth of an earlier historical literature on Africa, and of research methods suited to studying the past of places without institutionalized archives, meant that to establish the field of African history as an ongoing project, its pioneering practitioners found it useful to draw heavily on other disciplines – notably archaeology and social and cultural anthropology, as well as historical linguistics. Importantly, in doing this, Africanists made a wider range of research methods available to other historians.

Some of the Africanist works of these decades took a step towards "world history" by placing parts of Africa within frameworks that transgressed received area studies boundaries. Alpers's placement of East Africa within an Indian Ocean context is particularly notable in this regard. Yet even without this, by contesting the received division of humanity into peoples with and without history, this literature made a profound contribution to "working through" the discipline's institutionalized barriers to world history.

It is only in the last 15 or so years, however, that we find a number of books that presented themselves as world history and which have been taken, as a cluster, as making the case that it is possible for there to be a field of world history – and not just one-off works of singular, if high-status, outliers. R. Bin Wong's *China Transformed* (1997), John McNeill's *Something New under the Sun* (2000), and Kenneth Pomeranz's *The Great Divergence* (2000) all announced themselves as world history and all quickly gained prominence and stature. Not coincidentally, these authors occupied a similar structural position in the profession. All three had published first books that established significant reputations for their authors in their regional fields, and all three worked at solidly reputable but not top-tier universities. Pomeranz's book won the AHA's prize for East Asian history, a strong indication that doing "world history" need not be inconsistent with contributing to an areal field. Moreover, much as Bayly had argued for treating the canonically Western "age of democratic revolutions" as part of a world history produced by forces with many geographic origins, so too Wong, Pomeranz, and others have shifted the debate about the (equally canonically Western) "Industrial Revolution."[10] Within a few years of their publication, these three and other world history books began to appear on graduate (and undergraduate) "theory" reading lists and were recognized as important contributions to the wider discipline by prominent historians who were not identified with the world history movement (Eley 2005: 197; Hobsbawm 2010: 149–150).

A bit later, we began to see junior scholars in well-regarded and even major departments author *first* books that were framed and presented as works of world history: examples include Lauren Benton at New York University (NYU), Jeremy Prestholdt at University of California at San Diego, and Kerry Ward at Rice (Benton 2002; Prestholdt 2008; Ward 2009). Books by senior scholars also signaled and furthered the increased legitimacy of world history in the discipline. This included works by historians who had been early adopters of the world history label (e.g. Richards 2003) and works by others who had not (e.g. Burbank and Cooper 2010). Moreover, several leading departments that had not previously had world history graduate fields created them, in one form or other.[11] That there was now both a significant pool of well-received texts, as well as canonical debates for which one could hold students accountable, made this both easier and more legitimate than it had previously been.

Significant developments also emerged from US history – the largest and often most insular subfield in most departments in the United States. While "internationalizing US history" may seem an obvious move in retrospect – given both the role of empire in shaping the US and the role of the US in shaping globalization – it is only in recent years that this reframing of US history has itself been well established. Tyrrell's *Woman's World/Woman's Empire: The Woman's Christian Temperance Movement in International*

Perspective (1991) was an important early landmark, and among the many works that have followed, Rodgers's *Atlantic Crossings: Social Politics in a Progressive Age* (1998) and Manela's *The Wilsonian Moment: Self-Determination and the International Origins of Anticolonial Nationalism* (2007) are particularly noteworthy. Both come from scholars housed in departments of the highest prestige (Princeton and Harvard, respectively); both have won considerable professional acclaim; and both took stories that had previously been told in largely national terms and demonstrated that actors in multiple and dispersed sites mattered. Similarly salient for world history is work that contests the separation of settler and Native American histories, *contra* the entrenched practices of the US subfield (e.g., White 1991; Rath 2005; Hämäläinen 2011).

Nonetheless, world history's acceptance in the profession remains provisional and incomplete. Many leading departments do not teach it, even at the undergraduate level. At Berkeley, for instance, world history is in International Studies and largely taught by nonladder faculty; at Michigan, just how fully it will be embraced and institutionalized remains an open question. Graduate-level programs remain the exception rather than the rule; the recent National Research Council rankings of history departments did not list world history as a possible subfield. The pressures on graduate students to finish their programs rapidly have increased, which makes dissertations requiring multiple languages and visits to archives in multiple countries particularly difficult. And, of course, the intellectual tensions we have discussed above remain unresolved and deeply important. Even more than with new fields like environmental history and women's history, it seems likely that world history can only win full acceptance in the discipline if the discipline itself changes in significant ways.

Variations Now

What is striking about world history today – looking at both teaching and research – is the great variety of frameworks that are in use, and the continued difficulties of dealing with issues of geographic and temporal coverage, particularly in comprehensive projects.

The most inclusive approach of all – or so it may seem – is "big history," pioneered especially by David Christian. Christian seeks what he calls a "grand unified story" (a phrase modeled on the physicists' "grand unified theory") that places human history within the context of the development of the entire universe from the big bang forward (2011). Only this context, Christian argues, can enable us to break away from studying world history as an enlarged version, or syntheses, of national and/or civilizational histories, and thus allow us to frame questions appropriate to the history of the species – by asking, for instance, what actually distinguishes human history from the ways our "closest relatives," the chimpanzees, live in time (2004: 142). Christian argues that the answer to this question is "collective learning" which, over the long haul, results in human history moving in a clear direction: toward the building of ever more complex structures that depend on ever larger amounts of energy (2003). (See Spier, this volume.)

These are bold formulations, and "big history" courses have gained many adherents, shaking up assumptions of students and teachers alike.[12] Yet too much can be lost in Christian's single "big picture." First, while it is true that everything that is distinctly cultural, and thus distinctly human, about humans involves "collective learning," culture is also more than this. The languages we speak, for instance, are obtained by learning from others, but it misrepresents languages to think of them as "collective learning": languages are not nomenclatures. The more historical version or dimension of this same point is that while some of the movement of humans through time is defined by "collective learning," it is hard to see how this characterization applies to changes in, say, religious beliefs or artistic traditions. Moreover, it seems similarly reductive to think that humans ineluctably create increases in "complexity" that, even more specifically, ineluctably require ever larger amounts of energy. Here Christian seems to be both generalizing about the course of human existence primarily on the basis of the last two centuries, and using entropy, as defined in physics, too literally in thinking about cultural dynamics. Moreover, these mis-steps lead Christian to a profoundly circumscribed view of the contemporary moment and near future: on his view, either humanity will find a way to harness even more energy than it does now, on some sustainable basis, or the "complexity" that defines human history will collapse. That humans might instead, through collective action, respond to the dangers of climate change and exposure to radioactive materials by placing limits on further increases in energy consumption is an alternative future – a *complexity*, we would say – that Christian's theoretical apparatus rules out.

It is also unclear how useful this totalizing approach is for generating a range of distinctive and fruitful research agendas for historians. Charting flows of knowledge and trends in energy use fit within big history, but these would also fit within other versions of world, and even national, histories. Conversely, even though some very traditional topics might be placed in a "big history" frame – the trial of Galileo, for instance, can be seen as a case study of restraints on knowledge diffusion – it is not clear how the "big history" frame would change what one would say about this event. Thus, while provocative, "big history" does not have a strong purchase on research practices in the discipline.

By contrast, what is sometimes called "global history" in the United States has a much narrower temporal and topical agenda.[13] It traces the ongoing intensification of long-distance contacts, focusing particularly on the development of specifically modern institutions: multinational corporations, nongovernmental organizations concerned with specifically global issues (the environment, *human* rights as defined by supranational communities, and so on), and the United Nations. While acknowledging that long-distance contacts are not new, it emphasizes the purportedly unique and self-reinforcing character of these contacts in an era with technologies that allow for transcontinental interaction in something like real time (Mazlish n.d.). (See Bright and Geyer, this volume.) Whatever the merits of such a chronologically foreshortened and unabashedly teleological approach might be, it has relatively little to say to the large majority of historians who study people, places, and periods marked by very different conditions. And such an approach also offers little to those who pursue world history because they want to bring into historical study social orders and persons on the margins, or even outside, of states, markets, and so on.

Some similar issues arise with the attempt to frame world history along the lines suggested by world-systems theory. (See Chase-Dunn and Hall, this volume.) Scholars within this tradition differ over how far back in time they think one can detect a unified "world-system," with some going back far beyond the roughly 500-year timeline offered by Wallerstein (1974; Frank and Gills 1993; Chase-Dunn 1989; Chase-Dunn and Anderson 2005). Some, such as Arrighi, have also moved away from Wallerstein's view that, in modern times, a capitalist world-system centered in Europe became the sole motor of history; Arrighi (2007) has substituted a story built around the interaction of Atlantic and East Asian systems with distinct dynamics, thereby eliminating some of the Eurocentrism and determinism of Wallerstein's framework. Yet even in this more nuanced form, a world history that makes capital accumulation its master process has not proved congenial to large numbers of cultural, political, gender, and other sorts of historians – or to historians of times and places marginal to the rise of global capitalism. Moreover, even many historians who share the focus on economic history have been skeptical of world-systems models, particularly because of the small role accorded in them to technology. That said, many projects influenced by the world-systems tradition have made important contributions to world history. These include prominent works on "commodity chains" – which follow sugar, silk, coffee, cocaine, and other global goods across time and space (Mintz 1985; Gootenberg 1999). (See Levi, this volume.) However, research and teaching that embraces world-systems as an overall or master framework are probably much more common today in sociology than history departments.

A more widely embraced approach (and the subject of several chapters in this volume) has been to define world history around an emphasis on "connections" of diverse kinds – migration, trade, religious evangelism, warfare, crop diffusion, epidemics, technology transfers, and so on – without insisting on the primacy of any one kind of connection. (See Fernández-Armesto and following chapters, this volume.) In *Navigating World History*, for instance, Patrick Manning tells his readers: "I can state the basic nature of the world historical beast with some confidence: it is the story of past connections in the human community" (2003: 15). Jerry Bentley, lead author of the biggest-selling world history textbook, *Traditions and Encounters*, also gives connections priority in defining the field – a view he makes explicit in an essay (2003: 60). And John and William McNeill's very successful "bird's-eye view of human history," *The Human Web* (2003), makes the growth of long-distance connections its major theme. Our sense is that some version of a connection-centered view enjoys broad assent among scholars who say they do "world history": the contents of the *Journal of World History* and *Journal of Global History* certainly suggest as much.

This approach has had several advantages for gaining acceptance as a research field. It gives world history a specialized domain as one field of history among others: making it seem both more feasible and more respectful of the turf of other specialties than if it claimed to be comprehensive. Moreover, the turf it claims as its own is of growing contemporary interest, both for students and for the general public. Likewise, prioritizing connections over comparisons, without theorizing what constitutes a significant connection, privileges relations between geographically separated areas that seem to be objectively "there" rather than created by the scholar. This accommodates the discipline's attachment to empiricism, while avoiding head-on conflict with postmodern critiques of comparison, grand narratives, and generalized social theory. Overall, this focus on connections has generated much important work and, concomitantly, contributed to world history's legitimacy within the discipline. Yet, emphasizing "connections" as the sole distinction of world history risks limiting the project, and thus the benefits, of expanding the discipline's coverage to include the social orders that have most stubbornly been treated as being behind in, or outside of history.

Put simply, the problem with the focus on connections is that it treats the least connected social orders and persons as marginal to world history. The most obviously excluded are those in many small-scale communities, especially on islands or in difficult terrain. But even many people embedded in larger social orders have little personal experience of long-distance connections: many peasants in great agrarian empires, for instance. One important way of redressing this exclusion is to recognize that working with longer time-spans than is typical in historical research allows us to see and study flows that, particularly in earlier eras, proceeded at much slower rates. (See chapters by Yoffee and by Liu, this volume.) Yet even this usefully heightened knowledge of connections misses the intellectual importance of casting as wide a net as possible in order to avoid generalizations and explanations based on a restricted, and thus skewed, set of human histories.

It seems necessary, then, that world history recommit to broad comparison as well as a focus on connections. Granted, nobody would want to return to the mode of comparison in which essentialized "nations" or "civilizations" are treated as cleanly separated monads that could be compared without considering their interconnections or the fuzziness of their boundaries. Contemporary comparative strategies – whether the "encompassing comparisons" of Charles Tilly (1984), the "connected histories" of Sanjay Subramanyam (1997), or the "histoire croisée" of Michael Werner and Bénédicte Zimmermann (2006)[14] – all take into account that interconnections, and the effects of participation in some larger system, are part of what comparisons investigate. (See Adas, this volume.)

Insisting on the pursuit of both comparisons and connections makes it harder to define world history neatly; and it makes it harder to frame world history as a field that a graduate student could master and then, in producing a dissertation, work within and contribute to. In addition, insisting on more and broader comparisons will mean that world history will need to continue to draw on disciplines that have produced knowledge about the places and peoples that history has least attended to. In all of these ways, insisting on both comparison and connections is likely to sustain, rather than resolve, the sense that world history is in some tension with its disciplinary home. But this seems necessary if "world history" is to remain connected to the everyday meaning of *world* and, concomitantly, to the project of teaching at multiple levels of mass schooling; and too, if it is to be maximally effective at "doubting the absoluteness" of the familiar and of the sufficiency of any story in which modernity emerges from a single region of the globe (Boon 1982: 6).

Concluding Reflections

If the difficulties of defining world history have sometimes been an impediment to institutionalization, they also position the field to benefit from a wide range of scholarship and initiatives. It is important here to note that a commitment to inclusiveness does not mean that individual works must take the whole world as a unit of analysis to be world history; if it did, the field would remain very small. And insofar as the field hopes to demonstrate the insufficiency of national and civilizational stories, it makes sense that world history would embrace the growing numbers of studies that constitute regions for study not by claiming that the region shares a social or cultural essence, but by mapping multiple and shifting spaces in which diverse societies interact (Gilroy 1993; Thornton 1998; Chaudhuri 1985; Barendse 2002; Hamashita 2008). At least some studies of diasporic groups, professional and intellectual networks, and so on have also made important contributions to world history (for instance, Ho 2006; Aslanian 2011; Grove 1995; Liebersohn 2001). (See Ward, this volume.)

There are also important efforts to write global histories of processes abstracted from particular societies and, at least potentially, aggregated at the global level. One big project centered at the International Institute for Social History in Amsterdam aims to map the spread of wage labor (and changes in the amounts of other kinds of labor) around the world; a second project looks at migration rates; a third, based at the University of California at Davis, assembles wage and price data from around the globe (van der Linden 2008; Lucassen and Lucassen 2009; Global Price and Income History Group n.d.). Others, mostly focused on very recent times, count other important social phenomena such as institutionalized schooling, access to telecommunications, and so on.[15]

At this stage, such projects are largely concerned with definition, description, and quantification, but their participants hope that explanation will follow. Other projects, often based outside history, have attempted global histories of land use and deforestation, population and energy use, the state of the oceans and atmosphere, and other topics important to historians (Williams 2003; Richards 2003; Ellis 2003).

At the same time, such projects pose difficult questions. Their procedures – often involving large collaborative projects, and/or reliance on nontextual data – are alien to many historians. Even more importantly, deciding to assign some specific historical case to a general category such as "wage labor" often requires giving priority to the investigator's classificatory scheme over that of people within a particular society; thus historians of that society will often see it as distorting that group's lived experiences, as Feierman (1993) has argued in the case of certain African practices which he says have been placed too facilely in the familiar category, "slavery." At the very least, this insight shows the importance of taking such incommensurability into account when pursuing these macrohistorical studies.[16] (See Part III, this volume.)

One particularly important development for world history that began outside of the field is new work that looks at the history of science in a broader, and even global, context. Some of this has been comparative in a relatively conventional way, dealing with scientific traditions that had little or no interaction (or minimizing such interactions) (Huff 2003; Lloyd and Sivin 2002); some has dealt with the impact of Euro-American science and/or technology on other places (Elman 2005; Morris-Suzuki 1994; Curtin 1989; Chakrabarty 2000; and many others). However, there have also been increasing numbers of studies that emphasize the importance of extra-European locales for the growth of "modern science": as sources of stimulating ideas, puzzling and/or decisive data, as places where colonists could try experiments that European property-holders would not have tolerated, and so on. Richard Grove's pioneering work (1995) argues that colonial settings were crucial in all these ways for the origins of European and North American environmental sciences. But a global perspective can be highly illuminating even without all of the elements in Grove's analysis. Simon Schaffer (2009), for instance, has painstakingly traced the origins of all the empirical data in Newton's *Principia Mathematica* and found that a remarkable amount of it came from extra-European locales that had only recently become part of English trade routes. In particular, crucial data for Newton's explanation of tides – a mathematical breakthrough and a major factor in subsequent improvements in the accuracy of astronomical observations generally – came from the Gulf of Tonkin, the coast of Taiwan, and Cape Horn, and was provided by pilots employed by the East India Company, a venture in which Newton had made large investments.

This does not, of course, mean that either European scientific traditions or Newton himself had no independent significance. Yet – in concert with other work we have discussed, in which applying a world history frame unsettled received ideas about the French/democratic Revolution and the Industrial Revolution – it argues strongly that world history can reshape understandings of how the basic lineaments of the modern world came to be. Such ambitions suggest continued tension between world history and various other subfields, but also the possibility that those tensions could improve the questions behind histories pitched at myriad different spatial and temporal scales.

To end with this observation is to signal our judgment that we are observing world history at a moment when it remains emerging and in flux – that is, at a moment when it has not settled into what Thomas Kuhn would have called a normal science (1962). Not being "normal science," its acceptance remains incomplete, and its boundaries vague (which is one reason why we have not attempted a comprehensive survey of the field). But for the same reason, it still has great potential for surprising and unsettling the larger discipline.

Notes

1 Important examples include Jules Michelet, T.B. Macaulay, Heinrich von Treitschke, and F.J. Turner. "Past politics" is taken from the motto Herbert Baxter Adams chose in 1882 for the history seminar room at The Johns Hopkins University: "History is past Politics and Politics present History."
2 Prominent examples include H.G. Wells, Oswald Spengler, and Arnold Toynbee.
3 Courses at Harvard and Columbia were particularly influential models.
4 See Stavrianos (1959) and, in the Northwestern University archives, the L.S. Stavrianos Biographical File and the College of Arts and Sciences Records of Dean Simeon E. Leland, Series 11/1/2, Box 4, Folder 12 and Box 8, Folder 1.
5 Braudel (1981–1984) was published in French from 1967 to 1973 and then available in English in 1973, in an abridged edition. This work did, however, rely on essentialist notions of the "peoples" of different continents, as Feierman has persuasively argued (1993: 174–177).
6 Braudel (1972), published in French in 1949.
7 Said (1978) quickly became, and has remained, iconic of these critiques.
8 Sept. 19, 2010 email from Jerry Bentley, cited with permission.
9 Almost too neatly (given the location of the UC Los Angeles department in the discipline's prestige hierarchy), the participation of UCLA historians falls in between these two poles. The overall pattern is a rich, if painful, illustration of Bourdieu and Passeron (1977).
10 See also Frank 1998; Goldstone 2002; 2009. For a response that straddles this global approach and an older, British-centered approach, see Allen (2009).
11 Columbia, Penn, Brown, Duke, NYU, and Rice; others allow students to construct what is effectively a world history field. (See Streets-Salter, this volume.)
12 As of 2011, the movement of "big history" into secondary education has the benefit of funding from the Gates Foundation; Big History Project, at www.bighistoryproject.com (accessed May 8, 2011).
13 "Global history" has a different meaning outside the United States, as indicated by the contents of the British-based *Journal of Global History*.
14 There is a useful list of other formulations in Gould (2007: 766, nn 9 and 10).
15 See, for instance, Mapping Globalization, at www.princeton.edu/~mapglobe (accessed May 1, 2011).
16 A significant approach to world history that robustly registers such incommensurability, but that has had little uptake by historians to date, can be found in the work of Marshall Sahlins and other cultural anthropologists. Sahlins studies history as the interplay between culture

(understood as contingent categories and values) and experience (Sahlins 1991 is a key statement of his position). This suggests that different human communities will produce trajectories through time that exhibit distinctive forms (as Ortner 1989 emphasizes), with the variety of these forms being much richer than the binary of stasis or progress; it also suggests that colonial encounters involved complex interactions of distinctive cultural orders and meanings (as Robbins 2004 emphasizes).

References

Allen, R. 2009. *The British Industrial Revolution in Global Perspective*. Cambridge: Cambridge University Press.

Alpers, E. 1975. *Ivory and Slaves: Changing Pattern of International Trade in East Central Africa to the Later Nineteenth Century*. Berkeley: University of California Press.

Armitage, D., and S. Subrahmanyam, eds. 2010. *The Age of Revolutions in Global Context*. New York: Palgrave Macmillan.

Arrighi, G. 2007. *Adam Smith in Beijing: Lineages of the Twenty-First Century*. New York: Verso.

Aslanian, S. 2011. *From the Indian Ocean to the Mediterranean: The Global Trade Networks of Armenian Merchants from New Julfa*. Berkeley: University of California Press.

Barendse, R. 2002. *The Arabian Seas: The Indian Ocean World of the Seventeenth Century*. Armonk, NY: M.E. Sharpe.

Bayly, C. 1989. *Imperial Meridian: The British Empire and the World, 1780–1830*. New York: Longman.

Bentley, J. H. 2003. World history and grand narrative. In B. Stuchtey and E. Fuchs, eds, *Writing World History 1800–2000*, pp. 47–65. Oxford: Oxford University Press.

Benton, L. 2002. *Law and Colonial Cultures: Legal Regimes in World History, 1400–1900*. Cambridge: Cambridge University Press.

Boon, J. 1982. *Other Tribes, Other Scribes*. Cambridge: Cambridge University Press.

Bourdieu, P., and J. Passeron. 1977. *Reproduction in Education, Society and Culture*, trans. L. Wacquant. London: Sage.

Braudel, F. 1972. *The Mediterranean and the Mediterranean World in the Age of Philip II*, trans. Siân Reynolds. London: Collins.

Braudel, F. 1981–1984. *Civilization and Capitalism, 15th–18th Century*, trans. Siân Reynolds. New York: Harper & Row.

Burbank, J., and F. Cooper. 2010. *Empires in World History*. Princeton: Princeton University Press.

Chakrabarty, D. 2000. *Provincializing Europe*. Princeton: Princeton University Press.

Chase-Dunn, C. 1989. *Global Formation: Structures of the World-Economy*. Oxford: Blackwell.

Chase-Dunn, C., and E. Anderson. 2005. *The Historical Evolution of World-Systems*. New York: Palgrave Macmillan.

Chaudhuri, K. 1985. *Trade and Civilisation in the Indian Ocean: An Economic History from the Rise of Islam to 1750*. Cambridge: Cambridge University Press.

Christian, D. 2003. World history in context. *Journal of World History* 14 (4): 437–458.

Christian, D. 2004. *Maps of Time: An Introduction to Big History*. Berkeley: University of California Press.

Christian, D. 2011. A single historical continuum. *Cliodynamics* 2 (1) (Mar.): 6–26.

Cooper, F. 1980. *From Slaves to Squatters: Plantation Labor and Agriculture in Zanzibar and Coastal Kenya, 1890–1925*. New Haven: Yale University Press.

Cronon, W. 1983. *Changes in the Land*. New York: Hill and Wang.

Curtin, P. 1989. *Death by Migration: Europe's Encounter with the Tropical World in the Nineteenth Century*. Cambridge: Cambridge University Press.

Ehret, C., and M. Posnansky. 1982. *The Archaeological and Linguistic Reconstruction of African History*. Berkeley: University of California Press.

Eley, G. 2005. *A Crooked Line: From Cultural History to the History of Society.* Ann Arbor: University of Michigan Press.

Ellis, R. 2003. *The Empty Ocean: Plundering the World's Marine Life.* Washington DC: Island Press.

Elman, B. 2005. *On their Own Terms: Science in China, 1550–1900.* Cambridge, MA: Harvard University Press.

Feierman, S. 1990. *Peasant Intellectuals: Anthropology and History in Tanzania.* Madison: University of Wisconsin Press.

Feierman, S. 1993. African histories and the dissolution of world history. In R. Bates, V.Y. Mudimbe, and J. O'Barr, eds, *Africa and the Disciplines.* Chicago: University of Chicago Press.

Frank, A.G. 1998. *ReOrient: Global Economy in the Asian Age.* Berkeley: University of California Press.

Frank, A.G., and B. Gills. 1993. *The World System: Five Hundred Years or Five Thousand?* New York: Routledge.

Gilroy, P. 1993. *The Black Atlantic.* Cambridge, MA: Harvard University Press.

Global Price and Income History Group. n.d. At gpih.ucdavis.edu (accessed May 1, 2011).

Goldstone, J. 2002. Efflorescences and economic growth in world history: Rethinking the "Rise of the West" and the Industrial Revolution. *Journal of World History* 13 (2): 323–389.

Goldstone, J. 2009. *Why Europe? The Rise of the West in World History, 1500–1850.* Boston: McGraw-Hill.

Gootenberg, P. 1999. *Cocaine: Global Histories.* New York: Routledge.

Gould, E. 2007. Entangled histories, entangled worlds: The English-speaking Atlantic as a Spanish periphery. *American Historical Review* 112 (3): 764–786.

Grove, R. 1995. *Green Imperialism.* Cambridge: Cambridge University Press.

Hall, M. 1987. *The Changing Past: Farmers, Kings, and Traders in Southern Africa, 200–1860.* Cape Town: D. Philip.

Hämäläinen, P. 2011. Retrieving a continent: North American grand narrative after the localist turn. MS.

Hamashita, T. 2008. *China, East Asia, and the Global Economy,* ed. L. Grove and M. Selden. New York: Routledge.

Harms, R.W. 1981. *River of Wealth, River of Sorrow: The Central Zaire Basin in the Era of the Slave and Ivory Trade, 1500–1891.* New Haven: Yale University Press.

Hiskett, M. 1984. *The Development of Islam in West Africa.* New York: Longman.

Ho, E. 2006. *The Graves of Tarim: Genealogy and Mobility across the Indian Ocean.* Berkeley: University of California Press.

Hobsbawm, E. 2010. World distempers: Interview. *New Left Review* 61: 133–150.

Huff, T. 2003. *The Rise of Early Modern Science: Islam, China, and the West.* Cambridge: Cambridge University Press.

Kuhn, T. 1962. *The Structure of Scientific Revolutions.* Chicago: University of Chicago Press.

Liebersohn, H. 1988. *Aristocratic Encounters: European Travelers and North American Indians.* Cambridge: Cambridge University Press.

Lloyd, G., and N. Sivin. 2002. *The Way and the Word: Science and Medicine in Early China and Greece.* New Haven: Yale University Press.

Lockard, C.A. n.d. The rise of world history scholarship. MS, revised and expanded from chapter in K. Boyd, ed., *Encyclopedia of Historians and Historical Writing,* pp. 130–135. London: Fitzroy Dearborn, 1999.

Lucassen, J., and L. Lucassen. 2009. The mobility transition revisited, 1500–1900: What the case of Europe can offer to global history. *Journal of Global History* 4 (3): 347–377.

Manela, E. 2007. *The Wilsonian Moment : Self-Determination and the International Origins of Anticolonial Nationalism.* Oxford: Oxford University Press.

Manning, P. 2003. *Navigating World History: Historians Create a Global Past.* New York: Palgrave Macmillan.

Mazlish, B. n.d.. The new global history. At www.newglobalhistory.com/docs/mazlich-the-new-global-history.pdf (accessed May 1, 2011).

McNeill, J.R. 2000. *Something New under the Sun: An Environmental History of the Twentieth-Century World*. New York: W.W. Norton.

McNeill, J.R., and W.H. McNeill. 2003. *The Human Web: A Bird's-Eye View of World History*. New York: W.W. Norton.

McNeill, W.H. 1963. *The Rise of the West: A History of the Human Community*. Chicago: University of Chicago Press.

McNeill, W.H. 1976. *Plagues and Peoples*. Garden City, NY: Anchor Press.

Miller, J. 1976. *Kings and Kinsmen: Early Mbundu States in Angola*. Oxford: Clarendon Press.

Mintz, S. 1985. *Sweetness and Power: The Place of Sugar in Modern History*. New York: Viking.

Morris-Suzuki, T. 1994. *The Technological Transformation of Japan: From the Seventeenth to the Twenty-First Century*. Cambridge: Cambridge University Press.

Nurse, D., and T. Spear. 1985. *The Swahili: Reconstructing the History and Language of an African Society, 800–1500*. Philadelphia: University of Pennsylvania Press.

Ortner, S. 1989. *High Religion: A Cultural and Political History of Sherpa Buddhism*. Princeton: Princeton University Press.

Pomeranz, K. 2000. *The Great Divergence: China, Europe, and the Making of the Modern World Economy*. Princeton: Princeton University Press.

Pouwels, R. 1987. *Horn and Crescent: Cultural Change and Traditional Islam on the East African Coast, 800–1900*. Cambridge: Cambridge University Press.

Prestholdt, J. 2008. *Domesticating the World: African Consumerism and the Genealogies of Globalization*. Berkeley: University of California Press.

Rath, C. 2005. *How Early America Sounded*. Ithaca, NY: Cornell University Press.

Richards, J. 2003. *The Unending Frontier: An Environmental History of the Early Modern World*. Berkeley: University of California Press.

Robbins, J. 2004. *Becoming Sinners: Christianity and Moral Torment in a Papua New Guinea Society*. Berkeley: University of California Press.

Rodgers, D. 1998. *Atlantic Crossings: Social Politics in a Progressive Age*. Cambridge, MA: Harvard University Press.

Sahlins, M. 1991. The return of the event, again. In A. Biersack, ed., *Clio in Oceania*. Washington DC: Smithsonian Institution Press.

Said, E.W. 1978. *Orientalism*. New York: Pantheon.

Schaffer, S. 2009. Newton on the beach. *History of Science* 47 (3): 243–276.

Segal, D. 2000. "Western Civ" and the staging of history in American higher education. *American Historical Review* 105 (3): 770–805.

Stavrianos, L.S. 1959. The teaching of world history. *Journal of Modern History* 31 (2): 110–117.

Subrahmanyam, S. 1997. Connected histories: Notes towards a reconfiguration of early modern Eurasia. *Modern Asian Studies* 31 (3): 735–762.

Thornton, J. 1998. *Africa and Africans in the Making of the Atlantic World, 1400–1800*. Cambridge: Cambridge University Press.

Tilly, C. 1984. *Big Structures, Large Processes, Huge Comparisons*. New York: Russell Sage Foundation.

Tyrrell, Ian R. 1991. *Woman's World/Woman's Empire: The Woman's Christian Temperance Movement in International Perspective, 1880–1930*. Chapel Hill: University of North Carolina Press.

van der Linden, M. 2008. *Workers of the World: Essays toward a Global Labor History*. Boston: Brill.

Vansina, J. 1990. *Paths in the Rainforests: Toward a History of Political Tradition in Equatorial Africa*. Madison: University of Wisconsin Press.

Vaughan, M. 1991. *Curing Their Ills: Colonial Power and African Illness*. Cambridge: Polity.

Wallerstein, I. 1974. *Capitalist Agriculture and the Origins of the European World-Economy in the Sixteenth Century*. New York: Academic Press.

Ward, K. 2009. *Networks of Empire: Forced Migration and the Dutch East India Company*. Cambridge: Cambridge University Press.

Werner, Michael, and Bénédicte Zimmermann. 2006. Beyond comparison: Histoire croisée and the challenge of reflexivity. *History and Theory* 45 (1): 30–50.

White, R. 1991. *The Middle Ground: Indians, Empires, and Republics in the Great Lakes Region, 1650–1815*. Cambridge: Cambridge University Press.

Williams, M. 2003. *Deforesting the Earth: From Prehistory to Global Crisis*. Chicago: University of Chicago Press.

Wills, J.E. 1993. Maritime Asia, 1500–1800: The interactive emergence of European dominance. *American Historical Review* 98 (1) (Feb.): 83–105.

Wong, R.B. 1997. *China Transformed: Historical Change and the Limits of European Experience*. Ithaca, NY: Cornell University Press.

CHAPTER TWO

Why and How I Became a World Historian

Dominic Sachsenmaier

First Steps

Writing on the question of why and how I became a world historian comes to me as a rather unusual task. While I feel quite at home with putting my own viewpoints to paper, I have hardly ever written about myself, at least not in any kind of public forum. I must admit that the idea of sharing some aspects of my intellectual and professional development makes me feel somewhat worried about sounding too self-important and pompous. It is maybe for this reason that now even the term "world historian" sounds quite aggrandizing to my ears, and definitely too honorific to befit a person like myself who, after all, can look back at hardly a decade of postdoctoral academic work. When asked about my own field, I usually reply that I work on world history, global history, or transnational history. I use this variety of terms since I believe that their meanings significantly overlap with one another, particularly if we consider how scholars use them today.[1] Yet in no case would I ever come to confer upon myself the title of a "global historian" or a "world historian" – which, however, does not mean that I am not fairly pleased when others identify me as such.

In that sense, my following essay will mainly describe how I became involved with world-historical scholarship and what have become my key interests and agendas in this field. If I look back at my own family background, not much would point to a life between different continents and an interest in world-historical connections. Born and raised in a family with partly French roots in southwestern Germany, my childhood and teenage years were not "global" in any regard. Certainly, like many families, my kin included distant relatives in America, as well as long-deceased paradise birds like the professor of mathematics who was married to an opera singer and translated Chinese works into German as a pastime. But I never met them, and as so often it was hard to tell truth from fiction in our family history. All the relatives and friends I knew personally were European, and – since the Iron Curtain still divided the continent – Western European, for that matter. The same scopes characterized my high school education: there was not a single instant when I was exposed to anything that would remotely resemble "world history." Rather, our instruction was quite literally

A Companion to World History, First Edition. Edited by Douglas Northrop.
© 2012 Blackwell Publishing Ltd. Published 2012 by Blackwell Publishing Ltd.

Eurocentric – except for some homeopathic dosages of the US experience, the rest of the world remained blank in our history curriculum. The same was true for other high school subjects as well, if one disregards a few lessons on the "underdeveloped world" in our geography class.

Within such an environment, it is small wonder that after school, as a rather passionate reader of history books and what I considered to be "world literature," my intellectual horizons reached from Dostoevsky in the east to Steinbeck in the west. Anything else – China, India, sub-Saharan Africa, and many other parts of the world – just seemed too remote to even try to approach them. Nevertheless, in hindsight it may be possible to identify some factors in my early life that may have contributed to my later interest in exploring transnational and global connections. For example, many of the people round me in Germany during the 1970s and 1980s (my childhood and teenage years) professed to be highly critical of German and any other kind of nationalism. My parents, many of my teachers, and other influential figures in my early intellectual development belonged to the so-called generation of "68ers." Named after the student protests during that year, they distanced themselves sharply from their parents, whom they blamed for the atrocities of the Nazi past. Of course, it is a complex question how genuine this declared antinationalism actually was and how much it was embedded in truly transnational visions and political intentions. Still, the dominant climate of opinion in my particular surroundings made it highly unlikely that one would accept and assert the nation as the main frame of one's identities and intellectual interests.

In addition, for anyone with at least a slight interest in history and politics, developments during the late 1980s necessarily heightened the degree of transnational awareness, even perhaps global consciousness. There were, on the one hand, long-term transformations such as the deepening of European integration, which – at least in my memory – were then far more closely tied to the idea of historical reconciliation than is characteristic of the European Union today. There were also the growing peace and environmentalist movements that sought to alert the public to those key issues of global concern. But it was especially the momentous changes around the year of 1989 which seemed to make the world too small for me to be merely interested in Europe. After all, the year not only saw the fall of the Berlin Wall and the collapse of many Communist regimes in Eastern Europe, but also the election of F.W. de Klerk, which marked the beginning of the end of the apartheid system in South Africa, while student movements in China came to a sudden stop on Tiananmen Square. These experiences, as well as the ensuing debates surrounding new concepts such as "globalization," fostered my desire to learn, think, and interact on much larger geographical scales than the environment in which I had lived before. I was then an ambulance driver in Cologne, doing mandatory civil service (in lieu of joining the army), and that was when I started developing thoughts of embarking upon cross-civilizational research.

Nevertheless, I first decided to deepen my understanding of European traditions and so enrolled as an undergraduate student in ancient history, medieval history, and classics at the universities of St Andrews (UK) and Freiburg (Germany). Two years later, I had an opportunity to widen my focus: I received a scholarship to spend one year at the Mandarin Training Center of Shi-Ta University in Taipei/Taiwan. This intensive language program, targeted at students outside of Chinese studies, enabled me to reach a decent proficiency in modern spoken as well as written Chinese within 12 months. Since my scholarship covered private tutorials as well, I was even able to start learning classical Chinese. All this was a good basis from which I could further develop my skills in the Chinese language.

It is hardly an exaggeration to say that this year in Taiwan changed my life. What had been a young man's distant dream about global interactions now evolved into a more palpable set of possibilities. Upon my return to Freiburg University, I decided to change my undergraduate major to early modern/modern history and to add Sinology as a minor to my portfolio. Given my changed base of experience, I grew more conscious of the problems surrounding an educational system in which "history" was treated as largely equivalent to European history, and research on other parts of the world was usually relegated to small so-called "orchid" fields such as Sinology or Japanology. As some of my later professional agendas started taking shape, I became increasingly convinced that, in the future, transcultural and global historical work could prosper only if one worked to change academic structures as well.

In 1996, I was accepted into the Freiburg PhD program, with Wolfgang Reinhard, a historian of early modern Europe and European expansion, as my main supervisor. For my dissertation project I intended to draw on my familiarity with European and Chinese history as well as my language skills in modern and classical Chinese, Latin, German, French, and English. I was particularly attracted to the history of Sino-European cultural relations during the seventeenth century, a time that appeared to me to be far less fully framed by European supremacy than later periods, despite an overall global historical context of colonial expansionism and religious intolerance. More concretely, I became convinced that many aspects of the interaction between Chinese scholars and Jesuit missionaries (who chose to seek an accommodation with Confucian teachings) warranted further investigation.

Searching for an adequate dissertation topic, I followed a lead offered by David Mungello (now at Baylor University) and decided to focus my attention on Zhu Zongyuan, a low-level scholar who spent most of his life (1616–1660) in the Chinese province of Zhejiang and who had never been the subject of a detailed research project. As a member of the local elite, Zhu Zongyuan did not belong to the highest echelons of Chinese Catholicism, on which most previous research had focused. For this reason, I believed that his works provided important additional insights into the complex, multilayered history of Christianity in seventeenth-century China. As a Confucian-educated member of the provincial scholar-official class, Zhu's life and belief system were also rather close to the world of Chinese popular and folk religions. Yet, at the same time, his writings contain learned discussions of such diverse subjects as Confucianism, Buddhism, Christianity, European philosophy, science, and magic. From the beginning of my dissertation work, I was determined to produce more than a conventional intellectual biography of Zhu Zongyuan. I did not want to follow the most obvious methodological route and merely relate his oeuvre to the Christian literature of the Ming-Qing transition period. Rather, I was resolved to situate Zhu's work within the larger, partly transcultural intellectual, social, and political contexts of his time. Such a project, however, required analysis of both European and Chinese source materials.

For my dissertation research I traveled to places in China, France, Belgium, Germany, the Netherlands, and the United States, all enabled by generous support from the German National Academic Foundation. Most notably, I spent two years as a visiting PhD student and teaching fellow at the Harvard-Yenching Institute and one semester at Nanjing University in China. Parts of my dissertation and the resulting book (Sachsenmaier 2001) apply a combination of semantic and historical perspectives to investigate Zhu's presentation of various European religious contents and philosophical concepts to the Chinese reader.[2] The book also explores different sociopolitical constraints that shaped the translation of Christianity from one cultural context into another. Further, I examine how Zhu Zongyuan approached the question of cultural belonging and political allegiance in his philosophical musings. For instance, I discuss Zhu's unique and rather extensive writings in response to Chinese criticism of Christianity based on its foreign origins. I first situate these writings against a background of changing modes of regional and global consciousness within elite circles during the early seventeenth century. For example, the European colonization of the Philippines and Taiwan was a key factor underpinning growing concerns that Christianity and its missionaries were the precursors to a larger threat. In his writings, Zhu Zongyuan addressed such concerns by applying different lines of reasoning. Most notably, he sought to deconstruct the notion of a territorially bounded China by arguing that the inner core of the "Middle Kingdom" needed to be understood in civilizational, ethical, and universal terms. Given such daring statements, I also closely investigated Zhu's efforts to maneuver between the political expectations of the Chinese state and the Catholic Church – expectations which could become acutely problematic, even at the level of symbolic performances such as rites and liturgy.

Indubitably the scope of my book did not attempt a truly global perspective in a strict sense of that term, since it focused almost exclusively on a segment of specifically Sino-European interactions. Nevertheless, I see research projects such as this one as ascribable to "world history," since otherwise this field would have to be monopolized by large-scale narratives and global interpretations. Books for a general audience and textbooks of this kind, which necessarily rely on secondary literature, are an important aspect of world-historical writing. Yet I believe that at the same time the field needs to cultivate a diverse research landscape, particularly if it wants to further gain recognition from other historians. To do so, however, detailed world-historical research also needs to be based on primary source work and hence be grounded in specific areas of regional and linguistic expertise. (See Weinstein, this volume.) In that manner, world-historical research projects cannot possibly cover all parts of the world equally; rather, they need to focus on specific case studies that focus most closely on certain countries or world regions. According to this definition, world-historical research would be differentiated from other historical work by using several case studies to bring different parts of the world into an overarching perspective.

In this sense I see world history, global history, and transnational history as a research trend aiming at critical reconsideration of those conceptions of space that have been foundational to modern academic historiography. After all, much university-based historiography has been largely structured around regional or national expertise. In this division, the histories of China and India, for example, have been primarily studied as separate from the European experience, just as there has been a big gap between academic expertise on Latin America and sub-Saharan Africa. Now, with Oceanic history and many other branches of world history, case studies focus on their linkages and comparisons, areas that previous scholarship had long relegated to the background or margins. Certainly, the segmentation of territoriality in the historians' workshop varied between different fields of inquiry. For example, for an expert of the European Middle Ages, explorations of intra-European interactions were certainly not revolutionary, yet until recently investigations of historical dynamics between Islam and Christendom were hardly present in the field. By contrast, the action radius of many historians working on the modern period tended to be framed by the concept of the nation-state (Wigen and Lewis 1997; and Berger 2007). I regard it as an important development in current sociologies of knowledge that a growing number of historians are trained in different parts of the world, which will allow them to transgress institutional and linguistic boundaries in their future work.

A Growing Identification with Global History and World History

The question of whether my dissertation could be categorized as "world history" or under any other field designation was virtually absent from my mind while I was a graduate student. I was interested in my topic and only recognized that it was somewhat unusual to work on both Chinese and European materials. Actually at that time a number of Europeanists and Sinologists cautioned me that I might not be able to find a job if my research agenda fell between the cracks of regionally defined fields such as European history and Chinese studies. Yet I decided not to let fears about the future and overly strategic professional thinking narrow my intellectual pursuits. As my later appointments at the University of California, Santa Barbara, and Duke University showed, academia did in fact start becoming more interested in young scholars like myself who crossed such boundaries in their own work. In this sense I was fortunate that my somewhat nonchalant attitude towards my own field happened to intersect with an opening process at history departments, at least in the United States and some other countries.

It was only after I had received my PhD that I became increasingly drawn to world and global history as dynamic existing fields of scholarship that I needed to further understand and explore. After a brief venture into business consulting, I returned to the academic world in late 2001, first as a postdoctoral research scholar at Harvard University. In the Boston area a wide range of scholars such as Bruce Mazlish, Akira Iriye, Charles Maier, William Kirby, Peter Perdue, and Patrick Manning were working on transnational and global historical issues. The vibrant intellectual atmosphere in Cambridge, Massachusetts, with its lecture series, conferences, research seminars, and graduate student circles greatly encouraged, and funneled, my interest in the potentials and future of world history. In addition, the presence of scholars from all over the world helped me gain further insight into the commonalities and differences in university-based historiography all over the world. I grew increasingly convinced that it would take a new generation of detailed scholarship and theoretical debate to rethink many earlier assumptions about the past of nations, civilizations, and continents.

During these years, I became actively involved in scholarly communities in the United States, Germany, and East Asia through publications, talks, and conference projects. I observed that in these three parts of the world, there was a growing interest in global and transnational historiography, which faced similar constraints imposed by the disciplinary cultures and institutional parameters of existing historiography. More importantly, I came to realize that while many scholars developed an interest in exploring history from transnational or even global angles, their approaches were far from identical. Obviously, there was not one homogeneous "global history" emerging, and in spite of all the global academic entanglements, the research landscapes of the field in China, Germany, and the United States remained shaped by a variety of local factors.

Seen against this background, it struck me as particularly unfortunate that many theoretical and practical contributions to global history written in English tended to ignore related scholarly trends in other languages. Problems such as the fact that the particular patterns and rhythms of global historical research in many corners of the world differed from each other were plainly undertheorized. I became convinced that, particularly in Western academia, the growing importance of global and world history was a movement more characterized by an increasing interest in scholarship *about* the world rather than scholarship *in* the world. This struck me as problematic, since a research field exploring new zones of interaction should necessarily reflect upon the nature and implications of plural perspectives emanating from different parts of the world. At the same time, I was aware of the fact that local differences between historiographical practices could certainly not be explained by exoticizing non-Western approaches. I grew convinced that any attempt to map out the global landscapes of the field would necessitate the consideration of factors ranging from global commonalities in modern academic historiography to hierarchies in the international sociologies of knowledge.

All these questions pointed to a massive theoretical endeavor, a book-length study offering detailed, historically informed and politically aware assessments of scholarship in different parts of the world. I began working systematically on this project during my time as an assistant professor at the University of California, Santa Barbara. In the following years, my research took me to various locations in the United States, Germany, Austria, Switzerland, Mainland China, Hong Kong, and Taiwan. Various fellowships and research grants provided me with the time and resources to read studies from a wide variety of fields, collect materials, talk to scholars in many different countries and world regions, and to think carefully through some conceptual problems related to this topic.

This research resulted in my book *Global Perspectives on Global History: Paths in China, Germany, and the United States*, which was published in 2011. This work combines globally oriented chapters with separate case studies on global historical scholarship in the United States, Germany, and Mainland China. It proceeds from the idea that it would be intellectually incomplete to reflect upon the directions of global or world history without considering the current professional, social, and political landscapes of academic historiography. Within this framework, I emphasize that, ironically, the worldwide spread of national historiography during the modern age needs to be understood as a necessary precondition of today's border-crossing trends. Subsequently I delineate some key features of historiography as a global professional field that is characterized not only by similarities, but also by significant hierarchies between world regions and languages. It is not my goal, however, to demonstrate that the inequalities in the international academic system have remained frozen in time. Particularly during the past few decades, many developments such as new forms of intellectual migration and political decolonization have contributed to increasingly critical attitudes to both Eurocentric and nation-centered visions of the past, and they have done so in many different parts of the world.

My three case studies on the United States, Germany, and China not only discuss developments within university-based historiography but also, I hope, shed light on relevant forces in other academic fields, as well as in society at large. Looking for more general characteristics of what I define as a global and transnational trend in historical scholarship, I investigate a broad spectrum of research fields ranging from economic history to cultural history and from gender studies to colonial history. For all three countries, I also illuminate the significant epistemological and structural changes within established fields such as international history. As I show, it would be wrong to assume that the centers of gravity of global historical research have converged around the same questions and paradigms all over the world. My case studies demonstrate that while everywhere world-historical scholarship is fragmented into various subfields and engaged in intense transnational networks of exchanges, its conceptual fabrics and underlying forms of historical consciousness remain seasoned by national or regional contingencies. These range from institutional settings and the availability of funding to political influences, modes of memory, the nature of publicly discussed themes, and the overall intellectual climate. In that sense historiography never developed into an academic discipline that would – analogous to the natural sciences – come to work with a largely identical spectrum of methodological schools all over the world.

Yet this book is not only intended as a theoretical elaboration of the basic idea that local factors will continue to influence global historical visions, despite methodological diversity and intensifying international academic connections. I seek to make another intervention: to assert that it hardly suffices to think globally about history while leaving intact the national divisions and hierarchies that continue to characterize the international environments of historiography. If we take seriously the quest for multiple perspectives and global concerns, it is necessary to expand our current forms of transnational academic collaboration while also developing new forms of cooperation. In other words, I am convinced that conceptual changes are insufficient for world history if they are not accompanied by structural transformations. In fact, some aspects of the now-global institution of "universities" as they emerged during the nineteenth and twentieth centuries may be ill-equipped to support some of the intellectual tasks that global and transnational historians choose to take on. After all, from the nineteenth century, universities were first and foremost local communities and firmly grounded within specific nation-states. In the past, academic structures have provided rather limited opportunities to engage in sustained academic dialogues across different world regions – which has limited the outcome of international collaborative efforts to the occasional collective volume, published as simple collections of standalone, separate papers. In the future, global historical theorizing will depend on intensifying forms of transnational scholarly cooperation, which reach beyond the collaboration patterns that have thus far constituted the bulk of transnational projects (cf. Wallerstein *et al.* 1996: esp. 94–105).

Engaged in a Field

Since I am convinced that, to paraphrase the Ming dynasty thinker Wang Yangming, thinking and acting need to be one in today's world-historical scholarship, I have sought to contribute my share to building these new structures of transregional cooperation. This has involved fundraising, grant proposal writing and, most of all, many intercontinental flights as well as sleepless nights in hotels around the world. From an early point in my academic career, I initiated or co-organized dialogue forums between Chinese and European historians on themes ranging from "multiple modernities" to the global and local dimensions of social history.[3] Furthermore, I have been eager to experiment with rather uncommon modes of scholarly interaction. For example, together with Sebastian Conrad (Berlin), I chaired a transatlantic research network on "Conceptions of World Order (ca. 1880–1935): Global Historical Perspectives," which gave nine young historians with different regional expertise the opportunity to collaborate closely with each other in a series of five international workshops and conferences. This project was funded by the German National Research Foundation from 2003 to 2007, and the network jointly published a book whose chapters, we hope, are more closely attuned to each other than in a standard edited volume (Conrad and Sachsenmaier 2007).

More recently, I initiated with Sven Beckert a joint Harvard/Duke project entitled "Global History, Globally". The inaugural conference, which took place in 2008, brought together leading practitioners of global and world history from every continent. The group has since met two more times, and it is our objective to develop this project into a more sustained global forum to debate worldwide dynamics in the field of historiography and, what is more, to discuss current global issues from historically informed perspectives. Furthermore, we are planning several publications, starting with an edited volume, in which historians based in very different parts of the world discuss important challenges, themes, and problems surrounding the future of world-historical scholarship. We hope that our project will be able to make at least some contributions to widening the geographical parameters of the academic communities in which world-historical research and related debates take place. Other projects such as the Korea-based "Flying University"[4] or the "Global Economic History Network"[5] have been working in a similar direction. (See Lim, this volume.)

At the level of education, I have tried to make a modest contribution to the small but growing landscapes of academic exchange networks and transnational graduate programs in world history and adjacent fields. For instance, together with Matthias Middell (Leipzig) I established a faculty and graduate student exchange program in global studies/global history between the University of California, Santa Barbara, and later Duke, and *Erasmus Mundus*, a European consortium of universities consisting of the London School of Economics, the University of Vienna, the University of Wroclaw, and the University of Leipzig. (See Naumann, this volume.)

I find it extremely gratifying to witness students getting their first intercontinental experiences through such programs. It reminds me very much of my own experience as an undergraduate student in Taiwan, which as noted above, set my life onto a completely different path. I am convinced that world history, as a globally concerned endeavor, needs to train a future generation of scholars who have lived in different parts of the world and acquired transregional skills, competences, and bases of personal experience. I believe this will greatly strengthen the social carriers on which future transnational collaboration and dialogues in the field need to depend. In the long run, I hope that a group of intellectually open, globally aware, yet locally sensitive young scholars may act as a counterforce to some of the polarizing political as well as cultural tendencies of our time. As I personally find it difficult to believe in abstract visions of an alternative world order, I place my own hopes and energies on the growth of individuals who have the educational background and personal horizon to respond to the continued presence of stereotypes and the hardening of identities, which we currently observe in many parts of the world. And if any field of study can serve as an academic contributor to such ideals, it should be world history – more specifically a particular form of world history, which has left behind its legacy of national biases and Eurocentrism.

This may not be a fully elaborated utopian vision, but I hope it differentiates me from the cynical critic who fails to act according to his or her own values. Of course, I am not naive enough to trust that increasing levels of intellectual migration necessarily translate into higher levels of tolerance and mutual understanding. I am well aware that the growth of academic connections also opens up significant problem zones.[6] There is the possibility that new hierarchies of knowledge or competing forms of cultural imperialism will replicate the patterns of marginalization and exclusion in new forms and at different levels. While some areas, for example privileged universities in the West and East Asia, may strengthen their ties, others may become even less connected. Despite the growing modes of transnational cooperation, in other words, world historians are still far from producing a scholarly community which closes opportunity gaps between the peripheries and the centers of our global academic landscapes. There is also the danger that many countries and regions will be primarily represented by a thin veneer of globally connected scholars who are too detached from their academic home communities to serve as bridge builders between local and translocal debates surrounding the study of world history.

Certainly we cannot naively regard the deepening of transnational academic contacts as a panacea. Yet without expanding current forms of transnational academic cooperation and developing new ones, the field will not be able to adequately consider such crucial problems as, for instance, the inequalities in the worldwide sociologies of knowledge. Concerned thinkers have problematized these from a variety of angles and through a wide spectrum of terminological options.[7] If we take the quest for multiperspectivity and professional self-reflexivity seriously, it hardly suffices to raise challenging questions regarding historiography while leaving intact the national divisions and transnational hierarchies that have long discouraged a spirit of shared concern between different academic systems.

Recently I have spent much of my time working on wide-ranging theoretical issues and institution-building, and yet I have not lost my joy of "doing history" in the most immediate and most rewarding sense. While I have spent long hours on high-flying theoretical issues, I have never abandoned primary source work, even temporarily. Most importantly, I have cultivated global historical perspectives on political cultures in China and Central Europe in the aftermath of the Great War as an additional research field, which may eventually evolve into my third major book project. Based on archival work conducted over the past few years, I intend to investigate themes such as the transnationalization of ideologies, and cross-cultural critiques of progressivism, during the early 1920s. In this context, I am particularly interested in tracing the global intellectual milieus, transnational political movements, and interconnected camps of opinion that connected many seemingly separate groups of Chinese and European thinkers. This is particularly striking in the case of so-called "conservative" or traditionalist circles, who, as I intend to show, were in many cases sharing ideas across national and even continental boundaries.

My teaching does not always revolve around my ideas regarding the future possibilities and necessities of world history. It does, however, in graduate teaching, for example in a seminar I taught under the heading "Readings in Global Connections". (See Getz, this volume.) In this course I put an emphasis on theories of global history in China and the West, and I encouraged my students to take both sets of perspectives equally into consideration when forming their own judgments. I gave this course a transnational structure by entangling it with parallel graduate seminars at Fudan University (China) and the University of Leipzig (Germany). For three weeks, students from all three locations engaged in online chat-room discussions about such controversial topics as imperialism or the notion of multiple modernities. These debates proved reliably lively and stimulating, and have encouraged me to continue with experiments of this kind. In the future, I may tie this specific class format to one of the transnational graduate exchange programs that I am building, which means that after a semester of online communication, students will see each other in person during a summer workshop or a comparable meeting.

In all courses that I have taught thus far, I adhere to my understanding of world history as a field that needs to remain grounded on regional expertise and an appreciation of local contingencies. I habitually teach on world-historical themes by transcending national or continental boundaries rather than assembling them along a global storyline. Given my own expertise, in many courses I draw particular connections between Western and Chinese experiences, mainly by applying global historical perspectives to both world regions. This leads me to problematize holistic images of "China," "Europe," or the "West." For example, I taught an undergraduate seminar on "Images of the West in Chinese Politics, Literature, and the Media," which covers the time period from the seventeenth century to the present. Furthermore, I have designed lecture courses on topics such as "Modern Political Thought in China and Europe," which covers the period from the eighteenth century to the present. In this class I emphasize that – due to the importance of interactions and multilateral influences – much local history is impossible to understand without relating it to other parts of the world and global dynamics in general. For example, I discuss the transmission channels for the global spread of nationalism as a modern ideology while at the same time outlining the differences between its various Chinese and European manifestations.

Teaching on entanglements between Europe and China helps students break through the multifarious unquestioned assumptions and stereotypes about "self" and "other" that still characterize many worldviews. By shedding light on shared or entangled historical transformations that were experienced by parts of Europe and China, for example, I try to avoid exoticizing the latter while still allowing sensitivity to historical difference. As in my own research, so in my teaching, a major goal is to demonstrate that in the present age we can only convincingly address questions of cultural diversity if we include the dense networks of exchanges and other global dynamics into the picture. I see it as one of my principal pedagogical tasks to help students discover the complexity behind our visions and interpretations of the past. Above all, this requires teaching young students to question and relativize their own standpoints and develop more nuanced images of other societies. I am convinced that such skills are of crucial importance for the future. And here, I think, world history and world historians have much to give.

Notes

1 For a longer discussion of possible definitions of these and other field designations, see Sachsenmaier (2011: ch. 2).
2 An updated and extended English version of Sachsenmaier (2001) will be published by the University of Hawai'i Press.
3 One resulting publication was Sachsenmaier et al. (2002).
4 At http://www.h-net.org/announce/show.cgi?ID=174403 (accessed Mar. 2012).
5 The network involved cooperation between several universities and organized various international conferences as well as other scholarly exchanges. See http://www2.lse.ac.uk/economicHistory/Research/GEHN/Home.aspx (accessed Mar. 2012).
6 For academic networks in general, see Charle et al. (2004).
7 Important concepts are, for example, the ideas of a world-systemic geoculture, "coloniality of power," "subalterneity," "hegemony," or, more plainly, "the theft of history." See, for example, Mignolo (2000); Chakrabarty (2000); Mudimb (1988); and Goody (2007).

References

Berger, Stefan, ed. 2007. *Writing the Nation: A Global Perspective.* Basingstoke: Palgrave Macmillan.

Chakrabarty, Dipesh. 2000. *Provincializing Europe: Postcolonial Thought and Historical Difference.* Princeton: Princeton University Press.

Charle, Christoph, Jürgen Schriewer, and Peter Wagner, eds. 2004. *Transnational Intellectual Networks: Forms of Academic Knowledge and the Search for Cultural Identities.* New York: Campus.

Conrad, Sebastian, and Dominic Sachsenmaier, eds. 2007. *Competing Visions of World Order: Global Moments and Movements, 1880s–1930s.* New York: Palgrave Macmillan.

Goody, Jack. 2007. *The Theft of History.* Cambridge: Cambridge University Press.

Mignolo, Walter D. 2000. *Global Histories/Local Designs: Coloniality, Subaltern Knowledges, and Border Thinking.* Princeton: Princeton University Press.

Mudimbe, Valentin Y. 1988. *The Invention of Africa: Gnosis, Philosophy, and the Order of Knowledge.* Bloomington: Indiana University Press.

Sachsenmaier, Dominic. 2001. *Die Aufnahme europäischer Inhalte in die chinesische Kultur durch Zhu Zongyuan (ca. 1616–1660)* [Integration of Western elements into Chinese culture by Zhu Zongyuan (ca.1616–1660)]. Nettetal: Steyler.

Sachsenmaier, Dominic. 2011. *Global Perspectives on Global History: Theories and Approaches in a Connected World.* Cambridge: Cambridge University Press.

Sachsenmaier, Dominic, Jens Riedel, and Shmuel N. Eisenstadt, eds. 2002. *Reflections on Multiple Modernities: European, Chinese, and Other Approaches.* Leiden: Brill.

Wallerstein, Immanuel, *et al.* 1996. *Open the Social Sciences: Report of the Gulbenkian Commission on the Restructuring of the Social Sciences.* Stanford: Stanford University Press.

Wigen, Karen E., and Martin W. Lewis. 1997. *The Myth of Continents: A Critique of Metageography.* Berkeley: University of California Press.

Researching the world:
techniques and methods

CHAPTER THREE

Becoming a World Historian

The State of Graduate Training in World History and Placement in the Academic World

HEATHER STREETS-SALTER

Evaluating the state of graduate education in World History is not a straightforward affair. It is complicated enough to put accurate data together about the number of programs offering graduate training in world history, about program structure, and about student placement. Interpreting this often incomplete data is more complicated still. For example, what do we make of the surge in the number of graduate programs claiming to offer training in World History since the turn of the twenty-first century? What impact, if any, are these rapidly proliferating programs having on the academic world? Moreover, are most institutions that offer programs in World History producing students with a genuine research interest in world-historical questions, or should that even be their goal? Finally, should we be pleased by the percentage of graduate students trained in world history that find permanent employment, or should we be concerned that they have (thus far) not generally found employment at top-tier universities?

While I do not attempt to offer definitive answers to all of these questions in what follows, I do hope to provide enough data to spark an informed discussion about them. When I agreed to write this chapter, I thought – as director of one of the few programs to offer World History as a primary PhD field in the United States – that I knew a good deal about the state of graduate training in the field. I soon discovered, however, that this was an overstatement. I knew about the existence and structure of some programs, but not all; I had a general sense of placement rates, but it was not backed by hard data. I was only somewhat comforted to find that I was not alone in my fragmentary knowledge. In fact, there is no central clearing house (yet!) for data and information about graduate training in this rapidly growing field. Thus, even after much discussion with colleagues, research into programs, and correspondence, this chapter must still represent only a starting point in exploring the state of graduate training in World History. It seems to me vital to the future of the field that we continue the discussion and improve the data on which the discussion is based.

This first section of this chapter begins with an evaluation of the existing data for programs that offer training in World History in the United States, Canada and, to a

A Companion to World History, First Edition. Edited by Douglas Northrop.
© 2012 Blackwell Publishing Ltd. Published 2012 by Blackwell Publishing Ltd.

lesser extent, Europe.[1] I then offer a reassessment of the number and kinds of programs offering training in the field, based on my own research. Once I have presented these revised data, I offer some observations about how we might assess the impact of these programs. The second section of the chapter discusses the structure of World History programs in order to evaluate whether or not these programs generally have the same goals for producing scholars in the field. The third and final section will discuss the admittedly incomplete data on placement for students completing advanced degrees with training in world history, and what these preliminary impressions might mean for the field in the future.

Graduate Programs in World History

Of course it would be difficult to evaluate the state of graduate training in World History without first knowing exactly how many programs offer such training, and at what level. Yet compiling this information is not as simple as it might at first seem. First, there are problems and disagreements about the label "World History," which means that some programs that call themselves "World" do not offer what I would call a recognizable program, whereas some programs that self-consciously resist calling themselves "World" do in fact offer training that most world historians would immediately recognize as world-historical in nature.[2] Second, existing resources that maintain lists of World History graduate programs have not been able to keep up with the number of new programs that have developed in the last five years, and thus are out of date. Third, even the programs that are listed by these resources are about 50 percent inaccurate.

Let's begin with labels. What exactly *is* a World History program? Although there are no simple answers to this question, I realized I would have to create some criteria by which to assess both the many programs that claim to offer training in World History, and even some that do not. Thus, for the purposes of this chapter I determined that it is not enough to claim to offer training in World History without any specific coursework, designated faculty mentors, or a formally designated field. At the same time, I determined that some – but not all – programs that call their fields "Global" or "Global and Comparative" do indeed offer training that operates from a similar historiographical base to World History, and encourages students to engage with recognizably world-historical research questions. In order to "qualify" here as an institution that offers graduate training in World History, then, programs must meet the following criteria: (1) they must offer core courses in World (sometimes called Global) History, at least one of which familiarizes students with a broadly similar historiography of the field and the various methodological approaches that have characterized it; (2) they must have faculty that are specifically designated as mentors for the field; (3) they must offer the field as a structured, formal option. I did not split hairs about how *many* faculty needed to be available as mentors in the field, mainly because very few existing programs to date have more than one or two faculty members who are active in the field. In the future, however, it may be necessary to determine the viability of World History programs based on the strength of the faculty cohort with training in the field.

Guided by the above criteria, I did not count the many and growing numbers of programs that offer fields in transnational history, comparative empires, Atlantic World, or international history, as the historiographical base and/or theoretical concerns of these fields tend to be distinct from – though not unrelated to – world history. To be sure, this means that many programs currently offering exciting opportunities for graduate students to stretch the boundaries of traditional fields and to explore transnational, cross-cultural, or thematic projects have been left out. Yet if we are to realistically assess the state of graduate education in World History, it seems important not to inflate the numbers by creating criteria so all-encompassing that the category "World History" loses specific meaning.

Once I decided on criteria, I was better able to evaluate the existing resources that list programs offering graduate training in World or Global History. The most important (and accessible) resources for these purposes are maintained by the American Historical Association (AHA), which lists graduate programs by specialization, and the World History Association (WHA), which lists institutions that offer graduate programs in World History.[3] As of August 2010, the AHA listed 52 programs offering training in world history, while the WHA listed 26. Yet on closer inspection – including an examination of departmental websites and, when such websites were unclear, direct correspondence – it turned out that over half of the departments listed by the AHA do not in fact offer graduate training in world or global history (and many do not even claim to). Likewise, of the 26 programs listed by the WHA, 12 do not (or do not yet) offer such training, nor do some of them make that claim. In fact, some department chairs and graduate coordinators were quite surprised to learn that their programs were listed in this way. Moreover, several programs that do offer graduate training in world history were not on either list, mostly because they were created after the lists were originally compiled.

Once I realized the problems of taking the AHA and WHA lists at face value, I decided to start from scratch. My goal was to locate all programs that offer graduate training in world history at the PhD level (major or minor fields), the MA level (major or minor fields), and the DA (Doctor of Arts) level in the United States, Canada and, as far as possible, Europe.[4] My method began with a close investigation of all institutions listed on the AHA and WHA website as specializing in world or, in the case of the AHA, world and global history. This included going to each departmental website and looking at field offerings, coursework, and supporting faculty. In cases where the existence of a field in world history was unclear, I corresponded directly with graduate studies directors or department chairs.[5] I also relied upon the help and suggestions of colleagues in the field, as well as my own experience.[6] Finally, I sent a request via H-World, the world history discussion forum on H-Net, for information from those who either finished their degrees with world history training, or who currently run programs in the field. The request yielded 31 responses, many from representatives of programs I did not previously know about.[7]

The results were as follows: 6 institutions currently offer World History, by name, as a primary or major PhD field in the United States and Canada.[8] A further 7 institutions offer primary PhD fields in Global, Comparative Global, or Global and International Programs that appear to offer core coursework and structures that are closely related to World History.[9] In addition to major fields in World or Global history, 22 institutions offer a minor, secondary, or complementary field in World History, while a further 5 offer minor fields in Global or Comparative World History.[10] At the MA level, 20 institutions offer programs with concentrations or majors in World History, and 11 offer World History as a minor or secondary concentration.[11] Three further institutions offer MAs in Global History.[12] Finally, two institutions offer a Doctor of Arts (geared primarily to teaching) in World History, and three offer certificates in teaching World History.[13] (See Bain, this volume.) In addition to these existing programs, during the summer of

2010 Pat Manning organized, for the first time, an intensive two-week workshop for graduate students interested in pursuing world-historical research questions at the University of Pittsburgh.[14] Moreover, several institutions are in the process of developing graduate programs in World History, including Queen's University (Canada), the University of Maryland, the University of Michigan, and the University of Pittsburgh.

What are we to make of this data, and what can it tell us about the state of graduate training in World History? At its most basic, it tells us that 58 discrete institutions offer graduate training in World (or similar Global) History at the MA or PhD levels in the United States, Canada, and Europe.[15] Yet the meaning of these numbers is not entirely clear. On the one hand, 58 seems an astonishingly high number given that just over a decade ago only a handful of institutions in the world offered such programs.[16] Indeed, this means that nearly 50 World History programs have been created just since the turn of the twenty-first century, and we know that more are in the pipeline. This rapid growth in itself suggests that World History is increasingly regarded as a useful and valuable addition to graduate programs in a period when all historical fields seem to be moving toward transnational, globalized, and comparative perspectives.[17]

On the other hand, perhaps it is too early to celebrate World History's momentous breakthrough into the mainstream. While 58 programs represents a huge growth over the number of programs that existed prior to the twenty-first century, we must keep the numbers in perspective: after all, there are 341 postsecondary institutions in the United States that offer MA or PhD degrees, and another 30 in Canada.[18] More importantly, we need to look beyond institutional numbers and ask how many students, PhD or MA, have graduated from – or are currently enrolled in – such programs. When we do this, the picture is more sobering. For example, of the six institutions that offer World History as a major field, four have produced fewer than two graduates.[19] Northeastern University leads the way in the production of World History PhDs, with 20 awarded since the creation of the program in 1994.[20] Washington State University, whose program was created in 2003, has produced 5 PhDs so far, while Columbia University's International and Global History program has produced 1 graduate with a world historical dissertation. In total, and allowing for a small margin of error, this means that fewer than 30 students have completed programs with World History as a major field in the last 16 years. Even taking into account that there are at least 30 more PhD candidates poised to obtain their degrees in the next five years,[21] the numbers of PhDs trained with World History as a major field will remain relatively small for some time to come. This number seems especially small if we note that between 750 and 1,000 new History PhDs are awarded each year in all fields.

While certainly the number of PhDs who have graduated – and who will graduate – with a minor, complementary, or second field in World History is considerably higher than those who completed a primary field, the data here are much more fragmentary and incomplete. What data there are suggest that, since 1985 (when the field was first created at the University of Hawai'i-Manoa), at least 200 students have completed a second field in World History.[22] Moreover, at least 100 students now appear to be in the process of completing a field.[23] Again, while these numbers are truly significant for the field of World History, they make up only a tiny fraction of the more than 18,000 PhDs that have been awarded in all fields since 1985. Numbers for MA programs are even more fragmentary, especially for those who have already completed their degrees. What slim data I do have suggests that there are at least 100 students currently enrolled with major or minor concentrations in World History at the MA level.[24]

None of this is to say that proponents of graduate training in World History do not have much to be pleased about. Clearly, the data presented here suggest that more programs are offering such training to more students than ever before, and that both programs and numbers of students are likely to rise in the future. And as more students complete their training in World History, it is likely that at least some will establish World History programs in their own institutions, thus creating the opportunity for training new generations of world historians. Indeed, this phenomenon has already begun.[25] Finally, it may well be a sign of the increasing value placed on World History in the historical discipline that a number of Tier I universities have recently established programs of their own. While the majority of World History graduate programs have been developed at Tier II or Tier III universities, fully one-quarter of the institutions that offer graduate training in World History are now housed in top-tier universities.[26] Taken together, these developments indicate that world historians have carved out a clear and growing space in graduate training, and that World History programs will continue to proliferate in the immediate future.

The Structure of Graduate Programs in World History

Now that we have a better (though admittedly still incomplete) sense of the number and types of World History graduate programs that currently exist, it makes sense to explore what kind of "products" these programs intend to produce. In other words, do these programs primarily focus on World History as a teaching field, or are they expressly geared toward encouraging students to design research projects with world-historical questions in mind? This is an important distinction, because the first type of program broadens students' knowledge base for the purpose of teaching, but does not necessarily impact the shape and direction of their research. The second type of program focuses explicitly on producing scholars who engage with the concerns of the field at the level of research. Both types of programs are important, and of course they are not mutually exclusive, but the existence of these two emphases means that not all students who complete graduate training in World History identify with the field in the same way, or employ its methodologies and approaches in their own historical research.

At the PhD level, it is this focus on research that most sharply distinguishes those programs that offer World History as a primary field from those that offer it as a secondary field. In the former, the structure of the program tends to be geared toward generating world-historical research questions – and a world-historical dissertation – from the very start. For example, students who complete a major field in World History at Washington State University (my former institution) begin the program by taking a World History Theory and Methods course in their first semester.[27] In the same semester, the new cohort of students would work closely with me and the other three key faculty involved in the program not only to develop their areas of research interest, but to develop them in the context of world-historical approaches and methodologies. By the end of the first year, students – with the active guidance of a faculty member in World History – have mapped out a plan of coursework, directed readings, and qualifying exam fields that are expressly focused around their research interests. Before moving on to the dissertation stage, students must pass three qualifying exams. First, students complete a general, overarching exam field in World History, which is largely oriented to historiography and method and is linked to an extensive, uniform reading list that covers both formative works in the field (e.g., Oswald Spengler, William McNeill, Immanuel Wallerstein) and the wide corpus of monographs and articles that have been written in the field since the 1980s.[28] Second, students complete an equally extensive field in a regional (not national) area of expertise under the direction of a specialist – three of whom also have training in World History. Third, students complete a complementary field in either an additional region or a thematic area of study such as imperialism, war and peace, or gender history. Finally, students must also complete a minor, nonexamination field (which likewise may be defined geographically or thematically) as well as the language training necessary for their research. The graduate guidelines at Washington State stipulate that students pass these qualifying exams before defending a dissertation prospectus which explains the historical question a doctoral thesis will address, along with its theoretical framework, methodology, and historiographical contribution. Students in the World History program, however, are strongly encouraged both to make a preliminary research trip and to begin constructing the prospectus prior to taking the qualifying exams.[29] Ultimately, then, the program is geared toward producing scholars whose "first language" is associated with the questions, approaches, and methodologies of World History, but who are also deeply trained in at least one regional area of expertise.[30]

In contrast, many of the programs that offer minor, secondary, or complementary PhD fields in World History are geared toward producing scholars with a more narrowly defined teaching competency in World History.[31] World History is often – rightly, as it turns out – viewed as a strategic field for the job market, since so many colleges and universities (at least in the United States) now require new hires to teach the undergraduate survey as a basic service course. These programs, although their emphasis differs from those that offer World History as a major field, nevertheless are usually structured around a similar set of core courses, a selection of regionally focused classes, and some form of qualifying examination – many of which are however focused on teaching rather than research. At Louisiana State University, for example, students preparing a minor field in World History take a seminar in Comparative History, three courses from regions offered in East Asian, Latin American, South Asian, Middle Eastern, or African history, and a general examination based on the student's creation of a syllabus in either early or modern World History. Some institutions offer a modified version of the secondary field in the form of a "certificate" in teaching World History. At the University of Pennsylvania, for example, graduate students must take a course in the historiography of World History, two courses in comparative history, and two courses in regions outside the student's own regional area of concentration, but they do not complete a culminating examination.[32]

Whether as a minor field or as a teaching certificate, graduate programs that offer World History expressly for the purpose of teaching tend, de facto, to teach World History as an "additional" language rather than as a "first" language. What this means is that there need be no *necessary* connection between students' own research interests and the questions and concerns of World History as a research field. Partly this is because students completing a minor or second field in World History do not always have to complete coursework in the field as they are *beginning* their graduate study. As a result, the ability of world-historical questions to shape the direction of student research can be diminished if research projects are already well underway by the time students encounter the field.

That said, not all programs that offer second fields in World History appear geared primarily toward teaching. Some, indeed, are clearly intended to shape research interests, at least in addition to assisting with teaching competence. At the University of

Wisconsin-Madison, for example, students completing a field in Comparative World History take a seminar in Comparative World History, and then two further courses on a culture area or thematic topic outside their own area of specialization. Once the coursework is completed, students write a research paper "that demonstrates the student's competence to handle historical materials comparatively and to work in more than one cultural or geographical area of specialization."[33] Finally, students must take an oral exam based on the research paper.

MA programs in World History are generally geared toward one of two tracks: either they aim to produce students who wish to proceed to graduate study at the PhD level, or they aim to produce highly qualified teachers of World History at the secondary or community college level. In the first type of program, which includes the program at Washington State, MA students take the same core courses as PhD students in the field, and produce a Master's thesis designed around a manageable but nevertheless world-historical research question. In programs designed for future secondary or community college teachers, some emphasize the MA thesis, while others offer a choice between a thesis and exams. In the MA program at New York University, the thesis is required even though the program is geared toward educators. In this program, students take three core courses in World History, three courses in a major field, and two courses in a minor field.[34] Students then go on to write a MA thesis on thematic or comparative questions.[35] In other World History MA programs, such as one offered at Sacramento State University, students are given the choice of passing their major and minor fields either with written and oral exams or by writing a formal MA thesis.[36]

When we look at all the various types of graduate programs in World History, it seems clear that these programs intend to produce a variety of different "products," from researchers in the field to university teachers at the PhD level, and from future PhD students to secondary teachers at the MA level. How important are these different emphases? On the one hand, I believe that the division between training World History researchers and World History teachers is significant for the development of the research field, since there is no guarantee that students who complete a teaching field will incorporate world-historical questions into their research. On the other hand, the broad commitment of all of these programs to core coursework in the historiography of the field, as well as to coursework in comparative or transregional training, gives them recognizable identities as World History programs notwithstanding their different emphases. Furthermore, even when programs are designed primarily for teaching purposes, exposure to world-historical questions and methodologies has the potential to influence student research and future scholarship, while programs focused primarily on research also assist students in becoming better teachers of the undergraduate survey. Finally, as will become clear in the next section, placement data suggests that there is a need for both types of programs in order to meet the demands of the current job market.

Placement: Where Do Graduate Students Trained in World History Find Jobs?

It would be impossible to evaluate the state of graduate training in World History without attention to placement. Are students trained as world historians finding jobs, and are they finding jobs – at least in part – as world historians? Once again, the available data to answer this question are fragmentary, especially from institutions that offer second PhD fields or MAs in World History. Fortunately, there are specific data on most of the students who finished their PhDs with a primary field in World History since the mid-1990s. In addition, I have collected anecdotal evidence from a variety of recent PhDs and MAs with training in World History via a poll on H-World. From this data, three things seem reasonably clear: First, the relatively small number of students who have finished degrees with a primary field in World History have, for the most part, successfully found tenure-track employment in academia. Second, these same students have generally not found employment at top-tier research universities. Third, anecdotal evidence seems to indicate that hiring institutions have thus far found world history training most attractive for its usefulness in teaching rather than because of its research potential.

Of the 28 students who have completed PhDs with World History as a primary field in the United States, 20 have found permanent employment in higher education. Of these 20, 18 are at four-year colleges or universities in tenure-track positions, one is in a secure position at a community college, and one is in a secure position at an institution that does not grant tenure.[37] All but two of the 18 found employment in the United States.[38] Of the remaining eight, two chose to remain in secondary education, one is an instructor in a community college, one is in a visiting professor position at a Tier I university, one has postponed searching for a job because of military service, one entered the law profession, and two are unemployed. Overall, then, students who completed PhDs with a major field in World History (at universities in the United States) between 1997 and 2009 enjoyed a 71.4 percent placement rate.

At first glance, such a high placement rate seems truly stellar. We know that placement rates for History PhDs in all fields between 1990 and 2004 were dismal, hovering at around 42 percent for graduates from top-tier programs, and at about 30 percent for graduates from second-tier programs (Townsend 2005: fig. 5). And while the outlook for job placement improved between 2005 and 2007 (when placement rates jumped to near 50 percent), it turned sour again in 2008 as the US economy contracted. In 2008–2009, indeed, the number of jobs in all fields of History declined by 23.8 percent (Townsend 2010). In contrast to such numbers, then, the placement rate of World History PhDs seems exceptional.

Yet it would be premature to read too much into these numbers. Indeed, the number of PhDs who have completed primary fields in World History is so small that it is difficult to gauge whether such extraordinary placement rates will continue. According to *Perspectives*, the year 1999–2000 saw a spike in job advertisements for specialists in World/Non-West, up from an average of 27 or 28 per year from 1995 to 1999 to over 40 per year from 1999 to 2004 (Townsend 2005: table 1).[39] By 2006–2007, about 7 percent of jobs advertised in *Perspectives* were categorized as World/Transnational. However, along with the downturn in the US economy, jobs in this category fell by 20 percent in 2009 (Townsend 2010). So while the excellent placement rate of PhD graduates from programs offering primary fields in World History is encouraging, it is likely still too early to tell if this trend will continue, or how much the current economic decline will negatively impact the employment prospects of World History PhDs.

In any case, placement rates do not tell the whole story. It is also important to realistically assess the types of institutions where World History PhDs find employment. Thus far, all but two World History PhDs have found employment at second- or third-tier institutions rather than at top-tier research universities.[40] Moreover, with the exception of a few who were hired at small, private colleges, most World History PhDs were hired at public state colleges and universities. The reasons for this are not completely clear, although anecdotal evidence suggests that, for one, top-tier institutions remain less likely to offer jobs explicitly advertised as World History than lower-tier institutions. Second, since most of the World History PhDs produced so far have completed their degrees at second-tier universities, it is likely that they are less competitive for jobs at top-tier universities than their peers from elite institutions. In fact, anecdotal evidence from World History PhDs who have been on the job market indicates that in some cases, search committees advertising for world historians have opted to hire candidates from elite universities with no training in the field rather than candidates from second-tier universities with formal training. Third, and perhaps most importantly, state colleges and universities have been at the forefront of the move toward teaching World History at the undergraduate level. Thus, it is likely that PhDs with significant training in World History are particularly attractive to search committees at such institutions.

Indeed, the demand for experienced and qualified teachers to teach undergraduate World History courses seems to have been a significant factor in the hiring process for many of the PhDs who completed training in World History as either a major or minor field. For example, of the 55 PhDs who completed a second field in World History from the University of California, Irvine, roughly half reported that they were hired for jobs at least partially to teach World History.[41] Moreover, anecdotal evidence from stories by both Washington State University graduates and by those I polled on H-World suggests that the ability to teach World History in addition to a regional specialization was a critical factor in successful job placement.[42]

Although I am tempted to bemoan the fact that World History teaching seems to be valued so much more than world-historical research on the current job market, in the end I believe there is significant cause for optimism about the future of the field. First, provisional evidence indicates that those graduate programs offering World History as a secondary or teaching field are serving an important function, and that demand for such programs is likely to increase in the future. Second, given the successful placement of PhDs who completed a primary field in World History thus far, it seems hopeful that the attractiveness of these students to search committees at public, state institutions will continue to allow new scholars in the field to secure places in academia from which to conduct their scholarship. Third, as more top-tier institutions develop World History programs of their own in the future, it seems likely that the range of institutions willing to hire PhDs trained with a primary field in World History will increase as well.

Conclusions

In 2010, there were more programs offering graduate training in World History than had ever existed before, and this trend looks as though it will continue in the future. Although these programs exist to serve a variety of purposes, all seem to share a commitment to introducing students to the historiography of the field, and to encouraging them to think broadly about connections, comparative analysis, and transregional themes. Provisional data on placement rates seem to bear out the need for these programs at all levels, and many graduates insist that their ability to find work in a tight job market was enhanced, not diminished, by their formal training in the field. While the numbers of students who have completed graduate training in World History is still proportionately small, and while most graduates from these programs have so far not found employment in top-tier universities, nevertheless recent trends in both the numbers and types of institutions that have developed programs in the field indicate the increasing viability of World History training at the graduate level.

Notes

1   My focus on the United States and Canada is based on the amount of data available for North American programs, which at present greatly outweighs the amount in Europe and the rest of the world. The European programs described here include only those programs for which I was able to obtain data – others may exist. (See Naumann, this volume.) Several universities in China and Japan have begun to train students in world-historical programs, but as yet I do not have enough data to evaluate the nature of these programs. (See the chapters by Lim and by Zhang, this volume.) Australia is not included here because the one program that offered training to MA students in World History – at Macquarie University – is no longer active.

2   Part of the reason some programs have been reluctant to take on the label "World History" is that some scholars – particularly at Tier I universities – have mistakenly conflated the study of World History with teaching the World History survey. Take, for example, the primary field in Global History at the University of North Carolina (UNC) at Chapel Hill. The creators of the program explicitly state what they see as the differences between "global" and "world" history by quoting from John Headley, who wrote in 1998: "While maintaining a planetary reference, global history studies how diverse peoples and cultures contend with a specific issue such as disease, labor – free and unfree – population growth, interoceanic trade, the family, the missions of world religions, technology's advance and the environment's degradation. Problem or issue-oriented, global history in the elegance of its selectivity and of its analysis differs from world history, which is essentially narrative and descriptive in its aggregative effort to deal as a compendium with the totality of the past. Thus global history intrinsically has the capacity to examine common issues which heretofore have been treated in the parochial context of a region or nation or at best comparatively and are now examined in a more interconnected and comprehensive perspective." The program rationale, however, goes on to cite affinities with the World History Association, and with particular practitioners like Jerry Bentley, whom they call a global rather than a world historian. Yet as anyone familiar with the field of World History must realize, the conception of World History as narrative and descriptive described above flies in the face of most world-historical scholarship written in the last quarter-century. Indeed, world historians make the same claims about their field as Headley claims for Global History, and the UNC program looks very similar to several other World History programs in all but name. It was for these and similar reasons that I included some Global History programs along with other World History programs. Quote and comments from "The Global History PhD: Introduction," University of North Carolina at Chapel Hill, formerly at http://history.unc.edu/fields/globalhistory/globalhistoryphd.

3   For the AHA, see http://www.historians.org/projects/cge/PhD/Specializations.cfm; for the WHA, which includes Canadian programs, see http://www.thewha.org/graduate_programs.php (both accessed Mar. 2012). H-World also maintains a link to such programs, but it is completely out of date.

4   My focus on North America stems from both the current dominance of North American programs in this field and the lack of data from European programs compared to those in North America. Moreover, my research indicates that existing European programs tend to focus more narrowly on the phenomenon of globalization or on "Europe in the world," in contrast to North American programs that are more broadly defined. That said, a number of graduate students in these European programs – listed below in notes 11 and 12 – are working on exciting world-historical projects.

5   Most replied, but some did not, a fact that detracts from the accuracy of the data.

6   Pat Manning, formerly director of the World History program at Northeastern and now at the University of Pittsburgh, and Laura Mitchell at the University of California at Irvine were particularly helpful.

7   For H-World, see http://www.h-net.org/~world/ (accessed Mar. 2012). While I have tried to be as comprehensive as possible, there are bound to be a few inadvertent exclusions and a few mistaken inclusions. Directors of programs in either category should feel free to contact me via email at h.streetssalter@neu.edu.

8   These include, alphabetically, George Mason University; Northeastern University; University of California (UC), Irvine; University of Cincinnati; University of Manitoba; and Washington State University.

9   These include Columbia University's program in International and Global History (although not all students in this program elect to do world-historical topics); State University of New York (SUNY) at Albany's program in International, Comparative, and Global History; SUNY Binghamton's program in Global History; the University of North Carolina's program in Global History; the University of Rochester's program in Global History; and the University of Wisconsin, Milwaukee's concentration in Global History.

10 These include Emory University; George Mason University; Georgia State University; Indiana University; Louisiana State University; Ohio State University; Rice University; Southern Methodist University; Temple University; University of Arizona; UC Irvine; University of California, Riverside; UC Santa Barbara; UC Santa Cruz; University of Hawai'i at Manoa; University of Houston; University of Iowa; University of Manitoba; University of North Dakota; University of Texas, El Paso; Washington State University; and Wayne State University. The institutions offering minor or secondary fields in Global or Comparative World History include Rutgers University (Global and Comparative); SUNY Albany (International Comparative, and Global); University of Massachusetts (Global and Comparative); University of Wisconsin-Madison (Comparative World); and York University (Comparative, Global, and Transnational History).

11 The institutions that offer a concentration or major in the World History MA include Birkbeck College (University of London); Bowling Green State University (MAT only); Brunel University (London); the joint program between Columbia University and London School of Economics in International and World History; Florida Gulf Coast University; Fordham University; Monmouth University; New York University; North Georgia State College and University; Northeastern University; Northern Illinois University; Portland State University; Rochester University; Sacramento State University; San Francisco State University; SUNY Brockport; University of Cincinnati; University of Manitoba; University of Wisconsin-Madison (terminal MA in Comparative World); and Washington State University. The institutions that offer a minor concentration or field at the MA level include Arkansas Tech University; Bowling Green State University; Emory University; Florida Gulf Coast University; Georgia State University; Northern Illinois University; Portland State University; Sacramento State University; University of Houston; University of Utah; and Washington State University.

12 These are Erasmus University, Rotterdam (MA in Global History and International Relations); Jacobs University, Bremen (MA in Global History); and University of Heidelberg (MA in Global History).

13 The Doctor of Arts programs are at St Johns University and the University of North Dakota (Ancient World only). SUNY Binghamton, the University of Pennsylvania, and Wayne State University offer teaching certificates in World History.

14 Of the ten participants, seven were from US institutions, two were from European institutions (in the Netherlands and Italy), and one was from a Japanese institution. Faculty participants, in addition to Pat Manning, were Adam McKeown and Heather Streets-Salter.

15   Although some institutions offer both major and minor fields, they were only counted once. It should be clear that these numbers, although carefully researched, are not definitive, and some institutions may have been inadvertently excluded or mistakenly included.

16   The Comparative World History program at the University of Wisconsin, Madison, established by Philip Curtin, was the first graduate program to be developed in World History in 1959. Ohio State University, the University of Hawai'i, the University of Minnesota, the University of Manitoba, and UC Santa Cruz all developed World History Fields in the 1980s, while Northeastern, Georgia State University, UC Riverside, and UC Irvine developed fields in the 1990s. For a longer evaluation of programs developed prior to 2000, see Manning (2003: 327–330).

17   This trend was noted by AHA Committee on Graduate Education (2003).

18   Numbers are from American Historical Association (2010).

19   These four are UC Irvine (2), George Mason University (0), University of Manitoba (0), and University of Cincinnati (numbers are unknown, but the program only accepts one or two students each year in any field).

20   The first PhD from this program was awarded in 1997.

21   This estimate is based only on data from Northeastern University, Washington State University, Columbia University, and University of North Carolina at Chapel Hill, and therefore may need to be revised upward slightly.

22   These numbers are conservative, as they include data from only University of Hawai'i at Manoa, UC Irvine, Washington State University, and Rice University. They do not include the people who took part in the Comparative World History program under Philip Curtin.

23   Again, these data are conservative, since they include data from only Georgia State University, UC Riverside, and Washington State University.

24   This number must be taken as a stab in the dark, as it relies only on data from Georgia State University, Portland State University, North Georgia College and State University, Arkansas Tech University, Florida Gulf Coast University, and Birkbeck College.

25   Examples include Maryanne Rhett and Amitava Chowdhury, both PhDs in World History from Washington State University. Rhett has established an MA program at Monmouth University, and Chowdhury is in the process of setting up a program at the PhD level at Queen's University, Canada.

26   Top-tier criterion is based on membership in the Association of American Universities. Universities in this tier with programs in World or Global/Comparative History include Columbia University; Emory University; Indiana University; New York University; Ohio State University; Rice University; Stanford University; University of Arizona; UC Irvine; UC Santa Barbara; University of Iowa; University of Michigan; University of North Carolina; University of Pennsylvania; University of Rochester; University of Wisconsin-Madison.

27   The program at Washington State relied heavily on the model of Northeastern's program while it was under the direction of Pat Manning.

28   See Appendix below. Note this is not a definitive list, but merely one example of an effort to define current readings.

29   This part of the program structure is based on Pat Manning's experience at Northeastern, where students completed the prospectus prior to taking the qualifying exams (2003: 335). At Washington State, World History students have access to a scholarship fund for research, language training, and conference travel designated for their use only. This allows most of them to make preliminary research trips, usually overseas.

30   At Washington State University, "regions" are defined by existing faculty areas of expertise.

31   Programs that emphasize World History as a teaching field include, among others, those at University of Indiana, UC Riverside, University of Arizona, Louisiana State University, and Rutgers University. UC Riverside also offers its students the option to take either Early or Modern World History as a complementary (research) exam field. Currently, however, no students are exploring this option, while approximately 60 are taking it as a teaching field.

32 See the guidelines for the University of Pennsylvania's Certificate in World History at http://www.history.upenn.edu/grad/world-certificate.shtml (accessed Mar. 2012).
33 From "Graduate handbook, 2010–2011," p. 24.
34 Either the major or the minor field must be outside Europe or North America.
35 New York University Department of History, Masters Program, World History, see http://history.fas.nyu.edu/object/history.gradprog.worldhistory (accessed Mar. 2012).
36 Standard History MA Program Requirements, Sacramento State University, see http://www.csus.edu/hist/graduate/standardguidelines.html (accessed Mar. 2012).
37 Data come from Columbia University, Northeastern University, UC Irvine, and Washington State University, provided by Adam McKeown, Laura Mitchell, Pat Manning, and Heather Streets-Salter, respectively.
38 Of those employed outside the US, one is in Canada, and one is in Singapore.
39 The report does not specify what is meant by World/Non-West, so it is unknown how many of these positions would be recognized as World History jobs by those in the field.
40 Two exceptions include one World History PhD who is a visiting professor at Brandeis University, and one who is an assistant professor at Queen's University in Canada.
41 Data provided by Laura Mitchell, UC Irvine.
42 There were 20 responses to the poll I conducted on H-World. Of course, it is possible that those most likely to respond were also those most likely to believe that their World History credentials made them more marketable.

References

AHA Committee on Graduate Education. 2003. The education of historians for the 21st century. *Perspectives on History: The News Magazine of the American Historical Association* (*Oct.*). At http://www.historians.org/perspectives/issues/2003/0310/0310not1.cfm (accessed Mar. 2012).

American Historical Association. 2010. *Directory of History Departments, Historical Organizations, and Historians, 36th edition, 2010–2011*. Washington DC: American Historical Association.

Manning, Patrick. 2003. *Navigating World History: Historians Create a Global Past*. New York: Palgrave Macmillan.

Townsend, Robert B. 2005. Job market report 2004. *Perspectives on History: The News Magazine of the American Historical Association* (*Jan.*). At http://www.historians.org/perspectives/issues/2005/0501/0501new1.cfm (accessed Mar. 2012).

Townsend, Robert B. 2010. A grim year on the academic job market for historians. *Perspectives on History: The News Magazine of the American Historical Association* (*Jan.*). At http://www.historians.org/Perspectives/issues/2010/1001/1001new1.cfm (accessed Mar. 2012).

Appendix: World History Comprehensive Exam Reading List (Washington State University, 2010)

Abu-Lughod, Janet. *Before European Hegemony: The World System AD 1250–1350*. New York: Oxford University Press, 1989.

Adas, Michael. *Machines as the Measure of Men: Science, Technology, and Ideologies of Western Dominance*. Ithaca, NY: Cornell University Press, 1990.

Adas, Michael, and American Historical Association. *Islamic and European Expansion : The Forging of a Global Order*. Philadelphia: Temple University Press, 1993.

Adas, Michael, and American Historical Association. *Agricultural and Pastoral Societies in Ancient and Classical History*. Philadelphia: Temple University Press, 2001.

Adelman, Jeremy. Latin American and world histories: Old and new approaches to the pluribus and the unum. *Hispanic American Historical Review* 84 (3) (July 30, 2004): 399–409.

Archer, Christon. *World History of Warfare*. Lincoln: University of Nebraska Press, 2002.

Armitage, David. *The British Atlantic World, 1500–1800*. New York: Palgrave Macmillan, 2002.

Aydin, Cemil. *The Politics of Anti-Westernism in Asia: Visions of World Order in Pan-Islamic and Pan-Asian Thought*. New York: Columbia University Press, 2007.

Banner, Stuart. *Possessing the Pacific: Land, Settlers, and Indigenous People from Australia to Alaska*. Cambridge, MA: Harvard University Press, 2007.

Bayly, C.A. *The Birth of the Modern World: 1780–1914*. Oxford: Blackwell, 2003.

Beckwith, Christopher. *Empires of the Silk Road: A History of Central Eurasia from the Bronze Age to the Present*. Princeton: Princeton University Press, 2009.

Benjamin, Thomas. *The Atlantic World: Europeans, Africans, Indians and Their Shared History, 1400–1900*. New York: Cambridge University Press, 2009.

Benjamin, Thomas, Timothy Hall, and David Rutherford. *The Atlantic World in the Age of Empire*. Belmont, CA: Wadsworth, 2000.

Bentley, Jerry H. *Old World Encounters: Cross-Cultural Contacts and Exchanges in Pre-Modern Times*. New York: Oxford University Press, 1993.

Bentley, Jerry. Cross-cultural interaction and periodization in world history. *American Historical Review* 101 (3) (June 1996): 749–770.

Benton, Lauren. *Law and Colonial Cultures: Legal Regimes in World History, 1400–1900*. Cambridge: Cambridge University Press, 2002.

Benton, Lauren. No longer odd region out: Repositioning Latin America in world history. *Hispanic American Historical Review* 84 (3) (July 30, 2004): 423–430.

Besse, Susan. Placing Latin America in modern world history textbooks. *Hispanic American Historical Review* 84 (3) (July 30, 2004): 411–422.

Bessis, Sophie. *Western Supremacy: Triumph of an Idea?* London: Zed Books, 2003.

Black, Antony. *The West and Islam: Religion and Political Thought in World History*. New York: Oxford University Press, 2008.

Blaut, James. *The Colonizer's Model of the World: Geographical Diffusionism and Eurocentric History*. New York: Guilford Press, 1993.

Brooks, Pamela. *Boycotts, Buses, and Passes: Black Women's Resistance in the US and South Africa*. Amherst, MA: University of Massachusetts Press, 2008.

Buck, David. Was it pluck or luck that made the West grow rich? Review of *ReORIENT: Global Economy in the Asian Age* (Frank); *The Wealth and Poverty of Nations: Why Some Are So Rich and Some So Poor* (Landes); *China Transformed* (R. Bin Wong). *Journal of World History* 10 (2) (1999): 413.

Bulliet, Richard. *The Camel and the Wheel*. New York: Columbia University Press, 1990.

Bulliet, Richard. *Hunters, Herders and Hamburgers: The Past and Future of Human–Animal Relationships*. New York: Columbia University Press, 2007.

Burbank, Jane, and Frederick Cooper. *Empires in World History: Power and the Politics of Difference*. Princeton: Princeton University Press, 2010.

Chanda, Nayan. *Bound Together: How Traders, Preachers, Adventurers, and Warriors Shaped Globalization*. New Haven: Yale University Press, 2007.

Chaudhuri, K. *Trade and Civilisation in the Indian Ocean: An Economic History from the Rise of Islam to 1750*. New York: Cambridge University Press, 1985.

Chaudhuri, K. *Asia before Europe: Economy and Civilisation of the Indian Ocean from the Rise of Islam to 1750*. New York: Cambridge University Press, 1990.

Cheng, Yinghong. *Creating the "New Man": From Enlightenment Ideals to Socialist Realities*. Honolulu: University of Hawai'i Press, 2008.

Christian, David. *Maps of Time: An Introduction to Big History*. Berkeley: University of California Press, 2004.

Clarence-Smith, W. *The Global Coffee Economy in Africa, Asia and Latin America, 1500–1989*. New York: Cambridge University Press, 2003.

Clark, Gregory. *A Farewell to Alms: A Brief Economic History of the World*. Princeton: Princeton University Press, 2008.

Clark, Robert. *The Global Imperative: An Interpretive History of the Spread of Humankind*. Boulder: Westview, 1997.

Connelly, Matthew. *Fatal Misconception: The Struggle to Control World Population*. Cambridge, MA: Belknap, 2008.

Conrad, Sebastian, and Dominic Sachsenmaier. *Competing Visions of World Order: Global Moments and Movements, 1880s–1930s*. Annotated edn. New York: Palgrave Macmillan, 2007.

Crosby, Alfred. *Columbian Exchange: Biological and Cultural Consequences of 1492*. Westport, CT: Greenwood, 1972.

Crosby, Alfred. *Ecological Imperialism: The Biological Expansion of Europe, 900–1900*. New York: Cambridge University Press, 1986.

Crosby, Alfred. *Children of the Sun: A History of Humanity's Unappeasable Appetite for Energy*. New York: W.W. Norton, 2006.

Crossley, Pamela. *What Is Global History?* Cambridge: Polity, 2008.

Curtin, Philip. *Cross-Cultural Trade in World History*. New York: Cambridge University Press, 1984.

Curtin, Philip. *The World and the West: The European Challenge and the Overseas Response in the Age of Empire*. New York: Cambridge University Press, 2000.

Diamond, Jared. *Guns, Germs, and Steel: The Fates of Human Societies*. New York: W.W. Norton, 1998.

Diamond, Jared. *Collapse: How Societies Choose to Fail or Succeed*. New York: Viking, 2005.

Dikötter, Frank. *Cultures of Confinement: A History of the Prison in Africa, Asia and Latin America*. Ithaca, NY: Cornell University Press, 2007.

Dunn, Ross. *The Adventures of Ibn Battuta, a Muslim Traveler of the Fourteenth Century*. Berkeley: University of California Press, 1986.

Dunn, Ross, ed. *The New World History: A Teacher's Companion*. Boston: Bedford/St Martin's, 2000.

Falola, Toyin. *The Atlantic world, 1450–2000*. Bloomington: Indiana University Press, 2008.

Fernández-Armesto, Felipe. *Civilizations: Culture, Ambition, and the Transformation of Nature*. New York: Free Press, 2001.

Findley, Carter. *The Turks in World History*. New York: Oxford University Press, 2005.

Frank, Andre G. *ReORIENT: Global Economy in the Asian Age*. Berkeley: University of California Press, 2004.

Fritze, Ronald. *New Worlds: The Great Voyages of Discovery, 1400–1600*. Stroud, UK: Sutton, 2002.

Getz, Trevor, and Heather Streets-Salter. *Modern Imperialism and Colonialism: A Global Perspective*. Harlow: Pearson Longman, 2010.

Geyer, Michael. World history in a global age. *American Historical Review* 100 (4) (1995): 1034.

Gilbert, Erik, and Jonathan T. Reynolds. *Africa in World History: From Prehistory to the Present*. 2nd edn. Upper Saddle River NJ: Prentice Hall, 2008.

Goody, Jack. *The Theft of History*. New York: Cambridge University Press, 2006.

Gran, Peter. *The Rise of the Rich: A New View of Modern World History*. Syracuse, NY: Syracuse University Press, 2009.

Gunn, Geoffrey. *First Globalization: The Eurasian Exchange, 1500 to 1800*. Lanham: Rowman & Littlefield, 2003.

Headley, John. *The Europeanization of the World: On the Origins of Human Rights and Democracy*. Princeton: Princeton University Press, 2007.

Headrick, Daniel. *The Tentacles of Progress : Technology Transfer in the Age of Imperialism, 1850–1940*. New York: Oxford University Press, 1988.

Headrick, Daniel. *Power over Peoples: Technology, Environments, and Western Imperialism*. Princeton: Princeton University Press, 2010.

Hobson, John. *The Eastern Origins of Western Civilization*. New York: Cambridge University Press, 2004.

Hodgson, Marshall. *The Venture of Islam: Conscience and History in a World Civilization*. Chicago: University of Chicago Press, 1977.

Hodgson, Marshall. *Rethinking World History: Essays on Europe, Islam, and World History*. New York: Cambridge University Press, 1993.

Hopkins, A. *Globalization in World History*. New York: W.W. Norton, 2002.

Hopkins, A. *Global History: Interactions between the Universal and the Local*. New York: Palgrave Macmillan, 2006.

Hornborg, Alf. *Rethinking Environmental History: World-System History and Global Environmental Change*. Lanham: AltaMira Press, 2007.

Hughes, J. *The Face of the Earth: Environment and World History*. Armonk NY: M.E. Sharpe, 2000.

Hughes, Sarah. *Women in World History*. Armonk, NY: M.E. Sharpe, 1995.

Hughes-Warrington, Marnie, ed. *Palgrave Advances in World Histories*. New York: Palgrave Macmillan, 2005.

Hugill, Peter. *World Trade since 1431: Geography, Technology, and Capitalism*. Baltimore: Johns Hopkins University Press, 1993.

Jones, E. *The European Miracle: Environments, Economies, and Geopolitics in the History of Europe and Asia*. New York: Cambridge University Press, 1981.

Jones, E. *Coming Full Circle : An Economic History of the Pacific Rim*. Boulder: Westview, 1993.

Kicza, John. *Resilient Cultures: America's Native Peoples Confront European Colonizaton, 1500–1800*. Upper Saddle River, NJ: Prentice Hall, 2003.

Kiernan, Ben. *Blood and Soil: A World History of Genocide and Extermination from Sparta to Darfur*. New Haven: Yale University Press, 2007.

Landes, David. *The Wealth and Poverty of Nations: Why Some Are So Rich and Some So Poor*. New York: W.W. Norton, 1998.

Langer, Erick. Introduction: Placing Latin America in world history. *Hispanic American Historical Review* 84 (3) (July 30, 2004): 393–398.

Lewis, Bernard. *The Muslim Discovery of Europe*. New York: W.W. Norton, 1982.

Liu, Xinru. *Connections across Eurasia: Transportation, Communication, and Cultural Exchange on the Silk Roads*. Boston: McGraw-Hill, 2007.

Lucassen, Jan, Leo Lucassen, and Patrick Manning, eds. *Migration History in World History. Multidisciplinary Approaches*. Leiden: Brill, 2010.

Manela, Erez. *The Wilsonian Moment: Self-Determination and the International Origins of Anti-colonial Nationalism*. Oxford: Oxford University Press, 2007.

Manning, Patrick. The problem of interactions in world history. *American Historical Review* 101 (3) (June 1996): 771–782.

Manning, Patrick. *Navigating World History: Historians Create a Global Past*. New York: Palgrave Macmillan, 2003.

Manning, Patrick. *Migration in World History*. London: Routledge, 2004.

Manning, Patrick. *The African Diaspora: A History through Culture*. New York: Columbia University Press, 2009.

Marks, Robert. *The Origins of the Modern World: A Global and Ecological Narrative from the Fifteenth to the Twenty-First Century*. 2nd edn. Lanham: Rowman & Littlefield, 2007.

Martin, Eric Lane. World history as a way of thinking, *World History Connected* (May 2005), at http://worldhistoryconnected.press.uiuc.edu/2.2/martin.html (accessed Apr. 9, 2008).

Matossian, Mary. *Shaping World History: Breakthroughs in Ecology, Technology, Science, and Politics*. Armonk, NY: M.E. Sharpe, 1997.

Mazlish, Bruce. Comparing global history to world history. *Journal of Interdisciplinary History* 28 (3) (1998): 385.

McClellan, James. *Science and Technology in World History: An Introduction*. Baltimore: Johns Hopkins University Press, 1999.

McKeown, Adam. *Melancholy Order: Asian Migration and the Globalization of Borders*. New York: Columbia University Press, 2008.

McNeill, John. *Something New under the Sun: An Environmental History of the Twentieth-Century World*. New York: W.W. Norton, 2000.

McNeill, John. *The Human Web: A Bird's-Eye View of World History.* New York: W.W. Norton, 2003.

McNeill, William. *The Rise of the West: A History of the Human Community.* Chicago: University of Chicago Press, 1963.

McNeill, William. *Plagues and Peoples.* Garden City, NY: Anchor, 1976.

Meade, Theresa, and Merry Wiesner. *A Companion to Gender History.* Oxford: Wiley-Blackwell, 2006.

Moses, A. *Empire, Colony, Genocide: Conquest, Occupation, and Subaltern Resistance in World History.* New York: Berghahn, 2008.

Nehru, Jawaharlal. *Glimpses of World History: Being Further Letters to His Daughter, Written in Prison, and Containing a Rambling Account of History for Young People.* New Delhi: Jawaharlal Nehru Memorial Fund and Oxford University Press, 1999.

Northrup, David. *Africa's Discovery of Europe: 1450–1850.* New York: Oxford University Press, 2002.

Ó Gráda, Cormac. *Famine: A Short History.* Princeton: Princeton University Press, 2009.

Osterhammel, Jürgen, and Niels P. Petersson. *Globalization: A Short History.* Princeton: Princeton University Press, 2009.

Poe, Marshall. *The Russian Moment in World History.* Princeton: Princeton University Press, 2003.

Pomeranz, Kenneth. *The Great Divergence: China, Europe, and the Making of the Modern World Economy.* Princeton: Princeton University Press, 2000.

Pomeranz, Kenneth. *The World That Trade Created: Society, Culture, and the World Economy, 1400 to the Present.* 2nd edn. Armonk, NY: M.E. Sharpe, 2006.

Ralston, David. *Importing the European Army: The Introduction of European Military Techniques and Institutions into the Extra-European world, 1600–1914.* Chicago: University of Chicago Press, 1990.

Reynolds, David. *One World Divisible: A Global History since 1945.* New York: W.W. Norton, 2000.

Reynolds, Jonathan, and Erik Gilbert, *Trading Tastes: Commodity and Cultural Exchange to 1750.* Upper Saddle River, NJ: Prentice Hall, 2005.

Richards, John. *The Unending Frontier: An Environmental History of the Early Modern World.* Berkeley: University of California Press, 2005.

Rodney, Walter. *How Europe Underdeveloped Africa.* Rev. edn. Washington, DC: Howard University Press, 1981.

Schaeffer, Robert. *Understanding Globalization: The Social Consequences of Political, Economic, and Environmental Change.* Lanham: Rowman & Littlefield, 1997.

Seigel, Micol. World history's narrative problem. *Hispanic American Historical Review* 84 (3) (July 30, 2004): 431–446.

So, Alvin. *Social Change and Development: Modernization, Dependency, and World-Systems Theories.* Newbury Park, CA: Sage, 1990.

Spengler, Oswald. *The Decline of the West.* London: G. Allen & Unwin, 1934.

Stavrianos, Leften. *Global Rift: The Third World Comes of Age.* New York: Morrow, 1981.

Stavrianos, Leften. *Lifelines from Our Past: A New World History.* Rev. edn. Armonk, NY: M.E. Sharpe, 1997.

Stearns, Peter. *The Industrial Revolution in World History.* Boulder: Westview, 1993.

Stearns, Peter. *Gender in World History.* London: Routledge, 2000.

Stiglitz, Joseph. *Globalization and Its Discontents.* New York: W. W. Norton, 2002.

Thornton, John. *Africa and Africans in the Making of the Atlantic World, 1400–1800.* 2nd edn. New York: Cambridge University Press, 1998.

Tilly, Charles. *Big Structures, Large Processes, Huge Comparisons.* New York: Russell Sage Foundation, 1989.

Toynbee, Arnold, and Royal Institute of International Affairs. *A Study of History.* New York: Oxford University Press, 1947.

Vries, P. Should we really ReORIENT? *Itinerario (Leiden)* 22 (3) (1998): 19–38.

Wallerstein, Immanuel. *The Modern World-System.* New York: Academic Press, 1974.

Williams, Eric. *Capitalism and Slavery*. Chapel Hill: University of North Carolina Press, 1994.

Wolmar, Christian. *Blood, Iron and Gold: How the Railways Transformed the World*. London: Atlantic, 2009.

Wong, R. Bin. *China Transformed: Historical Change and the Limits of European Experience*. Ithaca: Cornell University Press, 1997.

Woodside, Alexander. *Lost Modernities: China, Vietnam, Korea, and the Hazards of World History*. Cambridge MA: Harvard University Press, 2006.

Wright, Donald. *The World and a Very Small Place in Africa: A History of Globalization in Niumi, the Gambia*. 2nd edn. Armonk, NY: M.E. Sharpe, 2004.

CHAPTER FOUR

The World Is Your Archive?
The Challenges of World History as a Field of Research

BARBARA WEINSTEIN

All historians are world historians now.

C.A. Bayly, *The Birth of the Modern World*

The field of world history is unusual among areas of specialization in the historical profession for having its origins primarily, if not exclusively, in pedagogical concerns. More specifically, the rapid rise of world history as a field is intimately tied to the decline of the canonical Western Civilization course (Levine 2000; Allardyce 2000).[1] Spurred by critiques of Eurocentrism within the academy and demands by various ethnic groups not descended from Europeans for representation within the university curriculum, history departments found it increasingly untenable to treat "Western Civ" as an appropriate gateway course for understanding human experience. The result has been a shift away from Western Civ and toward World History, an approach to the classroom that carries a mandate to be more representative of the range of human experiences.

Thus, for better or for worse, world history as a field is wedded to the demand for more culturally diverse and inclusive courses that every year introduce masses of newly arrived mostly North American college students to the history of "the world." This has periodically provoked a backlash against world history in university departments, where the standard complaint (and by no means exclusively from defenders of its predecessor, Western Civ) is precisely that world history is principally a pedagogical field. Not being a "research field" – I have even heard colleagues claim that it not only isn't but *can't* be a research field – it therefore should not be a subject offered at the college level. The implication is that teaching a course in a field outside or beyond our research-related expertise debases the historical profession and reduces us to the condition of (gasp!) mere high school teachers.[2] (See Bain, this volume.)

This critique of World History is unpersuasive in any number of ways, starting with its faulty assumption that most courses taught by university professors relate to their

A Companion to World History, First Edition. Edited by Douglas Northrop.
© 2012 Blackwell Publishing Ltd. Published 2012 by Blackwell Publishing Ltd.

research. A few privileged clusters of academics aside, most historians routinely offer courses that involve large amounts of material and many historical issues only remotely connected to their own research agenda. More worthy of serious consideration is the claim that world history is an "impossible subject" since nobody actually studies "the world." But here again, one could respond that it is a question of degree, not a qualitatively different endeavor, since it is also true that nobody studies – to take my field of specialization as an example – "Latin America." Typically, Latin American historians focus on a particular country or set of countries, and within those countries only specific periods and topics.

At the same time, it is useless to deny that there is a kernel of truth in this complaint about world history. Despite the multiplication of world history courses, and in the last two decades, the founding of MA and even PhD programs in World History,[3] only very recently have we begun to see job openings that specify that applicants should have training in world history as a research field (Townsend 2007). (See Streets-Salter, this volume.) Job ads (for other fields) do frequently say: "The ability to teach world history would be a plus." Typically, what is meant by "ability" is that the candidate, while a graduate student, served as a teaching assistant in a course on World History, whose principal instructor was likely someone who also had no prior expertise in World History. This "learning by doing" process may be adequate for preparing instructors to engage undergraduates' attention, and to teach them enough world history to, say, pass an exam that would license them as secondary school teachers, but it promises little for a research field in world history. One can imagine a proliferation of world history instructors without any intensification of the intellectual conversation around world history.

Fortunately, just as new research agendas produce curricular innovations, new course offerings generate new research interests. The field of world history – while still more pedagogically inclined than most – has also ramified into cohorts and publications (the World History Association, the *Journal of World History*) that are oriented toward exploring questions related to research as well as teaching. Moreover, journals such as the *American Historical Review*, which have no particular geographic focus, have increasingly taken up world-historical issues. While a modal "world history" publication might still be a multi-authored textbook intended for classroom use, there is a growing community of scholars who would define their *research* field as world history, and who envision a synergy between their classroom teaching and scholarly work.

Of course, this in and of itself does not mean that scholars of world history have silenced their critics. First of all, world historians have to define in a persuasive way what it would mean to do research in world history. Despite my earlier claim about it being more a quantitative than a qualitative distinction, according to the conventions of the historical profession, it is quite acceptable for me to say that I am a Latin Americanist who specializes in twentieth-century São Paulo, Brazil – no informed person would bat an eyelash. But if I said I was a world historian who specialized in twentieth-century São Paulo, Brazil, that would certainly raise eyebrows and prompt colleagues to ask what exactly I might mean when I called myself a world historian. In other words, world history is not a field where the part can easily stand in for the whole. Hence, scholars in the field have had to be far more thoughtful than most historians about how they would define the field and what it means to do research in it.

Developments in the field of history since the 1980s have tended to make matters even more complicated for scholars of world history, both as instructors and researchers. The historical concerns that prompted the shift from Western Civ to World History have also challenged those historical approaches that offered the most convenient pedagogical frameworks and methodological underpinnings for the field. World History, in its current paradigmatic form, is not conceived as a mere amplification of the "Western Civ" course; rather one of its principal purposes is to rethink the place of the West in the macrohistorical narrative. At the same time, the very notion of a master narrative has been challenged from a number of different theoretical directions – most vigorously, from those associated with postmodern and postcolonial interventions (Bentley 2003; Weinstein 2005). Historical researchers in a variety of subfields have turned away from the grand explanatory narrative as incurably teleological and Eurocentric, and in many instances, it has given way to a preference for "micronarrative" of brief duration, concentrated on a particular event that offers us a goldmine of cultural meanings (Darnton 2004). This anecdote-based approach to history (most famously exemplified by Robert Darnton's *The Great Cat Massacre*, 1984), has been quite fruitful in a number of scholarly contexts. But its fragmentation of historical narrative/interpretation presents special problems for those who teach World History, and for those who seek to promote research in that field. While the absence of a narrative framework would be challenging for any course curriculum, it seems particularly difficult to imagine constructing an effective syllabus for a world history course based on a series of unconnected incidents. Clearly, some explanatory narrative would be needed to link them in some way, to provide some connective tissue so that students gain some sense of why these events or stories are significant. But most of the anecdotal/historical literature will be of little help in that regard. Furthermore, I have argued elsewhere that the micronarrative approach does not so much challenge grand narratives, or even deny them, as it ignores and obscures them, and the influence they continue to exert in how both scholars and the public view the past and present (Weinstein 2005). Ultimately, the micronarrative will be of limited utility for the project of "provincializing Europe," to cite Dipesh Chakrabarty's pithy formulation of the problem (2000).

To clarify the dilemma facing a scholar of world history who wishes to eschew Eurocentrism, it is useful to consider both the criticisms and proposals that Chakrabarty makes in his highly influential book. Early on in *Provincializing Europe*, he critically revisits the canonical essay by E.P. Thompson on "Time, work-discipline and industrial capitalism" (1967). In this essay Thompson not only describes the process by which the English worker is obliged to internalize the discipline associated with industrial work rhythms, but also contends that the same is happening, or will happen, to the Third World worker, with the only difference between the English and, say, Indian worker being the passage of secular/historical time. Thus, Thompson's essay, though focused on the English worker, is replete with world-historical implications or claims made intelligible by a certain Marxist grand narrative. But for Chakrabarty, these claims exemplify the way in which "the modern" continues to be understood "as a known history, something which has already happened elsewhere, and which is to be [merely] reproduced ... with a local content" (2000: 48). In other words, if we followed Thompson's reasoning, the narrative of Indian industrialization and work-discipline would be nothing more than an echo of what had happened long before in England. From this perspective, to understand history, one *must* know the history of England; knowing the history of India is optional and, in some ways, superfluous.

What, then, does Chakrabarty propose as a way to undo the Eurocentric bias that can be found in even some of the very best historical writing? In four chapters he elaborates on aspects of Indian cultural and political life that he argues cannot be easily assimilated into the West's historicizing narrative. He begins his analysis by citing Paul Veyne's distinction between "singularity" and "specificity" (Veyne 1984: 56–57). The latter is an example of a general tendency, and thus can be easily articulated to a larger narrative. Chakrabarty, however, seeks out forms of sociability or social practice that are, in his view, singularities – that is, ones that *resist* assimilation into a historicist narrative (2000: 56). But it is precisely this feature of his historical (as opposed to metahistorical) chapters that makes them of limited use for the aspiring teacher and/or scholar of world history.

Chakrabarty's text, given his critique of historicism in general, may be a particularly sweeping example of the rejection of grand narratives, but I would cite his work as symptomatic of a larger turn toward singularities or meaning-laden anecdotes, and toward research questions that are synchronic, rather than diachronic. Whereas the world history course, and the research questions it produces, needs to have a capacious geographic and chronological span, many historians are busy slicing and dicing the past in ways that threaten to reduce us, once again, to teaching "one damn thing after another," though now it is more likely to be a discontinuous assortment of discursive representations or cultural constructions. The latter provide poor ammunition for attacking the stubbornly Eurocentric vision of history that undergraduates – at least North American ones – often bring to the classroom. Bold, coherent stories have great heuristic appeal, and it is difficult to convince students to be more skeptical toward a particular story line if we are not offering anything in its place.

One response to this dilemma has been the rise of "big history" – most readily associated with the work of Jared Diamond (1997) and David Christian (2005). (See Spier, this volume.) Inspired by scientific disciplines' search for a unified field of knowledge, these historians seek to construct the grandest of grand narratives, which can isolate a handful of factors (germs, the vote, a technological innovation) that broadly, even universally, explain historical trends. It is beyond the subject of this chapter to discuss the many big problems presented by "big history" – including a spectacular overreaching that serves to remind us why so many historians eschewed grand narratives in the first place. But for our purposes here, it is relevant to note two especially troubling aspects of "big history." One is that its treatment of the "modern world" is (irremediably) Eurocentric since it tends to be constructed around measures of success and failure, gauged on the basis of Western notions of economic growth and development. The other is the virtual impossibility of rooting "big history" in primary source research. No doubt a "big history" text could feature some documents that are relevant and illustrative of its arguments, but the very need to eliminate distracting countervailing evidence makes archival sources more of an impediment than an inducement to "big history."

In short, there is an ongoing tension between the pedagogical need for some sort of narrative coherence and the tendency of grand narratives to reproduce Eurocentric versions of world history. Keeping this dilemma in mind, in the remainder of this chapter I will discuss both well-established and recently initiated ways of organizing and conceptualizing research in world history. In evaluating the merits, drawbacks, limitations, and promises of different approaches, I consider their potential to contribute, on the one hand, to rethinking (not just shrinking) narratives, and on the other hand, to constructing a field that does not lapse into Eurocentrism – that does not ultimately define world history as "The West and the Rest." In addition, I will consider the practical aspects of any particular approach – that is, can research be done in this vein given the usual constraints that historians operate under in terms of time and resources? As a point of clarification, I should say that almost any historical research could make a contribution to the field of world history – as the epigraph from C.A. Bayly claims, we are now all, in a sense, doing world history. But such an expansive definition would render this discussion unmanageable. So at the risk of drawing a somewhat artificial line, I will be classifying as "world-historical research" work that deliberately attempts to transcend conventional geographic field borders.

Perhaps the first school of world history that went beyond "The West and the Rest" narrative was the civilizations approach, and despite a steady stream of criticism and revision, it is likely that the average world history instructor still organizes his or her syllabus and adopts a textbook based on this perspective. (See the chapters by Pomeranz and Segal, by Getz, and by McKeown, this volume.) The appeal of this approach is its placement of different societies – defined as civilizations – on a similar plane, and while it implies cultural and material hierarchies at particular moments in time, a focus on the rise and fall of civilizations means that the civilizations approach can serve to undermine the linear/progressive narrative of the Rise of the West. One of the foundational concepts of this school – the idea of an "axial age" in the ancient world – both contributes to the linear/progressive narrative and suggests some ways in which to undermine its Eurocentrism. An idea first articulated by Karl Jaspers and then endorsed by Shmuel Eisenstadt, the phrase "axial age" refers to a pivotal era in history when several different civilizations independently developed certain concepts deemed crucial to human progress (Eisenstadt 1986). In other words, these significant developments do not have a single originating point from which they radiate out, but rather multiple points of origin.

For our purposes here, there are two drawbacks of the civilizations school that are worthy of note. One is the intrinsic and probably unavoidable tendency of this approach to operate with normative and anomalous categories – to focus on "successful" societies/ empires and to marginalize groups both within and beyond the successful society that are judged to have failed in constructing a "world civilization." A sort of "greatest hits of human history," it all but inevitably implies failure, even degeneration, for a culture or society once its hour of greatness has passed, thus potentially reproducing a principal pillar of nineteenth-century imperial ideologies.[4]

As for advancing a research agenda in world history, one can readily perceive the problems that a civilizational approach poses. If the object of discussion or analysis is an entire "civilization," how could one do original research, based on primary sources? The scale of the questions and the resulting holistic approach seems to preclude significant primary research. The world historian, in this situation, has no choice but to rely on a synthesis of the research done by others. A scholar might contribute to the historical knowledge available about a particular civilization, but that would not necessarily translate into a contribution to world history as a field that is not merely additive – that is, a sum of many parts, equaling less than the whole.

There has been, however, at least one serious proposal for conceptualizing the civilizations approach in a way that would both allow for a research agenda *and* advance a deliberately "world-historical" conception of the research. The emphasis would be on the way in which trends or innovations – religious, technological, linguistic – in a particular social formation interact with or circulate within other societies. According to Marshall Hodgson, perhaps the most ambitious and innovative of "civilizations" historians, "it is precisely in terms of the effect of changes in one place and time upon changes elsewhere that historical questions became so fatefully interrelated" (1993: 254–255).[5] In his 1993 introduction to Hodgson's *Rethinking World History*, Edmund Burke

III observed that Hodgson, while remaining committed to a civilizational approach, presaged both Edward Said and J.M. Blaut in his effort to de-essentialize the notion of civilization and critique diffusionism (Burke 1993). And Ross Dunn, in his review of this volume, lamented that historians were so "captivated by the civilization as a thing of conceptual beauty and fixedness" that they could not conceptualize the fluidity and indeterminateness implied by intense connections and exchanges, and therefore could not fully embrace the implications of Hodgson's work (1996: 133). Some recent studies, such as C.A. Bayly's *The Birth of the Modern World* (2004), have taken up Hodgson's call to emphasize connectedness, while not entirely eschewing European exceptionalism (Hall 2004); Hodgson's insights also fueled the critique of received geography offered by Martin Lewis and Kären Wigen in *The Myth of Continents* (1997).

Several leading world historians have identified the comparative method "as a promising window onto the larger project of writing world history." According to Richard Eaton (1997), "comparative historians are especially well positioned to help free the profession from the sort of nationalist or civilizational straitjackets that have bedeviled so much history writing in the past. To the comparativist, the topic, the problem, or the process is the focus of attention, not the place." He then contends that comparing patterns of religious conversion from one society to another can illuminate the "mechanics of a worldwide process." There is, of course, a substantial comparative historical literature – on slave systems, revolutions, feminist movements, etc. – by scholars who were not necessarily thinking of their work as a contribution to the field of world history, and typically were only considering two or three societies. Even in this more limited context, the comparative method posed problems that have been widely debated in the historical discipline over the last decade. As a deliberate contribution to world history – which might require comparisons among multiple cases – the problems of the comparative method are likely to multiply.[6]

As a heuristic device – an aid to analytical thinking – comparison is not only useful but inevitable. What historical reasoning doesn't involve some sense of a process or event happening in one place, but not (or less so) in another? But it is when scholars structure a research agenda around explicit, systematic comparison that certain problems are likely to emerge. Perhaps the most serious challenge is to avoid the designation of one case as normative and the other(s) as deviant or anomalous. A related problem is the tendency, even the need, to (overly) homogenize each case being compared so as to heighten the contrast, thereby losing a sense of the heterogeneity within cases which may be more meaningful than the differences revealed by the comparison. Yet another problem that has been identified in studies that favor the comparative method is the inclination to treat the entities being compared (empires, nations, cities) as bounded and distinct, rather than involved in webs of communication, trade, and cultural exchange. As Micol Seigel points out in her trenchant critique of the comparative method, "comparison requires the observer to name two or more units whose similarities and differences she or he will then describe. This setup discourages attention to exchange between the two, the very exchange postcolonial insight understands as the stuff of subject-formation." Seigel then extends her critique, noting that "above all, setting up parallel objects for study obscures the exchange fostered by comparisons themselves" (2005: 65). The resulting comparative "insight" can become a constitutive element in the construction of national, gender or racial identities, so that an attempt to neatly compare two cases becomes fraught with difficulties.

One could argue, however, that these are perils and pitfalls that can be avoided or negotiated; they may be reasons to modify the comparative method, not to eschew it altogether. Eaton's nuanced and sophisticated approach to the phenomenon of religious conversion – focused on three different Naga communities in northern India – is a case where the scale of the study and the depth of the historian's knowledge make the comparative conclusion compelling.[7] It is when Eaton wants to shift the frame of reference from a particular region of India to a world-historical perspective that I find his claims less persuasive. First of all, extending the discussion of religious conversion beyond this region would require archival and ethnographic research in multiple locations that would be daunting for most historians, and would probably only be feasible for a team of researchers. But more important, a comparative project, to maintain coherence, has to identify certain variables that will be considered in diverse locations, yet it is precisely the particularities of the Naga's cosmological traditions that seem most noteworthy in this context, and searching for the presence or absence of similar beliefs elsewhere already promises to skew the historian's research mission.

Yet, even with all of these caveats about the comparative method, we need to acknowledge that Kenneth Pomeranz's *The Great Divergence* (2000) – a work of comparative history – has been among the most influential books in the years since its publication for world historians, and for historians seeking to undermine a certain teleological narrative of the "Triumph of the West" (see also Wong 2000). This study of the economic trajectories of China and Britain argues that even as late as the eighteenth century, the two empires were more similar in economic terms than they were different, and that it is only due to a particularly favorable conjunction of circumstances for Britain in the second half of that century that it was able to experience such massive economic growth and technological development in the subsequent century, while China languished. As with any controversial and important book, Pomeranz's study has been criticized on a number of counts. Perhaps the most common criticism from world historians is that he merely switches from a unipolar Western-dominated world to a bipolar world reduced to Western Europe and China. And the book undoubtedly displays some of the flaws that have bedeviled other comparative histories – overhomogenization of the units of comparison, unequal degrees of expertise on the part of the author, reliance on syntheses of other historians' research, inattention to interactions and exchanges, and to the role of other units/actors, and the need to focus on elements that are more easily comparable phenomena than what Veyne calls singularities. Yet none of these complaints has dulled the appeal of Pomeranz's study, which provides a powerful antidote to works that trumpet European exceptionalism. The book's success does not mean that it has avoided all the pitfalls of comparative research, but rather that it forcefully addresses a major question that a significant portion of the historical profession still sees as being answerable through this sort of large-scale comparison driven by secondary sources.

Both the civilizational and comparative approaches rely on a notion of fixed, bounded places to which a historian brings a world perspective, but increasingly scholars of world history are choosing something or someone mobile as their object of study. By "mapping" the trajectory and ramifications of a moving subject or object, historians can identify and study persons, processes, and commodities whose history cannot be confined to a single society. The study of bodies in movement across imperial or national boundaries is not particularly new – immigration has been a subject of historical research since the mid-twentieth century. (See Ward, this volume.) But in the past, most scholars of migration focused on the "receiving" society and folded the immigrant story into a national narrative, whereas world historians would be expected to pay equivalent attention to the entire route (including the ocean passage), and to view such human movements in terms of their transnational implications. Furthermore, certain groups – for example, anarchists or abolitionists – are particularly interesting to world historians because their routes of circulation often go beyond a point of departure and arrival, increasingly an outmoded way of conceptualizing human movements (Keck and Sikkink 1998; Appadurai 1996).

For obvious reasons, such studies have been especially prevalent among historians who define their "area" as at least partly oceanic – those who study the Atlantic world, the Pacific Rim, and the Indian Ocean, as well as those who focus on diasporic populations. Rebecca Scott has traced a particular mixed-race family, originally from Saint-Domingue (Haiti), whose members dispersed to Cuba, Louisiana, France, and Belgium (see Scott 2007). Aside from revealing an intriguing family saga, her study (and a similar one by Martha Hodes, 2003) allows us to follow the ways in which the identities of the various family members and generations change according to the moment and place in which we encounter them, how their legal prerogatives and restraints are determined and defined, and what it tells us about an emerging Atlantic world of rights and racism. Natalie Zemon Davis's *Trickster's Travels* (2006) explores the remarkable and peripatetic life of a Muslim born in Granada in the fateful year of 1492, who became one of the leading geographers of his era (known in the West as Leo Africanus). The historical anthropologist J. Lorand Matory (1999) follows the cultural circuits and exchanges of former slaves and their descendants from Salvador da Bahia, Brazil, whose "return" to West Africa allows them to acquire fluency in English (and hence become "The English Professors of Brazil"), but also spearhead a revival of "authentic" Yorùbá religious practices then flourishing in Bahia but nearly obliterated by decades of civil war and British colonialism in West Africa.

Aside from being intrinsically fascinating stories to any reader, these sorts of studies have a special appeal for the world historian. To be sure, the research requirements can be daunting. Historians often struggle to get funding to visit a single research site, never mind multiple sites in far-flung locations requiring an array of language skills (though such efforts can make a scholar doubly appreciative of what his or her subject endured in moving from one place to the next). But this approach does allow the world historian to rebut one of the standard criticisms of the field: the research in this vein is thoroughly rooted in primary sources. The sort of historical detective work that such studies involve relies fundamentally on archival material or memoirs and oral accounts, not secondary research by scholars in a particular subfield.

The subjects of such studies, if carefully selected or critically presented, can also contribute to undermining the Eurocentric narrative that typically locates the origins of (modern) ideas and practices in what Chakrabarty calls a "hyper-real" Europe, and then describes them as radiating out to the less dynamic precincts of the globe. The circuitous routes followed by the individuals or groups whose movements have been mapped by historians illustrate how problematic it is to regard "influence" as flowing in a single direction, as well as how much such assumptions rest on an essentialized view of the identity of bearers of ideas and practices. In addition, there is an often unacknowledged advantage to studying the movement of a body or bodies rather than, say, the circulation or peregrinations of an idea (for example, religious conversion). Although an individual or group's identity and subject position may change in moving from one place to another, we still assume a degree of continuity or continuous subjectivity that makes the project of following in their footsteps an intellectually compelling one. In contrast, when tracing the itinerary of an idea, given the appropriations and adaptations any concept will undergo in its travels, it becomes difficult to know whether the thing being studied bears any relation to the version of it with which the project started.[8] (See the chapters by Burton and by Vélez, Prange, and Clossey, this volume.)

For all their virtues, these studies of particular bodies moving over time and space present one substantial drawback with regard to the field of world history: they do not offer an adequate framework for a world history curriculum. One can imagine using such studies as stimulating supplements to more macrohistorical works, but a course entirely composed of such stories, no matter how well interpreted, is likely to leave the average classroom of North American undergraduates scratching their heads and wondering what they were supposed to derive from the course. These are, after all, microhistories – Scott actually entitled one version of her article "Micro-history set in motion" (2009) – and while they may contribute to a rethinking of macrohistorical questions, they can rarely support the entire weight of a wide-ranging historical narrative.

A potentially sturdier alternative is to map the application and expansion of particular institutions or forms of regulation. An especially notable example is Lauren Benton's *Law and Colonial Cultures: Legal Regimes in World History, 1400–1900* (2002). In this work, which she herself terms "institutional world history," Benton examines a variety of locations and moments that witnessed innovations, conflicts, and negotiations over legal definitions, jurisdictions, and authority as colonizing powers sought to institute or invoke their hegemony in their colonies. Working with the concept of legal pluralism, Benton demonstrates that expanding authority did not entail a uniform application of legal codes originating from the hegemonic power – indeed, often the primary intention was to place subject peoples beyond the boundaries of legal rights and obligations. Conversely, colonized peoples might in one instance seek to be exempt from the legal exactions of the colonizer, and at another, demand to be included within the juridical penumbra of the empire. And since colonial legal regimes involved multiple jurisdictions and cultural contexts, they were also fertile points of exchange. According to Benton, "the law worked both to tie disparate parts of empires and to lay the basis for exchanges of all sorts between politically and culturally separate imperial or colonial powers" (2002: 3).

The advantages of this approach to world history, from both a scholarly and peda-gogical vantage point, are many. Colonial legal regimes provide us with a coherent and capacious framework for thinking about diverse societies and their interactions, as well as enabling us to consider change over time as certain legal patterns – for example, evolving definitions of property rights – enact relations constitutive of intensifying capitalist eco-nomic arrangements. At the same time, the highly focused research method, with its emphasis on specific court cases or legal struggles, makes it possible for Benton to rely at least partly, and often heavily, on primary sources.[9] Moreover, Benton describes her approach as suggesting "an important reorientation of world historical narratives" and insists that its "perspective clearly challenges Eurocentric world histories that emphasize the unique, progressive character of European institutions or that view global change as emanating exclusively from the dynamics of Western development" (2002: 6). In sum, Benton's study fulfills all three of the "missions" outlined at the outset of this essay: (1) it draws on archival research and primary sources; (2) it maintains a concern with constructing a broad interpretive narrative, and (3) it challenges the established Eurocentric narrative of world history.

Benton's *Law and Colonial Cultures* may well come as close as I can imagine to providing us with a full-fledged model for world-historical studies. However, lest this section close with what seems like a completely unreserved endorsement, I do want to express one small but significant reservation – or cite the reservation expressed by Steven Feierman (1999) in a different but analogous context. After a largely positive appraisal of historical studies focused on the hybridity of African culture in the colonial and postcolonial eras, Feierman indicates some qualms about the defining role of colonialism in the recent African historiography:

> These innovative contributions are fascinating when taken individually, but they present a profound problem of historical representation when aggregated into a regional historical narrative. The studies of commodities (or of Christian sin) in one place, and then another, and then another can be aggregated only on the basis of their shared relationship to the relevant European category: they cannot be placed within a larger or more general African narrative. What is African inevitably appears in a form which is local and fragmented, and which has no greater depth than the time of colonial conquest, or the moment just before it. (1999: 185)

In her study Benton deliberately (and in my view, successfully) disputes a representation of European legal regimes as rational, uniform, and originating solely in the West, and refuses any invidious (and largely fictitious) contrast between customary law at the local level and philosophically informed legal precepts at the imperial level. But whenever European imperial expansion is the structuring historical process, we need to be especially alert to the dangers that Feierman identifies above.

There are currently two other areas of research that, while not avowedly operating in the realm of world history (indeed some of their practitioners overtly disavow any connection), are nonetheless producing work with obvious ramifications for world historians. One is the field of transnational history, and the other is the field of global history (or a particular version of it). Of the two, transnational history is by far the more influential and visible. A quick search for the term transnational in the 2010 program of the American Historical Association meetings produced 120 hits, and the 2011 program produced 135 hits. (A related but not identical trend is "trans-regional history," but it is interesting to note that a search of the 2011 program produced only four papers or panels that used the term trans-regional.)

As with any approach that has attracted so many practitioners, there is no single, agreed-upon definition of what we mean by "transnational," but I find particularly useful Micol Seigel's distinction between international history (with its emphasis on interaction between nation-states) and transnational history, which "examines units that spill over and seep through national borders." Indeed, Seigel contends that the core of the transnational approach "is the challenge it poses to the hermeneutic preeminence of nations" (2005: 63). Or to borrow Prasenjit Duara's engaging phrase, it promises to "rescue history from the nation" (1997) – not by ignoring the nation as a category, but by refusing it the primacy and unity it enjoys in the more traditional historiography.

The virtues of the transnational approach for the world historian seeking to contest Eurocentrism are particularly evident if we follow Seigel's reasoning and contrast it to international history. Virtually all current practitioners of world history would agree on the need to emphasize interaction and exchange, but if we are conceptualizing such interactions as taking place between fully formed and reified nations or societies, we are likely to end up focusing yet again on those nations that have traditionally dominated the historical landscape. One of the merits of the transnational approach is its inclination to go against this grain by demonstrating the way in which ideas, commodities, cultural forms, or political practices often associated with one (hegemonic) nation or set of nations actually reflect the innovations and adaptations worked by myriad groups in multiple locations. Whether we are discussing a cultural form such as jazz, or a controversial text such as Katherine Mayo's *Mother India*, or an identity such as "middle class," transnational history disposes us to cast our net widely, and to avoid automatically assigning greater historical significance to a particular actor or group of actors on the basis of their national location (Seigel 2009; Sinha 2006; López and Weinstein 2012).

At the same time, transnational history – to live up to its promise – requires a research plan that involves comparable degrees of engagement with primary sources in the different locales under discussion. To consult archival documents and print sources in one location and rely on syntheses of secondary sources elsewhere will surely produce a study that has a narrative/interpretive "core" and supplementary "peripheries." This, in turn, implies that transnational historians – unless collaborating with a team of colleagues – cannot cast their nets too widely without compromising their commitment to transcending the national/historical framework. It is not, on its own, a substitute for (modern) world history since it does not offer a narrative framework for either a world history course or a world-historical research agenda, nor is that the intention. But one can imagine a thematic world history course that could be constructed out of carefully selected examples of transnational historical studies (Seigel 2004).

Although many scholars casually treat global history as a synonym for world history, a vocal group of academics, including Bruce Mazlish and Wolf Schäfer, have insistently defined global history as a very different field of study. According to Mazlish, unlike world history (which he tendentiously defines as "the whole history of the whole world"), global history should be understood as the history of globalization. (See Bright and Geyer, this volume.) The latter field can then be broken down into two camps – a "weak" definition that studies globalization in its *longue durée* form, and a "strong" definition (Mazlish's position) that sees the history of globalization as dating from the second half of the twentieth century. Although Mazlish acknowledges globalization's longer roots, he argues that it is only since the 1970s that the degree of "synergy and synchronicity" has been sufficient "to justify the launch of a new periodization" (1998: 391).

The "weak" definition of global history could easily be folded into the larger enterprise of world history, but Mazlish and Schäfer contend that *their* definition of global history distinguishes it sharply from world history in two key respects.[10] First, they cite novel developments in telecommunications, transportation, and, most recently, cyberspace that have shrunk time and distance and allowed certain events and processes to be experienced, for the first time, on a genuinely global scale. Thus, instead of what he sees as world historians' interminably additive and undertheorized approach to the history of the world, Schäfer (1993) claims that the new global historians can construct a category of analysis that is "truly global" and engage with theoretical frameworks for understanding planetary phenomena. Second, according to Mazlish, global historians "know that each of the factors of globalization requires rigorous empirical study" and therefore "are trying to establish a more deliberate research agenda" (1998: 392).

These challenges and critiques are useful for world historians to ponder, but it strikes me that the global historians are both demanding too much theoretical and methodological coherence from the field of world history and claiming too much of it for themselves. Their argument about periodization has by no means been universally persuasive to their fellow historians, some of whom argue that there were equally intense processes of globalization in earlier periods (Bayly 2004), or counter that the world is actually becoming less "globalized" in the sense of increasingly fragmented cultures and deeply divergent standards of living (Cooper 2005). The very argument about synchronicity seems, itself, undertheorized: when Mazlish notes that over 3 billion human beings simultaneously watched the same Coca-Cola commercials during a recent Olympics, I immediately recall theories of reception and wonder to what extent we can say that they saw the *same* commercial, any more than we can claim that villagers undergoing conversion in different locations at different times embraced the same Christian god. And while I can easily envision doing empirical research on how Coca-Cola tailored its commercials to a vast global audience, and contributed to shaping the image of the global consumer, not even the most deliberate research agenda could adequately address the other side of the question on a global scale.

Perhaps more troubling is a certain tendency to treat contemporary globalization as a process that, by its very nature, reduces Eurocentrism. Aside from minimizing the significance of populations that are still stubbornly or unwillingly "off the grid," this view overstates the democratic character of recent technological and organizational innovations, and understates the extent to which globalization might reinforce processes of normalization. Among the factors of globalization that Mazlish mentions (1998: 393) as requiring rigorous empirical study are nongovernmental organizations, multinational corporations, and the United Nations, none of which would seem to challenge a Eurocentric vision of the world. He also notes that "with globalization has come the adoption of a uniform calendar," but treats this as a neutral development with no implications for reproducing hierarchies of power and authority. Scholars of world history may not have figured out how to dismantle the master narrative of the West civilizing the World, but at least they widely recognize the need to grapple with it.

The point of this chapter has been to consider some of the ways in which historians laboring in the field of world history have attempted to make it a research-based as well as pedagogical enterprise, and have sought to construct narratives that can allow both scholars and students to have a sense of broader historical processes without reproducing the Eurocentrism that World History, as a field, was intended to undo. As I suspect is immediately obvious, it is easier to sketch out the problems and pitfalls of various approaches than it is to suggest solutions to the intellectual quandaries facing the field. For one thing, many of the impediments to the fuller realization of world history as a research field stem from institutional structures and disciplinary traditions that are deeply entrenched and difficult to challenge. Topics that would prove impractical for an individual historian to pursue, whether in terms of linguistic requirements or travel to archives, might be feasible if historians could collaborate in research teams the way scientists typically do. In the humanistic disciplines, such efforts are extremely rare; even the multi-authored world history text commonly consists of discrete contributions with a similar "slant," rather than representing a genuinely collective undertaking that addresses a focused set of questions or phenomena. However appealing on the face of it, movement in the direction of more collective or collaborative research would require rethinking the historian's craft as well as professional practices ranging from research funding to evaluations for tenure and promotion.

Though it would surely be presumptuous to prescribe any single research method or interpretive framework for addressing such a wide and complex range of scholarly issues, I do have a sense that some research agendas are more likely to be fruitful than others. Once again I would cite Benton's *Law and Colonial Cultures* as indicating promising avenues for future research. Her argument about legal pluralism, on the one hand, and about an increasing state presence on the other, demonstrates how we can decenter a historical process without obscuring hierarchies of power and authority. Much the same approach is suggested in an essay that appeared in an issue of the *Radical History Review* devoted to rethinking world history: In "Pluralizing capital, challenging Eurocentrism" (2005) John Chalcraft argues for a de-essentialized and capacious definition of capitalism that can accommodate the variety of productive forms that have shaped the contours of capitalist economies, thereby moving away from a normative/linear model of capitalist development associated with the West. Once we shift to this more "generous" notion of productive relations, it becomes "too simple to say that Europe imposed the market and the commodity form on the rest of the world." Furthermore, he argues that "the market was one of the things that the rest of the world both made by itself and appropriated from Europe" (2005: 27).

Although Chalcraft's suggestive and somewhat polemical article cannot be compared to Benton's deeply researched and fully realized monograph, my point here is simply to highlight their common concern with pluralizing forms and with the implications of that "pluralism" for the historical processes in which they are embedded. Neither author is arguing simply for paying attention to "local variation" – an approach that typically leaves the "core" of the process largely untouched. Rather, both are insisting that these plural forms become dynamic elements in the process of historical change. Finally, they both indicate ways to focus our scholarly inquiries so that they can lead to a feasible research agenda, and allow us, at the end of the day, to imagine a narrative, or set of narratives, that can counter the Eurocentric story line that so many of our students still carry in their heads (Seigel 2004).

Notes

1 As Levine (2000) reminds us, the Western Civ course is itself a relatively recent curricular innovation, not something that could be defended as a venerable tradition.

2 Vinay Lal (2005), in a very different vein, denounces world history as just the latest in a series of epistemological efforts by the West to impose its knowledge/power on the rest of the world. Since this critique could be extended to virtually any intellectual trend associated with the Western academy, I will simply note it and move on.

3 The University of Hawai'i has a doctoral program in world history that emphasizes the study of transregional phenomena. It also specifically does not offer a master's in world history, a degree typically associated with classroom teaching rather than archival research. The University of Pittsburgh is also in the process of initiating a doctoral program in world history.

4 It seems obvious that there is a problematic ranking of societies involved in an approach that, for example, could easily incorporate material on the Aztec and Inca empires, but would be hard-pressed to include material on postindependence Latin America.

5 Given that Hodgson died in 1968 at the age of 46, the breadth and prescience of his work is simply astonishing.

6 For a much more extensive discussion of the comparative method and world history, see the chapter by Michael Adas, this volume.

7   It is worth noting, however, that Eric Van Young (1990; 2001), in his study, on a similar scale, of villages that did or did not join in the independence-era insurrections in Mexico, refuses any interpretive framework that could explain political behavior at the level of the individual community.

8   Another version of objects in motion is the commodity chain (Topik *et al.* 2006). In this case, the very point is to follow transformations and to use these to construct a narrative about the global economy. This makes the study of commodity chains an excellent pedagogical tool for world history courses, but this literature has not led to a significant rethinking of the Europe-centered "world-system."

9   The same applies to Seed (1995), although her analysis of rituals, legal and symbolic, through which European powers enacted their authority over conquered territories in the New World is narrower and more static than Benton's study.

10 It should be noted that Schäfer, in a subsequent article (2003), adopted a more conciliatory and collaborative stance toward the field of world history.

References

Allardyce, Gilbert. 2000. Toward world history: American historians and the coming of the world history course. In Ross E. Dunn, ed., *The New World History*, pp. 29–58. Boston: Bedford/ St Martin's.

Appadurai, Arjun. 1996. *Modernity at Large: Cultural Dimensions of Globalization*. Minneapolis: University of Minnesota Press.

Bayly, C.A. 2004. *The Birth of the Modern World, 1780–1914: Global Connections and Comparisons*. Oxford: Blackwell.

Bentley, Jerry. 2003. World history and the grand narrative. In B. Stuchtey and E. Fuchs, eds, *Writing World History*, pp. 47–65. New York: Oxford University Press.

Benton, Lauren. 2002. *Law and Colonial Cultures: Legal Regimes in World History, 1400–1900*. Cambridge: Cambridge University Press.

Burke, Edmund, III. 1993. Introduction: Marshall G.S. Hodgson and world history. In Marshall G.S. Hodgson, *Rethinking World History: Essays on Europe, Islam, and World History*, ed. Edmund Burke, III. Cambridge: Cambridge University Press.

Chakrabarty, Dipesh. 2000. *Provincializing Europe: Postcolonial Thought and Historical Difference*. Princeton: Princeton University Press.

Chalcraft, John T. 2005. Pluralizing capital, challenging Eurocentrism: Toward post-Marxist historiography. *Radical History Review* 91 (Winter): 13–39.

Christian, David. 2005. *Maps of Time: An Introduction to Big History*. Berkeley: University of California Press.

Cooper, Frederick. 2005. *Colonialism in Question: Theory, Knowledge, History*. Berkeley: University of California Press.

Darnton, Robert. 1984. *The Great Cat Massacre and Other Episodes in French History*. New York: Basic Books.

Darnton, Robert. 2004. It happened one night. *New York Review of Books* 51 (11) (June 24): 60–64.

Davis, Natalie Zemon. 2006. *Trickster's Travels: A Sixteenth-Century Muslim between Worlds*. New York: Hill & Wang.

Diamond, Jared. 1997. *Guns, Germs, and Steel: The Fates of Human Societies*. New York: W.W. Norton.

Duara, Prasenjit. 1997. *Rescuing History from the Nation: Questioning Narratives of Modern China*. Chicago: University of Chicago Press.

Dunn, Ross E. 1996. Review of Marshall G.S. Hodgson, *Rethinking World History*. *Journal of World History* 7 (1) (Spring): 131–133.

Eaton, Richard M. 1997. Comparative history as world history: Religious conversion in modern India. *Journal of World History* 8 (2) (Fall): 243–271.

Eisenstadt, Shmuel N. 1986. *The Origins and Diversity of Axial Age Civilizations*. Albany: State University of New York Press.

Feierman, Steven. 1999. Colonizers, scholars, and the creation of invisible histories. In Lynn Hunt and Victoria Bonnell, eds, *Beyond the Cultural Turn*, pp. 182–216. Berkeley: University of California Press.

Hall, Catherine. 2004. Review of C.A. Bayly, *The Birth of the Modern World, 1780–1914. Reviews in History*, at http://www.history.ac.uk/reviews/review/420 (accessed Feb. 2012).

Hodes, Martha. 2003. The mercurial nature and abiding power of race: A transnational family story. *American Historical Review* 108 (1): 84–118.

Hodgson, Marshall G.S. 1993. *Rethinking World History: Essays on Europe, Islam, and World History*, ed. Edmund Burke III. Cambridge: Cambridge University Press.

Keck, Margaret E., and Kathryn Sikkink. 1998. *Activists beyond Borders: Advocacy Networks in International Politics*. Ithaca, NY: Cornell University Press.

Lal, Vinay. 2005. Much ado about something: The new malaise of world history. *Radical History Review* 91 (Winter): 124–130.

Levine, Lawrence W. 2000. Looking eastward: The career of Western Civ. In Ross E. Dunn, ed., *The New World History*, pp. 18–25. Boston: Bedford/St Martin's.

Lewis, Martin W., and Kären E. Wigen. 1997. *The Myth of Continents: A Critique of Metageography*. Berkeley: University of California Press.

López, A. Ricardo, and Barbara Weinstein. 2012. *The Making of the Middle Class: Toward a Transnational History*. Durham: Duke University Press.

Matory, J. Lorand. 1999. The English professors of Brazil: On the diasporic roots of the Yorùbá nation. *Comparative Studies in Society and History* 41 (1): 72–103.

Mazlish, Bruce. 1998. Comparing global history to world history. *Journal of Interdisciplinary History* 28 (3): 385–395.

Pomeranz, Kenneth. 2000. *The Great Divergence: China, Europe, and the Making of the Modern World Economy*. Princeton: Princeton University Press.

Schäfer, Wolf. 1993. Global history: Historiographical feasibility and environmental reality. In B. Mazlish and R. Buultjens, eds, *Conceptualizing Global History*, pp. 47–69. Boulder: Westview.

Schäfer, Wolf. 2003. The new global history: Toward a narrative for Pangaea Two. *Erwägen Wissen Ethik* 14 (Apr.): 75–88.

Scott, Rebecca J. 2007. Public rights and private commerce: A nineteenth-century Atlantic creole itinerary. *Current Anthropology* 48 (2): 237–256.

Scott, Rebecca J. 2009. Microhistory set in motion: A nineteenth-century Atlantic creole itinerary. In G. Baca, A. Khan, and S. Palmié, eds, *Empirical Futures: Anthropologists and Historians Engage the Work of Sidney W. Mintz*, pp. 84–118. Chapel Hill: University of North Carolina Press.

Seed, Patricia. 1995. *Ceremonies of Possession in Europe's Conquest of the New World, 1492–1640*. Cambridge: Cambridge University Press.

Seigel, Micol. 2004. World history's narrative problem. *Hispanic American Historical Review* 84 (3): 431–446.

Seigel, Micol. 2005. Beyond compare: Comparative method after the transnational turn. *Radical History Review* 91 (Winter): 62–90.

Seigel, Micol. 2009. *Uneven Encounters: Making Race and Nation in Brazil and the United States*. Durham: Duke University Press.

Sinha, Mrinalini. 2006. *Specters of Mother India: The Global Restructuring of an Empire*. Durham: Duke University Press.

Thompson, E.P. 1967. Time, work-discipline and industrial capitalism. *Past and Present* 38 (1): 56–97.

Topik, Steven, Carlos Marichal, and Zephyr Frank. 2006. *From Silver to Cocaine: Latin American Commodity Chains and the Building of the World Economy, 1500–2000*. Durham: Duke University Press.

Townsend, Robert B. 2007. What's in a label? Changing patterns of faculty specialization since 1975. *Perspectives* 45 (1): 12–14.

Van Young, Eric. 1990. To see someone not seeing: Historical studies of peasants and politics in Mexico. *Mexican Studies/Estudios Mexicanos* 6 (1): 133–159.

Van Young, Eric. 2001. *The Other Rebellion: Popular Violence, Ideology, and the Mexican Struggle for Independence*. Stanford: Stanford University Press.

Veyne, Paul. 1984. *Writing History: Essay on Epistemology*. Manchester: University of Manchester Press.

Weinstein, Barbara. 2005. History without a cause? Grand narratives, world history, and the postcolonial dilemma. *International Review of Social History* 50: 71–93.

Wong, Roy Bin. 2000. *China Transformed: Historical Change and the Limits of European Experience*. Ithaca, NY Cornell University Press.

CHAPTER FIVE

What Are the Units of World History?

ADAM MCKEOWN

Imagine a textbook of United States history with the following table of contents:

America: From Continent to Nation

Part I: Early Societies in America
1. Alaska: The Bridge of Humanity
2. The Midwest and New England: Living with the Earth
3. New Mexico: Plateaus, River Canyons and the First Urbanization

Part II: Middle Grounds in the Middle Years, 1500–1776
4. New Mexico: A New Empire
5. The Midwest: Trappers and Confederacies
6. New England: Religion and Trade
7. Virginia: Home of Slavery and Liberty

Part III: A Nation Emerging, 1776–1914
8. New England: Immigrants and Elites
9. Virginia and Washington: Separate Traditions, Uncertain Unity
10. The Midwest: An Industrializing Heartland
11. California: The Western Shore

Part IV: Integration and Diversity, 1914–2010
12. Washington, DC: The Making of National Politics
13. New England: Tradition and Change
14. The Midwest: Rust and Race
15. California: The Flowering of New Cultures

Each chapter would cover important themes such as political institutions and ideologies, gender roles, economic development, technological achievements, and famous cultural

A Companion to World History, First Edition. Edited by Douglas Northrop.
© 2012 Blackwell Publishing Ltd. Published 2012 by Blackwell Publishing Ltd.

benchmarks. Maps would situate the regions and states in national context, and sidebars would provide documents and pictures that illustrate the cultural and social specificities of each region. And thought-provoking study questions would ask students to compare and connect material from the different chapters.

We can also imagine some of the objections to this textbook. The most basic critique would be that it does not convey a sense of the history of the nation as a whole, but is merely a collection of state and regional histories loosely arranged around a narrative of the rise of the East coast and subsequent spread and transformations of its institutions and cultures. Other critiques might challenge the elite Northeastern-centric narrative as being *too* totalizing and overdetermined, and challenge our book to include a greater diversity of perspectives.

We could respond to these critiques in subsequent editions. The revisions could include short prefaces for each section that draw attention to major themes and outline the broader narrative about the integration of the nation. Additional maps could show flows of people and communication networks across the continent. New sidebars could describe processes that linked the nation and distinguished its parts: Currents and Climate, Native American Migrations, The Constitution, The Mississippi River, Presidential Elections, From Postal Service to Internet, Democrats and Republicans, The Influenza Pandemic of 1918, The Nation Goes to War, "Houston, We Can See the Nation." Other sidebars could present primary materials that illustrate the perspectives of peoples such as the Navaho, Chinese-American laundrymen, French-Creole children, women's suffrage workers, Yippies, Samoan football players, and illegal Mexican immigrants. We could also write new chapters that make the scope of the text more inclusive:

The South: A Slave Society
Indian Reservations: Making a Multijurisdictional Nation
The Great Plains: From Passageway to Heartland
From Puerto Rico to Guam: Defining Inclusion

We could even introduce entire chapters on thematic topics, especially for the twentieth century when technology made the process of national integration even stronger and more irreversible (albeit still dividing these chapters into subsections that show how different regions reacted):

The Civil War: Integration by Force
Strengthening an American State: Progressivism and the New Deal
An American Century? America in the World from World War I to Iraq
From Beatniks to Tea Partiers: Postwar Culture and Politics

Such changes would have to be made carefully. Reviewers and concerned parents will complain that crucial events and processes are being sacrificed for the sake of trendiness or a political agenda. Overworked teachers may find it hard to integrate the revisions into syllabi and teaching plans that they have built up over years. And armchair pundits will complain of an increasingly incoherent narrative. In the most general sense, the critics would be right. It would be an unwieldy and difficult textbook.

Fortunately, actual American history textbooks are much better structured (Brinkley 2008; Foner 2008). The chapters are not divided according to geographical spaces, but by themes and chronology. Typical chapters center on topics such as slavery; Western expansion; the growth of markets and industrialization; wars such as the Revolution, Civil War and World War II; political moments and movements such as Reconstruction, the New Deal, or Civil Rights; and even "eras" such as the Jacksonian era, the Gilded Age, the Progressive Era, the Depression or the Sixties. Regional variations are acknowledged, but rarely fundamental to the structure of the histories being related. The basic units of American history in these texts are periods, events and themes that coalesce around a single narrative of how the nation came to be what it is.

But our imagined textbook is not entirely a fantasy. This structure still shapes most world history textbooks. The basic units of these texts are territorial: world regions, empires or civilizations. Chapters are loosely grouped into chronological order, but rarely organized into a compelling narrative of how the world came to be as it is. This has been even more the case over the past generation, as the Rise of the West narrative has fallen out of favor. Attempts to move away from that narrative have certainly created more inclusive texts. Thematic sidebars, introductions that attempt to summarize developments across multiple areas and, especially for the earliest and most recent periods of history, thematic chapters have all been introduced to emphasize connections, comparisons and broad processes in world history. But other than a general sense of growing interconnectedness, no compelling narrative has emerged to replace the Rise of the West (See Bright and Geyer, this volume.) And even in books where those innovations are most thorough, geographic units still hold sway through subheadings and document choices (e.g., Fernández-Armesto 2009; Tignor *et al.* 2010).

There are many good reasons why it is easier to subject US history (or any national history) to a chronological approach than world history. These include the existence of a single national government with national policies, a dominant language and religion, a relatively unified media and civic sphere, and over two centuries of tireless work by amateur and professional historians to pull the scattered threads into a single narrative. A different mix of these factors – with more colonialist politics and an even greater exercise of the imagination thrown in – has also worked to produce coherent Western Civilization textbooks, and their close cousins, the area studies courses. The chronological and thematic units are so predominant in Western Civilization that the stability of geographical units becomes irrelevant as the narrative gradually sweeps from the eastern Mediterranean to North America. The power and deep institutionalization of these narratives and units can be seen in the fact that even the last generation of historians who have so tirelessly critiqued nationalist histories and the construction of area studies still for the most part identify themselves as national historians and area studies practitioners.

These very same factors have made it difficult to establish a world-historical narrative. They have divided the world into national and regional containers of history, all of which share common methodologies grounded in detail and particularism. These make it hard to construct any broader generalizations about global processes (although colonialism is a significant exception – one that has been incorporated as a common context for many national histories outside the West. (See Sinha, this volume.) Moreover, the early prestige of European models of national history and, by the early twentieth century, the Western Civilization narrative has compounded the problem by leaving the Rise of the West narrative as their greatest legacy to world history. Resistance against this narrative has generated productive new research and historical questions, in what has been called the "New World History" (Dunn 1999). Some critics have even responded to this legacy by rejecting world history narratives *per se* as inherently totalizing and Eurocentric master narratives (Dirlik 2003; Lal 2005; chapters by Weinstein and by Northrop, this volume. But see also Dirlik 2005 for an analysis more similar to mine). Most world historians, however, remain skeptical of a retreat into equally one-sided localism (Bentley 2005). But they have internalized this critique enough to remain wary of rashly constructing new narratives, and alternatives to the Rise of the West story have yet to cohere.

Is world history thus doomed to remain an array of geographical units without narrative or conceptual coherence other than a loose commitment to comparisons, connections, contacts and climate change? It may well be that world history works best by posing problems and critiques, rather than new narratives. Research by scholars grounded in various sorts of area studies training has, after all, been a fertile source of new challenges, ideas and perspectives in world history (Pomeranz 2007).

The logic of this new research, however, pushes us past the limits of the geographical units in which it is still largely grounded. Connective and critical world histories have shown the limitations of the traditional units of empires, civilizations, oceans and regions in understanding global processes (Dirlik 2005; Lewis and Wigen 1997). And if history is ultimately about the question of change over time and how we came to be where we are, world history cannot avoid narrative explanations. Historical explanations are grounded in complex specificities rather than laws, which makes narrative a key mode of exposition (Gaddis 2004; Manning 2003). The comparison and juxtaposition of local narratives does not necessarily add up to a world-historical explanation. It may well be that certain historical questions require global explanations, such as how and why *Homo sapiens* spread around the world, the different geographical diffusions of Buddhism, Christianity and Islam, the effects of global population rise over the past 500 years, the origins and effects of the industrial revolution, or the spread of decolonization (Bentley 2003). But it is hard to imagine a genuinely global explanatory narrative emerging while our knowledge remains divided into familiar geographic units. The units that make up those narratives may instead have to be chronological, event-centered, network-centered, or rooted in geographical spaces other than those framed by area studies.

It is worth emphasizing that grand historical narratives – whether of a nation, a region or the world – are never meant to be a final explanation, or the sum of all knowledge. To be sure, the institutionalization of textbooks and history curricula sometimes makes it seem as if they are. But among practicing historians, narratives are most notable for their instability and incompleteness (see Getz, this volume). They are heuristic tools, under constant modification. They provide frameworks that help shape new questions and research problems. Few historians aim to merely reiterate a dominant narrative in their research. A successful work of history, at least as written by professional historians, generally aims to elaborate, modify, rethink, challenge and even undermine "dominant" narratives.

Here, we can take a lesson from work done under the rubric of national histories. Narratives of US history, for example, can create broad contexts and issues that invest local studies with greater significance. Those local studies, in return, earn much of their relevance by the extent to which they are able to modify our perception of these national narratives. A history of industrialization in Cleveland, the New York draft riots, Hmong immigrants in Wisconsin, or the spread of air conditioners may all be of interest to readers with a direct connection to those places or peoples, as well as to other readers with eclectic curiosities or theoretical concerns. But every one of these topics also gains greater relevance and reach by situating itself as a contribution to understanding better how the United States, as a whole, came to be what it is.

And this relevance need not come merely in the form of case studies that add detail and variation to our existing knowledge. Indeed, many of the best contributions aim to undermine or radically revise existing narratives. This has been the main achievement of the last four decades of social, ethnic and gender history – to incorporate slavery, women, Asians, popular culture and any other number of new dimensions into the grand narrative of American history. And it is precisely this concern with the grand narrative that has put these many specialized researches into conversation with one another as part of a larger project.

When engaging with a grand narrative, we must also remain aware of what can and cannot be known at different scales of analysis – both temporal and spatial – and what questions can best be answered at those scales. To some extent this is a matter of selectivity. Just as the historian of Potosí need not know the history of every mine, church and individual in the city in order to write a convincing narrative, so the historian of Bolivia need not know the history of every city in Bolivia, and a historian of the world need not know the histories of every nation, empire and trade diaspora. Similarly, nobody expects a generalization about industrialization in the United States to apply equally to Chicago, Georgia and the Hopi Indian reservation. Indeed, one may doubt that such a generalization could be applied to the Hopis at all. Nonetheless, it would be impossible to understand the Hopis without some awareness of the contexts of American (and global) industrialization (Pomeranz 2007).

This awareness also applies to temporal scales. Individual human decisions are of less relevance at longer and longer time scales, except as components of mass statistical aggregates. But many particularities, such as the divergence of national policies and individual wars, must ultimately be explained by human decisions – perhaps even those of single persons. These particularities all have had an effect over the subsequent course of history. But merely collecting examples of policy choices and decisions to go to war will not help us to understand the long-term processes of the creation of an international system or the buildup of conflicting interests that frames the possible choices and decisions. These have to be understood at a longer time frame, often beyond the life of a single, decision-making human.

This awareness of scale is about more than just different levels of generalization. Different scales of analysis also highlight different historical processes. The common criticism that grand narratives get the details of local histories wrong is often beside the point. A grand narrative looks at long-term trends and patterns. To claim the existence of a broad trend is not to claim that every place and everybody behaves the same. It is to claim that over time certain choices, actions, institutions and patterns become more and more likely, thus shaping the probable directions of subsequent change. Outliers, rebels and variations can coexist perfectly well with broad trends, and may even help instigate some of the most notable changes. Immanuel Kant commented on this in 1784, when he noted that actions such as marriage and birth may seem to be so dependent on human free will and contingency that they would be impossible to reckon in advance. And "Yet ... they occur according to laws as stable as [those of] the unstable weather" (Kant 1963).

At the same time, the grand narratives must take care not to go to the opposite extreme and discount local particularities. In part this is because the large-scale view often cannot account for local particularities and processes that may be of great importance in daily human life. But it is also because one of the major sources of historical change may well be specific and local events that, for whatever contingent reasons, cascade into developments of regional, national and global significance. The very methods of large-scale, aggregate analysis tend to obscure these possibilities.

Let me give an example from my own research on migration from the 1840s to 1930s to show how different processes emerge at different scales of analysis (McKeown 2010). At the largest aggregate levels of over 20 million journeys over a period of 100 years, mass migrations out of Europe, China and India showed remarkably similar cycles of return and female migration, patterns that converged over time. If we break down any one of those mass flows into smaller flows defined by destination or region of origin, the correspondence is much weaker and very little convergence can be observed. This disparity grows stronger when we move down to the levels of villages and extended family. And we finally come to a point of absolute difference when we compare the lifetimes of the individual brother who did not migrate with the brother who did.

No one of these scales of analysis is the "true" scale. Instead, each scale illuminates different processes. The largest mass scale shows the effects of an increasingly integrated world economy on migration. Fluctuations in the smaller regional flows more strongly reflect historical events, national policies and economic contingencies that impacted those migrations. At the level of village, these contingencies are even more strongly shaped by the fates and fortunes of individual migrants who were able to establish a beachhead and new migrant networks. Finally, at the level of two brothers with their entirely opposite responses to similar structural conditions, we must resort to psychology or the specifics of family dynamics if we are to offer any explanation. We could also further expand the scale temporally, beyond the specifics of mass migration in the age of industry, to attempt larger generalizations of humans as a "migratory species" (Manning 2005).

The division of labor in science offers a good metaphor to understand the nature of knowledge at different scales. The principles of quantum mechanics underlie the structure of atoms and molecules, which then make up chemicals, substances and tissues come together to form organs and organisms, which then form populations, ecosystems and human societies. Any change in quantum mechanical principles would surely alter the nature of ecosystems and human societies. But nobody would ever propose to study ecosystems through the principles of quantum mechanics. An understanding of how ecosystems operate depends on setting limits to relevant information, devising appropriate methods and formulating appropriate questions. The relevant units for ecosystems are not electrons, neutrons and photons, but populations, environments, symbiotic relationships and moments of evolutionary change.

The need for different questions and relevant information is equally true for different scales of historical analysis. His family life and education would be an indispensable part of a biography of Mao Zedong. It is of less significance in a history of China or of the Chinese Communist Party, and of almost negligible interest in a history of the global communist movement. By the same token, a history of the global communist movement, or even a history of China, cannot really explain why millions of students beat their teachers and millions of city dwellers were sent to the countryside in China in the 1960s. To understand this, we would have to highlight Mao's political tactics as part of the explanation, which might then bring us back to his personality and personal background. Although the questions, data, and assumptions (such as agency or structure as motive forces in history) at one scale of analysis do not always seem relevant, or even valid, at other scales, they are all linked through complex relationships.

Jared Diamond's popular book *Guns, Germs and Steel* (1999) offers another example of the different kinds of knowledge that emerge at different scales of analysis (see chapters by Yoffee and Adas, this volume). Diamond provides a well-constructed and plausible argument for why economic development was more probable in the east–west Eurasian axis than in other parts of the world. Briefly put, the Eurasian axis was a space that facilitated greater levels of interaction and mutual learning, which made development more probable. He develops this argument with a mix of epidemiological, evolutionary, environmental, geographical and historical evidence. He goes wrong, however, in the final chapter where he extends his method to explain why Europe rather than other parts of Eurasia had an industrial revolution. His methods and arguments fail at this smaller scale. More standard historical methods that pay attention to social, political, institutional, cultural and economic specifics are necessary at this scale. An engagement with Diamond on the 10,000-year Eurasian scale, on the other hand, would require different tools such as evolutionary theory, an ability to challenge Diamond's claims about the qualities of certain crops and animals, and an understanding of the long-term patterns and effects of cultural and technological interaction (Bulliet 2005).

For most historians, of course, a scale that encompasses the histories of different parts of Eurasia over a period of even 2,000 rather than 10,000 years is already well beyond their comfort zones. We are still a long way from any consensus on the narratives, questions and units that are appropriate for a world historical analysis. They will not necessarily be the same as those for national and regional histories. Topics like environment, climate, the global political order, the spread of religions and the movement of goods, peoples and ideas are sure to remain fundamental features of world-historical research. But we should not restrict ourselves to the most obviously global and connective topics and units.

The units we use to make sense of these processes are not necessarily the big units. We often tend to think in terms of a nested spatial hierarchy of units, from individuals to locales to nations to regions to the global, in which only the latter will be relevant to world history. But the specific units and topics of most relevance to world-historical research may often be quite small: a volcano eruption of a few days; a trading diaspora of a few hundred people; the construction and suppression of piracy; an international conference; a few maritime craftsmen, nomadic raiders or isolated missionaries; casual intimacies leading to the spread of syphilis; the history of passports; a multinational corporation; or the spread of the T-shirt. These may often seem to be, variously, of either negligible or enormous relevance to particular regional or national histories. But that should not be the metric by which we judge these topics. Rather, we should look at how they shape our understanding of the long-term processes that made the world as it is.

Periodization and chronology will also play a role in developing world-historical narratives, and temporal categories are no less crucial in writing world history. Debates over global periodization could revolve around questions such as the ebb and flow of nomadic power, the possibility of common cycles of state expansion and contraction, the relevance of the Black Death in producing new patterns of global interaction, the existence of a global seventeenth-century crisis, or the timing of the great divergence between Europe and the world. Such debates may often seem irrelevant to the questions formulated in the contexts of regional and local history. But again, that should not be the marker by which we judge their value. Rather it should be their potential to construct a better understanding of global history. Regardless of whether any particular periodization earns consensus, they are an excellent way to get scholars talking to each other across regional divides.

The geographic units of most relevance to world history may also be fundamentally different than those empires, civilizations and area studies units that still commonly divide world history textbooks. For example, the Kushan Empire, which existed in what is now Afghanistan and northern Pakistan from the second century BCE to the third century CE, had little political legacy and is rarely discussed in textbooks. But it was an important crucible for the mixing of Greek, Indic, Central Asian and Chinese cultures, and was a key space for facilitating the Silk Road trade and the formulation of Mahayana Buddhism as an expansive religion. Other geographical spaces, such as the highlands that cross Southeast Asia, China and India (especially for prehistoric periods), the network of early modern port cities that stretched from Amsterdam to Nagasaki, or the zone of Turkic-speaking peoples, are also examples of spaces that lie at the margins of most area studies but are of great importance to the processes and stories of world history.

Being historians who always build on the work of others, perhaps we should look to past and present practice in imagining appropriate units. What units and methods are now being used in world-historical research and teaching, and what are their potential and limitations? The following sections are not meant to be an exhaustive survey, but to give a sense of some of the broad possibilities in world-historical research.

Comparison and Connection

Comparison and connection are both deeply rooted in existing historical method and units. Both start with existing frames of historical knowledge and try to generate new understanding by juxtaposing and linking them. Diego Olstein (2009) calls comparative history the "pivot of historiography" because it brings together diachronic narratives of national history monographs with the more synchronic concerns of macrohistory and sociology (see also Tilly 1984). Connective histories, entangled histories and *histoire croisée* are the close siblings of comparative histories (Lepenies 2003; Manning 2003; Subrahmanyam 2005; Werner and Zimmermann 2004). They are a bit more daring in their greater willingness to transcend territorial boundaries and work from the bottom up. They sometimes present themselves as alternatives to comparative history. But the units to be connected are precisely those civilizational, national and regional units that make up comparative history.

Comparative and connective histories have been extremely fruitful in generating world-historical research and writing. William McNeill's *Rise of the West* (1963), generally seen as a founding text of the New World History, used both of these techniques in the service of a narrative focused on civilizations and how they responded to diffusing ideas and techniques. More recently, early modern historians have put these methods to effective use in challenging the "rise of the West" narrative. Comparative works have shown that economic activity, trade, living standards, legal formations, frontier expansion and cycles of state consolidation were far more similar across Europe and parts of Asia than had previously been appreciated (Bayly 1989; Benton 2002; Lieberman 2009; Pomeranz 2000; Richards 2006). Connective histories have brought non-European actors into the mix as important agents of interaction, and made provocative cases for the significance of early modern economic and cultural exchange in shaping the order of the early modern world (Alexandrowicz 1967; Flynn and Giráldez 2002; Fletcher 1985; Frank 1998; Subrahmanyam 2005). Taken together, this work has invested new life into questions about the origins of the industrial revolution, reduced the significance of Europeans as the main agents of early modern global integration, demonstrated the emergence of increasingly similar legal and political structures, and made the question of the ultimate rise of the West all the more perplexing.

Most of the historians engaged in this research were trained professionally in areas of Asian history. The conceptual advances against the old rise of the West narratives have not come in the form of cutting-edge, anti-Orientalist theorizing, but in the application of traditional methods of documentary analysis and political and economic history. The mere act of not starting from an assumption about European difference, but of testing that assumption, has produced astonishing results. It has also meant that questions and narratives developed in the context of European history nevertheless continue to project a long shadow over comparative and connective history.

The grounding of these historians in area studies also means that they tend to be conservative in making generalizations that cross the familiar civilizational borders. The best of this work is very nuanced in the choice of units to be compared, moving between smaller regions such as the English Midlands or the Yangtze Delta, and the broader context such as the European state system or Chinese empire when relevant (Goldstone 2002). But even the connective historians (with the exception of those trained in economics) are very wary about suggesting generalizations that cross the usual area studies boundaries or that might suggest a global historical narrative. The aim of most of these historians does not appear to be the construction of a world-historical narrative so much as using their regional histories as a basis from which to critique Europe-centered world-historical narratives and rethink their own regional histories using the tools derived from European historical questions. Comparative and connective history does not yet seem equipped to provide innovative new units and approaches that are appropriate to a global historical scale.

Zones and Systems

Connections are central to various proposals for alternative geographic units such as zones of interaction, ecumenes, middle grounds, borderlands, systems and world systems (Braudel 1996; Chaudhuri 1985; Hodgson 1993). These units tend to center on large empty places such as oceans and deserts (although rarely jungles and arctic zones) across which different peoples and states frequently interact. The vast scholarship surrounding the Atlantic and Indian Ocean worlds (and the anxieties about the coherence of these units that accompany this scholarship) are the best-developed examples in recent years, although the Mediterranean, Black Sea, Central Asia, Sahara, maritime Southeast Asia and Dar-al-Islam are not far behind. The virtue of these units is that they simultaneously draw attention to integration through interaction, and to the social and cultural diversity that persists and is even generated in the context of this interaction. They show that world history is as much about the framing of difference as about integration. Difference is taken for granted not as the product of isolated histories, but as the product of an interactive history.

World-systems theory, pioneered by Immanuel Wallerstein in the 1970s, is the most ambitious of these approaches, and still the most systematic attempt to establish a global historical narrative and scale of analysis (Flint and Taylor 2005; Wallerstein 2000). (See Chase-Dunn and Hall, this volume.) It posits a world divided between tribute and tribal systems until the sixteenth century, when a capitalist world-system emerged in

Europe. The modern capitalist system expanded to incorporate the entire world by the late nineteenth century (although see Frank 1991 and 1998 for an alternative narrative of a single system throughout history). The institutional and economic structures of all societies are fundamentally shaped by their position within this system. And those structures and relationships also change over time with the cycles of expansion and contraction within the system. In this way, world-systems approaches effectively transcend national and regional boundaries and places connections at the heart of world history.

World-systems theory has not, however, achieved an effective synergy with national and regional historical traditions. Regional historians resist what they see as the overly programmatic and structural account offered by world-systems theory, which often fails to produce good accounts of the complexities of local and mid-scale (under 50 years, or national units) histories. They also complain that it leaves little room for local agency and contingency. World-systems theorists have tended to respond by digging in their heels and further demonstrating the relevance of their models to understanding long-term trends. More recently, Wallerstein has also developed an extended critique of the forms of knowledge within the world-system. This includes an argument that the fragmentation of knowledge between the disciplines and area studies serves to obscure understanding of the system as a whole and uphold power relations (Wallerstein 2000). Compelling as these analyses may be, they only further close off the prospect of a working relationship between world-systems researchers and more mainstream historians and area scholars. Historians and world-systems theorists have reached a methodological impasse, each holding firm at opposite sides of the scalar divide.

More productive challenges have come from historians willing to work at a global level. For example, the early modern historians discussed above have seriously challenged the world-system narrative of a capitalist system that spread out from Europe to incorporate external areas from the sixteenth to the nineteenth century. They have shown that the economies beyond Europe and connections between Europe and Asia were much more dynamic and complex than depicted in Wallerstein's account. Indeed Wallerstein's history of the modern world-system is deeply rooted in the same form of a rise of the West narrative that he otherwise so thoroughly critiques in its substance. I suspect that historians of the nineteenth and twentieth centuries willing to work at a broader, aggregate level can also find discrepancies with the patterns described by world-systems theory (McKeown 2008). The hope is that, rather than being used to discredit world-systems theory, these findings can be used to develop a better narrative – a narrative that appreciates the power of world-systems in formulating questions, drawing attention to connections as a systemic context for the production of difference, and interrogating the ways in which standard categories of knowledge exist in collaboration with a fragmented world.

Other kinds of systemic and zonal approaches tend to be looser in their claims than world-systems theory, providing space for a variety of possible outcomes and complexities. But this comes at the expense of imagining a global history narrative. As is the case with area studies research, work on one zone tends to happen in isolation from work on other zones and the borders around those zones can become calcified rather quickly. Then we once again fall into the same cycle of trying to find connections between the established zones of interaction, and to bring places at the margins of those zones more into the center. Zonal research draws our attention to the kinds of dynamics that are crucial to world history, but stops short of reaching for the narratives and questions that are most appropriate for large-scale research.

Globalization

The idea of globalization offers an alternative to approaches that are rooted in geographic units. A history of globalization would focus attention on the diverse causes and consequences of connectivity, and is an inherently time-based narrative. It would have to be grounded in units other than the primarily geographical ones discussed above. These could include chronological units based on periodization, and content-based units focused on types of flows, such as investment, trade, people, ideas, communication networks, etc. A history of globalization could also be easily mapped on to concepts such as convergence, diffusion and divergence that have long shaped the work of global historians (Crossley 2008).

The idea of globalization brings much baggage, however, and few historians seem willing to adopt it (see Bright and Geyer, this volume). It is a highly presentist buzzword, often deployed in a way that insists on the newness of the phenomenon. It also evokes strong emotional and political reactions, both from those who see it as an agenda of exploitation, and from those who see it as an essentially benign process that brings the benefits of technology, information and free markets to all. Both of these reactions are grounded in images of homogenizing forces that overwhelm local histories. Even in more thoughtful accounts, globalization is often depicted as an undifferentiated bundle, as if flows of people, money, ideas, communication and goods naturally moved in conjunction with each other in all times and places.

This baggage, however, also carries some basic tools and opportunities. If historians want to be relevant to the contemporary world, how better than to critically engage with a concept that fundamentally shapes our understanding of the world today? Historians are the ones who can show the effects of past globalizations, moderate the hyperbole, add complexity to the more simplistic claims, and clarify what is specific about the current moment. At the same time, historians can also learn from some of the more nuanced analyses of contemporary globalization that show how processes of regionalization, differentiation and new identity formation come hand in hand with contact and interaction (Appadurai 1996; Robertson 1992).

An example of the kind of nuance a historical perspective can bring is the effects of flows of information about legitimate political forms in the nineteenth and twentieth centuries. The mid-twentieth century is often seen as a period of deglobalization, when the massive flows of goods, money and people in the late nineteenth and early twentieth centuries had receded. But if we look at the diffusion of political structures, the mid-twentieth century is actually one of the most powerful moments of globalization ever. As late as the 1900s, the world was still covered by a plethora of political forms: nation-states, city-states, empires old and new, dominions, protectorates, territories, colonies, princedoms, tribal areas, etc. But throughout the nineteenth and twentieth centuries, channels of information – as well as gunboats and colonizing armies – carried information about the institutions, symbols, practices and desirability of effective nation-states able to control their borders, engage in diplomatic relations, and otherwise engage in the same activities as similar states around the world. By the early 1960s, over 90 percent of the world was organized into nation-states of a kind that could be recognized by their peers and accepted into the United Nations. This was perhaps the most effective example of homogenizing globalization in human history. Yet it came hand in hand with the nationalist economic policies, border controls and restricted material flows that are often understood as the opposite of globalization (McKeown 2008; Thomas *et al.* 1987).

The idea of globalization has already generated productive debates about periodization. The early nineteenth century is seen as a crucial moment, often pointed to as the start of the great divergence and a new era of mass globalization characterized by expanding industrial markets, price convergence, rapidly increasing mass communications, the establishment of an international system of nation-states and an omnipresent conviction of living in a new era that the world had never experienced before (Hopkins 2002; McKeown 2007; O'Rourke and Williamson 2002). Such a periodization has significant effects on how we understand contemporary globalization. If the present can be understood as the continued unfolding of processes that have been in place for two centuries (which includes the consolidation of regional identities and borders, as well as the expansion of global flows), this should have serious consequences for our understanding of the effects and nature of current flows.

Acceptance of a nineteenth-century turning point will also have significant implications for how we interpret global connections in the earlier past. Were the global flows of silver, prestige items, weapons and soldiers, drugs, foods, new crops, trade diasporas, religious practices, ideas of kingship and common practices for treating foreigners actually not globalization? Or can they be understood as a different kind of globalization, one that grew hand in hand with a political landscape of universal empires and entrepôts rather than nation-states, one in which the cultural and social effects of interaction had dimensions other than the economic ones that dominate in the more recent era? And were the forms of exchange different in the Mongol era, during the age of classical empires, or earlier?

Such debates are crucial for the construction of a world history. Even if we ultimately jettison the idea of globalization (or, what is more likely, turn it into something that is entirely unrecognizable from its current form), consideration of that idea provides a context for productive discussions about processes that cross geographic boundaries. Out of these debates may come the rudiments of a narrative structure, some basic chronological and thematic units and, most importantly, further research questions at a scale different from those generated in area studies and European history.

Humanity

At first glance, humanity is both the most obvious and the most platitudinous unit of world history. Of course world history is about the history of human species, and how we came to be where we are. But this assertion gives us few guidelines about how to actually go about telling and analyzing that story.

This skeptical reaction perhaps says more about the limitations of historical method than about the category itself. Telling the history of humanity can actually be a most exciting challenge for world history, one that compels us to be interdisciplinary and search for new methods and modes of knowledge. This is the case when we understand the category of humanity not as defining the outer limits of our research, but as just a small part of a much larger living and physical environment.

The starting point for a compelling history of humanity is the question of what makes us human: when does "humanity" start, and how do we relate to other organisms and physical processes? These questions can never be definitively answered. But they are questions that can only be approached with knowledge of anthropology, evolution, linguistics, brain science, genetics, biology, environmental science and a host of other disciplines (Buchanan 2000; Bulliet 2005; Christian 2005; Smail 2008; Spier 2011; Wilson 2003).

They are questions that transform the scale of humanity from an overwhelmingly large and substanceless platitude, to just a small portion of the diversity of life and the universe.

Once the scale of humanity is reduced like this, it become more possible to see the kinds of units and questions that can help us to understand humanity as a life form. When and how did humans come to cover and transform the Earth? What are the effects of language and writing? How have humans transformed the environment and their fellow life forms, and vice versa? What forms of social organization and relationships are distinctive to humanity? (For example, humans tend to distribute their reproductive burdens relatively evenly across multiple families rather than delegating them to one or two queens – as with bees – or to a single dominant male with his harem.) How has cultural evolution and learning shaped our physical distribution and evolution?

Many of these questions can be found in world history textbooks. But they are usually restricted to a small portion of the first chapter, because they threaten to overwhelm the kinds of questions that concern most historians. This need not be the case. Situating human history as part of world history (with the world understood as something that includes more than just humans), or even as part of a "big history" that stretches beyond the Earth, provides the rudiments for a narrative about how humans have interacted with the nonhuman world (see Spier, this volume). Rather than minimizing the importance of humans, it highlights their impact, situates that impact in time and space, and even draws attention to the last 200 years of massive, sometimes exponential growth in energy and resource consumption (Christian 2005). This, then, establishes a context from which we can return to and generate extra significance for more familiar questions about globalization, the agricultural and industrial revolutions, patterns and effects of global trade, and global inequality.

Note

Thanks to the participants in the Summer Dissertation Workshop in World History, University of Pittsburgh, June, 2010 for helping me to think through the ideas in this chapter. As far as I can tell, few if any of them would agree with all of my arguments here, especially my neglect of empire. But their engagement and challenges helped me to think more clearly.

References

Alexandrowicz, C.H. 1967. *An Introduction to the History of the Law of Nations in the East Indies*. Oxford: Clarendon Press.
Appadurai, A. 1996. *Modernity at Large: Cultural Dimensions of Globalization*. Minneapolis: University of Minnesota Press.
Bayly, C.A. 1989. *Imperial Meridian: The British Empire and the World, 1780–1830*. London: Longman.
Bentley, J. 2003. World history and grand narrative. In B. Stuchtey and E. Fuchs, eds, *Writing World History, 1800–2000*, pp. 47–65. Oxford: Oxford University Press.
Bentley, J. 2005. Myths, wagers, and some moral implications of world history. *Journal of World History* 16: 33–82.
Benton, L. 2002. *Law and Colonial Cultures: Legal Regimes in World History, 1400–1900*. Cambridge: Cambridge University Press.
Braudel, F. 1996. *The Mediterranean and the Mediterranean World in the Age of Philip II*. 2 vols. Berkeley: University of California Press.
Brinkley, A. 2008. *American History: A Survey*. 13th edn. New York: McGraw-Hill.

Buchanan, M. 2000. *Ubiquity: The Science of History … or Why the World Is Simpler Than We Think*. London: Weidenfeld & Nicolson.

Bulliet, R. 2005. *Hunters, Herders, and Hamburgers: The Past and Future of Human–Animal Relationships*. New York: Columbia University Press.

Chaudhuri, K.N. 1985. *Trade and Civilization in the Indian Ocean: An Economic History from the Rise of Islam to 1750*. Cambridge: Cambridge University Press.

Christian, D. 2005. *Maps of Time: An Introduction to Big History*. Berkeley: University of California Press.

Crossley, P.K. 2008. *What Is Global History?* Cambridge: Polity.

Diamond, J. 1999. *Guns, Germs, and Steel: The Fates of Human Societies*. New York: W.W. Norton.

Dirlik, A. 2003. Confounding metaphors, inventions of the world: What is world history for? In B. Stuchtey and E. Fuchs, eds, *Writing World History, 1800–2000*, pp. 91–133. Oxford: Oxford University Press.

Dirlik, A. 2005. Performing the world: Reality and representation in the making of world histor(ies). *Journal of World History* 16: 391–410.

Dunn, R., ed. 1999. *The New World History: A Teacher's Companion*. New York: Bedford/St. Martin's.

Fernández-Armesto, F. 2009. *The World: A History*. 2nd edn. Upper Saddle River, NJ: Prentice Hall.

Fletcher, J. 1985. Integrative history: Parallels and interconnections in the early modern period, 1500–1800. *Journal of Turkish Studies* 9: 37–57.

Flint, C., and P. Taylor. 2005. *Political Geography: World-Economy, Nation-State and Locality*. Upper Saddle River, NJ: Prentice Hall.

Flynn, D., and A. Giráldez. 2002. Cycles of silver: Global economic unity through the mid-eighteenth century. *Journal of World History* 13: 391–428.

Foner, E. 2008. *Give Me Liberty! An American History*. 2nd edn. New York: W.W. Norton.

Frank, A.G. 1991. A plea for world system history. *Journal of World History* 2: 1–28.

Frank, A.G. 1998. *ReORIENT: Global Economy in the Asian Age*. Berkeley: University of California Press.

Gaddis, J.L. 2004. *The Landscape of History: How Historians Map the Past*. Oxford: Oxford University Press.

Goldstone, J. 2002. Efflorescences and economic growth in world history. *Journal of World History* 13: 323–390.

Hodgson, M. 1993. *Rethinking World History: Essays on Europe, Islam and World History*. Cambridge: Cambridge University Press.

Hopkins, A.G., ed. 2002. *Globalization in World History*. New York: W.W. Norton.

Kant, I. 1963. Idea for a universal history from a cosmopolitan point of view. In I. Kant, *On History*, trans L.W. Beck. Indianapolis: Bobbs Merrill,.

Lal, V. 2005. Much ado about something: The new malaise of world history. *Radical History Review* 91: 124–130.

Lepenies, W., ed. 2003. *Entangled Histories and Negotiated Universals: Centers and Peripheries in a Changing World*. Frankfurt: Campus.

Lewis, M., and K. Wigen. 1997. *The Myth of Continents: A Critique of Metageography*. Berkeley: University of California Press.

Lieberman, V. 2009. *Strange Parallels, vol. 2: Mainland Mirrors*. Cambridge: Cambridge University Press.

Manning, P. 2003. *Navigating World History: Historians Create a Global Past*. New York: Palgrave Macmillan.

Manning, P. 2005. *Migration in World History*. London: Routledge.

McKeown, A.M. 2007. Periodizing globalization, *History Workshop Journal* 63 (1): 218–230.

McKeown, A.M. 2008. *Melancholy Order: Asian Migration and the Globalization of Borders*. New York: Columbia University Press.

McKeown, A.M. 2010. Chinese emigration in global context, 1850–1940. *Journal of Global History* 5 (1): 95–124.

McNeill, W.H. 1963. *The Rise of West: A History of the Human Community*. Chicago: University of Chicago Press.

Olstein, D. 2009. Comparative history: The pivot of historiography. In B.Z. Kedar, ed., *New Ventures in Comparative History*, pp. 37–52. Jerusalem: Magnes Press.

O'Rourke, K., and J. Williamson. 2002. When did globalization begin? *European Review of Economic History* 6 (1): 23–50.

Pomeranz, K. 2000. *The Great Divergence: China, Europe, and the Making of the Modern World Economy*. Princeton: Princeton University Press.

Pomeranz, K. 2007. Social history and world history: From daily life to patterns of change. *Journal of World History* 18 (1): 69–98.

Richards, J. 2006. *The Unending Frontier: An Environmental History of the Early Modern World*. Berkeley: University of California Press.

Robertson, R. 1992. *Globalization: Social Theory and Global Culture*. London: Sage.

Smail, D.L. 2008. *On Deep History and the Brain*. Berkeley: University of California Press.

Spier, F. 2011. *Big History and the Future of Humanity*. Oxford: Wiley-Blackwell.

Subrahmanyam, S. 2005. *Explorations in Connected History: From the Tagus to the Ganges*. Oxford: Oxford University Press.

Thomas, G., J. Meyer, F. Ramirez, and J. Boli. 1987. *Institutional Structure: Constituting State, Society and the Individual*. Thousand Oaks, CA: Sage.

Tignor, R., J. Adelman, S. Aron, *et al.* 2010. *Worlds Together, Worlds Apart: A History of the World from the Beginnings of Humankind to the Present*. 3rd edn. New York: W.W. Norton.

Tilly, C. 1984. *Big Structures, Large Processes, Huge Comparisons*. New York: Russell Sage Foundation.

Wallerstein, I. 2000. *The Essential Wallerstein*. New York: New Press.

Werner, M., and B. Zimmermann, eds. 2004. De la comparaison à l'histoire croisée. Paris: Seuil.

Wilson, E.O. 2003. *Consilience: The Unity of Knowledge*. New York: Knopf.

Teaching the world:
publics and pedagogies

CHAPTER SIX

Meetings of World History and Public History

LESLIE WITZ

The first impetus for this chapter was the symposium of selected professional practitioners of world history convened under the auspices of the World History Network and the World History Association in Boston in 2006. Given calls to move World History out of its dominant location in the US academy and the ever-present crisis over what constitutes its field of study, the symposium's organizers set a seemingly ambitious task to define a disciplinary "research agenda." It became clear, though, that what was being sought was not a statement of consensus or direction, but rather a series of indications that research, writing and institutional organization of world history as a field might possibly take up (Christian *et al.*: 2–3, 12–13). For all this hesitancy there was an underlying prospect for world history that was continually evoked and sought: expansion of the field of practitioners, the archive and research themes. The general trend was always towards accumulative possibilities, to make "room for" and take "stock of different approaches to world history" within and outside the academy, leading perhaps to an "International Historiography Research Cluster" and an extension of the spatial and temporal scales of research. With such expansion there was the expectation that "interdisciplinary challenges" would open up, "novel insights" would materialize and "comparative themes" emerge (Christian *et al.*: 12–15). In effect, the priorities of world history research that were articulated were ones of creating abundance as a vehicle to revitalize the field and face disciplinary challenges.

In participating in these proceedings I felt like a little bit of a charlatan. Although I had taught world history in the 1990s at the University of the Western Cape in Cape Town, South Africa, in a first-year course entitled "The Making of the Modern World," my major area of research and teaching had turned to public history. In my short presentation, "World heritage and the challenges to world history," I tried to bring these concerns together by arguing for analyses of the different ways and means by which world heritage is produced, how notions of "world" come to be constituted in the public domain, and how claims to universality are made. But the more I reflected on my own presentation and listened to others the greater my sense of unease that the prospect of "unlimited

A Companion to World History, First Edition. Edited by Douglas Northrop.
© 2012 Blackwell Publishing Ltd. Published 2012 by Blackwell Publishing Ltd.

accumulation" was being presented as a model to "compensate for lack" (Rogoff 2002: 64). These processes of accumulation and incorporation were no guarantees of developing pathways that would inaugurate new and different pasts. How could I rethink a meeting between public history and world history that would not replicate this problem? This chapter is an attempt to set up such a meeting where it may be possible to enable movement away from a framework of accrual. I attempt to unlock the "world" and "history" from their moorings, and rather than seeking to situate them spatially, place them in a state of permanent tension by opening up a set of engagements around public pasts. This is not to stake a claim for a public history of world history that concerns itself with popularization, audiences and inclusion, but rather to question framings and methodologies, "clearing the ground" (Lalu 2008: 277) to reformulate the constitutions of world histories. The "world" of these histories neither denotes global linkages nor is it an ever-expanding incorporative spatial domain but refers to sites of appropriation and association in a range of productive settings where meanings are generated, transmitted, altered and contested. What becomes significant in this state of instability is how worlds and their pasts come "to be defined and re-defined ... negotiated, circulated and contested" in and between public and academic locales (Witz and Rassool 2008:15).

Defending History

Perhaps a way to begin proposing such a meeting is to think through, admittedly from an outsider's perspective, the uneasy relationships which both public history and world history have with the category of history as a "professional" pursuit, particularly within the US academy. Public history in the United States primarily has concerned itself with issues of audiences and accessibility, of taking the methods and results of research beyond the confines of universities. With history defined through "outreach," what has come under scrutiny from within the discipline are whether the methodology and a commitment to striving for objectivity can be retained when the key interest is with audiences. The initiation of public history programs at universities, establishing the National Council on Public History, and the founding of a journal, *The Public Historian*, are all endeavors to claim public history as a serious, professional pursuit (Stanton 2006: 8–13). World history seems to have faced similar challenges. The overall objective is to develop a "wide-angle historical lens," that investigates "large-scale historical processes" and seeks to connect the local to the global.[1] As with public history, many of its concerns have been with history beyond the academy, particularly in high schools, where survey courses that used to be categorized as "Western Civilization" are taught. It is as a result of this association with survey courses at high schools, community colleges and universities, with a constant seeking for linkages and relationships across vast regions, and sometimes a lack of intense, in-depth archival research, the supposed hallmarks of "real" history, that world history is placed in a very uneasy relationship with the academy and causes great anxiety about its objectives (Maracas 2006: 203–205). The World History Association, graduate programs in world history and the *Journal of World History* have over the last 20 years all sought to stake a claim for world history as an academic, respectable, specific field of research and analysis.

These assertions of professional pursuit have gone beyond the institutional terrain into insisting that historical methodologies remain the foundations of these enterprises. In public history this has been articulated to distinguish it from a category labeled as "heritage," where it is claimed that many who entered the latter field gave up "their search for objective truth," "surrendered their claims of expertise" and transferred "responsibility from the profession to the marketplace for determining whose version of history is most 'real.'" According to the president of the National Council on Public History in 2006, Robert Weible (2006: 14–15), while public history was a "movement" that concerned itself with making history meaningful outside the bounds of the academy, it had to adhere to the principles of "professional scrutiny," and present a past reality that was as dispassionate as possible. As "historians with a purpose" the public historians had to constantly maintain the dual objectives of public service and professional responsibility.

Weible's position on service and responsibility is not necessarily one on which there is consensus. Many public historians prefer to employ Michael Frisch's (1990) concept of "shared authority," where, to varying degrees, audiences, communities and organizations contribute with professionally trained historians in the construction of histories and meanings in the public domain. Sometimes this may lead to more meaningful engagements where there are constant struggles and negotiations over the temporal and spatial alignments of history in the intersections between the academy and a variety of stakeholders. But what still remains in place is a historian/audience dichotomy, where it is the historians who represent themselves as searching for "complexity" and "ambiguity," in contrast to those who seek singular and monolithic narratives for their audiences. The latter are attributed to forces like the heritage industry, globalization, multiculturalism, national states, political interests and tourist imperatives, where seemingly easy fits and simplistic narratives are generated to accord with specific interests (Walkowitz and Knauer 2009). So "the distinctions remain firmly in place. The public of this public history is already constituted, and the purpose of public history is to 'thicken,' 'deepen' and critically expand what is perceived as a thin, mythic, romanticized sentimental past at local levels from a professionally derived source." In effect, "the 'sharing of authority' is the production of authority" (Minkley *et al.* 2009: 18–19).

Similarly for many world historians in the academy it is the collection and interpretation of evidence that is held as sacrosanct in sustaining what is designated as the "profession." Most vociferously articulated by Jerry Bentley (2008: 137–139), the editor of the *Journal of World History*, at stake is something he calls "a continuing obligation" by world historians "to base their work on the best available historical evidence." He sees it as the "task for all historians," as they seek to expand their regional and temporal frameworks, to strike a "balance between the interests of historical meaning and professional demands for historical precision." While recognizing that world history can, and indeed should, encourage a variety of different perspectives, starting points, theoretical frameworks and objects of focus, the appeal to "foster and facilitate the articulation of multiple perspectives on the global past" is firmly located in advancing and increasing "the value of professional history" that "opens itself to examination and criticism from all angles" (Bentley 2005: 76). Meanings, connections and frameworks would be placed within the methodologies of history as a profession in order to form what Bentley calls the "canon of world history."[2]

There are several calls for world history to move away from universalizing frameworks that subsume locality and its knowledges. Bentley, alert to such critiques, has suggested an "ecumenical world history" where expansive temporal and spatial scales, rather than presenting a "totalizing metanarrative," can provide important historical contexts and cross-cultural understandings. A major concern is how, and indeed whether, academic historians can present interpretive pasts in different frameworks that do not coincide with the sometimes linear and circumscribed "Western" temporal and spatial models. Joseph Miller (2005) has argued for a multicentered approach to history that would destabilize "Western" models of society and progress that are often presented as universal. "My 'world history,'" writes Miller, would bring together "meaningful worlds in a multi-centric history of balanced, engaged autonomous strivings and misunderstandings." The starting point for this history would be the particular locality and "personal biographies of the people who made – and continue to make – history happen in Africa (or anywhere else!)." It would then proceed to build "multiple histories" by showing the "diverse strategies" which "drew on the broader contexts, or proceeded innocently of them while nonetheless being part of them." Dirlik (2005: 409) takes this a step further to argue that given the existence of different notions of the world and history, the only way to do world history is to do historiography. This is not merely a historiography of "taking stock" (Christian *et al.* 2008: 13) as a component of world history but an account of "different conceptualizations of the world" and importantly "different ways of conceiving the past."

Bentley's suggestion of ecumenical world history, Miller's call for history that is centered at a multiplicity of sites, and, to a lesser extent, Dirlik's notion of world history as historiography, remain very much reliant upon assertions of history as profession with a series of distinct modes of operation. Bentley's (2005: 78) ecumenical world history is one that relies upon an "empirical narrative" that constructs "empirical realities of global human experience." Miller's invocation of different knowledges is one for better and more nuanced disciplinary history that has as its starting point local knowledges and histories. In effect, for Miller, this is history that does not need the appellation of "world" to signify its operation of seeking multiple, specific, diverging and converging contexts. In Dirlik's (2005: 410) call for world history as historiography, there is a much greater sense of presenting a disciplinary challenge that goes beyond the "who, where, when" (and I would add the why). Instead it takes shifting and different spatializations and temporalities seriously, argues for their historicization and accounts for "processes of commonality and difference, unity and fragmentation, and patterns in motion of homogeneity and heterogeneity." Yet, what this operation of historicization would entail, beyond changes over time, is not clearly spelt out by Dirlik. It is almost as if there is a historical context in waiting that needs to be made available in order to destabilize and question prevalent explanatory frameworks that use categories of time and space as if they are immutable. In this project it is "the evidence of the past in all its prolific variation including variation over the meaning of the world and of history" that is advocated as world history's recovery project. This, though, is not a call for history that will smooth the contradictions. Instead it would help elucidate how the past becomes usable, showing changes in modes of action and representation (Dirlik 1999: 30).

World history and public history therefore meet each other as constantly attempting to secure and mark their space as academic pursuits by adhering to professional standards. What tends to be elided in staking these claims, though, is a concern over one of the most powerful settings where the world is made, the discipline of history. This is where claims to authority are asserted through rules of evidence, the structures of narration and the invocation of precedent (sometimes called historiography). Although almost always presented as tentative and constantly approaching (but never finding) realities, these operations provide the security for history-as-discipline, seemingly located beyond the operations of power. Yet, as many postcolonial critics have pointed out, these processes of knowledge formation do not only emerge from histories of violence and subjection (particularly of colonialism), but sustain a methodological structuring that continues to draw upon its modes of silencing and speaking as authoritative. A much more cautious and less programmatic response would possibly be to seek ways to disavow the foundational narratives of history, continually interrogate how its disciplinarity is constituted, examine how history creates its events, subjects, contexts and worlds, and critique the forms of power that both maintain and are maintained by the discipline. In effect, this would mean doing not less history but "more histories of concepts, discourses, representations, narratives and formations of subjectivities" (Lalu 2009: 258–259). One way to try and accomplish this would be to set up a different type of meeting between world history and public history that instead of seeking to secure their respective positions presents the possibilities of constantly challenging the structures, modalities, authorities and limits of the discipline.

Revisiting Public History

To set up this meeting I want to return to public history and take a somewhat different approach. Instead of twinning professional/public with responsibility/service I want to suggest a notion of public history that always questions expertise and thinks of public, not as audience, but as existing "only by virtue of address." One important aspect of making public discourse is that in order to constantly reconstitute itself it has to develop a poetic that "must characterize the world in which it attempts to circulate and it must attempt to realize that world through address" (Warner 2002: 87, 113–114). With audiences not self-evident, the key issue for public historians is not how to convey knowledge to the public but rather how to redefine one's practice in a field where one's "expertise ... is constantly being challenged, shaped and re-shaped" and "the mystique of scientific knowledge" (Rassool 2006: 307) is under severe pressure.

With Ciraj Rassool, I have argued that this notion, of engagement with publics as a series of transactions "where knowledge is negotiated and mediated," forces us to "rethink of our practices as historians and history educators" (Witz and Rassool 2008: 11–12). A productive concept to employ for these knowledge transactions is the idea of "museum frictions" proposed by Kratz and Karp (2006: 2) to explain contestations both within and outside the institutional bounds of the museum and how these impact upon each other. These frictions, they maintain, occur when "disparate communities, interests, goals and perspectives ... produce debates, tensions, collaborations, [and] conflicts of many sorts." Following this, Rassool and I have noted that a similar set of contests arise with historical practices as "claims to knowledge are asserted, substantiated and articulated across an ever increasing wider-range of communities and institutions." These "ongoing negotiations where different and competing narratives, claims and priorities come up against each other" we refer to as "history frictions." In effect "the historian has constantly to negotiate and mediate between histories across a range of disparate domains, genres and interests to ... 'make history'" (Witz and Rassool 2008: 12–13).

It is from this vantage of engaged contested public history that I suggest that a starting point for a meeting between public history and world history might be a consideration of histories where plurality is all-important. This is not the same as different interpretations of events past but rather that history practiced in academic settings is only one of many "multiple locations of historical knowledge" (Cohen 1994: 23) where different methodologies are used to process a range of pasts with their own genres of knowledge formation. Public inscriptions of and upon the landscape of pasts are means of producing history rather than sources of evidence for past events. In all these different locations one can then begin to examine how these different histories generate "representations and attribute value," through "notions of what the world is or should be" (Lidchi 1997: 160). The tasks of this meeting with public history would be then to think through the "politics of representation" where there are "debates about how particular topics, perspectives, and images become prominent, how their depictions are formed and inter-preted, and the social relations and inequalities reproduced through representational practices, including their institutional settings" (Kratz 2002: 220).

Although the word "world" is used here in the same sense as public rather than a spatial and/or temporal location, bringing the idea of world as an unstable, constantly addressed and readdressed public to "world history" may perhaps be a way to initiate the type of meeting I am proposing. Sometimes this may be a world that does make associations with assertions to universal, global, and international meanings and values. At other times that world may be one that is much more circumscribed but at the same time claims a wider imaginary unity called "the public" (Warner 2002: 114–117). To examine and analyze "world history" would therefore entail a consideration of the representation and circulation of public address to selected pasts as history.

But these movements and representations of worlds and their pasts do not emerge of their own accord. This opens up for exploration how these different sites of history-making are constituted, their various codes and conventions and how they articulate with each other so that "in approaching the 'production of history' one is also approaching history as production" (Cohen 1994: 23). Control, limitations, structuring, excisions, conventions and past histories are all significant components of the production of history. This would include

> the organizing sociologies of historicizing projects and events, including commemoration, the structuring of frames of record-keeping, the culturally specific glossing of texts, the deployment of powerfully nuanced vocabularies, the confronting of patterns and forces underlying interpretation, the workings of audience in managing and responding to presentations of historical knowledge, and the contentions and struggles which evoke and produce texts and which also produce historical literatures. (Cohen, 1994: 245)

Rather than presenting a narrative that seeks linkages and associations, and instead highlighting the different versions or fragments of histories, there is an emphasis on the looking for the unresolved, for history as uncertainty rather than points of closure and convergence (Cohen 2005: 246). To take a meeting with public history seriously is to look at ways it can open up more debates about the representations of pasts, and to study the different ways and means by which world histories are produced and competing knowledge claims are asserted.

Two "Backward Hamlets"

In suggesting representation, production, circulation and the making of space as place as concerns of a world history beyond accrual and inclusivity, I want to take up two examples that are usually not considered as sites that are "worth serious consideration" and may be depicted as "backward hamlet[s]."[3] The first pertains to the site which tops the list of major internet search engines when one looks for "museums world history." It leads one to the foothills of the Appalachian mountain range in the southern United

States in the northeast of the state of Alabama, where in the small town of Anniston is the only named Museum of World History. Secondly, I want to examine the township of Lwandle, South Africa, where one of the country's newest museums, a museum of migrant labor, is situated. Both of these localities have barely made it into the annals of written history and even then they hardly feature. In the case of Anniston there is little beyond a PhD dissertation, a personal reminiscence, a nostalgic assemblage of annotated photographs, a centennial commemorative album, the local newspaper's 125th anniversary publication and a social and economic history of Anniston's early years. A few recent journal articles on the museum, housing project reports, a master's thesis and two ethnographic studies, one dealing with childhood and another on personal safety and criminality, comprise the sum total of the formal historical writings on Lwandle. I want to propose that the museums in Anniston and Lwandle provide illustrative devices to begin thinking through how places and their histories come to be constituted and reconstituted in and along a variety of routes into pasts, where power and knowledge are mediated and where there are constant reappropriations of places and memories (Crashaw and Urry 1997: 177–179).

Adjacent to a former military base in the 185-acre John B. Lagarde Interpretive Park in Anniston, Alabama, the visitor is invited to go to the Museum of World History and "take a trip back in time ... [and] around the world" to "view ancient treasures and objects" (Berman Museum 2007). A notice at the entrance to the museum gives an account of origins, explaining how the "6,000 plus piece collection of objects of art and artefacts" were acquired by Colonel Farley Berman and his wife, Germaine, from the 1940s. Colonel Berman, the notice goes on to say, "wished to remain mysterious about how he acquired the collection. Some pieces he suggested might have made their way into his bedroll after World War Two. Others, he liked to say, simply appeared in his home." Inside, the museum largely frames its displays through military history, where exhibitions of uniforms, guns, knives and armor enable a world history that is in effect an aesthetic of technology. Probably the museum's main attraction is a set of artifacts related to Adolf Hitler: a personally autographed photograph of Adolf Hitler, a bust of Hitler, Hitler's plans for the invasion of Britain, and Hitler's silver tea service. The context of history that is provided for all these artifacts is one of wonder and curiosity, and perhaps astonishment that they are located in this museum. It would nonetheless be inaccurate to cast the displays in the museum entirely as reifying military technology as central to the making of world history. Most notably in the "American West" exhibition, which one enters on the ground floor, a social history is the mechanism for dispelling romantic myths of expansion. Whereas the rest of the museum relies on objects displayed on walls, in cases and on stands, here dioramas, photographs, artifacts and elaborate explanatory labels are the vehicles used to establish a version of the American West that is gender-sensitive, attempts to present the ways of lives of different social and cultural groupings, and lays bare the extreme violence of encounters in westward expansion. Although there are still several display cases with guns in the "American West" in Anniston, the use of a very different type of exhibitionary technology seeks to represent inclusivity.

Less than 100 meters away, in the Anniston Museum of Natural History, another type of world history is on display. The "wilds of Africa, the wonders of the North American Wilderness and the mysteries of 2300 year old mummies" based on the collection of the local textile merchant, H. Severn Reager, and mammal collector, John Lagarde, are offered as vehicles of interpretation, leading to an understanding of relationships between "humankind and the natural environment."[4] In contrast to the Museum of World

History, the exhibitions are explicitly much more didactic, experiential and make much greater use of an exhibitionary technique that emphasizes locality, explanatory text and recreated environments. Caves, trees, rocks, gravel and simulated earth tremors all form part of what the museum calls "NatureSpace."

But what is not featured in the world histories on display in what the city of Anniston's publicity department presents as "two world class museums" (City of Anniston 2010) are moments in the town's local pasts that have featured in national histories. The first relates to a broader national narrative of civil rights and the firebombing, on May 14, 1961, of a bus of Freedom Riders, who were testing the new federal laws forbidding segregation on transport between states, by a "white mob" on the outskirts of the city. The second occurred in the 1980s when the Monsanto Corporation contaminated the local river system with polychlorinated biphenyls (PCB), waste from a local manufacturing plant. Some 20 years later a class action suit was settled with $300 million paid out to the plaintiffs for the deleterious health effects caused by the plant.

Although not featured in the museums of Anniston, these events have been incorporated into local and national pasts. With the "burning bus," the city and the Alabama Historical Commission were initially reluctant to give the site of destruction an official marker, claiming that the incident took place outside the boundaries of the city and that there was no way to identify the exact location of the event, as road construction had subsequently occurred (Spears 2009). It was through the sponsorship of a black college fraternity who worked with the privately funded Alabama Historical Association that a marker was placed on the site in 2007. The text on the board concludes with words that "the incident served to strengthen the resolve of the civil rights movement." Similarly, environmental activists have sought to highlight the ways that inhabitants of Anniston both were affected by and fought against industrial pollution. Archived under the heading "Anniston PCB/Lead Site – Anniston, AL," the US Environmental Protection Agency on its website (2010) provides a set of documents on the case that in effect provide a virtual memorial marker of how Anniston's image was altered from the "Model City of the New South" to "Toxic Town U.S.A." Earthfirst rates the PCB poisoning in Anniston as number 7 in its "America's top ten worst man made environmental disasters" (Rogers 2010). And in a special hearing on Anniston in the Committee on Appropriations of the US Senate held on April 19, 2002, David Barker, the president of Community Against Pollution (Anniston, Alabama), invoked his somewhat outdated knowledge of world history to stake a claim for compensation for the effects of PCBs:."You understand that Anniston is not in South Africa, Rhodesia, or some other totalitarian country, that we are Americans, and we live in Anniston, Alabama, and all we want to do is live a normal life" (Committee on Appropriations 2003).

It would be relatively easy to situate the two events described above into world histories of the environment, transnational struggles for human rights and the making of race, for instance. Indeed, the "burning bus" has already been incorporated into world histories, through texts and images that "solicit our gaze" (Warner 2002: 87–89) and constitute a public of concern for rights that appear as universal. It has made it into the South African Grade 12 school curriculum in the section on the civil rights movement in the USA, where the Freedom Riders are discussed (SA History Online 2010). Such an inclusion is indicative of a dramatic shift in the way school history has been conceptualized in post-apartheid South Africa. One of the key practices in the school curriculum had been a division into two sections, South African and General History (or European History), with the former emphasizing the "advance" of "Western civilization" as an alibi for conquest, and the latter a world history that was produced as a lesson in "civilization." (See Simo, this volume.) In the new school curriculum this division has fallen away and South Africa is placed in a world history that deals with topics such as the Cold War, independence movements in Africa, and civil society protest in the 1960s and 1970s. It is in the last mentioned topic, where strategies of civil disobedience and nonviolent protest are discussed, that Anniston appears. In world history from South Africa, the photograph of smoke bellowing out of the bus is placed to show violent conservative reactions to nonviolent protests, which in turn makes it easier to put in place a post-anti-apartheid national narrative of repression and resistance.

Yet neither the burning bus nor the industrial pollution find a position in the histories of the world in Anniston's local museums. These museums are simultaneously sites that, through their collections, provide a map of the world, and, in their exhibitions, corridors and passageways, take visitors through "conceptual paths" of representation (Kirshenblatt-Gimblett 1998: 132). Their claims to knowledge of the world are through acquisition and then appropriation into the classificatory and exhibitionary modes of the museum. In a world made primarily through objects that claim these institutions as serious author-ities of collection and display, pasts that rely upon evocations of memory in pursuance of what are presented as moral universal obligations are largely bypassed. The museums' fiction is an uncritical acceptance of the "representational power of ordering and classification," where history is presented as a scientific pursuit counterposed to a memo-rial strategy of visual commemoration (Sherman 1995: 51–52). An ethical rendering of pasts does, though, start to appear in the global history of nature on display in Anniston, where a utopian future and a long gone past of adaptation is counterposed to a dystopian present. The category of natural history in the museum is partially wrenched from its nineteenth-century origins, where the reference was the collection and display of species, to one that embraces an identity of nature being endangered, and asserts ecological concerns and a green consciousness of equilibrium (Yanni 2005: 157).

If there is a divergence in the making of commemorative and museum pasts in Anniston, in South Africa in the late twentieth century these histories came together as a large number of new museums were constructed with the primary objective of displaying, recollecting and teaching about aspects of the violence and suffering of the system of apartheid. One of these institutions, the Lwandle Migrant Labour Museum, some 40 kilometers from Cape Town, has worked since 2000 to install a narrative of Lwandle as a primary example of apartheid's effects. Lwandle was established in 1958 entirely as a hostel labor compound for single male migrant workers in the municipal services of the seaside resort of Strand and the growing fruit and canning industry in the region. The number of people living in Lwandle increased dramatically in the 1980s as a result of limited reforms and increasing poverty in rural areas. Because it was marked as a "black spot" in a region designated for people classified as "white," the apartheid government decided to close down Lwandle. This process, though, had not taken place by the time of South Africa's first elections based on universal adult franchise in 1994. The inception of a Government of National Unity, headed by the African National Congress, altered Lwandle's future and the hostel compounds were reconstructed as family homes. And, in an extraordinary moment, as the hostels were reconfigured the executive of the local municipality decided to support a proposal to establish a museum in Lwandle.

The Lwandle Migrant Labour Museum, opened on May 1, 2000, has become the primary vehicle for revisualizing Lwandle and its history. Its collection and displays include reproductions of pass books (the identity document through which the lives of

Africans in urban areas were controlled), a beach sign indicating segregated facilities, artifacts used by migrant laborers, photographs of people and street scenes in Lwandle and selected photographs used to depict migrant labor, from poverty in the rural areas to influx control and resistance (Mgijima and Buthelezi 2006: 801–804). Lwandle was made visible by placing its residents into a visual history that conformed to a new post-apartheid national narrative of repression and resistance. The family houses and the establishment of the museum proclaimed the changing political scenario as the culmination of these "national" struggles, where now Lwandle was being installed as a significant example of the operations of apartheid and those who fought against and ultimately defeated it.

At the same time as it made a local/national past for Lwandle, the museum also engaged with different world histories, sometimes embracing them and at other times displaying a great deal of ambivalence. Most enthusiastically the museum inserts Lwandle's past into an international discourse of human rights as a site of conscience which, like similar sites worldwide, actively uses history "to promote humanitarian and democratic values." (International Coalition of Sites of Conscience 2010). Hostel 33, the one remaining hostel that was not converted into a house, has been used as an artifact by the museum to recall memories of apartheid and the migrant labor system (Mgijima and Buthelezi 2006: 799).

Effectively Hostel 33 performs the role of a "memorial museum." These are museums that usually use a specific site of repression and/or torture and/or massacre to evoke memories of suffering in the past. They are explicitly political, they provide historical interpretations within a "moral framework," and their defining characteristic is that they "function as a memorial." Although their collections are typically small, their greatest assets are "the stories entrusted to them and the confidence imparted to them by survivors, family members, and their descendants, who use them as both spaces of private mourning and public memory" (Williams 2007: 8, 184). It is by locating these stories into a wider circuit of internationalized memorialization that Lwandle's pasts become exemplars of worldwide human rights abuses. Linking to a location selected and designated as a typical example of "historical crimes against humanity," the museum, much like the Museums of Occupation in Estonia, Memory Park in Argentina and the genocide memorial centers in Rwanda, is a site of political activism, attempting to estab-lish a community of survivors, and ongoing educational programs that assert a moral legacy through making past–present linkages. These world histories do not maintain any façade of neutral detachment (Williams 2007: 21).

But the museum has become part of another set of world histories. From the very beginning one of its primary concerns was to become a tourist attraction in Cape Town, and it had to confront world histories emerging from an industry that relies upon and sustains images of the colonial enterprise that often paved the way for opening up "primitive" and "exotic" destinations. The promotion of South Africa as a place of exploration, where one encounters wildlife and ethnic indigeneity in comfortable, secure surroundings, draws precisely upon these metaphors of exploration and uncritically celebrates the development of colonial modernity (Rassool and Witz 1996). Placed in an extremely vulnerable position, with little or no possibility of funding on the immediate horizon, the museum, when it first opened, found that it "had to dance to the tune of tourism." In a "shift" the museum moved "from a preservationist to tourist rhetoric" and partly positioned itself into this internationalized knowledge system as an ethnically situated Xhosa place (Mgijima and Buthelezi 2006: 800).

While international tourism (as an industry) might continue offering a "safe haven" for "marketing a troubled history that glorifies colonial adventure and a repudiated anthropology of primitivism" (Kirshenblatt-Gimblett 1998: 136), the Lwandle Museum has been negotiating ways to alter the foundational images and narratives of tourism and at the same time develop new notions of a public citizenry through the construction of a new set of public pasts. The exhibitions in the old community hall have continually attempted to challenge stereotypical notions of the people of Lwandle that rely upon depictions of an essential rural timeless Africanness in an urban setting, often cast as ethnicity. A walking tour through the township organized by the museum became a visit to people's homes, not to see and gaze upon people, but to talk with and hear stories about their lives and histories. And the lives of people in Hostel 33 have become a focal point of the tour, conjoining histories with selected and crafted artifacts, making it possible for the museum to imagine, image and represent lives for visitors.

In the development of a historical narrative that makes use of histories as a methodology towards constructing and performing lives, the museum is placing Lwandle in the ever-growing field of international heritage tourism. Heritage has become one of the main ways in which "location becomes a destination" through signifying "hereness," by adding value, creating pastness, elaborating difference and invoking a virtual experience (Kirshenblatt-Gimblett 1998: 150–176). The performance of history through Hostel 33 parallels similar modes of history production through heritage tourism. One of the most prominent of these has been in the southern United States, and Alabama in particular, where African-American heritage tourism and the possibilities of associated culture-led urban regeneration has provided a major impetus for establishing civil rights memorial sites and museums (Brundage 2005: 304–313; Eskew 2006: 41–42). So, in Anniston an association of business and heritage interests in the town, under the title of the Spirit of Anniston, whose work has mainly been around a Main Street revitalization program, has begun to embrace the Freedom Riders/Burning Bus memorial project. It has been suggesting that the site become part of an Alabama Civil Rights Trail that would attract tourists as part of "low hanging fruit" (a means to keep visitors in Anniston as long as possible) (Bean 2009; McGhee 2009).

Conclusion

Appearing as somewhat "out-of-the-way places" it would seem that Lwandle and Anniston would have to either remain consigned to the margins of world history or else be recovered and placed within a larger past of linkages, associations, routes and economies, setting up a series of "local–global interconnections." (See Gerritsen, this volume.) Yet neither core nor margin is a stable spatial and temporal entity, and what might seem to be "local commentaries" are always involved in "wider negotiations of meaning and power" with more localized "stakes and specificities" in the making of histories (Tsing 1993: 9). What a meeting of world and public history would suggest, therefore, is not one of placement, accumulation or including "social history" or "the people without history" (Wolf 1982) into world history. It instead might enable one to reflect upon and investigate the paradoxes around how notions of "the world" come to be constituted in the public domain through circuits of international tourism, processes of museumization, activist politics, movements that assert global or universal values, and changing and competing sets of local knowledges. To varying degrees these all come into play in Anniston and Lwandle in the ways that differing local and world histories are claimed, evoked and contested. Contradictions emerge between and within the locality and the universal, suggesting questions about what constitutes history, historical time and the space of history. These instabilities of category, time, place and identity offer potential histories of what Scott (2004: 263–267) has called the production of "discontinuity" and "differentiation." A meeting between public history and world history may open up for examination how spaces come to be constituted, made, remade and moved into different types of worlds of public address. It can provide possibilities for interrogating existing frameworks and assumptions about how localities are represented and produced, and the manner in which different circuits of knowledge production conflict and coalesce.

Notes

1 Patrick Manning, panelist at roundtable session, New Directions in World History Morocco, 14th annual conference of the World History Association, Al Akhawayn University, Ifrane, Morocco, June 27–29, 2005. Notes taken by author.
2 Jerry Bentley, panelist at roundtable session, New Directions in World History.
3 Email correspondence between the author and the editor of the *Journal of World History*, Jan. 25, 2010.
4 Anniston Museum of Natural History, postcard, collage of animals, Anniston, 2007; Anniston Museum of Natural History, "Mission statement," photograph of exhibition by L. Witz, April 2007.

References

Bean, B. 2009. Anniston: a historic military and industrial town. At http://www.spiritofanniston. com/pages/?pageID=26 (accessed Feb. 2012).

Bennett, T. 1995 *The Birth of the Museum*. London: Routledge.

Bentley, J.H. 2005. Myths, wagers, and some moral implications of world history. *Journal of World History* 16 (1): 51–82.

Bentley, J.H. 2008. The *Journal of World History*. In P. Manning, ed., *Global Practices in World History: Advances Worldwide*, pp. 129–140. Princeton: Markus Wiener.

Berman Museum. 2007. Take a trip around the world … take a trip back in time. Pamphlet, Berman Museum of World History, Anniston.

Brundage, W.F. 2005. *The Southern Past: A Clash of Race and Memory*. Cambridge, MA: Harvard University Press.

Christian, D., M. Lake, and P. Swarnalatha. 2008. Mapping world history: Report on the World History research agenda symposium. In P. Manning, ed., *Global Practices in World History: Advances Worldwide*, pp. 1–16. Princeton: Markus Wiener.

City of Anniston. 2010. Welcome to Anniston, Alabama. At http://www.annistonal.gov/ (accessed Feb. 2012).

Cohen, D.W. 1994. *The Combing of History*. Chicago: University of Chicago Press.

Cohen, D.W. 2005. The uncertainty of Africa in an age of certainty. In M.D. Kennedy and D.W. Cohen, eds, *Responsibility in Crisis: Knowledge Politics and Global Publics*. Ann Arbor: Scholarly Publishing.

Committee on Appropriations. 2003. Hearing before a subcommittee of the Committee on Appropriations, United States Senate, One hundred seventh Congress, Second session, Special hearing, April 19, 2002 – Anniston, Alabama. Washington DC: US Government. At http://www.ewg.org/files/annistonsenatehearingtrans_0.pdf (accessed Nov. 28, 2010).

Crashaw, C., and J. Urry. 1997. Tourism and the photographic eye. In C. Rojek and J. Urry, eds, *Touring Cultures: Transformations of Travel and Theory*, pp. 176–180. London: Routledge.

Dirlik, A. 1999. Is there history after Eurocentrism?: Globalism, postcolonialism, and the disavowal of history. *Cultural Critique* 42: 1–34.

Dirlik, A. 2005. Performing the world: Reality and representation in the making of world histor(ies). *Journal of World History* 16 (4): 391–410.

Eskew, G. 2006. The Birmingham Civil Rights Institute and the new ideology of tolerance. In Renee C. Romano and Leigh Raiford, eds, *The Civil Rights Movement in American Memory*, pp. 28–66. Athens: University of Georgia Press.

Frisch, M. 1990. *A Shared Authority: Essays on the Craft and Meaning of Oral and Public History*. Albany: State University of New York Press.

International Coalition of Sites of Conscience. 2010. At http://www.sitesofconscience.org/about-us#section1 (accessed July 31, 2010).

Kirshenblatt-Gimblett, B. 1998. *Destination Culture*. Berkeley: University of California Press.

Kratz, C.A. 2002. *The Ones That Are Wanted: Communication and the Politics of Representation in a Photographic Exhibition*. Berkeley: University of California Press.

Kratz, C.A., and I. Karp. 2006. Introduction. In I. Karp, C.A. Kratz, L. Szwaja, and T. Ybarra-Frausto, eds, *Museum Frictions: Global Transformations/Public Cultures*, pp. 1–31. Durham: Duke University Press.

Lalu, P. 2008. When was South African history ever postcolonial? *Kronos: Southern African Histories* 32: 267–281.

Lalu, P. 2009. *The Deaths of Hintsa: Postaparthied South Africa and the Shape of Recurring Pasts*. Cape Town: HSRC Press.

Lidchi, H. 1997. The poetics and politics of exhibiting other cultures. In S. Hall, ed., *Representation: Cultural Representations and Signifying Practices*, pp. 151–222. London: Sage.

Maracas, M. 2006. Transcript of the World History Research Agenda Symposium. Boston, Nov. 11–12, 2006. At http://www.worldhistorynetwork.org/conference/Transcript_Symposium.pdf (accessed Aug. 13, 2010).

McGhee, W. 2009. Spirit of Anniston plans for sites on Alabama Civil Rights Trail; Group also wants to create "Alabama Museum of the Southern Small Town." *Anniston Star*, Sept. 4. At http://www.allbusiness.com/trade-development/economic-development-tourism/12826675-1.html (accessed Nov. 7, 2009).

Mgijima, B., and V. Buthelezi. 2006. Mapping museum: Community relations in Lwandle. *Journal of Southern African Studies* 32 (4): 795–806.

Miller, J. 2005. Beyond blacks, bondage and blame: Why a multi-centric World History needs Africa. Draft for a talk at Carleton College, Northfield, MN, Mar. 9.

Minkley, G., C. Rassool, and L. Witz. 2009. South Africa and the spectacle of public pasts: Heritage, public histories and post anti-apartheid South Africa. Paper presented at Heritage Disciplines symposium, University of the Western Cape, Oct. 8–9.

Rassool, C. 2006. Community museums, memory politics, and social transformation in South Africa: Histories, possibilities and limits. In I. Karp, C.A. Kratz, L. Szwaja, and T. Ybarra-Frausto, eds, *Museum Frictions: Global Transformations/Public Cultures*, 286–321. Durham: Duke University Press.

Rassool, C., and L. Witz. 1996. "South Africa: a world in one country": Moments in international tourist encounters with wildlife, the primitive and the modern. *Cahiers d'Études Africaines* 143 (36–3): 335–371.

Rogers, S. 2010. America's top ten worst man made environmental disasters. Earthfirst.com, at http://earthfirst.com/americas-top-10-worst-man-made-environmental-disasters/ (accessed Nov. 27, 2010).

Rogoff, I. 2002. Hit and run: Museums and cultural difference. *Art Journal* 61 (3): 63–73.

SA History Online. 2010. The Civil Rights Movement in the USA: Extra information on well-known events in the Civil Rights Movement. South African History Online, at http://www.sahistory.org.za/classroom/grade12/3-1-3-1d.htm (accessed Jan. 11, 2010).

Scott, J. 2004. After history? In K. Jenkins and A. Munslow, eds, *The Nature of History Reader*, pp. 259–270. London: Routledge.

Sherman, D.J. 1995. Objects of memory: History and narrative in French war museums. *French Historical Studies* 19 (1): 49–74.

Spears, E. 2009. Memorializing the Freedom Riders. *Southern Spaces*, June 29, at http://www.southernspaces.org/2009/memorializing-freedom-riders (accessed Feb. 2012).

Stanton, C. 2006. *The Lowell Experiment: Public History in a Postindustrial City*. Boston: University of Massachusetts Press.

Tsing, A. 1993. *In the Realm of the Diamond Queen*. Princeton: Princeton University Press.

US Environmental Protection Agency. 2010. Anniston PCB/lead site – Anniston, AL. At http://www.epa.gov/region4/foiapgs/readingroom/anniston/ (accessed Aug. 14, 2010).

Walkowitz, D.J., and L.M. Knauer, eds. 2009. *Contested Histories in Public Space: Memory, Race, and Nation*. Durham: Duke University Press.

Warner, M. 2002. *Publics and Counterpublics*. New York: Zone Books.

Weible, R. 2006. The blind man and his dog: The public and its historians. *Public Historian* 28 (4): 9–17.

Williams, P. 2007. *Memorial Museums: The Global Rush to Commemorate Atrocities*. Oxford: Berg.

Witz, L., and C. Rassool. 2008. Making histories. *Kronos: Southern African Histories* 34: 6–15.

Wolf, E. 1982. *Europe and the People without History*. Berkeley: University of California Press.

Yanni, C. 2005. *Nature's Museums: Victorian Science and the Architecture of Display*. Princeton: Princeton Architectural Press.

CHAPTER SEVEN

Challenges of Teaching and Learning World History

ROBERT B. BAIN

The popularity of a high school course often masks the challenges students and teachers face in learning its content. Such, I think, is the case with world history. While it is the fastest growing subject of the secondary social studies curriculum in the United States[1] – by 2005 over 75 percent of American secondary students were graduating having taken a course in world history, an increase of more than 125 percent in the last 30 years (Cavanagh 2007: 10) – world history is a course with distinctive and often unacknowledged challenges for secondary history teachers and students.

Obviously, one challenge is the amount of content "covered" in a course traversing all of human history. How can history teachers and students work with such a vast range and scope of content as studying the whole world's history seems to entail? "How am I supposed to teach all that stuff?" is the teachers' version of the students' "how am I supposed to learn all that stuff?" Frankly, with the average world history textbook weighing in at a bit over 7 pounds, that is a good question to consider. For teachers and students, it is not easy to bring the whole world's history into focus while avoiding the "one darn thing after another" approach, or the cultural cavalcade that plagues so much history instruction. The danger, of course, is a fragmentation of understanding – where students acquire knowledge in pieces, and are unable to weave what they learn into a coherent and usable picture of the past.

Of course, developing coherent history at a national, regional or even local scale is also a challenge. But it is a much more challenging task for teachers and students of world history because of the temporal and spatial scales nested within the world history enterprise. These require students to make connections among events and processes occurring across a vast range of time frames and within geographic settings of different sizes. To avoid fragmentation and to construct a coherent and usable understanding of the past requires world history teachers and students to learn to manage what Tom Holt (1995) has called "the levels problem," a complicated issue of "establishing the continuity between behavioral explanations sited at the individual level of human experience and those at the level of society and social forces." The historian's task, Holt

A Companion to World History, First Edition. Edited by Douglas Northrop.
© 2012 Blackwell Publishing Ltd. Published 2012 by Blackwell Publishing Ltd.

argues, and, by extension, I think the *history teacher's* task, is "to simultaneously grasp the manifestations of the very large and abstract structures and the transformations of the world in the small details of life" (1995: 8). Michael Adas (1998) agrees, arguing that world history must "infuse the contextual analysis of world systems and structures and aggregate socioeconomic transformations with serious attention to ideas, human agency, and contingency." Or to repurpose Emmanuel Le Roy Ladurie's semicryptic categorization of historians, world history requires historians – teachers and students – to be both parachutists and truffle hunters.[2] In this chapter, I argue that the intellectual capacity to move strategically among temporal and spatial scales is useful, even outright necessary, for both world history teachers and students if they are to avoid the fragmented approach of too many history courses that requires students to commit one fact after another to memory. A parachute and a nose for history's truffles are required to make sense of all the events and changes teachers and students encounter in studying the world's history. A small but instructive body of international research on teachers' and students' historical thinking suggests that without explicit instructional attention, thinking effectively across different scales is "unnatural" in both teachers and students.[3] This essay suggests that making meaningful connections among world-historical events and processes is particularly challenging, for three identifiable reasons.

First, the resources for teachers and students in world history reflect the fragmentation and incoherence that history education seeks to mediate or avoid. Standards and textbooks rarely present teachers or students with a coherent path through the blizzard of facts, concepts, eras and cultures that define courses in world history. School-standards documents, constructed as they are in lists of learning outcomes, rarely develop instructional connections to help teachers link content to particular classroom approaches. Textbooks and standards documents, at least as written in the United States, reflect confusion within both the scholarly and educational fields about what exactly constitutes "world history." There remains wide variation in the ways American state governments, curricular standards, published textbooks and working teachers present world history. Analysis of world history standards reveals sharp differences in periodization schemes, criteria used to judge historical significance, units of analysis, and the temporal-spatial scales that frame world history content. Although most American students graduate with a course labeled "world history" on their transcripts, in practice there are at least four variations for what this means, variations I define as (1) Western heritage, (2) serial area studies, (3) social science thematic history, and (4) global world history. Each has its own unique issues in helping students develop coherence. However, as common standards and mass-market textbooks are meant in part to help teachers develop these connections, the variation among models creates a complicating challenge. Further, and of fundamental intellectual as well as pedagogical importance, these models are not equal in their capacity to develop nested pictures of the world's history. Some focus particularly on one or more regions of the world, or on disconnected and often achronological themes. Thus the tools ostensibly designed to assist teachers often place a burden on them to make meaningful connections, both for themselves and for their students.

Second, there is increasing evidence that teachers' own knowledge of world history is also often in pieces, reflecting one or another of these models of history. Thus, teachers may also have difficulty moving fluidly across historical space or time, or among the various approaches to the global past. And finally, there is modest but informative work in the educational literature on the challenges students face in understanding changes that occur on large scales.[4] Such research suggests that students have difficulties "seeing" the past at different scales, of conceiving of causal agency outside of individual human actions, or moving among and between what Braudel (1980) called the events, structures and *longue durée*. Teaching and learning world history requires teachers and students to "grasp the manifestations of the very large and abstract structures and the transformations of the world in the small details of life" and to become more aware of the challenges they face in doing so – but success will increase the possibilities of our improving instruction in real-life world history courses. (See Getz, this volume.)

A Teaching Problem: Figuring Out the Story and Connections

To introduce the issue more concretely, I begin with a "thought experiment" that my colleague Lauren McArthur Harris and I have used in workshops with hundreds of history teachers over the past 10 years. We ask teachers to construct three- to five-minute histories of the United States, of Western civilization, and of the world. With only a few exceptions, the results are strikingly similar. When asked to craft a short history of the United States, teachers typically get right to work, identifying familiar eras and events, and explaining relationships between them. The structure of these US histories is usually remarkably similar, with common key events: Native American societies, European settlement and colonization, the War for Independence, Constitutional Convention, Civil War and Reconstruction, westward expansion and industrialism, World Wars, Depression and New Deal, Cold War, and the civil rights movement. Not only do the teachers string events together, but they often capture processes that link these events into a narrative that builds meaning. Likewise, teachers quickly develop a coherent short story of Western civilization, often marked by common turning points and events: River Valley civilizations, classical Greece and Rome, Dark and Middle Ages, the Renaissance, Reformation, Enlightenment, nation-states, exploration, democratic revolutions, industrialism, imperialism, World Wars and Cold Wars.

History teachers, ranging from relative novices to seasoned veterans, thus had readily available large-scale stories to frame change over time in the United States or in Europe. Quickly they decided what events to include and which to omit, and how to connect included details to the large events that defined their histories. However, when asked to craft a short history of the world, the reaction was very different. Few got right down to the task. Most struggled over the most basic matters: where to begin, what to include, and how to order what they included. Some tried to tell multiple short histories of India, China, and Europe. Others used European periodization schemes (e.g., Middle Ages, Renaissance) to situate different civilizations, such as China or India, against a European backdrop. Most said it was a difficult if not impossible task, one for which they were not well prepared. Unlike US or Western history, constructing frames large enough to organize their thinking of world history proved a challenge. Teachers reported feeling bogged down with details, unsure about what to include, what to leave out, and how things were connected to one another.

Here is the crux of world history's distinctive teaching and, consequently, learning problem. When confronted with lists of US or Western history standards or corresponding textbooks stuffed with details, most teachers appear to have a rough sense of key turning points and major events – a broad narrative on which they can hang the details. To use Ladurie's categorization scheme of historians, when approaching more familiar national or regional histories most teachers are like parachutists gliding over the historical landscape.

From that distance they can see the entire temporal and spatial topography *and* the relationships among large structures; and while floating down they are able to situate close-up detail as it comes into view. However, these teachers do not seem to approach world history from the grand perspective that distance allows, acting instead like Ladurie's truffle hunters, noses in the dirt sniffing out disconnected but precious details.

Sense-making in history requires both a parachute *and* the nose for truffles or, to shift metaphors, the ability to view history using different lenses, including the wide-angle, medium-range and close-up lenses. The turn of mind to move among and see the relationships between different temporal-spatial scales defines all history, surely; but particularly world history.

Now, this is not a cry for creating some grand world-historical narrative of progress or regress, but rather an attempt to underscore the importance of teachers having usable "big" pictures or frameworks to situate and connect a wide range of macro- and microhistorical details, details located across multiple temporal and spatial scales. Frankly, the more familiar national or regional containers, while necessary, are not big enough for the task. If world history teachers cannot construct, when necessary, coherent global pictures, then it is understandable why so much world history appears to be a cavalcade of different and disconnected cultures, civilizations or events. And without the knowledge and habits of mind needed to build global, cross-temporal and regional connections, it is difficult to imagine that teachers will be able to help their students make such meaning from all the "stuff."

Such is what Lauren McArthur Harris (2008) found in her study of 10 veteran and prospective world history teachers. Harris asked teachers to sort and build concept maps – big pictures – using a seemingly random stack of 18 historical events and concepts, such as the Atlantic Slave System, Bantu Migrations, the Renaissance, and the Cold War. The events and concepts Harris selected were located at different time spans and territorial scope. Some events crossed large expanses of time and huge regions of the world (e.g. Atlantic Slave System), while others lived in smaller bands of time and geographic area (Renaissance). As the teachers sorted and used these cards to build their concept maps of world history, Harris prompted them to talk aloud about their decisions. Thus, she not only saw how teachers used historical events to create a big historical picture, but was also able to hear their thinking for each move. Teachers did the card sort twice: first to capture their own understandings, and then to explain how (or if) they might structure these same events for students.

The differences among these 10 teachers were stunning. Using both chronology and temporal-spatial categories to sort and place the event cards on the developing concept map, the experienced teachers filled the space between cards with connecting lines and/ or language showing dynamic relationships among and between events, regardless of the region, time period or scale in which the teacher initially categorized the card. Some of the veteran teachers, all with specific training in global or world-scale history, developed complicated conceptual maps by building contextual, comparative, causal, or consequential relationships among and between the events (see Figure 7.1). Like a road map with many roadways linking cities or points of interest, these cognitive maps showed potential links among historical events. As they constructed the webs, these teachers operationalized levels of thinking as they described the continuities and discontinuities they saw among macro- and microhistorical events, swiftly moving among and across events at different temporal and spatial scales.

Listen to one of these teachers as she moves among global and regional events trying to figure out where to place them or how to connect them:

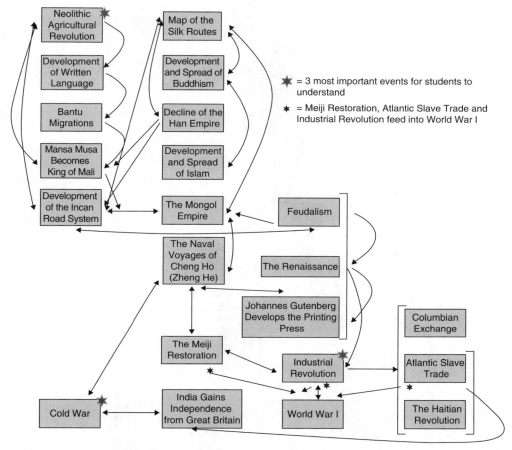

Figure 7.1   An expert teacher's concept map using multiple scales and multiple connections.
Source: Lauren McArthur Harris, "Building coherence in world history: A study of instructional tools and teachers' pedagogical content knowledge," PhD diss., University of Michigan, 2008, p. 305.

Well it's hard because these are so … I mean you're looking at a global perspective but then you put them into areas where … I have Africa and I have Europe … But then you have things like the Silk Route, which involves Asia, Africa, and Europe, so I would kind of piece that out on its own. And then, the Incas and the Haitians are in the same area, however, I wouldn't necessarily … I mean they don't connect. And then the Development of Written Language, Agricultural Revolution, again those are things that affected a large area, although occurring more in the Middle Eastern area. They have such an impact on Europe and Africa and Asia. So I'll put that … it all kind of interacts with one another, because when you're teaching world history you're looking at it not only from what happened in Africa or what happened in Europe but the global perspective of things. (Harris 2008)

Messy thinking to be sure, but thinking that displays both the knowledge and habit of mind to make meaningful, nested connections among events ranging across various time periods and located in different geographic space. Such thinking defined all the "experts" in Harris's study.

However, as shown in Figure 7.2, other, less experienced teachers constructed far less dynamic pictures, employing simple chronology to organize events or placing the cards

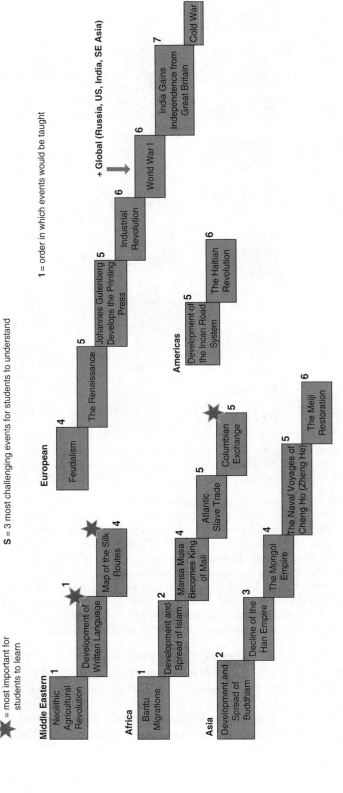

Figure 7.2 A novice teacher's concept map organized by region with few connections.
Source: Harris, "Building coherence in world history" (as Figure 7.1), p. 308.

into a handful of regional (e.g., Europe, Africa) *or* institutional categories (e.g., economic, political, or religious). Two key features differentiated these maps from the others discussed above. First, there were far fewer attempts to connect events, as the novice maps had significantly fewer connecting lines and language. Second, once an event landed in a category, teachers typically treated the event as an *example* of the category, such as government or trade. It lost historical specificity, although it is not clear to me whether these teachers initially had much detailed knowledge of the events to lose. Some novices drew connecting lines between categories, such as government and economy, but almost none between historical events. When they did make connections between events, novices rarely gave an explanation, and often drew the connections with hesitation. For example, a novice preservice teacher in Harris's study explained that in teaching the Meiji restoration, she would "say what feudalism is, and use the [Meiji] Restoration as an example, but I don't know how I'd do that."

All the teachers in Harris's study attempted to develop meaningful connections among the events of world history. And all the teachers did find ways to sort and group the historical events so that no event stood alone. However, only the first group of teachers explicitly situated events in their respective historical place, using global, interregional and regional scales, linking and nesting them, demonstrating multiple connections and pathways, and suggesting complicated understanding of change over time and space. Other teachers made significantly fewer connections, often using atemporal or aspatial categories to group the cards. And in discussing the events, these novices were more likely to treat them in isolation or to puzzle about how to connect them to others.

These differences, Harris argued, were not simply a matter of knowing the details of particular historical events, although that certainly played a role. Nor was the variation among participants related only to the raw number of years teaching world history or to specific courses taken. Rather, Harris speculated that participation in a curriculum and professional development *specifically* focused on world history at a global scale had helped prepared these "expert" world history teachers to see more useful conceptual schemes. Both knowledge of particular events and knowledge of possible connections spanning centuries, or millennia, across nations, continents or hemispheres, seemed to enable these teachers to develop more meaningful connections for themselves, and, Harris suspected, for their students.

Standards in World History

Ironically, some recent efforts in the United States to foster the growth of world history may have exacerbated this problem of developing a clear "framework" for teachers and students. In particular, the standards movement of the past 20 years has instantiated the tensions among frameworks described above. Although there has been modest change in the past 10 years, the main approaches to the subject continue to vary in periodization schemes, criteria used to measure historical significance, units of analysis, and the temporal-spatial scales that frame the world's history (Bain and Shreiner 2005; 2006; Marino and Bolgatz 2010). Although now almost ubiquitous in the US secondary-school curriculum, world history has taken on specific content that differs greatly from state to state, textbook to textbook, school to school, and likely even classroom to classroom.

While there may be agreement over the value of world history, that does not necessarily mean there is agreement on what history students should study. Indeed, scholars analyzing state standards have found distinct patterns to the shape of world history: although the names used to describe specifics vary, the general picture is the same. World history appears to be structured around *either* a Western civilization model, *or* a thematic social studies frame, *or* an area studies approach, *or* a global history frame. These unfold as follows.

Western civilization model

This model has its origins in the Western Civilization framework that became a staple in US history teaching as early in the 1920s (see Pomeranz and Segal, this volume). Western Civilization has a familiar narrative that traces the development of "civilization" westward from ancient river valleys to Greece and Rome; through an interregnum variously called the Dark or Middle Ages; followed by a cultural rebirth and Reformation; and then transformation created by enlightened and scientific thinking, the rise of the nation-state, growth of national economic systems, democratic revolutions, and industrialism. The narrative structure has a coherence populated with familiar and important political events (e.g., the rise and fall of Rome, the French Revolution) and famous people (e.g., Galileo, Bismarck), stressing the "rise" of the West.

The world history version of this narrative adds cultures and civilizations beyond Europe, but without dramatically shifting the key events or the underlying narrative structure (see McKeown, this volume). In adding important "non-Western" content, this curricular pattern nevertheless continues to place Europe in the center of study. Although states call this sort of standard and curriculum "world history," approximately 70 percent or more of the content is devoted to the study of Europe, and it relies upon Western Civilization's periodization schemes and organizing features.[5] This pattern appears to be the most dominant among American state standards documents today, with about 29 states adding non-Western content to what appears functionally to be a Western civilization model.

Thematic world history

There are a few states that use political or economic themes to shape world history. While on the surface these appear to offer an opportunity to develop the coherence on a global scale that the Western heritage model lacks, typically these thematic approaches also suffer from an almost exclusive focus on European events and thus reflect a regional rather than world approach. Marino and Bolgatz, for example, found that the topics and themes mentioned are almost always those that are standards in the Western Civilization course, such as "revolutions, nationalism, industrialization, imperialism, and world wars." They noted that while these topics could be "interpreted as global phenomena, they tend to be viewed here as distinctly European events" and when using non-Western topics, they are always situated in relationship to an event from European history (2010: 375). In focusing on large, grand generalizations and stressing broad themes or processes, these versions of "world history" draw attention to big ideas that appear to be global and crossing scales, but upon digging a bit deeper, reflect merely a different version of the regional, Europe-focused course structure.

Area studies history

A smaller number of state documents reflect features of a geographic or regional studies approach to world history. This pattern treats geographic regions of the world separately (e.g., Africa, Asia or the Middle East), often folding the history, geography and economics into one combined study. In many ways, this is analogous to the traditional Western

Civilization course model, now applied to civilizations or regions outside of Europe or the United States. While no state exclusively embraces this approach for high school history, we did find a number of states whose standards reflected significant features of the Regional History approach, particularly in the middle school years. Many school districts also use a Geographic/Regional History pattern in offering world history courses to students.

"Global" world history

The last pattern, Global World History, constitutes a self-conscious attempt to locate history at different scales of time and space, specifically adding transregional historical processes to the study of regions and civilizations. This approach often asks students to move among different scales of time and space – sometimes focusing on a person or group, at other times on the nation, civilization, region, transregion, or even the globe.

The Advanced Placement (AP) World History course is the best example of an approach in the US that combines transregional and civilizational studies, requiring students to look both at and across regions of the world. According to the AP World History Guide, one of the distinctive features of a global history course is that it requires students to study large patterns over time and space, "while also acquiring the ability to connect local developments to global ones and move through levels of generalizations from the global to the particular." For example, while studying the development of civilizations, the AP course also looks specifically at global processes and interactions, such as trade and migration across different types of societies over time. Because a global world history course, at times, unties school history from its typical mooring of the nation or civilization, AP provides specific guidance to teachers to help them balance attention to global processes with other features that constitute history. For example, AP limits its course of study to five chronological periods, five key themes, and the major civilizations within four regions. The AP course guide also specifies that "coverage of European history does not exceed 30 percent of the total course. This encourages increased coverage of topics that are important to Europe in the world and not just to Europe itself, as well as attention to areas outside Europe." Comparative history plays a significant role in the global approach as students compare different political, economic and social systems (e.g., "compare industrialism in Japan and Western Europe," or "compare Haitian, American, French, Mexican, or Chinese revolutions").

The AP World History course remains the best example of the global world history approach in practice, and it appears that more US states are now starting to use this framework to organize world history. The standards in at least eight states show significant global, comparative and chronological features of this pattern. Over the last few years, this number has increased slightly. Because of its growing popularity and increasing success among both school districts and students, the Global World History pattern as typified by AP World History is an important approach to consider for a possible national assessment in the school curriculum, even though its shape and content still differ greatly from state to state, textbook to textbook, and school to school.

Recently, a few states have moved toward a more global focus, but within an existing (other) framework. For example, New Jersey has begun to pepper its standards with issues of globalization and comparative history, where the comparisons typically involve relating cases across regions or sometimes across regions and over time (e.g., "Compare slavery practices and other forms of coerced labor or social bondage common in East Africa, West Africa, Southwest Asia, Europe and the Americas," or "Determine the global impact of increased population growth, migration, and changes in urban–rural populations on natural resources and land use") (Marino and Bolgatz 2010: 375). The new Michigan standards nest their content along three different temporal and spatial scales, called (a) Global and Cross-temporal, (b) Inter-regional, and (c) Regional. This approach "offers a way to connect specific historical content to broad concepts and ideas" situated at the global and interregional scales, yet the nesting of standards at three different levels – that is, the connections from the regional to the global and back again – are not always clearly articulated, and thus the Michigan standards represent a "hybrid" of the global, the thematic and the area studies approach to world history (Marino and Bolgatz 2010: 386).

Figuring Out How Students See the Story and Make Connections

Seeing bigger global pictures and being able to make connections among historical events is only one facet of the professional problem faced by teachers of world history. Their jobs are more complicated than simply understanding world history for them-selves, as they must also help students develop such understanding. Thus teachers have to understand how adolescents build meaning from events scattered over the grandest scope of time and space, and recognize the challenges students face in learning to see (or care about) the world from such distances.

Research suggests that adolescents are not typically parachutists, particularly when it comes to understanding historical change. A number of studies reveal a tendency for students to gravitate toward the "personal" to explain historical change, often pushing large-scale structural factors, such as economics, politics or ideology, aside. For example, Carretero and his colleagues (1997) asked sixth, eighth and tenth graders as well as graduate history majors to explain the causes of pivotal events in history that occurred in 1492. The researchers asked the students to put in rank order five types of historical explanations – personal, political, economic, ideological, or global – for the Columbian voyages, the European "discovery" of the Americas, and transformations in Spain. Only graduate history majors valued political, economic or global explanations (such as "changes in international trade generated new economic and political needs in Spain") over personal explanations of human wants or desires (such as "Columbus wanted personal wealth and glory"). Further, the graduate students attempted to locate personal actions *within* larger structural contexts. However, pre-collegiate students consistently ranked personal agency, that is, the intentions and desires of the historical actors, as the most compelling explanations for these historical changes. Most surprising was how little change in causal reasoning occurred between grades six and twelve.

This finding presents a powerful challenge for history teachers seeking to push their students to understand large-scale structural changes and their impact in history, a particularly important goal for world historians. However, if teachers do not intentionally engage students' tendency to see change as a byproduct of human agency alone, then students will be more likely to translate *all* structural trends into personal desires or to personify abstract categories, for example, "the middle class wanted *X*."

Hallden's research suggests that many students see history as the "the sum of the actions of each and every individual," with human agency as the central driving force. In short, for students in these studies, there was "no room for structures or structural expla-nations ... for formal constructs or impersonal structures" (Hallden 1997: 207).

Compared with world historians, who look to impersonal structures as well as the actions of individuals to account for historical events, and indeed have been criticized by other historians for relying too heavily on abstract structural approaches (see Northrop, introduction to this volume), students seem to persist in locating their explanations of events in the "actions, reactions, and intentions of individuals or individualized phenomena" (Hallden 1994: 35).

In one evocative study, Hallden interviewed and observed a teacher whose major focus during a unit was large-scale political change in Sweden. However, after instruction, this line of thinking was almost totally absent from the students' writing or their conversations about the class, obscured entirely by language such as "the middle class desired." In another study, Hallden described a class where the secondary teacher was attempting to analyze the terms of German surrender, but the students only seemed interested in the "psychological reactions of the German people" (Hallden 1997: 206):

Student 5 (S5): Yeah, it wasn't a treaty for them. They never agreed to it.
Teacher (T): Hitler said so, yes. But what I mean, it was after all the Treaty of Versailles.
S5: Yeah, but they weren't satisfied.
T: Why weren't they?
S: They were forced into it.
T: Yes, but what did the Treaty mean for Germany?
Student 8 (S8): They felt humiliated.
T: Yes, but what ... I mean, concretely?
S8: That everything was their fault.

Students appear to hold to a Great Man/Woman view of history, while these world history teachers seemed to want students to situate human agency within impersonal political or economic structures. Although participating in the same discussion, at times it appeared that the students and the teachers were playing a slightly odd game of *Jeopardy*, one where the questions and answers never quite matched. Hallden argued that "students try to contextualize given information through their personalized concept of history. However, the historical period as presented by the teacher was described, and the events explained, mostly by reasoning at the structural level. If the students try to interpret such information in a personalized concept of history, they are likely to get lost" (Hallden 1994: 39).

Teachers, then, should consider that students may be grafting new explanations for historical change onto an older, more familiar view that does not "entail structural conditions and structural reorganizations, but rather deals with individuals, personalized phenomena, and the actions performed by these agents" (Hallden 1994: 41). Students may not only act locally but also think locally. Such circumstances present a most difficult challenge precisely for those world historians who move with analytical facility along multiple structural levels, governed by a practice that the inquiry should embrace whatever geographical, social, or cultural field is appropriate (Dunn 2000).

Recent research in the United Kingdom also suggests the difficulties of students developing big-picture understandings of the past, and using that understanding to develop coherence and minimize fragmentation. For example, in a longitudinal study, Foster, Ashby and Lee found that most students see the past as "consisting of a catalogue of arbitrary and disconnected events." A small number of students moved beyond these "event-like" views of history, going beyond simple "recounting discrete and unconnected events" to establish a "process-like" view, employing the "conceptual apparatus that enabled them to make connections across time" (2008: 9). In analyzing adolescents' production of historical accounts across a range of tasks, Foster, Ashby and Lee found that students *had* historical content knowledge – thus belying the oft-heard claims, usually generated by standardized tests, that today's students "don't know any history" – but that they conveyed their knowledge as discrete events or concepts. For example, consider this typical event-like student response when asked to write a short history of England:

> Medevil times, battle of hastings 1066, william of Normandy, Shakespear, King Eward, Henry VIII and his 8 wives, tudors, stuarts, Queen elizabeth, victoria, Elizabeth 2nd, world war 1&2, jack the ripper, magret thatcher, golf war, cold war, vietcong, vietnam, nuclear bombs, hollywood, cinema, cars, planes, the moon, space travel, tony blair, George Bush, Iraq war, terrorism, £ V euro, euro all other currency in europe except £. (Foster *et al.* 2008: 26)

It is clear that this student *has* substantive knowledge, but it is "arbitrary and disconnected." Consider, however, a student who seemed to display similar conceptual or substantive knowledge but also had the conceptual tools to make connections over time scales:

> Timeline: Roman Invasion – dark Ages – Medieval ages – 1066 Norman invasion – Tudor era – Stuart era – Industrial Revolution – WWI – WWII – now (2007) War in Iraq. Britain was shaped, both socially and economically through numerous different countries. The multicultural Britain of today is the result of the Roman invasion, the Norman invasion, French influences, American influence, African influence. Socially, Britain is not British, it is a blend of numerous different cultures. Britain has been shaped by hundreds of wars, from the Roman invasion in the 1st century through to the civil war and relatively recently, both world wars. (Foster *et al.* 2008: 27)

Meeting the Challenges

As I have been arguing, world history teachers need a distinctive form of analytical flexibility to build curricular and instructional coherence. As world-historical *thinkers*, they need content knowledge of connections and interactions across multiple scales of time and space, and the turn of mind to analyze plausible connections among the personal, national, regional, interregional, and global. As world history *teachers*, they need an understanding of students' preinstructional ideas about change, agency and scale, and pedagogical ways to engage and challenge students' views. These may well be world history education's most characteristic and necessary intellectual and pedagogical attributes.

So what does this mean for historians, for history teacher-educators, and most importantly, for teachers charged with the responsibility of teaching world history, especially but not exclusively in the United States? I see three implications: first, for teacher preparation and professional development; second, for future research on student learning, and finally and most immediately, for the actual teachers and students of world history today.

First, teachers simply need more course work in world history. Deep knowledge of world history makes a self-evident difference, as teachers cannot teach well what they do not know well. States, universities and school districts should therefore extend opportunities to both preservice and inservice teachers to work with world historians.

However, simply requiring more course work may not be enough unless we also require that a portion – half – of the course work be specifically in world history.

However, it is important to remember that course work is only a proxy for what teachers will need to know to teach well. Studies of teachers' knowledge seem to show that the *quantity* of content knowledge – while necessary – is not sufficient. Indeed, many teachers know details about the events of world history, but are not able to fit the pieces together, or make them cohere around intellectual problems or big questions to drive inquiry. World history, as I have argued, is too often in the mind of teachers and students a fragmented study of civilizations and nation-states, with little attention to interconnections except for an occasional comparison that serves to emphasize political and cultural differences. Therefore, special courses for teachers focusing on connections and comparisons across multiple scales are needed. Further, history instructors must do more than teach history when working with teachers; they must also explain the intellectual moves and conceptual devices they use to develop coherence. History courses for teachers must go beyond teaching the "stuff" or merely using historian's general habits of mind, but must also make *visible* these ways in which historians make sense of the past and how they represent their understandings, so others may learn to do the same.

There are few models of instruction that make these pedagogical moves visible to learners *while* they are learning the content. At the University of Michigan, we designed such a course to accompany "Zoom: A History of Everything," Douglas Northrop's "big history" course for undergraduates (see chapters by Spier and by Ward, this volume). In addition to the large lecture and recitation section, interested students registered for an additional history section where the object of study was the instruction itself, both in the lecture and the recitation sections. Students kept pedagogical notebooks as well as content notebooks, looking for representations they thought particularly instructive (or not), the big questions or ideas that organized content, and the conceptual devices that signaled connections among different scales of time and space. The course asked the students to be trifocal in considering the content as students of world history, as world historians, and as world history teachers (see Ball *et al.* 2008; Ball 2000; Bain and Mirel 2006).

Second, we need to pay more attention to the experiences of students learning world history. We know very little about how students understand the relationships between macro- and micro-explanations of historical change, make formal comparisons, consider relationships between structure and culture, or pursue historical questions at different temporal-spatial scales. Yet, such is exactly what learning world history entails. Frankly, when it comes to student learning, our field is working in the dark.[6] We need more studies of students working in and on world history, and more of these studies available and accessible to teachers of world history.

Teachers with whom we work have met with historians to create concept maps out of the lists of standards. With the help of knowledgeable world historians, teachers can connect individual objectives to big ideas or, better still, to big historiographic problems that may organize instruction and drive student learning. For example, some world history teachers engage their students in extended investigations to weigh competing claims about Europe's altered position in the world between 1500 and 1900. Such work connects required content of great variety while forcing students to continually use content to develop and revisit previously developed arguments. Many world historians have taken up such questions, and their monographs and counter-monographs demonstrate ways teachers and students might move along multiple scales and use a wide range of events and processes to make historical arguments.

To help teachers see these large-scale, coherent frames for world history, we have used books such as David Christian's *This Fleeting World* (2008), a 90-page history of humanity, or John and William McNeill's *The Human Web: A Bird's-Eye View Of World History* (2003). Without claiming these books are *the* narrative, they do offer teachers *a* frame upon which they can hang the things they must teach. And since neither is a complete picture of the world's history – such is impossible – each is also open to critique and modification.

Teachers could make "scale" an explicit tool in their course, an intentional and visible feature of a course and of instruction. When I taught in a high school, I did this by – very early on – taking students out into the hall, where they took and compared two "mental pictures" of me, one when we were at opposite ends of the hall and the other when they were as close to me as was politely possible. We then compared the two pictures of "Bain in the Hall," with me asking students if one was better than the other, or what kind of information could be gleaned from each perspective, and whether the two views of me were connected or related to each other in any way. Thus, I introduced them to scale and the change in perspective that it entails. We used the hall as a cognitive tool and figuratively asked for each chapter in the text, or each primary source, or each map, "where in the hall" the author was standing in relationship to his or her subject. For students whose default perspective was the local, the hall became a tool to both remind them and enable them to shift or understand scale.

Of course, this is but one way to make scales a critical and visible feature of instruction. We have used films such as the *Powers of Ten* (Eames and Eames 1968) or the *History of the World in Seven Minutes* (WHFUA 2011) to offer students an experience with shifting scales. The key point is to avoid the assumption that students are with you, or the materials you use, when you shift scales – rather, make it always visible.

A final but related suggestion is to consider using different temporal-spatial "containers." In another recent study, Harris and I analyzed the impact on teachers who were using a global history curriculum (Bain and Harris 2010). We found that developing a conceptual frame large enough for other stories to come into focus was a critical step in designing coherent instruction. In particular, teachers learned to use "Afro-Eurasia" or the "Atlantic World" to burst through the usual nation-state or continental boxes and enable their students to see how human interactions and history went across the borders of our standard or familiar geographic containers.

If world history in schools is to become more than disaggregated bits and pieces of information, then teachers and students need to develop both a big-picture understanding of the past and multiple ways to connect the fragments to the big picture. This does not mean teachers and students should construct a grand narrative and then force all events to fit the framework, or ignore those that do not. The intentional and overt movement back and forth along varied temporal and spatial scales can enable students and teachers to consider how views from different "levels" of time and space illuminate those above and below, encouraging students both to use the big picture to assess the details *and* to use the details to evaluate and reassess the big picture. Critical judgment need not be abandoned as teachers and students work to develop coherent frameworks. Making visible the movement among and between historical explanations located at the level of human experience and those at the larger structural levels – intellectual movements that world historians can make with ease but that research suggests are very difficult for students and teachers alike – should help students develop a more coherent and usable picture of the past. Becoming aware of the challenges that such intellectual work demands is a first step toward meeting them.

Notes

1 With few exceptions, this chapter focuses on world history as taught in secondary schools in the United States, not globally.

2 Although it is often quoted by historians, I have never been able to find the place where Ladurie wrote or said this. Recently, J.H. Elliott reported that in a correspondence Ladurie urged Elliott to cite him as the source of these distinctions "with confidence" (Elliott 2009: xviii).

3 Sam Wineburg (2001) makes the compelling argument that the type of thinking in which historians engage needs to be taught: thinking practices such as sourcing, corroborating, contextualizing, or historical empathy are not things people generally "pick up."

4 See, for example, Shemilt (2000; 2009); Lee and Ashby (2000); Leinhardt *et al.* (1994); Lee (2005); Howson (2007); Foster *et al.* (2008); Bain (2000; 2005); Seixas (1996); Vosniadou and Brewer (1992).

5 For the issue of periodizing in world history, see Green (1998).

6 Of course, work by people such as Sam Wineburg (2001), Peter Lee (2000; 2005), Linda Levstik (2001), and Peter Seixas (1996) have deepened our understanding of students' thinking over the past 30 years. However, most if not all of this work has been done with students studying regional or national history. Few studies have focused on world history.

References

Adas, Michael. 1998. Bring ideas and agency back in: Representation and the comparative approach to world history. In P. Pomper, R. Elphick, and R.T. Vann, eds, *World History: Ideologies, Structures, and Identities*, pp. 81–104. Oxford: Blackwell.

Bain, Robert B. 2000. AP world history habits of mind: Reflecting on world history's unique challenge to students' thinking. In J. Arno, ed., *Teacher's Guide: AP World History*, pp. 237–243. Princeton: College Entrance Examination Board.

Bain, Robert B. 2005. They thought the world was flat? HPL principles in teaching high school history. In J. Bransford and S. Donovan, eds, *How Students Learn: History, Mathematics, and Science in the Classroom*, pp. 179–214. Washington DC: National Academies Press.

Bain, Robert B., and Lauren McArthur Harris. 2010. *External Evaluation: World History for Us All.* San Diego, CA: World History for Us All. At http://worldhistoryforusall.sdsu.edu/downloads/Long%20Beach%20Report%202010.pdf (accessed Mar. 2012).

Bain, Robert B., and Jeffrey E. Mirel. 2006. Setting up camp in the great instructional divide: Educating beginning history teachers. *Journal of Teacher Education* 57 (3): 212–219.

Bain, Robert B., and Tamara L. Shreiner. 2005. Issues and options in creating a national assessment in world history. *History Teacher* 38 (2): 241–272.

Bain, Robert B., and Tamara Shreiner. 2006. The dilemmas of a national assessment in world history: World historians and the 12th grade NAEP. *World History Connected* 3 (3), at http://www.historycooperative.org/journals/whc/3.3/bain.html (accessed Mar. 2012).

Ball, Deborah Loewenberg. 2000. Bridging practices: Intertwining content and pedagogy in teaching and learning to teach. *Journal of Teacher Education* 51 (3): 241–247.

Ball, Deborah Loewenberg, Mark Hoover Thames, and Geoffrey Phelps. 2008. Content Knowledge for Teaching. *Journal of Teacher Education* 59 (5): 389–407.

Braudel, Fernand. 1980. *On History.* London: Weidenfeld & Nicolson.

Carretero, Mario, Asunción López-Manjón, and Liliana Jacott. 1997. Explaining historical events. *International Journal of Educational Research* 27 (3): 245–253.

Cavanagh, Sean. 2007. World history and geography gain traction in class: Seeds of internationally themed lessons were planted in the 1980s. *Education Week* (Mar. 21): 10.

Christian, David. 2008. *This Fleeting World: A Short History of Humanity.* Great Barrington, MA: Berkshire.

Dunn, Ross E., ed. 2000. *The New World History: A Teacher's Companion*. Boston: Bedford/ St Martin's.

Eames, Charles, and Ray Eames, dirs. 1968. *Powers of Ten*. Short documentary film.

Elliott, John H. 2009. *Spain, Europe and the Wider World 1500–1800*. New Haven: Yale University Press.

Foster, Stuart, Ros Ashby, and Peter Lee. 2008. *Usable Historical Pasts: A Study of Students' Frameworks of the Past*. Technical Report, ESRC Award Number RES-000-22-1676. Swindon, UK: Economic and Social Research Council.

Green, William A. 1998. Periodizing world history. In P. Pomper, R. Elphick, and R.T. Vann, eds, *World History: Ideologies, Structures, and Identities*, pp. 53–68. Oxford: Blackwell.

Hallden, Ola. 1994. On the paradox of understanding history in an educational setting. In G. Leinhardt, I.L. Beck and C. Stainton, eds, *Teaching and Learning in History*, pp. 27–46. Hillsdale, NJ: Lawrence Erlbaum.

Hallden, Ola. 1997. Conceptual change and the learning of history. *International Journal of Educational Research* 27 (3): 201–210.

Harris, Lauren McArthur. 2008. Building coherence in world history: A study of instructional tools and teachers' pedagogical content knowledge. PhD diss., Educational Studies, University of Michigan.

Holt, Thomas C. 1995. Marking: Race, race-making and the writing of history. *American Historical Review* 100 (1): 1–20.

Howson, John. 2007. Is it the Tuarts then the Studors or the other way round? The importance of developing a usable big picture of the past. *Teaching History* 127: 40–47.

Lee, Peter J. 2005. Putting principles into practice: Understanding history. In J. Bransford and S. Donovan, eds, *How Students Learn History in the Classroom*, pp. 31–77. Washington DC: National Academy of Sciences.

Lee, Peter J., and Ros Ashby. 2000. Progression in historical understanding among students ages 7–14. In P. Stearns, P. Seixas, and S. Wineburg, eds, *Knowing, Teaching, and Learning History*, pp. 199–222. New York: New York University Press.

Leinhardt, Gaea, *et al.* 1994. Learning to reason in history: Mindlessness to mindfulness. In M. Carretero and J.F. Voss, eds, *Cognitive and Instructional Processes in History and the Social Sciences*, pp. 131–158. Hillsdale, NJ: Lawrence Erlbaum.

Levstik, Linda S. 2001. Crossing the empty spaces: Perspective taking in New Zealand. Adolescents' understanding of national history. In O.L. Davis, Jr, E.A. Yeager, and S. Foster, eds, *Historical Empathy and Perspective-Taking in the Social Studies*, pp. 69–96. Lanham: Rowman & Littlefield.

Marino, Michael, and Jane Bolgatz. 2010. Weaving a fabric in world history? An analysis of US state high school world history standards. *Theory and Research in Social Education* 38 (3) (Summer): 366–394.

McNeill, John Robert, and William Hardy McNeill. 2003. *The Human Web: A Bird's-Eye View of World History*. New York: W.W. Norton.

Seixas, Peter. 1996. Conceptualizing the growth of historical understanding. In D.R. Olson and N. Torrance, eds, *Handbook of Education and Human Development: New Models of Learning, Teaching and Schooling*, pp. 765–783. Oxford: Blackwell.

Shemilt, Denis. 2000. The Caliph's coin. In P. Stearns, P. Seixas, and S. Wineburg, eds, *Knowing, Teaching, and Learning History: National and International Perspectives*, pp. 83–101. New York: New York University Press.

Shemilt, Denis. 2009. Drinking an ocean and pissing a cupful: How adolescents make sense of history. In L. Symcox and A. Wilschut, eds, *The Problem of the Canon and the Future of History Teaching*, pp. 141–209. Charlotte, NC: Information Age.

Vosniadou, Stella, and W. Brewer. 1992. Mental models of the Earth: A study of conceptual change in childhood. *Cognitive Psychology* 24: 535–585.

WHFUA (World History for Us All). 2011. *History of the World in Seven Minutes.* Video for the Classroom, WHFUA project, San Diego State University and National Center for History in the Schools, University of California at Los Angeles.

Wineburg, Sam. 2001. *Historical Thinking and Other Unnatural Acts: Charting the Future of Teaching the Past.* Philadelphia: Temple University Press.

CHAPTER EIGHT

Teaching World History at the College Level

TREVOR GETZ

My experience at World History Association conferences has been that there is a deep divide between research and teaching in world history, despite the efforts of many to connect the two. Most of the instructors who do the grunt work of teaching world history, for example, eschew the kind of theoretical and epistemological discussions put forward by historians like Alun Munslow and Keith Jenkins. Yet their work has deep relevance for the kinds of discussions we should be having as world historians. Munslow and Jenkins have clearly identified three genres of historical scholarship: reconstruction, construction, and deconstruction (Munslow 2006; Jenkins and Munslow 2004). As teachers, we reconstruct the past for our students, and try to teach them the "best practices" of reconstruction as well. But we also construct stories and themes for our students, and aim to teach them to critically deconstruct the global histories presented to them out in the world, in books, in theater, in museums, and elsewhere in popular culture.

What we are perhaps least likely to do successfully, however, is to teach students to deconstruct their classroom learning, an act that would undermine our own authority and that of the material we are passing on to them. (See Bain, this volume.) Yet that is exactly what I mean to do in this chapter. Specifically, I am going to delve back into my own past as an instructor to explore how I have taught world history over the past decade. My objective is to explore the content, structures, and approaches of my courses over time, and to interpret the changes and continuities I find. The analysis of a course as something that changes over time might be surprising to students, who tend to understand a "course" as a static structure. In their brief encounter with it, a course seems complete and unchanging. Only the instructor, who encounters this course again and again, will have insight into it as a process rather than an event. Of course, the instructor is not an unbiased observer. Yet this does not mean that there is no value in a reflexive survey of one's own courses and how they have changed over time. This is a point that I will try to prove in the conclusion to this chapter – but to begin my story at the beginning …

A Companion to World History, First Edition. Edited by Douglas Northrop.
© 2012 Blackwell Publishing Ltd. Published 2012 by Blackwell Publishing Ltd.

Snapshot 1: World History Survey, University of New Orleans, 2000

In late August 2000, I gave my second lecture as a newly minted assistant professor in New Orleans. The pre-Katrina history department at the university was a pleasant place to teach. Courses were largely assigned to faculty by the department chair, but it was a benevolent dictatorship with the needs of the faculty and students carefully considered. Nevertheless, a weak union and strong administration meant that I ended up frantically writing lectures for both halves of the world history survey in my second semester. In my first lecture for the earlier half of world history (to 1500) I focused on "prehistory" and especially the Neolithic lifestyle. In the second hour, I took on the task of differentiating for my students between "Stone Age" lifestyles and the age of civilizations on which we would be concentrating for the rest of the semester. Thus I began the lecture by defining "civilization" which, in my view at the time, entailed the following:

- "centralized government" – civilizations show some type of complex governing structure;
- "expanded economic and technological capacities" – trade and possibly even currency, invention, sometimes written languages, new tools;
- "more elaborate social and cultural structures" – densely populated cities or towns, some type of social stratification, some type of structured religious or mythological practices.

Over the past decade I have read many definitions of civilization – old and new – which I find to be troubling. Some focus on separating "civilized" peoples from "barbarians" and "primitives" on the basis of some assumed racial or cultural characteristic.[1] Others merely position rigidly defined civilizational blocs against each other in ages-long struggles (e.g. Huntington 1993). While avoiding these overt misconceptualizations, my definition of 2000 was almost equally troubling. Drawing deeply on the work of Europe-centered archaeologists, historians, and dilettantes like V. Gordon Childe (1950), it ignored critiques from rebel scholars as diverse as Afrocentrists such as Cheikh Anta Diop, subaltern studies scholars like Vinay Lal, and leftist empiricists such as Andre Gunder Frank. For while my definition recognized that any people – regardless of race or ethnicity – could *achieve* civilization, it still posited such a civilization as a step forward on a teleological, universal staircase upward from barbarism to modernity. Thus while I can now applaud my then-self for seeking to define a term that would recur frequently in the course, I am chilled at how blithely I had internalized a singular notion of "civilization" that by definition cast as irrelevant or backward any people living without "centralized government" and "expanded economic and technological capacities."

Yet while this simple example suggests how dissatisfied I would now be with my first efforts at teaching world history, the student reviews from that semester reflect neither an awareness of my inexperience nor dissatisfaction with my approach. Some students may have noticed the inexperience, but most simply dutifully took notes and regurgitated them on the midterm and final exams. I sometimes wonder whether they were aware that they were guinea pigs in a half-formed new offering, and whether such knowledge would unsettle them. Would it scare students to find out that their instructors may completely change their understandings of core course contents over consecutive semesters? Such questions are likely unimportant to the average undergraduate student seeking only to survive their 15-unit course-load and probably a part-time job (or two).

Yet the history instructor cannot afford to ignore this question. History is often described as the study of "change over time." Almost all of us began our training by learning to take snapshots ("primary sources") and turn them into narratives of transformation ("secondary sources"). Thus it behooves us, especially, to examine our own changing understandings of the world and the profession. As a young world historian, I can remember being especially affected by William McNeill's self-examination of his own conversion as a researcher from celebrant of Westernness to global historian of connections in the 25 years following the publication of his ground-breaking *The Rise of the West* (see McNeill 1990). This brief essay was more valuable in explaining to me the debates and positions underpinning the field of world history than any book-length work. Can examining our teaching records in the same way help us to similarly understand a field as pedagogically rich as world history?

This broad question reverberates in my retrospective evaluation of this excerpt of the second lecture I gave as I started my academic career a decade ago. Like many of my peers, as I stood before that first world history class I was only just barely ahead of my students. This is not to say that I hadn't had a reasonably long relationship with "history," or even with global history. Jewish families like mine are notoriously diasporic, and that fact was reflected in the first stories about the past I can remember. These I encountered while on my grandfather's knee, listening as he explained how he and a few other Polish soldiers serving under British officers and with American equipment had stormed an Italian redoubt full of German troops. I listened to these stories in his apartment in South Africa, while on vacation from my American home.

One thing led to another, and my grandfather's (slightly exaggerated) stories led to reading *Time/Life* histories of World War II, and then to an undergraduate degree in history, and finally to graduate work. In the process, I also moved from military history to political history and finally to social history, and studied on three continents. I was, in fact, truly an individual example of the global scope of human experience. Yet in truth I knew nothing about global history, or my own place in it. Like many of my students, my personal feelings of heritage, tradition, and family seemed far distant from my academic understandings of History as a discipline.

Facing the teaching of a world history course for the first time, then, I found myself in the same situation as many of my peers. For one thing, I had no training in world history (still then a rarity as either an undergraduate or graduate course). I was, in fact, an "expert" really only in the nineteenth-century social history of two very small regions in West Africa. On the other hand, I had an ethical and political leaning towards cosmopolitanism that drove me towards a model of world history that focused on peace, interaction, environmental and social justice, and a shared human past (Allardyce 1990).

As a trained professional historian, I knew that I had to teach a history that had a narrative; one that showed the sort of positivistic notions of progress that were central to my being as a good, liberal American. But how was I to express this idea of progress without evaluating societies and differentiating among them? How could I even explain the differences among human societies without positing some as superior? I knew, of course, that the dreaded Eurocentrists were guilty of doing this.[2] Yet even Afrocentrists seemed to implicitly accept a consensual set of categories by which societies were to be evaluated, arguing, for instance, that ancient Africa was great through reference to its great monuments and mighty empires. Similarly, even the canonical world historians seemed to argue that early modern Asia was great by evaluating the sizes of its merchant fleets and economic capitalization (Pomeranz 2000; Frank 1998).

I finally found my (temporary) solution not in the work of a historian, but rather a physiologist. Jared Diamond (1997) seemed to be able to explain why and how societies diverged through a simple, provable environmental narrative. His argument – that some societies developed in more favorable environments than others – allowed for an exploration of the differential evolution of human societies while still expounding a unity – and fundamental equality – of humankind. This made it inherently attractive to cosmopolitans like myself. However, what made it attractive to the historian in me was its apparent empiricism and objectivity. Following what Patrick Manning has called the "scientific-cultural" path, it was a quintessential "big history," mobilizing evidence to refute the idea that Europeans were superior in any racial or cultural quality. However, it still embraced a notion of progress in its focus on the development of civilizations, exemplified by the city and by the kinds of social and economic transformations that came with it. Finally, Diamond's grand narrative sweep of history, with its decisive argument for environmental rather than racial determinism, and even a case for human unity, all fits neatly into a 15-week structure that covered the whole human history of world (to 1500) in an easily comprehensible package.

Snapshot 2: World History for Graduate Students, San Francisco State University, 2006

Yet while such neat packages are the stock-in-trade of the first-year survey, they tend to also provoke more issues than they resolve. Human history is not neat, but rather messy and complex. This is a lesson that I had learned on a theoretical level, but whose ramifications only really reached me during the next stage of my development as a "world historian." In 2002, I moved from New Orleans to California, to teach at San Francisco State University. The department of history at SFSU was (and still is) structured in a tripartite division familiar to many departments in the United States: US, Europe, and World. This was a result partly of a long process of internal negotiation and pressures from the strong ethnic studies college, which limited the department's abilities to offer strong coverage of areas seen as homelands for many of the university's students.

At the time that I began to teach at SFSU, the "World" division was still something of an academic ghetto for "the rest," that is, those who didn't fall into the two "traditional" categories. In other words, it comprised one scholar each for East Asia, Africa, and the Middle East, as well as two Latin Americanists. Unlike our US- and European-focused colleagues, who generated a multicourse curriculum for their areas divided chronologically and thematically, most of the courses for the World concentration were surveys of long periods of history for an entire continent.

Shortly before my arrival, however, William Issel had led an initiative to develop a truly transnational World concentration at both the undergraduate and graduate levels. Since there were not at the time many graduate students who studied Africa, I volunteered to teach a newly designed graduate course entitled "The World and the West" that would fit this transnational approach. I also briefly taught another newly developed course (History 701) required of all "world history" graduate students. In retrospect, the decision was not a mistake. By moving into "transnational" or global courses, I gained access to numerous readings and debates from other fields that later informed my research. Perhaps more importantly, I came into contact with many of the superb graduate students attracted by SFSU's MA program in history. Whether officially "World," "European," or "US" history students, the students were a varied group of high school teachers, former undergrads seeking a step upward to PhD programs, successful professionals returning to their passion, and aspiring community college instructors. Many of them were influenced to take the courses I offered by the State of California's transition from "Western civilization" to "world history" at the high school and community college levels.

In History 701, I assigned and therefore read for the first time such canonical works of world history as Ross Dunn's *The New World History* (2000) and Patrick Manning's *Navigating World History* (2003), as well as monographs by Janet Abu-Lughod, Kenneth Pomeranz, Andre Gunder Frank, and Alfred Crosby. Much of my understanding of these books came from the give-and-take of the seminar format, as students challenged my interpretations and those of their colleagues. In this respect, having a cross-section of fields represented in the class was a great advantage.

Consider part of my syllabus from this course, as I taught it in 2006:

World History for Graduate Students

Abstract
This research-oriented seminar addresses the connections between societies around the world in the modern era. Readings explore contrasting and complementary ecological, economic, political, and cultural narratives. The focus is a truly global understanding of this crucial phase of world history.

Student goals
Students who have completed this course:
- will be able to explain the principal issues, tropes, and themes of world history, and the challenges facing the development of world history as an independent field and a set of epistemological approaches;
- will have evaluated ecological, cultural, political, and sociocultural scholarship on the purported "rise of the west" in the sixteenth to the eighteenth centuries and will be able to present a critical and academically rigorous synthesis of these works;
- will be able to demonstrate an understanding of the ways in which societies, populations, and regions interact in the modern period (ca. 1350–present);
- will be able to demonstrate the advantages and limitations of thematic, comparative, and regional approaches to world history;
- will have evaluated core polemical works in world history and will be able to construct a synthesis that addresses the debate between these works.

As this brief excerpt demonstrates, my purpose was to teach students the models of world history put forward by the World History Association and its leading practitioners. Thus I embraced the definition of world history offered by Patrick Manning (2003), who wrote that it is defined by its focus on "the story of connections within the global human community" and that "the world historian's work is to portray the crossing of boundaries and the linking of systems in the human past."[3]

My attraction to this kind of world history was symptomatic of my growing cosmopolitanism and sense of social justice. In tandem with many other world historians, I embraced this approach to history as a way to express my commitment to humanitarianism and ethics by retelling the past through those themes. Such a connection has been expressed by leading world historians as far back as 1951, when Ralph E. Turner wrote of the desire to present an "objective, unbiased treatment ... [to] further the cooperation of peoples thus made aware of their common bonds, of the harmony resulting from natural contacts, and of a unity asserting itself in spite of apparent difference."[4] More recently the Italian scholar Luigi Cajani (with whom I shared a panel at the 2006 World History Association conference in Long Beach) has written optimistically:

> Historical ethnocentrism can be overcome by a world vision of history, a vision not from the bottom, from an ethnic center, but from the top, encompassing the human experience as a whole ... On the philosophical level, world history goes arm in arm with cosmopolitanism, as happened during the Enlightenment. Cosmopolitanism is now in a revival phase, linked to the debate on constitutional patriotism, human rights and globalization ... (2007: 7)

Not long before, Jerry Bentley, editor of the *Journal of World History*, had expressed the belief that: "Ecumenical world history has strong potential to serve larger social purposes much more constructively than the xenophobic and hyper-patriotic versions of the global past that are all too prominent in schools throughout the world, including the United States" (Bentley 2005).

In the middle years of the decade, I had imbibed these beliefs with my readings, and the way that I understood them was one that centered empiricism and rationality within a universal moral code. In other words, when I taught History 701 in 2006 I believed that a cosmopolitan world history was the *correct* and *accurate* world history as well as the most *desirable* one.[5] Thus my purpose in this course was to help students refute what I saw (and still see) as the myths of an internal, cultural superiority that led to the West's emergence as the center of a world-system or world-empire in the nineteenth century.[6] The approach I chose to take was to assign chauvinistic, Eurocentric histories like David Landes's *The Wealth and Poverty of Nations* (1998) alongside others like Andre Gunder Frank's *ReORIENT* (1998), and help students engage the debate between them. However, in doing so I firmly believed that students would find Frank's arguments more compelling than those of Landes, and I certainly did not teach the course in an unbiased manner.

Both the surface assertion of objective, empirical history and the undercurrent of bias are evident in the syllabus statement excerpted above. On the one hand, I called on students to "evaluate" scholarship and present "critical and academically rigorous syntheses" of both individual works and debates between them. Yet I was quite clear that the rise of the West was only a "purported" event. To be fair to myself, I did call on students to determine the limitations of "thematic" and "comparative" as well as "regional" approaches. Yet my entire approach to the class was to attempt to unveil the myths put forward by Landes through the use of Andre Gunder Frank and other world historians.

Snapshot 3: Twentieth-Century World History Survey, University of Stellenbosch, 2008

The world history that I was teaching in 2006 was in part an attack on a metanarrative of inevitable Western superiority. An older generation of historians like William McNeill and Alfred Crosby had challenged their protégés to question the received wisdom that underpinned the "rise of the West" thesis, and scholars such as A.G. Frank, Kenneth Pomeranz, and R. Bin Wong (2000) successfully produced and interpreted the kinds of evidence that allowed us to weave a much more complex and global story of the human past than those that came before.

As a US-based, rather leftist and internationalist historian, I had by 2006 become quite comfortable with global historical narratives of interdependence and exchange.

On a political level, these gave me tools to work against patriotic histories of the neoconservative right that reduced humanity to perpetually struggling "civilizations" in the service of their foreign policy goals (Huntington 1993). In the multicultural San Francisco State University classroom, they also allowed me to present my students with a shared history that included everyone's pasts within it. Yet as an Africanist, this universal narrative clashed with my evolving understanding of the role of History (the discipline) in relationship to the African societies I was studying. Scholars in the fields of African studies and African history were, during this same period, beginning to raise the questions of whether the work we did was relevant, helpful, or authentic to the people whose pasts we were portraying.[7] I was particularly moved by the arguments of Joseph C. Miller, who wrote that:

> Until "world" historians incorporate Africa on its own terms, and focus also on the unique aspects of other world regions that may be easier to force into the appearance of modern modes, the logic of progressive world history is condemned to obscure the dynamism of a truly global past – "global" in the historical sense of multiple and inclusive, rather than in the too-conventional sense of merely macro in scale, and hence singular in concept – behind visions of the modern West writ larger and larger, farther and farther back in time, and inscribed over and over again on the lives of people who in fact proceeded with very different agendas on their minds. It is to *them*, the Africans and many others, and *their* visions and strategies, that we must turn to realize the full potential of thinking distinctively as historians – ultimately, true to the centered nature of history, to do so productively about ourselves. (2005: 35)

These scholars echoed the critiques of other researchers, who argued that world history, emanating from North America and Europe, was an imperial or colonial act. (See chapter by Weinstein, this volume.) For example, Vinay Lal wrote:

> As far as I am able to judge, "world history" informs the greater part of the people in the world that the only history they have is to catch up to someone else's history, or else they themselves will become history. Such a history has every potential to be a form of "cultural genocide," politically disempowering, and destructive of the ecological plurality of knowledge and lifestyles. (2003: 288–289)

These arguments suggested to me that world historians would benefit from the "provincialization" of world history. That is to say, we needed to historicize it as a movement and a field, to examine from where we had created it and its political economy (Lal 2005).[8] In 2007, I set out to understand the domestic setting of world history within the United States, a country whose citizens dominate it as a subdiscipline and largely officer its structures, including the World History Association and the *Journal of World History*.[9] Yet this task proved too difficult to undertake entirely from "within." Thus I applied for and happily won a Fulbright grant to study global history in and from South Africa. This year abroad provided a unique opportunity to develop a fresh perspective. As a country that had recently been through a major political upheaval, South Africa was paying close attention to the portrayal of history (e.g. Stolten 2007). This was true not only within its disciplinary bodies and in schools, but also in terms of contests to define national heritage, tradition, memory, and even a sense of nostalgia for various constructed pasts. There were numerous sites in which these contests took place – cinema, newspapers, monuments, museums, and public events. (See Witz, this volume.) One important set of sites were the first-year history courses at South Africa's universities.

Within the university setting in postapartheid South Africa, multiracial democracy had led to a reversal of Eurocentric Western civilization histories and their replacement by courses approximating world history. Concurrently, however, the prevailing situation in South Africa also led to the questioning of History itself as the voice of the nation or of the people in studying African pasts. (See Simo, this volume.)

Because I knew and admired several South African historians who had participated in world history conferences and events, I arrived there expecting scholars and students to have strong opinions on the field. Instead, I found that world history was largely alien to most practitioners and students, with the exception of a small group of scholars. Thus I was frequently asked to explain what world history was. The excerpt below, from a lecture slide I used in a course at the University of Stellenbosch, is an example of my attempts to do so. Historically an Afrikaans-speaking university, Stellenbosch had a rich history of scholars engaged in determining the relationship between European and South African societies, but the history department was only beginning to become more globalized, partly through the work of Dr Sandra Swart, who had begun to offer a global environmental history course. I was able to participate in another young course on twentieth-century global history. My contribution was to give a historiology of twentieth-century history, including the development of the field of world history:

What Is World History?
- World Historians seek to tell stories of the world that don't focus on Europe or the "West" but rather the whole world.
- World History tells stories about trade, exchange, migration as the engines of historical change.
- World History largely comes out of the United States and Canada, and its focus reflects domestic issues in this region.
- World History is still recognizable as social science "History," obeying the rules of evidence, data, etc.

As this slide may show, by this point in my career I was beginning to think critically about the meanings inscribed upon the student by world history. By the time I wrote this lecture, six months into my stay in South Africa, I had reached some findings but also was left with a number of questions. The findings are largely reflected in this slide. Beyond the first two (widely accepted) points that world history is about connections and that it seeks to overturn a Eurocentric metanarrative, I was arguing two further points. The first was that world history as it then stood largely reflected political and sociocultural issues in the United States by serving as a rejoinder to both ethnic studies and right-wing patriotic histories of the world.[10] Second, I argued that world historians (with some exceptions) had largely sidestepped the issues raised by postcolonial and cultural studies practitioners.

Although not explicitly mentioned in these slides, my discussions of these issues with colleagues in South Africa had left me with several unresolved questions. Who decides the research agendas of world history? Who has the money and the power in the field? What constitutes "history" and who decides who qualifies as a historian? What is the relationship between world history and localized systems of historical consciousness? How does inclusion as subjects or objects of world history benefit the people of Africa? Together, I then believed, my findings and my questions constituted a critique of world history as a set of structures and an approach to studying the past.

Snapshot 4: The World and the West Seminar, San Francisco State University, 2010

However, criticism alone seldom makes for good scholarship. As Caroline Walker Bynum has written in *Perspectives on History*, historians have in the past decade or so made great strides in teaching our students to read sources critically, but this doesn't mean they are well prepared to become historians:

> We have taught them to be critical of where they find material; we have taught them to expect bias and to study authors for it; we have taught them to ask questions of their material, not just to "accumulate facts." All to the good. But in the process we have perhaps led them to think that when they have "critiqued" someone else's position, they have found one of their own; that the work of the historian is to find the flaws in how others put things … (Bynum 2009: 14)

For better or worse, historians don't merely deconstruct. We also construct and recon-struct. This was a reality of which I was reminded when I returned from South Africa with my array of conclusions about world history in the United States and my questions about the future of a global world history. In striving to catch up with the recent scholar-ship in my field, I found the "critical" works oddly unsatisfactory except where they were accompanied by sound research and well-rounded narratives. Thus, while I knew that I was no longer satisfied to teach the kinds of universal world histories I had taught in 2000 and 2006, I could not yet decide how to replace them.

One direction forward from the purely critical position was pointed out by Eva-Maria Swidler in her article "Defending Western Civ." Swidler's argument is not a defense of the traditional, celebratory Western Civilization course, but rather suggests that world history has raised the discursive system of the "West" to global prominence. As she writes:

> Western Civ in all its guises, whether taught by historians or by independent humanities programs, talks explicitly about scientific thinking and rationality, about democracy and individual liberties, about progress. But as historians we know that platitudes are not history. We must bring to bear the critical insights on these themes that history can offer: the questioning of absolute objectivity, the historical construction of knowledge, the socially determined construction of the self that varies so widely across space and time, the manifold ways beyond the modern liberal democracy that the world has seen for people to participate in political decision making. (Swidler 2007)

Contained herein is a powerful argument against resting any cosmopolitan history upon universal, empirical and purportedly anti-Eurocentric narratives. As Swidler notes, whether we like it or not the notion of the "West" is all around us. In order to understand the world, we need to understand the West not as an empirical reality but as a set of social constructions out of which people act. In our world today, anti-immigration sentiment, homophobia, racism, and the realities of business and politics are shaped by ideas of Westness. Any responsible world history, therefore, requires us also to understand this concept, where it came from, and the ways in which it is held. By extension, world history therefore should be a history of other worldings, or ways of understanding the world outside of the discourse of the West, as well.[11] What such an understanding of world history requires, therefore, is not *universality* but instead *multiplicity* and *plurality* (Nandy 1995).

This understanding has led me to reenvision all of my world history courses. At the undergraduate level, I no longer concentrate on developing a unified vision of the development and interactions of civilizations. While I still try to give students a framework for reconstructing "what happened," I only use this as a launching pad to encourage them to explore the different ways in which the world was understood by people in different places and times. I ask questions like "How did West Africans experience and talk about the Atlantic slave trade?" and "How did Mughal and Vijayanagaran subjects discuss the coming of British colonialism?"

Still, in order to get back to this key idea of multiple worldings it is important that students first understand the dominance of discourses of the West today, and begin to deconstruct them. This is the task at the center of the graduate seminar (History 740) that I was teaching in fall 2010. Consider the following syllabus excerpt:

This is a graduate-level research course that revolves around two main tasks:

1. The collective exploration of the historical processes through which the ideas and discourses of "the West" were formed and how it came to be placed in binary opposition to non-modernity, "people-without-history," and other formulations for the non-west.
2. Individual interaction with primary sources that help to illuminate some aspects of these processes through their historicization and interpretation.

The topics of students' papers and the sources on which they write are not limited to a specific location or time, so long as they engage the principal topics of the course. This does mean that some places and periods may not be appropriate to this course.

I continue to try to teach world history unbounded by region or geography, but now I construct it as a history of ideas and discourse. From the realm of social and economic history I am proposing to move students into the realm of cultural history, with the dual objectives of teaching students to conduct thick analyses of individual sources and to understand them as artifacts of a global process of constructing the "West" and, by extension, the "world."

In some respects, I thus find myself having moved away from my early teaching of world history survey courses, in which I concentrated on *reconstructing* a shared global past. In the middle years of the last decade I had instead been driven to share with my students my growing understanding of how world history has been *constructed* by historians and laypeople alike. More recently, I have come to work, with my graduate students at least, on *deconstructing* those histories through understanding the shifting meanings of common tropes like "the West."

Yet even while I teach this approach, I have also been learning its limits. As scholars as diverse as Carolyn Hamilton (1998) and Jan Vansina (1961) have written, discourse isn't invented out of nowhere. Rather, it has some discernible relationship to things that "actually happened," and clearly students still need to have some ability to reconstruct the past if they are also to deconstruct the sources produced out of it. Thus my challenge for future classes is figuring out how to combine these skills in approximately equal measure.

World History as a Work in Progress

Of course, I do not propose my current classes as the *right* way to teach world history. I would be a hypocrite if I did not appreciate the diverse ways of teaching this subject.

Rather, I accept that my world history courses even today are works in progress. As historians, we study "change over time" and we must acknowledge that we and the courses we teach are constantly shifting as well. I suspect these changes are usually, although not always, to the better.

World history, too, is a work in progress. From its North American/European roots to its dominance by US scholars, it is now moving into a phase in which it is truly globalizing under the confederated organizations brought together as NOGWHISTO (Network of Global and World History Organizations), and with many more voices like those included in Part III of this volume. What will happen as more Asian, African, and Latin American scholars find channels to input their global histories into the world history movement? This is an exciting moment, and one that cannot help but influence how we all teach world history. I look forward to reflecting upon it ten years from now.

Notes

1   The literature here is well known and too long to cite, but some disturbing takes and analyses include Fredrickson (1981); Bierstedt (1966); Freeman (1995).
2   See the critique from Blaut (2000).
3   Manning is President and Chairman of the Board of the World History Network, former editor of H-World, and has consulted for more than a dozen universities on their World History programs.
4   Ralph E. Turner, "Working Paper of the Plan for a Scientific and Cultural History of Mankind," 1951, quoted in Allardyce (1990: 28–29).
5   Bentley is not as clear on this, as he seems to admit in the first pages of "Myths, wagers" that World History is a "mythistory," but has defended it in other settings as uniquely "critical."
6   Immanuel Wallerstein's influence should be clear here.
7   The unpublished work of Esperanza Brizuela-Garcia has particularly influenced my thinking here.
8   Vinay Lal calls for an examination of world history's political economy in this article.
9   At the time of the writing of this chapter, all of the officers and council members of the World History Association, and all of its past presidents, hail from the United States. The WHA sponsors the publication of two journals – *Journal of World History* and *World History Connected* (online) – as well as a bulletin. The editors of all of these publications are similarly located in the US. Of course, a number of younger but important institutions have emerged outside of the US, such as the Europe-based *Journal of Global History* and the new Asian and African associations of world historians affiliated with the WHA.
10 I expand upon this in Getz (2012).
11 There are fields outside of history that are pursuing this line much more effectively than we are; e.g. Tickner and Waever (2009), Connery and Wilson (2007). (See chapter by Northrop, this volume.)

References

Allardyce, Gilbert. 1990. Toward world history: American historians and the coming of the world history course. *Journal of World History* 1: 23–76.

Bentley, Jerry. 2005. Myths, wagers, and some moral implications of world history. *Journal of World History* 16: 54–68.

Bierstedt, Robert. 1966. Indices of civilization. *American Journal of Sociology* 71: 483–490.

Blaut, James M. 2000. *Eight Eurocentric Historians*. New York: Guilford Press.

Bynum, Caroline Walker. 2009. Teaching scholarship. *Perspectives on History* 47 (9) (Dec.): 14–16.

Cajani, Luigi. 2007. Citizenship on the verge of the 21st century: The burden of the past, the challenge of the present. In L. Cajani and A. Ross, eds, *History Teaching, Identities, Citizenship*, pp. 1–12. Stoke-on-Trent: Trentham.

Childe, V. Gordon. 1950. The urban revolution. *Town Planning Review* 21: 3–17.

Connery, Christopher Leigh, and Rob Wilson. 2007. *The Worlding Project: Doing Cultural Studies in the Era of Globalization*. Berkeley: North Atlantic Books.

Diamond, Jared. 1997. *Guns, Germs, and Steel: The Fates of Human Societies*. New York: W.W. Norton.

Dunn, Ross E., ed. 2000. *The New World History: A Teacher's Companion*. New York: Bedford/St Martin's.

Frank, Andre Gunder. 1998. *ReORIENT: Global Economy in the Asian Age*. Berkeley: University of California Press.

Fredrickson, George M. 1981. *White Supremacy: A Comparative Study in American and South African History*. Oxford: Oxford University Press.

Freeman, Michael. 1955. Genocide, civilization and modernity. *British Journal of Sociology* 46: 207–223.

Getz, Trevor R. 2012. World history and the rainbow nation: Educating values in the United States and South Africa. In A. Diptee and D. Trotman, eds, *Memory, Public History and Representations of the Past: Africa and Its Diasporas*. New York: Continuum.

Hamilton, Carolyn. 1998. *Terrific Majesty: The Powers of Shaka Zulu and the Limits of Historical Invention*. Cambridge, MA: Harvard University Press.

Huntington, Samuel P. 1993. The clash of civilizations? *Foreign Affairs* 72: 22–36.

Jenkins, Keith, and Alun Munslow. 2004. *The Nature of History Reader*. New York: Routledge.

Lal, Vinay. 2003. Provincializing the West: World history from the perspective of Indian history. In B. Stuchtey and E. Fuchs, eds, *Writing World History, 1800–2000*, pp. 271–289. Oxford: Oxford University Press.

Lal, Vinay. 2005. Much ado about something: The new malaise of world history. *Radical History Review* 91: 124–130.

Landes, David S. 1998. *The Wealth and Poverty of Nations: Why Some Are So Rich and Some So Poor*. New York: W.W. Norton.

Manning, Patrick. 2003. *Navigating World History: Historians Create a Global Past*. New York: Palgrave Macmillan.

McNeill, William H. 1990. "The Rise of the West" after twenty-five years. *Journal of World History* 1: 1–21.

Miller, Joseph C. 2005. Beyond blacks, bondage, and blame: Why a multi-centric world history needs Africa. Draft originally prepared for a talk at Carleton College.

Munslow, Alun. 2006. *Deconstructing History*. New York: Routledge.

Nandy, Ashis. 1995. History's forgotten doubles. *History and Theory* 34 (2): 44–66.

Pomeranz, Kenneth. 2000. *The Great Divergence: China, Europe, and the Making of the Modern World Economy*. Princeton: Princeton University Press.

Stolten, Hans Erik, ed. 2007. *History Making and Present Day Politics: The Meaning of Collective Memory in South Africa*. Uppsala: Nordiska Afrikainstitutet.

Swidler, Eva-Maria. 2007. Defending Western Civ: Or how I learned to stop worrying and love the course. *World History Connected* 4, at http://worldhistoryconnected.press.illinois.edu/4.2/swidler.html (accessed Mar. 2012).

Tickner, Arlene B., and Ole Waever. 2009. *International Relations Scholarship around the World*. New York: Routledge.

Vansina, Jan. 1961. *Oral Tradition: A Study in Historical Methodology*. Chicago: Aldine.

Wong, R. Bin. 2000. *China Transformed: Historical Change and the Limits of European Experience*. Ithaca: Cornell University Press.

PART II

Categories and Concepts

Framing

CHAPTER NINE

Environments, Ecologies, and Cultures across Space and Time

I. G. SIMMONS

Every year a study is published which pushes back the horizon beyond which the world was without human influence. Even if we confine ourselves to the last 10,000 years, the chronicling of the changes in the planet's ecology and understanding them in historic terms present fearsome tasks of erudition and the explanation of complexity. If we think there may be relevance to today's issues, and maybe even those of tomorrow, then the undertakings are increased many-fold. Generalizations are essential but full of pitfalls, although there are some threads that can be followed through the labyrinth, some of which are outlined in this chapter. In particular, the whole of human history can be seen as a series of projects in harnessing the energy which is necessary to survive but also to break land for cultivation, to build pyramids, whether in Giza or San Francisco, to fire arrows or to launch nuclear missiles. Thus a broad-scale but effective history of humanity can follow the accumulation of harnessed energy sources from sunlight to the atom. Within such a framework there are many millions of interactions between the world of biophysical nature and that of human cultures, but again some themes shine through: the ways in which some of these ecologies have, to use today's anthropocentric terminology, proved "unsustainable" is one of them; another must surely be the driver of so much environmental metamorphosis, that of human population growth allied to demands for resources from the Earth. Yet it is clear to all that some changes are local whereas others affect the whole planet; there are both spatial and temporal scales of alteration.[1] To talk of all this past in a short space and a comprehensible vocabulary brings its own headaches but it is suggested here that the tension between worldwide forces of coalescence in culture–nature relations and those of fragmentation provides a space for the broadest of approaches without totally losing focus. Each of these three central themes – harnessing energy, scales of alteration, and nature–culture interactions – is given a condensed but still meaningful treatment below, followed by short discussions of these contending forces of coalescence and fragmentation.

A Companion to World History, First Edition. Edited by Douglas Northrop.
© 2012 Blackwell Publishing Ltd. Published 2012 by Blackwell Publishing Ltd.

Harnessing Energy

The chronicle of the human role in occupying the thin zone of the planet that can support life is well documented in broad outline (i.e., Hughes 2007; Mosley 2010), with many contributors to the detail. This sequence is treated more specifically in other chapters of this volume (especially Fred Spier's chapter on "big history," but also those by Yoffee, Chase-Dunn and Hall, and Adas). One intention here is to present an overview of the last 10,000 years as a narrative of human access to energy sources and the ways in which planetary manipulation has led to so many material (and indeed nonmaterial) changes.

The story starts with gatherer-hunters concentrating their take of solar energy by small acts of manipulation: finding out that plants set out in middens grew very well, or that periodic fire allowed the growth of food plants that also had an enriched protein content. Their only true domesticate, the dog, helped concentrate prey animals during the hunt. Most foraging techniques moved towards the taking of more calories per unit of area than before, a process intensified when domestication of plants and animals created the field and the herd, with more calories and protein per unit of area per unit of time becoming available to humans. Both types of economy lived off recent solar energy, with dead wood the main representative of this older ("banked") photosynthesis. One constraint on production in several climates was water supply to crop plants, which could be alleviated by irrigation, in the cause of which many water diversions were invented. The trend towards tapping more concentrated sources of energy took a leap when the potential of fossil fuels (first coal, then oil and natural gas) to release energy in large quantities, and especially to generate steam under pressure, spread from a few cradles to many "Western" countries and then to Japan. Such fuels underlie many of today's environmental relations, along with later additions to the repertoire in the form of nuclear power and the interest in "renewable" energy sources now that the finite availability of the fossil hydrocarbons has been realized. Though transitions from one era to the next are often gradual, by 8000 BCE there was no going back from agriculture; the world was set on its industrial trajectory around 1750 CE and a "postindustrial" state became possible after 1950, with energy embedded in materials and services available to individuals as never before (Simmons 2008).

Scales of Alteration

There are many environmental consequences of the skein interweaving human societies and the nonhuman. The scales of effect are sometimes obvious and may evoke a variety of responses, but equally not all are detectable except with sophisticated equipment and they may not enter the consciousness of any but a scientific interest group. Indeed, ideas with immense breadth like the Gaia hypothesis were for many years the scientifically unloved child of an individual (James Lovelock, 1919–); the bioaccumulation of pesticides was scarcely acknowledged in many countries until Rachel Carson (1907–1964) produced her catalytic book in 1962. But the microscale of interaction is present for us all, as when we swat a fly or mow a lawn. Yet nobody recorded the last Moa bird in Aotorea/New Zealand (ca. 1500) or the last dodo on Mauritius, ca. 1693. At a larger scale, there are regional changes that follow the deforestation of a watershed: not only are the trees replaced with lower-biomass species but the soil dynamics change, and often soil is lost downhill into runoff, which causes floods in the valleys and perhaps eventually

Table 9.1   Gross energy consumed by humans

Period	Number of years	Total energy consumption (joules)	Notes
50,000–8000 BCE	42,000	2.5×10^{15}	Largely gatherer-hunters; fire
8000 BCE–1 CE	8,000	49×10^{18}	Solar power, wind power, some irrigation and water power
1–1750 CE	1,750	14×10^{21}	Solar, wind, and water power but increasingly efficient
1750–1950	200	3.6×10^{21}	Major years of fossil fuel power
1950–2002	52	6.4×10^{21}	High population plus fossil fuels and other energy sources

Source: Data from Population Reference Bureau (Washington DC) based on the number of people who have ever lived multiplied by a representative figure for per capita consumption at each stage. So far the gross energy consumption and hence environmental impact is largest for the 1–1750 CE era.

delta formation in lakes and oceans. The loss of biodiversity is in large part due to habitat change rather than direct extirpation, often as an unintended result of environmental manipulation in the cause of the production of materials; its importance is being promoted as equivalent to that covered by the Intergovernmental Panel on Climate Change (IPCC) (Marris 2010; UNEP 2010). It is possible to change the ecology of almost a whole continent (although not at once) by eliminating a type of human–environment nexus, as when the dominant gatherer-hunters of North America were eliminated or took up other economic modes; few of the ecosystems of that continent present in 1500 were unchanged by 1900, and most of the metamorphoses involved the removal of pre-agricultural modes of subsistence. Table 9.1 makes the case for the era of agriculture (approximately 8000 BCE through 1750 CE) having had a major impact upon the Earth's systems.

Some alterations can be classed as worldwide, that is, they occur in all parts of the globe, although they are not necessarily connected into one system. Soil erosion is one example: it happens everywhere all the time, but in some places it is enhanced by land management systems that mobilize particulate matter. There is no evidence, however, to suggest the unification of the various inputs into one marine deposit. That is not true of molecules in suspension or solution in the oceans' water, for persistent chemicals from runoff have turned up thousands of kilometers from their source and have also undergone bioaccumulation which has further dispersed them: think of the range of an albatross, for example (one bird can cover 6,000 kilometers in 12 days). There are also some truly global instances of human-driven change which involve the atmosphere of the whole planet. These are well known and their representation concentrates on the buildup of "greenhouse gases" after the nineteenth century, and the models that predict "global warming." Even here, though, a greater historical depth is of value, since enhanced methane levels in the upper atmosphere may have been present ever since the introduction of wetland rice farming, about 8,000 years ago (Zong 2007; Ruddiman *et al.* 2008).

At all scales, some such trends are impermanent, whereas others seem irreversible. Shifting agriculture in forests seems to allow a more or less complete reversion to preexisting ecologies when a plot is abandoned, and it seems the "ozone hole" caused by CFCs may be repairable. On the other hand, extinction of species may not yield to the Jurassic Park treatment, in which modern technologies somehow bring back long-departed plants or animals. Current methane levels in the atmosphere are the highest in the last 400,000 years: at 1,850 parts per billion rather then the historically normal level of 600–700 ppb, they seem unlikely to diminish very soon (Shindell *et al.* 2009). The overall conclusion from the natural sciences seems to be that humans have been manipulators of species and ecosystems for much longer than has been implanted in the popular imagination, and they have been more penetrative than recognized by many scholars until perhaps quite recently.

Nature–Culture Interactions

The previous section only hints at the dauntingly long and complex list of linkages between humans and the nonhuman world, and at the ways in which changes have taken place over time. The idiosyncrasies of human culture have often led to diverse outcomes, so there is still controversy over why China did not develop industrialization in the way it happened in Europe; why early Islam rejected the wheel and printing; and even the reasons, long discussed, for the fall of complex cultures such as the Maya (Diamond 2005). In most of these there was an environmental component in the consequences, if not the causes, although the fall of Rome continues to be blamed on lead piping. Complex socio-ecological trains of causation like those proposed by Tainter (1988) are unusual: he hypothesizes that breakdowns occur when the energy of a group is largely consumed in feedback to keep the unit steady, rather than investing in innovation. So one difficulty in this historiography is that environmental components become simply existential elements of otherwise foregrounded historical processes, with which they compete for attention; when the strength of the king or the health of the peasants fails to convince, then "environmental factors" are a later resort. Even where the environment is the main focus, such matters become difficult across time and space and so very large-scale backdrops indeed have to be used: "the unending frontier" for early modern times, "something new under the sun" for industrialization (McNeill 2000; Richards 2003).

At the heart of any consideration of 10,000 years of human history there must surely be the driver of population growth. A species whose total number was perhaps 1 million gatherer-hunters in 8000 BCE became about 6.8 billion in 2010: perhaps 6 percent of all the people who have ever lived on Earth are alive today. The basic lesson for environmental change is the amount of energy to which succeeding eras have had access, and the use of this energy for environmental manipulation (Smil 1994). Although today's distribution is highly uneven, the delivery of almost any form of "development" involves access to more energy: consider the embedded energy in the mobile phone as well as the energy costs of satellite telecommunications. An industrial society today consumes about 20 times the amount of energy of a solar-powered economy. Back-of-the-envelope reckoning suggests that the world during the twentieth century CE used 10 times as much energy as it had in the thousand years before 1900 CE. In the 100 centuries between the dawn of agriculture and 1900, humanity used only about two-thirds as much energy as in the twentieth century. The inevitable conclusion is that environmental interaction is a function of population growth multiplied by a factor for resource use; energy availability is a reasonable measure of that factor. The historical consequences of such a formulation include conflicts in which access to oil has been or will be crucial.

Many historians have written explanatory accounts for all of the above: they cannot be accused of ignoring nature. Their attitudes have ranged from a simple kind of determinism in which societies simply adapted to the surroundings, through the possibilities and opportunities made possible by enterprising individuals or enhanced technologies, down to the renewal of determinism implicit in the models of climatic change set out by the IPCC. The "new" relevance of nature can be seen in titles that include phrases like "a global and ecological narrative" (Marks 2006). As a way of making the variety of social and ecological relations within an overall environment-population envelope more comprehensible, two opposing features of society and nature can be highlighted and drawn out for examination. These features, which have been in tension for much of the last 10,000 years, may be categorized as *coalescence* and *fragmentation*. Coalescence can be briefly defined as the coming together of features, either of the natural world, as by species migration and interbreeding, or of the social world through the spread of near-identical social practices. Fragmentation, by contrast, affects ecosystems through either extinction or sequestration as a reserve of some kind, paralleled by the stratification of societies by differential access to energy or other resources. Such general ideas, although admittedly dogged by a Western delight in binary opposites, may help provide a useful foundation for examining both current and historic dynamics in the relations between environments, ecologies, and cultures.

Environmental historians have indeed looked at the dynamics of "natural" ecosystems in time, assessed the roles of technologies in accessing natural resources, looked at the effects of environmental policies, and focused on cultural values and beliefs about the nonhuman world. Are there ways in which scholars might improve our understandings even further? So far there has been a relatively low level of use of the findings of the natural sciences, particularly those of ecology. Similarly, fluency in languages other than English would help to interpret cultural variations in assessing the role of nature. The "soft" side of social context is also uncertain ground for many historians: poetry, music, and myths may well underlie grand narratives.[2] (Think of how often news stories evoke Prometheus.) Many writers seem to find such comfort in their "discipline," as if the named crystallizations of the nineteenth century (anthropology, sociology, geography) had been there for all time. Much too frequently ignored is the dictum of John Amos Comenius (1592–1670), the Czech founder of modern education, that knowledge should be "universal, disgraced with no foul Casme."[3]

Coalescence

For the nonhuman world this term is interpreted to mean processes which bring together different phenomena and produce a wider spread of the resultant feature. A species may evolve in a unique temporal and spatial context but its spread carries its relationships over a wider area. (The archaeology of genus *Homo* demonstrates such diffusion.) The interaction of two species may produce a hybrid which is so successful as to colonize large areas: the salt-marsh grass *Spartina* x *townsendii* is one such case. At a more complex scale, ecosystems recovering from the Pleistocene ice ages extended their range and brought similarities to great tracts, as with the Boreal conifer forests or the temperate deciduous forests of the mid-Holocene. Where climate and weather are concerned, influence can be global: one obvious example is the massive volcanic eruptions whose particulate emissions produced a form of global dimming. One hypothesis suggests eruptions from the Lake Toba region of Indonesia some 70,000 years ago created a bottleneck in human populations, with subsequent genetic consequences. Indonesia also contributed eruptions of Mount Tambora that produced "the year without a summer" of 1815 and of Krakatoa in 1863, which reduced global temperatures by 1.2 degrees centigrade for about five years.

Analogous convergences in the social world are harder to find in gatherer-hunter groups since they mostly lived apart, but attention can be drawn to the ways in which some societies see no ontological distinction between human and "other" components: the Koyukon Indians lived in a world in which the surroundings had to be treated with respect since they were aware, sensate and personified; the cosmos simultaneously exhibited both being and sacredness (Nelson 1983; Ingold 1986). In preindustrial times the Silk Road might stand proxy for many convergences: rhubarb and silk and bubonic plague westwards, Buddhism and Islam eastwards. Of course, there were more complexities and some surprising distances, with Austronesians voyaging from Taiwan to Rapanui/Easter Island, and by the thirteenth century, a world system of trade circuits would have allowed the trade of expensive objects from England to Indonesia (Chase-Dunn and Grimes 1995). An inevitable common experience of humans thereafter was epidemic disease of the kind which brought exterminations of peoples in the Americas, Caribbean and Pacific. (See Pernick, this volume.) The appeal of new crops is well documented (sugar, tobacco, maize), and native flora and fauna were often replaced (most notably in the West Indies) by a relatively uniform set of introduced species (Watts 1987; Hobhouse 1999). No doubt the best-documented coalescences are those between Europe and the Americas (Bray 1993; Crosby 1993; Cronon 2003). If one adds concepts to the mix, then measurement of space and time led to map-making and navigation, and the establishment of empires with fixed ideas about faith, slavery, crops, and trade (Crosby 1997).

In later eras the application of steam power was seen as a universal blanket of change for good: "Every improvement of the means of locomotion benefits mankind morally and intellectually as well as materially," said Thomas Macaulay (1849: 370), and material transmissions certainly improved with the advent of the railway, steamship, electric telegraph, powered flight, and radio, with TV following closely after 1950. Backed up with firearms and quinine, Western ways carried finished goods, raw materials and accumulated capital and this made possible thousands of environmental alterations seen through the same spectacles, that of profit. But even here there were unexpected attempts at convergence: an African Research Survey set up in the 1930s had as one aim the standardizing of the colonial policies of Britain, France, Belgium and Portugal. It was abandoned in 1940 but had developed environmental attitudes in opposition to the usual colonial rejection of traditional ecological knowledge (Tilley 2003).

Science also brought about coalescences, nowhere more so than in the system of Linnaean nomenclature of plants and animals, published in the eighteenth century and influential ever since, although not currently adopted in detail, especially since the advent of DNA sequencing. The transfer of species between continents accelerated with trade, and many species took rides as stowaways. To list even a small fraction would be tedious, but recall the export of trout from the UK to at least six pieces of the British Empire, including the Falkland Islands, and California's 1860 contribution of *Phylloxera* to European winemaking. The general cure-all for plant diseases of dusting with sulfur or one of its compounds was part folk knowledge but also came from German science. Likewise, a more precise formulation of industrial fertilizers' need to contain nitrogen also emanated from German laboratories. The leading element in prescriptions for chemical death, at least until the 1960s, was chlorine, which was built up into a variety of chlorinated hydrocarbons (CHCs), the most famous of which was DDT. What was not predicted was that the group would have very low breakdown rates even outside the target organisms, and so would become subject to biological amplification. This meant that very low concentrations, for example in water, could become lethally high as they moved up a predator–prey food chain. Rachel Carson's book *Silent Spring* (1962) shone a bright light upon this trajectory. Many species became almost extinct until Western governments began to act. Residues of CHCs are distributed throughout the world's oceans (where they are still available for uptake) and thence via aerosol formation at the water–air interface may be rained out on land surfaces and on, for instance, the Antarctic ice. There is a case, therefore, for seeing this industrial residue as having a global distribution.

An even stronger claim can be made for waste gases that, having been let off into the atmosphere, are only slowly scavenged out. They remain long enough to affect the general processes of the atmosphere. The likelihood seems high that climate will be affected by gases which contribute to the effectiveness of retaining radiation within the Earth's system. In 1750, the concentration of carbon dioxide was about 280 parts per million and in 2010 it was 391 ppm, with a straight line of growth between these two estimations. Other industrial era emissions such as nitrogen oxides (270–285 ppm) and methane (700–1,850 ppb) followed the same trend between 1750 and today. Once in the atmosphere, moreover, their distribution is virtually homogeneous spatially: no matter who emits, everybody will receive consequences, although these may be to some extent spatially variable. This globalization is certainly material, is the subject of much intellectual activity, and is without doubt moral in its implications. Not all of it stems from the "means of locomotion," but the centrality of motors of many kinds cannot be evaded.

A key concept since the 1990s has been "globalization." In its material effects, this meant the human ability to transport and communicate worldwide, along with an added capacity to "use" the atmosphere and space. The development of satellites, (usually) reliable rocket propulsion, and instant electronic communication has produced a dominant technologically based culture with very few wishing to opt out. A related major cultural feature is commercial penetration, so that the same brand names are seen worldwide with only minor regional variations: Toyota and Coca-Cola are obvious examples, although the incidence of (unbranded) "pizza" seems to be even higher. Crisscrossing of the planet entrains all kinds of organisms and materials, not the least of which is the spread of disease, including phenomena like pandemics of influenza which emerge with panic-inducing rapidity.

All this commerce requires energy, and the world's superpower (the United States) is the biggest consumer of all, even though the energy needs of countries emerging into industrialization (notably India and China) are also immense (and growing). Burning carbon-laden fuels has led to emissions which have enhanced the capacity of the atmosphere to retain heat and thus produce the "greenhouse effect." The late twentieth-century emphasis on methane and CO_2 was preceded by concern about CFCs and their production of "ozone holes" over the poles. The nature of a warmer globe has been assessed in two ways. First, any current trends which seem to fit the idea are assigned to that cause. Thus the rise in global temperature at the end of the twentieth century is seen as one result, as are species shifts (the retreat of the cold-tolerant, and the advance of the warmth-seekers). Second, complex models predict likely effects and their regional variations, including complex feedback effects of such elements as cloudiness or the breakdown of tundra peats giving off methane. This process has been the subject of immense amounts of science and is constantly reviewed and presented with appropriate caveats. Thus it represents the best that the natural sciences can contribute to the question of the global environment.

Although there is now one world as never before, there have been at least three waves of integration of the world. It starts with migration and trade in the period before ca. 1500; integration is then catapulted to a new level by access to fossil fuels and the accompanying technologies; and all these processes are then outclassed by the post–World War II integration led by the United States (Reynolds 2003) and which, in the current "postindustrial" era, qualifies for the first time as "global." It is produced by a superpower, also, in the sense of access to energy applied through technology and driven by the distinctively high levels of consumption and the associated cultural-economic values of the United States.

Fragmentation

Here fragmentation is taken to mean processes such as the breaking up of ecosystems and the sequestration of species into reserves, or into the shields of patents, analogous to individuation within society, situations where an individual or small group can arrogate resources (in a broad sense) to themselves. For gatherer-hunters few internal examples are chronicled until relatively recent times, although there are the historic cases of groups which moved into and out of herding and farming. Some African hunters, for example, were once herders who had lost their cattle (Jolly 1966). In the colonial era from about 1800 to 1945, when the spread of industrial economies was accompanied by genocide, together with the loss of territory and autonomy, perhaps 50 million tribal people were killed, many of them gatherer-hunters. They were also subject to introduced diseases, such as those that killed 75 percent of the Yokut and Wintun people of California in 1830–1933, or those that contributed to the reduction in native Tasmanians from 5,000 to 111 in 30 years, with final extinction in 1876 (Bodley 1999). Even when European attitudes to hunting and gathering peoples became more protective, that way of life still diminished, not least because the thought patterns of the nation-state demanded assimilation, via school and mission. What was once the only way of life for humans is now confined to a few enclaves in remote and marginal environments, or is a barely recognizable form of it.

One of the abiding themes of the world's agricultural millennia must be the new separations that became possible. Certainly by the early seventeenth century, when John Donne wrote of his world "'tis all in pieces, all coherence gone," and when in ca. 1720–1740 J.S. Bach separated the fundamental harmonics of nature from those of a musical instrument in *The Well-Tempered Clavier*, the creative arts had latched onto a resonating theme in human history. Archaeological research shows how the fragmentation of objects, with parts being buried with the dead, both differentiated and cemented a social identity in Neolithic Europe. This suggests that there were social practices which brought about both tendencies at the same time (Chapman 2000). One major avatar of fragmentation in Western societies has been the growth of individualism, with the rise of the private sphere in Europe between 1000 and 1800 anticipating many trends of the twentieth and twenty-first centuries. This emergence had periods of acceleration, as in the wake of the Black Death, when there was less feudal control and the family unit became dominant. Much of this was cemented by the rise of the "artist" (as distinct from the artisan) in the Renaissance, and the affirmation of the standing of the individual human in the Reformation and the Enlightenment (Levine 2000). Few social historians fail to point out the way separations of role and withdrawals of behavior come alongside successful agriculture. It appears to hasten the dominance of men over women, for example, and sharpens the focus on the rich as they sequester resources which then appear as conspicuous displays of power. The grain surpluses of the Nile valley are thus transmogrified into the pyramids and other galaxies of treasure designed to procure eternal life. Smaller-scale actions have also attracted notice: the withdrawal of the lord and lady from a common hall of the medieval manor to their private room ("the solar") behind the dais, and the early modern development of the corridor in large houses. Increased wealth meant an ability to own and organize land for pleasure, as in hunting parks and landscape gardens, and to exclude the lesser folk from them by means of restrictive (indeed often draconian) laws.

Agriculture provoked a cultural evaluation of noncrop species, with many being regarded as "other" and therefore liable to be extirpated. "Predators," "weeds," and "pests" became sharply differentiated in a way not native to foragers. Inevitably, some became extinct. Our focus today is often on the visible loss of tree cover and its fauna (as in the Caribbean) or the disappearance of a noted species (as with the retreat of the elephants in China), but we need also to remember the multiplicity of fungi, bacteria and other micro-organisms and the complex communities in which they lived that were also farmed out of existence. The highest profile of all such retreats has been given to forest cover. The calculation that a hand-powered pitsaw can convert trees to planks at about 100–200 board feet per day, whereas a water-powered saw of 1621 can raise that figure to 2,000–3,000 bf/day, is indicative of the advance of technology, though it is eclipsed by the steam-powered band saw of 1876 at over 20,000 bf/day (Williams 2006). The other great change was in wetland habitats, with worldwide shifts in land cover and land use on a variety of spatial and temporal scales. Attention has been centered on massive schemes in Russia, China, Holland, England and the United States before steam power was available to pump up water – so drainage relied on gravity or windmills and, to a lesser extent, horse mills (Williams 1990).

Such lists are potentially endless but must include the seas, where for instance silt runoff from the land can affect the breeding success of fish or even the food webs of adults; overfishing could occur even in preindustrial times if a heavy effort coincided with alterations in water quality or with climatic shifts bringing about alterations in water temperatures. The advent of fossil fuel-powered technology changed almost everything in one way or another. This included indirect changes, as with the success of pharmacology in disease control, helping to contain death rates, a shift with considerable environmental consequences. Equally important, perhaps, was the ability of technology in about 1900 to impose the fractured time of the stopwatch on human movements and thus make an assembly line for all kinds of goods. Not least among these was the automobile, whose ascent into private ownership was one of the most environmentally pervasive technologies of the twentieth century. One of the coalescent forces of industrialization was the emplacement of marginal groups within a wider nation-state context, with new actors, structures, and networks that might bail them out if they ran into famine or disease epidemics. At the same time, the boundaries of the nation-state and its component units might well not be the best for resource management, a situation still true of water, for instance, in the Middle East and many of the oceans. Entities like Tokugawa Japan, which had deliberately cut themselves off from the world for 250 years (1603–1868), survived famine, tsunami and earthquake without any outside assistance, yet crumbled when confronted with an industrial world in the form of steamships with large guns.

The diminution of the public in favor of the private has also had many ecological consequences. One of these was the need for the public bodies to acquire land for wider use. Instead of common land, there was now public access land under the name of "park" in one form or another.[4] It was as though the rich preserved more nature (unless it could be the basis of tourist income) since they could call in resources from their economic periphery of poorer dependents. The poor had often no choice and either converted longstanding systems to cash crops for exports, at no matter what environmental cost, or transformed fragile ecologies into subsistence systems at great risk from environmental hazards such as floods, landslides, and even tsunami. The same industrial revolution which brought the world closer together, also estranged the human winners and losers, to say nothing of the nonhuman members of ecosystems. It begot multiple worlds, not all of which either understood or had sympathy for each other (Landes 1988). But they all stem from basic worldviews in which there were no overriding cultural reasons why nature should not be altered by breeding of species, by extirpation of pests, or by "improving" the land cover. Both agriculture and industrialism used technology as a pathway through which to direct human and solar energies, and there has been a broad acceptance of the social and environmental results that persists to this day.

One cultural evolution can be seen in the intellectual construct of modernism. Applied first to the arts between 1890 and 1914, it has come to express implications for the rational use of resources (as in town and country planning) and the styles of that rationality. The core of these ideas in the arts, politics, and science comes in the many spheres in which any element of continuity is broken up by the realization that the world and its representations are discontinuous. The atom was not a new idea in the nineteenth century, but its central role in physics and then indeed its fragmentation into smaller particles whose behavior is probabilistic comes from the twentieth century, as does the delineation of movement on film by capturing 16 individual frames per second in 1903. The early pictures of Piet Mondrian (1872–1944) show the representation of, for example, trees breaking up into fragments, and the *pointillisme* of Georges Seurat (1859–1891) makes every brush-stroke a series of dots. With words, James Joyce's *Ulysses* (conceived in 1907) was a series of episodes only resolved by the magnificent soliloquy of Molly Bloom which shifts tenses as often as a restless sleeper. In the concert hall, the atonalities of Schoenberg (1874–1951) and Webern (1883–1945) provide little clue about the next note. Politically, the invention of the concentration camp sequesters whole noncombatant populations "for their own good," a nostrum often credited to the British during the second Boer War (1899–1902) but more correctly the inspiration of Valeriano Weyler y Nicolau, a Spanish army officer in a Cuban war of independence, who constructed three *campos de reconcentración* in the province of Pinar del Rios in 1896 (Everdell 1997). This separation of function is also behind the analytic approach to planning which results in grid plans, outer suburbs, industrial zones and shopping malls, all with a single purpose.

In all these changes, two features need final emphasis. The first is the impact of colonialism (see Sinha, this volume) in so many regions of the world beyond the temperate zone: both wet and dry environments were subject to production systems and environmental management whose origins were in temperate areas and which might be imposed (although not always) irrespective of the different conditions. Thus shifting agriculture was often stigmatized as "primitive" and "wasteful," even though it was usually a rational response to soil–vegetation combinations. The second is a common response to fragmentation of ecologies in places with very fast change in the nineteenth and early twentieth centuries. The United States is a prime example, with many public policies developed in the wake of rapid ecological transformation of forests and grasslands. But note the instrumental theme: the US National Parks Service in the 1950s promulgated a "parks are for people" policy (Sellars 1999). Any ontological continuity between humanity and its coexisting entities had been lost.

Two linked processes have dominated environmental history and its potentials in the early twenty-first century: miniaturization and advanced biotechnology. "My music" on an MP3 player replaces the shared experience of a concert and avoids anything that might be unexpected. The mobile phone replaces the community's box; medication is formulated to a particular physiology, and "designer babies" will make it further into the world than the tabloid press. In such a setting, the rise of intellectual postmodernism, with its emphasis on avoiding the ubiquitous and the absolute in favor of the local and the relative, is not surprising (Sennett 2002; Bauman 2005). Being able to manipulate the basic material of the living cell has opened new vistas of tailoring. The main thrusts have been in matters of human health, such as replacement parts grown from embryonic stem cells, and the so-called GM ("genetically modified") crops in which resistance to disease or to a herbicide is implanted in the crop's genetic material. In 2012 it was clear that there is much more to be developed. Stem cell researchers largely brush off the ethical implications of their work ("we just do the science") and GM advocates concentrate on higher yields without worrying about the social implications of the associated cost and supply structure. Beyond both, there is the fear that uncontrollable harmful organisms will be released and that insufficient international protocols will ever be in place to guard against the "Frankenstein Effect" (Mannion 1995: ch. 10). In the immediate future, the development of a new species by GM means that it can be patented, a new development in the history of humans' relationship with the nonhuman. Biotechnology at the field level could mean coalescence as well, since many fewer crop varieties may dominate a region if a broad-spectrum tolerance is implanted.

A segmented market of individual choice militates for an analogous land-use pattern, with piecemeal conversions, for instance to supply seafood from shrimp farms at the expense of mangroves, soy-bean farms instead of tropical forest, and golf courses to replace agricultural land or pasture. On some coasts the makeover is virtually complete, with artificial islands extending the pleasure zone, as in Dubai. Thus "nature" becomes a separate category, with fences (often literally so) around "reserves"; the nonhuman world becomes in some cases (especially in National Parks) something recreational, to be entered or observed largely for pleasure – a reserve for tourism. Tiny cameras mean that no part of the life of a wild bird need be unobserved, on a TV screen; we are invited to "sponsor" an individual dolphin, panda, or tiger. There is a paradox in the sense that mini-cameras (and similar microtechnology) mean a heavier footprint and there has been little sense of decoupling the processes of the planet's ecology from those of human economies, still less of the somewhat vague notions of dematerializing the economies of the world.

Tensions

It is evident that there is a tension between ideas and processes of coalescence and fragmentation. The immediate setting for many of these issues is that of consumerism.

Former luxuries are now commonplace and so positional goods have to be sought, very often involving further environmental impact (Stearns 2001). In contrast, globalization has brought the limits to nature back into the frame, whereas in much of the nineteenth and twentieth centuries "environment" was simply a barrier between humanity and the modern world. The thinking may have changed but many of the forces associated with it (especially in terms of technology) continue to expand (Albrow 1997). It is a domain that exhibits many things at once, but the tension at its heart between rich and poor has many environmental consequences and all lead to an increased chance of instabilities of many kinds. These are likely to show greater amplitudes of fluctuation than in the past, and probably (in spite of the remarkable successes of modeling) predictable only imprecisely. Add to this the as yet unfathomable outcomes of biotechnology at the gene level and of nanotechnology, and history does not equip us at all well to deal rationally with such a world, even though it may help instill our sense of being members of a shared family. Humility is necessary, since this family includes the nonhuman. The Gaia hypothesis reminds everybody that there is no need to "save the planet": it will survive no matter what histories humans have inflicted on it.

Notes

1   I think there is a difference between "worldwide" and "global," with the wider term being reserved for phenomena that can occur in all the components of the planet, notably the deep oceans and the atmosphere.
2   Historians no less than almost everybody else probably subscribe to the myth that the species *Homo sapiens* will be here for ever.
3   Casme is an archaic spelling of "chasm."
4   The etymology of "park" is interesting since it connotes enclosure rather than availability.

References

Albrow, M. 1977. *The Global Age: State and Society beyond Modernity*. Stanford: Stanford University Press.
Bauman, Z. 2005. *Liquid Life*. Cambridge: Polity.
Bodley, J.H. 1999. Hunter-gatherers and the colonial encounter. In R.B. Lee and R. Daly, eds, *The Cambridge Encyclopedia of Hunters and Gatherers*, pp. 465–472. Cambridge: Cambridge University Press.
Bray, W., ed. 1993. *The Meeting of Two Worlds: Europe and the Americas 1492–1650*. Oxford: Oxford University Press for the British Academy.
Carson, R. 1962. *Silent Spring*. New York: Fawcett Crest.
Chapman, J. 2000. *Fragmentation in Archaeology: People, Places and Broken Objects in the Prehistory of South-Eastern Europe*. London: Routledge.
Chase-Dunn, C., and P. Grimes. 1995. World system analysis. *Annual Review of Sociology* 21: 387–417.
Cronon, W. 2003. *Changes in the Land: Indians, Colonists, and the Ecology of New England*. Rev. edn. New York: Hill & Wang.
Crosby, A.W. 1993. *Ecological Imperialism: The Biological Expansion of Europe 900–1900*. 2nd edn. Cambridge: Cambridge University Press.
Crosby, A.W. 1997. *The Measure of Reality: Quantification and Western Society 1200–1600*. Cambridge: Cambridge University Press.
Diamond, J.R. 2005. *Collapse: How Societies Choose to Fail or Succeed*. New York: Viking.

Everdell, W.R. 1997. *The First Moderns: Profiles in the Origin of Twentieth-Century Thought.* Chicago: University of Chicago Press.

Hobhouse, H. 1999. *Seeds of Change: Six Plants That Transformed Mankind.* London: Macmillan.

Hughes, J.D. 2007. *An Environmental History of the World: Humankind's Changing Role in the Community of Life.* 2nd edn. New York: Routledge.

Ingold, T. 1986. *The Appropriation of Nature: Essays on Human Ecology and Social Relations.* Manchester: Manchester University Press.

Jolly, P. 1966. Symbiotic interaction between black farming communities and the south-eastern San. *Current Anthropology* 37: 277–305.

Landes, D.S. 1998. *The Wealth and Poverty of Nations.* New York: W.W. Norton.

Levine, D. 2000. *At the Dawn of Modernity: Biology, Culture and Material Life in Europe after the Year 1000.* Berkeley: University of California Press.

Macaulay, T.B. 1849. State of England in 1685. In T.B. Macaulay, *History of England,* vol. 1, ch. 3. Leipzig: Bernard Tauchnitz.

McNeill, J.R. 2000. *Something New under the Sun: An Environmental History of the World in the 20th Century.* New York: W.W. Norton.

Mannion, A.M. 1995. *Agriculture and Environmental Change.* Chichester: John Wiley.

Marks, R.B. 2006. *The Origins of the Modern World: A Global and Ecological Narrative.* 2nd edn. Lanham: Rowman & Littlefield.

Marris, E. 2010. UN body will assess ecosystems and biodiversity. *Nature* 465: 859.

Mosley, S. 2010. *The Environment in World History.* London: Routledge.

Nelson, R.K. 1983. *Make Prayers to the Raven: A Koyukon View of the Northern Forest.* Chicago: University of Chicago Press.

Reynolds, D. 2003. American globalism: Mass, motion and the multiplier effect. In A.G. Hopkins, ed., *Globalization in World History,* pp. 243–260. London: Pimlico.

Richards, J.F. 2003. *The Unending Frontier: An Environmental History of the Early Modern World.* Berkeley: University of California Press.

Ruddiman W.F., *et al.* 2008. Early rice farming and anomalous methane trends. *Quaternary Science Reviews* 27: 1291–1295.

Sellars, R.W. 1999. *Preserving Nature in the National Parks: A History.* New Haven: Yale University Press.

Sennett, R. 2002. *The Fall of Public Man.* London: Penguin.

Shindell, D.T., *et al.* 2009. Improved attribution of climate forcing to emissions. *Science* 326: 716–718.

Simmons, I.G. 2008. *Global Environmental History: 10,000 BC to AD 2000.* Edinburgh: Edinburgh University Press.

Smil, V. 1994. *Energy in World History.* Boulder: Westview.

Stearns, P.N. 2001. *Consumerism in World History: The Global Transformation of Desire.* London: Routledge,

Tainter, J.A. 1988. *The Collapse of Complex Societies.* Cambridge: Cambridge University Press.

Tilley, H. 2003. African environments and environmental sciences. In W. Beinart and J. McGregor, eds, *Social History and African Environments,* pp. 109–130. Oxford: James Curry.

UNEP (United Nations Environment Programme). 2010. 2010: International year of biodiversity. At http://www.unep.org/iyb (accessed Mar. 2012).

Watts, D. 1987. *The West Indies: Patterns of Development, Culture and Environmental Change since 1492.* Cambridge: Cambridge University Press.

Williams, M., ed. 1990. *Wetlands: A Threatened Landscape.* Oxford: Blackwell.

Williams, M. 2006. *Deforesting the Earth: From Prehistory to Global Crisis.* Abridged edn. Chicago: University of Chicago Press.

Zong Y., *et al.* 2007. Fire and flood management of coastal swamp enabled first rice paddy cultivation in east China. *Nature* 449: 459–462.

CHAPTER TEN

Deep Pasts

Interconnections and Comparative History in the Ancient World

NORMAN YOFFEE

World history might be said to have begun when the first group of hominins left Africa about 1.9 million years ago and when subsequent migrations left Africa 500,000 to 300,000 years ago and then after 100,000 years ago (*Science Daily* 2010). The history of the world is a record of migrations, ecological adaptations, and social interactions over larger and shorter distances ever since.

Although all peoples have history, historians limit their purview severely, only considering history to refer to times when people produced written documents, that is, to the last 5,000 years, a mere twinkling in the history of human societies. Although some historians regard Herodotus, who lived in the fifth century BCE, as "the father of history," ancient historians study documents of ancient Mesopotamia, Egypt, the Levant, Iran, Anatolia, China, and South Asia that date well before the invention of the Greek alphabet (itself an adaptation from older scripts). These documents show the large interregional systems of interactions of ancient peoples as well as the distinctive qualities of several ancient states and civilizations.

Archaeologists have documented the history of the development of cities and states and of long-distance trade networks that flourished long before writing was invented in the Old World. (Levi, in this volume, discusses much more recent trade networks.) Thus, the exchange of obsidian (volcanic glass that could be used to make surgically sharp blades) has been traced from its sources in eastern Anatolia (Asiatic Turkey) into Mesopotamia, the Levant, and Egypt, starting at least as early as 8000 BCE. By 3500 BCE lapis lazuli, a turquoise-like stone, was brought from its sources in northeastern Afghanistan, into Iran, Mesopotamia, and Egypt. Weights that were used to measure precious metals were found in the Persian Gulf and Mesopotamia in the mid-third millennium BCE and were identical to those found in Harappan cities in South Asia, showing the presence and importance of long-distance trade between the regions (Potts 1997; 2007). Even the first writing, invented in Mesopotamia towards the end of the fourth millennium BCE, was quickly transported to Iran, Syria, Anatolia, and the Levant. History itself was a kind of export and import since Mesopotamian chronicles, epics, royal

A Companion to World History, First Edition. Edited by Douglas Northrop.
© 2012 Blackwell Publishing Ltd. Published 2012 by Blackwell Publishing Ltd.

inscriptions, and lexical lists/encyclopedias were learned in schools outside Mesopotamia as ways to teach scribes how to write and, necessarily, how to think about the past.

The Meaning and Mechanisms of Interconnections

Interconnections between regions in the ancient world are easily documented in the prehistoric archaeological record. These include the spread of farming from nuclear zones to nearer and farther areas. For example, in the Old World wheat moved from West Asia into Europe and into Africa, in the New World maize moved from southern Mexico south to South America and north to North America (Bellwood 2005; Smith 1995). Languages and the people speaking them moved from the Indo-European heartland, north of the Black Sea (Mallory and Adams 2006; Anthony 2007), eastward to South Asia and westward to Europe.

But what is the cause of the spread of domesticated plants and animals and people and their languages from one region to other regions, and what were the changes effected in cultures and social organizations that were the recipients of new products and folk? To a certain extent, this is a false question, since there was never a time when some people were localized and sealed from movements and contacts, and so the appearances of new things/people were integrated in existing cultures and environments in a variety of ways. However, there were certainly cases in which the long-distance movements of people resulted in the introduction of plants, animals, pests, and diseases in places where they were unknown before. An obvious example is the migration and colonization of Pacific islands. (See Salesa, this volume.)

Although popularizers of the effects of migrations across the globe, like Jared Diamond (1997), ascribe culture change to underlying geographic asymmetries, superior weaponry, and the catastrophic transfer of diseases, they tend to simplify the complex historical specificities of movements of people and culture change in favor of the inevitable triumph of the West (Blaut 2000). (See Simmons, this volume.) Close study, however, reveals the complexities of the movement of goods and the ensuing changes in cultures and social organizations.

In the American Southwest, archaeologists show that ancestral Puebloan people were in contact with Mesoamerican people to the south. Maize, domesticated in Mexico, was transported to the Southwest (roughly Arizona and New Mexico), macaws from the tropical jungles of southern Mexico and Guatemala were raised in northern Mexico and taken northward to the American Southwest, where their feathers were used in ceremonies and the birds themselves were carefully interred. Copper bells from Mexico were likewise taken to the Southwest, and recently chocolate and the kinds of beakers used to drink chocolate in Mesoamerica have been found in Chaco Canyon, New Mexico. These pots are identical to those used in Maya ceremonies, and the chocolate itself must have come from the Mesoamerican region (Crown 2009; Cordell 1997; Lekson 2009). Although it is impossible to understand the nature of prehistoric Southwestern cultures without reference to Mesoamerican cultures, it is equally clear that Southwestern cultures were, first, quite different from one another (Hohokam in southern Arizona and New Mexico being unlike Anasazi/ancestral Puebloans in the Four Corners region of Colorado, Utah, New Mexico, and Arizona), and, second, simply "peripheries" of Mesoamerica. And connections between these regions also worked in the other direction: Mesoamerican cultures, after acquiring turquoise from the American Southwest, incorporated the precious stones into their own ideas of decoration in their societies and rituals.

Thus, the situation in the ancient world was certainly not like the one described for the eighteenth century (CE) in *The World That Trade Created* (Pomeranz and Topik 2006: xi): Silver mined in the New World and taken to Spain was used to purchase coffee from Muslims trading in Yemen. The coffee was traded to European courts, where it was served on Chinese porcelain, sweetened with sugar from Brazil, and French soirées were followed by a smoke of Virginian tobacco. If this trade was part of a "world-system" (Wallerstein 1974; Mair 2006), the scale and penetration of goods throughout the ancient world was not comparable to the premodern world. Still, much production in the ancient world was not for local consumption but was intended for exchange, sometimes over very long distances (Kohl 1978; 1989; Sherratt 2000; 2006; Wengrow 2010). One cannot understand local affairs apart from a larger geographic context.

Since I am a Mesopotamian historian, I present some illustrations of the movements of goods and people to show the nature of these long-distance interactions. Interregional interactions in West Asia flourished in the fifth millennium BCE, the Ubaid period, as shown by the transfer of metals from their sources to the places where they are found in the archaeological record. David Wengrow has synthesized the evidence for smelting, forging, casting, and alloying on the southern shores of the Caspian Sea, in the Turkish highlands, and as far as the Negev Desert. Chemical analysis of a hoard of copper artifacts from a site in the Negev shows traces of arsenic and antimony which must have come from about 1,000 kilometers distant in eastern Turkey or Azerbaijan. Also, in the Ubaid period new farming practices were invented and disseminated. These new practices include grafting and artificial pollination and a resulting hybridization of new foods in which "unprecedented flavors, smells, and sensations" were the products of "what Andrew Sherratt has called the 'diversification of desire'" (Wengrow 2010: 59). In the Ubaid period also new techniques of ceramic production were invented and diffused, such as use of the slow potter's wheel, which afforded a greater and more standardized production of containers. Newly crafted stone seals impressed distinctive marks on the vessels. These marks denoted ownership of the contents of the pots and their point of origin.

At the end of the Uruk period (ca. 4000–3200 BCE) (Rothman 2001), cities suddenly appeared in Mesopotamia, both in the south and in the north (Emberling 1999). These cities, the best known of which is the site of Uruk itself (which gives its name to the prehistoric period) (Englund 1994; Liverani 2006) was populated by around 20,000 people in 2.5 square kilometers (1.1 square miles) and the immediately adjacent countryside. In Uruk, in southmost modern Iraq, there was a ceremonial center with several temples (one of which was nearly a football field in length), an ornately decorated sunken court, and other buildings. In this complex the first written tablets were found. Attendant to the first urbanization in Mesopotamia and the world, there was also a process of "ruralization," in which the countryside became depopulated as people moved into cities (Nissen 1988; Pollock 1999; Yoffee 2005).

If this demographic process could be called an "implosion" (from about 3200 to 2500 BCE), there was also an "explosion" in which the events in Uruk and other southern Mesopotamian cities affected far distant regions in Iran, Syria, and Anatolia. This is the so-called "Uruk expansion" (Algaze 2009) and it marks a new chapter in interregional relations in West Asia.

As a result of salvage excavations in Syria and Turkey that were launched in the 1970s to study sites that would be flooded in a new dam project, archaeologists discovered that several of these sites had material culture (building plans, especially of temples, and various kinds of artifacts) that was characteristic of the late Uruk period (ca. 3350–3100 BCE) in southern Mesopotamia. Guillermo Algaze (1989; 1993; 2009) has argued that these sites, including those in Syria and southern Turkey, about 500 miles up the Tigris and Euphrates rivers, as well as other sites into the Zagros Mountains of Iran, were part of an "Uruk phenomenon," or an "Uruk expansion," or even an "Uruk World System" (using Wallerstein's terminology and concepts). (See Chase-Dunn and Hall, this volume.)

Algaze proposed that the new cities in southern Mesopotamia required natural resources that were lacking in the south of Iraq but were found in "peripheral" regions, especially in the north. The southern Mesopotamian plain favored the growth of large cities because abundant water resources, rich aquatic life, and enormously productive agriculture – all of which could and did produce large surpluses – led to large concentrations of population. The hilly and mountainous areas to the north and east contained timber and stone for building, copper and silver, and semiprecious stones, and were near trade routes for more distant materials (such as gold and lapis lazuli). These regions, however, had less capacity to produce surplus agricultural products and to support cities.

Algaze proposed that southern Mesopotamian cities were manufacturing centers, especially of expensive woolen textiles, which were produced by specialized herders, fullers, dyers, and weavers – the latter being female captives. In southern Mesopotamian cities, which were socially and economically stratified, other industries developed to produce copper tools and jewelry. The southern Mesopotamian cities, which were politically centralized under kings and their officers, including military cadres, sent merchants and founded colonies, according to Algaze, in the underdeveloped periphery to assure themselves of a supply of raw materials.

Algaze's economic model of "the Sumerian advantage" (the earliest Mesopotamian texts from Uruk and other sites in the south were written in the Sumerian language), in which economies of scale privilege producers of goods over suppliers of raw materials, has been criticized (Emberling 2011). Some archaeologists have shown that some of the Uruk "colonies" in Syria and southern Anatolia were not dominated by southern Mesopotamians (Stein 1999; 2005; Frangipane 1997; 2001; 2002) – meaning that the Uruk material culture was restricted only to some parts of sites and in some instances local Anatolian rulers and local Anatolian material culture were dominant in sites which also had Uruk Mesopotamian presence.

Although Algaze's synthesis of the existence of southern Mesopotamian Uruk culture found well outside the cultural region of Mesopotamia is extremely valuable, new research has shown that the "margins" of Mesopotamia had their own historical trajectories. Large sites like Tell Brak and Hamoukar existed in Syria as early as if not earlier than Uruk and other cities in southern Mesopotamia, although the north was never the heartland of cities and Mesopotamian civilization. Furthermore, the Uruk expansion was marked by significant conflict in and among northern sites, the most important of which disappeared at the end of the Uruk period, as did several of the "Uruk colonies." Nevertheless, the experience of southern Mesopotamians in the north sets the stage for further interregional connections in West Asia.

The effects of Mesopotamians in Syria and Anatolia and Iran are seen in the use of the cuneiform script, first used to write Sumerian, then Akkadian, in Mesopotamia, for local languages of Syria, notably Eblaite (Huehnergard and Woods 2004), and in the Elamite language of southern Iran (Stolper 2004) during the third millennium BC. Around 2300

BCE Mesopotamian kings of the dynasty of Akkade campaigned in Syria and Iran, conquering sites and ruling territories, if only for a short time. Logically a prime goal in these campaigns was to acquire goods from regions that had been known for millennia to southern Mesopotamians.

In northern Mesopotamia, at the city-state of Assur, around 1900 BCE, another strategy shows how goods from Anatolia were obtained by (northern) Mesopotamians (Larsen 1976; Veenhof 2008; 2010). The texts recounting these activities come from an Assyrian trading colony, Karum Kanesh, which is in central Anatolia, nearly 500 miles from Assur (see Map 10.1). *Kārum* is the Akkadian word for "harbor, quay," a place where merchants lived in or near a Mesopotamian city, presumably originally along a river or canal. In Anatolia it denotes a settlement of Assyrian traders living outside the Anatolian town of Kanesh (and other towns as well). The remarkable finds of more than 20,000 clay tablets in Karum Kanesh document the activities of Assyrian merchants, and they allow us to write new chapters in economic and world history.

Assyrian merchants did not control the territory of the Anatolian colonies (there were several dozen Assyrian karums and smaller way-stations in Anatolia), which were colonies in the absence of colonialism. (See Sinha, this volume.) Rulers of Anatolian towns were the overlords of the Assyrian merchants. Assyrian trade consisted in the movement of textiles, produced in Assyria and obtained also from Babylonia to the south, and tin. The sources of this tin are obscure, perhaps from Afghanistan. Texts show only that the tin moved through Iran and central Mesopotamia to Assyria and then to Anatolia. In Anatolia the Assyrian traders exchanged these textiles and tin for silver and gold, which they shipped to Assur.

Assyrian merchants made a huge profit, moving goods from where they were plentiful to where they were scarce (Yoffee 2005: 150).[1] This profit was made solely on their organizational ability. In Assur, where silver was scarce and was used as the most important system of value, the silver to tin ratio was about 1:15, whereas in Anatolia, where silver was comparatively plentiful, the ratio was about 1:7. If 15 units of tin could be economically transported from Assur to Anatolia, by means of donkey caravans, 2 units of silver could be obtained. These 2 units of silver could then be brought to Assur and turned into 30 units of tin. Assuming a constant demand, the knowledge of where and how to get tin, and the technology of how to move the tin to Anatolia, great profits could be and were made by Assyrian merchants.

Long-term business contracts were negotiated whereby joint capital could be accumulated and continuity in business relations could be assured for decades. In one such document, an Assyrian state official sanctions the proceedings, thus attesting to the interest the Assyrian government had in trade. Indeed, some leading merchant families in Assur, which established "branches" in Anatolia, held high governmental ranks. The Assyrian state was in fact administered by councils of "great and small" at a "city-hall," and these councils coexisted with the city ruler and his court. Assyrian rulers also established treaties with potentates living along the trade routes so that Assyrian traders could ply their wares.

The Assyrian traders had to pay a variety of taxes to the local Anatolian ruler at Kanesh and to their own governmental organization in Karum Kanesh. Documents record that Assyrians tried to evade these taxes by smuggling goods, but merchants could suffer punishment if the Anatolian ruler caught them. The documents record profits and losses, various kinds of debts, lawsuits, and claims of economic injuries of various kinds. The traders were not officers of the state but private entrepreneurs. The Assyrian state was,

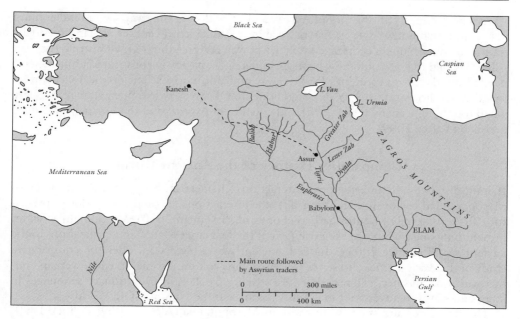

Map 10.1 Major sites in the Old Assyrian trading system.
Source: Based on M. Van De Mieroop, *A History of the Ancient Near East, ca. 3000–323 BC*, 2nd edn (Oxford: Wiley-Blackwell, 2007), map 5.2, p. 102.

however, not simply a disinterested spectator of the trade, but was concerned to promote trade, for example through treaties, because the merchants also paid taxes to the government in Assur.

The collapse of the lucrative system, which flourished for about 150 years, is related to the larger political structure of the entire region. After 2000 BCE, there was no territorial power in Mesopotamia, and one Assyrian king, Ilushuma, undertook a campaign to the southern cities of Babylonia, presumably to ensure access to Assyrian traders to Babylonian goods, such as rich textiles. Similarly, in the north itself, no city was supremely powerful, and Assur was one of a number of cities in the region. Finally, in the early days of the Assyrian trading system of the late twentieth to early eighteenth centuries BCE, there was no central power in Anatolia. Assyrian traders thus flourished in conditions when political interferences in the long-distance exchange system were few.

If the Assyrian trade in the early second millennium BCE was immensely profitable, it was also fragile. In the early eighteenth century BCE, the political constellation had changed. Hammurabi of Babylon established a central, regional state in Babylonia (southern Mesopotamia), an interloper seized the throne in Assur and conquered northern Mesopotamia, and a new group of people, the Hittites, were in the process of establishing their authority in central Anatolia. When unrestricted passage to trade was apparently constricted by political maneuvers and wars, long-distance trade suffered, and the prosperous trading families in Assur disappeared. When the new ruling family in Assur was defeated, the whole structure of the state became decentralized, and the region entered into a kind of dark age when not only trade but literate, urban traditions went into a centuries-long decline (Van De Mieroop 2007).

As a postscript to this history of Assyria and its traders in the early second millennium BCE, I note that a new state in Assyria rose in the fourteenth century BCE and gradually transformed itself into a centralized military power. As if reading its own history, Assyrian rulers decided that it would now be more efficient for its newly constituted army to seize needed goods from nearer and farther away and not worry about political vicissitudes that dictated how and when trade could flourish. Of course this military state met its fate when tough, new enemies allied with old enemies of Assyria, and the Assyrian state itself perished (Yoffee 2009).

Comparative History of the Ancient World

If long-distance and interregional interactions characterize the rise and character of Mesopotamian civilization and long-distance interactions flavored the worlds of prehistory, from the time of hunter-gatherers onward (Sassaman 2010), Mesopotamian states present only one example of the evolution of the first cities, states, and civilizations in the ancient world (Yoffee 2005).[2] Indeed, ancient world history includes the comparative study of the earliest cities and states (see Adas, this volume), some of which were in contact with one another, whereas there are striking parallels in evolutionary sequences in cities and states that were not in contact (such as in the New and Old Worlds).

The first cities and states were those in Mesopotamia (Algaze 2009; Pollock 1999) and Egypt (Wengrow 2006; Bard 2008). In Mesopotamia the first cities arose in the middle of the third millennium BCE, and in Egypt the city of Hierakonpolis (and others) flourished just after that time. In South Asia (Wright 2010), the cities of Mohenjo Daro and Harappa and other urban sites are dated to around 2600 BCE, and in China (Liu 2009) the first cities and states date to shortly after 2000 BCE. In the New World, the first Maya cities (Houston and Inomata (2009) grew in the pre-Classic period, by around 100 BCE, and Teotihuacan (Cowgill 2007) was an urban metropolis in south-central Mexico at about the same time, while in Andean South America (Silverman and Isbell 2008) cities appeared early in the first millennium CE. After the retreat of the last ice ages, about 12,000 years ago, in wetter and warmer climatic conditions there appeared the first villages and farming and eventually the rise of cities and states. This evolutionary process, the details of which are outside the purview of this chapter, is an important area of research in world history.

Over time the countryside of the earliest agricultural villages, along with new and spectacular ceremonial sites that were built by the earliest farmers or proto-farmers,[3] were transformed into landscapes with cities. In these cities social groups, themselves progressively internally differentiated and stratified, were recombined under new kinds of centralized leadership. This new kind of leadership was "legitimized" by new ideologies that insisted that the new leaders, kings and their minions, were not only possible but the only possibility. The new ideologies, which proclaimed that the first states included richer and poorer, elites and slaves, leaders and subjects were invented in the new urban centers. The first states that exercised authority over members of different groups, maintained the central symbols of the state, defended the state and guided its expansion, especially against other states, were very small. Indeed, the first states were in effect city-states or microstates (Hansen 2000).

These first cities evolved as nodal points of pilgrimages and ceremonies, sites for defense and warfare, places for the exchange of goods, storage facilities, and centers of invented rituals that connected rulers with newly created citizens and the gods. These rituals displayed and justified the supremacy and legitimacy of kings and reaffirmed command over the social order. The social roles and practices of citizens were routinized within the urban layout of monumental constructions, streets, pathways, walls, and courtyards. The newly built environments of cities demonstrated the superior access to knowledge and planning held by the rulers, ostensibly on behalf of all. Statecraft in the earliest cities involved providing an order to the present, which the rulers declared in literature and in a created landscape that overlay the unruliness of a society composed of many groups, each with its own interests and orientations.

The evolution of cities and states was rapid, at least as measured in the long history of humans as hunter-gatherers. Furthermore, the transition from agricultural villages to cities across the planet was not gradual, that is, with small villages getting larger and larger and finally becoming cities. Rather, modest villages, that is, of about 10 hectares (about 25 acres) and with a few hundred inhabitants, within the time of a few hundred years (a short time in prehistoric reckoning) became urban sites ranging from 150 hectares to more than 3,000 hectares (30 km^2, about 11.5 square miles), with 10,000 to more than 100,000 inhabitants (Yoffee 2005). These urban transformations were often supernovas that exploded from the environment of village life that preceded them. The new cities rerouted the experiences of everyday life, in cities and their countrysides, and incubated new ideologies in which economic and social differences and bases of power could be expressed and contested.

Let us look more closely at the histories of the areas of the world where the first cities and states appeared to determine both the general historical trends of development and also the particularities of cultures.

While cities emerged in ancient Egypt about the time they appeared in Mesopotamia, the relation between cities and states could not have been more different. In Egypt, the first cities, initially rivals, became quickly embedded in a politically centralized territorial state that was tube-like, flanking the Nile River. Egyptians perceived their world in terms of its frontiers, with national kings ensuring an ordered and unified polity, commanding and managing the production and distribution of resources. Egyptian cities were dedicated to displays of royal power and religious ceremony (especially in mortuary displays). The population of Egypt was relatively small, about a million people in the Old Kingdom (the pyramid age) and perhaps twice that in the New Kingdom (the time of kings Akhenaten, Tutankhamun, and Ramses II).

In Mesopotamia, on the other hand, cities were seldom incorporated in territorial states, and when one city managed to conquer others to form a regional state in early Mesopotamia, the centralized apparatus of governance did not last long and cities were soon able to reestablish their independence. Mesopotamian cities were multi-ethnic communities, and the cities themselves provided identifications of citizenship. There was, nevertheless, a common cultural construct that we term "Mesopotamian," in that the same high gods were worshiped in all Mesopotamian cities and the same literary texts were copied in schools in Mesopotamian cities, including the same lists of the gods, which has been called the Mesopotamian "stream of tradition" (Oppenheim 1964). In the political sense of the word, there was no Mesopotamian state, only a Mesopotamian culture (which, however, included ideas of what the state was and how kings were to behave in it).

The Maya cities in the New World were also independent microstates, like Mesopotamian city-states, with their dynastic lines of succession and histories. As in Mesopotamia, Maya cities continuously fought one another, occasionally forming larger territorial states, but ones that soon dissolved. In second millennium BCE China, the scene of the largest cities in the world at the time – at 1200 BCE, Anyang covered more than 30 km², with a population estimated at over 100,000 – territorial states were exceptional. Even the most powerful early state in China, the late Shang state with its center at Anyang, was, in the evocative words of David Keightley (1978), not solid like tofu but full of holes like Swiss cheese. Territorial organization did not come to China until the first emperor's unification of the country in the late third century BCE.

In ancient South Asia, in the modern states of Pakistan and India, there was, as in Mesopotamia and the Maya region, a number of cities that were politically independent, but there was also a cultural commonality that overlay them. This "Harappan civilization" included city-plans, a writing system (that remains undeciphered), a uniform set of weights (for measuring goods and precious metals), and similar styles of artifacts.

In the New World, Teotihuacan, in the Valley of Mexico, is an exception to our model of politically independent cities flourishing as part of a large cultural set of commonalities that we call "civilizations" (because, among other things, they contained cities). In fact Teotihuacan had no peer-cities, but dominated its region and was without serious rivals for centuries. Teotihuacan is an extreme example of "urban primacy," since its countryside became depopulated as the growth of the city "ruralized" the countryside in which many villages had existed. This phenomenon of ruralization characterizes the growth of cities also in Andean South America (for example, in the growth of the city of Wari, which was the capital of an expansionist state in the late first millennium CE). Thus, the countryside of the first cities and states was quite unlike the countryside before the evolution of the first cities. In the earliest states, villages had become dependent on the goals of political leaders in cities, supplying produce and labor for urban projects. As the cities grew, the countryside – which had at first been depopulated, for example in Mesopotamia, where archaeological surveys have been systematically accomplished – was repopulated in order to supply the needs of the early cities.

Although I could continue with observations of similarities and differences among the earliest cities and states of the world,[4] I must conclude this section of the comparative study of the ancient world with a subject that has taken on new and considerable meaning in the modern world, namely how and why the first cities and states collapsed. This subject is of interest today precisely because of claims by Jared Diamond (2005) and others that the leaders of ancient states destroyed their own environments.[5] Diamond's message is clear: if ancient states fell because they mismanaged environmental resources, then in our modern world we must learn the lessons of history and not mismanage our own resources.

The history of the collapse of ancient states, however, is not one of environmental mismanagement.[6] In Mesopotamia, cities and Mesopotamian culture, especially as denoted by the use of Mesopotamian languages, flourished from the mid-fourth millennium BCE to the first centuries CE. Writing first appeared about 3200 BCE, and the last dated text in the cuneiform script (used to write Sumerian and Akkadian) was written in 75 CE. Of course, there were various "collapses" of Mesopotamian states and dynasties, and the longest-lived city of all, Uruk, was itself abandoned for a short time around 1600 BCE, only to be repopulated and flourish into the first centuries CE. When one state collapsed, another took its place. The historical record is one of substantial instability of states and internal struggle among various social groups in Mesopotamia that led alternately to collapse and reformulation. In the northern part of Mesopotamia, Assyria, there was the largest state and empire in Mesopotamian history. It grew at the end of the second millennium BCE until it reached its apogee around 660 BCE. But its enemies soon put the Assyrian state to the sword, burned its cities, and killed many people. The Assyrian state and also Assyrian culture, that is, language, religion, literature, disappeared at a stroke at 610 BCE.

However, the story of the fall of Assyria was not as simple as new and old enemies allying to destroy the state (Yoffee 2009). In fact, the very success of the expansionist and militaristic state of Assyria was the main reason why the Assyrian state, like other Mesopotamian cities and states, did not regenerate. In order to control much of West Asia from Iran to Egypt in the first half of the first millennium BCE, Assyrian kings progressively transformed Assyrian society into an efficient fighting machine. In addition to disenfranchising the old-line nobility and gentry and rewarding generals, Assyrians increasingly deported conquered peoples (like the "Ten Lost Tribes of Israel," whom the Assyrian army defeated) throughout the Assyrian realm in order to increase agricultural production and to build new capitals for Assyrian kings. Thus, when Assyria was defeated, as all militaristic and imperial ancient states were fated to be, there was no way for the Assyrian state to be rebuilt along the Assyrian template of state. That is, there were no natural Assyrian hierarchies of villagers, gentry, nobles, and so forth left in Assyria. These ranks of Assyrians, which had existed before the transformation of the Assyrian state into a military machine, were destroyed by the most successful Assyrian kings themselves. In the countryside lived mainly people who were not Assyrians, did not worship the Assyrian gods, did not speak Assyrian (a dialect of Akkadian), or who had no attachment to Assyrian history.

In the south of Mesopotamia, Babylonia, the situation of collapse was quite different. Babylonia had been made subject to the Assyrian state and was one of the enemies of Assyria who allied with others (chiefly Medes and Persians from Iran) to defeat Assyria. The Babylonian state rushed to emulate the Assyrian empire, but its last king was defeated by Cyrus the Great of Persia in 539 BCE. Although the cities and people of Babylonia survived this conquest, thereafter no king of Babylonia was Babylonian. Persians ruled the country for about two centuries, after which Alexander the Great of Macedon/Greece conquered them, and Greeks (called Seleucids) ruled Babylonia. Progressively, citizens of Babylonia naturally found it advantageous to speak, write, and learn non-Babylonian languages and learn non-Babylonian cultures and, in effect, to abandon their identities as Babylonian. In the end, when the last dated tablet in Babylonian was written, only a few temples (and associated landholdings) clawed precariously for existence.

Naturally, this rather detailed account of the last days of Mesopotamia has nothing to do with the catastrophist scenarios of popular writers who create convenient histories about environmental mismanagement. The histories of other early states similarly show varieties of political struggles, abandonments of cities, and social and political changes, often dramatic in nature. For examples, in the Maya region (McAnany and Negrón 2009; Webster 2002) most of the extremely large Maya cities in the Petén region in Guatemala were abandoned over a century (roughly from 800 to 900 CE). Other Maya cities, especially in the north (e.g., in the Yucatán of Mexico), however, flourished as the nature of Maya culture was transformed as the result of contact with Mexican cultures. Whereas the Maya landscape was certainly transformed by intensive agricultural practices needed to support the large populations and ceremonials in Maya cities, human mismanagement of the environment (and a possible regionwide drought) does not explain why some cities were abandoned and others weren't. Rather, it seems that in the Yucatán, Maya society in an amalgam of sorts with Mexican cultures was resilient and survived. Indeed today there are about 5 million modern Maya who celebrate the continuities of their past in modern Hispanic societies. Whereas there is a large literature on the "Maya collapse," the story of Maya survival is at least as interesting, and certainly more important to the Maya of today.

The stories of social and political change can similarly be told of the earliest states and dynasties of ancient China, in which continuity to the present is a common theme. In South Asia, there are similarly continuities from the early Harappan cities to later cities and states in India, even as new languages, peoples, and beliefs were the result of migrations into the land. Other cases of collapse, resilience, and reformulation can be told.

There are two morals to these studies of collapse in the ancient world. First, ancient states were fragile, subject to decomposition either from external or internal stresses, or usually, a combination of both. Second, stories of environmental mismanagement in ancient states are gross exaggerations. Humans have altered their environments since the time one can speak of humans, and usually these anthropogenic environmental changes have not been happy ones. But in no instance in the deep past did human-caused environmental change result in the collapse of an entire state and certainly not an entire culture. If one considers that we must learn from history – and all historians believe this to some degree – the lesson is that ancient states, fragile as they were, did not have the power to destroy their environments, as we today in fact have. Global warming and environmental destruction of today have no parallels, no models in the past. Therefore, we must be the more vigilant and increasingly active in confronting the threats to our environment today.

The Verticality of Global History in the Ancient World

In the studies sketched in the preceding pages I have discussed a variety of interregional interactions in the ancient world and also aspects of the comparative study of the earliest cities and states. These are, for lack of a better term, "horizontal" components of ancient world history, but there are also "vertical" matters that require at least brief notice.

In my portrayal of the collapse of Assyria, the northern part of Mesopotamia, I noted that when the Assyrian state and empire were defeated, there could rightly be called the collapse of Assyrian civilization. To repeat: not only were the Assyrian kings and army defeated and cities destroyed, but also there was no regeneration of the Assyrian state or Assyrian culture. The Assyrian culture, that is, the beliefs and languages of Assyria, disappeared because the transformations of Assyria into a military machine reduced the traditional social system in Assyria, and then the inhabitants of Assyria, both in cities and in the countryside, were significantly composed of people conquered by the Assyrian army and deported into Assyria. They had no interest in rebuilding an Assyrian state on the template of Assyrian cultural norms.

This summary of the collapse of Assyria, insisting that Assyria disappeared from world history, is, however, wrong. As a result of the nineteenth-century excavations of Iraq, Assyrian palaces, buried for about 2,600 years, were brought to the light of day. Assyrian art – reliefs of battles and gardens, gigantic figures, part lion, bull, and man – fascinated the West and led to more excavations. Clay tablets in cuneiform script, preserved especially well in levels of fiery destruction, were soon deciphered, and the culture of the Assyrians, which had been only minimally described by biblical and classical writers, and for their own purposes (mainly to show how decadent Assyrians were in comparison to themselves), took on new meaning.

Although we mainly think of ancient Assyrians giving their name to the academic field of study "Assyriology," and becoming subjects of study by modern scholars, the meaning of ancient Assyrian civilization that was resurrected by archaeologists was deeply significant to a group of people who called their religion "the Church of the East." These were Nestorian Christians, a group of Aramaic-speaking Christians whose faith was one of the "heresies" of the mid-first millennium CE. These Christians, who lived in northern Iraq, Syria, southern Turkey, Iran, and elsewhere also called themselves "Assyrians." Indeed, they trace their origin to the region of ancient Assyria.

The Assyrian minorities in the Middle East have in the twentieth century largely migrated to Europe and North America. Whether the modern Assyrians are genetically connected to ancient Assyrians is perhaps a question for biological research. Their use of Aramaic in ritual may well connect them to those Aramaic-speaking peoples whom the Assyrians conquered and deported into Assyria. In Assyria itself, after the defeat of the last kings and capitals, the remaining Assyrians must have adopted Aramaic, which was the majority language of West Asia, the language of Jesus of Nazareth, for example. There is no question that modern Assyrians consider themselves descendants of ancient Assyrians, and they are proud of their long history as one of the major powers of the ancient Near East.

This story can be repeated in almost every area of the world, with appropriate variations. In India, certain political parties regard themselves as descendants of ancient Harappans. In Mexico and Guatemala ancient Maya are certainly part of the history of their countries, and as I mentioned, there are millions of Maya today.

In sum, the history of the ancient world is not an abstraction to many modern folk. The past is today hotly contested, its meaning debated. The past serves as means by which modern people partly form their self-identification, usually in opposition to other people who are the dominant element in their countries. It is impossible to study the modern world, the agendas of parties and leaders, allies and enemies, without an understanding of their deep pasts.

Notes

1 The section in this chapter follows my narrative in the referenced book.
2 Further information on these social evolutionary processes, including discussions of the debated terms "evolution" and "civilization," are found in Yoffee (2005). I provide here newer references to the development (and collapse) of the first cities and states.
3 Such as at Göbekli Tepe in eastern Anatolia (Schmidt 2006) or Poverty Point in Louisiana (Sassaman 2010).
4 One subject of modern cross-cultural interest is the origin, distribution, and demise of ancient languages and scripts; see Houston (2004) and Baines et al. (2008).
5 Diamond also claimed that a variety of societies, as in Easter Island, Chaco Canyon in the American Southwest, Norse Greenland, and others, destroyed their environments and so collapsed.
6 McAnany and Yoffee (2009). The collection of essays in this book also show that the other societies Diamond cities did not collapse because their leaders had ruined their environments.

References

Algaze, G. 1989. The Uruk expansion: Cross-cultural exchange in early Mesopotamian civilization. *Current Anthropology* 30: 571–608.
Algaze, G. 1993. *The Uruk World System: The Dynamics of Expansion in Early Mesopotamian Civilization.* Chicago: University of Chicago Press.

Algaze, G. 2009. *Ancient Mesopotamia at the Dawn of Civilization: The Evolution of an Urban Landscape*. Chicago: University of Chicago Press.

Anthony, D. 2007. *The Horse, the Wheel, and Language: How Bronze Age Riders from the Eurasian Steppes Shaped the Modern World*. Princeton: Princeton University Press.

Baines, J., J. Bennet, and S. Houston, eds. 2008. *The Disappearance of Writing Systems*. London: Equinox.

Bard, K. 2008. Royal cities and cult centers, administrative towns, and workmen's settlements in ancient Egypt. In J. Marcus and J. Sabloff, eds, *The Ancient City: New Perspectives on Urbanism in the Old and New World*, pp. 165–182. Santa Fe: SAR Press.

Bellwood, P. 2005. *First Farmers: Origins of Agricultural Societies*. Oxford: Blackwell.

Blout, J.M. 2000. *Eight Eurocentric Historians*. New York: Guilford Press.

Cordell, L. 1997. *Archaeology of the Southwest*. New York: Academic Press.

Cowgill, G.L. 2007. The urban organization at Teotihuacan, Mexico. In E. Stone, ed., *Settlement and Society: Essays Dedicated to Robert McCormick Adams*, pp. 261–295. Los Angeles: Cotsen Institute of Archaeology.

Crown, P. 2009. Chocolate drink used in rituals in New Mexico 1,000 years ago. *Science Daily*, Feb. 5, at http://www.sciencedaily.com/releases/2009/02/090203173331.htm (accessed Aug. 16, 2010).

Diamond, J. 1997. *Guns, Germs, and Steel: The Fates of Human Societies*. New York: W.W. Norton.

Emberling, G. 1999. Urban social transformations and the problem of the "first city." In M. Smith, ed., *The Social Construction of Ancient Cities*. Washington DC: Smithsonian Institution Press.

Emberling, G. 2011. On the early cities of Mesopotamia. Review of G. Algaze, *Ancient Mesopotamia at the Dawn of Civilization*. H-Net Reviews, at http://umich.academia.edu/GeoffEmberling/Papers/1130378/On_the_Early_Cities_of_Mesopotamia (accessed Feb. 2012).

Englund, R. 1994. *Archaic Administrative Texts from Uruk*. Berlin: Deutsches Archaeologisches Institut.

Frangipane, M. 1997. A fourth millennium temple/palace complex at Arslantepe/Malatya: north–south relations and the formation of early state societies in the northern regions of southern Mesopotamia. *Paléorient* 23: 45–73.

Frangipane, M. 2001. Centralization processes in greater Mesopotamia: Uruk expansion as the climax of systemic interactions among areas of the greater Mesopotamian region. In M. Rothman, ed., *Uruk Mesopotamia and Its Neighbors*, pp. 307–348. Santa Fe: SAR Press.

Frangipane, M. 2002. "Non-Uruk" developments and Uruk-linked features on the northern borders of greater Mesopotamia. In J.N. Postgate, ed., *Artefacts of Complexity: Tracking the Uruk in the Near East*, pp. 123–148. Warminster: Aris & Phillips.

Hansen, M.H. ed. 2000. *A Comparative Study of Thirty City-State Cultures*. Copenhagen: Royal Danish Academy of Sciences and Letters.

Houston, S. ed. 2004. *The First Writing: Script Invention as History and Process*. Cambridge: Cambridge University Press.

Houston, S., and T. Inomata. 2009. *The Classic Maya*. Cambridge: Cambridge University Press.

Huehnergard, J., and C. Woods. 2004. Akkadian and Eblaite. In R. Woodard, ed., *Cambridge Encyclopedia of the World's Ancient Languages*, pp. 218–287. Cambridge: Cambridge University Press.

Keightley, D. 1978. *The Late Shang State: When, Where, and What*. Berkeley: University of California Press.

Kohl, P. 1978. The balance of trade in Southwestern Asia in the mid-third millennium BC. *Current Anthropology* 19 (3): 463–492.

Kohl, P. 1989. The use and abuse of world systems theory. In C.C. Lamberg-Karlovsky, ed., *Archaeological Thought in America*, pp. 218–240. Cambridge: Cambridge University Press.

Larsen, M.T. 1976. *The Old Assyrian City-State and Its Colonies*. Copenhagen: Akademisk Forlag.

Lekson, S. 2009. *A History of the American Southwest*. Santa Fe: SAR Press.

Liu, Li. 2009. State emergence in early China. *Annual Review in Anthropology* 38: 217–232.

Liverani, M. 2006. *Uruk: The First City*, trans. Z. Bahrani and M. Van De Mieroop. London: Equinox. First published in 1998.

Mair, V. ed. 2006. *Contact and Exchange in the Ancient World*. Honolulu: University of Hawai'i Press.

Mallory, J.P., and D.Q. Adams. 2006. *The Oxford Introduction to Proto-Indo-European and the Proto-Indo-European World*. Oxford: Oxford University Press.

McAnany, P., and T. Gallerta Negrón. 2009. Bellicose rulers and climatological peril? Retrofitting twenty-first century woes on eighth-century Maya society. In P. McAnany and N. Yoffee, eds, *Questioning Collapse: Human Resilience, Ecological Vulnerability, and the Aftermath of Empire*, pp. 142–175. Cambridge: Cambridge University Press.

McAnany, P., and N. Yoffee, eds. 2009. *Questioning Collapse: Human Resilience, Ecological Vulnerability, and the Aftermath of Empire*. Cambridge: Cambridge University Press.

Nissen, H. 1988. *The Early History of the Ancient Near East 9000–2000 BC*. Chicago: University of Chicago Press.

Oppenheim, A.L. 1964. *Ancient Mesopotamia: Portrait of a Dead Civilization*. Chicago: University of Chicago Press.

Pollock, S. 1999. *Ancient Mesopotamia: The Eden That Never Was*. Cambridge: Cambridge University Press.

Pomeranz, K., and S. Topic. 2006. *The World Trade Created: Society, Culture, and the World Economy 1400 to the Present*. Armonk, NY: M.E. Sharpe.

Potts, D.T. 1997. *Mesopotamian Civilization: The Material Foundations*. London: Equinox.

Potts, D.T. 2007 Babylonian sources of exotic raw materials. In G. Leick, ed., *The Babylonian World*, pp. 124–140. London: Routledge.

Rothman, M. 2001. *Uruk Mesopotamia and Its Neighbors: Cross-Cultural Interactions in the Era of State Formation*. Santa Fe: SAR Press.

Sassaman, K. 2010. *The Eastern Archaic, Historicized*. Lanham: AltaMira Press.

Schmidt, K. 2006. *Sie bauten die ersten Tempel*. Munich: Beck.

Science Daily. 2010. New human species discovered: Mitochondrial genome of previously unknown hominins from Siberia decoded. Mar. 25. At http://www.sciencedaily.com/releases/2010/03/100325100848.htm (accessed July 28, 2010).

Sherratt, A. 2000. Envisioning global change: A long-term perspective. In R. Denemark, J. Friedman, B. Gills, and G. Modelski, eds, *World System History: The Social Science of Long-Term Change*, pp. 115–132. New York: Routledge.

Sherratt, A. 2006. The trans-Eurasian exchange: The prehistory of Chinese relations with the West. In V. Mair, ed., *Contact and Exchange in the Ancient World*, pp. 30–61. Honolulu: University of Hawai'i Press.

Silverman, H., and W. Isbell, eds. 2008. *Handbook of South American Archaeology*. New York: Springer.

Smith, B. 1995. *The Emergence of Agriculture*. New York: Scientific American Library.

Stein, G. 1999. *Rethinking World Systems: Diasporas, Colonies, and Interaction in Uruk Mesopotamia*. Tucson: University of Arizona Press.

Stein, G. 2005. The political economy of Mesopotamian colonial encounters. In G. Stein, ed., *The Archaeology of Colonial Encounters*, pp. 143–172. Santa Fe: SAR Press.

Stolper, M. 2004. Elamite. In R. Woodard, ed., *Cambridge Encyclopedia of the World's Ancient Languages*, pp. 60–94. Cambridge: Cambridge University Press.

Van De Mieroop, M. 2007. *A History of the Ancient Near East, ca. 3000–323 BC*. 2nd edn. Oxford: Wiley-Blackwell.

Veenhof, K.R. 2008. The Old Assyrian period. In K.R. Veenhof and J. Eidem, *Mesopotamia: The Old Assyrian Period*, ed. M. Wäfler: 13–263.

Veenhof, K.R. 2010. Ancient Assur: The city, its traders, and its commercial network. In J. Gommans, ed., *Empires and Emporia: The Orient in World Historical Space and Time*.

Jubilee issue of *Journal of the Economic and Social History of the Orient* 53 (1–2), pp. 39–82. Leiden: Brill.

Wallerstein, I. 1974. *The Modern World-System*. New York: Academic Press.

Webster, D. 2002. *The Fall of the Ancient Maya: Solving the Mystery of the Maya Collapse*. London: Thames & Hudson.

Wengrow, D. 2006. *The Archaeology of Early Egypt: Social Transformations in North-East Africa, 10,000–2650 BC*. Cambridge Cambridge University Press.

Wengrow, D. 2010. *What Makes a Civilization? The Ancient Near East and the Future of the West*. Oxford: Oxford University Press.

Wright, R. 2010. *The Ancient Indus: Urbanism, Economy, and Society*. Cambridge: Cambridge University Press.

Yoffee, N. 2005. *Myths of the Archaic State: Evolution of the Earliest Cities, States, and Civilizations*. Cambridge: Cambridge University Press.

Yoffee, N. 2009. Collapse in ancient Mesopotamia: What happened, what didn't. In P. McAnany and N. Yoffee, eds, *Questioning Collapse: Human Resilience, Ecological Vulnerability, and the Aftermath of Empire*, pp. 176–206. Cambridge: Cambridge University Press.

CHAPTER ELEVEN

Big History

FRED SPIER

What Is Big History?

In big history, the human past is placed within the context of the history of life, our planet, our solar system, our galaxy, and even the universe as a whole. Thus, in a radical departure from established academic ways of looking at human history, in big history our common past is viewed from within the whole of natural history ever since the beginning of the universe.

The term "big history" was coined by the historian David Christian. In 1989, Christian started a cross-disciplinary course at Macquarie University, in Sydney, Australia, in which academics ranging from astronomers to historians gave lectures about their portions of the all-embracing past. This course has become a model for other university courses in Australia, the United States, and the Netherlands, including the ones I have been teaching since 1994, first at the University of Amsterdam and later also at the Eindhoven University of Technology. In the 1970s and 1980s, other big history courses emerged independently, such as the ones pioneered by astrophysicist Eric Chaisson and astronomer George Field at Harvard University, historian John Mears at Southern Methodist University, and astrophysicist Siegfried Kutter at Evergreen State College in Washington State.

All these courses have attracted large numbers of enthusiastic students. The need for course materials soon led to the publication of an increasing number of big history books and articles, the most important of which are mentioned in the reference list.[1] The emergence of big history was a remarkable development during a period of time when the interest in large-scale overviews had almost disappeared in the humanities after French philosopher Jean-François Lyotard had famously declared in 1979 that what he called metanarratives had become obsolete (Lyotard 1984: xxiv–xxv).

A Companion to World History, First Edition. Edited by Douglas Northrop.
© 2012 Blackwell Publishing Ltd. Published 2012 by Blackwell Publishing Ltd.

Why Study Big History?

First of all, big history provides a modern scientific answer to the biggest question that can be posed about the past, namely how everything has become the way it is now. To be sure, big history cannot provide all the answers. But more than any other approach to history, big history shows how humans and human societies have become the way they are; how they have been influenced by their planetary and cosmic environment, as well as how they have changed it; and more in general, how both living and lifeless nature have become the way they are now. As a consequence, big history offers a fundamentally new understanding of the human past, which allows us to orient ourselves in time and space in a way no other form of academic history can match.

In the second place, big history allows us to see big patterns that escape attention when only smaller processes are studied. Very few historians, for instance, compare the history of humanity with the history of life. Yet doing so brings out striking similarities, such as the fact that in both cases increasing complexity went hand in hand with a division of labor among the parts that make up the whole. This was, for instance, the case during the emergence of more complex cells, the so-called eukaryotic cells, which later became the building blocks of all more complex organisms, such as plants and animals, including organisms like you and me. The formation of more complex cells and organisms caused a division of labor to emerge within and between these cells as well as between whole groups of cells. A very similar development took place during human history when the first state societies emerged. A growing division of labor led to different groups, most notably farmers, slaves, craftspeople, traders, bureaucrats, soldiers, priests and rulers, who all became dependent on each other. And in all cases one may wonder which parts have benefited the most, or the least, from this development. This is only one example of the great many patterns that become visible while one is studying big history.

Although extremely complicated in its details (in all academic studies the details are always complicated), thanks to these large patterns big history offers a surprisingly simple framework for all of the past. In fact, discovering these large patterns may have been one of the most unexpected and rewarding results of doing big history. I have explored this theme in two books (Spier 1996; 2010). Finding these patterns is rewarding, because they help to make history easier to understand. With the aid of these emerging large patterns, the grand sweep of history may now be summarized in rather simple terms.

In the third place, big history offers a straightforward structure within which all scientific knowledge can be accommodated. By marching through history from the beginning of the universe until today, we start with big bang cosmology, which explains how the universe itself emerged, including all the small particles that are the building blocks of all larger structures that have formed, from the tiniest molecules to clusters of galaxies. By looking at the history of our planet in relation to its closest neighbors, Venus and Mars, we discover the importance of its special position in the solar system, which has made possible the emergence and continued existence of life. While considering plate tectonics, we learn how this geological process, unique to Earth, has shaped the continents and the oceans for at least 2 billion years and, as a result, also Earth's climate and biological evolution. By examining the history of life, we encounter Darwin and Wallace's theory of evolution, which, in its modern form, is currently the best scientific explanation for how life evolved on our home planet. By tracing millions of years of early human history, we begin to understand how humans became different from all other species, in both a biological and a cultural sense. And by considering an overview of the last 10,000 years of human history, we become aware of the enormous importance of culture for shaping human societies into what they have become today.

While the big history enterprise may sound wildly ambitious, for its practitioners it has become a daily routine. Yet at the same time, big history has changed our perception of the world beyond recognition. I remember very well, for instance, that while studying biochemistry in the 1970s I often experienced an overwhelming and bewildering feeling in academic bookstores, wondering how these great many different forms of knowledge, from astronomy to small-scale histories, were all interrelated. Nobody could tell me then, and I could not figure it out myself either. Now I look at these publications and immediately know a fitting place for all of them within the overarching scheme of big history. This is a very relaxing and comforting sense which, I think, many people share after having been introduced to big history.[2]

In the fourth place, big history offers a very detached, and it is hoped to some extent a transcultural, version of history that may become acceptable all around the globe. Although all practitioners of big history are (like all humans) shaped by, and to some extent bound to, their own cultural background, looking at history from a cosmic point of view may make it possible to avoid many biases that result from studying history at smaller scales. My experience with students from all continents, as well as discussions with big history enthusiasts from many different cultural backgrounds, has been encouraging in this respect.

All modern academic forms of history, including big history, have emerged within urban settings which were usually well connected to other cities. These histories were developed by privileged city dwellers who had sufficient time and means of existence to create these stories and diffuse them, thanks to the demand from other urbanites. As a result, all forms of academic history cater mostly to the needs of city people, while the great many traditional farmers on this planet, as well as the few still-existing gatherers and hunters, may find them less interesting, if not totally useless, because they are not very helpful in orienting them in their very localized daily lives. Because in the twenty-first century more than 50 percent of all humans are living in cities for the first time in human history, the entire range of academic histories, including big history, may now become acceptable to a considerable portion of humanity. Today, in our rapidly urbanizing and ever more interconnected world, it is more important than ever to develop a coherent common history of humanity that is embedded within the wider history of the planet and the universe, because that will help urbanites to understand the full context of both their current lives and their past.

Last, but probably not least, big history may help us prepare better for the future. Although no one knows the future with any degree of certainty, it appears reasonable to suppose that some of the large trends that have existed in history will also continue into the immediate future. This includes, perhaps most importantly, the practices of energy extraction that are needed to produce all the forms of complexity that we make and use today, ranging from our daily food to airplanes. At the same time we have to get rid of the entropy, "mess," that we inevitable produce by doing all these things. Because today we are using a rapidly diminishing supply of fossil fuels to carry out all these tasks, a major issue for the near future is: How will humans survive and prosper after these energy supplies are gone forever?

How Old Is Big History?

Big history and its precursors may well represent the very oldest accounts of what we now call "history." As long as we can trace back such narratives, people have tried to answer the questions of where they came from, as well as how everything else they saw had come into being. Such accounts are now known as origin stories. The questions themselves are usually not made explicit in these stories; they only provide the answers.

The beginning of the Jewish Torah, for instance, known to Christians as Genesis, offers an excellent example of such an origin story. It starts with the well-known sentence: "In the beginning G-d created the heaven and the Earth." Apparently, for those who produced this document the first big question was how heaven and Earth had originated. The next big question was, apparently, how the shape of the Earth, as well as everything that was on it, had emerged (interestingly, with the exception of water). The next big question was where light had come from (explaining darkness does not seem to have been a problem). After having explained all of this by divine action, the next big question was why there was water both on the surface on the Earth and in the sky. And so it continues, all the way down to the question of how humans had emerged. This was apparently not the first big question for those who codified this story, which testifies to the degree of detachment and contemplation. From a modern scientific point of view, this origin story may be summarized as a series of answers to the question of how energy (light) and a great many forms of complexity had emerged, ranging from the heavens and the Earth to humans. In big history, this is currently becoming the general approach. The major difference is that in big history, divine action is not invoked as the underlying cause for how everything first emerged.

Another major difference with traditional origin stories is that in big history we seek to abstain as much as possible from setting judgmental norms or prescribing forms of desired behavior. Of course, choices have to be made all the time about what to include and what to omit in telling such a story. But we avoid stating what has been good or bad in history, or how people *should* have behaved. We leave those aspects to the judgment of our audience. All traditional origin stories, by contrast, include both normative and prescriptive aspects. These old stories functioned, therefore, not only as explanations of reality but also as rules of desired behavior. In doing so, they helped to orient people both in time and space. Here, too, big history has a similar goal – but one based on scientific knowledge, without normative or judgmental goals other than using basic scientific insights for providing the best possible overview of the past.

While the narrators of traditional origin stories often claim that their versions of history are "true," thoughtful big historians will never make that claim, aware as they are that scientific knowledge keeps constantly changing. Just as one's updated GPS navigation system may provide the newest road map, the latest version of big history is intended to offer the best possible (currently available) map of past reality, the largest scientific map of time and space that humans have yet produced.

When Did Academic Big History Emerge?

When scholars such as Eric Chaisson, John Mears, and David Christian began teaching big history in the 1970s and 1980s, they all thought that they were doing something fundamentally new. Elements of the big history approach are, however, much older. They are based on scientific knowledge that emerged in the sixteenth century (CE), while the first big historians *avant la lettre* wrote their seminal books in the first half of the nineteenth century. Two major pioneers were the Prussian scientist Alexander von Humboldt (1769–1859) and the Scottish entrepreneur Robert Chambers (1802–1871).

Alexander von Humboldt was as famous during his lifetime as Albert Einstein is today, first of all thanks to his daring five-year expedition through Spanish America, during which he undertook a wide range of scientific experiments, and later also because of his writings. Usually considered the father of modern geography, von Humboldt was interested in nearly everything – ranging from peoples and their cultures to the universe as a whole. After his epic voyage he spent the next 30 years, mostly in Paris, publishing his results. After moving to Berlin later in life, von Humboldt wrote a multivolume series called *Cosmos*, in which he tried to summarize in a coherent manner all the existing knowledge about nature, including humans. The first volume was published (in German) in 1845. Like his earlier works, these books set a new trend. They were widely read and translated into many languages. Unfortunately, von Humboldt died before he could finish this project. His descriptions in *Cosmos* were often rather static, because he refused to speculate about the history of nature beyond the available evidence, such as specific ages of rocks and fossils, which were simply unknown at the time.

A second pioneer of big history *avant la lettre* was the Scottish publisher and author Robert Chambers. Like von Humboldt, Chambers was familiar with the world of contemporary science, including, of course, the broader Scottish Enlightenment. He lived in an increasingly entrepreneurial society that was rapidly industrializing. The introduction of the steam press had made the publishing business more profitable, which is how Chambers made a living. His book *Vestiges of the Natural History of Creation* was anonymously published in London by John Churchill in 1844, because Chambers correctly foresaw some of the controversies that his book would generate. Only in 1884 was the identity of the author posthumously revealed.

In contrast to von Humboldt's mostly descriptive solid history of the universe, Chambers's *Vestiges* offered a dynamic and very speculative process history of everything, beginning with the origin of the universe in the form of a "fire mist," and ending with the history of humanity (see Chambers 1994). Some of his challenging hypotheses still look surprisingly modern, including the idea that matter emerged in a fire mist and that civilizations rose as a result of specific ecological and social constraints. But Chambers had also other ideas, less appealing today, such as a racial theory about the evolution of humans, which started at the lowest stage with black savages, leading ultimately to English Caucasian whites at the pinnacle of history.

It is not clear to what extent Chambers may have been influenced by von Humboldt's work. In England, Chambers's *Vestiges* and von Humboldt's *Cosmos* both appeared in print at more or less the same time, while von Humboldt had been lecturing about such issues for about 20 years. In either case, *Vestiges* caused a huge stir in Victorian Britain and sold very well. Following the works of the naturalists Charles Lyell and Alexander von Humboldt, among others, *Vestiges* suggested a time span for the history of Earth and of life that was far longer than the generally accepted biblical account allowed. *Vestiges* contributed substantially, therefore, to preparing the ground for Charles Darwin's and Alfred Russel Wallace's later work on the evolution of life.

During the second part of the nineteenth century, to my knowledge no new big histories were published. The academic world was splitting into clearly demarcated disciplines, and most emerging academic historians were oblivious to attempts to place humans within a wider terrestrial, let alone a cosmic, context. They focused instead on constructing patriotic histories and civilizational trajectories, as these helped to shape the identities of the emerging nation-states in Europe and the Americas. As a result, there seemed to have been little or no room for big history in academia. Yet there remained room for large-scale accounts within the wider walls of science. Nineteenth- and twentieth-century naturalists increasingly adopted historical approaches, for example, while at the same time the biblical account was losing credibility within academia as a literal historical source.[3]

In the twentieth century big history reemerged, first a little feebly and later with new force. The first pioneer was the English author H.G. Wells in his book published in 1920, *The Outline of History* (Wells 1930). The horrifying effects of World War I motivated Wells to write such an all-embracing history. He hoped it would foster a global identity which could contribute to preventing new wars. Because the universe was still seen as both stable and infinite, Wells concentrated his efforts on the areas in which change took place – namely the history of Earth, life and mankind (as he called it). Yet after this publication appeared, not much happened in terms of big history until the 1970s. I do not know why it took so long. Possibly, earlier twentieth-century big history texts have not yet been rediscovered.

During the 1970s most of today's key scientific paradigms (in the sense of Thomas Kuhn) relating to the history of the universe and Earth became accepted. This coincided with the introduction of novel techniques to determine the ages of rocks (and thus also of fossils) with the aid of radioactive decay measurements. Furthermore, new methods were devised or refined to determine the age of other objects and events, such as the counting of tree rings, the analysis of ice cores, genetic dating and the detection of electromagnetic radiation that originated in the early universe. All of this led to what David Christian (2009) calls a "chronometric revolution." As a result, scientists could construct much more precise accounts of the history of life, Earth, the solar system and even the entire universe. By that time, also the more distant view of the Earth resulting from the Apollo moon flights, as well as the ongoing globalization and industrialization, stimulated the idea of looking at things as a whole once again.

A few farsighted scholars started to synthesize this new knowledge in the classroom and in print. The first resulting account of big history known to me is a large volume titled *The Columbia History of the World* (1972), edited by John Garraty and Peter Gay. This book, written by a team of scholars from Columbia University, ran to more than 1,000 pages, 45 of which covered the period from the emergence of the universe to the rise of agriculture. The first modern university course to offer such a grand overview, designed by Eric Chaisson and George Field, started at Harvard University in 1975 and is still running today. Chaisson also wrote a stream of pioneering books and articles (1977; 1981; 1987; 1988; 2001; 2006). In 1977, NASA Apollo scientist Robert Jastrow wrote the book *Until the Sun Dies*, which covered everything from the beginning of the universe until the far future, namely the end of our solar system.

In 1980, the American astronomer Carl Sagan's 13-part television series *Cosmos* presented a magnificent view of the history of the universe, including the emergence of humans (see Sagan 1980). Other astronomers, such as Hubert Reeves, joined in this effort to synthesize cosmological knowledge and to explain it to a wider public audience; they all drew on earlier pioneers such as Harlow Shapley and Robert Jastrow (see Shapley 1959; 1963; Jastrow 1967; 1977; Reeves 1985; 1991; Reeves *et al.* 1998). In the same year as Sagan's television series, the Austrian philosopher Erich Jantsch developed the first systematic model for big history in his book *The Self-Organizing Universe* (Jantsch 1980). Jantsch died soon after its publication, a tragic fact that may partially explain why his book did not become better known in academic circles. In the Soviet Union, though, Jantsch's work served as a source of inspiration for many scholars, including the psychologist Akop Nazaretyan, to formulate their own approaches to universal history (i.e. Nazaretyan 2010). The fact that these scholars have published most of their work in Russian has not facilitated the globalization of their insights. (See Naumann, this volume.) Soon thereafter, also during the 1980s, other innovative American scholars, such as the geologist Preston Cloud at the University of Minnesota and the astrophysicist Siegfried Kutter at Evergreen State College, drew on this new knowledge to craft their own grand syntheses (Cloud 1978; 1988; Kutter 1987). Being natural scientists, they paid only limited attention to human history. In the 1990s, these large-scale accounts of natural and cosmic history began to fuse into a new genre, increasingly known as "big history" among historians in Australia, Western Europe and the United States, as "cosmic evolution" among astronomers and astrophysicists, and as "universal history" in Russia. Also in other countries, such as France, England, Colombia and Peru, broad-minded and intellectually gifted scholars began to write their own big histories, which have tended to be remarkably similar in approach. Today, such scholars may well be found in almost every country on Earth.

By the end of the 1980s, two pioneering academic historians began to teach the big story in a newly and thoroughly scientific way: David Christian at Macquarie University, in Sydney, and John Mears at Southern Methodist University in Dallas, Texas. While Mears took up the huge task of designing a big history course that he taught solo (see Mears 1986; 2009), David Christian designed a course model in which specialists from different academic disciplines were involved (1991; 2004; 2008). Astronomers taught about the history of the universe; geologists explained Earth history; biologists lectured on life and evolution; while archaeologists and historians covered human history. This course model not only produced the potential for synergy among the teachers, but has also served as an example for similar courses in Australia, the United States, and the Netherlands, where sociologist Johan Goudsblom and myself started such a course at the University of Amsterdam in 1994 (Spier 2005b), after Goudsblom had become familiar with Christian's initiative during a visit to Macquarie University in 1992. Christian himself later moved away from his collaborative teaching model. Finding that it was easier to tell a coherent story by doing all the lectures himself, Christian now usually teaches his big history course solo. In the Netherlands, however, we continue to use the co-teaching approach in our big history classes.

Who Is Doing Big History Today?

Despite this remarkable rise of big history, by the end of the 1990s only a handful of academics were actually active in this area (cf. Hughes-Warrington 2002).[4] Since 2005, however, there has been a considerable increase of big history scholars. An internet-based survey carried out in 2009 by the American big historians Barry Rodrigue and Daniel Stasko found big history courses being taught at 32 institutions in 7 countries, by 28 professors (or teams of professors) (2009: 1). Most of these courses were offered in the United States, scattered across 10 different states. The survey did not include the increasing number of courses, lectures, books, and websites in which large portions of history are told by astronomers, physicists, social scientists, or lay people. Grand historical narratives appear to be making an impressive comeback in the new millennium.

Let's now take a closer look at what a few of the major players in the field are doing today. While teaching big history at Macquarie University, and also at Ewha Woman's University in Seoul, South Korea, David Christian is working on the construction of a general paradigm for human history based on collective learning, which is intended to become the cultural equivalent of the theory of natural selection in biology. Together with Cynthia Brown and Craig Benjamin, Christian is writing a lower-division university level big history textbook planned for publication in 2012.[5] Furthermore, Christian and others have begun to develop an online syllabus for big history teaching at secondary schools. (See Bain, this volume.) This educational enterprise, called the Big History Project, is sponsored by Bill Gates, the co-founder of Microsoft, who became enthusiastic about big history after listening to an audio version of Christian's big history class in 2008.[6]

While teaching cosmic evolution (his version of big history) at Tufts University and Harvard University, Eric Chaisson promoted it also for decades through the Wright Center for Science Education that existed at Tufts University until 2011, and through the informative website *Cosmic Evolution*.[7] In his seminal books, Chaisson has elaborated an energy and complexity approach to all of history that has increasingly been adopted by other big historians (Chaisson 2001; 2006). He is now working on a new book on this subject.

In Russia, the psychologist Akop Nazaretyan is at the center of what Russians call "universal history," which he teaches at Dubna International University, not far from Moscow. Together with colleagues such as Leonid Grinin and Andrey Korotayev, Nazaretyan has organized a number of conferences and panels on universal history over the past 10 years. In 2002 this group of scholars also started the groundbreaking journal *Social Evolution and History*, which published a special issue on big history in March 2005.[8]

The geologist Walter Alvarez gained fame for his discovery, together with his father, the Nobel Prize winner Luis Alvarez, of an asteroid impact near the Mexican peninsula of Yucatán that caused the mass extinction of dinosaurs 65 million years ago. He now teaches big history from a geologist's perspective at the University of California at Berkeley, while also further promoting the web-based interactive time line ChronoZoom initially created by Roland Saekow, one of his students.[9]

Trained in anthropology, biology, history, and geography, Barry Rodrigue teaches big history at the University of Southern Maine. He is actively building a communications network among the global community of big historians. This includes a big history Facebook site and surveying who is doing big history today.

The astronomer Tom Gehrels, responsible for the imaging component of the NASA Pioneer missions to Jupiter and Saturn in the 1970s, the "Space Science" series from the University of Arizona Press in the 1980s, and electronic surveying of asteroids and comets in the 1990s, went on to teach big history both at the University of Arizona and in Ahmedabad, India, the latter as a part of a UN course for graduate students from Uzbekistan all the way to North Korea. Until his death in 2011, Gehrels, in addition to developing a new view of what happened in the early universe, was especially interested in the moral implications that he saw as arising out of big history (Gehrels 2007).

Since 1996, several important big history books and articles have appeared. Authors include the US-based writer Bill Bryson (2003), the Colombian scientist Antonio Vélez (1998), the UK-based scientist Robert Aunger (2007a; 2007b), the American astronomer Russell Genet (2007), the German scientists Harald Lesch and Harald Zaun (2008), and the Australian scientist Joseph Voros (2007). In 2008 the American scientist John Smart and the Belgian philosopher Clément Vidal started an organization for scholars interested in acceleration processes in the evolution and development of the universe.[10] In the Netherlands, a school teacher, Jos Werkhoven, has developed his big history method for primary schools, while in 2009 Bryson produced a children's version of his book.

A word about my own big history activities in the Netherlands: inspired originally by David Christian's course, I have been teaching big history since 1994 at the University of Amsterdam, since 2003 at Eindhoven University of Technology, and since 2009 also at Amsterdam University College. The realization in 1995 that by structuring a big history course I was also structuring big history itself led to my first book on big history. After becoming acquainted with Chaisson's work, I developed a theory that aims to explain all of history, first in an article and more recently in a book (see Spier 1996; 2005a; 2010). As the present chapter suggests, I am also very interested in the history of big history.

On August 20, 2010, during a big history meeting at the Coldigioco Geological Observatory in Italy, Walter Alvarez, Craig Benjamin, Cynthia Brown, David Christian, Lowell Gustafson, Barry Rodrigue and Fred Spier founded the International Big History Association (IBHA). The purpose of the IBHA is to promote the teaching and research of big history worldwide with the most up-to-date technological means.[11]

Different Approaches to Big History

During the reemergence of big history, a number of different approaches have been pursued. Scientists such as Eric Chaisson have placed great emphasis on natural science and, consequently, on the importance of energy for the emergence and continued existence of a great variety of forms of complexity, ranging from stars to human beings. Historians such as David Christian and Cynthia Brown (2007) have sought to combine scientific views and historical accounts within one large narrative with some attempts at rigorous theory that includes major aspects of Chaisson's work. Currently, the trend appears to be that all these approaches are converging into one single approach. This means that among big historians worldwide a large degree of agreement exists today about the major trends in history. This remarkable situation may have been caused by the fact that looking at history at the largest possible scale has suddenly rendered these trends and patterns visible, while they remained obscured as long as scholars were only studying more limited portions of history.

Big History and Religious Views

Because big history and traditional origin stories provide different answers to the same fundamental question of how everything has become the way it is now, a lively discussion is now taking place between proponents of these two different approaches to understanding the past. This has led to some interesting publications, including several by small teams of US scholars: one New Age-influenced book by the mathematical cosmologist Brian Swimme and the cultural historian and eco-theologian Thomas Berry (Swimme and Berry 1992); another by the astrophysicist Guillermo Gonzalez and the intelligent design advocate Jay Richards, in which they argue that our planet is so exceptionally well placed in the cosmos, fine-tuned for life as well as for observing our exceptional position, that it constitutes evidence for intelligent design (Gonzalez and Richards 2004); and an edited volume by the scientist-theologian Cheryl Genet, the astronomer Russell Genet, and others, which features contributions from a range of writers including priests, historians and astronomers (Genet et al. 2009).

From its own theological perspective, the Vatican has also actively fostered such discussions within its Pontifical Academy of Sciences, the body formerly directed by

Cardinal Joseph Ratzinger (later Pope Benedict XVI). As early as 1952, Pope Pius II declared that the big bang proved the existence of God (Pius II 1952). Since that time, discussions about these themes have been held at the Vatican, perhaps most notably in 2008, when the academy organized a Plenary Session on Scientific Insights into the Evolution of the Universe and of Life that featured world-famous scientists including Stephen Hawking, Martin Rees, Vera Rubin, Christian de Duve, Yves Coppens, and Luigi Cavalli-Sforza, who all explained modern scientific views (and who each, during the meeting, received the Pope's blessing). Through such efforts, the Vatican's motivation seems to be to explore where, in this modern scientific account, there may still be room for God.[12]

A final example of this development may be found in the fact that my big history Twitter account, on which I post news of developments in science that seem relevant for big history, is followed by a considerable number of fundamentalist Protestants in the United States, including for a while Rick Warren, the pastor who played a starring role in the inauguration of US president Barack Obama in 2009. Perhaps they wish to be kept updated to position themselves in this ongoing discussion. In any case, such interest points to a partial overlap, as well as some frictions between the proponents of traditional and modern origin stories.

While teaching big history from an academic point of view, however, in my opinion it seems wise to stick to the empirical scientific method and acknowledge the limits of our knowledge thus attained, such as the question of what came before the big bang, because we do not have any empirical evidence for such events. Anyone interested in exploring in religious terms what lies beyond the borders of scientific knowledge should, of course, feel free to do so.

Big History Research

Big history research has not yet been institutionalized as fully as other academic approaches, most notably for lack of sufficient funding. Because big history as a result of its wide-ranging interdisciplinary nature does not yet fit comfortably within any established academic slot where research grants can be obtained, big history scholarship has been limited to the work of a few privileged (usually tenured) academics.

Currently, there are at least three different major research themes. First of all, the discovery and analysis of general patterns characterizing big history as a whole, most notably in terms of energy, complexity and disorder, is pursued mostly by Eric Chaisson, David Christian, the Russian mathematician Sergey Grinchenko (2004; 2007), British scientist Robert Aunger and myself. In the second place, a few scholars are studying larger patterns within big history. This includes, most notably, Christian's work on collective learning and the chronometric revolution (Christian 2009). In the third place, smaller subjects are being placed within a big history framework. In this genre, increasingly known as "little big histories," researchers are tracing how their small subject can be understood better in terms of long-term processes, as well as similarities and differences with other processes, by placing it within a big history context. This may sound a little ambitious, but it is important to realize that, for instance, the abundance of chemical elements on the Earth of which everything consists (which thus conditions all "little histories") has come about as a result of cosmic and geological processes. Recent studies include Jonathan Markley's work on the history of grass (2009) and Esther Quaedackers's work-in-progress on why people build the way they do.

The Future of Big History: Opportunities and Constraints

Based on David Christian's illuminating ideas of what the future may bring for big history (2010), I venture a few bold predictions of my own, knowing full well that things may turn out very differently.

First of all, in the next 20 to 50 years big history approaches may well become common in universities, because increasing numbers of people will experience the physical limits of Earth and its resources while feeling more interconnected than ever before. Only big history provides a coherent academic narrative that helps people to orient themselves in such a situation. As a result, big history could become a standard introductory course for university students and secondary schools in many countries. This development has already started at one institution: Dominican University of California, where Cynthia Brown has been teaching big history since 1994. In the fall of 2010, this university became the first academic institution requiring all incoming freshmen to take a big history course – and then, in 2011, it went on to make big history a multidisciplinary centerpiece for the entire first-year curriculum.[13]

In addition to the enthusiastic reception of big history courses by students everywhere, signs of these developments can be found in the efforts mentioned above by David Christian, Cynthia Brown and Craig Benjamin to produce a big history textbook for university survey courses. Furthermore, it augurs well for big history that David Christian was invited to be a keynote speaker at the August 2010 Techonomy conference, where many high-profile US business leaders discussed future challenges, while he also delivered a TED lecture on big history in March 2011 as part of a session hosted by Bill Gates on the Knowledge Revolution, during which the online educational big history project was announced.[14]

Furthermore, the large patterns that show up in big history are very helpful for constructing scenarios for the future. As a result, the last class session of many big history courses is usually devoted to what the future may bring. A number of scholars, including the Dutch scientist Lucas Reijnders and sociologist Egbert Tellegen, the Australian futurologist Joseph Voros, along with big historians such as Barry Rodrigue and Cynthia Brown, have developed, or are preparing, courses dealing with the big future. I expect that such courses will also become standard over the next several decades. Increasingly, interdisciplinary university courses are addressing the enormous problems that humans will be facing in the immediate future on a planetary scale (see Spier 2009). Some of these courses are directly inspired by big history.

Institutionalizing big history, including research, at universities may prove to be much more difficult, given the stiff resistance from established disciplines in the ongoing struggle for limited university resources. Yet fortunate scholars may be sufficiently well positioned to pursue the big history research agendas mentioned above, most notably establishing a paradigm for big history as well as quantifying all aspects of big history in terms of energy flows and matter consumption, because this is what, in the final analysis, drives everything that has happened, and will happen, in the universe.

Notes

The author thanks Cynthia Brown, David Christian, and Douglas Northrop for their stimulating comments.

1   For a comprehensive overview of big history literature, see http://www.communities.uva.nl/bighistory under Literature (accessed Feb. 2012).

2 Although having enjoyed multidisciplinary education may certainly be helpful for practitioners of big history, it is not an absolute requirement. David Christian, Eric Chaisson, John Mears, Cynthia Brown, and Walter Alvarez, for instance, were trained as academic specialists, while others, such as Siegfried Kutter, Barry Rodrigue, and myself, have multidisciplinary backgrounds. Most important are a wide-ranging curiosity and interest and a willingness to become acquainted with types of academic knowledge that have been produced outside of one's own discipline.

3 Two, rather random, examples of nineteenth-century specialized naturalists who placed their subject in a large historical perspective include Flower (1891) and Weidman (1898).

4 There may have been similar initiatives that escaped our attention in language areas beyond our reach or by scholars without sufficient access to the internet.

5 Craig Benjamin teaches big history at Grand Valley State University in Michigan. He edited the October 2009 *Forum on Big History*, at http://worldhistoryconnected.press.illinois. edu/6.3/index.html (accessed Feb. 2012).

6 For the Big History Project sponsored by Bill Gates, see http://www.bighistoryproject.com (accessed Feb. 2012).

7 Cosmic Evolution website at https://www.cfa.harvard.edu/~ejchaisson/cosmic_evolution/docs/splash.html (accessed Feb. 2012).

8 On the *Social Evolution and History* website – http://old.uchitel-izd.ru/index.php?option= content&task=view&id=22&Itemid=51 (accessed Feb. 2012) – many articles can be downloaded for free.

9 Walter Alvarez's big history webpage is at http://learning.berkeley.edu/alvarez; the interactive time line ChronoZoom can be found at http://chronozoomtimescale.org (both accessed Feb. 2012).

10 Smart and Vidal's approach is at http://evodevouniverse.com (accessed Feb. 2012).

11 More information on the International Big History Association can be found at http://www. ibhanet.org (accessed Feb. 2012).

12 Pontifical Academy of Sciences website is at http://www.vatican.va/roman_curia/pontifical_ academies/acdscien/index.htm; the proceedings of the *Plenary Session on Scientific Insights into the Evolution of the Universe and of Life* can be downloaded at http://tinyurl.com/ yj3jwzy (both accessed Feb. 2012). For Ratzinger's views, see Ratzinger (1995).

13 This program involves many faculty and a range of big history-infused courses. See http:// www.dominican.edu/academics/big-history (accessed Mar. 2012).

14 For the Techonomy conference 2010, see http://techonomy.com (accessed Feb. 2012).

References

Aunger, Robert. 2007a. Major transitions in "big" history. *Technological Forecasting and Social Change* 74 (8): 1137–1163.

Aunger, Robert. 2007b. A rigorous periodization of "big" history. *Technological Forecasting and Social Change* 74 (8): 1164–1178.

Brown, Cynthia Stokes. 2007. *Big History: From the Big Bang to the Present*. New York: New Press.

Bryson, Bill. 2003. *A Short History of Nearly Everything*. London: Random House.

Bryson, Bill. 2009. *A Really Short History of Nearly Everything*. New York: Delacorte Books for Young Readers.

Chaisson, Eric J. 1977. The scenario of cosmic evolution. *Harvard Magazine*, Nov.–Dec., pp. 21–33.

Chaisson, Eric J. 1981. *Cosmic Dawn: The Origins of Matter and Life*. New York: W.W. Norton.

Chaisson, Eric J. 1987. *The Life Era: Cosmic Selection and Conscious Evolution*. New York: Atlantic Monthly Press.

Chaisson, Eric J. 1988. *Universe: An Evolutionary Approach to Astronomy*. Englewood Cliffs, NJ, Prentice Hall.

Chaisson, Eric J. 2001. *Cosmic Evolution: The Rise of Complexity in Nature*. Cambridge, MA: Harvard University Press.

Chaisson, Eric J. 2006. *Epic of Evolution: Seven Ages of the Cosmos*. New York: Columbia University Press.

Chambers, Robert. 1994. *Vestiges of the Natural History of Creation*. Reproduced in J.A. Secord, ed., *Vestiges of the Natural History of Creation and Other Evolutionary Writings*. Chicago: University of Chicago Press. First published in 1844.

Christian, David. 1991. The case for "big history." *Journal of World History* 2 (2): 223–228.

Christian, David. 2004. *Maps of Time: An Introduction to Big History*. Berkeley: University of California Press.

Christian, David. 2008. Big history: The big bang, life on Earth, and the rise of humanity. The Teaching Company, Course No. 8050, at http://www.teach12.com/ttcx/CourseDescLong2.aspx?cid=8050 (accessed Feb. 2012).

Christian, David. 2009. History and science after the chronometric revolution. In S.J. Dick and M.L. Lupisella, eds, *Cosmos and Culture: Cultural Evolution in a Cosmic Context*, pp. 441–462. Washington DC: National Aeronautics and Space Administration.

Christian, David. 2010. The return of universal history. *History and Theory* 49: 6–27.

Cloud, Preston. 1978. *Cosmos, Earth, and Man: A Short History of the Universe*. New Haven: Yale University Press.

Cloud, Preston. 1988. *Oasis in Space: Earth History from the Beginning*. New York: W.W. Norton.

Drees, Willem B. 2002. *Creation: From Nothing until Now*. London: Routledge.

Flower, William Henry. 1891. *The Horse: A Study in Natural History*. London: Kegan Paul.

Garraty, John A., and Peter Gay, eds. 1972. *The Columbia History of the World*. New York: Harper & Row.

Gehrels, Tom. 2007. *Survival through Evolution: From Multiverse to Modern Society*. Charleston, SC: BookSurge.

Genet, Cheryl, Russell Genet, Brian Swimme, Linda Palmer, and Linda Gibler. 2009. *The Evolutionary Epic: Science's Story and Humanity's Response*. Santa Margarita, CA: Collins Foundation Press.

Genet, Russell Merle. 2007. *Humanity: The Chimpanzees Who Would Be Ants*. Santa Margarita, CA: Collins Foundation Press.

Gonzalez, Guillermo, and Jay Wesley Richards. 2004. *The Privileged Planet: How Our Place in the Cosmos Is Designed for Discovery*. Washington DC: Regnery.

Grinchenko, Sergey N. 2004. *Sistemnaia pamiat' zhivogo*. Moscow: Institute of Informatics Problems of the Russian Academy of Sciences (IPI RAN).

Grinchenko, Sergey N. 2007. *Metaevoliutsiia*. Moscow: Institute of Informatics Problems of the Russian Academy of Sciences (IPI RAN).

Hughes-Warrington, Marnie. 2002. Big history. *Historically Speaking* 4 (2) (Nov.), at http://www.bu.edu/historic/hs/november02.html#hughes-warrington (accessed Feb. 2012); also in *Social Evolution and History* 4 (1) (Spring 2005): 7–21.

Humboldt, Alexander von. 1845. *Kosmos. Entwurf einer physischen Weltbeschreibung*, vol. 1. Stuttgart: J.G. Cotta'scher Verlag.

Jantsch, Erich. 1980. *The Self-Organizing Universe: Scientific and Human Implications of the Emerging Paradigm of Evolution*. Oxford: Pergamon.

Jastrow, Robert. 1967. *Red Giants and White Dwarfs: The Evolution of Stars, Planets and Life*. New York: Harper & Row.

Jastrow, Robert. 1977. *Until the Sun Dies*. New York: W.W. Norton.

Kutter, G. Siegfried. 1987. *The Universe and Life: Origins and Evolution*. Boston: Jones & Bartlett.

Lesch, Harald, and Harald Zaun. 2008. *Die kürzeste Geschichte allen Lebens. Eine Reportage über 13,7 Milliarden Jahre Werden und Vergehen*. Munich: Piper.

Lyotard, Jean-François. 1984. *The Postmodern Condition: A Report on Knowledge*, trans. G. Bennington and B. Massumi. Minneapolis: University of Minnesota Press.

Markley, Jonathan. 2009. "A child said, 'What is the grass?'" Reflections on the big history of the Poaceae. *World History Connected* 6 (3), at http://worldhistoryconnected.press.illinois.edu/6.3/markley.html (accessed March 11, 2010).

Mears, John A. 1986. Evolutionary process: An organizing principle for general education. *Journal of General Education* 37 (4): 315–325.

Mears, John A. 2009. Implications of the evolutionary epic for the study of human history. In C. Genet *et al.*, eds, *The Evolutionary Epic: Science's Story and Humanity's Response*, pp. 135–146. Santa Margarita, CA: Collins Foundation Press.

Nazaretyan, Akop P. (2010). *Evolution of Non-Violence: Studies in Big History, Self-Organization and Historical Psychology*. Saarbrücken: Lambert Academic.

Pius II, Pope. 1952. Modern science and the existence of God. *Catholic Mind* 49: 182–192.

Ratzinger, Joseph. 1995. *"In the Beginning ...": A Catholic Understanding of the Story of Creation and the Fall*. Grand Rapids, MI: Eerdmans.

Reeves, Hubert. 1985. *Atoms of Silence: An Exploration of Cosmic Evolution*. Cambridge, MA: MIT Press. Published in French in 1981.

Reeves, Hubert. 1991. *The Hour of Our Delight: Cosmic Evolution, Order, and Complexity*. New York: W.H. Freeman.

Reeves, Hubert, Joël de Rosnay, Yves Coppens, and Dominique Simonnet. 1998. *Origins: Cosmos, Earth and Mankind*. New York: Arcade.

Rodrigue, Barry, and Daniel Stasko. 2009. A big history directory, 2009: An introduction. *World History Connected* 6 (3), at http://worldhistoryconnected.press.illinois.edu/6.3/rodrigue.html (accessed Feb. 2012).

Sagan, Carl. 1980. *Cosmos*. New York: Random House.

Shapley, Harlow. 1959. *Of Stars and Men: Human Response to an Expanding Universe*. Boston: Beacon.

Shapley, Harlow. 1963. *The View from a Distant Star: Man's Future in the Universe*. New York: Basic Books.

Spier, Fred. 1996. *The Structure of Big History: From the Big Bang until Today*. Amsterdam: Amsterdam University Press.

Spier, Fred. 2005a. How big history works: Energy flows and the rise and demise of complexity. *Social Evolution and History* 4 (1): 87–135.

Spier, Fred. 2005b. The small history of the Big History course at the University of Amsterdam. *World History Connected* 2 (2), at http://worldhistoryconnected.press.uiuc.edu/2.2/spier.html (accessed Feb. 2012).

Spier, Fred. 2009. Big history: The emergence of an interdisciplinary science? *World History Connected* 6 (3), at http://worldhistoryconnected.press.uiuc.edu/6.3/spier.html (accessed Feb. 2012).

Spier, Fred. 2010. *Big History and the Future of Humanity*. Oxford: Wiley-Blackwell.

Swimme, Brian, and Thomas Berry. 1992. *The Universe Story: From the Primordial Flaring Forth to the Ecozoic Era: A Celebration of the Unfolding of the Cosmos*. San Francisco: HarperCollins.

Vélez, Antonio. 1998. *Del big bang al Homo sapiens*. Medellín: Universidad de Antioquia.

Voros, Joseph. 2007. Macro-perspectives beyond the world system. *Journal of Futures Studies* 11 (3): 1–28.

Weidman, Samuel. 1898. *A Contribution to the Geology of the Pre-Cambrian Igneous Rocks of the Fox River Valley, Wisconsin*. Madison: Wisconsin Geological and Natural History Survey, no. 3.

Wells, H.G. 1930. *The Outline of History: Being a Plain History of Life and Mankind*. New York: Garden City. First published in 1920.

CHAPTER TWELVE

Global Scale Analysis in Human History

CHRISTOPHER CHASE-DUNN AND THOMAS D. HALL

There are many perspectives on global scale analysis in human history (Benjamin 2009; Denemark *et al.* 2000; Friedman 2008; Harvey 2003; Hornborg and Crumley 2007; Hornborg *et al.* 2007; Robinson 2004; Sanderson and Alderson 2005; Sassen 2006; Sklair 2002; Turchin 2003). Because of this wide availability and our own areas of competence and expertise, we will focus on world-systems analysis (WSA) in this discussion (Chase-Dunn and Babones 2006; Wallerstein 2004). Virtually all of these approaches address many of the same questions and issues, although from different perspectives. The largest difference among types are those that focus on description of "what" and "how," versus those that seek to develop systematic, theoretical explanations for what happened and why. This difference is more complementary than oppositional. Of the theory-driven approaches, world-systems analysis addresses some questions that other approaches either cannot or do not ask. In this chapter we seek to highlight the contributions of a world-systems approach to global human history.

The comparative world-systems perspective is a strategy for explaining social change that focuses on entire intersocietal systems rather than single societies. Its main insight is that no society can be fully understood in isolation. All societies are shaped by, and shape, other societies through important interaction networks (trade, information flows, alliances, and fighting). These networks have woven polities and cultures together throughout human history. Explanations of social change thus need to take intersocietal systems (here, world-systems) as the units that evolve. This does not mean that individual societies are unimportant, or that local actors do not to some extent shape their own changes. Rather, it means that these actions take place within larger contexts which sometimes constrain and/or influence their actions. Intersocietal interaction networks were rather small when transportation was mainly a matter of walking. The expansion and intensification of interaction networks have been increasing for millennia, albeit unevenly, often cyclically. We begin to explore this idea with a general description.

A Companion to World History, First Edition. Edited by Douglas Northrop.
© 2012 Blackwell Publishing Ltd. Published 2012 by Blackwell Publishing Ltd.

World-systems are systems of societies. "Systemness" means that these societies are interacting with one another in important ways – interactions are two-way, necessary, structured, regularized, and reproductive. Systemic interconnectedness exists when interactions importantly influence the lives of people within societies, and have consequences for social continuity and/or social change. Systemness, or coherence, is itself a variable. Some systems are more coherent than others. World-systems, however, are not necessarily global. The word "world" refers to the importantly connected interaction networks in which people live, whether these are spatially small or large. That is, they are more or less self-contained "worlds."

Only the modern world-system has become planetary. It is a single economy composed of international trade and capital flows, transnational corporations that produce products on several continents, as well as all the economic transactions that occur within countries and locally. Culture and politics, too, are becoming increasingly global. The entire world-system is the whole system of human interactions, not only international trade and investment.

The modern world-system is structured politically as an interstate system, typically the main focus of the field of international relations, located within the academic discipline of political science. While the power of each state varies considerably, the overall world-system is multicentric. There is no world state. This is a fundamental feature of the modern system, and of many earlier smaller world-systems.

In order to compare different kinds of world-systems, the concepts used need to be sufficiently general to be applicable to all of them. For instance, a *polity* is any organization with a single authority that claims sovereign control over a territory or a group of people, such as bands, tribes, chiefdoms, or states. All world-systems are composed of interacting polities. This is a basis of comparison among modern world-systems, including those that have no states.

We follow current distinctions between "nations" and "states." Nations are groups of people who share a common culture and language; they identify with each other, have or perceive a shared history, and hold similar values. States have formal organizations, typically bureaucratic, and exercise legitimate violence within their territory. Occasionally, states coincide with one nation, though even today that is relatively rare (Laczko 2000). More typically, states are multinational entities which contain more than one nation. Statistically this has been the normal condition since the first known state, Ur, some five millennia ago (Hall 1998; McNeill 1986). In contrast, ethnic groups are subnations, usually minorities within states in which there is a larger national group. While sociologically similar, ethnic groups are typically demographic minorities. Rarely, a numerical minority may be the majority nation, as occurred under apartheid in South Africa.

Core/Periphery Hierarchy

The modern world-system is structured as a core/periphery hierarchy in which some regions contain economically and militarily powerful states while other regions contain polities that are much less powerful and less developed. The institutional features and processes of a world-system reproduce the socially structured inequalities of this core/periphery hierarchy.

Countries that are called "advanced," in the sense that they have high levels of economic development, skilled labor forces, high levels of income and powerful, well-financed states, are core powers, such as the United States, most countries in Europe,

Japan, Australia, and Canada. Conventionally, "core states" also have been called the first world, developed states, or global North.

The contemporary periphery includes relatively weak states that are not always strongly supported by their populations and have little power relative to other states. Until recently the colonial empires of the European core states constituted much of the periphery. These colonial empires broke down into formally sovereign states in waves of decolonization that began in the last quarter of the eighteenth century (the United States), and occurred through the early nineteenth century (former Spanish colonies), and in the twentieth century (Asia and Africa). Peripheral regions are usually economically less developed, having many subsistence producers, and industries with relatively low productivity and relatively unskilled labor. Peripheral agriculture typically employs simple tools, including animal and human labor, whereas in the core it is capital-intensive and employs machinery and inanimate forms of energy. Oil extraction and mining are often capital-intensive, but under the direct or indirect control of core capitalists. In the past, peripheral countries have been exporters of agricultural and mineral raw materials. Recently, even when they have developed some industrial production, it has usually been less capital-intensive and used less skilled labor. Contemporary peripheral countries include most of the countries in Asia, Africa, and Latin America – for example, Bangladesh, Senegal, and Bolivia.

The periphery is not "catching up" with the core. Rather both core and peripheral regions are developing, but most core states are developing faster than most peripheral states. By developing we mean, in a broad sense, becoming more complex socially, inventing new technologies or elaborating on old ones. In between there are countries, called the semiperiphery, that have intermediate levels of economic development or a mix of developed and less developed regions. Semiperipheral states have political/military power based in their large size; smaller semiperipheral countries typically are more developed than peripheral states.

A few other terms also require clarification. First, "the periphery" refers to all peripheral states or areas in total. Individual states or areas may be "peripheral states" or "peripheral areas." The boundaries between the core, semiperiphery, and periphery are generally not crucial, because there is a continuum of economic and political/military power that constitutes the core/periphery hierarchy. Indeed, we could make four or seven categories instead of three. However, we note that considerable research on the modern world-system does reveal three (sometimes four) major groups of countries. This is far less clear for earlier world-systems. These categories are mainly a convenient terminology to delineate international inequality.

There have been a few cases of upward and downward mobility in the core/periphery hierarchy, although most countries simply run hard to stay in the same relative positions. The United States is a spectacular and unusual case of upward mobility. In 300 years this territory was incorporated from outside the Europe-centered system to become a peripheral area, then a peripheral state, then a semiperipheral state, then a core state, then came to dominate the current system, although now it is declining slowly. The United Kingdom and Portugal are states that have likewise declined in the last century.

To compare different kinds of core/periphery hierarchies and relations, the concept also needs occasional subdistinctions. Analysts should not assume that all world-systems have core/periphery hierarchies. This is an empirical question. Treating the creation of hierarchy as a problematic issue facilitates comparisons and allows examination of how core/periphery hierarchies have emerged and evolved. To do so, it is helpful to distinguish between core/periphery differentiation and core/periphery hierarchy. Core/periphery differentiation means that societies with different degrees of population density, polity size, and internal hierarchy are interacting with one another. Village dwellers who interact with nomadic neighbors constitute an instance of core/periphery differentiation. Core/periphery hierarchy refers to the relationship between societies. Hierarchy exists when some societies exploit or dominate others, such as British colonization of India, or the Spanish colonization of Mexico. Core/periphery hierarchy is not unique to the modern Europe-centered world-system. The Roman, Chinese, and Aztec empires conquered and exploited peripheral peoples, and at times adjacent states.

This distinction allows an examination of situations in which larger and more powerful societies interact with smaller ones, but do not exploit them. It also allows the study of cases in which smaller, less dense societies may exploit larger societies, such as interactions between the nomadic pastoralists in Central Asia with agrarian states and empires in China and Western Asia, most spectacularly the Mongol Empire founded by Chinggis Khan. It also allows us to investigate how and why some instances of core/periphery differentiation became hierarchical.

The modern world-system is now a global economy with a global political system (the interstate system). It also includes all the cultural aspects and interaction networks of the human population of the Earth. Culturally the modern system is composed of several civilizational traditions (e.g., Islam, Christendom, Hinduism, etc.), nationally defined cultures, nations, and subcultures (e.g., technocrats or bureaucrats, etc.), and indigenous and minority ethnic groups within states. The modern system is multicultural in the sense that networks of interaction connect people who have different languages, religions, and other cultural characteristics. Most of the earlier world-systems also were multicultural.

Networks are defined by regular and repeated interactions among individuals and groups that may involve trade, communication (formal or informal), threats, alliances, migration, marriage, gift giving, and so on. A network is important if the interactions affect these individuals' and groups' everyday lives, access to food and necessary raw materials, their identities, and their security from or vulnerability to threats and violence. World-systems are fundamentally composed of interaction networks.

One of the important systemic features of the modern system is the rise and fall of a dominant core power, called the "hegemonic sequence." A hegemon is a core state that has a significantly greater amount of economic, political, and military power than any other core state, and that takes on the role of system leader. In the seventeenth century the Dutch Republic was the hegemon, in the nineteenth century Great Britain became the hegemon, and in the twentieth century the United States was the hegemon. The normal operation of the modern system – uneven economic development and competition among states – makes it difficult for a hegemon to sustain its dominant position, and so they tend to decline, as is currently happing to the United States. The decline is relative. Thus, the structure of the core oscillates back and forth between hegemony and hegemonic rivalry, a situation in which several roughly similar core states are contending for hegemony. Hegemonic rivalry is a dangerous condition, and system-wide wars are more common during this stage than in other times.

Spatial Boundaries of World-Systems

The modern world-system is distinctive in the spatial scale of its interaction networks, most of which are now global. In earlier, and especially smaller, systems there was a significant difference in spatial scale between networks in which food and basic raw materials (bulk goods) were exchanged and much larger networks of the exchange of luxuries such as spices, or jewels, silk, or bullion (prestige goods). (See Levi, this volume.) It is not economical to carry bulk goods far under premodern conditions of transportation. For foot transportation, the carrier will consume an amount of food equivalent to what he or she can carry over short distances, 50 miles or less. Occasionally food will be transported farther for some noneconomic reason. With domesticated animals or water transportation, this network can be much larger.

Prestige goods can be carried much further because of their high value-to-weight ratio, so this exchange usually constitutes a much larger network. Most early prestige goods trade was "down-the-line trade" in which goods are passed from group to group. For any particular group the effective extent of a trade network is that point beyond which nothing that happens will affect the group of origin. We note here that prestige goods and bulk goods are really poles of a continuum. Placement of any specific good on that continuum is a function of transportation technology, the relative value of the good, and supply and demand considerations. In short, whether a something is a prestige good or a bulk good is as much, if not more, a property of its context within an exchange system as a property of the good itself.

In order to bound interaction networks, we need to pick a place from which to start – a so-called "place-centric approach." Searches for actual breaks in interaction networks are often fruitless, because almost all groups of people interact with their neighbors. But by focusing on a single settlement, for instance the pre-European contact village of Onancock on the eastern shore of the Chesapeake Bay (near the current boundary between the US states of Virginia and Maryland), it is much easier to determine the spatial scale of the network by tracing how far food moved to and from it. Food came from some maximum distance, a bit beyond the groups that sent food directly. Two indirect jumps are probably sufficiently far that there would be little effect on Onancock. This sphere probably included villages at the southern and northern ends of the Chesapeake Bay.

Onancock's prestige goods network was much larger. Copper, for instance, may have come from as far away as Lake Superior. In between the size of bulk goods networks and prestige goods networks are the interaction networks in which polities make war and ally with one another. These are called political-military networks. For the sixteenth-century Chesapeake world-system, Onancock was one member of a regional, multivillage chiefdom. The Powhatan and the Conoy paramount chiefdoms across the bay were core chiefdoms that collected tribute from several smaller chiefdoms. Onancock was part of an interchiefdom system of allying and warmaking polities whose network included some indirect links. Thus the political-military network for Onancock extended to the Delaware Bay in the north and to what is now North Carolina to the south.

Information, like a prestige good, is light relative to its value. Information may travel far along trade routes and beyond the range of goods exchange, but it is subject to deterioration from decay of clarity. Thus information networks are usually as large as or larger than prestige goods networks. The actual spatial scale of important interaction needs to be determined for each world-system. Generally, the bulk goods nets are the smallest, the political-military nets are intermediate spatially, and the prestige goods nets and the information nets, while not coterminous, are the largest. There are exceptions to this general pattern. Thus the relative sizes of networks need to be determined empirically for each world-system.

Defined in this way, world-systems have grown from small to large over the past 12 millennia as societies and intersocietal systems have gotten larger, more complex and more hierarchical (see Chase-Dunn and Hall 1997: parts 2 and 3 for theoretical and empirical examples of this approach; Denemark *et al.* 2000 review most other grand scale approaches, and include statements by key thinkers). This spatial growth of systems has involved the expansion of some, and the incorporation of some into others. The processes of incorporation have occurred in several ways as systems distant from one another have linked their interaction networks. Because interaction nets are of different sizes, it is the largest ones that come into contact first. Thus information and prestige goods link distant groups long before they participate in the same political-military or bulk goods networks. The processes of expansion and incorporation brought different groups of people together and made the organization of larger and more hierarchical societies possible. In this sense globalization has been going on for thousands of years.

World-System Cycles: Rise and Fall, and Pulsations

Comparative research (e.g., Boswell and Chase-Dunn 2000; Chase-Dunn and Hall 1997) reveals that all world-systems exhibit cyclical processes of change. Two major cyclical phenomena are the rise and fall of large polities, and pulsations in the spatial extent and intensity of trade networks. Rise and fall corresponds to changes in the centralization of political/military power in a set of polities – an "international" system. Nearly all world-systems with hierarchical polities experience a cycle in which relatively larger polities grow in power and size and then decline.

Pulsation is a cyclical expansion and contraction in the spatial extent and intensity of exchange networks. Different kinds of trade usually have different spatial extents. They may also have different temporal sequences of expansion and contraction. It is an empirical question whether or not changes in the volume of exchange correspond to changes in spatial extent.

Egalitarian and small systems do not have cycles of rise and fall, but do experience pulsations as seen among sedentary foragers of Northern California (Chase-Dunn and Mann 1998). In the modern global system, trade networks cannot get larger because they are already global. But they might become denser, more intense, or faster. A good part of what has been called globalization is the intensification of larger interaction networks relative to the intensity of smaller ones. This is often seen to have occurred only in recent decades. However, research on trade and investment shows that there have been two recent waves of integration, one in the last half of the nineteenth century and the most recent since World War II (Chase-Dunn *et al.* 2000).

The simplest hypothesis regarding the temporal relationships between rise-and-fall and pulsation is that they occur in tandem. Whether or not this is so, and how it might differ in distinct types of world-systems, are problems amenable to empirical research. Chase-Dunn and Hall (1997) contend that the causal processes of rise and fall differ depending on the way in which wealth is accumulated. One major difference between the rise and fall of empires and the rise and fall of modern hegemons is in the degree of centralization within the core. We continue this discussion later.

The multiscalar method for regional bounding of world-systems as nested interaction networks is complementary with a multiscalar temporal analysis of the kind suggested by Fernand Braudel (see Braudel 1980 for an overview). Temporal depth, the *longue durée* (approximately, long duration), needs to be combined with analyses of short-run and middle-run processes to fully understand social change. Jared Diamond (1997) makes a strong case for the very *longue durée* in his study of the role of original zoological and botanical wealth in subsequent development. (See chapters by Yoffee, by Spier, and by Simmons, this volume.) The geographical distribution of species that could be easily domesticated explains a large portion of the variance regarding which world-systems expanded and incorporated other world-systems over millennia. Diamond also contends that the diffusion of domesticated plant and animal species occurs much more quickly along latitudinal dimensions (East/West) than along longitudinal dimensions (North/South). He uses this difference to explain why domesticated species spread so quickly to Europe and East Asia from West Asia, while the spread south into Africa was much slower, and why the North/South orientation of the American continents made diffusion much slower than in the Old World. Subsequent research supports Diamond's hypothesis (Turchin *et al.* 2006).

Much of contemporary social science and culture is not multiscalar and tends to have a shallow presentism that focuses on recent history of years or decades. Concentration on only one historical scale can lead to distorted understanding of multiscalar temporal processes (see Yang 2008 or Hall 1989 for extended examples).

Modes of Accumulation

All societies produce and distribute the goods that are necessary for everyday life. But the institutional means by which human labor is mobilized are very different in different kinds of societies. In order to comprehend the qualitative changes that have occurred in social evolution we need to conceptualize different logics of development and the institutional modes by which socially created resources are produced and accumulated.

Small and egalitarian societies rely primarily on normative regulation organized as shared understandings about the obligations of kin (in these societies kinship is reckoned far beyond what happens in contemporary core states). When a hunter returns with game there are definite rules about who should receive shares and how large those shares should be. Hunters want to be thought of as generous, but they must also take care of some people first. These rules, the "normative order," define the roles, obligations, norms, and values of kin relations. These are continually socially constructed and reconstructed in any kin-based mode of accumulation.

Accumulation involves the preservation and storage of food for scarce seasons. Status is based on one's reputation as a hunter, a gatherer, a family member, or a talented speaker. Group decisions are made by consensus, achieved through much discussion. The authority of leaders is based on their ability to convince others that they are right. These features are common (but not universal) in kin-based modes of accumulation.

As societies become larger and more hierarchical, kinship itself becomes hierarchically defined. Clans and lineages become ranked so that members of some families are defined as senior or superior to members of other families. Classical cases of ranked societies were those of the Pacific Northwest, in which the totem pole represents a hierarchy of clans. This tendency toward hierarchical kinship resulted in the eventual emergence of class societies (complex chiefdoms) in which a noble class owned and controlled key resources, and a class of commoners was separated from the control of important resources and had to rely on the nobles for access to them. Such a society existed in Hawai'i before the arrival of the Europeans.

However, normative power does not work well by itself as a basis for the appropriation of labor or goods by one group from another. Those who are exploited have a great motive to redefine the situation. On the one hand, nobles often elaborate a vision of the universe in which they are understood to control natural forces or to mediate interactions with the deities, thus obligating commoners to support these sacred duties by turning over their produce to the nobles or contributing labor to sacred projects. On the other hand, commoners will have an incentive to disbelieve unless they have only worse alternatives. Thus institutions of coercive power are invented to sustain the extraction of surplus labor and goods from direct producers. The hierarchical religions and kinship systems of complex chiefdoms became supplemented in early states by specialized organizations of regional control – groups of armed men under the command of the king, and bureaucratic systems of taxation and tribute backed up by the law and by institutionalized force. When institutional coercion became a central form of regulation for inducing people to work for the accumulation of social resources, the tributary mode of accumulation emerged. Various tributary modes of accumulation invented techniques of power that allowed resources to be extracted over great distances and from large populations. These are the institutional bases of states and empires.

The third mode of accumulation is based on markets. Markets can be defined as any situation in which goods are bought and sold. When competitive trading by large numbers of buyers and sellers is a major determinant of price, these are labeled price-setting markets. This is a situation in which supply and demand operate on price because buyers and sellers are bidding against one another. In practice there are very few instances in history or in modern reality where only markets set prices, because political and normative considerations quite often influence prices. But the price mechanism and resulting market pressures have become more important. These institutions were completely absent before the invention of commodities and money.

A commodity is a good that is produced for sale in a price-setting market in order to make a profit. A pencil is an example of a commodity. The capitalist mode of accumulation is based on commodity exchanges. Capitalism is the concentrated accumulation of profits by the owners of major means of the production of commodities in a context in which labor and the other main elements of production are commodified, that is things are treated as if they are commodities, even though they may not have been in the past. Land can be commodified even though it is a limited good that was not originally produced for profitable sale. There is only so much land on Earth, so it can never be a perfect commodity. This is also the case for human labor time.

The capitalist mode of production also required the redefinition of wealth as money. The first storable and tradable valuables were probably prestige goods (see Chase-Dunn and Hall 1997). These were used by local elites in trade with adjacent peoples, and eventually as symbols of superior status. Originally prestige goods were used only in specific circumstances by certain elites. This "proto-money" was eventually redefined and institutionalized as the so-called "universal equivalent" that serves as a general measure of value for all sorts of goods and that can be used by almost anyone to buy almost anything. The institution of money has a long and complicated history. Suffice it to say here that it has been a prerequisite for the emergence of price-setting markets and capitalism as increasingly important forms of social regulation. Once markets and capital become the predominant form of accumulation, we can speak of capitalist systems. Thus the Europe-centered world-system became fully capitalist during the Dutch hegemony in the seventeenth century, though to be sure there were pockets of capitalism in older world-systems (Chase-Dunn and Hall 1997). Other world-system scholars see capitalism developing in the fifteen and sixteenth centuries (Wallerstein 1974), or in the thirteenth and fourteenth centuries (Abu-Lughod 1989) or as having existed since the first states

(Frank and Gills 1993; for discussion of these and other approaches see Denemark *et al.* 2000). When the intensity of trade based on market prices is the major mode of exchange, the system has become a capitalist system. This does not mean, however, that all other forms of exchange, such as barter or tribute, have disappeared completely, only that they no longer are the major mode of exchange.

The various cyclical processes interact with the broader changes among modes of accumulation. In terms of rise and fall, tributary systems alternate between a structure of multiple, competing core states and core-wide (or nearly core-wide) empires. The modern interstate system experiences the rise and fall of hegemons, but a hegemon never conquers the other core states to form a core-wide empire. This is the case because modern hegemons are pursuing a capitalist, rather than a tributary form of accumulation.

Rise and fall works differently in interchiefdom systems because the institutions that facilitate the extraction of resources from distant groups are less developed. David G. Anderson's (1994) study of the rise and fall of Mississippian chiefdoms in the Savannah River valley provides an excellent and comprehensive review of the literature on what Anderson calls "cycling": the processes by which a chiefly polity extended control over adjacent chiefdoms and erected a two-tiered hierarchy of administration over the tops of local communities. At a later point these regionally centralized chiefly polities disintegrated back toward a system of smaller and less hierarchical polities.

Interchiefdom systems are highly dependent on normative integration and ideological consensus based on kinship. States developed specialized organizations for extracting resources: standing armies and bureaucracies. Tributary world-systems were more dependent on the projection of armed force over great distances than modern hegemonic core states have been. Capitalist systems are able to extract resources from faraway places with much less overhead cost because commodity production, mechanisms of financial control, and elaborations of bureaucratic power make such extraction more efficient.

Occasionally, during one of these cycles, people solve systemic problems in a new way that allows substantial expansion. This is how expansions, changes in systemic logic, and collapses occur. This can only be seen by comparing world-systems.

Patterns and Causes of Social Evolution

Here we explore how all these processes help explain the emergence of larger hierarchies and the development of productive technologies. These innovations often, but not always, come from semiperipheral societies. Semiperipheral societies are not constrained by sunk costs in specific resources or techniques to the same degree as older core societies. Thus, they are freer to implement new institutions. Occasionally by transforming a system a semiperiphery could become a new core society.

Marcher states are states that are spatially located out on the edge of a number of interacting states – in the "marchlands." Semiperipheral marcher states are better known than semiperipheral marcher chiefdoms. The largest empires have been assembled by conquerors who came from semiperipheral societies: the Achaemenid Persians, the Macedonians led by Alexander the Great, the Romans, the Ottomans, the Manchus, and the Aztecs. In other cases a semiperiphery may transform institutions, but does not take over. Semiperipheral capitalist city-states operated on the edges of the tributary empires, where they bought and sold goods in widely separated locations and encouraged people to produce a surplus for trade. Phoenician cities (e.g., Tyre, Carthage, etc.), as well as

Malacca, Venice, and Genoa, spread commodification by producing manufactured goods and trading them across great regions. They helped transform the world of the tributary empires without themselves becoming core powers.

All of hegemonic core states in the modern world-system – the Dutch, the British and the US – formerly had been in semiperipheral positions. Indeed, Europe had been a peripheral and then a semiperipheral region within the larger Afroeurasian world-system before it rose to become the new core of the multicore modern world-system.

Not all semiperipheries create transformations, nor do all transformations come from semiperipheral areas. Rather, semiperipheries have been unusually prolific sites for the invention of institutions that have expanded and transformed many small systems into today's global system. This could only be discovered within a conceptual apparatus of the comparative world-systems.

But why is this so? Some of the problems that needed to be solved were unintended consequences of earlier inventions, but others were very old problems that kept emerging again and again as systems expanded – such as population pressure and ecological degradation. These basic problems make it possible to specify a single underlying causal model of world-systems evolution. Figure 12.1 shows the links among demographic, ecological, and interactional processes that lead to the emergence of new production technologies, larger polities, and increased hierarchy.

This is an iteration model because it contains an important positive feedback mechanism in which the original causes are themselves consequences of the things that they cause. Thus the process goes around and around, which is what has caused the world-systems to expand to the global level. While the cycle can begin anywhere, we begin our account with population growth. All human societies contain a biological impetus to grow based on sexuality. This impetus is mediated by social institutions: infanticide, abortion, taboos on sexual relations, pronatalist ideologies, or support for large families. These means of regulation are costly. When food is relatively abundant, these controls tend to be eased. Thus, most societies experience periodic "baby booms." Over the long run, the population tends to grow despite institutional mechanisms that try to control it.

Population growth prompts greater efforts to produce food and other necessities, here labeled intensification. This usually leads to ecological degradation because all human production uses the natural environment through resource extraction and pollution, and eventually leads to environmental degradation. This has been a regular property of all states (Chew 2001). Only its global scale and intensity is new.

Following Diamond (1997), all locations did not start with the same animal and plant resources. Such exogenous factors affect the timing and speed of hierarchy formation and technological development, as do climate change and geographical obstacles that affect transportation and communications. The emergence of an early large state on the Nile was greatly facilitated by the ease of controlling transportation and communications in that linear environment, while the more complicated geography of Mesopotamia slowed stabilization of the system of city-states and slowed the emergence of a core-wide empire.

All of this changes the economics of production for the worse. According to Joseph Tainter (1988), after a certain point increased investment in complexity does not result in proportionately increasing returns. This phenomenon can be identified in the areas of agricultural production, information processing, and communication, including education and maintenance of information channels. Sociopolitical control and specialization, such as the military and the police, also develop diminishing returns. Tainter argues that

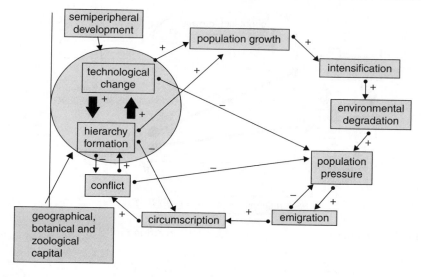

Figure 12.1 Basic iteration model of world-system evolution.

such decreasing marginal returns can occur in at least four instances: benefits constant, costs rising; benefits rising, costs rising faster; benefits falling, costs constant; benefits falling, costs rising. When herds are depleted the hunters must go farther to find game. The combined sequence from population growth to intensification to environmental degradation leads to population pressure. The growing effort needed to produce enough food is a major incentive for people to migrate. Migration eventually runs into barriers, called circumscription, limiting further migration: herds in all the adjacent valleys are depleted, or all alternative locations are deserts or high mountains, or all desirable locations are already occupied by people who can resist migration.

Circumscription combined with population pressure often leads to a rise in the level of intergroup and intragroup conflict. This is because more people are competing for fewer resources. All systems experience some warfare, but warfare becomes a focus of social endeavor that often has a life of its own. Boys are trained to be warriors and societies make decisions based on the presumption that they will be attacked or will be attacking other groups. Even in situations of seemingly endemic warfare, the amount of conflict varies cyclically. Because high levels of conflict reduce the size of the population as warriors are killed and noncombatants die because their food supplies have been destroyed or diminished, Figure 12.1 shows an arrow with a negative sign going from conflict back to population pressure. Some systems get stuck in a vicious cycle of population pressure and warfare.

Situations such as this are also propitious for the emergence of new institutional structures, especially through semiperipheral development as people tire of continual conflict. As shown in Figure 12.2, these institutional developments can produce streamlining, or shortcuts, in the iteration model. One solution is the emergence of a new hierarchy or a larger polity that can regulate access to resources in a way that reduces conflict. A larger polity usually is a result of conquest of several smaller polities by a semiperipheral marcher. The larger polity creates peace by means of an organized force that is greater than any force likely to be brought against it. The new polity reconstructs the institutions of

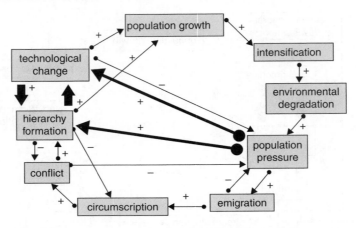

Figure 12.2 Temporary institutional shortcuts in the iteration model.

control over territory and resources, often concentrating control and wealth in a new elite. Also, larger and more hierarchical polities often invest in new technologies of production that change the way in which resources are utilized. They produce more food and other necessities through new technologies or intensification of old technologies. Either will increase the carrying capacity, the number of people that can be supported on a specific territory. This makes population growth more likely, so the iteration model is primed to go around again. It is important to note that circumscription does not cause new social inventions. Rather, it makes them more likely. Often they do not occur and the system collapses and cycles through growth again. Anderson (1994) notes that a chiefdom system can go through this cycle for a millennium or more before it invents a solution to it.

Thus, the iteration process is the basis of continual, if sporadic and cyclical expansion of world-systems, the development of new technologies, and new forms of regulation. Population growth resumes, which leads to new problems of ecological degradation and population pressure. The emergence of new institutions that change the economics of production creates new political organization and new technologies that allow the system to avoid the messy bottom end of the model.

This is not a teleological explanation. Rather, it suggests where and when change is most likely. Incidentally, this is also a time when human agency can be most effective in producing change. Often the first solution is not optimal; it merely works. As more systems find other solutions, a process of optimization begins. Eventually, however, even an optimal solution encounters the environmental degradation and population problem. Occasionally, however, the cycle is shortened. New technologies and/or new forms of hierarchy may allow some adjustments without increasing the level of systemic conflict. Still, the level of conflict may remain high because the rate of expansion and techno-logical change has increased.

It is difficult to understand why and where innovative social change emerges without a concept of a world-system. As we have seen, new organizational forms most often emerge in semiperipheral societies. Interestingly, all the hegemonic core states in the modern system had been semiperipheral (the Dutch, the British, the US). Such "semiperipheral development" (Chase-Dunn and Hall 1997) arguably includes organizational innovations in contemporary semiperipheral countries (e.g., China, Mexico, India, South Korea, Brazil) that may transform the current global system.

This approach requires that we think structurally. We must be able to abstract from the particularities of the game of musical chairs that constitutes uneven development in the system to see the structural continuities. The core/periphery hierarchy remains, though some countries have moved up or down. The interstate system remains, though the internationalization of capital has further constrained the abilities of states to structure their own economies. During such changes some states have been more successful at exploiting opportunities and protecting themselves from liabilities than others.

Thus, much that has been labeled "globalization" corresponds to recently expanded international trade, financial flows, and foreign investment by transnational corporations and banks. (See Bright and Geyer, this volume.) Too much of the globalization discourse assumes that until recently there were separate national societies and economies, and that these have now been superseded by an expansion of international integration driven by information and transportation technologies. Rather than a wholly unique and new phenomenon, it is an old world-systemic process. Recent research comparing the nineteenth and twentieth centuries shows that trade globalization both is cyclical and also follows a trend. For instance, Giovanni Arrighi (1994) has shown that finance capital has been a central component of the commanding heights of the world-system since the fourteenth century. The current floods and ebbs of world money are typical of the late phase of very long "systemic cycles of accumulation."

Most world-systems scholars contend that leaving out the core/periphery dimension or treating the periphery as inert are grave mistakes because the ability of core capitalists and their states to exploit peripheral resources and labor has been a major factor in deciding the winners of the competition among core contenders. Also, the resistance to exploitation and domination mounted by peripheral peoples has played a powerful role in shaping the historical development of world orders. Thus world history cannot be properly understood without attention to the core/periphery hierarchy. For instance, Yang (2008) shows that the two millennia long process of incorporation of what we now know as Yunnan into China can only be explained by examining the consequences of its participation in the Southern Silk Road – from Yunnan to Annam, Burma, and South Asia. Hall (1989) examines the interplay of local, regional, national, and global forces in a 500-year history of what we know today as the American Southwest. A key point for both authors is that it is the interactions of all of these levels that are crucial. Few other accounts of these regions examine the interplay of the extremes – the local and global – in their histories.

Philip McMichael (2003) has studied the "globalization project" – the abandoning of Keynesian models of national development, and a new (or renewed) emphasis on deregulation and opening national commodity and financial markets to foreign trade and investment. This approach focuses on the political and ideological aspects of the recent wave of international integration. This process has been called "neoliberalism," or "Reaganism/Thatcherism," or "the Washington Consensus." While the worldwide decline of leftist parties and movements began before the revolutions of 1989 and the demise of the Soviet Union, it was accelerated by these events. The structural basis of the rise of the globalization project is the new level of integration reached by the global capitalist class. The internationalization of capital has long been an important part of the trend toward economic globalization. Every modern hegemon has claimed to represent the general interests of business. Still, the integration of the interests of capitalists all over the world has very likely reached a historical peak.

This part of the theory of a global stage of capitalism must be taken most seriously, though this can be overdone. In the current world-system both the old interstate system, based on separate national capitalist classes, and new global institutions coexist, and are powerful simultaneously. Each country has a ruling class fraction that is allied with the transnational capitalist class. The major question is whether or not this new level of transnational integration will be strong enough to prevent competition among states for world hegemony from turning into warfare, as has always happened in past periods of hegemonic decline.

The discovery that capitalist globalization has occurred in waves, and that these waves are followed by periods of backlash has important implications for the future. Capitalist globalization increased both intranational and international inequalities in the nineteenth century and it has done the same thing in the late twentieth century (O'Rourke and Williamson 2000). Those countries and groups that have been left out of these changes either mobilize to challenge the hegemony of the powerful or try to retreat into self-reliance, or both.

Globalization protests emerged in the noncore with the riots of the 1980s against the International Monetary Fund. Several transnational social movements participated in the 1999 protest in Seattle brought globalization protest to the attention of observers in the core. This resistance to capitalist globalization has continued to grow despite the temporary setback that occurred in response to the terrorist attacks on New York and Washington in 2001 (Podobnik 2005).

There is an apparent tension between those who advocate deglobalization and delinking from the global capitalist economy and the building of stronger, more cooperative and self-reliant social relations in the periphery and semiperiphery, on the one hand, and those who seek to mobilize support for new or reformed institutions of democratic global governance. Self-reliance by itself, though an understandable reaction to exploitation, is not likely to solve the problems of humanity in the long run. The great challenge of the twenty-first century will be the building of a democratic and collectively rational global commonwealth. World-systems theory can be an important contributor to this effort.

References

Abu-Lughod, Janet. 1989. *Before European Hegemony: The World System AD 1250–1350.* New York: Oxford University Press.

Anderson, David. G. 1994. *The Savannah River Chiefdoms: Political Change in the Late Prehistoric Southeast.* Tuscaloosa: University of Alabama Press.

Arrighi, Giovanni. 1994. *The Long Twentieth Century.* London: Verso.

Benjamin, Craig, ed. 2009. Introduction to Forum on Big History. *World History Connected* 6 (3) (Oct.), at http://worldhistoryconnected.press.illinois.edu/6.3/index.html (accessed Feb 2012).

Boswell, Terry, and Christopher Chase-Dunn. 2000. *The Spiral of Socialism and Capitalism: Toward Global Democracy.* Boulder: Lynne Rienner.

Braudel, Fernand. 1980. *On History,* trans. Sarah Matthews. Chicago: University of Chicago Press.

Chase-Dunn, Christopher, and Salvatore J. Babones. 2006. *Global Social Change: Comparative and Historical Perspectives.* Baltimore: Johns Hopkins University Press.

Chase-Dunn, Christopher, and Thomas D. Hall. 1997. *Rise and Demise: Comparing World-Systems.* Boulder: Westview.

Chase-Dunn, Christopher, and Kelly M. Mann. 1998. *The Wintu and Their Neighbors: A Very Small World-System in Northern California.* Tucson: University of Arizona Press.

Chase-Dunn, Christopher, Yukio Kawano, and Benjamin D. Brewer. 2000. Trade globalization since 1795: Waves of integration in the world-system. *American Sociological Review* 65 (1) (Feb.): 77–95.

Chew, Sing C. 2001. *World Ecological Degradation: Accumulation, Urbanization, and Deforestation 3000 BC–AD 2000.* Walnut Creek, CA: Altamira Press.

Denemark, Robert A., Jonathan Friedman, Barry K. Gills, and George Modelski, eds. 2000. *World System History: The Social Science of Long-Term Change.* London: Routledge.

Diamond, Jared. 1997. *Guns, Germs and Steel: The Fates of Human Societies.* New York: W.W. Norton.

Frank, Andre Gunder, and Barry K. Gills, eds. 1993. *The World System: Five Hundred Years or Five Thousand?* London: Routledge.

Friedman, Thomas. 2008. *Hot, Flat, and Crowded: Why We Need a Green Revolution – and How It Can Renew America.* New York: Farrar, Straus & Giroux.

Hall, Thomas D. 1989. *Social Change in the Southwest, 1350–1880.* Lawrence: University Press of Kansas.

Hall, Thomas D. 1998. The effects of incorporation into world-systems on ethnic processes: Lessons from the ancient world for the contemporary world. *International Political Science Review* 19 (3) (July): 251–267.

Harvey, David. 2003. *The New Imperialism.* New York: Oxford University Press.

Hornborg, Alf, and Carole E. Crumley. 2007. *The World System and the Earth System: Global Socioenvironmental Change and Sustainability since the Neolithic.* Walnut Creek, CA: Left Coast Books.

Hornborg, Alf, J.R. McNeill, and Joan Martinez-Alier, eds. 2007. *Rethinking Environmental History: World-System History and Global Environmental Change.* Lanham: Rowman & Littlefield.

Laczko, Leslie S. 2000. Canada's linguistic and ethnic dynamics in an evolving world-system. In T.D. Hall, ed., *A World-Systems Reader: New Perspectives on Gender, Urbanism, Cultures, Indigenous Peoples, and Ecology,* pp. 131–142. Lanham: Rowman & Littlefield.

McMichael, Philip. 2003. *Development and Social Change: A Global Perspective.* 3rd edn. Thousand Oaks, CA: Pine Forge Press.

McNeill, William H. 1986. *Polyethnicity and National Unity in World History.* Toronto: University of Toronto Press.

O'Rourke, Kevin H., and Jeffrey G. Williamson. 2000. *Globalization and History.* Cambridge, MA: MIT Press.

Podobnik, Bruce. 2005. Resistance to globalization: Cycles and trends in the globalization protest movement. In B. Podobnik and T. Reifer, eds, *Transforming Globalization: Challenges and Opportunities in the Post 9/11 Era,* pp. 51–68. Leiden: Brill.

Robinson, William I. 2004. *A Theory of Global Capitalism.* Baltimore: Johns Hopkins University Press.

Tainter, Joseph A. 1988. *The Collapse of Complex Societies.* Cambridge: Cambridge University Press.

Sanderson, Stephen K., and Arthur S. Alderson. 2005. *World Societies: The Evolution of Human Social Life.* Boston: Allyn & Bacon.

Sassen, Saskia. 2006. *Territory, Authority, Rights: From Medieval to Global Assemblages.* Princeton: Princeton University Press.

Sklair, Leslie. 2002. *Globalization: Capitalism and Its Alternatives.* 3rd edn. Oxford: Oxford University Press.

Turchin, Peter. 2003. *Historical Dynamics.* Princeton: Princeton University Press.

Turchin, Peter, Jonathan M. Adams, and Thomas D. Hall. 2006. East–West orientation of historical empires and modern states. *Journal of World-Systems Research* 12 (2) (Dec.): 218–229.

Yang, Bin. 2008. *Between Winds and Clouds: The Making of Yunnan (Second Century BCE to Twentieth Century CE)*. New York: Columbia University Press; through Gutenberg-e, at http://www.gutenberg-e.org/yang/index.html (accessed Feb. 2012).

Wallerstein, Immanuel. 1974. *The Modern World-System: Capitalist Agriculture and the Origins of the European World-Economy in the Sixteenth Century*. New York: Academic Press.

Wallerstein, Immanuel. 2004. *World-Systems Analysis: An Introduction*. Durham: Duke University Press.

CHAPTER THIRTEEN

Region in Global History

PAUL A. KRAMER

Region has a peculiar status in the writing of world histories. Whereas the other principal scales of historical analysis – the local, the national, the global – each have a taken-for-granted meaning that has allowed them to be assembled in a convenient, nested triad, region fits uneasily. Of the four scales, it is arguably the most ambiguous and free-floating in its reach, able to embrace and define spaces from the just-larger-than-local to the multinational and continental. This is, perhaps, one of the main benefits of bringing an account of region to the writing of global histories: its very slipperiness and evasion of a single, agreed-upon definition points to the arbitrariness of scholars' spatial categories themselves. (See McKeown, this volume.) If the local, national, and global can some-times threaten to harden into reified realities, region's elusiveness brings with it fruitful, ontological disruption.

If there is a reason that region remains cloudy, it may be because historians have largely farmed out its definition to geographers, and because geographers have long been divided about what it means (Fledelius 1997). (See Simmons, this volume.) One way to think about these divisions is to turn to the origins of the term itself. Nathalie Cavasin (2005) notes region's dual etymological roots, in the Latin words *regio*, meaning "district" or "direction," and *regere*, meaning "to rule or direct." With perhaps not too much semantic stretching, one can use this conjoined origin to point to two different present-day academic approaches to region, which might be called positivist and constructivist. Positivist approaches, which can be associated with *regio*, take region as ontological fact: a territorial space that is internally similar, defined by a cluster of measurable traits that mark it as distinct from neighboring spaces; "nodal" approaches to region, for example, mark their "core" where these traits are manifested most densely, and their "peripheries" where they trail off into other sets of internal similarities. Here region is something like *regio*: a way of charting actually existing "districts" or "directions" in objective space (see, i.e., Grigg 1967). By contrast, constructivist approaches emphasize the historical production of regions: regions as imagined spaces generated and transformed through social and political processes across time.

A Companion to World History, First Edition. Edited by Douglas Northrop.
© 2012 Blackwell Publishing Ltd. Published 2012 by Blackwell Publishing Ltd.

Here region is more like *regere*: space defined less by its fixed, calculable elements and more by who "rules" it and how they define their rule and its internal and external boundaries. Constructivist approaches take region to be fundamentally processual, with region-making both the concerted and incidental result of migration, conquest, governance, cultural diffusion, and deliberate invention by history's mapmakers; regions are not found by scholars but made by history. In turn, it can be useful to divide constructivist approaches into two subcategories, one stressing the material and spatial constructedness of regions (and venturing closer to positivism in epistemological terms), and the other emphasizing their ideological, cultural, and discursive construction, the study of what Martin Lewis and Kären Wigen (1997) call "the myth of continents." While I mark a somewhat polar distinction here, my operating assumption is that when it comes to historical processes, these two dimensions of region-building are neither separable nor reducible one to the other.

This essay proceeds from constructivist premises: region as spatial and ideological practice. It does so with skepticism about the utility of "region" itself as an analytical frame or tool. This skepticism derives from my sense of region as a core element in the political and intellectual armature of modern state territoriality: it marks the outer limits of state efforts to homogenize space, registering (and sometimes institutionalizing and tapping into) differences that either are to be exploited, or cannot be made to go away. To the extent that "region" conveys a sense of physical and social coherence – the coterminous character of ecology, culture and sovereignty, for example – it was far less salient in premodern polities characterized by complex, overlapping domains. By contrast, it was somewhat organic to modernizing regimes dedicated to internalizing space by saturating it with fields of force, typologizing its diversities and harnessing its resources.[1] In some cases, region was built into modern territoriality as the residue of older forms of composite sovereignty; in other instances, particularly in the case of new states, it was installed in the territorial architecture of federalisms. Elsewhere, particularly in the late twentieth century, the term region (often followed by an -ism) was employed to characterize the embedding of individual states and national economies in multistate formations.

In all of these instances, if in very different ways, "region" remains tethered to state-centered modes of territory-making. Whether regions are defined as spatial components of larger polities, or conglomerates in which states situate themselves, region's implicit reference point is still the theoretically integrated, homogeneous, Westphalian state. It is telling, for example, that while both the region and the modern state are "surface" formations – bounded, cartographic imaginaries – they are, by definition, not coterminous: regions are critical enough to the triangulation of states that they cannot be rendered identical to them (Warf 2009).

With these caveats in place, this chapter will trace some of the ways constructions of region can be said to have played a role in global histories. Precisely because of the term's conceptual state-centeredness, I divide the piece into substate regions and multistate regions. Substate regions have been the by-product of either limited state-integrative capacities or federating strategies. Expressing either an unwillingness or incapacity to homogenize territory, here the "regional" marks both plurality and the presence of centrifugal, potentially fragmentary, forces. (Indeed, in common parlance, one way that areas become "regions" is to have territorial monopoly over them contested between adjacent states: Alsace-Lorraine and Kashmir would be examples in the twentieth and twenty-first centuries.)

Multistate regions have been brought into existence for a range of purposes: as trade blocs, defense pacts, systems of arbitration, or imperial systems, for example. They have varied along axes of institutional "thickness" (enmeshing their member states in dense or sparse networks of power and constraint), in their internal political balances (which have ranged from egalitarian to hierarchical), and their geopolitical objectives (which have varied from anticolonial to neocolonial purposes). Not all multistate structures and organizations, of course, identify and bound themselves in terms of the regional: for precisely this reason, the question of when and how states decide they comprise a "region," which notions of spatial connection they enlist, and to what ends, is a compelling one.

First, there are substate regions: territories within states that are characterized by their distinctiveness and multiplicity. Regional boundaries can be defined by particular natural elements, including physical barriers like mountain ranges, or by the presence of unique social and cultural practices and institutions, or by particular crossings of the social and the ecological, as in systems of agricultural production. Seen in this way, regions may or may not correspond to a government's territorial subcategories such as "provinces," "districts," or "states." In some cases, states have organized regions as a federalist strategy to absorb and stabilize separatist tendencies; in other cases, regionalization at the substate level has been a way to avoid overconcentrated state power. Substate regions can develop distinct ways of connecting to the global environment and this, in turn, can profoundly shape a region's relationship to the state of which it forms a part, while influencing that state's global trajectory.

In some cases, a region's intersections with world history run through political-economic and geopolitical channels. A good example is the US South. (That many of my examples here are drawn from the US context is a function of my expertise and its limitations, rather than any presumed exceptional relationship between the regional and the global.) While its distinctiveness as a region has been questioned, it is possible to identify the US South in broad terms as a region defined by racial slavery and struggles over legalized apartheid; staple crop production, capital dependence, and late industrialization; a volatile and resilient separatist politics; cultural formations defined by patriarchal authority, public religiosity and militarized honor; and, in the twentieth century, an intensity of militarization in the form of both basing and military-industrial development. The South's regional identity was and is a political-cultural project closely tied to proslavery ideology, Confederate secession and, in the twentieth century, segregationist resistance to a centralizing racial liberalism.

But the South's regionalism is also global, and its globalism regional. In the nineteenth century, its close ties to the British Empire as a cotton supplier to British textile mills encouraged secessionists to pursue a cataclysmic separatist path to a slave-based future. In the mid-twentieth century, large-scale migration from the Northwest and Midwest to the "Sunbelt" had a profound impact on US politics which, in an era of US global empire, had immense implications. In particular, this exodus – itself in part the result of Cold War investment patterns – shifted power towards polities that, both during and after the Cold War, tended to approach the world in highly unilateralist, manichean and militarized ways, inflected in the late twentieth and early twenty-first centuries by the region's energy politics.[2]

Substate regions also connect to the world in unique ways through large-scale migrations in which a critical mass of long-distance movement and settlement produces unique cultures defined in part through their population's ongoing ties to their "home" societies. (See Ward, this volume.) A good example of a substate region that is also a transborder region would be the US Southwest, a region governed by four states since the early nineteenth century. Initially incorporated into the orbits of global empire as the northern extensions of Spain's American dominion, it was transmuted into the massive, thinly populated provinces of Mexican independence, parts of it broken off into the separate nation of Texas, then conquered and annexed by the United States following the US-Mexican War of 1846–1848.

But the military detachment of Northern Mexico did not completely transform this territory as region: until the 1920s, the US–Mexico border as a state institution remained highly porous, allowing migrants to make seasonal back-and-forth journeys. Meanwhile, US railroad capital approached Northern Mexico and the US Southwest as a single region: profits were to be made, from paying travelers or long-distance exporters, by girding the region together with track. It was also a single, regional labor market for the American owners of mines and ranches, who relied heavily on transborder Mexican migrant labor and who would, for this reason, resist some efforts to harden the border. Even as the enforcement of the US–Mexico border intensified after the 1920s, culminating in its late twentieth-century militarization, transborder investment and infrastructure, labor recruitment and migration continued to fasten Mexico and the US Southwest, lending this part of the United States a distinct, regional character, despite nativist campaigns for separation (Sanchez 1993).

If some regions are defined as parts of states, others contain multiple states. These multistate regions involve projects in coordination, cooperation and alliance, the pursuing of advantage, especially economic or geopolitical, through the mobilization of imagined contiguity. These "regionalisms" – constructed proximities rendered into ideology and organizational practice – have often involved highly varying levels of institutionalization, from "thick" integration involving the formation of supranational political structures, to "thinner" forms involving looser, issue-specific agreements. Regionalisms of this kind have involved, to one degree or another, the invention of cross-national, integrative modes of identification that are both spatially broader and historically "deeper" than states, such as common language or folkways, ties to land, histories of oppression, or notions of shared cultural or racial "essence." Their shapes and strengths as formations have been determined by a number of factors: the infrastructural possibilities for cohesion, the convergence of economic and geopolitical interests across states, the prospects for ideological bridge-building, and the relative weakness of "outside" powers capable of fragmenting the would-be region and reorienting its parts "outward."

Some multistate regionalisms have come into being as campaigns to secure greater autonomy and escape from global dependence and subordination. An early example is mid nineteenth-century pan-Americanism: drawn together by revolt against Spanish colonialism, a desire to prevent further European intrusions, and a sense of creole distinctiveness, Latin American nationalists sought to preserve their new states' fragile independence through a defensive regionalism, a key example being Simón Bolívar's campaign for a confederacy of Spanish-American states. While early pan-Americanism helped organize regional treaties and the regulation of interstate legal issues, the scope of its success was limited by the vulnerability of the new states, the racial and class boundaries of creole nationalism, and by intraregional conflict, such as the War of the Triple Alliance of 1864–1870 between Paraguay and Argentina, Brazil and Uruguay. The question of whether the United States ought to participate in pan-American congresses or not, whether it was an ally or a threatening (and defining) other, was also fraught (Snyder 1984).

Another, later example of a decolonizing regionalism is pan-Africanism. Born in the nineteenth-century Caribbean and United States as a diasporic ideology and forged in a context of slavery, colonialism and segregation, early pan-Africanism emphasized the collective identity of African-descended peoples, harsh realities of white oppression, and the status of Africa as both homeland and site of civilizing redemption. Beginning in the early twentieth century, it took on an organizational life both in international congresses dedicated to the reform of European colonialism and the pursuit of greater African autonomy, and in mass movements exemplified by the Universal Negro Improvement Association. With the collapse of European colonialism after World War II, these ideologies informed multilateral African organizations created to combat older and newer forms of colonialism and to defend the sovereignty and territorial integrity of new nation-states and promote cooperation and mediation between them.

These values were promoted most actively by the Organization of African Unity (OAU), founded in May 1963, which achieved a membership of 53 states in 1994, prior to its disbanding and replacement by the African Union in 2002. As elsewhere, continent-wide regional unity in Africa faced divisions: the left-leaning Casablanca bloc favored political federation, for example, while the more conservative Monrovian bloc preferred economic cooperation short of federation. The OAU brought together and mediated between these factions. It took on a wide range of undertakings, but it dedicated its most focused energies toward the efforts that its members could most agree upon. It played a major role in the settling of territorial disputes between African states, sending selected African leaders to serve as agents of arbitration. It supported the emancipation of Africa from European colonialism through diplomatic support and the delivery of financial, military and logistical aid to liberation movements across the continent. It played a vital role in the isolation of apartheid South Africa, relentlessly campaigning to block its participation in international organizations and sending observer missions to oversee the first free elections in 1994. In the 1980s, with the winding down of the anticolonial struggle, the OAU turned its attention to questions of poverty and economic development, adopting the 1980 Lagos Plan of Action, which called for industrialization, a decreased reliance on extraction, and increased development aid, and the 1991 Abuja Treaty, which created the African Economic Community, with goals to create free trade zones, a central bank and a common currency (Leonard 2006).

While many decolonizing projects pursued regional scale and organization, so too did imperial politics, as illustrated in the twentieth century by US-dominated pan-Americanism and Japan-centered pan-Asianism. Both projects were predicated on the notion of a region united by common struggle against colonizing Europe; both ideologies rationalized the hegemony of regional powers by casting them as liberating vanguards, against European encroachment (in the American instance) and white colonialism (in the Asian one). While US pan-Americanism and Japanese pan-Asianism differed along multiple axes – the violence of the former was more sporadic but longer in overall duration, for example – both employed region as the scale and rationale for empire-building.

US exertions to direct "pan-American" politics dated back to the 1823 Monroe Doctrine, which asserted the exceptional role of the United States as guarantor of European noninterference in the Western hemisphere. Beginning in the late nineteenth century, US diplomats attempted to play a leading role in pan-American organizing, beginning with a conference in Washington DC in 1889–1890. From that point until the end of the twentieth century, US participation in pan-American regionalism developed in three basic stages. From 1890 through 1933, US diplomats defined intraregional "cooperation" in terms of the prevention of European interference in the hemisphere and US commercial access to Latin American markets and raw materials; "pan-Americanism" was fully compatible with US colonial rule in Puerto Rico, a neocolonial protectorate in Cuba, and Marine occupations in Haiti, Nicaragua, and the Dominican Republic. During the 1930s and 1940s, a desire to dampen Latin American criticism of US hegemony and build closer geopolitical ties to Latin America as a potential bulwark against fascist infiltration encouraged the pursuit of a "Good Neighbor" regionalism involving the end of military intervention and enhanced "cultural exchange"; the 1948 charter of the Organization of American States (OAS), successor organization to the Bureau of American Republics and Pan-American Union, upheld the "sovereignty" of all American states. Between the 1950s and the late 1980s, however, the OAS was profoundly shaped by Cold War politics, as the United States sought multilateral support for its interventions in Latin America; the OAS's 1962 decision to exclude Fidel Castro's Cuba from membership reflected this dynamic. US preeminence within pan-Americanism also faced challenges within Latin America across the twentieth century: in many respects, tensions between Bolívarean and Monrovian definitions of the Americas persisted (Snyder 1984).

Like pan-Americanism, pan-Asianism had its roots in an incipient anticolonial ideology, the work of late nineteenth- and early twentieth-century Asian intellectuals in pursuit of a unified past and present directed against Euro-American colonialism and white supremacy; in 1920, the first Pan-Asian Conference was held in Nagasaki. But organization was hampered by intraregional tensions, particularly involving Japan's imperial ambitions. Many Japanese pan-Asianists presumed Japan's leadership over a united Asia. Others were skeptical. Suspicions of Japan ran especially high in China, which advanced its own claims for regional dominance. Here, not unlike the pan-American case, one powerful state pursued regionalization as a way to advance its imperial interest. With Japan's invasion of Manchuria in 1931, pan-Asianism collapsed as a multilateral ideal and was fully absorbed into Japanese imperial ideology. From this point forward, pan-Asianism played a central role in the Japanese state's doctrine of regional "co-prosperity": the first among conquered equals, Japan would helm Asia's efforts to throw off the West's colonial yoke. (See Lim, this volume.) The intense violence of armed "co-prosperity" delegitimated pan-Asianism as regional ideology. After World War II, Asia was spatially recast along the lines of Cold War "alignment." Japan itself was integrated as the military and economic core of a US-dominated East Asia. The liberatory elements of early pan-Asianism were folded into the more global, aspirational solidarities of colonized peoples in Asia, Africa and the Middle East seeking an end to Western colonial rule that transcended Asia as region (Snyder 1984). (See Simo, this volume.)

Since World War II, regionalism in diverse institutional contexts has emerged as a core element of the global political order and capitalist world economy, developing at the intersection of a number of cross-cutting forces. It has taken shape as a structuring element of formally universal organizations like the United Nations. It has strong geopolitical dimensions: during the Cold War, both the Soviet Union and the United States cultivated what can be called strategic regionalisms, the former through the construction of a "Soviet Eurasia," the latter through the integration of Germany and Japan as the anchors of capitalist Western Europe and East Asia. Most recently, region-making has grown from competitive campaigns to aggregate resources and markets in a context of worldwide economic competition and, in particular, in response to European regionalization.

Despite its formal universalism, the United Nations built regionalism into its architecture at a number of levels from its beginning. At the insistence of Latin American and Arab states, the United Nations Charter included the right of self-defense at the level of multiple states as well as individual ones (Article 51) and the primacy of regional means of dispute settlement (Articles 33(1), 52(2) and 52(3)). The Charter also held open the possibility of regional subcommittees and a role for regional organizations as agents of UN action; regional distribution was to be a factor in the election of nonpermanent members of the Security Council. While regional substructures have not played a prominent role in the United Nations – five regional economic commissions being an important exception – regionalism has emerged in practice as a more significant feature than anticipated in the UN Charter, especially through the formation of caucuses that serve as settings for debate and consensus-building, mediating between the levels of individual states and the UN as a whole. The United Nations has also cooperated with external regional organizations, from the basic granting of observer status to joint exercises of military force (Schreurer 1995).

Between 1945 and 1991, however, the dominant regionalizing forces derived from Cold War competition, specifically, from Soviet and US efforts to create and integrate strategic geographies into their military, political and economic orbits. The USSR extended its control in Eastern Europe through military occupation, national communist parties, and the cultivation of highly selective linkages between its satellite countries, and formally organizing its regional dominance in the Warsaw Pact and Comecon; ideologically, constructing this region involved the Sovietization of earlier, pan-Slavic ideologies. Region-building by the United States was more global in scope, stretching from Western Europe to Latin America to East and Southeast Asia. It was also more pluralistic in character, involving the formation of multiple regional security pacts in Western Europe (North Atlantic Treaty Organization, NATO), Southeast Asia (South East Asia Treaty Organization, SEATO), and the Southern Pacific (Australia, New Zealand, United States Security Treaty). In each setting – in highly divergent ways – regional alliance structures extended US power globally, alongside military basing and overt and covert interventions in colonial and national politics. While US and Soviet globalisms were both anchored in regions, their ideologies transcended them, predicated on the exceptionalist status of the United States as first among "free world" equals and the Soviet Union's as first among socialist societies (Katzenstein 2005).

The forging of regions in geopolitical struggle is convincingly illustrated by the strange Cold War career of "Southeast Asia." As tracked by Donald Emmerson, the term was a comparative late arrival to scholarly, political and popular usage; while it was used sporadically and ambiguously prior to World War II, he argues, European colonial division shaped spatial and intellectual geographies in ways that erected barriers between colonies and fastened colonies to distant metropoles. Japan's destruction of these colonial states during World War II and Allied reconquest violently remapped these areas: "Southeast Asia" circulated officially as the designation of a theater of war (the South-East Asia Command or SEAC, created in 1943), and popularly on *National Geographic* maps. This process of strategic regionalization continued after the war, as the Americans caught up with the Europeans in their area studies. But where European scholars had approached "Southeast Asia" anthropologically, stressing "traditional" topics, the Americans emphasized the production of instrumental policy knowledge directed at a terrain presumed to be modern, organizing itself into nation-states, and an epicenter of Cold War military and ideological conflict and proxy war. Projects in regional organization reflected these geopolitical imperatives. Founded in 1954 in the neocolonial capital of Manila, SEATO defined the region in Cold War terms, limiting the treaty's ambit to areas threatened by perceived or actual Communist expansion. By the 1960s, local forces had taken the initiative in regional organization, but ASEAN (Association of Southeast Asian Nations), founded in 1967, still defined its boundaries in anti-Communist terms (Emmerson 1984).

As the terminological invention of "Southeast Asia" suggests, regions during the second half of the twentieth century were in important ways the by-products of new ways of organizing knowledge in the United States, at the intersection of the academy and state power. As sketched by Immanuel Wallerstein, beginning during World War II, American academics and officials observed that the breadth of US power now stretched geographically far beyond the scope of its expertise; this critical gap was one of "regional" or "area" knowledge. At mid-century, the social science disciplines were, for the most part, profoundly Eurocentric. The disciplinary outlier, anthropology, was primarily concerned with synchronic accounts, and "Oriental" studies within the humanities concentrated on premodern pasts; the two modes of scholarship which virtually monopolized research on what were increasingly called "developing areas" were, in other words, not very interested in these areas' contemporary development. A modern, global knowledge was deemed necessary if the United States was to successfully manage its postwar global "responsibilities," from anti-Communist containment to the negotiation of decolonization. Sponsorship of what would come to be known as "area studies" came from both private philanthropy (the Rockefeller, Carnegie and Ford Foundations) and the federal government. One key mechanism was Title VI of the 1958 National Defense Education Act, which funded faculty hiring, program-building and library collections under the area studies rubric. Within the academy, there have since been ongoing tensions between disciplinary and regional/areal modes of knowledge and over the policy instrumentality of "area studies" programs; the latter controversy took a decisive turn in the late 1960s, when scholars and activists politicized the crossings of area studies research and interventionist empire. For present purposes, what was particularly important about the advent of "area studies" was the way its framing of social inquiry through new spatial imaginaries led to the ontological grounding of region; given the scale of US cultural power and influence in the late twentieth century, these regional containers had global implications.[3]

The 1990s saw an increase in regional cooperation and organization in many parts of the world, a dynamic identified by some commentators as a "new regionalism" (Fawcett 1995; 2004; Guan 2005). This process derived in part from the fall of the Soviet Union and with it an unraveling of Cold War regionalisms. It was also driven by the formation of the European Union, the first experiment in supranational state-building and one that, through dynamics of interaction, emulation and competition, lent impetus to region-building elsewhere. Especially in North America and Southeast Asia, regionalist organization was driven by fears that European economic integration would close out foreign imports to the benefit of European producers. One response was the creation of counterregions like the North American Free Trade Agreement (NAFTA), competing commercial blocs achieved by lowering or abolishing barriers to trade.

European regional integration grew out of the tense, catastrophic conditions of World War II and the early Cold War, as elites in multiple states felt their way toward peace and survival. Early institutions reflected the hopes and preoccupations of double containment: the suppression of German warmaking, on the one hand, and the prevention of continental Soviet expansion, on the other. A desire to render another intra-European war impossible was manifest in the European Coal and Steel Community, which would prevent the national (and nationalist) control of critical warmaking resources. The goal of a joint defense against Soviet expansion was pursued through an (abortive) European Defence Community. The securing of human rights and the rule of law across national borders would be pursued by the Council of Europe. Economic recovery and the pooling of markets – especially crucial as decolonization destroyed systems of imperial trade preference – would be realized by the European Economic Community (EEC) which, when it was inaugurated in 1958, created a common market of 167 million people. These agencies received US encouragement. The Marshall Plan, for example, required European states to design joint recovery plans and work together within the Organization of European Economic Co-operation. In terms of strategic defense, the United States favored the integration of Europe along Atlanticist lines. When the European Defence Community collapsed, West German rearmament took place under NATO auspices and Western Europe emerged as the frontline US strategic regionalization.

As had been true of earlier region-building projects, there was nothing easy or fore-ordained about the making of a united Europe. Differences over the appropriate "depth" of integration emerged early, with Great Britain favoring a free trade area only, and France and Germany pushing for more intensive political and economic integration, for example. There were also struggles over the "internal" balance of power: under De Gaulle, France asserted its leadership over the continental bloc, pressing successfully for veto power over such key issues as agricultural policy, blocking British membership in the EEC twice, and alienating many other Europeans in the process. States brought particular and diverging interests to the European table, resulting in elaborate incentives and horse-trading compromises: underdeveloped Italy was encouraged by a European Investment Bank and the free movement of laborers, for example; the protectionist French accepted a common market in exchange for a leadership role in the development of atomic energy.

Despite these obstacles, European integration widened and deepened. Britain achieved EEC membership in 1973, and the 1980s saw a wave of southern enlargement, with Greece, Portugal and Spain joining as they emerged from authoritarian governments. Regionalism also thickened along several axes, with the formation of a customs union in 1968, a push toward direct democracy in the election of the European Parliament beginning in 1979, and the creation of a European Monetary System and the defining of a European Currency Unit in the late 1970s. Efforts at commercial integration culminated in the Single European Act of 1985–1986 which established a single European market by eliminating policy discrepancies between national economies. These region-making institutions did not simply connect otherwise integral nation-state components: rather, regionalization and the building of European nation-states were entangled processes, with the national units shored up and transformed by the institutional deepening of the regionalizing whole.

European regionalization intensified in the decades after the fall of the Berlin Wall and the collapse of the Soviet Union, events which also transformed it. The 1992 Maastricht Treaty became the founding charter of the European Union, providing for a common currency and a European Central Bank and enhancing the power of supranational European institutions. Maastricht was the result of compromises that left many unsatisfied: the British remained deeply skeptical, for example, and refused to join the common currency, and while the treaty was eventually ratified by all 12 member states, it passed by slim majorities in some instances. The biggest shift in European regionalism was, however, its eastern expansion, with 10 countries joining in 2004 and two more in 2007, many of them former Soviet satellites. The EU's population was now 493 million, of which 215 million lived in the original six signatories to the Rome Treaty (France, West Germany, Italy, Belgium, the Netherlands, and Luxembourg). As before, EU growth took place at the intersection of national and supranational interests: membership appealed to Eastern European states seeking access to rich markets and defense against outside powers (especially post-Soviet Russia), and to existing EU members eager for high growth rates, access to inexpensive labor forces and the stabilizing of Europe's edges.

In the first years of the twenty-first century, European integration faced numerous challenges. There were the ongoing difficulties of coordinating foreign policy, particularly when it came to engaging the United States. The consolidation of "European" modes of political identification remained shallow, with Europeans' disengagement – as measured in low levels of voting in European parliamentary elections – phasing into active hostility towards European regionalism. There was also a sharpening exclusionist politics: notions of "Europe" hardened around a xenophobia, crossed with class fears, directed against immigrant groups, many of them from Europe's former colonies and the Muslim world. It was ironic, perhaps, that a regional project born in the desolation of Nazi race war had resulted, a half-century later, in a Europe defined increasingly in terms of Christianity and "civilization" (Ludlow 2007; Christiansen 2001).

The formation of the European Union spurred regional organization in other parts of the world. This was primarily driven by economic competition: extra-European fears of being closed out of an economic Fortress Europe, and hopes of leveraging greater influence in multilateral institutions like the World Trade Organization. Asia-Pacific Economic Cooperation, founded in 1989, reduced tariffs and duties and coordinated economic policies between 34 countries. ASEAN, which dated back to the 1960s, expanded its membership in the 1980s and 1990s, pursuing stronger, joint negotiating positions with the larger economies of China, Japan and South Korea. MERCOSUR, inaugurated in 1991, abolished tariff barriers between South American states. NAFTA, from 1992, progressively lowered tariff barriers between the United States, Canada and Mexico. Each of these groupings faced internal divisions and controversies. ASEAN membership, for example, straddled neoliberal and socialist transition economies, dictatorships and democracies. NAFTA was blamed for facilitating North-to-South capital flight in pursuit of lower-wage labor forces and weaker environmental regulations; weak "side agreements" on labor standards did little to assuage these concerns. Viewed in broad, comparative terms, the EU's regionalist project was a trigger to regionalism elsewhere, but it was exceptional in its "thick" integration of economic, political and social levels. By contrast, the world's other region-building efforts secured the mobility of capital and goods, while continuing to bound human mobility and sociopolitical membership: what might be called corporate regionalisms, as contrasted with more sociopolitical regionalisms.

This chapter has attempted, somewhat paradoxically, to both account for region in global history and to deconstruct "region" itself as a category. While I have expressed skepticism about the assertion of region as an ontological reality, I have also attempted to suggest some ways that the study of region-making as a process with both material and ideological dimensions, unfolding both "beneath" and "above" the level of states, nonetheless presents possibilities to historians. While (not unlike nation-states) regions are to be approached with suspicion as analytical frames – why should scholars let past or present cartographers and their agendas gerrymander their maps of the world? – viewed as peculiar artifacts in larger histories of spatiality and territoriality, with complex roots, manifestations and effects, the ambiguity of which encourages a self-consciousness about spatial categorization, regions may, in fact, play a critical role in the writing of richer global histories.

Notes

1 Here I am thinking of the modern territorializing projects described by Maier (2006).
2 On the South from a diplomatic-historical perspective through the era of the Vietnam War, see Fry (2002).
3 On the emergence of area studies in the US academy, see Wallerstein (1998).

References

Cavasin, Nathalie. 2005. Region. In R.W. McColl, ed., *Encyclopedia of World Geography*, pp. 765–766. New York: Facts on File.

Christiansen, Thomas. 2001. European and regional integration. In John Baylis and Steve Smith, eds, *The Globalization of World Politics*, pp. 494–518. 2nd edn. New York: Oxford University Press.

Emmerson, Donald K. 1984. "Southeast Asia": What's in a name? *Journal of Southeast Asian Studies* 15 (1): 1–21.

Fawcett, Louise. 1995. Regionalism in historical perspective. In Louise Fawcett and Andrew Hurrell, eds, *Regionalism in World Politics: Regional Organization and International Order*, pp. 9–36. Oxford: Oxford University Press.

Fawcett, Louise. 2004. Exploring regional domains: A comparative history of regionalism. *International Affairs* 80 (3): 429–446.

Fledelius, Karsten. 1997. What is a region? What is regionalism?" *Regional Contact* 10: 15–18.

Fry, Joseph A. 2002. *Dixie Looks Abroad: The South and US Foreign Relations, 1783–1973*. Baton Rouge: Louisiana State University Press.

Grigg, David. 1967. Regions, models and classes. In Richard J. Chorley and Peter Haggett, eds, *Models in Geography*, pp. 461–507. London: Methuen.

Guan, Benny Teh Cheng. 2005. Regionalism. In R. W. McColl, ed., *Encyclopedia of World Geography*, pp. 766–769. New York: Facts on File.

Katzenstein, Peter. 2005. *A World of Regions: Asia and Europe in the American Imperium*. Ithaca, NY: Cornell University Press.

Leonard, Thomas, ed. 2006. *Encyclopedia of the Developing World*. New York: Routledge.

Lewis, Martin W., and Kären E. Wigen. 1997. *The Myth of Continents: A Critique of Metageography*. Berkeley: University of California Press.

Ludlow, Piers. 2007. Making the new Europe: European integration since 1950. In Gordon Martel, ed., *A Companion to International History 1900–2001*, pp. 327–339. Oxford: Blackwell.

Maier, Charles. 2006. Transformations of territoriality, 1600–2000. In Gunilla Budde, Sebastian Conrad, and Oliver Janz, eds, *Transnationale Geschichte. Themen, Tendenzen und Theorien*, pp. 32–55. Göttingen: Vandenhoeck & Ruprecht.

Sanchez, George. 1993. *Becoming Mexican American: Ethnicity, Culture and Identity in Chicano Los Angeles, 1900–1945*. New York: Oxford University Press.

Schreurer, Christoph. 1995. Regionalism v. universalism. *European Journal of International Law* 6 (1): 477–499.

Snyder, Louis. 1984. *Macro-Nationalisms: A History of the Pan-Movements*. Westport, CT: Greenwood.

Wallerstein, Immanuel. 1998. The unintended consequences of Cold War area studies. In Noam Chomsky *et al.*, eds, *The Cold War and the University: Toward an Intellectual History of the Postwar Years*, pp. 195–231. New York: New Press.

Warf, Barney. 2009. From surface to networks. In Barney Warf and Santa Arias, eds, *The Spatial Turn: Interdisciplinary Perspectives*, pp. 59–76. London: Routledge.

CHAPTER FOURTEEN

Scales of a Local
The Place of Locality in a Globalizing World

ANNE GERRITSEN

The business of the local historian is to re-enact in his own mind, and to portray for his readers, the Origin, Growth, Decline, and Fall of a local community. (Finberg 1952)

The careful practice of local history and the multiplication of monographs on specific regions may ... serve to destroy many of the general conceptions that once seemed so strong. (Goubert 1971)

As these two quotations show, there have long been divergent views of what local history should be. For H.P.R. Finberg, as he explained in his 1952 inaugural lecture for the University of Leicester, each local community was a "distinct and separate entity" that could and should be studied as a "cultural whole" (Samuel 1976: 197). The ultimate aim of local history for P. Goubert, on the other hand, was to reformulate "general conceptions" about the history of the nation. According to Goubert, local historians should always see themselves as making a difference to the writing of larger and ultimately more important units than the local (Goubert 1971). By the 1970s, critics of the practice of local history in England and elsewhere had begun to see the work in the field of local history as rather too narrative, "repetitive and inert," and based on documents that "vary remarkably little from place to place, and are heavily biased towards local government" (Samuel 1976). Local history was seen as merely chronicling the rise and fall of single, isolated communities, with little awareness of the dense connections between communities that scholars not long afterwards began to highlight. Goubert's suggestion that a multiplicity of local perspectives could challenge "general conceptions" previously considered unassailable foreshadowed critiques of the grand narrative that became popular in the 1980s.

Without claiming that communities could be studied in isolation, or that new grand narratives should be built on the basis of numerous single local studies, the local history of the last two decades has moved in new and interesting directions. Having received stimulating impulses from fields such as geography and sociology, local historians have

A Companion to World History, First Edition. Edited by Douglas Northrop.
© 2012 Blackwell Publishing Ltd. Published 2012 by Blackwell Publishing Ltd.

asked how communities came into being and developed through space and time, and how local communities looked from different perspectives of power and status (Massey 1995; Hindle 2000; 2008; Kurtz 2002). Robert Hymes, to take an example from the China field, studied a single prefecture in Song (960–1279) and Yuan (1279–1368) dynasty China to explore the shifts in elite allegiance away from the empire-wide level to the local level that occurred during this time (1986; 2002). In my own work on local history in early modern China, I have asked how various individuals positioned themselves as members of different networks in the southern Chinese prefecture of Ji'an (Ji'an Fu on Map 14.1) and in what ways these individuals sought to shape the local communities to which they imagined they belonged (Gerritsen 2007). But local history has become more sophisticated not only in its understanding of the units it studies, but in its approach to the units that surround it. Scholars working in the microhistorical tradition, radically reducing the scale of their research focus to a single individual or a single legal case, have shown how precisely the absence of representativeness could be instructive about their historical and political contexts. The ways in which a locality is unusual and deviates from the norm can tell us a great deal about that "normality," as we see in the case of Carlo Ginzburg's study of the miller Menocchio (1980). The local, however ordinary or unusual, can always tell us something about the wider context, especially as many local historians now work on the understanding that "places ... are always constructed out of articulations of social relations ... which are not only internal to that locale but which link them to elsewhere" (Massey 1995: 183). This idea becomes especially interesting as a topic for exploration when that "else-where" is conceived of as a world that is becoming more connected and integrated, as a "globalizing" world. This chapter is concerned specifically with the place of the local in such a globalizing world.

A "Globalizing" World?

Two questions present themselves immediately. What is a "globalizing" world, and when did the process implied by the word "globalizing" begin? Different meanings of the term have led to divergent answers to these questions, as several other chapters in this volume demonstrate. For Andre Gunder Frank and Barry Gills (1993), globalization refers to a world that is connected. They argue that the "world system" was created several millennia ago by competition over power and by cycles of economic rise and decline. Looking at the example of ceramics, one of the earliest traded goods to create global connections, then that exchange indeed goes back several millennia. Archaeological explorations have found evidence of ceramics made in China in sites in Southeast Asia, the Persian Gulf, and along the African Coast that date back to the Han dynasty (206 BCE–220 CE) (Finlay 2010). But a focus on ceramics also makes clear that from around 1300 CE, the intensity of that exchange increased significantly. Not only were larger quantities of Chinese ceramics shipped to Korea and Japan, Thailand and Cambodia by this time, merchants from Inner Asia and the Middle East were traveling to China via land and sea routes in far greater numbers than before. As Scott Levi discusses in his chapter, during the thirteenth and fourteenth centuries, the Mongol Empire created a more stable environment for trade and interaction across the Eurasian landmass than ever before. It was Muslim traders who brought Persian cobalt to the potters at Jingdezhen, and who transported large dishes with blue-and-white decorations back to consumers in Inner Asia and the Middle East. Finlay has suggested that the spread of porcelain across Eurasia during this period can serve as evidence for the first "sustained cultural encounter on a worldwide scale, perhaps even for indications of genuinely global culture" (1998: 143). Ceramics, and material culture more generally, were exchanged in large quantities and on a regular basis throughout Eurasia from around 1300. If we take material culture seriously as a medium for the global exchange of goods, knowledge and ideas, then we could see 1300 as the beginning of a globalizing world, an argument supported by, among others, Janet Abu-Lughod (1989), who locates the first world-system between 1250 and 1350.

Perhaps the most persuasive arguments for the beginnings of a globalizing world, however, have been made by those who see it emerging later, around 1500. One of the most vociferous proponents of this argument has been Immanuel Wallerstein (1974–1989; 2004), who argued that the growth of a capitalist mode of production during this time, and the accumulation of wealth in the hands of a relatively small group of European merchants, saw the emergence of a world-system. (See Chase-Dunn and Hall, this volume.) He acknowledged that there had been various world systems in place before 1500, but this world-system that operated as an integrated capitalist unit, with Europe at the center and Asia and the Americas in its periphery, only then came into being. Of course Asia had been present in European consciousness for much longer, for example through the luxury commodities that were transported each year from Asia along the Silk Routes to Europe via the Venetian merchants who met caravans in the Levant, and through the colorful descriptions in the ever popular accounts of the thirteenth-century traveler Marco Polo, but the Americas remained largely unknown to Europeans until sixteenth-century explorers followed Christopher Columbus (1451–1506) across the Atlantic Ocean. As Dennis Flynn and Arturo Giraldez have shown (2008), it was not until the Spanish extended their empire in the Americas across the Pacific Ocean by establishing a base in Manila in the Philippines in 1576 that the exchange of commodities and currency had a reach that literally circumnavigated the globe.

Beyond the intensification of trade and exchange leading to the emergence of capitalism around this time, and the growth of a European consciousness that spanned the entire globe, a number of other developments also converged around 1500. The Dutch, and later the English, the French and the Scandinavians, established trading companies with bases in Asia, from where they began to participate in the trade networks between Japan, China, Southeast Asia, and the Indian Ocean. Naval technology and military force, specifically guns, underpinned the expansion of these overseas empires and changed the nature of these extant trade networks fundamentally. (See Morillo, this volume.) Once the European companies had found ways to participate in this trade, thereby bringing Europe into global networks of trade, not only commodities but humans, crops and diseases began to be transported across vast distances and into new environments. (See Simmons, this volume.) Crops like the potato, corn, the tomato and the chili pepper, plants native to the Americas, thoroughly transformed both the agricultural practices and staple diets of Africans, Europeans and Asians. Along with humans and crops came germs and infectious diseases that killed vast numbers of "virgin" populations without resistance. Taking all these factors into consideration, one could argue that the world indeed became a globalizing world around 1500 (Stearns 2010).

Of course, many scholars have argued that the kinds of developments discussed above still do not amount to "globalization." (See Bright and Geyer, this volume.) For them, globalization refers to the connectedness of economic and financial institutions on the macro-level, a development they do not see in evidence before the so-called long nineteenth century (O'Rourke and Williamson 2002). They argue that from the nineteenth century, with the Industrial Revolution and the growth of imperialism, institutions like banks and corporations began to have influence far beyond the boundaries of the nation-state. Systems of transportation and communication, especially with the development of the steamship and telegraph, integrated the world and connected its inhabitants in ways that had not been possible before. The strength of the political and economic ties after the nineteenth century, they would argue, means that there are no longer any truly independent institutions or structures; local economies can no longer be separated from the larger units they form part of, and states do not have the political power to counteract the influence of the global market. Moreover, they note a cultural homogenization in the desire for consumer goods, brands, and images distributed by means of new media throughout the world. Globalization, thus, is often used to refer to recent developments that created the world as we know it today, with its global price convergences for commodities, instant communication technologies, worldwide migration patterns, and homogenized cultural icons (Osterhammel and Petersson 2005).

Conceptualizing the Local and the Global

The problem with these visions of the globalizing world is not just that there is a tendency to chart these developments from a Western perspective, and hence to see globalization emerge precisely at the time that Europe took center stage in terms of global economic development. This worldwide vision of development also leaves very little scope for exploring what happened at the local level. How did this global development and increasing connectedness look from a local perspective? By bringing in local perspectives from different parts of the world, this Eurocentric bias can, conceivably, also be redressed, so that we do not see globalization as merely a European or Western project.

A number of scholars of globalization have concerned themselves with the place of the local in larger processes of globalization. Ever since the late 1970s, when Jean-François Lyotard questioned the value of metanarratives and advocated the return to smaller, "localized" narratives (Lyotard 1984), social theorists have been interested in the diversity and multiplicity provided by the local perspective. For Lyotard, smaller, local narratives could provide a valuable counter to the universalizing tendency of larger narratives, although of course Lyotard was not concerned with the local *per se*, but with the local as the contingent, heterogeneous, fragmented and contextual (Rojek and Turner 1998).

When Anthony Giddens wrote his oft-quoted statement that "local transformation is as much part of globalization as the lateral extension of social connections across time and space" (1990: 64), he brought local transformation to the foreground of the study of globalization. What happens locally is determined not by local conditions but by global developments. Again, Giddens's focus is on understanding the forces of modernity and their impact on society and individuals, not the meaning of single localities within the wider context of globalization and modernity. Stuart Hall perhaps moves a step in that direction when he writes that "globalization might lead to a *strengthening* of local identities, or to the production of *new identities*" (1992: 308), although his emphasis is on identity, not locality. Hall sees the "return to the local" as a "response to globalization" (1991: 33); the local is what people take recourse to when they no longer understand the global.

The interconnectedness of the terms "global" and "local" seems thus to be beyond doubt, even if its conceptualization remains elusive. (See Northrop, last chapter in this volume.) The neologism "glocalization," initially brought into academic usage by the sociologist Roland Robertson in the early 1990s, suggests the existence of processes that are at once global and local. Robertson uses the term to critique the idea that globalization is "the triumph of culturally homogenizing forces" that "overrides the locality," and suggests that "what is often referred to as the local is essentially included within the global" (1995: 25–26, 35). Robertson understands globalization as the spatial process of compressing the world, whereby localities become more closely linked. In that very process of becoming linked, Robertson argues, they are also "invented" and "imagined" (1995: 35). In other words, the "production of locality" occurs precisely during this compression of time and space (Appadurai 1996: 178–199). Without taking recourse to the term glocalization, the anthropologist Arjun Appadurai arrives at a similar notion in *Modernity at Large*, where he argues vociferously against the idea that globalization is "the story of cultural homogenization" (1996: 11), seeing it instead as a "deeply historical, uneven, and even *localizing* process." As Appadurai argues, societies appropriate modernity in different ways, and thus localities merit study in terms of their "specific geographies, histories, and languages," but the histories through which localities emerge are "eventually subject to the dynamics of the global" (1996: 17–18). Locality, for Appadurai, is a "structure of feeling" rather than an existing social form, for which he uses the term "neighborhood." The latter has spatial and temporal dimensions, while the former is phenomenological, but both are under threat in Appadurai's vision: the neighborhood by being drawn increasingly into the dominant context of the nation-state, and locality by the growth of transnational movements and diaspora (1996: 188–189). More recently, sociologists like Mark Herkenrath have argued for more nuanced understandings of globalization by acknowledging the coexistence of divergence, convergence, and its hybrid form of glocalization (Herkenrath *et al.* 2005). Herkenrath's work seeks to recognize not only the cultural dimensions of globalization, but the diverse perceptions of and responses to globalization that exist at the local level (Herkenrath 2007).

Historicizing the Local and the Global

The brief discussion above sketches the contours of debates that involved numerous critical thinkers, and took place over more than 20 years across several disciplines. Yet this theorizing about the place of small-scale units, the locality, in the globalizing world rarely seems to have involved historians, or rather, historians seem to have played only tangential roles as observers and occasional consumers. One attempt to do more comes in a volume edited by Anthony Hopkins, entitled *Global History: Interactions between the Universal and the Local* (2006). For Hopkins, the historian has an almost moral duty to historicize globalization. Historians must provide the historical consciousness to support our global citizenship; historians have the task of writing metanarratives of universal significance by studying the ways in which individuals and local communities came to be drawn into larger units such as the region, the nation, the empire, and the global. The book is the result of Hopkins's exhortations of his colleagues to engage in this project. Each of the studies represents an exploration of the ways in which the local, in this case the particular topic studied by the author, is connected to the global. As Patrick O'Brien, a reviewer of this volume, writes, the "Austin model" of connecting the local to the universal is perhaps one of the most promising ways for encouraging historians "to engage seriously with globalisation" (2008). Without necessarily subscribing to the all

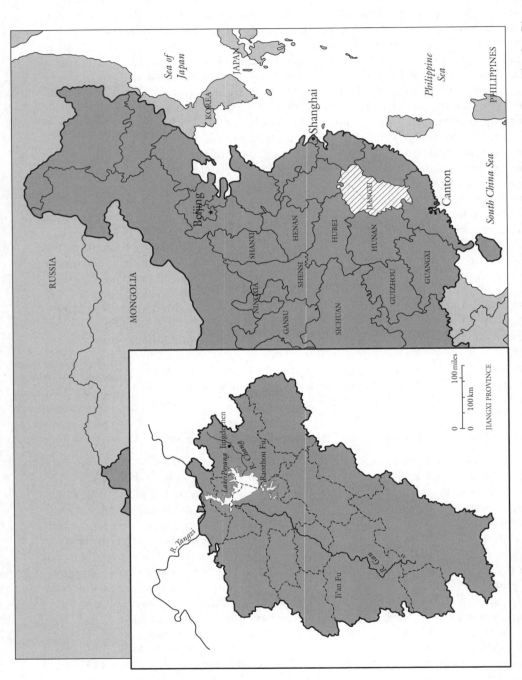

Map 14.1 Jiangxi province in late imperial China, showing its main prefectures and the wider regions to which it reached out. The Gan River forms a key transportation artery connecting locations in northern China via Lake Poyang to the south. One principal locality, Ji'an, lies on the Gan; the other, Jingdezhen, sits on the Chang, a shorter tributary of Lake Poyang to the north.

Source: Map of Jiangxi province based on China Historical Geographic Information System database, Version 3.0 (April 2005).

but missionary zeal of Hopkins and O'Brien to serve as the historical consciousness of global citizens, one can see that the studies included in Hopkins's *Global History* provide a way of conceptualizing the practice of global history. Without aiming to write the history of the global in its entirety, historians can make a contribution to the larger project by connecting the particular "local" they know about to larger analytical units. If historians approach their own area of expertise as having at least the potential of being connected to patterns of development and change that lie beyond their imagined boundaries, then even without making any claims for universality, their work will have a wider relevance. Historians of a particular locality have the linguistic skills and specialized knowledge that allow them to access the local sources, so the field of world history can only make substantial progress by drawing on their combined strengths, as Donald Wright (1997) shows in his study of the ways in which the micro-level developments in the Mandinka kingdom of Niumi in The Gambia in West Africa are shaped by but also shape the development of a global economy in the Wallersteinian sense. The integration of local and global in historical analysis, however, can do more than merely add an endless amount of local variation to global narratives. The study of locality in history can in fact be used to question the trajectory of the often uncritically assumed metanarrative of ever increasing connections and integrations. It can highlight the diversity and the heterogeneity that are as much part of the processes of becoming more globalized as the tendency to become more homogeneous.

Local Case Studies: Ji'an and Jingdezhen

To see how the local can be connected to the global in historical study, and how the local can reveal the particularities of global trajectories, it seems appropriate to put the idea into practice, by focusing on two case studies. The two places I will discuss briefly are localities of very different types. Both are located in the land-locked province of Jiangxi, in southeast China (see Map 14.1). Both are situated on important rivers: Ji'an on the Gan, which forms an important north–south artery, and Jingdezhen on the Chang, a much shorter river running from northeast to southwest in the north of the province, both ultimately flowing into Lake Poyang. This lake forms the northern boundary of the province and provides access to the Yangzi, southern China's most important river system connecting Tibet's mountainous plateau in the far west of China to Shanghai on the east coast. These extensive river-based transportation networks made it possible for inland towns like Ji'an and Jingdezhen to be connected to the high culture of scholars and officials in the capital as well as to the ever growing hub of trade with the wider world in Canton. The administrative structure of the Chinese empire, during the Ming (1368–1644) and Qing (1644–1911) dynasties was based on a strict hierarchy of places, with the county as the smallest administrative unit. Several counties together formed a prefecture, and several prefectures a province. Each unit was led by a group of centrally qualified and appointed administrators, who were never given posts in their home units so as to avoid favoritism and corruption. County magistrates, prefects and provincial governors therefore relied heavily on local elites to help with the day-to-day running of their areas.

Ji'an was both a county and the seat of the prefect, and thus administratively speaking the center of this entire region in the southwest of Jiangxi province. Its administrative importance, its proximity to fertile rice-growing hills and river-based transportation, and its rich heritage of sites of religious and philosophical significance all contributed to

Ji'an's attraction. From around the tenth century until at least the sixteenth century, in political, economic and sociocultural terms Ji'an was a thriving locality. More important perhaps than its material wealth was its intellectual wealth. It had some of the highest and most consistent success rates in the civil service examinations, and it had several academies known throughout the empire for their famous teachers and powerful lineages of students. Scholars and statesmen traded on their associations with Ji'an, however brief and however distant those associations might have been. They built cultural institutions such as schools, academies, and temple complexes that could accommodate large numbers of visiting scholars, monks and tourists, each leaving their records for posterity and in turn attracting new visitors. For a time, Ji'an even produced rather fine ceramics. These were mixed wares in a variety of colors and glazes, from small black and brown tea bowls sought after in Japan, to large vases decorated with bright paper-cut patterns. There is little evidence of ceramic production during the Ming dynasty, so it would seem that by the late thirteenth century, the ceramics production of Ji'an had already declined. Towards the mid-sixteenth century, Ji'an prefecture had started to lose out to another region, the lower Yangzi delta region, where economic development had surged ahead, making that the wealthiest, most urbanized, and most productive region of late-imperial China. A lingering reputation and the material traces of its erstwhile cultural splendor still remain in Ji'an to this day.

Throughout the centuries before its decline, Ji'an's identity as a locality was not constant. It is fruitful to ask how and where this identity was produced, how it changed over time, and how the locality was seen to fit into empire-wide and world-historical narratives. We are of course limited by the extant textual record in our explorations of local identity, but the most fruitful to date have been the repositories of local documents known as local gazetteers, the collections of writings created by the scholarly elites and administrators resident in the area, and the texts carved in stone and situated throughout the region at sites of cultural significance such as temples, shrines and academies. It is in such writings, I have argued elsewhere, that the identity of the locality and a sense of belonging were generated (Gerritsen 2007). Over time, such writings show, members of the elites found different ways of creating a sense of their locality, from telling the stories of local temples and shrines to compiling genealogies and emphasizing the importance of community institutions. The context within which the locality was produced also changed over time, as did the scale of the locality. In times of great wealth and cultural flourishing in the region, elite authors were proud to emphasize the individual unit of the county, stressing its separate identity, perhaps to an audience that was largely regional. When a new regime was established at the start of the Ming dynasty, on the other hand, the prefecture became the more important unit, and political leaders stressed its importance to an audience based at the central court. At no stage, however, were these individual counties or the prefecture as a whole situated in a context beyond the empire. In that sense, this locality, with its emphasis on administration and elite culture, seemed to remain entirely local in its outlook.

Jingdezhen, in contrast to Ji'an, was a manufacturing town that did not form part of the centrally administered hierarchy, and thus also did not have a resident administrator. Without an administrative center, there was little incentive for members of the local gentry to reside in the town. The sites of the area such as temples and academies rarely became the subject of the literary writings that placed such sites on the cultural map, and this failed to attract outside visitors. Culturally speaking, thus, Jingdezhen was very isolated, especially compared to Ji'an. The nearest county town and residence of a magistrate was Fuliang, about 10 kilometers upriver, and the nearest prefectural seat was Raozhou, more than 50 kilometers downriver. Although places like Jingdezhen were located outside of the administrative structure, and thus less visible in the official documentation generated by the administrative towns, they were important in terms of the manufacturing and trade, and thus crucial in the economic development of the empire (Von Glahn 2003). The imperial government also recognized the imperial and cultural significance of such places, and in particular of Jingdezhen, because during the Ming and Qing dynasties, it was responsible for the vast majority of the porcelain produced for the imperial court, for use throughout the empire, and for export. In order to ensure that the best porcelain continued to be produced here to the specifications of the emperor and within the financial regulations of the empire, representatives of the emperor were stationed in Jingdezhen as overseers. These overseers served as the eyes and ears of the emperor in the locality, and formed a crucial link between the porcelain production center and the imperial court. The overseer was also responsible for the communication of the emperor's wishes to the local producers. Important technological innovations were transmitted from the imperial court to Jingdezhen. The use of colored enamels on porcelain, for example, was unknown in China until missionaries and other court visitors brought samples from Europe, which inspired the emperor to demand the same from his court manufacturers based in Jingdezhen.

The production of porcelain for personal and ritual use by the emperor and his imperial household was clearly important, but it coexisted in Jingdezhen with a very active production of porcelain for the export market. In this sense, Jingdezhen manufactured a global product. White porcelains with blue decorations, "blue-and whites" for short, were produced in Jingdezhen and exported throughout the world. From the fourteenth-century Mongol capital in Karakorum to the court of Safavid Persia, from Ottoman Turkey to the Southeast Asian kingdoms, from royal and noble houses of Europe to the first settlements in the Americas, and along the Indian Ocean coasts, we find material traces of Jingdezhen production.

These two locations in Jiangxi province then, at first glance seem very different localities. (See Adas, this volume.) Ji'an produced a culture of knowledge and had an empire-wide reputation that rarely reached beyond the boundaries of the Chinese cultural realm. Jingdezhen produced porcelain and had a reputation that stretched through time and crossed many spatial and cultural boundaries. So how do these two localities fit into the wider discussion of global and local? Is it fruitful to think of places like Ji'an and Jingdezhen as either local or global, or are they situated somewhere along a local–global spectrum, where every place has varying degrees of both local and global elements? We need to explore the meaning of the term local in historical context in greater depth, to see how and where the local is produced, and how the local is connected to the global.

In Ji'an the production of locality was to some extent an elite project. Members of the Ji'an elite created a sense of the locality by writing about its institutions. Their descriptions of buildings and sacred sites, the histories they create for these sites in their narratives, and their accounts of their own roles within those histories are all part of the production of a sense of local identity. It is through these writings that they create and transmit an identity both for themselves as figures of local importance and for the area as significantly different from other locations. Interestingly, the involvement of the members of the Ji'an elite in such processes was strongest during times when these Ji'an men were actually located elsewhere. During the time when more men passed the civil service examinations than ever before, when more Ji'an men were located at the imperial capital and served in political positions with an empire-wide scope, their interest in the generation of such local identities increased (Dardess 1996). Their writings about the locality, however, were usually prefaced by a clear statement of their physical location at the capital. Their contribution to the production of local identity for Ji'an was predicated on the status they derived from being located at the imperial capital. At other times, when men from Ji'an were less likely to attain high status in the civil administration and drew their status instead from more local sources of prestige, the production of local identities seemed to be intended for a more local or regional audience. So even if the empire-wide by no means equates to the global, the local clearly exists in ever larger circles of context, and both the boundary of the local and the extent of the connections with the wider contextual circles that surround it change, depending on historical circumstances.

Where and how is the local identity of Jingdezhen produced? As Jingdezhen largely lacked a resident literary elite population, the rich textual sources available for Ji'an simply do not exist for Jingdezhen. Of course Jingdezhen produces objects, so arguably the bowls, cups, dishes and vases manufactured locally carry a kind of local identity. But the point about the popularity of Jingdezhen's wares is that they could so easily convey the tastes and demands of consumers elsewhere. Precisely because a consumer in the imperial Chinese court could order the highest-quality vase, or in fifteenth-century Samarkand could order a vast dish to serve large pieces of mutton, or in sixteenth-century Portugal could order a dish with his crest emblazoned under the glaze, or in seventeenth-century Holland could order a gin bottle or a butter dish, or in eighteenth-century Mexico could order a chocolatiere, Jingdezhen's factories were so in demand. Jingdezhen's wares sold globally because the producers could respond to consumer demand and make items that were completely alien to local taste and meaningless in local sensibility. Interestingly, another element of the appeal of all the wares I just mentioned is that they would have been identified as "oriental" or Asian, and perhaps even as Chinese, by all these different consumers. As objects they could fulfill both the specific requirements of different global consumers and the expectations of the exotic. They were inscribed with just enough "Chineseness" to make them attractive and distinctive without losing their usefulness and their fashionability. What they did not have, one might conclude, is a local, as in a Jingdezhen, identity. By being locally produced to the standards of global consumers the objects connected the local directly to the empire-wide and to the global context.

Another way in which one could argue that the local is produced in Jingdezhen is through the production of complex knowledge. Each object manufactured in Jingdezhen was the product of an extensive set of combined technologies. Without knowledge of the attributes of minerals and the potential of heat and water, the simple ingredients of stone, clay and cobalt ore could never have been transformed into porcelain. Much of that knowledge was contained within the minds and bodies of the workers in Jingdezhen: the many cogs in the connected processes that yielded porcelain. (See Burton, this volume.) But that this locally contained knowledge was extremely valuable was also identified very early on. The textual record of this accumulated knowledge goes back to the *Taoji* of the thirteenth century, and includes the extensive materials in the local gazetteer of the fifteenth century, the *Taoshuo* of the eighteenth century, and the nineteenth-century visual materials that chronicle the production processes of Jingdezhen. They also include extensive written documentation produced by foreign observers such as Johan Nieuhof and Olfert Dapper,

Daniel le Comte and Père d'Entrecolles. Ultimately, it was the combination of European knowledge about Chinese production processes and European inventiveness that gave initially the Germans, but soon all Europeans, the ability to produce porcelain, breaking the monopoly the Chinese had had over this knowledge for many centuries. Clearly, then, the written materials that document and transmit this local knowledge are, like the commodities themselves, produced for consumers located elsewhere, ranging from the emperor himself and his administrators sent to Jingdezhen to ensure protocols were followed and levies were paid, to foreign competitors seeking to outdo the Chinese manufacturers. Knowledge, then, also connects the local directly to the empire-wide and the global.

Both the objects themselves and the knowledge in circulation about the objects and their modes of manufacture are produced locally, for consumption beyond the boundaries of the locality. In that way, the local, which here takes shape in the material culture, that is, in the cultural complex that includes both the material objects and the technical know-how through which they are created, also produces the global. Arguably, then, we see here evidence of how the local produces the global and the global produces the local much as Robertson had described these processes in a very different spatial and temporal context. The local and the global are part of a set of scales, and neither is meaningful independently without attention to their places within these scales. The smaller the scale, the more visible the detail, but these local particularities do not seem to change the essence of even the largest scale, and could be seen merely to illustrate a wider story of ever increasing connectivity and convergence.

Ultimately, however, the picture that emerges from this approach is unsatisfactory. The local can do more than merely serve the narrative of homogeneity and convergence that is seen as part and parcel of the increase in globalization that may have started around 1400 or 1500. At the scale of the local we can also see the divergent, the heterogeneous, the fragmented, and the contingent. It is important not to let the powerful material traces of global connections hide local distinctiveness from view. We need to explore varied local sources to get at the aspects of locality that are not immediately connected to the global. The so-called *shufu* wares, a type of porcelain made in Jingdezhen during the fourteenth century, provide a useful example. *Shufu* wares, porcelains with matte white glazes, are generally assumed to have been made under orders of the imperial court. That assumption is based on the fact that many of these porcelains have been stamped on the inside with the characters "shu" and "fu," which refer to the Shumiyuan, the paramount central government agency in charge of all military affairs. These inscribed porcelains were presumably manufactured in Jingdezhen on the instruction of the highest echelons of the Yuan central government, and used within the imperial palace for ritual purposes. It was during this period that Central Asian merchants began to bring the cobalt ore from Persia to Jingdezhen to create blue decorations on white porcelains. The matte white of the *shufu* wares formed the perfect base for the blue decorations, and as soon as blue-and-whites became popular, *shufu* wares disappeared. They form, thus, a crucial transition between the simple monochrome tastes of the Song dynasty and the bright blue-and-white designs of the Ming and Qing dynasties. The first Mongol emperor to order blue-and-white ceramics from Jingdezhen was Togh Temur, who ruled over the Chinese realm from 1330 to 1333. These porcelains produced in Jingdezhen, both the *shufu* wares and the very early blue-and-whites, were arguably global products, circulating as they did in the Mongol empire that stretched from the eastern seaboard of China across Central Asia to the extremities of Europe. Imperial gifts of porcelain, together with the ubiquitous silk that formed such an important commodity in the steppe system of exchange, found their way throughout the Mongol empire.

While their consumption was to this extent global, their production was local. It was the local potters who had access to the resources (the stone and clay mixed to form the bodies, the limestone burnt with fern leaves for the glazes) and held the technological knowledge required to build kilns and regulate the temperatures and oxygen levels inside the kilns, and the local potters who knew about global markets to cater to them. Without local production, there could be no global consumption; local and global are inextricably connected. But local production does not merely serve global consumption, it also challenges and resists it. The emperors of the Yuan court who required Jingdezhen potters to make wares identified with imperial inscriptions and iconography such as the five-clawed dragon insisted these were produced for their exclusive use. Wares identified with imperial insignia but not of high enough quality to be selected for imperial use had to be destroyed and buried in Jingdezhen, so as to ensure they would not enter commercial circulation. Local archaeologists have found large quantities of purposefully broken pieces with five-clawed dragon decorations in Jingdezhen. *Shufu* wares, however, also associated with the imperial court, have been found throughout Southeast Asia and in Japan. Clearly, these were exported despite the imperial restrictions. As always, written legislation that prohibits the commercial circulation of imperial wares tells us very little about local practice, beyond the possibility of it being flouted. Local potters may or may not have acted in direct conflict with the regulations, but clearly local commercial interests that would not wish to lose the heavy investment required to fire a full kiln are part of the story. At the very least, the story of local production for global consumption should be complicated by the inclusion of local self-interest and alternative networks of circulation. Local and global have connected as well as individual stories to tell.

In conclusion, let me return to the question of the place of the locality in a globalizing world. On the one hand, as historians, we should follow the lead of sociologists and geographers and consider the scales of a globalizing world and think about how the local and the global are connected. There can be little doubt that at least from around 1400, the local became more integrated within the wider scale of the global, and thus, the local can tell important stories about the global. Objects like the blue-and-white ceramics manufactured in Jingdezhen are part of the story of global convergence; in very different locations all over the globe, the distinctive characteristics of these wares stood out and very few places in the world could completely resist the appeal of Chinese porcelains. But we also need to think about the localities that produced such global commodities, in terms of the technicalities of catering for global tastes in a land-locked early modern town, and the local perception of a global market. Local history can point us to the ways in which local particularities challenge the homogeneity of global narratives and where local practices point to divergence from the path to ever increasing connectedness. The place of the local is to remind us of the local diversity that flourished both because and in spite of the connections that shaped the early modern world. By reducing the scales of narration, we see not only more variation but, importantly, more deviation from the norms suggested by the macrohistorical perspective. In that sense, the opening quotes of Finberg and Goubert still have validity for us today. Even though Finberg's "Origin, Growth, Decline, and Fall of a local community" are perhaps not enough for us on their own terms, they do have a contribution to make in the context of an ever globalizing world, and may serve Goubert's challenge to "general conceptions" of globalization.

References

Abu-Lughod, Janet. 1989. *Before European Hegemony: The World-System, AD 1250–1350*. Oxford: Oxford University Press.

Appadurai, Arjun. 1996. *Modernity at Large: Cultural Dimensions of Globalization*. Minneapolis: University of Minnesota Press.

Dardess, John W. 1996. *A Ming Society: T'ai-ho County, Kiangsi, Fourteenth to Seventeenth Centuries*. Berkeley: University of California Press.

Finberg, H.P.R. 1952. The local historian and his theme. Introductory lecture delivered at the University College of Leicester, Nov. 6.

Finlay, Robert, 1998. The pilgrim art: The culture of porcelain in world history. *Journal of World History* 9 (2): 141–187.

Finlay, Robert. 2010. *The Pilgrim Art: Cultures of Porcelain in World History*. Berkeley: University of California Press.

Flynn, Dennis O., and Arturo Giraldez. 2008. Born again: Globalization's sixteenth-century origins (Asian/global versus European dynamics). *Pacific Economic Review* 13 (3): 359–387.

Frank, Andre Gunder, and Barry Gills. 1993. The 5,000-year world system: An interdisciplinary introduction. In A.G. Frank and B. Gills, eds, *The World System: Five Hundred Years or Five Thousand*, pp. 3–55. London: Routledge.

Gerritsen, Anne. 2007. *Ji'an Literati and the Local in Song-Yuan-Ming China*. Leiden: Brill.

Giddens, Anthony. 1990. *The Consequences of Modernity*. Cambridge: Polity.

Ginzburg, Carlo. 1980. *The Cheese and the Worms: The Cosmos of a Sixteenth-Century Miller*, trans. John Tedeschi and Anne Tedeschi. Baltimore: Johns Hopkins University Press.

Goubert, P. 1971. Local history. *Daedalus* 100 (1): 113–127.

Hall, Stuart. 1991. The local and the global: Globalization and ethnicity. In A.D. King, ed., *Culture, Globalization, and the World-system*, pp. 19–39. Basingstoke: Macmillan.

Hall, Stuart. 1992. The question of cultural identity. In S. Hall, D. Held, and T. McGrew, eds, *Modernity and Its Futures*, pp. 273–325. Cambridge: Polity.

Herkenrath, Mark. 2007. Introduction: The regional dynamics of global transformations. *International Journal of Comparative Sociology* 48 (2–3): 91–105.

Herkenrath, Mark, Claudia König, Hanno Scholtz, and Thomas Volken. 2005. Divergence and convergence in the contemporary world system: An introduction. *International Journal of Comparative Sociology* 46 (5–6): 363–382.

Hindle, Steve. 2000. A sense of place? Becoming and belonging in the rural parish, c.1550–1650. In A. Shepard and P. Withington, eds, *Communities in Early Modern England*, pp. 96–114. Manchester: Manchester University Press.

Hindle, Steve. 2008. Beating the bounds of the parish: Order, memory and identity in the English local community, c.1500–1700. In M.J. Halvorson and K.E. Spierling, eds, *Defining Community in Early Modern Europe*, pp. 205–227. Aldershot: Ashgate.

Hopkins, Anthony, ed. 2006. *Global History: Interactions between the Universal and the Local*. Basingstoke: Palgrave Macmillan.

Hymes, Robert. 1986. *Statesmen and Gentlemen: The Elite of Fu-chou, Chiang-hsi, in Northern and Southern Sung*. Cambridge: Cambridge University Press.

Hymes, Robert. 2002. *Way and Byway: Taoism, Local Religion, and Models of Divinity in Sung and Modern China*. Berkeley: University of California Press.

Kurtz, M. 2002. Re/Membering the town body: Methodology and the work of local history. *Journal of Historical Geography* 28 (1): 42–62.

Lyotard, Jean-François. 1984. *The Postmodern Condition: A Report on Knowledge*, trans. Geoff Bennington and Brian Massumi. Manchester: Manchester University Press.

Massey, Doreen. 1995. Places and their pasts. *History Workshop Journal* 39: 182–192.

O'Brien, Patrick. 2008. Review of *Global History: Interactions between the Universal and the Local*. *Reviews in History* 648, at http://www.history.ac.uk/reviews/review/648 (accessed Sept. 27, 2010).

O'Rourke, K., and J.G. Williamson. 2002. When did globalisation begin? *European Review of Economic History* 6: 23–50.

Osterhammel, Jürgen, and Niels Petersson. 2005. *Globalization: A Short History*. Princeton: Princeton University Press.

Robertson, Roland. 1995. Glocalization: Time-space and homogeneity-heterogeneity. In M. Featherstone, S. Lash, and R. Robertson, eds, *Global Modernities*, pp. 25–44. London: Sage.

Rojek, Chris, and Bryan Turner, eds. 1998. *The Politics of Jean-François Lyotard: Justice and Political Theory*. London: Routledge.

Samuel, Raphael. 1976. Local history and oral history. *History Workshop Journal* 1: 191–208.

Stearns, Peter. 2010. *Globalization in World History*. London: Routledge.

Von Glahn, Richard. 2003. Towns and temples: Urban growth and decline in the Yangzi Delta, 1100–1400. In P.J. Smith and R. von Glahn, eds, *The Song-Yuan-Ming Transition in Chinese History*, pp. 176–211. Cambridge, MA: Harvard University Asia Center.

Wallerstein, Immanuel. 1974–1989. *The Modern World-System*. 3 vols. New York: Academic Press.

Wallerstein, Immanuel. 2004. *World-Systems Analysis: An Introduction*. Durham: Duke University Press.

Wright, Donald. 1997. *The World and a Very Small Place in Africa*. Armonk, NY: M.E. Sharpe.

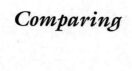

Comparing

CHAPTER FIFTEEN

Comparative History and the Challenge of the Grand Narrative

MICHAEL ADAS

Roughly two generations of comparative research and scholarship ago, in his preface to a collection of essays on *The Comparative Approach to American History*, C. Vann Woodward pronounced "historical comparison … notoriously dangerous and misleading" (1968: x). Clearly at cross-purposes with the efforts of the distinguished colleagues who had contributed to the edited volume and the apparent intent of the essays he was introducing, Woodward concluded that "historians as a rule are reluctant to make them." He did go on to concede, with a sense of resignation, that since comparisons – for reasons that were unclear given their problematical nature – were inevitably going to be made, "it would seem best that they be handled by expert historians." In effect dismissing decades of important theoretical and historical contributions by comparativists in other social science disciplines, he pronounced historians the "best qualified to point out the fallacies of comparisons, to distinguish between comparisons that are misleading and those that are illuminating, to warn against strained and unsophisticated experiments of the sort, and to call attention to new opportunities for fruitful comparative studies" (1968: x).

In his introduction and his concluding remarks, Woodward does not even attempt to define what comparative history might be or delineate the distinctive research and writing strategies the comparative approach entails. Nor does he have anything to say about the comparative methods deployed by the authors of the essays he seeks to frame. But that collective included some of the most distinguished historians of the time, among them Peter Gay, David Brion Davis, John Hope Franklin, and Arno Mayer. And they provided highly suggestive forays into subfields as diverse as slavery and revolution, urbanization and the Cold War, that presaged the emergence of the comparative approach as a major force in the historical profession in the 1970s and 1980s. This trend was clearly discerned by Raymond Grew (1980) just over a decade after the publication of Woodward's edited volume. Drawing on his remarkably wide-ranging mastery of contemporary historical scholarship and his stewardship of *Comparative Studies in Society and History*, Grew suggested a number of the ways in which comparative analysis had reshaped historical inquiry in both the United States and Europe in fields as disparate as

A Companion to World History, First Edition. Edited by Douglas Northrop.
© 2012 Blackwell Publishing Ltd. Published 2012 by Blackwell Publishing Ltd.

demography and literary expression.[1] Though he argued that no explicit or agreed upon method for doing comparative history had as yet emerged, he observed that many approaches had developed in ways that significantly enhanced the level of analysis and sophistication of theorizing in the discipline and cognate fields.

It is noteworthy that these and other early exchanges on the uses of comparison in historical enquiry rarely linked it to world or global history, which paralleled the comparative approach as a growing force in the discipline in these same decades. William McNeill's widely read *Rise of the West*, which was first published in 1963, began a sustained effort to recover the level of respectability that world history had not enjoyed within the transnational scholarly community since the time of Voltaire and Montesquieu. (See Pomeranz and Segal, this volume.) The enthusiastic reception of McNeill's path-breaking work and his *Plagues and Peoples* (1976), which followed just over a decade later, also served to reinstate the grand narrative as the predominant mode of doing world history. Although McNeill and other early advocates of the macronarrative were not purposeful, systematic practitioners of the comparative approach, their sweeping surveys of different aspects of the human experience shared an emphasis on patterns of interaction among civilizations and empires, nomadic and sedentary societies, and across culture zones and continents. But then, as now, world historians of the grand narrative persuasion diverged from those who identified themselves as comparativists in significant ways. The former were committed to tracing key themes and processes in a broad global perspective; the latter were intent on the rigorous application of a method of historical analysis that had long been nurtured mainly by fellow travelers in other social science disciplines. Although the two approaches have converged frequently over the past two or three decades – usually in works that have come to be labeled world history – practitioners in neither camp have given explicit attention to the differences between them. Consequently, there has been a dearth of dialogue devoted to explicating the ways in which the *conscious* cultivation and thorough incorporation of aspects of each of these options might enhance the work of scholars, teachers, and public intellectuals striving to improve our understandings of the cross-cultural interactions and transregional exchanges that are defining dimensions of both.

In this chapter, I explore key similarities and differences (with emphasis on the latter) between the two approaches and address the ways in which I believe comparative analysis can (and often does) add depth, focus and analytical rigor to our thinking about and writing world history in its various guises. Some of my arguments, and indeed many of the issues that I foreground, were first articulated nearly a century ago by Marc Bloch in a brilliant, seminal paper called "Pour une histoire comparée des sociétés européennes," presented in 1928 at the Sixth Annual Congress of Historical Sciences, Oslo (see Bloch 1969: 44–81). Reprinted in a number of languages, sometimes cited but seldom extensively invoked in rare discussions of methodology among world historians or in individual works on global themes, Bloch's exposition of the uses of comparison for historical scholarship tackles many of the challenges and obstacles that its practitioners have invariably had to grapple with. Often implicitly, he also provides credible rejoinders to the critiques or outright dismissals, such as those epitomized by C. Vann Woodward's introduction, that have been leveled for decades against both comparative and world history by more specialized, area studies-oriented researchers and scholars. Although the issues that I raise here go beyond and are at times at odds with aspects of the case for comparison made by Bloch, most of his interventions have stood the test of time remarkably well and remain in my view the obligatory starting point for anyone embarking on the serious study of history in either its comparative or global modes, or ideally any combination of the two.

In arguing his case for the advantages of in-depth comparative analysis, Bloch returns again and again to issues related to selection, perhaps the most fundamental dimension of the generic methodology that all professional historians are expected to master. From the cases that the comparativist seeks to probe in depth and decisions pertaining to evidence that will make this possible to the categories of analysis and different levels of variables deployed, the historian must make choices that will determine the extent to which her or his efforts at cross-cultural explanation will be credible and relevant for both world historians and theoretically minded scholars in a variety of social science disciplines. Once the comparativist has decided which cross-cultural themes, recurring patterns, global processes or theoretical propositions merit extended study, she or he must determine which case study examples are best suited to answer the questions likely to be posed. As Bloch insisted, several criteria need to be brought into play in determining which case histories will best test the causal arguments and overall hypotheses that he viewed as essential outcomes of fruitful comparison. To begin with, he assumed that extensive reliance on archival sources was obligatory, and consequently stressed the importance of at least a reading proficiency in languages appropriate for the societies, periods, and issues to be explored. Bloch advocated a mastery of both the published primary and archival sources for each of the case examples that approached monographic thoroughness. For comparison at this level to be feasible, Bloch concluded that the societies selected for case study examples ought to share significant historical connections, ranging from linguistic, institutional, epistemological and other cultural commonalities to ongoing interaction and exchanges over extended periods of time.

For some comparative and most world historians Bloch's prescriptions regarding case selection have proved problematic. In fact the demands they entail may explain why his pronouncements have been neglected. A book-length study with even two or three cases based on the depth of monographic mastery that Bloch had in mind could occupy the better part of a productive scholar's career. It is also likely that the case studies would not only come to make up the better part of the comparative study that resulted but possibly constrict the attention given to developing the themes, arguments and theoretical insights that transcend them. In actual practice even the best of comparative and world historians have tended to rely on a mix of archival, published primary and secondary sources in developing their case studies (for recent examples, see Lieberman 2003; 2009; Ward 2009; Hecht 2012). This approach has been especially fruitful for researchers working in the subfields of colonial expansionism, commercial diasporas, and slavery in which there are accessible, often abundant and well-cared-for archival repositories that make it possible to explore the convergence of multiple colonizers, diasporas and indigenous peoples (White 1983; 1991; Curtin 1984; Benton 2002; Schwartz 2008). Those who begin as area specialists producing closely argued monographic works have also productively and provocatively tackled major issues and controversies in cross-cultural and world historiography through a comparison of a core case example – based heavily on archival and published primary sources in their primary area(s) of expertise – and mainly secondary sources on one or more cases focused on other regions (Pomeranz 2000; Fredrickson 2002). At an even more ambitious level of argument, a number of the most widely read books in world history have resulted from cross-disciplinary combinations of decades of anthropological fieldwork in specific locales supplemented by secondary works ranging across diverse geographical and temporal settings (Wolf 1982; Diamond 1997).

Perhaps intentionally, Bloch had little to say about secondary sources beyond setting up a number of specialist monographs on French medieval history as foils for his demonstration of the ways in which comparison could expose false analogies, most notably the development of enclosures in France that resembled those in England. But secondary works have been central, hence critical, to almost all comparative and world history. For those undertaking either approach to cross-cultural analysis, broad surveys of relevant published works are essential for the task of determining which cases will provide the fullest and most appropriate evidence for exploring recurring or diverging patterns and causal connections. Coverage of the relevant secondary source literature can also uncover supplemental case examples for testing specific aspects of a comparativist's broader arguments, as well as counter examples that often complicate his or her interpretations in revealing ways. Extensive coverage of monographic studies and the theoretical literature available on the phenomena to be compared make it possible for the historian to formulate working arguments or hypotheses and an overall conceptual framework that can be tested and reworked in line with the evidence provided by archival and published primary documents. Bloch's confidence that the archives themselves would reveal the questions that needed to be posed is clearly at odds with the way that most historians work. As William Sewell has insisted (1967: 218), primary sources cannot "supply us with the explanations to be subjected to test: this is the task for the historical imagination." Perhaps more than monographic or narrative historians, comparativists need to enter the archives with at the very least tentative assumptions, questions to be asked, problems to be resolved and preliminary interpretations in order to select and make sense of the evidence to be examined.

With regard to both the questions they pose and the interpretations they advance, John Goldthorpe (1991) has argued that for historical sociologists, particularly those who undertake comparative analysis, a heavy reliance on secondary sources has been highly problematic. Without using primary documents, he contends, sociologists attempting to study historical phenomena are capable of only what he terms a "second order of interpretation." This means that their analysis and conclusions have been limited or skewed by the fact that they have not made use of written materials and other "relics" produced by actors and observers contemporaneous with the ideas and events they sought to analyze. Most crucially, in Goldthorpe's view, comparativists (as well as world historians of the grand narrative persuasion, whom he does not explicitly address) have been forced to "pick and choose" from the arguments and findings of other historians and rely on their interpretations of the extant primary sources, or at least the ones they have actually examined. Because broadly applicable causal explanations and theorizing have been central preoccupations of those who pursue comparative analysis, they have also been likely to privilege interpretations drawn from secondary works that buttress their own theoretical predilections and line of argument.

Barrington Moore Jr's *Social Origins of Dictatorship and Democracy* (1966) provides one of the more striking illustrations (though not one discussed by Goldthorpe) of this dubious outcome. In one of the most read and debated early comparative works, which was based on case examples focused on such extensively studied social upheavals as the English and French revolutions, Moore relied heavily on historians who stressed class divisions and material conditions that had long been seen by writers of the Marxist persuasion as critical causal factors behind social conflict. This reliance skewed Moore's handling of his case examples, and in turn his larger comparative framework and conclusions, in important ways. But, as Joseph Bryant pointed out in his nuanced rejoinder to

Goldthorpe's very contentious essay (Bryant 1994), ample alternative interpretations were readily available in the published works of non-Marxist historians. Thus, a comparativist or grand narrativist, such as Moore, can evaluate the evidence, arguments, and overall interpretations advanced in secondary works by advocates of differing theoretical persuasions and political proclivities, and fashion on that basis a less reductive, ideologically driven and narrowly conceived interpretation of comparative or global events and processes. Choices among well-researched and argued alternative interpretations are, of course, sometimes not available to historians drawing on case examples from areas, such as central Africa or Oceania, that have not received as much attention as France or China and do not have comparable historiographical traditions. In these cases greater reliance on primary source materials – often including oral testimony – becomes all the more imperative.[2] Thus, although levels of immersion may vary, the informed sampling of key primary sources (usually identified through extensive reading of the secondary literature) also enables comparativists not only to analyze more perceptively the periods and peoples under consideration, it allows them to choose among the relevant secondary works that usually – and necessarily – constitute the main evidence used in developing the case examples that undergird their thematic and theoretical arguments.

In addition to questions arising from Bloch's stress on the necessity of grounding comparative history in primary sources, his arguments for the importance of selecting case studies drawn from societies that share common origins and mutual interaction over extensive spans of time have proved contentious and perhaps daunting for those considering comparative options. In responding to the constraints Bloch's case study prescriptions would impose in this regard, William Sewell takes an extreme opposite view. He argues that the most productive comparisons are more likely to result from case examples drawn from societies which are geographically and historically distant from each other; for example tracing the rise of industrialization or right-wing political movements in Germany and Japan. But even a cursory survey of the more influential works published in recent decades in which the comparative method has been systematically applied to world history in a sustained manner suggests that insistence on either polar option is problematic in a number of ways. Comparisons of case examples that are linked in time and space, such as slave plantation societies in different Caribbean islands and mainland South America (Klein 1986; Blackburn 1997), women's work (Tilly and Scott 1989), labor in Latin America (Collier and Collier 1991), and nationalism in France and Germany (Brubaker 1992) have been very revealing. Equally transformative of the issues and approaches emerging in key historical subfields have been comparisons of institutions, including slavery and serfdom (Kolchin 1987), empires and colonization (Lang 1975; Doyle 1986; Abernathy 2000; Burbank and Cooper 2010), and settler societies (Solberg 1987; Weaver 2003), that develop in very different locales, largely independent of each other, and decades (and in some cases centuries) apart.

Although in terms of languages required and the accessibility of archival sources, research involving related cases may prove less time-consuming and arduous, the corpus of comparative historical works over the past half-century provides plenty of evidence indicating that the criteria for effective case selection have less to do with distance in time and space than with the questions the comparativist seeks to answer; the comparability of the kinds of social systems, institutions, movements, ideas or processes she or he seeks to analyze; and the availability of comparable evidence across cases. Depending, for example, on whether the historian is attempting to compare or contrast whole social systems or key elements within them, the broader phase or stage of development that potential case examples exemplify becomes a crucial factor in selection. Thus, Eugene Genovese's (1969) caution that in evaluating different slave-plantation systems it is essential to select case examples that exhibit comparable institutions, technologies, and commercial linkages, rather than the chronology of their rise and decline, is well taken if one seeks to explore the key commonalities of one type or phase. But comparisons stressing the differences between plantation societies in different phases of the South Atlantic System have been equally effective and more revealing of the forces behind shifts in this (regrettably) defining mode of early modern production for export over time.

The number and ordering of core case studies in works focusing on cross-cultural comparisons or global themes have also varied considerably. Though four or five fully developed cases have tended to be the upper limit, Victor Lieberman's magisterial, two-volume *Strange Parallels: Southeast Asia in Global Context* (2003; 2009) spans at least eight distinct culture areas (depending on how one counts), and Theda Skocpol's highly influential *States and Social Revolutions* (1979) compares and contrasts six. The predominant ordering of core cases has been to treat each of them in distinct chapters or sections, and then draw together broader patterns from each in conclusions that trace similarities and differences among them. Some comparativists and world historians have also endeavored to identify and set out what Theda Skocpol and Margaret Somers (1980) have aptly designated "middle level generalizations" (Wolf 1969; Goldstone 1991; Scott 1998). More challenging, but equally engaging and innovative in conveying patterns of cross-cultural interaction, have been comparative works that get at larger themes and processes by exploring converging cultures (White 1991) or mixing case study discussions within chapters defined by broader themes and key aspects of the general phenomena being explored (Degler 1971; Skocpol 1979; Adas 1979; Kolchin 1987; Fredrickson 1981; 1995).

However many cases are deployed and whatever ordering is adopted, all comparative historians are compelled, either implicitly or explicitly, to deal with the problem of "the nth case" that has bedeviled generations of practitioners in the other social sciences. Because there are clear limits to the number of case studies that can be compared in depth in a given study, the author and his or her audience are left to ponder whether and why possible alternative case examples have been missed or excluded. The sometimes highly contested answers to these questions often center on objections that core case studies have been deliberately chosen because they buttress an author's general hypotheses or line of argument, or, conversely, have been left out because much of what they reveal would run counter to the causal explanations and broader patterns he or she is attempting to introduce into scholarly discourse. At times, the more scrupulous of comparativists have published follow-up essays that set out categories of analysis and causal explanations that diverge significantly from their earlier work. Among the boldest and more revealing of these was Theda Skocpol's article (1982) on the Iranian revolution of 1978–1979, which stresses factors, such as human agency, ideology, and contingency, that have little place in her meticulously detailed *States and Social Revolutions*, which had done so much to shape scholarly discussion on the causes and course of revolutions for over a decade. There is no compelling remedy for this potential downside of the comparative approach, but careful and open-minded case selection based on a mastery of the relevant literature across disciplines and the deliberate selection of contrary or problematic core examples can at least mitigate the objections that evidence drawn from nth cases may summon.

As with any approach to analysis, the comparative method has yielded distinct advantages for its skilled practitioners while limiting possibilities that might have been better facilitated if they had pursued alternative options. In the realms of cross-cultural and world history, the grand narrative has proved to be the main contender in that regard. Among the more apparent pluses of the macronarrative is the fact that it allows the historian to tackle far greater swaths of time and space than comparativists – or at least those who build their studies on deeply contextualized case examples. Some of the more successful of the grand narratives encompass whole social systems and diverse aspects of the human experience across millennia (Pacey 1990; Bentley 1993; Allsen 2001), while others confine their temporal coverage of comparably diverse human endeavors while ranging across even more variable geographic locales and social systems (Bayly 2004; Darwin 2007). In both approaches, the case examples deployed and issues considered tend to shift in kaleidoscopic fashion, but in the best of the works of this genre this means that general patterns (both similar and contrasting), "big" questions and credible answers, and often underlying principles of historical development are fore-grounded. The relative paucity of explicit methodological interventions and strictures with regard to coverage means that the possibilities that the grand narrative approach offers for fast-paced, compelling overviews of historical processes, replete with dramatic flourishes, usually far exceed those available to the fully committed comparativist. The broader scope and bolder claims of the macronarrativist also contribute to the likelihood that their works will reach a larger audience, and very often one that extends beyond the historical profession and academe more generally. (See Witz, this volume.)

These and other, very considerable, merits of the grand narrative approach to world history need to be weighed against those garnered by the rigorous and deeply contextu-alized application of the comparative method to cross-cultural analysis and (necessarily) more narrowly construed swaths of global history. The emphasis placed by the compara-tivist on systematic and sustained exploration of a more modest number of case examples sacrifices the broader scope of the macronarrativist for more detailed attention to the complexities, contradictions and vagaries that arise from a more thorough mastery of the secondary and monographic literature in relevant specialist subfields and inevitably more extensive, but variable, reliance on primary and archival sources. The firmer command of a much broader source base for fewer case studies not only makes, as we have seen, for a surer handling of pivotal interpretive choices and ongoing debates within specialized fields, it forces the comparativist to grapple with the extent to which causal connections and conclusions based on a more superficial level of case study exploration need to be tested and perhaps modified in major ways. As Bloch found nearly a century ago with regard to attempts to lump agrarian enclosures in England and France (Bloch 1969: 49–51), in-depth comparisons may well reveal that rather different processes and outcomes are at work despite seeming similarities and historical connections across the societies and cultures being compared. They have the added advantage of deterring cross-cultural or world historians from building comparisons on the basis of categories of analysis and theoretical assumptions prompted by their field(s) of expertise, which is very likely to skew the reading of evidence drawn from other culture areas and sociopolitical contexts. Deep immersion in diverse and multiple cases is also perhaps the best antidote to Eurocentrism and other modes of privileging that have proved highly contentious for world historians.

Sustained comparisons among well-developed core cases also enhance the historian's capacity to recognize and avoid the pitfalls that very often punctuate the sweeping surveys and bold forays into generalized speculation that typify grand narratives. At the most basic level, they make it very unlikely that historians committed to cross-cultural analysis will opt for what Skocpol and Somers (1980) have labeled the Parallel Demonstration approach. Driven by the determination to support an *a priori* hypothesis or model, those who adopt this approach seek to identify and deploy as many case examples as possible. Hence, selection of case examples and sources is subordinated to the theoretical arguments or thematic patterns the author wishes to advance, and these in turn are often determined by the area expertise or extended fieldwork drawn upon for their core – and most detailed – comparisons. At its worst this approach can result in a proliferation of shallowly researched case examples that show little awareness of debates and differing interpretations in the secondary literature. It may also diminish an author's inclination to grapple with evidence that complicates or contradicts the main line of argument, and thus reduce the possibility of refinements or major revisions. Closer examination of works based on parallel demonstration also reveals that in many – if not a majority – of studies in this mode rather different categories of analysis would be more appropriate than those stressed by the author in question. It also becomes clear that seemingly similar causal connections work very differently – or in fact apply less well or not at all to some or even a majority of cases – than the author assumes. Consequently, the outcomes identified are disarmingly far more variable and contrary than the model or patterns that the comparison is intended to demonstrate would lead one to conclude (Worsley 1968; Paige 1975; Diamond 1997).

In-depth contextualization can also obviate problematic interpretive moves that are common not only to grand narrativists and comparativists but to historians more generally. If taken seriously, it could rid the discipline of what Carl Degler identified decades ago as "one-shot brief analogies" (1968) that crop up even in the most narrowly conceived monographic studies. Though often made with laudable intent of suggesting the broader applicability of single case findings, these asides are invariably simplistic and misleading. At the other end of the interpretive spectrum, well-developed case studies can serve to caution against explicating general patterns or causes in ways that suggest an underlying teleology that drives history. Though Jerry Bentley is right, for example, to argue for the need for world historians to analyze "big" processes, such as demographic fluctuations and the impact of technological innovation, that have been central to the human experience from its inception (2003), his approach suggests a progressive, evolutionary vision of history that has very often been called into question by the devastating reverses or destructive potential that, for example, technological innovation or rapid population growth has engendered.

This caution would also apply to the reductionism that is often found in works with world history perspectives as well as those based on conscious and serious comparative inquiry. Though reductionism and reification facilitate advancing broad and provocative conclusions, and especially developing general hypotheses, they can make short work of the contradictions and messy complexities that complicate the work of all serious historians and often undo those with cross-cultural ambitions. As Kenneth Pomeranz's *The Great Divergence* (2000), demonstrates, even the most rigorous and revealing of comparative works can raise major questions that arise from privileging selected events, kinds of causes and processes, or limiting the timespan that is brought into the account. His core assertion, that resources from the colonies and the accessibility of coal in Great Britain were the critical factors that explain (much of) Europe's capacity after ca. 1800 to break the high-level equilibrium bind that he and others (Elvin 2008) have argued led to Europe's surge and China's stagnation, is only somewhat persuasive, even if one focuses narrowly on economic indices of growth and social well-being. But confining the question to just that constricted range of causal variables, as Joseph Bryant (2006) has argued the most cogently, raises a multitude of problems regarding the nature and fit of the statistical data available on both (but particularly the Chinese) sides of the comparison. Perhaps more critical, Pomeranz's causal and temporal reductionism means that three centuries of European scientific breakthroughs and technological innovations *before* ca. 1800 that produced unprecedented transformations in areas of endeavor as diverse as weaponry and understandings of the natural world are not seriously taken into consideration. These advances, of course, contributed in major ways to the capacity for Western Europeans to acquire and exploit effectively the resources, including coal, of both the colonies and *Europe itself*, and they gave rise to societies in which growth was sustained and technological and scientific breakthroughs were systemic and proliferating. Hence, when contrasting cross-cultural social change of the pervasiveness and magnitude Pomeranz is trying to explain, it is imperative to take into account both diverse sectors and dimensions of the societies in question and the cumulative effects of change over a far longer durée than he envisions.

In-depth contextualization of a manageable number of core case studies allows the comparativist to make considerable use of the historicist techniques that Steven Greenblatt has so skillfully applied in his exploration of cross-cultural contacts and exchanges (1976; 1991). From recovering the meanings contemporaneous with earlier times of what appear to be familiar terms and expressions to understanding the significance of rituals, customs and everyday gestures, historicism depends to a significant degree on immersion in the languages, primary source materials and the sociocultural milieus in which cross-cultural history is enacted. Whether the comparativist or world historian is exploring interactions and exchanges associated with first or early contacts across cultures, or patterns of development within societies separated in time and space, it is also essential that serious attention is given to indigenous epistemologies, material artifacts, and the nuances of social differentiation, markers of status and conventions of command and deference. And without a strong grasp of the broader context in which these are formulated and deployed, they are very likely to be misinterpreted or passed over altogether.

Two rather different, but revealing, examples of missed signals in major comparative studies where case evidence is not fully contextualized, hence insufficiently historicized, underscore the importance of both. In analyzing the causes of the French Revolution, which serves as one of the core cases in *States and Social Revolutions*, Theda Skocpol makes quite extensive use of the ample published primary sources available. In surveying the agrarian disorders that contributed to the upheavals, she relies heavily on the *cahiers de doléances*, which are treated as first-hand compilations of peasant grievances (1979: 123–126). Further inquiry into the actual authorship of the information gathered in the *cahiers*, however, would have revealed that they were written by local notables and especially lawyers, and thus were as (or more) likely to reflect the views of landholders and professionals as those of the peasantry, which itself was divided into often quite distinct social strata. In a provocative essay on a very different form of social divisions, in this instance among European and Amerindian cultures in collision, Patricia Seed (1992) argues that European colonizers in the New World drew on distinctive ceremonies and different sorts of claims of possession in attempts to establish their authority over the indigenous peoples. Drawing on a command of European discourses, written in a number of languages, she seeks to establish the ideological underpinnings of these rituals and claims. But differing European perceptions and approaches to domination were also shaped by what they encountered in different areas of the Americas themselves. Whether land or people were paramount, for example, in the Europeans' efforts to provide legitimacy for their various colonizing schemes was surely determined in part by the numbers and sociopolitical organization of the indigenous peoples encountered and the environment and natural resources of the areas the colonizers sought to rule and exploit.

The pronounced tendency for world history written (and taught) in the grand narrative manner to privilege aggregates – whether population and migration trends, trading indices and levels of economic productivity, or wartime casualties and occurrences of social protest – can be offset in comparative studies that are to varying degrees grounded in fully developed case studies that allow for inclusion of human agency, ideology and contingency. Each of these not only provides ways of linking the specific to the general, the local to the global, but by interjecting individual and group experiences, ideas and pivotal events they offer the possibility of combinations of narratives infused with analyses that prove as compelling in terms of style as, and potentially more cogent and memorable in argument than, macronarratives. They also greatly enhance the cross-cultural or world historians' opportunities to recover the neglected or "lost" voices and agency of subaltern groups, especially those without written sources, which often become pawns to be manipulated, subjugated, and exploited, particularly in global history reified and abstracted by the structuralist, world-systems approach. Inga Clendinnen's work, particularly her superb article on "Fierce and unnatural cruelty" (1991), which compares Spanish and Aztec approaches to warfare, religion, conquest, and empire building, provides a superb example of the ways in which a thorough grounding in often difficult sources and sensitivity to both sides of cross-cultural encounters can yield detailed, gripping and highly revelatory accounts of pivotal events and processes in world history (on similar approaches to these same encounters, see the recent works cited in Townsend 2003). Clendinnen's essay is a remarkable tour de force that intersperses narrative of the maneuvers and combat from both sides' perspectives with reflections on topics of relevance to world and comparative historians as diverse as the rationales undergirding human social hierarchies, the problems of the extant documents dealing with the siege, and the contrast between each side's conceptions of warfare and its purposes.

Of all the many techniques the comparative method offers to advance our thinking, writing and teaching about world history, none are more critical than the analytical tools that it provides for causal analysis. The procedures involved in determining what Marc Bloch characterized as "real causes" (1969: 54) can infuse all approaches to cross-cultural history, including the grand narrative, with finely honed questions and clearly defined focus issues, as well as more coherently and rigorously developed explanatory hypotheses and conclusions. At the most basic level, comparison compels those who take it seriously to move well beyond mere description, which is the prevalent mode of most of the world history intended for popular consumption (Craton 1982; Watts 1997). Even more scholarly and indeed influential works, such as Janet Abu-Lughod's overview of what she argues was the first world system (1989; 1993), would have been more cogent and compelling if the forces that gave rise to and shaped the nature of the different trading nodes and network segments, whose structures she meticulously details, had been compared and analyzed. In this case, an exploration of causal dynamics is of particular importance because it might well have bridged the disconnect between her *description* of the trading networks, which occupies the greater part of her book and essays, and her *concluding speculations* about the decline of the first world system, which have little to do with what has gone before and are highly problematical.

Despite its positivistic assumptions and tone, Skocpol and Somers' essay on the "The uses of comparative history in macrosociological inquiry" (1980) remains the best summary available of the ways in which comparison can discipline, refine and underscore causal explanation in cross-cultural history. Though Marc Bloch is mentioned, and his certitude that facts and scientific inquiry are central to historical investigation are mirrored in Skocpol and Somers's critique of major approaches to comparative analysis, they build mainly on John Stuart Mill's logics of comparison. Broad categories of analysis (for example, economic inequities or types of social movements) and specific causal factors are not distinguished, but both are key aspects of thorough comparative analysis. Either or both can also serve as constants or grounds that insure the comparability of the case studies selected and the quality and depth of the sources available for each of them. Thus, significant similarities are critical not only for establishing comparability of cases (that, in popular parlance, oranges are being compared with oranges, not oranges with apples), but they are in addition very often the main focus of cross-cultural histories that seek to set out or reformulate recurring patterns of, for example, first contacts, systems of slavery, or peasant protest movements; to define types of political or social systems; or (more ambitiously) to argue for what Skocpol and Somers refer to as "middle level generalizations" that apply to institutions, ideologies and social systems, or historical processes.

In each case, Eugene Genovese's caution that the historian must be clear that the same outcome is being compared needs to be taken into account. Reflecting on decades of debate regarding the conditions endured by slaves in different New World plantation systems that had been initiated by Frank Tannenbaum's *Slaves and Citizens* (1947), Genovese (1969) observed that most of those engaged in these at times acrimonious controversies paid little attention to critical terminological questions, such as what did treatment or exploitation mean. He argued (contentiously in the view of many later scholars) that the *daily conditions* of slaves in the United States may have been better than those of their counterparts in Brazil, but due to higher manumission rates the possibility of being released from enslavement during one's lifetime in the latter system were higher.[3] In his view this meant that key, but neglected, causal factors – including timing, positioning in the global arena, and whether the system in question was still importing or no longer importing large numbers of slaves – needed to be taken fully into account. In each instance, the importance of deeply contextualized case analysis is underscored.

Although similarities and parallel developments have been stressed in perhaps a majority of the works on cross-cultural and world history, contrasting case examples have also proved a very effective way to identify and analyze causal factors. If diverging causes and outcomes are the focus of comparison, then commonalities in broader sociocultural contexts or analytical categories become critical to the viability of the comparison. Whichever approach is stressed, and most comparative studies exhibit a mix of parallels and contrasts, the weight or importance of different causal variables ought to inform both writing strategies and overall arguments and conclusions. Here again in-depth contextualization provides checks against construing causal variables too narrowly or selecting them with an *a priori* theoretical agenda in mind.

The methodological refinements of the last few decades on the comparative procedures that Marc Bloch advocated so eloquently nearly a century ago make it possible to test dominant paradigms, general hypotheses, persisting patterns, causal arguments, and even what has become received wisdom for those writing monographs in specialized fields. All of these tasks, which Bloch insisted comparison could best facilitate, can now be tackled with a good deal more consistency and analytical cogency than he could have imagined. In varying combinations these phenomena have been central to global grand narratives and cross-cultural history, and thus it is fair to assume that both approaches to world history can be advanced in significant ways through the rigorous application of the amended approaches to comparative analysis that build on Bloch's original formulations. This may well entail, particularly for the grand narrative, setting more modest parameters in terms of temporal and geographic scope. But it offers the possibility of significantly reducing the tendencies to excessive generalization, oversimplification, essentialism, and reification that area and subfield specialists often find so objectionable in macronarrative. In-depth case study comparisons could obviate the urge to clutter the historical narrative with clunky disquisitions on the proper comparative method and overly explicit and rigid frameworks of analysis. The conscious and sustained melding of the comparative method and the grand narrative ought to produce hybrids that enjoy short-term spikes in sales as well as a long shelf life, and become obligatory reading for historians across subfields and a broader, nonacademic audience. Because they are more likely to draw evidence and techniques from other social science and humanities disciplines, they are also more likely to shape scholarship in fields beyond history in pivotal ways that range from testing paradigms to challenging assumptions about the preconditions that gave rise to contemporary global processes. Even though perhaps most historians, and even many colleagues in these cognate disciplines, no longer share Bloch's confidence regarding the "scientific" nature of the comparative method (1969: 75), it remains the most productive approach devised thus far for writing and teaching enduring global or cross-cultural history.

Notes

1   Grew's disproportionate attention to studies of these two regions reflected the state of both world and comparative history at the time. These trends were exemplified by Barrington Moore Jr's ambitious *Dictatorship and Democracy: Lord and Peasant in the Making of the Modern World* (1966), which uses the United States, Britain and France as its core cases, and Theda Skocpol's just-published *States and Social Revolutions* (1979) in which four of six main cases are European, and fit best within her conceptual framework.
2   For perhaps the most cogent reflections extant on these issues of central importance for the historical method, see Collingwood (1946).
3   As many authors of works on slavery have pointed out, manumission did not necessarily mean a better or longer life for the individual released from bondage.

References

Abernathy, David B. 2000. *The Dynamics of Global Dominance: European Overseas Empires, 1415–1980.* New Haven: Yale University Press.

Abu-Lughod, Janet. 1989. *Before European Hegemony: The World System AD 1250–1350.* New York: Oxford University Press.

Abu-Lughod, Janet. 1993. The world system in the thirteenth century: Dead-end or precursor? In Michael Adas, ed., *Islamic and European Expansion: The Forging of a Global Order,* pp. 75–102. Philadelphia: Temple University Press.

Adas, Michael. 1979. *Prophets of Rebellion: Millenarian Protest Movements against the European Colonial Order.* Chapel Hill: University of North Carolina Press.

Allsen, Thomas. 2001. *Culture and Conquest in Mongol Eurasia.* Cambridge: Cambridge University Press.

Bayly, C.A. 2004. *The Birth of the Modern World, 1780–1914: Global Connections and Comparisons*. Oxford: Blackwell.

Bentley, Jerry H. 1993. *Old World Encounters: Cross-Cultural Contacts and Exchanges in Pre-Modern Times*. New York: Oxford University Press.

Bentley, Jerry. 2003. World history and the grand narrative. In B. Stuchtey and E. Fuchs, eds, *Writing World History*, pp. 47–65. New York: Oxford University Press.

Benton, Lauren. 2002. *Law and Colonial Cultures: Legal Regimes in World History, 1400–1800*. Cambridge: Cambridge University Press.

Blackburn, Robin. 1997. *The Making of New World Slavery: From the Baroque to the Modern, 1492–1800*. New York: Verso.

Bloch, Marc. 1969. *Land and Work in Medieval Europe: Selected Papers by Marc Bloch*, trans. J.E. Anderson. New York: Harper & Row.

Brubaker, Rogers. 1992. *Citizenship and Nationhood in France and Germany*. Cambridge, MA: Harvard University Press.

Bryant, Joseph M. 1994. Evidence and explanation in history and sociology: Critical reflections on Goldthorpe's critique of historical sociology. *British Journal of Sociology* 45 (1): 3–19.

Bryant, Joseph M. 2006. The West and the Rest revisited: Debating capitalist origins, European colonialism, and the advent of modernity. *Canadian Journal of Sociology* 31 (4): 403–444.

Burbank, Jane, and Frederick Cooper. 2010. *Empires in World History: Power and the Politics of Difference*. Princeton: Princeton University Press.

Clendinnen, Inga. 1991. "Fierce and unnatural cruelty": Cortés and the conquest of Mexico. *Representations* 33 (Winter): 65–100.

Collier, Ruth B., and David Collier. 1991. *Shaping the Political Arena: Critical Junctures, the Labor Movement, and Regime Dynamics in Latin America*. Princeton: Princeton University Press.

Collingwood, R.G. 1946. *The Idea of History*. Oxford: Oxford University Press.

Curtin, Philip. 1984. *Cross-Cultural Trade in World History*. Cambridge: Cambridge University Press.

Craton, Michael. 1982. *Testing the Chains: Resistance to Slavery in the British West Indies*. Ithaca, NY: Cornell University Press.

Darwin, John. 2007. *After Tamerlane: The Rise and Fall of Global Empires, 1400–2000*. London: Penguin.

Degler, Carl N. 1968. Comparative history: An essay review. *Journal of Southern History* 34 (4): 425–430.

Degler, Carl N. 1971. *Neither White nor Black: Slavery and Race Relations in Brazil and the United States*. Madison: University of Wisconsin Press.

Diamond, Jared. 1997. *Guns, Germs, and Steel: The Fates of Human Societies*. New York: W.W. Norton.

Doyle, Michael W. 1986. *Empires*. Ithaca: Cornell University Press.

Elvin, Mark. 2008. Defining the *explicanda* in the "West and the Rest" Debate. *Canadian Journal of Sociology* 33 (1): 168–185.

Fredrickson, George M. 1981. *White Supremacy: A Comparative Study in American and South African History*. New York: Oxford University Press.

Fredrickson, George M. 1995. *Black Liberation: A Comparative History of Black Ideologies in the United States and South Africa*. New York: Oxford University Press.

Fredrickson, George M. 2002. *Racism: A Short History*. Princeton: Princeton University Press

Genovese, Eugene D. 1969. The treatment of slaves in different countries: Problems in the application of the comparative method. In L. Foner and E. Genovese, eds, *Slavery in the New World*. Englewood Cliffs, NJ: Prentice Hall.

Goldstone, Jack A. 1991. *Revolution and Rebellion in the Early Modern World*. Berkeley: University of California Press.

Goldthorpe, John H. 1991. The uses of history in sociology: Reflections on recent tendencies. *British Journal of Sociology* 42 (2): 211–230.

Greenblatt, Stephen. 1976. Learning to curse: Aspects of linguistic colonialism in the sixteenth century. In Fred Chiappelli, ed., *The Impact of the New World on the Old*, pp. 561–580. Berkeley: University of California Press.

Greenblatt, Stephen. 1991. *Marvelous Possessions: The Wonder of the New World*. Chicago: University of Chicago Press.

Grew, Raymond. 1980. The case for comparing histories. *American Historical Review* 85 (4): 763–778.

Hecht, Gabrielle. 2012. *Being Nuclear: Africans and the Global Uranium Trade*. Cambridge, MA: MIT Press.

Klein, Herbert S. 1986. *African Slavery in Latin America and the Caribbean*. Oxford: Oxford University Press.

Kolchin, Peter. 1987. *Unfree Labor: American Slavery and Russian Serfdom*. Cambridge, MA: Harvard University Press.

Lang, James. 1975. *Commerce and Conquest: Spain and England in the Americas*. New York: Academic Press.

Lieberman, Victor. 2003. *Strange Parallels: Southeast Asia in Global Context, c. 800–1830, vol. 1: Integration on the Mainland*. Cambridge: Cambridge University Press.

Lieberman, Victor. 2009. *Strange Parallels: Southeast Asia in Global Context, c. 800–1830, vol. 2: Mainland Mirrors: Europe, Japan, China, South Asia, and the Islands*. Cambridge: Cambridge University Press.

McNeill, William H. 1963. *The Rise of the West*. Chicago: University of Chicago Press.

McNeill, William H. 1976. *Plagues and Peoples*. Garden City, NY: Anchor.

Moore, Barrington, Jr. 1966. *Social Origins of Dictatorship and Democracy: Lord and Peasant in the Making of the Modern World*. Boston: Beacon.

Pacey, Arnold. 1990. *Technology in World Civilization: A Thousand-Year History*. Cambridge, MA: MIT Press.

Paige, Jeffery M. 1975. *Agrarian Revolution: Social Movements and Export Agriculture in the Underdeveloped World*. New York: Free Press.

Pomeranz, Kenneth. 2000. *The Great Divergence: China, Europe, and the Making of the Modern World Economy*. Princeton: Princeton University Press.

Schwartz, Stuart. 2008. *All Can Be Saved: Religious Tolerance and Salvation in the Iberian Atlantic*. New Haven: Yale University Press.

Scott, James C. 1998. *Seeing Like a State: How Certain Schemes to Improve the Human Condition Have Failed*. New Haven: Yale University Press.

Seed, Patricia. 1992. Taking possession and reading texts. *William and Mary Quarterly* 49 (2): 183–209.

Sewell, William H. 1967. Marc Bloch and the logic of comparative history. *History and Theory* 6 (2): 208–218.

Skocpol, Theda. 1979. *States and Social Revolutions: A Comparative Analysis of France, Russia and China*. Cambridge: Cambridge University Press.

Skocpol, Theda. 1982. Rentier state and Shi'a Islam in the Iranian revolution. *Theory and Society* 11 (3): 265–283.

Skocpol, Theda, and Margaret Somers. 1980. The uses of comparative history in macrosocial inquiry. *Comparative Studies in Society and History* 22 (2): 174–197.

Solberg, Carl E. 1987. *The Prairies and the Pampas: Agrarian Policy in Canada and Argentina*. Stanford: Stanford University Press.

Tannenbaum, Frank. 1947. *Slave and Citizen: The Negro in the Americas*. New York: Vintage.

Tilly, Louise A., and Joan Scott. 1989. *Women, Work, and Family*. New York: Routledge.

Townsend, Camilla. 2003. Burying the white gods: New perspectives on the conquest of Mexico. *American Historical Review* 108 (3): 659–687.

Ward, Kerry. 2009. *Networks of Empire: Forced Migration in the Dutch East Company*. New York: Cambridge University Press.

Watts, Sheldon. 1997. *Epidemics and History: Disease, Power and Imperialism*. New Haven: Yale University Press.

Weaver, John C. 2003. *The Great Land Rush and the Making of the Modern World, 1650–1900*. Montreal: McGill-Queen's University Press.

White, Richard. 1983. *The Roots of Dependency: Subsistence, Environment and Social Change among the Choctaws, Pawnees, and Navajos*. Lincoln: University of Nebraska Press.

White, Richard. 1991. *The Middle Ground: Indians, Empires, and Republics in the Great Lakes Region, 1650–1815*. Cambridge: Cambridge University Press.

Wolf, Eric. 1969. *Peasant Wars of the Twentieth Century*. New York: Harper & Row.

Wolf, Eric. 1982. *Europe and the People without History*. Berkeley: University of California Press.

Woodward, C. Vann. ed. 1968. *The Comparative Approach to American History*. New York: Basic Books.

Worsley, Peter. 1968. *The Trumpet Shall Sound: A Study of "Cargo" Cults in Melanesia*. New York: Harper.

CHAPTER SIXTEEN

The Science of Difference
Race, Indo-European Linguistics, and Eurasian Nomads

XINRU LIU

The field of Indo-European linguistic studies emerged in the late eighteenth century, at roughly the same time that the British were taking the initial steps that ultimately led to their colonization of the Indian subcontinent. Since then, those who have engaged in Indo-European linguistic studies have not only sought out all the languages that belong to this family, but also those thought to be somehow related to it. Furthermore, given its early emergence, the study of Indo-European languages could be considered the vanguard of all modern linguistic studies. While searching for the original homeland of Indo-European speakers and the subsequent spread of their descendants, scholars realized that they had migrated over long distances and spread out over vast areas, and that they invariably had interacted with and exchanged various vocabularies with other branches of the family as well as with languages outside the system. The results of such studies soon demonstrated that a tool had been developed that allowed historians to trace human migrations, including those that took place in a prehistorical context where written records of such population movements are not available. This new tool also helped historians expand their horizons from areas whose populations were sedentary agricultural and urban societies to the vast Eurasian steppe where nomadic societies were more prevalent.

By the nineteenth century, when Indo-European linguistic studies had extended its reach to subjects other than languages, some Indo-European intellectuals began promoting the idea that their cultural and physical ancestry had given birth to a special and superior population that was fit to colonize other peoples' lands and rule over their populations. In India and then in Iran, some of these modern intellectuals also became enamored of the word "Arya," a title that ancient elites in both countries had bestowed upon themselves. Thereafter, scholars used this ancient term when presenting their concept of an "Aryan race," a concept that eventually became associated with light-skinned European peoples whom they believed were the most excellent human beings on the planet. This concept then flourished as a "race science," a field viewed as a credible natural science in the nineteenth century and the early twentieth century. However,

A Companion to World History, First Edition. Edited by Douglas Northrop.
© 2012 Blackwell Publishing Ltd. Published 2012 by Blackwell Publishing Ltd.

twentieth-century developments in the biological sciences undermined this vision of the various races. In recent decades, scientists have traced all human beings back to a common ancestral group, a development which turned out to be the last straw for the already declining race science. Indeed, the repudiation of race science also challenged aspects of Indo-European linguistic studies. Thus, this field of language study is now taking up the challenges created by modern science and is thereby remaking itself. Historians, as well, now need to take advantage of the arduous work done by the linguists and archaeologists in Indo-European studies so that they too can explore key questions such as the Indo-European migrations and the interactions among populations living in forests, on the steppe, and in agricultural zones.

From William Jones to Max Müller

William Jones (1746–1794) was the first British scholar to discover that the British and their subjects in India shared a common ancestral language (1807, vol. 3: 34–35). At a young age, before he set out for India in 1784, Jones had already become an established orientalist scholar who had translated works in Persian, Arabic and Turkish into English. In order to support himself financially he had also studied law and was thus able to join the East India Company as a judge. This happened soon after the British East India Company took over the province of Bengal from the Mughal Empire. Although the empire's rulers were Turkic-speaking Muslims whose ancestral homelands were in Central Asia, they chose Persian as an imperial language with which to rule over their Indian possessions. Thus, the British in India found Jones's language skills very useful, given that they were dealing with a multinational and unruly merchant community, as well as a Mughal government still nominally sovereign over the British East India Company. Jones, however, soon discovered that most people in India spoke various dialects of Hindustani, and the majority of the population belonged to sects of Hinduism whose religious language was Sanskrit. Jones thus could rely on his knowledge of Persian to learn Sanskrit, as most Hindu Brahman intellectuals knew both languages. Among Jones's many important studies of Sanskrit texts, his English translation of the Dharmashastra of Manu, Institutes of Manu, was especially useful to the English speakers who would be governing India.

Jones was only one of the numerous orientalists who studied Asian cultures and languages under colonial patronage. He was, however, the first among them to point out links between Sanskrit and Greek, and then, through Greek, to most of the European languages. Although many more languages were added to the Indo-European family after Jones's death, he established the system's basic structure, and the geographical scope covered by this language family. It was Max Müller, a German-born scholar and a professor of comparative philology at Oxford University, who linked Indo-European language speakers to the "Aryan race." Living during the Victorian era, as British imperial glory reached its apex, Müller never so much as set foot in India. Nevertheless, he felt a deep affinity for Indian culture and especially the Sanskrit language. He argued that Indians who spoke languages descended from Sanskrit demonstrated that their ancestors had had similar – if not higher – intelligence levels to Europeans; that thus they both must have come from the same race, and were "Aryan Brethren" (Müller 1847 quoted in Trautmann 1997: 176). A major challenge to Müller's theory of brotherhood between the British colonial elite and colonized Indians seemed to be the simple fact that India was an extremely diverse country, linguistically and ethnically. Furthermore, the caste system divided the population into numerous hierarchically ordered communities. Müller thus offered a two-race theory to explain India's caste hierarchy. A group of people of the Aryan race, sharing intellectual properties and blood with their brothers in Europe, invaded India and established themselves as the Brahman caste and maintained their Indo-European languages. The dark-skinned indigenous people in India became their slaves, or at least belonged to low-ranking castes (Trautmann 1997: 174–175). This racial explanation of India's social structure is full of flaws, but Müller could not see them, in spite of his good intentions to put the Hindu intellectual elite on a social par with its British rulers.

Indian intellectuals, especially those in the Hindu upper caste, soon embraced the theory, presumably because it made them equal to their rulers, at least intellectually. But other European scholars doubted that they shared ancestors with the dark-skinned Indians who had submitted to British rule. For these scholars, who called themselves "ethnologists," the differences between races were physical, not linguistic, and they tried to diminish, and sometimes bluntly to deny, similarities between European and South Asian languages. To them, the superiority of fair skin and other Caucasian physical features seemed the very essence of European racial dominance over other people on the planet.

The Bible and Darwin

Throughout the years that William Jones was studying languages, he always assumed that all human beings on the planet were the descendants of the biblical Noah, whose three sons Shem, Ham, and Japhet departed from the holy land after the flood and thereby began the repopulation of the rest of the world. Based on the belief that all the Earth's inhabitants who had not been on Noah's ark died during this flood, studies of biblical chronology provided a relatively recent birth date for the current human race, not much more ancient than 6,000 years ago. Indeed, most scholars of the eighteenth and nineteenth centuries believed that the biblical flood had been part of a divine plan for human redistribution. Only the subordinate question of which of Noah's sons had fathered which human stock remained a topic of debate. Jones believed that Japhet fathered the peoples who lived in northern parts of Eurasia, specifically those who lacked literacy and became nomadic pastoralists. By contrast, he believed that Ham's descendants were the most cultivated people, and that they became the Indo-European speakers who settled in various "civilized" lands such as India, Egypt, and Europe. The children of Shem, lastly, became the Arabs and Jews who settled around the Red Sea. Jones saw them as a people who did not have much history, except for this descent from Abraham (Trautmann 1997: 51–52). Here, his reliance upon the Old Testament's Book of Genesis, which provided the same creationist vision shared by Christians, Jews, and Muslims, prevented him from identifying candidates for the honor of being named the earliest speakers of Indo-European languages, languages that he considered the most intelligent ones on the Earth.

Max Müller, on the other hand, gave the laurels for being the earliest Indo-European or Aryan speakers to what he thought to be the most chivalric of human lines, the "Japhetic race," which he believed had conquered and enslaved an indigenous Negro race in India (Trautmann 1997: 175). Although Müller was a passionate advocate for using intelligence (which he measured by the language that a people spoke) as a true identifier of the Aryan race, his use of a two-race notion to explain the complexities of

South Asian languages and ethnicity opened the door to a linkage of race to language. In other words, the fair-skinned, intelligent Aryans conquered dark-skinned savages and subsequently built a civilized, albeit hierarchical society. Müller lived in the middle of the nineteenth century, when some scholars in the natural sciences in Europe were starting to abandon the biblical version of human origins. Charles Darwin, for example, published *On the Origin of Species by Means of Natural Selection* in 1859. It is no wonder that his tracing of human origins to apes shocked Christian societies in Europe, even though other natural scientists had also been moving toward a more rational interpretation of human origins than that presented in the Book of Genesis. In their analysis of botanical and animal species around the globe, they were concluding that the world must have existed much longer than suggested by the biblical chronology, and that human beings had lived on the Earth far earlier than any interpretation of the Book of Genesis could allow. For many of them, Darwin's idea of natural selection of survivors was a more logical explanatory framework for the existence of humans.

The debate between religious and scientific interpretations of human origins is still underway. Indeed, the two sides have never stopped debating. To skeptics, one of the subjects that cannot be easily explained through natural selection is the existence of physical differences between ethnic groups. The environment may explain such phenomena as dark skin in tropical regions and fair skin near the North Pole, the argument goes, but natural selection alone cannot explain all the various physical differences among humans. In *The Origin of Species* Darwin did not offer any explanation for differences among races because he realized that not all seemed to be related to survival in particular natural environments (Darwin 1979). Later, he did try to understand such physical differences in another book, *The Descent of Man, and Selection in Relation to Sex*. In this later book he suggested that differences in the aesthetic values of various groups in a species, including the human species, especially when choosing mates, could create and reinforce different physical traits that are not visibly related to survival (Darwin 1871). In recent decades, Jared Diamond, among others, has revisited this issue of physical differences among human populations, and enriched Darwin's argument with more data (1992: 111–121).

The Failure of Race Science

During an age when there was high demand in "white" Europe for a moral justification of colonial rule over others, Darwin's "sexual preference" explanation of racial differences could not be popular among those convinced that the success of modern Europe had been divinely predestined. Peoples of the Aryan race, who possessed the most intelligent languages and thus made up the most intelligent race, also had to be physically different from the less intelligent races. Armed with modern scientific methods, race scientists thus painstakingly searched for physical differences that distinguished Aryans from Jews and Arabs, who speak non-Aryan languages but do not look very different. Meanwhile, such race scientists categorized people in Africa, East Asia and the Americas as subhumans, as demonstrated either through their dark complexions or through other features that marked them as visibly different. In Europe and in the colonized lands, census officers busily took measurements of skulls, noses, arms and legs, and described the various shades of colonial subjects' skin, the shapes of their body parts and even the characteristics of their hair, all to separate populations into races and subraces. Similarly, archaeologists worked all over the world taking the measurements of ancient human skeletons in order to determine which races had been the builders of various civilizations. In short, scholars of the Victorian era and the early twentieth century meticulously and scientifically accumulated a tremendous amount of data regarding human racial features.

Nearly all scientific observers today denounce such work, and dismiss it in its entirety. A scientifically valid race science never did emerge.[1] Recently, such works as Barbara Katz Rothman's *Genetic Maps and Human Imagination: The Limits of Science in Understanding Who We Are* (1998) and Stefan Arvidsson's *Aryan Idols: Indo-European Mythology as Ideology and Science* (2006) have addressed this issue from a modern perspective. Simply put, Rothman says, the race scientists wanted to answer an impossibly elusive question. Despite their invocation of all the possible scientific means of physical anthropology, biology and paleobiology, statistics, and ultimately genetic distributions, they could not come up with any conclusive answers. Essentially, the nineteenth-century European imperial use of physical difference as a tool to distinguish discrete "races" turned out to be no more than an effective way to denigrate black Africans, as well as brown and yellow Native Americans and Asians. In the United States, too, during and after the Civil War, white Americans also grappled with racial tensions. They also used the tools of race science to divide people into ostensibly distinct groups that had, they said, different levels of intelligence and should thus occupy a different status in society.

Arvidsson, a Swedish scholar of Indo-European studies, has also addressed the question of why this nineteenth-century race science failed. Race, he says, was an issue studied not only by those in the physical sciences, but also by specialists in languages, religions, and cultures. Arvidsson's study thus considers many of the other intellectual trends that contributed to the creation of the Aryan myth. For instance, peoples whose physical types seemed less obviously distinctive from European whites, in particular Jewish people, posed a difficult problem for these race scientists. Even more troublesome, the ancestral language of the Jews, Hebrew, was not Indo-European, and thus a language closely associated with the roots of Christianity could not be categorized as Indo-European. Whether or not they were devout Christians, European thinkers of the nineteenth and early twentieth centuries generally agreed that the values of Protestant Christianity had helped white people, including Americans, to further advance their already superior race. Another logical problem was that Christianity had not originated in Europe. Europe's Indo-European ancestors, finally, had been barbarians on the edges of ancient civilized societies, such as the Roman Empire, whose peoples had worshiped an entire pantheon of gods. Arvidsson's book discusses the many controversies caused by such inconvenient historical facts. And it points out that ultimately Nazi scientists were the ones who endeavored to solve the intrinsic contradictions of race science to create a more perfect theory of the supreme Aryan race, and who subsequently promoted Nordic-type, blond whites as the icons of the Aryan race.

Indo-Europeans/Aryans: Barbarians and Nomads

The failure of race science in general, and Aryan race theories in particular, did not in the end appreciably hinder the development of Indo-European linguistic studies. As a matter of fact, the search for answers to the wrong question led to an exploration of the human past that inadvertently provided the field with a much larger geographical and social scope. It also enriched the study of languages by providing more comprehensive studies of the people living on and moving across the Eurasian landmass. Although Nazi scientists tried to make a Nordic type emblematic of the model Aryan race among Indo-European speakers, they could not deny that the Germans had been barbarians in the eyes of classical Romans, even though the latter had darker hair and were shorter. And even if those Germans could somehow be called exemplars of the Aryan race, they were still indubitably latecomers to the civilized, urban Mediterranean world. Even the very term "Indo-European" was coined not by reference to the Germans, but to describe the complex relationship between Sanskrit and both Greek and Latin. Nevertheless, the search for a geographical origin of the Indo-European languages expanded the field's knowledge from the Mediterranean and the Indian Ocean to western and northern Europe, and then to the Eurasian steppe. From the perspective of classical historians, the Celts and Germans were barbarians, a term they used for people whose speech seemed incomprehensible. Essentially they were deemed uncivilized "others." Nevertheless, because they had now been classified as Aryans and thus spoke languages that shared roots with Greek and Latin, modern race scientists believed they had to have had special qualities that allowed them to conquer even the most civilized societies. Archaeologists and paleophilologists traced Indo-European/Aryans back to the second millennium BCE and discovered that the Mitanni, and probably the Hittites who replaced the Assyrians as Middle Eastern hegemons, had also been Indo-European speakers. Subsequently, Gordon Childe, a well-known archaeologist and historian, summarized a wide range of material-cultural data gathered by archaeologists and used it to provide a world history narrative in his book, *What Happened in History* (1942). Childe confirmed that these early Indo-European/Aryan populations should be seen as both barbaric and valiant. He concluded that the ancient Aryans, including both the Mitanni and the Hittites, had been associated with horses and horse chariots, and that they were able to monopolize the production of iron weaponry, a skill that gave them a key military and technological edge. Indeed, he concluded that the Aryans started the Iron Age (1942: 170, 175–177, 185, 191). Although Childe distanced himself from those scholars who identified languages with particular races, he did endorse the theory that all the Indo-European languages – Vedic Sanskrit, Persian, Greek, Latin, Celtic, and the various Slavonic tongues, Italian, Spanish, French, and Portuguese, as well as others – were descended from a "parent tongue" (1942: 176).

When tracing these earliest Indo-European speakers, of course, linguists quickly entered a domain without written records. Childe's outline of the early world, although incomplete, became a model for those seeking to use material culture to reconstruct history. In the second half of the twentieth century, many archaeologists and historians likewise depicted these early Indo-European speakers as warriors fighting from horse-drawn chariots. Their writings generally agreed that the nomadic Indo-Europeans had transformed themselves from barbaric, illiterate hordes into semisedentary, agricultural and pastoral communities once they came into contact with sedentary peoples, and more often than not the conquerors became rulers of sedentary societies. *The Coming of the Greeks: Indo-European Conquests in the Aegean and the Near East* by Robert Drews (1988) is one such book that depicts the transition of horse-chariot-riding Mycenae into vine-growing and seafaring Greeks. Using archaeological data from the northern frontier of the Roman Empire, *Barbarians Speak* by Peter Wells (1999) similarly describes both the hostilities and the mutual dependence of Barbaric Germans and the Roman Empire. The archaeologists thus reconstructed at least some of the history of peoples who left few if any written records, largely because they could mine the written records kept by contemporary literate societies.

Reconstructing the ancestry of Indo-European languages depends also on fragmentary information gleaned from preserved vocabulary. Linguists have established patterns based on changes in sounds and syntax, and used them to determine how close the relationship is between different branches of the languages. They also analyze words in a language's vocabulary that reflect the material cultures of the people who seem to have spoken the language. However, matching a language with material cultural assemblages poses serious problems both practically and theoretically. Consider, for instance, the association of the horse and chariots with Indo-European people. Linguists noticed that all known early Indo-European languages, though often geographically far distant from one another, used the same vocabulary when speaking about horses, horse gear, and horse chariots. Therefore, they posited that it had been Indo-Europeans who brought about a "chariot revolution" during the second millennium BCE, when steppe nomads developed this powerful weapon to conquer urban centers. The horse chariot became a focus of both Eurasian studies (archaeology) and Indo-European studies (linguistics). In particular, scholars wanted to know who were the first makers and drivers of horse chariots. The question could be phrased in two different ways. Had their developers been Indo-European speakers or people in some other linguistic group? Or, were they nomadic pastoralists who domesticated and trained horses on the steppe, or a sedentary people who manufactured sophisticated spoke-wheeled chariots? Associating the horse chariot exclusively with Indo-European speakers – the linguistic approach – soon reached a dead end. Though early Indo-European chiefs and kings, such as the Mycenae who entered Greece around 1600 BCE and the Vedic tribes who entered South Asia around 1500 BCE, all loved horse chariots and adopted names related to horses and chariots, other rulers, who did not speak Indo-European languages, seemed equally fond of horse chariots. For example, the Hyksos, who first brought horse chariots to Egypt, had a heterogeneous ethnic composition, and the Shang rulers in China (who literally took their chariots with them into the grave, believing that they would carry them to another world) were plainly not Indo-European speakers.

Asking whether nomads or sedentary peoples invented horse chariots, on the other hand, was a more productive question. A reasonable hypothesis is that nomadic people on the steppe invented the horse gear, including the reins, and that carpenters and bronze smiths in sedentary societies developed the sophisticated spoke wheels and chariot bodies. This would suggest that the invention of horse chariots most likely happened on some borderland that lay between the steppe and sown lands, in a place with ample quantities of timber and bronze. During the 1950s a discovery of 23 vehicles including chariots at Lchashen, on Lake Sevan in Armenia, almost confirmed this hypothesis (Cotterell 2005: 45). Lake Sevan is located in the highlands, where tree-covered mountains offered plenty of timber to make wooden parts of the vehicles, while just north of the mountains horses were readily available on the steppe. Not far to the south lay Mount Ararat and, beyond it, ancient agricultural lands. The chariots found at the site have been dated to circa 1500 BCE, but the four-wheeled wagon and the carts with solid wheels seem even older. In other words, Lchashen appears to be a virtual museum of vehicle development during the second millennium BCE.

Nevertheless, the significance of this Armenian site has recently been overtaken by an even more astonishing discovery farther to the northeast. In 1992 a book entitled *Sintashta* was published in Russia. It described the discovery of early industrial settlements located east of the Ural Mountains on the northern steppe, far from any ancient agricultural-urban regions. The first site found was a fortified circular settlement filled with bronze metallurgy workshops. Several similar settlements, including a well-preserved site at Arkaim, were also discovered by Russian archaeologists. To date, at least 16 chariot graves have been discovered in nine separate cemeteries in the Sintashta-Arkaim complex, which has been dated to 1900–1750 BCE. For more than a decade information about these important discoveries remained accessible only to those who could read Russian. Now, however, readers of English can also find this information in David Anthony's well-researched book, *The Horse, the Wheel, and Language: How Bronze-Age Riders from the Eurasian Steppes Shaped the Modern World* (2007).[2] Indeed, the evidence uncovered in these horse chariot graves deep in the steppe suggests that scholars will be forced to abandon both the assumption that nomads could not produce their own manufactured products, and the core idea that they had to be constantly on the move. It is now clear that ancient peoples living on the steppe (see Map 16.1) were not only the inventors of sophisticated products, but also could create and sustain settlements, albeit relatively short-lived, to promote their own mobility.

So who were these innovative nomads? In particular, were they Indo-European speakers? David Anthony thinks so. As an archaeologist, he defends the field of Indo-European linguistic studies. He concedes that languages have nothing to do with human racial types, and that any correlation between a specific, archaeologically discovered material culture and a specific language is extremely difficult to establish. However, he proposes a new approach to analyzing the relationship between archaeological finds and linguistic reconstructions. He argues that even though one cannot directly link a certain kind of material culture or a certain physical type to a language, nevertheless a persistent, robust cultural frontier does seem to indicate the coexistence of two different cultures and two different languages. Furthermore, the shifting of such a frontier could suggest complicated interactions between the two peoples as well as migrations, and thus the spread of at least one of the languages to the other side (Anthony 2007: 106). Using this methodology, Anthony gathered a large amount of Eurasian archaeological data, including the Russian data mentioned above, and then he arranged it to create a historical narrative of the spread of Indo-European languages. Unlike most historians, he approaches the interface between the Eurasian steppe and various agricultural zones from the perspective of the steppe's foragers and herders, instead of viewing it from the angle of ancient urbanites. His analysis gives a clearer picture of the development of a mutual dependency, as well as the existence of a volatile relationship, between these two zones.

In his chapter "The opening of the Eurasian steppes," Anthony discusses the spread of the horse and then the horse chariot from the steppe to various Bronze Age states in the Middle East, as well as to other peoples living south of the steppe. In particular, the discovery in recent decades of the Bactria-Margiana archaeological complex (located in present-day northern Afghanistan and eastern Iran) reveals that agricultural oases and agricultural colonies had been established within this realm around 2100 BCE. Its people could thus provide way-stations for nomads driving horse chariots (thus good candidates for being Indo-European speakers) who migrated from the northern steppe toward the west and the south. The people who lived in this archaeological complex of walled towns and oases imported horses from the northern steppe, and traded with their contemporaries in urban western Asia. The language they spoke has yet to be determined. Sometime around 1800 BCE the population living in this complex began to decline, but the people who remained there did not abandon their sedentary agricultural-pastoralist society. Two or three centuries later, Vedic speakers arrived in South Asia with their horses and chariots, probably by way of this buffer zone.

If horse chariots are used as the gold standard, there is still a glitch in this picture of the spread of Indo-European-speaking nomads along with their material culture. The

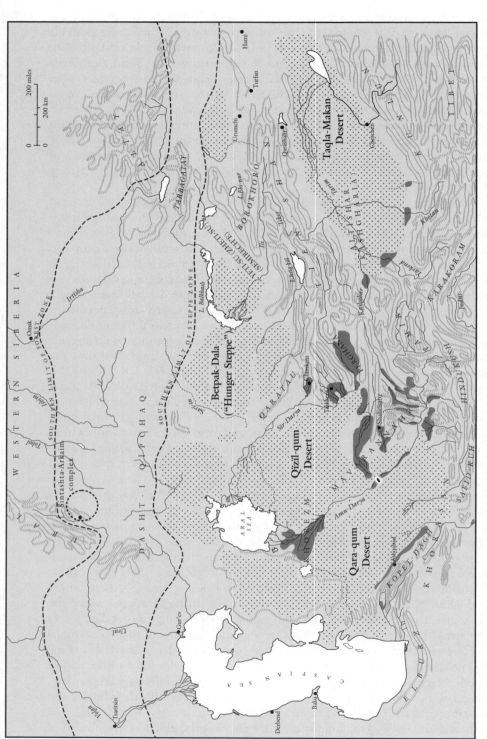

Map 16.1 Central Asia, the land early Indo-European peoples once roamed. Note the location of the Sintashta-Arkaim complex, north of the Aral Sea. Other Bronze Age sites, including a number of copper mines, have also been found at a similar latitude, stretching from the Don River (just off this map's western edge) to the Ishim River (east of Sintashta). These sites, taken together, offer compelling archaeological evidence for the presence of Indo-Iranian groups in the steppe between ca. 2100 BCE and 1800 BCE.

Source: Map of Central Asia based on Yuri Bregel, *An Historical Atlas of Central Asia* (Leiden: Brill, 2003), map 1.

odd exception is the distribution of the Tocharian language family. This language was discovered and named in the early twentieth century, when many Tocharian manuscripts written on palm leaves and wooden tablets were discovered in the oases of the Tarim Basin (in present-day Xinjiang, northwestern China). It was one of several previously unknown languages deciphered from these manuscripts, and it seems to have been used mostly for writing Buddhist texts and commercial documents from the sixth to the eighth centuries CE. Tocharian clearly differed from other Indo-European languages found in this region (such as Khotanese and Sogdian) in that it was associated not so much with the eastern branches of Indo-European (such as Iranian and Sanskrit), but with Celtic and German. Indeed, it even has some features related to Hittite. Scholars have thus searched for the migration routes of these Tocharian speakers. One line of research has convincingly linked the Tocharian with the Yuezhi people, who migrated west from the northwestern border of agricultural China to a bank of the Oxus River, which they crossed into Bactria to eventually establish the Kushan Kingdom. Since then this region has been called the land of Tuharans, or Tokharistan. This migration is best explained by Craig Benjamin in his book *The Yuezhi: Origin, Migration, and the Conquest of Northern Bactria* (2007). While Benjamin's book focuses on the Yuezhi people themselves, *Connections across Eurasia: Transportation, Communication, and Cultural Exchange on the Silk Roads*, co-authored by Xinru Liu and Lynda Shaffer (2007), addresses the interactions among nomadic peoples, including the Xiongnu, the Yuezhi, the Turks, and the Mongols, as well as their relationship with sedentary societies such as China, India, Persia, the lands around the Mediterranean shores, and the oases in Central and Western Asia. These works reveal both the mutual economic dependence and the hostility between two quite different kinds of people who lived in two different ecological zones. Among the nomads under study, the Yuezhi, or more generally, the Tocharians, the Sakas, and the Scythians, were likely Indo-Europeans. Nomadic people who spoke languages other than Indo-European, such as the Xiongnu, the Hephthalites, and the Mongolians, also seem to have been excellent horse breeders, valiant warriors, and savvy politicians.

In recent decades many dried corpses, dated from the second millennium BCE to the first millennium CE, have also been excavated along the rims of the Tarim Basin. Some of the corpses have high noses and socketed eyes, that is, the features of a "Caucasoid." Those dated to the second millennium BCE, or the Bronze Age, have attracted the attention of both linguists and physical anthropologists. Although the skin color of these corpses, dried by the climate of the Taklamakan desert, has been hard to determine, the possibility of some linkage to European whites, or to speakers of the western branches of Indo-European languages, has been suggested. Some linguists think they may have spoken Tocharian, given that these people migrated to this location along steppe routes during the early second millennium BCE (Mair 1995; Mallory and Mair 2000: esp. ch. 9). This possible identification of a Tocharian-speaking Caucasoid or "Europoid" people living in the Tarim Basin has now been tentatively accepted by scholars of Eurasian studies.

Yet a more recent discovery in the same region, a burial ground on the bank of the dry bed of the Xiaohe ("Small River" – *Chin.*) near Loulan, Xinjiang, has raised questions about the Tocharian identification of the Europoid people who resided near agricultural China during the second millennium BCE. The corpses in this cemetery are so well preserved that their skin is still pale and their hair is still blond and thus there is no doubt that they were Europoid. They were buried in boat-shaped coffins, wearing fur hats, and were surrounded by baskets filled with wheat, millet and some gruel (Mair 2006). (Wheat was domesticated in western Asia, and millet was from China.) There is, however, no evidence of any horses or chariots, an important indicator of Indo-European speakers, according to David Anthony. These Europoid-looking people, living on the Xiaohe oasis between steppe and desert, would appear to have been farmers rather than horse-riding nomads. A peculiar phenomenon associated with these burials is that

> Twigs and branches of ephedra were placed on or beside the body of every single person buried at SRC5. Some of the deceased were literally smothered in small bundles of ephedra and little bags of ephedra (as well as grains of wheat, millet, or barley) were sometimes tied along the edges of the capes wrapped around the bodies of the deceased. (Mair 2006: 299)

Both ephedra and hemp have been discovered in the Bactria-Margiana archaeological complex, and both are thought to be ingredients in the ritual intoxicant called "soma" in the Vedas and "homa" in Avesta Persian texts. If the ephedra indicates that the Xiaohe people were Indo-European in origin, they would most likely have spoken one of the eastern branches of the language family associated with Indo-Iranian, rather than Tocharian. In short, given what is now known, it is too early to say with certainty that Tocharian-speaking people migrated eastward along the steppe routes to the Tarim Basin during the second millennium BCE, or that their descendants were the Yuezhi who lived in the Tarim Basin and became famous for their horses, and then migrated westward to Bactria/Tokharistan where they built the Kushan Empire. Studies of the migration of Indo-European speakers in both prehistorical and historical times demonstrate that they could be city-dwellers, farmers, or horse-riding nomads. Likewise, they could be pale-skinned or dark-skinned. The association of a race with any particular language, in other words, has reached a dead end. On the other hand, using material cultures to match language affiliations is a more plausible approach, even though potholes often appear on this path as well.

Aryans and Brahmans

Although Max Müller spoke enthusiastically about the blood affinity between Europeans, including the British, and their Indian subjects, Victorian-age British and European race scientists continued to deny their equality with any dark-skinned Indo-European speakers in South Asia. Members of the Indian intellectual elite, on the other hand, more often than not Brahmans, entertained this racist interpretation of the caste hierarchy. Because of their Sanskrit heritage, they believed they were just as Aryan as their colonial overlords. Even though their identification with the Aryan race became a part of the nationalist discourse that condemned colonial rule, it also served as a defense of the privileged status of upper-caste Hindus, especially Brahmans. After the early twentieth-century discovery of ancient Indus Valley urban cultures, the archaeologist Mortimer Wheeler offered a new boost to the theory that invading Vedic tribes had become the upper castes in South Asia. The Indus Valley urban culture began to flourish around 2500 BCE, and started to decline in the early second millennium BCE. Excavations at Mohenjo Daro, one of the major cities on the Indus River, revealed what he thought was the scene of a "last massacre," at the top level of the site. In a celebrated book, *The Indus Civilization*, first published in 1953, he portrayed the Aryans as successful invaders who wiped out the last of the Indus cities (Wheeler 1968: 131–132). This hypothesis seemed plausible and rational and was accepted by academics, and thereafter quickly made its way into Indian history textbooks.

In this "coherent picture," the invading Aryan Vedic people and thus their descendants, the Brahmans and Kshatriyas, shared a similar physical appearance with European whites, while the indigenous Indus people were of a flat-nosed (i.e. ugly) variety. Physical anthropologists started busily measuring skeletons excavated from Indus Valley urban sites and trying to determine their racial types. They soon became mired, however, in the same sort of problems that had proved fatal to race science in other regions. The comprehensive data they accumulated provided no definite conclusions regarding the racial type of the Indus residents. Using the categories of race science, they found that the ancient Indus people belonged to a variety of races, including "Proto-Australoid," "Alpine," and "Mongoloid." One particular skeleton had features that could have placed it within several different racial categories. Later, when the field of race science was waning, archaeologists reexamined the physical features of the ancient Indus people while studying their adaptation to the ecological environment and urban-agricultural life. This approach proved much more productive. They discovered that physically the ancient population on the Indus was not much different from the current one, and generally could have been linked to several large groups of people living in many places between the eastern Mediterranean and the western parts of Asia (Kennedy 1984).

Another fatal flaw found within the Aryan invasion theory was the inaccurate dating of the decline and disappearance of the Indus urban sites. After archaeologists began using carbon-14 to date the sites, they revised the time for the complete demise of Indus urban sites to circa 1700 BCE or even earlier. This made it clear that there had been at least a 200-year gap between the demise of the Indus civilization and the arrival of Vedic people. It also became apparent that the mid-second millennium date for the arrival of Vedic people in the Indus Valley was nothing more than an assumption. Given the lack of any datable archaeological remains for these 200 years, the linguistic dating of the Vedic arrival could not be pushed any earlier than circa 1500 BCE. Thus it is now clear that when the Vedic people who worshipped Indra arrived on the banks of the Indus River, they may have found the 200-year-old ruins of a city, but no people there to conquer.

No matter what language or languages were spoken by the ancient people in the Indus Valley and northern India in general, the arrival of a Vedic-speaking population led to an encounter between a pastoral nomadic population and a sedentary agricultural society. Indo-European linguistic studies and textual research on ancient documents have revealed some of the complexity of this encounter. In her book *From Lineage to State* (1984), Romila Thapar demonstrates that the Vedic language picked up a considerable amount of vocabulary from South Asia's indigenous farmers. The warfare recorded in the Rg Veda and other epics seems to have occurred mostly between various Vedic lineages, and not so much with the "flat-nosed" Dasas or Dasyus. Indeed, local clans that had lived in India long before the Vedic people arrived were known to have joined with a Vedic lineage in order to pursue fights with another local lineage.

More recently, the linguist Asko Parpola has compared the Vedas with Avesta Persian texts and has concluded that the Iranian line of the Indo-Iranian branch and the Vedic line had actually been adversaries in Central Asia, and it was internal conflicts among these groups that caused the migrations of both lines to their later homes. *Ashuras*, demons in the Vedic culture, were *Ahuras* (gods) in the Zoroastrian religion; and *Devas* who were divine in the Hindu tradition were enemies of *Ahuras* in the Zoroastrian faith (Parpola 2002). Parpola also argues that the Vedic-speaking tribes were not the first

Indo-European speakers to enter South Asia, and that Classical Sanskrit did not have its roots in the Vedic language, but was actually a continuation of another line of Indo-Iranian speakers who had arrived in India even earlier than the Vedic people. A battle over who would be dominant in northern India had broken out among various Indo-European lines and was recorded in the Rg Veda. Parpola argues further that the *Dasas* and *Dasyus* were not indigenous to India, although they had arrived there prior to the Vedic peoples. Indeed he argues that the word "Das-" was of Indo-European origin. However, an article by the linguist J.P. Mallory, published in the same volume, disagrees with this view of the Indo-European origin of *Dasa* and *Dasyu*. Instead he suggests that the Bactria-Margiana archaeological complex was a way-station for Indo-European migrations to South Asia. Thus the chariot-driving Vedic people could have stayed in the agricultural and non-Indo-European-speaking zone of Bactria-Margiana, where they could have picked up some vocabulary or even some people, including the *Dasa* and *Dasyu*, on their way southward (2002: 38).

The history of Indo-European linguistic studies is a significant part of the intellectual history of the modern world. Early in its development it became entangled with the search for human origins and the resulting tensions between religious and scientific views of the world and its peoples. The discovery of linguistic similarities between the British colonizers and their Indian subjects gave birth to a false race science, but the search for the homeland of the Indo-European languages led to a study of nomadic peoples living on the vast Eurasian steppe and brought about the realization that the nomads were a well-integrated component of the human community. One limitation of Indo-European studies, in this regard, is that Indo-European speakers were not the only nomads who lived on the steppe and invaded and dominated sedentary lands. In their historical studies of nomads, scholars in this field often seem to forget or neglect the roles played in world history by those nomads who did not speak Indo-European languages. Nevertheless, one can easily understand why this happens, given the extraordinary amount of territory and time covered by these scholars, and the large quantity of important scholarship that this field produces.

Notes

1 This argument is developed more fully in Liu (2011), which also draws on some of these same sources.
2 Anthony discusses these Sintashta-Arkaim cemeteries, and their dating, on p. 397.

References

Anthony, David. 2007. *The Horse, the Wheel, and Language: How Bronze-Age Riders from the Eurasian Steppes Shaped the Modern World*. Princeton: Princeton University Press.

Arvidsson, Stefan. 2006. *Aryan Idols: Indo-European Mythology as Ideology and Science*, trans. Sonia Wichmann. Chicago: University of Chicago Press.

Benjamin, Craig G.R. 2007. *The Yuezhi: Origin, Migration, and the Conquest of Northern Bactria*. Turnhout: Brepols.

Childe, Gordon. 1942. *What Happened in History*. Harmondsworth: Penguin.

Cotterell, Arthur. 2005. *Chariot: From Chariot to Tank, the Astounding Rise and Fall of the World's First War Machine*. New York: Overlook Press.

Darwin, Charles. 1871. *The Descent of Man, and Selection in Relation to Sex*. London: John Murray.

Darwin, Charles. 1979. *On the Origin of Species by Means of Natural Selection*. New York: Random House. First published 1859.

Diamond, Jared. 1992. *The Third Chimpanzee: The Evolution and Future of the Human Animal*. New York: HarperCollins.

Drews, Robert. 1988. *The Coming of the Greeks: Indo-European Conquests in the Aegean and the Near East*. Princeton: Princeton University Press.

Jones, William. 1807. *The Works of William Jones*, ed. Anna Maria Jones. 13 vols. London: John Stockdale & John Walker.

Kennedy, Kenneth A.R. 1984. A reassessment of the theories of racial origins of the people of the Indus Valley civilization from recent anthropological data. In Kenneth A.R. Kennedy and Gregory L. Possehl, eds, *Studies in the Archaeology and Palaeoanthropology of South Asia*, pp. 97–107. New Delhi: Oxford & IBH.

Liu, Xinru. 2011. Cong Yalian Ren dao Ouya Youmu Minzu, Tansuo Yinouyuxi de Qiyuan [From "Aryan" to Eurasian nomadic – Exploration of the origin of Indo-European languages], Lishi Yanjiu. *Studies of History*, 6: pp. 156–67.

Liu, Xinru, and Lynda Norene Shaffer. 2007. *Connections across Eurasia: Transportation, Communication, and Cultural Exchange on the Silk Roads*. New York: McGraw-Hill.

Mair, Victor. 1995. Prehistoric Caucasoid corpses of the Tarim Basin. *Journal of Indo-European Studies* 23 (3 and 4): 281–307.

Mair, Victor. 2006. The rediscovery and complete excavation of Ördek's necropolis. *Journal of Indo-European Studies* 34 (3 and 4): 274–318.

Mallory, J.P. 2002. Archaeological models and Asian Indo-Europeans. In Nicholas Sims-Williams, ed., *Indo-Iranian Languages and Peoples*, pp. 19–42. Oxford: Oxford University Press for the British Academy.

Mallory, J.P., and Victor Mair. 2000. *The Tarim Mummies: Ancient China and the Mystery of the Earliest Peoples from the West*. London: Thames & Hudson.

Müller, Max. 1847. On the relation of the Bengali to the Arian and Aboriginal languages of India. *Report of the British Association for the Advancement of Science*, 349: 319–350.

Parpola, Asko. 2002. From the dialects of old Indo-Aryan to Proto-Indo-Aryan and Proto-Iranian. In Nicholas Sims-Williams, ed., *Indo-Iranian Languages and Peoples*, pp. 43–102. Oxford: Oxford University Press for the British Academy.

Rothman, Barbara Katz. 1998. *Genetic Maps and Human Imaginations: The Limits of Science in Understanding Who We Are*. New York: W.W. Norton.

Thapar, Romila. 1984. *From Lineage to State*. Delhi: Oxford University Press.

Trautmann, Thomas. 1997. *Aryans and British India*, Berkeley: University of California Press.

Wells, Peter. 1999. *Barbarians Speak*. Princeton: Princeton University Press.

Wheeler, Mortimer. 1968. *The Indus Civilization*. 3rd edn. Cambridge: Cambridge University Press. First published in 1953.

CHAPTER SEVENTEEN

Projecting Power
Empires, Colonies, and World History

MRINALINI SINHA

Is the United States of America an empire or is it a global hegemon? If the US is not an empire, then would it be a good thing for the US and the world were it to become one? And what has the US to learn, if anything, from empires past? These are some of the questions that suddenly burst on public consciousness at the end of the Cold War and continue to have traction well into the era of what has been called the "War on Terror." These questions, prompted by such developments as the dramatic changes that followed the collapse of the Soviet Union – often referred to as the "last empire" – and the preemptive war on Iraq led by the United States, reflect the changing fortunes of the term. The "E" and the "I" words, *empire* and *imperialism*, as Giovanni Arrighi notes, are definitely back on people's minds again (2005: 23). The terms, whose contemporary meanings have been shaped most recently by the history of the overseas European colonial empires, had in the wake of the post–World War II era of decolonization acquired typically pejorative connotations of unilateral power. The stakes in the revival of "empire talk" in the closing decades of the twentieth century thus reflect the political ambivalence of this history.

The contemporary public discourse on empire, joined by politicians and academics alike, displays several common threads. These include an invocation of empire as a metaphor for unbounded power; debates over precise definitions of empire to cover political forms from antiquity to the present; an accounting of the balance sheet of empires in the morally charged terms of good and bad; and an acknowledgment of a shift in the role of US power in the present. At the same time, the historiographical field of empire studies has undergone both an enormous transformation and a renaissance. This has by and large been obscured by the raucous terms of the public debate on empire.

From roughly the last quarter of the twentieth century, the traditional historiography of empire has been substantially overhauled. Take the following example. Scholars had for long understood European colonial empires as the expression of European national power: hence the hitherto dominant framework of the "expansion" of Europe. However, as much recent scholarship has shown, European empires were not an expression of

A Companion to World History, First Edition. Edited by Douglas Northrop.
© 2012 Blackwell Publishing Ltd. Published 2012 by Blackwell Publishing Ltd.

some prior superiority that enabled Europe to dominate the rest of the world. Rather, Europe's dominant position in the world was itself the result, or the product, of empire.

The initial impetus for reexamining imperial history came from efforts to redress what Frederick Cooper has called "the nonreckoning that accompanied and followed the end of empires" (2005: 54). The most important work was that of literary critic Edward Said, whose book *Orientalism* (1978) taught generations of scholars to pay attention to the cultural and intellectual legacies of empire that were typically underestimated in Marxist and neo-Marxist economic theories of imperialism. Said's book spawned a loosely defined field known as postcolonial studies, as well as what has been called the "new imperial history," which drew its momentum largely from studies of the erstwhile European colonial empires (Howe 2009). New attention also followed, in the wake of the breakup of the Soviet Union, on the continental land empires of Europe, as reflected in Dominic Lieven's *Empire: The Russian Empire and Its Rivals* (2000). While the need for a better accounting of the legacy of the European empires of the past prompted much of the initial historiographical revolution, the continued vitality of the field has had much to do with interest in understanding the US, especially the place of American power in the emerging new century. The latter, for example, has also prompted a resurgence of a variety of Marxist and neo-Marxist economic theories of imperialism. Explorations of the changing conditions of capital accumulation are thus once again emerging center-stage (Arrighi 1994; Harvey 2003). The growing receptiveness of this new historiography of empire to the contributions of non-Western historiographies and of "area studies" programs, which in the US have traditionally housed the interdisciplinary scholarship on the non-European parts of the world, has further helped to make the remit of this field more global. These multiple, and often unrelated, strands have come together to make empire studies into a thriving field, especially in the US academy, only a short time from the moment when historians were bemoaning the obsolescence of a field that had begun to lose steam – just like the retreating European empires that had once been its primary objects of study.

This rejuvenated field – quite different from the sterile debates that have bogged down much of the public discourse about empire – has far-reaching implications for the study of world history. The obvious affinity of empire studies with world history, of course, is its attention to the exercise of power in and through large-scale structures. Yet what distinguishes an empire from other political forms, such as city-states, republics, kingdoms, and nation-states, is not only a matter of scale. Empires, as current scholarship is reminding us, were functionally differentiated polities with a variety of heterogeneous political and administrative arrangements and with complex patterns established for negotiating diversity among its population. But attempts at actually arriving at a single definition of empire – as a transhistorical and abiding political state-form from antiquity into the present – have proven notoriously difficult, if also misguided. Empire, a word that can be traced to the Roman *imperium*, has historically meant a number of different things: a one-size-fits-all definition of empire would simply never do. Some scholars prefer to work with various loose taxonomies of empires, such as the longstanding distinction between the far-flung seaborne empires and the contiguous land empires, not to mention a third type: the decentralized nomad empires, like the Mongol empire (Barfield 2001). Add to this, the renewed attention in recent years to early or premodern empires as a distinct imperial form (Bayly and Bang 2003). Others have offered a range of functionalist explanations – based on what states have sought and how they have behaved – to arrive at certain family resemblances among empires, an "imperial minimum," as it were, for the purpose of making comparisons across time and space (Maier 2006). The definitional inexactitude constitutive of the term has led still others to suggest that the concept of empire may be more useful as a loose descriptive category than as a tight analytical one.

The crux of the analytical purchase of empire, however, especially for the student of world history, may lie elsewhere. The eschewing of pointless debates over the formal properties of empires, and the resulting corollary about whether particular states could be named properly as "imperial" or not, as well as of the opposite, and mistaken, temptation of identifying empire too loosely as simply a metaphor for unbounded power, can actually be quite liberating. It enables a better engagement with the contributions made by the historiography of empires. This, at its best, has provided enormously generative ways of thinking for world history. The value of the new empire studies thus does not rest on providing a textbook definition of empire to fit this or that historical case; rather, it rests on the new lines of enquiry that the attention to empire in historical scholarship has enabled. Empire, in this sense, is important precisely because it has been "good to think." The reference, of course, is to Claude Lévi-Strauss's distinction between that which is merely the subject of description and that which provides the basis or tools for thinking and theorizing (1963: 89).

There have been several ways in which empires have proved especially good to think with. First, empires have been extremely useful in thinking about connections in world history. The history of empires has provided some of the most useful ways of thinking about what scholars are calling connected histories, entangled histories, or *histoires croisées*. (See Fernández-Armesto, this volume.) Individuals writing from such diverse political perspectives as John Seeley, the doyen of imperial history in Britain, and Frantz Fanon, the Martinique-born French anticolonial writer, had long acknowledged that empire bound together the histories of the imperial powers and their colonies (Seeley 1883; Fanon 1963). Yet it took until the last quarter-century before either imperial historiography or nation-based historiographies began to take this insight systematically to heart. This shift in the historiography of empire has not only brought together "domestic" (read national) and "imperial" history within the same framework, but has also pointed to their coproduction or mutual constitution in an "imperial social formation."

To be sure, this challenge to hermetically sealed national historiographies has not gone entirely uncontested. Several scholars have mounted a rearguard action to protest that because historical actors themselves were often blissfully inattentive to empire, empire could not be said to have had a "fatal impact" on national history (Porter 2004). Yet this line of argument, even aside from its flawed logic, has failed to gain much traction in the face of mounting evidence of the ways in which empire shaped not just the colonies or the imperial peripheries, but also the imperial centers or the metropoles. Indeed, it is this reversal of the traditional understanding of the flow of imperial influence – from center to periphery – that has been the most controversial and also, perhaps, the most rewarding.

Not surprisingly, therefore, the substitution of the familiar centripetal model with a centrifugal model of imperialism has had the greatest impact on the national historiographies of erstwhile European metropolitan powers. Modern British history especially, but also French, Dutch, German, Russian, Spanish, and even US history, have begun to look very different once the constitutive role of empire is acknowledged. The entangled or connected history of the imperial metropole and the colonial periphery has done much to put paid to familiar narratives of the "rise of the West" as well as to its corollary of "first in the West and then in the rest." The following two examples should suffice.

Long ago the historian Eric Williams (1944) drew attention to the impact of the slave economy in the Caribbean on the causes of the first "Industrial Revolution" in Britain. Since then legions of scholars have argued with, and against, Williams's thesis. While that thesis has been considerably modified, as scholars take into account a combination of internal and external factors, in the causes of the industrial revolution, this story can no longer be told as a purely internalist or entirely autochthonous British or European development (Inikori 2002). Likewise, scholars of Asia have suggested that the "great divergence" between Britain and much of Asia, especially China, occurred only as late as the 1800s, and that the chance "windfall" provided by the land and resources of the Americas and Africa was critical to this outcome (Pomeranz 2000). Even though the debate on the "rise of the West" has not been fully settled, its terms have undoubtedly been transformed (Bryant 2006).

Following on the pioneering work of another famous scholar from the Caribbean, C.L.R. James, who first put the eighteenth-century Haitian Revolution alongside the French Revolution, scholars have begun to revise the received history of universal human rights as a European idea gradually extended to peoples and places outside Europe (James 1938). Central aspects of this history, usually seen as a product of an exclusively European intellectual and political project, were in fact forged in the struggles for emancipation fought by slaves and their descendants in the Caribbean. To the "black Jacobins" of Saint Domingue we may owe much of what we have hitherto connected to the legacy of an exclusively continental revolution (Dubois 2004). The entangled histories that the new attention to empire has thrown up have made it difficult to sustain the neat compartmentalization between the West and the Rest that was once the staple of our historiography.

If thinking through empires helps to defamiliarize the history of an entity called "the West," as well as the national histories of individual European metropolitan powers, by the same token it also helps revise our understanding of the histories of the colonized world. To the more familiar narrative of the impact of the political and economic violence of imperialism, for example, scholars have added attention to colonialism's "epistemological violence": that is, to the role of colonial knowledge in the exercise of power. (See Simo, this volume.) The strategies of colonial rule relied on the accumulation and categorization of knowledge of the subject societies and peoples. The desire to "know" subject populations was a source of perennial anxiety and vulnerability for colonial rule; but it was also the basis for colonial intervention and interference in the name either of defending or reforming what colonial authorities frequently, if often mistakenly, assumed were the true and authentic customs and practices of indigenous peoples (Cohn 1996). Through such mechanisms as the census, ethnographic classifications, the codification of religious practices, and medical science, as well as more cynical "divide and rule" policies, albeit to different degrees in different locations, colonialism both constructed knowledge of indigenous peoples and often became complicit in local processes of the "invention of traditions." Colonial era accounts of "tribes" and chiefs, of castes and "communalism" (the term used for the politics of religious sectarianism in India), and even of the subordination of women, although these had their own prior histories in the societies of Asia and Africa, were seldom merely neutral reflections of the perduring remnants of precolonial cultures. In fact, colonial knowledge-practices, more often than not, were actively involved in recasting these. The supposedly timeless and "traditional" aspects of indigenous cultures turn out, on further scrutiny, to be often quite "modern" after all.

Colonialism, indeed, involved more than military conquest, economic domination, and the loss of political sovereignty: it was also a complex cultural project that remade indigenous societies, albeit not unilaterally, nor out of whole cloth, and certainly not always as originally intended. When in 1829 the East India Company abolished the practice of the self-immolation of widows on their husband's funeral pyre, commonly referred to as *sati*, from its territories in India, for example, this was not a straightforward story of the modern civilizing force of empire triumphing over the benighted traditions of the natives. European commentaries on the practice, as well as the protracted debates about the wisdom of colonial interference in this matter in the years prior to the legislation, tell a far more complicated story. These contributed to the process of converting an indigenous practice, which was supposed to be restricted to only a certain class of women and that was practiced in only certain parts of the country, into an enduring symbol of Hindu *qua* Indian culture. The subsequent debates between the supporters and opponents of legislative interference – and both camps had their share of Indians and Europeans – put "Indian" culture on trial.

Women, as Lata Mani famously puts it, were neither the subject nor the objects of the ensuing debate on the abolition of sati; they were instead merely the ground on which competing views of tradition and culture came to be debated (Mani 1987). The debate, moreover, came to be framed within the terms of a colonial understanding of a "textualized" version of Hindu culture: an understanding that privileged the authority of ancient canonical texts over the evolution of customary practices. Even though a process of "hierarchizing textualization" of elite forms of knowledge was already underway in India before the advent of colonial rule, as Sheldon Pollock reminds us (1993: 97), these trends were considerably exacerbated by colonial policies. One of the legacies of this pioneering social legislation of the colonial era was thus also the strengthening of a "textualized" understanding of Hindu culture that would circumscribe subsequent debates over the status of women in colonial India.

Such an expanded understanding of the legacy of European colonial empires – for both the European metropole and its colonies – has revised substantially our understanding of the modern world. Indeed, the real challenge of a focus on the constitutive role of empire is to make evident that the mere addition of non-Western history to Western history courses is not sufficient: the histories of both, instead, need to be rethought in the crucible of their unequal, but mutually constitutive, interactions.

The emphasis of this new historiography has been on the cultural project of empire, both in response to, and sometimes at the cost of, an earlier emphasis on political and economic factors; its major concern has been in tracing the processes by which colonial rule established mastery over colonized society through control of its natural, human, and cultural resources. This scholarship, to be sure, has challenged the simple binary opposition between the metropole and the colony and between colonizers and colonized, demonstrating in the case of the latter the enormous sociocultural work of class, race, and gender that was necessary, in the first place, to construct, and then to police the boundaries between the two (Stoler 1989). Yet an emphasis on the power of colonial knowledge and on the production of "difference" has also inadvertently tended to reify the very oppositions it sought to undo. Sometimes colonial categories of knowledge appear more powerful than they were and are assumed to have had a free hand in remaking colonized societies. The implication is that colonial knowledge operated on a *tabula rasa*, or that colonial intentions had a constancy and durability that remained largely impervious either to the dictates of particular exigencies or to the impact of indigenous responses (Cooper 2005). In effect, then, certain longstanding concerns about the top-down and the metropolitan-centered approach of imperial history linger even in some of its newer manifestations.

Similarly, the historiography of European colonial empires has too frequently remained locked within a singular metropolitan–colony axis at the cost of delineating other forms of connections and interactions that spilled over this divide. Hence the recent shift to notions of imperial "webs" and "networks" (Ballantyne 2002; Lester 2001). These latter help trace lateral connections between different colonial sites, beyond the vertical metropolitan–colony axis, as well as between rival empires. So particular colonial sites – such as Britain's Indian empire – themselves became nodes in a subimperial network (Metcalf 2007). The strategies of colonial rule as well as of anticolonial resistance, more-over, moved promiscuously within and between empires (Lake and Reynolds 2008). The impact of a comparative turn in the scholarship – to a consideration of European seaborne empires alongside contemporaneous European and non-European continental empires, as well as attention to a longer global history of empires before the modern period – has gone a long way in opening further lines of enquiry as well as in redressing some of the concerns that continue to plague empire studies.

Comparison, indeed, is a second way in which empires have proved good to think. (See Adas, this volume.) The comparative study of empires, along with offering a con-siderably expanded temporal and spatial dimension to the field, offers some perspective-altering insights. The widening of the time and space of empires has done much to reorient a field dominated by the study of European colonial empires. One obvious, yet important, contribution of this wider perspective is a reminder that for much of human history empires have been, as John Darwin (2007) puts it, the "default" form of politi-cal organization and thus hardly the "original sin" of Europeans perpetrated on the rest of the world.

The global and *longue durée* perspective on empires has been generative of new paradigms and avenues of research. It has certainly reminded scholars of the potential of comparative histories of empires: between whole empires; between component parts of individual empires; as well as between particular themes, say, religion, or the military, or court culture, across different empires. Empires are especially fertile grounds for comparative histories both because of the idea of *translatio imperii*, by which empires often claim "succession" by invoking earlier empires, and because of a related set of ideas, institutions, and practices – an "imperial repertoire," as it were – that were often subscribed to by, and freely exchanged between, rival empires. This much, perhaps, is already well known. The further point is the conceptual break-throughs that have come from the engagement with not just the histories, but also with the historiographies of empires in times and places other than those of nine-teenth- and twentieth-century European colonial empires. The disorienting perspec-tive this provides both puts the European colonial empires in their proper place and uproots, once and for all, the residual "national" frameworks that continue, often by default, even in the field of empire studies.

Take for example the conceptual rewards of bringing together the large continental land empires – such as the Romanov, Habsburg, Qing, and Ottoman empires – with that of the European seaborne empires with which they were contemporaneous. The historiographical liberation from Eurocentric conceptual categories, in no small part enabled by the attention of scholars to deconstructing colonial practices of constructing knowledge, has allowed these continental land-based and dynastic empires to emerge as more than just "archaic" and premodern hangers-on or misfits that some-how managed to persist into an era supposedly shaped by the "national" empires of northwestern Europe. Building on the work of generations of scholars of China, of Russia, and of the Ottoman empire, who have countered the myth that the nineteenth- and twentieth-century histories of these empires were one long story of inexorable "decline," comparative empire studies is breaking down many of the conceptual barriers that divided the field. These supposedly premodern empires, in fact, shared with European colonial empires many features of colonial knowledge production and of the construction of "difference" at particular moments and in relation to particular regions within their empires. The evidence of such "modernizing" trends suggests a need to revise the "sick man" narrative of these empires, barely hanging on, on life support, and to acknowledge the shared temporal and conceptual space they occupied with European colonial empires.

Even more importantly, perhaps, the engagement with the historiography of the continental empires as modern in their own right helps to question the inevitability (reflecting a teleology built into nationalism) of the substitution of empires by nation-states (Burbank and Cooper 2010). Here some of the scholarship on the breakup of the Ottoman empire (1326–1922) at the end of World War I is especially apposite. Contrary to what scholars had long assumed, an imperial Ottomanism, based, after the Balkan Wars, on an integrative Islamism, continued to be a viable political option for opponents of the imperial state up until the outbreak of the war. The "Young Turks," as Hasan Kayali (1997) suggests, may thus be something of a misnomer: they were, at least in the early years, more Ottoman, perhaps, than Turkish. The fact that rival Arabic and Turkish nationalisms ultimately took the place of an imperial Ottomanism was not foreordained: this outcome was the product of several contingent forces, including the impending threat from European powers, in the years leading up to the war. Here, as in the Austro-Hungarian empire that was also reconstituted into separate nation-states at the end of the war, the surprising longevity of imperial ideals and of imperial visions of the polity, alongside more "national" alternatives, suggests that the "transition" to the political form of the nation-state cannot be simply assumed or taken for granted.

The scholarship on early modern empires has likewise been disorienting for understanding both the place of European empires and of the retroactive "national" framing of the history of empires. The concept of the "early modern," a period roughly from the 1500s to the 1800s, has already done much to dislodge the idea of modernity from an exclusively European provenance (Eisenstadt and Schluchter 1998; Dussel 2000). Many of the political, economic, and social changes associated with this period were very widespread and, in fact, quite global in their scope; and, more importantly, the subsequent global dominance of Europe could not always be read back in a direct line, necessary and inevitable, from the developments during this period. So it was with early modern empires.

The dynamism of imperial expansion in the early modern period was not confined only to the overseas European empires. Central Eurasia, for example, was the site of an intense imperial rivalry between three empires, the Russian (1613–1917), Qing China (1644–1911), and the Zunghar empire (1671–1760), the last of the important pastoral-ist empires in the region. The Qing defeat of the Zunghars and the resulting conquest of modern Xinjiang, as Peter C. Perdue (2005) has shown, closed the ancient Eurasian frontier in an event that was no less momentous (according to scholars since Frederic Jackson Turner) than the closing of the American frontier. The state mobilization that was necessary for the successful conquest of the steppe region put the Chinese very much alongside the state-building efforts of European states at the time.

At the other end of the world, and in the very midst of European overseas empire-building, the Comanche Indians built an "American empire that, according to conventional histories, did not exist" and that, nevertheless, lasted from the mid-eighteenth century to about the second half of the nineteenth century (Hämäläinen 2008: 1). This "indigenous empire," with its own history of conquest on the southern plains of North America and its own aggressive imperial project at least until the second half of the nineteenth century, managed not only to counteract European imperialism, but also to have a decisive role in the outcome of the United States's westward expansion. Europeans were not the only, and for much of this period at least, certainly not the most dominant empire-builders.

The history of early modern European empires also highlights their later and retroactive construction as "national" projects. The early modern Spanish empire, as Henry Kamen has demonstrated, was hardly "Spanish" in any simple way. Kamen (2003) reconstructs the "international" collaboration that made possible the Spanish colonial enterprise. The Spanish empire, especially in the early years, was truly international: the contributions of the Portuguese, Italians, Catalans, and Jews as well as of African slaves supplemented those of Castilians and Aragonese. Even the actual conquest of the Americas was facilitated by the exploitation of dissension that already existed within American societies and by strategic alliances with the peoples whom the "conquistadors" encountered. These "multinational" foundations of the Spanish empire raise questions about the extent to which even overseas European empires could be considered purely "national" projects.

At its most challenging, moreover, the comparative study of empires has done much to shrink the length of the period of history in which the nation-state has been the dominant political form. The traditional view of the nation-state as the dominant political form of the modern age, starting with the Treaty of Westphalia in 1648 and coming into its own with the revolutions of the eighteenth and early nineteenth centuries, has taken a considerable beating. The empire-state remained a viable political form well into the twentieth century. In fact, as John Kelly and Martha Kaplan have argued, it was arguably not until the post–World War II era of decolonization that the nation-state came to be institutionalized as the dominant political form in the interstate system established in the United Nations (Kelly and Kaplan 2001).

This has opened up the history of the modern period – the era of the supposedly "national" European colonial empires – to revisionist interpretations. Scholars are beginning to reconsider, for example, the extent to which even the modern British and the French states were proper nation-states as opposed to imperial states (Wilder 2005). France, as this argument goes, did not become a fully "national" polity – that is, delimited to its territorial boundaries in Europe – until 1962 with the loss of Algeria. Empires, as this line of research seems to suggest, did not beget nation-states just in former colonized parts of the world or in the Ottoman and Austro-Hungarian lands, about which we have long known. Also, more controversially, the nation-state may be a more belated political form – created in the aftermath of decolonization – even in some of the "core" states of the modern world. The more "national" models of empire-building may have come, in fact, relatively late in the game and with the imperial latecomers – pioneered, according to Prasenjit Duara, by Japan in Manchukuo but also, perhaps, by the Germans at the turn of the nineteenth century and taking different forms in the Soviet Union's "empire of nations" or the United States's post–World War II anticolonial imperialism that operated precisely through an interstate order of nation-states (Duara 2003; Hirsch 2005).

This line of thinking has also been extremely productive for reappraising the diversity of anticolonialism. Not all forms of anticolonial resistance, for example, took the form of the demand for a separate nation-state. Even as late as the 1940s and 1950s, as Frederick Cooper's (1996) work on French West Africa demonstrates, labor and political leaders were using postwar French imperial notions of Greater France to make a powerful claim on the government: equality of wages and benefits for all whom the government asserted to be French. The logic of this claim proved ideologically and politically dangerous for the government to dismiss, even as metropolitan constraints also made the demands impossible to fulfill. Scholars have begun to explore the full range of anticolonial movements beyond demands made on behalf of a particular community. These include attempts to completely transform the structure of the imperial polity, as in the case of the demands made by labor and political leaders of French West Africa above, as well as movements that were not territorially defined: Pan-Islamic; Pan-Slavic; Pan-African and so on. This has also produced a vigorous new body of work that is drawing attention to the ideas of "universalism" and of "cosmopolitanism" as articulated in a variety of anti-colonial thoughts and practices hitherto seen largely within particularistic nationalist frames (West *et al.* 2009).

Recent scholarship on "premodern" empires – variously called archaic, early, agrarian, or tributary empires – has opened up a further set of questions of general and field-altering import. Comparisons between the Roman empire (ca. 200 BCE–395 CE, for the unified empire) and the roughly contemporaneous Han empire in China (221 BCE–220 CE), the two largest agrarian empires of antiquity, have become especially popular (Schiedel 2009). They go a long way to countering the privileging of Greco-Roman history in the study of the ancient world. (See Liu, this volume.)

The scholarship on premodern empires, moreover, has also reopened in interesting ways the familiar debate on the definition of "empire." Consider Sheldon Pollock's provocative argument about the divergent instantiations of the empire-form in antiquity. Empires, as he argues, have involved historical imitations. The Achaemenid empire (ca. 550 BCE to ca. 330 BCE), considered the "first political world-empire," provided the model for the emergence of successor empires in both Rome and early South Asia, but these two forms were radically different, especially the relationship in each between culture and power. (See Yoffee, this volume.) To take one example: while the early Indian polity was expansive culturally, unlike Rome it did not subscribe to an ideology of limitless territorial expansion (Pollock 2005). What are the implications of the conceptual dominance of the "Roman model" – as opposed to the "Indian model" – in our understanding, and identification, of empires elsewhere?

This question is especially relevant because it was against the background of the European colonial empires, which themselves self-consciously imitated the Roman model, that many a non-European precolonial state was first "discovered" and, then, conferred with an imperial identity. How has this "conceptual Eurocentrism" (in the identification of empires) influenced the study of, say, the Vijayanagara empire (1336–1646) in South India or the Songhay empire (1464–1591) in Western Sudan? Does the process of constructing ideological supremacy within empires, for example, look different when viewed from the perspective of imperial Songhay, where Islamic concepts of political legitimacy, especially under the Askiya rulers, came to be accepted as the norm, even though the major centers of the religion lay beyond the empire (Tymowski 2003–2004)? These are some of the lines of inquiry that are facilitated once the paradigmatic status of the Roman model is brought under scrutiny and the various instantiations of the empire-form in different places and in different times given their due.

The renewed attention on early empires or "tributary" empires as distinct imperial forms is also challenging the teleology, implicit or explicit, that has hitherto measured them in relation to modern industrial society. Hence "modernizers" focused on identifying both proto-modern forces and forces that blocked the full transition to modern capitalist society, while "primitivists" emphasized a sharp distinction between ancient agrarian-aristocratic society and industrial-capitalistic modernity. Challenging this intellectual *cul de sac*, Peter Bang draws attention to the institutional structures of "tributary" empires that reorients comparisons with modern industrial society in favor of more cross-cultural and trans-epochal comparisons among tributary empires. He thus places the Roman empire not in relation to early modern Europe, but in relation to other tributary empires: the Mughal, Ottoman, and Chinese empires. This move makes it easier not only to "abandon the tyranny of Europe over Rome," but also to reprise some of the characteristics associated with "tributary" empires (Bang 2008: 59). Such old chestnuts as the nature of patrimonial authority, the role of trade, and the relationship between the state and market formations in early empires are thus receiving a fresh look. The reappraisal of agrarian or preindustrial empires is opening the way for a better accounting of the economic and state institutions of premodern empires in their own terms, as well as of the precise nature of the rupture associated with the advent of modern industrial society.

Ultimately, the expansion of the temporal and the spatial scope of empire studies has helped dispel a powerful myth about empires, common both in popular and some academic discourses, about their unbounded power. The legitimacy and longevity of empires depended to a large extent on their ability to work with a range of intermediaries, especially local elites, who were critical to their functioning. At one end of the spectrum, for example, was the Mughal empire (1526–1858) in northern India. This Turkic Muslim dynasty, which started out in Herat and Kabul, could not consolidate its rule by force alone in a territory where the majority of the population was non-Muslim. The "Mughal compromise," as Sanjay Subrahmanyam puts it, was one "in which the ruler would take on attributes and practices that appealed to his non-Muslim subjects, while Mughal rule would then proceed on the basis of a progressive Persianization of elite culture and the incorporation of extensive territories through recognizably Mughal fiscal and administrative institutions" (2006: 84). The composite Mughal ruling elite was made up of Indian Hindus and Muslims, but also of Iranians and Central Asians. Even among contemporaries, like the Ottoman empire with its "multinational" ruling elite, the Mughal empire stands out for the substantial presence of non-Muslims in the highest ranks of the ruling elite. At the other end was British rule in India, which took up the mantle of imperial rule from the Mughals. The British colonial empire, at its height, rested on a much sharper separation from the subject populations, with the result that the incorporation of local elites into the higher ranks of the ruling class remained extremely limited and fitful. Even such "modern" colonial empires, however, could not entirely escape the necessity of balancing between incorporating, and differentiating themselves from, subject populations.

This new attention to the limits on imperial power has been largely salutary. It has brought more attention to imperial practices, as opposed to ideologies and intentions, and to the actual working out of empire on the ground. By emphasizing the role of local interlocutors and of local exigencies, including precolonial historical processes, scholars are demonstrating that the colonial mastery of modern European empires was limited even at their heights. Geography – as in oceans, mountains, rivers, and islands – was also a factor, as Lauren Benton suggests, in the exercise of imperial sovereignty. (See Simmons, this volume.) European overseas empires, she suggests, were actually quite "lumpy," consisting of "narrow bands or corridors, and ... enclaves and irregular zones around them" (2009: 2). The jurisdictional authority of empires was strongest at the nodes, in the corridors and enclaves, and a lot weaker in other areas. If imperial historiography's emphasis from the 1980s onwards was on the coproduction of the histories of the colonizing and colonized worlds, and on colonial knowledge and power, then the more recent emphasis has shifted to the contingency of imperial practices and to the various limits to the exercise of imperial and colonial power.

Comparative empire studies has thus qualified considerably the popular vision of empire as a juggernaut capable of laying waste to all in its wake. Empires had to coexist, and to make their peace, with historical processes that often predated any individual empire. At the same time, this comparative turn in the scholarship – especially when combined with a contrast between the "multiculturalism" of empires with the relative conformism of nation-states – can verge on an uncritical imperial nostalgia. The violence and inequality endemic to empires should caution against any overly rosy views. By the same token, the shift in the current scholarship from colonialism to empire has also raised some legitimate concerns about the elision of the specificity of modern colonialism. More attention, indeed, is needed to spell out carefully the features that made colonial empires distinctive: that is, in the particular forms of political, economic, and cultural relationships that they established between the metropolitan center and the periphery. The return of careful attention to the changing conditions of capital accumulation – prompted in part by contemporary forms of noncolonial imperialisms – also serves as a reminder of the need to bring the history of capitalism back to greater prominence in the scholarship on empires. These are minor caveats about a historiography that has made thinking through empires extremely generative for world history. The study of empires – through its contributions to a history of both connections and comparisons – provides a useful basis from which to think narratives for world history.

Empires, finally, and above all, are also good to think about the spatial units that structure the narratives of world history. (See McKeown, this volume.) Scholars increasingly reject the legitimacy of "civilizations" and of "nation-states" as adequate spatial units for structuring the narrative of world history, while offering a range of alternatives in their place. The "world" and the "globe" may offer useful horizons for scholarship. However, as units of analysis that anchor actual historical narratives, they can remain problematic: the tendency of the bird's eye view to flatten and totalize the diversity and contingency of human experience is real. On offer, therefore, are a variety of intermediate scales below the level of the global that combine both macro- and microhistorical processes. These include renewed attention to some of the following: the history of regions (albeit regions with porous boundaries that take into account cross-regional interaction); histories of oceans that emphasize mobility across maritime spaces that cut across bounded geographical regions; and the history of networks, with their various nodes and interacting systems that chart the transnational flow of goods, peoples, ideas, plants, and microbes. An emphasis on empires does not preclude these alternative approaches, but, in fact, is both enriched by them and, in turn, enriches them.

To be sure, empires are not the only networks of transfer and interaction. There have always been alternative networks – pilgrimage routes, trade diasporas, lines of intellectual and cultural exchange – that both predate, and persist beyond, any individual empire. Consider, for example, an old diaspora of Arabs from Hadramawt, Yemen, spread across the Indian Ocean, which for the past half-millennium has been drawn into both conflict and cooperation with a succession of empires that have come and gone. The latest chapter in this interlocked history of a transnational Muslim diaspora and empire, as Engseng Ho reminds us, is currently being played out in the "War on Terror." This pits a new noncolonial or anticolonial US empire against an enemy that was personified by Osama bin Laden, a member of the same Hadrami diaspora. Here "empire through diasporic eyes," as Ho (2004) puts it, provides a perspective from which to analyze the working both of different imperial power relations and of the various forms of resistance to them. Indeed, an attention to empire itself as a type of network, alongside diasporas as well as other cross-regional and oceanic networks and flows, helps to ensure that the "imperial ship of state" is not rendered invisible even as scholars do more to make visible the "smaller boat[s] sailing the same seas" (Ho 2004: 213). Imperial social formations remain useful precisely because they are explicit about the asymmetries of power: they have the potential to offer a historical narrative with, as it were, the "politics left in."

Empires also overlap and work with recently reconfigured regional histories. (See Kramer, this volume.) The idea of "autonomous" regions that was once the basis for traditional area-studies programs in the US has come in for legitimate criticism over the years. However, acknowledging afresh some of the strengths of the traditional area-studies programs, some scholars have been loath to throw out the baby (of intensive training in a region's languages and cultures) with the bathwater (of "civilizational" thinking as filtered through Cold War, and now post–Cold War, self-contained geographical categories). Take, for example, Sugata Bose's call to reconceive the geographical boundaries of South Asian area studies as "South Asia without Borders" (2010). The danger of retaining the name without its territorial coordinates, however arbitrary these were, is to risk endowing a cultural fixity to "South Asianness" that perdures no matter where it appears. Empires, as descriptive or as analytical categories, need not preclude the kind of close attention to languages and sources promoted in area studies programs: they offer, in addition, a way out of fixed notions of culture and identity that still too often stick to attempts to rethink regional categories.

Consider the case of "Eurasia," a new name for the area roughly between Germany and Japan that is being adopted by many former Soviet studies programs in the US academy in these post-Soviet times. "Eurasia," according to Stephen Kotkin (2007), is a problematic category, not just because of the checkered history of "Eurasianism" in the interwar period, but, even more importantly, because it retains lingering associations with concerns about identities. Kotkin proposes that scholars eschew such associations – still at work in reimagined region-based categories – in favor of a greater attention to institutions and to issues of governance. He turns to the formative framework of empires, taking his cue from the colossally disruptive and constitutive impact of the Mongol empire to revise the understanding of the field. Significantly, however, he does not propose the notion of a Mongol Commonwealth (with its connotations of a Mongol-centric Eurasia at the cost both of other empires and of nonimperial networks), but the notion of *ab imperio* (from empire). The point, as Kotkin explains, is not to impose an imperial coherence over the region in place of any alleged geographical, religious, linguistic, or geopolitical coherence. The work done for him by the cross-regional notion of *ab imperio* (a term he borrows from the journal of that name published in Kazan), then, is precisely to counterbalance a preoccupation with identities, of individuals, groups, and of regions, with an emphasis on processes of exchange and institutions of governance.

Thinking with empires, then, is not about imperial nostalgia. Empires, more often than not, were a nasty business. The exchanges that they facilitated were often coercive and always unequal. Violence was never very far away from empires. Empires, after all, are always about power, both real and desired. Yet empires are never omnipotent: they coexist with, and are survived by, alternative networks of exchange, whether by land or across maritime spaces; and, further, they always remain subject to contestation both from within and from outside. Because networks of interactions midwifed the world, including the cultures and identities that we have inherited, warts and all, and because these operated under conditions of asymmetrical power, empires still remain some of the most useful categories with which to think world history.

References

Arrighi, G. 1994. *The Long Twentieth Century*. London: Verso.

Arrighi, G. 2005. Hegemony unravelling 1. *New Left Review* 32: 23–80.

Ballantyne, T. 2002. *Orientalism and Race*. London: Palgrave Macmillan.

Bang, P.F. 2008. *The Roman Bazaar*. New York: Cambridge University Press.

Barfield, T.J. 2001. The shadow of empires. In S.E. Alcock, T.N. D'Altroy, K.D. Morrison, and C.M. Sinopoli, eds, *Empires: Perspectives from Archaeology and History*, pp. 10–41. Cambridge: Cambridge University Press.

Bayly, C., and P.F. Bang. 2003. Introduction: Comparing premodern empires. *Medieval History Journal* 6 (2): 169–187.

Benton, L. 2009. *A Search for Sovereignty*. Cambridge: Cambridge University Press.

Bose, S. 2010. South Asia without borders. Presentation at International Institute Symposium, Oct. 29, University of Michigan.

Bryant, J. 2006. The West and the Rest revisited. *Canadian Journal of Sociology* 31 (4): 403–444.

Burbank, J., and F. Cooper. 2010. *Empires in World History*. Princeton: Princeton University Press.

Cohn, B. 1996. *Colonialism and Its Forms of Knowledge*. Princeton: Princeton University Press.

Cooper, F. 1996. *Decolonization and African Society*. Cambridge: Cambridge University Press.

Cooper, F. 2005. *Colonialism in Question*. Berkeley: University of California Press.

Darwin, J. 2007. *After Tamerlane*. London: Bloomsbury.

Duara, P. 2003. *Sovereignty and Authenticity*. Lanham: Rowman & Littlefield.

Dubois, L. 2004. *Avengers of the New World*. Cambridge, MA: Harvard University Press.

Dussel, E. 2000. Europe, modernity, and Eurocentrism. *Nepantla* 1 (3): 465–478.

Eisenstadt, S.N., and W. Schluchter. 1998. Introduction: Paths to early modernities. *Daedalus* 127 (3): 1–18.

Fanon, F. 1963. *The Wretched of the Earth*, trans. Constance Farrington. New York: Grove. First published as *Les damnés de la terre*, 1961.

Hämäläinen, P. 2008. *Comanche Empire*. New Haven: Yale University Press.

Harvey, D. 2003. *The New Imperialism*. Oxford: Oxford University Press.

Hirsch, F. 2005. *Empire of Nations*. Ithaca, NY: Cornell University Press.

Ho, E. 2004. Empire through diasporic eyes. *Comparative Studies in Society and History* 46 (2): 210–246.

Howe, S., ed. 2009. *New Imperial Histories Reader*. London: Routledge.

Inikori, J.E. 2002. *Africans and the Industrial Revolution in England*. Cambridge: Cambridge University Press.

James, C.L.R. 1938. *Black Jacobins*. London: Secker & Warburg.

Kamen, H. 2003. *Empire*. New York: HarperCollins.

Kayali, H. 1997. *Arabs and Young Turks*. Berkeley: University of California Press.

Kelly, J., and M. Kaplan. 2001. *Represented Communities*. Chicago: University of Chicago Press.

Kotkin, S. 2007. Mongol Commonwealth? *Kritika* 8 (3): 487–531.

Lake, M., and H. Reynolds. 2008. *Drawing the Global Colour Line*. Cambridge: Cambridge University Press.

Lester, A. 2001. *Imperial Networks*. London: Routledge.

Lévi-Strauss, C. 1963. *Totemism*, trans. Rodney Needham. Boston: Beacon. First published as *Le Totémisme aujourd'hui*, 1962.

Lieven, D. 2000. *Empire*. London: John Murray.

Maier, C. 2006. *Among Empires*. Cambridge, MA: Harvard University Press.

Mani, L. 1987. Contentious traditions. *Cultural Critique* 7: 119–156.

Metcalf, T. 2007. *Imperial Connections*. Berkeley: University of California Press.

Perdue, P. 2005. *China Marches West*. Cambridge, MA: Harvard University Press.

Pollock, S. 1993. Deep Orientalism? In C. Breckenridge and P. van der Veer, eds, *Orientalism and Postcolonial Predicament*, pp. 76–113. Philadelphia: University of Pennsylvania Press.

Pollock, S. 2005. Axialism and empire. In J. Arnason, S. Eisenstadt, and B. Wittrock, eds, *Axial Civilizations and World History*, pp. 397–450. Leiden: Brill.

Pomeranz, K. 2000. *The Great Divergence*. Princeton: Princeton University Press.

Porter, B. 2004. *The Absent-Minded Imperialists*. Oxford: Oxford University Press.

Said, E. 1978. *Orientalism*. New York: Pantheon.

Schiedel, W., ed. 2009. *Rome and China*. Oxford: Oxford University Press.

Seeley, J.R 1883. *The Expansion of England*. London: Macmillan.

Stoler, A.L. 1989. Rethinking colonial categories. *Comparative Studies in Society and History* 31 (1): 134–161.

Subrahmanyam, S. 2006. A tale of three empires. *Common Knowledge* 12 (1): 66–92.

Tymowski, M. 2003–2004. Use of the term "empire" in historical research in Africa: A comparative approach. *Afrika Zamani* 11 and12: 18–26.

West, M.O., W.G. Martin, and F.C. Wilkins. eds. 2009. *From Toussaint to Tupac*. Chapel Hill: University of North Carolina Press.

Wilder, Gary. 2005. *The French Imperial Nation-State: Negritude and Colonial Humanism between the Two World Wars*. Chicago: University of Chicago Press.

Williams, E. 1944. *Capitalism and Slavery*. Chapel Hill: University of North Carolina Press.

CHAPTER EIGHTEEN

The Body in/as World History

ANTOINETTE BURTON

For Muslim veils in France to seem out of place, we need to forget that Charles Martel stopped 'Abd-al-Raman only 300 miles south of Paris, two reigns before Charlemagne.

Michel-Rolph Trouillot, "The perspective of the world"

the body itself balks account

Walt Whitman, "I sing the body electric"

If you were to do an ethnography of world history textbooks with an eye to assessing how well they account for women, gender and sexuality across time and space, I suspect that even historians who have no truck with those subjects of inquiry would be surprised by what a comparatively slight impression they have left on the grand narratives that many of us in the United States use to help us teach the global past. Indexes are a rich and remarkable archive in this regard. The category "women" generates the most hits, typically in the form of a long sublist: one page for "Hittites," one page for "during war," two pages for "Islamic," and three – three! – for "feminism." "Mass politics" might generate a few pages, as might "education of" and "between 1650 and 1750." If you are lucky the textbook index will also direct you to "see gender" or "see feminism" and will specify people such as Mary Wollstonecraft or Marie Antoinette or Eleanor Roosevelt. "Marriage" might also be a category, and subjects like women and gender and sexuality might be embedded in "clothing," "Christianity" or "hijabs." Any of the above might lead to an illuminating photograph, which is where women often appear to support a claim – over there in the main text – about religion, politics, science or the law. While it would require a more sustained study, I'd venture a guess that women are to be found most commonly in world history textbooks at the margins, popping up here and there to complement a section on revolution or trade or cultural contact or what have you. Despite the work that has been done to decenter Europe and to move world history

A Companion to World History, First Edition. Edited by Douglas Northrop.
© 2012 Blackwell Publishing Ltd. Published 2012 by Blackwell Publishing Ltd.

away from the Western Civilization models whence it partly derived – and regardless of whether the text takes a civilizational or an integrative approach – women tend to act mainly as buttresses to larger narrative claims, even when the narrative turns microhistorical. Histories of women or gender rarely, if ever, drive histories of the global except when those histories are themselves about recovering women.

The latter project is a worthy cause, and it has absorbed the energies of some of the most distinguished practitioners of women's and gender history coming out of, and in turn shaping, the second wave of academic feminism (Berger *et al.* 1988). Some of them, such as Lynn Hunt and Bonnie Smith, have even turned their attention to general textbooks, with decidedly better results for the incidence of women in both the index and the narrative (see Hunt *et al.* 2005). But this largely leaves aside the question of how to sediment both women as *regular* historical subjects, and gender and sexuality as *historical* systems in introductory narratives of the past. The stakes of such an undertaking are undoubtedly high. Undergraduate students in the US are increasingly required to take world history as part of their liberal arts curriculum, and AP (Advanced Placement) exam preparation is an increasing staple feature of a high school education, at least for the college- and university-bound. The comparative failure of best-selling world history textbooks to do more than glancingly address these subjects – serious and practically uncontested ones in intellectual and disciplinary terms – is even more astonishing when we consider the vast scholarship, both historical and interdisciplinary, that has been produced in the field, even when we delimit that field simply as "women's history."[1] And if we acknowledge that women's and gender history has long been transnational and comparative (with all the pros and cons those approaches entail), it seems incredible that they can have left so little mark on major textbooks in world history, one of the few growth industries in early twenty-first century academic publishing and one of the major delivery systems of knowledge about "the global," if not the only one, to which institutions of secondary and tertiary education in the US share a commitment. In the face of world history's role as both handmaiden to and gadfly on contemporary globalization, it is tempting to tweak Dipesh Chakrabarty's (1992) ontological lament and observe that the project of gendering the global past refers to a history that does not yet exist, because it presumably cannot exist without accounting somehow, anyhow, for these critical dimensions of the human experience via more than an indexical trace.

Do women, gender and sexuality have a place in world histories other than as supplements and ornaments – functions which may be said to neatly summarize how women as such have been viewed by civilizations, Western or not, across the landscape of human and geophysical time that accounts of the global past(s) aim to capture? Yes and no. In this chapter, one of the few in this volume to nominate anything that might be related to these questions in its title, I want to think this problem less through an additive or inclusive framework than through a strategic one. Drawing on the insight of feminist historian Kathleen Canning, who coined the phrase "body as method," as well as on the work I have done with Tony Ballantyne, I suggest that in addition to recovering embodied histories across landscapes of civilizations, regions, empires and/or "the world," we ought to think about the body as a strategy – in this case, a strategy for how we structure introductory level courses and train graduate students in the field (Canning 1992; Ballantyne and Burton 2005). A locus of discipline, spectacle and power; a screen onto which fantasy and violence are projected, literally and otherwise; a carrier of biopower across space and place; a recurrent tool of rulers and ruled – these are just a few of the possibilities the body offers as the ground for thinking with and through the global. And no matter which approach you take to conceptualizing "globality" – via civilizations, webs, war, religion, trade networks, the environment, events, material culture, catastrophes – the body is arguably indispensable for understanding how power was imagined, aspired to, and executed in specific times and places and across them as well. More than just the addition of women and sexuality to the syllabus, attention to bodies as technologies of resistance and rule and much in-between illuminates virtually any topic or thematic you might wish to cover: it is a strategy as much as a subject *per se*. In a very real sense, the body as method seeks company with many of the preoccupations shared by scholars and teachers of world history in the last 20 years. If we think of the body itself as an access point, an index not only of specific women or genders and sexual practices but as a dynamically interconnective historical force, contingent on time and place; absorbent and irritating; vulnerable to exploitation and contagion yet hardy and resourceful; dangerous to would-be hegemons and a carrier of all kinds of power – if, in other words, we rethink the body as a kinetic and malleable agent, actor and acted upon – we might just be able to realign it with the project of world history and, in the process, persuade our students of its transformative impact on that enterprise, and the worlds they live in as well.

Acts of Relegation, Acts of Repositioning

It is tempting to rehearse that simple refrain of first-wave women's history when confronted with the dearth of sustained attention to women *qua* women in world history narratives: Women were there. They were in the streets during various phases of the French Revolution, with its global antecedents and reverberations; they were there in the worlds that trade has made across wide swaths of the early modern, modern and late modern worlds; their labor, both physical and reproductive, was at the heart of the slave system wherever it occurred (in ancient Greece and Rome, in Eurasia, in the Atlantic world and the Pacific Rim, in the Indian Ocean world, and in the southern hemisphere); they were a key symbol of social and sexual order in imperial regimes of all kinds; they played consequential roles in anticolonial nationalism; they have shaped bodies of law, sacred and secular; and they have been critical to the historical forces of migration and religious practice and war from one millennium to the next. Choose any topic, any temporal frame, any geographical unit, any spatial ecumene, any scale of history. Not only can you address the impact of women, you can access a sizable body of historiography that can help you integrate women into any given lecture, as well as across your syllabus as a whole.

Why, then, are women *per se* not more visible in world history textbooks? It's partly a matter of omission, partly a matter of genre. With few exceptions, and despite the widely acknowledged impact of women's and gender history on the content and practice of History (capital H), these topics remain the specialty of only a medium-sized proportion of the profession in North America – and I will be so bold as to say that when they appear, they remain a drop-in feature of much historical work, whether monographic or grand narrative in form. In the case of world history, this is certainly intelligible, especially if we understand "the history of women" or of "gender" as specific examples of "larger" phenomena – as a dimension, if you will, of Andean peasant culture or the May Fourth Revolution in China. And, taken on their own terms, the kinds of macronarrative schemes to which world history textbooks are usually committed preclude the possibility of too much particularity or too much dimensionality; or, rather, there is so much to cover, there is not enough time and space for "drilling down" to the local example, of which women are often considered to be a species. This is equally, if differentially, true for people of color and other subjects – laborers, for example, who are often women and people of color – perceived to be "at the bottom" of world history. They erupt at the sightline of big events or as dimensions of global processes, to recede again until the next big political crisis or economic transformation or subsection of that chapter that deals with social and/or cultural matters. When we visualize the work that individuals or people do to move accounts of world history forward we see a dotted landscape, where the landscape itself is not just a horizon but marks the ground of historical visibility, the threshold to which legitimate subjects, of all kinds, must rise in order to be recognized and cited as such. Women are most often, if not always, relegated to a kind of subliminal zone until they are called on to deepen our understanding of the main event.[2]

And this is fine in many respects. Who has not used Ibn Battuta or Marco Polo or Zheng He or Isabella of Spain or Emmeline Pankhurst or Archduke Franz Ferdinand and his wife, Sophie, or W.E.B. DuBois or Chica Da Silva to humanize colossal moments and phenomena in a world history lecture? As Natalie Zemon Davis (1997) has shown, even individual women admittedly "at the margins" – in her case, Glikl Bas Judah Leib, Marie de l'Incarnation, and Marie Sybilla Merian – can illuminate entire worlds, multiple worlds in all their simultaneity. World history cannot, perhaps, afford to be interested in individual accomplishments or lives except instrumentally. And yet teachers of world history must call on many things instrumentally. I, for one, use empire as a structuring device: a way to track connectivity, its limits and possibilities, and the many historical phenomena it makes hypervisible (war, capital, migration). Practitioners of world history have to cop to the necessity of such selective and partial frames, or else they would not be able to craft any narratives at all. And frames invariably occlude and exclude. Choices must be made and those choices close out wide swaths of planetary experience. Our choices also involve making arguments about proportionality: When is empire an important explanatory device, when is it not? When does it drive global processes, and under what specific circumstances? What are the limits, indeed, of any analytical frame or subject for historicizing what we are consolidating as world history?

If the same questions were applied to women and gender, they might or might not yield a revision of your syllabus, depending on where you have relegated them initially in your course. Even if you want to give a human face to world history, it is likely that unless you are a historian of women, gender or sexuality by training, you will not be easily convinced that women, whether as individuals or in aggregate, have exerted enough of a force on world history to make their histories a consistent feature of your course plan, or even that it is possible to do more than add gender and sexuality at specific moments. This is both ironic and vexing, because feminist historians have not just been producing work that models "connective comparisons," they have been the vanguard of thinking globally, as the scholarly work of the last three decades – and the careers of the two major Anglophone journals in the field, *Gender and History* and the *Journal of Women's History* – amply illustrate.[3] Their relatively newer equivalents in the field of world and global history have struggled, in contrast, to register women, gender and sexuality as subjects of research and teaching in their table of contents more than sporadically. Recourse to the body – not merely as a subject but as a method for apprehending historical processes, vectors of power, capillaries of circulation and materialities of violence and struggle – is one alternative to this impasse, an impasse that I, for one, am not content to allow simply to endure as an occupational hazard of world history teaching. Using the body as a (re)positioning device challenges the add-women-and-stir mentality that characterizes much world history pedagogy by capturing women, gender, sexuality not as identities or dimensions of the past but as historical forces that have to be reckoned with if students are to come away with an appreciation of what "history" is and what thinking about it in a global way actually entails.

What do I mean when I say the body? I mean a complex of material and symbolic properties that do not exist *a priori* but are produced and consolidated by their collision with historically specific events, formations and experiences. Emphatically not a universal or transhistorical category, the body is neither self-evident nor static. To borrow from Judith Butler (1993: 9), it is not a site or surface in the passive sense of those terms, in part because it is always being brought into being as a subject by the historical contexts that animate it. As a complex or a matrix – and in contradistinction to accounts that render it mainly a supine subject – the body is an agent, a force, which *indexes* historical processes that, in turn, help to stabilize it as an object of violence, a resource for labor, a vessel of reproduction, an instrument of pleasure, and above all, a mode of power. As such it is an invaluable archive of history at work, with the capacity not simply to represent identities (women, men) or reflect "what happened" (women shaped the suffrage debate) but to render visible historical conditions in-the-making and to throw the dynamism of historical processes into bold relief as well. And in the context of world history, the body has the capacity to register circulation, mobility, processes of exchange and trade, political economies in all their scope and scale – to dramatize, in short, the very connective tissue of globality in its myriad micro and macro forms.

Take one of the most commonly taught subjects in world history, the trade in slaves. There are all kinds of ways to convey its global character – in terms of maps, in terms of numbers, in terms of personal testimony by slaves and slavers alike. A focus on the body in this context arguably encompasses all of these modes of inquiry, allowing you to capture the massive corporal movement at the heart of the trade and to make a case for slavery as the first, if not the paradigmatic, modern global system. In this particular instance, you can mobilize bodies not as passive subjects but as historical forces that index a variety of dynamic factors: capital, sexuality and empire, among others. Doing so allows you, and your students, to appreciate slaves as people who were turned into com-modities, who were *made body* in commercial and symbolic terms – a racializing and sexualizing process that unfolds differently in different times and places and helps to account for the discrepant relationships between bondage and indenture and to track the shades of meaning and practice that attached to those designations from the Atlantic to the Indian Oceans. Here the body functions as an aggregate but also as the driver: the maps, the demographics, even the slave narratives (where they exist) are contingent on it not just as an analytical category but as a social, political or economic actor. Once you've established it as a point of departure, the framework of your narrative, you can, of course, unpack the body and move your story in any number of directions, again to underscore the global character of slavery and its correlatives as a system. You can use the slave ship as an example of how and under what conditions bodies were transported and, in the case of the Middle Passage, transformed in transit, most often from living into dead but also from Mandinkan into Carolinian or boy into man. You can talk about the shift from slavery to indenture as a kind of bodily refit; you can focus on the body at work on plantations, in flight via runaway slave ads, in rebellion in Haiti, in childbirth wherever estate and other records permit you to see and/or imagine it. The body is both an abstraction and an opportunity for interpreting lived reality, however speculatively. And it can provide opportunities for understanding both what roles women (as well as men) played and how gender and sexuality worked as well.

Jennifer Morgan's *Laboring Women* (2004) is exemplary here, emphasizing as it does how women of African descent were transformed into slaves by the exigencies of colonial profit in early colonial Barbados and South Carolina. Her skepticism about the inherent nature of women's historical experience – a refusal to take the body as self-evident or *a priori* – is crucial. She argues that neither their femaleness nor their blackness was a given: as bodies, they accrued specific meanings and functions in the service of local and global economies but equally as a result of planters' recognition of their tremendous labor/reproductive power. Both their womanness and their blackness were produced by what Morgan calls their "enslaveability"; those properties were historically, contingently, produced through the fact of New World slavery and they cannot be understood outside of those specific contexts of production. Nor was it only as slaves that African women manifested as bodies, as sexualized and racialized beings: they were also "free laborers … wives of traders and settlers and … travelers in their own right," who either circulated widely in the Atlantic world or who occasioned, via their work and their value, much of the global mobility that characterized this region (Morgan 2004: 1–2). Whiteness was also dramatically produced, gendered and sexualized in such contexts (Jones 2007). "Women" don't just have a history, they offer ways into the workings of History itself. And when I mobilize Morgan's research in my own world history teaching, it is not as a local example of a global phenomenon. Rather, by establishing the body as a method for apprehending the global effects of slavery, we have the opportunity to see the striations of historical event and process writ large and small on either aggregates or individuals.

Although this strategic use of the body can lead to the "recovery" of individual women and their experiences, it is not a magic bullet. Recourse to bodies does not produce "voices" or speaking subjects any more than brief and generalized invocations of women in textbooks can do. The majority of enslaved women left no discursive trace, though scholars like Morgan and others have striven to read planters' wills and other kinds of documentation to recreate their worlds; they have even engaged in historically informed speculation as to how such women may have felt about their children, their daily lives, their fates. If anything, the body as method complicates the idea that women can simply be restored to history *qua* women. As Morgan's work so effectively shows, gender was never the only variable at work. Enslaved women were also imagined as black or "colored" or "mulatto" – racialized *assignments* that were part of the complex of gender, the modality in which it was lived, but that were ultimately inseparable from the slave's identity as "woman." For scholars of women and gender and sexuality committed, as many of us are, to thinking sex/gender as a system rather than as an identity *per se*, attention to the body makes more complicated – and historically dynamic – accounts of "women's experience" not only possible but inevitable. In this sense, the body is as critical for feminist histories on a global scale as it is for world history as a genre or a practice. In methodological terms – and somewhat paradoxically – taking the body seriously in and as world history means both rematerializing gender/sexuality as a historical system *and* refusing to reduce histories of women simply to the sexed and gendered body. It means acknowledging, in other words, that bodies have histories that depend in part on their sexual capacity but that they function in a variety of other domains – economic, social, political – as well (see Butler 1998).

As a method, the body is protean and eminently portable. Want to understand Mughal court life in the age of Akbar? Think about the centrality of the harem to its management and hegemony. A "domestic" spatial arrangement that assigned specific domains to specific bodies, it mapped both the conditions of daily life and the dynastic ambitions of the emperor himself. As Ruby Lal's work on the subject suggests, the harem was neither static nor fixed: it assigned women to certain spaces and regulated men's contact with them, but it was continually on the move – producing what she calls a "peripatetic world" of court politics and an increasingly, if unevenly, gendered and sexualized sovereign subject in the body of Akbar himself. Given the emphasis on his genealogy, his divinity and the "fortified masculinity" of his body in Mughal chronicles – and given the stakes of these for his sovereign power – it is frankly hard to imagine how one could talk about Akbar absent attention to these questions (Lal 2005: 152). They are not simply ethnographic, though they do offer some window into the daily life of the court and the monarch's place in it. As in the case of Louis XIV – whose ceremonial morning levee was a performance of the most intimate bodily detail and the highest political magnitude – attention to the body affords us entry to a whole set of historical processes, allowing us to slice politics and political economies wide open and access their protocols and modes of operation. Even if women are not the subject, or their individual historical experiences are not accessible, an embodied view of dominant forms offers insight into how power worked, and how inseparable it was from civilizational aspiration – even when such aspiration was thwarted or went unrealized.

Can the body as method really get at the big and/or traditional subjects of world history? Revolution is perhaps exemplary in this regard; to what extent is the body a useful strategy for its global histories? One very useful feature of this approach is the way the body can serve as a scalar standard, an index of how far ostensibly catastrophic events reach and what impact they have across populations, as collectivity and in the particular. Douglas Northrop's (2004) work on struggles over the veil as a means of extending Soviet revolutionary power into Muslim Central Asia is a perfect example here, not least because it engages body politics in a very expansive way, illustrating how critical the family and specifically women and girls were to Moscow's ideological and economic programs. His study allows us to see with particular vividness how linked local struggles against the unveiling campaign were to longer histories of Russian colonization and how readily the body might be reappropriated as a terrain of resistance or accommodation. As in the example of slave women, we see here with particular vividness how a political and cultural identity – "the Soviet woman," "the Uzbek family" – is being forcibly assigned to certain subjects as part of a larger historical process; those designations do not exist *a priori* and in fact emerge directly from historical struggle. Depending on your predilections, this story could attach to a more conventional lecture on the Russian Revolution; it could be linked with narratives of how gender worked to shape the Mexican Revolution; or it could be used to remap what counts, in geographical terms, as Soviet territory into the interwar period, with the veil/body a kind of mercury trail for the success and limits of Sovietization as a globally aspirant ideology.[4] At the very least, the impact of "revolution" on the body politic – as measured by the old and new regimes' visions for the sociosexual order – is an indicator of the extent to which claims of historical transformation of the kind to be found in revolutionary rhetoric may actually have obtained. The body is, then, a litmus test for the scale of change – a critical indicator of a canonical disciplinary concern, for world history no less than any other. In part because students can be as hostile as anyone else to them in such settings, it is a litmus test you might not be able to employ with as much rhetorical or persuasive force if you employed "women" or even "gender," although attention to these are clearly enabled by the body as method. (See chapters by Bain and by Getz, this volume.) Indeed, it would take some effort *not* to account for women and gender once you have mobilized the body as a strategy.

My examples so far have, admittedly, been quite particular. Let's take a wider swath of times and places and see how the body as method might play out as an explanatory framework for a larger portion of a world history syllabus. What follows is a rationale for how I conduct the part of my world history syllabus I call "Global Economies and Uneven Developments," in which I strive self-consciously to globalize a kind of core European narrative of modernity and progress, prizing it open to and for histories of empire both east and west, both above and below. I operate under the presumption that since the publication of volume 1 of Michel Foucault's *The History of Sexuality* in 1979, a scholarly consensus has emerged about the centrality of the body to modern Western regimes of discipline and punishment, to the political economies of production and consumption, and indeed, to the history of liberal democracy and its discontents as well. As over a quarter of a century of research across a variety of Euro-American contexts has illustrated, it is not simply that the exigencies of biopower were foundational to the emergence of modern state bureaucracies, or even that governmentality, in its strictest sense, was predicated on the presumption that bodies, in all their messiness, be rationalized as citizen/subjects. The enduring though often overlooked insight offered by Foucault's conceptual apparatus is rather that the body has had a distinctively *political* career entailed by its ideological and material work as a vector of labor and violence, reproduction and atrocity, alterity and civility. Bodies serve, in short, as lightning rods for politics – sexual and otherwise – across spaces small and vast. The body is nothing more nor less than the scandal of the state, in many senses of the term (Sunder Rajan 2003). For whether hegemonic or not, the agencies of modern power have struggled with, and often failed in, the project of fixing bodies, striving to make them legible *to* dominant forms of power and *as* stable and stabilizing sites of legitimacy. In doing so, state power has most often violated, reshaped and otherwise deformed the body: most commonly in the name of progress and civilization and with a very specific, if always unfolding, iteration of a "universal" white, male and middle-class model in view. Whether we begin the story of modernity in the 1350s, the 1490s or the 1750s, we must admit to the body as more than incidental to the fate of polities, nations and empires.[5] In both the aggregate and the particular, bodies have consistently, and most often insistently, shaped the forms and meanings of the modern world in ways we have only begun to fully countenance.

Indeed, one way to approach the modern is as a set of symbolic and material practices that were made with, through and against the bodies of colonial subjects, however limited we may ultimately deem their agency. As students of other empires have been quick to point out, neither this temporal/causal relationship nor the category of colonial modernity itself is unique to Western empires. It is an observation that throws the exceptionality of the European experience into question and raises doubts about the segregation of the Western imperial body politic from Asian and Eurasian imperial histories. These are subjects that limits of space, regrettably, prevent me from taking up here (but see Barlow 2007; Sinha, this volume). In any case, if we heed the work of postcolonial histories and take colonial modernity as our point of departure, Foucault's terms of embodiment are invariably *colonial* biopower, *colonial* governmentality, and *colonial* subjectivity; and the injunction is to understand body and its *geopolitical* careers as entangled in and by the multifaceted histories of empire as well. Subsections that dwell on "Working bodies: slavery and geopolitics, 1750–1900," "Body politics: suffrage and citizenship, 1850–1920" and "Bodies for the nation: racial purity, imperial war and the 'international' order, 1870–1940" might ensue.

Clearly there is no single approach to the body as method. I see that as one of its many virtues: rather than an additive, it is a repositioning device (Ahmed, 2006) that can serve to restructure how we think about world history and offer us a set of procedures for thinking through the global. In elaborating some possibilities as I have done here, I want to offer a few caveats. First, if the body is to be a strategy for teaching world history, it must not stand still, as it were. It should be used wherever possible to forward arguments about interconnectedness rather than only to provide an example of or at a particular location. Some practitioners in the field may well disagree with me, but it is all too easy – especially in the US – to imagine a world history syllabus in which "it is Tuesday, so it must be East Asia." Plotting syllabi that capture the dynamic interconnectedness of places and spaces, that attempt to map exchange and circulation and mobility, is one of the huge but highly motivating challenges of doing world history. Bodies can enhance the argument about connectivity but examples must be chosen that do that work, if not only that work. So my use of the veil in Central Asia in a world history lecture would not be simply to touch down on a local example but to dramatize the interregional ambit of Soviet state projects and/or to make comparisons with contemporary examples that look similar or dissimilar. Making visible the reticulate histories of whatever we nominate as a subject is nothing more nor less than the task of world history itself, however idiosyncratically we enact it in various professional venues. On the other hand, I also understand world history in its most critical, self-engaged form to be committed to assessing the limits of such interconnectedness, rather than arguing for a transhistorical globality of the kind we most often see unfolding across the cable news networks and other mainstream media venues. For the body is as useful a marker of the breakdown of linkages and the limits of circulation or exchange. One of my favorite texts to teach is Shula Marks's *Not Either an Experimental Doll* (1998), which tells the story of the worlds of three South African women in the late 1940s, the moment of the onset of apartheid. At the heart of the story is the relationship between a young Xhosa girl, Lily Moya, and her would-be white patron, Mabel Palmer. Though their "friendship" is framed by all kinds of "worldly" forces – global empire, the transnational Christian civilizing mission, intertribal and linguistic economies, and Lily's own determined mobility – what prevents their connection is the hard fact of racially segregated space designed to keep black and white bodies apart. I do not use the book as either a story of female solidarity thwarted or, just as problematic, a specifically African instance of body politics – although students invariably reach for both of those interpretation frames, sometimes at once. Rather, I set the evidence Marks provides alongside the partition of Pakistan, the creation of the state of Israel and the birth of the iron curtain as metaphor and reality, tracking the body/politic in and through all of those temporally simultaneous and variegated sites to make an argument about the limits placed on mobility, even in a postwar era known for its unmoored subjects, its refugees and displaced persons. It is a very challenging narrative and I am still perfecting it. But these very challenges are a perpetual reminder to me and to the students who grapple with it that neither "the body" nor "the world" of world history is self-evident. The subjects thrown up by them have to be understood not only (if ever) as "representatives" of specific histories but as artifacts of often broad, geospatially linked or divergent historical processes and epistemes that we need to learn how to make sense of.

So far I have been working inside what might be called some fairly canonical frameworks, both geographical and temporal. This has as much to do with the limits of my own expertise as it does with anything else. But there are all manner of frames and architectures in the vast field of "world history" that are emergent and, as contributors in this volume attest, that are in urgent need of being called into being. For my part, I am acutely aware of my own North American location, and of its impact on how I see "the global," which "globals" I have access to, and how naturalized some can look to me and to my students in east central Illinois in the second decade of the twenty-first century. This is what I think of, following Adrienne Rich (1991), as the "where do we see it from" question. The emphasis on geopolitics that can underwrite world history narratives in textbooks and source books is equally an issue, and has a huge impact on what kind of body we see and use as we develop and implement our methods. World environmental history, in which I am an interested but occasional reader at best, is one of the most innovative in this regard. At its most radical it offers challenges to all the narrative forms I have proffered in this chapter, because it offers new ways to historicize and render proportional the role of human agency at the heart of most history writing, even if we think of that agency as collective, social, civilizational. Sea and ocean worlds, as Jerry Bentley remarked over a decade ago now, might reasonably displace nation-states and empires as frameworks for historical analysis (Bentley 1999), with the result that the bodies we should privilege are salty and every bit as dis/integrative as any other methodological instrument we might choose to use to navigate world history. (See Salesa, this volume.) In the age of the BP disaster, who could disagree?

I submit that even allowing for such shifts – which are in any case not new, having enjoyed a long life thanks to scholars of the Pacific and Indian ocean worlds – the (human) body remains a useful and indeed an indispensable method for "following nature across time and place." This is especially true as conventional "primary" sources for such a project do not abound for the pure environmental historian any more than they do for the scholar of the body. I would suggest that what Michael Egan so eloquently argues for historicizing "natural agency" – that is, that "historians read the physical environment as an active participant in human history, not just a backdrop" (2010: 112) – can readily be applied to the body as I have been outlining it here. Our projects share a conviction about the dialogic relationship between history and our primary subjects. Like Egan, I'd like to see more imaginative engagements with the processes of collision rather than a focus on the sovereign status of the "matter" at hand, whether nature or body. It is their motility that interests me because it reminds us that historical "matters" are rarely static or given, in part because their motile properties (even if they remain just potentialities) make them candidates for apprehending the very historicity of what we call "the global." I would also like to see scholars like Egan attend to the body as an index of what he calls "mercury's web" to describe the history of mercury's global impact in the twentieth century. Toxins are carried in part by bodies and have ramifications for consumption, reproduction, labor, energy, biopower. Engagement with those interfaces requires, in turn, a commitment to reading and encouraging the production of body histories on all of our parts, because without it, we are not in a position to make anything like an informed set of claims about what constitutes world history.

Conclusion: The Body as World System?

Although I opened this chapter with a musing on women and world history textbooks, I am less interested in how these questions I have mooted are dealt with in grand narratives that students read (or don't!) than I am in how they are addressed in the courses we actually teach. What is the world, for whom, and how do we begin to apprehend it and relay it in our classrooms? I open one of the first lectures in my 100-level world history course by quoting Immanuel Wallerstein, who defines a world-system as follows:

> [it is] a social system, one that has boundaries, structures, member groups, rules of legitima-tion, and coherence. Its life is made up of the conflicting forces which hold it together by tension and tear it apart as each group seeks eternally to remold it to its advantage. It has the characteristics of an organism, in that it has a life-span over which its characteristics change in some respects and remain stable in others. One can define its structures as being at different times strong or weak in terms of the internal logic of its functioning. (1976: 229)

While the body as I mobilize it does not fulfill all of these schematics, it is enough of a workable approximation to warrant asking whether the body might not be included in our consideration not of what a world-system *looks like* (its identity) but *what* a world-system *does* (its material and ideological work). And the organicism that Wallerstein's notion of world-system conjures reminds us, again, of how "naturally" the body can and should serve as a ground for thinking globally in historical terms. This returns me to the distinctions I drew earlier between identity versus function, dimen-sion versus index, when assessing the place of women, gender, sexuality and the body in our narratives of world history. My antipathy to the identitarian impulse grows, as I hope have made clear, from my conviction that bodies are not simply to be found in history, they are produced: they are the consequential effects of the collision of people and systems with a variety of contingent histories. If these processes are inveterately human, they also draw a boundary between homo sapiens and the rest – a peculiarly "humanist" effect with its own environmentally global histories.[6] In any case, bodies are not outside or below the sightline of History, they are one of its material and discursive agents: kinetic evidence of its vitality, its power, its grandeur, its intimacy, its cruelty, its indifference.

   Or perhaps the body is better understood as a genre, where genre means not taxon-omy but a means of access to some historical aspects of global experience that other methods do not provide. In rhetorical terms, the body has a dynamic energy in part because it is an open system, capable of registering the evolution of new forms of embod-iment and of older, decaying ones as well.[7] A capacious hold-all in many respects, the body has the capacity to act in aggregate and to disaggregate specific examples; it can be "about women" but it is also about race and class and age and status and labor and order and pain and mobility and disease and birth and death. Bodies can illuminate connection and exhibit its real and deadly limits. If the body has limitations as an analytical category, if it telescopes too much or too little, it does so no more and no less than the other categories we work with (politics, religion, militarism, trade), and which we should surely subject to as much critical scrutiny. World history may look inclusive, but it has its own axes of power, its evidentiary standards, its blind spots. This is especially true given its predominantly North American provenance and its function in US curricular arenas, state and local, public and private, in an age of hyper-trophic globalization. The body as method, even the body as world-system, is by no means a way out of these conundrums. But it does offer an angle of vision on the problem of world history as a struggle over the very form and content of that enterprise.

Notes

The author thanks Adele Perry, Emily Skidmore and Siobhan Somerville for their feedback.

1 I understand "women's history" as a practice that engages questions of gender and sexuality, without necessarily being coterminous with them.
2 I draw here on Sarah Ahmed's notion of "acts of relegation" (2006: 31).
3 For connective comparison see Weinbaum *et al.* (2008). For an account of the first 20 years of women's history journal work, see Allman and Burton (2008).
4 For Mexico see Olcott *et al.* (2007).
5 For possible chronologies for the onset of modernity and/or European hegemony see Abu-Lughod (1991); Frank (1998).
6 I am indebted to Siobhan Somerville for this point, and for raising the question of organicism as well.
7 Here I borrow from and reshape arguments from Miller (1984: 151, 53). Thanks to Asha Varadharajan for this reference.

References

Abu-Lughod, Leila. 1991. *Before European Hegemony: The World System AD 1250–1350.* Oxford: Oxford University Press.

Ahmed, Sara. 2006. *Queer Phenomenology: Orientations, Objects, Others.* Durham: Duke University Press.

Allman, Jean, and Antoinette Burton. 2008. Editors' note. *Journal of Women's History* 20 (1): 8–13.

Ballantyne, Tony, and Antoinette Burton, eds. 2005. *Bodies in Contact: Rethinking Colonial Encounters in World History.* Durham: Duke University Press.

Barlow, Tani E., ed. 2007. *Formations of Colonial Modernity in East Asia.* Durham: Duke University Press.

Bentley, Jerry. 1999. Sea and ocean basins as frameworks of historical analysis. *Geographical Review* 89: 215–224.

Berger, Iris, *et al.* 1988. *Restoring Women to History: Teaching Packets for Integrating Women's History into Courses on Africa, Asia, Latin America, the Caribbean, and the Middle East.* Bloomington: Indiana University Press.

Butler, Judith. 1993. *Bodies That Matter: On the Discursive Limits of Sex.* New York: Routledge.

Butler, Judith. 1998. Merely cultural. *New Left Review* I/227: 33–44.

Canning, Kathleen. 1999. The body as method? Reflections on the place of the body in gender history. *Gender and History* 11 (3): 499–513.

Chakrabarty, Dipesh. 1992. Postcoloniality and the artifice of history: Who speaks for "Indian" pasts? *Representations* 37: 1–26.

Davis, Natalie Zemon. 1997. *Women at the Margins: Three Seventeenth-Century Lives.* Cambridge, MA: Harvard University Press.

Egan, Michael. 2010. Mercury's web: Some reflections on following nature across time and place. *Radical History Review* 107: 111–126.

Frank, Andre Gunder. 1998. *ReORIENT: Global Economy in the Asian Age.* Berkeley: University of California Press.

Hunt, Lynn, *et al.* 2005. *The Making of the West: Peoples and Cultures.* New York: Bedford/St. Martins.

Jones, Cecily. 2007. *Engendering Whiteness: White Women and Colonialism in Barbados and North Carolina, 1627–1865.* Manchester: Manchester University Press.

Lal, Ruby. 2005. *Domesticity and Power in the Early Mughal World.* Cambridge: Cambridge University Press.

Marks, Shula, ed. 1998. *Not Either an Experimental Doll: The Separate Worlds of Three South African Women*. Bloomington: Indiana University Press.

Miller, Carolyn R. 1984. Genre as social action. *Quarterly Journal of Speech* 70: 151–167.

Morgan, Jennifer. 2004. *Laboring Women: Reproduction and Gender in New World Slavery*. Philadelphia: University of Pennsylvania Press.

Northrop, Douglas. 2004. *Veiled Empire: Gender and Power in Stalinist Central Asia*. Ithaca, NY: Cornell University Press.

Olcott, Jocelyn, Mary Kay Vaughan, and Gabriela Cano, eds. 2007. *Sex in Revolution: Gender, Politics, and Power in Modern Mexico*. Durham: Duke University Press.

Rich, Adrienne. 1991. *An Atlas of the Difficult World*. New York: W.W. Norton.

Sunder Rajan, Rajeswari. 2003. *The Scandal of the State: Women, Law and Citizenship in Postcolonial India*. Durham: Duke University Press.

Trouillot, Michel-Rolph. 2002. The perspective of the world: Globalization then and now. In E. Mudimbe-Boyi, ed., *Beyond Dichotomies: Histories, Identities, Cultures and the Challenge of Globalization*, pp. 3–20. Albany: State University of New York Press.

Wallerstein, Immanuel. 1976. *The Modern World-System: Capitalist Agriculture and the Origins of the European World-Economy in the Sixteenth Century*. New York: Academic Press.

Weinbaum, Alys Eve, *et al.* 2008. *The Modern Girl around the World: Consumption, Modernity, and Globalization*. Durham: Duke University Press.

Whitman, Walt. 1904. *Leaves of Grass*. Boston: Small, Maynard.

CHAPTER NINETEEN

Benchmarks of Globalization
The Global Condition, 1850–2010

CHARLES BRIGHT AND MICHAEL GEYER

Globalization: Ever since it came into common use during the 1980s, the word itself has been both the problem to explain and its own explanation – a puzzle and a prediction. Wonderment or dismay, even horror, ran through the burgeoning literature, conveying a vertiginous sense of looking over the edge of a precipice into we know not what. That sticky little suffix "-ization" calls to attention something very much in process – not yet history and, possibly, beyond history. Implicit here is the notion of a destination – where historical processes were headed – or, alternatively, the triumphant assertion of a posthistorical age, in which movement is everything but nothing ever changes (Fukuyama 1992). Global-ization became a condition that is always becoming and also forever not yet. As prophecy it bore a distancing relationship to the past, carried along by a shallow language of "er" words – faster, denser, deeper – that cascaded through the present toward a future of both imminent fulfillment and unlimited transformation.

Among historians, marveling over the new and untoward met with resistance and has subsided somewhat under the weight of scholarly analysis and the application of tried and true terminologies that stress continuities and recurrence. But what is lost in the more sober inquiries into globalization is that sense of disorientation that arises from our direct and often chaotic experience of the global condition in the present. What a global history must seek to explain is the shocking reality of what is – how we got to where we are, and how we deal with a condition in which who we are and what we might become are irreversibly linked, for good and bad, with everybody else. First, there is the acceleration of world-crossing interaction with its attendant mobility of people, things and ideas that is transforming economies, societies and cultures in untoward ways and with incredible speed. Second, there is the engagement of all with all that has stripped away buffering layers of protection and security, once safeguarded by distances of space and time. Third, there is the exploration and exploitation of nature to the farthest extent of the globe, so that we have come to live in a habitat overwhelmingly defined by the human-made imprint. Finally, there are the ways we make meaning of this condition of wholesale transformation in time, space, and nature; for globalization is ultimately what people make of it – not in emoting a global consciousness, but in the most immediate sense of working with and being in a global world (Mazlish 2006). We need a conceptual hold on the experience of a world that is defined by its globality.

What a History of the Present Can Do

In taking up the problem of globalization in the present, historians have turned to the deep past of world history, developing a running start on the present by highlighting long-term continuities and recurring patterns. Some have championed a deep history of multiple civilizations (see McKeown, this volume), while others have stressed the ingrained nature of human communication and exchange and the interconnectivities these sustain (Bentley 1993; 2002; Curtin 1984; McNeill 1991). Its subject is the "human community" (McNeill 1997). While "new" global history may stretch back to the global "event" of Mongol expansion (Abu-Lughod 1989), its preferred site has been centered on the early modern period (see chapters by Levi and by Fernández-Armesto, this volume). This scholarship presents us with a complicated world full of linkages and patterns of exchange, movements of goods and ideas, flows of people, often over vast distances and in broad diasporas, and the migration of biomoral products (bodily ointments, remedies, and adornments) appropriated by elites in disparate and distant places. Work on what Chris Bayly has called "archaic" or "proto-" globalization has effectively accomplished two things (Bayly 2002; 2005). It has displaced the older stand-by narratives in world history that were concerned with the "rise of the west," decisively disconnecting world history from European history and re-placing – and resituating – Europe in a larger, multicentered story in which Asia was once the center of a global economy (and may soon be so again) and Islam was the nexus of a cultural universe and a wide-reaching system of faith, knowledge, and exchange long before anything like Wallerstein's "modern" (and Western) world-system may be said to exist (Wallerstein 1974–1989; Wolf 1982).

Comparative historians like Pomeranz and Wong, with their pivot in East Asia, have effectively done what Chakrabarty calls the provincialization of Europe, contextualizing it and reducing its specialness (Chakrabarty 2000; Pomeranz 2000a; Wong 1997). They have shown that the world as a whole remained bounded by the limits of the biological old regime of agrarian life and natural cycles well into the nineteenth century, and that efforts to transcend these biological limits of human existence can be found everywhere in "industrious revolutions" throughout the world (Wong 2002). The European breakout along an industrializing path based on fossil fuels that transformed nature and the human relationship to it came suddenly and relatively late – only during the course of the nineteenth century (Burke and Pomeranz 2009).

It is telling, however, that the best works in this genre stop well short of the present (Bayly 2004; Osterhammel 2003; 2009). The assumption seems to be that, having congealed in the ever deepening interconnectivity of the eighteenth and nineteenth centuries CE, the subsequent "modern world" is familiar history. The "great divergence" of the West from the rest is now much later and more contingently understood and the rise of the "modern" world (with its stately and gradualist overtones) has been replaced with a birth (with its implied suddenness, even a scream), but the history of connections ends with European empires girdling the Earth and binding all into a single world. As global histories move into the twentieth century, rupture talk loses out to more-of-the-same, as global connections become denser, faster, fuller, more sustained and continuous, and an ever greater accretion of interconnectivity shapes the terrain of globalization (and even defines it), bringing us to the present on an accumulating wave of ever more of what has long been.

This history may be "globalizing," but does it tell us "when the problems which are actual in the world today first take visible shape?" (Barraclough 1967: 9). As the deep history of connections among the world's regions gets swept up in the onward march of twentieth-century globalization, it loses an analytic and narrative grasp on the distinct features of the entangled history of a world that has become global. The problem with the predominant mode of writing is that it looks at global history from the vantage point of its beginnings moving forward, as if the forward movement were a mere extension of these origins. It is unable to capture the transformations unleashed by globalization itself and even the most daring and complete of these histories peter out in the 1910s and 1920s (Osterhammel 2009; Pomeranz 1993; 2000b).

The resulting (short) twentieth century (Hobsbawm 1996) becomes a strangely "lost" period of disconnection in a longer history of globalization. The world economic crisis gets treated as an interruption in the forward movement of globalization, a turn away from nineteenth-century integration and free trade, and global conflict becomes a form of backsliding from the putative cosmopolitanism of the nineteenth century (James 2001). To capture late twentieth-century upheavals, the forward narration is salvaged by adding another phase to the globalizing sequence, as Hopkins (2002) does by amending Bayly's trilogy (archaic, proto-, and modern globalization) with a fourth, "postcolonial globalization" since 1945, to go along with the postmodern, postindustrial, post–Cold War language that telegraphs above all an inability to connect the present to the recent past except in terms of what it is not any longer. The new global history rewrites the prehistory of the present, but the road still runs out short of it and, like the proverbial road-runner, we zoom off beyond the precipice at the end of history.

How then to narrate the transformations unleashed by globalization? We might start with the simple observation that what we see and what we experience today is not connectivity in the making, but connectivity as a done deal. The world does not need to be discovered; distance no longer shelters the unknown; wherever we go, we are already there. Rather than a world being explored and connected, we live in an interior space of manifold and inescapable entanglements, thoroughly interconnected. What we want to know is when this *condition* of the world as a connected or entangled space became a palpable reality and what this condition entailed for those living in it.

Two things matter here. First, globalization was happening – and happening with striking simultaneity around the world – long before a global *condition* of enmeshment could set in. As analogy, we speak of industrial*ization* as a series of disparate local processes reaching back into the eighteenth century, and we debate at length its occurrences, comparing localities around the world and drawing distinctions between industrious and industrial revolutions. But an "industrial condition" can only be said to be reached with the mutual entanglement and reciprocal reinforcement of these local processes. The same is the case with globalization. What matters is the requisite threshold of cumulative critical interaction needed to set in motion a self-reinforcing process of transformation that sucks in the entire world. Rather than a series of "takeoffs," with some regions leading others who must wait awhile or get bumped, the more adequate image is one of an explosive chain reaction, a moment when continuities of long duration kick over into a rupture of cascading effects. Hence, in the spirit of Barraclough, the more productive historicization of the present goes back in time, not to find the origins of globalization, but in search of the threshold when globalization processes working themselves out over time began generating a chain reaction of consequences and effects that had a (new) life of their own.

In short, we suggest resituating in time the process of globalization. The most crucial and, indeed, breathtaking insight we take away from the path-breaking work of Bayly and Osterhammel is that the extended period of multicentric, imperial and commercial expansion and interconnectivity across the seventeenth and eighteenth centuries that enabled disparate power centers, buffered in time and space, to reproduce themselves while in continuous connection with one another – all of which gets bracketed in this literature with the prefix "proto-" – was in fact the real thing: an *age of globalization*. Tracing globalization back in time obscures the import of this history at the other end: globalization as a process of becoming was a done deal by the middle decades of the nineteenth century.

Second, the outcome of this process was a condition of entanglement on a global scale. This "global condition" was initially quite thin and it got thicker only in spurts. It was also limited in space; it never covered everything and everybody in the world. But there is a critical moment when this condition took hold and, once this threshold was crossed, the effects reverberated throughout the world. At this point, a history of connections linking disparate parts of the world must give way to a connected history of the world.[1] This is emphatically not a call for a history of the whole (world, humanity, Earth) or a new world-systems theory (see Chase-Dunn and Hall, this volume), but for a history of the effects of connectedness as a global condition. The latter can always entail more connections, of course, but it will focus on the partial, yet entangled histories of already connected people, places, things, ideas and images. These connections were always uneven and unequal; many are left out (un- or disconnected, though still actors in a connected history). A global history must also capture the sheer violence, the grim tensions and utter disorientation that come with this age of globality. Above all, we need to understand the explosive dynamism and often catastrophic instabilities – the "turbulences" (Rosenau 1990; 2008) – of this condition; how people have organized their lives and their polities within this condition or gone crazy trying (Comaroff and Comaroff 2001); and how and with what effect the natural world is transformed and eaten up by it (Kinkela and Maher 2010).

The Time of the Global

If we treat a broad swathe of time, across the seventeenth and eighteenth centuries, as the age of globalization, its end-game came quite rapidly in the late eighteenth to the mid-nineteenth centuries. This was a time of upheaval and revolution, and not just in the transatlantic world. Its outcome was a global entanglement of the world. By the 1870s/1880s, we are no longer in an age of multicentered globalization or "proto-globalization," but in an age of global entanglement. What happened in the middle decades of the nineteenth century was both transitional and transformative.

Global historians tell the story of the beginning of the modern world as the history of a "great divergence," which they date from the late eighteenth century extending across the first half of the nineteenth (Pomeranz 2000a). This is the moment when the West – or narrow pieces of it – broke through the limits of the old regime and rapidly gained significant comparative advantages vis-à-vis all other regions of the world. While the new global history has pushed this story deep into the nineteenth century, once the familiar features of the modern world have congealed and been let loose upon the world, it seems content to ride along. In so doing, these global historians allow Western initiatives to take over global history, following the trajectory of the great divergence. (See chapters by Adas and by Zhang, this volume.) While there is no gainsaying the explosive acceleration of Western powers of production and destruction, which, when coupled with the improved technologies of transportation and communications, the new sources of energy in fossil fuel and steam, and medical and scientific advances, provided a very few societies with enormous new capabilities for global projections of power into and over the rest of the world, it is a misstep to make this the crux of the story. For the "great divergence" of capabilities generated an equally powerful convergence – indeed a massive collision, forcing deep, mind-wrenching entanglements – that pushed beyond and challenged imperial superiority.

A far better starting point is the general crisis of "old rule" that ran like parallel wild-fires from one end of the world to the other (Bayly 2004; Osterhammel 2009). These convulsions and regime crises were accumulating from the late eighteenth century across the first half of the nineteenth, but timing matters here. Among the great land-based empires of Eurasia – all expanding through the eighteenth century – it was during the second and third quarters of the nineteenth century (1830s–1870s) that accumulating premonitions of all kinds (in the biological limits of the old regime, the recurrent rebellion of peasants, the breakaway of provincial subordinates, the weakening of central administrations, and the disintegration of tax structures and military capacities) kicked over, in one place after another, into a full-blown crisis of confidence in political coherence and legitimacy – even of civilization itself: in China with military defeat, the Taiping rebellion of the 1850s and the long civil war that followed; in the Ottoman Empire with the Egyptian breakaway and the overhaul of administrative and military bureaucracies in the Tanzimat reforms; in India with the great "Mutiny" of 1857 and the collapse of the East India Company, followed by the reinvigoration of British rule and, from the 1860s, the rapid expansion of commodity exports; in Russia after the Crimean defeat in the 1850s, with the overhaul of the tsarist administration and the emancipation of serfs. And it was in the third quarter of the nineteenth century that political renovation and constitutional crises in regimes of the Atlantic world were also played out – most often in conjunction with struggles over slavery. The civil war in north America that remade the (re)United States into an industrial power, the realignment of the settler societies of the southern hemisphere toward export-led growth as primary producers in a British-centered world economy, and the forced reconfiguration of the slave-trading conquest states of West Africa are just the most vivid examples.[2]

Both the simultaneity of these crises, and the fact that they ran in parallel and were largely coeval with the "great divergence" of industrial Europe and the dramatic tilting of the regional balance of power in the world in favor of European-based empire, meant that aggressive assertions of Western power – themselves products of the great upheavals in Europe after 1848 – everywhere encountered *not* settled societies coolly aloof and indifferent or passively waiting around to be dominated, but a world in upheaval, fully in motion and scrambling to overcome local and regional crises of social order and authority. Unsettlement – the mobilization of people, things, and knowledge on a global scale – became the signature of the age. Everyone was running faster – scrambling to shore up and conserve or salvage and renew themselves through measures of self-strengthening. Whether the scrambles for self-renewal succeeded, or collapsed under (or into) new over-lays of Western power, they *began* as proactive responses to specific regional crises – they *developed* in a competitive synchronicity that lifted regional interactions to a new plane of global entanglement – and they *continued* within and under the constraints and the unequal conditions of the imperial domination that was rapidly consolidated in the last third of the nineteenth century.[3]

Crucially, what came to an end in the course of these middle decades of the nineteenth century was that world of autonomous regions and arms'-length appropriations of distant goods and knowledge that had enabled disparate power centers and cultures to draw from exchange with each other the means necessary to carry on in their own, distinct ways. Distance, and the time it took to traverse distance, had remained crucial and foundational throughout the long "age of globalization." The hallmark of that era had been the continuing capacity of disparate regions to produce autonomous histories – that is, to shape the articulations of power, production and social reproduction as well as ecology within their own terms, largely from their own resources, and in the adaptation of "other" techniques, goods and knowledges only inasmuch as local conditions facilitated or warranted assimilation (Cooper 1980). These buffers of space, time, and nature collapsed in the course of the nineteenth century, and most especially in its middle decades.

This mid nineteenth-century passage was born of the moment when the *effects* of globalizing processes began to shape destinies on all sides; when the cushions of distance, time and environment no longer protected; when "all" were forced, with a new immediacy, to secure and maintain control over their futures by means of a greater, more sustained engagement with all others; and when, in deepening engagement, the capacity for the production of discrete or autonomous histories, on all sides, imploded. It was in this passage that the global condition took shape as a multisided, if unequal engagement in a distinctively interior space of sustained enmeshment that was, in principle, and increasingly in fact, conducted in real time and that was, in principle and increasingly in practice, an engagement of all with all. It was in this moment that we enter a condition in which globality proved the tangible context of action, of political decisions and social practice, for all.

Contemporaries experienced this condition as a crisis of survival, which is not far-fetched if we think of the human-made catastrophes of the global age (Moses 2008). But it is more useful to think of globality as a series of choices about how to change in order to keep pace with, hold out against, or adapt to a world of continuous and inescapable interactivity and to appropriate from it those "tools of continuation" necessary for survival. Here the challenge was how to position oneself in a many-sided scramble so as to continue being oneself – how (as the Chinese said in the 1850s) to learn from the barbarian in order to defeat the barbarian (Harootunian 2000a).

The bottom line was this: to position oneself anywhere in this world of entanglements, one could only remain the same by transforming oneself. This chain reaction – and we would advocate thinking of it as an imperative for self-transformation – profoundly shaped the development of the global condition from the mid-nineteenth to the end of the twentieth century. Much of the energy that drove self-transformation across this epoch derived from the dream of recapturing the autonomy of a previous age that, in fact, proved irretrievable (Sahlins 1992). In consequence, over the course of the long twentieth century, the struggle became less and less a matter of whether or not to be a part of a global history and more and more a contestation over the terms of that engagement and over one's placement in it. It is this global condition rather than globalization that should be the object of a connected history of the twentieth century.

Global Actors and Spaces of Action

What then defines the "after-history" of a world already globalized? Who makes this history and where does it take place? We need to specify the spaces of engagement available and the actors who, on all sides, devised strategies to grapple with a condition that they both found and helped generate (Sewell 1996). This is a history as much of (re) settlement as it is a history of unsettlement and the (im)balances between them. If the quintessential history of settlement is one of empire, the quintessential history of unsettlement is the formation of cross-border or transnational spaces cutting across imperial regimes and epistemologies. Neither suffices on its own to capture the global condition in the long twentieth century. In collision with each other, settlement and unsettlement propelled actors and actions across the long twentieth century.

A world of enmeshment put the question of settlement onto an entirely new plane. Most simply, the question was how to organize the putative engagement of all with all? Who had the power and who had the authority to exercise control? What regimes of order might congeal? In whose interests? Within what ideological conventions? With what effects and with what exclusions?

For Europeans in their moment of ascendency, empire was a logical first response. Visions of hierarchical power, organizing capacious systems of exchange, controlling human and territorial resources in imperial divisions of labor, and deploying rules and mandates of behavior flowed easily from a long history of overseas expansion. Centered projections of top-down control, stabbing at the means for ordering the whole – with Britain and the United States being perhaps the most successful, if only briefly – generated tremendous global power and extraordinary wealth, but never established stable authority or sustainable control.[4] The problem with empires in the global age was both their strength (which attracted imitators and rivals) and their limited capacity for exercising authority (which required legitimacy as opposed to dominion) (Bright and Geyer 2005). Historians have tended to attribute this problem to generic features of empire such as imperial overstretch or the absence of a social contract of consent (Kennedy 1987; Lundestad 1998; Westad 2005). However, the global condition, while enabling extraordinary accumulations of wealth and power, also made it extraordinarily difficult for anyone or any combination to organize a regime of global order. There would be no universal empire.

This was certainly not due to a lack of trying. But all efforts to establish dominance dissipated in the multiplying spaces of action and were overwhelmed by the multitude of actors crowding into them. Four of these arenas bear close scrutiny: the proliferation of national formations that sought to encompass and organize people on the basis of territoriality; the formation of territories of industrial production, which expanded within national states, but were also interlocked in inter- and transnational exchanges; the social and cultural lifeworlds that sought to organize meaning in and responses to the fragmented ways global enmeshment was picked up locally; and the expansion, the peopling, and the institutionalization of transnational spaces in between and across nations and empires that sought to shape and influence the very process of enmeshment that affected all.

The intensity of competition among imperial powers promoted what Charles Maier has called the growing territorialization of state power – the congealing of the territorial nation in deliberate, high-stakes efforts to mobilize the resources and manpower of the nation (and of colonial preserves or dependent Cold War satellites) as a vehicle for survival in a global competition that often appeared to contemporaries as a zero-sum game within a closed geopolitical arena (Maier 2000; 2006). The territorializing impulse led to a wholesale restructuring of "old empires," as the Ottomans, Persians, Russians, and Chinese turned themselves into nations or sought to manipulate the national idiom to fend off global pressures or to engage in competition, setting off, in the process, the major revolutions of the twentieth century. But the real heat of territorialization came from so-called young nations – the United States, Germany, Italy, and Japan, which scrambled for place in a world in which competition for territory had shifted from violent annexation to systematic organization. This model for securing competitive place through self-mobilization (even self-exploitation), in turn, spilled back into colonial competition with the twentieth-century projects of imperial development, and these, in another turn, were picked up by anticolonial and nationalizing movements that struggled to recapture independence by pursuing national projects of self-determination and economic development through import substitution and state-led industrialization (Hamashita 2008; Rothermund 2000; Woo-Cumings 1999). In all, nation-making – the organization and self-mobilization of territorial entities – became the dominant political vector of the twentieth century, and the principal means by which political actors around the world sought to engage the global condition and to challenge empire (Paine 2010).

Territorialization also proved a crucial motor in the relentless and uneven industrialization of the world in the long twentieth century. The narrative of the "great divergence" was premised on the industrialization of a few corners of the globe and the accumulating advantages these new productive powers accorded the few over the rest, as global agriculture and primary production were attached to the engines of industrialization at the "core." To be industrial was a mark of superiority, of white skin and a capitalist ethos, open to only a few (Adas 1989). For others to industrialize was, it was thought, a difficult and destabilizing project, one that had to be driven by modernizing elites and posed awesome challenges of coordination and control – the Soviet "catch-up" being treated, almost necessarily, in terms of heroic struggle and staggering cruelty. In all, industrialization was a national project and what mattered were national capacities to organize, mobilize, and suppress (Adas 2006; Cowen and Shenton 1996; Engerman 2003). Yet even the most single-minded and state-centered drives to industrialize were planned and sustained in a transnational infrastructure of exchange – whether of people or goods, of technologies or knowledge, or, not least, of social models for and comparisons of the possible ways of industrialized life. And the territories of industrial production within territorial nation-states were linked and interconnected with one another. Like nations, industrialization was a product of, and a response to, a global condition, and in its development, it deepened and intensified global entanglements. And because both nationalizing and transnationalizing forces were built into the process of industrialization, its progress proved extremely volatile.

Yet, while this history might well be written as a contest between "territorialists" and "globalists" (Maier 1997), the ultimate arena of struggle in industrialization was not between nations, or between nationalism and globalism, but in a worldwide division of labor between city and countryside. The subordination of the countryside was pivotal in the process of industrialization around the world (Rothermund 1992; 1996). All efforts at industrialization in the long twentieth century put pressure on the countryside and on ecology. In some of the more febrile and force-fed efforts at industrial transformation, as in the Soviet Union, this pressure turned into an all-out war on the peasantry and on nature. Even in less dramatic cases, and despite periodic upswings in prices or improvements in the terms of trade, the ever more efficient transfer of surpluses from agriculture to industry fostered a systemic impoverishment of the countryside and a spoilage of environments. Agrarian crisis was an abiding characteristic of the global condition, from the periodic panics, price depressions, and famines of the late nineteenth century, to the evacuation of rural communities with mechanization and consolidated farming in the mid-twentieth, to the late twentieth-century flight from an impoverished and ecologically depleted countryside into megacities of the global South (Davis 2004). The deepening squeeze on livelihoods and, as often, the grim struggle for survival imposed by these processes concentrated poverty in rural areas and associated it with absolute want. This subordination of agriculture and the fundamental divide it imposed between the priorities of the city and the needs of the countryside were a hallmark of the global condition in the long twentieth century – amounting, we would argue, to a kind of global civil war in the peak struggles of the 1930s to the 1950s, and framing the agendas of revolution and development in the postcolonial world of the 1960s.

These struggles framed a problematic epistemology. The notion of "catching up" or modernization, which informed the language of empire and nation-making, of industrialization and development, with such profligacy, is not a meaningful way to describe the accelerated state of self-transformation that overtook everyone, everywhere, as a global condition shaped options and strategies. Simply to "catch up" was a recipe for self-dissolution. The key to success for local actors was always survival and this meant engaging ascendant power on their own terms. In point of fact, people imitated and adapted all the time, and they learned very fast, taking up ideas, beliefs, images, and practices from wherever they found them, if and as these seemed to work to their own advantage (Beckert 2005). None of this ever made them uniform. If indeed what matters are strategies of self-preservation and self-improvement across the long twentieth century, then what needs to be explained are the multiple and competing tools of mimicking, adapting, rejecting, appropriating, and developing ways of life – vernacular modernities (Hansen 1999) – and the redifferentiation of social and cultural spaces that were generated in the contentious engagements of the global condition. If the real story of the last century and a half is one of self-transformation in which continuous change proved necessary in order for all to persevere as distinct selves, then we should remember that homogeneity makes people disappear, whereas difference – or, in fact, the reproduction of difference – enables them to persist.

The struggle over lifeworlds is best captured if we take the contraction of time and space seriously and explore the synchronicity of the challenge of the modern everywhere (Harootunian 2000b; Mitchell 2000). (See Northrop, last chapter in this volume.) How (and whether) to dress "modern" was a matter of grave concern in Shanghai and Mexico City, every bit as much as it was in Berlin and Paris. How to use the new means of an emergent leisure society, such as cinema or photography, posed problems around the world and virtually simultaneously. How to organize labor for mass-scale production was not a problem faced and solved in the industrial centers of the West and then applied to or adapted by the rest, but one that was framed and addressed in many places, from Lancashire to Mumbai to Osaka and São Paulo, at once. In short, we cannot presume the universalizing conceit of the West spilling over into the rest of the world. Rather, in the vortex of the global transformation, all societies – the West and the rest – were thrown into nerve-wracking processes of radical self-transformation that remade them, from the inside out, by recombining themselves and their ways with adaptations and imports from all sides.

Without the possibility of autonomous histories, all actors formulated their present in reference to and in contestation with all others (Aydin 2007). Finding place in these new conditions was a global problem, a source of endless fascination, but also of deep uncertainty, recurring panics, and outbursts of extreme violence. The synchronicity of grappling with the modern and the simultaneity of these labors of self-transformation are measures of a global condition confronting everyone – including, one should emphasize, the Western world, catching up with itself: for the challenges to tradition and old ways were as ubiquitous and contentious in Germany, Japan, and the United States as anywhere else and the deep strains – the uneasy and politically dangerous processes of "Westernization" in the West – were everywhere apparent in the industrial core and a source of tremendous cultural stress and internal violence for these societies. The destabilization of lifeworlds was general. Simultaneity and synchronicity – rather than the time lapses of catch-up and falter – help us see the long twentieth century as a connected, global history.

Nations could be torn apart by industrial and cultural transformations, and this fact animated imperial imaginings and the presumption that empires could control the spaces in between the territories of nations, industries, and lifeworlds – entangled spaces, as well as the people, money, things, knowledge, and images that populated them. And so it might have appeared. Empire in its new guise of imperialism seemed to swallow up the proliferating spaces in-between and organize the transfers among them. (See Sinha, this volume.) Imperialism thrived on making transnational spaces accessible, regulating them, and reaping handsome rewards from maintaining them. It fostered a club of civilized nations and a privileged civil society of transnational experts (Geyer and Paulmann 2001; Gong 1984). And yet transnational spaces proliferated and they were crowded by nonstate actors with minds of their own;[5] multilateral arrangements and transnational institutions (International Labour Organization, United Nations Conference on Trade and Development) slipped beyond imperial control (Maul 2007); the establishment of transnational, rules-based governance (United Nations) advanced the struggle for equality on a global scale quite contrary to the intent of its initiators (Mazower 2006). Moreover, the deployment of imperial regimes of control created links and vectors for ever more robust counterimaginings that proposed alternative ways of composing human relations in this era: transnational leagues, federations, and movements calling for peace and disarmament, international law and human rights, socialist solidarity across national and class divisions, racial, religious, and women's equality and the overthrow of colonial empire – all finding restatements and inflections in local contexts that spoke back to imperial pretensions and limited them (Evangelista 1999). In all, competition, cooptation, and contestation in this transnational arena crimped and contained imperial bids to order the whole.

Reframing the Global Condition

How well do the narrative tropes and epistemological framings that might organize a history of the global condition since the mid-nineteenth century hold up when viewed from the vantage point of the late twentieth or early twenty-first century (Wallerstein 1991)? Looking back at this history, not in order to plot a future trajectory of global*ization*, but to specify the shifting terms of global entanglement, it would seem that the shifts, even ruptures, of recent decades mark, not the "emergence" of the global or a sudden acceleration of a directional global*ization*, but a dramatic realignment in the terms of engagement – really a redivision of globality and a reordering of this interior space.

The "great divergence" – tracing the weakening of the "rest" next to the ascending "West" – does not project well to the end of the century, when China and India have ceased to be abject before, or objects of, Western organizing power, and trajectories that began in relative weakness now push toward a new division of power. Also narratives of a "great convergence" – the intense struggles for self-transformation and modernity within a global condition – have been losing cogency and descriptive power, at least since the 1970s, as it becomes increasingly presumptuous, if not impossible, to specify the sources and the trajectories of modernity in the old binary terms of the rest catching up with and copying the West. A century of self-transformation has made modernity – whatever it may have meant in the global history of the long twentieth century – a "fact of life" at its end, one that generates, not sudden global*ization*, but a deeper and more effective (because no longer weak) engagement of all with all that is, at the same time, rapidly reorganizing – even reordering – the terms under which this engagement may develop.

The same may be said for industrialization. Viewed from the vantage point of the early twenty-first century, it is evident that the industrialization of the world is largely a done deed. The once seemingly impenetrable boundaries of the industrial world have been giving way with surprising speed since the 1970s, including in places like China or India, long paragons of arrested development. The "great divergence" which, from the mid-nineteenth century, had made the development of "the rest" in the shadow of "the West" appear hugely challenging, if not impossible, has run its course and lost its utility as a historian's trope. The old imagery of "catch-up" as a model for global industrialization has also been strikingly twisted by the parallel fact that the industrialization of the world has proceeded in tandem with a broad deindustrialization of the very regions that were once the seemingly permanent core spaces of industrial development, as movements offshore have disaggregated production into streams of supply and assembly under transnational coordination.

Inequalities of wealth and power have not declined, and abject poverty, powerlessness, and social injustice remain widespread and even spreading. But these can no longer be mapped so easily onto an imperial division of labor with its core clusters of (industrial) nations and wide swatches of primary-exporters, or between the West and the rest, white and colored, advanced and backward (Lake and Reynolds 2008). Indeed the very meaning of development has been transformed, from an emphasis on the parallel (and presumably convergent) trajectories of national self-improvement to highly competitive and deeply fragmenting scrambles to find sustainable niches in global markets on a transnational plane of competition. In the process, the threefold division of the world into first, second, and third worlds that the Cold War authorized have vanished. Gone too are the spatially defined, geographic terms of "core" and "periphery" as meaningful devices for analyzing the arcs of poverty and affluence, development and marginalization, that now girdle the globe. Everywhere there is underway a redivision of impoverishment that relocates the centers of poverty from the countryside to the slums of megacities – revamping survival strategies and in the process literally overwhelming the old division of urban and rural, backward and advanced that once ordered the scales of human want.

Finally, nation-making – the consolidation and self-mobilization of territorial states – has taken a surprising turn. The stunning rise of the nation-state as a worldwide device for societies and peoples to organize themselves for survival reached a high point (accompanied by extraordinary hopes and expectations) in the chronological middle of the twentieth century. Yet seen from the millennial vantage point, it is apparent that territorially based nations, pursuing national strategies of economic development under the guidance of modernizing elites linked, politically, with broad segments of domestic populations and producing subjectivities bounded geographically by national borders, have given way, in many places and to varying degrees over the last quarter-century, to new configurations of an expanded space for production and accumulation separate from territoriality and transcending national frames. If the political organization of the world remains national, as economic, social and cultural practices become more transnational the principal role of politics has become one of absorbing the changes and adjusting domestic alignments to the requirements of global capital. States do not vanish, but they must figure out how to act transnationally, and their principal tasks become accordingly different, having less to do with the integration of national populations than with the segmentation of their own peoples. The pressure on societies to remake themselves in a global image, with exogenous elements and resources, has proven immense and immensely destabilizing.

In all these – and other – dimensions it seems apparent that the basic contours that framed a connected history of the global condition in the long twentieth century are now undergoing fundamental reorganization. The historical opportunities of one epoch have been played out. On the one hand, the projects of self-reliance that aimed at achieving self-renewal or self-mobilization in the name of successfully engaging the global condition are no longer relevant responses to that condition. On the other hand, centered, hegemonic projects of top-down ordering, cohering around a single imperial power and hierarchically imposed rules, have not been viable means of addressing the questions of global order. Transnational spaces have dramatically grown and proven to be beyond the control of any single actor, yet are ever more critical to assuring their capacity to act. The possibilities opened up in the mid nineteenth-century passage have been played out, and modes of explanation authorized by that passage no longer explain what is happening.

In retrospect from this vantage point, several things become clear. First, we can describe a discrete historical era of globality – the first in world history. The chronology of a long twentieth century is reasonably established: a global condition, congealing in the middle passage of the nineteenth century, experienced two periods of extraordinarily intense acceleration in the movement of goods, people, information, and knowledge (the 1880s to the 1910s and the 1980s to the 2010s), during which, arguably, production and exchange outweighed restriction and control. These periods were punctuated by a long middle period (1920s through the 1970s) of contestation among rival empires, protracted civil and international war, and economic instability during which, arguably, great – at times utopian – faith was reposed in state power and nationalized production. We mark in this, not a forward march (with inevitable backsliding and retreat) of globalization, but protracted, open-ended struggles over the terms of an enmeshment in which various strategies and essays of engagement were tried, tested, consolidated and reproduced or, alternatively, defeated and cast aside.

Secondly, while it may seem that the initial responses to this condition were competitive, even defensive ones – preclusive nationalism, protected industry, the reproduction of cultural difference – they were all, in fact, inherently transnational expressions – made by people in awareness of others, drawing on the examples of others, and pursuing separate survival through a deeper engagement with all others. Throughout the entire period, at every level, state strengthening, protected industrialization, and cultural renovation went hand in hand with, and depended upon constant transnationalization – understood not simply as "flows" and exchanges, but as a vital facilitating force (technology transfer), a mediating and enabling energy (capital), a regulating power (standards setting), an enabling imaginary (comparisons and roadmaps), and even a utopian dreamworld (the desire for consumption and the modeling of identities). And the habits, institutions, rules and practices that congealed from these struggles – from conflict, competition, and cultural warfare – only deepened the entanglement that first required and then shaped strategies of engagement. At the end of this era of global history, looking back, it is clear that global enmeshment remains, even as initial strategies and responses exhaust themselves, and that global entanglement is the principal subject of a connected history of the global condition.

Finally, without reverting to prophecy or assuming that we can anticipate the future by extrapolations from the past, we may begin to discern the new contours of globality that will shape the history of the next century. Most strikingly, human beings have taken over the entire Earth – not just in numbers that may exceed the carrying capacity of the planet, a concern of 30 years ago, but also in the sense that the world we inhabit is now entirely man-made, a human device. It is not just that human activity transforms nature; there is really no natural world left, save in man-made preserves. Nor is it simply a question of finite natural resources and when they will run out, another concern of 30 years ago. The gradual amplification of an environmental awareness has made plain the scale of the planetary human footprint which is permanently compromising ecosystems and the atmosphere. (See Simmons, this volume.) These are principal effects of the competitive struggles and the sociopolitical solutions of the last century and a half. Similarly, grappling with modernity in an effort to cope with and make meaningful the vertiginous movement of global forces has, in recent times, moved into new realms of spirituality – fundamentalist faiths being prominent – turning away from the materiality of the global condition in the absence of earthly answers toward less secular, and often less worldly, solutions to the human and now totally global condition. (See Vélez, Prange, and Clossey, this volume.) These changing parameters of debate and contestation become new arenas of engagement that cut through the familiar ligatures of globalization as it is imagined: the transformation of production and finance, the speedy networks of communication and information retrieval, the circuitry of consumption (inclusion) and desperation (exclusion), and the new patterns of sub- and transnational violence that shape conflicts over self-provisioning or ultimate ends. The condition of globality which congealed in the nineteenth century has irreversibly changed human history in the last 150 years, and the contours of that condition are now being transformed. There is openness in this moment, of a specific kind: will this man-made world turn into a wasteland or be made a habitable place by human effort? It is a global question, in which the conditions of entanglement and the question of global order remain on the table.

Notes

1   See our early efforts in this direction (Geyer and Bright 1987; 1995).
2   We have attempted a synoptic analysis of this mid-century cataract in Geyer and Bright (1996).
3   Burma and Argentina are good examples for subordinate integration into empire; German East Africa for the persistence of resistance. The uneasy entanglement of global and local actors is best seen in the development of maritime logistics in the Indian Ocean. "Break-ins" to the charmed circle of imperial nation-states were rare, Japan being the obvious example.
4   We leave aside the distinction between imperial (hard power) as opposed to hegemonic (soft power) bids, because neither of them was capable of commanding or ordering global interaction for long.

5 International lawyers are among these experts; see Koskenniemi (2002) and so are engineers (Mitchell 2002). Recent treatment sees them as exponents or instruments of an imperialism of rules; see Goodale (2005).

References

Abu-Lughod, J.L. 1989. *Before European Hegemony: The World System AD 1250–1350*. New York: Oxford University Press.

Adas, M. 1989. *Machines as the Measure of Men; Science, Technology, and Ideologies of Western Dominance*. Ithaca, NY: Cornell University Press.

Adas, M. 2006. *Dominance by design: Technological imperatives and America's civilizing mission*. Cambridge, MA: Belknap.

Aydin, C. 2007. *The Politics of Anti-Westernism in Asia: Visions of World Order in Pan-Islamic and Pan-Asian Thought*. New York: Columbia University Press.

Barraclough, G. 1967. *An Introduction to Contemporary History*. Harmondsworth: Penguin.

Bayly, C.A. 2002. "Archaic" and "modern" globalization in the Eurasian and African arena, ca. 1750–1850. In A.G. Hopkins, ed., *Globalization in World History*. New York: W.W. Norton.

Bayly, C.A. 2004. *The Birth of the Modern World, 1780–1914: Global Connections and Comparisons*. Oxford: Blackwell.

Bayly, C.A. 2005. From archaic globalization to international networks, circa 1600–2000. In J.H. Bentley, R. Bridenthal and A.A. Yang, eds, *Interactions: Transregional Perspectives on World History*. Honolulu: University of Hawai'i Press.

Beckert, S. 2005. Cotton: A global history. In J.H. Bentley, R. Bridenthal and A.A. Yang, eds, *Interactions: Transregional Perspectives on World History*. Honolulu: University of Hawai'i Press.

Bentley, J.H. 1993. *Old World Encounters; Cross-Cultural Contacts and Exchanges in Pre-Modern Times*. Oxford: Oxford University Press.

Bentley, J.H. 2002. The new world history. In L. Kramer and S. Maza, eds, *A Companion to Western Historical Thought*. Oxford: Blackwell.

Bright, C., and M. Geyer. 2005. Regimes of world order: Global integration and the production of difference in twentieth-century world history. In J.H. Bentley, R. Bridenthal and A.A. Yang, eds, *Interactions: Transregional Perspectives on World History*. Honolulu: University of Hawai'i Press.

Burke, E., and K. Pomeranz, eds. 2009. *The Environment and World History*. Berkeley: University of California Press.

Chakrabarty, D. 2000. *Provincializing Europe: Postcolonial Thought and Historical Difference*. Princeton: Princeton University Press.

Comaroff, J., and J.L. Comaroff. 2001. *Millennial Capitalism and the Culture of Neoliberalism*. Durham: Duke University Press.

Cooper, F. 1980. *From Slaves to Squatters: Plantation Labor and Agriculture in Zanzibar and Coastal Kenya, 1890–1925*. New Haven: Yale University Press.

Cowen, M.P., and R.W. Shenton. 1996. *Doctrines of Development*. London: Routledge.

Curtin, P.D. 1984. *Cross-Cultural Trade in World History*. Cambridge: Cambridge University Press.

Davis, M. 2004. Planet of slums: Urban involution and the informal proletariat. *New Left Review* 26 (Mar.–Apr.): 5–34.

Engerman, D.C., ed. 2003. *Staging Growth: Modernization, Development, and the Global Cold War*. Amherst: University of Massachusetts Press.

Evangelista, M. 1999. *Unarmed Forces: The Transnational Movement to End the Cold War*. Ithaca: Cornell University Press.

Fukuyama, F. 1992. *The End of History and the Last Man*. New York: Free Press.

Geyer, M., and C. Bright. 1987. For a unified history of the world in the twentieth century. *Radical History Review* 39: 69–91.

Geyer, M., and C. Bright. 1995. World history in a global age. *American Historical Review* 100 (4): 1034–1060.

Geyer, M., and C. Bright. 1996. Global violence and nationalizing wars in Eurasia and America: The geopolitics of war in the mid-nineteenth century. *Comparative Studies in Society and History* 38 (4): 619–657.

Geyer, M.H., and J. Paulmann, eds. 2001. *The Mechanics of Internationalism: Culture, Society, and Politics from the 1840s to the First World War*. Oxford: Oxford University Press.

Gong, G.W. 1984. *The Standard of "Civilization" in International Society*. Oxford: Clarendon Press.

Goodale, M. 2005. Empires of law: Discipline and resistance within the transnational system. *Social and Legal Studies* 14 (4): 553–583.

Hamashita, T. 2008. *China, East Asia and the Global Economy: Regional and Historical Perspectives*. London: Routledge.

Hansen, M. 1999. The mass production of the senses: Classical cinema as vernacular modernism. *Modernity/Modernism* 6 (2): 59–77.

Harootunian, H.D. 2000a. *History's Disquiet: Modernity, Cultural Practice, and the Question of Everyday Life*. New York: Columbia University Press.

Harootunian, H.D. 2000b. *Overcome by Modernity: History, Culture, and Community in Interwar Japan*. Princeton: Princeton University Press.

Hobsbawm, E.J. 1996. *The Age of Extremes: A History of the World, 1914–1991*. New York: Vintage.

Hopkins, A.G. 2002. The history of globalization – and the globalization of history. In A.G. Hopkins, ed., *Globalization in World History*. New York: W.W. Norton.

James, H. 2001. *The End of Globalization: Lessons from the Great Depression*. Cambridge, MA: Harvard University Press.

Kennedy, P. 1987. *The Rise and Fall of the Great Powers: Economic Change and Military Conflict from 1500 to 2000*. New York: Random House.

Kinkela, D., and Maher, N., eds. 2010. *Transnational Environments: Rethinking the Political Economy of Nature in a Global Age*. Special issue, *Radical History Review* 107.

Koskenniemi, M. 2002. *The Gentle Civilizer of Nations: The Rise and Fall of International Law, 1870–1960*. Cambridge: Cambridge University Press.

Lake, M., and H. Reynolds, eds. 2008. *Drawing the Global Colour Line: White Men's Countries and the International Challenge of Racial Equality*. Cambridge: Cambridge University Press.

Lundestad, G. 1998. *Empire by Invitation: The United States and European Integration, 1945–1997*. Oxford: Oxford University Press.

Maier, C.S. 1997. Territorialisten und Globalisten. Die beiden neuen "Parteien" in der heutigen Demokratie. *Transit* 14: 5–14.

Maier, C.S. 2000. Consigning the twentieth century to history: Alternative narratives for the modern era. *American Historical Review* 103 (3): 807–831.

Maier, C.S. 2006. Transformations of territoriality, 1600–2000. In G. Budde, S. Conrad, and O. Janz, eds, *Transnationale Geschichte: Themen, Tendenzen und Theorien*. Göttingen: Vandenhoeck & Ruprecht.

Maul, D. 2007. *Menschenrechte, Sozialpolitik und Dekolonisation. Die Internationale Arbeitsorganisation (IAO) 1940–1970*. Essen: Klartext.

Mazlish, B. 2006. *The New Global History*. New York: Routledge.

Mazower, M. 2006. An international civilization? Empire, internationalism, and the crisis of the mid-twentieth century. *International Affairs* 82 (3): 553–556.

McNeill, W.H. 1991. *The Rise of the West: A History of the Human Community; with a Retrospective Essay*. Chicago: University of Chicago Press.

McNeill, W.H. 1997. *A History of the Human Community: Prehistory to the Present*. 5th edn. Upper Saddle River, NJ: Prentice Hall.

Mitchell, T., ed. 2000. *Questions of Modernity*. Minneapolis: University of Minnesota Press.

Mitchell, T. 2002. *Rule of Experts: Egypt, Techno-politics, Modernity.* Berkeley: University of California Press.

Moses, D.A., ed. 2008. *Empire, Colony, Genocide: Conquest, Occupation, and Subaltern Resistance in World History.* New York: Berghahn.

Osterhammel, J. 2003. In search of the nineteenth century. *GHI Bulletin* (German Historical Institute, Washington DC) 32 (Spring): 9–32.

Osterhammel, J. 2009. *Die Verwandlung der Welt. Eine Geschichte des 19. Jahrhunderts.* Munich: Beck.

Paine, S.C.M., ed. 2010. *Nation Building, State Building, and Economic Development: Case Studies and Comparisons.* New York: M.E. Sharpe.

Pomeranz, K. 1993. *The Making of a Hinterland: State, Society, and Economy in Inland North China, 1853–1937.* Berkeley: University of California Press.

Pomeranz, K. 2000a. *The Great Divergence: Europe, China, and the Making of the Modern World Economy.* Princeton: Princeton University Press.

Pomeranz, K. 2000b. Re-thinking the late imperial Chinese economy: Development, disaggregation, and decline, 1730–1930. *Itinerario* 2 (3–4): 29–75.

Rosenau, J.N. 1990. *Turbulence in World Politics: A Theory of Change and Continuity.* Princeton: Princeton University Press.

Rosenau, J.N. 2008. *People Count! Networked Individuals in Global Politics.* Boulder: Paradigm.

Rothermund, D. 1992. *India in the Great Depression, 1929–1939.* New Delhi: Manohar.

Rothermund, D. 1996. *The Global Impact of the Great Depression, 1929–1939.* London: Routledge.

Rothermund, D. 2000. *The Role of the State in South Asia and Other Essays.* New Delhi: Manohar.

Sahlins, M. 1992. The economics of develop-man in the Pacific. *Res* 21: 12–25.

Sewell, W.H., Jr. 1996. Historical events as transformation of structures: Inventing revolution at the Bastille. *Theory and Society* 25: 841–881.

Wallerstein, I.M. 1974–1989. *The Modern World-System,* vols 1–3. New York: Academic Press.

Wallerstein, I.M. 1991. *Unthinking Social Science: The Limits of Nineteenth-Century Paradigms.* Cambridge: Polity.

Westad, O.A. 2005. *The Global Cold War: Third World Interventions and the Making of Our Times.* Cambridge: Cambridge University Press.

Wolf, E.R. 1982. *Europe and the People without History.* Berkeley: University of California Press.

Wong, R.B. 1997. *China Transformed: Historical Change and the Limits of European Experience.* Ithaca: Cornell University Press.

Wong, R.B. 2002. The search for European difference and domination in the early modern world: A view from Asia. *American Historical Review* 107: 447–469.

Woo-Cumings, M., ed. 1999. *The Developmental State.* Ithaca, NY: Cornell University Press.

Connecting

CHAPTER TWENTY

Networks, Interactions, and Connective History

Felipe Fernández-Armesto with Benjamin Sacks

Global history, strictly understood, is the history of what happens worldwide – across the planet as a whole, as if viewed from a cosmic crow's nest, with the advantages of immense distance and panoptic range. Sometimes global events arise beyond the reach of human agency. Climatic lurches or microbial mutations or seismic convulsions or the dispersion or extinction of some nonhuman species can affect all the world's peoples more or less simultaneously. Usually, however, cultures change because of their own internal dynamic or because of what, for purposes of this chapter, I shall call "connections": transmutative contacts with other cultures. Historians sometimes use the word to mean something else: similarities or commonalities arising not from genuine connections but from parallel experiences or related environmental influences or supposed evolutionary effects. Examples include the independent development of agriculture, the state, and the city in various unlinked places, "connected," if at all, only by involvement in supposedly universal processes, such as progress or Providence or "development" or increasing complexity or "class struggle." "Connections," in these usages, do not appear in these pages because the changes they denote, while important in themselves, are most helpfully designated by their own names (Mazlish 1993; 2004; 2005; 2006; 2009).

Connections properly understood – those made, and those severed – are important because they serve to document and calibrate the most pervasive processes detectable in the history of the world: the processes of divergence and convergence, which make cultures at different times more and less like each other. Understanding those processes is worthwhile because, if we can achieve it, we can see how and perhaps why humans differ from other cultural animals: the range of cultural variation is immeasurably greater in homo sapiens than in any other cultural creature we know of – including, most notably, extinct species of the genus homo and the more remotely kindred primates who, among surviving animals, most resemble us in other respects. Broadly speaking, if we accept that our species has a common origin in a small community of culturally uniform human creatures in East Africa, perhaps around 200,000 years ago, it follows that the astonishing, prolific multiplication of human cultures since then has

A Companion to World History, First Edition. Edited by Douglas Northrop.
© 2012 Blackwell Publishing Ltd. Published 2012 by Blackwell Publishing Ltd.

been the result of many episodes of divergence. Some cultural differentiation arose in the course of migrations into new environments, which demanded or imposed adaptations of the migrants' ways of life. Other instances occurred as a result of cultures' relative mutual isolation in a patchily inhabited world. Others again, presumably, may have been the result of conscious self-differentiation between neighboring or sometime-neighboring peoples. Other changes, which contributed to divergence, may have been visionary or optative in nature, arising in the minds of the people who espoused or imposed them.[1]

Convergence has happened alongside divergence and, increasingly, has become the dominant trend, as sundered cultures have reestablished contacts and influenced each other. Whenever we see languages, religions or ideologies, food and foodways, technologies, kinship systems, political and economic institutions, laws, and tricks or habits of thought spread across cultural frontiers, we usually find that specific connections underlie the trends. Culturally effective changes, which historians generally like to call "transmissions," happen with greatest impact or intensity when human vectors bear them – most commonly, migrants, sojourners, settlers, warriors, envoys, missionaries, merchants, pilgrims, explorers, colonial administrators, wandering scholars, disinterested travelers. Instances of all these demand attention, but first it may be helpful to look at how artifacts can pass from place to place and so can exercise cultural influence beyond the reach of individual human journeys.

Material Culture

That texts can transmit or affect culture, independently of the people who carry them and even, at times, of those who write them or interpret them in their places of origin, is a statement unlikely to provoke dissent or demand exemplification. But all material objects have, potentially, the same capacity. They can travel, by emporium trading, beyond the range of human travelers; they can shape culture by conveying meaning, inspiring imitation or awe, or igniting social, economic, and technological innovations. Ochre, certainly, and fire, salt, and shells, probably, were among the earliest commodities traded over relatively long distances. Communities that received them could imitate those that supplied them. The commodities empowered the individuals through whose hands they passed.[2] The anthropologist Mary W. Helms has – without much acknowledgment from historians – done the most important work on the subject of how material objects exercise cultural influence over distances untraversed by human agents. In *Ulysses' Sail* and other work she has documented receptivity to the exotic on a global scale. "Not only exotic materials," she points out, "but also intangible knowledge of distant realms and regions can be politically valuable 'goods,' both for those who have endured the perils of travel and for those sedentary homebodies who are able to acquire such knowledge by indirect means and use it for political advantage" (1993b: 4). In *Craft and the Kingly Ideal* she showed how "the symbolism or meanings associated with things obtained from distant places by acts of long-distance trade are comparable to the symbolic associations that accompany things created by acts of skilled crafting" (1993a: 91). Objects from afar arrive at their destinations touched, at least, with rarity value and often by sacrality: an association with the divine horizon. (See also Helms 1975; 1983.) Sanctity accumulates with travel. The power of "cargo cults" in the recent history of some Pacific island peoples demonstrates this dramatically. Objects acted independently in transmitting some of the greatest, long-range, transmutative influences of modern history, bringing oriental models and materials to the makers of the Renaissance and the Enlightenment. The role of objects in forging cultures has become a commonplace of historical, anthropological, and sociological literature.[3]

The Stranger-Effect

For objects, it seems, cultural frontiers are easily permeable. Individuals often find alien cultures harder to penetrate. Hostility or suspicion in the face of strangers and unwillingness to recognize them as fellow beings are widespread, readily comprehensible, self-protective habits. Like artifacts, however, in some cultures humans can acquire numinous connotations in proportion to their unfamiliarity, and can, in consequence, have transformative impacts; a phenomenon best called the "stranger-effect" or, as I have written elsewhere,

> the experience of welcome, which may include deference of various kinds, accorded in some societies to newcomers who are not easily classifiable in the terms of the approached community, except as strangers, outsiders, foreigners or by some roughly equivalent term … One would expect strangers to be massacred, and they often are. More interesting, however, are the frequency of the exemptions and the depth of collaboration between strangers and host-communities, such as often ensues. (Fernández-Armesto 2000: 80–81)

Without the force of the stranger-effect, it is hard to imagine the reception of the bearers of Christianity to the New World or of Islam in sub-Saharan Africa or around the Indian Ocean, or of Buddhism in China, Tibet, Japan, and southeast and central Asia.[4] Most preindustrial empires could not have functioned as arenas of long-range cultural exchange without the willing acceptance of stranger-colonists and of strangers as traders, arbitrators, sexual partners, and rulers, since empires of that period were essentially weak, limited by geography, and without adequate technology to enforce obedience or even – on the very large scale of the global seaborne empires that grew from the sixteenth century onward – the means of making their commands known rapidly or effectively (see Caldwell and Henley 2008).

Sometimes an entire culture can exercise influence analogous to the stranger-effect by commanding admiration and imitation beyond its own boundaries. China's influence is the most striking example, shaping contiguous and neighboring cultures and transmitting models and patterns, especially in technology, even further afield to Europe and Africa. In Central Asia, steppe-based dynasties borrowed Chinese courtly models, rituals, and political ideas: when they invaded China, as they often did, it was, in some measure, always an act that arose from admiration. As early as the third century BCE, Chinese visitors had reached Malaya, Indonesia, Kampuchea, and Formosa. In Japan, during the Yayoi period (ca. 250 BCE–250 CE), the magnetism of China brought the idea of coinage, the pottery wheel, bronze materials, and, most importantly, the rice crop that became critical to the Japanese diet. By the beginning of the eighth century, in Japan and Korea, T'ang dynastic law, calligraphy, literature, poetry and architecture were widely accepted and reshaped to suit local needs and tastes. Even the Chinese moniker for the Japanese islands was adopted: *Je-pen*, "land of the rising sun," was translated into Japanese as *Nippon*. Music too, did not escape the influence of China. With the spread of Buddhism and Chinese commerce, Han drums and strings filtered into Japanese and Korean folk life and state ceremony.

To a lesser extent, the diffusion of the influence of classical Greek culture, primarily via the media of Roman and Christian imitators and assimilators, has had a comparable effect in the West. "Greek revival" architecture in the nineteenth-century United States owed nothing to the travels of individual Greeks, but was a distant reflection of the adulation – sometimes amounting to thralldom – that ancient Greek models of life and thought had attracted in Europe at intervals from the time of the Roman Empire onwards. That Western philosophy can be, with only some exaggeration, routinely characterized as "footnotes to Plato" exemplifies this fascination. So does the medieval tradition of exalting Aristotle as "the" philosopher. So does the scientific tradition of coining technical terms by transliteration from approximate Greek cognates. So does the dependence of Western political discourse on adaptations of Greek terms such as "democracy" and "tyranny." European and North American influence, in its turn, has helped to transmit Greek models worldwide. When eighteenth-century Britons became rulers in Bengal, they built the Hindu College of Calcutta in what they took to be the style of the Lyceum or Academy in ancient Athens. Similarly, nineteenth-century New Englanders constructed public rotundas, supported with Corinthian columns, to debate abolitionism, temperance, religion, women's rights, and human evolution. Postmodern architecture – which includes the latest "Renaissance" in the history of the world – has helped spread pedimented buildings as far afield as Tokyo (Tzonis and Giannisi 2004; Malacrino 2010).

In recent times, the only close parallel to the magnetism of ancient Greece in the West or China in East and Southeast Asia is that of the United States, which has exerted transforming magnetism, by way of example, on cultures it has barely touched in other ways. The twentieth century is widely known as "the American century" because of the way other countries have aped and bought US popular culture – especially in music and film – as well as US economic and political values, exemplified by the worldwide triumphs of capitalism and representative democracy toward the century's end. At the very inception of the history of the US, the Declaration of Independence evoked global resonance. Even before "the American century," American social values, folk tales, literature on liberty, democracy, and government and dreams had long chaperoned cotton from the Carolinas, textiles from Massachusetts and New Hampshire, furniture from New York and Pennsylvania, and coal and tobacco from Virginia to European and Asian ports (see Armitage 2008). Near-instantaneous communication followed the merchant ships; in 1866 the transatlantic telegraph cable was completed, enabling for the first time rapid cultural exchange between New York and London. Nineteenth-century European visitors to the US, such as Alexis de Tocqueville, Charles Dickens, Anthony Trollope, and James Bryce, journeyed consciously in search of the future – of models for the Old World to follow. In Tocqueville's and Bryce's cases, especially, they succeeded in getting Old World elites to adjust first their ideas and then their countries' respective constitutions to reflect American influence.[5]

In politics, the United States launched, nurtured, or revised some ideas of enormous and growing influence in the world – including, notably, democracy and socialism – but it is hard to find a movement of any significance in the arts, literature, science, or philosophy that started in the United States before the 1890s. Then, however, the flood began, as European composers discovered the wonders of American ragtime. The projection of the US as the principal model for global admiration and imitation is often said to have begun with World War I, when 3 million US troops "over there" acted as highly effective vectors of culture, alerting the world to the superpower status of their homeland. But the phenomenon really began a couple of decades earlier, with the

Chicago and St. Louis World's Fairs of 1893 and 1904, respectively. Skyscrapers, Coca-Cola, hamburgers, ragtime and jazz all began to change the world towards the end of the nineteenth century and in the early years of the twentieth.

The structures within which the stranger-effect is usually exercised overlap and are ultimately inseparable: exploration, peaceful migration, war, empire-building, trade, and religious proselytization. But for the sake of convenience they can be dealt with in turn – necessarily, in each case, by a few conspicuous but not comprehensive examples.

Exploration

Exploration logically comes first, because explorers have been responsible for finding the routes of encounter between formerly sundered cultures. Our knowledge of the process in the ancient world is only fragmentary: evidence, for instance, of Egyptian exploration of the upper Nile in the twenty-third century BCE, which made the pharaonic court aware of the cultures of the forest region, or the slaving missions of the Garamantes across the Sahara, or of Phoenician and Greek voyagers in the worlds of the Atlantic and Indian Oceans, or of the maritime heroes of early Buddhist Jatakas, or of Chinese monks in search of Buddhist texts in India. But the scale of the connections explorers reestablished from the late fifteenth century onward eclipsed all of these earlier cases. The New World became a warped simulacrum of Europe thanks to the efforts Columbus and his successors initiated. The modern "world system" of global economic specialization in production and interconnection by trade developed in these explorers' wakes (see Fernández-Armesto 2006; Cunliffe 2001; Frank *et al.* 1993).

Peaceful Migration

Peaceful migrations have been, by some measure, even more effective in forging connections. It is hard to imagine philhellenism ever getting underway in the West if Greek colonization had not preceded it along and across the Mediterranean, or Christianity taking root in Rome if that city had not already housed one of the many Jewish communities that peaceful migrations had scattered across the Roman world. As far as we can tell, in the present state of knowledge, largely peaceful migrations of Bantu-speaking peoples out of West Africa were partly responsible for spreading agriculture across the continent. The most prolific peaceful colonists in the history of the world have been Chinese. In the mid-1200s, indigenous inhabitants of present-day Guangxi, Hainan, and Guangdong provinces introduced Han migrants to the process of irrigating, cleaning, and weaving cotton. The Han, in turn, shared this knowledge with the invading Mongols, who established cotton as a key Chinese industry. Even after the death of the expansionist, flag-waving Yongle emperor in 1424, Chinese merchants and farmers transformed bazaars and communities from Zanzibar to Persia and Java, sending remittances – and the beliefs and customs of the lands they visited – back to their families. In the nineteenth century, Chinese migration became a genuinely global phenomenon. Early modern Batavia and Manila were, in demographic terms, overwhelmingly Chinese colonies that happened to be under European leadership. From 1834, when the British Empire abolished slavery, until the eve of World War I in 1914, 4 million workers, mainly from India and China, kept the empire supplied with cheap labor. They and their counterparts left an indelible cultural imprint in the continental New World, select European cities, and East Africa. Nineteenth-century Chinese migrants sought work in the United States, constructing railroads and telegraph networks, working in factories and mills; they developed key socioeconomic centers at Vancouver, San Francisco and Los Angeles, and fashioned "Chinatowns" in many of the world's largest metropolitan areas. By 1890, over 100,000 Chinese were working in the United States alone.[6]

Massive migration of free labor was the final factor that helped to reshape the world's labor force. Population increase – so great as to overspill from some areas – combined with improved, cheap, long-range communications to make unprecedented migration rates possible. Russian and Chinese migration into northern Asia illustrates this well. Russia's population exceeded 167 million in 1900 – an increase of nearly 20 million in the last two decades of the nineteenth century. Siberia relied on convict labor until the 1870s, but by the end of the century, almost all the migrants living there were free. Nearly a million settlers entered Siberia during the 1890s while the Trans-Siberian Railway was under construction (Marks 1991). About 5 million followed in the first decade or so of the twentieth century, when the railway was complete. Much like San Francisco or Denver, Vladivostok, Khabarovsk, and Irkutsk became energetic boom towns. Chinese colonization of Manchuria increased after 1860, when the Qing relaxed the rules restricting it. Although Armenians, Jews, Lebanese, and Roma were of enormous importance in particular desti-nations and economic niches, China was still the world's most prolific source of long-range colonists – even if one takes the involuntary colonists enslaved in Africa into account. The age-old Chinese diaspora in Southeast Asia gathered pace, rising to a total of almost 14 million in the 1890s and leaping further in the years before World War I.

Meanwhile, the steamship trade, which also facilitated coolie migration, helped to populate underexploited frontiers in the Southern Hemisphere and the North American West, and to provide labor for North American industrialization. Europe, because of its exceptional rise in population, was the main source of free migrants. "New Europes," areas with similar climates and environments to those the migrants left behind, were the most attractive destinations. There were areas of this kind in North America, the southern cone of South America (particularly popular with Germans and the Welsh), Australia, New Zealand, Algeria, and South Africa. Transatlantic routes were the most popular and carried the most traffic, chiefly because of the economic opportunities that North American expansion created.

The United States gained more than 128,000 migrants in the 1820s and over 500,000 in the 1830s. Numbers trebled in the next decade. Until then, most migrants came from Germany, Britain, and Ireland. A further leap in the 1880s brought the total to over 5.25 million, from all over Europe and especially from Scandinavia, Italy, Central Europe, and the Russian Empire. This was the manpower that fueled continental expansion and industrialization (see Dinnerstein 2009; Daniels 1990; Cannato 2009).

War and Empire

War and empire have forged connections and created enormous arenas for the exchange of culture. (See chapters by Morillo and by Sinha, this volume.) Rome is a familiar example in Western history. Rome's influence can be measured in the uniform archaeology of villas, cities, and monumental engineering, and still resonates in many European languages, as well as in the predominance of Christianity. The Arab conquests from the seventh century onward had a similar effect where they occurred, transmitting Islam and Arabic as well as a great deal of intellectual culture inherited from parts of the Roman Empire that Arabs or their allies overran. On a Eurasian scale, the Mongols remain the most conspicuous empire-builders, facilitating the transmission of Chinese ideas and techniques to southwest Asia and Europe in the thirteenth and fourteenth centuries. In southwest Asia, Sayyid 'āl Hamadānī's scholarship profited from extensive contact with Chinese, Indian, and Mongol academics and travelers, the ability to import seeds, spices, and documents from far beyond Persia, and from his period as a minister to Ghazan Khan, a position that permitted experimentation in Tabrīz and Sultāniyya. Under Mongol rule in China, Buddhism, Taoism, and Confucianism flourished; by the fifteenth century Buddhism was exported back to the Mongol heartland around Karakorum, where Tibetan monks successfully blended Buddhism with local shamanism. The revival of empiricism in Europe, and the appearance or proliferation there of such new technologies as gunpowder, paper, the compass, the rudder and the blast furnace are all outcomes of enhanced contact across Eurasia. The revolutionary experiences of the West at the time – the technical progress, the innovations in art, the readjustment of notions of reality through the eyes of a new kind of science – were owed, in part, to influences transmitted along routes the Mongols maintained. The steppe became a highway of fast communication, linking the extremities of the landmass and helping transfer culture across two continents. Without the Mongol peace, it is hard to imagine any of the rest of world history working out as it did, for these were the roads that carried Chinese ideas and technology westward and opened up European minds to the vastness of the world. The importance of the Mongols' passage through world history does not stop at the frontiers of their empire. It resonated across Eurasia (Fielding 2009; Robinson 2009).

Of later examples, European seaborne empires founded from the sixteenth through twentieth century forged even wider connections, roughly indicated on today's world map by the reach of imperial languages, especially Spanish, Portuguese, English, French, and to a lesser extent Dutch. Most such empires, including that of the United States in continental North America, also acted as vicarious agents for the transmission of culture out of Africa, borne by the people enslaved and forcibly resettled in pursuit of imperial economic strategies (see Carney and Rosomoff 2009). Above all, the empires were spaces in which "ecological exchange" took place, as biota formerly restricted to particular places were carried all over the world: cultural traits associated with the preparation and consumption of foodstuffs or the treatment of diseases accompanied ecological exchange (Newell 2010; Fernández-Armesto 2001: 282–284 (on Polynesia), 384–385 (on ecological imperialism); and also chapters by Simmons and by Pernick, this volume). The role of French revolutionary and Napoleonic armies in spreading values associated with the European Enlightenment was more restricted geographically – affecting only continental Europe and the Ottoman Empire – but left visceral changes in the laws and political traditions of almost every country that formed part of the Napoleonic empire or neighbored it. In recent times, war has played a part in connecting parts of the world with the US. Millions of American soldiers in Europe during the two world wars bore US popular customs with them, permanently altering the European cultural landscape. In the early twenty-first century, US leaders dissatisfied with their influence in some parts of the world – notably Iraq and Afghanistan – followed precedent in attempting to impose that influence by force of arms.

Religion

Religious proselytization and communication has made three religions, which are universal in their aspirations, genuinely or nearly global in their reach. (See Vélez, Prange, and Clossey, this volume.) Buddhism was able to forge cross-cultural connections in its early centuries, spreading from India to China, Japan, Tibet, and Central and Southeast Asia. But it shrank in its heartlands and stagnated elsewhere until, at Altan Khan's invitation, the Dalai Lama visited Mongolia in 1576 and 1586. He guided reform of Mongol customs. Human sacrifices were forbidden, and blood sacrifices of all sorts stopped. The *ongons* – the felt images in which spirits resided, except when the rites of shamans liberated them – were to be burned and replaced by Buddhist statues. The new religion was at first limited to the aristocracy. But over the next century, Buddhism spread through society and outward across the Mongol dominions. Expanding Manchu political power, after they conquered China in 1644, reinforced the Buddhist mission. The Manchu emperors perceived Buddhist missionaries as pacifiers and potential agents of imperial policy. They appointed Tibetan lamas to instruct the Mongols, presumably in part to reconcile the Mongols to Chinese rule. Like Catholic missions in the New World, Buddhist missions in northern Asia were shadowed and disfigured by political conquests and violence. The leading missionary Neyici Toyin burned before his tent a bonfire of ongons 10 tent frames high in the 1630s. In practice, the old gods reemerged as Buddhist deities, just as in Christian America the Native American gods survived as saints and representations of the Virgin Mary. In both Mongolia and the Americas, the old gods continued to mediate between humans and nature.[7]

Islam displayed even more remarkable cultural elasticity in appealing beyond its heartlands to congregations in Africa and in and around the Indian Ocean in the Middle Ages and the early modern period. The means of conversion were fourfold: commerce, deliberate missionary effort, holy war, and dynastic links. Merchants and missionaries spread Islam together. Trade shunted pious Muslims from city to city and installed them as port supervisors, customs officials, and agents to local rulers. Missionaries followed: scholars in search of patronage, discharging along the way the Muslim's obligation to convert unbelievers; spiritual athletes in search of exercise, anxious to challenge native shamans in contests of conspicuous austerity and supernatural power. In some areas, Sufis made crucial contributions. In Southeast Asia, Sufis congregated in Melaka, and after the city fell to the Portuguese in 1511, they fanned out from there through Java and Sumatra. In the late sixteenth and seventeenth centuries, the sultanate of Aceh in northwest Sumatra in modern Indonesia was a nursery of Sufi missionaries of sometimes dubious Islamic orthodoxy, such as Shams al-Din, who saw himself as a prophet of the end of the world and whose books were burned after his death in 1630. Even peaceful Muslim missionaries tended to see themselves as warriors of a sort, waging a "jihad of words." During the seventeenth century, perhaps under the goad of competition from Christianity, the "jihad of the sword" grew in importance, and the extension of the frontier of the Islamic world depended increasingly on the aggression of sultans, especially from central Java (Hodgson1974; Fregosi 1998; Lewis 2008; Sonn 2010; Ruthven 2004).

In West Africa, merchant clans or classes, like the Saharan Arabs known as Kunta, who made a habit of marrying the daughters of holy men, were the advanced guard of Islam. The black wandering scholars known as the Torokawa incited revivalism and jihad in Hausaland in modern Nigeria from the 1690s. Schools with a wide curriculum played a vital part in diffusing Islam among the Hausa, scattering pupils who in turn attracted students of their own. A sheikh who died in 1655 was able, at school in Katsina, near the present border of Niger and Nigeria, to "taste to the full the Law, the interpretation of the Quran, prophetic tradition, grammar, syntax, philology, logic, study of grammatical particles, and of the name of God, Quranic recitation, and the science of meter and rhyme" (Fernández-Armesto 1996: 270). Paid by donations according to pupils' wealth, the master of such a school sat on a pile of rugs and sheepskins before his niche of books, equipped with his tray of sand for tracing letters with his finger. He might have had his brazier filled with burning charcoal to warm him in winter, and his spittoon for the husks of kola nuts that were eaten for their caffeine content. Students' manuscripts survive, smothered in annotations from the teacher's commentary, which was often in a native language instead of Arabic, the language of the Quran. At the end of this course, the student acquired a certificate, emblazoned with a long pedigree of named teachers going back to Malik ibn Anas, the eighth-century codifier of Islamic law.

Christianity has, so far, been the most culturally adaptive or elastic of the great world religions. The Reformation helped stimulate Catholics to intensified activity in the wider world and, in the long run, aroused Protestant missionary societies to emulate the Catholic religious in mission fields. Christian missionaries acted as both envoys and scholars, at once representing the whims of church and state (which were often the same), and adapting their teachings for local consumption. The result was the establishment of a global religion – but with countless local interpretations and expressions. In Latin America, "Andean religion" is recognizably a form of Catholicism, albeit distinguished by aberrations and continuities with pre-Christian religious sensibilities (MacCormack 1990; 1991). Today, on the Yucatan Peninsula, Christians venerate both Jesus Christ and Mayan idols. Other cults, such as that of Maximon are local constructs (Pédron-Colombani 2004). Indeed, Maximon seems equally at home nestled next to the Virgin Mary, or with a cigar in his mouth, or adorned with Guatemalan shawls and European hats. Other New World religions sometimes called "syncretic," such as Candomblé and Voodoo, combine transmissions from Africa with Christian influence, or in the case of Pentecostalism, match Christian faith with sensibilities often characterized as originating in African tradition.[8] The success of Christianity beyond its Middle Eastern and Western heartlands has not depended on imperial contexts. The success of Catholicism in early modern China and Japan, though interrupted by the hostility of states, demonstrates that, as does the flourishing of Christianity in postcolonial Africa and in some places that never experienced Western imperialism, notably Korea.[9]

Trade: Land Routes

In the long run, sea routes were more important for making the connections of global history than land routes. They carried a greater variety of goods faster, more economically, and in greater amounts. Nevertheless, in the early stages, most Eurasian long-range trade was small scale – in goods of high value and limited bulk. Goods moved through a series of markets and middlemen. (See Levi, this volume.) In the first millennium BCE, the land routes that linked Eurasia were as important as the sea routes in establishing cultural contacts: bringing people from different cultures together, facilitating the flow of the ideas of the axial-age sages, transmitting the works of art that changed taste and the goods that influenced lifestyles.

From around the mid-first millennium BCE, Chinese silks appeared here and there across Europe – in Athens, and at present-day Budapest in Hungary, and in a series of south German and Rhineland burials. By the end of the millennium, we can trace the flow of Chinese manufactured goods from the southern Caspian to the northern Black Sea, and into what were then gold-rich kingdoms in the southwest stretches of the Eurasian steppe. Meanwhile, roads that kings built and maintained crossed what is now Turkey and Iran, penetrated Egypt and Mesopotamia, reached the Persian Gulf, and, at their easternmost ends, touched the Pamir Mountains in Afghanistan and crossed the Indus River. The silk roads were by no means safe. Bandits hid in the dangerous terrain, preying on wearied, heat-exhausted merchants. An eighth-century Mongol painting depicted one such robbery in progress. Robbers wielding long, blood-tipped swords blocked the path of the caravans, demanding fees and goods from their victims.[10]

The silk roads were, nonetheless, the most convenient means of transport between Europe and China, active as early as the third-century BCE. From this avenue of trade, culture flowed across Eurasia. To function, an avenue of communications needs people at either end of it who want to be in touch. The Eurasian steppe was like a dumbbell, with densely populated zones and productive economies at either end. For people in Europe, Southwest Asia, and North Africa, access to the products of South, Southeast, and East Asia was highly desirable. For the suppliers of spices, drugs, fine textiles, and luxury products in the east, it was good to have customers who paid in silver.[11]

In the Americas, there was no chance to reproduce such relationships. The North American prairie is aligned on a north–south axis, across climatic zones, whereas the Eurasian steppe stretches from east to west. Plants and animals can cross the steppe without encountering impenetrable environments. Seeds can survive the journey without perishing and without finding, at the end of the road, an environment too sunless or cold to thrive in. In North America, it took centuries longer to achieve comparable exchanges. Transmissions of culture across latitudes are much harder to effect than those that occur within latitudes, which have relatively narrow boundaries and where climate and conditions are familiar. Elsewhere in the Americas, the concentrations of wealth and population were in two regions – Mesoamerica and the Andes – that neither grasslands nor any other easily traveled routes linked. Though societies in other parts of the hemisphere drew lessons, models of life, technologies, and types of food from those areas, the results were hard to sustain because communications between these areas and outlying regions were difficult to keep up. Without the horse – extinct in the Americas for 10,000 years – the chances of an imperial people arising in the prairie or the pampas to do the sort of job the Mongols did in Europe were virtually zero.[12] (See chapters by Yoffee, by Liu, and by Sinha, this volume.)

In Africa, the constraints were different. The Sahel might have played a role similar to that of the steppes in Eurasian history. There was a viable corridor of communication between the Nile and Niger valleys. In theory, an imperial people might have been able to open communications across the continent between the civilizations of East Africa, which were in touch with the world of the Indian Ocean, and those of West Africa, which the trade routes of the Sahara linked to the Mediterranean. But it never happened. For long-range empire building, the Sahel was, paradoxically, too rich compared with the Eurasian steppe. The environment of the Sahel was more diverse. Agrarian or partly agrarian states had more opportunity to develop, obstructing the formation of a Sahel-wide empire. Although pastoral peoples of the western Sahel often built up powerful empires, invaders from the desert always challenged and sometimes crushed them. While they lasted, moreover, the empires of the Sahel never reached east of the region of Lake Chad. Here states grew up, strong enough to resist conquest from outside, but not strong enough to expand to imperial dimensions themselves: states like Kanem and Bornu – which were sometimes separate, sometimes united.

Despite the lack of east–west connectivity across Africa, the "gold routes" across the Sahara linked the cultures of the Mediterranean with those of the Niger valley, from the mid-first millennium BCE. Medieval sources are copious enough for us to be able to reconstruct something of the nature of the connections made or reinforced in that period. The location of West Africa's gold mines was a closely guarded commercial secret, but it was probably in Bure, around the upper reaches of the Niger River and the headwaters of the Gambia and Senegal rivers. Muslims – presumably traders – had their own large quarter in or near the Ghanaian capital Kumbi Saleh, but were kept apart from the royal quarter of the town. The Soninke fought off Almoravid armies until 1076. In that year, Kumbi fell, and its defenders were massacred. The northerners' political hold south of the Sahara did not last, but Islam was firmly implanted in West Africa.

By the middle of the next century, Arab writers regarded Ghana as a model Islamic state, whose king revered the true caliph in Baghdad and dispensed justice with exemplary openness. They admired his palace, with its objects of art and windows of glass; the huge natural ingot of gold that was the symbol of his authority; the gold ring by which he tethered his horse; his silk clothes; his elephants and giraffes. This magnificence did not last. After a long period of stagnation or decline, pagan invaders overran the Soninke state and destroyed Kumbi. But Islam had spread so widely by then among the warriors and traders of the Sahel that it retained its foothold south of the Sahara for the rest of the Middle Ages. The merchants of Mali handled the gold trade but never controlled its production. The mansa took nuggets for tribute – hence the image on Cresques Abraham's famous map. The gold bought salt. Mali was so rich in gold and so short of salt that the price of salt reputedly tripled or quadrupled in the kingdom's markets (Rosander and Westerlund 1997; Clarke 1982; Hunwick 1999).

Trade: Sea Routes

What Indian mapmakers in antiquity called the Seas of Milk and Butter were, to Greek merchants, "the Erythraean Sea," from which traders brought back aromatics – especially frankincense and myrrh – and an Arabian cinnamon substitute called cassia. Important ports for long-range trade lined Arabia's shores. At Gerrha, for instance, merchants unloaded Indian manufactures. Nearby, Thaj also served as a good place to warehouse imports. Egyptian merchants endowed Egyptian temples with incense in the third century BCE. The reason for the long seafaring, sea-daring tradition of the Indian Ocean lies in the regularity of the monsoonal wind system. Above the equator, northeasterlies prevail in winter; but when winter ends, the direction of the winds reverses. For most of the rest of the year, the winds blow steadily from the south and west, sucked toward the Asian landmass as air warms and rises over the continent. By timing voyages to take advantage of the predictable changes in the direction of the wind, navigators could be confident of a fair wind out and a fair wind home.

It is a fact not often appreciated that, overwhelmingly, the history of maritime exploration has been made into the wind, presumably because it was at least as important to get home as to get to anywhere new. This was how the Phoenicians and Greeks opened the Mediterranean to long-range commerce and colonization. The same strategy enabled South Sea Island navigators of this period to explore and colonize islands of the Pacific. (See Salesa, this volume.) The monsoonal wind system in the Indian Ocean freed navigators from such constraints. One must try to imagine what it would be like, feeling the wind, year after year, alternately in one's face and at one's back. Gradually, would-be seafarers realized how the changes of wind made outward ventures viable. They knew the wind would change and so could risk an outward voyage without fearing that they might be cut off from returning home. Maps 20.1, 20.2, and 20.3 show the wind patterns of the world's major oceans, which shaped all of these key maritime routes.

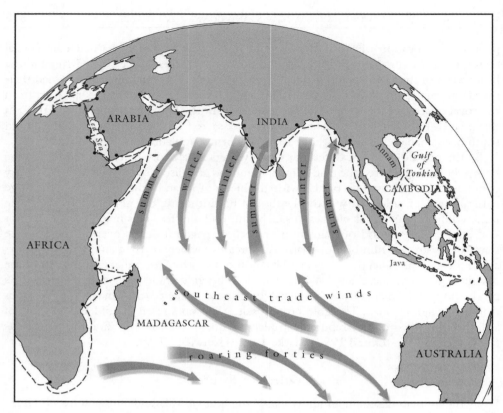

Map 20.1 The Indian Ocean: wind and weather patterns, with trade routes.
Source: Based on maps in Felipe Fernández-Armesto, *Pathfinders: A Global History of Exploration* (New York: W.W. Norton, 2006).

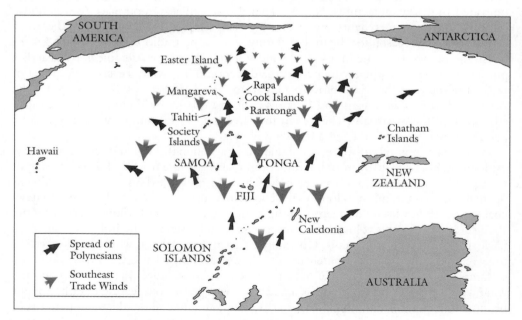

Map 20.2 The Pacific: wind patterns and population movements.
Source: Fernández-Armesto, *Pathfinders* (as Map 20.1).

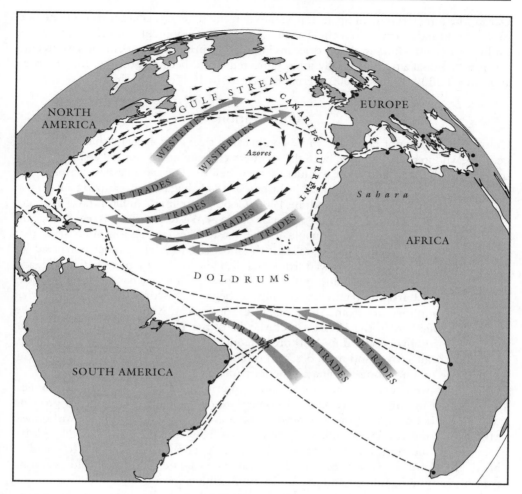

Map 20.3   The Atlantic: wind patterns and trade routes.
Source: Fernández-Armesto, *Pathfinders* (as Map 20.1).

Fixed-wind systems have proved harder for navigators to negotiate. The Mediterranean Sea was, nonetheless, a vital site of cultural exchange. In antiquity, a large trade existed between the Roman and Greek empires, the Arab civilizations that hugged the Mediterranean's eastern shores, Egypt, and North Africa. Kenneth Clark noted that "if you had gone into the square of any Mediterranean town in the first-century you would hardly have known where you were, any more than you would in an airport today" (1969: 3). The Mediterranean remained a "corrupting sea" even after the fall of the Roman Empire ended the political unity that spanned its shores. A similar zone of navigation, with a measure of cultural unity, developed along Europe's Atlantic face in antiquity. Gradually, with increasing intensity from the twelfth century onward, regular navigation connected the two zones. The Atlantic *espace* created by European navigation, imperialism, slaving and trade in the early modern period was, in a sense, an outgrowth of this process. Highlights in the process of connecting up the oceans of the world were the late fifteenth-century and early sixteenth-century decoding of the Atlantic wind-system and the discovery that the westerlies of the South Atlantic provided a link to the Indian

Ocean; the long struggle of Spanish navigators in the sixteenth century to find practical routes back and forth across the Pacific; and the development, especially by Dutch explorers, of routes linking all three oceans in a world-girdling network in the seventeenth century. A globalizing, universally interconnected world became possible. (See Horden and Purcell 2000; Braudel 2002; Fernández-Armesto 1987; 2006: ch. 10.)

Globalization

Cultural exchange got faster and more complicated than ever. In part, this was because people – who in every age have been the most effective agents of cultural change – could travel farther, faster, and more frequently than before. The world's first travel agent, Thomas Cook & Company, founded in Britain in 1841, began by organizing a local trip for a temperance society in England. By 1900, Cook was selling 3 million travel packages a year. Cultural exchange, however, was not one-way Westernization. What Europeans considered exotic became fashionable in the West. The Japanese-inspired style that Western designers called "Japonisme" was the most striking case. Monet portrayed his wife in a kimono. Puccini borrowed from what little he knew of Japanese, Chinese, and even Native American music and put it in his operas. These exchanges took in wider influences, too. European painters and sculptors began to discover the wonders of what they called primitive art from Africa and the South Seas. Some exchanges bypassed the West altogether. In the 1890s, Chief Mataka of the Yao – deep in the East African interior – made his people don Arab dress, launched Arab-style ships on Lake Nyasa, planted coconut groves and mangoes, and rebuilt his palace in the mixed Arab-African Swahili style that had long dominated the East African coast.[13]

Not only were cultures becoming more intermingled; so too were economies. Globalization meant the increasing economic interdependence of a world of growing trade. In the last quarter of the twentieth century, in line with the worldwide withdrawal of the state from economic regulation, businesses were able to drive an expanding global economy by operating internationally with greater freedom than ever before – and to imperil global prosperity by irresponsible risk-taking, as a series of colossal failures among credit institutions in Europe and the US in 2008–2009 showed.

More trade and increased intercommunication promoted peace, increased prosperity, and stimulated cultural exchange. The benefits of globalization, however, were unevenly distributed. A relatively few vast business corporations, most of them centered in the United States, handled a disproportionate amount of the world's economic activity. Shunting their assets around the world, those businesses evaded regulation by individual governments. Powerful countries – the United States above all – were able to demand free trade where and when it suited them, but retain protective tariffs or subsidies for businesses they favored. To some extent, globalization perpetuated the old colonial pattern of the world economy – peasants and sweatshop labor in impoverished countries supplied rich ones with cheap goods, twisting the poverty gap into a poverty spiral.

Information traveled globally even more freely than trade. In 1971, the world's first microprocessor appeared, enabling the transmission of billions of units of information along a fiber-optic cable every second. Radio transmission made virtually every item of information from every part of the world universally accessible. By the end of the century, the world had over 2.5 billion telephones and over 500 million computers. The way people handled information changed. Miniaturization redefined individualism, enabling the like-minded from all over the world to form cyberspace communities. The trend was unstoppable. China, for instance, tried to control internet access, especially after demonstrators coordinated their activities by computer in what almost turned into a revolution in 1989. But China nonetheless had 30 million internet users by 2000. Worldwide censorship became difficult – for a while. But in the early twenty-first century, major servers began to impose filters, at first to black out pornography. Of course, the success of American culture as a global model has depended on the multiplication of the means of cultural transmission, with increasing pace, in recent times: efficient locomotion, broadcasting, cinema, and, in the late twentieth century, information microtechnology have made cultural transmission easy, and instantly communicable across the globe. (See chapters by Bright and Geyer, and by Northrop, this volume.)

The internet promoted globalization in the strongest sense of the world: the global spread of uniform culture. In reality, in a plural world, this was not a threat to cultural diversity, though people often perceived it as such. If there ever were to be a global culture, it would probably not replace diversity, but would rather supplement it.

Notes

1   Goudsblom *et al.* (1996) is important for early long-range exchanges, as are Goudsblom (2004) and Erlichman (2010).
2   On ochre see Wreschner (1976; 1980; 1981). On fire, see Goudsblom (1992) and Wrangham (2009).
3   Jardine (1996); Morena (2009); Impey (1977). On material culture generally see Porter and Brewer 1994); Douglas (1996); Trentmann (2008; 2009; 2010).
4   Smith (2010) focuses on twentieth- and twenty-first century transmutations and "culture clashes."
5   Evans (1998; 2004); Chafe (2009). On Tocqueville see Brogan (2007); Elster (2009). On Bryce, see Seaman (2006). See also Fernández-Armesto (1999).
6   Gerne (1996: 195–205); Fernández-Armesto (2006: 113–116; 1996: 315–323). See Blussé (1986; 2000; 2008). The classics in the field are Needham *et al.* (1956–) and Lach (1965–1999).
7   For bibliographical data see Fernández-Armesto (2009).
8   On the problems of syncretism in general, see Leopold and Jensen (2004). On religions of blacks see Métraux (1972); Naro *et al.* (2007); Bastide (2007).
9   Brockey (2008); Massarella (1990; 2008). On Korea, see Kane and Park (2009).
10 "Eighth-century bandits holding up merchants on the Silk Road," ink on paper, Hispanic Society of America, New York; see Fernández-Armesto (2006: 75).
11 Wood (2002) is an excellent guide for students and researchers; Whitfield (2001).
12 For example, Jared Diamond calculated that food production spread much more rapidly from the Philippines to Polynesia and from Southwest Asia toward Europe and North Africa than from Mexico to central and western North America. See Diamond (1999: 177–179, fig. 10.1). He attributed this, in large part, to the north–south orientation of the Americas, versus the east–west orientation of Eurasia and, by geographical extension, North Africa.
13 On Chief Mataka see Helms (1993a). On tourism, see Brendon (1991); Douglas-Hamilton (2005); Hyde (1975).

References

Armitage, David. 2008. *The Declaration of Independence: A Global History*. Cambridge, MA: Harvard University Press.
Bastide, Roger. 2007. *The African Religions of Brazil: Toward a Sociology of the Interpenetration of Civilizations*. Baltimore: Johns Hopkins University Press.

Blussé, J. Leonard. 1986. *Strange Company: Chinese Settlers, Mestizo Women, and the Dutch in VOC Batavia*. Dordrecht: Foris.

Blussé, J. Leonard. 2000. *Bridging the Divide: 400 Years, the Netherlands–Japan*. Leiden: Hotei.

Blussé, J. Leonard. 2008. *Visible Cities: Canton, Nagasaki, and Batavia and the Coming of the Americans*. Cambridge, MA: Harvard University Press.

Braudel, Fernand. 2002. *Memory and the Mediterranean*. New York: Random House.

Brendon, Piers. 1991. *Thomas Cook: 150 Years of Popular Tourism*. London: Secker & Warburg.

Brockey, Liam Matthew. 2008. *Journey to the East: The Jesuit Mission to China, 1579–1724*. Cambridge, MA: Harvard University Press.

Brogan, Hugh. 2007. *Alexis de Tocqueville: A Life*. New Haven: Yale University Press.

Caldwell, Ian, and David Henley. 2008. Stranger-kings in Indonesia and beyond. *Indonesia and the Malay World* 36 (105).

Cannato, Vincent J. 2009. *American Passage: The History of Ellis Island*. New York: HarperCollins.

Carney, Judith Ann, and Richard N. Rosomoff. 2009. *In the Shadow of Slavery: Africa's Botanical Legacy in the Atlantic World*. Berkeley: University of California Press.

Chafe, William Henry. 2009. *The Rise and Fall of the American Century: United States from 1890 to 2009*. Oxford: Oxford University Press.

Clark, Kenneth. 1969. *Civilisation*. Harmondsworth: Penguin.

Clarke, Peter B. 1982. *West Africa and Islam: A Study of Religious Development from the 8th to the 20th Century*. London: Edward Arnold.

Cunliffe, Barry. 2001. *Facing the Ocean: The Atlantic and its Peoples, 8000 BC–AD 1500*. Oxford: Oxford University Press.

Daniels, Roger. 1990. *Coming to America: A History of Immigration and Ethnicity in American Life*. New York: HarperCollins.

Diamond, Jared. 1999. *Guns, Germs, and Steel: The Fates of Human Societies*. New York: W.W. Norton.

Dinnerstein, Leonard. 2009. *Ethnic Americans: A History of Immigration*. New York: Columbia University Press.

Douglas, Mary. 1996. *The World of Goods: Towards an Anthropology of Consumption*. London: Routledge.

Douglas-Hamilton, Jill. 2005. *Thomas Cook: The Holiday-Maker*. Stroud, UK: Sutton.

Elster, John. 2009. *Alexis de Tocqueville: The First Social Scientist*. Cambridge: Cambridge University Press.

Erlichman, Howard J. 2010. *Conquest, Tribute, and Trade: The Quest for Precious Metals and the Birth of Globalization*. Amherst, NY: Prometheus.

Evans, Harold. 1998. *The American Century*. New York: Knopf.

Evans, Harold. 2004. *They Made America*. New York: Little, Brown.

Fernández-Armesto, Felipe. 1987. *Before Columbus: Exploration and Colonisation from the Mediterranean to the Atlantic, 1229–1492*. London: Macmillan.

Fernández-Armesto, Felipe. 1996. *Millennium*. London: Black Swan.

Fernández-Armesto, Felipe. 1999. A role without an empire: Problems of super-power status in the twentieth century. In J. Guest, ed., *The American Century from Afar*, pp. 49–62. Melbourne: Boston, Melbourne, Oxford Conversazioni on Culture and Society.

Fernández-Armesto, Felipe. 2000. The stranger effect in early modern Asia. *Itinerario* 24 (2): 80–103.

Fernández-Armesto, Felipe. 2001. *Civilizations: Culture, Ambition, and the Transformation of Nature*. New York: Free Press.

Fernández-Armesto, Felipe. 2006. *Pathfinders: A Global History of Exploration*. New York: W.W. Norton.

Fernández-Armesto, Felipe. 2009. Conceptualizing conversion in global perspective: From late antique to early modern. In C.B. Kendall, O. Nicholson, W.D. Phillips, Jr., and M. Ragnow, eds, *Conversion to Christianity from Late Antiquity to the Modern Age: Considering the Process in Europe, Asia, and the Americas*. Minneapolis: Center for Early Modern History, University of Minnesota.

Fielding, Ann. 2009. *The Mongols in the Making of Europe 1220–1500.* Folkestone, UK: Global Oriental.

Frank, Andre Gunder, Barry K. Gills, and David Wilkinson, eds. 1993. *The World System: Five Hundred Years or Five Thousand?* London: Routledge.

Fregosi, Paul. 1998. *Jihad in the West: Muslim Conquests from the 7th to the 21st Centuries.* Amherset, NY: Prometheus.

Gernet, Jacques. 1996. *A History of Chinese Civilization,* trans. J.R. Foster and C. Hartman. 2nd edn. Cambridge: Cambridge University Press.

Goudsblom, Johan. 1992. *Fire and Civilization.* London: Allen Lane.

Goudsblom, Johan. 2004. *Humans and Their Habitats in a Long-Term Socio-ecological Perspective: Myths, Maps and Models.* Amsterdam: Amsterdam University Press.

Goudsblom, Johan, Eric L. Jones, and Stephen Mennell, eds. 1996. *The Course of Human History: Economic Growth, Social Process, and Civilization.* Armonk, NY: M.E. Sharpe.

Helms, Mary W. 1975. *Middle America: A Cultural History of Heartland and Frontier.* Upper Saddle River, NJ: Prentice Hall.

Helms, Mary W. 1983. Miskito slaving and culture contact: Ethnicity and opportunity in an expanding population. *Journal of Anthropological Research* 39 (2): 179–197.

Helms, Mary W. 1993a. *Craft and the Kingly Ideal: Art, Trade, and Power.* Austin: University of Texas Press.

Helms, Mary W. 1993b. *Ulysses' Sail: An Ethnographic Odyssey of Power, Knowledge, and Geographical Distance.* Austin: University of Texas Press.

Hodgson, Marshall G.S. 1974. *The Venture of Islam.* 3 vols. Chicago: University of Chicago Press.

Horden, Peregrine, and Nicholas Purcell. 2000. *The Corrupting Sea: A Study of Mediterranean History.* Oxford: Blackwell.

Hunwick, John O. ed. 1999. *Timbuktu and the Songhay Empire: Al-Sa'dī's Ta'rīkh al-Sūdān down to 1613 and Other Contemporary Documents.* Leiden: Brill.

Hyde, Francis. 1975. *Edwin Cunard and the North Atlantic, 1840–1973: A History of Shipping and Financial Management.* Atlantic Highlands, NJ: Humanities Press.

Impey, Oliver. 1977. *Chinoiserie: The Impact of Oriental Styles on Western Art and Decoration.* Oxford: Oxford University Press.

Jardine, Lisa. 1996. *Worldly Goods: A New History of the Renaissance.* New York: Doubleday.

Kane, Danielle, and Jung Mee Park. 2009. The puzzle of Korean Christianity: Geopolitical networks and religious conversion in early twentieth-century East Asia. *American Journal of Sociology* 115 (2): 365–404.

Lach, Donald F. 1965–1999. *Asia in the Making of Europe.* 3 vols. Chicago: University of Chicago Press.

Leopold, Anita M., and Jeppe Sinding Jensen, eds. 2004. *Syncretism in Religion: A Reader.* London: Equinox.

Lewis, David L. 2008. *God's Crucible: Islam and the Making of Europe, 570 to 1215.* New York: W.W. Norton.

MacCormack, Sabine. 1990. *Children of the Sun and Reason of State: Myths, Ceremonies and Conflicts in Inca Peru.* Baltimore: University of Maryland.

MacCormack, Sabine. 1991. *Religion in the Andes: Vision and Imagination in Early Colonial Peru.* Princeton: Princeton University Press.

Malacrino, Carmelo G. 2010. *Constructing the Ancient World: Architectural Techniques of the Greeks and Romans.* Los Angeles: Getty Museum.

Marks, Steven G. 1991. *Road to Power: The Trans-Siberian Railroad and the Colonization of Asian Russia, 1850–1917.* Ithaca, NY: Cornell University Press.

Massarella, Derek. 1990. *A World Elsewhere: Europe's Encounter with Japan in the Sixteenth and Seventeenth Centuries.* New Haven: Yale University Press.

Massarella, Derek. 2008. Revisiting Japan's "Christian century." *Casahistoria* (Jan.).

Mazlish, Bruce. 1993. *Conceptualizing Global History.* Boulder, CO: Westview.

Mazlish, Bruce. 2004. *Civilization and Its Contents*. Stanford: Stanford University Press.

Mazlish, Bruce. 2005. *The Global History Reader*. London: Routledge.

Mazlish, Bruce. 2006. *The New Global History*. London: Routledge.

Mazlish, Bruce. 2009. *The Idea of Humanity in a Global Era*. Houndmills: Palgrave Macmillan.

Métraux, A. 1972. *Voodoo in Haiti*. New York: Schocken.

Morena, Francesco. 2009. *Chinoiserie: The Evolution of the Oriental Style in Italy from the 14th to the 19th Century*. Florence: Centro Di.

Naro, Nancy Priscilla, *et al.* eds. 2007. *Cultures of the Lusophone Atlantic*. New York: Palgrave Macmillan.

Needham, Joseph, *et al.*, gen. eds. 1956–. *Science and Civilisation in China*. Cambridge: Cambridge University Press.

Newell, Jennifer. 2010. *Trading Nature: Tahitians, Europeans, and Ecological Exchange*. Honolulu: University of Hawai'i Press.

Pédron-Colombani, Sylvie. 2004. *Maximon: A Guatemalan Cult*. Berkeley: Periplus.

Porter, Roy, and John Brewer, eds. 1994. *Consumption and the World of Goods*, London: Routledge.

Robinson, David M. 2009. *Empire's Twilight: Northeast Asia under the Mongols*. Cambridge, MA: Harvard University Press.

Rosander, Eva E., and David Westerlund, eds. 1997. *African Islam and Islam in Africa: Encounters between Sufis and Islamists*. Athens: Ohio University Press.

Ruthven, Malise. 2004. *Historical Atlas of Islam*. Cambridge, MA: Harvard University Press.

Seaman, John T. 2006. *A Citizen of the World: The Life of James Bryce*. London: I.B. Taurus.

Smith, Patrick. 2010. *Somebody Else's Century: East and West in a Post-modern World* New York: Pantheon.

Sonn, Tamara. 2010. *Islam: A Brief History*. Oxford: Wiley-Blackwell.

Trentmann, Frank. 2007. Citizenship and consumption. *Journal of Material Culture* 7 (2): 147–158.

Trentmann, Frank. 2008. *Free Trade Nation: Consumption, Civil Society and Commerce in Modern Britain*. Oxford: Oxford University Press.

Trentmann, Frank. 2009. Crossing divides: Consumption and globalization in history. *Journal of Material Culture* 9 (2): 187–220.

Trentmann, Frank. 2010. The long history of contemporary consumer society: Chronologies, practices, and politics in modern Europe. In Alan Warde, ed., *Consumption*. London: Sage, vol. 2, chap. 20.

Tzonis, Alexander, and Phoebe Giannisi. 2004. *Classical Greek Architecture: The Construction of the Modern*. Paris: Flammarion.

Whitfield, Susan. 2001. *Life along the Silk Road*. Berkeley: University of California Press.

Wood, Frances. 2002. *The Silk Road: Two Thousand Years in the Heart of Asia*. Berkeley: University of California Press.

Wrangham, Richard. 2009. *Catching Fire*. New York: Basic Books.

Wreschner, Ernst E. 1976. The red hunters: Further Thoughts on the evolution of speech. *Current Anthropology* (Dec.).

Wreschner, Ernst E. 1980. Red ochre and human evolution: A case for discussion. *Current Anthropology* (Oct.).

CHAPTER TWENTY-ONE

Objects in Motion

Scott C. Levi

Consumers in today's global market regularly shop in a virtual bazaar, using the internet to survey and compare a vast array of merchandise available at warehouses across the world. Relying on online descriptions, digital photographs and reports posted by other consumers, we trade the opportunity to physically see, touch, smell and taste for an exponentially larger selection and a convenience unimaginable just a few years ago. With the click of a button, the consumer sets in motion a chain of events. An order is logged into a computer database and an item packed in cardboard and plastic, sitting on a shelf in a warehouse in Shanghai, or Mumbai, or Atlanta, is almost immediately packed into a box, tagged, loaded onto a truck, and then placed on a cargo jet, to be delivered to the consumer's doorstep in Europe, North America, or most anywhere else around the globe, in just a few short days.

Globalization is a modern phenomenon, but long-distance trade is not. The transregional exchange of commodities among peoples of distant civilizations has been a persistent feature of world history since the early stages of human civilization. For millennia, merchant groups have overseen the transportation of goods available in abundance in one place and in demand elsewhere. Already during the fourth millennium BCE, even before the Bronze Age (3000–1200 BCE), archaeologists have noted nearly synchronous developments in pottery and material production among the ancient peoples of the Indus Valley, Central Asia, Mesopotamia, and the Nile River Valley, indicating a high degree of transregional engagement. (See Yoffee, this volume.) Additional material evidence from the Bronze Age demonstrates a vibrant commercial exchange in a variety of goods: lapis lazuli from Afghanistan and other precious and semiprecious stones; Indian indigo and other dyes; cloth made of flax, wool and cotton; wheat, barley and other grains; salt, salt-cured and dried foods; tin and copper, and the bronze they were combined to make; farming implements, tools, and other objects made of metal; special varieties of wood; and, of course, gold and silver.

Throughout recorded human history, nearly every commodity imaginable – both the precious and the mundane – has been harvested, mined, or manufactured, and then

A Companion to World History, First Edition. Edited by Douglas Northrop.
© 2012 Blackwell Publishing Ltd. Published 2012 by Blackwell Publishing Ltd.

packed, transported across great distances, and exchanged for other commodities. Camels, donkeys, bullocks, horses and other beasts of burden, as well as ships great and small, have transported aromatic spices, incense, luxurious silks, magnificent porcelains, and gold and silver jewelry, coins, and ingots. But at least as important as the trade in luxury goods was the trade in the everyday necessities of life: livestock, leather, wool and other animal products, salt, grains, fruits both fresh and dried, base metals, textiles, medicinal plants, and so on. The totality of transregional commodity exchange, or "objects in motion," through human history is too vast even to begin to summarize. This chapter directs attention to a few of the key commercial systems that have emerged over the past two millennia to facilitate this trade, from the trans-Eurasian Silk Road of antiquity to the colonial economy of the nineteenth-century industrializing world. This survey addresses technology, environment, and the spirit of exploration as we chart the gradual movement toward the global economy of today.

The Silk Road

In the first decade of the third century BCE, two rival powers in East Asia came into being. (See Liu, this volume.) In northern China, the Han Dynasty (206 BCE–220 CE) emerged following the collapse of the Qin (221–206/7 BCE). Nearby, in the open grasslands to the north and west, the nomadic Xiongnu established a powerful steppe empire, the rise of which is typically attributed to the charismatic leader Modu Chanyu (r. 209–174 BCE). In subsequent decades, as the territory of the nomadic Xiongnu expanded to cover much of the northern steppe, the Han conducted a lucrative exchange with their nomadic neighbors. The Chinese commodity that the Xiongnu most desired was silk, which the nomadic nobility valued as a symbol of prestige. In exchange for their bolts of silk, the Xiongnu provided the Chinese with many thousands of horses and other livestock. This "silk diplomacy" was an effective means to appease the Xiongnu nobility, but the Han simultaneously worked to strengthen their defenses by continuing earlier Qin efforts to link the various walls that earlier states had constructed into a singular "Great Wall." Even at this early date Chinese rulers knew well that peaceful relations with their nomadic neighbors were both desirable and temporary (Di Cosmo 2002).

Some decades later the Han Emperor Wudi (r. 141–87 BCE) sent a young man named Zhang Qian westward to the court of another nomadic confederation, the Yuezhi, hoping to establish an alliance with them against the Xiongnu, their mutual enemy. The Xiongnu twice captured the unfortunate emissary, and kept him as a captive for more than a decade. But the young man escaped both times, and eventually made his way back to the Han court, having traveled as far as the Ferghana Valley, in modern Uzbekistan. The mission was technically a failure, as the Yuezhi balked at the notion of taking up arms against the much stronger Xiongnu. But Zhang Qian submitted an official report to the emperor, the surviving portions of which include abundant information about the lands and peoples of the west, as well as detailed descriptions of the rich luxuries and merchandise available in those lands. The imagination of the Han aristocracy appears to have been ignited by tales of the regal, legendary, supposedly blood-sweating horses of Ferghana.

Meanwhile, Emperor Wudi grew strong enough to take an offensive position against the Xiongnu, and in 133 BCE he unleashed an overwhelming military force against the nomadic troops occupying the lands to the north of his capital at Chang'an (modern Xi'an). The victory was decisive, and it turned out to be only the first of many. During

Emperor Wudi's long reign, Han armies annexed a substantial amount of territory in virtually all directions, and they made their way far to the west, where, for the first time, Chinese rulers extended their control over the desert oases of modern Xinjiang. In subsequent decades, Emperor Wudi and his successors extended the Great Wall and established military garrisons to protect merchants and other travelers moving along the northern Hexi (or Gansu) corridor, a narrow strip of fertile land wedged between the Qilian Mountains and the Gobi Desert that connected Chang'an with urban centers to the west. This put China in contact with new neighbors and, as caravan towns grew along this new trade route, gave rise to the first great commercial system to emerge and facilitate the movement of commodities between East and West: the Silk Road (see Map 21.1).

That said, precisely what is meant by the term Silk Road requires some explanation. The German geographer Baron Ferdinand von Richthofen (1833–1905) first coined the term "Seidenstrassen" (or Silk Routes) in 1877 to refer to the movement of Chinese luxury goods, most notably silk, along the overland caravan routes that connected Han China with the Roman Empire. References to the Silk Road, or even Silk Roads (or Routes), are quite often accompanied by a map of Eurasia (like this one) that illustrates the horizontal movement of merchandise along what appears to be a premodern superhighway of sorts. Beginning at the Han capital of Chang'an and moving westward, the "Silk Road" diverges to skirt either the northern or southern rim of the inhospitable Tarim Basin, after which it passes through Central Asia and Persia on its way to the shores of the Mediterranean. Some versions of this map add a southern branch of the Silk Road that passes through Afghanistan, connecting Central Asia to the markets of north India.

The term "Silk Road" conjures, for many, a romantic image: dusty, turban-clad Central Asian merchants leading long caravans of hundreds of richly decorated camels with bells jingling as they wend their way along isolated desert trails. The travelers walk for months under a hot sun as they gradually make their way the full distance of 4,000 miles to Rome. Upon reaching the bustling entrepôts on the shores of the Mediterranean, these merchants unload their camels, take razor-sharp knives in hand and cut open the bales to reveal thousands of bolts of exquisite Chinese silk. Local wholesalers excitedly line up to inspect this exotic merchandise and, in no time at all, the Eastern merchants exchange their silk for silver and gold. The caravan then disappears back into the desert, beginning the long journey home to China, where local artisans are already hard at work producing more silk for the merchants to purchase – and thus the process begins anew.

This is a compelling image, or succession of images, but it is also an oversimplified fiction that has at least partly been perpetuated by those who have approached the study of the Silk Road as a subject of cultural, not commercial inquiry. The commercial network popularized as the "Silk Road" has been a medium for some scholars to investigate the mechanisms by which travelers exported Buddhism from India to Central Asia and China, where it found a remarkably receptive audience. Others have looked into the transmission of other faiths along the Central Asian caravan routes (Manichaeism, Nestorian Christianity and, later, Islam), or the transfer of technologies, artistic styles, knowledge and information, and more.[1] Scholars of such subjects found little need to complicate the simplistic commercial model presented above. But those more familiar with the dynamics of the Silk Road trade itself all recognize that this simplified narrative is inadequate to explain the structures and mechanics of overland Eurasian trade. This subject requires further explanation in its own right.

To begin, it must be noted that the term "Silk Road" is itself a misnomer. First, the commodities that constituted the overland Eurasian caravan trade were in no way limited

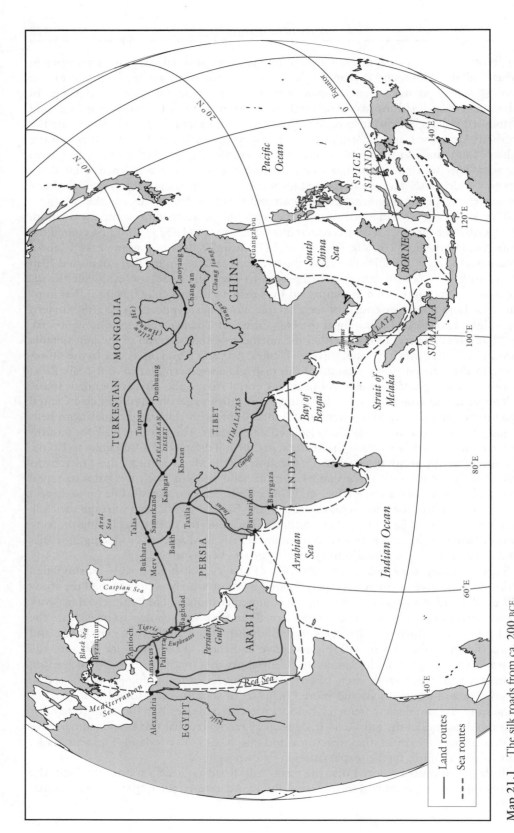

Map 21.1 The silk roads from ca. 200 BCE.

Source: Based on J.H. Bentley and H.F. Ziegler, *Traditions and Encounters*, 5th edn (New York: McGraw-Hill, 2010), p. 237.

to, or even dominated by, silk (although the value associated with the luxurious textile did earn it a special place in the historical record). Even in the early centuries BCE, caravan traders dealt also in spices, perfumes, foodstuffs, animals and animal products, and nearly every other commodity mentioned above. Additionally, while it was possible for a trader to travel the full distance from Chang'an to the Mediterranean, it would have been a truly exceptional occurrence. In general, merchandise passed through many hands as it made its way from producer to consumer, with value and cost increasing every step of the way. This provided important opportunities for many merchant families based in China, Central Asia, and elsewhere to profit handsomely by placing family members at key locations along the most vibrant commercial networks.[2]

Furthermore, while the routes mentioned above represented several "trunk roads" of primary importance, the caravans that moved along them by no means carried all, or even most, of the goods that moved along the overland Eurasian caravan routes. There was indeed an increase in China's westward trade following the Han conquests, but there was nothing uniform about it. During the Han period, as before and after, caravan traders utilized an elaborate network of roads that crisscrossed and connected virtually every human settlement in the Eurasian landmass. Travelers relied on fresh water supplies, mountain passes and other natural features to facilitate travel. They also thirsted for intelligence about security. When travel along a route or through a territory became for any reason inhospitable, whether from the threat of robbers or political instability, merchants would opt for an alternate route. Envisioned this way, instead of an unpaved superhighway connecting East and West, one might conceptualize the overland caravan network as an ever evolving web that expanded and contracted depending upon the historical vicissitudes of the time. The importance of this commercial system continued in subsequent centuries, and it gave rise to multiple mediatory commercial networks, with multiple centers, in the vast expanse between Europe and China. But this is only part of the story.

Long before the rise of the overland "Silk Road" trade during the Han Dynasty, merchants also relied on maritime routes to move goods and people across great distances. Peoples used ships to transport heavy commodities as early as the Bronze Age, when new metal tools enabled craftsmen to build stronger seagoing vessels. Ancient Greek mariners confidently sailed the Mediterranean, and Herodotus (484–425 BCE) reports that they regularly ventured to the northern shores of the Black Sea.[3] Well before his time, Greek traders had established a series of trading colonies there that supplied Greece with grains produced in the fertile Pontic steppe of modern Ukraine.

Navigating the Mediterranean and crossing the Black Sea was one thing, but early ship captains were generally less eager to venture into the open waters of the Indian Ocean. This was partly because of the limitations they faced in navigational technology, and partly because of the larger and more dangerous waters. Nevertheless, trade continued. Ships loaded with all varieties of merchandise gradually made their way from one port to the next, skirting the shores of the Indian Ocean and connecting the markets of China, Indonesia and India with those in the Mediterranean and beyond. Ancient authors, including Pliny the Elder (23–79 CE), report persistent Roman demand for silks, spices, cotton textiles and incense originating in China, Southeast Asia, India and Arabia, which the Romans paid for partly with their own merchandise, but largely with exports of gold and silver acquired from their mines in Iberia, Macedon, Gaul and elsewhere, as well as their trade with Africa (Bostock and Riley 1855, vol. 2: 63). In the first centuries of the Common Era, when the Silk Road was still young and flourishing, Roman sailors in the Indian Ocean added to the earlier Greek genre of travel literature known as the *periplus* tradition, enriching it with their own experiences. The most famous of these, the *Periplus Maris Erythraei*, provides abundant information pertaining to the geography of the Red Sea and the Indian Ocean, as well as the merchandise available in Indian port cities (Casson 1989).

The Mongol World Empire

In the history of the premodern world, the Mongol conquests of the early thirteenth century stand out as arguably the single most disruptive force to existing commercial networks and institutions the world had ever seen. But in the later thirteenth century, as the Mongols' focus shifted from conquest to governance of the world's largest ever contiguous empire, the Mongol leadership instituted a series of highly successful policies deliberately designed to encourage long-distance trade and communication across Eurasia.

The Mongol conquests were both rapid and devastating. (See Morillo, this volume.) They began under the leadership of Temujin (ca. 1167–1227), an extraordinarily talented military strategist who united the nomadic tribes of Mongolia and, from 1206, ruled them as Chinggis (Genghis) Khan. China at the time was governed by three rival states: the Xi Xia and the Manchurian Jin in the north, and the considerably larger, more populous, and more powerful Sung Empire in the south. In 1209, Chinggis Khan's nomadic warriors defeated the Xi Xia and by 1215 forced the Jin to abandon their capital of Zhongdu (modern Beijing). Chinggis Khan's attention at the time was focused squarely on China, but it was soon drawn to Central Asia, where the regional ruler, the Khwarezmshah, represented a potential threat. In 1219, Chinggis Khan broke from his campaigns against the Jin to lead a large-scale invasion of Central Asia. As was usual Mongol policy, those cities that submitted willingly were looted and made subject to Mongol governance. Those that resisted were completely demolished and, with few exceptions, depopulated.

The Mongols swept through Central Asia and, in 1221, returned northward to resume their campaigns against the Jin. Chinggis Khan died in 1227, but his sons and successors continued these efforts and achieved victory over the Jin in 1236. The Mongol armies next directed their attention westward and, from 1236 to 1241, they defeated a variety of Slavic princes (including those of Muscovy), and made their way into Europe, reaching as far as Poland and Hungary. Further expansion stopped temporarily with news of the great khan's death, and the subsequent contest for succession. But in the late 1250s, the Mongol conquests began again, with one force quickly occupying the Middle East while another began the long process of completing the conquest of China. It took nearly 20 more years, but with the defeat of the Sung in 1279, the Mongols ruled an empire that stretched from Europe to the Pacific Ocean, and from the Himalayan Mountains to Syria.[4]

Our sources describe the devastation: millions of people killed, irrigation canals and agricultural territory laid to waste, and great cities of antiquity destroyed, with their monuments tossed to the ground and libraries burned to ashes. The Mongol destruction was cataclysmic, but it was also uneven. Some regions were incorporated into the empire relatively unscathed. Additionally, as the nomadic conquerors transformed into governing administrators, they developed an appreciation for the importance of encouraging agricultural production, technological advancements, trade, and communication across their empire. Regions that were not devastated soon flourished, and, with some notable exceptions (e.g. northeastern Iran), areas that had been demolished recovered. Industrial centers and commercial entrepôts across the empire were, in some key ways, bound together in a single economy. The historically unprecedented dichotomy between this period and the one before it has led some to characterize the century from 1250 to 1350 as the Pax Mongolica: the Mongol Peace.

Much like "Silk Road," the term "Pax Mongolica" is a compact and descriptive label that is also an oversimplification subject to exaggeration. Emphasizing the destructive component of the Mongol conquests, in the first edition of his classic treatment of the Mongol Empire, historian David Morgan dismisses the term as hyperbolic. Illustrating his point, he recalls the words of the Roman historian Tacitus (d. 117): "They make a desolation, and call it peace" (Morgan 1986: 73). To be sure, the century following the conquests witnessed continued wars, rebellions, criminal activity, a bloody and highly destructive civil war at the Mongol court (1259–1264), and more. But in the updated second edition of his work, Morgan recognized that more recent scholarship lends credence to the notion of a "Mongol peace" (2007: 194–196; see esp. Allsen 1997; 2001). Especially when compared to the half-century immediately preceding it, from 1250 to 1350 peoples and states across Eurasia did indeed enjoy a lengthy period of growth and prosperity.

Surveying evidence of the vibrant regional economies of this time in both Europe and Asia, Janet Abu-Lughod (1991) has sought to demonstrate that this century witnessed the emergence of the first world system: a period of profound Eurasian commercial integration and dynamic growth that, following an interlude, gave rise to Immanuel Wallerstein's more famous "modern world-system," which he argues first developed in sixteenth-century western Europe. (See Chase-Dunn and Hall, this volume.) Without understating the importance of later European achievements, Abu-Lughod notes that, from the middle of the thirteenth century, both overland and maritime routes were heavily trafficked with Sung porcelains and silken textiles, Southeast Asian spices, golden brocade and other "Islamic" cloth, Flemish textiles, precious stones and precious metals, and all other varieties of luxury and bulk commodities. After the Sung finally succumbed to Mongol attacks in 1279, the Mongols of the Yuan Dynasty (1279–1368) oversaw an even more centralized expansion in the Chinese silk and porcelain industries. Some world historians, including the late Andre Gunder Frank, have taken issue with Abu-Lughod's periodization and her distinction between two discrete "world systems," which, he argues, were essentially one and the same (1998: 57, 328–329). Indeed, Frank went so far as to argue in favor of a unified Afro-Eurasian economic system dating back some 5,000 years. Be that as it may (and Frank's view of an ancient global system is far from agreed), Abu Lughod's conclusions regarding the systemic character of Eurasian commercial integration in the thirteenth- and fourteenth-century economy have been generally accepted.

Abu-Lughod's view is supported by the fact that medieval travelers from various parts of Europe to the "exotic East" returned home with firsthand reports that such precious commodities as pepper, cloves, nutmeg, cinnamon and more – goods worth nearly their weight in gold in Europe – were available in distant entrepôts at a small fraction of their European market value. Such reports were abundant, and they collectively sparked the imagination and provided tangible motivation for the adventurous to travel eastward in search of these precious commodities. Marco Polo is a familiar name in this context, but he is only the most famous of the many travelers to take advantage of the improved safety of long-distance travel in the Mongol age. Indeed, one might argue that the only thing truly remarkable about the celebrated Italian merchant's long journey from Venice to Yuan China and back is that, by sheer coincidence, he found himself imprisoned in Genoa with Rustichello of Pisa, a novelist, who took advantage of the long passing days to commit the merchant's account to paper (with some embellishment). Partly because of its association with an author of romances, many contemporaries dismissed Rustichello's *Il Milione*, known today as *The Book of Ser Marco Polo*, as fantasy. But it remained popular nevertheless and, as we shall see, drew considerable attention among later generations of explorers.

To those attuned to such things, the feverish trade and economic vitality of the Mongol era must have seemed an unstoppable force, even as the Mongol Empire itself fragmented. But the extended period of economic growth did eventually meet with a reversal brought about by the onset of epidemic disease. A highly contagious plague, first observed in the 1320s, spread across China in the 1330s and, from there, passed westward across the Eurasian trade routes. In 1347, the plague reached the Italian trading outpost of Caffa on the Crimean Peninsula. Transmitted to people by the bites of fleas that lived on rats, the disease was unwittingly carried by Italian sailors to the Mediterranean. Estimates suggest that as much as one-third of the populations of both Europe and China succumbed to the disease. Urban centers were hit hardest, with mortality estimates for some cities reaching as high as 90 percent.[5] Within just a few years all seemed lost.

The Age of Exploration

There was a recovery, of course, but it was slow and its progress was hampered by the tendency of the plague to revisit regions that it had already devastated. Depopulation in Europe had contributed to the collapse of the medieval feudal system and, although the subject rests safely beyond the boundaries of our present discussion, it is worth noting that some argue the sustained trauma of the Black Death to have been a catalyst that led to the revolutionary rebirth of European civilization, the Renaissance. For decades, too, famine also spread across China, prompting peasant rebellions that eventually developed into a different sort of revolution. The Ming dynasty (1368–1644) emerged from the ashes of the Yuan, and by the beginning of the fifteenth century China once again started to enjoy a new era of economic strength and cultural efflorescence. As the population recovered, China again became a leader in the production and exportation of fine silks, ornately decorated porcelains, tea, and other merchandise in great demand across Eurasia.

Demand for spices and other "luxury" (i.e. nonessential) goods in both China and Europe – indeed across the whole of Eurasia – increased dramatically from around 1400 (Chaudhuri 1985). This continued to such an extent that from the fifteenth century, Southeast Asian producers increasingly began cultivating as a cash crop first pepper and then other spices, rather than harvesting them from the wild as previously (Reid 1993: 15, 32–36). As demand within Europe increased and Italian mediatory merchants grew wealthier and more influential, others began to recognize the commercial advantage that could be had by circumventing the Italians and achieving direct access to Asian markets. This motivated certain European powers to invest in maritime exploration, primarily by building stronger and faster ships and equipping them with state-of-the-art gunpowder weapons. In Europe, the Age of Exploration had begun.

Over the course of the fifteenth century, the Iberian Catholic kingdoms of Spain and Portugal became the primary competitors in the race to bypass the Italians (Ringrose 2001). Already in the 1430s, the Portuguese began establishing a network of fortresses progressively farther down the coast of West Africa. One aim in doing so was to reach the Indian Ocean, but the African trade itself was quite lucrative, and these fortresses developed into highly profitable commercial outposts where Portuguese merchants exchanged European weapons, textiles and other manufactured items for African gold and slaves. Finally, in 1488, the Portuguese explorer Bartholomew Dias (1451–1500) reached the southernmost limits of Africa and sailed around it. (See Fernández-Armesto, this volume.) His success made him the first European to make his way into the Indian Ocean, but his crew refused to sail on to India, leaving him with no choice but to return to Lisbon.

As news of Dias's achievement spread, it provided a strong motivation for the Spanish rulers Ferdinand and Isabella to gamble on the proposal made by another explorer. The Genoese captain Christopher Columbus (Cristoforo Colombo, 1451–1506) argued vehemently (if incorrectly) that he could put his benefactors in contact with Asia using a shorter, more direct route that entailed sailing westward across the Atlantic. It was generally understood at the time that if one were to sail far enough to the west one would eventually reach Asia. Critics of Columbus's plan argued (correctly) that he had dramatically underestimated the circumference of the Earth and that Asia was much farther from Europe than Columbus believed. Nevertheless, having studied a number of available sources, including *The Book of Marco Polo*, and with the support of his Spanish benefactors, in 1492 Columbus sailed westward into the unknown (Pomeranz and Topik 1999: 21). After several months he returned to announce that he had been successful: he had reached land and encountered Indians. Columbus led three more voyages to "India" (1493, 1498, and 1502) and died without recognizing, as others soon did, that those whom he referred to as "Indians" were in fact a completely different people living on a continent that existed between Europe and Asia.

As was the case in the so-called "Old World," the Aztecs, Incans, Mayans and other peoples inhabiting the Americas at the time of Columbus's voyage were similarly bound together by an elaborate network of trade routes, and had been for many centuries. In addition to the urban and pastoralist populations of North America, there were tens of millions of people inhabiting the islands of the Caribbean and agrarian civilizations across Central and South America. Some elite members of these societies traded in precious stones, gold and silver jewelry, fine cotton textiles and some other materials that would be considered "luxury goods." But significantly more important was the exchange in ordinary cotton and woolen textiles, metal tools, leather and other animal products, maize, and a great variety of other food items. Here, too, it was the everyday exchange of the mundane that kept people alive and societies healthy.

Within a few years of Columbus's initial voyage, Spanish explorers, missionaries and conquistadors ventured from the islands of the Caribbean into the mainland and found that the location and its inhabitants were not all that was new. This "New World" was also rich with all varieties of unfamiliar plants and animals, as well as an abundance of gold and silver. In subsequent decades the shipping lanes across the Atlantic became much more heavily trafficked, as increasing numbers of Spanish and Portuguese ships passed from Europe to one or another slave trading outpost in West Africa, and then to the Americas, before returning to Europe to begin the circuit anew. Following the work of Crosby (1972), historians have come to refer to this triangular trade as the Columbian

Exchange, a commercial network that rapidly transformed the lives of peoples across the globe. Discussions pertaining to the movement of people, knowledge, technologies, and diseases between the "Old World" and the Americas are addressed sufficiently elsewhere in this volume. (See chapters by Ward, by Pernick, and by Vélez, Prange, and Clossey, this volume.) The following discussion will therefore remain focused on commodities.

The ever more rapid movement of people and commodities across the Atlantic resulted in the introduction of new plants and animals, and other goods, to both regions. Horses were among the many animals that Spaniards brought across the Atlantic, greatly facilitating the Europeans' military conquests and revolutionizing mobility in the Americas. Other domesticated animals that Europeans introduced into indigenous American diets and lifestyles include cattle and chickens. The very long list of Old World plants taken to the Americas includes such modern staples as coffee, bananas, oranges and other citrus fruits, peaches, pears, carrots, lettuce, garlic, onions, rice, sugarcane and wheat. In exchange, Europeans brought back to the Old World a number of animals, including turkeys, as well as legumes, blueberries, cocoa, corn (maize), chili peppers, peanuts, potatoes, tomatoes, tobacco, and a superior variety of long-fiber cotton.

This exchange added what must have been a wonderful richness and diversity to regional diets across the globe – introducing the tomato to Italian cuisine, for example, the potato to Ireland, chili peppers to India and China, and coffee to Columbia. More important, however, is that the introduction of new foods enabled farmers to diversify their crops and experiment with nutritious and drought-resistant alternatives. This had a positive and sustained impact on caloric intake across the globe, which decreased mortality rates and contributed to population growth and recovery in both Europe and China. It eventually brought recovery in the Americas as well, where the introduction of new crops occurred alongside the introduction of a smallpox epidemic that almost completely obliterated the indigenous communities.

In the meanwhile, just five years after Christopher Columbus made his maiden voyage to the New World, in 1497 the Portuguese captain Vasco da Gama led four ships from Lisbon down the coast of Africa.[6] In 1498, Gama successfully rounded the Cape of Good Hope, entered the Indian Ocean, and, with the help of a pilot, whom Subrahmanyam notes was probably, although not certainly, an Indian from Gujarat, navigated the trade winds to arrive at Calicut on May 20, 1498 (Subrahmanyam 1997: 121–128). This achievement ushered in a new era of European activity in the Indian Ocean. Upon meeting the ruler of Calicut the Portuguese famously asked for two things: Christians and spices. They were disappointed not to find Christians, but the Portuguese mission was a success nonetheless. The ruler of Calicut permitted the Portuguese to exchange their relatively paltry merchandise, consisting primarily of textiles and agricultural goods, for pepper and cinnamon (Subrahmanyam 1993: 56–62).

In the wake of this initial success the Portuguese rapidly went to work building more and better ships and, within a few years, the Portuguese Estado da India was a new maritime power in the Indian Ocean. Benefiting from the addition of cannons, something never before affixed to Asian ships, the Portuguese approach was "to trade where possible, to make war where necessary" (Subrahmanyam 1993: 60). Within just a few years they managed to conquer key commercial entrepôts throughout the Indian Ocean, from East Africa to Hormuz at the entrance of the Persian Gulf, to Goa on the southwest coast of India, to Malacca in Southeast Asia. The Portuguese encountered some stiff resistance, but by the 1571, the Estado da India was in control of approximately 40 trading outposts dotting the Indian Ocean coastline and beyond, stretching from Sofala in Mozambique as far as Macao in China and Nagasaki in Japan (Russell-Wood 1992: 22).

By all accounts, the initial intent of the Portuguese Estado da India was to achieve direct access to the spice trade and to monopolize the movement of pepper, cloves, nutmeg, mace, cinnamon, cardamom and other spices to Europe. While earlier scholarship credited the Portuguese with doing just that, more recent work has determined that the Portuguese were never able to achieve much more than to become a relatively minor player in a much older and much larger commercial arena. They were the primary European commercial interest in the Indian Ocean, but throughout the sixteenth century indigenous networks centered in China, India and Arabia consistently outpaced them (Frank 1998: 179). Even in the movement of spices to Europe, as late as 1585 Asian merchants using the old Red Sea route to the Mediterranean transported approximately four times more spices than Portuguese ships traveling to Europe by the Cape route (Frank 1998: 179; see also Subrahmanyam 1993: 74–78). As their efforts to achieve a monopoly failed, the Portuguese adapted by taking a more active role in the inter-Asian trade: purchasing Chinese merchandise and transporting it to markets in Africa, for example, where they exchanged it for gold and other merchandise which they traded in the markets of India, Indonesia, their new colonial territory of Brazil, and elsewhere (see Russell-Wood 1992: 123–147).

The Spanish and Portuguese movement around the globe had a direct and profound impact on the trajectory of world history: Iberian explorers established colonial empires; their movement of crops and domesticated animals revolutionized agrarian economies; and they ushered in the age of European expansion, tightening the bonds that connected the regional economies across Eurasia and, for the first time, connecting them to the Americas as well. China and Oceana had long ago boasted large-scale, powerful seafaring technologies (see Levathes 1997). Engineers now developed new models of Spanish galleons and Portuguese carracks and caravels to transport larger quantities of a great variety of commodities around the globe.[7] In this long list, one commodity takes precedence as being, arguably, the single most important: silver.

In the Americas, Europeans amassed a vast amount of gold by trading, looting, stealing, and, especially, forcing indentured laborers and slaves to mine it from the ground. But in both quantity and value, silver far exceeded gold. This is partly because of the extraordinary richness of silver ore in such American locations as Potosí, Bolivia. But also, unlike gold, silver had a substantially higher purchasing power in Asian markets than in Europe and it was therefore the Europeans' preferred medium for offsetting their trade deficits in Asia (see Flynn and Giráldez 2002: 396–397). In Spanish territories, colonizers rapidly developed political institutions that facilitated the exploitation of indigenous populations, frequently by using them to extract silver from an expanding network of mines in Bolivia, Peru, Mexico and elsewhere. (See Ward, this volume.) The figures involved in this trade are staggering. During the sixteenth and seventeenth centuries, Spanish galleons exported thousands of tons of silver from the Americas. In the eighteenth century, more American silver was mined than in the sixteenth and seventeenth centuries combined (Frank 1998: 143; Flynn and Giráldez 2002: 407).

Much of this silver was taken directly to Europe, where it circulated in regional economies before making its way further on to markets in the Indian Ocean. Following Magellan's voyage across the Pacific in 1520–1521, much was also shipped westward from the Americas to markets in China, moving through the entrepôt of Manila in the Philippines, a Spanish possession from 1571. This sustained injection of precious metals into the global economy intensified the economic system that connected regional economies in Europe, Africa, Asia and the Americas, leading to economic growth in some markets and, depending upon circumstances, provoking inflation and crisis in others. Over the centuries, Asian production expanded in response to growing demand, and Europeans used American silver to buy their way into the Asian markets (Frank 1998: 258–320, 356).

The pace of global trade accelerated further from the beginning of the seventeenth century, as two new groups of explorers from northwest Europe joined the Iberians. In the year 1600, the English East India Company was chartered with the primary objective of outmaneuvering the Portuguese and establishing a direct line of trade with Asian markets. Two years later, the Dutch VOC (Verenigde Oostindische Compagnie) joined the English. While the Spanish and Portuguese commercial interests were intended to be royal monopolies, the Companies were both joint stock ventures that were organized as a way for private interests to pool their capital to invest in the Asia trade. The Dutch and English Companies financed the construction of large numbers of ships that easily outpaced the Portuguese, and within a few decades the Dutch emerged as the dominant European power in the spice-producing regions of Southeast Asia while the English focused their commercial interests to the west, in India.

Prior to moving on to the final part of our discussion, we should note that the dramatic increase of Europeans' commercial activities in the Indian Ocean was accompanied by more continuity than change in the overland trade along the Eurasian caravan routes. Although some have argued that the European maritime traders usurped the caravan trade, those arguments have been based on assumptions rather than evidence.[8] This perception at least partly stems from an imbalance in the sources. Historians of Dutch and English maritime trade have long benefitted from an abundance of Company records archived in Amsterdam and London, while there is no analogous resource for historians of overland trade.

To be sure, there was little need for caravan traders to transport Chinese silks and porcelains the full distance from China to the Mediterranean. But as noted above, the east–west "Silk Road" trade in luxury commodities represented only one element of a much more complex overland Eurasian network of exchange. Recent research has demonstrated that the early modern overland trade remained quite active, with caravans consisting of thousands of pack animals – camels, horses, donkeys and bullocks – regularly making their way between commercial centers throughout the Eurasian interior.[9] Rather than luxury goods, this trade consisted primarily of more mundane items such as cotton textiles and dyes, Chinese tea, both fresh and dried foodstuffs, animals, and animal products. Still, it must be recognized that European commercial interests in the Indian Ocean did gradually grow in influence, and in specific places at certain times, there were disruptions in continental commercial patterns. In general, as shown in Maps 21.2 and 21.3, during the period from the sixteenth century through the nineteenth century there was an extraordinary increase in the overall movement of merchandise across the globe, associated especially with the expansion of European trade posts (in Afro-Eurasia) and political conquests (in the Americas).

The Industrial Age

During the initial centuries of European activity in the Indian Ocean, with few exceptions European merchants represented little more than new participants in a vibrant commercial arena dominated by much larger indigenous Asian enterprises. Europeans were increasingly active in Asian markets in this period, but the Portuguese, Dutch, English,

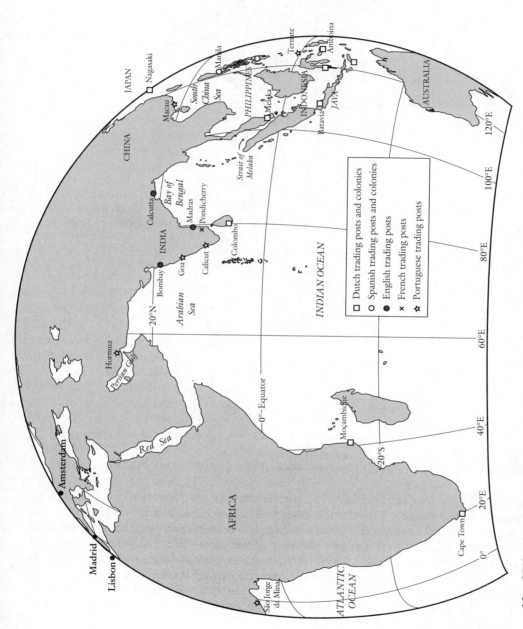

Map 21.2 Going global: European trade contacts in Africa and Asia, ca. 1700.
Source: Based on Bentley and Ziegler, *Traditions and Encounters* (as Map 21.1), p. 479.

Map 21.3   Europeans in the Americas, ca. 1700.
Source: Based on Bentley and Ziegler, *Traditions and Encounters* (as Map 21.1), p. 530.

and others did not achieve anything that resembled the expansive Spanish colonial empire in the Americas. Even if it had been their aspiration to do so, they simply did not have the economic resources, military strength, and manpower to achieve anything of the sort. It was not until the early decades of the nineteenth century that European powers began to extend colonial authority across nearly all of Africa and Asia. When this process did begin to unfold, it did so rapidly and with great effect. Even China, which escaped outright European colonization, was soundly subjugated following the First Opium War (1839–1842) and found its role in global trade to be ever more directly dictated by European demand.

Since even before McNeill's classic study, *The Rise of the West* (1963), world historians have endeavored to reach an improved understanding of the various factors behind this epoch-making shift in global power dynamics.[10] (See Adas, this volume.) In recent years, researchers have made some progress in determining when it was that Western powers achieved relative economic and military superiority over China, India, and other Asian powers, and they have directed attention to a number of factors that contributed to this development. The most critical element in this equation is the Industrial Revolution, which began, in most accounts, with the mechanization of the textile industry in England during the second half of the eighteenth century (see Bayly 2004). Precisely why it took place when and where it did remains a matter of ongoing debate. It is clear, however, that the mechanization of production and the rapid expansion of an industrial infrastructure had a profound impact on global trade, first in cotton textiles and then in every other manufactured commodity (see Stearns 2007). For purposes of expediency, we will focus attention on cotton and extrapolate from this one case larger implications relating to global trade patterns.

As noted above, English East India Company merchants came to India in the early seventeenth century looking primarily for spices. From 1619, the English began to establish a growing number of trading "factories" at key locations along the South Asian coastline. English merchants stationed at these well-defended trading warehouses purchased a wide variety of merchandise, including especially pepper and other spices, but also a variety of handmade cotton textiles including muslin, calico and chintz, which were growing more popular in European markets. In subsequent years, as the Dutch focused their efforts on the spice trade, Indian cotton textiles came to represent one of the most important commodities in the English East India Company's commercial portfolio. By 1684, Company merchants purchased an estimated 18 million yards of Indian cloth and injected a substantial amount of cash into the Indian economy in exchange (see Levi 2002: 74–76, 242–243).

The onset of the Industrial Revolution brought about a complete inversion of European trade relations with the nonindustrialized world. As textile factories in Great Britain rapidly expanded their production, instead of finished textiles Company merchants developed an insatiable appetite for raw materials. Already in 1760, Great Britain imported 2.5 million pounds (in weight) of raw cotton. That number increased to 42 million pounds by 1800, and to 366 million pounds by 1840. Rather than precious metals, the Company increasingly offset these enormous purchases by exporting Britain's own finished textiles and other manufactured merchandise to foreign markets. In the early decades of the nineteenth century, the British purchased Indian cotton and shipped it to textile factories in Great Britain, where power looms would turn it into cloth. They then transported this same cloth back to India, where it could be sold at a lower price than India's own handmade textiles. In terms of the Indian textile trade, the tipping point in this equation can be dated to 1816, the year that Indian merchants purchased more textiles from Great Britain than they sold. In 1824, Indian merchants imported approximately 1 million yards of cotton cloth produced in British factories. By 1837, this had increased to 64 million yards.

Such a radical transformation in global trade patterns had profound political implications as well. Governments of industrializing, urbanizing nations, such as Great Britain, recognized that it was imperative for them to achieve a reliable supply of raw materials from abroad in order to keep factories open and keep their increasingly urban populations at work. The need to sustain growing industrial economies led such states to invest heavily in their militaries, which they used to force open markets in some places (e.g. China) and conquer territories in others (e.g. India and Africa). European colonial administrations frequently operated at a loss when comparing taxation revenues from their colonial subjects to the expenditures that supported the empire. Significantly more important, however, was that they supervised a steady flow of necessary raw materials to industrial centers in the homeland. Industrial capitalists also used tariffs and other mercantile measures to control access to their own colonial markets. In the nineteenth century, these factors, as well as growing competition among industrializing states for access to resources and markets, precipitated the rapid expansion of European colonial authority over much of Africa and Asia. (See Sinha, this volume.)

The exponential increase in the industrial powers' demand for raw materials led to a corresponding increase in the production of "cash crops" across the globe, largely by means of a dramatic expansion of increasingly specialized plantation economies. From the turn of the nineteenth century, producers across the globe began to set aside more diverse and self-sufficient agricultural models in favor of highly specialized plantations that produced exclusively crops for export – items that were in demand on a global market. As the labor involved in such ventures could be extraordinarily expensive, this was achieved largely by relying on the labor of untold numbers of indentured servants and millions of African slaves. To reference just a few examples, farmers found the hot and humid climate of the American South suitable for cotton and tobacco. Hoping to establish their own reliable supply of raw cotton, Russian colonial authorities expanded irrigation agriculture in Central Asia and eventually established a cotton monoculture in the region. Agriculture in the Caribbean was turned over largely to sugarcane. Nearby, in Central America, some economies were based on coffee plantations, while others, the "banana republics," produced little else. In Europe as well, Poland and Ukraine focused on wheat production at the expense of other agricultural goods, and became known as the "breadbasket of Europe." Meanwhile, other European regions that had previously produced wheat shifted their focus to industrial production or other more lucrative (for them) economic activities, agricultural or otherwise.

Conclusion

The pace of globalization continues to increase into the twenty-first century. With a global population that is increasingly urban and has grown by more than 300 percent in the past century to reach nearly 7 billion people, agricultural producers and manufacturers have struggled to increase productivity correspondingly and devise new methods to move their merchandise more quickly and efficiently. Instead of caravans, carracks and caravels, goods are now loaded onto railroad cars, semitrailers, freighters and cargo planes and rapidly transported to nearly every market around the world. And instead of merchants and merchant families, it is now multinational corporations that oversee the production and transportation of goods worldwide. As notions of regional self-sufficiency and agricultural diversity gradually became a thing of the past, the world is no longer only bound together by a network of exchange: it has become utterly dependent upon it. (See chapters by Bright and Geyer, and by Simmons, this volume.)

Building upon recent technological developments, globalization has even transcended the movement of tangible objects to include the trade in information and technical services. To cite one common example: a consumer's question regarding the operation of a computer made by a US company with parts from across the globe and assembled in China leads to a phone call to an English-speaking customer service agent in India. If there is one defining feature of this globalizing trend it is that it is limited only by the speed of the objects in motion.

Notes

1 The literature on the Silk Road is abundant. For two recent studies of religious transmission along the Silk Road, see Foltz (2000) and Elverskog (2010).
2 For an excellent study of Central Asian merchants in this context, see Vaissière (2005).
3 Herodotus, IV, 8, 17–18.
4 For an up-to-date bibliography of literature on the Mongol Empire, see Morgan (2007).
5 See the classic studies by McNeill (1976) and Gottfried (1983), and the more current one by Cohn (2002).
6 For a detailed historiographical discussion of the life and career of Vasco da Gama, see Subrahmanyam (1997).
7 For a discussion of the various types of ships and other modes of transport employed in this trade, see Russell-Wood (1992: 27–57).
8 One recent example is Beckwith (2009: 232–263).
9 For a more detailed discussion of this subject, see Levi (2002: 21–84).
10 In addition to McNeill (1963) and Frank (1998), see especially Goldstone (2008), Pomeranz (2000), and Wong (2000).

References

Abu Lughod, J. 1991. *Before European Hegemony: The World System A. D. 1250–1350*. New York: Oxford University Press.

Allsen, T. 1997. *Commodity and Exchange in the Mongol Empire: A Cultural History of Islamic Textiles*. Cambridge: Cambridge University Press.

Allsen, T. 2001. *Culture and Conquest in Mongol Eurasia*. Cambridge: Cambridge University Press.

Bayly, C.A. 2004. *The Birth of the Modern World, 1780–1914*. Oxford: Blackwell.

Beckwith, C.I. 2009. *Empires of the Silk Road: A History of Central Eurasia from the Bronze Age to the Present*. Princeton: Princeton University Press.

Bostock, J., and H.T. Riley, trans. 1855. *The Natural History of Pliny*. 2 vols. London: Taylor & Francis.

Casson, L., trans. 1989. *The Periplus Maris Erythraei*. Princeton: Princeton University Press.

Chaudhuri, K.N. 1985. *Trade and Civilisation in the Indian Ocean: An Economic History from the Rise of Islam to 1750*. Cambridge: Cambridge University Press.

Cohn, S. 2002. *The Black Death Transformed: Disease and Culture in Early Renaissance Europe*. Oxford: Oxford University Press.

Crosby, A.W. 1972. *The Columbian Exchange: Biological and Cultural Consequences of 1492*. Westport, CT: Greenwood.

Di Cosmo, N. 2002. *Ancient China and Its Enemies: The Rise of Nomadic Power in East Asian History*. Cambridge: Cambridge University Press.

Elverskog, J. 2010. *Buddhism and Islam on the Silk Road*. Philadelphia: University of Pennsylvania Press.

Flynn, D.O., and A. Giráldez. 2002. Cycles of silver: Global economic unity through the mid-eighteenth century. *Journal of World History* 13 (2): 391–428.

Foltz, R. 2000. *Religions of the Silk Road*. New York: St Martin's Press.

Frank, A.G. 1998. *ReORIENT: Global Economy in the Asian Age*. Berkeley: University of California Press.

Goldstone, J. 2008. *Why Europe? The Rise of the West in World History, 1500–1850*. Boston: McGraw-Hill.

Gottfried, R.S. 1983. *The Black Death*. London: Collier Macmillan.

Levathes, L. 1997. *When China Ruled the Seas: The Treasure Fleet of the Dragon Throne, 1405–1433*. Oxford: Oxford University Press.

Levi, S.C. 2002. *The Indian Diaspora in Central Asia and its Trade, 1550–1900*. Leiden: Brill.

McNeill, W.H. 1963. *The Rise of the West*. Chicago: University of Chicago Press.

McNeill, W.H. 1976. *Plagues and Peoples*. Garden City, NY: Anchor.

Morgan, D.O. 1986. *The Mongols*. 1st edn. Oxford: Blackwell.

Morgan, D.O. 2007. *The Mongols*. 2nd rev. edn. Oxford: Wiley-Blackwell.

Pomeranz, K. 2000. *The Great Divergence: China, Europe, and the Making of the Modern World Economy*. Princeton: Princeton University Press.

Pomeranz, K., and S. Topik. 1999. *The World That Trade Created: Society, Culture, and the World Economy, 1400 to the Present*. Armonk, NY: M.E. Sharpe.

Reid, A. 1993. *Southeast Asia in the Age of Commerce, 1450–1680*, vol. 2: *Expansion and Crisis*. New Haven: Yale University Press.

Ringrose, D.R. 2001. *Expansion and Global Interactions, 1200–1700*. New York: Addison Wesley Longman.

Russell-Wood, A.J.R. 1992. *A World on the Move: The Portuguese in Africa, Asia, and America, 1415–1808*. New York: St Martin's Press.

Stearns, P. 2007. *The Industrial Revolution in World History*. 3rd edn. Boulder: Westview.

Subrahmanyam, S. 1993. *The Portuguese Empire in Asia, 1500–1700: A Political and Economic History*. London: Longman.

Subrahmanyam, S. 1997. *The Career and Legend of Vasco da Gama*. Cambridge: Cambridge University Press.

Vaissière, Étienne de la. 2005. *Sogdian Traders: A History*, trans. J. Ward. Leiden: Brill.

Wallerstein, I. 1974. *The Modern World-System*. New York: Academic Press.

Wong, R.B. 2000. *China Transformed: Historical Change and the Limits of European Experience*. Ithaca, NY: Cornell University Press.

CHAPTER TWENTY-TWO

People in Motion

KERRY WARD

My somewhat tongue-in-cheek one-sentence definition of world history is: People on the move, whether they want to or not. Movement, communication, connection, exchange – physical, temporal, spatial, and conceptual – makes us human. To examine people in the context of world history is to engage with motion. World historians adopt various approaches to describe people in motion and this chapter posits four registers of scale as an analytical framework, using a few specific examples, to examine some of these approaches. Needless to say, it is not meant to be comprehensive in coverage. In using scale as an organizing principle I have been inspired by Douglas Northrop's University of Michigan undergraduate world history course "Zoom," which, as the title suggests, zooms in from the broadest to the narrowest perspective to create a coherent "history of everything." Using a "nesting" of scales in a set of four, from the largest possible dimension of human motion to the smallest, each scale in this chapter directly narrows the focus of the former. The purpose of this approach is to show what comes into view and what is obscured by adopting a particular scale of analysis in examining migration in world history. Although the chapter focuses on a limited number of historians and their methodologies as their work demonstrates each scale, for the most part world historians are all cognizant of the "big picture" even when they are writing at the smallest scale – a biography of an individual. Likewise, while "big history" examines humans within the context of the whole cosmos, the individual is not irrelevant to the narrative even if they are not a point of focus. These issues of scale have been particularly challenging for historians writing world history textbooks for high school and undergraduate students. (See Bain, this volume.) Individual narratives are not only inserted into textbooks to enliven and illustrate narratives that encompass the entirety of human history, the shift in scale demonstrates to students that individual subjectivity and experience lies at the heart of human society and the production of sources which we examine as evidence. "Zooming" in this chapter implicitly recognizes that the entire spectrum of human mobility, encounters, and exchange exists simultaneously throughout time, but explicitly uses different scales as an ordering principle to examine people in motion.

A Companion to World History, First Edition. Edited by Douglas Northrop.
© 2012 Blackwell Publishing Ltd. Published 2012 by Blackwell Publishing Ltd.

Scale One, the Cosmos: Big History and Life on Earth

"Like merchants in a huge desert caravan, we need to know where we are going, where we have come from, and in whose company we are traveling. Modern science tells us that the caravan is vast and varied, and our fellow travelers include numerous exotic creatures from quarks to galaxies." In this evocative opening to *Maps of Time* (2004: 1), David Christian at once tells us the core of his argument – big history is a "modern creation myth." As an approach to world history, it is designed to integrate now generally accepted scientific knowledge about the origins of the universe with commonly held understanding about the evolution of humans as a species.[1] (See Spier, this volume.)

At the scale of big history essential binaries frame the cosmos – being and nothingness; energy and entropy; order and chaos; simplicity and complexity. Contained in each of these binaries is the notion of movement and change. The only point at which stasis is contemplated is the infinitesimal moment of origin more than 13 billion years ago, which scientists call Planck time, when the "big bang" created the universe. At this moment, essential forces and elements came into being out of which the universe, and eventually humans, were created. Humans are therefore linked directly to the origins of the universe in a physical dimension and are part of the dynamic harnessing of energy generated and expended in increasingly complex ways. Four and a half billion years ago, gravitational forces caused the sun and our solar system to emerge from a cloud of matter. Less than a billion years later, through a process of natural selection, organic chemicals stabilized into living single-celled organisms able to reproduce, and then diversified, around 3 billion years ago, and began to form multicellular organisms. Species diversification emerged as life developed on Earth; it took 7 million years of evolution, for instance, from the appearance of the first bipedal hominines to the appearance of modern humans. The evolution of human language and humans' unique capacity for collective, inherited learning enabled our species to store and utilize information about each other and the surrounding environment. Harnessing the energy of collective learning and resource exploitation is the hallmark of human society. Humans as a species have embodied the gravitational forces of the cosmos through processes of migration that have generated larger and more complex urban centers and societies. Historians of precolonial Southeast Asia aptly named these societies "galactic polities," but the global trend transcends region. About 250,000 years ago modern humans began migrating out of Africa and this process of movement, combined with increasingly diverse and far-reaching forms of communication, collective action, and exploitation of the natural environment, has accelerated ever since. The human twentieth (into the twenty-first) century stands – even at a cosmic scale, when measured against the entire history of the universe – as a period of escalating and accelerating complexity, societal diversity, movement and change, combined with exponential growth of humans' impact on the biosphere. This period, merely an instant in the cosmos's history, returns the narrative full circle: the production and consumption of multiple forms of energy by humans of course contains the potential for our own extinction as well as that of other species and, indeed, the entire planet.

The great achievement of big history is the interdisciplinary integration of the study of humanity with natural history in a coherent historical narrative. In employing the methodologies that explore the largest possible chronological scope, big history paradoxically also relies on methodologies that examine some of the smallest possible scales – such as chemical evolution, because the argument is based on the universality of matter being organized into structures that (at every scale) require the expenditure of energy. The result is an astonishing connection of humans as a life form not only with all other life forms but with all other forms of matter in a state of constant movement and change. Our commonalities with the cosmos are greater than our differences, resulting in a historical narrative where people are a miraculous chance combination of carbon and hydrogen producing and expending energy. Given the trajectory of increasing complexity through evolution and chance innovation alongside the general trend towards entropy, the ultimate fate of humanity is yet to be determined.

David Christian takes big history one step further by projecting his analysis into the future, thereby fulfilling one of the core criteria of a creation myth. At the largest scale of the cosmos, scientific predictions point towards infinite expansion. Less certain is the future of Earth and, in a relatively immediate time frame, humans as a species. One scenario contemplated by Christian continues the pattern of energy and movement at the center of big history: "Humans may migrate to planets or moons within the solar system, and perhaps even farther afield ..." (2004: 491). The logic of this argument makes it impossible to conceptualize humans as static and confined in space. Big history points to an inherent need as a species to expand our horizons. It also offers a cautionary tale. Humans appear as but a brilliant spark of energy in the brief exuberant springtime of the lifetime of our universe.

In Christian's hands, big history also explores humans' own quests for creation myths over time and in different cultures, linking these spiritual quests with the quest for all forms of knowledge, including the scientific knowledge upon which his own methodology rests. It is fascinating at this broad sweeping scale to note the commonalities in these myths and forms of knowledge. Humans as a species are united at one level despite all the differences and divisions that constitute the usual scale of human history.

Big history perhaps inevitably loses sight of individuals in this grand vision of the universe through the examination of progressively smaller but more complex periods of time to our present. But contemplating big history narratives as a creation myth is simultaneously an intensely individual experience, and this contemplation of the meaning of life has been shared by people throughout human history.

Scale Two, the Earth: Peopling the World

The scale of the entirety of human history constitutes the foundation of world history. The challenge of constructing a narrative that encompasses this entirety has resulted in a variety of approaches to human history constructed on the edifice of specific themes and metaphors, as shown by many of the chapters in this book. It is also at this scale of world history that academic and trade monographs meet textbooks and encyclopedias. Particularly in the United States education system, the content of world history curricula remains hotly contested alongside the huge growth in the Advanced Placement World History course and examination. One of the major conceptual divisions in this debate is between the "Western Civilization" trajectory that first developed after World War I and the proliferation, in the late twentieth century, of more fluid approaches to the analysis of changing patterns in world history that are not based on civilization models. (See Pomeranz and Segal, this volume.) The first posits a trajectory from the emergence of human civilization to its apotheosis in contemporary American (and European) society and the triumph of this "Western model" as the basis of the new globalized world order and the embodiment of a human ideal. The second is more open-ended in the examination of multiple perspectives on culture and history in which humans are not locked into single cultural identities from which they view the world, interactions with others, and the past (Dunn 2000). Each of these approaches focuses on the emergence of distinctive peoples, their movement over time and through space, and their interaction with other peoples within and between complex social formations like cities, states, empires, and modern nations – culminating in the contemporary global era when borders are often still porous despite states' attempts to police them. At this scale, humans are not examined as a species but as culturally and historically diverse peoples. (See McKeown, this volume.)

Academic monographs and textbooks aside, the most famous example of the civilizational approach is Jared Diamond's *Guns, Germs, and Steel: The Fates of Human Societies* (1997), which won a Pulitzer Prize in1998 and remains probably the most widely read popular work on world history. (See the chapters by Yoffee, by Chase-Dunn and Hall, and by Simmons, this volume.) Diamond has been criticized for presenting a geographically deterministic argument that Eurasian dominance over other societies was inevitable. In *this* march of civilization, Eurasians were able to move faster, over more favorable terrain, than others, and this resulted in their ability to eventually overrun slower, more sedentary folk. The book raises some of the problems of scale embedded in conceiving human history along a trajectory of emergence to the present because it inevitably leads to generalizations that stereotype civilizational models – in Diamond's case this is particularly problematic in the loose and inconsistent definition of "Eurasia."

In general, "Western Civ" approaches in textbooks have increasingly eschewed arguments about the inherently superior nature of Europeans in favor of more complex explanations about the "rise of the West" – even if the baton race of Western civilization, starting from the emergence of human society and passing along a progression of societies ending with the contemporary United States, is still embedded in the narrative. Two examples of alternative approaches to "peopling the Earth" suffice to illustrate a different narrative of people on the move. The first is Jerry Bentley and Herbert Ziegler's *Traditions and Encounters: A Global Perspective on the Past* (published in its fifth edition in 2011) and the second is Valerie Hansen and Kenneth Curtis's *Voyages in World History* (2010). Both traverse the complex terrain of comprehensive coverage of human history from the evolution of modern humans to the globalized present, not losing sight of individuals or the production of historical texts within this macronarrative. *Traditions and Encounters*, as the title suggests, simultaneously stresses the two themes of the evolution of individual societies and the cross-cultural encounters between different peoples. Central to these encounters is the theme of human movement in various forms – travel, exploration, trade, migration, and invasion. Covering similar content, *Voyages in World History* forefronts individual travelers and their journey narratives. Its primary theme of "movement" also stresses cross-cultural interaction through the eyes of the travel narrative, yet contact is embedded in the connection between different societies. Again the narrative trajectory is towards the increasing ease of travel for humans, the mass migration from rural to urban areas, alongside opportunities and obstacles for migration between states.

The overarching theme at this scale of world history is the relentless movement of humans and their quest for mastery over their environment, themselves, and each other. As in big history, narratives of peopling the world accelerate the pace of movement and change towards the present. Most of these narratives, whether monograph or textbook, begin with a discussion of the evolution of various species of hominids in Africa and the slow movement of *Homo erectus* into Eurasia and throughout the eastern hemisphere. These early migrations were mirrored by the emergence of *Homo sapiens* (modern humans) from central-southern Africa, but unlike their predecessors, modern humans traveled not only on foot but also by boat, eventually populating the entire habitable world.

"Peopling the world" approaches to world history beg one obvious question: who constitutes a people? The evolution of human language and communication, which sets us apart as a species, involves the evolution of linguistic communities that become the basis of different "peoples"; ergo these are said to become the foundation of civilizations. Debates still rage about whether human languages have a single origin in Africa or appeared simultaneously and diversely in multiple sites in Afro-Eurasia. Whatever the origin of human language, though, distinctive linguistic groups indisputably become a basic unit of analysis for human society. (See Liu, this volume.) These societies create boundaries of human communication while simultaneously being transformed from within and through interaction over space and time. Patrick Manning argues that "human migration portrays migratory movement as a human habit and as a thread running through the full extent of our history as a species" (2005: x). The encounter of people speaking different languages as they migrate over small and large distances, and then learn to communicate with each other through language transmission, remains a constant feature of the human condition, one that is still shaping our existence. Despite the current globalization of English in modern forms of mass communication, linguistic differences are still relevant for cultural identity in the contemporary world.

The increasing scale and pace of human interaction through various forms of movement invoke the metaphor of webs of connection. John and William McNeill employed this metaphor in their book *The Human Web: A Bird's-Eye View of World History* (2003). While the avian metaphor indicates viewing humans from not too high a vantage point, the narrative has much in common with the scale of peopling the world: from the evolution of humans as a species, to the emergence of multiple webs of civilizations, to the thickening of these webs of connections into the first worldwide web in the early modern period. From this point onward, the human web is depicted as one interconnected system of cooperation and competition. The worldwide web has consistently increased in density through revolutionary changes that have occurred in production and consumption; population growth, migration and the commodification of labor; and political and social changes. All of these forms of communication, cooperation, and competition have also generated profound ecological transformations. The human web is a set of connections that link people to one another. In all such relationships, people communicate information and use that information to guide their future behavior. What drives history is the human ambition to alter one's conditions to match one's hopes (McNeill and McNeill 2003: 3). *The Human Web* depicts the peopling of the world as a process of increasing density and intensity of interaction, based on movement and communication – fueled particularly by mass rural–urban migration as a phenomenon of contemporary globalization.

Scale Three, Modern Human Society: Globalizing Encounters and Migrations, 1500–1900

There are few current terms so widely used and so little understood as "globalization," a word much invoked in both world history narratives and many other realms besides. In the domain of world history, it often underlies writers' efforts to construct narratives of human history at a planetary scale, especially during the modern period. Frederick Cooper, a historian who is strongly skeptical of such efforts, bluntly states: "There are two problems with the concept of globalization, first the 'global,' and second the '-ization.'" In criticizing the implicit claim that "systems of connection" have penetrated the entire globe and that this is essentially a contemporary process, Cooper dismantles what he sees as the presentist bias of concepts of "the global," further arguing that to look for the moment of globalization is fundamentally misguided. Globalization narratives, he argues, posit an image of increasing fluidity of movement without examining the limitations and unevenness of connections, or historicizing how these connections and disconnections have reconfigured, dissipated or consolidated over time (2009: 32).

Equating the moment of globalization with the era of European voyages of "exploration" leading to Columbus and the "discovery" of the "New World," and culminating in Magellan and the circumnavigation of the globe, moreover, has proved a particularly powerful narrative convention in world history textbooks and classes. These oceanic voyages are often presented as the most significant turning point in world history. They often structure the conceptual and chronological "break" in world history literally by physically marking the dividing point between two volumes in an otherwise unwieldy textbook, or between two semesters in a year-long sequence course. This narrative break also separates the premodern from the early modern and modern – with implications that modernity is newly global in scope and reach, and that it is, by virtue of its association with changes that developed after ca. 1500, a process emanating from Europe.

Chronological terminology itself becomes challenging in world history narratives, and no other periodization illustrates this better than the designation of "early modern." The beginning of the early modern period in European history is also hotly contested, to be sure, but how do world historians make sense of this term in relation to, for example, sixteenth-century Bali? What does the "early modern" mean for examining people on the move? The emphasis is often placed instead on maritime expansions directly linking peoples in new ways. Global patterns of connection through maritime voyages were forged between peoples who had not previously come into contact with each other, as in the initial encounter between peoples of southern and western Europe, the Americas and the Caribbean, and west and central Africa in the making of the "Atlantic World." Simultaneously, European maritime powers – first the Spanish and Portuguese, then the Dutch, English and French (and a few Danes) entered into and altered the diverse, and in some cases ancient, maritime trading networks linking African, Arab, Indian, and Southeast and East Asian maritime trading societies in the Indian Ocean and the South China Sea. Polynesian and Melanesian voyages of exploration and migration across the Pacific were eventually followed by European maritime powers creating new networks across the Pacific to the South China Sea and onwards to the Indian and Atlantic Oceans. The emergence of new imperial, colonial, and state formations and an intensification of competition between them, marked the emergence of an era that connected much of the world through maritime networks. While continental trade routes and migrations are not ignored in this narrative, the emphasis is oceanic – although the experience of people on ships is often ignored. (See Salesa, this volume.) Rather, it is the transfer of people from one place to another, often in large numbers, and their encounters with resident societies in the forging of ("modern") trading posts, colonies and empires that constitute the main focus of these narratives.

One of the major theoretical approaches to world history, world-systems analysis, developed by Immanuel Wallerstein, also posits the origins of the modern world-system which now dominates the globe as being in the sixteenth century with the emergence of capitalism in Western Europe and the Americas (Wallerstein 2004).[2] (See Chase-Dunn and Hall, this volume.) Although world-systems analysis focuses on relationships of exchange and processes of commodification, including the commodification of labor, it does not focus on migration *per se*. The basic structure of this theory is the division of the world into core, semiperiphery, and periphery – emerging within empires and adapting to the modern state system. Exchange in the modern world-system is fundamentally unequal, with the core areas disproportionally and continuously accumulating capital at the expense of the semiperiphery and periphery.

Nevertheless, even if one refuses to adopt either the "discovery of the New World" or the inauguration of the modern world-system as the key turning point in world history, it can be argued that the period from 1500 to 1900 represented a shift in patterns and scales of human migration that connected parts of the globe previously isolated or marginally visited, and that in the course of these mass migrations much of the world was transformed. (See Bright and Geyer, this volume.) This period witnessed the creation of new routes and networks created by oceangoing vessels of increasing size and speed, which together with the evolution of railways in the nineteenth century facilitated an unprecedented movement of people around the globe. Bearing in mind Cooper's admonition regarding the ruptures and limitations of global patterns of connection, it is still difficult to argue against the character of people on the move during this period as something new under the sun. Although all mass population movements of course took place in regional and continental contexts, the remainder of this section will focus on transoceanic exchanges to illustrate the scale of this modern human movement through evolving maritime technology.

The chronological scale of 1500 to 1900 is not the typical temporal framework for world history narratives – many break around the end of the eighteenth century with the Atlantic world revolutionary period. I am suggesting a different chronological unit to demonstrate how combining these four centuries can bring into view new aspects of human mobility. Most crucially, mass human movement during this period exists along a spectrum of free and forced migration. As David Eltis suggests: "Generally, large-scale and systematic coerced migration began with European expansion and ended when free and contract migrants became more willing – or in the Russian empire were allowed – to replace slaves and prisoners. In effect the predominance of slave, serf, and prisoner migrants was sandwiched chronologically between long periods when voluntary migration was the norm" (2002: 11).

The initial period of substantial migrations from Europe and Africa to the Americas and Caribbean, beginning in the fifteenth century, involved interaction between people from societies and environments which had had no previous contact, and it wrought profound short-term and long-term transformations. This process was first described by Alfred Crosby in 1972 as "the Columbian Exchange" (Crosby 2003). The term has passed into common usage for the cultural and ecological change set in motion by the forging of contacts between peoples around the Atlantic Ocean. Crosby extended his argument in 1986 to examine the global consequences of the expansion of European empires, migration, and contact (Crosby 2004). Such arguments posit that migration and contact between people from the Americas, the Caribbean, Europe, and Africa resulted in the exchange of diseases, plants, animals, and goods that transformed all of these cultures and environments. The argument is by now familiar, so three quick examples will suffice. First, diseases borne by the Spanish, particularly smallpox, resulted in the devastation of Amerindian peoples, initially in the densely populated Aztec and Incan empires and the smaller-scale Caribbean societies because they had no preexisting immunities. Second, the introduction of American native staple crops, especially corn and potatoes, eventually transformed the diets of people in much of Afro-Eurasia, resulting in significant population increases. Finally, the introduction of horses from Europe to the Americas facilitated state formation in the North American plains. (See the chapters by Pernick, by Simmons, and by Morillo, this volume.)

European sailing ships, settlements, and colonies were peopled by a range of willing and unwilling travelers and migrants. The Portuguese constructed the first global network of settlements peopled by male and female convicts, orphans, soldiers, free migrants, and slaves from Europe, Africa, and Asia. Likewise the Dutch East India Company operating in the Indian Ocean – and its Atlantic counterpart, the Dutch West India Company – used penal transportation as well as free migration and the slave trade in peopling their ships, settlements, and colonies. After the establishment of colonies in North America based on both free and forced migration from Britain, Britain's expanding empire constructed global ethnic and regional networks of migration, largely determined by ethnicity. When the American Revolution cut off penal transportation from Britain, for instance, new colonies in Australia were founded on the basis of British convict labor (Ward 2009; Christopher *et al.* 2007). The complex spectrum of freedom and coercion in networks of migration during this period belies any attempt to stereotype forms of migration through a simple dichotomy of free or slave. At the global scale, one discerns a pattern: the numbers of coerced migrants outnumbered free migrants in transoceanic voyages until the end of the legalized global slave trade in the nineteenth century.

The slave trade from Africa to the Americas and the Caribbean across the Atlantic Ocean, from the early sixteenth century until the second half of the nineteenth century, ranks as the most massive transfer of people categorized primarily in terms of their race and status in human history. "The Voyages: Trans-Atlantic Slave Trade Database," a cooperative research project, has documented almost 35,000 slaving voyages carrying over 10 million African men, women, and children as slaves to the Americas and Caribbean (Voyages 2009). David Eltis (2007) estimates that in total there were more than 43,600 voyages carrying approximately 12.5 million African slaves between 1514 and 1866. Historians have long speculated about the extent of the trans-Atlantic slave trade, which brought African slaves as forced migrants and shaped the development of societies throughout the Americas and the Caribbean. The effect of this mass population transfer on the African societies from which they were taken is still widely debated, and may be impossible to fully determine. What is clear is that African slaves shaped the colonial societies of the Americas and Caribbean as profoundly as European migrants and indigenous Amerindians.

The experience of the trans-Atlantic slave trade is often termed "the Middle Passage." Recently, this term has been reinterpreted to include multiple forms of transoceanic forced migration, particularly in the period 1500 to 1900. In this broader context, two distinct global networks of the mass movement of people come into view: penal transportation and indentured servitude. Imperial networks of penal transportation from the fifteenth and sixteenth centuries evolved from the Spanish, Portuguese and English policy of using prisoners to provide labor for military posts and proto-colonies in foreign territories. The establishment of a number of British colonies in North America was facilitated by penal transportation and indentured servitude as forms of unfree labor that were eventually displaced by slave labor. The expansion of intra-imperial networks of penal transportation resulted in specific patterns of population transfers. Clare Anderson, for example, has written the history of Indian convicts being transported by the British East India Company to Mauritius, Southeast Asia, and the Andaman Islands in the Indian Ocean from the late eighteenth century (Anderson 2000). Simultaneously, the British government began sending convicts from its own territory halfway around the world to establish penal colonies in the distant continent of Australia. These networks of penal transportation also became intra-imperial with convicts transported between colonies. However, the British government implemented a policy to restrict penal transportation to the Australian colonies only to convicts of European origin. Australia was thereby incorporated into the British Empire through the establishment of a series of settler colonies reserved primarily for white free and forced migrants. (See Sinha, this volume.)

The decline of global transoceanic slave trades and penal transportation networks in the nineteenth century coincided with shifting patterns of mass migration, with significant increases in free migration motivated by labor shortages in recipient societies and economic depression in societies of origin. These new and expanded networks of global migration were also facilitated by the development of maritime steam technology, which considerably lessened the perils and duration of transoceanic voyages. Alongside the growth of free migration, slave emancipation globally stimulated demands for other forms of cheap labor which were fulfilled by the mass migration of people, overwhelmingly from South Asia and China, who were contracted as indentured workers. Indentured servitude was only partially free, and evidence is widely available that in many cases people were coerced and deceived into signing contracts that restricted their freedom as migrant laborers. It can therefore be analyzed along a spectrum running from free to forced migration. Imperial networks were conduits for indentured labor migration, which had the effect of completely altering the population of many smaller colonies and states. This was the case particularly for island colonies that were dependent on plantation agriculture. For example, Indian indentured servants went in their hundreds of thousands to sugar-producing colonies such as Trinidad and Tobago in the Atlantic, Fiji in the Pacific, and Mauritius in the Indian Ocean. Unlike in the slave trade and free migration, the gender pattern of indentured servitude was overwhelmingly male. Some of these men, if they survived their terms, often sought to remain as migrants after their service contracts and to establish families through migration of women from their homelands. Others returned home. Indentured servitude of South Asians and Chinese workers was phased out in the early twentieth century, as abuses of the system, which at its worst constituted a form of slavery, brought it into disrepute.

But increasingly from the late nineteenth century, as Adam McKeown (2008) points out, global migration was as much about monitoring borders and enforcing exclusion as it was about attracting labor and migrants. Restrictions on immigration were initially implemented by states that sought to severely curtail migration of people from Asia. The creation of border controls as a foundation of modern sovereignty demonstrates Cooper's critique of globalization as a process of increasingly unimpeded flows and connections. By the end of the nineteenth century, all forms of forced migration had become illegal in most parts of the world, and free migration had been increasingly channeled through assertions of state sovereignty that granted the right of entry (or refused it) to people as either members of an ethnic group, citizens of a particular state, and/or individuals.

Scale Four, Microhistory and Biography: Individual Lifespans and Journeys

Most individual human beings are in constant motion, of course, even if they stay in the same dwelling space their entire lives – the human lifespan on a temporal level is a form of movement that, on the one hand, is profoundly intimate and, on the other, brings my narrative of people in motion full circle, back to the cosmological character of existence. Aging, after all, is a form of energy expenditure and entropy. Humans have recognized this metaphysical perspective on life in their quest for the meaning of existence. (See Vélez, Prange, and Clossey, this volume.) Buddhist philosophy takes the idea of constant change one step farther, positing that reality itself is not fixed and that humans are continually in flux. Biological imperatives aside, examining people in motion on the scale of the individual inevitably raises questions of self-identity and its shifting nature in the context of changing circumstances – temporal and spatial. World historians have engaged with biographical writing as a way to engage with the complexities of human experience in a global context. Biographies seem to present historians with a limited chronological framework, but one that can enable a microhistorical examination of experience, context and change. (See Gerritsen, this volume.)

One way to overcome the chronological limitation of biography – and to stretch its temporal scale – is through family history. Rebecca Scott's approach to the transregional, even global microhistory of the Tinchant family goes beyond showing how individuals are embedded in familial relationships and traces how radically the status of individuals and the scope of family networks can change over a relatively brief period of time. Her narrative focuses on "a single peripatetic family across three long-lived generations, from enslavement in West Africa in the eighteenth century through emancipation during the Haitian Revolution in the 1790s to emigration to Cuba, Louisiana, France, and Belgium in the nineteenth century" (Scott 2009: 84). While Scott's aim is to trace the emergence of an Atlantic vernacular public-rights framework as expressed by members of this family, the breadth of geographical residence within this family over generations shows how the movement of individuals simultaneously constructs intimate global connections. Although an individual's self-identity shifts with life stages and is particularly shaped by changing circumstances and mobility, family history can amplify this combination of micro- and macroscales of analysis.

In closing, therefore, I will zoom in on the lives of two individuals who were born in the mid-eighteenth century during the heyday of complex networks of free and forced migration that included global slave trades. Each of them experienced aspects of free and forced migration on a global scale, which makes their life stories illustrative of these broader patterns. Not coincidentally, both individuals also wrote and published autobiographies which have provided rich detail about their lives. While biographical research and writing is experiencing a resurgence as a promising methodology for world history, autobiographies are much trickier – as few can meet the field's core criterion of engaging with a wider world. So these two individuals, Olaudah Equiano and Elizabeth Marsh, are at once extraordinary because their experiences with capture and enslavement warranted an audience for their stories, but also ordinary in the sense that their lives were shaped by contexts experienced by many others. Both individuals have been the subject of biographies as well (and in the case of Equiano, multiple biographies that have made their way into world history textbooks). It is fair to say that Equiano was famous in his own lifetime as a result of his autobiography and political involvement and has become an iconic figure in narratives of the trans-Atlantic slave trade. Elizabeth Marsh received considerable attention around the publication of her autobiography, but this did not shape the remainder of her life. She was neither famous nor, much less desirable for a woman of her era, infamous. Her story has been reproduced by historians extensively in the context of similar stories in the "captive narrative" genre (Colley 2003). She has, however, been the subject of only one biography, written by Linda Colley and aptly titled *The Ordeal of Elizabeth Marsh: A Woman in World History* (2008).

Olaudah Equiano published his *Interesting Narrative of the Life of Olaudah Equiano, or Gustavas Vassa, the African* in 1789. It immediately became a bestseller, launching the author into public view, where he became an outspoken critic of the slave trade and slavery during the ascendancy of the Abolitionist movement. Equiano's autobiography was the first detailed account of the shock of enslavement as a boy captured from his family home in West Africa, the horrors of the middle passage on a slave ship, and the iniquities of slavery as he experienced them in multiple contexts in the Americas. It was also a redemption story: Equiano found God and freedom and vowed to praise both for the remainder of his life. He rose to the status of a gentleman in England and, having married a local woman and raised a family, he left his daughters with a considerable inheritance upon his death. Equiano's talent as a writer enabled him to describe, graphically and movingly, his experiences and perspectives on the Atlantic world in the late eighteenth century, which he traveled during most of his adulthood as a sailor before arriving in England and eventually becoming a spokesperson for the Abolitionist movement. This, at least, has been the received version of Olaudah Equiano's life story since the appearance of his *Interesting Narrative* (Equiano 2001).

Yet recently, Vincent Carretta has raised questions about the accuracy of Equiano's self-presentation. Although there is no doubt that Equiano is the author of the narrative, which he assertively stated was "Written by Himself," it is less clear that the contents reflect his lived experiences as an "Atlantic creole" born in Africa. All autobiographies are acts of self-fashioning, of course, but Carretta claims to have uncovered evidence in the form of baptismal and naval records to prove Equiano was born a slave in South Carolina. "The available evidence suggests that the author of *The Interesting Narrative* may have invented rather than reclaimed an African identity. If so, Equiano's literary achievements have been vastly underestimated" (Carretta 2005: xiv). It appears likely that Olaudah Equiano constructed a fictive autobiography by drawing on composite narratives told to him by other slaves or through written accounts of the experiences he depicts as his own. Carretta's findings have proved controversial, as they bring into question the most iconic life narrative of the middle passage. One could argue that even if Carretta is correct, this does not undermine the significance of Equiano's autobiography or his achievements in his own lifetime. What it does suggest, though, is that even at the intimate level of self-representation through autobiography, it is the ability of a life story to connect with the experiences of others or the broader context of its time that gives such narratives lasting power. The horrors of the middle passage and of the experience of slavery were indeed brought to life by Olaudah Equiano to an increasingly literate and book-buying public in Europe who were expanding their global awareness by reading popular travel and biographical narratives.

Elizabeth Marsh decided to write about her experiences of capture by Barbary pirates in 1756 and potential enslavement in the seraglio of the Sultan of Morocco, Sidi Muhammad, much later in her life. By the time she penned *The Female Captive* and published it anonymously in 1769, while still assertively declaring it was "Written by Herself," Marsh was a respectable married woman with children. Her husband was in the service of the British East India Company in Dhaka. Linda Colley's depiction of Elizabeth Marsh's life in the context of her familial connections "charts a world in a life and a life in the world. It is also an argument for re-casting and re-evaluating biography as a way of deepening our understanding of the global past" (2008: xix).

Marsh spent much of her life traveling on British naval and merchant ships, movements at first controlled and then later facilitated by her male relatives. Her story simultaneously reveals the social and economic restrictions imposed on women, and how individuals and families strategized to maintain or improve social status and security across generations in the context of global opportunities of trade and empire. (See Burton, this volume.) While Marsh's *Female Captive* describes a moment of extreme vulnerability for a young Englishwoman in a precarious position as a hostage in Morocco, it is Linda Colley's extraordinary achievement in tracing archival records pertaining to her extended family, particularly the business and official records left by her male relatives, that fashions a life for Elizabeth Marsh. Although her account shows her as an extraordinary and captivating woman, Marsh was nevertheless confined by her gender role and her desire to ensure her own financial and social security as well as that of her children. Her own mother migrated from the Caribbean with her father, and Colley speculates that she may have been a creole. Depicting a very different experience of slave societies in the Americas than her contemporary Equiano, Marsh came from a family belonging to the slave-owning colonial elite. They were, however, not members of the British elite, but occupied a somewhat precarious aspiring middle-class position facilitated by naval and merchant global networks providing the basis of employment for menfolk and profit for the family. Marsh asserted her independence through oceanic and colonial travel and her range of itineraries was extraordinary. She clearly had a restless streak. Elizabeth Marsh and her family experienced both the opportunities and constraints of her time. As Colley suggests:

> This micro-strategy – using the perspectives on the past afforded by a family – becomes paradoxically more, and not less, valuable when dealing with historical developments that extend over vast territorial and oceanic spaces … I have sought to reveal the many and diverse connections that existed between "impersonal and remote transformations" on the one hand and, on the other, "the most intimate features of the human self." (2008: 300)

For historians, trained in close archival reading, the digital revolution has created access to sources of evidence worldwide that has reinvigorated biographical writing and expanded the possibilities of writing world histories on an individual scale. This is the value of biography in world history.

Notes

1   The next section is a summary of Christian (2004).
2   For the full articulation of world-systems analysis, see Wallerstein (1974–2011).

References

Anderson, C. 2000. *Convicts in the Indian Ocean: Transportation from South Asia to Mauritius 1815–1853.* London: Macmillan.
Bentley, J., and H. Ziegler. 2011. *Traditions and Encounters: A Global Perspective on the Past.* New York: McGraw-Hill.

Carretta, V. 2005. *Equiano the African: Biography of a Self-Made Man.* Athens: University of Georgia Press.

Christian, D. 2004. *Maps of Time: An Introduction to Big History.* Berkeley: University of California Press.

Christopher, E., C. Pybus, and M. Rediker, eds. 2007. *Many Middle Passages: Forced Migration and the Making of the Modern World.* Berkeley: University of California Press.

Colley, L. 2003. *Captives: Britain, Empire and the World 1600–1850.* New York: Random House.

Colley, L. 2008. *The Ordeal of Elizabeth Marsh: A Woman in World History.* New York: Anchor.

Cooper, F. 2009. Space, time, and history: The conceptual limitations of globalization. In G. Baca, A. Khan, and S. Palmié, eds, *Empirical Futures: Anthropologists and Historians Engage the Work of Sydney W. Mintz.* Chapel Hill: University of North Carolina Press.

Crosby, A. 2003. *The Columbian Exchange: Biological and Cultural Consequences of 1492.* Westport, CT: Greenwood. First published in 1972.

Crosby, A. 2004. *Ecological Imperialism: The Biological Consequences of Europe 900–1900.* Cambridge: Cambridge University Press. First published in 1986.

Diamond, J. 1997. *Guns, Germs, and Steel: The Fates of Human Societies.* New York: W.W. Norton.

Dunn, R., ed. 2000. *The New World History: A Teacher's Companion.* Boston: Bedford/St Martins.

Eltis, D. 2002. Introduction: Migration and agency in global history. In D. Eltis, ed., *Coerced and Free Migration: Global Perspectives.* Stanford: Stanford University Press.

Eltis, D. 2007. A brief overview of the trans-Atlantic slave trade. In Voyages: The Trans-Atlantic Slave Trade Database, at http://www.slavevoyages.org/tast/assessment/essays-intro-01.faces (accessed Nov. 11, 2010).

Equiano. O. 2001. *The Interesting Narrative of the Life of Olaudah Equiano, or Gustavus Vassa, the African. Written by Himself. Authoritative Text, Context and Criticism,* ed. W. Sollors. New York: W.W. Norton.

Hansen, V., and K. Curtis. 2010. *Voyages in World History.* Boston: Wadsworth.

Manning, P. 2003. *Navigating World History: Historians Create a Global Past.* New York: Palgrave Macmillan.

Manning, P. 2005. *Migration in World History.* London: Routledge.

McKeown, A. 2008. *Melancholy Order: Asian Migration and the Globalization of Borders.* New York: Columbia University Press.

McNeill, J., and W. McNeil. 2003. *The Human Web: A Bird's-Eye View of World History.* New York: W.W. Norton.

Scott, R. 2009. A nineteenth-century Atlantic creole itinerary. In G. Baca, A. Khan, and S. Palmié, eds, *Empirical Futures: Anthropologists and Historians Engage the Work of Sidney W. Mintz.* Chapel Hill: University of North Carolina Press.

Voyages. 2009. The Trans-Atlantic Slave Trade Database. At http://www.slavevoyages.org (accessed Mar. 2012).

Wallerstein, I. 1974–2011. *The Modern World-System.* 4 vols. Berkeley: University of California Press.

Wallerstein, I. 2004. *World-Systems Analysis: An Introduction.* Durham: Duke University Press.

Ward, K. 2009. *Networks of Empire: Free and Forced Migration in the Dutch East India Company.* New York: Cambridge University Press.

CHAPTER TWENTY-THREE

Religious Ideas in Motion

KARIN VÉLEZ, SEBASTIAN R. PRANGE, AND LUKE CLOSSEY

What moves in world history? Armies, slaves and migrants, technologies, commodities and capital, plants, animals and microbes all have journeys neatly mapped out in world history textbooks. Ideas are entangled with each of these roving facets of human experience, but their itineraries are more difficult to chart. Consider Islam, for instance. Older textbooks almost always include confident maps that represent the spread of Islam through boldly swung arrows that point outwards from Mecca in all directions. These vectors are plotted along the routes of conquest and commerce, with the sites of battles and ports of trade as their coordinates. Convenient and conventional as it is, this linking of the movement of ideas with that of more tangible changes and exchanges has its pitfalls. It hinges on a facile trope of diffusion whereby one place, a core, supplies a pure and intact notion to another place, a periphery, that passively receives it. It also conceals the need to ask how ideas traveled in practice and how, in turn, their movement affected the ideas themselves. In the case of Islam, focusing attention on how the tenets of this faith were transported calls into question the simple conflation of the spread of Islam with the political expansion of the caliphate.

The transit of ideas can rarely be adequately represented by unidirectional arrows. Ideas in motion are more meaningfully visualized as multiple ouroboric circuits that are continuously rearticulated and reshaped. The complicated dynamics of their journeys are what make them both difficult and useful as modes of analysis. One must address the multiplicity of ways in which ideas interlock and transfer. They travel in hearts and minds, prayers and practices, books and stories, and artifacts both artistic and everyday. As ideas move through time and space, they expand, collide, are contested, or collapse. They arrive in one form and soon take flight in another, with variations between new and old often difficult to discern. Acknowledging the fantastic mobility, permeability and connectivity of ideas is the first step towards comprehending their global reach.

World historians are showing a growing interest in the circulation of scientific, artistic, and religious thought across the planet. This chapter focuses primarily on ideas that are religious in nature.[1] In part this is because of its authors' particular interests, but there

A Companion to World History, First Edition. Edited by Douglas Northrop.
© 2012 Blackwell Publishing Ltd. Published 2012 by Blackwell Publishing Ltd.

are less omphaloskeptical reasons to shine the spotlight on religion when considering ideas in motion. Among all global modes of thought (*Anschauungen*), religious ideas have arguably traveled the farthest and lasted the longest. This scope and longevity may be rooted in the unapologetic intent found in many religious traditions to have their ideas move and be moved. Religious ideas are usually conceived and presented with the explicit purpose of transforming the beliefs – and consequently the lives – of many people. This is most evident in the commission in some religions to proselytize. Religious ideas are also worthy of our attention because of the importance religion attains as it is lived and the extent to which it permeates so many aspects of life from birth to death (and, according to most religions, also thereafter). For this reason, the engagement with religious ideas can give substance to some startling analogies. We might, for instance, compare current commitments to secularism to earlier religious doctrines, or examine the global dissemination of the scientific worldview (and, at times, the fervor of its proponents) in light of the transplantation of religions. Over the last century, science itself has expanded to become the dominant creed of the modern age, allowing it to share in the historically insidious mobility of religion. Akin to the manner in which, say, medieval Christians took it for granted that religious icons could move of their own volition, science is nowadays widely regarded as a universal truth that exists in a timeless, all-encompassing sphere autonomous of human intervention. We offer this survey of recent scholarship of religious ideas in motion with an eye for such analogies.[2] Cumulatively, the works described below demonstrate the value of historicizing the movement of all types of ideas, and highlight the potential benefits of studying them in the context of global patterns of exchange, social networks, and human agency.[3]

As world historians, we are committed to considering the big picture and the long term. When it comes to religions, however, this macrohistorical approach often translates into studying them as organized systems of thought (or orthodoxies) that render their followers as identifiable groups through shared norms and behaviors. From this broad perspective, we risk losing sight of an essential aspect of religion that distinguishes it from mere philosophy or ideology: its adherents' *faith* in a spiritual realm or deity that accounts for, and lends meaning to, human existence. Historically, the movement of ideas derived much of its motivation and momentum from such personal conviction, or what sociologists term "religiosity." While religion is often practiced in communal and performative ways, it is ultimately vested in a personal commitment to certain beliefs about history, human nature, and the cosmos. At the same time, it is important to remind ourselves that the assumption of an invariable, deep-rooted spiritual dimension to everyday life in the past is no less essentialist – and erroneous – than the projection of an unwaveringly rational, Laodicean post-Enlightenment individual. Such an approach risks forever positing the "religious" premodern as inherently irrational and, therefore, effectively unknowable. Moreover, adherents to a common faith do not necessarily understand or articulate their beliefs in the same way. Religious ideas, then, are on the one hand inherently personal, while on the other hand their acquisition, transmission, and articulation are necessarily shaped by social, economic, and political contexts. As a result, it is always problematic to generalize about the wider historical resonance of religious ideas. They undoubtedly suffuse the worldly experience of many people, past and present, but they may not be in themselves the key to understanding it.

There is a further obstacle to reconciling the acculturation of religious ideas with their personal and confidential (in the word's original sense of "fully trusting") quality. The world historian of religion is also confronted with the challenge of meaningful classification.

The most general categories into which religions are conventionally grouped are "world" and "primal."[4] "World" religions are characterized by written scripture, the notion of salvation, and a universal mandate, whereas "primal" religions are defined by the opposite qualities of oral transmission, a focus on mundane existence, and an identification with a specific ethnic group or territory. As a result of this contradistinction, those belief systems that have not been reified into "world" religions are often treated as perennially "traditional," as stuck in time and place and largely unresponsive to the great currents of world history. (See the chapters by Yoffee and by Pomeranz and Segal, this volume.) "World" religions are assumed to move more or less intact; "traditional" religions are held not to move at all. This categorization does not do justice to either grouping. For "primal" religions, whether described as shaman, animist, totemic or pagan, the blanket category fails to grasp the vast range of religious ideas that have marked the last 250,000 years of human history, with an astounding diversity of religious artifacts and spiritual rituals.[5] The same shortfall presents itself with regard to "world" religion. In recent years, for example, the field of Indian religious history has been abuzz with studies describing the multitude of local and temporal variants of the Hindu tradition, thereby challenging the notion of one coherent and continuous pan-Indian Hinduism (Saberwal and Varma 2005). Such rebuttals to the notion of stable, perduring, monolithic religions alert us to the historical complexities not only of individual but also of collective religious identities.

These formidable challenges in studying religion from a world-historical perspective are, in our view, more than offset by the immense promise this endeavor holds. Historians who are currently studying religion-in-motion are leading the charge to understand how ideas of all types can go global. In this chapter, we flag some of their most innovative contributions over the past decade or so. The most noteworthy trend among these scholars is their insistence on broadening the geographic frame of analysis. They also explore the portability of sacred intangibles like space and belief, the networks of people who carry religion far afield, negotiations and reverberations between the local and the global, and the latest encroachments of religious ideas in modern life. This selective overview of recent English-language scholarship bearing on the world history of religious ideas is not intended to be comprehensive or representative. For instance, we deliberately present Christianity-centered works alongside those focused on other religions. This is to compensate for the lingering academic emphasis on Western-prescribed Christianity as the defining example of a world religion (Lindenfeld 2007; Sinitiere 2007). In this small way, our brief survey stands as an exercise in the new, adamantly world-historical arena of religious studies.

The Call for a Global Frame

The intensified call to action for researchers to consider religion in the context of the wider world has prompted study of how religious ideas spread and travel between regions. The plea for global perspective has come from several quarters. Among the most vocal are historians of the early modern Catholic Church. Simon Ditchfield (2004) has sharply articulated the need to reconfigure studies of Catholicism to show the interdependency and conciliation between Catholic Church administrators in Rome and local practitioners. In "A Catholic Atlantic," Allan Greer and Kenneth Mills – historians of French North America and Spanish South America respectively – second this move by calling attention to the "dialectical relationship" between European promoters of

Catholicism and the "reconfiguring recipients" of the religion in the Americas (2007: 13). Europe is not jettisoned or decentered in the approach these scholars advocate. Rather, the sphere of religious interaction is widened to span the Atlantic and the world. Discussions of religious ideas beyond the halls of the Roman papacy are shown to matter deeply, and to reshape the whole.

Outside the discipline of history, too, there has also been interest in the push-and-pull between authorities and lived practice, as played out on a global stage. Social anthropologist Harvey Whitehouse has put forward a cognitive theory of religion based on his fieldwork on a "cargo cult" in Papua New Guinea in the 1990s. Whitehouse (2000) proposes two mixed modes of religiosity, one "doctrinal," counterintuitive and centrally managed, the other "imagistic," ritual-based and intuitive. His separation of modes has provoked a flurry of debate over religions as chronologically disparate as early antique Mithraism and the nineteenth-century Lutheran revivalist movements in Finland (Whitehouse and Martin 2004). Like Ditchfield, Greer, and Mills, Whitehouse wants to understand religion's appeal, or what allows it to transcend place and time. This includes both fixed teachings and flexibility on the ground.

In his survey of textbooks on the history of religion, David Lindenfeld (2007) notes that their narratives still take as normative the lossless transmission of text-based teachings. This preoccupation with texts privileges faiths with strong scriptural traditions – an attitude encapsulated in one such text, the Qur'an, that accords special status to Jews and Christians as "people of the book." It also tends to emphasize the opinions and experiences of a small scholarly elite that defined and disputed these texts in writing. This tendency is especially pronounced because a scriptural religion typically finds early expression and elaboration in one particular language: for instance, Sanskrit for Hinduism, Latin for Catholicism, and Arabic for Islam. These languages themselves came to be regarded as sacred, and command of them became not only a status marker but often a necessary standard for explicating social and political dictums. In *The Language of the Gods in the World of Men* (2006), Sheldon Pollock describes how Sanskrit became transformed from a purely religious language into a medium for literary and political expression that tied elites across much of southern Asia into a "Sanskrit cosmopolis." Even though most scriptural religions eventually underwent a process of vernacularization, historians of Hinduism, Catholicism or Islam are still most likely to be trained in these traditions' dominant languages and therefore to pay greater attention to discourses written in them.

Phillip Sinitiere exhorts world historians to temper this bias by choosing a different index, by looking at the "translatability and indigenization" of world religions rather than their universalistic clamor (2007: 13). Vernacularization and translation are not simply the transfer of a stable set of meanings into new idioms but authorial acts: to translate is to create anew. (See Northrop, final chapter in this volume.) For example, the emergence of Persian as the political language of Islam in much of the eastern Islamic world "acted as a potent agent of assimilation" in which multiple meanings could emerge, compete, and coexist (Alam 2004: 142).[6] Increasingly historians recognize that ideas might move best and farthest when they are not the sole province or static purveyance of any one group. Studying religions from the perspective of mobility, at moments of transference and translation that enabled their global reach, highlights change, not constancy, as a key feature of religious ideas in world history. In short, it is not enough to set a wider scope and to note the presence of a religious idea in multiple places in the world; we should also ask how it has been altered to have resonance in new settings and how this transmutation, in turn, affected these religious traditions as a whole.

Space and Beliefs in Motion

There is an immediate challenge posed by this double quest to assess the extent of a religious idea's global presence as well as its variability: how do we track an idea on the move? Trevor Johnson (1996) has done so by tying ideas to transient objects. His study of the seventeenth-century relic trade in bones, exhumed from Christian catacombs in Italy and shipped north to Bavaria, demonstrates how sacred identities of saints were mapped onto tangible and transferable items. (See Levi, this volume.) More recently, scholars have trailed sacred articles whose portability is not so immediately obvious: namely, temples. Joanne Punzo Waghorne charts how the Hindu urban middle class replicated sacred space in London and Washington DC in the 1960s, and long before then in Chennai (Madras) in the 1640s. Waghorne describes the "conservative creativity" these displaced Hindus employed to create new sites for communal worship (2004: 34). Jualynne Dodson looks at the variety of altars assembled by practitioners of the Afro-Cuban religions of Palo Monte, Vodú, Espiritismo, and Muertéra Bembé de Sao. She too detaches sacred spaces from specific landscapes to redefine them as "constructed assemblages of shared awareness" (2008: 62). Johnson, Waghorne, and Dodson each track circumforaneous objects to show how religious ideas are shifted and renovated.

Stuart Schwartz set himself the even more audacious task of pursuing religious ideas along the trajectory of a concept rather than through the itinerary of an object. In *All Can Be Saved*, he considers how the amorphous notion of religious tolerance traversed and persisted within the Iberian Atlantic world during the centuries of the dreaded Inquisition. Schwartz trails the ideas of tolerance and salvation as they surface in a repeated refrain, "Each person can be saved by his or her own religion" (2008: 1). This phrase was mustered as a defense by ordinary Iberians arrested by Inquisition courts in Spain, Portugal, the Canary Islands, Brazil, Peru, Mexico, and Colombia between 1500 and 1700. Schwartz is able to trace the concept of tolerance across much of the world because of its durability in a particular genre of legal documents. Charles Keyes (2007) also follows a recurring idea – violence – among practitioners of Theravada Buddhism in Sri Lanka, Burma, Thailand, Cambodia, and Laos over the last 23 centuries. He demonstrates how the rise of Buddhist nationalism and fundamentalism embroiled Buddhists in the politics of their different countries and led to the intrusion of an aberrant idea, violence, into the Buddhist religious sphere. Keyes thus follows corpses while Schwartz follows words. Both are interested in how local politics activate a charged concept – be it tolerance or violence – and cause it to take hold with a particular religious group of people. Movement, for these writers, is chronological, evidenced in a latent and enduring idea being passed like a baton to fresh runners.

Networks of Carriers

Other historians are just as curious about the people who carried religious ideas as about the ideas themselves. What united these carriers and helped them succeed in broadcasting their faith? Francesca Trivellato (2009) argues that carefully cultivated trust, not kinship or religion, was what held together the trade diaspora of Sephardic Jewish merchants in the early modern era. Sebastian Prange (2009) returns to the importance of religion as a link for Muslim merchants in the Indian Ocean, whose contributions to spreading Islam are often overlooked. Alongside traders, Muslim spiritual orders known as Sufi brotherhoods played a key role in the propagation of Islam across much of Asia. In the case of India, their study reveals the remarkable degree to which individual saints were revered by Muslims, Hindus, Sikhs, and, at times, Christians alike (Ernst and Lawrence 2002). Anthropologist Pnina Werbner (2003) describes this phenomenon in the contemporary period, using the example of a Sufi cult centered on a living saint from northwestern Pakistan that extends globally to Europe, the Middle East, and Southern Africa. Looking at another set of missionaries, the Catholic Society of Jesus, Luke Clossey (2008) shows that when studied from a world-historical perspective, even professional messengers of religious ideas like the Jesuits emerge not as a centrally directed order but as interconnected (and often unmediated) regional networks whose currencies were relics and hard coin as much as doctrine and a shared desire to save souls. Clossey, Prange, and Trivellato overturn the stereotype of a lone missionary or remote merchant carting his beliefs overseas by highlighting the role of solid but imperfect networks tied together by movement and faith.

Some of the more neglected networks of religious conveyors to be brought to light recently are composed of women. (See Burton, this volume.) M. Whitney Kelting (2001) has analyzed the stavan songs of a group of Jain women and found that women used these songs as a public forum for theologizing and commenting on religion. The negotiation and leadership that Kelting witnessed among Jain women in the 1990s has also been noted by Haruko Narata Ward (2009) among Japanese female converts to Catholicism in the 1600s. Ward compares early modern Shinto-Buddhist and Christian beliefs to consider the unique benefits each afforded to Japanese women in particular situations. She also observes how Japanese women converts acted as teachers and catechists alongside Portuguese Jesuits. Aviva Ben-Ur (2009) also focuses on the interface between women and male religious leaders in early modern Suriname. There, mulatto daughters of Jewish landowners were assigned a second-class status but nonetheless found ways to contribute to Suriname's Jewish community. Writing of a more recent century, Tayba Sharif (2005) reports on how Iraqi Shiite women thrown together in refugee camps in Saudi Arabia and then in the Netherlands worked through their grief collectively in lamentation sessions to commemorate Zaynab, a granddaughter of the prophet Muhammad. They used sacred narrative to connect themselves and their experiences with their foremothers, and to support each other. These informal religious associations between women show that "networks [can] free individuals. They are more affiliative than filiative" (Belghazi 2005: 277).

Several recent studies have endeavored to show individuals, whether women or men, maneuvering between or outside of networks. Jon Sensbach (2005) tells the story of Rebecca Protten, a slave on the Danish island of St Thomas who converted to Protestantism, joining the Moravian Brethren and preaching to fellow slaves, and eventually traveling to Europe and Africa. Natalie Zemon Davis (2006) describes the African and European journeys of the Muslim al-Hasan al-Wazzan. His capture by Mediterranean pirates and captivity in Rome led him to convert to Catholicism and become a protégé of the pope, only to return later in his life to Muslim North Africa. Sensbach and Davis call attention to larger political and economic forces acting upon individuals and pushing them towards one religion or another. Remarkably, these individuals – like the networks they skirted between – united mobility and faith. The movement of religious ideas around them bumped them onto new life paths.

Negotiations and Reverberations

In attempting to describe the lives of individuals like Protten or al-Wazzan, who lived in zones of intense religious contact, many scholars are wary of using terms with historically negative connotations such as pure "orthodoxy" versus muddied "syncretism." Still, there is a need to describe the dynamics of encounter between the contesting and neighboring apples and oranges we lump together as "religions." Michael Carrithers (2000) offers the term "polytropy," or "spiritual cosmopolitanism," as an alternative to explain an experience of the Digambar Jain in South Asia. In contrast to the monopoly some traditions insist upon, the notion of polytropy seeks to describe situations in which people appropriate and combine elements from (seemingly) discrete religious traditions. In a similar vein, Nicolas Standaert (2008) asks how a missionary credal religion adapted to a polytropic society. His examination of Christian burial rites in seventeenth-century China shows that intercultural contact brought together European and Chinese forms of religiosity, giving rise to new, hybrid religious identities. Focus on ritual, local faiths, and lived religion has recently become a popular way to look at the overlap of religious practices. Jennifer Scheper Hughes (2010) tells of the lived religion that sprang up among Catholics of Mexico around the cross of the Cristo Aparecido. After its discovery in the 1540s, this cross took on a multiplicity of meanings, ranging from a friar's early (and unpopular) claim that it symbolized human sinfulness, to a sense of local ownership by recently converted Indians of Totolapan. These conflicting meanings came to a head in the 1580s, when Augustinian friars and Indian Christians of Mexico City together witnessed the cross coming to life. Shared experience obscured the lines between Christian miracle and Indian animism, combining the different strands of meaning for the object and thereby multiplying its resonance.

Often it is not old and new religions that need to be reconciled locally, but textual authorities and ritual practitioners. Although designed to stifle contrarian religious ideas, prescriptions and persecutions by priests, shamans, brahmans, mullahs, popes or rabbis frequently served to propel the dissemination of supposed heresies, sometimes along unexpected routes. The complex (and largely peaceful) processes by which Zoroastrian Iran became an Islamic territory, for example, not only engendered the establishment of a sizable Zoroastrian diaspora in India but also had profound effects on Islam itself: in the words of one expert, the "Islamic conquest of Iran was counterbalanced by the Iranian conquest of Islam." (Stausberg 2008: 581). Harjot Oberoi (1994) identifies such transformations born of tension in the early development of the Sikh religion. First, he describes how Sikhism, Hinduism, and Islam did not begin as well-demarcated units of religious identity. The early days of Sikhism were marked by recognition of multiple, competing forms of ritual practice drawn from many traditions. Only later, in the late 1800s with the emergence of the Singh Sabha movement among the Sikhs and the administrative consolidation of the British Raj, did the category of Sikh become reified from within and without.[7]

Oberoi's provocative argument is partly couched in a regional distinction between South Asia and Europe, with South Asia as a realm of religious pluralism and Europe (and the wider Christian West) as the domain of monolithic and centralized religion. However, William Taylor's (2005) study of two competing shrines in colonial Mexico calls such regional characterizations into question by describing a different sort of interplay between text and practice in a Christian sphere, also at a late consolidating moment like Oberoi's. Taylor uncovers a case of crossed claims over a miracle-working relic, the large crucifix of the Cristo Renovado. In 1623, the cross was removed from Mapethé, a small mining community near Mexico City, and taken to the capital for safe-keeping. Sixty years later, a priest wrote a history of the relic's translation to Mexico City, which was read by Otomí Indians from Mapethé. In the 1740s, a full century after the Cristo Renovado was relocated,

Otomí leaders renovated the church at Mapethé and petitioned that the relic be returned to them. Their request was not granted, but Mapethé began to draw pilgrims in its own right as the original home of the Cristo Renovado. Here, textual authority inadvertently blurred and extended categories of ritual ownership rather than ossifying them. Faith fractured and multiplied across two centers instead of becoming pinned on one.

Another fascinating global dynamic becomes evident when internal religious negotiations are stretched out over continents and oceans rather than playing out in a single location. What happens when a "local faith" revisits its ancient cradle? Returns are the crowning flourish of the mobile. There have been several recent studies on new recipients of a religion reaching back to reconnect with old donors in unanticipated ways. Toni Huber (2008) considers how Buddhists in Tibet have reinvented India as the birthplace of their religion. Through pilgrimage and exile, modern Tibetans have reenvisioned India's sacred geography around themselves. Similarly, Karin Vélez (2011) writes on the Catholic Huron of the Jesuit mission of Lorette who sent gifts across the Atlantic Ocean to their namesake Italian shrine of Loreto and to several other Catholic sanctuaries. The shared name of Lorette inspired the Huron neophytes to approach European and American religious sites as fellow Catholics.

One of the greatest annual movements inspired by religious devotion is the *hajj*, the pilgrimage to Mecca all able Muslims are urged to perform at least once in their lifetime. For over 1,300 years, the *hajj* has brought together Muslims from all corners of the world, generating a regular, multitudinous exchange of ideas (as well as texts, goods, and diseases) that reached far beyond the purely religious. Michael Pearson's (1996) study of the *hajj* from India during the early-modern period, for instance, highlights the centrality not so much of its destination, Mecca, but of the pilgrimage itself in routinely connecting Muslims across the Indian Ocean world. Also focusing on the Indian Ocean, Engseng Ho considers how inherited names preserved in genealogies created a sense of connection between the dispersed Muslims from the Hadhramawt region in Yemen. These names tied people to graves back in Tarim to which some of them returned on pilgrimage. The process of the Hadhrami diaspora making a circuit outwards and back home again is held up by Ho as an example of how "the idea of mobility becomes an interpretive key" (2006: xxv, 29). Indeed, the reverberations caused by returns challenge our sense of how and where religions are defined, and by whom. Instead of being laid out in one heartland by controlling elites, in these works religions appear to form and reform on the road, on the fly, at the hands of drifters in active transit around the world.[8]

New Spheres for Religion

An old adage identifies the two most common plots of fiction: someone goes on a long journey, and a stranger comes to town. The global history of religion is taking shape along similar storylines. Some historians stake out ports and crossroads, to wait for the ideas to come to them. Others stalk their prey across all borders, breaking with the old custom of ending the chase at a coastline or national border, like a sheriff helplessly watching outlaws escape into a neighboring jurisdiction. Persisting in the pursuit sometimes creates odd geographical units of analysis: Clossey's 2008 study of Jesuit networks between the Holy Roman Empire, Ming China, and Spanish Mesoamerica is likely the first (and just as likely the last) work of Sino-Germano-Mexican history. At times historians can take advantage of contemporary geopolitics to work within more coherent, but no less vast, geographical boundaries, as Fernando Cervantes and Andrew Redden do in their project on angels and demons in the colonial Hispanic world (forthcoming). Those historians working within the broad geographies of expanding civilizational languages – Greek and Latin, Persian and Arabic, Sanskrit and Chinese, to name a few – have increasingly taken care to balance the wealth of documents in the expansive language with the scanter and often more difficult indigenous sources, which often require painstaking discovery and reconstruction (e.g. Burkhart 2001).

Some mobile ideas wind up in places so unexpected that their movement causes us to rethink the stability even of geographies traditionally thought least permeable. Brandon Marriott, for instance, traces millenarian ideas from Jewish pens in the Ottoman empire into the minds and hearts of Puritans in the British Atlantic World; here Jews and Christians think from the same fountain (Marriott forthcoming). Studies like his problematize the conventional demarcations not only of Judaism and Christendom but also of European Enlightenment. It was during this period of European intellectual history, amidst such unexpected circumambulations of religious ideas across an expanding world, that religion came to be conceived as the primitive counterpart to modern reason. As scholars from different disciplines have rightly pointed out, this hugely pervasive discourse requires us to properly historicize the epistemological category of religion itself in both research and teaching (e.g. Kippenberg 2002).

The recasting of religious thought in terms of mobility begs the question of where religion will move to next. Some promising recent work has been done on the impact of the internet and mass technology on Islam. Carl Ernst (2005) has studied how the technologies of printing and recording have made previously secret classical Sufi texts widely available, even to non-Muslim and foreign consumers. This shift has eroded the traditional Sufi hierarchy of authority. H. Samy Alim is beginning to look at how Muslim hip-hop artists and pop stars are positioning themselves as "the most cutting-edge conveyors of contemporary Islam" (2005: 272). Jonathan James (2010) describes the phenomenon of Hindu televangelism in contemporary India and its surprising linkages to a globalized brand of Charismatic Christianity. The presence of religious ideas at the forefront of globe-reaching initiatives like music, satellite television, and the world wide web is neither surprising nor novel. At a similar moment of technological acceleration in the nineteenth century, thousands of ordinary Christian laypeople linked themselves to popular science, for instance, frequenting lectures on astronomy, anatomy, alchemy, and geology (Numbers 1997).

Thus we come full circle to where we began, adrift in a planet-spanning sphere of ideas in motion, with science, art and religion as peripatetic bunkmates. It becomes clear that religion is not the static antagonist of a mobile modernity, but rather a transformative vector crisscrossing through world history. Might we go so far as to claim that within the ricocheting trajectories of religious ideas, world historians can find one of their strongest mandates to justify studying the past in its global dimensions? We believe so. Religious ideas motivated immense journeys and pilgrimages, fueled contacts and conquests, and even propelled some faithful onto heroic quests or fool's errands of global proportions. Members of religious communities may be regarded as "the oldest of the transnationals: Sufi orders, Catholic missionaries, and Buddhist monks carried word and praxis across vast spaces before those places became nation-states or even states" (Rudolph 1997: 1). Religious ideas in motion are closely intertwined with global dynamics that world historians study – be they commerce, migration, diaspora, imperialism, capitalism, or any other outlined in this volume – and in many instances exemplify the state of the art in world history methodology.

Amidst this blaze of discovery and reconfiguration, it behooves us to momentarily look beyond this spotlight on mobility to ask whether we, and perhaps world historians in general, have been too intent on identifying and tracing ideas that were transmitted, transported and transformed translocally, while neglecting those that refused such processes. For instance, it has been said that if the great panoply of indigenously sub-Saharan religious ideas that are conventionally subsumed under the umbrella term "animism" all share one single characteristic, it is their "almost total refusal to countenance *unlocalized*, unembodied, unphysicalized gods and spirits" (Garuba 2003: 267, emphasis added).[9] Studying religious ideas from the vantage point of world history means not only to demarcate their reach but also to emplace them in differing everyday spaces.[10] Along with the great insights we gain from the emergent world history of religious ideas that is beginning to displace the staid history of "world" religions, we must remember that ostensibly global exchanges and trends were – and, arguably, continue to be – both self-selective and selectively exclusionary. In this aspect too, then, studying religious ideas mirrors the wider challenges that world history faces as a field: to reconcile the personal with the collective, transformative moments with long-term trends, agency with structure, the local with the global. Were this chapter to submit anything resembling a dogma, it would be a profession of faith that persisting in this endeavor is both wise and good.

Notes

1 For examples of diverse global approaches to the history of science, see Bala (2006), Joseph (2000), Safier (2008), Scharfstein (1998).
2 The authors note that the study of religious ideas in motion, surveyed here as part of a section on "Connecting," is only one of many current world-historical approaches to religion. One might attempt comparison, as in Sharot (2001), or focus on rupture and splintering, as does Wellman (2007).
3 With regard to agency, we suggest that religious ideas do not (solely) exist in some ethereal realm that people tapped into at different times and in different places, but that their effectuation and transmission are contingent historical processes. It is contingency, not credo, that we believe in *quod ubique, quod semper, quod ab omnibus* (everywhere, always, and by everyone), to revise St Vincent of Lérin's famed expression of the eternal nature of Catholic doctrine.
4 The category of "primal" (at times expressed in terms of "traditional," "archaic," "indigenous," or "tribal") is nowadays seen as less objectionable than the older designation of "primitive"; unchanged, however, is the connotation of an evolutionary stuntedness in comparison to more "advanced" (or "scriptural," "modern," "world") religions.
5 The scarcity of evidence for the prehistoric period allows scholars to use what few sources that do exist as inkblot diagrams on which to project their own assumptions and anxieties. Whether this is religion at all is not entirely clear. For a responsible treatment, see Insoll (2004).
6 The intermingling of religious and imperial projects in the early modern world was, of course, not limited to the Mughals but a remarkably widespread feature of the period; see Clossey (2007).
7 Oberoi's work raises further questions about what happens when scholarship reaches a wider public. For a discussion of this issue see Barton and James (2010), and Witz, this volume.
8 Other recent studies of pilgrimage include Kaufman (2005) and Stopford (1999).
9 For a discussion of the global spread of the apparently non-global Yoruba religion to Brazil, Cuba, and elsewhere in the Americas during the nineteenth century as a consequence of the slave trade, see Manning (2009: 173–175.) (Also see Gerritsen, this volume.)
10 Other disciplines grapple with similar methodological challenges of unifying global religious phenomena with their highly localized manifestations; see for instance Vásquez (2008).

References

Alam, Muzaffar. 2004. *The Languages of Political Islam in India,* c. *1200–1800.* Chicago: University of Chicago Press.

Alim, H. Samy. 2005. A new research agenda: Exploring the transglobal hip hop *umma.* In M. Cooke and B.B. Lawrence, eds, *Muslim Networks from Hajj to Hip Hop,* pp. 264–274. Chapel Hill: University of North Carolina Press.

Bala, Arun. 2006. *The Dialogue of Civilizations in the Birth of Modern Science.* New York: Palgrave Macmillan.

Barton, Keith C., and Jennifer Hauver James. 2010. Religion in history and social studies. *Perspectives in History* 48 (5).

Belghazi, Taieb. 2005. Afterword. In M. Cooke and B.B. Lawrence, eds, *Muslim Networks from Hajj to Hip Hop,* pp. 275–282. Chapel Hill: University of North Carolina Press.

Ben-Ur, Aviva. 2009. A matriarchal matter: Slavery, conversion, and upward mobility in Suriname's Jewish community. In R. Kagan and P. Morgan, eds, *Atlantic Diasporas: Jews, Conversos, and Crypto-Jews in the Age of Mercantilism, 1500–1800,* pp. 152–169. Baltimore: Johns Hopkins University Press.

Burkhart, Louise. 2001. *Before Guadalupe: The Virgin Mary in Early Colonial Nahuatl Literature.* Albany, NY: Institute for Mesoamerican Studies.

Carrithers, Michael. 2000. On polytropy: Or the natural condition of spiritual cosmopolitanism in India: The Digambar Jain case. *Modern Asian Studies* 34 (4) (Oct.): 831–861.

Cervantes, Fernando, and Andrew Redden, eds. Forthcoming. *Angels, Demons and the New World: Spanish America, 1524–1767.* Cambridge: Cambridge University Press.

Clossey, Luke. 2007. Faith in empire: Religious sources of legitimacy for expansionist early-modern states. In C. Ocker, M. Printy, P. Starenko, and P. Wallace, eds., *Politics and Reformations: Histories and Reformations: Essays in Honor of Thomas A. Brady, Jr,* pp. 571–587. Leiden: Brill.

Clossey, Luke. 2008. *Salvation and Globalization in the Early Jesuit Missions.* New York: Cambridge University Press.

Davis, Natalie Zemon. 2006. *Trickster Travels: A Sixteenth-Century Muslim between Worlds.* New York: Hill & Wang.

Ditchfield, Simon. 2004. "Of dancing cardinals and mestizo madonnas": Reconfiguring the history of Roman Catholicism in the early modern period. *Journal of Early Modern History* 8 (3–4): 386–408.

Dodson, Jualynne. 2008. *Sacred Spaces and Religious Traditions in Oriente Cuba.* Albuquerque: University of New Mexico Press.

Ernst, Carl W. 2005. Ideological and technological transformations of contemporary Sufism. In M. Cooke and B.B. Lawrence, eds, *Muslim Networks from Hajj to Hip Hop,* pp. 191–207. Chapel Hill: University of North Carolina Press.

Ernst, Carl W., and Bruce B. Lawrence. 2002. *Sufi Martyrs of Love: The Chishti Order in South Asia and Beyond.* New York: Palgrave Macmillan.

Garuba, Harry. 2003. Explorations in animist materialism: Notes on reading/writing African literature, culture, and society. *Public Culture* 15 (2): 261–285.

Greer, Allan, and Kenneth Mills. 2007. A Catholic Atlantic. In J. Cañizares-Esguerra and E.R. Seeman, eds, *The Atlantic in Global History, 1500–2000,* pp. 3–19. Upper Saddle River, NJ: Pearson/Prentice Hall.

Ho, Engseng. 2006. *The Graves of Tarim: Genealogy and Mobility across the Indian Ocean.* Berkeley: University of California Press.

Huber, Toni. 2008. *The Holy Land Reborn: Pilgrimage and Tibetan Reinvention of Buddhist India.* Chicago: University of Chicago Press.

Insoll, Timothy. 2004. *Archaeology, Ritual, Religion.* New York: Routledge.

James, Jonathan D. 2010. *McDonaldisation, Masala McGospel and Om Economics: Televangelism in Contemporary India.* New Delhi: Sage.

Johnson, Trevor. 1996. Holy fabrications: The catacomb saints and the Counter-Reformation in Bavaria. *Journal of Ecclesiastical History* 47 (2): 274–297.

Joseph, George Gheverghese. 2000. *The Crest of the Peacock: Non-European Roots of Mathematics*. 2nd. edn. London: Penguin.

Kaufman, Suzanne K. 2005. *Consuming Visions: Mass Culture and the Lourdes Shrine*. Ithaca, NY: Cornell University Press.

Kelting, M. Whitney. 2001. *Singing to the Jinas: Jain Laywomen, Mandal Singing, and the Negotiations of Jain Devotion*. New York: Oxford University Press.

Keyes, Charles F. 2007. Monks, guns, and peace: Theravada Buddhism and political violence. In J.K Wellman, ed., *Belief and Bloodshed: Religion and Violence across Time and Tradition*, pp. 145–164. Lanham: Rowman & Littlefield.

Kippenberg, Hans G. 2002. *Discovering Religious History in the Modern Age*, trans. B. Harshav. Princeton: Princeton University Press.

Lindenfeld, David. 2007. The concept of "world religions" as currently used in religious studies textbooks. *World History Bulletin* 23 (1): 6–7.

Manning, Patrick. 2009. *The African Diaspora: A History through Culture*. New York: Columbia University Press.

Marriott, Brandon. Forthcoming. Religious community and cross-religious communication beyond the Atlantic world: The lost tribes in the Americas and Mecca. In J. Corrigan, ed., *Religion and Space in the Atlantic World*. Bloomington: Indiana University Press.

Numbers, Ronald L. 1997. *Science and Christianity in Pulpit and Pew*. New York: Oxford University Press.

Oberoi, Harjot. 1994. *The Construction of Religious Boundaries: Culture, Identity and Diversity in the Sikh Tradition*. Chicago: University of Chicago Press.

Pearson, Michael N. 1996. *Pilgrimage to Mecca: The Indian Experience, 1500–1800*. Princeton: Markus Wiener.

Pollock, Sheldon. 2006. *The Language of the Gods in the World of Men: Sanskrit, Culture, and Power in Premodern India*. Berkeley: University of California Press.

Prange, Sebastian R. 2009. Like banners on the sea: Muslim Trade networks and Islamization in Malabar and maritime Southeast Asia. In R.M. Feener and T. Sevea, eds, *Islamic Connections: Muslim Societies in South and Southeast Asia*, pp. 25–47. Singapore: Institute of Southeast Asian Studies.

Rudolph, Susanne H. 1997. Introduction: Religion, states, and transnational civil society. In S.H. Rudolph and J.P. Piscatori, eds, *Transnational Religion and Fading States*, pp. 1–24. Boulder: Westview.

Saberwal, Satish, and Supriya Varma. 2005. *Traditions in Motion: Religion and Society in History*. New Delhi: Oxford University Press.

Safier, Neil. 2008. *Measuring the New World: Enlightenment Science and South America*. Chicago: University of Chicago Press.

Scharfstein, Ben-Ami. 1998. *A Comparative History of World Philosophy: From the Upanishads to Kant*. Albany: State University of New York Press.

Scheper Hughes, Jennifer. 2010. *Biography of a Mexican Crucifix: Lived Religion and Local Faith from the Conquest to the Present*. New York: Oxford University Press.

Schwartz, Stuart B. 2008. *All Can Be Saved: Religious Tolerance and Salvation in the Iberian Atlantic World*. New Haven: Yale University Press.

Sensbach, Jon F. 2005. *Rebecca's Revival: Creating Black Christianity in the Atlantic World*. Cambridge, MA: Harvard University Press.

Sharif, Tayba Hassan Al Khalifa. 2005. Sacred narratives linking Iraqi Shiite women across time and space. In M. Cooke and B.B. Lawrence, eds, *Muslim Networks from Hajj to Hip Hop*, pp. 132–154. Chapel Hill: University of North Carolina Press.

Sharot, Stephen. 2001. *A Comparative Sociology of World Religions: Virtuosos, Priests, and Popular Religion*. New York: New York University Press.

Sinitiere, Phillip Luke. 2007. Of borders and boundaries: World history, world Christianity, and the pedagogy of religion. *World History Bulletin* 23 (1): 7–13.

Standaert, Nicolas. 2008. *The Interweaving of Rituals: Funerals in the Cultural Exchange between China and Europe*. Seattle: University of Washington Press.

Stausberg, Michael. 2008. On the state and prospects of the study of Zoroastrianism. *Numen: International Review for the History of Religions* 55 (5): 561–600.

Stopford, J., ed. 1999. *Pilgrimage Explored*. Woodbridge, UK: York Medieval Press.

Taylor, William. 2005. Two shrines of the Cristo Renovado: Religion and peasant politics in late colonial Mexico. *American Historical Review* 110 (4): 945–974.

Trivellato, Francesca. 2009. *The Familiarity of Strangers: The Sephardic Diaspora, Livorno, and Cross-Cultural Trade in the Early Modern Period*. New Haven: Yale University Press.

Vásquez, Manuel A. 2008. Studying religion in motion: A networks approach. *Method and Theory in the Study of Religion* 20 (2): 151–184.

Vélez, Karin. 2011. "A sign that we are related to you": The transatlantic gifts of the Hurons of the Jesuit Mission of Lorette, 1650–1750. *French Colonial History* 12: 31–44.

Waghorne, Joanne Punzo. 2004. *Diaspora of the Gods: Modern Hindu Temples in an Urban Middle-Class World*. New York: Oxford University Press.

Ward, Haruko Narata. 2009. *Women Religious Leaders in Japan's Christian Century, 1549–1650*. Burlington, VT: Ashgate.

Wellman, James K., Jr, ed. 2007. *Belief and Bloodshed: Religion and Violence across Time and Tradition*. New York: Rowman & Littlefield.

Werbner, Pnina. 2003. *Pilgrims of Love: The Anthropology of a Global Sufi Cult*. Bloomington: Indiana University Press.

Whitehouse, Harvey. 2000. *Arguments and Icons: Divergent Modes of Religiosity*. New York: Oxford University Press.

Whitehouse, Harvey, and Luther H. Martin, eds. 2004. *Theorizing Religions Past: Archaeology, History, and Cognition*. New York: Altamira Press.

CHAPTER TWENTY-FOUR

Diseases in Motion

MARTIN S. PERNICK

Introduction: Germs Don't Travel Alone

When diseases travel, the results can be catastrophic. The arrival of plague from Asia in 1347–1349 killed close to half of Europe's population. Smallpox and other newly imported childhood infections slaughtered about 80 percent of the Aztec Empire by the mid-1500s. The reimportation of yellow fever after a two-generation absence literally decimated Philadelphia in 1793. The global spread of the previously "Asiatic" cholera produced a terrifying series of nineteenth-century pandemics. Well into the twentieth century, Arctic Native villages were devastated by the importation of tuberculosis, while the arrival of measles and influenza nearly depopulated previously isolated Pacific Islands. The echoes of such past disasters still reverberate in current fears of the global spread of new or previously geographically isolated microbes (W.H. McNeill 1976; Garrett 1994).[1]

Recognition that these disasters resulted from transcontinental disease importation played a key role in the evolution of world history as a discipline. Seminal works, such as William McNeill's *Plagues and Peoples*, Alfred Crosby's *The Columbian Exchange*, and Jared Diamond's *Guns, Germs, and Steel* not only established disease as a crucial component of the history of global exchanges, but also used disease to demonstrate the dramatic importance of the new field of world history (McNeill 1976; Crosby 1972; Diamond 1997).[2]

Many early histories portrayed epidemics as the seemingly inevitable effect of transplanting new germs in "virgin soil." Mass death seemed to be the horrific but unavoidable result of introducing new microbes among people who had no prior opportunity to develop "natural defenses." However, such common interpretations of how diseases travel are seriously flawed. First, simply moving a microbe to a new location is rarely sufficient to trigger a catastrophic new disease. Although a few new germs did lead to some of the most devastating disease outbreaks in history, the vast majority of new germs fall on infertile soil (Gladwell 1995). If every novel microbe caused an epidemic, humanity would not have survived the invention of the ocean liner. Second, the

A Companion to World History, First Edition. Edited by Douglas Northrop.
© 2012 Blackwell Publishing Ltd. Published 2012 by Blackwell Publishing Ltd.

same new germ often produced significantly different effects in different physical and cultural environments. Third, diseases travel to new locations by the importation of environmental, social, and cultural changes, along with, or even sometimes without, the introduction of novel germs. In other words, the arrival of new germs does not determine whether a devastating new disease will result. New germs are neither sufficient, nor even necessary, to produce new epidemics. Rather, the importation of a new disease results from the interaction of new germs with new environmental, economic, and cultural changes.[3]

Early histories of global disease transmission also initially focused on a few of the most dramatic imported disease outbreaks, especially the Black Death and other bubonic plague epidemics in Asia and Europe, and smallpox epidemics among Native Americans. Other devastating transported diseases, including yellow fever, malaria, cholera, and influenza, have been well examined in individual locations, but are only just beginning to receive sustained attention in their global dimensions, as is the global spread of noninfectious diseases.

This chapter will examine a few selected examples – one extensively studied and several other less familiar diseases in motion – to show how specific pathogens interacted with other physical and cultural changes to produce enormous differences in the mortality and the cultural effects of imported diseases.

Imported Epidemics and the Decimation of Native Americans

Five centuries ago, the Americas were first colonized by people who were accompanied by the viruses of smallpox, measles, and other childhood infections common throughout the rest of the world. The ensuing epidemics devastated Native American populations from the Arctic to the Andes, while largely sparing the arriving Europeans and Africans. Measured by the mortality rate, the proportion of the population killed, the result was the biggest medical catastrophe in recorded history.

Most explanations for this disaster emphasize that because these germs were newly imported, Native Americans lacked immunity to them. Immunity results when an individual who has been exposed to a specific germ, and who survives the initial encounter, thereafter produces antibodies and specifically sensitized blood cells that protect against subsequent infection with that germ. Acquiring immunity requires individual personal exposure to a specific antigen; it is not hereditary. The number of generations without infection does not affect the level of immunity; even one generation without exposure will produce a completely non-immune population.

Native Americans prior to 1492 had no exposure to these germs and thus none of them were immune. They lacked exposure because these germs could not have been transported by the slow-moving, small, and isolated groups who initially populated the Americas from Asia. Any childhood disease virus initially present in such a population would have killed some and left the remainder immune. Without a critical mass of newborns to infect, the germs then would have died out and never reached the Americas.

By contrast, among densely populated and more interconnected regions of Europe, Africa, and Asia, enough children were born to provide the germs with a steady supply of new hosts. The germs remained always present, despite the fact that most who survived to adulthood became immune. These were childhood diseases, not because the germs specifically targeted children, but because it was mostly children who were not yet immune.

Childhood diseases were hardly benign in Europe; about a fourth of all newborns died before the age of five (Bideau *et al.* 1997). Nor were Native Americans living in a disease-free natural paradise prior to 1492; they suffered health problems, from crop failures to dysentery, that produced periodic fluctuations and perhaps an overall decline in pre-Columbian populations (Mann 2006). But for specific childhood infections, Native Americans lacked the immunity that adults elsewhere usually acquired in childhood.

Does this lack of immunity to new germs fully explain the devastation many Native American populations experienced after European contact? Many historians have assumed so. One 1940s book was titled *The Effect of Smallpox on the Destiny of the Amerindian* (Stearn and Stearn 1945). In an intentionally provocative 1990s college textbook, an eminent historian summarized this interpretation for student debate: "The doom of the Indians was sealed the moment outsiders began to set foot in America. ... The people of the Old World had developed immunities to a wide variety of diseases, but the native Americans had not. ... [N]othing the newcomers did, apart from simply being there, had anything to do with the demise of the native American" (McDonald 1991).

However, recent scholarship emphasizes that lack of immunity to new germs was only part of the story. Lack of immunity meant that Native Americans were likely to get sick when new germs were introduced, but it did not determine why some died while others recovered, nor did it determine whether or not the survivors rebuilt their population levels or preserved their cultures. Despite the fact that all Native Americans in 1492 lacked immunity, there were enormous differences in the severity and duration of the effects once new germs were introduced. Such differences in outcomes cannot be explained by immunity; they resulted from the interaction of biology, environment, and culture (Kelton 2007; Jones 2004).

Some social conditions promoted the rapid spread of new germs, such as population density, trade, and war. Such environments made it likely that a high proportion of the population would get sick simultaneously, thus increasing the initial deaths from famine, lack of nursing care, panic, and social disintegration. However, these same factors often promoted long-term recovery. After the initial outbreaks, the immune survivors in a large urban society would have enough children to keep the germs in circulation as childhood diseases, with high childhood mortality but few adult epidemics. Complex hierarchical Native American societies also may have had greater resources for cultural adaptation to survive European conquest.

The physical and emotional condition of those infected likewise altered the odds of their recovering. The question is not whether it was "guns or germs" that caused the decimation of Native Americans. Guns and germs interacted synergistically (see Morillo, this volume). Sick Native Americans were easier to shoot; and getting shot made it harder to recover from disease.

For example, in large densely populated urban-centered empires such as the Aztecs of central Mexico or the Incans of the Andes, the initial contact epidemics were especially devastating, but the population levels eventually rebounded and significant elements of Native language and culture survived. In the decades following the first Spanish attack in 1519, epidemics, a siege-induced famine, internal political conflicts, and the enslavement of many Indians combined to reduce the indigenous population of central Mexico by an estimated 80 percent. But by the seventeenth century the Native American population had recovered to pre-Columbian levels in central and southern Mexico, as it did in the Andes a century later (Cahill 2010: esp. 229–231; Cook 1998).[4]

Conversely, among smaller, more isolated, migratory hunters living in what is today the US Great Plains, initial contact epidemics tended to be limited to single villages or bands. Too distant and poor to attract conquest prior to the nineteenth century, these groups first encountered new germs brought by other Indians fleeing epidemics further east, or by individual European explorers, missionaries, or traders. Outbreaks might decimate the villages in which they struck, but prior to the 1830s, they usually remained localized. Even the Upper Missouri smallpox epidemic of 1837–1838, which devastated whole villages of Blackfoot and Mandan, barely affected neighboring Crow and Gros Ventres (Jones 2004: 105–107). With their less complex division of labor compared to Aztecs or Incans, the Plains Indians also experienced fewer deaths due to epidemic-induced social disruption or loss of vital cultural skills. Furthermore, the introduction of European horses to the Plains actually resulted in a population increase, with improved hunting, mobility, and military abilities more than offsetting the effects of new germs. However, the small size and isolation of Plains Indian villages made it less likely that they could develop the childhood disease pattern in which most adults would grow up immune. As a result, these small, isolated groups were susceptible to repeated adult epidemics as each new generation grew up without immunity.

The indigenous population of the Great Plains only began to decline in the nineteenth century, when better plows, water pumps, and railroads made it possible for white settlers to farm the prairie, and when precious metals were discovered from California to the Black Hills. The resulting increase in outside contact was followed by conquest, elimination of the buffalo, and forced concentration on reservations that often lacked adequate food. These policies produced an increase in disease deaths far greater than the initial effects of the introduction of European germs (Allen 1975).

Recent scholarship provides many other examples of how differences in physical and cultural contexts resulted in vastly different patterns of disease and outcomes when different specific Native American peoples encountered new germs. In the colonial Carolinas, enslavement, not merely the presence of new germs, produced the greatest Native American mortality (Kelton 2007). In the Southwest, new germs decimated the densely concentrated populations of pueblo dwellers. However, that devastation helped make possible a significant increase in population of the geographically more dispersed sheep-herding Navajo. Imported infections only reversed this Navajo population growth in 1864–1869, when thousands were confined to Fort Sumner on the Bosque Redondo Reservation in New Mexico, where disease, deprivation, and despair combined (Barrett 2002; Kunitz 1983: chs 1–2).

New germs thus played a crucial role in the decimation and conquest of Native Americans, but they alone did not determine the outcome. Although all Native Americans in 1492 lacked immunity to European childhood diseases, the effects varied enormously, depending on the interaction of germs, environment, and culture. It is not possible to separately measure the relative contributions of germs and environment, because the two reinforced each other synergistically. War and deprivation made germs more lethal; germs made war and deprivation more deadly.

Comparing the arrival of the Black Death in Europe with the effects of European diseases in the Americas, the historian Alfred Crosby in 2003 revised his earlier emphasis on the role of new germs in determining the outcome of new diseases, writing:

> [V]irgin soil epidemics often do produce high mortality rates, but if left alone the population will recover in numbers. Europe, for instance, lost one-third of its population to the Black

Death in the fourteenth century and recovered in time.[5] [But] if the Black Death had been accompanied by the arrival of Genghis Khan's hordes ... I think it is unlikely that I would be writing this ... in an Indo-European language. (2003: xxii)

Moving Environments and Moving Germs: Malaria and Cholera

Malaria, a widespread, deadly and debilitating disease marked by recurring cycles of fever and chills, is now known to be caused by several different species of the parasite Plasmodium, transmitted by the bite of an infected female Anopheles mosquito. For much of medical history, such fevers were associated with specific geographic places, climates, and atmospheric conditions. (See Simmons, this volume.) Such diseases were generally assumed to stay put in particular locations, and many doctors believed they were solely local rather than imported in origin. However, from the classical Hippocratic work on Airs, Waters, and Places, to nineteenth-century American physicians such as the pioneer medical educator Daniel Drake, doctors recognized that changing the environment might spread or reduce the geographic range of malarial fevers.

Recent historians of malaria have built on these premicrobial insights to emphasize that the spread of malaria globally and intraregionally required not just the movement of parasites and mosquitoes, but the movement of environmental conditions that favored the interaction of microbes, insect vectors, and susceptible hosts. For example, while malaria parasites probably crossed the Atlantic with the importation of slaves from Africa, the successful spread of the disease also resulted from the decision to employ slaves in tasks that created environments favorable to mosquito breeding, such as the importation of African rice agriculture. Throughout the history of malaria, its movement from place to place involved not only the transport of germs but the transit of cultural practices and physical environments conducive to human contact with mosquitoes. From the first industrial revolution, which spread the building of mill dams where mosquitoes bred, to the late nineteenth-century global market for beef, which provided nonhuman alternative blood sources for mosquitoes, nineteenth-century global economic trends disseminated a variety of environmental conditions that first spread and then restricted the geographic distribution of human encounters with malaria mosquitoes.[6]

The global spread of cholera, among the most widely feared pandemic diseases of the nineteenth century, also resulted not just from importation of the germs, but from the global diffusion of conditions favorable for transmitting the germs. However, unlike recent histories of malaria, studies of cholera still focus on specific outbreaks in specific regions, rather than tracing the global dimensions of the disease. The global history of cholera has only just begun to be studied.[7]

The infectious agent of cholera is the bacterium Vibrio cholerae, transmitted by food or drink contaminated with excrement from an infected person. The disease causes sudden, massive and painful diarrhea, which can produce rapid extreme dehydration, circulatory collapse, and death within a day. Until the nineteenth century, cholera had been largely endemic to a few densely populated river systems in Asia, especially the Ganges Valley in India. Because people harbor the germ only briefly before they elimi-nate it or it eliminates them, cholera could not move further inland than an infected person could travel in a few days. So long as overland travel required human or animal power and took a day of hard physical effort to move 10 or 15 miles, cholera could not spread much beyond the river.

In the nineteenth century, a combination of changes in the technology and organiza-tion of transportation first made it possible for large numbers of cholera-infected people to travel long distances. Railroads, clipper ships, and steamboats provided the technol-ogy. In addition to these new machines, cholera's mobility also depended on a new model of business organization, the invention of cheap mass transit. For the first time, transport companies organized frequent and regularly scheduled trips, supported by recruiting large numbers of travelers, made possible by offering cut-rate no-amenities fares (Chandler 1977). The post-Napoleonic expansion of the British Empire in India utilized these new forms of transport to move troops and commerce between Asia and Europe, while the famines and revolutions of mid nineteenth-century Europe produced waves of refugees who used the new means of transport to cross the Atlantic. (See Ward, this volume.)

Not only did the nineteenth century produce new ways to move the cholera germ, it also disseminated new social conditions in which the germs could cause disease. Untreated cholera can kill up to half the people who develop symptoms. The vast majority of healthy people who ingest vibrios, however, excrete them without any signs of disease. Conditions that increase the chances of disease include repeated high levels of exposure and prior malnutrition. Poor, hungry, crowded people may be unable to avoid contaminated food and water, while those already marginally malnourished can least afford to lose more nutrients to diarrhea. Cholera was thus especially likely to devastate poor crowded cities that had outgrown their previous food, water, and sanitary infrastructures. While nineteenth-century epidemics were not limited to cities, the rapid urbanization of Europe and the Americas in the nineteenth century produced environ-ments and populations especially susceptible to the germ.

As a result, world-wide pandemics of cholera were a distinctly nineteenth-century phenomenon, with at least five transcontinental outbreaks between 1817 and 1892. The most deadly and widespread pandemic, in 1831–1832, killed about 2 percent of the population of many cities across Europe and the Americas.

Although the German physician Robert Koch eventually identified Vibrio as the disease's infectious agent in 1892, cities around the world began to reduce their cholera rates as early as the 1847–1852 outbreaks, following British physician John Snow's identification of contaminated water as a source of the disease, and the development of new institutions of city government with the power and resources to improve living conditions for the poor. Thus the global spread of cholera was made possible by the diffusion of early nineteenth-century social conditions, and it was ended by a later nineteenth-century spread of new social responses (Rosenberg 1962).

Diseases That Traveled without New Germs

Sometimes infectious diseases travel to new locations without any importation of new germs, but simply by the introduction of physical and cultural practices that allow previously existing, relatively insignificant, parasites to cause newly widespread human disease. An excellent example is hookworm. This intestinal parasite was identified as the cause of a growing epidemic in the US South, the Mediterranean, Latin America, and Africa in the early twentieth century. With recognition of its global importance, hook-worm became the target of the first international disease control campaign, begun by the Rockefeller Foundation in the 1910s. The foundation's efforts focused on ways to kill the worms inside the body and to prevent their spread. Researchers assumed that the appearance of the disease in a new region meant that infected individuals had imported the parasites.

However, recent work by historian Steven Palmer demonstrates that hookworm disease outbreaks often spread, not by transporting worms, but by transporting the conditions favorable for already existing worms to multiply and to cause infections. The international diffusion of mining technologies and other industrial practices that concentrated large numbers of impoverished, poorly clothed migrant workers in frontier areas with wet soil enabled already present hookworms to start causing massive outbreaks of disease (Palmer 2009). Similarly, global demand for mining products and the introduction of new mining practices also spread outbreaks of tuberculosis (Packard 1989).

Another epidemic that spread across continents without any movement of the causative germ was paralytic poliomyelitis. During World War II, when soldiers from Britain and America landed in North Africa, dozens at a time fell victim to unprecedented polio epidemics. The source of these outbreaks puzzled and alarmed doctors and military planners. While paralytic polio epidemics were increasingly common in the United States and Western Europe, in North Africa polio was a mild and rare disease of infants. Deadly epidemics among adults were unknown there. A US Army Commission, led by Yale virologist John R. Paul, solved the mystery, by showing that the polio virus caused much milder or unapparent infections in infants than in adults. They found that the virus was so widespread in North Africa that in this environment most of the population got a mild infection and thus became immune shortly after birth. Thus, they concluded, the wartime epidemics resulted from importing non-immune European and American soldiers into settings where the virus was already widespread, not by importing the virus (Paul 1971: 348–366).

One key environmental factor in the movement of infections has been famine. Malnutrition lessens resistance to, and slows recovery from, new pathogens; while the physical and emotional impact of an epidemic can undermine the ability and the will to produce food or even eat (Benedictow 2004: 263). Furthermore, famines, like epidemics, spread by the interaction of biological and social causes. The Irish famine of 1848 resulted from both the importation of potato-blight fungus and British land policy. In turn, the famine made the population especially susceptible to cholera, while it spurred a mass diaspora that furthered the global spread of the epidemic.[8]

Finally, while the best-known and fastest-spreading diseases that travel are usually infections, historians are just beginning to realize that some of the deadliest recent diseases to spread globally are not germ diseases at all. Global industrialization contributes to the spread of modern epidemics from lung diseases induced by air pollution to heavy metal and radiation toxicity. The globalization of high-fat, high-sugar diets seems to be causing a global increase in heart disease, obesity, and diabetes. And the post-1945 export of American cigarettes is clearly producing a global pandemic of heart and lung diseases. Allan Brandt's recent history of American cigarettes concludes with a section titled "Globalization: exporting an epidemic," which documents the basis for the World Health Organization projection that by 2030, 70 percent of tobacco-related deaths will be in the developing world (Brandt 2007: section V, see chart on p. 451).

The importation of new diseases has also often spurred the spread of new medical treatments and preventive measures. Plague epidemics, for example, produced a diffusion of government health boards, pest-houses, and quarantines from city to city across Europe and beyond (Cipolla 1981). The arrival in 1721 of epidemic smallpox in Boston prompted the Reverend Cotton Mather to introduce the practice of preventive inoculation, based upon the African experience of his slave Onesimus, and the news of Ottoman practice as disseminated by the Royal Society of London (Hopkins 1983: 248). In the early twentieth century, the Rockefeller Foundation's international campaign against hookworm disease became a model for subsequent international health agencies – from the Pan American Health Organization to the League of Nations and the World Health Organization (Palmer 2009).

Conclusion

When diseases travel, mass death can result. Some of history's most deadly new diseases involved the importation of new microbes. The fear of such deadly new microbes remains deeply resonant in mass culture, including popular films like *The Andromeda Strain* (1971), *Outbreak* (1995), and *Contagion* (2011). But new germs are rarely either sufficient or necessary to transport new diseases. The most deadly diseases in human history have arrived most often where newly introduced pathogens are accompanied by the spread of new social and cultural disease environments.

Notes

1   Estimating premodern disease rates involves applying sophisticated demographic tools to limited and fragmentary evidence. Diseases have evolved, data are incomplete, and past diagnoses don't correspond to modern disease categories. There is thus considerable uncertainty and controversy over these numbers (e.g. Benedictow 2004). This chapter focuses on diseases that modern science sees as having been transported. For examples of the history of responses to diseases that people in the past perceived as imported, see Kraut (1994); Markel (2004); Pernick (2002); Wald (2008).

2   These authors differ significantly in the extent to which they see germs alone as sufficient causes, and in their accounts of the role of cultural and environmental factors, but all give primacy to the arrival of new microbes.

3   Histories of world diseases that emphasize social factors include Watts (1998); Hays (1998); Kiple (1993).

4   There is however great debate and uncertainty about the magnitude and timing of these statistical estimates.

5   More recent, detailed estimates place the Black Death mortality at over 50 percent: see Benedictow (2004: ch. 33).

6   For global histories of malaria see Packard (2007); Webb (2009). An important early environmental history was Ackerknecht (1945). Other historians taking this environmental approach include J.R. McNeill (2010); Valencius (2002); Grob (2002: 129–133); Humphreys (2001); Nash (2006). For analysis of Alexis de Tocqueville's insightful early nineteenth-century comments linking rice and fevers, see Pernick (2012). There are many similarities between malaria and another mosquito-borne disease, yellow fever. A few historians who have studied both malaria and yellow fever do make the connection: Humphreys (1992); J.R. McNeill (2010); Peard (1999).

7   See Hamlin (2009). Important local studies include Rosenberg (1962); Kudlick (1996); Evans (1987); Arnold (1986).

8   Famines can have a complex relation to epidemics. The spread of the Black Death of 1347 followed the Great Famine of 1315, but the specific places most devastated by famine were not necessarily hardest hit by plague (Kelly 2005: 60–64).

References

Ackerknecht, E.H. 1945. *Malaria in the Upper Mississippi Valley, 1760–1900.* Baltimore: Johns Hopkins University Press.

Allen, V. 1975. The white man's road: Physical and psychological impact of relocation on the Southern Plains Indians. *Journal of History of Medicine and Allied Sciences* 30 (2): 148–163.

Arnold, D. 1986. Cholera and colonialism in British India. *Past and Present* 113: 118–151.

Barrett, E. 2002. The geography of the Rio Grande Pueblos in the seventeenth century. *Ethnohistory* 49: 123–169.

Benedictow, O.J. 2004. *The Black Death, 1346–1353: The Complete History.* Woodbridge, UK: Boydell.

Bideau, A., B. Desjardins and H.P. Brignoli. 1997. *Infant and Child Mortality in the Past.* Oxford: Clarendon Press.

Brandt, A.M. 2007. *The Cigarette Century: The Rise, Fall, and Deadly Persistence of the Product That Defined America.* New York: Basic Books.

Cahill, D. 2010. Advanced Andeans and backward Europeans: Structure and agency in the collapse of the Inca Empire. In P. McAnany and N. Yoffee, eds, *Questioning Collapse: Human Resilience, Ecological Vulnerability, and the Aftermath of Empire*, pp. 207–238. Cambridge: Cambridge University Press.

Chandler, A.D. 1977. *The Visible Hand: The Managerial Revolution in American Business.* Cambridge, MA: Belknap.

Cipolla, C.M. 1981. *Fighting the Plague in Seventeenth-Century Italy.* Madison: University of Wisconsin Press.

Cook, N.D. 1998. *Born to Die: Disease and New World Conquest 1492 to 1650.* Cambridge: Cambridge University Press.

Crosby, A.W. 1972. *The Columbian Exchange: Biological and Cultural Consequences of 1492.* Westport, CT: Greenwood.

Crosby, A.W. 2003. *The Columbian Exchange: Biological and Cultural Consequences of 1492.* 30th anniversary edn. Westport, CT: Praeger.

Diamond, J. 1997. *Guns, Germs, and Steel: The Fates of Human Societies.* New York: W.W. Norton.

Evans, R.J. 1987. *Death in Hamburg: Society and Politics in the Cholera Years 1830–1910.* Oxford: Clarendon.

Garrett, L. 1994. *The Coming Plague: Newly Emerging Diseases in a World Out of Balance.* New York: Farrar, Straus & Giroux.

Gladwell, M. 1995. The plague year. *New Republic*, July 17, pp. 38–46.

Grob, G.N. 2002. *The Deadly Truth: A History of Disease in America.* Cambridge, MA: Harvard University Press.

Hamlin, C. 2009. *Cholera: The Biography.* Oxford: Oxford University Press.

Hays, J.N. 1998. *The Burdens of Disease: Epidemics and Human Response in Western History.* New Brunswick, NJ: Rutgers University Press.

Hopkins, D. 1983. *Princes and Peasants: Smallpox in History.* Chicago: University of Chicago Press.

Humphreys, M. 1992. *Yellow Fever and the South.* New Brunswick, NJ: Rutgers University Press.

Humphreys, M. 2001. *Malaria: Poverty, Race, and Public Health in the United States.* Baltimore: Johns Hopkins University Press.

Jones, D. 2004. *Rationalizing Epidemics: Meanings and Uses of American Indian Mortality since 1600.* Cambridge, MA: Harvard University Press.

Kelly, J. 2005. *The Great Mortality: An Intimate History of the Black Death.* New York: HarperCollins.

Kelton, P. 2007. *Epidemics and Enslavement: Biological Catastrophe in the Native Southeast, 1492 to 1715.* Lincoln: University of Nebraska Press.

Kiple, K. ed. 1993. *The Cambridge World History of Human Disease*. Cambridge: Cambridge University Press.

Kraut, A. 1994. *Silent Travelers: Germs, Genes, and the "Immigrant Menace."* New York: Basic Books.

Kudlick, C.J. 1996. *Cholera in Revolutionary Paris: A Cultural History*. Berkeley: University of California Press.

Kunitz, S. 1983. *Disease Change and the Role of Medicine: The Navajo Experience*. Berkeley: University of California Press.

Mann, C.C. 2006. *1491: New Revelations of the Americas before Columbus*. New York: Vintage.

Markel, H. 2004. *When Germs Travel: Six Major Epidemics That Have Invaded America since 1900 and the Fears They Have Unleashed*. New York: Pantheon.

McDonald, F. 1991. Debate: Were the Indians victims? In V. Bernhard, D. Burner, and E. Fox-Genovese. *Firsthand America: A History of the United States*, p. 54. 1st edn, combined. St. James, NY: Brandywine Press.

McNeill, J.R. 2010. *Mosquito Empires: Ecology and War in the Greater Caribbean, 1640–1914*. New York: Cambridge University Press.

McNeill, W.H. 1976. *Plagues and Peoples*. Garden City, NY: Anchor/Doubleday.

Nash, L.L. 2006. *Inescapable Ecologies: A History of Environment, Disease, and Knowledge*. Berkeley: University of California Press.

Packard, R.M. 1989. *White Plague, Black Labor: Tuberculosis and the Political Economy of Health and Disease in South Africa*. Berkeley: University of California Press.

Packard, R.M. 2007. *The Making of a Tropical Disease: A Short History of Malaria*. Baltimore: Johns Hopkins University Press.

Palmer, S. 2009. Clinics and hookworm science: Peripheral origins of international health, 1840–1920. *Bulletin of the History of Medicine* 83: 676–709.

Paul, J.R. 1971. *History of Poliomyelitis*. New Haven: Yale University Press.

Peard, J.G. 1999. *Race, Place, and Medicine: The Idea of the Tropics in Nineteenth-Century Brazilian Medicine*. Durham: Duke University Press.

Pernick, M.S. 2002. Contagion and culture. *American Literary History* 14: 858–865.

Pernick, M.S. Forthcoming 2012. Disease and the racial division of labor in America. The 2011 Garrison Lecture of the American Association for the History of Medicine. *Bulletin of the History of Medicine*.

Rosenberg, C.E. 1962. *The Cholera Years: The United States in 1832, 1849, and 1866*. Chicago: University of Chicago Press.

Stearn, E.W., and A.E. Stearn. 1945. *The Effect of Smallpox on the Destiny of the Amerindian*. Boston: B. Humphries.

Valencius, C.B. 2002. *The Health of the Country: How American Settlers Understood Themselves and Their Land*. New York: Basic Books.

Wald, P. 2008. *Contagious: Cultures, Carriers, and the Outbreak Narrative*. Durham: Duke University Press.

Watts, S. 1998. *Epidemics and History: Disease, Power and Imperialism*. New Haven: Yale University Press.

Webb, J.L.A. 2009. *Humanity's Burden: A Global History of Malaria*. Cambridge: Cambridge University Press.

CHAPTER TWENTY-FIVE

Bullets in Motion

STEPHEN MORILLO

One premise of this book is that world history's dynamism and complexity as a research field need to be demonstrated more broadly to mainstream historians, who are not as aware as they might be of the field's recent developments. The same could be said – indeed, has recently been said (Morillo 2006; Black 2004) – of military history. Both fields suffer from negative stereotypes among academic historians: world history from the perception that it is a teaching field and thus the preserve of textbook writers, military history that it is practiced far too much by retired generals or popularizers (never mind war being politically suspect). In other words, both are caricatured as somehow not really professional, "serious" history.

The intersection of world history and military history therefore suffers from a double burden of negative images. What's worse, those negative stereotypes arise from within the two subfields themselves. Many military historians are accustomed to working within a Euro-American historical framework, and are thus both suspicious of the breadth of world history and unsure of its relevance. Many world historians, informed by approaches in social and cultural history (Pomeranz 2007), are equally suspicious of the methodologies and supposed ideology of military history.

The result is that world military history is not just the intersection of two somewhat marginalized subfields, it is a fairly tiny intersection. But it is an intersection that is not only growing with the expansion of world history generally: it is, contrary to the stereotypes imposed upon it from within and without, yet another dynamic and sophisticated field of research filled with potential for conceptual breakthroughs and new discoveries.

Audiences

World military history faces a number of issues as it moves forward. The first is, if not unique to military history (whether global or not), at least more acute than it is for other fields of historical writing. This is that publishing in military history aims at three distinct audiences with different demands and expectations. This diversity, while presenting

A Companion to World History, First Edition. Edited by Douglas Northrop.
© 2012 Blackwell Publishing Ltd. Published 2012 by Blackwell Publishing Ltd.

opportunities for researchers, contributes to the complicated image and status of world military history within the larger historical profession.

The first audience, and the primary one at which this book is aimed, is the community of academic historians. Some of the issues outlined below, of effectively globalizing approaches to military history and working out reasonable terms of comparison and conceptualization, arise from the demands of this audience for a world military history that fits with the methods and understandings of the broader fields of world history and of academic history generally.

Two other audiences, however, make publishing in military history, especially world military history, more complicated than in some other specialties. First, military history appeals to a large popular audience, as any stroll through the history shelves of mass-market bookstores demonstrates immediately. The American Civil War and World War II each constitute substantial franchises in military history; at least the latter has an inherently global orientation, even as the European theater of conflict tends to dominate the lists. What publishers want for this audience and what scholars produce do not overlap perfectly. (See Witz, this volume.) This is not to say that all the books produced for popular consumption have no academic value: Williamson Murray and Allan Millett's *A War To Be Won: Fighting the Second World War* (2001), for example, presents a truly global and nuanced interpretation of the war. But more common are books that, while academically sound, present condensed summaries of broad (sometimes even global) topics, copiously illustrated in a glossy format (e.g., Dawson 2002; Bouchard 2009), or that apply sound scholarship to the "big event, famous person" genre of military history that thereby excludes much in the way of a world history approach (e.g., Strauss 2005; 2009). And of course the potential profits of the popular market do spawn some books that contribute to the dubious academic reputation of military history.

The final audience for military history is military professionals, working in the armed services of many different countries, who are engaged as students or teachers in Professional Military Education (PME). While the goals of academic historians and PME are somewhat different, there is much more potential for synergy and understanding between the two groups than the cultural differences between them make evident. And while PME is in many ways nationalistically oriented – national military academies are at the foundation of PME – there is nothing in that teaching structure that precludes a global perspective. Indeed, the global nature of contemporary military problems encourages both global approaches and the globalization of audiences for military history. The publisher of a major military world history textbook (Morillo *et al.* 2009), for example, has contracted to publish translations in Chinese, Arabic, and Dari, the latter specifically for use at the Afghanistan National Military Academy.

Issues: Globalization

The continuing globalization of military history, however, faces two challenges in terms of established patterns of analysis in the field: military Eurocentrism, and a disparity in the sources available for doing military history in different regions – itself partly a cause of military Eurocentrism, and partly a result of the very cultural differences that gave rise to that Eurocentrism.

The most common form of military Eurocentrism in popular military history, although probably the least creditable in professional academic circles, is the "Western way of war" argument first put forward by Victor Davis Hanson (1989). Hanson argues for a uniquely effective "Western" culture of war based in a combination of what he calls "civic militarism" and a willingness to kill face-to-face in decisive battles, a combination that originated, he says, with the city-state warfare of the classical Greeks. Numerous scholars have questioned various aspects of this argument, starting with whether the paradigm even describes classical Greek warfare very well (Van Wees 2004). There are a number of other deep problems with the thesis. Whether there was a continuous military culture as described by Hanson is seriously in doubt: "civic militarism," in particular, describes neither late imperial Rome nor most of medieval Europe very well; and there is little evidence for the unique effectiveness of European arms before the industrialization of warfare in the nineteenth century. At the deeper, more philosophical levels that most interest world historians, Hanson's definition of "Western" is vague to the point of evanescence (Rome, geographically east of Carthage, is the "Western" power in the Punic Wars, and Rome's lineal descendant, Byzantium, is apparently not Western because it was not, in the end, victorious). Indeed, events since 2001 also call into question the unique effectiveness of any "Western way of war," even if that idea is defined simply as the way of war practiced by current "Western" powers. At the level of defining cultures of war and their impact, John Lynn's *Battle* (2003) also makes important points about the malleability of cultures generally and military cultures in particular that tell against Hanson's thesis.

For in fundamental ways Hanson's argument depends upon a caricature of "Eastern" ways of war as not only averse to decisive battles and face-to-face combat, and grounded in despotism rather than civic participation, but as essentially unchanging. Here the steady expansion of recent work in military history into non-Western regions provides the most effective disproof of Hanson's picture of world history. Histories of steppe nomadic peoples highlight the terribly effective military forces they raised – usually more effective, man for man, than almost any army raised by any sedentary state, never mind European ones, from their origins perhaps 4,000 years ago down into the sixteenth century – while nomadic social and political patterns seem a perfect instantiation of "civic militarism," although not a version that a modern democratic society would wish to embrace. The burgeoning field of Chinese military history, meanwhile, shows clearly the dynamism and creativity of military forces and leaders throughout Chinese history, simultaneously lifting the veil of Confucian-bureaucratic idealizations in Chinese historiography and debunking any Orientalist notions of an "unchanging East" at its heart (e.g., Lorge 2005; Graff 2002).

Ancient Chinese history, as well as recent work in Japanese military history, also undermines another conceptual manifestation of military Eurocentrism, the "Military Revolution" paradigm. This idea is not as inherently Eurocentric as Hanson's thesis. The landmark book that brought the Military Revolution debate to mainstream history by implicating military change in broad processes of state formation and regional dominance is Geoffrey Parker's *The Military Revolution: Military Innovation and the Rise of the West* (1988). It advertises its focus on the rise of Europe in a subtitle, but in the text acknowledges that China underwent a similar revolution, in witnessing a shift away from small, elite-based and largely cavalry forces towards massed infantry armies, fortifications, wars of territorial conquest, and centralized states supported by absolutist ideologies, during the Warring States era (475–221 BCE) (see also Lewis 1992). Still, despite this case and others, such as the military transformation of sixteenth-century Japan (Morillo 1995) and Bronze Age changes (Drews 1993) that have been called "military revolutions," the emphasis remains on "Western" military innovation. This is especially true of work on the early modern military revolution and its modern analogue about a "Revolution in Military Affairs" (RMA). All of this, it should be said, is laid over deeper questions of whether "military revolutions" really exist, an interesting philosophical-historiographical problem that has, potentially at least, truly global possibilities for analyzing military change.

Overcoming military Eurocentrism is not simply a matter of recognizing the philosophical problem and placing global comparative perspectives at the center of military world history, however. European military history benefits from a long historiographical tradition that dates back to the classical historians of Greece and Rome. This has made the writing of accounts of military actions a commonplace since Herodotus, Thucydides, and Caesar. When this practice is combined with a record-keeping culture, the result is that European military historians have had readier access to a larger store of relevant primary source materials than military historians elsewhere. Furthermore, the recent dominance of Western academics has made the linguistic barrier to studying or disseminating non-European military history higher as well. But recognition of the philosophical problem, as well as the globalization of modern military affairs and conceptions of military effectiveness, have begun to prompt efforts to redress the balance. The already noted explosion of Chinese military historiography builds on much work by Chinese historians, which in turn builds on the copious sources provided by another record-keeping culture. The cultural orientation of Chinese literati and record-keepers means that less detail on matters of tactics and leadership has survived in the sources, but the connection between military action and political policy is, by contrast, often clearer than in European accounts of glorious battles. Japanese military history can also draw on a tradition and sources quite comparable in amount and cultural orientation to those of Europe. On the other hand, world military historians will simply never be able to know as much about the history of societies whose cultural orientation made writing about military affairs unimportant, or whose literate and historical traditions focused on warfare but were aborted (as, for example, with the Mayas and Aztecs). Nonliterate societies, meanwhile, will be as underrepresented in military history as in any other subfield.

Issues: Problems of Analysis

World historians generally face problems of methodology in constructing transregional or transcultural analyses and comparisons, including issues of appropriate units of analysis, comparing like phenomena, and distinguishing terminology from underlying reality (to the extent that we can get at that slippery target). (See Adas, this volume.) Military world history faces its own versions of each of these issues.

To begin, the globalization of military history highlights the fact that much military history has been uncritically state-centric, without "the state" necessarily having been clearly defined or delineated as an analytical concept. It is too often simply assumed, partly as a consequence of the long shadow Clausewitz casts over modern military analysis: his dictum that "war is the continuation of policy with an admixture of other means" assumes state-directed warfare. As a result, the varieties of forms taken by states globally, including most monarchies in which "policy" was essentially a synonym for "the whims of the ruler," and the many regions and time periods in which state-level societies did not exist or in which formal state mechanisms of governance were secondary to informal social and cultural means of exercising power, have often led to their patterns of warfare being ignored or their rationales being rendered opaque by traditional state-centered military analysis. Even for Eurocentric military history, state-centrism is problematic for analyzing much medieval warfare. For world military history, then, the concept of the state must become part of the problem, not an assumed part of the answer.

This is not to say that warfare is unconnected to issues of state formation (and state collapse). It is simply to recognize that wars between fully state-level complex societies probably constitute a minority of the war that fills the pages of world history. Even attention to intrastate wars, including civil wars and other internecine power struggles, does not capture the rich complexity of the topic. Violence and armed force may be at the heart of many complex societies in one way or another, but histories of state-raised and state-directed armies, even those acting as the tax-collecting arms of the state, must sit beside analyses of the place of warrior elites in social structures and the existence of warfare as a lifestyle – at times, as on the Eurasian steppes, of whole peoples, not just warrior elites – rather than as a tool of state policy. Much of the warfare in global history may indeed be a tool of policy, but the policy was informal, unstated, and social: to keep warrior (and other) elites themselves in power, not to defend "the state."

This issue has become more visible since 2001 as the armed forces of the United States and the North Atlantic Treaty Organization face nontraditional enemies, and more generally as the World War/Cold War paradigm of major state wars increasingly gives way to substate conflict, nonstate actors, and the rising importance, in perception and reality, of guerrilla, irregular, and what is termed "asymmetric" warfare. This has already prompted new interest in colonial wars of the nineteenth century, wars largely ignored even at the time by military analysts for whom confrontations between major European powers were all that really mattered militarily, and in the sorts of warfare conducted by, for example, the Romans around their borders in the imperial period, when threats from other states outside the Parthian or Persian Empire were rare. But the very use of the terms "irregular" and "asymmetric" betray the state-centric bias ingrained in much modern military analysis.

And in fact, modernity may be the larger issue here. State-centrism is simply part of a wider present-centrism in much military analysis and therefore in a good deal of history. Certainly in terms of weight of research and publication, the last two centuries predominate in military history. While this may be justified in terms of popular book-market demand, it pushes the terms of analysis toward modern concepts and issues. This includes not just the centrality of the state, but also a fascination with and focus on technology, and some deep assumptions about military rationality that reflect a difficulty for modern military history in escaping its own cultural framework.

The rapid technological changes of the last two centuries, including significant changes not just in weaponry but in nonmilitary technologies with militarily significant applications, such as railroads and steamships, have brought technology to the fore in popular perceptions of warfare. The history of the twentieth century, in particular, with its naval arms races, tanks, airplanes, missiles and atomic and nuclear bombs, can make war seem like a battle for the best weapons, from the introduction of bronze and iron to the spread of early gunpowder weapons. Put in more philosophical terms, technological determinism becomes a real danger in explaining the course of warfare in world history – many forms of the early modern military revolution thesis view it as the direct consequence of the introduction of cannon and effective gunpowder small arms. But careful analysis of the longer history of the preindustrial world, and even of the last two centuries globally, shows that technology is almost always a dependent variable, not an independent one, whose effects are shaped by the contexts into which it is introduced.

That the "obvious" advantages of new military technologies were not always obvious to those exposed to them reminds us that people's cultural frames of reference are one of the contexts not just for the reception of technology but for the evaluation of past military action. Here again, the modern tendency for military analysis to see the world through a cultural frame that emphasizes, at least in the major industrial powers, materialist if not outright economic factors, and that sees politics and power in "rational" (again, largely material) terms, can lead to serious misunderstanding of warfare waged not just by past peoples with very different frames of reference but by modern enemies for whom materialism may be a central threat rather than a "natural" assumption about how people operate in the world. Rationality, in other words, is culturally constructed: some medieval battle-seeking strategies that seem to make no sense from a modern materialist perspective (battle avoidance looks safer and more likely to achieve positive material results) were, in a cultural framework based on divinely judged trial by battle, the only "rational" choice of action. Abandoning the modern materialist myth of a universal military rationality complicates the project dear to some aspects of military analysis, especially those aimed at a PME audience interested in learning timeless lessons about the "art of war." But the corresponding gain comes in understanding past military cultures and actions more accurately on their own terms, a goal more in harmony with academic approaches to the study of history. In general, one of the challenges posed by the globalization of military history is how to incorporate a more careful and nuanced approach to culture broadly, and to varying cultures of war specifically, into the field.

What these problems of present-centrism demonstrate, finally, is that the globalization of military history demands a sophisticated approach to the problem of cross-cultural comparison. Strategic and operational "art of war" principles are not the only place where comparison based in unexamined modern concepts and terminology threatens to "shoehorn" past evidence into misleading containers. The problem of translating terms for types of soldiers provides a good example of these potential pitfalls. Even terms as apparently straightforward as "infantry" and "cavalry" are loaded, in modern English, with assumptions that may not be appropriate for different times and places. Each is built from different vectors of meaning that point in different directions: functional (whether a soldier fights on foot or horseback at any particular moment); organizational (how the unit a soldier belongs to "normally" fights or is designed to fight); and social (with soldiers on horseback usually, though not always, having higher social status). Thus, Roman legionnaires and modern US foot soldiers may actually be "infantry" in about the same mixture of functional, organizational and social ways, but for Anglo-Norman writers *pedites* would describe any soldier fighting on foot, regardless of class and with no organizational component possible (there being no permanent units in Anglo-Norman armies), while the Japanese term *ashigaru*, often translated as "infantry," is really a social term denoting low status. Similarly, the term "mercenary" contains all sorts of assumptions about nationalistic identity and the operation of market economies that do not fit the realities of most past societies, calling for a more nuanced definition of soldier types that combines mode of payment with measures of social embeddedness to more usefully distinguish soldier types from one another (Morillo 2001; 2007). Again, the expectations of professional military audiences and the demands of popular audiences complicate the challenges posed by globalizing academic military history.

Themes: Global Patterns of War

Taking the optimistic view that the challenges outlined above are not an obstacle to advances in world military history but considerations that will produce better histories when they are accounted for, what topics, themes, or questions currently generate the most controversy or hold the most promise for future investigations?

Not surprisingly, much of the extant work at the still small intersection of world and military history has focused on surveys and on outlining long-term global patterns in the history of war. Among surveys, the dated but still surprisingly useful *Encyclopedia of Military History* (Dupuy and Dupuy 1970), although Eurocentric, is truly global in coverage and narrative-chronological in organization. *World History of Warfare* (Archer *et al.* 2002) is similarly dated and Eurocentric, though it attempts a more coherent analysis. By contrast, various encyclopedias organized alphabetically by topic (e.g. Cowley and Parker 1996; Martel 2012) are useful as references but offer an overview only in mosaic form. *War in World History* (Morillo *et al.* 2009), a military world history textbook, offers the most up-to-date interpretive survey that is as globally balanced and comparative as the available sources allow; it focuses on setting warfare in its socioeconomic, political and cultural contexts. Less detailed as surveys but attempting a grander sort of synthetic overview are John Keegan's *A History of Warfare* (1993) and Azar Gat's more successful *War in Human Civilization* (2006). All such surveys address, to one extent or another, basic questions about the origins of war, the causes of wars, the relationship of war to state formation, culture, and society. What this body of work shows is that much more work remains to be done on these questions in the global and comparative perspectives provided by world-historical approaches.

The question of the origins of war is one of the most contentious. The sparseness of the archaeological record makes reaching definitive conclusions difficult, and arguments from evidence of contemporary hunter-gatherer groups are fraught with methodological issues. Essentially, two opposing positions have emerged. On the one hand, some argue for a very early emergence of warfare – at least with the emergence of the modern human species around 190,000 years ago, if not before. Indeed, disputed evidence about warfare between chimpanzee groups, our closest surviving relatives, is cited in support of a "war instinct" in humans, in addition to abundant archaeological evidence for war around the globe (see e.g. Keeley 1996). On the other hand, supporters of a late date for the invention of warfare point out that none of the definitive archaeological evidence actually dates to earlier than about 8000 BCE, and that when it does appear, it is in conjunction with the whole set of conditions associated with the origins of agriculture: sedentary communities, emergent social complexity, and possibly climate change as a trigger. (See Yoffee, this volume.) Thus, in this view, warfare is a product of (and then spur to greater) hierarchical social organization – a cultural invention with no antecedents in the long history of the species or its ancestors or close relatives (see e.g. Ferguson 2005). These two positions tend to align roughly with political positions on the possibilities for preventing or mitigating conflict in the modern world, but the cases ultimately stand on their own merits, with the cultural construction position having for now somewhat the better of the argument.

In any case, once war appeared in the historical record, it rapidly became a pervasive phenomenon, indicating that however destructive it is, it also proved both highly successful as a communal survival strategy, and one that usually demanded a response in kind even from those disinclined to follow the path of organized violence. Broad global histories of warfare since its emergence (whatever the earlier antecedents) tend to focus on what might be called "technological-tactical" landmarks to provide some periodization. Thus, from the earliest clear signs of (relatively) large-scale communal violence in the Neolithic, several subsequent turning points are commonly cited. The introduction of metallurgy into warfare, first bronze and then iron, made for more effective weapons and body armor. At least as important and occurring at roughly the same period, the domestication of the horse made for the tactical and strategic advantages of mobility, and when combined with powerful composite bows invented on the Eurasian steppes (where horse riding also originated) made for a powerful and lasting weapons system that put the pastoralists of the steppes at the center of Eurasian warfare, at least, for two and a half millennia (Anthony 2007; also Liu, this volume).

The decline of steppe cavalry is then associated with the invention and spread of increasingly effective gunpowder weapons, which came to affect patterns of warfare not only on land but perhaps more significantly at sea after 1500. Finally, the entire suite not just of rapidly developing technologies but of socioeconomic organization and political revolution stemming from the Industrial Revolution sets the last two centuries off from its preindustrial history as much in the global history of warfare as in any other aspect of world history.

There is certainly value in this broad periodization, and there is no denying that the great division between sedentary agrarian societies and their infantry-dominated armies against the nomadic pastoralist societies of horsemen was a central one in large-scale patterns of war, and one determined by a combination of technology (taking the domestication of the horse as a technological achievement) and geography. But this periodization's emphasis on technological and tactical factors holds the danger of over-emphasizing material factors and particularly weaponry over deeper political, social, and cultural patterns in the history of war. Arguably, the most significant development in those terms was the "invention" of what might be called the "modern" combination of strong, centralizing political authority and effective administration that could support mass armies of various complementary troop types, armies which in turn backed up the central authority's claims to dominance. The Assyrians and the Qin were the first to independently invent this powerful combination with all its implications for state-building, though one could also argue that it was only with the addition of an ideological framework that made the workings of such a machine acceptable to those whom it came to rule – achieved by the immediate successors to both inventors, the Persians and the Han – that this sort of socio-political-military establishment reached its full potential. The advantage of an analytical scheme that subordinates technology to broader social developments is that it brings more of the world's societies into the discussion. Whereas a technologically based outline relegates regions that did not have metal weapons, horses, or later gunpowder to a sort of teleological backwater, emphasis on organization sheds light, for example, on the achievement of the Incas, who arrived, much later but completely independently, at something resembling the Persian-Han synthesis of political-military organization with effective ideology. It also connects pre-gunpowder and preindustrial state-level societies more clearly to their industrial successors, as from this perspective the Persian-Han formula differs from the nationalist-inspired mass conscript armies of the last two centuries only by degree, not by type. An emphasis on social and cultural factors also casts the decline of the steppe nomads in a different, less gunpowder-dominated light, as it was the slow accumulation of demographic and organizational advantages by the successors of the Persians and the Han that eventually contained and then swallowed the steppe nomadic threat.

Emphasis on political, social, and cultural factors brings other patterns obscured by a technological focus to light as well. The steppe–sedentary divide, for example, was not just a technological and geographic divide, and an economic one based on technology and geography, but a social and cultural one as well. But instead of the opposition set up by viewing the two worlds through the lens of technology, a cultural perspective highlights the interactions across frontier zones, processes of mutual or at least semi-mutual acculturation, and dynamics of synthesis and political interrelationship. Thus, the gradual closing of the steppes between 1500 and 1700 may have been powered by the slow advance of the demographic and technological advantages that centralized sedentary states following the Persian-Han model could deploy. But the actual polities that accomplished the closing – the Qing Dynasty in China, the Ottomans, and even Muscovy and the Mughals – represented in another way the last assertion of steppe power, as each combined cavalry forces whose origins and cultures of war arose on the steppes with the administration and mass infantry armies of a major sedentary state, in every case except Muscovy under leadership that was from the steppes or identified itself culturally as nomadic. More broadly, the "divide" itself was hardly a simple dichotomy. "Horse zones" spread out from the epicenter of the steppes. An inner circuit of Eurasian societies facing the steppes directly depended far more on cavalry as part of their mix of troops than an outer circuit of regions, especially western Europe and Japan, that were somewhat insulated from the steppes. In that outer circuit, cavalry tended more to be the preserve of small mounted warrior elites working alongside infantry forces that could assume a larger role in warfare. This may have had consequences for the spread of gunpowder technology (Chase 2003); it was certainly a development with clear consequences for social structure and status as much as for tactics and weaponry. Beyond that lay numerous different "no-horse zones" where horses were either absent (the Americas)[1] or did not thrive for climatic and disease reasons (the tropics generally) and so had no influence on war and the social dynamics connected to waging war.

Similarly, and in fact connected to the decline of the steppes, a social-cultural perspective on patterns of war places more prominence on naval warfare, especially the globalization of naval power after 1500, because of its deep connections to trade and the early modern history of cultural contact and exchange (see chapters by Fernández-Armesto and by Levi, this volume). It also highlights in that history the contexts in which new technologies of naval power, above all the cannon-bearing full-rigged ship, were generated by and worked as part of socioeconomic dynamics and cultural outlooks in western Europe, and that it was these contexts, not the technologies themselves, that distinguished the European maritime world. Put another way, European naval forces came to prominence as much through lack of opposition as through their own efforts.

In a broader but more diverse way, social and cultural factors also constantly influenced the practices of war, creating patterns subject to comparative analysis that are not necessarily subject to chronological periodization. Strategic patterns of battle-seeking and battle-avoidance in the preindustrial world can be explained in terms of the intersection between practical matters of logistics on one hand and culturally determined goals on the other, for example (Morillo 2002). These topics, potentially fruitful areas for cross-cultural analysis, may be divided for convenience into "war and society" and "war and culture" questions.

Themes: War and Society

Studies of "war and society" are a well-established genre in military history. It was largely through examination of the impact of war on society that military history built a larger presence in the mainstream of academic history starting in the 1960s. While this work is still mostly Euro-American in orientation, its quality provides models for extending such investigations to other areas of the world, a project already underway. Routledge's War and History series provides a number of fine examples of such work (e.g., Haldon 1999; Friday 2004). Since the 1970s, "war and society" has come to mean not just the impact of war on society but also the converse: the impact of society, including class and gender, on armies and warfare. Though initially open to the criticism that the institutional and social orientation of such studies made for "military history without warfare," by now the integration of context and events is more typical, even routine.

One of the first major themes of war and society studies was the importance of logistics to patterns of campaigning. This involved for starters the recognition that available sources of water and stores of food, founded in local agricultural productivity and transportation, were perhaps the major constraint on the movement of armies that often constituted, in the magnitude of their demands, something like cities on the march. Donald Engels's pioneering study of the logistics of Alexander the Great (1978) and Martin van Creveld's broader study of more modern logistics (1977) opened up a rich field for comparative studies that could take account of different agricultural systems, including different crops and seasonal patterns – the logistical constraints on Aztec warfare, for example, created their own patterns of campaigning (Hassig 1988). How armies actually gathered supplies on campaign probably constituted, for much of history, the key moment of interaction between states and local populations outside of tax collection. Whether armies plundered, requisitioned, paid in markets, or brought along their own supplies clearly had significantly different implications for the relationship of peasants to armies. Thus, the different methods employed are one of the most useful windows into different military administrations and the broader topic of state–society relationships.

A crucial question about the state–society relationship in the context of logistics is whether military establishments and campaigning damaged a society's economy or stimulated production and led to improvements in infrastructure. Clearly, both happened in different times and places, but comparative studies of which effect predominated in particular cases, and what factors were involved, could reveal interesting patterns about economic development and state formation (or deformation). Taken beyond individual societies, there is fruitful work to be done on the connections between war, trade, and network flows (including not just material goods but cultural encounters and exchanges more generally). Avner Offer's innovative work on the role of global food production and imperial trade in the success of the British war effort in World War I provides an instructive exemplar here (1991).

Finally, war and society studies have explored the impact of armed violence on societies broadly. Here, too, the transregional network connections highlighted by world history can contribute to such analyses. War was long associated, especially in the premodern world but in evolving ways even after industrialization, with slavery and the slave trade. Thus, established patterns of sub-Saharan African warfare, in which slave-taking was one common result, formed part of the link between African societies and the Islamic world's demand for domestic slaves; later and more infamously African warfare also supplied the Atlantic slave trade. Questions of war and slavery inevitably also raise issues of the division between combatants and noncombatants and how that division has been constructed through time in different places, as well as of the impact of armed violence on women and children – with child warriors in recent African warfare highlighting the complexities of such topics. (See Ward, this volume.)

While the impact of war on society is a well-established field, less work has been done on the impact of society on war. One issue open to further investigation in cross-cultural context is how the interactions of social structure, ideology, and state power produce different types of troops, from warrior elites and militia to stipendiaries, volunteer armies, and mercenaries, in various combinations. Two central factors are prominent in this analysis. First, there are variations in terms of service, extending from purely political or coercive sorts such as conscription to purely economic incentives that draw volunteers, with a whole range of combinations in between. Second, there is the question of whether the soldiers who make up an army are more or less socially embedded in the society of the state that employs them, a sometimes clear reflection of the relationship of state to society and the legitimacy of state power. Analyzed in this way, it turns out that true mercenary service – soldiers drawn by pay in a free market for military manpower and with no social connection to the society of their employing state – is quite rare in history (Morillo 2007). But the distribution of other sorts of military service over time and place could be revealing about deeper patterns of social and political development. Under what political and economic conditions does paid service appear? Is there a global trend in terms of common soldier types? These are unanswered questions that would repay comparative investigation. And are terms of service and social embeddedness adequate as factors of analysis? Might social status provide another vector of fruitful analysis? The complex interaction of social class, economic development, and political participation with mass conscription is relatively well studied in nineteenth- and early twentieth-century Europe, for example, and the problems of creating a modern mass army have been studied for some non-European societies (Ralston 1990). Even broader comparative work is possible, however.

In addition to class, the subject of war and gender has attracted recent important research (Goldstein 2001; Lynn 2008), with John Lynn's study of women, "campaign communities," and the life of early modern European armies establishing especially questions for investigation in other societies. The relationship of warfare and the construction of gender roles, especially notions of masculinity, is one of the central themes of Goldstein's work. (See Burton, this volume.) Questions of gender and warfare have been addressed through examinations of gendered violence, especially rape, in wartime, but one of the lessons of Lynn's work is that women were not just passive victims of military violence. Women in combat may have particular relevance to modern armed forces (Krylova 2010), but studies of women in command roles in medieval warfare, particularly but not exclusively in siege warfare, indicates that more remains to be explored.

Themes: War and Culture

Construction of gender roles creates a segue from questions of war and society to those about war and culture. Cultural analysis has not been one of the strengths of traditional military history, as Lynn notes in his study of women and warfare. It holds great promise, however. Given the social and political importance in many traditional, preindustrial cultures of warrior elites, surprisingly little critical work has been done on the impact of warrior cultures on broader cultural developments, or even in a comparative way of the similarities and differences among the world's various traditional warrior cultures. A critical question here concerns the transition from preindustrial to industrial era patterns. Warrior elites as such arguably disappeared with the spread of industrial mass society and the new forms of mass politics industrialization created. But in many ways the values of traditional warrior cultures have transitioned neatly into the bureaucratic, institutional settings of modern military forces, as one look at television recruiting advertisements for, say, the United States Marine Corps demonstrates instantly. How well cultural values with roots in the coercive, hierarchical structures of preindustrial complex societies fit into the more egalitarian, democratic and market-based socioeconomic and political structures of modern societies is an open question seriously in need of careful historical scholarship with a global perspective (see, e.g., Enloe 2007).

More broadly, variations in cultures of war offer a tantalizing field for further investigation. Warrior elites were not the only social group with input into the construction of such cultures. In the preindustrial world, the interaction of warrior values with religion produced among other things theories about Just War, most famously in the formulations of Augustine that Aquinas refined and systematized in the Christian tradition that have strong parallels in Islamic just war theory, but also in different ways in other traditions (Brekke 2005). Crusading theory is exhaustively studied in medieval European scholarship, but the topic of holy war more generally would benefit from a broader, more global and comparative approach. The modern parallel with such topics is the intersection between war and nationalism over the last two centuries, nationalistic ideology having largely displaced (or in some cases reoriented) religion as the most important ideological framework for conflict both between and within states.

Finally, consideration of war and culture brings us back to some of the methodological issues explored early in this chapter from a different perspective. In his brilliant examination of epistemologies of military experience, reporting, and historiography, *The Ultimate Experience: Battlefield Revelations and the Making of Modern War Culture, 1450–2000* (2008), Yuval Harari analyzes how, at least in Western culture, there was a shift in such epistemologies that has vital implications for the writing of military history today, implications that gain even greater force when set in a complex, multicultural context. Briefly, Harari shows that in medieval and early modern Europe, war, like most other human experiences outside mystical revelation, was subject to an "eye-witness" epistemology: information was gained through seeing events; that information could then be narrated. Narration passed on the eye-witness's information to others, including experts – those with moral (or academic/professional) authority to interpret information and create knowledge. But the rise during the later eighteenth century and into the nineteenth century of Romanticism, with its at least partial rejection of the dominance of Reason in favor of direct emotional experience and sensation, gave rise to what Harari calls an epistemology of "flesh-witnessing." The crucial claim of flesh-witnessing is that the experiences of a flesh-witness (to combat, especially, the "ultimate experience" of Harari's title) cannot be transferred by narration. As the saying goes, "you had to be there": a listener may come to know the events the flesh-witness experienced, but it is the experiential aspect itself that is crucial, so the claim goes, so the hearer's new information is worthless. As a consequence, only flesh-witnesses can claim the authority to interpret what the combat experience means. Flesh-witnessing, as Harari shows, has underlain the claims of both militarists (Hitler, the former corporal, being a prime example) and pacifists (Erich-Maria Remarque's *All Quiet on the Western Front,* from the same war).

In either form, however, acceptance of flesh-witnessing as the epistemological foundation of military analysis removes debate about war – and by extension about the history of war – not just from academic analysis but from the public sphere altogether, with serious implications for the democratic debate about policy of which the writing of history is arguably an important part. Thus, what Harari's analysis reveals is the danger of flesh-witnessing as an epistemology. By implication, it therefore shows the importance of world history, and especially, in this context, of world military history, to the globalizing public sphere of a connected world in which there is no shortage in the capacity and the will for global conflict.

Note

1   Ironically, horses evolved in the Americas, but after spreading across the Bering land bridge to Asia went extinct in their place of origin before humans arrived there from Asia. They did not reappear until imported by the Spanish in the 1500s.

References

Anthony, David W. 2007. *The Horse, the Wheel and Language*. Princeton: Princeton University Press.
Archer, Christon I., John R. Ferris, Holger H. Herwig, and Timothy H.E. Travers. 2002. *World History of Warfare*. Lincoln: University of Nebraska Press.
Black, Jeremy. 2004. *Rethinking Military History*. London: Routledge.
Bouchard, Constance, ed. 2009. *Knights in History and Legend*. Buffalo, NY: Firefly Books.
Brekke, Torkel. 2005. *The Ethics of War in Asian Civilisations: A Comparative Perspective*. London: Routledge.
Chase, Kenneth. 2003. *Firearms: A Global History to 1700*. Cambridge: Cambridge University Press.
Cowley, Robert, and Geoffrey Parker, eds. 1996. *The Reader's Companion to Military History*. Boston: Houghton Mifflin.
Dawson, Doyne. 2002. *The First Armies*. New York: Cassell.
Drews, Robert. 1993. *The End of the Bronze Age: Changes in Warfare and the Catastrophe ca. 1200 BC*. Princeton: Princeton University Press.
Dupuy, R. Ernest, and Trevor N. Dupuy. 1970. *The Encyclopedia of Military History from 3500 BC to the Present*. London: Macdonald. 3rd edn 1993 (New York: HarperCollins)..
Engels, Donald. 1978. *Alexander the Great and the Logistics of the Macedonian Army*. Berkeley: University of California Press.
Enloe, Cynthia. 2007. *Globalization and Militarism: Feminists Make the Link*. New York: Rowman & Littlefield.
Ferguson, Brian. 2005. Archaeology, cultural anthropology, and the origins and intensifications of war. In E. Arkush and M. Allen, eds, *Violent Transformations: The Archaeology of Warfare and Long-Term Social Change*. Gainesville: University of Florida Press.
Friday, Karl. 2004. *Samurai, Warfare and the State in Early Medieval Japan*. London: Routledge.
Gat, Azar. 2006. *War in Human Civilization*. Oxford: Oxford University Press.
Goldstein, Joshua. 2001. *War and Gender: How Gender Shapes the War System and Vice Versa*. Cambridge: Cambridge University Press.
Graff, David. 2002. *Medieval Chinese Warfare, 300–900*. London: Routledge.
Haldon, John. 1999. *Warfare, State and Society in the Byzantine World, 565–1204*. London: Routledge.
Hanson, Victor Davis. 1989. *The Western Way of War: Infantry Battle in Classical Greece*. New York: Knopf.

Harari, Yuval. 2008. *The Ultimate Experience: Battlefield Revelations and the Making of Modern War Culture, 1450–2000*. New York: Palgrave Macmillan.

Hassig, Ross. 1988. *Aztec Warfare*. Norman: Oklahoma University Press.

Keegan, John. 1993. *A History of Warfare*. New York: Knopf.

Keeley, Lawrence. 1996. *War before Civilization*. Oxford: Oxford University Press.

Krylova, Anna. 2010. *Soviet Women in Combat: A History of Violence on the Eastern Front*. Cambridge: Cambridge University Press.

Lewis, Mark Edward. 1992. *Sanctioned Violence in Early China*. Albany: State University of New York Press.

Lorge, Peter Allan. 2005. *War, Politics and Society in Early Modern China, 900–1795*. London: Routledge.

Lynn, John. 2003. *Battle: A History of Combat and Culture*. Boulder: Westview.

Lynn, John. 2008. *Women, Armies, and Warfare in Early Modern Europe*. Cambridge: Cambridge University Press.

Martel, Gordon, ed. 2012. *The Encyclopedia of War*. Oxford: Wiley-Blackwell.

Morillo, Stephen. 1995. Guns and government: A comparative study of Europe and Japan. *Journal of World History* 6: 75–106.

Morillo, Stephen. 2001. *Milites*, knights and samurai: Military terminology, comparative history, and the problem of translation. In B. Bachrach, ed, *The Normans and Their Adversaries at War: Essays in Memory of C. Warren Hollister*, pp. 167–184. Woodbridge: Boydell & Brewer.

Morillo, Stephen. 2002. Battle seeking: The contexts and limits of Vegetian strategy. *Journal of Medieval Military History* 1: 21–41.

Morillo, Stephen. 2006. *What is Military History?* Cambridge: Polity.

Morillo, Stephen. 2007. Mercenaries, mamluks and militia: Towards a cross-cultural typology of military service. In John France, ed., *Medieval Mercenaries*, pp. 243–260. Brill: Leiden.

Morillo, Stephen, Jeremy Black, and Paul Lococo. 2009. *War in World History: Society, Technology, and War from Ancient Times to the Present*. New York: McGraw Hill.

Murray, Williamson, and Allan Millett. 2001. *A War To Be Won: Fighting the Second World War*. Cambridge, MA: Harvard University Press.

Offer, Avner. 1991. *The First World War: An Agrarian Interpretation*. Oxford: Oxford University Press.

Parker, Geoffrey. 1988. *The Military Revolution: Military Innovation and the Rise of the West, 1500–1800*. Cambridge: Cambridge University Press.

Pomeranz, Kenneth. 2007. Social history and world history: From daily life to patterns of change. *Journal of World History* 18: 69–98.

Ralston, David. 1990. *Importing the European Army: The Introduction of European Military Techniques and Institutions into the Extra-European World, 1600–1914*. Chicago: University of Chicago Press.

Strauss, Barry. 2005. *The Battle of Salamis: The Naval Encounter that Saved Greece – and Western Civilization*. New York: Simon & Schuster.

Strauss, Barry. 2009. *The Spartacus War*. New York: Simon & Schuster.

van Creveld, Martin. 1977. *Supplying War: Logistics from Wallenstein to Patton*. Cambridge: Cambridge University Press.

Van Wees, Hans. 2004. *Greek Warfare: Myths and Realities*. London: Duckworth.

PART III

Many Globes

Who Writes the World?

CHAPTER TWENTY-SIX

The World from Oceania

DAMON IEREMIA SALESA

The largest single feature in the world, fully one-third of its surface, is the Pacific Ocean. So vast that all the land in the world would fit inside its perimeter, the Pacific is virtually incomparable. Though only a small fraction of the world's people make the Pacific their home – Oceania – those people speak around a quarter of the world's languages. The people of Oceania inherit some of the most ancient histories of humankind and some of its most singular achievements. Ancient civilizations that pioneered agriculture and horticulture, cultures that built some of the world's most beautiful and impressive artifacts and monuments, and the greatest mariners of human history, the history of Oceania seems, to those who know it, as rich as in significance, complexity, achievement and human experience as any region on Earth. Yet outside of its bounds, and on the continents particularly, it is little known, marginalized, disavowed or excised. In world histories, as even in world maps, the biggest thing on Earth actually manages to be omitted or divided or occluded.

The *Atlas of World History* from Oxford University Press (2003, rev. edn 2010) can stand in for most historical works and their approach to the history of Oceania. A magnificent volume, the *Atlas* contains literally *hundreds* of maps in its over 300 pages. In all of these hundreds of maps, however, there is not a single one of the Earth that is Pacific-centered, nor are there any that actually offer a depiction where one can see the entire Pacific Ocean. On all the maps that depict the "whole" Earth, the Pacific Ocean is literally at the margins, dissected and excised, the bookends of the significant world. If one did not know it already, it would be impossible to surmise that a substantial proportion of the globe is absent from *every single map*: as is, for the most part, one of the continents, Antarctica. But unlike Antarctica, people inhabit the Pacific, and it is an ancient and necessary space for any world history. Of these hundreds of maps, only four have any interest in Oceania. One two-page spread depicts the peopling of Oceania over 11,000 years – although with most of the Ocean cropped out and many major archipelagoes unidentified; much later, readers find a two-page spread on Australia and New Zealand after 1790 (2010: 26–27, 202–203). This is hardly to single out the *Atlas*;

A Companion to World History, First Edition. Edited by Douglas Northrop.
© 2012 Blackwell Publishing Ltd. Published 2012 by Blackwell Publishing Ltd.

its treatment of Oceania is typical. The *Atlas* simply makes visible and striking exactly what most world histories do in text: marginalizing, minimizing or occluding Oceania to the point of actually having to fundamentally misrepresent the Earth – even when their representations are in scales and projections of their own choosing. These representations are both powerfully silent and uninterested in Oceania.

Yet the histories of Oceania offer important challenges to many of the central tropes and narratives of world history. It is commonplace for world histories to be fashioned around divisions, categories and metaphors that cannot account for or describe Oceania, its peoples, cultures, or past. This is not simply a case of parochialism among specialists; as some have begun realizing, Oceania can restructure our understandings of many different scales and registers of the past. Any serious attempt to cast a world history that makes Oceania's histories visible must grapple with the ways in which most "world histories" remain Eurasian-centric, land-centric and logocentric. Little wonder, then, that most such histories are unable to seriously engage or comprehend an extra-Eurasian, oceanic, and chiefly nonliterate immensity of human history. In these and other ways, global historians have tended to constitute their subject in ways that are unable to address the Pacific, or make it legible or visible. The answer is not simply to add the Pacific to an already defined world, to assimilate or annex it: but rather to understand how the trouble that Oceania presents is instructive in some of the blindspots and quiet hegemonies of world history.

Terms with which to talk about the Pacific are not straightforward among specialists, either. The complexity and vastness of Oceania mean that long-established categories for describing its geography and populations are generally unsatisfactory. The received tripartite division of the Pacific, where its peoples and lands are divided into Polynesia, Melanesia, and Micronesia, remains popular, not least because many contemporary people in these places share public identities that have partly been fashioned around these ideas. But the distinctions of Polynesia ("many islands"), Micronesia ("small islands") and Melanesia ("black islands") not only turn on crude nineteenth-century racial distinctions, but elide people, territory, language and culture in ways that are often either inaccurate and unhelpful. (See chapters by Liu and by Kramer, this volume.) These categories, for instance, are troubled even on their own terms by Fiji, which shares qualities, and is on the putative "border," of Polynesia and Melanesia. Likewise such distinctions are substantively confounded by the presence throughout Melanesia of peoples, cultures and languages that are identified as "Polynesian" (usually called "the Polynesian outliers"). Rather than recognize the complexity that creates such situations, the usual answer is to stress that these people are, in a sense, out of place. Specialists may argue about the utility, as well as the analytical and political stakes, of these categories: but they remain in ordinary usage, and continue to order the self-views of most of Oceania's people.

Other scholars of the Pacific have searched for different schemes to describe its peoples and places. Many of these distinctions are tuned to particular purposes, and do not claim fully to describe every combination of territory, people and culture/language. Of particular importance is the categorical distinction between "Near Oceania" and "Remote Oceania" (see Map 26.1), pioneered chiefly by Roger Green and other prehistorians and archaeologists. Along with the recognition of the continental shelves – where the outlines of Sunda and Sahul were once revealed by different sea-levels – these chart the great fields of human expansion into, and then throughout, Oceania. Near and Remote Oceania recognize this spatial and historical difference, as human relationships

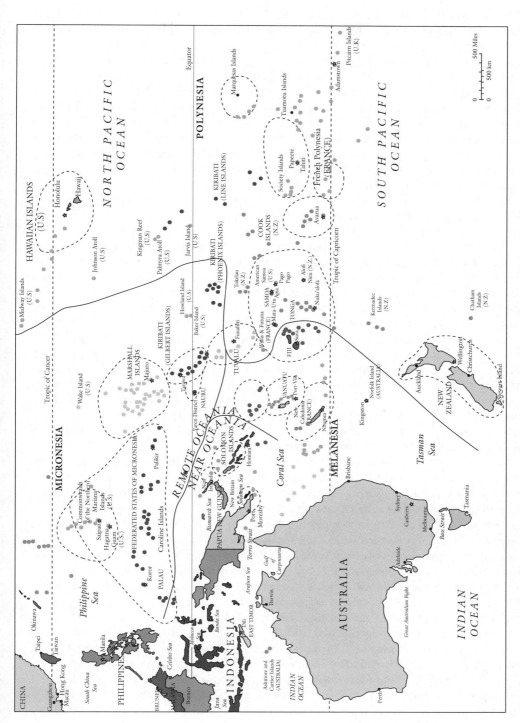

Map 26.1 Oceania, showing the major island groups and Near and Remote Oceania. Areas in close voyaging contact are within dotted lines.
Source: Based on map from Perry-Castañeda Library Map Collection, University of Texas at Austin, at http://www.lib.utexas.edu/maps/.

with each area hinge on the large break in time and space between them: between those that were settled at least 40,000 years ago, and those settled only in the last 3,000–4,000 years. Near Oceania is part of the chain of lands that stretched from island southeast Asia to the Pacific, and most of these islands could be seen from each other. Those that were not intervisible required voyages of around 150–200 kilometers – at the time of their settlement, probably the longest voyages humans had yet undertaken. But these great voyages paled against the magnitudes of the maritime task in moving from the Solomon Islands into Remote Oceania. The voyages grew longer and longer, and the targets mostly smaller. At this point, around 3,500 years ago, human voyaging began its deep-water history, with passages that began at over 350 kilometers and ended in the prodigious voyages to Rapanui (Easter Island), Hawai'i and New Zealand – surely among the great human achievements.

Yet because the variety of people and lands *within* Remote and (especially) Near Oceania is staggering, these categories are often too broad to tell stories accurately. In terms of language, for example, "Melanesia" remains the most diverse place in the world, with hundreds of languages of diverse origins. It exemplifies the difficult task of characterizing diversity in ways that are accurate but also usable to nonspecialists or at larger scales. Consequently, other distinctions are often mobilized: one common approach among linguists is to distinguish between the two groups of Oceanian languages – Austronesian and Papuan. In other cases, slippery terms appear to identify a historical population of people (and their culture) through material culture, such as a kind of pottery – for instance, "Lapita people." These can be useful terms, but as with all terminological schemes they also present potential pitfalls to the comprehension and analysis of Oceania. Specialists in the region's history have to stay on their toes when thinking through, and using, any particular terms (Clark 2003). Other disciplines underscore this need for care: genetic studies of the Pacific demonstrate in a different register just how complicated and interwoven the ancestry (as well as languages, technologies and cultures) of this region are. Although found on islands, the peoples of Oceania are enormously difficult to put into boxes.

This struggle to "come to terms" with the Pacific, and to find adequate ways to talk about its specificities and vastness, has another, perhaps more imposing opponent: the recent adoption of terms such as "Asia-Pacific" and the "Pacific Rim." These common categorizations sit over Oceania, and serve to obscure and minimize it, fundamentally appending Oceania to a more populous but spatially smaller region (Asia), one that is *already* visible in – and often central to – standard renditions of the world. In a single imperious move Oceania is made at once less visible and distinctive, and incorporated into Asia as part of "Asia-Pacific" or the Pacific Rim. This makes little sense historically, but is useful as it meshes and supports, rather than troubles, standard projections of the globe. "Oceania," the name I (like many other specialists) choose to use, places an opposite emphasis on the islands of the Pacific, exclusive of Asia and the Philippines. The term "Oceania" has its own problems, mostly due to its provenance in the same nineteenth-century moment as "Polynesia," "Melanesia," and "Micronesia," and it has its own vagaries – in some iterations it includes Australia and New Zealand, while in others it does not. Though an old term, coined elsewhere, Oceania now bears the standard for a new approach to the region, and has recently been reappropriated by Pacific and Pacific Islander scholars as a way to represent their reimagining and reinvigoration of the region.

In older models of world history – "Western Civilization plus" – there was virtually no place for the Pacific region. Insofar as the Pacific could be positioned in these kinds of narratives, it was either to gesture to the full arc of human settlement, or to describe the reach of modern empires, especially the British Empire. (See Sinha, this volume.) In such views Australia and New Zealand were consequently worthy of some attention, but only *after* James Cook or the British, not for the 40,000 or so years prior. The Pacific as prelude, and Europeans as the beginning of history: such a structure of "inclusion" is a well-worn treatment for histories outside Eurasia (and for many within). At any rate, it was rare for Oceania to be given more than a few sentences, even in books of prodigious size. The dominant theme was, effectively, that of invisibility. Recent world histories typically constitute their narratives very differently, and have been more robustly inclusive. But while this inclusion is apparent through a drawing in of non-Western civilizations, examples and features, whether Asian, African or Native American, this spirit of inclusivity usually dries up short of the coasts of the Pacific. In the ordinary phrasing of the global past, Oceania merits not even a passing mention.

No history can be total, and most world histories understand many of their own limitations. But the absence of Oceania and the Pacific is peculiar in at least two senses: not only is Oceania commonly invisible, and seemingly illegible, in most global narratives, but outside scholars rarely feel any compunction to rectify this. (Compare the increasing inclusion of, for instance, African civilizations.) The sources for this are evidently not only historiographical, but political and institutional, and are conspicuous in institutional and disciplinary arrangements. By these lights the marginalizing of Oceania is of a different order from that of either Africa or the (Native) Americas – which still literally and figuratively appear on the map, or in faculty corridors in Europe and North America. Outside of the Pacific region, ignorance of the history of Oceania seems congenital, but is also still entirely normalized. One world historian, for instance, whose work I otherwise enjoy, can obliviously declare that "there has not yet emerged an organized scholarly community focused on Pacific history" (Benton 2004: 427). This would come as news to the many centers specializing in Pacific history and culture, or the editors of any of the monograph series or journals, including, for instance, the *Journal of Pacific History* (established 1966) or the members of the Pacific History Association: just as it does to scholars, such as myself, who consider themselves Pacific historians. Oceania is demonstrably *not* an absence waiting to be called into history.

Thankfully, not all world historians are so silent towards Oceania, so a different engagement is evidently possible. This fact suggests that the marginality of Oceania owes less to selectivity, and more to limitations in historians' knowledge or imagination. When world historians know more about the Pacific, they – for the most part – also become less convinced of its marginality. Jerry Bentley's oeuvre is perhaps the best example of this point (Bentley and Ziegler 2008), also evident in the work of David Christian, who is oriented more to the Pacific as he teaches Big History from Australia, and incorporates far more elements of Oceania into his narrative than is customary or expected (Christian 2008). Likewise, J.R. McNeill, who has researched and written about Oceania, co-wrote a world history that includes and interpolates Oceania in ways that strongly distinguish it as a volume from others like it, and this is also evident in the well-known volume he jointly authored with his father (McNeill 2001; McNeill and McNeill 2003).

Scholars of the Pacific, meanwhile, have not stood still, and have been engaged with the turn towards global/world history from its outset. One obvious marker of this investment is the centrality of the University of Hawai'i in the institutional circles of world history, both as a point of origin for "world history" and as the home of both the World History Association and the *Journal of World History*. Yet, in many ways, this is largely due to the guiding efforts of particular individuals (Jerry Bentley, again). Moreover, the pages of the *JWH* are far from overflowing with articles on the Pacific (and it has not been a preferred publishing outlet for scholars of the Pacific). Indicative of both the limits and possibilities of an engagement between "world history" and scholars of the Pacific is a *JWH* article by Ben Finney, entitled "The other one-third of the globe" (1994). Finney, an esteemed scholar and a public intellectual well known throughout the Pacific for catalyzing and helping sustain the reinvigoration of ancestral Polynesian voyaging, wrote this essay as an accessible primer on over 40,000 years of Oceania's history. Obviously, as his title suggests, he still saw the Pacific as neglected in the pages of the *JWH*, positing it as the lost third of the world.

A range of scholars of the Pacific have consciously responded to the rising challenges posed by world history, interest in it, and its increasing status. Ian Campbell, Tony Ballantyne, Rainer Buschmann, Andrew Pawley, and Paul D'Arcy all trained as Pacific specialists and have written substantially about world history (if, as with many world historians, as a second field), or about Oceania in ways that are inflected towards world history (Buschmann 2011; Campbell 1997; Pawley 2010). Paul D'Arcy's *The People of the Sea* (2006) is particularly congenial to the scales and tasks of world history, but seems to have been little read by world historians. Incisive interventions by Tony Ballantyne, more directly engaging the historiography and problematics of world history, do so critically and from a perspective steeped in the Pacific (Ballantyne and Burton 2005; 2009; Ballantyne and Moloughney 2006). This raft of work pursues world history in ways that are recognizable by, and reflective of, traditions particular to those in Pacific history discussed above.

A very different angle of vision, but one at once global and centered on the Pacific, comes from a scientist who long worked in the Pacific. Jared Diamond's stunningly popular *Guns, Germs, and Steel* (1997) is organized around a question putatively posed to him by a man from New Guinea, Yali: "Why is it that you white people developed much cargo and brought it to New Guinea, but we black people had little cargo of our own?" The central argument of *Guns, Germs, and Steel* is that the answer to "Yali's question" has little to do with individual or cultural choices, but is preponderantly due to differences in environment, which become amplified into technological, biological, and political differentials. As Diamond himself later summarized it, his book was about "the differing rates of buildup of human societies on different continents over the last 13,000 years" (Diamond 2005). Diamond's intent seems to be not just to produce a decentered, counterintuitive history, but also an antiracist and anti-Eurocentric argument. He argues that the differences Yali noted are the result not of inequalities in the potential of individuals or societies, but of originary differences in geography, biota, and other environmental factors. (See Simmons, this volume.) "Yali's question" anchors Diamond to a particular nonmetropolitan space, and to the real-world concerns of peoples almost always excluded from history's grand narratives. Such an environmentalist argument is not new, and Diamond's claim to distinction is rather more that of synthesis and popularization than innovation, but his contribution remains nonetheless noteworthy. Diamond has offered a Pacific-centered vision of global history, where Oceania is treated as demonstrative, even exemplary, and where historiography (or historical narratives and plots) can begin and end in the islands, and with its peoples.

Yet *Guns, Germs, and Steel* has not been well received by Pacific Island specialists. Typically the harshest critics of Diamond were historians, many of whom have been exercised by what they consider his environmental determinism. (See chapters by Adas,

Chase-Dunn and Hall, McKeown, and Yoffee, this volume.) But in the Pacific his strongest critics have been anthropologists: most academic Pacific historians, by contrast, have seemed uninterested. Some of these Oceanian critiques have been substantial and salient; others are familiar from, say, criticisms of Alfred Crosby's work. But Diamond's work in Oceania has also been scrutinized for his research methodology and accuracy (Errington and Gewertz 2004). This renewed scrutiny revealed much about Diamond's work, including that the Yali in question was not the famous "cargo cult" leader, Yali, as had been assumed for years by all Pacific specialists, and which Diamond had done nothing to correct. Moreover, it seemed as if some of the interviews that Diamond used in his work had been misquoted, combined or fictionalized without attribution (Shearer *et al.* 2009). These critiques seemed to unmoor Diamond from much that was innovative about his work, and weakened the Oceanian edge that had been in some ways so striking.

Yet, although Diamond's work has critical complications, its undeniable success – both in gaining a readership and composing a compelling narrative originating in Oceania – is proof positive that the current treatment of Oceania is not without alternatives. World histories centered on, originating in, or rich with Oceania will, almost by definition, be innovative. But there is more than simple novelty at stake, for there is much that is distinctive about the practice of history – teaching, writing, research, communal engagement – in the Pacific. Even the canonical, academic arm of Pacific history is far from standard when held against its European and North American counterparts. Although the serious, rigorous and specialized study of the histories of the Pacific is only about 50 years old, it has produced a dazzling array of works, many unrivaled in their quality, and many of which speak to scales of history larger even than the Pacific itself.

"Pacific history" as a subdiscipline has a distinctive genealogy. Typically it claims a specific point of origin: the assumption by James W. Davidson of the first chair of Pacific History at the Australian National University in 1949–1950. In the context of this time, Davidson's vision amounted to a radical departure from previous academic efforts to study Oceania. Institutionally he represented a sharp departure from the previous situation, where amateurs and colonial officials had amounted to the only historians interested in the Pacific. Under Davidson, Pacific history professionalized: it took form around a PhD program (then still unusual in the Commonwealth world), and became research-driven. But these institutional arrangements merely brought the field's practices into alignment with first-world institutions; what made Pacific history more distinctive, even radical, lay in its intellectual investments, the protocols of research and writing, and the political consciousness and commitment to decolonization foregrounded in historians' work.

By the time Pacific history formally began, centuries of foreign empires in the Pacific had profoundly shaped the historiography of Oceania. Indicative of the kinds of denigration integral to imperial claims and colonial rule was the disparagement or erasure of a sense of value in the Pacific's indigenous past. In the Pacific the sole subjects in which ("Western") historians were interested were ones delimited by the activities of empires, Euro-American foreign policy, and the acts of a very small class of persons, almost solely foreign, white men. The only counterpoints to these narrow visions were located outside "history" *per se*: the historiographical efforts of missionaries, the vanguard of ethnographers, archaeologists and anthropologists, and a few travelers or white residents or indigenous writers. Few island or cultural groups had acquired written histories in a Western form; this was not simply a sign of a lack of interest, but of a disavowal by Euro-American scholars that Pacific Island cultures and peoples either had a history, or had one of any importance. This disavowal was precisely the first ground on which Pacific history had to struggle, to make the case that Pacific Islanders actually *had* histories, and that these histories were interesting and important. Pacific history had to reconstitute the subject of Pacific history so that it actually included Pacific islanders and cultures.

Pacific history as a disciplinary field thus made Pacific Island histories visible, and insisted that Pacific Islanders were subjects and actors in their own histories. To substantiate this reframing and reconstitution of histories hitherto ignored or invisible to foreigners, Pacific historians turned to innovative historical techniques. The most obviously distinctive step was the adoption of what Davidson called "participant observation," an insistence that historians' fieldwork was not only in the archives, but in the islands of which they were writing. This necessitated a deeper engagement with local languages and cultures, and aligned parts of Pacific history with what was elsewhere being called "ethnohistory." Pacific history's interdisciplinarity went well beyond anthropology, though, engaging archaeology, geography, the environmental sciences, political science, linguistics, and law. This interdisciplinarity, in confluence with historians' accepted practices of archival rigor, always kept Pacific history from becoming narrow: Pacific historians had always to make their way to, and through, imperial and metropolitan archives, and empires remained central characters in modern Pacific history (Munro and Lal 2006).

Pacific history's engagement with outside empires sat alongside, and in tension with, its deep commitment to locality and culture. In many instances it was the latter that seemed the most urgent, and before long there was some lamentation that Pacific historians were turning out monograph after monograph, and ultimately turning Pacific island groups into isolates. With few exceptions the first decades of these Pacific histories did seem to be suffering from what Kerry Howe called "monograph myopia." There were few histories that tackled subjects that crossed or incorporated separate island groups, no synthetic overviews, and only one or two works that grappled with the largest scales or the interconnections that characterized living in Oceania. In this there seemed a parallel with anthropology, and it likewise meant that Pacific history did not present itself as easily assimilable to larger scales of history. (See Northrop, final chapter in this volume.) For decades the catchword in Pacific history was "agency," a legacy of the struggle to reconstitute and revalue the subject of Pacific history, and one that tended to bring individuals and particular events into focus, but was less useful for capturing larger scales, structures, or comparisons. It severed rather than joined histories.

But there was an enormous exception to these isolated histories: one that turned Pacific historians to connectivities between and among islanders. This move was precipitated by the work of Andrew Sharp, which directly challenged the assumption historians, archaeologists and anthropologists had made about the sailing and exploratory prowess of Pacific Island ancestors. This view, typified in Te Rangihiroa Peter Buck's *Vikings of the Sunrise* (1938), was singularly attacked by Sharp's *Ancient Voyagers in the Pacific*, which recast these ancestors not as Te Rangihiroa had depicted them – heroic voyagers skillfully traversing the Pacific – but as gamblers taking their chances in a punitive lottery of sea, wind and current (Sharp 1957). This criticism was galvanizing, and drove a generation of scholarship that revisited and substantiated in great detail what technologies and knowledge lay behind the original exploration and discovery of Oceania. Sharp's argument and analysis was systematically criticized and dismantled by later historical research – especially by Ben Finney and David Lewis, using contemporary sailing investigations with "traditional" Pacific island navigators (who do not use charts, compasses or other instruments) and a host of other techniques from archaeology to computer simulations (Lewis 1972a; 1972b; Finney 2003). Yet Sharp's intervention proved to be the most powerful catalyst towards a better understanding of the variety of changing webs that connected and reconnected islands and archipelagoes: connections established before any Europeans had made any notable blue water voyages. This connectivity has become a defining feature of recent Pacific history, one through which the metaphors and narratives of the Pacific have been reimagined.

Pacific history has always grasped, and grappled with, the political nature and consequences of history and historiography, and as a result is already sensitized to some of the consequences of global history. This sensitivity was enhanced by the recency of the arrival of historiography in the Western-style – national textbooks, archives, historians, and so on – usually only since the 1960s. Given the sustained efforts required to achieve even this, it seems appropriate to be suspicious of moves that seem once again to marginalize or exclude Pacific Islanders from the "history club." And while the explicit claims of world historians are inclusive, it is apparent that the key metrics of inclusion are decided upon by a very narrow group of practitioners, and that even compared to the profession at large these practitioners are disproportionately white, male, and metropolitan. These metrics of inclusion remain similar to those of earlier generations of world historians, and they have reinscribed the marginality or irrelevance of the Pacific to these narratives. Moreover, although the partiality seems so raw, patent and potent to those situated in Oceania, the language of these practitioners is yet again universalist: they are writing the history of "the human species," our shared story – without, it seems, sharing the storytelling, telling the story in different ways, or asking if (or how) different peoples wish to be represented. Oceania now gets to be a part of the story, but still sings in the rear of the chorus, quietly, and to a tune chosen by far distant choirmasters.

On the one hand this is a familiar story about which *local* most powerfully gets to advance its claims to be *global*. (See Gerritsen, this volume.) The familiar political and economic strategies are, of course, conjoined with diverse cultural means, including the characterization and emplotment of the past. The choice of narratives by many world historians makes it clear that the cost of inclusivity in their grand narratives is high: because their measures of value so often remain calibrated to ethnocentric measures of "civilization," technology and culture, Oceania's histories appear to have little utility. Even now one finds that the Pacific is so profoundly disruptive to these grand narratives, it can still only be placed in a timeless "now," where Pacific Islanders are seen as survivals of an earlier time: out of time and place in the contemporary world – living archives of an otherwise defunct earlier history. (See Pomeranz and Segal, this volume.) Most Pacific scholars (or African and Native American scholars for that matter) thought such notions had been put to bed, but they seem to retain currency in some realms, including world history.

Robert Strayer's *Ways of the World* (2010), for instance, a popular US-based world history textbook, illustrates its first chapter (in a section titled "The ways we were," subsection "The first human societies") with one of its few mentions of Oceania. When it comes to some people, time, it seems, is of no matter: in a discussion of the deep human past, Strayer quotes a description of Australian aboriginals from 1770, placing it next to a photograph of present-day Aboriginal women and children (who are, according to the caption, digging for food). Flattening 1770, the present, and ancient times, Strayer explicitly casts Aboriginals as people without history, living in the present as relics of the past, out of time and place. Ironically, although the image is supposed, somehow, to represent a "Paleolithic" past, in it an older woman digs dirt with what appears to be a steel pole, wearing a green sweatshirt, while two young boys in shorts look on – one holds a mass-produced shovel and the other wears a baseball cap. Digging in the dirt is a shared characteristic of many systems of food production – including contemporary capital-intensive industrial horticulture – and presumably sweatshirts and baseball caps were uncommon in "Paleolithic societies." No doubt Strayer did not consider putting a contemporary white American hunter, wearing camouflage clothing and holding an assault rifle or compound bow, as an illustration of the persistence of a Paleolithic hunting lifestyle. Yet he uses an image that could easily have been captioned "Australian woman digs hole: boys look on with shovel." The salient feature, evidently, is the race of those photographed: and this example serves perhaps as another hint of why Oceania remains illegible in so many world history narratives.

If one challenge for world historians today is to learn about and engage Oceania, for Oceania's scholars it remains a challenge to take what is distinctive about Oceania and renovate other kinds of large-scale history. Central to this task is the challenge of changing the narrative, to offer different kinds of emplotment, and to introduce a different range of characters. Currently, the subjects of world histories figure a fairly narrow range of political, environmental and regional actors: these are histories that value size and state actors, and a few other abstractions or aggregations that are visible through their methodologies and narratives. But world history seems to handle rather poorly the peoples whose lives are largely conducted "outside" of particular political or state formations. These are not "the people without history," but peoples with "other" histories. In the Pacific many of these people live in polities and communities – small, but overlapping or intertwined – that are amazingly durable, politically congenial, and in key ways self-sufficient: yet which have always been engaged with distant places, foreigners, innovation and exchange. I have in mind the nu'u ("villages") of Sāmoa or the kolo ("towns") of Tonga: political, cultural and economic communities that have histories that cohere across many, many centuries. Always articulated with larger regional spheres, they were also tied to particular places, histories and cultures, and have become increasingly articulated and mobilized regionally and globally. Sāmoan and Tongan understandings were, however, always contextualized in the largest of known scales, and this persists today, where few places are more evidently global or transnational than Sāmoa and Tonga, with populations as large overseas as at "home," and with their deep attuning to many different developments and places (Macpherson and Macpherson 2009; Besnier 2011). These, and similar places, offer unique occasions through which to reimagine world histories: they are indeed old, with deep histories of human achievement; but their durability in environments that are far from easy to inhabit offers a narrative of sustainability that is both remarkable and humbling (Macpherson and Macpherson 2009; Besnier, 2011). Even as these places sit on the "edge of the global," longstanding styles of life – in agriculture, arts, politics and domesticity – are evidently *not* going away, and they remain vibrant, sustainable, dynamic and connected.

Each historical account, whether of the world or of Oceania, is redolent with views of the present. For decades the scholarly status quo, as well as that of development experts and metropolitan policymakers, has been that Pacific Island people, in their states, cultures and nations, were destined only for a position of global marginality, one where they would be dependent on the largesse of the world's powerful and wealthy countries. By this view, Pacific Island nations, communities and peoples are small, weak, poor, remote, marginal and dependent. One influential characterization was that they were "MIRAB" societies, dependent for their lives on "Migration, Remittances, Aid and Bureaucracy" (Bertram and Watters 1985; Poirine 1998). This kind of analysis is also common among historians, including some specialists in the Pacific. As one Pacific historian declared in his recent survey of Oceania in world history, "Oceania and Australasia remain on the margins of world history," their destinies being only to "generally modify the impact of these external forces rather than hope to shape them." In his view, the peoples of Oceania (and Australasia) had been and would remain marginal, destined to be fought over by others, receptors rather than makers of global history, "linked to processes beyond its area over which they have no influence" and, at least in this view, with no hope to change (D'Arcy 2011).

Yet indigenous scholars, in particular, have challenged these ominous visions of dependency, powerlessness and marginality. The most often cited work in this vein, Epeli Hau'ofa's "Our sea of islands," was an explicit response to such assertions (chiefly of outsiders and elites) that Oceania is marginal, small, remote, hopeless and powerless. In making an argument that many Pacific scholars find visionary – especially indigenous scholars of the Pacific – Hau'ofa's "Our sea of islands" contends that instead of seeing the Pacific Islands as remote and isolated "islands in a far sea," it is more accurate to see them in the ways that Islanders have lived on them: as an ocean filled with islands, "a sea of islands" (Hau'ofa 1994). This view fits the term "Oceania," and the argument also reconciles the largest and smallest of scales, seeing Oceania's past and present in terms contrary to those who insist on the islands' marginality and hopelessness. Oceania was not isolated but mobile, and not small, powerless or dependent, but expansive, agentive and substantially independent.

Hau'ofa remains the most widely read, but he was neither the first nor the only Pacific Islander to make such arguments. Such a view is in accord with the heroic creation accounts common in many Pacific Island cultures, and the daring and far-reaching – often cosmological – acts of the ancestors; and was no less evident in the work of modern Pacific writers. These writers, perhaps best characterized by the broad-based "Pacific Way" movement of the 1960s and 1970s, included Te Rangihiroa Sir Peter Buck, and a raft of other writers such as 'Okusitino Mahina, Grace Molisa, Tuiatua Tupua Tamasese Taisi Efi, Konai Helu Thaman, Futa Helu, and especially the Sāmoan novelist and historian Albert Wendt.

Wendt (1976) was the first explicitly to reenvision the island Pacific as a "New Oceania" – in ways that were different from but compatible with Hau'ofa's. This broadened, connected, islander-centered and politicized analysis of the Pacific present and past, which has at its heart interwoven archipelagic visions, recontextualized understandings of both local and large-scale histories of the Pacific Islands. Such an analysis has not been evenly embraced by metropolitan or foreign critics and scholars, but it has proven momentous for Pacific Islander students and scholars. Revealingly, while the numbers of indigenous Pacific Islanders working in disciplinary subfields of history (even in Pacific history) have remained sparse and fragile, indigenous Pacific Island students and scholars have been strongly attracted to the interdisciplines where these new analyses of Oceania – that are almost always historical in some way – prevail.

Increasingly, this archipelagic sensibility seems to characterize much that is distinctive about writings produced in the Pacific, but even more striking has been the recent emphasis on the ocean-going vessels that joined these archipelagoes. Pacific historians since Davidson have thought through a sense of islands and archipelagoes, using these metaphors and tropes to shape their narratives. If anything represents the newest trend among scholars of the Pacific, it has been this recentering around canoes and vessels: as subjects of study, as metaphors, tropes and symbols, but most particularly as implicit historical actors integrating the broad horizons of the Pacific. This new emphasis on connectivity is evident in ways that range very far from traditional types of maritime history. The touchstone collection *Vaka Moana*, the writings of Pa Tuterangi Ariki Sir Tom Davis, Dame Anne Salmond, Ben Finney and David Lewis, films such as *Sacred Vessels* (directed by Vince Diaz), or even my own work about the indigenous mobilities that dynamically constituted what might be called a "Brown Pacific," all advance this sense of deep, expansive, durable yet changing connections over great distances and in large scale (Diaz 1999; Howe 2006; Salesa 2003; Salmond 2003; Davis 1992). In such a vein, canoes become vessels, not just for journeying across the ocean, between islands and islanders, but across time and scale as well.

In the multiplex ways of analysis this reframing of Oceania has inspired, the standard casting of Oceania as marginal or insubstantial has proven fundamentally contestable. If, as many different historians have persuasively argued, there is little analytical utility in crude center/margin metaphors, the world is better understood as meshes of relationships, as webs or "nested scales" or in other more complicated, distributed, ways. Scholars of the Pacific have, for instance, often shown how encounters in the Pacific were mutually formative with distant developments, whether this meant historical European ways of thinking about, experiencing and seeing the world (in a critical book, Bernard Smith called this the "European Vision" (1960)), or whether it meant more recent developments, from nuclear technologies (an industry critically active in the region) to anthropology, tourism and, not least, global militarism. In these realms the disposition of Pacific Islanders, their nations, cultures and states will remain critical and decisive in the next decades of global political arrangements: just as it has in the last. Guam, for instance, a critical pivot in American war planning through most of the twentieth century, is again absolutely vital, and informally referred to by US military personnel as "the tip of the spear." The two great threats to Guam's utility for the United States constitute very different kinds of challenge: on the one hand the military of its Asian competitor (China), and on the other the Chamorro nationalists and antimilitarism activists who seek to free Guam from US plenary power and the militarism it enables (Camacho and Monnig 2010). By such lights Oceania is less a margin than a frontier, a place where contestation and difference meet, where the stakes are higher and meanings are concentrated.

From such angles, answers to the challenges that world history and Oceania present to each other are not simply to append or include the Pacific, or to broaden the edges of the map so that its presence and people can be brought into focus. Even though recentering the world on unexpected locales, like Oceania, would at moments be very useful for its own sake, it seems far more important that to properly engage Oceania requires a reimagining of the fundamental narratives, categories, and subjects of world history. Oceania offers not just a disruption to (putatively) global narratives, but an invitation to remake them, and in key ways a suggestion of how this disruption might be undertaken. Arising from, perhaps, the world's only truly Oceanic peoples, the archipelagic histories of Oceania both reveal, and potentially reorient, not only received histories but visions of the present. In this sense, a greater engagement with the Pacific and Oceania is not just additive or inclusive, but if undertaken fully may actually prove transformative. Quite literally, the world looks different when the Pacific is in it; and maps of time, and the world, also change shape when not just the Pacific, but Oceania, appears.

References

Ballantyne, T., and A.M. Burton. 2005. *Bodies in Contact: Rethinking Colonial Encounters in World History*. Durham: Duke University Press.

Ballantyne, T., and A.M. Burton. 2009. *Moving Subjects: Gender, Mobility, and Intimacy in an Age of Global Empire*. Urbana: University of Illinois Press.

Ballantyne, T., and B. Moloughney. 2006. Asia in Murihiku. In T. Ballantyne and B. Moloughney, eds, *Disputed Histories: Imagining New Zealand's Pasts*, pp. 23–34. Dunedin: Otago University Press.

Bentley, J.H., and H.F. Ziegler. 2008. *Traditions and Encounters: A Global Perspective on the Past*. New York: McGraw-Hill.

Benton, L.A. 2004. No longer odd region out: Repositioning Latin America in world history. *Hispanic American Historical Review* 84: 423–430.

Bertram, G., and R. Watters. 1985. The MIRAB economy in South Pacific microstates. *Pacific Viewpoint* 26: 497–519.

Besnier, N. 2011. *On the Edge of the Global: Modern Anxieties in a Pacific Island Nation*. Stanford: Stanford University Press.

Buck, P. 1938. *Vikings of the Sunrise*. New York: Frederick A. Stokes.

Buschmann, R.F. 2011. The Pacific Ocean basin to 1850. In J.H. Bentley, ed., *The Oxford Handbook of World History*. Oxford: Oxford University Press.

Camacho, K.L., and L.A. Monnig. 2010. Uncomfortable fatigues: Chamorro soldiers, gendered identities and the question of decolonization in Guam. In S. Shigematsu and K. Camacho, eds, *Militarized Currents: Toward a Decolonized Future in Asia and the Pacific*. Minneapolis: University of Minnesota Press.

Campbell, I.C. 1997. Culture contact and Polynesian identity in the European age. *Journal of World History* 8: 29–55.

Christian, D. 2008. *This Fleeting World: A Short History of Humanity*. Great Barrington, MA: Berkshire.

Clark, G., ed. 2003. *Dumont d'Urville's Divisions of Oceania: Fundamental Precincts or Arbitrary Constructs?* Special issue of *Journal of Pacific History* 38 (2).

D'Arcy, P. 2006. *The People of the Sea: Environment, Identity, and History in Oceania*. Honolulu: University of Hawai'i Press.

D'Arcy, P. 2011. Oceania and Australasia. In J.H. Bentley, ed., *The Oxford Handbook of World History*, pp. 546–563. Oxford: Oxford University Press.

Davis, T. 1992. *Vaka: Saga of a Polynesian Canoe*. Suva: Institute of Pacific Studies, University of the South Pacific.

Diamond, J. 1997. *Guns, Germs, and Steel: The Fates of Human Societies*. New York: W.W. Norton.

Diamond, J.M. 2005. *Collapse: How Societies Choose to Fail or Succeed*. New York: Viking.

Diaz, V., dir. 1999. *Sacred Vessels: Navigating Tradition and Identity in Micronesia*. Honolulu: Pacific Islanders in Communication.

Errington, F.K., and D.B. Gewertz. 2004. *Yali's Question: Sugar, Culture, and History*. Chicago: University of Chicago Press.

Finney, B. 1994. The other one-third of the globe. *Journal of World History* 5: 273–297.

Finney, B.R. 2003. *Sailing in the Wake of the Ancestors: Reviving Polynesian Voyaging*. Honolulu: Bishop Museum Press.

Hau'ofa, E. 1994. Our sea of islands. *Contemporary Pacific* 6: 147–161.

Howe, K.R., ed. 2006. *Vaka Moana: Voyages of the Ancestors: The Discovery and Settlement of the Pacific*. Auckland: David Bateman.

Lewis, D. 1972a. The Gospel according to St Andrew. *Journal of Pacific History* 7: 223–225.

Lewis, D. 1972b. *We, the Navigators: The Ancient Art of Landfinding in the Pacific*. Honolulu: University of Hawai'i Press.

Macpherson, C., and L.A. Macpherson. 2009. *The Warm Winds of Change: Globalisation in Contemporary Samoa*. Auckland: Auckland University Press.

McNeill, J.R. 2001. *Environmental History in the Pacific World*. Aldershot: Ashgate.

McNeill, J.R., and W.H. McNeill. 2003. *The Human Web: A Bird's-eye View of World History*. New York: W.W. Norton.

Munro, D., and B.V. Lal. 2006. *Texts and Contexts: Reflections in Pacific Islands Historiography*. Honolulu: University of Hawaii Press.

Pawley, A. 2010. Prehistoric migration and colonisation processes in Oceania: A view from historical linguistics and archaeology. In J. Lucassen, L. Lucassen, and P. Manning, eds, *Migration History in World History: Multidisciplinary Approaches*, pp. 77–112. Leiden: Brill.

Poirine, B. 1998. Should we hate or love MIRAB? *Contemporary Pacific* 10: 65–105.

Salesa, T.D.I. 2003. "Travel-happy" Samoa: Colonialism, Samoan migration and a "Brown Pacific." *New Zealand Journal of History* 37: 171–188.

Salmond, A. 2003. *The Trial of the Cannibal Dog: Captain Cook in the South Seas*. London: A. Lane.

Sharp, A. 1957. *Ancient Voyagers in the Pacific*. Wellington: Polynesian Society.

Shearer, R.R., M. Kigl, K. Keleba, and J. Elapa. 2009. Jared Diamond's factual collapse: New Yorker mag's Papua New Guinea revenge tale untrue, tribal members angry, want justice. At http://www.stinkyjournalism.org/latest-journalism-news-updates-149.php (accessed Oct. 30, 2011).

Smith, B. 1960. *European Vision and the South Pacific, 1768–1850: A Study in the History of Art and Ideas*. Oxford: Clarendon Press.

Strayer, R. 2010. *Ways of the World*. New York: Bedford/St Martin's.

Wendt, A. 1976. Towards a New Oceania. *Mana Review* 1: 49–60.

CHAPTER TWENTY-SEVEN

The World from China

WEIWEI ZHANG

In China, "world history" as a notion or a concept was introduced from the West in the course of cultural exchange between China and the outside world in modern times. China has had a long tradition of Sinocentric historiography ever since Sima Qian (ca. 140–86 BCE), in which the rest of the world near and far was treated either as barbarians or tribute-payers to the Middle Kingdom or the Central Empire. "World history," in China, has thus usually meant "foreign history/ies"; "world history" in the sense of this volume – as a disciplinary subfield – has in China generally been seen as West/Eurocentric from the very beginning, simply because it was created in and introduced from the West/Europe. Furthermore, in modern times, Chinese "world historians" have been trained in the arguably Eurocentric literature and scholarship of world history while under the influence of such an inferiority complex that "world history" has been seen not as "ours/Chinese," but as "theirs/foreign." Therefore, the reasoning goes, "we/Chinese" do not have the firsthand resources to study "world history," even though China has, of course, always been part of the world and world history – and has been at least as important as any other part, although this fact has sometimes been ignored or forgotten. That world history, as a category, has more often been treated within China as a synonym for "foreign history" also can be seen from the fact that there are two volumes of "Foreign history" and three volumes of "Chinese history" in the 32-volume Encyclopedia of China (*Zhongguo da bai ke quan shu*) (2009). In short, "Chinese history" and "world/foreign history" have been two separate disciplines in China from the very beginning, notwithstanding the presence of some brief Chinese history in published discussions of world history.

The first Chinese world historians were mostly those who studied abroad in the West (Europe and the United States) and Japan and returned to China to offer history courses under the heading of *Xi Yang Shi*, "a history of the West," or *Dong Yang Shi*, "a history of the East" (history/ies of Japan and other countries to the east of China). They had been trained in the scholarship of Western and Japanese writers and then introduced these world/foreign history/ies into China. Their Chinese students took over what they had learnt abroad and followed these approaches to lay the foundation of world history in China, in which "world history" and Chinese history developed into two institutionally separate disciplines/fields, in terms of resources, traditions, methodologies, theories, and frameworks.

At first, world history served mostly as a brief introduction to the history/ies of the rest of the world beside China, defined by major regions such as Europe, Asia, Africa, and the Americas (northern America, especially the United States, and southern/Latin America), or particularly important countries such as Britain, France, Germany, the United States, Japan, India, Egypt (or others, according to individual teachers' specialty and expertise). After the establishment in 1949 of the People's Republic of China, more and more importance was laid on world history for both ideological and educational reasons. In the 1950s, notions of wider world history through a social evolutionary lens came to be introduced from the Soviet Union, both by Russian/Soviet scholars who came to China to teach short, intensive courses in world history framed by Marxism and Leninism, and by Chinese scholars who had gone to the Soviet Union to be trained in this revolutionary scholarship. This new generation of world historians criticized their predecessors' ideology as "liberal" or "bourgeois/capitalist." The new world history was taught and studied in the light of Marxism-Leninism-Maoism, with an overriding emphasis on class struggle, international conflict and ideological confrontation. In the early 1960s, *A General History of the World* (Zhou and Wu 1962), written by Chinese world historians, was published in four volumes (ancient, medieval, modern, and contemporary times). It was the first world history textbook written by Chinese world historians – trained as they had been in Soviet scholarship and based on Soviet interpretations of world history.

In the decade of the Great Cultural Revolution from 1966 to 1976, world history textbooks (like much other prior scholarship) came under critique, and these first publications were reexamined in the light of new ideas about "antirevisionism" and "anti-imperialism." The first generation of Chinese world historians was criticized and mistreated for its supposedly bourgeois ideology and revisionism. From an academic perspective, world history teaching and studying in China was again "revolutionized" and cut off totally from international academic exchange during the subsequent ideological phobia (on both sides) during the Cold War. In China, "world history" became a closed knowledge system about the rest of the globe, defined either regionally or nationally, in which every question was assigned a standardized answer – one that was deemed correct, politically and ideologically. The task of "academic research/study" was to find these answers, and to write them correctly according to the terms of Marxism, Leninism and Mao Zedong Thought. The task of "teaching/education," unsurprisingly, was to transmit and instill these answers in students, who could be tested and judged entirely on the basis of how well they remembered the correct answers. This approach to education sent the message that there is only one correct answer to everything and the only thing people need to do is to memorize it through a rote kind of research/study. During the Cultural Revolution, all universities and colleges were closed to "do revolution," and most professors/teachers found themselves sent to factories or the countryside, where they were reeducated and revolutionized for several years. The gap between world history in China and that in international academic circles widened greatly thanks to the diminution of academic exchanges and the near-total lack of interaction in different ideological contexts.

Thanks to changes in state policy since the 1970s, particularly the move to new forms of "reform" and specifically an "opening-up policy," world history in China has changed dramatically again, this time under the pressure of modernization and globalization. It is safe to say that much academic writing in world history as well as contemporary social sciences in China has been developed in efforts to understand – out of a sort of inferiority complex – why it was the West, not China, that achieved modernization first, especially if "much of modern social science originated in efforts by late nineteenth- and twentieth-century Europeans to understand what made the economic development path of western Europe unique" (Pomeranz 2000: 3), a comparison sometimes considered by Chinese writers in terms of superior psychology. Ever since the differences between China and the West in terms of socioeconomic development and science and technology were finally realized empirically, Chinese social scientists, including world historians and Chinese historians, have tried their utmost to find out "what went wrong" in China and Chinese history from a consciously self-critical approach. And scholars in world history focused on what made the West unique and different from China in socioeconomic development and modernization to identify their/West/European "advantages" in comparison with our/Chinese "disadvantages." These efforts have resulted in the introduction of much famous Western scholarship to China, and in the rewriting of world history and foreign national histories according to or based on Western literature. For example, books written by L.S. Stavrianos, William H. McNeill, G. Barraclough, Immanuel Wallerstein, Andre Gunder Frank, J.H. Bentley, Kenneth Pomeranz, David Christian, and many others have been introduced into China and some of them have been published in Chinese translations. New textbooks of world history written and edited by famous Chinese world historians such as Wu Yujin, Qi Shirong, and others were published in the late 1980s and early 1990s, and a series on modernization edited by Luo Rongqu was published in the 1990s.

Comparative studies between China and the West in general, or "big powers" around the globe, have grown very popular in the context of this anxiety about modernization (or a "modernization complex"), as Chinese writers worked with the goal of finding out what China could learn from the West/Western countries in their experience of modernization, ideally so that shortcuts could avoid the mistakes made by or experienced in the developed countries. There was even a book (Tang Jin 2006) and a major 12-part TV series made by China Central Television on *The Rise of the Great Powers* in 2006 to explain why and how those "great powers," Portugal, Spain, the Netherlands, England, France, Germany, Russia, the United States, and Japan, came to be "modernized." This kind of research is misleading; it is not helpful to offer a utilitarian comparison of this sort and compare incomparable parts of global history. (See Adas, this volume.) So, it has been easy for Chinese world historians to adopt West/Eurocentrism as the mainstream theory or dominant paradigm and to overemphasize Western advantages, even though they simultaneously bristle at the marginalization and underestimation of China and other non-European countries produced in such narratives of global/world history. Academic research has been much more utilitarian and pragmatic than theoretic and original under these conditions. Most writers followed the Western ideas of concept, theory and pattern to explore Western advantages that had already been identified by Western scholars and forgot a simple fact: China had functioned differently in the same global context, and hence some local advantages might have been disadvantages in global interaction, and vice versa. For instance, China was an advanced and modernized empire in European eyes during the Middle Ages and early modern times. But the disadvantages of some small European countries became advantages in modern global stories of interaction, while the advantages of some big Asian countries such as China, India and the Ottoman Empire turned out to be disadvantages when seen from a noncentric and holistic perspective (about which, more below).

Since there are more academic exchanges today in global/world history between China and the rest of the world, especially with the West, Chinese global/world historians are trying their best to narrow the academic gap developed during the Cold War. Many world history textbooks, monographs and articles on histories of particular countries, especially those in Western Europe and the United States, have been published recently, and research is proceeding on foreign areas alongside Chinese history – from many different perspectives in a more global context. Centers for world history, or for area and national studies, have been established in most universities and most of these centers work on national or provincial research projects or programs sponsored by central or provincial governments. For example, at my own institution, Nankai University, there are sites such as the Center for Modern Global History (where I am a fellow), the Center for Chinese Social History, the Center for Latin American Studies, the Institute of American History and Culture, and other smaller centers based in the College of History, and also an independent Institute of Japanese Studies. Similar centers and institutes for historical study are present in most top universities, including Peking (Beijing) University, Tsinghua (Qinghua) University, People's University of China, Capital Normal University, Beijing Normal University, Guangzhou University, Wuhan University, Nanjing University, Fudan University, and Northeast Normal University, to name only a few.

National associations of world history and foreign national history, as well as those of specialized methodological/disciplinary areas such as economics, foreign relations, culture, religion, and so on, have been set up to encourage cooperative research and academic exchange. There are provincial and local associations for history, too. Most of these associations are supported or sponsored by the Chinese government, the Ministry of Education in particular. More and more scholars of world/foreign history are going abroad to study and do research, and more and more academic exchanges are underway, both individually and cooperatively. Scholars trained overseas, and with academic experience abroad, especially in the West, have been introducing the latest scholarship into China. At the same time, more foreign scholars in world history and other fields are coming to China to teach and give lectures. International academic conferences on world history in general, and various area or national studies in particular, have been held every year at different levels throughout China, with the participation of scholars from all over the world. More Chinese world historians, too, have gone abroad to attend international conferences and workshops. In short, the gap between Chinese world historians and foreign world historians has narrowed, even though there are still many differences in theory, methodology, structure, focus, interpretation and narrative. But global/world history in China is being Westernized in both resources and scholarship.

As a student of global/world history in China for more than 30 years, I have experienced and witnessed most of these changes in theory, methodology, structure and focus of both textbooks and scholarship. I have developed a suspicion about what I have been taught, and about what I am teaching about global/world history, because I too can become confused whenever I change my perspective from a national to a global one. The more I read and think, the more I find out that a "glober" perspective is badly needed – for a global history for all "globers," my name for all people living on the globe. (I choose not to use "global citizens," because "citizen" is a modern concept, intertwined with ideas of nationalism, and there are still many globers who do not have any "citizenship" of a particular nation on the globe.) I have always had the sense that something is wrong or missing in global/world history because of the preoccupations with, and prejudices of, nationalism, and also the fuzziness of what I call "centrism" in global/world history.

I started with the question "Is global history centered?" when I wrote to Andre Gunder Frank to criticize his simple replacing of Eurocentrism with Sinocentrism in *ReORIENT* (Frank 1998). Instead I have argued for "a noncentric and holistic approach to global history," initially in a presentation at Northeastern University's World History Center in December 2002, and later developed this idea into a chapter, "Teaching modern global history at Nankai: A noncentric and holistic approach" (in Manning 2007), with the assistance of Frank, and also of Patrick Manning, Alfred Andrea, Andrea McElderry, Jerry Bentley, and Peter Gran.

In my view, there has been no globally received single center for most of global history, but instead many "centers" of civilization are to be found, scattered or distributed here and there all over the globe (e.g., Christendom, the Islamic world, the Chinese/Confucian world, to name only a few). It is understandable that human beings are self-oriented and egocentric, a kind of cultural narcissism. So the view of "centrality" attached to a race/nation, a nation-state, or a culture/civilization is, in a sense, a form of cultural narcissism. This may be one of the reasons why global/world history has been understood, explained, taught or written in different "centric" perspectives. Egocentrism can be naturally developed into racial, national, and cultural/civilization-centric perspectives. This is seen fully in the cases of Sinocentrism, West/Eurocentrism or any other centrisms in global history. A person or people feels superior or inferior in comparing themselves with others, either consciously or unconsciously, from an egocentric or centric perspective. These psychological responses matter in global history because these feelings determine what the elite and the masses are seen to do in global history and everyday life in a kingdom/empire/nation-state, according to their perceived superiority or inferiority (based on their place and function in a given regional or global context).

In the modern period, centrism has been a product of newly born nationalisms in those "big countries" or "nation-states" competing for global hegemony. It is a difficult task for global historians to take a "glober" perspective because it means pursuing real de-centrism and de-nationalism from a noncentric and holistic perspective. Global historians' own nationalist identities and standpoints have led to particular approaches and methods. When we were discussing "nationalism" and the "international," Andre Gunder Frank made a similar point when he wrote to me:

> And there are hardly any nation states. The job of historians – what they are paid for – is to create and implant a "nationalism" which is in fact a "statism." The state pays them to do that and to invent nations/nationalities that don't even exist. Of the nearly 200 United "Nations" – all are states, and not more than a handful, a dozen, have only one, or even a dominant, nation. (email, Dec. 13, 2002)

This so-called nationalism prevents global historians from developing a "glober" perspective on global history, because they have been tasked to demonstrate their "national" or regional superiorities and advantages – consider, for example, such instances as *The Rise of the West* (McNeill 1963), *The European Miracle* (Jones 1981), the "core–periphery" in *The Modern World-System* (Wallerstein 1974), *The Wealth and Poverty of Nations* (Landes 1998), *The Clash of Civilizations* (Huntington 1996),

The Great Divergence (Pomeranz 2000), and the recent "Rise of China" and "Chinese Miracle" in the ongoing global crisis and global disequilibrium. How can one understand global history objectively from a "nationalist" perspective?

It is senseless to talk about centrism whenever an organic system is taken as a whole – within which it matters that interdependence, interaction, contingency and conjuncture of parts functioned differently for the development of the whole in general and each part in particular. In the case of the field of global history, all the forces of social physics work together to create a global disequilibrium that changes global history contingently. What happens in global history, in what I call a "socialquake," is a result of all social forces – far more than the "core/center" – just as an earthquake is caused by an interaction of physical forces from other places. Here I draw inspiration from Zhuangzi's idea of *You Dai Er Ran* (interdependence/contingence),[1] Engels's concept of the "resultant" in 1890 (Engels 1958), Nash's "game theory," and Hawking's "theory of the universe," as well as "chaos theory," "fuzziology," "holism," and "physics." The noncentric and holistic approach argues that global history has been determined by an all-inclusive global disequilibrium caused by many, various social forces. Global disequilibrium is a disorder or a crisis caused by the combined result of all forces (ecological, economic, political, military, social, cultural, religious, psychological, etc.) in global history. In other words, the global disequilibrium is a global crisis.

The Chinese translation of "crisis" is two characters. One, *Wei*, means "chaos," and the other, *Ji*, "chance," indicating that chaos provides a chance for change. It is global disequilibrium that has forced development and shaped global history as well as national histories. For instance, the Pax Mongolica, the westward expansion of the Islamic Ottoman Empire, Europe's trade imbalance with the East, socioeconomic problems caused by natural and man-made disasters (the Black Death, wars, religious conflicts, etc.) in Europe, as well as the psychological temptation of the Orient occasioned by Marco Polo's book in Europe, and many other changes combined to create a global result that led to global disequilibrium: a combination of mutual attraction and exclusion (racial, cultural, religious, economic, political, military, etc.) among various civilizations because of the struggle for survival. Several poor and small West European countries – Spain, Portugal, the Netherlands, and England in particular – had to go to sea in order to survive. The result was worldwide exploration, and thereafter the domino effect of modern history. Obviously, however, those small countries were not initially a global "core/center" in any meaningful sense. Pomeranz is correct in saying: "Our perception of an interacting system from which one part benefited more than others does not in itself justify calling that part the 'center' and assuming that it is the unshaped shaper of everything else. We will see, instead, vectors of influence moving in various directions" (2000: 10).

It is problematic to ask what made the west "the West," or, to put it another way, what made the West "rise." Recently, there has been a tendency to deconstruct this hermetic "West" in such scholarship such as *The East in the West* (Goody 1996) and *The Eastern Origins of Western Civilization* (Hobson 2004) – writings aiming to demonstrate the presence of Oriental or non-European elements interwoven into "the West." Goody and Hobson highlighted this mixed nature of "Western civilization." And neither are the East, the South, and the North isolated "civilizations" in cultural origin and composition. They are all hybrid mixes, and what makes them different is their unique composition and development in an ever-changing global context: "globers" have always moved around all over the globe to find better places to live since the very beginning of human history. Global migration and interchange between and among civilizations have made each modern "nation-state," or culture/civilization/race/ nation/people/state/country, a unique mix. None is pure, but each is unique. The diversity of any individual nation in race and culture is a special and specific result of historical contingency. Where did "the English" come from? Who are "the Chinese"? Is there a "typical" national citizen of the United States? Questions like these are difficult to deal with academically and practically. "The Oriental West" (Hobson 2004) thus has its counterparts in the East, the North and the South. Current manifestations of culture, or "civilizations," are only a unique mix developed contingently in a regional/global context of diversity in unity. (See McKeown, this volume.)

During the half-century since its initial publication, McNeill's *The Rise of the West* has been challenged from many different perspectives. Toynbee frankly pointed out in his later years:

> The West's ascendancy over the rest of the world during the last three centuries has been reflected in the recent Western way of looking at mankind's history as all leading up to the modern West. I think this West-centered view of history is a palpable case of subjectivism; it seems to me to misrepresent the reality and, in so far as it distorts it, to make it unintelligible. (1974: 34–35)

Frank and Marks tried to recast this view of the West by approaching it from an oriental context, as in Frank's subtitle, *Global Economy in the Asian Age* (Frank 1998; Marks 2007). And Peter Gran tried to go *Beyond Eurocentrism* (1996) and replace "the rise of the West" with *The Rise of the Rich* (2009) in a more global perspective. Yet ironically, even Chinese world historians today are still for the most part Eurocentric, because of their training and the geopolitical/cultural inferiority complex mentioned above. For example, some recent Chinese world historians have written: "In the fifteenth and sixteenth centuries, when the old China was racing ahead in the Middle Ages, the West somehow caught up and stood silently beside us on the same starting-line" (Mao Lei *et al.* 1991: 1). And then they have tried to find out why and how China was left behind, and how the West surpassed the East, in an analysis similar to that offered by Pomeranz in *The Great Divergence* (2000). In my view, by contrast, China and the West have never been "on the same starting-line," and thus there is no comparability between China and the West because it is an interpretive dead end to compare two incomparable parts of global history. They functioned differently in the division of labor of global economy/ history, just as different as the proverbial trunk, leg, ear, tusk or stomach of an elephant. How can we compare two incomparable parts of a whole?

In global history, several socialquake "bands" were formed from the internal interaction of parts within the globe. For instance, the changing balance of power between civilizations during the period 1500–1900 resulted from global disequilibrium, which shaped the histories of its parts (empire/kingdom/newly born nation-state) in particular, in the light of the social physics of convergence, contingency, conjuncture, interdependence, and interaction of various forces in various parts in the globe. This resulted in socialquakes contingently arising along the coasts of Western Europe, the Atlantic coast of the Americas, western and sub-Saharan Africa, the Pacific basin (China, Japan, Southeast Asia, the western Americas, and Australia), and the Indian Ocean basin (India, southeast Asia and eastern Africa). In other words, what happened in Western Europe was not a European phenomenon or an internal development in Europe but a contingent result of interaction of all parts in the globe in a three-dimensional global history.

Having suggested a theory contrary to the received concept that the "'Fall of the East' preceded the 'Rise of the West'" (Abu-Lughod 1989: 361), I further argue that the "general rise of socialquake bands" that caused global disequilibrium facilitated the "rise of the West" as only part of a general rise. From the sixteenth to the mid-nineteenth centuries, there was a "general rise" along those bands, in which most "Oriental" countries/empires rose to their peaks either relatively or absolutely. For example, the Ottoman Empire, the closest "Oriental" country to the West, was expanding westwards, growing into a huge empire embracing parts of Asia, Europe and Africa around the Mediterranean. The Moghul Empire (1526–1707) in India had long been attractive to Westerners because of its wealth. China in the Ming (1368–1644) and the Qing (1644–1911) dynasties was enjoying one of the golden ages in Chinese history. Japan developed rapidly in the Tokugawa Shogunate (1603–1867). In my view it is the "rise of Oriental empires" in general that pushed and facilitated the oft-discussed "rise of the West." And the subsequent exploitations and colonization of African coasts and American hinterlands, along with the "rise of the United States" and the establishment of Latin American countries, also helped to further impel the "rise of the West." Could you image a modern England or any "nation-states" in Western Europe without thinking of what happened in the rest of the globe? Hence I cannot agree with most Chinese world historians in their interpretations of nationalist modernization approached in a way defined by the "big countries."

From this noncentric and holistic perspective, the structure of "center" and "core–periphery" is neither reasonable nor persuasive when the question becomes: what is the "center/core" and what is the "periphery" in "the rise of the West" and Eurocentrism? For instance, during the early stages of "the rise of the West" (circa 1400–1800), those "small" countries, Portugal, Spain, the Netherlands and England in particular, were all in a position of "periphery" in the wider Afro-Eurasian landmass, geographically, culturally, and economically (in terms of chain of demand–supply and consumer–producer). Actually, they functioned only as the middlemen between the producers in the East and the consumers of manufactured luxury goods (cotton cloth, silk, porcelain, tea and spices, to select only a few) in the West, recalling what the English East India Company and the Dutch East India Company did and how they made their fortunes. When small Western European countries developed and "modernized" their economies as their functional position changed in global markets and interstate balances of power, they were still parts of a wider global interdependence in which they relied much more on the rest of the globe than the other way around in terms of global capital, markets, resources and labor.

From the perspective of global social history, then, it was Indian cotton weavers, Chinese silk-makers and porcelain producers, and many other manufacturers who forced some Europeans, some English people to be specific, to be creative and to devise import substitutes or knock-offs of oriental goods that had produced the long-existing trade imbalance between the West (especially England) and the East. Only colonial producers in the Americas and Africa could provide Europeans with the needed silver, gold and other products to buy or exchange luxury goods from the East. As a matter of fact, labor, that is, workers, farmers or slaves, built the base for daily life and hence should not be marginalized or peripheralized in global history.

In my view "the West" was, for most of this period, only a small part of the global picture. Its superiority to the Muslims, the Indians and the Chinese was problematic at best, and its "centric/core/dominant" position was no better than arguable. Just think of how many heavy pressures Western Europe faced from the East in terms of economy, trade, military, culture and politics, and how long it took for the Europeans to grasp opportunities to catch up or to be "modernized" during the processes dubbed by later historians Renaissance, Reformation, Exploration, Enlightenment, Industrial Revolution, Democratic Revolution, and social improvement. This gives us a better understanding of global disequilibrium in global history in a full picture as well as in its 3-D image. In other words, crises of this global disequilibrium provided an opportunity for the "rise of the West" along the wider Atlantic socialquake band.

Although I do not wish to overstate the role that the West/Europe has played in global history, one could fairly say that it has had a positive and significant position, fully as important as those of the rest of the globe. When I expressed disagreement with Frank's efforts to challenge Eurocentrism by overemphasizing Asia and thus underestimating Europeans' activities and functions as "part and parcel of a single global world economy," Frank replied, "Yes, but prior to my book all others claimed the opposite, which is much less true. I err a bit perhaps in overemphasizing what has previously been totally neglected" (email exchange, Dec. 13, 2002). Frank went on to argue that

> Britain was NOT the workshop of the world – with an export deficit, growing every year from 1816 to 1913, and the "rise" of the Brits was due to its favored position in the multi-lateral trade system of interlinked trade triangles of which the China–India–Britain opium triangle was of course the most important if only because it was the drain from India that supported the whole system including European investment in the USA and the Brit Dominions and Argentina. (letter to author, early 2001)

The global disequilibrium I perceive between 1900 and 1950 could be portrayed as a military Armageddon under an ideological cover in the light of political, military and economical conflicts. The game began with a contest between "democracy" and "autocracy" among "capitalist" countries but ended "accidentally," with a confrontation between "capitalism" and "socialism/communism." Many "backward" countries, led by the USSR, made their own way in the chaos of war, and grasped the opportunities in the crisis to establish a bloc of socialist countries – and in exchange obtained rapid development and expansion. On the other hand, "capitalist" countries, neither winners nor losers, were badly hurt and faced the tough task of rebuilding in a shrinking bloc. In this global interaction, who was the "center" and who was the "periphery"?

As a crucially important element/force of "social physics," psychology interacts with other elements contingently and interdependently. For example, people often overreact in an emergency or crisis when they are scared, as in a stock market crash or financial chaos that shakes markets and causes job losses nationally or globally. Those overreactions – selling shares and protectionism – can only make things worse and cause a vicious cycle. What is more terrible than real economic difficulties is that people lose their confidence during a depression. "The only thing we have to fear is fear itself," as Franklin Roosevelt put it. Those who live on credit and hope for future gains are suffering psychologically as well as physically in global crisis. It is not easy for them to get away from the shadow of depression.

Global history demonstrates that superiority or inferiority is but a temporary and passing psychology and phenomenon. As an actor, each part of the globe has its designated position in terms of superiority or inferiority at any given time. It is only a matter of time, but the timing matters. After the Cold War, global changes developed new balances of power both regionally and globally, and have brought about a new global disequilibrium as well as new attitudes of superiority or inferiority.

We are now amidst this process of global disequilibrium, which is shaping our common human future dramatically and significantly. The global economic crisis, which started from the United States, is changing people's attitudes of superiority or inferiority and their prospects or predictions about the future, producing new invocations of optimism and pessimism. Perhaps, this time, people from all the world's nations can realize that all people and peoples, just like those in Noah's Ark, are but collaborators in a common venture and go on to establish a fully "glober" identity. We as globers should learn from a better understanding of those previous global disequilibriums which resulted in new balances of power or new global orders in the past, and seize the present opportunity. In any event, to cope with today's global issues together, we globers must understand our common past first – to help each other tide over the crisis, to realize we are all on the same boat, and to work for our common future and gain a new confidence as globers rather than in terms of national superiority or inferiority.

One of the primary historical missions arising from the study of global history is to establish this glober identity or a wider vision associated with such a noncentric and holistic perspective. Global historians aim to do this by providing a better understanding and explanation of global history, from a glober perspective.

Recently, globers have been haunted by so many worldwide issues that they are very worried about the future of humanity. Where are we heading? What does our future hold? It is a truism to say that there are many possibilities and myriad uncertainties. As Wallerstein wrote in 1999:

> The third premise is that the modern world-system, as a historical system, has entered into a terminal crisis and is unlikely to exist in fifty years. However, since its outcome is uncertain, we do not know whether the resulting system (or systems) will be better or worse than the one in which we are living, but we do know that the period of transition will be a terrible time of troubles, since the stakes of the transition are so high, the outcome so uncertain, and the ability of small inputs to affect the outcome so great. (1999: 1)

This prospect seems different from what he wrote 25 years earlier, when he predicted: "This would constitute a third possible form of world-system, a socialist world government" (1974: 348). He grew more despondent during the most recent global economic crisis when he repeatedly emphasized that at the end of the current world-system, 25 years hence, there would be nothing particularly good to follow; that one could only hope for the lesser of evils (see his speech at the international conference on Andre Gunder Frank's Legacy of Critical Social Science, held at the University of Pittsburgh in April 2008).

The growing role of the G8 and the wider G20 groups of countries at the turn of the twenty-first century has meant further important developments in this global disequilibrium/crisis. It has been posited, and widely accepted, that the G8 is "the core/center" of the world that controls world affairs. In the middle of the 1990s, I asked a group of world-systems specialists whether they thought China would be among the core states in 50 years. (This was at a conference convened by a group of scholars from Wallerstein's center who were paying a visit to Nankai University.) The answer was negative: these scholars did not think China or any other peripheral countries would become a core state, even over such a protracted timeframe, despite the already evident changes in China since the reform and opening-up policies. They instead emphasized that the core states had been Western countries (at least if Japan is included as a sort of Westernized oriental one) since the formation of the core–periphery structure – and thus they were likely to be Western countries for a long time. Actually, the global disequilibrium/crisis itself facilitates the development of G20 and a new approach to global affairs and issues, one in which the core–periphery perspective does not work very well in shedding light on global issues such as financial crises, global warming, terrorism, trade wars, and many others. Is the G20 "the core/center" of the globe? Does the G20 provide a new forum to discuss and solve global issues from an approach other than a core–periphery one?

The foregoing noncentric and holistic approach mainly analyzes the formation and structure of our current global disequilibrium. Global history is neither a sum of histories of separate nation-states nor a compilation of thematic histories (of economy, politics, society, diplomacy, the military, culture, science and technology, etc.). It is, instead, focused on the cause and effect of interdependence/contingency and interaction/conjuncture of various forces from a global perspective – to offer a proper understanding and description of the overall trajectory of global history as a whole, and as seen in three dimensions. So, the causes of global disequilibrium are explored in a global context rather than nationalist perspectives. It deals with a mix of various forces of diversity in unity, and concentrates on their interdependence and interaction: a mix of relations of production, a mix of social relations, a mix of political systems, a mix of cultures, a mix of religions, a mix of races, a mix of ideologies, etc. The internal contradictions of global history have been based on these mixes, which generate conflict and cooperation and form global equilibriums and disequilibriums. Coexistence and civilizational conflicts in the biosphere have also changed the ecological environment, with a strong impact on global history.

Global history is a contemporary understanding, explanation and description of what happened across the globe as a whole. Notably, most of the terminologies, notions, concepts and theories for global history were developed in Europe in the eighteenth and nineteenth centuries, and thus originate from a Eurocentric perspective, thus inevitably expressing temporal, regional, racial, class and ideological limitations. For example, "the West," "the East," "Modern History," "the Old World," and "the New World" may all be problematic/debatable in the light of a global history. When I, for example, used the word "international" in a paper, Andre Gunder Frank wrote to me:

> The very language is wrong. It refers to inter-nations that don't exist. And it supposes that we start with pieces/parts A & B that then take up inter-relations between them. Of course this is totally counterfactual and anti-historic. But we don't even have a vocabulary to express the globe from which we start and which breaks down into parts. (email, Dec. 13, 2002)

Frank is correct: we need to develop a new terminology and theory to enable a better understanding of global history.

In China, too, world/global history is at a similar crossroads, one that provides possibilities for new development and improvement. Mainstream structures and theories introduced from the West still have strong influences on textbooks and scholarship. Recent changes in the field of world/global history are still new to most Chinese world historians trained under Western (Eurocentric) notions, because the educational and knowledge system is relatively closed. Global history in China should include Chinese history, of course, and Chinese historians who can understand Chinese history in a global context instead of only through a nationalist perspective. Global history in China needs to be globalized, rather than Westernized, in a process of academic exchanges between Chinese global historians and their counterparts in the rest of the world – especially in overlooked issues and blind spots of global history as a whole. Meanwhile, global history itself also needs to be globalized – to share and express a global identity rather than many national ones.

Global history is a huge project that needs to include not only the wisdom of the West and the East, but also that of the South and the North. This is a task for all global historians, who need to find proper approaches and methods to cooperate with scholars of other fields in both social sciences and natural sciences. It seems that scholars in all relevant fields hold pieces of a jigsaw puzzle, one that can form a three-dimensional big global history. Globalized global histories are what we need. History, both national and world/global, has often highlighted rulers, elites, the rich, the strong, winners, celebrities, the core/center, and the unique. It is time for global historians to more fully incorporate the ruled, the poor, the weak, the losers, the marginalized, and the masses; without these social forces, the picture of global history is not complete or perfect. The newly founded Network of Global and World History Organizations (NOGWHISTO, July 2008), which combines other bodies – the WHA (World History Association), ENIUGH (European Network in Universal and Global History), AAWH (Asian Association of World Historians) and ANGH (African Network in Global History) – is certainly a great step towards the creation of such a globalized global history.

Note

1   "Shade said to Shadow, 'A little while ago, you were moving; and now you are standing still. A little while ago, you were sitting down; and now you are getting up. Why all this indecision?' Shadow replied, 'Don't I have to depend on others to be what I am? Don't others also have to depend on something else to be what they are? My dependence is like that of the snake on his skin or of the cicada on his wings. How can I tell why I do this, or why I do that?'" (Zhuangzi 1974: 48).

References

Abu-Lughod, Janet L. 1989. *Before European Hegemony: The World System AD 1250–1350*. New York: Oxford University Press.

Encyclopedia of China. 2009. *Zhongguo da bai ke quan shu*. 2nd edn. Beijing: Encyclopedia of China Publishing House.

Engels, Frederick. 1958. To J. Bloch, London, September 21–22, 1890. In Karl Marx and Frederick Engels, *Selected Works in Two Volumes*, vol. 2, p. 489. Moscow: Foreign Languages Publishing House.

Frank, Andre Gunder. 1998. *ReORIENT: Global Economy in the Asian Age*. Berkeley: University of California Press.

Goody, Jack. 1996. *The East in the West*. Cambridge: Cambridge University Press.

Gran, Peter. 1996. *Beyond Eurocentrism: A New View of Modern World History*. Syracuse, NY: Syracuse University Press.

Gran, Peter. 2009. *The Rise of the Rich: A New View of Modern World History*. Syracuse, NY: Syracuse University Press.

Hobson, John M. 2004. *The Eastern Origins of Western Civilization*. Cambridge: Cambridge University Press.

Huntington, Samuel P. 1996. *The Clash of Civilizations and the Remaking of World Order*. New York: Simon & Schuster.

Jones, Eric. 1981. *The European Miracle: Environments, Economies, and Geopolitics in the History of Europe and Asia*. Cambridge: Cambridge University Press.

Landes, David S. 1998. *The Wealth and Poverty of Nations: Why Some Are So Rich and Some So Poor*. New York: W.W. Norton.

Manning, P., ed. 2007. *Global Practice in World History*. Princeton: Markus Wiener.

Mao Lei *et al.*, eds. 1991. *Zhong xi wu bai nian bi jiao* [China/West comparative studies in the last 500 years]. Beijing: Chinese Workers' Publishing House.

Marks, Robert B. 2007. *The Origins of the Modern World: A Global and Ecological Narrative from the Fifteenth to the Twenty-First Century*. 2nd edn. New York: Rowman & Littlefield.

McNeill, William H. 1963. *The Rise of the West*. Chicago: University of Chicago Press.

Pomeranz, Kenneth. 2000. *The Great Divergence: Europe, China, and the Making of the Modern World Economy*. Princeton: Princeton University Press.

Tang Jin. 2006. *Daguo jueqi* [The rise of the great powers]. Beijing: People's Publishing House.

Toynbee, Arnold J. 1974. *Toynbee on Toynbee: A Conversation between Arnold J. Toynbee and G.R. Urban*. Oxford: Oxford University Press.

Wallerstein, Immanuel. 1974. *The Modern World-System, vol. 1*. New York: Academic Press.

Wallerstein, Immanuel. 1999. *The End of the World As We Know It: Social Science for the Twenty-First Century*. Minneapolis: University of Minnesota Press.

Zhou Yiliang and Wu Yujin, eds. 1962. *Shi jie tong sh* [A general history of the world], vols 1–4. Beijing: People's Publishing House.

Zhuangzi [Chuang Tsu]. 1974. *Inner Chapters*, trans Gai-Fu Feng and Jane English. New York: Vintage.

CHAPTER TWENTY-EIGHT

Historicizing the World in Northeast Asia

JIE-HYUN LIM

The Configuration of the National and the Global

Marc Bloch's saying that "all history is comparative history" hints at the transnationality of the nationalist imagination, for comparative history throws into relief the peculiarities of a given national history and thus helps to essentialize it. Indeed a nationalist imagination can be fed only in the transnational space. National history is also a product of worldwide cultural interactions and transnational discourses, which demand "an attempt at a globalized (not total) description" (Said 1994: 233). It would be more appropriate to stress the configuration of national *and* world history rather than an either/or rivalry. This configuration helps to position national histories sequentially in a linear developmental trajectory of historicism. In the sequence of national histories, at least as these came into being in academic history-writing during the nineteenth century, Western countries occupy the higher positions, to be followed and taken as models by backward Easterners.[1] Thus, making national histories in East Asia was not conceivable without referring to a world history based on the dichotomy of "normative" Western History and a "deviated" Eastern variation. (See Pomeranz and Segal, this volume.)

A history of cultural encounters between "East" and "West" shows how non-Europeans have been obliged to respond to the conceptual categories brought into play by "Western" modernity. Conscripted to modernity at large, willingly or unwillingly, "Easterners" rendered themselves the objects and agents of Western modernity, which was thought to become global over time. East Asian historians have tried to evidence their civilizational potential by finding European elements such as rationalism, science, freedom, equality, and industrialism in their own national histories. Any national history that suggested a lack of "Western" modernity could be branded as the history of "history-less people." Modern historiography in Japan and Korea was thus partly a struggle for recognition of the national *raison d'être* by showing up their national potential for modernist development against skeptical Westerners. This struggle for recognition could be successful only when it was written in a way that was intelligible and

A Companion to World History, First Edition. Edited by Douglas Northrop.
© 2012 Blackwell Publishing Ltd. Published 2012 by Blackwell Publishing Ltd.

appealing to Western readers. In order to satisfy their expectations, the East and the West, the Orient and the Occident had to be configured and structured into a grammar familiar to European history.

The struggle for Western recognition gave rise to a consequential Eurocentrism in the East. Writing national history in East Asia was a voluntary act of inscribing Eurocentrism on its own past (Lim 2008). Even in search of anti-colonial nationalist agendas and historical peculiarities, East Asian historians have turned the European past into a hegemonic mirror reflecting their own national past. The trajectory of modern historiography of *and* in East Asia is imprinted with the traces of "the attempt to posit the identity of one's own ethnicity or nationality in terms of the gap between it and the putative West, that is, to create the history of one's own nation through the dynamics of attraction and repulsion from the West" (Sakai 1997: 50). The configuration of norm and deviation, of East and West, and of the national and the global is crucial to understanding the historicist complicity of national history and world history. Paradoxically, therefore, world history functioned as a nationalist rationale in East Asia. However, the accommodation of national history or even the promotion of nationalist agendas through world history is hardly unique to East Asia.

The question of "why wasn't Germany England," posed by Ralf Dahrendorf in the German *Sonderweg* debates, originated in the same schematic configuration: English history of a universal/normal/democratic path had been posited as a yardstick against which to measure German history of a particular/abnormal/fascist path. Viewed from a "problem space" rather than a geopositivistic sense, the demarcation of normative modernity in England and deviated modernity in Germany overlaps the boundary of "West" and "East" (Lim 2010). "Western Civilization," designed as a part of the core curriculum of many American universities, is another good example. The "Western Civilization" course was created to encourage the national integration of massive numbers of new immigrants of diverse nationalities during World War I. The history of "Western Civilization" presented the United States as the culmination of a civilized "Western" tradition and imprinted the American national identity with more "Western" than European identities (Dunn 2007). This "patriotic world history" to highlight and celebrate American political and ideological values and its parochial understanding of humankind's history has a century-long tradition (Bentley 2005).

In parallel with Eurocentric world history, Asia-centric world history also contributed to consolidating a nationalist rationale in East Asia. Confronted by the dilemma of a consequential Eurocentrism in making national histories, East Asian historians appealed repeatedly to the historico-political slogans of anti-Western Occidentalism, perhaps best represented by Asiatic internationalism. (Examples include the pre–World War II discourses of "pan-Asianism" and a "Greater East Asia Co-Prosperity Sphere," and the postwar discourses of an Asiatic value-system and East Asian Community.) From the beginning, discourses of an internationalist Asia have been loaded with nationalist repugnance, impulses, and aspirations. What is most revealing in the trajectory of regional histories is the discursive complicity between the Eurocentric Orientalism of "Western Civilization" and the anti-Western Occidentalism of "Asian Civilization" in promoting the idea of civilization as a self-regulating entity. This reflection suggests the urgent task of problematizing the trilateral complicity of national, regional (Oriental) and world (Western) history in abusing history for a nationalist rationale.[2] This chapter thus explores world history as a domain of both scholarship and education in Japan and Korea in conjunction with their respective national histories.

From World History to National History

World history came to Japan in the 1870s with the *Meiji Ishin* (Meiji Regeneration). The Japanese government took the initiative to introduce world history in the name of *Bankokushi*, meaning "the history of all countries of the world." The stress was laid on providing information about current world affairs rather than on studying the histories of others. Its aim was to introduce Western things to Japan in order to help the Japanese nation adapt to new conditions and enter the gate of civilization as quickly as possible. Among the various books of "world history" and "universal history," the most popular one initially was *Bankokushi* (1876), a Japanese translation of Samuel Goodrich's *Universal History on the Basis of Geography* (1870). This book was a simple compilation of many histories, dealing with every region on Earth, like a travel guidebook. Other *Bankokushi* books carried the Eurocentric messages more explicitly than Goodrich's book. For example, William Swinton's *Outlines of World History* viewed world history as the histories of the European people (Aryan races) that led the progress of civilization. (See Liu, this volume.) The Swinton line of *Bankokushi* was called "Civilization History" and its Eurocentric interpretation of world history became dominant in Japan during the 1880s (Minamizuka 2007: 190–191).

These world history textbooks thus preceded the first national history textbooks. It was at the request of the bureau of the Paris International Exhibition that the first national history of Japan, *Nihonshiryaku* (A brief history of Japan), appeared in 1878. The finalized version of the text, *Kokushigan* (View of national history), was adopted as an official history textbook in 1888 by the newly created history department of Tokyo Imperial University. Thus, the first Japanese national history and official history textbook had "Western readers" as its primary target. The first book on the history of Japanese art, *Histoire de l'art Japon*, was actually published first in French, at the request of the International Exhibition bureau in 1900 (Takagi 1989: 74). The motivation was to glorify the Japanese state by highlighting its national heritage and encouraging "our own artistic spirit" to keep abreast of European standards. The cognitive sequence from the world to the nation was demonstrated also by the work of Fukuzawa Yukichi. This champion of modernity in Meiji Japan uttered the famous dictum that "knowledge of oneself develops in direct proportion to the knowledge of others: the more we know about them (the West), the more we care about our own destiny" (Kondo 2007: 117).

The Japanese scholar Kuroita Katsumi personifies this idea. Contrary to his contemporary reputation as the founder of positivist scientific history in the 1880s and 1890s, he was not afraid to declare that if historical sites can stimulate the people's patriotic emotion, then they deserve to be protected as historically important sites – regardless of their historical value. (See Witz, this volume.) In his opinion it was just as important to encourage national sentiments and patriotism as it was to promote objective historical study. Kuroita's encounter with the European way of making nations drove his passion for national history. What impressed him most during his visit to Europe in 1908–1910 was the story and historical sites of William Tell. Kuroita was not concerned with whether this reflected the historical truth or not. He believed that insofar as it inspired patriotism among the common people in Switzerland, this history could serve the state (Lee 2004). Japanese positivistic historiography, influenced by the methods of Leopold von Ranke, would develop in parallel with this sort of political commitment to the nation-state. The myth of an "objective truth" in history, in other words, presumed that the nationalist inclination was real.

Japanese intellectuals of the Enlightenment thus found themselves in a dilemma: the more they became familiar with European history, the wider the gap grew between Japan and Europe. The more they tried to find symmetrical equivalents to the history of the West, the more they had to suffer from the sense of a lack. When historicism changed vertical evolutionary time into the horizontal space of an "imaginative geography," for example, Japan discovered that it lagged behind the unilinear development scheme of world history, and it had to be placed in the Orient in comparison with Europe. To escape from this dilemma, Japanese modern historiography adopted its own Orientalist strategy of highlighting the Japanese differences from the rest of Asia. Inventing its own "Orient" – of Asian neighbors – was a way to make up for that lack. By inventing Japan's own Orient, Japanese historians let China and Chosŏn (a historical name of Korea between 1392 and 1897) take the place of Japan (in Western views), and allowed Japan to join the West in the imaginative geography of the period. Thus, *toyoshi* (history of Orient) was established as a Japanese version of Orientalism. It aimed at removing the Japanese image of the invented Orient by capturing European elements in Japanese history and inventing its own Orient of China and Chosŏn.

Toyoshi as a regional history was intended to mediate between national/Japanese and world/Western history, but in fact it was Japan's own formulation of the "Orient." In 1894 Naka Michiyo proposed a division of world history into Occidental and Oriental history in the middle school curriculum, and the Ministry of Education accepted this proposal in 1896. Perhaps not coincidentally, the establishment of *toyoshi* had the Sino-Japanese War as its historical background, an episode which served to enhance Japanese national pride because of the victory over a traditional Great Power. Following the subsequent victory in the Russo-Japanese War (1904–1905), historical pedagogy came to be divided into three departments: national, Asian, and Western history (Tanaka 1993). This tripartite structure of history helped to elevate the strategic location of Japan into closer connection with the "West." That noble dream of de-Asianizing and Europeanizing Japan could be well imagined through a trilateral discursive complicity of national (Japanese), regional (Oriental/Asian), and world (Occidental/Western) history. This tripartite structure still dominates the institutions of historical research and education in Japan and Korea today.

World history was also thriving in late nineteenth-century Korea, but here it was based on the crisis, not the surge into prominence, of the nation. The first world history textbook written in Korean was *The Short History of the World*, published in 1896. Many other works of Western history were published in translation, including *The Outline of English History* (1896), *A Short History of Russia* (1898), *History of American Independence* (1899), *History of the Fall of Poland* (1899), *A History of Modern Egypt* (1905), *History of the Independence of Italy* (1907), *World Colonial History* (1908), and biographies of Napoleon, Otto von Bismarck, and Peter the Great. World history was promoted as a way to inspire patriotism and justify "civilization and enlightenment" (*munmyŏng kaehwa*). In this regard, Korea stands as a predecessor to America in creating a "patriotic world history." The dual historical tasks of modernization and independence urged Korean intellectuals to study world history in the belief that the joint advancement of globalism and nationalism would define their path toward "civilization." (See McKeown, this volume.)

The newly acquired knowledge of world history provoked comparisons between Korea and the Great Powers, and between East and West. From a Korean point of view, world history (with its Western accent) signaled the deconstruction of the traditional

Sinocentric world order and repositioning of East Asia in the new international order. Korean Enlightenment intellectuals adopted the Japanese approach to Orientalist thinking in order to decenter and provincialize China. For Korean nationalist intellectuals, making China an Asian province was an appealing means of appropriating the Western concept of civilization in the interest of national sovereignty. The repositioning went so far as claims by Korean journalists that China would soon be shamed even by Denmark. Contrasts with the West were inherent in these representations of China. By shaking the Sinocentric world order, world history helped to promote the national sovereignty of Korea. In both Korea and Japan, public history – civic history-writing – was much more active than official, or professionally written, history in decentering China. Writing world history was a very political project.

World history, however, simultaneously served to reinforce a Eurocentric definition of a historically inferior East by replacing the traditional Sinocentrism with Eurocentrism (Schmid 2002: 32–36, 56–59, 80). The configuration of Korea and the West underscored Korea's potential for following and catching up to the West, but also presented Korea as lacking or backward. Korea was frequently compared to Western countries of two or three centuries ago by a temporalization of space into a homogeneous and unified time of "History." Compared to a generic "Western farmer," for example, a Korean peasant was depicted as 500 years behind. Here we see the cognitive sequence from the world to the nation as present in Korean historical thought. The sequence of "first world history, then national history" reflects the "first in Europe, then elsewhere" structure of global historicist time that accommodates the Eurocentric diffusionism of a unilateral flow from Europe to the "Rest" (Chakrabarty 2000: 7). This explains why Korean national history based on the configuration of East and West gave rise to a consequential Eurocentrism. Furthermore, the dichotomy of world history and national history was soon to be complicated by the advent of pan-Asianist regional history.

Overcoming Western History

Along with the Japanese Orientalist discourse of *toyoshi* (Asian History) discussed above, visions of peace and unity within a racially defined Asia were intermittently heralded by "East Asian" intellectuals. Influenced by social Darwinism, the struggle for national survival was translated into a racial struggle between "white people" and "yellow people." The ideal of pan-Asianism as an antithesis of the European imperialist racism was shared by some enlightened intellectuals in both China and Korea. (See Zhang, this volume.) They supported pan-Asianism as an ideology to assure their own national independence and regional security against Western imperialism. Upon the colonial conquest of Taiwan and annexation of Korea, however, pan-Asianism revealed what some observers took to be its hidden agenda of Japanese regional hegemony, seeming to serve the multinational integration of colonial subjects into the Japanese empire. Later, it proved to be a stepping stone towards the transnational ideal of the "Greater East Asian Co-Prosperity Sphere" to bring colonial subjects more fully into a total war system of "voluntary mobilization."

One obviously peculiar aspect of historical discourses in imperial Japan, then, was the cohabitation of these notions of pan-Asianism and Japanese Orientalism. In parallel with pan-Asianist regional history, "studies of colonial policies" (*shokuminji seisakugaku*) represented the vulgar version of Orientalist *toyoshi* discourse. If *toyoshi* focused mainly on China, Chosŏn-Korea was the main target of Japanese "studies of colonial policies." While historians elaborated on *toyoshi*, however, social scientists led the "studies of colonial policies," armed with the framework of the German historical school of national economy. Fukuta Tokujo, a pioneer of social policies in Japan, argued that Japan had developed along a historical path formulated by Karl Bücher and had now reached the final stage of economic progress: the stage of national economy. As in other historical discourses, "studies of colonial policies" was also based on the configuration of East and West. In this schema, Fukuta foregrounded the contrast between East and West with the presupposition that Japan stood outside the East (Kang 1997: 94–95). Interestingly, in Japan, the German historical school of national economy became a seedbed for a Marxist vein of developmentalist history. Thus, the concept designated for the *Sozialpolitik* to forestall the emerging socialist movement in Germany played a very different role when transferred to Japan.

Japanese nationalist discourse in the colonial era fluctuated between multicultural nationalism and exclusive ethnic nationalism, which foreshadowed the tension between transnational and national historiographies. However, the transnational variant in imperial Japan differed from the first iteration of world history as written in the late nineteenth century. Transnational history during the imperial period could be accommodated insofar as it served the *kokuminka-kominka* (nationalization of colonial subjects) policy in the colonies. World history tended to be supplanted by a pan-Asianist regional history in colonial Korea, and to a lesser extent in imperial Japan, but the grand narrative of pan-Asianist regional history was oversimplified and one-directional. Petty actors, everyday practices, minor events, and historical ambiguities all escaped from this grand narrative. The reciprocal relations between colonizers and colonized, and between the colonies and the Japanese metropole were simply disregarded for abstract pan-Asianism. (See Sinha, this volume.) Pan-Asianist regional history could not articulate that the empire (Japan) was also made by its imperial projects (Stoler and Cooper 1997).[3]

The structure of the history department at Keizo (Seoul) Imperial University, the only university in colonial Korea (opened on May 1, 1926), indicates this problem. In his inaugural speech, Hattori Unokichi, the first president of the university, emphasized the academy's duty to serve the state. In parallel with the basic policy line of the imperial university, he announced a blueprint to make Keizo a center for Oriental studies. Based on this Orient-centered research strategy, the history department was composed only of three Oriental history tracks: national (Japanese) history, Chosŏn (Korean) history, and Oriental history. Kaneko Kosuke taught Western history at the university from 1928, but there was no official Western history track in the history department. What distinguished Keizo from other imperial universities in the Japanese archipelago was that Western history had been replaced by Korean history. Of its 80 history graduates between 1929 and 1941, 18 students majored in Japanese history, 34 in Oriental history and 28 in Korean history (Park 2009: 217–234). In fact, Seoul National University (the postliberation successor to Keizo Imperial) had no professor lecturing on Western history until 1962.

The outbreak of World War II in the Pacific hastened the decline of world history in East Asia. As the war against the West began, Japanese national "modernists against modernity" stopped looking to "Western Civilization" as a model for Japan's future. Under the brash philosophical slogan of "overcoming modernity," the West became an object to be overcome by Japanese national culture (Harootunian 2000). "Asian Civilization," as represented by Japan, was thought to deserve much more serious investigation than Western history. National history, under the slogan of pan-Asianism or "overcoming modernity," simply overwhelmed Western/world history. World history was thus diagnosed with infection by the Western disease. Japanese intellectuals who supported this idea of "overcoming modernity" lamented the distortion of the Japanese spirit by Western modernity and sought opportunities to remedy the perceived ills of Westernization. The Kyoto school postulated an alternative world history based on a new "Asian" world order, through which European dominance could be overcome in world history. This alternative approach to world history meant one that emanated from the Japanese empire. The intellectual project of "overcoming modernity" was the theoretical lever devised to lift Asia into the context of world history, yet to make a world history of "overcoming Western history." An Asia-centric new kind of world history was much discussed, but never fully articulated, structured or written.

Alongside the discourse of "overcoming modernity," another potential resource for alternative world history was Marxist historiography, with its criticism of capitalist modernity. A history of the complex cultural transfers and interactions of Marxist ideas, in Asia and elsewhere, shows clearly that a vast range of movements and ideologies have been developed and invoked in the name of Marx. When Marx's *Das Kapital* was translated into Russian, for example, the Russian bourgeoisie was second to none in welcoming it, because they read from Marx the historical necessity of capitalist development in Russia. In other global peripheries, socialism under the slogan of "the creative application of Marxism-Leninism" became a development strategy of rapid industrialization to catch up and overtake advanced capitalism, even at the cost of the working masses. To many East Asian intellectuals suffering from the schizophrenia between Westernization and the national identity, socialism came as a two-birds-with-one-stone solution. Socialism could solve the historical dilemma of anti-Western modernization through its vision of an anti-imperialist national liberation and rapid industrialization from above (Lim 2001). In search of an alternative modernity, however, Marxist historiography in imperial Japan and colonial Korea remained also the offspring of Eurocentric world history.

What distinguished Marxist historiography was its comparative history of capitalist development on a global scale. Consider the well-known Marxist controversy over the *Meiji Ishin* of 1868 and subsequent capitalist developments, specifically the debate between the *Kōza-ha* (Lecture's faction) and the *Rono-ha* (Labour-Peasant faction). While the *Kōza-ha* saw the "Meiji Restoration" as the transition to an absolutist state, the *Rono-ha* interpreted it as a bourgeois revolution. Thus *Rono-ha* Marxists insisted that the socialist revolution in Japan was imminent, given the universal interwar crisis of world capitalism. The *Kōza-ha* Marxists, on the other hand, emphasized Japanese backwardness and the peculiarities of military and semifeudal capitalism in Japan as indications that Japanese Marxists should first complete the bourgeois democratic revolution. Caught by the Marxist unilinear schema of socioeconomic development, both factions presumed that every country must experience a bourgeois revolution. The *Kōza-ha*'s definition of Japanese capitalism closely resembles Lenin's description of the "Prussian path" of capitalist development. The contrast between Japan's supposedly distorted and crooked capitalist development, on the one hand, and English autogenous capitalism, or the similar contrasts between the Prussian and American paths, were also imprinted with historicist Eurocentrism.

Marxist historiography in colonial Korea was also not free of the Eurocentric vision of world capitalist development in a unilinear schema, despite its creative attempts to combine a nationalist agenda with the Marxist history of world capitalism. Among the various Marxist views, Paik Namwoon periodized Korean history as corresponding exactly with the Marxist model of development stages: primitive commune → slave economy → Asiatic feudalism → capitalism. In his book, the most influential historical study from a Marxist perspective written in colonial Korea, Paik vehemently opposed any particularistic interpretation of Korean history and instead located Korean history within the universal history of Marxism (Bang 1992). By relying on the unilinear schema of world capitalist development, Paik also invoked a consequential Eurocentrism. But the Eurocentrism inherent in his universalist conception of history was a "weapon of criticism" to be wielded against red Orientalism, which argued for a view of Korea as stagnant (as characteristic of the "Asiatic mode of production"). It is intriguing to witness how the Eurocentric unilinear development model in the end undergirded this view of autogenous capitalist development of the colonized against the colonizer's theory of stasis and stagnancy. Confronting red Orientalism under colonial circumstances, in other words, Marxist universal history and its consequential Eurocentrism was able to accommodate the nationalist rationale.

Overcome by Western History

The end of World War II was a watershed historical event in both Japan and Korea (and of course for the rest of the world). World history as a form of both scholarship and pedagogy went through a sea change that was most visible in the postwar school curricula, influenced most directly by the American military government. Korea was much more receptive to this change than Japan because the new school curriculum was deemed to be a departure from the Japanese colonial legacy. World history was introduced in 1946 to the new school curriculum of postcolonial Korea. World history was integrated into "Social Studies" along with geography, politics, economics, ethics, etc., in Korean primary (grades 1–6) and middle school (grades 7–9). James Harvey Robinson's conception of the "New History," aligned with the educational reform of American Progressivism, was the force behind this change. (See Bain, this volume.) History as a form of education stopped being "art for art's sake" and became a subject self-consciously intended for promoting democratic citizenship. History also remained a part of the "Social Studies" program in high school (grades 10–12) (Cha 1988: 138–152).

Within this new field of "Social Studies," however, history courses in middle school retained the colonial legacy of the Japanese tripartite structure of "Oriental history," "Occidental history," and "national history." The division of world history and national history, into two parts rather than three, was introduced only in the high school curriculum. Notably, there the terms "world civilization" and "Korean civilization" were used instead of world history and Korean history.[4] In the postcolonial turbulence immediately following liberation, too, Koreans could not produce their own world history textbooks. They had to translate and adopt a modified version of "World Civilization," a text originally written for American GIs.

In postwar Japan, despite the peculiar tripartite structure of professional historiography and education at the university level, middle and high school history education kept the division of "world history" and "Japanese history" in line with American military government after 1949. Education reforms in Japan took more time after the Supreme Command of Allied Powers (SCAP) issued an order on December 31, 1945 for a complete "blacking out" of textbooks in history, ethics and geography (Nozaki 2008: 3).

World history thus came back to postwar East Asia as an educational project at the implicit behest of American military authorities. It became a required subject at the middle and high school levels in Japan, and part of the required high school curriculum in Korea, during the educational reforms that took place immediately after World War II. Although world history's status did shift periodically in Korea (as later curricular reforms meant it was sometimes optional, and sometimes required) it remained a consistently required subject in Japan. Overall, stress was laid on world history as part of a history education, but it was still conceived as a very West-centered history. Some world history textbooks in the late 1940s and early 1950s clearly show these unbalanced proportions: Western history overwhelms Eastern history with a ratio of about three to one. Course periodizations were also based on European historiography: the progression of stages from ancient → medieval → modern → contemporary. Liberalism, democracy, bourgeois revolution, industrial revolution, nationalism, etc. were singled out as the most popular problematics in world history textbooks, which in turn reinforced a Eurocentric understanding of world history. And this framing emphasis did not stop at the textbook level: research and education about world history were, and have remained, entangled in bilateral cause–effect chain relationships.

The shift of emphasis from national history to world history in Korean and Japanese postwar school curricula were the results, respectively, of historical reflections on the colonial past in Korea and the wartime defeat in Japan. The dominant discourse in the historical evaluation of Japanese modernity was that Japanese militarism and colonial expansion could be attributed to pathological factors of an immature civil society, semifeudal backwardness and authoritarian political culture, all seen as inherent in its "premodern residues." Postwar Japan thus had to be reformed to eliminate premodern irrationality and complete the democratic revolution. This diagnosis was the partial convergence of the SCAP's official view of the "Pacific War" and the *Kōza-ha* Marxist faction's interpretation of Japanese modernity (Koschmann 1998: xi–xii).

Democratic liberals joined in this interpretation mainly through the work of Ōtsuka Hisao, who bridged the gap between *Kōza-ha* Marxists and modernization theory. Around 1960 Walter Rostow's theory of "modernization" was introduced in Japan, and postwar Japan's rapid economic growth seemed to provide evidence for Rostow's argument. Contrary to any view of sharp ideological antagonisms, Rostow's theory of the stages of historical growth was similar to a Marxian concept of unilinear history. Developmental historicism explains why world history books in Japan, especially in the 1950s and 1960s, were full of tropes necessitating the "follow and catch up" strategy of the peripheries (Geto 2006: 166).

This peculiar amalgam of Marxist historicism and the Rostovian take-off model of economic growth was also influential in postwar Korean historiography. The cohabitation of the stubborn Marxist interpretation of the French Revolution of 1789 and the ardent advocacy of Rostow's modernization theory could even sometimes be seen in the same person, such as Seok-Hong Min, who was the first professor of Western history at Seoul National University (Yook 2009: 331–348). The desire for modernity – in both of these ways – was a locomotive to drive the study and education of world/Western history. In this context, though, world history meant exclusively Western history, because the apparently failed project of modernization in Asia could not at the time be used as a development model. Its underlying assumption was to find a reasonable model to serve postwar Korean development.

As a result, the field's research subjects concentrated heavily on Western history, and specifically on the transition from feudalism to capitalism. Issues such as the rise of capitalism, the Renaissance and Reformation, German peasant wars, the English Revolution and gentry debates, the American Revolution and slavery, Enlightenment and the French Revolution, agrarian reforms in Prussia, and the Industrial Revolution were among the most popular topics for Western-oriented world historians. Eurocentric world history was promoted to accelerate the historical process of industrialization, political democracy and modern nation-building in East Asia. Japanese historians, relatively free of Cold War imposition, could also expand their research frontiers to Eastern Europe, Latin America, the Middle East and Africa in the 1970s, and since then leftist critical historiography has been quite strong in Japan.

Conversely, Korean historians, deprived of academic freedom under the anti-Communist dictatorship of the 1970s and 1980s, struggled to pursue "history from below." The postcolonial generation, born in the 1950s and attending university in the 1970s, were eyewitnesses of a typical process of primitive accumulation of capital under the South Korean developmental dictatorship. A sort of enclosure movement, not by force, but by a market manipulation of keeping low prices for agrarian products, a massive migration of peasants to the city as a reserve army of labor, the misery of the working masses, the mobilization of worker-peasants to the project of modernizing the fatherland and social patriotism – all these phenomena of nineteenth-century European social history seemed to recur in twentieth-century South Korea. In these circumstances, it is not surprising to see the emergence of Korean *narodniks* and their concern for "history from below" (in Europe).[5] By transposing the national epic from the field of high politics to that of everyday life, however, "history from below" contributed to the making of national history within Korea (Lim 1990).

Indeed, Marxist historiography has never been an exception to this configuring of East and West in historical thinking and writing. When Marx said in *Das Kapital* that the "country that is more developed industrially only shows, to the less developed, the image of its own future," he proclaimed the manifesto of Marxist historicism. If Marx is viewed as a theorist of modernity, it can easily be found that "Marx's account of modernisation was inextricably a description of Westernisation, and therefore that his view of global history was a general history of the West" (Turner 1994: 140). At the moment when Korean and Japanese Marxists began to stress universal history or the universal laws of world history, they became dependent on Eurocentric historical narratives and plunged into the discursive pool of "red Orientalism." Yet the location of Korean history in Marx's Eurocentric, universalist scheme was also the result of a desperate effort by Asians to deny the stagnancy of an "Asiatic mode of production."

It is not surprising that the dominant Marxist historical narrative in Korea focuses on the thesis of "sprouts of capitalism" and an "endogenous development of capitalism." New national historiography in postcolonial Korea tried very hard to locate the polarization of the rural population and the emergence of "enlarged scale farming," a historical process that produced an agrarian bourgeoisie and proletariat in the premodern Chosŏn period. They then sought a blueprint for utopia in historical phenomena such as the development of commercial production of specialized crops, the development of wholesale commerce, handcraft industries that relied on merchant capital in the putting-out system, mercantilism, and modernist thought. Along with emerging capitalist relations of production, this line of historical inquiry looks back to ancient and medieval history to find a slave and feudal society. The major currents in Korean Marxist historiography preferred the Marxian universalist scheme to the Asiatic mode of production, precisely to avoid justifying Japanese colonialism. However, neither the "Asiatic mode of production" nor the Eurocentric universalist scheme could escape from the charge of "red Orientalism."

The landing of dependency theory in Korea in the late 1970s signified a rupture in the intellectual milieu dominated by Eurocentric discourses of both right and left. It stressed the unrequited transfer of capital from the colony to the metropole and the additional transfer of surplus to the metropolis through the process of unequal exchange between the center and periphery. Dependency theorists approached colonial history with the basic premise that at the heart of colonialism lay surplus appropriation from the colony to the metropolis. In Korean historiography, dependency theory became entangled with postwar Japanese historiography of the total war system in blaming the backwardness and catastrophe on "premodern" residues and "deviated modernity." Ōtsuka Hisao's economic history of Kōza-ha Marxism and modernization theory heavily influenced this postliberation Korean Marxist historiography.

Dependency theory and its aftermath did not shatter the dichotomy of the normative West and the deviated East, or of model modernization and deviated modernization, in historical scholarship. With its sharp criticism of the unequal exchange and unilateral surplus transfer between center and periphery, dependency theory and its historical arguments were often based on an oversimplified opposition between East and West, and essentialized regional differences represented by the concept of the "Third World." Thus, they failed to notice the historical tensions inherent in any historical unit of either peripheries or centers. They tend to essentialize the homogeneity and heterogeneity among historical units, whether of the nation-state or the region. In the final instance, dependency theory and its worldview also came to serve world history as a nationalist rationale, by justifying the accumulation of capital by the nation-state for rapid industrialization. Once again both modernist and Marxist world history had been overcome by Western history in postwar East Asia.

Decentering World History

Since its introduction to Japan and Korea in the late nineteenth century, world history has fluctuated between Eurocentric world history and an Asia-centric world vision. This swinging pendulum of world history pedagogy and scholarship can be located within the intellectual history of competing ideas of "overcoming modernity" and being "overcome by modernity." Eurocentric world history was dominant in the intellectual milieus that favored Western-oriented modernization during the Meiji Ishin, Enlightened Reformism and the post–World War II era. The focus was on Western rather than Asian history in this period, but an Asia-centric world vision can be found in the various discourses of "pan-Asianism" in the late nineteenth century, through "overcoming modernity" in the colonial period, and into contemporary discussions of the "East Asian Community."

These versions of world history have been in conflict, but both have also been complicit with visions of national history. The antagonistic stance between Eurocentric and Asia-centric world history evaporates on this point, and in fact they are different forms of the same nationalist agenda: a European path or an Asian (peculiar) path of modernization in the capitalist world system. Both versions of world history presuppose that capitalist development is inevitable on a worldwide scale. In fact "the appeal to world history emphasized not a spatial but a temporal category" (Conrad 2010: 171). The emphasis on uniform historical time and a unilinear development of world history was shared by Marxists and nationalists, which led to the Eurocentric diffusionism of a unilateral flow from Europe to the "Rest." This configuration of national history and world history gave rise to what I have called a consequential Eurocentrism in postwar Japan and Korea.

Pluralizing world history demands deconstructing the historicist scheme to temporalize spaces and to locate them in a unilinear historical time. Rather than criticizing historicism *per se*, Korean historians' efforts to pluralize world history were concentrated on criticizing Immanuel Wallerstein's single capitalist world-system and its Eurocentric connotation. (See Chase-Dunn and Hall, this volume.) Various other discourses that sought to pluralize and decentralize world systems in human history were of course also introduced by non-Korean scholars in the first decade of the twenty-first century: Andre G. Frank and Barry K. Gills's "five thousand year world system," Janet Abu-Lughod's arguments about proto-capitalist systems in the thirteenth century, Patrick Manning's multipolar world system with a focus on West Africa, and David Ludden's focus on South Asia can all be included on this list. Many of the Korean writers who introduced (and popularized) these recent trends in world or global history were not trained especially in the field, but began their academic careers as researchers of Western history (Hankook Sŏyangsahakhoi 2009).

Historians of Asian history joined them by introducing the California School's works, such as the writings of Kenneth Pomeranz and Bin Wong. Among their many revealing arguments, Pomeranz's and Wong's demonstrations of the Chinese economy's preponderance over the European economy as late as the eighteenth century provoked a serious interest among many historians across different fields of research. If contemporary Chinese nationalist historians and intellectuals have appropriated these arguments for their own purposes, some Korean nationalists read the California School as evidence of the wider superiority of Eastern civilization over Western civilization – which confirms these nationalists' Occidentalist worldview. At the same time, scholars of history education have been concerned about world history or global history for pedagogical reasons. They have written about worldwide new trends in global history and introduced contemporary debates on how to write world history. The urgent task of writing world history textbooks inclined them to keep abreast of the newest trends in world history. In this regard it is particularly noteworthy that a "Big History" course has been taught by David Christian at the summer session at Ewha Women's University. (See Spier, this volume.)

The influence of these path-breaking studies in world history on Korean historiography is not yet clear. Korean historians are on the threshold of a brand new world history, one that is neither Orientalist nor Occidentalist. From the perspective of the Korean academy, world history looks double-edged. Any critic of Eurocentrism risks Occidentalism as a reversed form of Orientalism, which justifies nationalist politics (Chen 1995). The trend that currently looks most impressive is a transnational history project run by RICH, the Research Institute of Comparative History and Culture based at Hanyang University in Seoul. If world/global history in Korea focuses on the introduction and translation of recent studies from overseas, RICH's transnational history has produced innovative studies within Korea, of the mass dictatorship as a working hypothesis for comprehending the twentieth-century dictatorships on a worldwide scale (Lim and Petrone 2011). The "Flying University of Transnational Humanities," organized by RICH, is also an important new academic structure, and a matrix for transnational history scholars and graduate students in search of a world history that is neither Orientalist nor Occidentalist.[6]

The Japanese historiography of world history has likewise been singularly productive: it is in global economic history that it has produced the most impressive work. The rise of the East Asian economy has been a driving force of the development of a new Asian economic history on the platform of global history. What distinguishes this new global economic history from preexisting comparative economic histories is its focus on relationships, linkages, encounters and various networks of merchants and migration. With a wider regional framework of analysis, it tries to locate each individual Asian country in the context of an integrated Asian regional economy and constructs the entangled history of empires (especially the British Empire) and the Asian regional economy. In one such study, the Sinocentric world system based on a tributary trade system has been used to explain the indigenous roots of Asian regional economies. As a criticism of the Eurocentric world system, a globally linked system of cotton supply and its final demand have also been explored fruitfully, and a unique chain of the global linkage comprising Japan, China, British India, Burma, the Dutch East Indies and Great Britain and other European countries has also been mapped (Akita 2008).

In line with the development of this new global economic history, Japanese world history textbooks, particularly since 1989, have begun to emphasize cultural interconnectedness and trade networks between different cultural spaces. World history textbooks in Japanese high schools now come in two varieties: one written for "World History A" (a course for students in the vocational system) and a second for "World History B" (intended for those headed toward university). "World History A," although its textbook is shorter, has a more impressive structure and narrative, perhaps partly because it is not intended as part of a university entrance examination. What is most striking in both of these textbooks is that they disregard the conventional periodization of ancient–medieval–modern. Instead of a vertical chronological structure, this subject stresses horizontal networks as the historical space of cultural interactions and supraregional trade. Modernity stops being Eurocentric in this perspective. It is a global modernity that Europe, Africa, America and Asia coproduced through interregional networks and interactions (Shibata Michio *et al.*: 2007). (See Bright and Geyer, this volume.) The solid academic accumulation of global economic history written in Japan made this world history textbook possible – and remarkable.

In sum, world history is on the verge of blossoming in Japan and Korea. This brand new world history or global history has been freed in the last two decades from the bias of Eurocentric world history as a nationalist rationale to promote Westernization or modernization, although it may remain vulnerable to devolving into a particular kind of Asia-centric world history because of its regional accent. There arises a necessity of "worlding" instead of "regionalizing." "Worlding" history would bring local, national and regional history into the world and bring the world into local, national and regional history (Dirlik 2007). (See Gerritsen, this volume.) But worlding history should also be followed by decentering world history. This sequential combination may give us a clue to finding an exit from the vicious circle of Eurocentric and Asia-centric world history and reconstructing world history *per se*.

Notes

1 It is noteworthy that *Daguo jueqi* (The rise of great powers), a popular Chinese history documentary on China Central Television to justify the contemporary modernization project, deals with nine foreign countries in sequence: Portugal, Spain, the Netherlands, Great Britain, France, Germany, Japan, Russia, and United States.
2 From context to context I will use the terms of "world history" and "Western history" alternately because world history has been often identified with Western history as a hegemonic discourse in East Asia.
3 This sentence is a paraphrase of Cooper and Stoler on imperial history.

4   This civilizational dichotomy was changed later, in 1955, into the division of "world history" and "national history."

5   The original *narodniks* arose in mid nineteenth-century Russia, as populist intellectuals oriented toward the peasantry as a likely source of socialist revolution. Their name derives from the Russian word *narod* ("people," "nation").

6   See http://www.rich.ac/eng/fly/program.php (accessed Feb. 2012).

References

Akita, Shigeru. 2008. World history and the creation of a new global history: Japanese perspectives. In *Conference Reader of "Global History, Globally,"* Harvard University, Feb. 8–9.

Bang, Kijung. 1992. *Hankook gunhyundai sasangsa yŏngu* [A study of modern thought in Korea]. Seoul: Yŏksabipyungsa.

Bentley, Jerry. 2005. Myths, wagers, and some moral implications of world history. *Journal of World History* 16 (1): 51–82.

Cha, Hasoon. 1988. *Sŏyangsahakui suyonggwa baljeon* [A historiography of Western history in Korea]. Seoul: Nanam.

Chakrabarty, Dipesh. 2000. *Provincializing Europe: Postcolonial Thought and Historical Difference.* Princeton: Princeton University Press.

Chen, Xiaomei. 1995. *Occidentalism.* Oxford: Oxford University Press.

Conrad, Sebastian. 2010. *The Quest for the Lost Nation,* trans. Alan Nothnagle. Berkeley: University of California Press.

Dirlik, Arif. 2007. Contemporary perspectives on modernity: Critical discussion. Special lecture delivered to East Asian Academy at Sŏngkyunkwan University.

Dunn, Ross E. 2007. Rethinking civilizations and history in the new age of globalization. In *Proceedings of the 34th International Symposium of the National Academy of Sciences,* Seoul, Oct. 12.

Geto, Yuji. 2006. Ilbonui segyesa gyogwasŏ [Japanese world history textbook]. In Nakamura Satoru, ed., *Dongasia yŏksa gyogwasŏnun ŏttŏge suyeoittulka?* [How have East Asian history texts been written?], pp. 151–176. Seoul: Editor.

Hankook Sŏyangsahakhoi, ed. 2009. *Europejungsimjooui segyesarul nŏmŏ* [Beyond a Eurocentric world history]. Seoul: Purunyŏksa.

Harootunian, Harry. 2000. *Overcome by Modernity: History, Culture, and Community in Interwar Japan.* Princeton: Princeton University Press.

Kang Sang-jung. 1997. *Orientalism No Kanatae* [Beyond Orientalism], trans. S.M. Lim. Seoul: Isan.

Kondo, Kazuhiko. 2007. The studies of Western history in Japan and the understanding of modernity. In *Proceedings of the Conference on Commemorating the Fiftieth Anniversary of the Korean Society for Western History,* Seoul National University, July 5–6.

Koschmann, J. Victor. 1998. Introduction. In Y. Yamanouchi, J.V. Koschmann, and R. Narita, eds, *Total War and "Modernization",* pp. xi–xvi. Ithaca, NY: Cornell University Press.

Lee, Sung-si. 2004. Shokuminchi bunka seisaku no kachi wo tsuujite mita rekishi ninsiki [The value of colonial cultural production seen through historical awareness]. Paper presented to Kyoto Forum of Public Philosophy, Mar. 13.

Lim, Jie-Hyun. 1990. Hankook sŏyangsahakui bansunggwa jŏnmang [Reflections and prospects of Western history in Korea]. *Yŏksabipyung* 8: 99–122.

Lim, Jie-Hyun. 2001. Befreiung oder Modernisierung? Sozialismus als ein Weg der anti-westlichen Modernisierung in unterentwickelten Ländern. *Beiträge zur Geschichte der Arbeiterbewegung* 43 (2): 5–23.

Lim, Jie-Hyun. 2008. The configuration of Orient and Occident in the global chain of national histories: Writing national histories in Northeast Asia. In S. Berger, L. Eriksonas, and A. Mycock, eds, *Narrating the Nation: Representations in History, Media and the Arts*, pp. 290–308. New York: Berghahn.

Lim, Jie-Hyun. 2010. A postcolonial reading of *Sonderweg*: Marxist and modernist historicism revisited. Paper presented to conference on Postcolonial Reading of *Sonderweg*, Research Institute of Comparative History and Culture, Hanyang University, Seoul, Dec. 3–4.

Lim, Jie-Hyun, and Petrone, Karen, eds. 2011. *Gender Politics and Mass Dictatorship: Global Perspectives*. Basingstoke: Palgrave Macmillan.

Minamizuka, Shingo. 2007. How to overcome Euro-centrism in the Western history in Japan: Some lessons from *Bankokushi* in the Meiji era. In *Proceedings of the Conference on Commemorating the Fiftieth Anniversary of the Korean Society for Western History*, Seoul National University, July 5–6.

Nozaki, Yoshihiko. 2008. *War Memory, Nationalism and Education in Postwar Japan, 1945–2007: The Japanese History Textbook Controversy and Ienaga Saburo's Court Challenge*. London: Routledge.

Park, Gwanghyun. 2009. Sikminji Chosŏnesŏ dongyangsahakun ŏttŏke hyungsongdoiŏttna? [How was East Asian history formulated in colonial Chosŏn?]. In Do Myunhoi and Yoon Haedong, eds, *Yŏksahakui Segi*, pp. 217–246. Seoul: Humanist.

Said, Edward W. 1994. *Culture and Imperialism*. London: Vintage.

Sakai, Naoki. 1997. *Translation and Subjectivity: On "Japan" and Cultural Nationalism*. Minneapolis: University of Minnesota Press.

Schmid, Andre. 2002. *Korea between Empires, 1895–1919*. New York: Columbia University Press.

Shibata, Michio, *et al.* 2007. *Sekaino rekishi* [World history]. Tokyo: Yamakawashuppan.

Stoler, Ann Laura, and Frederick Cooper. 1997. Between metropole and colony: Rethinking a research agenda. In F. Cooper and A.L. Stoler, eds, *Tensions of Empire*, pp. 1–56. Berkeley: University of California Press.

Takagi, Hiroshi. 1995. Nihon bijutsushi no seiritsu/Shiron [History of the establishment of Japanese art history]. *Nihonshi Kenkyu* 400: 74–98.

Tanaka, Stefan. 1993. *Japan's Orient: Rendering Past into History*. Berkeley: University of California Press.

Turner, Bryan S. 1994. *Orientalism, Postmodernism and Globalism*. London: Routledge.

Yook, Youngsoo. 2009. Kukga/gŭndaehwa gihoekurosŏui sŏyangsa [Western history as a national modernization project]. In *Yŏksahakui Segi*. Seoul: Humanist.

CHAPTER TWENTY-NINE

Writing Global History in Africa

DAVID SIMO

The writing of global history is always the consequence and the product of a consciousness of that reality. This reality today is one of great compression of time and space, of intense mobility and of a permanent exposure, through the media, to human experiences in all corners of the world. But it is practiced from institutions and in a discourse that function according to some mechanisms which are themselves inscribed in a given tradition. While the product of globalization, the writing of global history as a university practice seeks to be part of a tradition it wants, indeed, to modify or to transform.

This writing intends to provide a platform for a plural narration of subjective experiences of the past of all human groups, but each group has its own mode of narration of past experiences. That is why it is important to bear in mind what the Indian economist G. Balachandran writes: "New is not the same as distinct. Hence it is also necessary to be alert to whether, in encountering global history/ies, we are hearing distinct new voices narrating their own stories as they experience/d them. Or are we in the presence of a master ventriloquist re-telling a master narrative in several seemingly different voices?" (2011: 7)

Some analysts such as Abolade Adeniji (2005), who scrutinize African historiography and African intellectual history in search of examples of global history writing, too quickly conclude that there was no such tradition. This follows an approach that favors a particular model of writing history. As Mamadou Diouf (2000) stresses, there are several ways to deal with the past and we should avoid creating too tight a bulkhead between writing history in universities and other forms of narrating experiences. So here I am interested in any attempt to structure the past in order to submit seemingly chaotic events to an interpretative work that recreates them and elucidates the structures or relational systems of implication between them. I will be taking into account the narratives that implicitly or explicitly integrate Africa into the history of humankind, or into the history of the given *oikoumene* Africans were confronted with, or which compare implicitly or explicitly African history with that of other peoples. Such an undertaking cannot claim or even aim to be exhaustive. The examples I present here do not intend to

A Companion to World History, First Edition. Edited by Douglas Northrop.
© 2012 Blackwell Publishing Ltd. Published 2012 by Blackwell Publishing Ltd.

reconstruct a full tradition, merely to indicate traditions; they are not used in a normative sense to indicate what is suitable and what is problematic. My aim is simply to make visible some efforts by Africans to think the globality of their different times, and to position themselves in that globality. My aim is also to make intelligible their constraints and objectives when they do this work. Some believe that we should reconstruct a genealogy of the writing of history in Africa which includes all intellectuals of African descent, including early Christian theologians like St Augustine and theorists of American modernity like W.E.B. DuBois. I will not follow this path and I shall address narratives developed on African soil, preferably by Africans.

Conversion, the Emergence of a New Cosmology and Self-Rewriting

Throughout its history, Africa has been embedded in several projects of globalization that have confronted it with new universalist and teleological visions. We often underestimate the intellectual challenge posed by these adventures. Several authors have stressed the almost anthropological desire of any group to create symbolic orders to position and orientate themselves in the world. The desire to create coherence in order to escape the vertigo of chaos forces one to continuously update the narrative of the self, its trajectory, and its objectives.

If a dominant narrative emerges, especially one that ignores or marginalizes you, there is an almost natural reflex to reject this narrative or to rephrase it so as to position yourself in it. In general, the narrative of the self intends to strengthen internal consistency and establish a sense of solidarity; in situations where there is a challenge or even a total dismissal of the prevailing narrative, the narrative of self enters into a debate with the new powerful and dominating discourse.

Africa has gone through three major globalizing processes which integrated it brutally into a new world order in which it found itself relegated to the periphery. These processes were Islamization, Christianization, and colonization. Africans clearly have produced narratives of resistance and rejection of these new orders, but they have also engendered a reformulation of new symbolic orders which reproduced the logic and the language of the dominant discourses, while modifying them to include Africa and the African in a more honorable position in the new world order. These reformulations must necessarily be regarded as part of an original mode of global history writing by Africans – even though they use a narrative matrix borrowed from the dominant discourse and seem to focus on parochial experiences. I will present here two examples of such narratives, reacting first to the Islamization of parts of Africa in the sixteenth century, and then to the Christianization of other parts in the nineteenth century.

The first example is the *tarikh* ("chronicle") genre which emerges in the second half of the seventeenth century and which is emblematic of the manuscripts of Timbuktu. The tarikh genre was "centered upon the task of making historical sense of the political and social upheavals brought about by the Moroccan invasion of 1591" (Moraes Farias 2008: 97). Two famous documents pertaining to this new literary genre are the Tarikh al-Sudan (Chronicle of the Sudan) by Abd al-Rahman al-Sadi (1653) and the Tarikh al-fattash (Chronicle of the Researcher) by Mahmud b. al-Mutawakil Kati (1657–1669). To these manuscripts, which are well known and still preserved in Timbuktu, we shall add other written chronicles which are not currently available, but which have been used by some African historians, for example those of the Mande and of the Fulani of Futa Jallon or Fouta Toro.

In a lecture delivered in Timbuktu in 1997 on Islam and West Africa, Seydou Camara mentioned a text from the historical tradition of the Mande people in which the Jabati from the Kela Centre formulated a new history of the Mande people as constituted by the following phrases (1997: 117):

The creation of the Universe and the origin of Humanity.
The conquest of Khaybar.
The beginning of the mansaya (monarchy) in the Mande.
The saga of Sunjata.
The mottos and genealogies of the heroes of the main Mande clans.
The list of the thirty Mande "families."
The settlement and hegemony of the Keyita Kandasi in the Niger Valley.

As we can see, such a cosmology mixes historical fact and myths of origins and reconstructs a history of Mandes to integrate them into a trajectory corresponding to an Islamic vision of teleology. Thus a connective logic appears whose final objective is to legitimize the ruling dynasty and to reconcile it with the dominant order. Diagne observes:

> In the rewriting of their origins, the Mande present themselves as the descendants of the royalty from Khaybar who converted to Islam after their military defeat. The function of this narrative is quite clear. First, it transforms the conversion of the Mande to Islam and its cosmology into an epic which took place at the very beginning of the Muslim religion, as part of the early Islamic saga in the Arabian Peninsula. Second, it legitimizes the mansaya as the continuation of an ancient tradition of royalty in Khaybar (a process of legitimization which is the usual role of myths). (2008: 21)

Some historians have interpreted this rewriting as a sign of a break with the pagan origins of Mandes and a willingness to reinvent oriental ancestors to fit within the new *oikoumene*, centered in the Middle East. Diagne denied such a narrow interpretation and instead emphasized the overall significance of a new cosmology, which was to anchor the community through a new historical narrative in a global Islamic world, that is to say the *umma*, which implies a new geography, new places of memory, new memory of places, a new temporality.

For Diagne, the text of the Mande, like other manuscripts of Timbuktu which mix dynastic developments, biographies, genealogies, collective developments, and sociological considerations, creates a new philosophy of time: as creative movement, as the idea of becoming, in short, as teleology. Diagne quotes another Timbuktu scholar whose views show clearly that the intellectual endeavor expressed in the chronicles is not just a reproduction of a given narrative, but also its criticism and its modification. Ahmad Baba writes in his work, *Mi'raj al-su'ud*, "There is no difference between one race and another." This is an unequivocal dismissal of Islamic narratives which pretend that the enslavement of black people was a natural consequence of some curse against the descendant of Ham, one son of Noah, a narrative which naturalizes slavery and leads to "disparagingly calling black people *'abid* (slaves), as is even today the case" (Diagne 2008: 26).

The second example of Africans reformulating processes of globalization comes from a historiography that developed in the nineteenth century, with two leading scholars who created a genre that others then perpetuated. The first scholar was Carl Christian Reindorf, pastor of the Basel Mission, who published in 1895 a document entitled *History of the Gold Coast and Asante: Based on Traditions and Historical Facts, Comprising a Period of More Than Three Centuries from about 1500 to 1860.* The second author was the Reverend Samuel Johnson, who completed a manuscript in 1897, published only after his death, with the title "The history of the Yoruba, from the earliest time to the beginning of the British protectorate." From these titles, it is clear that the two pastors intended to reconstruct the history of their respective peoples, the Ashanti and Yoruba. How can micronational history be regarded as a kind of global history writing? For the same reasons as the chronicles discussed above. Indeed, the project of writing a history of a people is here an attempt to position oneself in a new cosmology and a new global community. As noted by Diagne, "conversion is not only entering a new religion with its creed, dogmas and rituals. As the Latin etymology indicates, to convert is to get totally turned around. That means a new self-reappraisal following the adoption of a new cosmology. One visible aspect of conversions has been a radical change in the discourse of identity" (2008: 21).

The writing of the history of their people by new converts and pastors is inscribed in this logic. It aims at positioning themselves in a new trajectory charted by the new religion. Unlike the tarikh genre, the two pastors do not mix facts and myths. On the contrary, they are concerned about accuracy, authenticity and truth, all of the requirements they internalized by reading historians, anthropologists and other observers, including Europeans who had written about their people and whom they quote extensively. But they also realize the importance of the hermeneutic problems of understanding the "facts." They are also aware of the difficulty of access to sources and conclude by arguing that a greater legitimacy should be accorded to their own narration of their people's history. Thus Reindorf wrote in his preface:

> A history of the Gold Coast written by a foreigner would most probably not be correct in its statements, he not having the means of acquiring the different traditions in the country and comparing them with those which he may have gathered from a single individual. Unless a foreigner writes what he witnesses personally, his statements will be comparatively worthless, as it is the case with several accounts of the Gold Coast already published. Hence it is most desirable that a history of the Gold Coast and its people should be written by one who has not only studied, but has had the privilege of initiation into the history of its former inhabitants and writes with true native patriotism. (1895: iii–iv)

As we can see very clearly, there are already in this text the different requirements that nationalist writings of African history would later assert. To write this kind of history becomes an act of patriotism. But unlike other approaches that are part of the resistance and rejection of the new symbolic order and of the new cosmology, the goal here is only to restore the truth of this history, without questioning the new colonial perspective. The author then states: "If a nation's history is the nation's speculum and measure-tape, then it brings the past of that nation to its own view, so that the past may be compared with the present to see whether progress or retrogression is in operation; and also as a means of judging our nation by others, so that we may gather instruction for our future guidance" (1895: iv).

The writing of the past here does not at first sight correspond to a desire to work out glorious ancestries, but corresponds to the presentation of a reality which has to be transformed. The knowledge seems to be serving the project of integration into a new Christian and colonial order. Even if writing History is focusing on oneself, it is already a conversation with the Other and with the ongoing process of globalization. Patriotism is not here nativistic, in the sense of being based on the defense and protection of endangered values. This, in any case, is how his fellow European missionaries read Reindorf's text. J.G. Christaller, who published the manuscript at the time, wrote in an introductory note:

> But the superstitions, cruelties, horrors and atrocities in the private and public life of heathenish nations are also brought to view in too many instances of this History of the Gold Coast, and this ought to impress natives and Europeans with thankfulness for the changes already effected and with the conviction of the necessity of continuing and increasing every effort to bring the various tribes more under the influence of true Christian religion and civilization. (Reindorf 1895: ix)

The writing of history thus brings elements of Christian legitimization for present and future. But this writing of history is not confined to the development of a new teleology in which the past would be a step beyond, a goal which has to be achieved. It also reveals the existence and the presence of a *history* and as such is a challenge to Christian cosmology since that tended to hold a thesis of the absence of a history and culture for these peoples. The requirement of accuracy and the claim of a right to tell one's own story stems from a critique of the dominant discourse. Why would people fight to restore the truth of the past if they did not believe there was something important they had to know about it and perhaps even save? In this sense, these pastors and historians were revising the new dominant cosmology and teleology, and it is on the basis of these revisions that African theology could later claim the enculturation of Christianity: its transformation to take into account traditional cultural practices in Africa. The project in which these historians were engaged, then, is a global history for two reasons. It is a *comparative* history, since their history of the African peoples was written in comparison with a Christian history of Christianity which provided the categories and trajectory. It corresponds at the same time to *mimicry* in the sense of Homi K. Bhabha (1994), because it seems to reproduce a narrative, but in fact it transforms it to record its own intentionality, its own objectives and its own teleology.

Defining Africa's Position in the World as Permanent Preoccupation

The examples we have analyzed so far are symptomatic of the evolution of historiography in the twentieth century, especially since independence. Today, as in the past, several departments of African universities claim to teach the history, culture, geography, and politics of different regions of the world. Different social sciences departments indeed offer courses on Europe, Asia, and America, according to their various fields. But in general these areas do not constitute real fields of research within the African academy. The reason for the general lack of interest shown by African academic institutions and African intellectuals in writing about and teaching other parts of the world is quite simple. After independence, most African intellectual energy has been focused on researching African sociopolitical, historical, cultural, and geographical reality. This activity has appeared to be urgent and indispensable. Achille Mbembe summarizes the objectives of this endeavor in the following critical words:

> The first ritual contradicts and refutes Western definitions of Africa and Africans by pointing out the falsehoods and bad faith they presuppose. The second denounces what the West has done (and continues to do) to Africa in the name of these definitions. And the third provides ostensible proofs that – by disqualifying the West's fictional representations of Africa and refuting its claims to have a monopoly on the expression of the human in general – are supposed to open up a space in which Africans can finally narrate their own fables. This is to be accomplished through the acquisition of a language and a voice that cannot be imitated, because they are, in some sense, authentically Africa's own. (2002a: 244)

To do research on Europe, for example, was perceived by many as an activity that perpetuated, in some sense, the colonial extraversion which was about to be overcome and which would keep Africans away from themselves. This largely explains the fact that there are so few experts on Europe or other parts of the world in the African academic disciplines just mentioned.

Interestingly, however, in the philological disciplines there is a true tradition of research on different parts of the world. This philological domain is not my focus in this essay, but in these disciplines there is a serious attempt to discuss and historicize not only European discourses but also American ones. (See Northrop, final chapter of this volume.) Until now, most of these philological departments were oriented towards American, Commonwealth, French, English, Spanish, and Arabic studies. There are also different projects to create Chinese departments throughout Africa. Such a department is already functioning in the University of Witwatersrand in South Africa and in the University of Maroua in Cameroon. The creation of these Chinese departments is motivated by the growing political and economic relations between most of the African states and China. These departments are funded by the respective African states, but they are supported by the Chinese state, which sends teachers. The evolution and the importance of these departments cannot yet be appreciated. Anyway, from this philological perspective, there is a true attempt to develop a discourse from an African point of view on some parts of the world. But even these discourses are mainly interested in the evaluation of the general historical relationship between Africa and the world, and participate in the general effort of positioning Africa in the world.

Since talking about oneself is conceived as self-positioning in the world, what place have Africans assigned themselves in the world and what is the idea of the world that prevails? In African historiography and other African discourses, it is possible to identify two basic modalities of defining the being-in-the-world of Africa and the Africans. The writing of global history has thus favored two major discourses on self and the world and two major ways of writing history itself. Generally speaking, the first way is interested in what the world and more especially Europe has done to Africa, while the second is interested in what Africans have done in the world.

What the World Has Done to Africa

Africa as product of world history

What are the basic assumptions of this approach? The worldliness of Africa, its being-in-the-world, is not seen as the result of an African initiative or will, but as the result of different universalizing projects initiated and conducted by forces which come from elsewhere. The three main forces, as I noted in the opening section of this chapter, are Islam, Christianity, and colonization. To these forces, which gained power over the structuring of imagination, bringing social, economic and political transformations and therefore producing an empirical reality to be observed in the daily life of Africa today, should be added the slave trade, which is also a modality of linking Africa to the rest of the world. If we consider only these four moments as modalities through which Africa became part of the world and was integrated in the world history, Africa indeed appears as a product of world history and not as its agent. When approached from this perspective, the history of the worldliness of Africa begins in the fifteenth century.

It must also be stated once more that this approach is not inscribed in the paradigm governing mainstream historiography in Europe, which is based on the geopolitical myth of the uniqueness and centrality of the North Atlantic world. But it is oriented towards what the world has done to Africa and not towards what Africa has done in the world. As such, of course, this approach has consequences in the way Africa and the Africans are defined. It thus has serious implications for the way Africans perceive themselves in the world: the way they see themselves in world history. This focus on the last five centuries, and especially on events and forces like the slave trade, Islam, Christianity, and colonization as central modalities of African participation in world history, has nurtured a perception of history as traumatic experience and a process of loss.

Books like *How Europe Underdeveloped Africa* (Rodney 1973) are very characteristic of this discourse. Just at the beginning of colonization, as the first Africans were converted to Christianity, there were some African voices, as we have seen, presenting European influences as positive, as something that would help Africa move towards civilization and culture. But very rapidly the tonality changed. As soon as Africans took up the dialogue and could emancipate themselves from the colonial discourse, they started developing a critical appraisal of what was happening to them. Being-in-the-world was, from this point onward, experienced mostly as traumatic, as violence.

History as a discipline, but also literature and other forms of the academic arts and humanities, have worked out different forms and modes of violence that were at the basis of the colonial experience and the way Africans experienced it. This violence was economic, political, social, and physical. There are extensive writings on the way Africans were exploited, deprived of their land, subjugated, killed, harassed, and so on. Many historical studies focus on the ways foreign rule restructured African economy, society, and juridical systems. There are many novels, poems, theatrical plays, and essays presenting psychological and physical suffering, humiliation, depersonalization, and loss of freedom, dignity and orientation due to colonial action and to the exposure to a wider world it made possible. The history of Africa's integration into the capitalistic world economy and into the international world political system appears clearly as a history of suffering and loss. Africa and Africans appear as victims of the world. All these well-documented facts and experiences have founded a general discourse of victimization. This discourse systematizes historical facts and experiences and works out a fundamental logic which underlines the history of Africa in the world. Even new developments leading to what is called "globalization" are interpreted to confirm the general principle that Africa is not a subject of world history but its object and victim. Any exposé which shows how slavery, colonization and globalization have deprived Africa of any initiative, autonomy and opportunity for action, then, will be generally considered by an African audience as an accurate and correct analysis of historical reality.

But there are some critical voices that challenge this way of thinking. The most powerful is that of Mbembe (2002a). He characterizes the discourse of victimization as a vision of history as sorcery. The idea of sorcery implies a conception of life where forces beyond one's control represent a permanent danger to one's autonomy and life. Mbembe seems to offer three critiques of this mainstream mode of self-writing and conception of world history. The first critique is aimed at what he calls the "fixation on the past and the frenetic claim to the status of victim" (2002b: 635). In his polemical approach, Mbembe seems at times to criticize historical approaches and to privilege a synchronic approach to reality. But he himself constantly proceeds to a genealogical analysis of present reality (Mbembe 2000). He is surely aware of this ambiguity. That is why he adds a second critical point where he questions the interpretation of facts in the discourse of victimization. Mbembe challenges the claims of this discourse to provide the only way of giving sense to past facts, and instead proposes other modes of decoding them and developing different visions of history. We will present and discuss this mode later.

The third critique by Mbembe is philosophical and ideological. He questions the state of mind and the type of attitude favored in the discourse of victimization. He interrogates the status of the African subject when the world is decoded in such a way that the "African subject cannot express him- or herself in the world other than as a wounded and traumatized subject. What does it mean if we stress that nothing is happening in Africa because history (the slave trade, colonization, and apartheid) has already happened and anything more would be nothing but a repetition of those originary events?" (2002b: 630). In order to answer these questions, Mbembe refers to the concept of "slave morality" as developed by Nietzsche. He is not ready to establish a total equivalence between the state of mind structured by the discourse of victimization and the "slave morality," but he postulates the proximity of both.

But this critique is excessive and does not take into account the variety of responses given to the process of depravation and reification. Not all discourses which treat the integration of Africa in the world economy and world politics as successive acts of violence and dispossession can be considered as having a view of history as sorcery, where Africans do not demonstrate any will, where they are only victim and not actors. The assertion of what has been done to Africa does not necessarily implicate a slave mentality, or the consciousness that history repeats itself eternally and cannot be given a new direction. This assertion of wounds inflicted by history is, most of the time, more likely to be a dialectical moment which founds another moment, that of resistance.

Global history as history of resistance

In his preface to Frantz Fanon's *The Wretched of the Earth*, Jean-Paul Sartre, the French philosopher, suggests three steps towards the emancipation of colonized peoples, and especially of Africans (Sartre 1963). In fact he is mostly interested in analyzing elite discourses, where the signs of this emancipation are visible. In the first step, Sartre says, the colonized confront the colonizers with their contradictions. The colonized person reproaches Europeans with their own inhumanity: in other words, he or she has assimilated Europeans' own principles of humanity sufficiently to use them as criteria to judge Europeans themselves. Although they are critical, these voices thus bear witness to the deeper European success in changing the mind of the colonized, and making colonial subjects adopt European ideals.

In the second step, according to Sartre, "a new generation came to the scene, which changed the issue" (Sartre 1963: 8). The writers and poets of this generation were most interested in showing the difference between Europeans' values and their own identity. The most radical change then came with the third generation, which developed a nationalist and revolutionary discourse and challenged Europe directly.

For Sartre the main change in this discourse is neither the tone of expression nor the character of the claim. It is rather the target group of the speech, those to whom it is directed. Whereas in the first two steps the speech is directed to Europeans, in the third it is directed to the colonized themselves.

> For the fathers, we alone were the speakers; the sons no longer even consider us as valid intermediaries: we are the objects of their speeches. Of course, Fanon mentions in passing our well-known crimes: Sétif, Hanoi, Madagascar: but he does not waste his time in condemning them; he uses them. If he demonstrates the tactics of colonialism, the complex play of relations which unite and oppose the colonists to the people of the mother country, it is for his brothers; his aim is to teach them to beat us at our own game. In short, the Third World finds *itself* and speaks to *itself* through his voice. (Sartre 1963: 16)

This is a very interesting way to read different discourses in Africa. They appear as different steps towards emancipation, as difference modes of resistance, each having its shortcomings, but each demonstrating the will of Africans to become the subjects of history. Therefore the different discourses from Negritude to Fanon, from Fanon to Mundimbe and from Mundimbe to Mbembe, from pan-Africanism to African Renaissance, from nationalism to cosmopolitanism, can be read historically as different ways of posing and treating Africa's inscription in world history by examining possibilities of overcoming marginality and reification.

One could interpret in a similar vein this discourse, not only to reconstruct a genealogy of critical writings as sign of Africans' own presence, but also to reconstruct the continuity of different forms of resistance, cultural resistance, military resistance, political and intellectual resistance to subjugation and imperialism.

This approach might be considered as a "polemical definition" of Africa's relationship to the world (Mbembe 2002a), but not every polemic about relationship to the world ends up in nativism.

What Africa Has Done in the World

The Afrocentric approach

The father of the Afrocentric definition of the worldliness of Africa is the Senegalese scholar Cheikh Anta Diop. His most influential book, *Nations nègres et culture*, was written in the 1950s. Its contributions were then extended in the 1960s by other books which have also become classics in Africa. Cheikh Anta Diop has also attained great influence in some circles in America – those calling themselves "Afrocentric," and whose members have developed a full theory of Afrocentrism which goes beyond the theses of Cheikh Anta Diop.

What are these theses and their underlying theoretical links? Cheikh Anta Diop addressed the following basic topics:

- The African and negroid origin of humankind and civilization.
- The Negro origins of Egypt and Numid civilizations.

- The importance of Negro thought for the emergence and development of Western civilization, especially in the sciences, literature, and arts.
- The identification of migration-streams and the formation of ethnic groups in Africa.
- The linguistic relationship (of lineal descent) between Egypt and black Africa.
- The "true" origin of the Semitic world.
- The delimitation of a black cultural world which extends as far as West Asia in the Indus Valley.
- The formation of African states on the whole continent – after the decline of Egypt.
- The continuity of historical and cultural links between Egypt and other African states from the ancient period through today.
- The existence of a common artistic foundation in Africa.
- The capability of African languages to express scientific and philosophic thoughts.

There are at least three ways of analyzing this historical narrative. The first is what we might identify as a realist epistemological approach. The second is a relativistic approach, while the third could be called the discursive analytical approach.

The first of these alternatives, the realist epistemological approach, asks questions about the scientific basis of the narrative. And in this regard there is an ongoing discussion, especially since the publication of Martin Bernal's several books (1987; 1991; 2006) under the general title *Black Athena*, in which some critics reject Afrocentrism generally as mythical and ideological and therefore nonscientific (Howe 1998; Fauvelle-Aymar *et al.* 2000), while other critics are more balanced in their appreciation (van Binsbergen 2000). Most critics agree about the poor scholarship of many Afrocentric publications. They note that conclusions are often largely contained in the opening pages, and that authors develop the tendency thereafter to fill the gaps with assumptions that derive from the already-defined central theme. But there are some voices that ask us to consider Afro-centrism as at least a testable hypothesis, and to confront it with empirical facts and not simply to dismiss it out of hand as contradicting hegemonic paradigms (Van Binsbergen 2000).

The second approach, of relativism, does not engage in this discussion of the objectivity or nonobjectivity of narratives, but rather stresses the point that knowledge formation is *always* political and historically contextual. In this sense, every historical narrative is strategic and therefore more or less mythical. The Afrocentric narrative is thus compared to other historical narratives and especially to the Eurocentric whitening of ancient Greece, which, according to Martin Bernal (1987), followed the same logic as the Afrocentric narrative. Through a process of selection of historical facts, Greece is presented as an autonomous culture which emerges out itself, and with this myth thus constructed, Europe could be made to appear as the cradle of civilization.

The third approach, which I label discursive, follows Foucault in simply suspending the question of truth. It is, rather, interested in the premises that render a narrative true for some people and, even more, why this narrative is elaborated. By developing a long-term perspective, the Afrocentric approach opens the opportunity of analyzing the impact of the last few centuries as merely a periphery of its own – once seen in the context of the overall history of Africa – a periphery which has had an undeniable impact on the contemporary position of Africa in the world but doesn't definitively push it to the margins of overall world history. This approach makes it possible to think of continuities that have not been annihilated by the momentary situation of today. It also makes it possible to think about Africa's relationship to other continents and other cultures not as a relation of pure exteriority. It follows a logic that transcends the economy of alterity, and postulates that nothing developed in Europe, Asia and America is actually totally alien or strange to Africa, since it, too, has its deeper roots in Africa. It makes it possible to think of the globality of the world as in this sense nonproblematic. But such possibilities are not always consequently thought, because this discourse is contaminated by another logic, that of difference and alterity.

Changing the shape of the world

The subtitle to *The Wretched of the Earth*, the English version of Frantz Fanon's *Les damnés de la terre*, is *The Handbook for Black Revolution That Is Changing the Shape of the World*. The intent of this subtitle is to indicate the epochal importance of decolonization. African nationalism and even anticolonial struggle have come under critical scrutiny. Their contradictions, their expectations and especially their results, the emergence of postcolonial states, have been analyzed, and the judgments provided are often rather negative. But the importance of decolonization and of its underlying ideas cannot be overestimated as far as world history is concerned. It was the end of an epoch. It was a process that changed the shape of the world. And the actors in this process were people of the global South: a category that includes Africans too.

In the writings of Fanon, but also in those of Amilcar Cabral (1975) and other African nationalists and theoreticians of liberation, the central impetus is not hate, nor is it rejection of the other. The emancipation movement is not driven by the will to cut oneself off from the world or to seek a place outside the international net. On the contrary, most theoreticians in Africa consider the emancipation of colonized peoples as a universal project. The aim was not merely to gain sovereignty in the former colonies, but also to change the world and to inaugurate another type of international relations. The last sentences of Fanon's book are very clear on this point:

> But if we want humanity to advance a step further, if we want to bring it up to a different level than that which Europe has shown it, then we must invent and we must make discoveries ... Moreover, if we wish to reply to the expectations of the people of Europe, it is no good sending them back a reflection, even an ideal reflection, of their society ... For Europe, for ourselves, and for humanity, comrades, we must turn over a new leaf, we must work out new concepts, and try to set afoot a new man. (1963: 315)

Of course, it is fair to ask if this proposition has been realized; but that is not my point here. I wish simply to indicate the spirit that animated some actors and legitimated the writing of world history by some scholars who have stressed the central role of the Third World in world history over the past 50 years. The Kenyan writer, playwright, and scholar Ngugi wa Thiong'o (1993) has proposed a view of world history centered on changes in perspectives, on the development of new ideas and a consciousness to which writers from the South have contributed. He summarizes this process in the expression "moving the center."

Ngugi interprets the history of the world since the 1960s "as a struggle to shift the base from which to view the world from its narrow base in Europe to a multiplicity of centers" (1993: 6). For him the achievement of this struggle has been the successful challenge to Eurocentrism, a development which has contributed first of all to a freeing, at least to a certain extent, of the "genuinely universal" (1993: xvii) "in the West imprisoned by Eurocentrism" and to an opening of spaces for new narrations. This movement between nations or continents had been prolonged by "the need to move the centre from all minority class establishments within nations to the real creative centres among the working people in conditions of gender, racial and religious equality" (1993: xvii).

Ngugi thus links the different international efforts towards increased freedom and equality with internal national struggles for changes in social relationships and personal mentalities. What he proposes is a writing of world history wherein global processes both engender and boost local processes. And in these processes, Africans among others will play a central role. Resistance and opposition to hegemony and homogenization in the global scene, which he considers as still present, are the prerequisites for this international and internal emancipation and progress, since "conditions of external domination and control, as much as those of internal domination and oppression, do not create the necessary climate for the cultural health of any society" (1993: xvi).

The view of this Kenyan writer is universalist. It doesn't oppose the local and the global, but rather combines both levels to construct a vision of the shared history and projection of humanity as a whole.

> I am an unrepentant universalist. For I believe that while retaining its roots in regional and national individuality, true humanism with its universal reaching out, can flower among the peoples of the earth, rooted as it is in the histories and cultures of the different peoples of the earth. Then, to paraphrase Marx, will human progress cease to resemble the pagan idol who would drink nectar but only from the skulls of the slain. (1993: xvii)

The insistence on the role of the Third World and especially Africa on reshaping the world through a process of moving the center is simply one way of inscribing oneself as actor in world history. The second way, which does not contradict, but rather completes or prolongs it, is the idea of coproduction of the modern world. Ngugi wa Thiong'o expresses this clearly: "The modern world is a product of both European imperialism and of the resistance waged against it by the African, Asian and South American peoples" (1993: 4). This idea is central to the postcolonial discourse which renews and reorients different discourses emerging in the 1950s and 1960s and aims at challenging central Western philosophical epistemes. One of these epistemes is a conception of history as a process of influence and diffusion, as a teleological movement in which humankind is steadily remade and transformed, moving towards perfection and progress. These principles structure narratives in which the Western world is the main if not the unique actor of these transformations. In these narratives, the relation between the Western world and the rest of the world can only be that of conversion, transformation, and assimilation. Imperialism was thus legitimized as a burden, as a duty to transform the other and to integrate him or her in the historical process.

The idea that the modern world is a coproduction of imperialism and the resistance of the South challenges these Eurocentric conception of world history and tries to interpret the encounter of Europeans with others in the colonial process as an active enterprise on both sides.

Postcolonial historiography is concerned with analyzing changes over time not only in the colonized world but also in the North by relating them explicitly or implicitly to the heritage of colonialism. But these changes are interpreted not as influence and dissemination, but rather as the result of a tension between two forces. The forces on the side of the colonized world are called resistance and one of these forces, in Africa, is what Mbembe calls "heretical spirit."

In *Afriques indociles*, published as early as 1988, Mbembe developed a position in opposition to the then common assumption that Africa had been thoroughly transformed by colonialism and suffered mightily from this transformation. He developed the thesis that it is rather the African who transformed the principles and ideas that European colonialists tried to inculcate. Especially with regard to Christianity, he defended the idea that Africans installed their meanings in the very heart of Christians' dogmas and symbols and therefore transformed them thoroughly.

Since then he has developed this idea of an African "heretical spirit" to propose a reading and writing of the archive of the present. He, for example, examines what has become of the three major universalizing projects whose aim was not only to propose a system of knowledge, but also to have authority over what "Africa" signifies and therefore to "state the conditions under which Africa could become part of the universalizing project of modernity" (Mbembe 2002b: 632). All these projects, of course, wanted to transform Africa. But what happened? Mbembe takes the example of Islam and shows the same heretical spirit still at work:

> Likewise, Africans have responded to the Islamic project by means of creative assimilation. In these cultures marked by orality, the hegemony of the Book is made relative. The doctrinal core is interpreted and recited in a way that largely leaves open to negotiation the question of what constitutes an Islamic society or government. ... Two factors explain this fluidity. The first involves the ability to extend and disperse across space – and thus negotiate long distances. In West Africa, for example, several networks link the Arab-Berber and the Negro-African Worlds. The brotherhoods are dispersed around geographical poles from which they can extend outwards. Migrations and long-distance trade are therefore organized across borders and even across continents. (2002b: 637)

From this analysis it appears plain that the original universalizing project of transformation and integration of Africa in a modernizing teleology was actually transformed into an African globalization project which reinvented its objectives and established new networks. The purpose of Mbembe is to counter the nativistic – what he calls Afro-radical – discourse, which he criticizes as fixated on the past, and instead to formulate a "correlation between geography (an accident) and destiny" (2002b: 636). Instead of a thesis that the encounter between Africa and the world is an "open wound," a destabilizing and totally negative experience, Mbembe asserts that the effective practice of social actors proceeded according to the principle of composition. He therefore defends the idea that contemporary cultural abilities allow Africans to treat the past as a kind of open-ended negotiation.

Mbembe thus develops a conception of world history as shared history, as a process of entanglement which produces not only negative effects, like asymmetry and hegemony, but also creativity, new possibilities. World history, in his hands, is therefore not teleology, but an open-ended process.

I have presented here several different modalities, different ways Africans both experience the world and write about it. Not all modalities are discussed here, of course; and even those presented are not discussed in full detail. But this discussion shows, it seems to me, how reading and writing the relation between local and global has been fully part of Africans' experience of international processes, and also an anticipatory discourse that aims at defining what should become of these processes – while working to transform them.

References

Adeniji, Abolade. 2005. Universal history and the challenge of globalization to African historiography. *Radical History Review* 91 (Winter): 98–103.

Balachandran, G. 2011. Writing global histories: Claiming history beyond nations. At http://graduateinstitute.ch/webdav/site/international_history_politics/shared/working_papers/WPIHP-Balachandran.pdf.

Bernal, Martin. 1987. *Black Athena: The Afroasiatic Roots of Classical Civilization*, vol. 1: *The Fabrication of Ancient Greece, 1785–1985*. New Brunswick, NJ: Rutgers University Press.

Bernal, Martin. 1991. *Black Athena: The Afroasiatic Roots of Classical Civilization*, vol. 2: *The Archaeological and Documentary Evidence*. New Brunswick, NJ: Rutgers University Press.

Bernal, Martin. 2006. *Black Athena: The Afroasiatic Roots of Classical Civilization*, vol. 3: *The Linguistic Evidence*. New Brunswick, NJ: Rutgers University Press.

Bhabha, Homi K. 1994. Of mimicry and man: The ambivalence of colonial discourse. In H.K. Bhabha, *The Location of Culture*, pp. 85–92. London: Routledge.

Cabral, Amilcar. 1975. *Unité et lutte. L'arme de la théorie*. Paris: Maspero.

Camara, Seydou. 1997. Islam et tradition historique au Manden. In *La culture arabo islamique en Afrique au sud du Sahara. Cas de l'Afrique de l'Ouest*, pp. 115–120. Proceedings of an international conference held in Timbuktu. Zaghouan, Tunisia: Fondation Temimi.

Diagne, Souleymane Bachir. 2008. Toward an intellectual history of West Africa: The meaning of Timbuktu. In Shamil Jeppie and Souleymane Bachir Diagne, eds, *The Meanings of Timbuktu*, pp. 19–27. Cape Town: HSRC Press.

Diouf, Mamadou. 2000. Des historiens et des histoires, pourquoi faire? L'histoire africaine entre l'État et les communautés. *Canadian Journal of African Studies* 34 (2): 337–374.

Fanon, Frantz. 1963. *The Wretched of the Earth*. New York: Grove. First published as *Les damnés de la terre* in 1961.

Fauvelle-Aymar, François-Xavier, Jean-Pierre Chrétien, and Claude-Hélène Perrot. 2000. *Afrocentrismes. L'histoire des Africains entre Égypte et Amérique*. Paris: Karthala.

Howe, Stephen. 1998. *Afrocentrism, Mythical Pasts and Imagined Homes*. London: New Left Books.

Mbembe, Achille. 1988. *Afriques indociles. Christianisme, pouvoir et État en société postcoloniale*. Paris: Karthala.

Mbembe, Achille. 2000. *De la postcolonie. Essai sur l'imagination politique dans l'Afrique contemporaine*. Paris: Karthala. Trans. as *On the Postcolony*, Berkeley: University of California Press, 2001.

Mbembe, Achille. 2002a. African modes of self-writing. *Public Culture* 14 (1): 239–273.

Mbembe, Achille. 2002b. On the power of the false. *Public Culture* 14 (3): 629–641.

Moraes Farias, Paulo F. de. 2008. Intellectual innovation and reinvention of the Sahel: The seventeenth-century Timbuktu chronicles. In Shamil Jeppie and Souleymane Bachir Diagne, eds, *The Meanings of Timbuktu*, pp. 95–108. Cape Town: HSRC Press.

Ngugi wa Thiong'o. 1993. *Moving the Centre: The Struggle for Cultural Freedoms*. London: Heinemann.

Reindorf, Carl Christian. 1895. *History of the Gold Coast and Asante: Based on Traditions and Historical Facts, Comprising a Period of More Than Three Centuries from about 1500 to 1860*. Basel. At http://www.archive.org/stream/historyofgoldcoa00rein/historyofgoldcoa00rein_djvu.txt (accessed Mar. 2012).

Rodney, Walter. 1973. *How Europe Underdeveloped Africa*. London: Bogle-L'Ouverture.

Sartre, Jean-Paul. 1963. Preface. In Frantz Fanon, *The Wretched of the Earth*, pp. 7–34. New York: Grove.

van Binsbergen, Wim. 2000. Le point de vue de Wim van Binsbergen. *Politique Africaine* 79 (Oct.): 175–180.

CHAPTER THIRTY

Islamicate World Histories?

Huri Islamoğlu

Historians of different regions view world history in relation to how they situate their regions in that history. In a very broad sense, world history writing since the nineteenth century originated in the "West," with European expansion into and colonization of non-European regions. Western world histories, with some notable exceptions, have told the story of European domination in the world – casting the histories of non-European regions in terms of categories that tended to universalize European (and later American) concerns and perceptions related to that domination. These concerns varied over time with the twists and turns in the European presence in the world, ranging from demonstrations of the essential cultural superiority of the West, to sentimental bemoaning of its decline, to regrets over the sins of European trade expansion in the subjugation of non-European regions, resulting in their underdevelopment and backwardness, and finally, when European domination has been challenged in the early twenty-first century, to attempts to relativize the success of the West, exploring the historical or environmental contingencies that may have accounted for it, and asking whether it could have happened – or will happen – elsewhere.

Engagements of historians of non-European lands with world history have generally taken the form of turning inwards to write or rewrite regional or national histories, responding or reacting to the presuppositions of European world historical writings about their society and history. On the other hand, regional or national histories written from a comparative point of reference, measuring the history of a given region against that of Europe, could be considered as much world history as European world histories had been – with their focus on European concerns, and with non-European regions serving as a contrastive backdrop to an essentially European story. All this, of course, suggests a fundamental question: Is world history possible? Is it perhaps time to set aside the hefty claim to "world history" and simply and more humbly talk about comparative history? (See Adas, this volume.) This chapter addresses the various engagements of historians in one part of the Islamicate world: in the former Ottoman territories encompassing the Arab Middle East, Anatolia, the Balkans and the Caucasus. In doing so, it

A Companion to World History, First Edition. Edited by Douglas Northrop.
© 2012 Blackwell Publishing Ltd. Published 2012 by Blackwell Publishing Ltd.

explores the conceptual bottlenecks in imaginings of world history that have been ingrained in existing world historical thinking in relation to the history of Ottoman territories. It suggests that if historians could distance themselves from such habits of mind, it may perhaps be possible to write a genuine "world history."

First, however, an explanatory word about the term "Islamicate." This term was coined in the 1960s by the historian Marshall Hodgson.[1] It represented a challenge to the existing, Orientalist world historical vision that condemned the history of Islamic lands to one of continued decline and stagnation following Arab cultural florescence from the ninth through the twelfth centuries CE. Hodgson objected to this erasure of the modern history of Islam, which amounted to a rejection of its universalistic, cosmopolitan reach. "Islamicate" referred to its distinctly universal dimension, to the world historical "venture of Islam" (as Hodgson titled his major work) that swept across Eurasia from Spain to North Africa, the eastern Mediterranean, Iran and Central Asia, merging the diverse societal, cultural, and religious legacies of these lands from medieval to modern times. Hodgson challenged scholars to rewrite world histories and to restore to the histories of Islamicate lands their place in world history, that is, to write the histories of these lands in terms *other* than those of their subordination to the West. Historians of the Ottoman lands have not, for the most part, taken up his challenge. In fact, most regional or national histories of the region ignored Hodgson's work, taking Western histories (and their basic categories) as an underlying frame of reference.[2] This chapter attempts again to nudge historians in the direction Hodgson suggested.

The position of Ottoman territories within Western world histories varied over time, shifting with changes in world conditions, just as historians within the Ottoman territories changed their views of their societies' place in the world and in relation to the West. Of the many such shifts that could be described, this essay will focus first on four Western modes of interpretation: (1) the Orientalist/liberal perceptions of the nineteenth century, an approach that still lingers in perceptions of the formerly Ottoman territories; (2) the Braudelian moment; (3) the world-system perspectives of the 1970s; and (4) the antistatist new liberalism of the 1990s. Reactions or responses by historians working within these lands also varied, from nationalist histories rejecting the Ottoman past in favor of imagined ancient (pre-Islamic) national legacies, to secular, statist formulations embracing the Ottoman past. They also included conceptions of Ottoman territories as victims of European trade expansion, or as an idealized oasis of premodern societal harmony. Some, lastly, conceived the empire's modern historical trajectory since the fifteenth century in a world-historical context of trade expansion and interstate competition, an approach that underscored convergences rather than divergences with the outside world, and between the East and the West. In relation to this latter understanding of the Ottoman Empire as part of a shared world history of modern transformation that has characterized all of Eurasia since the fifteenth century, the conclusion suggests some possibilities of writing truly world histories that will not be so overshadowed by Western concerns and perceptions.

In the Wake of Defeat and Humiliation:
Tortuous Dialogues with Orientalist Visions

Following the collapse of the Ottoman Empire at the end of World War I, historical writing in the former Ottoman lands became a key part of the processes of nation-building and the creation of new social and political identities: national, secular, Western, and Islamic. The histories written during this period tell us as much about their authors' personal commitments and the societies they inhabited as they do about their ostensible subject matter. Often historians' commitments were rooted in a profound sense of pathos in the wake of military defeat, of European colonization, of societies torn apart as millions of people were compelled to leave their homes in the former imperial territories to pursue dreams of creating new societies, and of restoring dignities lost to defeat, humiliation, and colonization at the hands of Europeans. Indeed, historians and the postimperial elites they belonged to can be said to have lived with a sense of failure as late as the 1960s, with their scholarly work driven by the urgent need to rewrite history to establish a firm distance from that failure, one that came to be identified with Ottoman rule and/or Islam. Yet both the Ottomans and Islam were embraced under conditions of other defeats by the West, this time represented by Israel, and of global market developments heralding new ways of imagining Europe, the Ottomans and Islam.

Elites in the former Ottoman lands often resorted to Orientalist conceptions, articulated in a binary vision of world history, for explanations and solutions of the condition of their society. This was especially true of the Ottoman bureaucratic elites who, following the empire's collapse, governed in the new Turkish republic that had been established in its Anatolian provinces. Historical writing of the 1920s and 1930s in Turkey thus largely assimilated Orientalist depictions of the Ottoman Empire, highlighting some Orientalist assertions while ignoring others. For the Orientalists, the Ottoman Empire as part of an Islamic civilization in decline since the twelfth century was characterized by economic backwardness, without the rule of law and ruled by despots. Islam, its law, its political theory recognizing the legitimacy of a *de facto* ruler, all were held responsible for the Ottoman deprivation, while Europe (in contrast) epitomized modern civilization – economic progress, the rule of law, participatory government, and rational and secular thinking.[3] As such, Europeanization was the solution; it amounted to becoming civilized. This Orientalist perspective on world history haunted historical writing in the independent Turkish republic.[4] History became an arena for venting all kinds of self-hatred and for the making of national, secular and Westernist identities often in conflict with each other. Universally, though, it meant a rejection of the Ottoman past.

This rejection of the Ottoman/Islamic past led these historians to other domains of world history, most importantly to that of Turkic lands and the peoples of Central Asia.[5] M.F. Koprulu, for instance, a prominent member of the Ottoman elites, while dismissing the Islamic component, retold the story of the rise of the Ottoman Empire by tracing it to tribal movements out of Central Asia,[6] and the subsequent "civilizing" of the tribes through exposure to the Byzantine institutional environment (Ersanli 1993; Koprulu 1988). In this way, Koprulu sought a reconciliation of the nationalist story (the Turkic) with the Western element (Byzantine); an encounter of the primitive with the "civilized" perhaps pointing to the future adoption of European institutions. On the other hand, for H. Inalcik, this "civilizing" dimension is sought not in Europe (via Byzantium) but in a non-European context – pre-Islamic Iran – through a focus on the uniqueness of Ottoman civilization as rooted in the institutions of Iranian statecraft.

Yet the overriding emphasis of Turkish republican elites on a critique of Islam and on secularism was paralleled by a tendency to overlook the liberal strand in that thinking. The latter idea refers to a critique of Oriental despotism and its detrimental effects on economic development and progress. Historians and elites of the Turkish republic did not engage with the antistatist dimensions of Orientalist discourse. This was particularly so in the wake of global economic depression in the 1930s, when statist economic policies prevailed in Turkey and widely throughout the world. In this context, Ottoman history was reconceived as part of a nationalistic and secularist discourse. Hence, for Inalcik (1992), secular law, propagated by the state, had enabled a more just distribution of resources – notably of land. This process was, however, interrupted by the introduction of Islamic law and its precept of individual landownership – which, according to Inalcik, partly caused the social unrest that led to the end of the secular golden age of the Ottomans, starting in the late sixteenth century.

By contrast, in the Arab lands which, unlike Turkey, were colonized by European powers, rejection of Ottoman history took a liberal turn. Consigning Ottoman rule to the wider domain of colonial history, Arab historians built a nationalist vision of the past by turning to an idealized Arab history, one inseparable from that of Islam. At the same time, in the 1930s an attempt was made to derive a "secular" civil code from Islamic law, wherein jurists drew a distinction between the moral and religious dimension of the law, on the one hand, and its legal dimension, on the other (Hill 1987).[7] The anticolonialist approach prevailed in Arab history writing, and in the 1960s Israeli aggression sparked a widespread perception in Arab regions that colonial administrations had divided up a singular area, one united by Ottoman societal and administrative networks, into smaller units that then became the different nation-states.[8] Increasingly the Ottoman past was dissociated from the region's colonial past and became part of a more indigenous form of modern history.

A similar process, a repatriation of Ottoman history, took place in the Balkans following the Balkan wars of the 1990s. In this region Orientalist visions had not so much been rooted in a critique of Islam (given the local predominance of Christianity) but rather concentrated on the mosaic character of Balkan society – depicting it, that is, as an unruly society of disconnected communities held together only by the iron rule of an Oriental despot. Both nationalist and socialist histories later sought an interpretive cohesion of the different regions through recourse to pre-Ottoman Slavic pasts and to a universal history of socialism, respectively. Yet following the collapse of socialist regimes and the outbreak of ethnic and religious conflict alongside the rise of dictators, the earlier conception reappeared, depicting (in both the historical past and the violent present) a view of the Balkans as a mosaic-like society ruled by despots. In countering such images of fragmented societies, where violence reigns supreme unless countered by the iron hand of a ruler, recent historiography has turned to Ottoman history in search of historical connections among the different communities that make up these societies, to recover a broader societal identity (see, e.g., Todorova 2009; Blumi 2003).

Europe: Coveted Object of Desire, and of Alienation

Orientalist world historical visions cast the relationship between Europe and the Ottoman lands in contrasting images of prosperity and deprivation, law and tyranny, civilized and uncivilized. Such contrasts had not only been internalized by elites (including historians) but also by wider populations. This vision in time became part of a popular discourse, a societal auto-critique, a constant reminder that equality with Europe was unattainable unless and until society abandoned its essential (i.e. distinctive) cultural features and adopted European ones. From the 1960s onwards, world developments, including the Vietnam War, conditions of economic underdevelopment in postcolonial areas, including former Ottoman territories in Arab lands, Israeli aggression and invasion of Arab lands, and Israel's identification with the West, all led to notions of the difference between the West and the rest as cast more in structural economic and political terms, and less in terms of culture. The divide between the East and the West thus came to be expressed more tangibly, in ways that either suggested the divide was permanent and insurmountable, or that (as in Latin America) one could find political possibilities for engaging with it.

During World War II, a time of deep crisis in Europe that underscored the shift of world economic power to America, Fernand Braudel wrote a world history of the sixteenth-century Mediterranean – when that majestic sea was the center of a world economy. He found a geographic and economic unity of the Mediterranean region, in other words, precisely as the center of the world economy was shifting to the Atlantic. Braudel wanted to suggest that Europe should be united rather than divided, and his work (and the deeper idea of *Mediterranean*) became an inspiration for the later European Community.

Historians of the Ottoman Empire saw in Braudel's conception the possibility of bringing Ottoman territories' history back into Europe (where it had been) and thus into the mainstream of world history. Nineteenth-century European culturalist perspectives, by siting the Ottoman Empire within a separate, Islamic civilizational unit, had contributed to its isolation. Braudel, by contrast, viewed the Ottoman territories as part of a wider geographical/economic landscape of the Mediterranean world, as part of the global historical drama of the shifting of world trade routes to the Atlantic; a broader story, one beginning in the seventeenth century, and that accounted for the dramatic world-economic marginalization of both the Spanish Habsburgs *and* the Ottomans.

To this end, Braudel had formed a team of researchers at the École des Hautes Études en Sciences Sociales to study population and production trends in the western Mediterranean. Historians of the Ottoman Empire, most notably O.L. Barkan, sought to collaborate in this project, assembling in the 1950s a group of researchers at the University of Istanbul to publish hundreds of Ottoman tax registers from which population and production data for the Ottoman eastern Mediterranean regions could be gleaned. This was a glimpse of genuine world-historical work. (See Weinstein, this volume.) For the secular and Western-oriented historians of the early Turkish republic, it had the additional value of psychologically reestablishing ties with the empire's European territories in the Balkans and in Crimea, the study of which had been neglected in favor of a nationalistic focus on Anatolia and its linkages to Central Asia.[9] Braudel's conception of world history as expressed in the sixteenth-century Mediterranean was the first step in the de-Orientalization of the Ottoman Empire and its territories – in relation to both nationalistic and Orientalist historical writings.

In the 1970s, a world-system perspective, following Braudel, also situated the Ottoman territories in the world historical context of European world trade. (See Chase-Dunn and Hall, this volume.) In doing so, it too challenged culturalist views of civilizational isolation, which (in either Orientalist or nationalist forms) had resulted in a fragmentation of the history of the empire and in erasures of the multiple connectivities (networks of trade, administration, educational and religious institutions, or societal relations) that made the empire a viable economic and social unit, as well as a political and cultural one.[10]

However, the world-system perspective – not unlike earlier liberal/Orientalist world histories – also set out to tell the story of European world domination. Granted, it did not portray that domination as part of Europe's mission to civilize the non-European world. To the contrary, world-system scholars traced the roots of economic backwardness and poverty in postcolonial regions (including the former Ottoman territories) to

European trade expansion and the incorporation of these regions into a European world economic system. The world-system perspective presented a vision of world history that rested on the emergence, starting in the sixteenth century, of a global division of labor between a European center and a non-European periphery. The former specialized in the production of manufactured goods, where high-cost wage labor prevailed, and strong states developed industrial production and trade. What sustained the European center was its trade with non-European regions. These latter areas specialized in the production of raw materials, and in them forms of coerced or serf-like cheap labor prevailed; as weak states, their practices enabled the incorporation process but had little initiative beyond that. In fact, this "peripheralization" character-ized a process whereby the non-European regions or societies (and ultimately their histories) were placed at the mercy of world markets, responding to, and continually shaped by, the exigencies of European demand for primary goods, while also providing markets for European manufactured goods. Peripheral regions had practically no say in the determination of this division of labor, nor could they determine its effects on labor organization or production patterns. The history of the periphery was thus understood to be one of submission: of the processes and institutions, that is, that enabled its submission to the demands of European trade.

The Ottoman territories had thus been designated as part of the world periphery, their incorporation into the world system having begun in the late sixteenth century. During the 1970s and 1980s, a significant number of historians adopted this perspective to explore the history of peripheralization in the Ottoman Empire's territories in Anatolia, and in its Arab lands in the eastern Mediterranean. Historians studied changing structures of trade, the ways European demand affected new patterns of organization of rural agricultural and industrial production, and most significantly, the organization of European trade in port cities, and the activities of non-Muslim Ottoman merchants there (see especially Kasaba 1988).

Above all, for historians of the Ottoman Empire, the world-system perspective provided an opening from their previous position of culturalist isolation, and it permit-ted their entry into the wider domain of world history. It also allowed different ways of thinking about "underdevelopment" and economic backwardness from which regions of the former empire suffered. Many prescriptions for modernization that had been intro-duced by the World Bank and other agencies blamed Islam and/or authoritarian political culture for contemporary economic and social ills. The world-system perspective provided relief from this brand of self-hatred that had been imposed on these societies: now Europe was to be blamed, not individuals in the formerly Ottoman lands, and not their culture either. As a result, Ottoman history began to make a new kind of sense in the context of the anti-imperialist struggles of the 1960s and 1970s. The writing and teaching of Ottoman history from this perspective gained considerable institutional trac-tion, and came to be most prominently expressed in two major universities in Turkey: Middle Eastern Technical University (Ankara) and Bogazici University (Istanbul).[11]

The world-system perspective also contributed to the reinstating of Ottoman history in the writing of wider histories of the region. Studies of the incorporation of different regions – especially in Anatolia and the Arab eastern Mediterranean – found similarities in the institutional infrastructure throughout the empire that had been exposed to common pressures from European trade. This discovery encouraged historians to think in terms of commonalities among the histories of different regions. Historical research increasingly pointed to a totality of Ottoman history as being about a peripheral area; in doing so, at least from the perspective of Arab lands, the Ottoman era was no longer viewed as part of the region's colonial history. Scholarly networks and organization of workshops, providing historians with opportunities to exchange insights and information, all contributed to a reconceptualization of the Ottoman Empire as a viable object of historical inquiry, and returned it to a place in world history – albeit a peripheral one.[12]

Yet conceptualizing Ottoman history in relation to the categories of the world-system, attempting to fit that history into the straitjacket of peripheralization or the status of the periphery, implied that historical inquiry had to sacrifice an attention to the specific internal dynamics of these regions to the broader dynamics of European trade and its assumed transformative effects. This emphasis meant a significant narrowing of the domain of historical inquiry, and a parochializing of the history of the Ottoman regions. They, along with other world peripheral regions in Africa and Asia, had thus been assigned a separate historical trajectory, one different from that of the West, or the center. The center had its own story, one to which the periphery could only be linked in a relationship of subordination. It also meant that these regions were always peripheral to world history, in the sense of never having any agency: their structures, societies, and economies were condemned lastingly to be subject to the transformative logic of European trade, condemned to a certain history, to a certain kind of world history.[13]

The world-system perspective primarily focused on the transformative effects of European trade on non-European societies – societies they assumed to have been stagnant before the advent of that trade. Thus, existing regional and interregional trade was understood to have been one of distributive channeling of surpluses – which were collected as taxes, and met only the basic requirements of both rural and urban populations, not allowing for any capital accumulation. The latter was assumed to have been a unique feature of European trade. In the case of the Ottoman territories, however, regional and interregional trading networks (both land-based and maritime) had been a key source of capital accumulation invested in urban as well as rural manufacturing, in state financing (most notably through tax-farming arrangements), and, crucially, in external trade – both European and non-European. One simply cannot talk about external trade – either European or non-European – without its linkages to the empire's internal trade.[14] Nor is it possible to assign a particular prominence to non-Muslim merchants in these interlocking trade activities. No doubt European states and trading interests, by pressuring the Ottoman government in the nineteenth century, *sought* such prominence, but this effort should not (and did not) mean that Ottoman Muslim merchants ceased to participate in trade.[15] Interregional and regional trade flourished into the nineteenth century, sustaining important inland trading cities in Anatolia, Arab east Mediterranean areas, and the Balkans, with both Ottoman Muslim and non-Muslim merchants participating. Finally, the distinction between external and internal trade needs to be problematized even farther, considering that "European" trade had from the late eighteenth century onwards included areas that were part of the Ottoman Empire in the northern Black Sea, the Caucasus, and the Balkans. After these regions came under Russian or Austrian control, trade continued, largely maintaining the integrity of earlier exchange networks.

On the other hand, the effect of increased commercial demand on societal relations, or on the wider developmental trajectories of the Ottoman territories, was largely determined (or mediated through) political power relations centered on the state. The Ottoman state in the nineteenth century, in fact, was far from the weak state that world-system analysts assumed it to be. Such a depiction primarily focuses on the concessions European governments extracted in the form of reform edicts, including privileges for European trade representatives (non-Muslim Ottoman subjects). State practices responded not only to the demands of European traders and states, though, but also to merchants in internal trade, and to rural and urban producers. That the European trade did not result in the transformative trajectories – semi-servile rural labor, agricultural large estates, or deindustrialization – predicted by world-system analysis was largely due to state actions and initiatives that testify to an institutional innovativeness rather than a desperate accommodation to a growing mosaic of external demands.[16] For instance, legislation on land and commercial transactions, which shaped the developmental trajectories of rural production relations and ownership, was attentive both to local political and economic tensions and to state interests in taxation and security. The resulting pattern did not favor large estates but rather smallholdings, with cultivators maintaining a tenacious hold on use-rights in various forms, including legally sanctioned, permanent tenancies. In other cases, by contrast, state inaction could be determining. For instance, the state bureaucracy – notwithstanding pressure from the British government – did not intervene in the activities of rural textile manufacturers, an approach that served to limit the import of European cloth.

What is at issue here is how historians assign agency to state actors and others in shaping the direction of societal transformations. Both the liberal/Orientalist perspective and the later world-system view assigned such agency, in the Ottoman case, to European actors – either states or merchants. They did so because they understood a modern transformation to have originated – for either historical or cultural reasons – in Europe, while the rest of the world sat on the receiving end of impulses from the West. In this sense, world histories written from these perspectives remained essentially European histories.

Global Capitalism, Contested Western Hegemony, and New World Historical Visions

In the 1990s, amid a burgeoning global market economy and the rapid emergence of China as a possible economic rival to the West, new world-historical writing appeared. These histories, published mostly in the United States, questioned the Eurocentric character of earlier accounts. Employing the terminology of the prevailing market discourse, A.G. Frank pointed to the competitive superiority of China as well as of Ottoman and Mughal regions in world trade and industrial production prior to the eighteenth century, at which point Europe gained a competitive edge and achieved world domination. Historical inquiry thereafter focused on the question of what accounted for this European, or more specifically British, "divergence." (See Adas, this volume.) Recent explanations have highlighted environmental and economic features affecting factor endowments – most notably, coal and labor – in Britain and in the East.[17] This is tantamount to a relativization of Western world domination, pointing first to other historical eras when different regions had the lead, then suggesting that the West may have had its moment, and that now the East may be gearing up for a renewed domination.

Historians of the Ottoman Empire did not directly engage with these world-historical visions of the 1990s, except for a few historians schooled in world-system analysis who shifted their emphasis away from the process of peripheralization to the identification of multiple historical trajectories of different regions in competition, in keeping with a wider spirit of market liberalism (Kasaba 2009; Emrence 2008). More prominently, however, historical writing on the Ottoman past in the 1990s turned toward a broadly culturalist agenda under the general rubric of postmodernism, an offshoot of the free-trade infused global environment, and with an eye on widespread societal liberations in the wake of the dismantling of communist states in the Soviet bloc, and the retreat of welfare states in the West and developmentalist states in the Third World. Above all, postmodernist thinking resting on a rejection of the "modern" governmental state from the nineteenth century onward, and it turned back to the early modern era in search of forms of civil society which modern state practices were thought to have done away with. To historians of the former Ottoman territories, the emphasis on early modernity offered an opportunity for distancing the post-nineteenth-century history of a weakening empire, and its consequent Westernization via secular state formations. The modern state and its practices were thus blamed for all the aspects in Ottoman society which Orientalists (both in the nineteenth century and again in the late twentieth and early twenty-first centuries, especially following the September 11, 2001 attacks in the United States) claimed had been lacking in Ottoman society: the rule of law, legitimate state power, institutions responsive to changing conditions, and abilities to negotiate ethnic and religious differences. Moreover, as the modern state was similarly maligned in European historiography (also under the sway of this postmodern trend), it seemed Ottoman historiography finally had acquired an intellectual legitimacy in the eyes of dominant world historiography. Significant numbers of students – most notably Americans, but also students from these formerly Ottoman territories who went to study Ottoman history at US universities – have adopted this perspective.

For historians from the former Ottoman territories, this postmodern turn to early modernity to recover a civil society of multiple religious and ethnic communities, a society with a tolerance of diversity, a personalized state that negotiated with individuals and accommodated their needs, offered a number of possibilities. One, the almost idyllic imaginings of an early modern society, became a way of marshaling an intellectual defense against the onslaught of authoritarian and militaristic governments, variously nationalist, secular, and Westernist.[18] Secondly, in the wake of eruptions of ethnic and religious conflict, especially in the former Yugoslavia, visions of an early modern Ottoman society that was a "mosaic" of diverse ethnic and religious communities provided new ways of imagining the past and perhaps hope for the future (Todorova 2009).

Thirdly, reimagining the early modern past and its social diversity also provided an inspiration for exploring new identities or ways of being in the increasingly transnational context of global capitalism. One such context was that of the European Union. Pluralistic conceptions of Ottoman early modernity resonated with searches for multiculturalist identities in the EU. At the same time, Islamic identity – as one that had been suppressed by modern states – has emerged as a cosmopolitan and transnational framework, one enabling networks of economic and societal cooperation.

From the perspective of situating Ottoman territories into the terrain of world history writing, the postmodern turn displays a certain involution, a rather self-satisfied withdrawal into remote and cozy utopias where the virtues of Ottoman history could be defended against Western (Orientalist) preconceptions, while, at the same time, rendering that history "precious" and incomparable in its cultural specificities – whether of its legal or state cultures. This culturalism, however, results in erasures of all the tensions and conflicts both within the Ottoman imperial entity and arising in its interactions in the wider world, in broader contexts of which the Ottoman Empire was an integral part. Put differently, it sacrifices history at the altar of a cultural early modern fantasy which is granted admission into a gallery of similar fantasies about European societies. Instead of a comparative early modern *world* history, one obtains a colorful display of cultural narratives – the Ottoman narrative serving as a welcome exotic addition. Moreover, the seeming challenge posed by the postmodern turn to Orientalism, is only seeming: unlike earlier contestations of Orientalist categories (e.g. world-systems analysis), which represented a challenge to the Orientalist methodology of culturalism, the postmodern turn is totally subsumed by that methodology.

One important focus of this new liberal trend in the writing of Ottoman history has been studies of Ottoman legal culture, its meditational and negotiative character. For instance, E. Akarli (2005) emphasizes that law, as it was practiced at local courts – and at the imperial high court as well – addressed the concerns of individuals and communities in different localities, accommodating customary practices and the laws of different religious communities and guilds. This approach allowed each their own ways of settling disputes, with judges intervening only when custom failed to resolve a dispute. Such practices, according to Akarli, contributed to harmonious relations in the society and were pivotal in building a consensus in support of the ruler's power among society's many diverse elements. Yet, on the other hand, this legal culture – pervasive and cohesive – was also steeped in Islam, and its transcendent quality vis-à-vis other religions. The modern bureaucratic state, with its secular, Westernist aspirations and nonnegotiable law that required no consensus for its authority, is then held responsible for disrupting this utopia's seamless blending of pious law and political authority. We are thus presented with a view in which society has been wronged in history, a story told as "morality tale,"[19] a tale of lost worlds projected into a world-historical context of passages to modernity. It is also a story that distances "modernity" from the actually existing modern society, through a total erasure of all the social tensions produced by challenges of commercial expansion and state demands. For instance, there is no sign of the perennial tension between judges at Islamic courts of law, also members of the religious establishment which controlled large resources (most importantly lands), and the state bureaucracy that wished to extract revenues from these lands. Such tensions crystallized both secular and religious claims, and one cannot simply expel the "secular" to a yonder domain of alien modernity, with its associated evils.

This culturalist perspective also prevails in characterizations of the state. For instance, Pamuk (2004) explains the longevity of the Ottoman state by referring to a culture of pragmatism, which enabled the state to accommodate societal conflicts. Hence, while subscribing to (or taking on faith) the nineteenth-century liberal/Orientalist presupposition that the conflict between state and commercial interests was the key difference between Ottoman and European environments, Pamuk argues that the flexibility of state practices meant commercial interests could prevail until the nineteenth century, when such flexibility finally reached its limits and more oppressive practices took over. A similar fetishization of accommodation and negotiation as key aspects of early modern society, as practices lost to modernity (this time in relation to empire), characterizes the work of Karen Barkey. (See Sinha, this volume.) Barkey (2008) accounts for the persistence of an Ottoman society of multiple and diverse religious and ethnic communities by framing the empire as a negotiated enterprise, one motivated by a culture of tolerance that waned once the empire confronted European attacks on its territories. Such attacks forced it onto the defensive, and tolerance came to an end. In the process, the empire (it is not clear here how Barkey differentiates empire from the state) falls afoul of commercial interests, conjoined with tax-farming processes, which realize their own form of indigenous modernity – as the empire drifts toward oppressive management practices, and ultimately extinction. True to the precepts of nineteenth-century liberalism, Barkey, like Pamuk, underscores the essentially conflicting interests of empire (state?) and merchants. Yet it still appears that the latter group, comprising both Muslims and non-Muslims, needed the empire's negotiating environment to sustain itself.

Most significantly, as noted above, the postmodern turn represents a withdrawal from the wider history of a modern transformation that encompassed both European and non-European societies. Such a withdrawal is infused with a theoretical critique of the modern governmental state. Central to the crucial divide this approach posits between early modern and late modern, a divide meant to replace the earlier distinction between East and West, is the notion of negotiation. "Negotiation" is taken as the defining feature of early modern society, whereas the uncompromising modern state does not allow any negotiation of its practices. Hence, this notion is a fundamental principle used to explain virtually all kinds of state actions. It results in the definition of two ideal types (i.e., early modern states and late modern states), which are locked into their respective definitions. Yet taking this concept of negotiation as an object of inquiry, not as something assumed, would allow for evaluations of the different contexts in which negotiations take place, and for the careful tracing of shifts in these contexts, precisely as early modern states transformed into modern ones.[20] This approach, crucially, would allow history writing to move beyond ideal types, and would thereby make possible a more historicized vision of modernity, one that emerges in its complicated continuities and changes, from at least the fifteenth century. Instead, what is proposed is a horizontally integrated view of the early modern histories of Europe and non-European societies, which are portrayed with certain shared features, both contrasted with similarly defined late modern histories. It appears as if the postmodern turn took both European *and* non-European regions out of the bounds of historical inquiry; it developed an internalized moral mapping of a remote imagined past, alongside an ostensibly failing future, one full of strife, and with the laudably flexible cultures of legal, religious, and state tolerance long gone.

Can We Write World Histories That Are Genuinely "World Histories"?

I conclude this chapter by venturing that finally the time may have come to address world history writing in a new way: by giving full weight to the histories of different world regions and *not* subsuming these histories in a story of Western world domination. Our present history at least suggests that it is time to look beyond that domination.

A genuine rethinking of world history implies transcending the binaries of West and non-West, European center and non-European periphery, premodern and modern. It implies questioning the identification of modernity with the West, whereby institutions emerging from Western history represented universal attributes of modernity, merely imported or adopted or resisted by non-Westerners. Insofar as it exists as a discrete and recognizable entity, though, "modernity" is a *universal* historical process, one with a history not confined to that of the West. It refers to the continuous processes of exploring new institutional configurations to cope with the challenges of commercial expansion and state formation/interstate competition underway throughout Eurasia (and later the Americas and other continents) since the fifteenth century (Islamoğlu and Perdue 2009). The Ottoman Empire – as well as the Ming Empire in China, the Habsburgs in Spain, and others – emerged out of this world-historical context. They were all born into this world-historical environment: the survival of any depended on the ability of different actors (including states, merchants, artisans, and cultivators), to generate innovative institutions (financial instruments, land tenure systems, statecraft, weapon technologies, agricultural techniques). In all of these efforts can be traced a shared history of different regions, responding to the demands of a new world-historical context and, in doing so, relating to and linking with each other. (See Bright and Geyer, this volume.)

Decades ago, Marshall Hodgson remarked that without the rich cumulation of institutional innovations in the Afro-Eurasian *oikoumene* – including those in the Islamicate lands of the Ottoman, Mughal and Safavid empires – the Western transmutation would have been "unthinkable" (Hodgson 1993: part I). That transmutation, he said, was itself part of world-historical processes, representing mostly an acceleration of these processes in the late eighteenth century, in such a way as to result in Western world domination. This did not mean that other regions stopped being institutionally innovative (that, after all, was part of merely surviving in the modern world), but they did so at a different pace; nor did it mean that other societies did not have their high points or moments of domination; nor, by implication, does it mean they will not have their moments again.

For Hodgson, this concerted effort to respond to changing conditions through institutional innovation – to find new ways of ordering production, property rights, commercial transactions, and state administration – represented the "unity of history." That view of unity, however, implied that different regions shaped and contributed to the core content of this history. Hence, it is important to ask, *how* did different societies meet the challenge of modern transformation, what institutional solutions did they produce? By whom and through what means? What, then, were the different trajectories of this common modern transformation in various societies? How did these trajectories interact with each other? When seen in a world-historical context of shared challenges faced by different regions, the answers should ignore the perennial issue that has previously distracted historians, that is, which area is "modern," and which is not. *All* the regions throughout Eurasia have been involved in the historical processes of modern transformation, and these processes have been constitutive of social, political, and economic practices in the different regions. Various areas responded to the core challenges of modern history in different ways, thus partly accounting for their different historical trajectories. Such variations speak to the more general issue of locating human or societal agency in the making of specific, contingent historical trajectories. On the other hand, specific institutional responses were also simultaneously shaped through continuous interactions across regions. In this sense, we cannot speak of hermetically sealed universes of "regional" responses to "external" (world-historical) phenomena either, but rather need to suggest an assimilation of those phenomena into the very fabric of their specific institutional trajectories.

Historically, states representing various configurations of political power relations have been central to the exercise of societal agency (as have communities of merchants, artisans, and cultivators). As such they have played a key role in these modern transformations. Most importantly, state power referred to an ability to order societal realities, that is, initiating and defining particular institutional solutions in response to changing conditions. In the Ottoman context, as in other territorial empires, this work focused on securing social peace to ensure (among other things) commerce, production, and resource collection.

Statecraft or rulings drawing on Islamic law as well as Roman law, even ancient Sassanid traditions of statecraft, had been the chief means for crafting such institutional solutions. However, these solutions also created further terrains for deliberations among and contestations by multiple actors in this world region. In the nineteenth-century Ottoman empire, for instance, rulings about landed property and the rules of commercial transactions were subject to continuous debate among different actors, including state administrators, commercial interests and tax-farmers who had ownership claims, cultivators who had use-rights, and urban producers and pastoralists. Property rulings as well as rules of commercial transaction bore the traces of such struggles, often accounting for differences in various places and times, often related to shifting power relations among the different actors. Yet one may nevertheless speak of an underlying unity of the institutional environment: of the state (its sovereign status) represented through a set of general principles to address what were fundamentally the moral concerns of the government.[21] These concerns – which in Ottoman parlance were expressed through a language of "justice" – were shared throughout Eurasia. They aimed to achieve a balance between freedom (representing the ever-expanding commercial environment) and power, or the responsibility of the state to mediate the adverse affects of freedom on the larger community.[22]

The political character of the state and its statecraft or law ultimately contributed to the particular developmental trajectories of this world region and thus ultimately to the shaping of a wider world-historical context, as each state in turn interacted with others. This could take the shape of war and peace, of assimilating institutions, of understandings of government and its role. One could speak – in the spirit of Joseph Fletcher – of the ways steppe empires linked the Chinese and Ottoman state formations, transmitting techniques of government between East Roman (Byzantine), Iranian, Chinese, and Turkic traditions.[23] To Europeans, Ottoman statecraft appeared as the visible face of this body of knowledge, and it was assimilated into the Renaissance ideal of governance. Machiavelli's *Prince* approximated an idealized image of the Ottoman ruler, possibly more than the glorious Medici. Later, as centralizing European states looked to Frederick the Great's "well-ordered police state" or *Rechtsstaat* and the subjecting of governments themselves to the rule of law, the Ottoman Empire and the Mughal state, as well as the Chinese Middle Kingdom, became contrasting metaphors for despotism, mirrors for a critique of the absolutist practices of European rulers (Islamoğlu and Perdue 2009). Finally, one could refer to state actions affecting worldwide trade flows, movements of people, and production levels worldwide.

Western world-historical writing, however, has long denied the centrality of states or political power relations to the process of modern transformation, instead focusing extensively – almost exclusively – on commercial relations (Frank, Pomeranz) or by denying state effectiveness to non-European regions, Islamicate areas in particular. By doing so they have distanced the latter histories from a shared history of modernity. The world-system perspective, for instance, assimilated Orientalist visions to identify the Ottoman state with the figure of an oriental despot who ruled over but did not govern the multiple and diverse communities of traders, people of different religious faiths, fraternities of artisans, religious sects, trading communities, villages, cities – all coexisting but quite unrelated to each other. The despot's rule was not rooted in societal relations, supposedly, but on coercive relations of taxation. In the nineteenth century this perception justified European interventions in Ottoman governance, including the introduction of European-inspired reform packages and legislation that aimed to establish "modern institutions."[24] Ottoman statesmen of the nineteenth century understood the intent of these proposals: they saw the introduction of the French civil code, for example, as an impingement on their right to govern, that is, to generate their own institutional responses to political and economic conditions. For them, such intrusions were tantamount to denial of the political identity or the sovereign existence of the empire (Mardin 1946). In response, Ottoman jurists drafted the Land Code, including new definitions of landed property rights, and a Civil Code containing new rules for commercial transactions. Both legislative changes drew on the categories of Islamic *fiqh* as well as a rich legacy of customary practices.

Above all, the rethinking of world history as one that is *not* bifurcated into domains of domination and subordination, East and West, center and periphery, allows for human or societal agency in different world regions, whereby multiple actors are continually engaged in crafting institutionally innovative responses to changing conditions. They do so in a common world-historical context of continuous interactions across regions through trade, war, and exchange of ideas. Specific institutional responses were shaped through such interactions. What accounted for the persistence of different non-European formations – for instance, Chinese and Ottoman – were the abilities of states as well as other actors to initiate institutional solutions in specific relation to particular patterns of societal relations within individual regions and worldwide. As such, their survival cannot be explained through recourse to any overly specific cultural features, such as their particular abilities to accommodate and tolerate.

In this context, one could refer to changes in the relative positioning of different regions, with changes in the power relations among them or within a given world region. Similarly, one could talk about varied forms of production system, property rights, or the unintended results of societal power relations worldwide. Hence, world history should no longer be imagined as a yet-to-be-realized liberal utopia of the nineteenth century (or its late twentieth-century analogue), as part of a liberal/Orientalist vision. Nor is it one of dependent but irreconcilable separations, as world-system analysts assumed it to be. If histories of non-European regions are not overdetermined by histories of their subjugation to the West, it makes it possible to imagine positioning them in a new kind of world history, according them a compatible space to that of Europe, judging them not simply by outcomes, but evaluating them in relation to the world-historical processes they were part of and to which they responded – or failed to respond.

Notes

1   This work of Hodgson's from the 1960s has been republished more recently in *Rethinking World History* (Hodgson 1993), parts I and II.

2   For instance, Hodgson's *magnum opus*, *The Venture of Islam* (1974), was initially translated into Turkish in the early 1980s by a small Islamist publishing house and was largely ignored. From 2002, after an Islamic political party came to power, its intellectuals turned to world historians favored by their secularist counterparts – including world histories by I. Wallerstein and A.G. Frank. Hodgson's interest in transcending the usual binaries of East and West, religious and secular, did not resonate in the post-2002 Turkish political context. Similarly, P. Gran's work on multiple paths of historical development, also critical of the East/West

divide, resonated with Egyptian historians such as Nelly Hannah but not with Turkish historians. Finally, it was primarily due to a labor of love by Edmund Burke that Hodgson's work came back to the attention of Western world historians in the 1990s; it thereafter contributed largely to the rapidly consolidating field of "world history" in the United States.

3   In this relation it is important to keep in mind Talal Asad's (2003) distinction between the secular and secularism – the latter referring to a modern self-definition or ideology, while the former describes a societal/historical phenomenon.

4   Identification of Europe with a civilizing project to which to aspire has been a central theme in discussions of Turkey's European Union membership, especially by the secular intelligentsia in the 1990s and early 2000s.

5   This reflected the influence of émigré intellectuals, who came to the Ottoman Empire both in the wake of Russian colonization of the Caucasus and Central Asia and following the Bolshevik takeover, on Turkish understandings of a Turkic world history. Most notable was Zeki Velidi Togan, a leader of the *basmachi* movement in Central Asia, who wrote a major world history, *The General History of the Turks*.

6   He was partaking of another favorite theme in Orientalist discourse: the tribe as a representation of primitive society that would be civilized by Europeans (Asad 1973).

7   For an excellent discussion of this distinction in the civil code drafted by al-Sanhuri see Johanssen (1999).

8   This perspective is epitomized in the work of A. Hourani, for instance Hourani (1968).

9   The de-Orientalization of the empire – by claiming its uniqueness and by linking it to the history of Mediterranean Europe – no doubt had a salience for historians such as Barkan and Inalcik, who traced their origins to the Balkan provinces and Crimea, respectively.

10 Two articles in particular introduced the world-system perspective to the study of the Ottoman territories: Islamoğlu and Keyder (1977); Wallerstein *et al.* (1987).

11 A number of world-system historians received their PhDs at the State University of New York-Binghamton, where Immanuel Wallerstein launched the world-system project in the mid-1970s.

12 In this respect R. Owen's efforts were crucial. His scholarly output and his textbooks (*The Middle East in the World Economy*, see Owen 1993) as well as numerous workshops he organized (with Talal Asad and Sami Zubaida) contributed to an integration of Arab lands into the Ottoman imperial unit.

13 Conforming to this vision of dependent but separate histories, in the 1970s there was a proliferation of comparative Third World histories. See Amin (1990).

14 For instance, Damascene Greek Orthodox merchants who had been active in the Hawran wheat trade in northern Syria invested in overseas trade with the Philippines. For this example I am grateful to William Gervase Clarence-Smith, who is currently working on a book on these global linkages.

15 See Hannah (2011) for the internal coffee trade that linked to European trade.

16 For the accommodationist perspective, see Pamuk (2004).

17 Similarly, K. Pomeranz pointed to the compatibility of developmental trajectories in China and Britain with respect to trade, population and production trends, and industrial innovation until the Industrial Revolution, when the trajectories of the East and the West began to diverge (Burke and Pomeranz 2009: Introduction). For Pomeranz (2000), greater availability of coal in England, as compared with the Yangzi Delta in China, played a crucial role.

18 In the Turkish historiography, recent critiques of the nineteenth-century Ottoman state have been extended to that of the Turkish secular, Westernist state in the 1980s. The military coup d'état in Turkey in 1980, however, while emphasizing the secular, nationalist, Westernist premises of the state, also was instrumental in laying the groundwork for a global market economy by removing all the obstacles or resistance to global flows of capital, e.g., cutting trade union power as well as silencing civil society institutions, including universities and professional associations. Postcolonial historians have approximated the practices of the

nineteenth-century Ottoman state to those of colonial European states (Deringil 1999). For the practices of the colonial modern state in Egypt, see Mitchell (1988).

19   Appropriately the title of a book by Leslie Pierce, *Morality Tales* (2003), whose work represents one of the best examples of this genre of history writing.

20   I am grateful to Baber Johansen for his analytical distinction between negotiation as an explanatory category and as an object of inquiry.

21   For instance, in the sixteenth-century formulation of the principle of state ownership in land (Inalcik 1992).

22   In this regard, see the extensive literature on the "social question" in Europe in the early nineteenth century.

23   I thank James Millward for his eloquent comment on this point, presented at the workshop on Shared Histories of Modernity: State Transformations in the Chinese and Ottoman Contexts, Seventeenth through Nineteenth Centuries, at the Kevorkian Center for Near Eastern Studies, New York University, April 1999.

24   In fact, a perception of a liberal governmental state (a ghost of Bentham perhaps?) appears to loom large behind Smithian free-tradist formulations (Bevir and Trentman 2004).

References

Akarli, E. 2005. Law in the market place: Istanbul 1730–1840. In, M. Masud, R. Peters, and D. Powers, eds, *Dispensing Justice in Islam: Qadis and Their Judgements*, pp. 245–270. Leiden: Brill.

Amin, S. 1990. *Delinking towards a Polycentric World*. New York: Zed Books.

Asad, T. 1973. *Anthropology and the Colonial Encounter*. New York: Humanities Press.

Asad, T. 2003. *Formations of the Secular: Christianity, Islam, Modernity*. Stanford: Stanford University Press.

Barkey, K. 2008. *Empire of Difference: The Ottomans in Comparative Perspective*. Cambridge: Cambridge University Press.

Bevir, M., and F. Trentman. 2004. *Markets in Historical Contexts: Ideas and Politics in the Modern World*. Cambridge: Cambridge University Press.

Blumi, I. 2003. *Rethinking the Late Ottoman Empire: A Comparative Social and Political History of Albania and Yemen, 1878–1918*. Istanbul: ISIS.

Burke, E., III, and K. Pomeranz. 2009. *The Environment and World History*. Berkeley: University of California Press.

Deringil, S. 1999. *The Well-Protected Domains: Ideology and Legitimation in the Ottoman Empire*. London: I.B. Tauris.

Emrence, C. 2008. Imperial paths, big comparisons: The late Ottoman empire. *Journal of Global History* 3: 289–311.

Ersanli, C. 1993. *Iktidar ve Tarih. Turkiye'de "Resmi Tarih" Tezinin Olusumu (1929–1937)* [Power and history: the makings of "official history" in Turkey, 1929–1937]. Istanbul: Afa.

Hannah, N. 2011. Artisans in Cairo 1600–1800: An alternative framework for the early modern economic history of Egypt. MS.

Hill, E. 1987. *Al-Sanhuri and Islamic Law: The Place and Significance of Islamic Law in the Life and Work of Abd-al-Razzaq Ahmad al-Sanhuri, Egyptian Jurist and Scholar, 1895–1971*. Cairo: American University of Cairo Press.

Hodgson, M.G.S. 1974. *The Venture of Islam*. 3 vols. Chicago: University of Chicago Press.

Hodgson, M.G.S. 1993. *Rethinking World History: Essays on Europe, Islam and World History*, ed. and introd. E. Burke, III. Cambridge: Cambridge University Press.

Hourani, A. 1968. Ottoman reform and the politics of notables. In W.R. Polk and R.L. Chambers, eds, *Beginnings of Modernization in the Middle East: The Nineteenth Century*, pp. 41–68. Chicago: University of Chicago Press.

Inalcik, H. 1992. Islamization of Ottoman laws on land and land tax. In C. Fragner and K. Schwarz, eds, *Festgabe an Josef Matuz: Osmanistik, Turkologie, Diplomatik*, pp. 100–116. Berlin: Klaus Schwarz.

Islamoğlu, H., and C. Keyder. 1977. Agenda for Ottoman history. *Review* (Journal of the F. Braudel Center) 1 (1): 37–55.

Islamoğlu, H., and P. Perdue. 2009. Introduction. In H. Islamoğlu and P. Perdue, eds, *Shared Histories of Modernity: China, India and the Ottoman Empire*, pp. 1–20. London: Routledge.

Johanssen, B. 1999. *Contingency in Sacred Law: Legal and Ethical Norms in the Muslim Fiqh*. Leiden: Brill.

Kasaba, R. 1988. *Ottoman Empire and the World Economy in the Nineteenth Century*. Albany: State University of New York Press.

Kasaba, R. 2009. *A Movable Empire: Ottoman Nomads, Migrants and Refugees*. Seattle: University of Washington Press.

Koprulu, M.F. 1988. *Osmanli Devletinin Kurulusu* [Foundation of the Ottoman state]. Ankara: TTK.

Mardin, E. 1946. *Medeni Hukuk Cephesinden Ahmet Cevdet Paşa (1822–1895)* [Ahmet Cevdet Pasa and civil law (1822–1895)]. Istanbul: Istanbul University Press.

Mitchell, T. 1988. *Colonizing Egypt*. Berkeley: University of California Press.

Owen, R. 1993. *The Middle East in the World Economy, 1800–1914*. Rev. edn. London: I.B. Tauris.

Pamuk, S. 2004. Institutional change and the longevity of the Ottoman Empire, 1500–1800. *Journal of Interdisciplinary History* 35 (2): 225–247.

Pierce, L. 2003. *Morality Tales: Law and Gender in the Ottoman Court of Aintab*. Berkeley: University of California Press.

Pomeranz, K. 2000. *The Great Divergence: China, Europe, and the Making of the Modern World Economy*. Princeton: Princeton University Press.

Todorova, M. 2009. *Imagining the Balkans*. Oxford: Oxford University Press.

Wallerstein, I., H. Decdeliand, and R. Kasaba. 1987. Incorporation of the Ottoman Empire into the world economy. In H. Islamoğlu, ed., *The Ottoman Empire and the World*. Cambridge: Cambridge University Press.

Chapter Thirty-One

The World from Latin America and the Peripheries

Eduardo Devés-Valdés
(Translated by Sarah Hamilton)

Statement of the Problem

(1) To think from the periphery is to think from otherness. It is to think in another manner, and to think in order to leave the peripheral condition (which is a sort of exile from history) to locate oneself in a centrality, which offers the possibility of abandoning pariah status. To think from otherness is to think about other modes of emancipation, understood as the ways to leave the marginal state and to settle in a place of equality in the world space; that is, to think of ways to leave that otherness, understood as marginality.

   The peripheral condition is a consciousness and a fact, to put it somewhat schematically. This chapter is about the "constitution" of the consciousness: the ways in which the intellectual agents of the peripheries, mainly American, have assumed an eidetic position with respect to their place in the world – "constituting" (rather than "building," because it was not usually a conscious process) a notion of the world in which they place themselves in the periphery. This story then leads to the recollection of the process of constitution of that consciousness.

   However, this narrative leads, on the other hand, towards the necessary rupture with this consciousness, as a step towards the rupture with the peripheral condition, since the peripheral dilemma has transformed itself into a theoretical prison or straightjacket in that it blocks out other ways, the opening of other horizons, seeing from other perspectives. The constitution of the peripheral consciousness is also a process that entraps or encapsulates the peripheries, making of that very consciousness a barrier that prevents them from abandoning the condition of being segregated from history. To break with the manner of thinking that is expressed in the peripheral dilemma (be-like-the-center versus be-like-ourselves) is to advance towards a break with one's own peripheral status. The consciousness that was a manner of understanding the new situation created after European expansion was transformed into a prison, in a sort of intellectual cloistering that came to inhibit the development of other possibilities. The constitution of the

A Companion to World History, First Edition. Edited by Douglas Northrop.
© 2012 Blackwell Publishing Ltd. Published 2012 by Blackwell Publishing Ltd.

peripheral consciousness is a process, albeit not necessarily a process that goes from error to truth, nor necessarily a process of positive maturation, nor the construction of a heroic consciousness. In a certain sense, criticism of the ideas and the peripheral dilemma is also criticism of the peripheral condition and the possibility of overcoming it.[1] In this sense, to think from the periphery is to take on the direction of thought conceived in the peripheries and to capitalize on, project and overcome it, going beyond it to stop thinking peripherally and to stop being periphery.

(2) Key to the construction of the peripheral consciousness is the notion of difference from the center, a difference that can be located on several levels, but which is always relational. There are concepts that refer to geocultural, historical differences, and others that are created by economic difference. Some are understood simply as difference, others as difference produced by the actions of the center.

The construction of the idea of "different peoples," with respect to those Europeans who showed the power of their expansion, was early. It was produced largely independently from one society to the other, although it has always been a dialectic between the intellectual construction of a peripheral region and the image delivered by the agents of the center, to which are added contributions from other peripheries.

In this process of creating an awareness of the periphery there are at least two subperiods: in one, the image of a society is constructed, passing from the "naive" ancestral vision of being the center of the world to the new notion of periphery-of-a-new-center; in the other, it is the image of difference.

Concepts such as "colonial regions," "non-Europeans," "non-Christianity" are some of the proto-conceptions that contribute, from the center, to the origins of this idea. But these concepts, which are not principally economic, will gradually acquire a more economic tone, assuming aspects that were not in the proto-conceptions and leaving aside others that were key there, such as religious affiliation.

Thus, concepts such as "Third World," "South," "poor countries," "periphery" are intended to characterize a majority, nonprivileged segment of humanity, at least in terms of economics and power.

(3) To account for the constitution of the peripheral consciousness it is important to take into account the history of intellectual networks in which this consciousness developed and prospered, for example: Ibero-American enlightenment, peripheral romanticism, neo-Salafism, pan-Asianism, anti-imperialism, pan-Africanism, Eurasianism, Third Worldism, and the socioeconomic sciences of development. Figures such as G.M. Jovellanos, F. Miranda, P. Olavide, S. Bolívar, A. Khomiakov, A. Mickiewicz, D.F. Sarmiento, F. Bilbao, A. Herzen, Y. Fukusawa, E.W. Blyden, J. Rizal, I. Gasprinski, J. el Din Afghani, N. Kemal, S. Williams, R. Tagore, Sun Yat-sen, V.R. Haya de la Torre, Gabriela Mistral, M. Sultan-Galiev, M. Abduh, M. Hatta, V.I. Lenin, M. Gandhi, N. Trubetskoi, R. Prebisch, G. Padmore, L. Zea, K. Nkrumah, F. Herrera, P. Freire, J. Nyerere, C. Furtado, M. ul Haq, S. Amin, and F.H. Cardoso, among many others, are incomprehensible without those networks.[2]

The networks are normally formed and/or expressed through important meetings. These include the meeting of the 1893 Parliament of the World's Religions in Chicago, the pan-African conferences between 1901 and 1945 in several cities in Europe and the

United States, the 1911 Universal Race Conference in London, the 1920 Congress of the Peoples of the East in Baku, the 1925 anti-imperialist meeting in Paris, and especially the 1927 meeting of the Anti-Imperialist League in Brussels. These meetings are frequently organized by agents from the center and take place in important cities, but they allow peripheral intellectuals to meet, which otherwise would have been impossible at certain times. Even the pan-African meetings would not be in Africa until after Independence.

Proto-history: The Difference of the Partialities with Respect to the Center

The "proto-history" of the peripheral consciousness is composed of three expressions. Key to all three is that their diverse definitions of the periphery itself are always defined by their relation to the center. That is, people do not conceive of themselves simply as Guaraníes, Incas, Chinese or Arabs, but rather formulate a definition of their own society in relation to the center. (See Zhang, this volume.)

A first expression in the constitution of a peripheral consciousness consists of the notion of belonging to a large group, to a large set of peoples that are different from the center, although they do not conceive of themselves as exploited or oppressed by the center, but rather simply ethnoculturally different. A very early case that exemplifies the peripheral consciousness can be seen in the Peruvian Garcilaso Inca who, as early as the seventeenth century, understood some of the American identity in contrast to the center, highlighting its Spanish-American character, as Indian, as Mestizo, and differentiating it from the mainland Creoles.

Simón Bolívar, in the second decade of the nineteenth century, defined Spanish-colonized America as composed of a people that "is not European nor North American; it is more a composite of Africa and America than an emanation from Europe," a sort of "little human species," because

> we are neither Indian nor European, but a species midway between the legitimate proprietors of this country and the Spanish usurpers. In short, though Americans by birth we derive our rights from Europe, and we have to assert these rights against the rights of the natives, while at the same time we must defend ourselves against the invaders.

By 1850, Senegalese Pierre David Boilat and Argentinian D.F. Sarmiento conceived of their respective regions as barbarous and wild relative to Europe, while Nigerian Samuel Crowther defined his people as pagans. These are other ways of marking a difference, clearly situating the Western European model as an alternative (Devés 2008b).

The Slavic discourse in the first half of the nineteenth century is very important in this regard. The Slavic-Slavophile discourse is built from elements such as a conflict between the Slavic world and Western Europe. Adam Mickiewicz contrasted the rationalism that dominated Western Europe with the spiritual character of the Slavs. The Slavs retained certain "living truths" able to lead humanity to a moral revival, which should form a sort of equilibrium (Floryńska-Lalewicz 2003). A highly developed approach to marking differences is that of Aleksei Khomiakov, one of the few who understood Russia's difference to be associated with its Asian and not just its Slavic dimension in the first decades of the nineteenth century – a Russia composed not only of Slavs, but also of peoples of other ethnicities, languages, customs, and religions, but all united in the sense that they were different from Western Europe.

Another version of these large alliances comes from black or sub-Saharan African thought, in its pan-African, pan-Negro, and Blackness aspects. It originated on the basis of eidetic constructions present in the black world of the second half of the nineteenth century, such as Ethiopianism, Bookerism, racial-identism of E.W. Blyden, pan-Africanisn, pan-Negroism and Blackness. These trends initially considered difference on the basis of ethnic characteristics, which was associated with cultural essentialism from 1870 onwards with the works of Blyden, J.E. Casely-Hayford, and the young Aimé Césaire and Leopold Senghor. The consciousness of difference is constructed on a geo-ethnic dimension: Africa and Africanness is thought of as land, climate, race. This telluric-ethnocentric view operates from Blyden to Senghor (Devés 2008b).

Yet another version arises from Turkism, pan-Turkism and pan-Turanism. For example, Ahmed Midhat Efendi presented the history of pre-Ottoman Turks and their role in the development of world civilization, making an effort to rule out any connection of the Ottomans with Greek civilization (Shaw and Kural-Shaw 1988: 263). For his part, Ahmed Vefik Pasha defended the old Turkish customs and lifestyle, and opposed Westernization and the constitutional regime (Berkes 1998: 315). (See İslamoğlu, this volume.)

A second expression is produced when sets of people form in the peripheral regions that are distinguished not only by their cultural differences but also because they see themselves as threatened, marginalized or exploited, and thus needing to defend themselves against an invasive center, albeit without raising the similarities among themselves or proposing any collective action.

The Ottoman I. Muteferrika, writing in the 1730s, perceived things in this manner in his understanding of the precarious situation of the Ottomans, then marginalized by the European (Christian) powers. In his 1731 book on the "Rational bases for the polities of nations" (in Turkish), he asked "Why did Europeans, who were so weak in the past compared to the Muslim nations, begin to dominate so many territories in modern times, and even defeat the once-victorious Ottoman armies?" (cited by Berkes 1998: 42).

In the first generation of pan-Africanism, that of Henry Sylvester Williams in 1900, the idea of pan-African solidarity was still partial, as it referred only to those who belonged to the "African race." Progressively, Blackness and pan-Africanism are becoming more sociopolitical and less ethnocultural. George Padmore, Kwame Nkrumah and Frantz Fanon, among others, foster this eidetic change.

A third expression is the formation of a large set of peripheral regions that do not belong to a single geocultural sphere, but whose similarities arise, rather, from their marginality. "France, you whom we have loved so much, what have you done?" asked Francisco Bilbao, in *The American Gospel*, in 1864:

> Betray and bomb Mexico. England, oh England! What is this nation of powdered wigs and rapacious lords doing in India? Blood and exploitation, tyranny and conquest. It appears in Mexico for a time and offers three ships to Maximilian … Down with so-called European civilization. Europe cannot even civilize itself and it would civilize us. Europe, with its social and political action, with its dogma, its morality, its diplomacy, with its institutions and doctrines, is the antithesis of America. (quoted in Zea 1976: 56)

These sets of regions accept the difference of power, but at the same time they come to terms with a certain solidarity between peoples that transcends ethnicity and language, though not always to the same extent. More restricted positions include Marcus Garvey's "Negroes of the world, unite", Pixley K. Isaka Seme's call for the union of all southern Africans despite their differences, and the members of the Indian National Congress, who were also open to a union across ethnicities, languages and religions, within the boundaries of English dominion on the subcontinent (Devés 2008b). Broader positions include some of those belonging to the Arielists, whose innovation is that, positioning themselves as Latin Americans, they simultaneously succeed in creating a common cause with non-Latin American peoples who find themselves in similar situations of peripheralness, despite belonging to other cultural horizons.

Luís Ross-Mugica, in his *Más allá del Atlántico* (Beyond the Atlantic) (1909), adopts a view of the similarity between Latin Americans and North Africans, who fought for independence from European plunder. He sets the European way of life ("civilized") against that of the Moors. He wonders where civilization is in all the invasions and exploitations to which Europe is subjecting Morocco. "And civilization? Ah! Civilization is the mudguard: Morocco is in anarchy; there are two sultans instead of one; the exalted religious passions and the wild love of independence of the Kabyle have increased. It is no exaggeration to say 'Europe, the impotent civilizer'" (1909: 192). He then notes the similarity between "some of those new peoples, victims of European greed." He believed that they would erase the old civilization and create a new era: "Turkey, Persia, India and some South American countries are humanity's future" (1909: 199).

For example, by 1910, Manuel Baldomero Ugarte was maintaining that "the peace of recent years was maintained at the expense of the weak countries of Asia, Africa, and America. The force of expansion was diverted or canalized onto defenseless cores, thereby opening an era of colonial conquests or of undeclared protectorates, during which the large nations made, in a manner, a bloc against the small nations" (quoted in Hodge 2010: 98).

In this manner, a way of thinking about identity aiming at the unity of the Hispano-American space, understood as Latinness against Saxonness, was expressed in one version with a certain anti-US Americanism and anti-imperialism, associated more with the political-cultural than the economic. This discourse, with new emphases and new hybridizations, would transform from Latinism to mestizophilia and indigenism, from anti-US Americanism to anti-imperialism, and from cultural integrationism to economic and political integrationism.

Another tendency at this same level of consciousness is the classic Eurasianism of the 1920s, with its proposals about Russia as a multi-ethnic and multicultural society, clearly different from the center in many senses, where even the understanding of the Slavophiles who considered it a Slavic society fell very short. Trubetskoi's classical or first generation Eurasianism, specifically Russia's claiming of its Eurasianism, can serve as a guide for colonial peoples that resist against Europe. That is why he mentions Russia's adoption of Eurasian identity with such emphasis. It is precisely now, Trubetskoi says, that the elemental face (the national specificity and the half non-European, half Asian character of Russia-Eurasia) has become more visible than ever. The genuine Russia, historic Russia, old Russia can be seen, not an invented "Slavic" or "Slavic-Varangian" Russia, but a real, Russo-Turanic Russo-Eurasia, the legacy of Genghis Khan (Laruelle 2005).

In short, these notions are the expressions of intellectuals who aim to describe the difference, either as a simple difference or as the product of the action of the center, either as a confirmation of this contrast or to generate a defensive position against the dangers of the center. These views are articulated over time, thus creating the idea of a certain fellowship based on the pan-African, anticolonialist and anti-imperialist struggles that allow distant and different peoples to see themselves as united in the common project of defense of certain interests and principles, overcoming national, linguistic, ethnic, and religious differences which until then had set up different identities among them. In this new manner of understanding things, "being oppressed by the same power" is what allows them to consider themselves united in a struggle for liberation.

If one can speak of any progress in the development of the peripheral consciousness, it is in advancing the understanding of the peripheral condition as something shared by all peoples outside the center, moving precisely towards the notion of an excluded middle: it is either the center or it is the periphery. In this sense, Eurasianists' broadened conception of Russia as varied, multi-ethnic and multicultural, and in almost every way different from the center, is expressive, as is José Vasconcelos's extension of Latin American mestizophilia, indigenism, and Negroism (Devés 2000–2004, vol. 1) into a region of mixed race and "cosmic race."

History: Since the Formation of a Global Center and Periphery

A new collection of expressions, representing a qualitative leap, is manifested in the notion of the excluded middle, either center or periphery. This is achieved to the extent that the center is conceived of as exploitative and, therefore, the generator of the peripheral condition of all the peoples to which it reaches out.

It may be said that there has been a change from the notion of difference to the notion of periphery. During the twentieth century, the consciousness of the need to think about difference was consolidated, achieved by thinking about and of oneself as the periphery. In this line, major meetings were important because they permitted, at least partially, intellectuals from different parts of the periphery to meet and recognize each other.

What follows is a further development upon some of the kernels of thought that have been crucial to the constitution of the peripheral consciousness itself, in seven separate institutional and/or intellectual instantiations. These, however, must in no way be considered as a progression towards truth or even necessarily a full and proper understanding of the peripheral dimension.

First expression

A first expression of this is the theory of imperialism, in its specifically Leninist form or in others. This is a key concept that has produced many variants, not all of them orthodox, but all marked by the basic distinguishing feature that the labor of the center generates and maintains the peripheral condition. These positions emphasize economic and political elements much more than cultural ones, and are stated in historical analysis. The theory of imperialism is key because it conceives of the rest of the world (or most of it) as a unified body different from the center. It is the first notion that allows us to think of an economic similarity outside of any other condition and, simultaneously, to imagine a joint action or, even better, concerted action on the part of the peripheries. Concepts developed primarily during the years of World War I, perceiving that the capitalists divided the world among themselves, that capitalism is manifested in a handful of especially rich and powerful countries plundering the rest of the world (1916, see Lenin 1963), that "the so-called Great Powers have long been exploiting and enslaving a whole number of small and weak nations. And the imperialist war is a war for the division and redivision of this kind of booty" (1918, see Lenin 1952), are what enable us to think of a global division that divides the entire world into a few exploiter-class countries and many more exploited-class countries.

The meeting of the Anti-Imperialist League in 1927 was an important event in the constitution of an almost complete intellectual and political network inspired by these ideas. In Brussels, a meeting of individuals of the greatest importance was arranged. Among others, participants included Soong Qing-ling, the widow of Sun Yat-sen, Lamine Senghor, Mohamed Hatta and Sen Katayama, Jawaharlal Nehru, V.R. Haya de la Torre and Julio Antonio Mella. Mohandas Gandhi was invited, although he did not attend.

In Latin America and the Caribbean during the 1920s, on the basis of eidetic beginnings arising from anti-US American Arielism, theosophy, anti-imperialism, and proto–Third World nationalism, a vision of the region's situation and its role in the global space matured. It was developed by, among others, J. Vasconcelos, M. Ugarte, Gabriela Mistral, V. Haya, and J.C. Mariátegui, and expressed through a series of publications, of which the *Repertorio Americano* was the most important (Devés 2000–2004, vol. 1). In this context they discussed the role of capitalism, European expansion as a world question, racial confrontations between whites and "brown races," and of the World War as a war between imperialisms vying for the world. Like the American Popular Revolutionary Alliance (APRA), it proposed concerted action against US imperialism, for the political unity of Latin America, for the nationalization of lands and industries, for the internationalization of the Panama Canal, and for the solidarity of all the peoples and oppressed classes of the world (Haya de la Torre 1990: 22–23).

This contrast between the peripheries (Latin America-Caribbean, Asia, and Africa) and the center was marked by the accentuation of otherness, not only economic but in the assertion of ethnocultural otherness: the nonwhite, in formulas such as mestizo, Indian, Afro, and Oriental. Indigenism, pan-Africanism, Blackness, pan-Asiaticism, and Orientalism are forms of expressing the claims of the others of the world (Kodera Kenkichi, Vasconcelos, Gabriela Mistral, Leopold Senghor, Marcus Garvey, Aimé Césaire).

Second expression

A second expression is that of the center/periphery of the Economic Commission for Latin America (ECLA). The ideas of R. Prebisch/ECLA since 1949 have helped to form a conceptualization that, from a non-Marxist Latin American perspective (albeit with vague Marxist inspirations), contributed to the idea of a world divided in two, where a certain solidarity among the underdeveloped countries was important to overcome this situation.

The peripheral condition was seen as marginal, inferior, and subordinated with respect to a center that benefited from and maintained deteriorating terms of trade, the hetero-geneous distribution of science and technology, the financial management of the world economy, and thus the center–periphery relationship and with it underdevelopment.

These notions, with a basic scientific criterion of the deterioration of the terms of trade and almost no "philosophies" or "ideologies," allowed for dialogue between agents who were thus able to set aside racialisms, socialisms, tellurisms, religious criticisms, and other principles that had previously disqualified and excluded many potential partners.

Third expression

Another expression is Third Worldism, a trend that was based on very diverse intellectual heritages with little relation to each other: pan-Africanism, pan-Asianism, Eurasianism and anti-imperialism. It dealt with the political unity of all those who were "different": segregated, defeated, exploited, and despised. This has enabled identitarianisms, nationalisms, tellurisms, and racialisms (and even racisms) that are often exclusive to coexist, articulated on the basis of the idea that the center is primarily responsible for their woes.

One future result of the 1927 Anti-Imperialist League's meeting was the Bandung meeting in 1955. After Bandung,[3] progress was made in the constitution of the Non-Aligned Movement, one of whose key motives, giving rise to the name, consisted of nonparticipation in the Cold War. The group was organized on the basis of Nehru's five principles and it was he who, in large part, shaped the movement. These principles, which had been previously designed for relations between India and China, were mutual respect for territorial integrity and sovereignty, nonaggression, noninterference with domestic affairs, equality and mutual benefit, and peaceful coexistence. The basic formulation of Nehru's five principles is very pragmatic, but it is not sufficient to constitute Third World thought itself.

In his 1955 speech in Bandung, Ahmed Sukarno said:

> In political terms, what is the highest code of morality? It is the subordination of everything to the well-being of mankind ... We are united, for instance, by a common detestation of colonialism in whatever form it appears. We are united by a common detestation of racialism. And we are united by a common determination to preserve and stabilize peace in the world ... We are often told "colonialism is dead." Let us not be deceived or even soothed by that. I say to you, colonialism is not yet dead. How can we say it is dead, so long as vast areas of Asia and Africa are unfree ... Colonialism has also its modern dress, in the form of economic control, intellectual control, actual physical control by a small but alien community within a nation. It is a skilful and determined enemy, and it appears in many guises ... What can we do? We can do much! We can inject the voice of reason into world affairs. We can mobilize all the spiritual, all the moral, all the political strength of Asia and Africa on the side of peace ... The five Prime Ministers did not make threats. So, let this Asian-African Conference be a great success! Make the "live and let live" principle and the "Unity in Diversity" motto the unifying force which brings us all together – to seek in friendly, uninhibited discussion, ways and means by which each of us can live his own life, and let others live their own lives, in their own way, in harmony, and in peace. (Sukarno 1955)

The "hard core" of Third Worldism is very small, while its aggregates are extensive. In fact, the first true constitution possessed a strong anti-imperialist component, with essentially Leninist roots, but also brought together various other nationalist components: Indian, Indonesian, West African, Arab-Baathist, and socialist, and even more unorthodox, Nasserism, third- and fourth-generation Pan-Africanism, Titoism, and Maoism. Nehru, Zhou Enlai, Nkrumah, Nasser, and Sukarno contributed to this from the Bandung Conference; and in the 1960s, Ho Chi Minh, Fanon of the Algerian National Liberation Front, Prebisch from the United Nations Conference on Trade and Development (UNCTAD), Leopold Senghor, Celso Furtado, and Fidel Castro.

Fourth expression

A fourth expression is the theory of neocolonialism. The past versions were enriched, in the early 1960s, with notions of neocolonialism. Taking elements of Marx, Lenin, and Owen Lattimore, Nkrumah argued that neocolonialism represents the final stage of imperialism. Neocolonialism is the worst form of imperialism: for those who practice it, it means power without responsibility, and for those who suffer it, it is exploitation without redress (1965: 3–5). This observation, with the prior observations of Mamadou Dia and Frantz Fanon, constitutes one of the first critiques or self-criticisms of the new situation of post-Independence Africa.

Nkrumah believes that complete independence and continental integration are necessary prerequisites for economic development. Borrowing from imperialism theory, Nkrumah aims to understand the difference between countries that are merely "formally" independent but trapped in the web of financial and diplomatic dependence, and truly independent countries (1965: 232–233). The essence of neocolonialism is that the subject state is, in theory, independent and has all of the external trappings of international society, but usually they are small states, Balkanized by imperialism, and unable to cope. If Africa was united, no large power bloc would attempt to subdue it (1965: 3–4). Because of their failure to unite, the Latin American countries had suffered disastrous consequences from the beginning of the nineteenth century to the present (1965: 250). This should be a lesson to the Africans. (See Simo, this volume.)

Fifth expression

A fifth expression is manifested in the foundation of UNCTAD in 1964,[4] and in the ideas of the deterioration in the terms of trade, the heterogeneous distribution of science and technology, the center/periphery notion, and the "syndicalism" of the underdeveloped countries, aimed at a New International Economic Order. In this, the ECLA ideas of center/periphery and others converged with the Third Worldism of Bandung and with the ideas of anti-neocolonialism.

UNCTAD was created at the behest of ECLA and Prebisch, who was its first Secretary General. Prebisch's ideas strongly influenced the strategies and policies for economic and social development in developing countries. Among his many achievements, he called the attention of the international community to the need for a significant change of attitudes about relationships between developed and developing countries, and for substantial modifications in the traditional patterns of the international division of labor. From UNCTAD, Prebisch promoted trade negotiations between rich and poor countries and encouraged the evolution of new approaches to multilateral development diplomacy (Love 2010: 5).[5]

In his famous "Five stages in my thinking on development," Prebisch notes that

> the fourth stage, related to my work at UNCTAD, was oriented toward matters of international cooperation ... Despite the great differences between the countries of the world periphery, there were many common denominators ... This was the beginning of the North–South dialogue ... One of the main arguments prevailing in the developed countries was that the developing countries should take adequate measures to deal with their own internal development problems. (1984: 21)

Thus, Prebisch established a trio of opposites: center/periphery, North/South, developed countries/developing countries. This trio of concepts was key to understanding the global economy in the framework of thought that inspired UNCTAD.[6]

Sixth expression

A sixth version is that of the Third World Forum (TWF), a group whose aim was to develop a specific form of thought for the Third World.[7]

If UNCTAD was constituted as an intergovernmental forum, with all the potential and limitations this entails, the Forum was also created as an instance of civil intellectual society, one of the merits of which was that it was the first meeting independent of state organs that brought together important intellectuals from three continents: Africa, Latin America, and Asia. Gathered there, among other people, were Samir Amin and M. ul Haq, J. Bagwhati, F.H. Cardoso, O. Sunkel, E. Iglesias, Nurul Islam, and J. Rweyemamu, helping to strengthen links between socioeconomic experts in Asia and Africa.

The Forum was envisioned as a think-tank of the underdeveloped world, generating a dialogue about the eidetic needs of the Third World. It suggested that the world had changed, as could be observed by the depletion of the international order, the emergence of the decolonized states and the deterioration in terms of trade, increasing inequalities and progressive indebtedness, the dangers posed by multinational companies through their political action and/or the introduction of technologies that create new dependencies. In connection with this is the idea of a New International Economic Order, which aims to overcome the differential levels of privilege accorded to some (but only some) of the world's states, thereby achieving greater equality, unity, and integration.

This group of socioeconomic experts conceived of itself as destined to resolve issues such as the fact that the Third World actually feeds on conceptions of development that are created externally and are therefore inadequate (Santiago Declaration, Third World Forum 1973), since the ideas and ideologies for the Third World should come from within (Desai 1973: 63). To change this, it would be necessary to generate relevant and appropriate research (Santiago Declaration). In other words, self-reliant intellectual institutions should be established (Third World Forum 1975). To advance this process of intellectual self-reliance, socioeconomic experts of the Third World must have a platform to exchange ideas (Santiago Declaration); Third World intellectuals should organize an environment conducive to an equitable national and international order (Third World Forum 1975). All of that is synthesized in the need to wage a permanent intellectual revolution, to overcome the dependence of the Third World and the profound changes in the internal and external order facing developing countries today.

The "Charter" of the Forum stated: "We, the social science experts and other intellectuals of the Third World, desiring to make a more constructive and significant contribution to the peoples of our countries, are convinced that for now the best form to achieve this is through the foundation, organization, and support of a 'TWF.'" (Third World Forum 1975: 1). The principal functions are providing a platform for exchanging views; providing intellectual support to the countries of the Third World; stimulating and organizing cooperative research between developing countries; and presenting opinions about international questions that affect the Third World (1975: 1–2).

Seventh expression

A seventh version is the one developed by the South–South Commission. Yet another contribution was that of the conceptualization produced within many international bodies and commissions, synthesized by Julius Nyerere and a large team in coordination and discussion in the 1980s around the notions of South–South and North–South dialogue. The expression North–South came to complement, but mainly to rephrase, expressions such as development/underdevelopment, center/periphery, and even imperial-capitalist/exploited. In this scheme, the South emerged as the underdeveloped world, as the underdog in the economy, the historical subaltern.

The Commission of the South was established in 1987, largely inheriting the approaches created within the UNCTAD and the Third World Forum. Its members included leading figures from the South of various backgrounds and political outlooks.[8] Developing countries funded its work for a period of three years, but Commission members worked as individuals, not as representatives of any particular country.

During this three-year period, the Commission issued declarations on external debt obligations, and also on the Uruguay Round of trade negotiations. It also issued a final report, *The Challenge to the South*, in which it summarized this work and urged further efforts for "self-reliant, people-centered development strategies" (South Commission 1990). The developing countries, it maintained, could overcome disadvantageous trade, finance, and technological relationships by working together in negotiations with the North. Growing global interdependence, in fact, suggested that *all* countries – not just those of the South – would benefit if developing countries could be helped out of poverty.

The Commission then gave way to a new "South Centre."[9] Within that framework, the Centre was created to investigate and analyze the common problems and matters of interest to the developing countries; to promote cooperation, networking and solidarity among the peoples and countries of the South; to remain "intellectually autonomous" and to act as "think tank" and "network" for the South; to provide timely political analysis and develop Southern views on major policy issues. Its objectives included promoting South–South cooperation, coordinating the participation of the countries of the South in international forums, contributing to the convergence of the countries of the South, and improving understanding and collaboration between the South and the North (Centro Sur 1995b).

Conclusion

This chapter has tried to sketch the constitution of the peripheral consciousness. To do so, it has described a varied proto-consciousness with three different expressions and then a more fully expressed consciousness in seven separate guises. This has been done primarily from the perspective of Latin American thought, but with numerous connections to other regions. Some writers have explicitly proposed the need to think about the peripheries in this way, and have sought to constitute this consciousness in an organized manner, but they are few in number. A shared interest in knowledge production brings these authors together: how to think of the periphery, how to recover peripheral thought, how to overcome various obstacles to articulate it fully, how better to understand the comparative parallels and similarities, how to gauge which are the correct formulas and which the incorrect. In most cases, however, these writers do not even know each other, and certainly they do not conceive of themselves as a whole, nor do they see their work as an articulated or joint project.

Intellectual contributions from many sources thus converge on an awareness of difference and, later, of forming part of a great world periphery, although clearly not all contributions offer a consistent definition of difference or the peripheral condition.

The "awareness of difference" associated with a "peripheral condition" is based on ancient notions that distinguished the various empires or regions of the known world for every society. Some intellectuals of great peripheral empires, such as the Russian or the Ottoman, come to terms with this "difference" more easily than do those who belong to independent states, such as Latin Americans. Membership in empires makes it easier to see the difference as, at the same time, membership in multi-ethnic and multicultural empires allows a certain similarity between distant peoples on the periphery of the Western European hub. (See Sinha, this volume.) During the eighteenth century it was possible, from the proto-periphery, to see Europe, although not to imagine non-Europe. For example, the Russian or Ottoman intelligentsia, which were seen as distinctly non-European, did not conceive of themselves as associated with Africans, Indians, or Orientals. Prior to the nineteenth century, there were very few people capable of conceiving, from the periphery, an area that transcended that of their own people; that is, to see sets of people that transcended borders, mountain ranges, and oceans. In the nineteenth century, some ideas on this, such as those of Khomiakov, timidly appeared.

However, unlike the Hegelian consciousness that marks progress when each dialectical moment represents the overcoming of the last, in this case we are simply showing cases that are found on the same level and that represent different expressions of the feeling of being and existing on the periphery. If some elements of earlier expressions are incorporated and others excluded, this is nonetheless not a dialectical progression.

Notes

1 In general, the intelligentsia of the center (and in large part, the reason that it is the center) are more vital and sophisticated than the intelligentsia of the peripheral regions, and these intelligensia of the center have been those that denominated the non-center. These intelligentsia members also, and this is no small thing, possess the capacity to find themselves atop the watchtower of the center, and to see from there the entirety of the lands and the seas. The peripheral intelligentsia, lower down and at times crushed, are barely able to understand their own regions and the metropolis through which they are articulated to the world.

2 It is true that on many occasions the networks have been loose, with sporadic relations, and populated by a minimum density so that they have not been able to constitute themselves in environments capable of generating a weight in ideas. In this sense, the role that some international levels have played has been relevant, whether interstate organizations or parts of civil society in the process of articulating regional and continental energies towards larger and, above all, more permanent and higher density organizational spaces (such as UNESCO, international policies, the World Council of Churches, and other institutions like the World Social Forum).

3 The driving group consisted of Nehru from India, Sukarno from Indonesia, Tito from Yugoslavia, Nasser from Egypt, and Nkrumah from Ghana. The first meetings of the Non-Aligned Movement were Belgrade 1961, Cairo 1964, Lusaka 1970, and Algiers 1973.

4 According to its official mission statement, UNCTAD is "the principal organ of the United Nations for the integrated study of trade, development and interrelated issues in the areas of finances, technology, investment and sustainable development. UNCTAD is a forum for intergovernmental deliberations aimed at building consensus on priority issues for developing countries."

5 Joseph Love notes that "Prebisch became an itinerant preacher to spread the UNCTAD evangel. He took his message on unequal exchange, the Trade Gap, concessionary financing and export-substitution industrialization to Africa and Asia, as well as to Latin America. Between 1964 and 1969 he logged 600,000 miles giving speeches and meeting heads of government and their ministers. On the force of his ideas and personality, Prebisch attempted to strengthen and expand the Group of 77 as an effective voice on trade and development" (Love 2010: 8–9).

6 Salvador Allende, in his inaugural address to UNCTAD III in Santiago de Chile, in 1972, complemented Prebisch's triad, adding "we," "Third World," "poor peoples," "backward nations," and, in opposition, "imperialist domination" and "rich peoples" (Allende 1972).

7 This section reproduces, with some corrections and elaborations, passages from Devés 2006.

8 President: Julius Nyerere (Tanzania); Secretary General: Manmohan Singh (India); Members: Ismail Abdalla (Egypt); Abdlatif Al-Hamad (Kuwait); Evaristo Arns (Brazil); Solita Collas-Monsod (Philippines); Eneas Comiche (Mozambique); Gamani Corea (Sri Lanka); Aboubakar Diaby-Ouattara (Ivory Coast); Aldo Ferrer (Argentina); Celso Furtado (Brazil); Devaki Jain (India); Simba Makoni (Zimbabwe); Michael Manley (Jamaica); Jorge Navarette (Mexico); Pius Okigbo (Nigeria); Augustin Papic (Yugoslavia); Carlos Andrés Perez (Venezuela); Jiadong Qian (China); Shridath Ramphal (Guyana); Carlos Rafael Rodriguez (Cuba); Abdus Salam (Pakistan); Marie-Angélique Savane (Senegal); Tan Sri Shafie (Malasia); Tupuola Tupua Tamasese (Samoa); Nitisastro Widjojo (Indonesia); Layachi Yaker (Algeria).

9 South Centre: An Intergovernmental Think Tank of Developing Countries, at http://www.southcentre.org/ (accessed Feb. 2012). "It is the responsibility of the South," said Mugabe in 1995, "to fund this Centre, and a test of the seriousness and the commitment we make to the South Centre is the extent to which we can make it financially sustainable ... We must show our support for the goals we have set. If all of us in the South give at least a small amount to this good cause ... we will have made a great investment and also demonstrated our commitment to the cause ... The countries of the South should follow the example of industrialized countries which, despite the many support mechanisms, still employ more than 2,000 people in the OECD, hosted in Paris, to investigate and discuss matters of common interest, and help coordination of the trading platform of the North and South. The countries of the South are in a much weaker position and need a stronger support mechanism" (Centro Sur 1995a).

References

Allende, Salvador. 1972. *Discurso inaugural UNCTAD III*. Comisión Chilena para la UNCTAD III, Santiago.

Berkes, Niyazi. 1998. *The Development of Secularism in Turkey*. London: Hurst.

Centro Sur. 1995a. Cooperación y negociación. *Tercer Mundo Económico* 73 (Oct. 1–15), at http://www.redtercermundo.org.uy/tm_economico/texto_completo.php?id=2180 (accessed Mar. 2012).

Centro Sur. 1995b. Necesidad de actuar en forma concertada. *Tercer Mundo Económico* 73 (Oct. 1–15). At http://www.redtercermundo.org.uy/tm_economico/texto_completo.php?id=2179 (accessed Feb. 2012).

Desai, Padma. 1973. Third World social scientists in Santiago. *World Development* 1 (9): 57–65.

Devés, Eduardo. 2000–2004. *El Pensamiento Latinoamericano en el Siglo XX. Entre la modernización y la identidad*, vol. 1: *Del Ariel de Rodó a la ECLA (1900–1950)*; vol. 2: *Desde la ECLA al neoliberalismo*; vol. 3: *Las discusiones y las figuras del fin de siglo. Los años 90*. Buenos Aires: Biblos.

Devés, Eduardo. 2006. Los cientistas económico sociales chilenos en los largos 1960s y su inserción en las redes internacionales. La reunión del Foro Tercer Mundo en Santiago en abril de 1973. *Universum* (University of Talca) 21 (1): 138–167. At http://www.scielo.cl/scielo.php?pid=S0718-23762006000100009&script=sci_arttext (accessed Feb. 2012).

Devés, Eduardo. 2008a. La circulación de las ideas económico-sociales de Latinoamérica y el Caribe en Asia y África ¿Cómo llegaron y como se diseminaron? (1965–1985). *Universum* (University of Talca) 23 (2): 86–111.

Devés, Eduardo. 2008b. *O pensamento africano sul-saariano. Conexoes e paralelos com o pensamento Latino-Americano e Asiático. Um esquema*. Rio de Janeiro: CLACSO- EDUCAM.

Floryńska-Lalewicz, Halina. n.d. Adam Mickiewicz. At http://www.culture.pl/web/english/resources-literature-full-page/-/eo_event_asset_publisher/eAN5/content/adam-mickiewicz (accessed Oct. 2011).

Haya de la Torre, Víctor R. 1990. *El antiimperialismo y el APRA*. Santiago: Ercilla.

Hodge, Eduardo. 2010. El pensamiento internacional de Manuel Baldomero Ugarte y Víctor Raúl Haya de la Torre. Una aproximación hacia sus ideas sobre integración latinoamericana, anti-imperialismo y defensa continental (1900–1939). Masters' thesis, University of Santiago.

Laruelle, Marlene. 2005. La triangulaire "Russie", "exil russe", "culture d'accueil". Le prisme occidental inassumé de l'eurasisme. In *Les Premières Rencontres de l'Institut européen Est-Ouest*, pp. 197–217. Lyon: European Institute of East–West Relations, at http://russie-europe.enslyon.fr/IMG/pdf/communications.pdf (accessed May 2012).

Lenin, Vladimir Ilyich. 1952. *The State and Revolution*. In V.I. Lenin, *Selected Works*, vol. 2, part 1. Moscow: Foreign Languages Publishing House. First published in 1918.

Lenin, Vladimir Ilyich. 1963. *Imperialism, the Highest Stage of Capitalism*. In V.I. Lenin, *Selected Works*, vol. 1, pp. 667–766. Moscow: Foreign Languages Publishing House. First published in 1917.

Love, Joseph. 2010. Latin America, UNCTAD, and the postwar trading system. In H.S. Esfahani, G.J.D. Hewings, and G. Facchini, eds, *Economic Development in Latin America*, pp. 22–33. New York: Palgrave Macmillan. First published in 2001.

Nkrumah, Kwame. 1965. *Neo-colonialism, the Last Stage of Imperialism*. London: Nelson.

Prebisch, Raúl. 1984. Five stages in my thinking on development. In G.M. Meier and D. Seers, eds, *Pioneers in Development*, pp. 175–191. New York: Oxford University Press.

Ross Múgica, Luis. 1909. *Más allá del Atlántico*. Valencia: Sempere.

Shaw, Stanford, and Ezel Kural-Shaw. 1988. *History of the Ottoman Empire and Modern Turkey*, vol. 2: *1808–1975*. Cambridge: Cambridge University Press.

South Commission. 1990. *The Challenge to the South: The Report of the South Commission*. Oxford: Oxford University Press.

Sukarno, Ahmed. 1955. Speech at the opening of the Bandung Conference, April 18, 1955. At http://www.fordham.edu/halsall/mod/1955sukarno-bandong.html (accessed Feb. 2012).

Third World Forum. 1973. Santiago Declaration. In Third World Forum folder, Library, Economic Commission for Latin America.

Third World Forum. 1975. Karachi press release. In Third World Forum folder, Library, Economic Commission for Latin America.

Zea, Leopoldo. 1976. *El pensamiento Latinoamericano*. Barcelona: Ariel.

CHAPTER THIRTY-TWO

(Re)Writing World Histories in Europe

KATJA NAUMANN
(Translated by Anne Berg)

World and global history can undoubtedly look back on a long tradition in European scholarship. Europe and European historians figure prominently in the accounts of the ancient and early modern periods. However, they increasingly disappear in the descriptions of the decades after World War II and contemporary trends. A perfunctory glance at the footnotes of recently published works reveals the predominance of North American authors. With considerable self-confidence, American scholars refashion the historiography of contemporary topics and developments. In fact, it seems that the world as written by Europeans is relegated to a prehistory of sorts. European contributions are rarely discussed after the 1960s and more often function as a negative foil against which twenty-first century scholars map global processes of the past in a new key. Curiously, perhaps, this phenomenon is not limited to North American authors. Even some European historians, such as R.I. Moore (1997), dutifully replicate the pervasive habit of their transatlantic compeers when sketching the development of the field.

Yet at the same time, historians on the European side of the Atlantic have engaged in lively debates on, and diverse practices of, world history, a selection of which I will review in the first part of this chapter. This renewed interest in world historical approaches, paralleled by similar trends elsewhere (Sachsenmaier 2011), ought to be understood in the context of a more general attentiveness to global developments after the implosion of the Cold War world order. In the years after 1989–1991, a politically integrated Europe constituted a new actor on the stage of international relations. Scholarly perspectives shifted in parallel with the rapid increase of global entanglements and new interdependencies. Just as events of the mid-nineteenth century, the *fin de siècle*, and again World War II pressed historians of the day to understand their changing world in its historicity, the 1990s similarly directed European writers' attention toward global processes and developments. Apparently, and perhaps not surprisingly, world historical writing is contingent upon cycles of global transformations; it reacts to changes in cultural connections and global configurations. As a result historians have not only radically rethought world history over the

A Companion to World History, First Edition. Edited by Douglas Northrop.
© 2012 Blackwell Publishing Ltd. Published 2012 by Blackwell Publishing Ltd.

past two decades, but the field itself has undergone a thoroughgoing institutionalization in academia, a development I will discuss in the second part of this chapter. Obviously, intellectual developments are often concurrent with, and in any case related to, social processes. To underscore these interactions and to highlight the parallels between cognitive innovations and institutional changes, these developments are discussed in the two separate parts of this chapter.

Meanwhile, historians across Europe are widening their perspectives and writing history that crosses regional, national and continental boundaries. It is worth stressing that the manifold if equally novel approaches they employ hardly constitute *one* version of world history. In their multiplicity, these histories neither produce an epistemological, methodological or thematic consensus, let alone because some scholars base their writings on a critical reflection on their Europeanness while others do not address their own perspective and position, nor do they differ recognizably from approaches prominent in other world regions. Owing to the heterogeneity of European societies and their equally different historiographical traditions, an identifiably European history is unlikely to develop. In fact, such uniformity would only gratuitously narrow current research trends, which benefit from multifarious cooperation with scholars from other parts of the world. Fortunately, plurality prevails in both approach and perspective (O'Brien 2006).

Nonetheless, certain general trends characterize the disciplinary developments of recent years. The reasons are at least twofold. For one, scholars discuss world historical problems in a wider European context: that is they trace historical developments more readily across national and linguistic boundaries. Without doubt English has been in use as a lingua franca. Recently, however, due to a rising interest in world historical explorations in France, and to a lesser extent in Spain, it has become more common to read contributions in French and Spanish. This definitely leads to a more differentiated debate since semantic and conceptual subtleties come to the fore. Multilingualism has a long tradition on the European side of the Atlantic. Nowadays it follows the rule, especially at congresses, that everyone chooses from among the main languages the one they prefer, and if translation is necessary it is provided from the audience. This is not surprising considering the transnationality of European debates. From the almost 200 conferences and workshops in the field that took place between 2008 and 2010, only 6 saw participants from only one country. In half of them, scholars of between 6 and 23 nationalities joined in the exchange (Middell and Naumann 2010). Publications that include several languages are still the exception, but they can well be expected to become more popular. Secondly, the European Union's crucial financial sponsorship of academic work in the arts and sciences, and especially its priority to reposition Europe in the world, has provided clear incentives to universities to encourage globally oriented studies.

Characteristic of recent world history writing in Europe is the vehement renunciation of Eurocentrism. Whereas much of the historiography of the nineteenth and early twentieth centuries postulated Europe's superiority, nowadays scholars no longer view Europe as a model, trailblazer or benchmark for non-Western societies. Instead historians who are historicizing global and transnational pasts (and less so the mainstream of the profession) agree that Europe was hardly an immutable instigator of world history. They concede that non-Western cultures developed according to their own principles and thus decisively affected European development. It is equally beyond dispute now that global dynamics cannot be grasped by linear or teleological narratives. Instead, postcolonial and poststructural approaches are rapidly replacing philosophies of history that postulated the unity of the world. As Michael Geyer and Charles Bright explain:

> humanity no longer comes into being through "thought." Rather, humanity gains existence in a multiplicity of discrete economic, social, cultural, and political activities. In the past such humanity has been the dream of sages and philosophers and, not to be forgotten, of gods, but now it has become the daily work of human beings. This world needs its imagination. (1995: 1060)

In this vein, a consensus focuses around a shared commitment to ground the myriad processes of global integration and cultural cross-fertilizations empirically, and to trace their effects on the history of numerous places simultaneously.

Still, important differences remain even in the abounding rejections of the universalism characteristic of earlier approaches to world history. While Margrit Pernau and Corinne Pernet, to name only two, attempt to defy Eurocentrism by glossing over the history of Europe in favor of the pasts of non-Europeans, historians such as Hans Heinrich Nolte and Peter Feldebauer follow more closely in the footsteps of Wallerstein's world-systems theory. (See Chase-Dunn and Hall, this volume.) Rejecting monocentric perspectives, they focus on the multiple polarities of past and present world orders, precisely because they understand world history as histories of interactions. However, both strategies run the risk of reemploying dated concepts of space that remain impervious to the so-called spatial turn. Moreover, both approaches tend to rely on comparative methods and diffusionist theories reminiscent of equally dated conventions. (See Adas, this volume.) More recently, historians point to the potential pitfalls of comparison and insist that cross-cultural encounters necessarily alter civilizations on either side of the postulated divide. Hence, spirited debates about alternatives to diffusionist and comparative approaches are rife. In my view, this dialogue constitutes one of the most intellectually stimulating challenges of current world-historical practice in Europe. Hence, these debates will lie at the center of my discussion of this rediscovered, and newly reinvigorated, field, although I will discuss neither the numerous world historical syntheses nor the voluminous specialized research of the past few years.

I should say that I do not aim for comprehensiveness in the examples I give, an impossible task in any case. "Coverage" and the related question of which parts of Europe to include are thus of less concern in this chapter: Russia is mentioned only briefly, Turkey omitted, and the West is considered only as far as Spain.

Toward a New Consensus

This new European world history reconstructs intricate intercultural entanglements, global exchange processes and a wide range of social phenomena across national and geographic boundaries. In doing so, it traces connections between historical actors from diverging cultures as a function and cause of change over time. It emerged from three epistemological criticisms that took shape within Europe and later crystallized into different conceptual approaches.

In the mid-1980s Espagne and Werner explained the complex relationships between different societies in terms of "cultural transfer" (*transferts culturels*). They challenged the dominant notion according to which cross-cultural exchange reproduces hegemonic constellations (Espagne and Werner 1988; Espagne 1999). Instead of studying encounters as unidirectional imprints of one culture's ideas and practices onto another, cultural transfer studies foreground *interactions*. To make this argument Michel Espagne contended: "To transfer is not to transport." Instead he likened cultural transfer to a metamorphosis, and argued that "the term cannot by any means be reduced to the poor and very banal question of cultural exchange." He further insists: "It is not so much the circulation of cultural goods as the reinterpretation that is in question" (Espagne 2011). Historians now carefully outline the roles of concrete historical agents in the active appropriation and adaptation of goods, ideas, knowledge and customs, whereas these same agents figured merely as passive recipients in earlier diffusionist models. Cultural transfer studies, moreover, sharpen our awareness of the pitfalls of comparing ostensibly discrete objects. These objects are themselves constructed and hardly possess the stable and separate identities that comparisons invariably postulate, in particular when civilizations are classified along a hierarchical continuum of cultural progress. Imposing a comparative framework necessarily obstructs other contextual references that might obscure the mutual constituency and interconnectedness of the compared entities (Middell 2000).[1] Cultural transfer studies focus instead on the respective interfaces between different cultures and place reciprocal encounters in precisely these larger contexts. In particular, they unpack the complicated processes of integration that take place in a multipolar world. As a result, the historiography of cultural transfers relativizes above all the notion of the center. Thus it becomes possible to recognize cross-cultural relations as the cause for historical change, as the motor for dynamic, large-scale integration. (See chapters by Fernández-Armesto and by Zhang, this volume.) The majority of studies reconstructing the transfer of ideas, people, and goods now demonstrate that different cultures developed as a result of intricate relations with precisely those aspects, people, and places they consciously excluded. The demarcation of regional difference is an essential part of forging national coherence. In other words, both national differentiation and internal coherence are the result of intricate relationships and exchanges that are not marginal, but lie at the center of these developments.

Sociologists, and then human geographers, came to view the category of space, second only to time, as a socially produced and continuously changing construct rather than an immutable constant (Lefebvre 1974; Foucault 1986; Harvey 2001). Contrary to common assertions of the compression and dwindling significance of space and time as a result of modern mass communication, close scrutiny has revealed that location and spatial organization continue to acutely impact the experience of social reality. As a result of the reconceptualization of space and its relation to time as prefigured in the spatial turn of the 1990s, historians in Europe have generally accepted the premise that spatial relations are socially produced: whether drawing political boundaries, controlling (im)migration, developing new markets or managing the flows of goods and capital, social agents construct spatial realities (Döring and Thielmann 2008). Recognizing that the nation-state had grown to dominate political organizations only in the nineteenth and twentieth centuries, historians investigated the conditions under which particular forms of spatial organization crystallized and thrived. Claims regarding the ostensibly universal trajectory of development from the imperial to the national state were the first to collapse. More recently, historians have argued that spatialization needs to be understood in its multitudinous varieties, since even dominant locations have always existed in tension with competing spatial allegiances (Revel 1996). At any rate, scholars no longer postulate spatial organizations as fixed or linear. Since space is not an empty vessel to contain social reality, spatial relations can hardly be grasped as part of a predefined hierarchical progression from local to global. Instead, spatial organization is the result of interlocking, and mutually constitutive, social relations. Accordingly, nationalization and nation-state formation must appear as a reaction to global constellations, as McKeown reiterates in his contribution to this volume.

The two approaches already discussed experienced a dynamic boost with the advent of a third perspective, one that more radically challenged established patterns of thought. In the context of decolonization, scholars began to systematically investigate the trajectory and meaning of European power. Beginning with the colonial period, Shalini Randeria, Andreas Eckert and others scrutinized European hegemony, calling into question the validity of polarizing analyses (dividing the world into Orient and Occident) along with modernization theories in general. They thus leveled sustained criticism at Western epistemologies and corresponding research practices (Randeria and Eckert 2009). Subaltern and postcolonial scholars strove to come to terms with historically existing Eurocentrism, and attempted to overcome its contemporary variants. On the one hand, their work bears out the structural inequalities that have characterized Europe's relations to other world regions. On the other hand, precisely because they seek to emphasize agency and subaltern voices, scholars such as Sebastian Conrad and Ulrike Freitag draw attention to the impact colonial encounters had on European metropoles. As postcolonial analyses highlighted interdependencies germane to any cultural contact and documented the myriad interactions between colonial power and its subjects, they clearly positioned themselves against diffusionist models (Blaut 1993). Thus they provided a critical impulse for historians to probe more deeply into the complicated transfers between Western and non-Western societies and opened a way to study more general global developments in light of cross-cultural relations.

Together, the notion of cultural transfers, the realization that spatial organization is socially constructed, and the insights facilitated by postcolonial studies anchor recent European contributions to world history. These shifts redirect historical questions toward interactions between different cultures and social groupings. Linear, let alone teleological, narratives appear increasingly problematic. Instead, postcolonial and post-structural approaches have rapidly gained ground and replaced the historical philosophies that postulated the unity of a globe.[2] In contrast, these newer approaches empirically demonstrate concrete connections and cross-cultural imbrications to understand historical processes that affect various places simultaneously. Recognizing processes of exchange and interaction to be central to historical developments, historians now widely accept the interdependency of nation-state building, regionalization, and globalization (David *et al.* 2007). Nonetheless, scholars continue to ponder the advantages of differentiating between world and global history on the one hand and transnational approaches on the other (*Revue d'Histoire* 2007). While the boundaries separating the various subcategories of a burgeoning field remain somewhat fluid, debates about descriptors and delimitations are avid.

Transnational history offers a particularly illustrative example in this respect. While Kiran Klaus Patel, for example, scrutinizes transnational connections for the modern period and is thus able to offer a more nuanced view of the concrete national histories in question, Michael Geyer argues that reconstructing the crossing of national boundaries is an essential step in decentering the nation-state and foregrounding specific transnational processes in the nineteenth and twentieth centuries (Patel 2005; Geyer 2012). Taken from a different angle: in the cases of Spain, France and Great Britain, where national histories are deeply, directly and obviously linked to imperial pasts, historians readily investigate the impact of non-Western regions on the metropole. The same holds true for countries in which nation-building and colonial expansion were inextricably linked, as in Germany and Italy (Stuchtey and Fuchs 2003). Meanwhile, the transnational history of East/Central Europe continues to foreground inter-European entanglements and exchange processes with immediate national neighbors. Only recently, and rather hesitantly, have European historians started to account for Central Europe's imperial pasts (Hadler and Mesenhöller 2007; Kasianov and Ther 2009).[3]

The disputes over the definition of transnational history are more complicated still. Philipp Ther, among others, insists on a clear distinction between the history of diplomatic relations and transnational history. In contrast, scholars such as Pierre-Yves Saunier make a compelling argument for studying state actors and nonstate actors simultaneously, to avoid reifying the problematic separation of political and diplomatic history from social and cultural experiences (Iriye and Saunier 2009). Gerhard Haupt and Jürgen Kocka (2010) address transnational history primarily as a history of comparison, whereas Eric Vanhaute (2009) pleads for the meticulous integration of multiple approaches, including world-system theory, comparison, and transfers. In light of this, it is hardly surprising that the wealth of perspectives on transnational history is mirrored by a similar multitude of approaches to world and global histories. From a bird's-eye view, these various approaches acquire different contours as they oscillate between two ideal types: relatively rigorous distinctions between world history, global history and transnational history contrast with more fluid conceptualizations of the field. One example of each pole will serve to outline the spectrum of approaches.

Jürgen Osterhammel insists on a clear distinction between transnational, world-historical, and global approaches. Transnational history, Osterhammel suggests, is primarily concerned with inter-European relationships and their transatlantic connections. Moreover, transnational history generally examines shorter time periods and is less concerned with universal patterns of connectivity. Notwithstanding its careful attention to historical multiplicity, world history (*Weltgeschichte*), in contrast, aims specifically to explicate such general tendencies. Hence, or so Osterhammel argues, it examines developments over the *longue durée* and across much larger regions as it privileges transcultural relations. He then conceives global history (*Globalgeschichte*) in much narrower terms: as an approach that historicizes global entanglements. Thus it examines developments that originated in the middle of the nineteenth century, and which still characterize the interconnectedness of the world today. Osterhammel carefully distinguishes global history, then, from the history of globalization. While the former in his view explores the contacts and interactions between various global networks, the history of globalization suggests a master narrative chronicling the continuous intensification of exchange and interdependencies (Osterhammel 2001; 2005).

Unlike Osterhammel, Sebastian Conrad, Andreas Eckert, and Ulrike Freitag – perhaps representative of a more integrative approach – stress the common elements between world, global, and transnational histories. Whether they are inspired by world-system theory, analyze different civilizations, insist on multiple modernities, write the history of globalization, or build on postcolonial studies, they reject modernization theory and seek to reconstruct "modernity" as a fully relational category; after all, they are specialists in non-European history. Moreover, they insist, world and global history no longer postulates a universal past, no longer means a teleological view of historical development, and no longer attempts to represent the world in its spatial and temporal totality. Because this new world history is primarily interested in recording a multiplicity of interactions and exchange, it resituates national histories in complex global contexts (Conrad *et al.* 2007). But even among those who conceive the field of world and global history in such fluid terms, debates remain: for example, the precise onset of globalization remains contested (Grandner *et al.* 2005). Such disputes notwithstanding, historians taking a more integrative perspective generally view the various methods, approaches and foci as essentially compatible. Further, they concern themselves only peripherally with the question of whether there is much intellectual gain in excluding the history of globalization from the field of global history.

This conceptual debate is by no means restricted to German-speaking contexts. For example Michael Geyer (Chicago), Michael Espagne (Paris) and Matthias Middell (Leipzig) collaborate in integrating the argument concerning the emergence of a "global condition" in the middle of the nineteenth century with the study of cultural transfers and the analysis of processes of territorialization. In focusing on spaces of globalization they give the conceptual debate – and the writing of transnational and global history – another twist (Mann and Naumann 2010).

Is this new European world history characterized by a multiplicity of approaches distinctive to the European region, or by ways that are emblematic of the discipline more generally? Are the contours of world history, for that matter, defined by the personal motivations, thematic preferences and temporal foci that also underwrite, say, social, cultural or regional history? There is no doubt that individual and departmental considerations play a role as well, but more pressing conceptual issues are at stake.

First, in delineating a field of world history, European historians insert themselves into the debates on world history and global development currently perceived as dominated by US-based historians. Very recently, for example, historians in France have begun to stake out their position in the field vis-à-vis North American historiography and to debate the extent to which American scholars' predominance can be seen as part and parcel of a wider imperialist project (Maurel 2009; Grosser 2011). In the United States, of course, world history's attempts to emancipate the modern era from its European roots has long been oriented toward presenting an alternative history of Western civilization. As early as the 1880s, in fact, the first president of the American Historical Association, Andrew White (1886), argued for a decidedly American perspective, insisting that the history of the world "must be rewritten from an American point of view ... to help build up a new civilization." Throughout two world wars, a similar ideological landscape inspired historians to theorize the "rise of the West" as a result of the cultural affinity (if not identity) between Western Europe and the United States. In the second half of the twentieth century, the processes of decolonization in Asia and Africa shifted the focus of historians in the United States to other parts of the world. During the Cold War the so-called Third World became especially relevant to the geopolitical interests of the United States (Levine 1996). In response, and alongside Europe's dwindling potential to disturb the emerging US hegemony, scholars of world history criticized the discipline's unremitting Eurocentrism and redirected their gaze toward the pasts of non-European peoples and societies, being shaped by very different trajectories of the study of world regions in European academia.

Within Europe, by contrast, historians attempted simultaneously *both* to provincialize the history of the continent, by engaging with extra-European developments, *and* to recast the history of the world without relapsing into traditional narratives of superiorities and exceptions (*Sonderwege*). Exemplary in this regard is the research network

"Tensions of Europe" at Eindhoven University of Technology. Focusing on infrastructure and technological innovation, historians there recast the history of European integration from circa 1850 to today, exploring the impact of cultural transfer from former colonies (and the United States) on the development of a uniquely European set of outlooks and behaviors (van der Vleuten and Kaijser 2006; Schot 2007; Badenoch and Fickers 2010). The group of researchers known as "Homo Europeaus" stresses even more vehemently the importance of external developments for the crystallization of a European identity (von Hirschhausen and Patel 2010). Even historians of premodern Europe insist that a global perspective is indispensable (Drews and Oesterle 2008 and others). To put this more bluntly: On the one side of the Atlantic historians search for the world by circumventing Europe, on the other side of the Atlantic, Europe's provincialization (as Chakrabarty 2000 put it) holds the key to understanding the world.

Obviously, location affects point of view. Societies negotiate the effects of globalization in different ways. Depending on where they find themselves in the matrix of global power structures, they formulate specific answers in the attempt to explain the ways in which the precise set of entanglements developed in the first place. Accordingly, European historiography of the world reviews exchanges and connections of particular significance for societies in Europe. And here topics that are of little (or no) significance to US-based historians figure centrally – be they the integration of the Baltic states, intercultural encounters in the Mediterranean, West European relations with Russia, or interactions between Central Europe and its southeastern neighbors.

Similarly diverging perspectives negotiate the constitution of today's globalized world, and (world-)political interests undeniably leave their mark. For, as historians order societies as part of global networks, they attribute significance and inescapably structure the scope of political action in the present. In the words of Arif Dirlik, "World history, then, is inevitably about world-making" (2003: 92).[4] What is presented as "the world" in world histories always bears an undeniable connection to the societies for whom they are written. Taken to extremes, ideas about an effective world order after 1989–1991, or even after 9/11, almost appear *naturally* different in Europe than in the United States.

Secondly, and very practically, Europe-based historians who are trained in European or Western history bargain with their colleagues in area studies over limited departmental resources and thereby negotiate the parameters of world historical programs. Such intra-disciplinary repositioning extends beyond resource distribution, however. The standing of world history largely depends on its grounding in empirical knowledge, and hence its integrity is contingent on the expertise provided by area studies scholars. Questions about the feasibility of developing and deploying overarching and transcultural conceptual categories lie at the heart of such intra-disciplinary discord and negotiation (Pernau 2007). Such questions of course have analogues in the professionally complicated position of world/global historians in North American historical circles, and in other world regions too. (See Pomeranz and Segal, this volume.)

Thirdly, the different approaches produce diverging narratives of modern integration that contrast with previously universalist accounts. World histories analyze the extent of globalization today as the outcome of processes and interactions that developed over centuries if not millennia. Global histories, in contrast, generally postulate a caesura, whether they place the development of new entanglements in the 1500s or locate it in the nineteenth century. In yet another vein, the new global history, in Europe as elsewhere, largely restricts its scope to the past century (Middell 2005). Debates over periodization are more than ritualized bickering: the structuring of time is, in fact, a central concern. (See Bright and Geyer, this volume.) Choosing a particular timeframe will determine which cast of historical actors occupies center stage, and can redefine their sphere of action.[5] Among others, Andrea Komlosy has pointed out the challenge of correlating local, regional, national, and worldwide chronologies in global interpretations. After all, different spaces each have their own time, as do cross-cultural interactions. While the stability, quantity and quality of intraregional and long-distance contacts guides the periodization of global history, a chronology of worldwide integration must remain sensitive to the particular temporality of individual spaces and their social organization (Komlosy 2005).

The plurality in approach and perspective of world historical studies sketched above is mirrored in the equally complex research praxis of European world historians. (See Weinstein, this volume.) To describe these in merely a few sentences risks conjuring a map in which white spots markedly outnumber concrete places, names, and publications. Nevertheless, by way of sketching world histories of European origin, I will briefly introduce four dominant practices.

Particularly in the realm of economic history, global approaches can look back on a long tradition both on the Continent and in the British Isles, and they are well represented in institutional contexts. Largely thanks to the efforts of Patrick O'Brien, the Department of Economic History at the London School of Economics has since the mid-1990s developed as a center for the study of world economic processes. The Global Economic History Network, established there in 2003, now encompasses nearly 50 researchers from the British Isles, the Netherlands, Italy, Germany and Turkey. Together with colleagues from the United States, India and Japan, they have begun to outline a global history of economic processes that utilizes resources and findings from many disciplines. For example, Gareth Austin and Peer Vries have taken up and carried on the debates over divergent economic developments in Europe and Asia instigated and vigorously pursued by Bin Wong, Kenneth Pomeranz, and Andre Gunder Frank in the United States. Austin, based in Geneva, differentiates between land-, labor-, and capital-based industrialization and postulates these as distinct types observable only in global comparison. In Vienna, Vries redirects the focus to China and demonstrates that the development of industrialization is intimately connected to the organization of statehood. In Amsterdam, meanwhile, a research colloquium under the direction of Marjolein 't Hart explores the interface between economic and political history, suggesting that global power dynamics reflect the compounding coexistence of fiscal and military efficiencies (Sugihara and Austin 2011; Vries 2003).

The rather hesitant European ventures into world political history correspond to a more general disciplinary trend, if one ignores for a moment studies on international organization and diplomacy. (See Northrop, final chapter in this volume.) Innovations here mainly focus on two subject areas. First, the key term "world order" invites divergent and often conflicting interpretations of global relationships and the mechanisms of their implementations (Conrad and Sachsenmaier 2008). On the other hand, historians have also begun to outline a political history of globalization. Sebastian Conrad, who works in Berlin, understands the formation of the German Empire in this way as a reaction to global integration. He suggests that increasing transnational connections between 1880 and 1914 did not obliterate national differences but rather made them ever more salient (Conrad 2006). Matthias Middell and Ulf Engel, both from Leipzig, also explore the interrelation between nationalization and globalization, but integrate it into a general history of sovereignty (one sensitive to cultural and economic organization) that focuses on its spatialization. In other words, they foreground processes of de- and reterritorialization. Middell and Engel join others to argue that the worldwide correlation of economic, cultural, social and political spaces emerged in the middle of the nineteenth century, thereafter challenging existing territorialization within a nation-state framework. Since then, a balance has had to be found between preserving sovereignty, on the one hand, and autonomy, on the other, as national demarcation of power and identity had to be reconciled with global entanglements and interactions. Sometimes this dialectic produces stable territorial entities, while at other times, the same dialectic accounts for their dissolution. When established patterns of territorialization lose their effectiveness, crises ensue. Furthermore, when these crises solidify, they pose a structural challenge to the world order. Middell and Engel describe these phenomena as "critical junctures of globalisation" (Engel and Middell 2010).

For quite some time, a global perspective has also informed social history – itself a longstanding field in European scholarship. While labor and labor conditions still stand at the center of social historical approaches, world history has contributed to a rejuvenation of the subfield. The changed focus of the International Conference of Labour and Social History, founded in Vienna in 1964, is a compelling example. Since the end of the 1990s, explicitly comparative and transnational projects have dominated the conference program. Around the same time, Marcel van Linden opened the Amsterdam-based International Institute of Social History (IISH), a center for the study of labor history, in relation to world historical questions, and conceptualized a research program for a global history of work. Two thematic emphases are now particularly prevalent. First, research in "global labor history" focuses on international manifestations of organized labor reform movements, the history of labor in the global South, and global transformations of working conditions in their plurality. In cooperation with the Institute of Social and Economic History at the University of Vienna, historians study, for example, the myriad types of work (Global Collaboratory on the History of Labour Relations 1500–2000). The history of migrants and migration is also a key arena of research, as are global flows of goods and commodity chains.[6] Secondly, "global economic history" also focuses on a previously ignored topic in world history: the story of price and wage developments (van Zanden n.d.). As in Amsterdam, historians explore the scope of free and unfree labor ranging from slavery, indentured labor and sharecropping to free wage labor and self-employment. Similarly, labor migration and commodity chains provide a useful lens for global historical entanglements across state boundaries (Stanziani 2008; Pries 2001). Most recently, several European universities have focused on the history of slavery, such as the exemplary Institute for the Study of Slavery at Nottingham University. New globally oriented questions concerning the history of labor are also a central focus of the International Research Center for Work and Human Life Cycles in Global History, founded at Humboldt University in Berlin in 2009. Finally, Eric Vanhaute and his research team in Ghent explore the complicated global contexts of agricultural labor (Vanhaute 2008).

Again following more general trends of the discipline, cultural history now figures centrally in world-historical studies within Europe. Since the mid-1990s, the Centre National de la Recherche Scientifique at the École Nationale Supérieure in Paris has been home to Michel Espagne and his research team, whose work grounds the general theory of cultural transfer in empirical studies. Their work concentrates on the transnational complexities of the humanities and the circulation of discourses on art and literature, as well as the places and actors central to these exchange processes. Whereas intra-European cultural relations constituted the original focus of this work, historians now increasingly trace connections to non-European societies. Furthermore, in 2008 a group of researchers from Berlin, Hamburg, Bremen, Edinburgh, Florence and Zurich launched a study of "actors of cultural globalization, 1860–1930." In contrast to most globalization studies, they concentrate on social actors, whether individuals or collectives. One of their core questions is how these actors articulated notions of difference and structured the globalization process, which in turn defined and limited their room to maneuver. To cite a final example of current practice, Dan Diner's work recasts the transnational history of East European Jews as a central dimension of historical developments. His work emphasizes mobility as a long-term characteristic of Jewish history and carefully outlines the globally relevant particularities of the region (i.e. Eastern Europe), which remains a blind spot in most world histories (Diner 1999).

Taken together, European scholars interested in history on a global scale place historical actors center stage, work in a poststructuralist framework, employ a constructionist understanding of space, and emphasize connections, transfer, and intercultural exchange from a perspective shaped by postcolonial studies. To the extent that these positions are not driving the field in other regions, world history writing in Europe has its own shape.[7]

Carving Out an Institutional Home

These newer studies on transfer and exchange processes owe their existence in large part to the methodological and theoretical debates reviewed above. However, their disciplinary impact would have been much smaller without the wide-ranging institutional changes which opened academia to world-historical perspectives in European research and teaching – to an extent unparalleled even in the United States. Had I been asked to sketch the institutional landscape of world history in Europe at the beginning of the 1990s, it would not have been possible to foreground the work of more than a few individuals and even fewer places. In 1991, an international conference on Conceptualizing Global History (Mazlish and Buultjens 1993) and the Verein für Geschichte des Weltsystems (Association for the History of the World System) (founded in 1992) were the lone contenders for institutional representation. Apart from these, I would have had to stress the resurgence of questions and approaches related to historicizing the nation. Today, in contrast, the countless programs of academic study, research centers, networks and forums on world-historical problems and issues constitute a dense web within Europe. A fully detailed map of the proliferating institutionalization of world history, which lies beyond the scope of this chapter, would underscore the previously established multifariousness of approaches, methods and questions. Instead, here I will provide only a snapshot of the dramatic developments that have marked the past decade.

The institutionalization of world history in academic structures proceeded along two main paths. Of these, the establishment of new research centers and university institutes clearly predominates. The somewhat unhurried expansion of area studies within existing history departments initially opened the field to a younger generation of historians, who in turn introduced world-historical questions to the history classroom. Despite the fact that the traditional focus on national history has been called into question, and scholars now increasingly explore transnational connections to extra-European world regions, the overall transformation of institutionalized history departments proceeds more sluggishly. The replacement of existing professorships with world historians, as happened recently at the ETH Zurich (Eidgenössische Technische Hochschule, or Swiss Federal Institute of Technology, Zurich), at Leiden University, at Salzburg University and in Bamberg, Bremen and Vienna, remains the exception. Even the integration of extra-European expertise is far from universal at this level (Sachsenmaier 2010). Slightly more room to maneuver exists in mid-level academic positions, but since tenure-track positions remain the exception in Europe (they play a significant role only in Great Britain and Scandinavia), mid- and entry-level jobs present younger historians with only limited, and at times fragile, opportunities. Therefore, the following discussion focuses on the more dominant path of integrating world-historical practice into academia through the rapid proliferation of new institutions.

At least two factors underpin this institutional development. First, the newly created institutional landscape reflects the changed interest of financial sponsors. National research foundations, such as the DFG (Deutsche Forschungsgesellschaft) in Germany or the ANR (Agence Nationale de la Recherche) in France, and the European Union even more powerfully, increasingly urge and foster projects that integrate global perspectives into the disciplines comprising the social sciences and humanities.[8] Secondly, the model prevalent in the United States, and which also existed in the socialist countries, namely a twofold structure of national and world history within individual history departments, did not take hold in a West European context, nor is it presently even discussed as an option.

Thus the newly founded institutions distinguish themselves through their interdisciplinarity. The Global History and Culture Centre at the University of Warwick and the Centre for Transnational History at St Andrews University are illustrative cases, with, further, the cluster of excellence on "Asia and Europe in a Global Context: Shifting Asymmetries in Cultural Flows," at Heidelberg University, the "Laboratoires d'Excellence: Transferts Matériels et Culturels, Traduction, Interfaces," at the École Normale Supérieure, Paris, as well as the research group around Martti Koskenniemi at the Erik Castrén Institute of International Law and Human Rights at the University of Helsinki.

Institutional change was often a first response to the growing number of scholars working on non-European topics and collaborating with colleagues in area studies. The School of Oriental and African Studies at the University of London, the more recently established Department of History and Area Studies at Aarhus University, and the Center for Area Studies at the University of Leipzig have also played a prominent role in shaping world-historical questions and research agendas. Much less common are initiatives that originate in the social sciences and explore global phenomena in historical detail, but Roskilde University is a noteworthy exception here.

Such generalizations cannot easily be extended to East and Central Europe, where area studies are much less prominently represented in university structures than in former colonizers such as Great Britain or France. (See Sinha, this volume.) Accordingly, postcolonial perspectives have suggested themselves with less urgency, and comparative approaches remain more prominent in East and Central Europe. Nevertheless, studies foregrounding multi-ethnic experiences, overlapping developments, and the often fluid ethnic, religious, and linguistic identities and boundaries occupy a central role in the historiography of these regions, even if scholars rarely present themselves as engaged in world or global history (Antohi *et al.* 2007). Historians in the East and Central European countries have rediscovered their own world-historical traditions, reading these older works through a new lens, and expanding on them with a refined theoretical apparatus

(Sosnowska 2004). The global dimensions of East and Central European pasts have inspired countless new studies, primarily in the following four fields.

First, Jewish history, particularly well grounded in Polish institutions, perforce crosses political boundaries. Secondly, the study of minorities and their diasporas requires a broader perspective, exemplified by the attempt of scholars at the Research Institute of Ethnic and National Minorities at the Hungarian Academy of Sciences in Budapest to trace the migrations of Slovaks, Romanians, and Roma. Similarly, the International Center for the Problems of Minorities and Intercultural Relations (IMIR) in Sofia as well as the Center for Transylvanian Studies and the Center for Population Studies in the Romanian city of Cluj-Napoca are committed to developing a more comprehensive narrative that explains the multicultural history of this area (Brunnbauer 2004). Thirdly, diplomatic history is experiencing its own revival, for example at the Teleki László Institute in Budapest, where scholars analyze the place of Hungary in international and global processes. Lastly, Balkan Studies has recently developed into a new field that explores numerous transnational and global problems, and that ultimately also revisits the question of "Europeanness," in light of the region's history as a vassal of the Ottoman Empire. Even though disciplinary traditions and foci are different in East-Central Europe, and though they focus less often on extra-European developments, the trajectories of institutional development and change are remarkably similar. Scholars at newly founded institutions and research centers are just as likely now to pursue globally focused projects. The establishment of numerous new universities after the implosion of socialism in 1989 (of which the Central European University in Budapest is certainly the best known) played a decisive role. But, as in Western Europe, new venues for the practice of world history also extend outside academia, not least as a result of the creation of the Center for Advanced Studies in Sofia.

Again different is the situation in Russia, which has its own long tradition in world history writing. This is despite the fact that relatively little recent attention has been paid to it within Russian university departments. There has, however, been a vigorous research program within the Academy of Sciences, especially the Institute of World History.

Similarities notwithstanding, the institutionalization of world history, its relationship to related disciplines and approaches, its internal alignment, its inclusion in curricula, and its resources undoubtedly vary from place to place. In some locations the newly established venues prove immensely successful, whereas elsewhere their efforts have collapsed after only short periods of time. This continuous renewal of diversity is characteristic for the field of world history in Europe. In the United States, in contrast, world history has established itself successfully in a handful of institutions. As discussed by Heather Streets-Salter in this volume, however, PhD programs in world history remain the exception, and other scholars, such as Patrick Manning, have expressed pessimism about the field's institutional standing.

In Europe, world and global history has recently become a booming subfield of the discipline, one that depends on the work of young academics and accordingly is particularly notable in current patterns of graduate education. Since the mid-1990s, structured doctoral programs have become the norm in Germany, for example, and no fewer than seven graduate programs explicitly explore global and transnational issues where historians, area-studies scholars and exponents of the social sciences engage in fruitful exchange.[9] Central European University awards doctoral degrees in comparative Central, East, and Southeast European history. Moreover the program ENGLOBE (Enlightenment and Global History) boasts nine cooperating universities in Portugal, Spain, Ireland, France, Poland, and Germany. In addition, several programs offer master's degrees in world history, for example the Erasmus Mundus Program, "Global Studies: A European Perspective," which is a cooperative venture between the universities of Leipzig, Vienna, Roskilde, and Wroclaw, along with the London School of Economics and partner universities in Canada, China, India, Australia, South Africa, and the United States. Lastly, one should also mention the program in Modern Global History at the Jacobs-University Bremen in this context. (For developments in primary and secondary education, see Schissler and Nuhoglu Soysal 2005.)

Research groups and networks, often with an international and interinstitutional character, are of particular relevance for the debate over methods and thematic approaches. They continue earlier efforts to compose collectively authored world histories (like the *Propyläen Weltgeschichte*, edited by Walter Goetz, 1931–1933, or the several editions of the *History of Mankind*, edited by UNESCO). In doing so they extend, and offer homage to, one sort of perspective inherent within globally oriented historiography. Furthermore they stand in contrast to the recent wave of syntheses written by single authors (for example, works by Christopher Bayly and Jürgen Osterhammel), which offer thought-provoking interpretations but are inevitably based on a narrower scope of empirical and literary evidence.

In addition to previously mentioned groupings, historians based in Göttingen, Basel, Münster and Bonn organized a working group in 2006 that focused on premodern transcultural history (so far, historians have only just begun to produce syntheses that cross established epochal boundaries for the history of world markets and transcontinental trade). (See chapters by Levi, by Yoffee, and by Liu, this volume.) Two years later, historians Bo Strath and Hagen Schulz-Forberg founded the Nordic Global History Network, to which area studies scholars and historians from the universities of Aarhus, Helsinki, Malmš and Roskilde contribute. Together they direct their attention to discourses of modernization and seek to compare global upheavals. Likewise, they examine the circulation of categories, terms and conceptual models between different cultures.

Every other year since 2006, the European Social Science History Conference provides a forum for more general exchanges and regular contact between the practitioners of world history: part of its program is organized by the Network of World History. The European Network in Universal and Global History (ENIUGH), established in 2002, orchestrates a European Congress on World and Global History. Since 2005 this triennial congress has brought together 200–300 scholars from the social sciences and humanities to discuss projects in transnational and global history. ENIUGH's primary purpose is to facilitate efficient cooperation and multilingual communication between scholars within Europe. It also provides an opportunity to connect with colleagues from other world regions. Seeking to transcend the Eurocentric, teleological and universalist assumptions characteristic of previous approaches, ENIUGH encourages the continued provincialization of Europe from a global perspective. It promotes research in world, global, comparative and transnational history by publishing articles, book reviews, conference announcements, and shorter debates about methods and theoretical approaches. The network edits two peer-reviewed journals, the paper-based *Comparativ: A Journal of Global History and Comparative Studies* and the electronic *geschichte.transnational*. Counting the *Journal of Global History* (based in London, and founded in 2007) and the *Zeitschrift für Weltgeschichte*, Europe now boasts four major scholarly journals devoted to the study of a global past.

This proliferation continues in other arenas. Numerous book series – six based in Vienna alone – provide ample opportunity for scholars to publish their own research and keep abreast of their colleagues' work. For example, the series "Expansion, Interaktion, Akkulturation" expands on world-system theory and positions itself against the traditional emphasis that postulated a world-system dominated by the West. The series moreover calls into question diffusionist models that reduce the complexity of cultural contacts to a simple inequality, and seeks to critically reexamine Europe's own place in the world. The same publisher produces the series Weltregionen, focused on the intensification of global relations, while Mittelmeerstudien (Magnus Verlag) mirrors the growing interest in European regions that have principally shaped intercultural exchange.

Again through ENIUGH, which is a founding member of the wider international Network of Global and World History Organizations (NOGWHISTO), world historians in Europe have the opportunity to cooperate with the full range of non-European institutions in the field. NOGWHISTO, which has been approved as an international organization affiliated with the Comité International des Sciences Historiques, provides a formal space for cooperation and exchange among members of the World History Association (WHA), the Asian Association of World History (AAWH), the African Network in Global History/Réseau Africain d'Histoire Mondiale (ANGH/RAHM) and ENIUGH.

In light of these continuously expanding institutional as well as intellectual topographies, there can be no doubt that world and global history is a dynamic and institutionally grounded field of research in Europe. The existing diversity, in the arena of world history praxis and institutionalization, should be seen as a sign of success rather than fragility. The selective examples provided in this chapter attest to the energy and enthusiasm of a field whose raison d'être now lies beyond contestation. Calling for an inclusion of the recent work of European world historians in accounts of the field, I certainly do not intend to reassert the dominance of a previous center. Turning a blind eye to it and its new shape, however, would itself only serve to assert a new center, a move that would be rather anachronistic in today's multipolar world.

Notes

The author would like to thank the working group on "Global History" at the Global and European Studies Institute of the University of Leipzig for their critical comments and supportive discussions.

1 The heated debates on the pitfalls and benefits of comparative approaches are outlined by Kaelbe and Schriewer (2003) and Haupt and Kocka (2010). The empirical evidence further underscores the reductionist implications of traditional comparative approaches and promotes a sustained dialogue about the fundamental incompatibility of historical comparison with cultural transfer studies (Espagne 1994).

2 For an excellent example of the break with metaphysical models of interpretation, in favor of empirically grounded world historical practice, see Tortarolo (2000).

3 The imperial history of Russia has also entered research agendas, in Russia itself and in other European historiographies. Consider especially the journal Ab Imperio, founded in 2000 in Kazan (Tatarstan), and for an overview see Aust (forthcoming).

4 Marnie Hughes-Warrington and Ian Tregenza (2008) illustrate the extent to which Australian emancipation from Great Britain influenced the development of Australian world history and its attempt to strengthen Australia's geopolitical position. Jerry Bentley (2005) has sketched

the political import of global approaches in the United States, and Hartmut Bergenthum (2004) has highlighted the nexus of world-historical approaches to the German Empire and its colonial expansionism prior to World War I.

5   Marshall Hodgson's critique of William McNeill's *The Rise of the West* illustrates this: "McNeill displays a persistent Western bias, despite his very sincere attempt to get beyond it … This lack is reflected … most significantly in his choice of the time of demarcating modern from pre-modern. The choice of 1500 instead of 1600 as the round number here is disastrous. It causes him … to treat Portuguese expeditions not as one more venture within an essentially agraria-nate-level historical complex, which was rather readily contained in the course of the 16th century by other peoples in the Indian Ocean …" (Hodgson 2002: 92).

6   See in particular the contribution to the book series Studies in Global Social History (Brill) issued since 2008 by Marcel van der Linden. For the research program at Amsterdam consult van der Linden (2002).

7   One telling example: the approach of big history, prominent in North America, is hardly followed in Europe (excepting a few scholars such as Fred Spier, represented in this volume). In the same vein, European approaches to periodization generally concentrate on shorter periods, finding shifts and changes in the eighteenth to twentieth centuries; world histories written in the US tend to stress a transformation around the year 1500. And finally, while historiography – in the sense of the history of the historical discipline – is a well-established subfield within Europe, and analyses of world history writing have thus also become a subject of this branch, such professional self-reflection is less widespread elsewhere.

8   The Seventh Framework Program for Research and Technological Development of the European Union for 2007–2013, equipped with 50 billion euros, serves as a telling example since it places the sponsorship of the humanities under the heading Europe in the World. For the impact of the European Commission (through its funding schemes) on higher education in Europe, see Batory and Lindstrom (2011).

9   Graduate students pursue world historical questions in Bielefeld (Weltgesellschaft – Die Herstellung und Repräsentation von Globalität), in Leipzig (Bruchzonen der Globalisierung), in Gießen (Transnationale Medienereignisse von der Frühen Neuzeit bis zur Gegenwart), in Rostock (Kulturkontakt und Wissenschaftsdiskurs), in Mainz and Hildesheim (Transnationale Soziale Unterstützung), in Frankfurt (Oder) (Transnationale Räume), and in Greifswald (Baltic Borderlands: Shifting Boundaries of Mind and Culture in the Borderlands of the Baltic Sea Region).

References

Antohi, Sorin, Balázs Trencsényi, and Péter Apor, eds. 2007. *Narratives Unbound: Historical Studies in Post-Communist Eastern Europe*. Budapest: Central European University Press.

Aust, Martin. Forthcoming. Á la recherche d'histoire impériale: Histories of Russia from the nineteenth to the early twenty-first century. In M. Middell and L. Roura, eds, *World, Global and European Histories as Challenges to National Representations of the Past*. Basingstoke: Palgrave Macmillan.

Badenoch, Alexander, and Andeas Fickers, eds. 2010. *Materializing Europe: Transnational Infrastructures and the Project of Europe*. Basingstoke: Palgrave Macmillan.

Batory, Agnes, and Nicole Lindstrom. 2011. The power of the purse: Supranational entrepreneurship, financial incentives, and European higher education policy. *Governance* 24 (2): 311–329.

Bentley, Jerry. 2005. Myths, wagers, and some moral implications of world history. *Journal of World History* 16 (1): 51–82.

Bergenthum, Hartmut. 2004. *Weltgeschichten im Zeitalter der Weltpolitik. Zur populären Geschichtsschreibung im wilhelminischen Deutschland*. Munich: Martin Meidenbauer.

Blaut, James M. 1993. *The Colonizer's Model of the World: Geographical Diffusionism and Eurocentric History*. New York: Guilford Press.

Brunnbauer, Ulf, ed. 2004. *(Re)Writing History: Historiography in Southeast Europe after Socialism*. Münster: LIT.

Chakrabarty, Dipesh. 2000. *Provincializing Europe: Postcolonial Thought and Historical Difference*. Princeton: Princeton University Press.

Conrad, Sebastian. 2006. *Globalisierung und Nation im deutschen Kaiserreich*. Munich: C.H. Beck.

Conrad, Sebastian, Andreas Eckert, and Ulrike Freitag, eds. 2007. *Globalgeschichte. Theorien, Ansätze und Themen*. Frankfurt am Main: Campus.

Conrad, Sebastian, and Dominic Sachsenmaier, eds. 2008. *Competing Visions of World Order: Global Moments and Movements, 1880s–1930s*. New York: Palgrave Macmillan.

David, Jérôme, Thomas David, and Barbara Lüthi, eds. 2007. *Globalgeschichte/Histoire globale/ Global History*. Special issue, *Traverse: Zeitschrift für Geschichte/Revue d'Histoire* (Zurich) 14 (3).

Diner, Dan. 1999. *Das Jahrhundert verstehen. Eine universalhistorische Deutung*. Munich: Fischer.

Dirlik, Arif. 2003. Confounding metaphors, inventions of world: What is World History for? In B. Stuchtey and E. Fuchs, eds, *Writing World History, 1800–2000*, pp. 91–133. Oxford: Oxford University Press.

Döring, Jörg, and Tristan Thielmann, eds. 2008. *Spatial Turn. Das Raumparadigma in den Kultur- und Sozialwissenschaften*. Bielefeld: Transcript Verlag.

Drews, Wolfram, and Jenny Oesterle, eds. 2008. *Transkulturelle Komparatistik. Beiträge zu einer Globalgeschichte der Vormoderne*. Issue of *Comparativ. Zeitschrift für Globalgeschichte und vergleichende Gesellschaftsforschung* 19 (Leipzig).

Engel, Ulf, and Matthias Middell, eds. 2010. *Theoretiker der Globalisierung*. Leipzig : Leipziger Universitätsverlag.

Espagne, Michel. 1994. Sur les limites du comparatisme en histoire culturelle. *Genèses* 17: 112–121.

Espagne, Michel. 1999. *Les transferts culturels franco-allemand*. Paris: Presses Universitaires de France.

Espagne, Michel. 2011. The notion of cultural transfer. Opening lecture at the Third ENIUGH Congress on World and Global History, London School of Economics, Apr. 14–17.

Espagne, Michel, and Michael Werner, eds. 1988. *Transferts. Les relations interculturelles dans l'espace franco-allemand*. Paris: Recherche sur les Civilisations.

Foucault, Michel. 1986. Of other spaces. *Diacritics* 16: 22–27.

Geyer, Michael. 2012. The new consensus. In M. Middell, ed., *Transnationale Geschichte als transnationale Praxis*. Göttingen: Vandenhoeck & Ruprecht.

Geyer, Michael, and Charles Bright. 1995. World history in a global age. *American Historical Review* 100 (4): 1034–1060.

Grandner, Margarete, Dietmar Rothermund, and Wolfgang Schwenkter, eds. 2005. *Globalisierung und Globalgeschichte*. Vienna: Mandelbaum.

Grosser, Pierre. 2011. L'histoire mondiale/globale. Une jeunesse exubérante mais difficile. *Vingtième Siècle* 110 (Apr.–June): 3–18.

Hadler, Frank, and Mathias Mesenhöller, eds. 2007. *Vergangene Grösse und Ohnmacht in Ostmitteleuropa. Repräsentationen imperialer Erfahrung in der Historiographie seit 1918*. Leipzig: Akademische Verlagsanstalt.

Harvey, David. 2001. *Spaces of Capital: Towards a Critical Geography*. Edinburgh: Edinburgh University Press.

Haupt, Heinz-Gerhard, and Jürgen Kocka, eds. 2010. *Comparative and Transnational History: Central European Approaches and New Perspectives*. New York: Berghahn.

Hodgson, Marshall. 2002. Doing world history. In M. Hodgson, *Rethinking World History: Essays in Europe, Islam, and World History*, ed. E. Burke, III. Cambridge: Cambridge University Press.

Hughes-Warrington, Marnie, and Ian Tregenza. 2008. State and civilization in Australian New Idealism, 1890–1950. *History of Political Thought* 29 (1): 89–108.

Iriye, Akira, and Pierre-Yves Saunier, eds. 2009. *The Palgrave Dictionary of Transnational History*. Basingstoke: Palgrave Macmillan.

Kaelbe, Hartmut, and Jürgen Schriewer, eds. 2003. *Vergleich und Transfer. Komparatistik in den Sozial- und Geschichts- und Kulturwissenschaften*, pp. 469–493. Frankfurt am Main: Campus.

Kasianov, Georgiy, and Philipp Ther, eds. 2009. *A Laboratory of Transnational History. Ukraine and Recent Ukrainian Historiography*. Budapest: Central European University Press.

Komlosy, Andrea. 2005. Weltzeit – Ortzeit. Zur Periodisierung von Globalgeschichte. In M. Grandner, D. Rothermund, and W. Schwenkter, eds, *Globalisierung und Globalgeschichte*, pp. 83–114. Vienna: Mandelbaum.

Lefebvre, Henri. 1974. *La production de l'espace*. Paris: Anthropos.

Levine, Lawrence W. 1996. *The Opening of the American Mind: Canons, Culture, and History*. Boston: Beacon.

Mann, Michael, and Katja Naumann. 2010. 1989 in a global perspective. Report of conference, Leipzig, Oct. 14–16, 2009. *Comparativ* 20 (3): 105–116.

Manning, Patrick. 2007. Nordamerikanische Ansätze zur Globalgeschichte. In B. Schäbler, ed. *Area Studies und die Welt. Weltregionen und neue Globalgeschichte*, pp. 59–89. Vienna: Mandelbaum.

Maurel, Chloé. 2009. La world/global history. Questions et débats. *Vingtième Siècle* 104 (Oct.–Dec.): 153–166.

Mazlish, Bruce, and Ralph Buultjens, eds. 1993. *Conceptualizing Global History*. Boulder: Westview.

Middell, Matthias. 2000. Kulturtransfer und Historische Komparatistik. Thesen zu ihrem Verhältnis. *Comparativ* 10 (1): 7–41.

Middell, Matthias. 2005. Universalgeschichte, Weltgeschichte, Globalgeschichte, Geschichte der Globalisierung – ein Streit um Worte? In M. Grandner, D. Rothermund, and W. Schwentker, eds, *Globalisierung und Globalgeschichte*, pp. 60–82. Vienna: Mandelbaum.

Middell, Matthias, and Katja Naumann. 2010. Global history 2008–2010. Empirische Erträge, konzeptionelle Debatten, neue Synthesen. In M. Middell, ed., *Die Verwandlung der Weltgeschichtsschreibung*. Issue of *Comparativ* 20 (6): 93–133.

Moore, R.I. 1997. World history. In M. Bentley, ed., *Companion to Historiography*, pp. 941–959. London: Routledge.

O'Brien, Patrick K. 2006. Historiographical traditions and modern imperatives for the restoration of global history. *Journal of Global History* 1 (1): 3–40.

Osterhammel, Jürgen. 2001. *Geschichtswissenschaft jenseits des Nationalstaates. Studien zur Beziehungsgeschichte und Zivilisationsvergleich*. Göttingen: Vandenhoeck & Ruprecht.

Osterhammel, Jürgen. 2005. Weltgeschichte. Ein Propädeutikum. *Geschichte in Wissenschaft und Unterricht* 56: 452–479.

Patel, Kiran Klaus. 2005. Transnationale Geschichte – ein neues Paradigma? *geschichte.transnational*, Feb. 2, at http://geschichte-transnational.clio-online.net/forum/id=573&type=artikel (accessed Feb. 2012).

Pernau, Margrit. 2007. Transkulturelle Geschichte und das Problem der universalen Begriffe. Muslimische Bürger im Delhi des 19. Jahrhunderts. In B. Schäbler, ed., *Area Studies und die Welt. Weltregionen und neue Globalgeschichte*, pp. 117–150. Vienna: Mandelbaum.

Pries, Ludger, ed. 2001. *New Transnational Social Spaces: International Migration and Transnational Companies in the Early Twenty-First Century*. London: Routledge.

Randeria, Shalini, and Andreas Eckert, eds. 2009. *Vom Imperialismus zum Empire. Nicht-westliche Perspektiven auf Globalisierung*. Frankfurt am Main : Suhrkamp.

Revel, Jacques. 1996. *Jeux d'échelles. La micro-analyse à l'expérience*. Paris: EHESS.

Revue d'Histoire. 2007. *Histoire globale, histoires connectées*. Supplement to *Revue d'Histoire Moderne et Contemporaine* 54 (4 bis).

Sachsenmaier, Dominic. 2010. European history and questions of historical space. In W. Eberhard and C. Lübke, eds, *The Plurality of Europe: Identities and Spaces*, pp. 521–535. Leipzig: Leipziger Universitätsverlag.

Sachsenmaier, Dominic. 2011. *Global Perspectives on Global History: Theories and Approaches in a Connected World*. Cambridge: Cambridge University Press.

Schissler, Hanna, and Yasemin Nuhoglu Soysal. 2005. *The Nation, Europe, and the World: Textbooks and Curricula in Transition*. Oxford: Berghahn.

Schot, Johan. 2007. Globlisering en Infrastructuur. *Tijdschrift voor Sociale en Economische Geschiedenis* 4 (3): 107–128.

Sosnowska, Anna. 2004. *Zrozumie zcofanieć. Spory historyków o Europę Wschodnią, 1947–1994* [Understanding backwardness: historians arguing on Eastern Europe, 1947–1994]. Warsaw: Trio.

Stanziani, Alessandro. 2008. Free labor–forced labor: An uncertain boundary? The circulation of economic ideas between Russia and Europe from the eighteenth to the mid-nineteenth century. *Kritika: Explorations in Russian and Eurasian History* 9 (1): 1–27.

Stuchtey, Benedikt, and Eckhardt Fuchs, eds. 2003. *Writing World History, 1800–2000*. Oxford: Oxford University Press.

Sugihara, Kaoru, and Gareth Austin, eds. 2011. *Labour-Intensive Industrialization in Global History*. London: Routledge.

Tortarolo, Eduardo. 2000. World Histories in the twentieth century and beyond. *Storia della Storiografia* 38: 129–137.

van der Linden, Marcel. 2002. Globalizing labour historiography: The IISH approach. Position paper, International Institute of Social History, Amsterdam.

van der Vleuten, Erik, and Arne Kaijser, eds. 2006. *Networking Europe: Transnational Infrastructures and the Shaping of Europe 1850–2000*. Sagamore Beach, MA: Science History.

van Zanden, Jan Luiten. n.d. On global economic history: A personal view on an agenda for future research. Paper. At http://socialhistory.org/sites/default/files/docs/jvz-research_1.pdf (accessed Feb. 2012).

Vanhaute, Eric. 2008. The end of peasantries? Rethinking the role of peasantries in a world-historical view. *Review* (Fernand Braudel Center) 31 (1): 39–59.

Vanhaute, Eric. 2009. Who is afraid of global history? Ambitions, pitfalls and limits of learning global history. In P. Vries, ed., *Global History*. Issue of *Österreichische Zeitschrift für Geschichtswissenschaften* 20 (2): 22–39.

von Hirschhausen, Ulrike, and Kiran Klaus Patel. 2010. Europeanization in history: An introduction. In M. Conway and K.K. Patel, eds, *Europeanization in the Twentieth Century: Historical Approaches*, pp. 1–18. Basingstoke: Palgrave Macmillan.

Vries, Peer. 2003. *Via Peking Back to Manchester: Britain, the Industrial Revolution, and China*. Leiden: Leiden University.

White, Andrew D. 1886. On studies in general history and the history of civilizations. *Papers of the American Historical Association* 1: 49–72. At http://www.historians.org/info/AHA_History/adwhite.htm (accessed Feb. 2012).

CHAPTER THIRTY-THREE

Other Globes
Shifting Optics on the World

DOUGLAS NORTHROP

"Give me a place to stand," Archimedes reportedly said while contemplating a lever in the third century BCE, "and I will move the world." The quotation may be dubious: the remark first appears in manuscripts written hundreds of years after Archimedes had died, and it has been translated in different ways from the Greek. But the words lived on, and have spread far beyond Archimedes' own fields of interest, mathematics and engineering. The phrase has been invoked, and its underlying idea applied metaphorically, by such varied figures as Plutarch, René Descartes, Joseph Conrad, Leon Trotsky, and Al Gore. To historians such a long pathway might suggest, first, the complexities of tracing utterances through space and time, finding a tapestry of shifting meanings and resonances along the way – moving beyond questions of simple fact ("Did Archimedes really say that?") to particular contexts and social practices ("Why did Trotsky use a lever to describe the Bolshevik Revolution?"). Yet Archimedes' attributed words still do conceptual work for scholars, suggesting the importance of choosing one's starting point with care. Put simply, much depends on where a writer stands, and how she or he begins to work. A starting point frames whatever follows: it shapes where readers of a history book, for example, will be taken in space or time; what they will be shown as legitimate and persuasive evidence; and what an author's guiding principles, concepts, and questions will be.

The present volume closes by asking readers to consider explicitly where *they* should begin – in conceiving new directions for teaching and scholarship. It does so by reaching outside the discipline of History. Complementing the foregoing essays on world and global history as seen from outside the institutional settings of Anglophone academia, how *else* might globally inclined historians think differently about their subject? How else could one conceive a "world"? How could we benefit from knowing about other forms of globally oriented work, and how might it infuse historical thinking about the human past? Scholars are wrestling with the global in other disciplinary terrains – all the more as "disciplines" bleed into one another, with neither space nor time the sole province of historians (not by a long way). Many other academic fields face similar issues:

A Companion to World History, First Edition. Edited by Douglas Northrop.
© 2012 Blackwell Publishing Ltd. Published 2012 by Blackwell Publishing Ltd.

responding to globalization – a universally recognized, but contradictorily defined, phenomenon; displacing the nation-state as a presumptively fundamental category for scholarly analysis; evaluating the trade-offs of big-picture analysis, with its macro-scaled perspectives, against the risks of metanarratives; overcoming the cultural parochialism of longstanding disciplinary and institutional practices; and dealing with problems of inclusivity at multiple scales of inquiry. What optics have other intellectual terrains produced to see the world? What other starting points exist, and how might they enrich the global dimensions of historical teaching and scholarship?

Practitioners of world and global history have prided themselves on having an expansive view, an insistent openness to breaking through the predefined categories that structure disciplinary history. This includes perspectives generated at greater scales of space and time, and emphasizes approaches that cut across national, state, and regional boundaries. But it simultaneously includes a willingness to use new forms of evidence, and new ways of pursuing historical knowledge. World historians show an almost gleeful inclination to cross the borders of academic discipline as well as geographic space and temporal period. Such studious indiscipline may explain some of the skittishness among other ("traditional") historians, especially when disciplinary borrowings draw on positivistic methods and the natural sciences (e.g., attempts to apply evolutionary biological notions such as "natural selection" to human history). Fred Spier's chapter on Big History discusses these natural-science approaches, so I will not address them at greater length here.[1] For reasons of space I restrict myself to the social sciences and humanities, surveying recent work from five such approaches – five "other globes."

The sketches offered here illumine disciplines ranging from the self-consciously "hard" (defined by practitioners as "scientific," that is, positivist, experimental, and/or quantitative) to "soft" (empirically based, but using "fuzzier" qualitative methods, relativistically framed or contextually oriented). Each has the potential to cross-fertilize writing in world and global history. Readers will conclude which approaches are the most germane or promising – and I hope they will also go on to explore other domains of globally inflected work (film studies, dance, philosophy, public health, international security, information sciences, or chaos theory, to name a few).[2]

The five areas chosen have clear, almost self-evident, connections to the core concerns of world and global history, but are also places where the scholarly literatures have not yet been fully interwoven.[3] Trade relationships, first, are a central, ongoing focus of world historians (see chapters above by Levi and by Fernández-Armesto); they produce copious sources (documents from merchants, trading companies, tax registers, etc.), and offer a straightforward way for historians to theorize exchanges and encounters among peoples from different parts of the world. The first sketch thus briefly asks how *economists*, a group ranging from abstract theorists to applied business economists, address issues of trade at interregional-to-global scales. Second, politics – in a broad sense, incorporating social and institutional power relations within, between, and prior to the entities we call "states" – likewise plays a key role for scholars of world history (see chapters by Morillo and by Sinha). How do *political scientists*, especially those writing about comparative politics and international relations, see a globe of political interactions? Can they shed light on state-based social hierarchies, military mobilizations, or interregional empires? Third, *anthropologists* – like historians – set out to study cultural practice and social relationships around the world (see chapters by Vélez, Prange, and Clossey, by Burton, and by Ward), while being generally more self-aware: much ethnographic writing shows how an author's presuppositions, choices, and mere presence can have a dramatic effect on the subject being investigated. Much anthropological work has focused on contextual, self-reflective "thick descriptions" written at relatively small scales. Recently, however, cultural and linguistic anthropologists have developed new forms of more geographically stretched "global ethnography." Fourth, scholars conventionally use the moment in time that written texts appeared as a way to divide "history" (practiced by historians) from "prehistory" (the turf of archaeologists and biological anthropologists) (see chapters by Yoffee and by Liu). But documents – with written words – do not only belong to historians. What happens to texts, whether ancient or modern, when they cross borders and move into new places, and are translated into new languages? How can specialists in *comparative literature* help us to understand global approaches to writing, reading, and publishing? Fifth, what about the visual (see chapter by Witz)? What happens when images, or other intentionally created objects, move through space and time – when motifs and techniques cross borders to influence artists in faraway places, artwork finds buyers on the other side of the world, and collections of supposedly emblematic objects are displayed in "global" museums? How do *art historians* think about nontextual materials, whether representational or abstract in form? Is it possible to discuss aesthetic questions at supranational or global scale?

A few caveats to begin. The authors I cite occupy a broad variety of methodological approaches and political positions, but obviously hardly begin to cover the full range of any single discipline, let alone to encompass the humanities and social sciences. In using them as exemplars of their "globes," I mean only to suggest some of the approaches that can be taken by using the tools of each discipline. Each of these domains obviously develops, and is constrained by, its own theoretical and analytical tools. Every author has already navigated a professional trajectory of intellectual, institutional, and interpersonal interactions, and it can be hazardous to abstract their work from these contexts. Doing so risks losing its embeddedness within theoretical and methodological vocabularies, ignores its institutional locations, and elides the interactive, iterative character of scholarly debate. (Do globally inclined specialists in other fields, for example, occupy marginal positions, or have as fraught a relationship with gatekeepers of disciplinary standing, as world historians perceive themselves to do? Sometimes yes, sometimes no.)

This point suggests the need for richly contextual disciplinary reading: a need that I can voice but not adequately observe. Without such contextual understandings, though, one faces the danger of cherry-picking ideas at an abstract or metaphorical level (such as Archimedes' lever) that are qualified and circumscribed in their original domains. Hence the sketches offered here should not be taken as definitive, but rather as suggesting areas for further reading. Take the headings as a roadmap, encouragement to pursue further investigation. Historians should not simply invoke these ideas – or rely on their halos of theoretical authority – without delving more deeply into the frameworks that produce and sustain them. Big Historians using notions of "complexity," for instance, need serious training in the mathematics of dynamical systems ("chaos theory") and the physics of entropy. Without it, a reader might fairly ask, how can they evaluate the use of concepts drawn from cosmic (or subatomic) spaces, or judge whether such notions are applicable to human society? How far can such scales speak to one another if they are studied by separate disciplines – each with its own understandings of evidence, institutional structures of authority, modes of argumentation, and conventions of proof?

Global Economics: International Trade and Business

Thomas Carlyle first dubbed economics "the dismal science" in 1849, and wags have quoted him ever since. Economists long since tired of the quotation, but still welcome part of the characterization: the idea that economics is a science. They see themselves as social *scientists*, investigating general "laws" of economic behavior – seeing people, all people, as unknowing actors in what amounts to a vast experiment. Many economists, although believing "economics" a universal human phenomenon, study it through the norms and practices of modern industrial capitalism – using a mix of experimental work, mathematical modeling, and quantitative analysis. Their methods include large-n studies, based on mathematical evaluation of aggregated data from thousands, even millions or billions, of transactions. At the other extreme of disciplinary economics one finds methods drawn from behavioral psychology: small-group experiments that undercut ideas of humans as rational-choice actors (in which consumers, investors, or business executives are seen as consistently motivated by self-interest and profit). Non- and precapitalist forms of economy are largely absent from either approach to economic research – as is economic history, especially of the deeper (preindustrial) human past, meaning the millennia before 1750 CE.[4] Economists and business professors aim instead to produce work of immediate, practical relevance to policymakers, businesses, and investors *today*; their disciplinary success rises if they can demonstrate a predictive ability. Does a particular analysis, in other words, accurately predict swings in stock-market prices, unemployment rates, or trade-account balances?

Historians do not set out to predict the future, nor do they generally talk about their subjects as part of a vast (nonrepeatable) experiment. World historians, however, are often more willing than others to think about "relevance," and do not always shy away from present-day questions and concerns. And here, surely, the data-focused approach of business economists could undergird a particular approach to, and perspective on, the globe. As one example, consider *World 3.0*, a recent book by Pankaj Ghemawat, a business economist now working in Spain. In it Ghemawat reaches an unusual set of conclusions, the details of which are by no means accepted by all economists; but his work – published in 2011 by the Harvard Business Review Press – usefully shows economic methods applied at global scale.

Ghemawat sets out ambitiously to investigate the actual meaning of "globalization" in today's world. To do so he adopts the perspective of industrial organization economics, which studies market failures and regulation, and also uses the empirical methods of international economics to evaluate how difference, and distance, affect trade. His analysis proceeds from the point of view of concrete actors – individual firms – not vague trends or abstract entities like "markets." At every step he asks how business professionals evaluate potential gains or losses from trading with partners across borders. *World 3.0* sets this analysis in the context of a (very) brief overview of human history, covering most of the human story in a half-dozen pages. Careful nuance on the deep past (labeled "World 1.0" and "World 2.0") is clearly not the goal, so Ghemawat moves quickly to his main point: testing the widespread assertion made by authors (such as Thomas Friedman, in *The World is Flat*, 2005) and policymakers (in speeches at meetings of the G5, G8, G20 countries, and so on) that we live in an unprecedentedly "global" world. Pundits and politicians alike say that today's world is far more interconnected than ever before, with economic relationships playing a key role to pull people from far-flung places together in freshly interdependent ways (whether they wish it or not). This discourse of unprecedented and omnipresent global exchange and dependence, in Ghemawat's contrarian view, is vastly overblown – more rhetoric than reality – and he calls it "globaloney."

Ghemawat argues that we live in a world that is as (at most) "semi-globalized." He even quantifies this assertion, concluding that depending on how one looks, today's world is only between 10 and 25 percent "globalized." He hopes this figure will grow: like many economists, he wants to encourage more and fuller market integration across ever larger areas. Disciplinary economics, in his view, proves that integration inevitably brings about an overall increase in prosperity (2011: 22). Nevertheless Ghemawat does not support unleashing the power of a completely free market at global scale. Instead he says that long-term global integration will require *more* market regulation, not less, and much of it is bound to happen at the level of national states. Nation-states remain more central to people's lives than "globalthink" suggests, for the ostensibly universal human reason that "trust and sympathy decline dramatically with difference" (2011: x). He offers a general rule of thumb that applies this principle everywhere: a 1 percent increase in distance between two potential partners produces a 1 percent reduction in trade between them (2011: 57). Ghemawat sees this rule as persisting throughout human history, and he finds it in today's world through empirical tests – specifically, lots of counting. He looks for things that cross state borders (objects, capital, information, people), and uses these as proxies for the "global." He then counts how many of these things move, but *not* across frontiers. With each set of numbers in hand, simple ratios show the proportion of each good that has been "globalized" – that is, the fraction of each economic activity that is practiced across national-state lines.

By this definition of globalization, the conclusions are stark. Against the views of such figures as Henry Ford (who said that cars and planes were inexorably "binding the world together"), or Martin Heidegger ("everything is equally far and equally near"), Ghemawat finds that first-generation immigrants represent only 3 percent of the world's population. Overseas students are just 2 percent of the world's university population. About 90 percent of the world's people never leave the country of their birth. Even the internet stays surprisingly close to home: between 2006 and 2008, only about 17–18 percent of electronic traffic crossed any national border. These striking findings are echoed in his specifically economic data: fewer than one in a hundred American companies have any operations overseas, and only a fifth of venture capital leaves its country of origin. "Global" companies usually seek profit by selling locally differentiated products, not aiming to impose uniform goods. They shy away from trying to homogenize the world: McDonald's use of different spices in Mexico, or its stress on selling vegetarian (rather than beef) burgers in India, would be an obvious example. Only 20 percent of the world's aggregated GDP involves cross-border export transactions, and this slice of economic activity is the first to be reversed in downturns. During the deep crisis of 2008, for instance, foreign direct investment fell abruptly (by nearly half), and multinational corporations suddenly and dramatically shortened their supply chains.

They did so by pulling back into core geographic spaces, precisely the places where people already felt deep ties of culture and proximity. Ghemawat thus comes back to the powerful, continuing effects of national borders, and with them, the lasting psychological/cultural power and institutional/bureaucratic frameworks of states – even in an ostensibly multinational, global era – through structuring practices like treaties, tariffs, or passports. (See chapter above by McKeown.) Such practices shape global trade, Ghemawat finds, in ways not captured by aggregated global statistics. Sharing a common language – such as English – increases two countries' trade substantially (by 42 percent); a common currency – such as the euro – is still more powerful (114 percent); most important of all is the historical experience of a shared colonial past (188 percent). Yet notwithstanding such lubricants to economic activity, even where trade should flow freely across interstate borders, it often stops. By way of example, *World 3.0* considers at length the US-Canadian frontier: a place with geographic proximity, a shared language (Quebec excepted), a largely shared history, even formal treaties that guarantee free trade (the North American Free Trade Agreement). If globalization is "ripping through people's lives" (Arundhati Roy), in other words, surely it can be found here. Yet instead Ghemawat finds a long list of impediments: after 9/11, for instance, triple the previous time was abruptly required for trucks to cross. Even in such apparently smooth and well-oiled locations, the onrushing global economy has a long way to go.

Global Politics: International Relations and Comparative Politics

Political science offers another avowedly scientific approach to general patterns ("laws") of human social behavior. Its practitioners – at least in the most "global" subfields of international relations (IR) and comparative politics (CP)[5] – share with economists the goal of generating testable (falsifiable), empirically grounded knowledge. Many political scientists pursue large-n comparative and quantitative analyses, seeking to understand cross-cultural and global phenomena (such as "democracy," or "authoritarianism," or "party politics"). Others use qualitative methods to study such issues in narrower view, using smaller samples and paying more attention to contextual factors.[6] Both groups seek to balance theoretical parsimony and completeness. Parsimony – an ideal also pursued by natural scientists – means elegance: finding the simplest model, mathematical or conceptual, that explains or predicts a given phenomenon. Completeness, on the other hand, reduces the number of outlying or excluded cases, incorporating contextual variables and considering the explanatory role of case-specific factors such as local structures, historical legacies, or individual leaders' traits. Such inclusiveness complicates (or, to critics, muddles) the overall picture, and makes it harder to reach straightforward, unambiguous conclusions. Given that the world is a complicated place, though, the recognition of particular and contingent factors also makes it possible to explain actual outcomes more compellingly. In either case, most political scientists agree that knowledge should be practically useful and relevant: they are much more likely than historians to pursue present-focused and policy-linked questions (such as water conflicts, religious conflicts, epidemics, poverty, or development initiatives). Disciplinary standing accrues to those whose ideas are clearly applicable to, and ideally predictive of, politics in the here and now – whether at a local, domestic, interstate, or global level.

"International relations" and "comparative politics" appear perfect candidates to generate optics for global analysis. IR's very name suggests attention to worldwide connections, specifically cross-state and interregional interactions, while CP raises anew the potential of comparative approaches. (See chapter by Adas.) Until recently, however, both subfields defined their objects of study in a way that, like Ghemawat, privileged the political practices of modern national states. They thus tended to presuppose a state framework, focusing on national-level institutions as key actors, not asking about wider "global" categories in ways world historians might welcome. Political science's distinction between "large-n" and "small-n" approaches usually rested on the number of *national* cases scholars incorporated into a study (large-n work compared dozens of countries;

small-n approaches could involve just three or four, sometimes from the same region). CP scholarship often presupposed the national scale in defining units to be "compared," while IR focused on inter*national* relations, that is, interactions of *states*. This meant that countries usually appeared as irreducible units, acting like billiard balls bouncing into each other: ricocheting in new directions, yes, but remaining basically self-contained. In the judgment of disciplinary observers like Navnita Behera, the Westphalian state still serves fundamentally as "the epistemological base of IR" (Tickner and Waever 2009: 35). One could qualify such broad-brush statements, of course, but they hold more than a grain of truth.

Especially in IR, though, this state-centered approach has been shifting, and recent work shows political scientists developing more genuinely global methods. More than a generation ago one group of IR scholars started to pose questions similar to those asked in this book. To wit: whose "globe"? How far has an ostensibly general disciplinary perspective ("international relations") been shaped by unrecognized forms of institutional, cultural, and intellectual provincialism? How different would "international relations" be as an academic domain if IR had not been defined by professors at a small subset of Western/Northern (especially US) universities? In 2003 the International Studies Association convened IR scholars from around the world to explore the powerful role of "geocultural epistemologies" in shaping the field. This group of critics within IR has since shown the potential benefits of "worlding" a discipline – and the costs of not doing so.

In a classic article from 1984, republished a quarter-century later with new data, Thomas Bierstecker (2009) demonstrated that US-based IR scholars occupy a position of theoretical hegemony, yet are often not even aware of the parochialism of their interests – how their agenda (and thus, the priorities of the "field") is deeply shaped by American methodological predispositions and US government priorities. (See also Marlin-Bennett 2011.) As American journals, universities, and foundations set the agenda for disciplinary debate, theoretical disputes that matter in the US tend to be deemed of general interest. This has meant that rationalist, positivist, and quantitative approaches dominate the disciplinary core of IR. When Bierstecker canvassed the field's top 10 PhD programs (all at US universities), such approaches represented more than two-thirds (69 percent) of the programs' assigned readings. Most had been written by men (in proportions from 65 percent to 92 percent), and nearly all – with only rare exceptions, such as Thucydides – published in the last 15 years. Every single required reading at all 10 programs, moreover, had been assigned in English; only one top department (MIT) assigned as much as 3 percent of its readings to works that originated in other languages. Most striking, nearly all of this canonical scholarship had been written by US-based specialists (an overwhelming average of 94 percent). By this measure Harvard ranked as exemplarily cosmopolitan: its corpus of required readings was merely 89 percent US-authored. The most extreme case, the University of Michigan, assigned its PhD students fully 99 percent American-written materials. US scholars' ideas were widely known around the world, Bierstecker concluded, and were cited routinely by colleagues in Europe, Asia, and Africa, but the reverse was far from true.

It is easy to see the problems that result from an "intellectual condominium" so fully dominated by Anglophone and US scholars.[7] In Bierstecker's full-throated critique,

it is easy to be content as a US scholar of international relations. You do not have to "bother" with other languages. Everyone speaks your language (English), and appears to be using your principal frameworks and theoretical understandings. You can travel throughout the world making references to IR theory entirely produced by other American scholars, and most of your audience will be familiar with the basic texts, if not all of the latest arguments. The problem is, however, that "they" can speak in languages and discourses that "we" Americans cannot understand. They may also have important insights and adaptations of our arguments that we cannot comprehend or benefit from, either due to linguistic or epistemological barriers. English has become the global lingua franca, not only for global business, but for global academia. While everyone may be speaking the same language, however, the core concepts and ideas may not always have the same meaning in translation. Identical concepts may be interpreted or understood differently, and these differences can at times be profound. Thus, there is a danger that by reading only other American scholars, by assigning virtually no translations of works published in other parts of the world, and by operating largely within a single rationalist and positivist theoretical framework, American International Relations will be less able to perceive counter-hegemonic developments, trends, resistances, and tendencies in the world. (2009: 324)

Similar issues are evident in comparative politics, where they again produce ethno-centric assumptions and unstated provincialism, even in self-declared attempts to globalize the field. The point does not need to be belabored, but take one recent example from CP, the latest book by the prominent American scholar Francis Fukuyama. In *The Origins of Political Order* (2011) Fukuyama sets out explicitly to use a global, transhistorical approach to explain the core story of modern politics: the rise of human particularism and difference, conceived around the nation-state. Unlike IR scholars who look for politics happening *outside* the state, or on a global scale, Fukuyama keeps the national frame at the center of his story. His book moves historically, tracing the appearance of states and the rise of nations around the world. The long-term trajectory is plain: more and more of the world is moving inexorably toward "modern liberal democracy" – the type of state already on display in the United States, Canada, Australia, and others descended from a (West) European lineage. This model is widely copied, he argues, for the simple reason that it is the most powerful, and also most attractive, form of political organization the world has ever seen.

Fukuyama defines modern liberal democracy – the entity he sees as the destination of world politics – as a tripartite combination of state power (measured at the national level), rule of law, and governmental accountability. The effectiveness, and the appeal, of such a combination, he says, is attributable to fundamental human nature: people are both social and competitive beings, and this system best meets their needs. It evolved, though, only by fits and starts, in different places over thousands of years. China is the key starting point for Fukuyama's comparative history, as state power began there, driven largely by military necessity. Chinese state power, however, lacked legal constraints on the ruler, so in the end it created only "high-quality authoritarianism" (2011: 313). Law started in India, with its more "sophisticated" religious ideas, yet there lacked a strong state (a South Asian failure Fukuyama explains by way of social and religious differences such as caste, and a mysterious lack of protracted warfare). The Islamic Middle East then combined these two elements, although Fukuyama says its Arab parts subsequently lost their connection to law. (Given the vast corpus of Muslim legal scholarship, one wonders about this assertion.) Only in Western Europe did legal accountability begin, thanks to the continent's unique combination of geographic, economic, social, and cultural factors (2011: 22, 160).

Origins thus uses a "global" approach, with a world-spanning argument that covers several thousand years. Yet not all globes are created equal: Fukuyama ends by placing

US-style politics as an endpoint of world political history. (He is now writing a second volume, covering the industrial era and presumably explaining a similar spread of capitalist economies.) Leaving aside the Whiggish teleology, though, and not belaboring the reductionism that posits simple "essences" of each society (e.g., "China" is lastingly authoritarian), note instead how Fukuyama treats the nation-state – approaching it not as an intellectual obstacle or a hindrance to globally oriented scholarship, but as the perfect framework for worldwide comparative study. As such he serves as a counterweight to many other scholars mentioned here, who as a group try to reconceptualize a world *without* the primacy of national identities or necessarily seeing "countries" as the self-evident scale at which human social life should be studied.

Fukuyama concedes little to such objections, seeking rather to refocus attention on the nation-state. He acknowledges the importance of very few border-crossing actors (such as the Catholic Church or the Islamic caliphate). His tale of global politics unfolds almost entirely through self-contained, separate cases. As he unapologetically explains,

> Almost all of the stories told in this book involve single societies and the interplay among different domestic political actors within them. International influences appear largely as a result of war, conquest or the threat of conquest, and the occasional spreading of religious doctrines across borders. ... But looking at the globe as a whole, development tended to be highly compartmentalized by geography and region. (2011: 476)

Only in today's world, ironically, does Fukuyama see global borders as notably flexible or porous – as countries everywhere are now, at last, able to emulate the superior Euro-American model of liberal democracy.

Not all comparativists keep the nation-state so central, of course, nor do all IR specialists frame their work as investigating only state-to-state diplomatic or policy interactions. To see some of the other possibilities, consider a very different recent publication in political science. *Who Governs the Globe?*, co-edited in 2010 by Deborah Avant, Martha Finnemore, and Susan Sell, showcases scholarship on "governance" that uses a global lens to reconceive the core subject and methods of IR. Avant, Finnemore, and Sell openly criticize previous state-centered theories, which by staying focused on governmental structures at the national level and facilitating the billiard-ball-type view of state interactions make it too easy for IR analysts to treat a messy, complicated world as simple and predictable. Instead, they look at the globe in a more complex way. This involves seeing the world at once – as a whole – but also moving continually up and down in scales of analysis, crossing levels and weaving back and forth (2010: 368). Actual actors – dubbed "global governors," that is, "authorities who exercise power across borders for purposes of affecting policy" (2010: 2) – stay in view at every step. Such governors vary widely in form, size, location, and purpose; they include international organizations, multinational corporations, and advocacy groups, among others. They also interact – competing, collaborating, sharing workloads, and fighting over the outcomes of policy debates – at every level of scale.

This variation, and the idea of pursuing "governors" across spatial scales, is a key contribution to IR methodology, and it has obvious ties with world-historical scholarship.[8] Contributors to *Who Governs the Globe?* use this flexibility to study how global systems take shape (one essay considers air-traffic control rules; another looks at worldwide regulation of electrical standards for home appliances). They use a range of methods, from statistical analysis and probit regressions through abstract theories of club organization. But every author keeps *agency* in each story, thus addressing a key objection to any globally scaled study, including in world history. Concrete people and identifiable groups, not faceless "forces," make things happen: they set agendas, define issues, write rules, implement and enforce norms, make states act, and monitor and adjudicate outcomes.

In one exemplary essay, for instance, Clifford Bob (2010) traces the emergence of small-arms trafficking as an international issue. To do so he charts competition among two networks of states, nongovernmental organizations, and advocacy groups, each trying to mobilize authority for its cause. On one side, he finds the United Nations, the International Action Network for Small Arms, and many governments, mostly European and African. On the other, he discusses the World Forum on the Future of Sport Shooting Activities, advocacy groups like the National Rifle Association (NRA), and a group of other governments, especially the US. Perhaps not surprisingly, one finds conflict at every level, with competing efforts to find allies and secure binding legal outcomes. Rational deliberation, and efforts to persuade audiences of the merits of one's case, play at most a secondary role in the face of deep transnational and ideological divisions. Crucially, the ultimate outcome – as seen in the IR arena of international politics – only makes sense if one considers the interlocking roles of actors on all these levels. The globe is more than the sum of its parts – yet simultaneously, each part is also always shaped by that globe.

Global Anthropology: Ethnographies of the World

To a wider public, anthropologists are self-evidently "global" – journeying around the world to study the inner workings of obscure tribes and ostensibly alien peoples. Such efforts, frequently in remote places like Nepal or Papua New Guinea, chronicle the full tapestry of human behavior, in all its variability and complexity, showing few if any traits to be universal ("human nature"). Although some anthropologists actually work much closer to home (e.g., writing an ethnography of an American high school) they still take nothing for granted, placing subjects into a wider framework and working to relativize the apparently familiar. Cultural and linguistic anthropologists, the practitioners of the subfields upon which I concentrate, share with political scientists and economists a broader identity as social scientists. Yet relying on methods of "participant observation" – rather than databases or calculations at a distance – makes them more sensitive to their personal effects on the knowledge they produce. People act differently, first of all, when anthropologists are around; and anthropologists then make sense of what they see through categories that make sense to *them*. Cultural, social, and linguistic anthropologists address such issues by generating knowledge that is self-reflective, qualitative, particular, and contextual.[9] They have much in common with historians, occupying a middle position among the five "globes," roughly halfway between the hard social sciences and more humanistic and artistic approaches.

Global thinking in anthropology has its own deeper history (Handler 2009; Brettell 2009). In the nineteenth century, as "anthropology" took shape as a separate discipline, some of its most prominent figures maintained that human societies were developing along a common, evolutionary trajectory. They looked for global patterns of human development, and debated local cultural practices in terms of their origins: for example, had behaviors diffused outward from a single point, or had similar behaviors arisen independently in different places? This work involved a range of comparisons, holding the lifeways of one group up against another. Such approaches fell into disfavor after 1900, thanks especially to the work of Franz Boas, who argued strongly against evolutionary frameworks – contending that anthropologists should not see all human societies as marching in common patterns of development (which meant some would be "leading" and some "backward"), but instead should focus on the careful study of individual cultures, at much smaller levels of scale. Some anthropologists did still pursue the sorts of large-n statistical methods that became prominent in political science (as in the anthropological Human Relations Area Files, which started at Yale in the 1940s). Structural and functionalist approaches, especially in Britain, also undertook cross-cultural comparisons. Most anthropologists, however, thought too much detail was lost in making such comparisons across space; some went so far as to call the act of generalization itself "oppressive."[10] By the 1970s the field had moved away from large-scale analysis and increasingly toward the production of finely grained, rigorous "thick descriptions" (as Clifford Geertz put it) of particular cases.

Such a shift pushed cultural anthropologists toward more fragmented kinds of analysis, and away from explicitly global questions. Why, then, is the field relevant for world historians today? Partly because anthropological training remained global, in a simple but important sense pointed out by Daniel A. Segal: students learned about the field by reading about people, places, and issues from all over the world. (In a stark contrast with disciplinary history, where PhD students could qualify by reading hundreds of books and then writing a dissertation, all focused on just one small place, e.g. a part of Europe.) By mid-century, too, the cultural formations anthropologists studied started to lose some of their boundedness. Topics that spilled over regional or national borders, such as international migration or diasporas, emerged as legitimate areas for anthropological-ethnographic study. Eric Wolf went farther: in a now-classic book, *Europe and the People without History*, he set out to write nothing less than "global anthropology," using Marxian ideas of structure to focus on "interlocking networks of human interaction" that stretched around the world (1982: 24). James Clifford (1997) wrote about cultures themselves "traveling," becoming deterritorialized and hybrid. Arjun Appadurai's (1996) work on globalization (already discussed in Anne Gerritsen's chapter) focused on *new* cultures created in transnational spaces, where people are connected by cross-border flows (of people, machines, money, information, or ideas). Still other scholars, such as Michael Wesch (2009), have taken up these elements to explore new global domains through "digital ethnography," in which human interconnections of far-flung individuals can emerge from, be mediated by, and be formed through newly created electronic forms. Comparison also rebounded to some degree, albeit usually focused on small-n studies, more carefully contextualized and better able to withstand the variabilities of scale and time (Gingrich and Fox 2002; de Munck 2000).

Another strand of anthropological work, perhaps less well known to historians than Wolf or Appadurai and thus worth highlighting here, has particular relevance to connective approaches in world and global history. Growing out of a wider debate about "multi-sited ethnography," cultural and linguistic anthropologists have developed methods to produce geographically dispersed – and variably scaled – ethnographic analysis. George Marcus, with whom the term "multi-sited ethnography" is most closely associated, has described (1995) the benefits of going beyond classic single-sited ethnography. The traditional approach, he pointed out, encourages anthropologists to see fieldsites in hermetic terms, more or less self-contained bubbles; it risks ignoring interactions with a wider, even global world system. (See also Ferguson 2006.) In its place Marcus proposed tracking *mobility* – of things, people, ideas – *between* places. Putting "circulation" at the center of ethnographic study required scholars to think about simultaneously analyzing different places, and seeing their mutually shaping interactions – similar to the approaches of connective world history. (It also produced a firestorm of debate among anthropologists, some of whom saw the multi-sited idea as methodologically suspect, even dangerous, not unlike the critique of world historians for undercutting their discipline's ideas about rigorous archival scholarship.[11])

The work of Anna Tsing offers a fine example of such an approach put into practice, standing as an important contribution to both cultural and linguistic anthropology. Her monograph *Friction* (2005), subtitled *An Ethnography of Global Connection*, is the logical place to begin. Tsing, a veteran of fieldwork in southeastern Asia, starts the book in Indonesia, asking why local communities in a forest area, the Meratus mountains of South Kalimantan, suddenly saw their trees felled, and village social relationships upended, during the 1980s and 1990s. Her conclusion, like Marcus's, is that such outcomes cannot be understood through study in Kalimantan alone, or even only in Indonesia, but through a "connective ethnography" that ties together various geographic arenas – and different scales of human activity. Village inhabitants played a key role, yes, along with illegal loggers who suddenly appeared in the Meratus from other parts of Indonesia; but also state officials in Djakarta who struggled through political revolution in 1998, and had to rethink national-level development policies; multinational corporations in Canada that launched lumber and mining projects halfway around the world to impress shareholders; and transnational constituencies of environmental activists who brought political templates from Brazil and financial pressures to bear in the United States.

Tsing works at each of these levels, following stories (she calls them "packages") from place to place, employing methods that are, in turn, ethnographic, journalistic, and archival – and paying careful attention to how the stories change. She is particularly interested in ideas that purport to stretch beyond their points of origin, staking ostensibly universal claims (about "prosperity," for instance, or freedom, or environmental justice) and how these are translated into new forms at different social levels. Such packages, she says, are special: they are "scale-making projects" (2005: 57–58), and they tie together the globe. For Tsing, scale amounts to much more than a useful scholarly category. Scale itself – specifically, humans' claims about it – actually *produces* the globe. She argues that one can see the globe by studying this process of claims-making.

Another crucial idea (embedded in the book's title) is that all of this motion around the world does not simply "flow," in the facile terms of market theorists and no small number of historians. Rather, as stories, people, objects, and money move, they encounter different terrains. In some they thrive, and in others they falter; in any case, the packages shift, taking on new codings and resonances before traveling onward. This neverending process she calls "friction," in which *all* the world's cultures are brought into being only through their encounters with others. The "traction" that packages gain in various places shows, first, the ongoing interactions between all layers of scale. Yet these interactions also preserve cultural diversities of all kinds – leaving the differences always to "simmer within global connections" (2005: xiii). The worldwide human story is thus never reducible to one of homogeneity or sameness. The picture that emerges is admittedly fragmentary: but this fact, for Tsing, is precisely the point. Fragments may not be systematic, but neither are they random or happenstance, mere flotsam on a global sea. Their fragmentary character is instead productive, "interrupting" smooth master narratives of global power and development. Friction shows the concreteness of awkward human encounters – bumps in the road of actual, lived global interaction (2005: 271).

Tsing has also coedited a collection of essays (with a Japanese historian, Carol Gluck) that extends this method and pushes it in explicitly cross-disciplinary directions; it thus serves as a good transition to the next "globe" (of comparative literature). Tsing and Gluck's book *Words in Motion: Toward a Global Lexicon* (2009) tracks words – individual words – as they move through space and time, around the world. Words move between languages and political systems, across borders and within societies and institutions. Some of these words may be big ("democracy"), some appear smaller ("commission"), while others sit in the ideological margins ("adat" in Indonesia, "secularism" in Morocco). Tsing contends that by following individual words, and seeing what happens as they travel, scholars can productively deploy their expertise and deep knowledge about particular places and peoples (something traditionally trained historians would welcome), but that adopting the method of word-tracing enables them to do so without reifying any of the customary units or social frameworks (culture, nation, race, "area").

Words appear concrete, graspable, firm: the ability to document precise words in primary documents is, after all, what historians take as hard evidence. When someone uses a word, orally or on paper, it is easy to think that on some basic level readers (or listeners) know what they mean. Tsing and Gluck, however, argue that in practice, this certainty rapidly blurs. Words accumulate meanings and resonances. They work differently at different scales and in disparate social arenas. Their spatial motion maps a dizzying array of pathways around the world. Tsing contends that words (like "packages," but smaller) interlock scales, as they travel from national to global arenas and percolate down to street level. Yet every street is different: Tsing argues that the entanglement of words thus unfolds into an unpredictable multitude of global stories, not a common narrative (Tsing and Gluck 2009: 11–17). *Words in Motion*'s essays on Southeast Asia, Turkey, and Japan, for example, stress the mutability of words; but articles about Europe and the Arabic Middle East focus on stabilization and impositions of meaning. Words – a perhaps unexpected entrée into global study – show the communicative motion that is everywhere inherent in human life, but without imposing unitary views of a homogeneous globe.

Global Texts: Comparative Literature and Worlds of Translation

Specialists in literature wrestle with similar questions, but from a different disciplinary perspective. They share with historians basically similar source materials: words preserved in texts.[12] Yet they approach texts quite differently. Treating a document as "literature" means analyzing it in an artistic/expressive/aesthetic sense, not principally to understand the historical contexts of a particular place and time. Historical context is valuable in literary scholarship, but from a reverse perspective: insofar as it sheds better light on a literary story. Literary texts, moreover, are usually written to reach an *audience* (of readers and other writers), some of whom respond with their own texts. Literary scholarship relies on this dialogic, interactive character – literature is comprised of individual works, but also is a conversation that develops through time. Hence literary scholars focus on texts that are circulated to audiences, rather than private materials such as diaries or letters. (They use such materials too, but again, mostly to illumine literary issues.)

The field of comparative literature (CL), a subdomain within this wider universe of literary scholarship, approaches textual materials in a distinctively cross-cultural, cross-regional, and even global manner. In recent years its influence has percolated widely, stretching the work customarily structured along lines of nation, ethnicity, and region: in departments of English, Slavic, Romance, or Asian languages and literatures, for instance. CL should therefore be well positioned to offer fresh ways of thinking and asking (literary) questions about the globe. Specialists in CL – especially in the subfield of "world literature" – are aware of world historians' work, and draw on it while seeking also to broaden its content.

Most obviously this takes the form of arguing that world history as a field omits literature (and, more broadly, cultural life) at its peril. As Giles Gunn (2001) points out, Wallerstein's theory of the modern world-system is typical in stressing the centrality of economic-political exchange and interdependencies. In Gunn's view, however, such exchanges and interdependencies are cultural and aesthetic phenomena; for him, exchanges of *meaning* lie at the core of human history. Recognizing this fact would avoid what he sees as Wallerstein's radical simplification, foreshortening, even misreading of the human story. Culture is more than the surface mystification of "real," underlying systems or structures – it after all determines how such structures are understood, enacted, and ultimately undone.

> The exchange not only of commodities and people but also of ideas, customs, rituals, technologies, religions, and perhaps, above all, languages, this expanding zone of communication, interaction, and eventual interdependence – which permitted circuits of meaning … was largely dependent on human capacities to create and inhabit, as well as challenge and revise, symbolic universes of shared, or at any rate sharable, meaning. (2001: 20–21)

Few world historians would dispute the potential enrichment of adding new source materials – paying more attention to cultural and literary materials alongside the political, social, and economic questions that are at the heart of world-historical writing. Beyond the add-and-stir benefits of including literature, however, I want to focus on three further ideas arising from a literary approach.[13] First, what makes a particular work of writing approachable as "*world* literature," and thus, how does CL think about the analytic category of world/global study? Second, how does a literary approach deal with the issue of *translation*: the cross-cultural movement of words and texts around the globe, not merely spatial/geographic mobility but also the epistemological shifts that come in new linguistic locations? What happens when words are translated, and inhabit new semantic spaces? Beyond that, how does CL assay the broader process of what might be called macrotranslation, in which quanta of meaning much larger than individual words move? How are full texts, authors, even entire genres "translated" into new places? Third, how does a literary approach allow us to think about *time* – can it put places around the world, and peoples long dead, into new comparative and connective relations? What fresh interlinkages and chronologies appear that historians may have overlooked?

David Damrosch addresses the first question squarely in his book *What Is World Literature?* (2003), a helpful overview on which I lean here. Scholars have offered many answers since 1827, when Goethe coined the term "world literature" (*Weltliteratur*). Goethe had in mind a small network of authors like himself – high-level, elite, mostly male – who read and reacted to each other's work. This network stretched beyond any one language or place, although not everywhere: Goethe admitted the near-total absence of writers from, say, China or India. De Stael later developed a more nationalized model of literary study, one that had a lasting institutional impact. (Even writings that appeared before the existence of modern nations are now read, taught, and studied as part of "national heritages.") In the twentieth century literary critics such as Northrop Frye (1957) took a different tack, looking around the globe to identify literary patterns or motifs that existed across cultures ("archetypes"), not unlike pre-Boasian approaches in anthropology or large-n efforts in political science. The consensus in CL today, however, is that such approaches lead mostly to empty generalities, not helpful insights into literary practices around the world.

Damrosch defines "world literature" neither as reducible to a collection of discrete national traditions, nor as a vast amalgam, an infinitude of everything that has ever been written – a "global babble" (as Janet Abu-Lughod memorably put it). Instead, he defines it as "a mode of circulation and of reading," one that can be applied as readily to classics as to new publications, whole collections of texts as individual items. The key criteria are that texts must first be deemed *literature* (that is, not just any form of mass culture will do – a distinction ultimately based on standards and aesthetic judgments) and then that they *circulate* (that is, move outward into the world). Specifically, literary writing becomes "world literature" when it moves "beyond its linguistic and cultural point of origin" (2003: 5–6). The ambit of specialists in world literature is to study what happens when literature *moves* – what happens to Goethe's work, for instance, when it is translated into English and read on the American prairie, or into Portuguese and read in Rio de Janeiro.

"World literature" is therefore oriented toward the crossing of borders, and the reading and rereading of texts in different global settings – giving rise to a vision of the world in multiplicity, not one captured by a master narrative, or reducible to known patterns. For Damrosch and like-minded scholars, there is no single "world literature" with a fixed, identifiable canon.[14] Literary scholars need instead to move within the multiplicities, to be both multicultural and multitemporal. The temporal – historical – logic is crucial, as literature circulates for hundreds and even thousands of years. World literature therefore makes a strong argument for time depth as well as cultural breadth (Damrosch himself covers 4,000 years). As in world history, this does not mean world literature needs to cover absolutely everything. Choices have to be made, and I spell out some principal themes below. The starting point, though, as Vilashini Cooppan puts it, is to see world literature as a special kind of writing: one that is both "locally inflected and translocally mobile" (2001: 33).

As texts move away from their point of origin and cross into new cultures, they are read, reread, learned and argued about. This process happens in widely separated places, where the text's original author, and his or her intentions, may be completely unknown. For Damrosch, this simple fact presents an argument against the sweeping objections of specialists – who long criticized world literature as shallow, shown (they asserted) by its propensity to get the details (as known to these specialists) wrong. Such critiques kept world literature marginal in the discipline of CL, relegated mostly to a pedagogical realm: perhaps appropriate for undergraduate survey classes, but hardly an area for serious scholarship.[15] Yet a deep knowledge of Chinese culture, to take one example, would become less crucial when a Chinese poem moves overseas. Yes, knowing China's literary history, with expertise in Chinese language and motifs, allows one to see how a text in its new locale diverges from its originary practices. One should learn texts' original language if possible, and if this is not an option, get the details right by careful and diligent reading of specialized scholarship. National-cultural marks and forms persist when writings travel – Damrosch, Cooppan, and Gunn agree that national literatures are not on the verge of fading away. But world literature, fundamentally, calls for striking a balance: recognizing that specialists' deep knowledge of particular places is essential, but it is not everything. It may not be much help in making sense of how a text is accepted into, and reworked by, foreign cultures, in ways shaped by their own traditions, forms, customs, and motifs.

World literature aims at a different purpose – one just as legitimate, and that complements rather than supplants national literary scholarship. Very few works are created entirely outside national traditions (*The Thousand and One Nights*, created by many different authors, may be one). Most begin within such a tradition, but are then "refracted" as they move. In the case of the hypothetical traveling poem from China, this refraction is world literature's focus: it does not end matters merely to point out that a text would no longer count as a poem "back home." As Damrosch points out:

> Not only is this something that those of us who don't read Chinese cannot judge; it is actually irrelevant to the poem's existence abroad. *All* works cease to be the exclusive products of their original culture once they are translated; all become works that only "began" in their original language. The crucial issue for the foreign reader is how well the poems work in the new language ... works of world literature take on a new life as they move into the world at large, and to understand this new life we need to look closely at the ways the work becomes reframed in its translations and in its new cultural contexts. (2003: 21, 24)

World literature treats such texts as "the locus of negotiation between two different cultures," potentially subject to a "double refraction," continually moving between them. Damrosch sees it as an ellipse, "with the source and host cultures providing the two foci that generate the elliptical space within which a work lives as world literature, connected to both cultures, circumscribed by neither alone" (2003: 283).[16]

Saying that literature is "refracted" as it moves is another way of saying that texts need to be translated. *Translation*, in all senses (linguistic, cultural, allegorical), thus also underpins the study of world literature – and translation studies is a well-developed theoretical and methodological arena in its own right, full of possibilities for world historians (Venuti 2004).[17] World literature treats the process of translation as "a negotiation between 'source' and 'target' cultures," illuminating literary values on each side and the triangulations that have to happen for meanings to move between them. Sometimes scholars examine successive translations of a single work (Damrosch traces an Egyptian poem's forms through different translations, and follows wildly divergent readings of Mechtild, a thirteenth-century mystic). Sometimes they focus on a single translator working out how to bring a text to life (Nabokov, for instance, translating Lewis Carroll into Russian). Some contemporary works are said to be "born translated," in Rebecca Walkowitz's phrase: authors such as J.M. Coetzee, Kazuo Ishiguro, or Jamaica Kincaid publish books simultaneously in many languages, being "designed to travel" (Walkowitz 2009: 570–571).

A translation can range from the very literal (retaining as many details as possible from the source culture, with explanatory footnotes, even at the risk of "foreignizing" a text) to the very flexible (attempting to assimilate the text entirely to its new surroundings, finding not just equivalent words but also corresponding accents, images, and references in the target culture).[18] The choices translators make vary along this spectrum, and therein lies the tale. Dryden, for example, sought to translate Virgil into English "as he himself would have spoken" – yet English did not exist in Virgil's time, 2,000 years ago (Damrosch 2003: 167–168). What to do? The decisions he made tell world literary scholars something important about Dryden – and perhaps about Virgil too.

   This type of translation studies looks at the movement of words, sentences, thoughts, from one language into another. A different sort of translation happens when texts are read around the world, but in shared languages not identified with the local culture. Think of publications in Arabic, Spanish, or French: they spread without the need for formal cross-linguistic translation. As geographically dispersed tongues, each is spoken – admittedly with regional/dialectal differences – by different regional, ethnic, racial, and national groups. English is the most extreme case. As the world's first truly global language, today it is spoken to some degree in more than 100 countries, and has spread its influence through forms such as the novel.[19] Some scholars of comparative literature decry this pervasiveness as a straightforward sign of power in global culture – the cultural corollary to, and outgrowth of, European colonialism and corporate-industrial capitalism. This view emphasizes the coercive aspects of widespread English, and applauds the propagation of texts in other languages (Owen 1990). Such critics point out that actually existing "world literature" today is less grandly inclusive than its pretensions, given authors' need to translate texts into English to reach a global audience. Because the circulation of texts varies greatly by language of origin, too, writers are helped hugely by their proximity to economic, political, and institutional centers.[20]

   Yet this critique, valuable as it is, only goes so far – since power never works only in one direction. Exploring concrete translations, at all levels of scale, allows scholars to see the unexpected complications – the bumpy literary encounters that recall Tsing's "friction." Chinua Achebe, to take one prominent example, writes as an African, and in English, to reach a worldwide audience. In doing so, however, he intends nothing less than to remake English itself. As he puts it:

> The price a world language must be prepared to pay is submission to many different kinds of use. The African writer should aim to use English in a way that brings out his message best without altering the language to the extent that its value as a medium of international exchange will be lost. He should aim at fashioning out an English which is at once universal and able to carry his particular experience. ... I feel that English will be able to carry the weight of my African experience. But it will have to be a new English, still in full communion with its ancestral home but altered to suit its new African surroundings. (1975, quoted by Damrosch 2003: 225–226)

   Alexander Huang deals with a different level of metatranslation – beyond the level of words or individual texts, to an authorial corpus and beyond – to show the complexities of global literary movement. Taking Shakespeare, the English literary icon par excellence, as an example of "culture that moves," he studies Shakespearean drama as it crosses borders, specifically into China. He finds nothing like a straightforward tale of English prestige or power crushing Chinese forms and voices. Instead, his book *Chinese Shakespeares: Two Centuries of Cultural Exchange* shows an ongoing process of adaptation – "the mutually constitutive grammar of the global and the local" (2009: 5–6) – in which Shakespeare is brought into China, translated, but completely reworked. The Shakespearean corpus was integrated into preexisting Chinese dramatic forms, such as *xiqu* (stylized regional theaters, sometimes called "Chinese opera") and *huaju* (spoken dramatic theater). It surely influenced their development. But the plays, too, changed, departing from their modes of presentation in the Anglophone West. They took on new lives in Asia: Huang cites a political debate in November 2006 in Taiwan (a place never subjected to English colonial rule) in which the premier, Su Tseng-chang, quoted *Julius*

Caesar to demonstrate support for the president, Chen Shui-bian. Other (remarkably literate) politicians then cited different passages from the same play to express their agreement or disagreement about Taiwan's future policy direction.

As Shakespeare's plays were staged in China, they became emblematic of groups within the Chinese artistic scene, who then reexported them to the world. Chinese Shakespeare plays thus serve as exemplars of Chinese – but also global – culture, and they ultimately influenced Shakespearean theater outside China too. Huang sees it as a collaborative process, in which Shakespeare and China serve as interacting "syntactical categories" that generate new meanings. Such collaborations happen in concrete, specific places – "global localities" – where Shakespeare's plays now reside in an interstitial space, between the texts' point of origin and the cultural terrains they came to inhabit (2009: 21–23).

This in-betweenness produces complicated outcomes. Huang cites the 1997 staging of a multilingual *King Lear* – with English subtitles, but in which the characters spoke different (Asian) languages. "The power-thirsty eldest daughter (performed cross-dressed) spoke only Mandarin and employed *jingju* chanting and movements," whereas Lear "spoke only Japanese and walked the stage in the solemn style of [Japanese] *no* performance." The performance was hugely controversial in Asia – for reasons that would have entirely escaped Western-trained Shakespearean experts. "Seen afar from the European perspective, the contrasts between the Asian languages and styles were flattened by their similarities. However, seen from an Asian perspective, the difference between Asian cultures was accentuated by the performance" (2009: 3–4). Asian audiences read the performance as politically inflected, and powerful: as making a sharp comment on Chinese-Japanese differences, today and in the recent past (the World War II era).

Genre – whether the multi-act stage plays of Shakespeare, the novel, or haiku – serves as an even grander structuring element of literature, accompanying texts as they move through space and time. Global genres connect readers in wildly different places, beyond a specific text or even the best-known authors: once one knows its form, a novel (or a sonnet, or a play) can reach audiences separated by hundreds of years or thousands of miles, and in dozens of languages. Or so it appears to readers who think they know how to decipher these forms (Walker 1994). What does it mean to think about translating genres, the largest scale of literary metatranslation? How can scholars trace changes in, and influences on, the edges and forms of genres? These genre-based questions ultimately suggest the most radical ideas from comparative literature, at least from a historian's perspective: that scholars can forget their conventional norms of historical *time*.

The literary critic Fredric Jameson is closely associated with this line of thought. Jameson's writings are too complex to distill here, but, long influenced by Marxian ideas, he has argued (against postmodern and structuralist critiques) that texts cannot be fully divorced from their social and cultural contexts – an idea that would be welcome to most historians. His idea of "postmodern hyperspaces" suggest a means by which to make sense of cross-border flows, and he has analyzed the "disjointedness of time" in modern global life (see Jameson and Miyoshi 1998). He is interested in genre, too, and specifically its link to temporality (as well as culture). Genres, as Ian Baucom has summarized this aspect of Jameson's thought, "travel through time. Synchronically present in a given moment, genres also link that moment, diachronically, to earlier moments, earlier times. At the level of form … genre is the presence of the past in the present" (2001: 163). Baucom goes on to call dominant genres, such as the novel, "an epistemological structure" that spreads throughout the globe. It seems to subordinate future texts to itself, by forcing them to conform – yet simultaneously it is "haunted by a ghost language" (the ideology of past generations) as an imprint, or aftereffect, of that same form.

By dropping linear notions of chronology and tracking literary forms around the world, world literature can propose startling new juxtapositions. Cooppan uses genre to teach her students to read across national borders – intentionally setting up juxtapositions ("polychronic encounters between texts" (2001: 31)) to illuminate the globe in motion, through these migrations of form. She calls her method "globalized reading," and uses it to query the idea of a "canon" or "center" in world literature, showing instead an ongoing array of multiple influences. Students read the *Pancatantra*, a Sanskrit collection of stories about the natural world, alongside medieval European fables and the *Thousand and One Nights*; the *Odyssey* appears alongside Ralph Ellison's *Invisible Man*. Damrosch likewise suggests triadic juxtapositions to bring new comparisons and connections to light. Why, he asks, put together distant texts – such as *Antigone*, *Shakuntala*, and *Twelfth Night*? Because studying them together does something that intense investigation of them alone could never manage:

> The effect of these combinations is very different from what we gain from a semester devoted to medieval Japan or to seventeenth-century France, and it is even different from the net effect of a semester on Japan followed by a semester on France. Immersion in a single culture represents a mode of relatively direct engagement with it, aptly symbolized by efforts to acquire "near-native fluency" in the culture's language. Reading and studying world literature, by contrast, is inherently a more detached mode of engagement; it enters into a different kind of dialogue with the work, not one involving identification or mastery but the discipline of distance and of difference. We encounter the work not at the heart of its source culture but in the field of force generated among works that may come from very different cultures and eras. (2003: 299)

Literature transports readers to new worlds – to mental times and places far remote from their own. To some scholars this mind-altering aspect of literature justifies, even necessitates, combining authors who might never have been linked in the "real" world. Baucom (2001: 170), drawing on Althusser, suggests that literature is well positioned to rethink basic notions of temporality (here historians may grow queasy). We are misled in thinking of history as a series of "synchronic slices of time," he says; such a view assumes that dispersed events and people all coexist according to a common clock and calendar, and are thus meaningfully contemporaneous "in the one and same present." But what if there *is* no singular global moment, either now or in the past or future – what if there is no "homogenizing, leveling, everywhere available time of modernity"? Time could be better seen as complexly constituted, through overlapping and intersecting arrays of many different local chronologic regimes, each with its "peculiar rhythms." These are, surely, not always separate; but it is only if and when they do confront and perturb one another that we see a "globe," or at least part of one. Scholars should thus seek these sites of mixing, where life is simultaneously of different "centuries," with mixed tongues and genres ("heteroglossic, heterochronic language[s]"), from novels to consumer capitalism to Marxist deconstruction. Baucom thinks that in such locales we start to see the globe.

Wai Chee Dimock goes yet farther in juxtaposing texts across time. In an article called "Literature for the planet" (2001), she uses the fact that the poet Osip Mandelstam always carried with him a copy of Dante's *Divine Comedy* as more than an interesting tidbit. She argues it shows literature is a continuum stretching across time and space, and that authors – like these from the fourteenth and twentieth centuries, living in completely different cultures – can be "inseparable." "Literary space and time," she writes, "are conditional and elastic; their distances can vary, can lengthen or contract, depending on who is reading and what is being read. ... Two thousand years and two thousand miles can sometimes register as near simultaneity; ten years and ten miles can sometimes pose an unpassable gulf" (2001: 174). She agrees with Baucom that there is no single universal present, no temporal plane that synchronizes the globe. A book may be being read "right now" by thousands of readers, but the readings do not line up neatly; and the words, as they are encountered by many eyes, elicit thousands of separate resonances, antecedents, and meanings.

Dimock concentrates on this "temporal disunity among readers," which underpins her view of Dante and Mandelstam – in which the *Divine Comedy* effectively resides throughout time. It exists, she says, not just in many places but also in different *centuries*, present anywhere (and anywhen) its meanings gain traction with readers. Dimock then comes back to the geographic dimension (the reach of global readership) to argue that literature has an unparalleled, sweeping worldwide power. Unlike Benedict Anderson, who famously held that literature (and print culture generally) stitched together vernacular spaces and turned them into nations, Dimock maintains the reverse: that literature deeply unsettles the nation-state. Books can be burned, but literature is tough: it outlasts political units, and gives readers horizons that "play havoc with territorial sovereignty." Dimock ultimately portrays literature as "an artificial form of 'life' – not biological like an organism or territorial like a nation but vital all the same," and "a species tougher than most" (2001: 175). Literature, stretching thousands of years and all around the globe, is, in this telling, glue for the deepest human story.

Global Art: Aesthetics across Cultures

Finally, humans see. That biological fact – the normative sightedness of the human body – suggests that "the visual" is a realm with transhistorical, transcultural resonance. The details vary, of course, but eyes are crucial for navigating the tasks of everyday human life. Not surprisingly, the metaphors of sight permeate human languages. Blindness is a tragedy, a divine punishment, or a "disability"; when violently inflicted, it ranks among the most egregious attacks that one person can visit upon another. When people encounter others with whom they cannot speak – with whom they share no written or oral language – they may start by using visual signs and gestures to communicate. Think of colonial sources describing initial interactions with "savages" – or the way humans (at least those at NASA) represented our species to extraterrestrial beings, in drawings of human bodies and scientific symbols (as shown in Figure 33.1) that were bolted onto the Pioneer 10 and 11 spacecraft in 1972–1973 and rocketed out of the solar system.

This essay, too, relies throughout on metaphors of lenses and the visual; so I end with the disciplines of seeing, to consider how the idea of "optics" is itself culturally bound. Art history, my focus here, arose as an academic discipline to study, interpret, and analyze the products of visual artists – those producing physical objects with aesthetic aims.[21] Given the global universality of sight and the visual, and of human creativity, one might expect art historians to be far ahead in thinking through questions of world-scaled study. In the academy, though, art history has in fact only just started to explore the globe. In

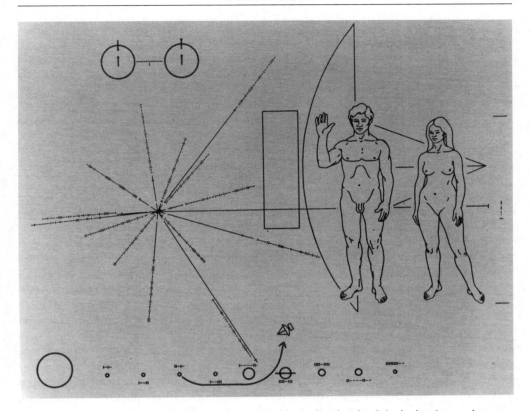

Figure 33.1 Our world's visual greeting. This gold-anodized, 6-by-9-inch aluminum plaque, co-designed by Carl Sagan, uses graphics to tell possible alien viewers who we, humans, are. The symbols aim to show what we look like, how large we are, where we come from (in space), what we know (via chemical and mathematical notation), and when the spacecraft carrying the plaque was launched. Note the culturally bound aspects of an ostensibly universal image (e.g. using a raised hand as a gesture to connote goodwill).
Source: National Aeronautics and Space Administration (NASA), at http://nssdc.gsfc.nasa.gov/image/spacecraft/pioneer_plaque.jpg.

the words of James Elkins, who in 2006 named "going global" one of the field's most pressing issues, world art studies remains a field in formation, at best "entrancingly disorganized." Strikingly, in 2007 he found not a single scholar able or willing to write an overarching historical introduction to his book *Is Art History Global?*[22]

Disciplinary art history long told the story of human art through a heavily Eurocentric core narrative, one reminiscent of "Western Civ"-style tellings of human history. Most art history textbooks began with cave art, moved rapidly to Egypt and ancient Greece, and then skipped onward to medieval Europe. They lingered on early Gothic cathedrals and then slowed dramatically to trace the ebbs and flows of style, and the aesthetic conversations that ensued, among mostly European artists. "World art history," when the term was even used, meant an agglomeration of national or regional stories, a few of which lay outside this European core. Although still overwhelmingly focused on Europe, the field widened after 1950 – such that by 2000 one could find many excellent studies of Chinese, or African, or Islamic art. Yet each tended to be studied as a world unto itself, with "histories" unfolding in developmental trajectories driven by internal aesthetic concerns and the innovations of individual artists. Most scholarship, even when it concerned the non-European world, still used Western themes and started with existing definitions of art and aesthetics – core notions hardly troubled by occasional encounters with art from elsewhere. No one even attempted a "full account of the interrelationships of visual cultures," seeing such efforts as doomed both practically and epistemologically. By the 1990s art historians, as David Carrier puts it (2008: xxiii–xxv), had skipped straight from the old Eurocentrism to a new skepticism of large-scale metanarratives – and were not interested in synthesizing, connecting, or asking how the various parts might function together as part of wider artistic stories.

Recently this situation has changed, with promising global art-historical developments in both practice and theory. A small group of scholars is creating a new kind of "world art history," drawing upon and extending global scholarship in other disciplines (Ziljmans and Van Damme 2008). One shared interest is the cross-cultural movement of art – how it is made, bought, sold, and displayed across national boundaries. The global art market today, and the sudden appearance of "global museums," suggest that the contemporary art scene includes cross-border elements (Elkins *et al.* 2010).[23] Sometimes this involves the purchase, repatriation, or traveling display of artworks as exemplars of national traditions (Chinese vases or terracotta soldiers, for instance). But beyond traveling exhibits or efforts to reclaim national patrimonies, contemporary art also now features artists who set out directly to confront issues of globalization. Some draw explicitly on influences that are "foreign" (that is, from places other than their own), while others use motifs and forms that are self-consciously deterritorialized and transnational. In either case, art historians see such moves as building a new kind of contemporary art: one that develops across, not within, borders, and that requires new modes of production, sponsorship, collecting, marketing, display, and analysis (Belting and Buddensieg 2009).

A few scholars are also reflecting critically on how art history as a field has long been shaped, intellectually and institutionally, by ethnoculturally framed points of departure. The discipline still exists mostly in the United States and Europe, with only a comparative handful of institutions elsewhere. This produces real difficulties in generating scholarship that vigorously engages issues of art and the aesthetic from non-European, non-American points of view. Elkins notes that scholarship in English is not often translated into other languages. Given the power of Euro-American scholars to define field-wide issues (as in IR), this Anglophone dominion effectively creates its own "lag," putting speakers of Chinese, Hindi, Arabic and other languages into a position of "belatedness" without access to publications. Textbooks around the world, moreover, are still deeply nationalistic, structured to serve curricula that rarely reach outside the nation-state (students in Istanbul study Turkish and Ottoman Art, students in Mumbai, Indian Art, etc.). Most problematically, even in non-Western contexts, art history still usually "depends on Western conceptual schemata." In China, for example, scholars "study Chinese art using the same repertoire of theoretical texts and sources – psychoanalysis, semiotics, iconography, structuralism, anthropology, identity theory. They frame and support their arguments in the same ways Western art historians do: with abstracts, archival evidence, summaries of previous scholarship, and footnoted arguments" (Elkins 2007: 19).

The first institutional signs of change are small and very recent. In 2005 programs in world art history started at Leiden and East Anglia. In 2009 Heidelberg hired a chair in "global art history," intending to break beyond the hermetic, regionally framed analytic approaches that characterize the field. It launched a "cluster initiative" that replaced fixed regions with the idea of "mobile contact zones with shifting frontiers," and concentrated research on migratory artists and public aesthetic spheres that could be linked to local and canonical as much as national discourses. The overall aim was to high-light artistic "entanglements" that lay beyond any individual nation, hoping instead to see "art and visual practices as polycentric and multivocal processes."[24]

Alongside the institutional shifts, scholarship in world and global art history is starting to crystallize. The Sterling and Francine Clark Art Institute, long known for its collection of Euro-American (especially French Impressionist) masterworks, held a major conference in late 2011 on the theme: In the Wake of the Global Turn: Propositions for an Exploded Art History without Borders. Some speakers came from India and Brazil, serving as proxies for the "world"; most presenters still came from European and American univer-sities. But all gathered to discuss a basic issue: Could art be redefined as a sphere of global interactivity? Could disciplinary art history be restructured along lines of regional inter-actions or interregional collaborations, rather than as separate nation-state stories, or a center–periphery model? What would it do to the field to design a "radically decentered" world art history (as opposed to one recentered on a new place, e.g. Africa)?

Such gatherings clearly draw inspiration from other disciplines, not least from world historians who have already pursued border-crossing connectivity, modes of interaction, and analytic units that reach outside the nation-state. In art history, though, a few scholars are starting to use this global reorientation more fundamentally: to rethink the entire field, in a basic theoretical way. What does it means to rethink the field's core ideas – art and the aesthetic – in ways that do *not* presuppose European-derived categories? Such a question would be tantamount to world historians asking (as they are only starting to do): How does the global view make one rethink the entire historical enterprise? Does the world-historical perspective force scholars to redefine "sources," reconceive chronology, or redesign History's basic methods? What are historians looking for in the archives, where else might they look – and how will they know what it means?

For theoretical art historians, stepping back to reconsider first principles means asking whether the visual itself, at least the visual sphere of "art," is universal (global, human), or whether it too is inescapably culturally bound. Is it possible to talk about a global aesthetic? One group of art historians has addressed these questions by moving across disciplinary lines toward the natural sciences. Engaging biological questions of eyes and seeing, they argue that art scholars can draw productively on brain science to understand how people – all people – process and make sense of visual information. Proponents of this approach – such as John Onians (2008), who coined the term "Neuroarthistory" – contend that neuroscience could make art history global and non-ethnocentric by beginning with the underlying biology of how artists, and nonartists, perceive and process their surroundings.

For those inclined to more humanistic approaches, James Elkins has suggested that some ideas like space or time may be sufficiently universal to "travel," relate to all cul-tures, and thus to reach beyond Western theories or narratives. David Summers has offered the most serious effort to date to theorize such an approach. In a massive book, *Real Spaces* (2003), he ambitiously aims to provide a theoretical basis for studying all human art, in all times, around the world. Summers does not focus on interregional interaction, nor does he compare different cultures' art or look for grand patterns. He does draw on biology, but only briefly, and in a less technical or scientific mode than Onians (he stays away from neuroimaging studies). Summers starts with the notion that all human bodies share a basic spatiotemporal character – they are always located finitely in space and time. From that kernel he spins out a complicated theory of global art. His approach encompasses and, he asserts, supersedes previous theories of "the visual" and aesthetics, all of which are ultimately based on foundational notions of *space*.

Summers draws a key distinction between "real" spaces (physical places in the actually-existing world) and "virtual" spaces (representations of those physical spaces, created through human actions, as for example in drawings, which depict – but cannot capture – real space). He then traces all human creations through a cross-cultural approach he calls "metaoptical" space, which stretches general ideas of "aesthetics" around the globe and into deep time. For Summers, "art" can be expansively defined – potentially including anything made by a human being, anywhere, ever. The ultimate goal of *Real Spaces* is to situate all cultures alongside one another, in a common framework for discussion, not to privilege the terms of any one aesthetic realm as setting the terms for all others. Once an equal playing field is achieved, Summers holds, art history can explore the art that is actually produced around the world – both in specific places and in the interactive and comparative senses already discussed.

Summers's book is widely admired as impressive and pioneering, but his universalizing argument has not been universally accepted. James Elkins, perhaps the most prominent advocate of "world art history" today (hence not an obvious foe), published a 30-page review of *Real Spaces*. It praised Summers's care and insight, but also used Aztec, Indian, Swedish and other specific cases to question the transhistorical, transcultural applicability of Summers's ideas about space.[25] Elkins wrote that in the end *Real Spaces* remains bound to Western categories – that it ultimately expands and reworks classical (European) ideas of space to better accommodate artwork from other parts of the world.

Elkins has sketched other approaches that hold still more radical potential for global scholarship in art history. Some, such as Nancy Munn's (1996) investigation of Australian Aboriginal ideas about landscape and place, or Wu Hung's (1995) study of Chinese systems for classifying artifacts, may not appear "global," but begin by seeking terms, categories, and ideas that emerge outside Western semantic or philosophical contexts. Most daunting of all are approaches that explicitly exclude any and all Western concepts. Scholars such as Cao Yiqiang (1997; 2008) want to begin with entirely different starting points – questioning the very Westernness of art history as an enterprise. This means abandoning shared disciplinary protocols such as citation practices; engaging new narrative structures such as those in ancient Indian or Chinese texts; and looking for new, non-Europeanate ways to conceive and depict the globe and modernity itself. (See also Henry 1994.) This approach, which echoes the objections of Vinay Lal (1999; 2003) (see chapter by Weinstein, above) and other radical critics of disciplinary world history, stands as the most eye-opening of all – holding the potential for a genuinely thoroughgoing and multicultural remaking of not just art history, but academia writ large. It also poses the starkest challenge to disciplinary coherence, by frontally questioning the very *existence* of "art history," or for that matter "history," as common enterprises that can be shared by scholars around the world.

Many Globes: Seeing a World

Many academic fields are engaging the globe – thinking about how to study a human world in all its global dimensions. Even the nonhistorical disciplines are reaching broadly, not just into contemporary manifestations of global encounter, but also deep into time. Some of these efforts will be useful to historians, others may not. Some authors in other fields are following paths that have already been traveled, and found wanting, by earlier generations of world historians. But others have found new approaches. This disciplinary excursion shows the potential for looking outside History's own "globe" as historians seek new ways to compare, to connect, and to understand the human past. Other globes are also stretching space and time, drawing on theoretical arenas that range from the familiar (economics and culture) to the alien (neuroscience or aesthetics).

These efforts face some common obstacles, starting with the practical. First, given the wealth and institutional/intellectual hegemony of American and European universities, how can ideas about the world come from more parts of the world? Calls to involve many places are often heard but difficult to realize, given barriers of language, method, and resources. It is not clear, moreover, that scholars everywhere will see "the global" in the same pressingly urgent terms as Western theorists – indeed, critics of world history portray the recent rush into global thinking as another case of Western intellectual imperialism. Second, given that scholars are still trained in national and "area-studies" frameworks, how can any one person know enough about many places to speak globally? Exhortations to encourage multi-authored, collaborative scholarship are likewise easy to find in many different disciplines. As in disciplinary history, however, such calls have not gained much traction, thanks largely to the interlocking constraints of the actually-existing institutional world. (These include, prominently, tenure and promotion practices at Euro-American universities, and the power of disciplinary gatekeepers, which keep a firm emphasis on single-authored, monographic scholarship.) Even when such efforts take root – as in the International Studies Association's seeding of work on IR's "geo-cultural epistemologies," or the International Comparative Literature Association's three-decades-long support of a multi-authored collection on the world's literature (Valdés and Hutcheon 1994) – they remain on the intellectual edges of disciplines, not overturning their terms.

Nevertheless these global approaches share a key proclivity both to challenge the existing institutional structures of academic work, and to introduce new intellectual categories of analysis – not to destroy their associated disciplines, but to enrich them. Globally scaled scholarship, in each of these "globes," aims to generate new knowledge, for a particular set of purposes. The proponents of each "globe" see the benefits of taking a bird's-eye view, contending that certain issues can only be seen at this level. Such a view is easy to maintain in an era of global climate change, capital mobility, and the World-Wide Web. Few if any, however, maintain that world-scaled perspectives should be *exclusively* used. For the most part these global writings also draw – diligently and rigorously – on the best scholarship at other levels too. Many scholars discussed here work simultaneously at *multiple* scales – not merely from a bird's-eye view. They struggle to keep individuals, and their families, neighbors, and friends, in focus alongside grand forces and abstract structures. How can "local," "global," and intervening middle levels coexist, their interlocking influences be teased out, while reifying none as fixed or all-explanatory? The global scholarship sketched here suggests various answers, but collectively it introduces this wider scale as a key perspective among many – not to replace other views, such as that of national history, but to enrich and broaden their reach.

Obviously other disciplines are already pursuing their own crossings; the lines drawn here between five distinct "globes" are too stark. Tsing and Gluck's *Words in Motion* is a good example, bringing together anthropologists, historians, and literary specialists to explore questions of translation, movement, and culture. Elkins's seminars on world art history – to which speakers such as Fredric Jameson have been invited, intentionally infusing internal conversations with extradisciplinary perspectives – are another. From the perspective of world history, this essay's brief journey through different visions of the globe aims to do something similar: to open pathways for fresh historical thinking. What would it mean to codesign classes with colleagues in literature? How would books on world history change if conceived around aesthetic categories of style? How can we, all of us, think more productively across lines of discipline as well as space and time?

Notes

1   Attempts by natural scientists to move in the other direction, addressing the concerns of disciplinary history, are less common: see Aunger (2007a; 2007b); or Gordon's tongue-in-cheek "Colonial studies" (2010).

2   Each domain deserves its own essay. Consider the uses of "infographics" and global statistics to improve international development policy: www.gapminder.org/world (accessed Mar. 2012); or "world music" and musicological studies of the interactions between local and global motifs, performers, markets, and listeners (Tenzer 2006).

3   This may be partly the result of internal disciplinary conversations framed by discourses of "globalization" (see chapter above by Bright and Geyer), often in unapologetically presentist terms – a starting point toward which historians display a professionally visceral allergy. I exclude the disciplines of geography and sociology, which are already more "baked in" to world history. In this volume, for example, Simmons, McKeown, and Kramer draw heavily on geography, while Chase-Hall and Dunn offer a kind of sociological analysis, directly on display. Gerritsen's chapter is one of several that rely on sociological theory – in her case, Roland Robertson's idea of "glocalization" to depict interlocking scales (see Robertson 1990), and Mark Herkenrath's related notions of divergence, convergence, and hybrid forms. Historical sociologists – from Janet Abu-Lughod (1991) to Charles Tilly (2006) and Immanuel Wallerstein (2004) – occupy more or less canonical status in world history, as do historical geographers such as Kären Wigen and Martin Lewis (1997).

4   A recent exception, attempting to merge economics with evolutionary psychology, is Frank (2011). More typically, Acemoglu and Robinson (2006; 2012), while positing a 500-year-plus time depth for their analysis, aim mostly to explain modern forms of state power (democracy, dictatorship) and contemporary economic issues (poverty, prosperity).

5   Specialists in other areas, such as Michael Shapiro in political theory, are also doing globally oriented work (see Der Derian and Shapiro 1989; Shapiro and Alker 1995). IR and CP also overlap the ostensibly interdisciplinary field of "international studies."

6   The dividing line is not quite so stark: some political scientists mix these approaches. But in the discipline as a whole, quantitative work has become more prominent.

7   Phrase from Kalevi J. Holsti (1985: 103), cited by Cox and Nossal (2009: 287).

8   For a cross-disciplinary example, see van Schendel and Abraham (2005), which likewise questions the centrality of the state, calls for multiscalar perspective, and argues that border spaces are good places to see flows and fluidity.

9   Work in other anthropological fields also stretches across geographical space and deep into time – one might consider archaeologists or evolutionary/biological anthropologists such as Robin Fox (2011) or Robin Dunbar (2004). These subfields, which obviously do not use methods of participant observation, are more aligned with positivist approaches.

10 Patricia Greenfield, quoted by Brettell (2009: 655).

11 The anxieties focused on losing touch with real people and especially with subaltern subjects – and also about stretching ethnography too far into macro scales, thereby losing the flavor of fieldwork. For recent contributions, see Falzon (2009) or Coleman and von Hellermann (2011).

12 I leave aside here nontextual, and also nonliterary, mass-culture materials. "Art" is discussed further below, but otherwise these fall into the bailiwick of "cultural studies," a sprawling interdisciplinary approach that has developed its own veins of global thinking. See Wilson and Connery (2007).

13 Comparative literature's very name obviously suggests a deep link with comparative approaches generally, the trade-offs of which have already been well covered by the chapter by Michael Adas. As in anthropology or comparative politics, recent work in CL has also reflected on the blurring of units used for study. I will not re-cover either topic here.

14 As Damrosch notes (2003: 25), other approaches, descended from Frye, go in different directions. For example, Itamar Even-Zohar (1990) is a translation theorist who uses a "poly-systems" approach to encompass all the world's literature. Franco Moretti mapped the global spread of a literary form (the European novel), at a high level of abstraction, without *any* close readings of particular texts – and then (2005) issued a manifesto for an entirely "abstract" literary history. This amounts to methodological heresy in literary scholarship, akin to some world historians' assertion that global history can be written with only secondary materials, rather than through recourse to primary documents.

15 To be fair, Damrosch notes (2003: 282) that comparatists returned the disregard, seeing their broader vision as tantamount to overcoming specialists' scholarly pedantry and their nation-alistically narrow linguistic training. Some even presented world literature as a chief hope for world peace and intercultural understanding. Parallels could be drawn with world history, in the rhetoric of its critics as well as some of its converts.

16 He notes that these texts will overlap – so the ellipses spread ever farther.

17 Think of historical intermediaries such as missionaries, merchants, notaries, as well as literal translators: Burns (2010).

18 Consider the Asterix series of comic books, which originated in French but have been translated into more than 100 global languages. Anthea Bell, their co-translator into English, has spoken about the challenge of recalibrating interwoven puns, songs, names, and pictures, see Bell (1999); also http://web.archive.org/web/20060327011137/http://www. literarytranslation.com/workshops/asterix/ (accessed Mar. 2012).

19 Crystal (2003: 4–5) notes that only a dozen or so countries use English as a "mother-tongue," but the language nevertheless has a special status, often legally recognized, in about 70. In more than 100 countries, English is the most commonly taught foreign language.

20 Werner Friedrich criticized "world literature" as being, in practice, "NATO literatures." Damrosch (2003: 110–113) admits a "dramatically uneven balance of literary trade," similar to the situation in IR. In 1987, for instance, 1,500 translations of American books were published in Brazil – but only 14 Brazilian books appeared in English translation.

21 I leave aside the wider approach of "visual studies" – a broad interdisciplinary domain, with a relationship to art history similar to that of cultural studies to literature.

22 Elkins (2007: 3–4); he goes on to declare, "Far and away the most pressing problem facing the discipline is the prospect of world art history" (2007: 41).

23 See, for example, an online exhibit on globalization mounted by the Museum für Kommunikation, Frankfurt, at www.globalmuseum.de (accessed Mar. 2012).

24 See www.asia-europe.uni-heidelberg.de/en/research/cluster-professorships/global-art-history.html (accessed Mar. 2012).

25 Originally published in 2004, the review was reprinted in Elkins (2007: 42–71).

References

Abu-Lughod, J. 1991. *Before European Hegemony: The World System AD 1250–1350.* New York: Oxford University Press.

Acemoglu, D., and J. Robinson. 2006. *Economic Origins of Dictatorship and Democracy.* Cambridge: Cambridge University Press.

Acemoglu, D., and J. Robinson. 2012. *Why Nations Fail: The Origins of Power, Prosperity, and Poverty*. New York: Crown.

Achebe, C. 1975. The African writer and the English language. In C. Achebe, *Morning Yet on Creation Day: Essays*, pp. 91–103. Garden City, NY: Anchor.

Appadurai, A. 1996. *Modernity at Large: Cultural Dimensions of Globalization*. Minneapolis: University of Minnesota Press.

Aunger, R. 2007a. Major transitions in "big" history. *Technological Forecasting and Social Change* 74: 1137–1163.

Aunger, R. 2007b. A rigorous periodization of "big" history. *Technological Forecasting and Social Change* 74: 1164–1178.

Avant, D.D., M. Finnemore, and S.K. Sell, eds. 2010. *Who Governs the Globe?* Cambridge: Cambridge University Press.

Baucom, I. 2001. Globalit, Inc.: Or, the cultural logic of global literary studies. *PMLA* 116 (1): 158–172.

Bell, Anthea. 1999. Asterix, my love. *Daily Telegraph*, Feb. 25.

Belting, H., and A. Buddensieg, eds. 2009. *The Global Art World: Audiences, Markets, and Museums*. Ostfildern: Hatje Cantz.

Biersteker, T.J. 2009. The parochialism of hegemony: Challenges for "American" international relations. In A.B. Tickner and O. Waever, eds, *International Relations Scholarship around the World*, pp. 308–327. London: Routledge. First published in 1984.

Bob, C. 2010. Packing heat: Pro-gun groups and the governance of small arms. In D.D. Avant, M. Finnemore, and S.K. Sell, eds, *Who Governs the Globe?*, pp. 183–201. Cambridge: Cambridge University Press.

Brettell, C.B. 2009. Anthropology, migration, and comparative consciousness. *New Literary History* 40: 649–671.

Burns, K. 2010. *Into the Archive: Writing and Power in Colonial Peru*. Durham: Duke University Press.

Carrier, D. 2008. *A World Art History and Its Objects*. University Park: Pennsylvania State University Press.

Clifford, J. 1997. *Routes: Travel and Translation in the Late Twentieth Century*. Cambridge, MA: Harvard University Press.

Coleman, S., and P. von Hellermann, eds. 2011. *Multi-Sited Ethnography*. New York: Routledge.

Cooppan, V. 2001. World literature and global theory: Comparative literature for the new millennium. *symplokē* 9 (1–2): 15–44.

Cox, W.S., and K.R. Nossal. 2009. The "crimson world": The Anglo core, the post-imperial non-core, and the hegemony of American IR. In A.B. Tickner and O. Waever, eds, *International Relations Scholarship around the World*, pp. 287–307. London: Routledge.

Crystal, D. 2003. *English as a Global Language*. Cambridge: Cambridge University Press.

Damrosch, D. 2003. *What Is World Literature?* Princeton: Princeton University Press.

De Munck, V. 2000. Introduction: Units for describing and analyzing culture and society. *Ethnology* 39 (4): 279–292.

Der Derian, J., and M.J. Shapiro, eds. 1989. *International/Intertextual Relations: Postmodern Readings of World Politics*. Lexington, MA: Lexington Books.

Dimock, W.C. 2001. Literature for the planet. *PMLA* 116 (1): 173–188.

Dunbar, R.I.M. 2004. *The Human Story: A New History of Mankind's Evolution*. London: Faber & Faber.

Elkins, J. ed. 2007. *Is Art History Global?* New York: Routledge.

Elkins, J., Z. Valiavicharska, and A. Kim, eds. 2010. *Art and Globalization*. University Park: Pennsylvania State University Press.

Even-Zohar, I. 1990. *Polysystem Studies*. Durham: Duke University Press.

Falzon, M.-A., ed. 2009. *Multi-sited Ethnography*. Farnham: Ashgate.

Ferguson, J. 2006. *Global Shadows: Africa in the Neoliberal World Order.* Durham: Duke University Press.

Fox, R. 2011. *The Tribal Imagination: Civilization and the Savage Mind.* Cambridge, MA: Harvard University Press.

Frank, R.H. 2011. *The Darwin Economy: Liberty, Competition, and the Common Good.* Princeton: Princeton University Press.

Friedman, T. 2005. *The World Is Flat: A Brief History of the Twenty-First Century.* New York: Farrar, Strauss, & Giroux.

Frye, N. 1957. *Anatomy of Criticism: Four Essays.* Princeton: Princeton University Press.

Fukuyama, F. 2011. *The Origins of Political Order: From Prehuman Times to the French Revolution.* New York: Farrar, Strauss, & Giroux.

Ghemawat, P. 2011. *World 3.0: Global Prosperity and How to Achieve It.* Cambridge, MA: Harvard Business Review Press.

Gingrich, A., and R.G. Fox 2002. *Anthropology, by Comparison.* Routledge, New York.

Gordon, D.M. 2010. Colonial studies. *Boston Review* 35 (5): 59–62.

Gunn, G. 2001. Introduction: Globalizing literary studies. *PMLA* 116 (1): 16–31.

Handler, R. 2009. The uses of incommensurability in anthropology. *New Literary History* 40: 627–647.

Henry, G. 1994. Can an ancient Chinese historian contribute to modern Western theory? *History and Theory* 33 (91): 20–38.

Holsti, Kalevi J. 1985. *The Dividing Discipline: Hegemony and Diversity in International Theory.* Boston: Allen & Unwin.

Huang, A.C.Y. 2009. *Chinese Shakespeares: Two Centuries of Cultural Exchange.* New York: Columbia University Press.

Hung, W. 1995. *Monumentality in Early Chinese Art and Architecture.* Stanford: Stanford University Press.

Jameson, F., and M. Miyoshi, eds. 1998. *The Cultures of Globalization.* Durham: Duke University Press.

Lal, V. 1999. Gandhi, the civilizational crucible, and the future of dissent. *Futures* 31: 205–219.

Lal, V. 2003. Provincializing the West: World history from the perspective of Indian history. In B. Stuchtey and E. Fuchs, eds, *Writing World History 1800–2000,* pp. 271–290. Oxford: Oxford University Press.

Marcus, G. 1995. Ethnography in/of the world system: The emergence of multi-sited ethnography. *Annual Review of Anthropology* 24: 95–117.

Marlin-Bennett, R., ed. 2011. *Alker and IR: Global Studies in an Interconnected World.* London: Routledge.

Moretti, F. 2005. *Graphs, Maps, Trees: Abstract Models for a Literary History.* New York: Verso.

Munn, N. 1996. Excluded spaces. *Critical Inquiry* 22: 446–465.

Onians, J. 2008. *Neuroarthistory: From Aristotle and Pliny to Baxandall and Zeki.* New Haven: Yale University Press.

Owen, S. 1990. What is world poetry? *New Republic* 203 (21): 28–32.

Robertson, R. 1990. Mapping the global condition: Globalization as the central concept. *Theory, Culture, and Society* 7 (2): 15–30.

Shapiro, M.J., and H. Alker, eds. 1995. *Challenging Boundaries: Global Flows, Territorial Identities.* Minneapolis: University of Minnesota Press.

Summers, D. 2003. *Real Spaces: World Art History and the Rise of Modernism.* London: Phaidon.

Tenzer, M., ed. 2006. *Analytical Studies in World Music.* Oxford: Oxford University Press.

Tickner, A.B., and O. Waever, eds. 2009. *International Relations Scholarship around the World.* London: Routledge.

Tilly, C. 2006. *Big Structures, Large Processes, Huge Comparisons.* New York: Russell Sage Foundation.

Tsing, A.L. 2005. *Friction: An Ethnography of Global Connection*. Princeton: Princeton University Press.

Tsing, A.L., and C. Gluck, eds. 2009. *Words in Motion: Toward a Global Lexicon*. Durham: Duke University Press.

Valdés, M., and L. Hutcheon. 1994. Rethinking literary history – comparatively. Occasional Paper No. 27. American Council of Learned Societies, New York.

Van Schendel, W., and I. Abraham, eds. 2005. *Illicit Flows and Criminal Things: States, Borders, and the Other Side of Globalization*. Bloomington: Indiana University Press.

Venuti, L. 2004. *The Translation Studies Reader*. New York: Routledge.

Walker, J. 1994. Reading genres across cultures: The example of autobiography. In S. Lawall, ed., *Reading World Literature: Theory, History, Practice*, pp. 203–235. Austin: University of Texas Press.

Walkowitz, R. 2009. Comparison literature. *New Literary History* 40: 567–582.

Wallerstein, I. 2004. *World-Systems Analysis: An Introduction*. Durham: Duke University Press.

Wesch, M. 2009. YouTube and you: Experiences of self-awareness in the context collapse of the recording webcam. *Explorations in Media Ecology* 8 (2): 19–34.

Wigen, K., and M.W. Lewis. 1997. *The Myth of Continents: A Critique of Metageography*. Berkeley: University of California Press.

Wilson, R., and C. Connery, eds. 2007. *The Worlding Project: Doing Cultural Studies in the Era of Globalization*. Berkeley: New Pacific Press.

Wolf, E.R. 1982. *Europe and the People without History*. Berkeley: University of California Press.

Yiqiang, Cao. 2008. World art studies and the historiography of Chinese art. In Kitty Zijlmans and Wilfried van Damme, eds, *World Art Studies: Exploring Concepts and Approaches*. Amsterdam: Valiz, pp. 119–133.

Yiqiang, Cao, and Fan Jingzhong. 1997. Ershi shiji Zhongguohua: Chuantong de yanxu yu yanjin [Chinese painting and the twentieth century: creativity in the aftermath of tradition]. Hangzhou: Zhejiang Renmin Meishu Chubanshe.

Zijlmans, Kitty, and Wilfried van Damme, eds, 2008. *World Art Studies: Exploring Concepts and Approaches*. Amsterdam: Valiz.

Bibliography

Abernathy, D.B. 2000. *The Dynamics of Global Dominance: European Overseas Empires, 1415–1980*. New Haven: Yale University Press.

Abu Lughod, J. 1991. *Before European Hegemony: The World System AD 1250–1350*. New York: Oxford University Press.

Abu-Lughod, J. 1993. The world system in the thirteenth century: Dead-end or precursor? In M. Adas, ed., *Islamic and European Expansion: The Forging of a Global Order*, pp. 75–102. Philadelphia: Temple University Press.

Achebe, C. 1975. The African writer and the English language. In C. Achebe, *Morning Yet on Creation Day: Essays*, pp. 91–103. Garden City, NY: Anchor.

Acemoglu, D. and J. Robinson. 2006. *Economic Origins of Dictatorship and Democracy*. Cambridge: Cambridge University Press.

Acemoglu, D. and J. Robinson. 2012. *Why Nations Fail: The Origins of Power, Prosperity, and Poverty*. New York: Crown.

Ackerknecht, E.H. 1945. *Malaria in the Upper Mississippi Valley, 1760–1900*. Baltimore: Johns Hopkins University Press.

Adas, M. 1979. *Prophets of Rebellion: Millenarian Protest Movements against the European Colonial Order*. Chapel Hill: University of North Carolina Press.

Adas, M. 1989. *Machines as the Measure of Men: Science, Technology, and Ideologies of Western Dominance*. Ithaca, NY: Cornell University Press.

Adas, M. 1998. Bring ideas and agency back in: Representation and the comparative approach to world history. In P. Pomper, R. Elphick, and R. T. Vann, eds, *World History: Ideologies, Structures, and Identities*, pp. 81–104. Oxford: Blackwell.

Adas, M. 2006. *Dominance by design: Technological imperatives and America's civilizing mission*. Cambridge, MA: Belknap.

Adas, M. and American Historical Association. 1993. *Islamic and European Expansion: The Forging of a Global Order*. Philadelphia: Temple University Press.

Adas, M. and American Historical Association. 2001. *Agricultural and Pastoral Societies in Ancient and Classical History*. Philadelphia: Temple University Press.

Adelman, J. 2004. Latin American and world histories: Old and new approaches to the pluribus and the unum. *Hispanic American Historical Review* 84 (3) (July 30): 399–409.

A Companion to World History, First Edition. Edited by Douglas Northrop.
© 2012 Blackwell Publishing Ltd. Published 2012 by Blackwell Publishing Ltd.

Adeniji, A. 2005. Universal history and the challenge of globalization to African historiography. *Radical History Review* 91 (Winter): 98–103.

AHA Committee on Graduate Education. 2003. The education of historians for the 21st century. *Perspectives on History: The News Magazine of the American Historical Association* (Oct.). At http://www.historians.org/perspectives/issues/2003/0310/0310not1.cfm (accessed Mar. 2012).

Ahmed, S. 2006. *Queer Phenomenology: Orientations, Objects, Others*. Durham: Duke University Press.

Akarli, E. 2005. Law in the marketplace: Istanbul 1730–1840. In M. Masud, R. Peters, and D. Powers, eds, *Dispensing Justice in Islam: Qadis and Their Judgements*, pp. 245–270. Leiden: Brill.

Akita, S. 2008. World history and the creation of a new global history: Japanese perspectives. In *Conference Reader of "Global History, Globally,"* Harvard University, Feb. 8–9.

Alam, M. 2004. *The Languages of Political Islam in India, c. 1200–1800*. Chicago: University of Chicago Press.

Albrow, M. 1977. *The Global Age: State and Society beyond Modernity*. Stanford: Stanford University Press.

Alexandrowicz, C.H. 1967. *An Introduction to the History of the Law of Nations in the East Indies*. Oxford: Clarendon Press.

Algaze, G. 1989. The Uruk expansion: Cross-cultural exchange in early Mesopotamian civilization. *Current Anthropology* 30: 571–608.

Algaze, G. 1993. *The Uruk World System: The Dynamics of Expansion in Early Mesopotamian Civilization*. Chicago: University of Chicago Press.

Algaze, G. 2009. *Ancient Mesopotamia at the Dawn of Civilization: The Evolution of an Urban Landscape*. Chicago: University of Chicago Press.

Alim, H.S. 2005. A new research agenda: Exploring the transglobal hip hop *umma*. In M. Cooke and B.B. Lawrence, eds, *Muslim Networks from Hajj to Hip Hop*, pp. 264–274. Chapel Hill: University of North Carolina Press.

Allardyce, G. 1990. Toward world history: American historians and the coming of the world history course. *Journal of World History* 1: 23–76.

Allen, R. 2009. *The British Industrial Revolution in Global Perspective*. Cambridge: Cambridge University Press.

Allen, V. 1975. The white man's road: Physical and psychological impact of relocation on the Southern Plains Indians. *Journal of History of Medicine and Allied Sciences* 30 (2): 148–163.

Allende, S. 1972. *Discurso inaugural UNCTAD III*. Comisión Chilena para la UNCTAD III, Santiago.

Allman, J. and A. Burton. 2008. Editors' note. *Journal of Women's History* 20 (1): 8–13.

Allsen, T. 1997. *Commodity and Exchange in the Mongol Empire: A Cultural History of Islamic Textiles*. Cambridge: Cambridge University Press.

Allsen, T. 2001. *Culture and Conquest in Mongol Eurasia*. Cambridge: Cambridge University Press.

Alpers, E. 1975. *Ivory and Slaves: Changing Pattern of International Trade in East Central Africa to the Later Nineteenth Century*. Berkeley: University of California Press.

American Historical Association. 2010. *Directory of History Departments, Historical Organizations, and Historians, 36th edition, 2010–2011*. Washington DC: American Historical Association.

Amin, S. 1990. *Delinking towards a Polycentric World*. New York: Zed Books.

Anderson, C. 2000. *Convicts in the Indian Ocean: Transportation from South Asia to Mauritius 1815–1853*. London: Macmillan.

Anderson, D.G. 1994. *The Savannah River Chiefdoms: Political Change in the Late Prehistoric Southeast*. Tuscaloosa: University of Alabama Press.

Anthony, D.W. 2007. *The Horse, the Wheel, and Language*. Princeton: Princeton University Press.

Antohi, S., B. Trencsényi, and P. Apor, eds. 2007. *Narratives Unbound: Historical Studies in Post-Communist Eastern Europe*. Budapest: Central European University Press.

Appadurai, A. 1996. *Modernity at Large: Cultural Dimensions of Globalization*. Minneapolis: University of Minnesota Press.

Archer, C.I., J.R. Ferris, H.H. Herwig, and T.H.E. Travers. 2002. *World History of Warfare.* Lincoln: University of Nebraska Press.

Armitage, D. 2002. *The British Atlantic World, 1500–1800.* New York: Palgrave Macmillan.

Armitage, D. 2008. *The Declaration of Independence: A Global History.* Cambridge, MA: Harvard University Press.

Armitage, D. and S. Subrahmanyam, eds. 2010. *The Age of Revolutions in Global Context.* New York: Palgrave Macmillan.

Arnold, D. 1986. Cholera and colonialism in British India. *Past and Present* 113: 118–151.

Arrighi, G. 1994. *The Long Twentieth Century.* London: Verso.

Arrighi, G. 2005. Hegemony unravelling 1. *New Left Review* 32: 23–80.

Arrighi, G. 2007. *Adam Smith in Beijing: Lineages of the Twenty-First Century.* New York: Verso.

Arvidsson, S. 2006. *Aryan Idols: Indo-European Mythology as Ideology and Science,* trans. S. Wichmann. Chicago: University of Chicago Press.

Asad, T. 1973. *Anthropology and the Colonial Encounter.* New York: Humanities Press.

Asad, T. 2003. *Formations of the Secular: Christianity, Islam, Modernity.* Stanford: Stanford University Press.

Aslanian, S. 2011. *From the Indian Ocean to the Mediterranean: The Global Trade Networks of Armenian Merchants from New Julfa.* Berkeley: University of California Press.

Aunger, R. 2007. Major transitions in "big" history. *Technological Forecasting and Social Change* 74 (8): 1137–1163.

Aunger, R. 2007. A rigorous periodization of "big" history. *Technological Forecasting and Social Change* 74(8): 1164–1178.

Aust, M. Forthcoming. Á la recherche d'histoire impériale: Histories of Russia from the nineteenth to the early twenty-first century. In M. Middell and L. Roura, eds, *World, Global and European Histories as Challenges to National Representations of the Past.* Basingstoke: Palgrave Macmillan.

Avant, D.D., M. Finnemore, and S.K. Sell, eds. 2010. *Who Governs the Globe?* Cambridge: Cambridge University Press.

Aydin, C. 2007. *The Politics of Anti-Westernism in Asia: Visions of World Order in Pan-Islamic and Pan-Asian Thought.* New York: Columbia University Press.

Badenoch, A. and A Fickers, eds. 2010. *Materializing Europe: Transnational Infrastructures and the Project of Europe.* Basingstoke: Palgrave Macmillan.

Bain, R.B. 2000. AP world history habits of mind: Reflecting on world history's unique challenge to students' thinking. In J. Arno, ed., *Teacher's Guide: AP World History,* pp. 237–243. Princeton: College Entrance Examination Board.

Bain, R.B. 2005. They thought the world was flat? HPL principles in teaching high school history. In J. Bransford and S. Donovan, eds, *How Students Learn: History, Mathematics, and Science in the Classroom,* pp. 179–214. Washington DC: National Academies Press.

Bain, R.B. and L.M. Harris. 2010. *External Evaluation: World History for Us All.* San Diego, CA: World History for Us All. At http://worldhistoryforusall.sdsu.edu/downloads/Long%20 Beach%20Report%202010.pdf (accessed Mar. 2012).

Bain, R.B. and J.E. Mirel. 2006. Setting up camp in the great instructional divide: Educating beginning history teachers. *Journal of Teacher Education* 57 (3): 212–219.

Bain, R.B. and T. Shreiner. 2005. Issues and options in creating a national assessment in world history. *History Teacher* 38 (2): 241–272.

Bain, R.B. and T. Shreiner. 2006. The dilemmas of a national assessment in world history: World historians and the 12th grade NAEP. *World History Connected* 3 (3), at http://www. historycooperative.org/journals/whc/3.3/bain.html (accessed Mar. 2012).

Baines, J., J. Bennet, and S. Houston, eds. 2008. *The Disappearance of Writing Systems.* London: Equinox.

Bala, Arun. 2006. *The Dialogue of Civilizations in the Birth of Modern Science.* New York: Palgrave Macmillan.

Balachandran, G. 2011. Writing global histories: Claiming history beyond nations. At http://graduateinstitute.ch/webdav/site/international_history_politics/shared/working_papers/WPIHP-Balachandran.pdf (accessed Mar. 2012).

Ball, D.L. 2000. Bridging practices: Intertwining content and pedagogy in teaching and learning to teach. *Journal of Teacher Education* 51 (3): 241–247.

Ball, D.L., M.H. Thames, and G. Phelps. 2008. Content Knowledge for Teaching. *Journal of Teacher Education* 59 (5): 389–407.

Ballantyne, T. 2002. *Orientalism and Race*. London: Palgrave Macmillan.

Ballantyne, T. and A.M. Burton. 2005. *Bodies in Contact: Rethinking Colonial Encounters in World History*. Durham: Duke University Press.

Ballantyne, T. and A.M. Burton. 2009. *Moving Subjects: Gender, Mobility, and Intimacy in an Age of Global Empire*. Urbana: University of Illinois Press.

Ballantyne, T. and B. Moloughney. 2006. Asia in Murihiku: Towards a transnational history of colonial culture. In T. Ballantyne and B. Moloughney, eds, *Disputed Histories: Imagining New Zealand's Pasts*, pp. 23–34. Dunedin: Otago University Press.

Bang, K. 1992. *Hankook gunhyundai sasangsa yŏngu* [A study of modern thought in Korea]. Seoul: Yŏksabipyungsa.

Bang, P.F. 2008. *The Roman Bazaar*. New York: Cambridge University Press.

Banner, S. 2007. *Possessing the Pacific: Land, Settlers, and Indigenous People from Australia to Alaska*. Cambridge, MA: Harvard University Press.

Bard, K. 2008. Royal cities and cult centers, administrative towns, and workmen's settlements in ancient Egypt. In J. Marcus and J. Sabloff, eds, *The Ancient City: New Perspectives on Urbanism in the Old and New World*, pp. 165–182. Santa Fe: SAR Press.

Barendse, R. 2002. *The Arabian Seas: The Indian Ocean World of the Seventeenth Century*. Armonk, NY: M.E. Sharpe.

Barfield, T.J. 2001. The shadow of empires. In S.E. Alcock, T.N. D'Altroy, K.D. Morrison, and C.M. Sinopoli, eds, *Empires: Perspectives from Archaeology and History*, pp. 10–41. Cambridge: Cambridge University Press.

Barkey, K. 2008. *Empire of Difference: The Ottomans in Comparative Perspective*. Cambridge: Cambridge University Press.

Barlow, T.E., ed. 2007. *Formations of Colonial Modernity in East Asia*. Durham: Duke University Press.

Barraclough, G. 1967. *An Introduction to Contemporary History*. Harmondsworth: Penguin.

Barrett, E. 2002. The geography of the Rio Grande Pueblos in the seventeenth century. *Ethnohistory* 4: 123–169.

Barton, K.C. and J.H. James. 2010. Religion in history and social studies. *Perspectives in History* 48 (5).

Bastide, R. 2007. *The African Religions of Brazil: Toward a Sociology of the Interpenetration of Civilizations*. Baltimore: Johns Hopkins University Press.

Batory, A. and N. Lindstrom. 2011. The power of the purse: Supranational entrepreneurship, financial incentives, and European higher education policy. *Governance* 24 (2): 311–329.

Baucom, I. 2001. Globalit, Inc.: Or, the cultural logic of global literary studies. *PMLA* 116 (1): 158–172.

Bauman, Z. 2005. *Liquid Life*. Cambridge: Polity.

Bayly, C.A. 1989. *Imperial Meridian: The British Empire and the World, 1780–1830*. New York: Longman.

Bayly, C.A. 2002. "Archaic" and "modern" globalization in the Eurasian and African arena, ca. 1750–1850. In A.G. Hopkins, ed., *Globalization in World History*, pp. 45–72. New York: W.W. Norton.

Bayly, C.A. 2004. *The Birth of the Modern World, 1780–1914: Global Connections and Comparisons*. Oxford: Blackwell.

Bayly, C.A. 2005. From archaic globalization to international networks, circa 1600–2000. In J.H. Bentley, R. Bridenthal, and A.A. Yang, eds, *Interactions: Transregional Perspectives on World History*, pp. 14–29. Honolulu: University of Hawai'i Press.

Bayly, C.A. and P.F. Bang. 2003. Introduction: Comparing premodern empires. *Medieval History Journal* 6 (2): 169–187.

Bayly, C.A., S. Beckert, M. Connelly, I. Hofmeyr, W. Kozol, and P. Seed. 2006. AHR conversation: On transnational history. *American Historical Review* 111 (5): 1441–1464.

Bean, B. 2009. Anniston: A historic military and industrial town. At http://www.spiritofanniston.com/pages/?pageID=26 (accessed Feb. 2012).

Beckert, S. 2005. Cotton: A global history. In J.H. Bentley, R. Bridenthal, and A.A. Yang, eds, *Interactions: Transregional Perspectives on World History*, pp. 48–63. Honolulu: University of Hawai'i Press.

Beckwith, C.I. 2009. *Empires of the Silk Road: A History of Central Eurasia from the Bronze Age to the Present*. Princeton: Princeton University Press.

Belghazi, T. 2005. Afterword. In M. Cooke and B.B. Lawrence, eds, *Muslim Networks from Hajj to Hip Hop*, pp. 275–282. Chapel Hill: University of North Carolina Press.

Bell, A. 1999. Asterix, my love. *Daily Telegraph*, Feb. 25.

Bellwood, P. 2005. *First Farmers: Origins of Agricultural Societies*. Oxford: Blackwell.

Belting, H. and A. Buddensieg, eds. 2009. *The Global Art World: Audiences, Markets, and Museums*. Ostfildern: Hatje Cantz.

Benedictow, O.J. 2004. *The Black Death, 1346–1353: The Complete History*. Woodbridge, UK: Boydell.

Benjamin, C.G.R. 2007. *The Yuezhi: Origin, Migration, and the Conquest of Northern Bactria*. Turnhout: Brepols.

Benjamin, C.G.R. ed. 2009. Introduction to Forum on Big History. *World History Connected* 6 (3) (Oct.), at http://worldhistoryconnected.press.illinois.edu/6.3/index.html (accessed Feb. 2012).

Benjamin, T. 2009. *The Atlantic World: Europeans, Africans, Indians and Their Shared History, 1400–1900*. New York: Cambridge University Press.

Benjamin, T., T. Hall, and D. Rutherford. 2000. *The Atlantic World in the Age of Empire*. Belmont, CA: Wadsworth.

Bennett, T. 1995. *The Birth of the Museum*. London: Routledge.

Bentley, J.H. 1993. *Old World Encounters: Cross-Cultural Contacts and Exchanges in Pre-Modern Times*. Oxford: Oxford University Press.

Bentley, J.H. 1996. Cross-cultural interaction and periodization in world history. *American Historical Review* 101 (3): 749–770.

Bentley, J.H. 1996. *Shapes of World History in Twentieth-Century Scholarship*. Washington DC: American Historical Association.

Bentley, J.H. 1999. Sea and ocean basins as frameworks of historical analysis. *Geographical Review* 89: 215–224.

Bentley, J.H. 2002. The new world history. In L. Kramer and S. Maza, eds, *A Companion to Western Historical Thought*, pp. 393–416. Oxford: Blackwell.

Bentley, J.H. 2003. World history and grand narrative. In B. Stuchtey and E. Fuchs, eds, *Writing World History, 1800–2000*, pp. 47–65. Oxford: Oxford University Press.

Bentley, J.H. 2005. Myths, wagers, and some moral implications of world history. *Journal of World History* 16 (1): 51–82.

Bentley, J.H. 2007. Why study world history? *World History Connected* 5 (1), at www.historycooperative.org/journals/whc/5.1/bentley.html (accessed Feb. 2012).

Bentley, J.H. 2008. The *Journal of World History*. In P. Manning, ed., *Global Practices in World History: Advances Worldwide*, pp. 129–140. Princeton: Markus Wiener.

Bentley, J. and H.F. Ziegler. 2008. *Traditions and Encounters: A Global Perspective on the Past*. New York: McGraw-Hill.

Benton, L. 2002. *Law and Colonial Cultures: Legal Regimes in World History, 1400–1900.* Cambridge: Cambridge University Press.

Benton, L. 2004. No longer odd region out: Repositioning Latin America in world history. *Hispanic American Historical Review* 84 (3): 423–430.

Benton, L. 2009. *A Search for Sovereignty.* Cambridge: Cambridge University Press.

Ben-Ur, A. 2009. A matriarchal matter: Slavery, conversion, and upward mobility in Suriname's Jewish community. In R. Kagan and P. Morgan, eds, *Atlantic Diasporas: Jews, Conversos, and Crypto-Jews in the Age of Mercantilism, 1500–1800*, pp. 152–169. Baltimore: Johns Hopkins University Press.

Bergenthum, H. 2004. *Weltgeschichten im Zeitalter der Weltpolitik. Zur populären Geschichtsschreibung im wilhelminischen Deutschland.* Munich: Martin Meidenbauer.

Berger, I. *et al.* 1988. *Restoring Women to History: Teaching Packets for Integrating Women's History into Courses on Africa, Asia, Latin America, the Caribbean, and the Middle East.* Bloomington: Indiana University Press.

Berger, S., ed. 2007. *Writing the Nation: A Global Perspective.* Basingstoke: Palgrave Macmillan.

Berkes, N. 1998. *The Development of Secularism in Turkey.* London: Hurst.

Berman Museum. 2007. Take a trip around the world … take a trip back in time. Pamphlet, Berman Museum of World History, Anniston.

Bernal, M. 1987. *Black Athena: The Afroasiatic Roots of Classical Civilization*, vol. 1: *The Fabrication of Ancient Greece, 1785–1985.* New Brunswick, NJ: Rutgers University Press.

Bernal, M. 1991. *Black Athena: The Afroasiatic Roots of Classical Civilization*, vol. 2: *The Archaeological and Documentary Evidence.* New Brunswick, NJ: Rutgers University Press.

Bernal, M. 2006. *Black Athena: The Afroasiatic Roots of Classical Civilization*, vol. 3: *The Linguistic Evidence.* New Brunswick, NJ: Rutgers University Press.

Bertram, G. and R. Watters. 1985. The MIRAB economy in South Pacific microstates. *Pacific Viewpoint* 26: 497–519.

Besnier, N. 2011. *On the Edge of the Global: Modern Anxieties in a Pacific Island Nation.* Stanford: Stanford University Press.

Besse, S. 2004. Placing Latin America in modern world history textbooks. *Hispanic American Historical Review* 84 (3) (July 30): 411–422.

Bessis, S. 2003. *Western Supremacy: Triumph of an Idea?* London: Zed Books.

Bevir, M. and F. Trentman. 2004. *Markets in Historical Contexts: Ideas and Politics in the Modern World.* Cambridge: Cambridge University Press.

Bhabha, H.K. 1994. Of mimicry and man: The ambivalence of colonial discourse. In H.K. Bhabha, *The Location of Culture*, pp. 85–92. London: Routledge.

Bideau, A., B. Desjardins, and H.P. Brignoli. 1997. *Infant and Child Mortality in the Past.* Oxford: Clarendon Press.

Bierstecker, T.J. 2009. The parochialism of hegemony: Challenges for "American" international relations. In A.B. Tickner and O. Waever, eds, *International Relations Scholarship around the World*, pp. 308–327. London: Routledge. First published in 1984.

Bierstedt, R. 1966. Indices of civilization. *American Journal of Sociology* 71: 483–490.

Black, A. 2008. *The West and Islam: Religion and Political Thought in World History.* New York: Oxford University Press.

Black, J. 2004. *Rethinking Military History.* London: Routledge.

Blackburn, R. 1997. *The Making of New World Slavery: From the Baroque to the Modern, 1492–1800.* New York: Verso.

Blaut, J.M. 1993. *The Colonizer's Model of the World: Geographical Diffusionism and Eurocentric History.* New York: Guilford Press.

Blaut, J.M. 2000. *Eight Eurocentric Historians.* New York: Guilford Press.

Bloch, M. 1969. *Land and Work in Medieval Europe: Selected Papers by Marc Bloch*, trans. J.E. Anderson. New York: Harper & Row.

Blumi, I. 2003. *Rethinking the Late Ottoman Empire: A Comparative Social and Political History of Albania and Yemen, 1878–1918*. Istanbul: ISIS.

Blussé, J.L. 1986. *Strange Company: Chinese Settlers, Mestizo Women, and the Dutch in VOC Batavia*. Dordrecht: Foris.

Blussé, J.L. 2008. *Visible Cities: Canton, Nagasaki, and Batavia and the Coming of the Americans*. Cambridge, MA: Harvard University Press.

Blussé, J.L., W. Remmelink, and I. Smits, eds. 2000. *Bridging the Divide: 400 Years, the Netherlands–Japan*. Leiden: Hotei.

Bob, C. 2010. Packing heat: Pro-gun groups and the governance of small arms. In D.D. Avant, M. Finnemore, and S.K. Sell, eds, *Who Governs the Globe?*, pp. 183–201. Cambridge: Cambridge University Press.

Bodley, J.H. 1999. Hunter-gatherers and the colonial encounter. In R.B. Lee and R. Daly, eds, *The Cambridge Encyclopedia of Hunters and Gatherers*, pp. 465–472. Cambridge: Cambridge University Press.

Boon, J. 1982. *Other Tribes, Other Scribes*. Cambridge: Cambridge University Press.

Bose, S. 2010. South Asia without borders. Presentation at International Institute Symposium, Oct. 29, University of Michigan.

Bostock, J. and H.T. Riley, trans. 1855. *The Natural History of Pliny*. 2 vols. London: Taylor & Francis.

Boswell, T. and C. Chase-Dunn. 2000. *The Spiral of Socialism and Capitalism: Toward Global Democracy*. Boulder: Lynne Rienner.

Bouchard, C., ed. 2009. *Knights in History and Legend*. Buffalo, NY: Firefly Books.

Bourdieu, P. and J. Passeron. 1977. *Reproduction in Education, Society and Culture*, trans. L. Wacquant. London: Sage.

Brandt, A.M. 2007. *The Cigarette Century: The Rise, Fall, and Deadly Persistence of the Product That Defined America*. New York: Basic Books.

Braudel, F. 1972. *The Mediterranean and the Mediterranean World in the Age of Philip II*, trans. S. Reynolds. London: Collins.

Braudel, F. 1980. *On History*, trans. S. Matthews. Chicago: University of Chicago Press.

Braudel, F. 1981–1984. *Civilization and Capitalism, 15th–18th Century*, trans. S. Reynolds. New York: Harper & Row.

Braudel, F. 1996. *The Mediterranean and the Mediterranean World in the Age of Philip II*. 2 vols. Berkeley: University of California Press.

Braudel, F. 2002. *Memory and the Mediterranean*. New York: Random House.

Bray, W., ed. 1993. *The Meeting of Two Worlds: Europe and the Americas 1492–1650*. Oxford: Oxford University Press for the British Academy.

Brekke, T. 2005. *The Ethics of War in Asian Civilisations: A Comparative Perspective*. London: Routledge.

Brendon, P. 1991. *Thomas Cook: 150 Years of Popular Tourism*. London: Secker & Warburg.

Brettell, C.B. 2009. Anthropology, migration, and comparative consciousness. *New Literary History* 40: 649–671.

Bright, C. and M. Geyer. 2005. Regimes of world order: Global integration and the production of difference in twentieth-century world history. In J.H. Bentley, R. Bridenthal, and A.A. Yang, eds, *Interactions: Transregional Perspectives on World History*, pp. 202–238. Honolulu: University of Hawai'i Press.

Brinkley, A. 2008. *American History: A Survey*. 13th edn. New York: McGraw-Hill.

Brockey, L.M. 2008. *Journey to the East: The Jesuit Mission to China, 1579–1724*. Cambridge, MA: Harvard University Press.

Brogan, H. 2007. *Alexis de Tocqueville: A Life*. New Haven: Yale University Press.

Brooks, P. 2008. *Boycotts, Buses, and Passes: Black Women's Resistance in the US and South Africa*. Amherst: University of Massachusetts Press.

Brown, C.S. 2007. *Big History: From the Big Bang to the Present*. New York: New Press.

Brubaker, R. 1992. *Citizenship and Nationhood in France and Germany*. Cambridge, MA: Harvard University Press.

Brundage, W.F. 2005. *The Southern Past: A Clash of Race and Memory*. Cambridge, MA: Harvard University Press.

Brunnbauer, U., ed. 2004. *(Re)Writing History: Historiography in Southeast Europe after Socialism*. Münster: LIT.

Bryant, J.M. 1994. Evidence and explanation in history and sociology: Critical reflections on Goldthorpe's critique of historical sociology. *British Journal of Sociology* 45 (1): 3–19.

Bryant, J.M. 2006. The West and the Rest revisited: Debating capitalist origins, European colonialism, and the advent of modernity. *Canadian Journal of Sociology* 31 (4): 403–444.

Bryson, B. 2003. *A Short History of Nearly Everything*. London: Random House.

Bryson, B. 2009. *A Really Short History of Nearly Everything*. New York: Delacorte Books for Young Readers.

Buchanan, M. 2000. *Ubiquity: The Science of History … or Why the World Is Simpler Than We Think*. London: Weidenfeld & Nicolson.

Buck, D. 1999. Was it pluck or luck that made the West grow rich? Review of *ReORIENT: Global Economy in the Asian Age* (Frank); *The Wealth and Poverty of Nations: Why Some Are So Rich and Some So Poor* (Landes); *China Transformed* (R. Bin Wong). *Journal of World History* 10 (2): 413.

Buck, P. 1938. *Vikings of the Sunrise*. New York: Frederick A. Stokes.

Bulliet, R. 1990. *The Camel and the Wheel*. New York: Columbia University Press.

Bulliet, R. 2005. *Hunters, Herders, and Hamburgers: The Past and Future of Human–Animal Relationships*. New York: Columbia University Press.

Burbank, J. and F. Cooper. 2010. *Empires in World History: Power and the Politics of Difference*. Princeton: Princeton University Press.

Burke, Edmund, III. 1993. Introduction: Marshall G.S. Hodgson and world history. In M.G.S. Hodgson, *Rethinking World History: Essays on Europe, Islam, and World History*, ed. Edmund Burke, III. Cambridge: Cambridge University Press.

Burke, E., III and K. Pomeranz. 2009. *The Environment and World History*. Berkeley: University of California Press.

Burkhart, Louise. 2001. *Before Guadalupe: The Virgin Mary in Early Colonial Nahuatl Literature*. Albany, NY: Institute for Mesoamerican Studies.

Burns, K. 2010. *Into the Archive: Writing and Power in Colonial Peru*. Durham: Duke University Press.

Burton, A., ed. 2003. *After the Imperial Turn: Thinking with and through the Nation*. Durham: Duke University Press.

Buschmann, R.F. 2011. The Pacific Ocean basin to 1850. In J.H. Bentley, ed., *The Oxford Handbook of World History*, pp. 564–580. Oxford: Oxford University Press.

Butler, J. 1993. *Bodies That Matter: On the Discursive Limits of Sex*. New York: Routledge.

Butler, J. 1998. Merely cultural. *New Left Review* I/227: 33–44.

Bynum, C.W. 2009. Teaching scholarship. *Perspectives on History* 47 (9) (Dec.): 14–16.

Cabral, A. 1975. *Unité et lutte. L'arme de la théorie*. Paris: Maspero.

Cahill, D. 2010. Advanced Andeans and backward Europeans: Structure and agency in the collapse of the Inca Empire. In P. McAnany and N. Yoffee, eds, *Questioning Collapse: Human Resilience, Ecological Vulnerability, and the Aftermath of Empire*, pp. 207–238. Cambridge: Cambridge University Press.

Cajani, L. 2007. Citizenship on the verge of the 21st century: The burden of the past, the challenge of the present. In L. Cajani and A. Ross, eds, *History Teaching, Identities, Citizenship*, pp. 1–12. Stoke-on-Trent, UK: Trentham.

Caldwell, I. and D. Henley, eds. 2008. *Stranger-kings in Indonesia and Beyond*. Special issue, *Indonesia and the Malay World* 36 (105).

Camacho, K.L. and L.A. Monnig. 2010. Uncomfortable fatigues: Chamorro soldiers, gendered identities, and the question of decolonization in Guam. In S. Shigematsu and K. Camacho, eds,

Militarized Currents: Toward a Decolonized Future in Asia and the Pacific, pp. 147–179. Minneapolis: University of Minnesota Press.

Camara, S. 1997. Islam et tradition historique au Manden. In *La culture arabo-islamique en Afrique au sud du Sahara. Cas de l'Afrique de l'Ouest*, pp. 115–120. Proceedings of an international conference held in Timbuktu. Zaghouan, Tunisia: Fondation Temimi.

Campbell, I.C. 1997. Culture contact and Polynesian identity in the European age. *Journal of World History* 8: 29–55.

Cannato, V.J. 2009. *American Passage: The History of Ellis Island*. New York: HarperCollins.

Canning, K. 1999. The body as method? Reflections on the place of the body in gender history. *Gender and History* 11 (3): 499–513.

Carney, J.A. and R.N. Rosomoff. 2009. *In the Shadow of Slavery: Africa's Botanical Legacy in the Atlantic World*. Berkeley: University of California Press.

Carretero, M., A. López-Manjón, and L. Jacott. 1997. Explaining historical events. *International Journal of Educational Research* 27 (3): 245–253.

Carretta, V. 2005. *Equiano the African: Biography of a Self-Made Man*. Athens: University of Georgia Press.

Carrier, D. 2008. *A World Art History and Its Objects*. University Park: Pennsylvania State University Press.

Carrithers, M. 2000. On polytropy: Or the natural condition of spiritual cosmopolitanism in India: The Digambar Jain case. *Modern Asian Studies* 34 (4) (Oct.): 831–861.

Carson, R. 1962. *Silent Spring*. New York: Fawcett Crest.

Casson, L., trans. 1989. *The Periplus Maris Erythraei*. Princeton: Princeton University Press.

Cavanagh, S. 2007. World history and geography gain traction in class: Seeds of internationally themed lessons were planted in the 1980s. *Education Week* (Mar. 21): 10.

Cavasin, N. 2005. Region. In R.W. McColl, ed., *Encyclopedia of World Geography*, pp. 765–766. New York: Facts on File.

Centro Sur. 1995. Cooperación y negociación. *Tercer Mundo Económico* 73 (Oct. 1–15). At http://www.redtercermundo.org.uy/tm_economico/texto_completo.php?id=2180 (accessed Mar. 2012).

Centro Sur. 1995. Necesidad de actuar en forma concertada. *Tercer Mundo Económico* 73 (Oct. 1–15). At http://www.redtercermundo.org.uy/tm_economico/texto_completo.php?id=2179 (accessed Feb. 2012).

Cervantes, F. and A. Redden, eds. Forthcoming. *Angels, Demons and the New World: Spanish America, 1524–1767*. Cambridge: Cambridge University Press.

Cha, H. 1988. *Sŏyangsahakui suyonggwa baljeon* [A historiography of modern thought in Korea]. Seoul: Nanam.

Chafe, W.H. 2009. *The Rise and Fall of the American Century: United States from 1890 to 2009*. Oxford: Oxford University Press.

Chaisson, E.J. 1977. The scenario of cosmic evolution. *Harvard Magazine*, Nov.–Dec., pp. 21–33.

Chaisson, E.J. 1981. *Cosmic Dawn: The Origins of Matter and Life*. New York: W.W. Norton.

Chaisson, E.J. 1987. *The Life Era: Cosmic Selection and Conscious Evolution*. New York: Atlantic Monthly Press.

Chaisson, E.J. 1988. *Universe: An Evolutionary Approach to Astronomy*. Englewood Cliffs, NJ: Prentice Hall.

Chaisson, E.J. 2001. *Cosmic Evolution: The Rise of Complexity in Nature*. Cambridge, MA: Harvard University Press.

Chaisson, E.J. 2006. *Epic of Evolution: Seven Ages of the Cosmos*. New York: Columbia University Press.

Chakrabarty, D. 1992. Postcoloniality and the artifice of history: Who speaks for "Indian" pasts? *Representations* 37: 1–26.

Chakrabarty, D. 2000. *Provincializing Europe: Postcolonial Thought and Historical Difference*. Princeton: Princeton University Press.

Chalcraft, J.T. 2005. Pluralizing capital, challenging Eurocentrism: Toward post-Marxist historiography. *Radical History Review* 91 (Winter): 13–39.

Chambers, R. 1994. *Vestiges of the Natural History of Creation.* Reproduced in J.A. Secord, ed., *Vestiges of the Natural History of Creation and Other Evolutionary Writings.* Chicago: University of Chicago Press. First published in 1844.

Chanda, N. 2007. *Bound Together: How Traders, Preachers, Adventurers, and Warriors Shaped Globalization.* New Haven: Yale University Press.

Chandler, A.D. 1977. *The Visible Hand: The Managerial Revolution in American Business.* Cambridge, MA: Belknap.

Chapman, J. 2000. *Fragmentation in Archaeology: People, Places and Broken Objects in the Prehistory of South-Eastern Europe.* London: Routledge.

Charle, C., J. Schriewer, and P. Wagner, eds. 2004. *Transnational Intellectual Networks: Forms of Academic Knowledge and the Search for Cultural Identities.* New York: Campus.

Chase, K. 2003. *Firearms: A Global History to 1700.* Cambridge: Cambridge University Press.

Chase-Dunn, C. 1989. *Global Formation: Structures of the World-Economy.* Oxford: Blackwell.

Chase-Dunn, C. and E. Anderson. 2005. *The Historical Evolution of World-Systems.* New York: Palgrave Macmillan.

Chase-Dunn, C. and S.J. Babones. 2006. *Global Social Change: Comparative and Historical Perspectives.* Baltimore: Johns Hopkins University Press.

Chase-Dunn, C. and P. Grimes. 1995. World system analysis. *Annual Review of Sociology* 21: 387–417.

Chase-Dunn, C. and T.D. Hall. 1997. *Rise and Demise: Comparing World-Systems.* Boulder: Westview.

Chase-Dunn, C., Y. Kawano, and B.D. Brewer. 2000. Trade globalization since 1795: Waves of integration in the world-system. *American Sociological Review* 65 (1) (Feb.): 77–95.

Chase-Dunn, C. and K.M. Mann. 1998. *The Wintu and Their Neighbors: A Very Small World-System in Northern California.* Tucson: University of Arizona Press.

Chaudhuri, K. 1985. *Trade and Civilisation in the Indian Ocean: An Economic History from the Rise of Islam to 1750.* Cambridge: Cambridge University Press.

Chaudhuri, K. 1990. *Asia before Europe: Economy and Civilisation of the Indian Ocean from the Rise of Islam to 1750.* New York: Cambridge University Press.

Chen, X. 1995. *Occidentalism.* Oxford: Oxford University Press.

Cheng, Y. 2008. *Creating the "New Man": From Enlightenment Ideals to Socialist Realities.* Honolulu: University of Hawai'i Press.

Chew, S.C. 2001. *World Ecological Degradation: Accumulation, Urbanization, and Deforestation 3000 BC–AD 2000.* Walnut Creek, CA: Altamira Press.

Childe, V.G. 1942. *What Happened in History.* Harmondsworth: Penguin.

Childe, V.G. 1950. The urban revolution. *Town Planning Review* 21: 3–17.

Christian, D. 1991. The case for "big history." *Journal of World History* 2 (2): 223–228.

Christian, D. 2003. World history in context. *Journal of World History* 14 (4): 437–458.

Christian, D. 2004. *Maps of Time: An Introduction to Big History.* Berkeley: University of California Press.

Christian, D. 2008. Big history: The big bang, life on Earth, and the rise of humanity. The Teaching Company, Course No. 8050, at http://www.teach12.com/ttcx/CourseDescLong2. aspx?cid=8050 (accessed Feb. 2012).

Christian, D. 2008. *This Fleeting World: A Short History of Humanity.* Great Barrington, MA: Berkshire.

Christian, D. 2009. History and science after the chronometric revolution. In S.J. Dick and M.L. Lupisella, eds, *Cosmos and Culture: Cultural Evolution in a Cosmic Context*, pp. 441–462. Washington DC: National Aeronautics and Space Administration.

Christian, D. 2010. The return of universal history. *History and Theory* 49: 6–27.

Christian, D. 2011. A single historical continuum. *Cliodynamics* 2 (1) (Mar.): 6–26.

Christian, D., M. Lake, and P. Swarnalatha. 2008. Mapping world history: Report on the World History research agenda symposium. In P. Manning, ed., *Global Practices in World History: Advances Worldwide*, pp. 1–16. Princeton: Markus Wiener.

Christiansen, T. 2001. European and regional integration. In J. Baylis and S. Smith, eds, *The Globalization of World Politics*, pp. 494–518. 2nd edn. New York: Oxford University Press.

Christopher, E., C. Pybus, and M. Rediker, eds. 2007. *Many Middle Passages: Forced Migration and the Making of the Modern World*. Berkeley: University of California Press.

Cipolla, C.M. 1981. *Fighting the Plague in Seventeenth-Century Italy*. Madison: University of Wisconsin Press.

Clarence-Smith, W. 2003. *The Global Coffee Economy in Africa, Asia, and Latin America, 1500–1989*. New York: Cambridge University Press.

Clark, G., ed. 2003. *Dumont d'Urville's Divisions of Oceania: Fundamental Precincts or Arbitrary Constructs?* Special issue of *Journal of Pacific History* 38 (2).

Clark, G. 2008. *A Farewell to Alms: A Brief Economic History of the World*. Princeton: Princeton University Press.

Clark, K. 1969. *Civilisation*. Harmondsworth: Penguin.

Clark, R. 1997. *The Global Imperative: An Interpretive History of the Spread of Humankind*. Boulder: Westview.

Clarke, P.B. 1982. *West Africa and Islam: A Study of Religious Development from the 8th to the 20th Century*. London: Edward Arnold.

Clendinnen, I. 1991. "Fierce and unnatural cruelty": Cortés and the conquest of Mexico. *Representations* 33 (Winter): 65–100.

Clifford, J. 1997. *Routes: Travel and Translation in the Late Twentieth Century*. Cambridge, MA: Harvard University Press.

Clossey, L. 2007. Faith in empire: Religious sources of legitimacy for expansionist early-modern states. In C. Ocker, M. Printy, P. Starenko, and P. Wallace, eds., *Politics and Reformations: Histories and Reformations: Essays in Honor of Thomas A. Brady, Jr*, pp. 571–587. Leiden: Brill.

Clossey, L. 2008. *Salvation and Globalization in the Early Jesuit Missions*. New York: Cambridge University Press.

Cloud, P. 1978. *Cosmos, Earth, and Man: A Short History of the Universe*. New Haven: Yale University Press.

Cloud, P. 1988. *Oasis in Space: Earth History from the Beginning*. New York: W.W. Norton.

Cohen, D.W. 1994. *The Combing of History*. Chicago: University of Chicago Press.

Cohen, D.W. 2005. The uncertainty of Africa in an age of certainty. In M.D. Kennedy and D.W. Cohen, eds, *Responsibility in Crisis: Knowledge Politics and Global Publics*, pp. 225–263. Ann Arbor: Scholarly Publishing.

Cohn, B. 1996. *Colonialism and Its Forms of Knowledge*. Princeton: Princeton University Press.

Cohn, S. 2002. *The Black Death Transformed: Disease and Culture in Early Renaissance Europe*. Oxford: Oxford University Press.

Coleman, S. and P. von Hellermann, eds. 2011. *Multi-Sited Ethnography*. New York: Routledge.

Colley, L. 2003. *Captives: Britain, Empire and the World 1600–1850*. New York: Random House.

Colley, L. 2008. *The Ordeal of Elizabeth Marsh: A Woman in World History*. New York: Anchor.

Collier, R.B. and D. Collier. 1991. *Shaping the Political Arena: Critical Junctures, the Labor Movement, and Regime Dynamics in Latin America*. Princeton: Princeton University Press.

Collingwood, R.G. 1946. *The Idea of History*. Oxford: Oxford University Press.

Comaroff, J. and J.L. Comaroff. 2001. *Millennial Capitalism and the Culture of Neoliberalism*. Durham: Duke University Press.

Committee on Appropriations. 2003. Hearing before a subcommittee of the Committee on Appropriations, United States Senate, One hundred seventh Congress, Second session, Special hearing, April 19, 2002 – Anniston, Alabama. Washington DC: US Government. At http://www.ewg.org/files/annistonsenatehearingtrans_0.pdf (accessed Nov. 28, 2010).

Connelly, M. 2008. *Fatal Misconception: The Struggle to Control World Population*. Cambridge, MA: Belknap.

Connery, C.L. and R. Wilson. 2007. *The Worlding Project: Doing Cultural Studies in the Era of Globalization*. Berkeley: North Atlantic Books.

Conrad, S. 2006. *Globalisierung und Nation im deutschen Kaiserreich*. Munich: C.H. Beck.

Conrad, S. 2010. *The Quest for the Lost Nation*, trans. A. Nothnagle. Berkeley: University of California Press.

Conrad, S., A. Eckert, and U. Freitag, eds. 2007. *Globalgeschichte. Theorien, Ansätze und Themen*. Frankfurt am Main: Campus.

Conrad, S. and D. Sachsenmaier, eds. 2007. *Competing Visions of World Order: Global Moments and Movements, 1880s–1930s*. Annotated edn. New York: Palgrave Macmillan.

Cook, N.D. 1998. *Born to Die: Disease and New World Conquest 1492 to 1650*. Cambridge: Cambridge University Press.

Cooper, F. 1980. *From Slaves to Squatters: Plantation Labor and Agriculture in Zanzibar and Coastal Kenya, 1890–1925*. New Haven: Yale University Press.

Cooper, F. 1996. *Decolonization and African Society*. Cambridge: Cambridge University Press.

Cooper, F. 2005. *Colonialism in Question: Theory, Knowledge, History*. Berkeley: University of California Press.

Cooper, F. 2009. Space, time, and history: The conceptual limitations of globalization. In G. Baca, A. Khan, and S. Palmié, eds, *Empirical Futures: Anthropologists and Historians Engage the Work of Sydney W. Mintz*, pp. 31–57. Chapel Hill: University of North Carolina Press.

Cooppan, V. 2001. World literature and global theory: Comparative literature for the new millennium. *symplokē* 9 (1–2): 15–44.

Cordell, L. 1997. *Archaeology of the Southwest*. New York: Academic Press.

Cotterell, A. 2005. *Chariot: From Chariot to Tank, the Astounding Rise and Fall of the World's First War Machine*. New York: Overlook Press.

Cowen, M.P. and R.W. Shenton. 1996. *Doctrines of Development*. London: Routledge.

Cowgill, G.L. 2007. The urban organization at Teotihuacan, Mexico. In E. Stone, ed., *Settlement and Society: Essays Dedicated to Robert McCormick Adams*, pp. 261–295. Los Angeles: Cotsen Institute of Archaeology.

Cowley, R. and G. Parker, eds. 1996. *The Reader's Companion to Military History*. Boston: Houghton Mifflin.

Cox, W.S. and K.R. Nossal. 2009. The "crimson world": The Anglo core, the post-imperial non-core, and the hegemony of American IR. In A.B. Tickner and O. Waever, eds, *International Relations Scholarship around the World*, pp. 287–307. London: Routledge.

Crashaw, C. and J. Urry. 1997. Tourism and the photographic eye. In C. Rojek and J. Urry, eds, *Touring Cultures: Transformations of Travel and Theory*, pp. 176–180. London: Routledge.

Craton, Michael. 1982. *Testing the Chains: Resistance to Slavery in the British West Indies*. Ithaca, NY: Cornell University Press.

Cronon, W. 2003. *Changes in the Land: Indians, Colonists, and the Ecology of New England*. Rev. edn. New York: Hill & Wang.

Crosby, A.W. 1993. *Ecological Imperialism: The Biological Expansion of Europe 900–1900*. 2nd edn. Cambridge: Cambridge University Press.

Crosby, A.W. 1997. *The Measure of Reality: Quantification and Western Society 1200–1600*. Cambridge: Cambridge University Press.

Crosby, A.W. 2003. *The Columbian Exchange: Biological and Cultural Consequences of 1492*. 30th anniversary edn. Westport, CT: Praeger.

Crosby, A. 2006. *Children of the Sun: A History of Humanity's Unappeasable Appetite for Energy*. New York: W.W. Norton.

Crossley, P.K. 2008. *What Is Global History?* Cambridge: Polity.

Crystal, D. 2003. *English as a Global Language*. Cambridge: Cambridge University Press.

Cunliffe, Barry. 2001. *Facing the Ocean: The Atlantic and its Peoples, 8000 BC–AD 1500*. Oxford: Oxford University Press.

Curtin, P. 1984. *Cross-Cultural Trade in World History*. Cambridge: Cambridge University Press.

Curtin, P. 1989. *Death by Migration: Europe's Encounter with the Tropical World in the Nineteenth Century*. Cambridge: Cambridge University Press.

Curtin, P. 2000. *The World and the West: The European Challenge and the Overseas Response in the Age of Empire*. New York: Cambridge University Press.

Damrosch, D. 2003. *What Is World Literature?* Princeton: Princeton University Press.

Daniels, R. 1990. *Coming to America: A History of Immigration and Ethnicity in American Life*. New York: HarperCollins.

D'Arcy, P. 2006. *The People of the Sea: Environment, Identity, and History in Oceania*. Honolulu: University of Hawai'i Press.

D'Arcy, P. 2011. Oceania and Australasia. In J.H. Bentley, ed., *The Oxford Handbook of World History*, pp. 546–563. Oxford: Oxford University Press.

Dardess, J.W. 1996. *A Ming Society: T'ai-ho County, Kiangsi, Fourteenth to Seventeenth Centuries*. Berkeley: University of California Press.

Darnton, R. 1984. *The Great Cat Massacre and Other Episodes in French History*. New York: Basic Books.

Darnton, R. 2004. It happened one night. *New York Review of Books* 51 (11) (June 24): 60–64.

Darwin, C. 1871. *The Descent of Man, and Selection in Relation to Sex*. London: John Murray.

Darwin, C. 1979. *On the Origin of Species by Means of Natural Selection*. New York: Random House. First published 1859.

Darwin, J. 2007. *After Tamerlane: The Rise and Fall of Global Empires, 1400–2000*. London: Penguin.

David, J., T. David, and B. Lüthi, eds. 2007. *Globalgeschichte/Histoire globale/Global History*. Special issue, *Traverse: Zeitschrift für Geschichte/Revue d'Histoire* (Zurich) 14 (3).

Davis, M. 2004. Planet of slums: Urban involution and the informal proletariat. *New Left Review* 26 (Mar.–Apr.): 5–34.

Davis, N.Z. 1997. *Women at the Margins: Three Seventeenth-Century Lives*. Cambridge, MA: Harvard University Press.

Davis, N.Z. 2006. *Trickster Travels: A Sixteenth-Century Muslim between Worlds*. New York: Hill & Wang.

Davis, T. 1992. *Vaka: Saga of a Polynesian Canoe*. Suva: Institute of Pacific Studies, University of the South Pacific.

Dawson, D. 2002. *The First Armies*. New York: Cassell.

De Munck, V. 2000. Introduction: Units for describing and analyzing culture and society. *Ethnology* 39 (4): 279–292.

Degler, Carl N. 1968. Comparative history: An essay review. *Journal of Southern History* 34 (4): 425–430.

Degler, Carl N. 1971. *Neither White nor Black: Slavery and Race Relations in Brazil and the United States*. Madison: University of Wisconsin Press.

Denemark, R.A., J. Friedman, B.K. Gills, and G. Modelski, eds. 2000. *World System History: The Social Science of Long-Term Change*. London: Routledge.

Der Derian, J. and M.J. Shapiro, eds. 1989. *International/Intertextual Relations: Postmodern Readings of World Politics*. Lexington, MA: Lexington Books.

Deringil, S. 1999. *The Well-Protected Domains: Ideology and Legitimation in the Ottoman Empire*. London: I.B. Tauris.

Desai, P. 1973. Third World social scientists in Santiago. *World Development* 1 (9): 57–65.

Devés, E. 2000–2004. *El Pensamiento Latinoamericano en el Siglo XX. Entre la modernización y la identidad*, vol. 1: *Del Ariel de Rodó a la ECLA (1900–1950)*; vol. 2: *Desde la ECLA al neoliberalismo*; vol. 3: *Las discusiones y las figuras del fin de siglo. Los años 90*. Buenos Aires: Biblos.

Devés, E. 2006. Los cientistas económico sociales chilenos en los largos 1960s y su inserción en las redes internacionales. La reunión del Foro Tercer Mundo en Santiago en abril de 1973. *Universum* (University of Talca) 21 (1): 138–167. At http://www.scielo.cl/scielo.php?pid=S0718-23762006000100009&script=sci_arttext (accessed Feb. 2012).

Devés, E. 2008. La circulación de las ideas económico-sociales de Latinoamérica y el Caribe en Asia y África ¿Cómo llegaron y como se diseminaron? (1965–1985). *Universum* (University of Talca) 23 (2): 86–111.

Devés, E. 2008. *O pensamento africano sul-saariano. Conexoes e paralelos com o pensamento Latino-Americano e Asiático. Um esquema.* Rio de Janeiro: CLACSO-EDUCAM.

Di Cosmo, N. 2002. *Ancient China and Its Enemies: The Rise of Nomadic Power in East Asian History.* Cambridge: Cambridge University Press.

Diagne, S.B. 2008. Toward an intellectual history of West Africa: The meaning of Timbuktu. In S. Jeppie and S.B. Diagne, eds, *The Meanings of Timbuktu*, pp. 19–27. Cape Town: HSRC Press.

Diamond, J. 1992. *The Third Chimpanzee: The Evolution and Future of the Human Animal.* New York: HarperCollins.

Diamond, J. 1997. *Guns, Germs, and Steel: The Fates of Human Societies.* New York: W.W. Norton.

Diamond, J. 2005. *Collapse: How Societies Choose to Fail or Succeed.* New York: Viking.

Diaz, V., dir. 1999. *Sacred Vessels: Navigating Tradition and Identity in Micronesia.* Honolulu: Pacific Islanders in Communication.

Dikötter, F. 2007. *Cultures of Confinement: A History of the Prison in Africa, Asia, and Latin America.* Ithaca, NY: Cornell University Press.

Dimock, W.C. 2001. Literature for the planet. *PMLA* 116 (1): 173–188.

Diner, D. 1999. *Das Jahrhundert verstehen. Eine universalhistorische Deutung.* Munich: Fischer.

Dinnerstein, L. 2009. *Ethnic Americans: A History of Immigration.* New York: Columbia University Press.

Diouf, M. 2000. Des historiens et des histoires, pourquoi faire? L'histoire africaine entre l'État et les communautés. *Canadian Journal of African Studies* 34 (2): 337–374.

Dirlik, A. 1999. Is there history after Eurocentrism? Globalism, postcolonialism, and the disavowal of history. *Cultural Critique* 42: 1–34.

Dirlik, A. 2002. History without a center? Reflections on Eurocentrism. In E. Fuchs and B. Stuchtey, eds, *Across Cultural Borders: Historiography in Global Perspective*, pp. 247–284. Lanham: Rowman & Littlefield.

Dirlik, A. 2003. Confounding metaphors, inventions of the world: What is world history for? In B. Stuchtey and E. Fuch, eds, *Writing World History 1800–2000*, pp. 91–133. Oxford: Oxford University Press.

Dirlik, A. 2005. Performing the world: Reality and representation in the making of world histor(ies). *Journal of World History* 16 (4): 391–410.

Dirlik, A. 2007. Contemporary perspectives on modernity: Critical discussion. Special lecture delivered to East Asian Academy at Sŏngkyunkwan University.

Ditchfield, S. 2004. "Of dancing cardinals and mestizo madonnas": Reconfiguring the history of Roman Catholicism in the early modern period. *Journal of Early Modern History* 8 (3–4): 386–408.

Dodson, J. 2008. *Sacred Spaces and Religious Traditions in Oriente Cuba.* Albuquerque: University of New Mexico Press.

Döring, J. and T. Thielmann, eds. 2008. *Spatial Turn. Das Raumparadigma in den Kultur- und Sozialwissenschaften.* Bielefeld: Transcript Verlag.

Douglas, M. 1996. *The World of Goods: Towards an Anthropology of Consumption.* London: Routledge.

Douglas-Hamilton, J. 2005. *Thomas Cook: The Holiday-Maker.* Stroud, UK: Sutton.

Doyle, M.W. 1986. *Empires.* Ithaca, NY: Cornell University Press.

Drees, W.B. 2002. *Creation: From Nothing until Now.* London: Routledge.

Drews, R. 1988. *The Coming of the Greeks: Indo-European Conquests in the Aegean and the Near East*. Princeton: Princeton University Press.

Drews, R. 1993. *The End of the Bronze Age: Changes in Warfare and the Catastrophe ca. 1200 BC*. Princeton: Princeton University Press.

Drews, W. and J. Oesterle, eds. 2008. *Transkulturelle Komparatistik. Beiträge zu einer Globalgeschichte der Vormoderne*. Issue of *Comparativ. Zeitschrift für Globalgeschichte und vergleichende Gesellschaftsforschung* 19 (Leipzig).

Duara, P. 1997. *Rescuing History from the Nation: Questioning Narratives of Modern China*. Chicago: University of Chicago Press.

Duara, P. 2003. *Sovereignty and Authenticity*. Lanham: Rowman & Littlefield.

Dubois, L. 2004. *Avengers of the New World*. Cambridge, MA: Harvard University Press.

Dunbar, R.I.M. 2004. *The Human Story: A New History of Mankind's Evolution*. London: Faber & Faber.

Dunn, R.E. 1986. *The Adventures of Ibn Battuta, a Muslim Traveler of the Fourteenth Century*. Berkeley: University of California Press.

Dunn, R.E. 1996. Review of Marshall G.S. Hodgson, *Rethinking World History*. *Journal of World History* 7 (1) (Spring): 131–133.

Dunn, R.E., ed. 2000. *The New World History: A Teacher's Companion*. New York: Bedford/ St. Martin's.

Dunn, R.E. 2007. Rethinking civilizations and history in the new age of globalization. In *Proceedings of the 34th International Symposium of the National Academy of Sciences*, Seoul, Oct. 12.

Dupuy, R.E. and T.N. Dupuy. 1993. *The Encyclopedia of Military History from 3500 BC to the Present*. London: Macdonald. 3rd edn. New York: HarperCollins.

Dussel, E. 2000. Europe, modernity, and Eurocentrism. *Nepantla* 1 (3): 465–478.

Eames, C. and R. Eames, dirs. 1968. *Powers of Ten*. Short documentary film.

Eaton, R.M. 1997. Comparative history as world history: Religious conversion in modern India. *Journal of World History* 8 (2) (Fall): 243–271.

Egan, M. 2010. Mercury's web: Some reflections on following nature across time and place. *Radical History Review* 107: 111–126.

Ehret, C. and M. Posnansky. 1982. *The Archaeological and Linguistic Reconstruction of African History*. Berkeley: University of California Press.

Eisenstadt, S.N. 1986. *The Origins and Diversity of Axial Age Civilizations*. Albany: State University of New York Press.

Eisenstadt, S.N. and W. Schluchter. 1998. Introduction: Paths to early modernities. *Daedalus* 127 (3): 1–18.

Eley, G. 2005. *A Crooked Line: From Cultural History to the History of Society*. Ann Arbor: University of Michigan Press.

Elkins, J., ed. 2007. *Is Art History Global?* New York: Routledge.

Elkins, J., Z. Valiavicharska, and A. Kim, eds. 2010. *Art and Globalization*. University Park: Pennsylvania State University Press.

Elliott, J.H. 2009. *Spain, Europe and the Wider World 1500–1800*. New Haven: Yale University Press.

Ellis, R. 2003. *The Empty Ocean: Plundering the World's Marine Life*. Washington DC: Island Press.

Elman, B. 2005. *On their Own Terms: Science in China, 1550–1900*. Cambridge, MA: Harvard University Press.

Elster, J. 2009. *Alexis de Tocqueville: The First Social Scientist*. Cambridge: Cambridge University Press.

Eltis, D. 2002. Introduction: Migration and agency in global history. In D. Eltis, ed., *Coerced and Free Migration: Global Perspectives*, pp. 1–32. Stanford: Stanford University Press.

Eltis, D. 2007. A brief overview of the trans-Atlantic slave trade. In Voyages: The Trans-Atlantic Slave Trade Database, at http://www.slavevoyages.org/tast/assessment/essays-intro-01.faces (accessed Nov. 11, 2010).

Elverskog, J. 2010. *Buddhism and Islam on the Silk Road*. Philadelphia: University of Pennsylvania Press.

Elvin, M. 2008. Defining the *explicanda* in the "West and the Rest" debate. *Canadian Journal of Sociology* 33 (1): 168–185.

Emberling, G. 1999. Urban social transformations and the problem of the "first city." In M. Smith, ed., *The Social Construction of Ancient Cities*, pp. 254–268. Washington DC: Smithsonian Institution Press.

Emberling, G. 2011. On the early cities of Mesopotamia. Review of G. Algaze, *Ancient Mesopotamia at the Dawn of Civilization*. H-Net Reviews, at http://umich.academia.edu/GeoffEmberling/Papers/1130378/On_the_Early_Cities_of_Mesopotamia (accessed Feb. 2012).

Emmerson, D.K. 1984. "Southeast Asia": What's in a name? *Journal of Southeast Asian Studies* 15 (1): 1–21.

Emrence, C. 2008. Imperial paths, big comparisons: The late Ottoman Empire. *Journal of Global History* 3: 289–311.

Encyclopedia of China [*Zhongguo da bai ke quan shu*]. 2009. 2nd edn. Beijing: Encyclopedia of China Publishing House.

Engel, U. and M. Middell, eds. 2010. *Theoretiker der Globalisierung*. Leipzig: Leipziger Universitätsverlag.

Engels, D. 1978. *Alexander the Great and the Logistics of the Macedonian Army*. Berkeley: University of California Press.

Engels, F. 1958. To J. Bloch, London, September 21–22, 1890. In Karl Marx and Frederick Engels, *Selected Works in Two Volumes*, vol. 2, p. 489. Moscow: Foreign Languages Publishing House.

Engerman, D.C., ed. 2003. *Staging Growth: Modernization, Development, and the Global Cold War*. Amherst: University of Massachusetts Press.

Englund, R. 1994. *Archaic Administrative Texts from Uruk*. Berlin: Deutsches Archaeologisches Institut.

Enloe, C. 2007. *Globalization and Militarism: Feminists Make the Link*. New York: Rowman & Littlefield.

Equiano, O. 2001. *The Interesting Narrative of the Life of Olaudah Equiano, or Gustavus Vassa, the African. Written by Himself. Authoritative Text, Context and Criticism*, ed. W. Sollors. New York: W.W. Norton.

Erlichman, H.J. 2010. *Conquest, Tribute, and Trade: The Quest for Precious Metals and the Birth of Globalization*. Amherst, NY: Prometheus.

Ernst, C.W. 2005. Ideological and technological transformations of contemporary Sufism. In M. Cooke and B.B. Lawrence, eds, *Muslim Networks from Hajj to Hip Hop*, pp. 191–207. Chapel Hill: University of North Carolina Press.

Ernst, C.W. and B.B. Lawrence. 2002. *Sufi Martyrs of Love: The Chishti Order in South Asia and Beyond*. New York: Palgrave Macmillan.

Errington, F.K. and D.B. Gewertz. 2004. *Yali's Question: Sugar, Culture, and History*. Chicago: University of Chicago Press.

Ersanli, C. 1993. *Iktidar ve Tarih. Turkiye'de "Resmi Tarih" Tezinin Olusumu (1929–1937)* [Power and history: the makings of "official history" in Turkey, 1929–1937]. Istanbul: Afa.

Eskew, G. 2006. The Birmingham Civil Rights Institute and the new ideology of tolerance. In R.C. Romano and L. Raiford, eds, *The Civil Rights Movement in American Memory*, pp. 28–66. Athens: University of Georgia Press.

Espagne, M. 1994. Sur les limites du comparatisme en histoire culturelle. *Genèses* 17: 112–121.

Espagne, M. 1999. *Les transferts culturels franco-allemands*. Paris: Presses Universitaires de France.

Espagne, M. 2011. The notion of cultural transfer. Opening lecture at the Third ENIUGH Congress on World and Global History, London School of Economics, Apr. 14–17.

Espagne, M. and M. Werner, eds. 1988. *Transferts. Les relations interculturelles dans l'espace franco-allemand*. Paris: Recherche sur les Civilisations.

Evangelista, M. 1999. *Unarmed Forces: The Transnational Movement to End the Cold War.* Ithaca, NY: Cornell University Press.

Evans, H. 1998. *The American Century.* New York: Knopf.

Evans, H. 2004. *They Made America.* New York: Little, Brown.

Evans, R.J. 1987. *Death in Hamburg: Society and Politics in the Cholera Years 1830–1910.* Oxford: Clarendon Press.

Even-Zohar, I. 1990. *Polysystem Studies.* Durham: Duke University Press.

Everdell, W.R. 1997. *The First Moderns: Profiles in the Origin of Twentieth-Century Thought.* Chicago: University of Chicago Press.

Falola, T. 2008. *The Atlantic World, 1450–2000.* Bloomington: Indiana University Press.

Falzon, M.-A., ed. 2009. *Multi-sited Ethnography.* Farnham: Ashgate.

Fanon, F. 1963. *The Wretched of the Earth,* trans. Constance Farrington. New York: Grove. First published as *Les damnés de la terre,* 1961.

Fauvelle-Aymar, F.-X., J.-P. Chrétien, and C.-H. Perrot, eds. 2000. *Afrocentrismes. L'histoire des Africains entre Égypte et Amérique.* Paris: Karthala.

Fawcett, L. 1995. Regionalism in historical perspective. In L Fawcett and A. Hurrell, eds, *Regionalism in World Politics: Regional Organization and International Order,* pp. 9–36. Oxford: Oxford University Press.

Fawcett, L. 2004. Exploring regional domains: A comparative history of regionalism. *International Affairs* 80 (3): 429–446.

Feierman, S. 1990. *Peasant Intellectuals: Anthropology and History in Tanzania.* Madison: University of Wisconsin Press.

Feierman, S. 1993. African histories and the dissolution of world history. In R.H. Bates, V.Y. Mudimbe, and J. O'Barr, eds, *Africa and the Disciplines: The Contributions of Research in Africa to the Social Sciences and Humanities,* pp. 167–212. Chicago: University of Chicago Press.

Feierman, S. 1999. Colonizers, scholars, and the creation of invisible histories. In L. Hunt and V. Bonnell, eds, *Beyond the Cultural Turn,* pp. 182–216. Berkeley: University of California Press.

Ferguson, B. 2005. Archaeology, cultural anthropology, and the origins and intensifications of war. In E. Arkush and M. Allen, eds, *Violent Transformations: The Archaeology of Warfare and Long-Term Social Change,* pp. 469–523. Gainesville: University of Florida Press.

Ferguson, J. 2006. *Global Shadows: Africa in the Neoliberal World Order.* Durham: Duke University Press.

Fernández-Armesto, F. 1987. *Before Columbus: Exploration and Colonisation from the Mediterranean to the Atlantic, 1229–1492.* London: Macmillan.

Fernández-Armesto, F. 1996. *Millennium.* London: Black Swan.

Fernández-Armesto, F. 1999. A role without an empire: Problems of super-power status in the twentieth century. In J. Guest, ed., *The American Century from Afar,* pp. 49–62. Melbourne: Boston, Melbourne, Oxford Conversazioni on Culture and Society.

Fernández-Armesto, F. 2000. The stranger effect in early modern Asia. *Itinerario* 24 (2): 80–103.

Fernández-Armesto, F. 2001. *Civilizations: Culture, Ambition, and the Transformation of Nature.* New York: Free Press.

Fernández-Armesto, Felipe. 2006. *Pathfinders: A Global History of Exploration.* New York: W.W. Norton.

Fernández-Armesto, F. 2009. Conceptualizing conversion in global perspective: From late antique to early modern. In C.B. Kendall, O. Nicholson, W.D. Phillips, Jr, and M. Ragnow, eds, *Conversion to Christianity from Late Antiquity to the Modern Age: Considering the Process in Europe, Asia, and the Americas.* Minneapolis: Center for Early Modern History, University of Minnesota.

Fernández-Armesto, F. 2009. *The World: A History.* 2nd edn. Upper Saddle River, NJ: Prentice Hall.

Fielding, A. 2009. *The Mongols in the Making of Europe 1220–1500.* Folkestone, UK: Global Oriental.

Finberg, H.P.R. 1952. The local historian and his theme. Introductory lecture delivered at the University College of Leicester, Nov. 6.

Findley, C. 2005. *The Turks in World History*. New York: Oxford University Press.

Finlay, R. 1998. The pilgrim art: The culture of porcelain in world history. *Journal of World History* 9 (2): 141–187.

Finlay, R. 2010. *The Pilgrim Art: Cultures of Porcelain in World History*. Berkeley: University of California Press.

Finney, B.R. 1994. The other one-third of the globe. *Journal of World History* 5: 273–297.

Finney, B.R. 2003. *Sailing in the Wake of the Ancestors: Reviving Polynesian Voyaging*. Honolulu: Bishop Museum Press.

Fledelius, K. 1997. What is a region? What is regionalism? *Regional Contact* 10: 15–18.

Fletcher, J. 1985. Integrative history: Parallels and interconnections in the early modern period, 1500–1800. *Journal of Turkish Studies* 9: 37–57.

Flint, C. and P. Taylor. 2005. *Political Geography: World-Economy, Nation-State and Locality*. Upper Saddle River, NJ: Prentice Hall.

Flower, W.H. 1891. *The Horse: A Study in Natural History*. London: Kegan Paul.

Flynn, D.O. and A. Giráldez. 2002. Cycles of silver: Global economic unity through the mid-eighteenth century. *Journal of World History* 13 (2): 391–428.

Flynn, D.O. and A. Giráldez. 2008. Born again: Globalization's sixteenth-century origins (Asian/global versus European dynamics). *Pacific Economic Review* 13 (3): 359–387.

Foltz, R. 2000. *Religions of the Silk Road*. New York: St. Martin's Press.

Foner, E. 2008. *Give Me Liberty! An American History*. 2nd edn. New York: W.W. Norton.

Foster, S., R. Ashby, and P. Lee. 2008. *Usable Historical Pasts: A Study of Students' Frameworks of the Past*. Technical Report, ESRC Award Number RES-000-22-1676. Swindon, UK: Economic and Social Research Council.

Foucault, M. 1986. Of other spaces. *Diacritics* 16: 22–27.

Fox, R. 2011. *The Tribal Imagination: Civilization and the Savage Mind*. Cambridge, MA: Harvard University Press.

Frangipane, M. 1997. A fourth millennium temple/palace complex at Arslantepe/Malatya: North–south relations and the formation of early state societies in the northern regions of southern Mesopotamia. *Paléorient* 23: 45–73.

Frangipane, M. 2001. Centralization processes in greater Mesopotamia: Uruk expansion as the climax of systemic interactions among areas of the greater Mesopotamian region. In M. Rothman, ed., *Uruk Mesopotamia and Its Neighbors*, pp. 307–348. Santa Fe: SAR Press.

Frangipane, M. 2002. "Non-Uruk" developments and Uruk-linked features on the northern borders of greater Mesopotamia. In J.N. Postgate, ed., *Artefacts of Complexity: Tracking the Uruk in the Near East*, pp. 123–148. Warminster, UK: Aris & Phillips.

Frank, A.G. 1991. A plea for world system history. *Journal of World History* 2: 1–28.

Frank, A.G. 1998. *ReORIENT: Global Economy in the Asian Age*. Berkeley: University of California Press.

Frank, A.G. and B. Gills. 1993. The 5,000-year world system: An interdisciplinary introduction. In A.G. Frank and B. Gills, eds, *The World System: Five Hundred Years or Five Thousand*, pp. 3–55. London: Routledge.

Frank, A.G. and B.K. Gills, eds. 1993. *The World System: Five Hundred Years or Five Thousand?* London: Routledge.

Frank, R.H. 2011. *The Darwin Economy: Liberty, Competition, and the Common Good*. Princeton: Princeton University Press.

Fredrickson, G.M. 1981. *White Supremacy: A Comparative Study in American and South African History*. Oxford: Oxford University Press.

Fredrickson, G.M. 1995. *Black Liberation: A Comparative History of Black Ideologies in the United States and South Africa*. New York: Oxford University Press.

Fredrickson, G.M. 2002. *Racism: A Short History*. Princeton: Princeton University Press.

Freeman, M. 1955. Genocide, civilization and modernity. *British Journal of Sociology* 46: 207–223.

Fregosi, P. 1998. *Jihad in the West: Muslim Conquests from the 7th to the 21st Centuries.* Amherst, NY: Prometheus.

Friday, K. 2004. *Samurai, Warfare and the State in Early Medieval Japan.* London: Routledge.

Friedman, T. 2005. *The World Is Flat: A Brief History of the Twenty-First Century.* New York: Farrar, Straus, & Giroux.

Friedman, T. 2008. *Hot, Flat, and Crowded: Why We Need a Green Revolution – and How It Can Renew America.* New York: Farrar, Straus & Giroux.

Frisch, M. 1990. *A Shared Authority: Essays on the Craft and Meaning of Oral and Public History.* Albany: State University of New York Press.

Fritze, R. 2002. *New Worlds: The Great Voyages of Discovery, 1400–1600.* Stroud, UK: Sutton.

Fry, J.A. 2002. *Dixie Looks Abroad: The South and US Foreign Relations, 1783–1973.* Baton Rouge: Louisiana State University Press.

Frye, N. 1957. *Anatomy of Criticism: Four Essays.* Princeton: Princeton University Press.

Fukuyama, F. 1992. *The End of History and the Last Man.* New York: Free Press.

Fukuyama, F. 2011. *The Origins of Political Order: From Prehuman Times to the French Revolution.* New York: Farrar, Straus, & Giroux.

Gaddis, J.L. 2004. *The Landscape of History: How Historians Map the Past.* Oxford: Oxford University Press.

Garraty, J.A. and P. Gay, eds. 1972. *The Columbia History of the World.* New York: Harper & Row.

Garrett, L. 1994. *The Coming Plague: Newly Emerging Diseases in a World Out of Balance.* New York: Farrar, Straus & Giroux.

Garuba, H. 2003. Explorations in animist materialism: Notes on reading/writing African literature, culture, and society. *Public Culture* 15 (2): 261–285.

Gat, A. 2006. *War in Human Civilization.* Oxford: Oxford University Press.

Gehrels, T. 2007. *Survival through Evolution: From Multiverse to Modern Society.* Charleston, SC: BookSurge.

Genet, C., R. Genet, B. Swimme, L. Palmer, and L. Gibler. 2009. *The Evolutionary Epic: Science's Story and Humanity's Response.* Santa Margarita, CA: Collins Foundation Press.

Genet, R.M. 2007. *Humanity: The Chimpanzees Who Would Be Ants.* Santa Margarita, CA: Collins Foundation Press.

Genovese, E.D. 1969. The treatment of slaves in different countries: Problems in the application of the comparative method. In L. Foner and E. Genovese, eds, *Slavery in the New World.* Englewood Cliffs, NJ: Prentice Hall.

Gernet, J. 1996. *A History of Chinese Civilization*, trans. J.R. Foster and C. Hartman. 2nd edn. Cambridge: Cambridge University Press.

Gerritsen, A. 2007. *Ji'an Literati and the Local in Song-Yuan-Ming China.* Leiden: Brill.

Geto, Y. 2006. Ilbonui segyesa gyogwasŏ [Japanese world history textbook]. In Nakamura Satoru, ed., *Dongasia yŏksa gyogwasŏnun ŏttŏge suyeoittulka?* [How have East Asian history texts been written?], pp. 151–176. Seoul: Editor.

Getz, T.R. 2012. World history and the rainbow nation: Educating values in the United States and South Africa. In A. Diptee and D. Trotman, eds, *Memory, Public History and Representations of the Past: Africa and Its Diasporas.* New York: Continuum.

Getz, T. and H. Streets-Salter. 2010. *Modern Imperialism and Colonialism: A Global Perspective.* Harlow: Pearson Longman.

Geyer, M. 2012. The new consensus. In M. Middell, ed., *Transnationale Geschichte als transnationale Praxis.* Göttingen: Vandenhoeck & Ruprecht.

Geyer, M. and C. Bright. 1987. For a unified history of the world in the twentieth century. *Radical History Review* 39: 69–91.

Geyer, M. and C. Bright. 1995. World history in a global age. *American Historical Review* 100 (4): 1034–1060.

Geyer, M. and C. Bright. 1996. Global violence and nationalizing wars in Eurasia and America: The geopolitics of war in the mid-nineteenth century. *Comparative Studies in Society and History* 38 (4): 619–657.

Geyer, M.H. and J. Paulmann, eds. 2001. *The Mechanics of Internationalism: Culture, Society, and Politics from the 1840s to the First World War.* Oxford: Oxford University Press.

Ghemawat, P. 2011. *World 3.0: Global Prosperity and How to Achieve It.* Cambridge, MA: Harvard Business Review Press.

Giddens, A. 1990. *The Consequences of Modernity.* Cambridge: Polity.

Gilbert, E. and J.T. Reynolds. 2008. *Africa in World History: From Prehistory to the Present.* 2nd edn. Upper Saddle River, NJ: Prentice Hall.

Gilroy, P. 1993. *The Black Atlantic.* Cambridge, MA: Harvard University Press.

Gingrich, A. and R.G. Fox 2002. *Anthropology, by Comparison.* Routledge, New York.

Ginzburg, C. 1980. *The Cheese and the Worms: The Cosmos of a Sixteenth-Century Miller,* trans. J. Tedeschi and A. Tedeschi. Baltimore: Johns Hopkins University Press.

Gladwell, M. 1995. The plague year. *New Republic,* July 17, pp. 38–46.

Global Price and Income History Group. n.d. At http://gpih.ucdavis.edu (accessed May 1, 2011).

Goldstein, J. 2001. *War and Gender: How Gender Shapes the War System and Vice Versa.* Cambridge: Cambridge University Press.

Goldstone, J.A. 1991. *Revolution and Rebellion in the Early Modern World.* Berkeley: University of California Press.

Goldstone, J.A. 2002. Efflorescences and economic growth in world history: Rethinking the "Rise of the West" and the Industrial Revolution. *Journal of World History* 13 (2): 323–389.

Goldstone, J.A. 2008. *Why Europe? The Rise of the West in World History, 1500–1850.* Boston: McGraw-Hill.

Goldthorpe, J.H. 1991. The uses of history in sociology: Reflections on recent tendencies. *British Journal of Sociology* 42 (2): 211–230.

Gong, G.W. 1984. *The Standard of "Civilization" in International Society.* Oxford: Clarendon Press.

Gonzalez, G. and J.W. Richards. 2004. *The Privileged Planet: How Our Place in the Cosmos Is Designed for Discovery.* Washington DC: Regnery.

Goodale, M. 2005. Empires of law: Discipline and resistance within the transnational system. *Social and Legal Studies* 14 (4): 553–583.

Goody, J. 1996. *The East in the West.* Cambridge: Cambridge University Press.

Goody, J. 2007. *The Theft of History.* Cambridge: Cambridge University Press.

Gootenberg, P. 1999. *Cocaine: Global Histories.* New York: Routledge.

Gordon, D.M. 2010. Colonial studies. *Boston Review* 35 (5): 59–62.

Gottfried, R.S. 1983. *The Black Death.* London: Collier Macmillan.

Goubert, P. 1971. Local history. *Daedalus* 100 (1): 113–127.

Goudsblom, J. 1992. *Fire and Civilization.* London: Allen Lane.

Goudsblom, J. 2004. *Humans and Their Habitats in a Long-Term Socio-ecological Perspective: Myths, Maps and Models.* Amsterdam: Amsterdam University Press.

Goudsblom, J., E.L. Jones, and S. Mennell, eds. 1996. *The Course of Human History: Economic Growth, Social Process, and Civilization.* Armonk, NY: M.E. Sharpe.

Gould, E. 2007. Entangled histories, entangled worlds: The English-speaking Atlantic as a Spanish periphery. *American Historical Review* 112 (3): 764–786.

Graff, D. 2002. *Medieval Chinese Warfare, 300–900.* London: Routledge.

Gran, P. 1996. *Beyond Eurocentrism: A New View of Modern World History.* Syracuse, NY: Syracuse University Press.

Gran, P. 2009. *The Rise of the Rich: A New View of Modern World History.* Syracuse, NY: Syracuse University Press.

Grandner, M., D. Rothermund, and W Schwenkter, eds. 2005. *Globalisierung und Globalgeschichte.* Vienna: Mandelbaum.

Green, W.A. 1998. Periodizing world history. In P. Pomper, R. Elphick, and R.T. Vann, eds, *World History: Ideologies, Structures, and Identities,* pp. 53–68. Oxford: Blackwell.

Greenblatt, S. 1976. Learning to curse: Aspects of linguistic colonialism in the sixteenth century. In F. Chiappelli, ed., *The Impact of the New World on the Old*, pp. 561–580. Berkeley: University of California Press.

Greenblatt, S. 1991. *Marvelous Possessions: The Wonder of the New World*. Chicago: University of Chicago Press.

Greer, A. and K. Mills. 2007. A Catholic Atlantic. In J. Cañizares-Esguerra and E.R. Seeman, eds, *The Atlantic in Global History, 1500–2000*, pp. 3–19. Upper Saddle River, NJ: Pearson/Prentice Hall.

Grew, R. 1980. The case for comparing histories. *American Historical Review* 85 (4): 763–778.

Grigg, D. 1967. Regions, models and classes. In R.J. Chorley and P. Haggett, eds, *Models in Geography*, pp. 461–507. London: Methuen.

Grinchenko, S.N. 2004. *Sistemnaia pamiat' zhivogo* [System memory of life]. Moscow: Institute of Informatics Problems of the Russian Academy of Sciences (IPI RAN).

Grinchenko, S.N. 2007. *Metaevoliutsiia* [Metaevolution]. Moscow: Institute of Informatics Problems of the Russian Academy of Sciences (IPI RAN).

Grob, G.N. 2002. *The Deadly Truth: A History of Disease in America*. Cambridge, MA: Harvard University Press.

Grosser, P. 2011. L'histoire mondiale/globale. Une jeunesse exubérante mais difficile. *Vingtième Siècle* 110 (Apr.–June): 3–18.

Grove, R. 1995. *Green Imperialism*. Cambridge: Cambridge University Press.

Guan, B.T.C. 2005. Regionalism. In R.W. McColl, ed., *Encyclopedia of World Geography*, pp. 766–769. New York: Facts on File.

Gunn, G. 2001. Introduction: Globalizing literary studies. *PMLA* 116 (1): 16–31.

Gunn, G. 2003. *First Globalization: The Eurasian Exchange, 1500 to 1800*. Lanham: Rowman & Littlefield.

Hadler, F. and M. Mesenhöller, eds. 2007. *Vergangene Grösse und Ohnmacht in Ostmitteleuropa. Repräsentationen imperialer Erfahrung in der Historiographie seit 1918*. Leipzig: Akademische Verlagsanstalt.

Haldon, J. 1999. *Warfare, State and Society in the Byzantine World, 565–1204*. London: Routledge.

Hall, C. 2004. Review of C.A. Bayly, *The Birth of the Modern World, 1780–1914*. *Reviews in History*, at http://www.history.ac.uk/reviews/review/420 (accessed Feb. 2012).

Hall, M. 1987. *The Changing Past: Farmers, Kings, and Traders in Southern Africa, 200–1860*. Cape Town: D. Philip.

Hall, S. 1991. The local and the global: Globalization and ethnicity. In A.D. King, ed., *Culture, Globalization and the World-System*, pp. 19–39. Basingstoke: Macmillan.

Hall, S. 1992. The question of cultural identity. In S. Hall, D. Held, and T. McGrew, eds, *Modernity and Its Futures*, pp. 273–325. Cambridge: Polity.

Hall, T.D. 1989. *Social Change in the Southwest, 1350–1880*. Lawrence: University Press of Kansas.

Hall, T.D. 1998. The effects of incorporation into world-systems on ethnic processes: Lessons from the ancient world for the contemporary world. *International Political Science Review* 19 (3) (July): 251–267.

Hallden, O. 1994. On the paradox of understanding history in an educational setting. In G. Leinhardt, I.L. Beck, and C. Stainton, eds, *Teaching and Learning in History*, pp. 27–46. Hillsdale, NJ: Lawrence Erlbaum.

Hallden, O. 1997. Conceptual change and the learning of history. *International Journal of Educational Research* 27 (3): 201–210.

Hämäläinen, P. 2008. *Comanche Empire*. New Haven: Yale University Press.

Hämäläinen, P. 2011. Retrieving a continent: North American grand narrative after the localist turn. MS.

Hamashita, T. 2008. *China, East Asia and the Global Economy: Regional and Historical Perspectives*. London: Routledge.

Hamilton, C. 1998. *Terrific Majesty: The Powers of Shaka Zulu and the Limits of Historical Invention*. Cambridge, MA: Harvard University Press.

Hamlin, C. 2009. *Cholera: The Biography*. Oxford: Oxford University Press.

Handler, R. 2009. The uses of incommensurability in anthropology. *New Literary History* 40: 627–647.

Hankook Sŏyangsahakhoi, ed. 2009. *Europejungsimjooui segyesarul nŏmŏ* [Beyond a Eurocentric world history]. Seoul: Purunyŏksa.

Hannah, N. 2011. Artisans in Cairo 1600–1800: An alternative framework for the early modern economic history of Egypt. MS.

Hansen, M. 1999. The mass production of the senses: Classical cinema as vernacular modernism. *Modernity/Modernism* 6 (2): 59–77.

Hansen, M.H., ed. 2000. *A Comparative Study of Thirty City-State Cultures*. Copenhagen: Royal Danish Academy of Sciences and Letters.

Hansen, V. and K. Curtis. 2010. *Voyages in World History*. Boston: Wadsworth.

Hanson, V.D. 1989. *The Western Way of War: Infantry Battle in Classical Greece*. New York: Knopf.

Harari, Y. 2008. *The Ultimate Experience: Battlefield Revelations and the Making of Modern War Culture, 1450–2000*. New York: Palgrave Macmillan.

Harms, R.W. 1981. *River of Wealth, River of Sorrow: The Central Zaire Basin in the Era of the Slave and Ivory Trade, 1500–1891*. New Haven: Yale University Press.

Harootunian, H.D. 2000. *History's Disquiet: Modernity, Cultural Practice, and the Question of Everyday Life*. New York: Columbia University Press.

Harootunian, H.D. 2000. *Overcome by Modernity: History, Culture, and Community in Interwar Japan*. Princeton: Princeton University Press.

Harris, L.M. 2008. Building coherence in world history: A study of instructional tools and teachers' pedagogical content knowledge. PhD diss., Educational Studies, University of Michigan.

Harvey, D. 2001. *Spaces of Capital: Towards a Critical Geography*. Edinburgh: Edinburgh University Press.

Harvey, D. 2003. *The New Imperialism*. New York: Oxford University Press.

Hassig, R. 1988. *Aztec Warfare*. Norman: Oklahoma University Press.

Hau'ofa, E. 1994. Our sea of islands. *Contemporary Pacific* 6: 147–161.

Haupt, H.-G. and J. Kocka, eds. 2010. *Comparative and Transnational History: Central European Approaches and New Perspectives*. New York: Berghahn.

Haya de la Torre, V.R. 1990. *El antiimperialismo y el APRA*. Santiago: Ercilla.

Hays, J.N. 1998. *The Burdens of Disease: Epidemics and Human Response in Western History*. New Brunswick, NJ: Rutgers University Press.

Headley, J. 2007. *The Europeanization of the World: On the Origins of Human Rights and Democracy*. Princeton: Princeton University Press.

Headrick, D. 1988. *The Tentacles of Progress: Technology Transfer in the Age of Imperialism, 1850–1940*. New York: Oxford University Press.

Headrick, D. 2010. *Power over Peoples: Technology, Environments, and Western Imperialism*. Princeton: Princeton University Press.

Hecht, G. 2012. *Being Nuclear: Africans and the Global Uranium Trade*. Cambridge, MA: MIT Press.

Helms, M.W. 1975. *Middle America: A Cultural History of Heartland and Frontier*. Upper Saddle River, NJ: Prentice Hall.

Helms, M.W. 1983. Miskito slaving and culture contact: Ethnicity and opportunity in an expanding population. *Journal of Anthropological Research* 39 (2): 179–197.

Helms, M.W. 1993. *Craft and the Kingly Ideal: Art, Trade, and Power*. Austin: University of Texas Press.

Helms, M.W. 1993. *Ulysses' Sail: An Ethnographic Odyssey of Power, Knowledge, and Geographical Distance*. Austin: University of Texas Press.

Henry, G. 1994. Can an ancient Chinese historian contribute to modern Western theory? *History and Theory* 33 (91): 20–38.

Herkenrath, M. 2007. Introduction: The regional dynamics of global transformations. *International Journal of Comparative Sociology* 48 (2–3): 91–105.

Herkenrath, M., C. König, H. Scholtz, and T. Volken. 2005. Divergence and convergence in the contemporary world system: An introduction. *International Journal of Comparative Sociology* 46 (5–6): 363–382.

Hill, E. 1987. *Al-Sanhuri and Islamic Law: The Place and Significance of Islamic Law in the Life and Work of Abd-al-Razzaq Ahmad al-Sanhuri, Egyptian Jurist and Scholar, 1895–1971.* Cairo: American University of Cairo Press.

Hindle, S. 2000. A sense of place? Becoming and belonging in the rural parish, *c*.1550–1650. In A. Shepard and P. Withington, eds, *Communities in Early Modern England*, pp. 96–114. Manchester: Manchester University Press.

Hindle, S. 2008. Beating the bounds of the parish: Order, memory and identity in the English local community, *c*.1500–1700. In M.J. Halvorson and K.E. Spierling, eds, *Defining Community in Early Modern Europe*, pp. 205–227. Aldershot: Ashgate.

Hirsch, F. 2005. *Empire of Nations.* Ithaca, NY: Cornell University Press.

Hiskett, M. 1984. *The Development of Islam in West Africa.* New York: Longman.

Ho, E. 2004. Empire through diasporic eyes. *Comparative Studies in Society and History* 46 (2): 210–246.

Ho, E. 2006. *The Graves of Tarim: Genealogy and Mobility across the Indian Ocean.* Berkeley: University of California Press.

Hobhouse, H. 1999. *Seeds of Change: Six Plants That Transformed Mankind.* London: Macmillan.

Hobsbawm, E.J. 1996. *The Age of Extremes: A History of the World, 1914–1991.* New York: Vintage.

Hobsbawm, E.J. 2010. World distempers: Interview. *New Left Review* 61: 133–150.

Hobson, J.M. 2004. *The Eastern Origins of Western Civilization.* Cambridge: Cambridge University Press.

Hodes, M. 2003. The mercurial nature and abiding power of race: A transnational family story. *American Historical Review* 108 (1): 84–118.

Hodge, E. 2010. El pensamiento internacional de Manuel Baldomero Ugarte y Víctor Raúl Haya de la Torre. Una aproximación hacia sus ideas sobre integración latinoamericana, anti-imperialismo y defensa continental (1900–1939). Master's thesis, University of Santiago.

Hodgson, M.G.S. 1974. *The Venture of Islam.* 3 vols. Chicago: University of Chicago Press.

Hodgson, M.G.S. 1993. *Rethinking World History: Essays on Europe, Islam, and World History*, ed. and introd. E. Burke, III. Cambridge: Cambridge University Press.

Hodgson, M.G.S. 2002. Doing world history. In M.G.S. Hodgson, *Rethinking World History: Essays in Europe, Islam, and World History*, ed. E. Burke, III. Cambridge: Cambridge University Press.

Holsti, K.J. 1985. *The Dividing Discipline: Hegemony and Diversity in International Theory.* Boston: Allen & Unwin.

Holt, T.C. 1995. Marking: Race, race-making and the writing of history. *American Historical Review* 100 (1): 1–20.

Hopkins, A.G., ed. 2002. *Globalization in World History.* New York: W.W. Norton.

Hopkins, A.G. 2002. The history of globalization – and the globalization of history. In A.G. Hopkins, ed., *Globalization in World History.* New York: W.W. Norton.

Hopkins, A.G., ed. 2006. *Global History: Interactions between the Universal and the Local.* Basingstoke: Palgrave Macmillan.

Hopkins, D. 1983. *Princes and Peasants: Smallpox in History.* Chicago: University of Chicago Press.

Horden, P. and N. Purcell. 2000. *The Corrupting Sea: A Study of Mediterranean History.* Oxford: Blackwell.

Hornborg, A. 2007. *Rethinking Environmental History: World-System History and Global Environmental Change.* Lanham: AltaMira Press.

Hornborg, A. and C.E. Crumley. 2007. *The World System and the Earth System: Global Socioenvironmental Change and Sustainability since the Neolithic*. Walnut Creek, CA: Left Coast Books.

Hornborg, A., J.R. McNeill, and J. Martinez-Alier, eds. 2007. *Rethinking Environmental History: World-System History and Global Environmental Change*. Lanham: Rowman & Littlefield.

Hourani, A. 1968. Ottoman reform and the politics of notables. In W.R. Polk and R.L. Chambers, eds, *Beginnings of Modernization in the Middle East: The Nineteenth Century*, pp. 41–68. Chicago: University of Chicago Press.

Houston, S., ed. 2004. *The First Writing: Script Invention as History and Process*. Cambridge: Cambridge University Press.

Houston, S. and T. Inomata. 2009. *The Classic Maya*. Cambridge: Cambridge University Press.

Howe, K.R., ed. 2006. *Vaka Moana: Voyages of the Ancestors: The Discovery and Settlement of the Pacific*. Auckland: David Bateman.

Howe, S. 1998. *Afrocentrism: Mythical Pasts and Imagined Homes*. London: New Left Books.

Howe, S., ed. 2009. *New Imperial Histories Reader*. London: Routledge.

Howson, J. 2007. Is it the Tuarts then the Studors or the other way round? The importance of developing a usable big picture of the past. *Teaching History* 127: 40–47.

Huang, A.C.Y. 2009. *Chinese Shakespeares: Two Centuries of Cultural Exchange*. New York: Columbia University Press.

Huber, T. 2008. *The Holy Land Reborn: Pilgrimage and Tibetan Reinvention of Buddhist India*. Chicago: University of Chicago Press.

Huff, T. 2003. *The Rise of Early Modern Science: Islam, China, and the West*. Cambridge: Cambridge University Press.

Hughes, J.D. 2000. *The Face of the Earth: Environment and World History*. Armonk, NY: M.E. Sharpe.

Hughes, J.D. 2007. *An Environmental History of the World: Humankind's Changing Role in the Community of Life*. 2nd edn. New York: Routledge.

Hughes, S. 1995. *Women in World History*. Armonk, NY: M.E. Sharpe.

Hughes-Warrington, M. 2002. Big history. *Historically Speaking* 4 (2) (Nov.), at http://www.bu.edu/historic/hs/november02.html#hughes-warrington (accessed Feb. 2012); also in *Social Evolution and History* 4 (1) (Spring 2005): 7–21.

Hughes-Warrington, M., ed. 2005. *Palgrave Advances in World Histories*. New York: Palgrave Macmillan.

Hughes-Warrington, M. and I. Tregenza. 2008. State and civilization in Australian New Idealism, 1890–1950. *History of Political Thought* 29 (1): 89–108.

Hugill, P. 1993. *World Trade since 1431: Geography, Technology, and Capitalism*. Baltimore: Johns Hopkins University Press.

Humboldt, A. von. 1845. *Kosmos. Entwurf einer physischen Weltbeschreibung*, vol. 1. Stuttgart: J.G. Cotta'scher Verlag.

Humphreys, M. 1992. *Yellow Fever and the South*. New Brunswick, NJ: Rutgers University Press.

Humphreys, M. 2001. *Malaria: Poverty, Race, and Public Health in the United States*. Baltimore: Johns Hopkins University Press.

Hung, W. 1995. *Monumentality in Early Chinese Art and Architecture*. Stanford: Stanford University Press.

Hunt, L., T.R. Martin, B.G. Smith, B.H. Rosenwein, and R.P.-C. Hsia. 2005. *The Making of the West: Peoples and Cultures*. 2 vols. New York: Bedford/St. Martin's.

Huntington, S.P. 1993. The clash of civilizations? *Foreign Affairs* 72: 22–36.

Huntington, S.P. 1996. *The Clash of Civilizations and the Remaking of World Order*. New York: Simon & Schuster.

Hunwick, J.O., ed. 1999. *Timbuktu and the Songhay Empire: Al-Sa'dī's Ta'rīkh al-Sūdān down to 1613 and Other Contemporary Documents*. Leiden: Brill.

Hyde, F. 1975. *Edwin Cunard and the North Atlantic, 1840–1973: A History of Shipping and Financial Management*. Atlantic Highlands, NJ: Humanities Press.

Hymes, R. 1986. *Statesmen and Gentlemen: The Elite of Fu-chou, Chiang-hsi, in Northern and Southern Sung*. Cambridge: Cambridge University Press.

Hymes, R. 2002. *Way and Byway: Taoism, Local Religion, and Models of Divinity in Sung and Modern China*. Berkeley: University of California Press.

Impey, O. 1977. *Chinoiserie: The Impact of Oriental Styles on Western Art and Decoration*. Oxford: Oxford University Press.

Inalcik, H. 1992. Islamization of Ottoman laws on land and land tax. In C. Fragner and K. Schwarz, eds, *Festgabe an Josef Matuz: Osmanistik, Turkologie, Diplomatik*, pp. 100–116. Berlin: Klaus Schwarz.

Ingold, T. 1986. *The Appropriation of Nature: Essays on Human Ecology and Social Relations*. Manchester: Manchester University Press.

Inikori, J.E. 2002. *Africans and the Industrial Revolution in England*. Cambridge: Cambridge University Press.

Insoll, T. 2004. *Archaeology, Ritual, Religion*. New York: Routledge.

Iriye, A. and P.-Y. Saunier, eds. 2009. *The Palgrave Dictionary of Transnational History*. Basingstoke: Palgrave Macmillan.

Islamoğlu, H. and C. Keyder. 1977. Agenda for Ottoman history. *Review* (Journal of the F. Braudel Center) 1 (1): 37–55.

Islamoğlu, H. and P. Perdue. 2009. Introduction. In H. Islamoğlu and P. Perdue, eds, *Shared Histories of Modernity: China, India and the Ottoman Empire*, pp. 1–20. London: Routledge.

James, C.L.R. 1938. *Black Jacobins*. London: Secker & Warburg.

James, H. 2001. *The End of Globalization: Lessons from the Great Depression*. Cambridge, MA: Harvard University Press.

James, J.D. 2010. *McDonaldisation, Masala McGospel and Om Economics: Televangelism in Contemporary India*. New Delhi: Sage.

Jameson, F. and M. Miyoshi, eds. 1998. *The Cultures of Globalization*. Durham: Duke University Press.

Jantsch, E. 1980. *The Self-Organizing Universe: Scientific and Human Implications of the Emerging Paradigm of Evolution*. Oxford: Pergamon.

Jardine, L. 1996. *Worldly Goods: A New History of the Renaissance*. New York: Doubleday.

Jastrow, R. 1967. *Red Giants and White Dwarfs: The Evolution of Stars, Planets and Life*. New York: Harper & Row.

Jastrow, R. 1977. *Until the Sun Dies*. New York: W.W. Norton.

Jenkins, K. and A. Munslow. 2004. *The Nature of History Reader*. New York: Routledge.

Johanssen, B. 1999. *Contingency in Sacred Law: Legal and Ethical Norms in the Muslim Fiqh*. Leiden: Brill.

Johnson, T. 1996. Holy fabrications: The catacomb saints and the Counter-Reformation in Bavaria. *Journal of Ecclesiastical History* 47 (2): 274–297.

Jolly, P. 1966. Symbiotic interaction between black farming communities and the south-eastern San. *Current Anthropology* 37: 277–305.

Jones, C. 2007. *Engendering Whiteness: White Women and Colonialism in Barbados and North Carolina, 1627–1865*. Manchester: Manchester University Press.

Jones, D. 2004. *Rationalizing Epidemics: Meanings and Uses of American Indian Mortality since 1600*. Cambridge, MA: Harvard University Press.

Jones, E. 1981. *The European Miracle: Environments, Economies, and Geopolitics in the History of Europe and Asia*. Cambridge: Cambridge University Press.

Jones, E. 1993. *Coming Full Circle: An Economic History of the Pacific Rim*. Boulder: Westview.

Jones, W. 1807. *The Works of William Jones*, ed. A.M. Jones. 13 vols. London: John Stockdale & John Walker.

Joseph, G.G. 2000. *The Crest of the Peacock: Non-European Roots of Mathematics*. 2nd edn. London: Penguin.

Kaelbe, H. and J. Schriewer, eds. 2003. *Vergleich und Transfer. Komparatistik in den Sozial- und Geschichts- und Kulturwissenschaften*, pp. 469–493. Frankfurt am Main: Campus.

Kamen, H. 2003. *Empire*. New York: HarperCollins.

Kane, D. and J.M. Park. 2009. The puzzle of Korean Christianity: Geopolitical networks and religious conversion in early twentieth-century East Asia. *American Journal of Sociology* 115 (2): 365–404.

Kang, S. 1997. *Orientalism No Kanatae* [Beyond Orientalism], trans. S.M. Lim. Seoul: Isan.

Kant, I. 1963. Idea for a universal history from a cosmopolitan point of view. In I. Kant, *On History*, trans L.W. Beck, pp. 11–26. Indianapolis: Bobbs Merrill.

Kasaba, R. 1988. *Ottoman Empire and the World Economy in the Nineteenth Century*. Albany: State University of New York Press.

Kasaba, R. 2009. *A Moveable Empire: Ottoman Nomads, Migrants and Refugees*. Seattle: University of Washington Press.

Kasianov, G. and P. Ther, eds. 2009. *A Laboratory of Transnational History: Ukraine and Recent Ukrainian Historiography*. Budapest: Central European University Press.

Katzenstein, P. 2005. *A World of Regions: Asia and Europe in the American Imperium*. Ithaca, NY: Cornell University Press.

Kaufman, S.K. 2005. *Consuming Visions: Mass Culture and the Lourdes Shrine*. Ithaca, NY: Cornell University Press.

Kayali, H. 1997. *Arabs and Young Turks*. Berkeley: University of California Press.

Keck, M.E. and K. Sikkink. 1998. *Activists beyond Borders: Advocacy Networks in International Politics*. Ithaca, NY: Cornell University Press.

Keegan, J. 1993. *A History of Warfare*. New York: Knopf.

Keeley, L. 1996. *War before Civilization*. Oxford: Oxford University Press.

Keightley, D. 1978. *The Late Shang State: When, Where, and What*. Berkeley: University of California Press.

Kelly, J. 2005. *The Great Mortality: An Intimate History of the Black Death*. New York: HarperCollins.

Kelly, J. and M. Kaplan. 2001. *Represented Communities*. Chicago: University of Chicago Press.

Kelting, M.W. 2001. *Singing to the Jinas: Jain Laywomen, Mandal Singing, and the Negotiations of Jain Devotion*. New York: Oxford University Press.

Kelton, P. 2007. *Epidemics and Enslavement: Biological Catastrophe in the Native Southeast, 1492 to 1715*. Lincoln: University of Nebraska Press.

Kennedy, K.A.R. 1984. A reassessment of the theories of racial origins of the people of the Indus Valley civilization from recent anthropological data. In K.A.R. Kennedy and G.L. Possehl, eds, *Studies in the Archaeology and Palaeoanthropology of South Asia*, pp. 97–119. New Delhi: Oxford & IBH.

Kennedy, P. 1987. *The Rise and Fall of the Great Powers: Economic Change and Military Conflict from 1500 to 2000*. New York: Random House.

Keyes, C.F. 2007. Monks, guns, and peace: Theravada Buddhism and political violence. In J.K Wellman, ed., *Belief and Bloodshed: Religion and Violence across Time and Tradition*, pp. 145–164. Lanham: Rowman & Littlefield.

Kicza, J. 2003. *Resilient Cultures: America's Native Peoples Confront European Colonizaton, 1500–1800*. Upper Saddle River, NJ: Prentice Hall.

Kiernan, B. 2007. *Blood and Soil: A World History of Genocide and Extermination from Sparta to Darfur*. New Haven: Yale University Press.

Kinkela, D. and N. Maher, eds. 2010. *Transnational Environments: Rethinking the Political Economy of Nature in a Global Age*. Special issue, *Radical History Review* 107.

Kiple, K. ed. 1993. *The Cambridge World History of Human Disease*. Cambridge: Cambridge University Press.

Kippenberg, H.G. 2002. *Discovering Religious History in the Modern Age*, trans. B. Harshav. Princeton: Princeton University Press.

Kirshenblatt-Gimblett, B. 1998. *Destination Culture*. Berkeley: University of California Press.

Klein, H.S. 1986. *African Slavery in Latin America and the Caribbean*. Oxford: Oxford University Press.

Kohl, P. 1978. The balance of trade in Southwestern Asia in the mid-third millennium BC. *Current Anthropology* 19 (3): 463–492.

Kohl, P. 1989. The use and abuse of world systems theory. In C.C. Lamberg-Karlovsky, ed., *Archaeological Thought in America*, pp. 218–240. Cambridge: Cambridge University Press.

Kolchin, P. 1987. *Unfree Labor: American Slavery and Russian Serfdom*. Cambridge, MA: Harvard University Press.

Komlosy, A. 2005. Weltzeit – Ortszeit. Zur Periodisierung von Globalgeschichte. In M. Grandner, D. Rothermund, and W. Schwenkter, eds, *Globalisierung und Globalgeschichte*, pp. 83–114. Vienna: Mandelbaum.

Kondo, K. 2007. The studies of Western history in Japan and the understanding of modernity. In *Proceedings of the Conference on Commemorating the Fiftieth Anniversary of the Korean Society for Western History*, Seoul National University, July 5–6.

Koprulu, M.F. 1988. *Osmanli Devletinin Kurulusu* [Foundation of the Ottoman state]. Ankara: TTK.

Koschmann, J.V. 1998. Introduction. In Y. Yamanouchi, J.V. Koschmann, and R. Narita, eds, *Total War and "Modernization,"* pp. xi–xvi. Ithaca, NY: Cornell University Press.

Koskenniemi, M. 2002. *The Gentle Civilizer of Nations: The Rise and Fall of International Law, 1870–1960*. Cambridge: Cambridge University Press.

Kotkin, S. 2007. Mongol Commonwealth? *Kritika* 8 (3): 487–531.

Kratz, C.A. 2002. *The Ones That Are Wanted: Communication and the Politics of Representation in a Photographic Exhibition*. Berkeley: University of California Press.

Kratz, C.A. and I. Karp. 2006. Introduction. In I. Karp, C.A. Kratz, L. Szwaja, and T. Ybarra-Frausto, eds, *Museum Frictions: Global Transformations/Public Cultures*, pp. 1–31. Durham: Duke University Press.

Kraut, A. 1994. *Silent Travelers: Germs, Genes, and the "Immigrant Menace."* New York: Basic Books.

Krylova, A. 2010. *Soviet Women in Combat: A History of Violence on the Eastern Front*. Cambridge: Cambridge University Press.

Kudlick, C.J. 1996. *Cholera in Revolutionary Paris: A Cultural History*. Berkeley: University of California Press.

Kuhn, T. 1962. *The Structure of Scientific Revolutions*. Chicago: University of Chicago Press.

Kunitz, S. 1983. *Disease Change and the Role of Medicine: The Navajo Experience*. Berkeley: University of California Press.

Kurtz, M. 2002. Re/Membering the town body: Methodology and the work of local history. *Journal of Historical Geography* 28 (1): 42–62.

Kutter, G.S. 1987. *The Universe and Life: Origins and Evolution*. Boston: Jones & Bartlett.

LaBianca, Ø.S. and S.A. Scham, eds. 2006. *Connectivity in Antiquity: Globalization as a Long-Term Historical Process*. London: Equinox.

Lach, D.F. 1965–1999. *Asia in the Making of Europe*. 3 vols. Chicago: University of Chicago Press.

Laczko, L.S. 2000. Canada's linguistic and ethnic dynamics in an evolving world-system. In T.D. Hall, ed., *A World-Systems Reader: New Perspectives on Gender, Urbanism, Cultures, Indigenous Peoples, and Ecology*, pp. 131–142. Lanham: Rowman & Littlefield.

Lake, M. and H. Reynolds. 2008. *Drawing the Global Colour Line: White Men's Countries and the International Challenge of Racial Equality*. Cambridge: Cambridge University Press.

Lal, R. 2005. *Domesticity and Power in the Early Mughal World*. Cambridge: Cambridge University Press.

Lal, V. 1999. Gandhi, the civilizational crucible, and the future of dissent. *Futures* 31: 205–219.

Lal, V. 2003. Provincializing the West: World history from the perspective of Indian history. In B. Stuchtey and E. Fuchs, eds, *Writing World History 1800–2000*, pp. 271–289. Oxford: Oxford University Press.

Lal, V. 2005. Much ado about something: The new malaise of world history. *Radical History Review* 91 (Winter): 124–130.

Lalu, P. 2008. When was South African history ever postcolonial? *Kronos: Southern African Histories* 32: 267–281.

Lalu, P. 2009. The *Deaths of Hintsa: Postapartheid South Africa and the Shape of Recurring Pasts*. Cape Town: HSRC Press.

Landes, D.S. 1998. *The Wealth and Poverty of Nations: Why Some Are So Rich and Some So Poor*. New York: W.W. Norton.

Lang, J. 1975. *Commerce and Conquest: Spain and England in the Americas*. New York: Academic Press.

Langer, E. 2004. Introduction: Placing Latin America in world history. *Hispanic American Historical Review* 84 (3) (July 30): 393–398.

Larsen, M.T. 1976. *The Old Assyrian City-State and Its Colonies*. Copenhagen: Akademisk Forlag.

Laruelle, M. 2005. La triangulaire "Russie", "exil russe", "culture d'accueil". Le prisme occidental inassumé de l'eurasisme. In *Les Premières Rencontres de l'Institut européen Est-Ouest*, pp. 197–217. Lyon: European Institute of East–West Relations, at http://russie-europe.ens-lyon.fr/IMG/pdf/communications.pdf (accessed May 2012).

Lee, P.J. 2005. Putting principles into practice: Understanding history. In J. Bransford and S. Donovan, eds, *How Students Learn History in the Classroom*, pp. 31–77. Washington DC: National Academy of Sciences.

Lee, P.J. and R. Ashby. 2000. Progression in historical understanding among students ages 7–14. In P. Stearns, P. Seixas, and S. Wineburg, eds, *Knowing, Teaching, and Learning History*, pp. 199–222. New York: New York University Press.

Lee, S. 2004. Shokuminchi bunka seisaku no kachi wo tsuujite mita rekishi ninsiki [The value of colonial cultural production seen through historical awareness]. Paper presented to Kyoto Forum of Public Philosophy, Mar. 13.

Lefebvre, H. 1974. *La Production de l'espace*. Paris: Anthropos.

Leinhardt, G., C. Stainton, S.M. Virji, and E. Odoroff. 1994. Learning to reason in history: Mindlessness to mindfulness. In M. Carretero and J.F. Voss, eds, *Cognitive and Instructional Processes in History and the Social Sciences*, pp. 131–158. Hillsdale, NJ: Lawrence Erlbaum.

Lekson, S. 2009. *A History of the American Southwest*. Santa Fe: SAR Press.

Lenin, V.I. 1952. *The State and Revolution*. In V.I. Lenin, *Selected Works*, vol. 2, part 1. Moscow: Foreign Languages Publishing House. First published in 1918.

Lenin, V.I. 1963. *Imperialism, the Highest Stage of Capitalism*. In V.I. Lenin, *Selected Works*, vol. 1, pp. 667–766. Moscow: Foreign Languages Publishing House. First published in 1917.

Leonard, T., ed. 2006. *Encyclopedia of the Developing World*. New York: Routledge.

Leopold, A.M. and J.S. Jensen, eds. 2004. *Syncretism in Religion: A Reader*. London: Equinox.

Lepenies, W., ed. 2003. *Entangled Histories and Negotiated Universals: Centers and Peripheries in a Changing World*. Frankfurt: Campus.

Lesch, H. and H. Zaun. 2008. *Die kürzeste Geschichte allen Lebens. Eine Reportage über 13,7 Milliarden Jahre Werden und Vergehen*. Munich: Piper.

Lester, A. 2001. *Imperial Networks*. London: Routledge.

Levathes, L. 1997. *When China Ruled the Seas: The Treasure Fleet of the Dragon Throne, 1405–1433*. Oxford: Oxford University Press.

Levi, S.C. 2002. *The Indian Diaspora in Central Asia and its Trade, 1550–1900*. Leiden: Brill.

Levine, D. 2000. *At the Dawn of Modernity: Biology, Culture, and Material Life in Europe after the Year 1000*. Berkeley: University of California Press.

Levine, L.W. 1996. *The Opening of the American Mind: Canons, Culture, and History*. Boston: Beacon.

Levine, L.W. 2000. Looking eastward: The career of Western Civ. In R.E. Dunn, ed., *The New World History*, pp. 18–25. Boston: Bedford/St. Martin's.

Lévi-Strauss, C. 1963. *Totemism*, trans. R. Needham. Boston: Beacon. First published as *Le Totémisme aujourd'hui*, 1962.

Levstik, L.S. 2001. Crossing the empty spaces: Perspective taking in New Zealand. Adolescents' understanding of national history. In O.L. Davis, Jr, E.A. Yeager, and S. Foster, eds, *Historical Empathy and Perspective-Taking in the Social Studies*, pp. 69–96. Lanham: Rowman & Littlefield.

Lewis, B. 1982. *The Muslim Discovery of Europe*. New York: W.W. Norton.

Lewis, D. 1972. The Gospel according to St Andrew. *Journal of Pacific History* 7: 223–225.

Lewis, D. 1972. *We, the Navigators: The Ancient Art of Landfinding in the Pacific*. Honolulu: University of Hawai'i Press.

Lewis, D.L. 2008. *God's Crucible: Islam and the Making of Europe, 570 to 1215*. New York: W.W. Norton.

Lewis, M.E. 1992. *Sanctioned Violence in Early China*. Albany: State University of New York Press.

Lewis, M.W. and K.E. Wigen. 1997. *The Myth of Continents: A Critique of Metageography*. Berkeley: University of California Press.

Lidchi, H. 1997. The poetics and politics of exhibiting other cultures. In S. Hall, ed., *Representation: Cultural Representations and Signifying Practices*, pp. 151–222. London: Sage.

Lieberman, V. 2003. *Strange Parallels: Southeast Asia in Global Context, c. 800–1830*, vol. 1: *Integration on the Mainland*. Cambridge: Cambridge University Press.

Lieberman, V. 2009. *Strange Parallels: Southeast Asia in Global Context, c. 800–1830*, vol. 2: *Mainland Mirrors: Europe, Japan, China, South Asia, and the Islands*. Cambridge: Cambridge University Press.

Liebersohn, H. 1988. *Aristocratic Encounters: European Travelers and North American Indians*. Cambridge: Cambridge University Press.

Lieven, D. 2000. *Empire*. London: John Murray.

Lim, J. 1990. Hankook sŏyangsahakui bansunggwa jŏnmang [Reflections and prospects of Western history in Korea]. *Yŏksabipyung* 8: 99–122.

Lim, J. 2001. Befreiung oder Modernisierung? Sozialismus als ein Weg der anti-westlichen Modernisierung in unterentwickelten Ländern [Liberation or modernization? Socialism as a means of anti-Western modernization in underdeveloped countries]. *Beiträge zur Geschichte der Arbeiterbewegung* 43 (2): 5–23.

Lim, J. 2008. The configuration of Orient and Occident in the global chain of national histories: Writing national histories in Northeast Asia. In S. Berger, L. Eriksonas, and A. Mycock, eds, *Narrating the Nation: Representations in History, Media and the Arts*, pp. 290–308. New York: Berghahn.

Lim, J. 2010. A postcolonial reading of *Sonderweg*: Marxist and modernist historicism revisited. Paper presented to conference on Postcolonial Reading of *Sonderweg*, Research Institute of Comparative History and Culture, Hanyang University, Seoul, Dec. 3–4.

Lim, J. and K. Petrone, eds. 2011. *Gender Politics and Mass Dictatorship: Global Perspectives*. Basingstoke: Palgrave Macmillan.

Lindenfeld, D. 2007. The concept of "world religions" as currently used in religious studies textbooks. *World History Bulletin* 23 (1): 6–7.

Liu, L. 2009. State emergence in early China. *Annual Review in Anthropology* 38: 217–232.

Liu, X. 2011: Cong Yalian Ren dao Ouya Youmu Minzu, Tansuo Yinouyuxi de Qiyuan [From "Aryan" to Eurasian Nomadic: Exploration of the origin of Indo-European languages]. *Lishi Yanjiu* [Studies of History] (Beijing) 6: 156–167.

Liu, X. and L.N. Shaffer. 2007. *Connections across Eurasia: Transportation, Communication, and Cultural Exchange on the Silk Roads*. New York: McGraw-Hill.

Liverani, M. 2006. *Uruk: The First City*, trans. Z. Bahrani and M. Van De Mieroop. London: Equinox. First published in 1998.

Lloyd, G. and N. Sivin. 2002. *The Way and the Word: Science and Medicine in Early China and Greece*. New Haven: Yale University Press.

Lockard, C.A. n.d. The rise of world history scholarship. MS, rev. and expanded from chapter in K. Boyd, ed., *Encyclopedia of Historians and Historical Writing*, pp. 130–135. London: Fitzroy Dearborn, 1999.

López, A.R. and B. Weinstein. 2012. *The Making of the Middle Class: Toward a Transnational History*. Durham: Duke University Press.

Lorge, P.A. 2005. *War, Politics and Society in Early Modern China, 900–1795*. London: Routledge.

Love, J. 2010. Latin America, UNCTAD, and the postwar trading system. In H.S. Esfahani, G.J.D. Hewings, and G. Facchini, eds, *Economic Development in Latin America*, pp. 22–33. New York: Palgrave Macmillan. First published in 2001.

Lucassen, J. and L. Lucassen. 2009. The mobility transition revisited, 1500–1900: What the case of Europe can offer to global history. *Journal of Global History* 4 (3): 347–377.

Lucassen, J., L. Lucassen, and P. Manning, eds. 2010. *Migration History in World History: Multidisciplinary Approaches*. Leiden: Brill.

Ludlow, P. 2007. Making the new Europe: European integration since 1950. In G. Martel, ed., *A Companion to International History 1900–2001*, pp. 327–339. Oxford: Blackwell.

Lundestad, G. 1998. *Empire by Invitation: The United States and European Integration, 1945–1997*. Oxford: Oxford University Press.

Lynn, J. 2003. *Battle: A History of Combat and Culture*. Boulder: Westview.

Lynn, J. 2008. *Women, Armies, and Warfare in Early Modern Europe*. Cambridge: Cambridge University Press.

Lyotard, J.-F. 1984. *The Postmodern Condition: A Report on Knowledge*, trans. G. Bennington and B. Massumi. Minneapolis: University of Minnesota Press.

Macaulay, T.B. 1849. State of England in 1685. In T.B. Macaulay, *History of England*, vol. 1, ch. 3. Leipzig: Bernhard Tauchnitz.

MacCormack, S. 1990. *Children of the Sun and Reason of State: Myths, Ceremonies and Conflicts in Inca Peru*. Baltimore: University of Maryland at College Park.

MacCormack, S. 1991. *Religion in the Andes: Vision and Imagination in Early Colonial Peru*. Princeton: Princeton University Press.

Macpherson, C. and L.A. Macpherson. 2009. *The Warm Winds of Change: Globalisation in Contemporary Samoa*. Auckland: Auckland University Press.

Maier, C.S. 1997. Territorialisten und Globalisten. Die beiden neuen "Parteien" in der heutigen Demokratie. *Transit* 14: 5–14.

Maier, C.S. 2000. Consigning the twentieth century to history: Alternative narratives for the modern era. *American Historical Review* 103 (3): 807–831.

Maier, C.S. 2006. *Among Empires*. Cambridge, MA: Harvard University Press.

Maier, C.S. 2006. Transformations of territoriality, 1600–2000. In G. Budde, S. Conrad, and O. Janz, eds, *Transnationale Geschichte: Themen, Tendenzen und Theorien*, pp. 32–55. Göttingen: Vandenhoeck & Ruprecht.

Mair, V. 1995. Prehistoric Caucasoid corpses of the Tarim Basin. *Journal of Indo-European Studies* 23 (3 and 4): 281–307.

Mair, V., ed. 2006. *Contact and Exchange in the Ancient World*. Honolulu: University of Hawai'i Press.

Mair, V. 2006. The rediscovery and complete excavation of Ördek's necropolis. *Journal of Indo-European Studies* 34 (3 and 4): 274–318.

Malacrino, C.G. 2010. *Constructing the Ancient World: Architectural Techniques of the Greeks and Romans*. Los Angeles: Getty Museum.

Mallory, J.P. 2002. Archaeological models and Asian Indo-Europeans. In Nicholas Sims-Williams, ed., *Indo-Iranian Languages and Peoples*, pp. 19–42. Oxford: Oxford University Press for the British Academy.

Mallory, J.P. and D.Q. Adams. 2006. *The Oxford Introduction to Proto-Indo-European and the Proto-Indo-European World*. Oxford: Oxford University Press.

Mallory, J.P. and V. Mair. 2000. *The Tarim Mummies: Ancient China and the Mystery of the Earliest Peoples from the West*. London: Thames & Hudson.

Manela, E. 2007. *The Wilsonian Moment: Self-Determination and the International Origins of Anticolonial Nationalism*. Oxford: Oxford University Press.

Mani, L. 1987. Contentious traditions. *Cultural Critique* 7: 119–156.

Mann, C.C. 2006. *1491: New Revelations of the Americas before Columbus.* New York: Vintage.

Mann, M. and K. Naumann. 2010. 1989 in a global perspective. Report of conference, Leipzig, Oct. 14–16, 2009. *Comparativ* 20 (3): 105–116.

Manning, P. 1996. The problem of interactions in world history. *American Historical Review* 101 (3): 771–782.

Manning, P. 2003. *Navigating World History: Historians Create a Global Past.* New York: Palgrave Macmillan.

Manning, P. 2005. *Migration in World History.* London: Routledge.

Manning, P., ed. 2007. *Global Practice in World History: Advances Worldwide.* Princeton: Markus Weiner.

Manning, P. 2007. Nordamerikanische Ansätze zur Globalgeschichte. In B. Schäbler, ed. *Area Studies und die Welt. Weltregionen und neue Globalgeschichte*, pp. 59–89. Vienna: Mandelbaum.

Manning, P. 2009. *The African Diaspora: A History through Culture.* New York: Columbia University Press.

Mannion, A.M. 1995. *Agriculture and Environmental Change.* Chichester: John Wiley.

Mao L. *et al.*, eds. 1991. *Zhong xi wu bai nian bi jiao* [China/West comparative studies in the last 500 years]. Beijing: Chinese Workers' Publishing House.

Maracas, M. 2006. Transcript of the World History Research Agenda Symposium. Boston, Nov. 11–12, 2006. At http://www.worldhistorynetwork.org/conference/Transcript_Symposium.pdf (accessed Aug. 13, 2010).

Marcus, G. 1995. Ethnography in/of the world system: The emergence of multi-sited ethnography. *Annual Review of Anthropology* 24: 95–117.

Mardin, E. 1946. *Medeni Hukuk Cephesinden Ahmet Cevdet Paşa (1822–1895)* [Ahmet Cevdet Pasa and civil law (1822–1895)]. Istanbul: Istanbul University Press.

Marino, M. and J. Bolgatz. 2010. Weaving a fabric in world history? An analysis of US state high school world history standards. *Theory and Research in Social Education* 38 (3): 366–394.

Markel, H. 2004. *When Germs Travel: Six Major Epidemics That Have Invaded America since 1900 and the Fears They Have Unleashed.* New York: Pantheon.

Markley, J. 2009. "A child said, 'What is the grass?'" Reflections on the big history of the Poaceae. *World History Connected* 6 (3), at http://worldhistoryconnected.press.illinois.edu/6.3/markley.html (accessed Mar. 11, 2010).

Marks, R.B. 2007. *The Origins of the Modern World: A Global and Ecological Narrative from the Fifteenth to the Twenty-First Century.* 2nd edn. New York: Rowman & Littlefield.

Marks, S., ed. 1998. *Not Either an Experimental Doll: The Separate Worlds of Three South African Women.* Bloomington: Indiana University Press.

Marks, S.G. 1991. *Road to Power: The Trans-Siberian Railroad and the Colonization of Asian Russia, 1850–1917.* Ithaca, NY: Cornell University Press.

Marlin-Bennett, R., ed. 2011. *Alker and IR: Global Studies in an Interconnected World.* London: Routledge.

Marriott, B. Forthcoming. Religious community and cross-religious communication beyond the Atlantic world: The lost tribes in the Americas and Mecca. In J. Corrigan, ed., *Religion and Space in the Atlantic World.* Bloomington: Indiana University Press.

Marris, E. 2010. UN body will assess ecosystems and biodiversity. *Nature* 465: 859.

Martel, G., ed. 2012. *The Encyclopedia of War.* Oxford: Wiley-Blackwell.

Martin, E.L. 2005. World history as a way of thinking. *World History Connected* (May), at http://worldhistoryconnected.press.uiuc.edu/2.2/martin.html (accessed Apr. 9, 2008).

Massarella, D. 1990. *A World Elsewhere: Europe's Encounter with Japan in the Sixteenth and Seventeenth Centuries.* New Haven: Yale University Press.

Massarella, D. 2008. Revisiting Japan's "Christian century." *Casahistoria* (Jan.), at http://www.casahistoria.net/japanchristaincentury.pdf (accessed May 27, 2012).

Massey, D. 1995. Places and their pasts. *History Workshop Journal* 39: 182–192.

Matory, J.L. 1999. The English professors of Brazil: On the diasporic roots of the Yorùbá nation. *Comparative Studies in Society and History* 41 (1): 72–103.

Matossian, M. 1997. *Shaping World History: Breakthroughs in Ecology, Technology, Science, and Politics*. Armonk, NY: M.E. Sharpe.

Maul, D. 2007. *Menschenrechte, Sozialpolitik und Dekolonisation. Die Internationale Arbeitsorganisation (IAO) 1940–1970*. Essen: Klartext.

Maurel, C. 2009. La world/global history. Questions et débats. *Vingtième Siècle* 104 (Oct.–Dec.): 153–166.

Mazlish, B. 1993. *Conceptualizing Global History*. Boulder: Westview.

Mazlish, B. 1998. Comparing global history to world history. *Journal of Interdisciplinary History* 28 (3): 385–395.

Mazlish, B. 2004. *Civilization and Its Contents*. Stanford: Stanford University Press.

Mazlish, B. 2005. *The Global History Reader*. London: Routledge.

Mazlish, B. 2006. *The New Global History*. New York: Routledge.

Mazlish, B. 2009. *The Idea of Humanity in a Global Era*. Basingstoke: Palgrave Macmillan.

Mazlish, B. n.d.. The new global history. At www.newglobalhistory.com/docs/mazlich-the-new-global-history.pdf (accessed May 1, 2011).

Mazlish, B. and R. Buultjens, eds. 1993. *Conceptualizing Global History*. Boulder: Westview.

Mazower, M. 2006. An international civilization? Empire, internationalism, and the crisis of the mid-twentieth century. *International Affairs* 82 (3): 553–556.

Mbembe, A. 1988. *Afriques indociles. Christianisme, pouvoir et État en société postcoloniale*. Paris: Karthala.

Mbembe, A. 2000. *De la postcolonie. Essai sur l'imagination politique dans l'Afrique contemporaine*. Paris: Karthala. Trans. as *On the Postcolony*, Berkeley: University of California Press, 2001.

Mbembe, A. 2002. African modes of self-writing. *Public Culture* 14 (1): 239–273.

Mbembe, A. 2002. On the power of the false. *Public Culture* 14 (3): 629–641.

McAnany, P. and T.G. Negrón. 2009. Bellicose rulers and climatological peril? Retrofitting twenty-first century woes on eighth-century Maya society. In P. McAnany and N. Yoffee, eds, *Questioning Collapse: Human Resilience, Ecological Vulnerability, and the Aftermath of Empire*, pp. 142–175. Cambridge: Cambridge University Press.

McAnany, P. and N. Yoffee, eds. 2009. *Questioning Collapse: Human Resilience, Ecological Vulnerability, and the Aftermath of Empire*. Cambridge: Cambridge University Press.

McClellan, J. 1999. *Science and Technology in World History: An Introduction*. Baltimore: Johns Hopkins University Press.

McDonald, F. 1991. Debate: Were the Indians victims? In V. Bernhard, D. Burner, and E. Fox-Genovese, *Firsthand America: A History of the United States*, p. 54. 1st edn, combined. St. James, NY: Brandywine Press.

McGhee, W. 2009. Spirit of Anniston plans for sites on Alabama Civil Rights Trail; Group also wants to create "Alabama Museum of the Southern Small Town." *Anniston Star*, Sept. 4. At http://www.allbusiness.com/trade-development/economic-development-tourism/12826675-1.html (accessed Nov. 7, 2009).

McKeown, A.M. 2007. Periodizing globalization. *History Workshop Journal* 63 (1): 218–230.

McKeown, A.M. 2008. *Melancholy Order: Asian Migration and the Globalization of Borders*. New York: Columbia University Press.

McKeown, A.M. 2010. Chinese emigration in global context, 1850–1940. *Journal of Global History* 5 (1): 95–124.

McMichael, P. 2003. *Development and Social Change: A Global Perspective*. 3rd edn. Thousand Oaks, CA: Pine Forge Press.

McNeill, J.R. 2000. *Something New under the Sun: An Environmental History of the Twentieth-Century World*. New York: W.W. Norton.

McNeill, J.R. 2001. *Environmental History in the Pacific World*. Aldershot: Ashgate.

McNeill, J.R. 2010. *Mosquito Empires: Ecology and War in the Greater Caribbean, 1640–1914.* New York: Cambridge University Press.

McNeill, J.R. and W.H. McNeill. 2003. *The Human Web: A Bird's-Eye View of World History.* New York: W.W. Norton.

McNeill, W.H. 1963. *The Rise of the West: A History of the Human Community.* Chicago: University of Chicago Press.

McNeill, W.H. 1976. *Plagues and Peoples.* Garden City, NY: Anchor Press.

McNeill, W.H. 1982. A defence of world history: The Prothero Lecture. *Transactions of the Royal Historical Society,* Fifth Series 32: 75–89.

McNeill, W.H. 1986. *Polyethnicity and National Unity in World History.* Toronto: University of Toronto Press.

McNeill, W.H. 1990. "The Rise of the West" after twenty-five years. *Journal of World History* 1: 1–21.

McNeill, W.H. 1991. *The Rise of the West: A History of the Human Community; with a Retrospective Essay.* Chicago: University of Chicago Press.

McNeill, W.H. 1997. *A History of the Human Community: Prehistory to the Present.* 5th edn. Upper Saddle River, NJ: Prentice Hall.

Meade, T. and M. Wiesner. 2006. *A Companion to Gender History.* Oxford: Wiley-Blackwell.

Mears, J.A. 1986. Evolutionary process: An organizing principle for general education. *Journal of General Education* 37 (4): 315–325.

Mears, J.A. 2009. Implications of the evolutionary epic for the study of human history. In C. Genet, R. Genet, B. Swimme, L. Palmer, and L. Gibler, eds, *The Evolutionary Epic: Science's Story and Humanity's Response,* pp. 135–146. Santa Margarita, CA: Collins Foundation Press.

Metcalf, T. 2007. *Imperial Connections.* Berkeley: University of California Press.

Métraux, A. 1972. *Voodoo in Haiti.* New York: Schocken.

Mgijima, B. and V. Buthelezi. 2006. Mapping museum: Community relations in Lwandle. *Journal of Southern African Studies* 32 (4): 795–806.

Middell, M. 2000. Kulturtransfer und Historische Komparatistik. Thesen zu ihrem Verhältnis. *Comparativ* 10 (1): 7–41.

Middell, M. 2005. Universalgeschichte, Weltgeschichte, Globalgeschichte, Geschichte der Globalisierung – ein Streit um Worte? In M. Grandner, D. Rothermund, and W. Schwentker, eds, *Globalisierung und Globalgeschichte,* pp. 60–82. Vienna: Mandelbaum.

Middell, M. and K. Naumann. 2010. Global history 2008–2010. Empirische Erträge, konzeptionelle Debatten, neue Synthesen. In M. Middell, ed., *Die Verwandlung der Weltgeschichtsschreibung.* Issue of *Comparativ* 20 (6): 93–133.

Mignolo, W.D. 2000. *Global Histories/Local Designs: Coloniality, Subaltern Knowledges, and Border Thinking.* Princeton: Princeton University Press.

Miller, C.R. 1984. Genre as social action. *Quarterly Journal of Speech* 70: 151–167.

Miller, J. 1976. *Kings and Kinsmen: Early Mbundu States in Angola.* Oxford: Clarendon Press.

Miller, J. 2005. Beyond blacks, bondage and blame: Why a multi-centric World History needs Africa. Draft for a talk at Carleton College, Northfield, MN, Mar. 9.

Minamizuka, S. 2007. How to overcome Euro-centrism in the Western history in Japan: Some lessons from *Bankokushi* in the Meiji era. In *Proceedings of the Conference on Commemorating the Fiftieth Anniversary of the Korean Society for Western History,* Seoul National University, July 5–6.

Minkley, G., C. Rassool, and L. Witz. 2009. South Africa and the spectacle of public pasts: Heritage, public histories and post anti-apartheid South Africa. Paper presented at Heritage Disciplines symposium, University of the Western Cape, Oct. 8–9.

Mintz, S. 1985. *Sweetness and Power: The Place of Sugar in Modern History.* New York: Viking.

Mitchell, T. 1988. *Colonizing Egypt.* Berkeley: University of California Press.

Mitchell, T., ed. 2000. *Questions of Modernity.* Minneapolis: University of Minnesota Press.

Mitchell, T. 2002. *Rule of Experts: Egypt, Techno-politics, Modernity.* Berkeley: University of California Press.

Moore, B., Jr. 1966. *Social Origins of Dictatorship and Democracy: Lord and Peasant in the Making of the Modern World*. Boston: Beacon.

Moore, R.I. 1997. World history. In M. Bentley, ed., *Companion to Historiography*, pp. 941–959. London: Routledge.

Moraes Farias, P.F. de. 2008. Intellectual innovation and reinvention of the Sahel: The seventeenth-century Timbuktu chronicles. In S. Jeppie and S.B. Diagne, eds, *The Meanings of Timbuktu*, pp. 95–108. Cape Town: HSRC Press.

Morena, F. 2009. *Chinoiserie: The Evolution of the Oriental Style in Italy from the 14th to the 19th Century*. Florence: Centro Di.

Moretti, F. 2005. *Graphs, Maps, Trees: Abstract Models for a Literary History*. New York: Verso.

Morgan, D.O. 2007. *The Mongols*. 2nd rev. edn. Oxford: Wiley-Blackwell.

Morgan, J. 2004. *Laboring Women: Reproduction and Gender in New World Slavery*. Philadelphia: University of Pennsylvania Press.

Morillo, S. 1995. Guns and government: A comparative study of Europe and Japan. *Journal of World History* 6: 75–106.

Morillo, S. 2001. *Milites*, knights and samurai: Military terminology, comparative history, and the problem of translation. In R. Abels and B. Bachrach, eds, *The Normans and Their Adversaries at War: Essays in Memory of C. Warren Hollister*, pp. 167–184. Woodbridge, UK: Boydell & Brewer.

Morillo, S. 2002. Battle seeking: The contexts and limits of Vegetian strategy. *Journal of Medieval Military History* 1: 21–41.

Morillo, S. 2006. *What is Military History?* Cambridge: Polity.

Morillo, S. 2007. Mercenaries, mamluks and militia: Towards a cross-cultural typology of military service. In John France, ed., *Medieval Mercenaries*, pp. 243–260. Brill: Leiden.

Morillo, S., J. Black, and P. Lococo. 2009. *War in World History: Society, Technology, and War from Ancient Times to the Present*. New York: McGraw-Hill.

Morris, I. 2010. *Why the West Rules – For Now: The Patterns of History, and What They Reveal about the Future*. New York: Farrar, Straus, & Giroux.

Morris-Suzuki, T. 1994. *The Technological Transformation of Japan: From the Seventeenth to the Twenty-First Century*. Cambridge: Cambridge University Press.

Moses, A.D., ed. 2008. *Empire, Colony, Genocide: Conquest, Occupation, and Subaltern Resistance in World History*. New York: Berghahn.

Mosley, S. 2010. *The Environment in World History*. London: Routledge.

Mudimb, V.Y. 1988. *The Invention of Africa: Gnosis, Philosophy, and the Order of Knowledge*. Bloomington: Indiana University Press.

Müller, M. 1847. On the relation of the Bengali to the Arian and Aboriginal languages of India. *Report of the British Association for the Advancement of Science*, 349: 319–350.

Munn, N. 1996. Excluded spaces. *Critical Inquiry* 22: 446–465.

Munro, D. and B.V. Lal. 2006. *Texts and Contexts: Reflections in Pacific Islands Historiography*. Honolulu: University of Hawai'i Press.

Munslow, A. 2006. *Deconstructing History*. New York: Routledge.

Murray, W. and A. Millett. 2001. *A War To Be Won: Fighting the Second World War*. Cambridge, MA: Harvard University Press.

Nandy, A. 1995. History's forgotten doubles. *History and Theory* 34 (2): 44–66.

Nandy, A. 1998. History's forgotten doubles. In P. Pomper, R. Elphick, and R.T. Vann, eds, *World History: Ideologies, Structures, and Identities*, pp. 159–178. Oxford: Blackwell.

Naro, N.P., R. Sansi-Roca, and D.H. Treece, eds. 2007. *Cultures of the Lusophone Black Atlantic*. New York: Palgrave Macmillan.

Nash, L.L. 2006. *Inescapable Ecologies: A History of Environment, Disease, and Knowledge*. Berkeley: University of California Press.

Nazaretyan, A.P. 2010. *Evolution of Non-Violence: Studies in Big History, Self-Organization and Historical Psychology*. Saarbrücken: Lambert Academic.

Needham, J. *et al.*, gen. eds. 1956–. *Science and Civilisation in China*. Cambridge: Cambridge University Press.

Nehru, J. 1999. *Glimpses of World History: Being Further Letters to His Daughter, Written in Prison, and Containing a Rambling Account of History for Young People*. New Delhi: Jawaharlal Nehru Memorial Fund and Oxford University Press.

Nelson, R.K. 1983. *Make Prayers to the Raven: A Koyukon View of the Northern Forest*. Chicago: University of Chicago Press.

Newell, J. 2010. *Trading Nature: Tahitians, Europeans, and Ecological Exchange*. Honolulu: University of Hawai'i Press.

Ngugi wa Thiong'o. 1993. *Moving the Centre: The Struggle for Cultural Freedoms*. London: Heinemann.

Nissen, H. 1988. *The Early History of the Ancient Near East 9000–2000 BC*. Chicago: University of Chicago Press.

Nkrumah, K. 1965. *Neo-colonialism: The Last Stage of Imperialism*. London: Nelson.

Northrop, D. 2004. *Veiled Empire: Gender and Power in Stalinist Central Asia*. Ithaca, NY: Cornell University Press.

Nozaki, Y. 2008. *War Memory, Nationalism and Education in Postwar Japan, 1945–2007: The Japanese History Textbook Controversy and Ienaga Saburo's Court Challenge*. London: Routledge.

Numbers, R.L. 1997. *Science and Christianity in Pulpit and Pew*. New York: Oxford University Press.

Nurse, D. and T. Spear. 1985. *The Swahili: Reconstructing the History and Language of an African Society, 800–1500*. Philadelphia: University of Pennsylvania Press.

Oberoi, H. 1994. *The Construction of Religious Boundaries: Culture, Identity, and Diversity in the Sikh Tradition*. Chicago: University of Chicago Press.

O'Brien, P. 2006. Historiographical traditions and modern imperatives for the restoration of global history. *Journal of Global History* 1: 3–39.

O'Brien, P. 2008. Review of *Global History: Interactions between the Universal and the Local*. *Reviews in History*, 648, at http://www.history.ac.uk/reviews/review/648 (accessed Sept. 27, 2010).

Offer, A. 1991. *The First World War: An Agrarian Interpretation*. Oxford: Oxford University Press.

Ó Gráda, C. 2009. *Famine: A Short History*. Princeton: Princeton University Press.

Olcott, J., M.K. Vaughan, and G. Cano, eds. 2007. *Sex in Revolution: Gender, Politics, and Power in Modern Mexico*. Durham: Duke University Press.

Olstein, D. 2009. Comparative history: The pivot of historiography. In B.Z. Kedar, ed., *New Ventures in Comparative History*, pp. 37–52. Jerusalem: Magnes Press.

Onians, J. 2008. *Neuroarthistory: From Aristotle and Pliny to Baxandall and Zeki*. New Haven: Yale University Press.

Oppenheim, A.L. 1964. *Ancient Mesopotamia: Portrait of a Dead Civilization*. Chicago: University of Chicago Press.

O'Rourke, K.H. and J.G. Williamson. 2000. *Globalization and History*. Cambridge, MA: MIT Press.

O'Rourke, K. and J.G. Williamson. 2002. When did globalization begin? *European Review of Economic History* 6 (1): 23–50.

Ortner, S. 1989. *High Religion: A Cultural and Political History of Sherpa Buddhism*. Princeton: Princeton University Press.

Osterhammel, J. 2001. *Geschichtswissenschaft jenseits des Nationalstaates. Studien zur Beziehungsgeschichte und Zivilisationsvergleich*. Göttingen: Vandenhoeck & Ruprecht.

Osterhammel, J. 2003. In search of the nineteenth century. *GHI Bulletin* (German Historical Institute, Washington DC) 32 (Spring): 9–32.

Osterhammel, J. 2005. Weltgeschichte. Ein Propädeutikum. *Geschichte in Wissenschaft und Unterricht* 56: 452–479.

Osterhammel, J. 2009. *Die Verwandlung der Welt. Eine Geschichte des 19. Jahrhunderts*. Munich: Beck.

Osterhammel, J. and N. Petersson. 2005. *Globalization: A Short History*. Princeton: Princeton University Press.

Owen, R. 1993. *The Middle East in the World Economy, 1800–1914*. Rev. edn. London: I.B. Tauris.

Owen, S. 1990. What is world poetry? *New Republic* 203 (21): 28–32.

Pacey, A. 1990. *Technology in World Civilization: A Thousand-Year History*. Cambridge, MA: MIT Press.

Packard, R.M. 1989. *White Plague, Black Labor: Tuberculosis and the Political Economy of Health and Disease in South Africa*. Berkeley: University of California Press.

Packard, R.M. 2007. *The Making of a Tropical Disease: A Short History of Malaria*. Baltimore: Johns Hopkins University Press.

Paige, J.M. 1975. *Agrarian Revolution: Social Movements and Export Agriculture in the Underdeveloped World*. New York: Free Press.

Paine, S.C.M., ed. 2010. *Nation Building, State Building, and Economic Development: Case Studies and Comparisons*. New York: M.E. Sharpe.

Palmer, S. 2009. Clinics and hookworm science: Peripheral origins of international health, 1840–1920. *Bulletin of the History of Medicine* 83: 676–709.

Pamuk, S. 2004. Institutional change and the longevity of the Ottoman Empire, 1500–1800. *Journal of Interdisciplinary History* 35 (2): 225–247.

Park, G. 2009. Sikminji Chosŏnesŏ dongyangsahakun ŏttŏke hyungsongdoiŏttna? [How was East Asian history formulated in colonial Chosŏn?]. In D. Myunhoi and Y. Haedong, eds, *Yŏksahakui Segi*, pp. 217–246. Seoul: Humanist.

Parker, G. 1988. *The Military Revolution: Military Innovation and the Rise of the West, 1500–1800*. Cambridge: Cambridge University Press.

Parpola, A. 2002. From the dialects of old Indo-Aryan to Proto-Indo-Aryan and Proto-Iranian. In N. Sims-Williams, ed., *Indo-Iranian Languages and Peoples*, pp. 43–102. Oxford: Oxford University Press for the British Academy.

Patel, K.K. 2005. Transnationale Geschichte – ein neues Paradigma? *geschichte.transnational*, Feb. 2, at http://geschichte-transnational.clio-online.net/forum/id=573&type=artikel (accessed Feb. 2012).

Paul, J.R. 1971. *History of Poliomyelitis*. New Haven: Yale University Press.

Pawley, A. 2010. Prehistoric migration and colonisation processes in Oceania: A view from historical linguistics and archaeology. In J. Lucassen, L. Lucassen, and P. Manning, eds, *Migration History in World History: Multidisciplinary Approaches*, pp. 77–112. Leiden: Brill.

Peard, J.G. 1999. *Race, Place, and Medicine: The Idea of the Tropics in Nineteenth-Century Brazilian Medicine*. Durham: Duke University Press.

Pearson, M.N. 1996. *Pilgrimage to Mecca: The Indian Experience, 1500–1800*. Princeton: Markus Wiener.

Pédron-Colombani, S. 2004. *Maximon: A Guatemalan Cult*. Berkeley: Periplus.

Perdue, P. 2005. *China Marches West*. Cambridge, MA: Harvard University Press.

Pernau, M. 2007. Transkulturelle Geschichte und das Problem der universalen Begriffe. Muslimische Bürger im Delhi des 19. Jahrhunderts. In B. Schäbler, ed., *Area Studies und die Welt. Weltregionen und neue Globalgeschichte*, pp. 117–150. Vienna: Mandelbaum.

Pernick, M.S. 2002. Contagion and culture. *American Literary History* 14: 858–865.

Pernick, M.S. Forthcoming 2012. Disease and the racial division of labor in America. The 2011 Garrison Lecture of the American Association for the History of Medicine. *Bulletin of the History of Medicine*.

Pierce, L. 2003. *Morality Tales: Law and Gender in the Ottoman Court of Aintab*. Berkeley: University of California Press.

Pius II, Pope. 1952. Modern science and the existence of God. *Catholic Mind* 49: 182–192.

Podobnik, B. 2005. Resistance to globalization: Cycles and trends in the globalization protest movement. In B. Podobnik and T. Reifer, eds, *Transforming Globalization: Challenges and Opportunities in the Post 9/11 Era*, pp. 51–68. Leiden: Brill.

Poe, M. 2003. *The Russian Moment in World History*. Princeton: Princeton University Press.

Poirine, B. 1998. Should we hate or love MIRAB? *Contemporary Pacific* 10: 65–105.

Pollock, S. 1993. Deep Orientalism? In C. Breckenridge and P. van der Veer, eds, *Orientalism and Postcolonial Predicament*, pp. 76–113. Philadelphia: University of Pennsylvania Press.

Pollock, S. 1999. *Ancient Mesopotamia: The Eden That Never Was*. Cambridge: Cambridge University Press.

Pollock, S. 2005. Axialism and empire. In J. Arnason, S. Eisenstadt, and B. Wittrock, eds, *Axial Civilizations and World History*, pp. 397–450. Leiden: Brill.

Pollock, S. 2006. *The Language of the Gods in the World of Men: Sanskrit, Culture, and Power in Premodern India*. Berkeley: University of California Press.

Pomeranz, K. 1993. *The Making of a Hinterland: State, Society, and Economy in Inland North China, 1853–1937*. Berkeley: University of California Press.

Pomeranz, K. 2000. *The Great Divergence: China, Europe, and the Making of the Modern World Economy*. Princeton: Princeton University Press.

Pomeranz, K. 2000. Re-thinking the late imperial Chinese economy: Development, disaggregation, and decline, 1730–1930. *Itinerario* 2 (3–4): 29–75.

Pomeranz, K. 2007. Social history and world history: From daily life to patterns of change. *Journal of World History* 18 (1): 69–98.

Pomeranz, K. and S. Topik. 1999. *The World That Trade Created: Society, Culture, and the World Economy, 1400 to the Present*. Armonk, NY: M.E. Sharpe.

Porter, B. 2004. *The Absent-Minded Imperialists*. Oxford: Oxford University Press.

Porter, R. and J. Brewer, eds. 1994. *Consumption and the World of Goods*. London: Routledge.

Potts, D.T. 1997. *Mesopotamian Civilization: The Material Foundations*. London: Equinox.

Potts, D.T. 2007 Babylonian sources of exotic raw materials. In G. Leick, ed., *The Babylonian World*, pp. 124–140. London: Routledge.

Pouwels, R. 1987. *Horn and Crescent: Cultural Change and Traditional Islam on the East African Coast, 800–1900*. Cambridge: Cambridge University Press.

Prange, S.R. 2009. Like banners on the sea: Muslim trade networks and Islamization in Malabar and maritime Southeast Asia. In R.M. Feener and T. Sevea, eds, *Islamic Connections: Muslim Societies in South and Southeast Asia*, pp. 25–47. Singapore: Institute of Southeast Asian Studies.

Prazniak, R. 2000. Is world history possible? An inquiry. In A. Dirlik, V. Bahl, and P. Gran, eds, *History after the Three Worlds: Post-Eurocentric Historiographies*, pp. 221–240. Lanham: Rowman & Littlefield.

Prebisch, R. 1984. Five stages in my thinking on development. In G.M. Meier and D. Seers, eds, *Pioneers in Development*, pp. 175–191. New York: Oxford University Press.

Prestholdt, J. 2008. *Domesticating the World: African Consumerism and the Genealogies of Globalization*. Berkeley: University of California Press.

Pries, L., ed. 2001. *New Transnational Social Spaces: International Migration and Transnational Companies in the Early Twenty-First Century*. London: Routledge.

Ralston, D. 1990. *Importing the European Army: The Introduction of European Military Techniques and Institutions into the Extra-European World, 1600–1914*. Chicago: University of Chicago Press.

Randeria, S. and A. Eckert, eds. 2009. V*om Imperialismus zum Empire. Nicht-westliche Perspektiven auf Globalisierung*. Frankfurt am Main: Suhrkamp.

Rassool, C. 2006. Community museums, memory politics, and social transformation in South Africa: Histories, possibilities and limits. In I. Karp, C.A. Kratz, L. Szwaja, and T. Ybarra-Frausto, eds, *Museum Frictions: Global Transformations/Public Cultures*, pp. 286–321. Durham: Duke University Press.

Rassool, C. and L. Witz. 1996. "South Africa: a world in one country": Moments in international tourist encounters with wildlife, the primitive and the modern. *Cahiers d'Études Africaines* 143 (36–3): 335–371.

Rath, C. 2005. *How Early America Sounded*. Ithaca, NY: Cornell University Press.

Ratzinger, J. 1995. *"In the Beginning ...": A Catholic Understanding of the Story of Creation and the Fall.* Grand Rapids, MI: Eerdmans.

Reeves, H. 1985. *Atoms of Silence: An Exploration of Cosmic Evolution.* Cambridge, MA: MIT Press. Published in French in 1981.

Reeves, H. 1991. *The Hour of Our Delight: Cosmic Evolution, Order, and Complexity.* New York: W.H. Freeman.

Reeves, H., J. de Rosnay, Y. Coppens, and D. Simonnet. 1998. *Origins: Cosmos, Earth, and Mankind.* New York: Arcade.

Reid, A. 1993. *Southeast Asia in the Age of Commerce, 1450–1680,* vol. 2: *Expansion and Crisis.* New Haven: Yale University Press.

Reindorf, C.C. 1895. *History of the Gold Coast and Asante: Based on Traditions and Historical Facts, Comprising a Period of More Than Three Centuries from about 1500 to 1860.* Basel. At http://www.archive.org/stream/historyofgoldcoa00rein/historyofgoldcoa00rein_djvu.txt (accessed Mar. 2012).

Revel, J. 1996. *Jeux d'échelles. La micro-analyse à l'expérience.* Paris: EHESS.

Revue d'Histoire. 2007. *Histoire globale, histoires connectées.* Suppl. to *Revue d'Histoire Moderne et Contemporaine* 54 (4 bis).

Reynolds, D. 2000. *One World Divisible: A Global History since 1945.* New York: W.W. Norton.

Reynolds, D. 2003. American globalism: Mass, motion and the multiplier effect. In A.G. Hopkins, ed., *Globalization in World History,* pp. 243–260. London: Pimlico.

Reynolds, J. and E. Gilbert. 2005. *Trading Tastes: Commodity and Cultural Exchange to 1750.* Upper Saddle River, NJ: Prentice Hall.

Rich, A. 1991. *An Atlas of the Difficult World.* New York: W.W. Norton.

Richards, J. 2003. *The Unending Frontier: An Environmental History of the Early Modern World.* Berkeley: University of California Press.

Ringrose, D.R. 2001. *Expansion and Global Interactions, 1200–1700.* New York: Addison Wesley Longman.

Robbins, J. 2004. *Becoming Sinners: Christianity and Moral Torment in a Papua New Guinea Society.* Berkeley: University of California Press.

Robertson, R. 1990. Mapping the global condition: Globalization as the central concept. *Theory, Culture, and Society* 7 (2): 15–30.

Robertson, R. 1992. *Globalization: Social Theory and Global Culture.* London: Sage.

Robertson, R. 1995. Glocalization: Time-space and homogeneity-heterogeneity. In M. Featherstone, S. Lash, and R. Robertson, eds, *Global Modernities,* pp. 25–44. London: Sage.

Robinson, D.M. 2009. *Empire's Twilight: Northeast Asia under the Mongols.* Cambridge, MA: Harvard University Press.

Robinson, W.I. 2004. *A Theory of Global Capitalism.* Baltimore: Johns Hopkins University Press.

Rodgers, D. 1998. *Atlantic Crossings: Social Politics in a Progressive Age.* Cambridge, MA: Harvard University Press.

Rodney, W. 1981. *How Europe Underdeveloped Africa.* Rev. edn. Washington DC: Howard University Press.

Rodrigue, B. and D. Stasko. 2009. A big history directory, 2009: An introduction. *World History Connected* 6 (3), at http://worldhistoryconnected.press.illinois.edu/6.3/rodrigue.html (accessed Feb. 2012).

Rogers, S. 2010. America's top ten worst man made environmental disasters. Earthfirst.com, at http://earthfirst.com/americas-top-10-worst-man-made-environmental-disasters/ (accessed Nov. 27, 2010).

Rogoff, I. 2002. Hit and run: Museums and cultural difference. *Art Journal* 61 (3): 63–73.

Rojek, C. and B. Turner, eds. 1998. *The Politics of Jean-François Lyotard: Justice and Political Theory.* London: Routledge.

Rosander, E.E. and D. Westerlund, eds. 1997. *African Islam and Islam in Africa: Encounters between Sufis and Islamists.* Athens: Ohio University Press.

Rosenau, J.N. 1990. *Turbulence in World Politics: A Theory of Change and Continuity*. Princeton: Princeton University Press.

Rosenau, J.N. 2008. *People Count! Networked Individuals in Global Politics*. Boulder: Paradigm.

Rosenberg, C.E. 1962. *The Cholera Years: The United States in 1832, 1849, and 1866*. Chicago: University of Chicago Press.

Ross Múgica, L. 1909. *Más allá del Atlántico* [Beyond the Atlantic]. Valencia: Sempere.

Rothermund, D. 1992. *India in the Great Depression, 1929–1939*. New Delhi: Manohar.

Rothermund, D. 1996. *The Global Impact of the Great Depression, 1929–1939*. London: Routledge.

Rothermund, D. 2000. *The Role of the State in South Asia and Other Essays*. New Delhi: Manohar.

Rothman, B.K. 1998. *Genetic Maps and Human Imaginations: The Limits of Science in Understanding Who We Are*. New York: W.W. Norton.

Rothman, M. 2001. *Uruk Mesopotamia and Its Neighbors: Cross-Cultural Interactions in the Era of State Formation*. Santa Fe: SAR Press.

Ruddiman W.F., Z. Guob, X. Zhoub, H. Wud, and Y. Yu. 2008. Early rice farming and anomalous methane trends. *Quaternary Science Reviews* 27: 1291–1295.

Rudolph, S.H. 1997. Introduction: Religion, states, and transnational civil society. In S.H. Rudolph and J.P. Piscatori, eds, *Transnational Religion and Fading States*, pp. 1–24. Boulder: Westview.

Russell-Wood, A.J.R. 1992. *A World on the Move: The Portuguese in Africa, Asia, and America, 1415–1808*. New York: St. Martin's Press.

Ruthven, M. 2004. *Historical Atlas of Islam*. Cambridge, MA: Harvard University Press.

Saberwal, S. and S. Varma. 2005. *Traditions in Motion: Religion and Society in History*. New Delhi: Oxford University Press.

Sachsenmaier, D. 2001. *Die Aufnahme europäischer Inhalte in die chinesische Kultur durch Zhu Zongyuan (ca. 1616–1660)* [Integration of Western elements into Chinese culture by Zhu Zongyuan (ca. 1616–1660)]. Nettetal: Steyler.

Sachsenmaier, D. 2010. European history and questions of historical space. In W. Eberhard and C. Lübke, eds, *The Plurality of Europe: Identities and Spaces*, pp. 521–535. Leipzig: Leipziger Universitätsverlag.

Sachsenmaier, D. 2011. *Global Perspectives on Global History: Theories and Approaches in a Connected World*. Cambridge: Cambridge University Press.

Sachsenmaier, D., J. Riedel, and S.N. Eisenstadt, eds. 2002. *Reflections on Multiple Modernities: European, Chinese and Other Interpretations*. Leiden: Brill.

Safier, N. 2008. *Measuring the New World: Enlightenment Science and South America*. Chicago: University of Chicago Press.

Sagan, C. 1980. *Cosmos*. New York: Random House.

Sahlins, M. 1991. The return of the event, again. In A. Biersack, ed., *Clio in Oceania*, pp. 37–100. Washington DC: Smithsonian Institution Press.

Sahlins, M. 1992. The economics of develop-man in the Pacific. *Res* 21: 12–25.

Said, E.W. 1978. *Orientalism*. New York: Pantheon.

Said, E.W. 1994. *Culture and Imperialism*. London: Vintage.

Sakai, N. 1997. *Translation and Subjectivity: On "Japan" and Cultural Nationalism*. Minneapolis: University of Minnesota Press.

Salesa, T.D.I. 2003. "Travel-happy" Samoa: Colonialism, Samoan migration and a "Brown Pacific." *New Zealand Journal of History* 37: 171–188.

Salmond, A. 2003. *The Trial of the Cannibal Dog: Captain Cook in the South Seas*. London: Allen Lane.

Samuel, R. 1976. Local history and oral history. *History Workshop Journal* 1: 191–208.

Sanchez, G. 1993. *Becoming Mexican American: Ethnicity, Culture and Identity in Chicano Los Angeles, 1900–1945*. New York: Oxford University Press.

Sanderson, S.K. and A.S. Alderson. 2005. *World Societies: The Evolution of Human Social Life*. Boston: Allyn & Bacon.

Sartre, J.-P. 1963. Preface. In F. Fanon, *The Wretched of the Earth*, pp. 7–34. New York: Grove.

Sassaman, K. 2010. *The Eastern Archaic, Historicized*. Lanham: AltaMira Press.

Sassen, S. 2006. *Territory, Authority, Rights: From Medieval to Global Assemblages*. Princeton: Princeton University Press.

Schaeffer, R. 1997. *Understanding Globalization: The Social Consequences of Political, Economic, and Environmental Change*. Lanham: Rowman & Littlefield.

Schäfer, W. 1993. Global history: Historiographical feasibility and environmental reality. In B. Mazlish and R. Buultjens, eds, *Conceptualizing Global History*, pp. 47–69. Boulder: Westview.

Schäfer, W. 2003. The new global history: Toward a narrative for Pangaea Two. *Erwägen Wissen Ethik* 14 (Apr.): 75–88.

Schaffer, S. 2009. Newton on the beach. *History of Science* 47 (3): 243–276.

Scharfstein, B.-A. 1998. *A Comparative History of World Philosophy: From the Upanishads to Kant*. Albany: State University of New York Press.

Scheper Hughes, J. 2010. *Biography of a Mexican Crucifix: Lived Religion and Local Faith from the Conquest to the Present*. New York: Oxford University Press.

Schiedel, W., ed. 2009. *Rome and China*. Oxford: Oxford University Press.

Schissler, H. and Y.N. Soysal. 2005. *The Nation, Europe, and the World: Textbooks and Curricula in Transition*. Oxford: Berghahn.

Schmid, A. 2002. *Korea between Empires, 1895–1919*. New York: Columbia University Press.

Schmidt, K. 2006. *Sie bauten die ersten Tempel*. Munich: Beck.

Schot, J. 2007. Globalisering en Infrastructuur. *Tijdschrift voor Sociale en Economische Geschiedenis* 4 (3): 107–128.

Schreurer, C. 1995. Regionalism v. universalism. *European Journal of International Law* 6 (1): 477–499.

Schwartz, S.B. 2008. *All Can Be Saved: Religious Tolerance and Salvation in the Iberian Atlantic World*. New Haven: Yale University Press.

Scott, J. 2004. After history? In K. Jenkins and A. Munslow, eds, *The Nature of History Reader*, pp. 259–270. London: Routledge.

Scott, J.C. 1998. *Seeing Like a State: How Certain Schemes to Improve the Human Condition Have Failed*. New Haven: Yale University Press.

Scott, R.J. 2007. Public rights and private commerce: A nineteenth-century Atlantic creole itinerary. *Current Anthropology* 48 (2): 237–256.

Scott, R.J. 2009. Microhistory set in motion: A nineteenth-century Atlantic creole itinerary. In G. Baca, A. Khan, and S. Palmié, eds, *Empirical Futures: Anthropologists and Historians Engage the Work of Sidney W. Mintz*, pp. 84–118. Chapel Hill: University of North Carolina Press.

Seaman, J.T. 2006. *A Citizen of the World: The Life of James Bryce*. London: I.B. Tauris.

Seed, P. 1992. Taking possession and reading texts. *William and Mary Quarterly* 49 (2): 183–209.

Seed, P. 1995. *Ceremonies of Possession in Europe's Conquest of the New World, 1492–1640*. Cambridge: Cambridge University Press.

Seeley, J.R. 1883. *The Expansion of England*. London: Macmillan.

Segal, D. 2000. "Western Civ" and the staging of history in American higher education. *American Historical Review* 105 (3): 770–805.

Seigel, M. 2004. World history's narrative problem. *Hispanic American Historical Review* 84 (3): 431–446.

Seigel, M. 2005. Beyond compare: Comparative method after the transnational turn. *Radical History Review* 91 (Winter): 62–90.

Seigel, M. 2009. *Uneven Encounters: Making Race and Nation in Brazil and the United States*. Durham: Duke University Press.

Seixas, P. 1996. Conceptualizing the growth of historical understanding. In D.R. Olson and N. Torrance, eds, *Handbook of Education and Human Development: New Models of Learning, Teaching and Schooling*, pp. 765–783. Oxford: Blackwell.

Sellars, R.W. 1999. *Preserving Nature in the National Parks: A History.* New Haven: Yale University Press.

Sennett, R. 2002. *The Fall of Public Man.* London: Penguin.

Sensbach, J.F. 2005. *Rebecca's Revival: Creating Black Christianity in the Atlantic World.* Cambridge, MA: Harvard University Press.

Sewell, W.H., Jr. 1967. Marc Bloch and the logic of comparative history. *History and Theory* 6 (2): 208–218.

Sewell, W.H., Jr. 1996. Historical events as transformation of structures: Inventing revolution at the Bastille. *Theory and Society* 25: 841–881.

Shapiro, M.J. and H. Alker, eds. 1995. *Challenging Boundaries: Global Flows, Territorial Identities.* Minneapolis: University of Minnesota Press.

Shapley, H. 1959. *Of Stars and Men: Human Response to an Expanding Universe.* Boston: Beacon.

Shapley, H. 1963. *The View from a Distant Star: Man's Future in the Universe.* New York: Basic Books.

Sharif, T. 2005. Sacred narratives linking Iraqi Shiite women across time and space. In M. Cooke and B.B. Lawrence, eds, *Muslim Networks from Hajj to Hip Hop,* pp. 132–154. Chapel Hill: University of North Carolina Press.

Sharot, S. 2001. *A Comparative Sociology of World Religions: Virtuosos, Priests, and Popular Religion.* New York: New York University Press.

Sharp, A. 1957. *Ancient Voyagers in the Pacific.* Wellington: Polynesian Society.

Shaw, S. and E. Kural-Shaw. 1988. *History of the Ottoman Empire and Modern Turkey,* vol. 2: *1808–1975.* Cambridge: Cambridge University Press.

Shearer, R.R., M. Kigl, K. Keleba, and J. Elapa. 2009. Jared Diamond's factual collapse: New Yorker mag's Papua New Guinea revenge tale untrue, tribal members angry, want justice. At http://www.stinkyjournalism.org/latest-journalism-news-updates-149.php (accessed Oct. 30, 2011).

Shemilt, D. 2000. The Caliph's coin. In P. Stearns, P. Seixas, and S. Wineburg, eds, *Knowing, Teaching, and Learning History: National and International Perspectives,* pp. 83–101. New York: New York University Press.

Shemilt, D. 2009. Drinking an ocean and pissing a cupful: How adolescents make sense of history. In L. Symcox and A. Wilschut, eds, *The Problem of the Canon and the Future of History Teaching,* pp. 141–209. Charlotte, NC: Information Age.

Sherman, D.J. 1995. Objects of memory: History and narrative in French war museums. *French Historical Studies* 19 (1): 49–74.

Sherratt, A. 2000. Envisioning global change: A long-term perspective. In R. Denemark, J. Friedman, B. Gills, and G. Modelski, eds, *World System History: The Social Science of Long-Term Change,* pp. 115–132. New York: Routledge.

Sherratt, A. 2006. The trans-Eurasian exchange: The prehistory of Chinese relations with the West. In V. Mair, ed., *Contact and Exchange in the Ancient World,* pp. 30–61. Honolulu: University of Hawai'i Press.

Shibata, M. *et al.* 2007. *Sekaino rekishi* [World history]. Tokyo: Yamakawashuppan.

Shindell, D.T., G. Faluvegi, D.M. Koch, G.A. Schmidt, N. Unger, and S.E. Bauer. 2009. Improved attribution of climate forcing to emissions. *Science* 326: 716–718.

Silverman, H. and W. Isbell, eds. 2008. *Handbook of South American Archaeology.* New York: Springer.

Simmons, I.G. 2008. *Global Environmental History: 10,000 BC to AD 2000.* Edinburgh: Edinburgh University Press.

Sinha, M. 2006. *Specters of Mother India: The Global Restructuring of an Empire.* Durham: Duke University Press.

Sinitiere, P.L. 2007. Of borders and boundaries: World history, world Christianity, and the pedagogy of religion. *World History Bulletin* 23 (1): 7–13.

Sklair, L. 2002. *Globalization: Capitalism and Its Alternatives.* 3rd edn. Oxford: Oxford University Press.

Skocpol, T. 1979. *States and Social Revolutions: A Comparative Analysis of France, Russia and China.* Cambridge: Cambridge University Press.

Skocpol, T. 1982. Rentier state and Shi'a Islam in the Iranian revolution. *Theory and Society* 11 (3): 265–283.

Skocpol, T. and M. Somers. 1980. The uses of comparative history in macrosocial inquiry. *Comparative Studies in Society and History* 22 (2): 174–197.

Smail, D.L. 2008. *On Deep History and the Brain.* Berkeley: University of California Press.

Smil, V. 1994. *Energy in World History.* Boulder: Westview.

Smith, B. 1960. *European Vision and the South Pacific, 1768–1850: A Study in the History of Art and Ideas.* Oxford: Clarendon Press.

Smith, B. 1995. *The Emergence of Agriculture.* New York: Scientific American Library.

Smith, P. 2010. *Somebody Else's Century: East and West in a Post-modern World.* New York: Pantheon.

Snyder, L. 1984. *Macro-Nationalisms: A History of the Pan-Movements.* Westport, CT: Greenwood.

So, A. 1990. *Social Change and Development: Modernization, Dependency, and World-Systems Theories.* Newbury Park, CA: Sage.

Solberg, C.E. 1987. *The Prairies and the Pampas: Agrarian Policy in Canada and Argentina.* Stanford: Stanford University Press.

Sonn, T. 2010. *Islam: A Brief History.* Oxford: Wiley-Blackwell.

Sosnowska, A. 2004. *Zrozumieć zcofanie. Spory historyków o Europę Wschodnią, 1947–1994* [Understanding backwardness: historians arguing on Eastern Europe, 1947–1994]. Warsaw: Trio.

South Commission. 1990. *The Challenge to the South: The Report of the South Commission.* Oxford: Oxford University Press.

Spears, E. 2009. Memorializing the Freedom Riders. *Southern Spaces*, June 29, at http://www. southernspaces.org/2009/memorializing-freedom-riders (accessed Feb. 2012).

Spengler, O. 1934. *The Decline of the West.* London: G. Allen & Unwin.

Spier, F. 1996. *The Structure of Big History: From the Big Bang until Today.* Amsterdam: Amsterdam University Press.

Spier, F. 2005. How big history works: Energy flows and the rise and demise of complexity. *Social Evolution and History* 4 (1): 87–135.

Spier, F. 2005. The small history of the Big History course at the University of Amsterdam. *World History Connected* 2 (2), at http://worldhistoryconnected.press.uiuc.edu/2.2/spier.html (accessed Feb. 2012).

Spier, F. 2009. Big history: The emergence of an interdisciplinary science? *World History Connected* 6 (3), at http://worldhistoryconnected.press.uiuc.edu/6.3/spier.html (accessed Feb. 2012).

Spier, F. 2010. *Big History and the Future of Humanity.* Oxford: Wiley-Blackwell.

Standaert, N. 2008. *The Interweaving of Rituals: Funerals in the Cultural Exchange between China and Europe.* Seattle: University of Washington Press.

Stanton, C. 2006. *The Lowell Experiment: Public History in a Postindustrial City.* Boston: University of Massachusetts Press.

Stanziani, A. 2008. Free labor – forced labor: An uncertain boundary? The circulation of economic ideas between Russia and Europe from the eighteenth to the mid-nineteenth century. *Kritika: Explorations in Russian and Eurasian History* 9 (1): 1–27.

Stausberg, M. 2008. On the state and prospects of the study of Zoroastrianism. *Numen: International Review for the History of Religions* 55 (5): 561–600.

Stavrianos, L.S. 1959. The teaching of world history. *Journal of Modern History* 31 (2): 110–117.

Stavrianos, L. 1981. *Global Rift: The Third World Comes of Age.* New York: Morrow.

Stavrianos, L. 1997. *Lifelines from Our Past: A New World History.* Rev. edn. Armonk, NY: M.E. Sharpe.

Stearn, E.W. and A.E. Stearn. 1945. *The Effect of Smallpox on the Destiny of the Amerindian.* Boston: B. Humphries.

Stearns, P. 2000. *Gender in World History*. London: Routledge.

Stearns, P. 2001. *Consumerism in World History: The Global Transformation of Desire*. London: Routledge.

Stearns, P. 2007. *The Industrial Revolution in World History*. 3rd edn. Boulder: Westview.

Stearns, P. 2010. *Globalization in World History*. London: Routledge.

Stearns, P. 2011. *World History: The Basics*. New York: Routledge.

Stein, G. 1999. *Rethinking World Systems: Diasporas, Colonies, and Interaction in Uruk Mesopotamia*. Tucson: University of Arizona Press.

Stein, G. 2005. The political economy of Mesopotamian colonial encounters. In G. Stein, ed., *The Archaeology of Colonial Encounters*, pp. 143–172. Santa Fe: SAR Press.

Stiglitz, J. 2002. *Globalization and Its Discontents*. New York: W.W. Norton.

Stoler, A.L. 1989. Rethinking colonial categories. *Comparative Studies in Society and History* 31 (1): 134–161.

Stoler, A.L. and F. Cooper. 1997. Between metropole and colony: Rethinking a research agenda. In F. Cooper and A.L. Stoler, eds, *Tensions of Empire*, pp. 1–56. Berkeley: University of California Press.

Stolten, H.E, ed. 2007. *History Making and Present Day Politics: The Meaning of Collective Memory in South Africa*. Uppsala: Nordiska Afrikainstitutet.

Stopford, J., ed. 1999. *Pilgrimage Explored*. Woodbridge, UK: York Medieval Press.

Strasser, U. and H. Tinsman. 2010. It's a man's world: Bringing masculinity to world history, in Latin American studies for example. *Journal of World History* 21 (1): 75–96.

Strauss, B. 2005. *The Battle of Salamis: The Naval Encounter that Saved Greece – and Western Civilization*. New York: Simon & Schuster.

Strauss, B. 2009. *The Spartacus War*. New York: Simon & Schuster.

Strayer, R. 2010. *Ways of the World*. New York: Bedford/St. Martin's.

Stuchtey, B. and E. Fuchs, eds. 2003. *Writing World History, 1800–2000*. Oxford: Oxford University Press.

Subrahmanyam, S. 1993. *The Portuguese Empire in Asia, 1500–1700: A Political and Economic History*. London: Longman.

Subrahmanyam, S. 1997. *The Career and Legend of Vasco da Gama*. Cambridge: Cambridge University Press.

Subrahmanyam, S. 1997. Connected histories: Notes towards a reconfiguration of early modern Eurasia. *Modern Asian Studies* 31 (3): 735–762.

Subrahmanyam, S. 2005. *Explorations in Connected History: From the Tagus to the Ganges*. Oxford: Oxford University Press.

Subrahmanyam, S. 2006. A tale of three empires. *Common Knowledge* 12 (1): 66–92.

Sugihara, K. and G. Austin, eds. 2011. *Labour-Intensive Industrialization in Global History*. London: Routledge.

Sukarno, A. 1955. Speech at the opening of the Bandung Conference, April 18, 1955. At http://www.fordham.edu/halsall/mod/1955sukarno-bandong.html (accessed Feb. 2012).

Summers, D. 2003. *Real Spaces: World Art History and the Rise of Modernism*. London: Phaidon.

Sunder Rajan, R. 2003. *The Scandal of the State: Women, Law, and Citizenship in Postcolonial India*. Durham: Duke University Press.

Sutherland, H. 2007. The problematic authority of (world) history. *Journal of World History* 18 (4): 491–522.

Swidler, E.-M. 2007. Defending Western Civ: Or how I learned to stop worrying and love the course. *World History Connected* 4, at http://worldhistoryconnected.press.illinois.edu/4.2/swidler.html (accessed Mar. 2012).

Swimme, B. and T. Berry. 1992. *The Universe Story: From the Primordial Flaring Forth to the Ecozoic Era: A Celebration of the Unfolding of the Cosmos*. San Francisco: HarperCollins.

Tainter, J.A. 1988. *The Collapse of Complex Societies*. Cambridge: Cambridge University Press.

Takagi, H. 1995. Nihon bijutsushi no seiritsu/Shiron [History of the establishment of Japanese art history]. *Nihonshi Kenkyu* 400, pp. 74–98.

Tanaka, S. 1993. *Japan's Orient: Rendering Past into History.* Berkeley: University of California Press.

Tang Jin. 2006. *Daguo jueqi* [The rise of the great powers]. Beijing: People's Publishing House.

Tannenbaum, F. 1947. *Slave and Citizen: The Negro in the Americas.* New York: Vintage.

Taylor, W. 2005. Two shrines of the Cristo Renovado: Religion and peasant politics in late colonial Mexico. *American Historical Review* 110 (4): 945–974.

Tenzer, M., ed. 2006. *Analytical Studies in World Music.* Oxford: Oxford University Press.

Thapar, R. 1984. *From Lineage to State.* Delhi: Oxford University Press.

Thomas, G., J. Meyer, F. Ramirez, and J. Boli. 1987. *Institutional Structure: Constituting State, Society, and the Individual.* Thousand Oaks, CA: Sage.

Thompson, E.P. 1967. Time, work-discipline and industrial capitalism. *Past and Present* 38 (1): 56–97.

Thornton, J. 1998. *Africa and Africans in the Making of the Atlantic World, 1400–1800.* 2nd edn. Cambridge: Cambridge University Press.

Tickner, A.B. and O. Waever, eds. 2009. *International Relations Scholarship around the World.* London: Routledge.

Tignor, R., J. Adelman, S. Aron, S. Kotkin, S. Marchand, G. Prakash, and M. Tsin. 2010. *Worlds Together, Worlds Apart: A History of the World from the Beginnings of Humankind to the Present.* 3rd edn. New York: W.W. Norton.

Tilley, H. 2003. African environments and environmental sciences. In W. Beinart and J. McGregor, eds, *Social History and African Environments,* pp. 109–130. Oxford: James Currey.

Tilly, C. 1984. *Big Structures, Large Processes, Huge Comparisons.* New York: Russell Sage Foundation.

Tilly, L.A. and J. Scott. 1989. *Women, Work, and Family.* New York: Routledge.

Todorova, M. 2009. *Imagining the Balkans.* Oxford: Oxford University Press.

Topik, S., C. Marichal, and Z. Frank. 2006. *From Silver to Cocaine: Latin American Commodity Chains and the Building of the World Economy, 1500–2000.* Durham: Duke University Press.

Tortarolo, E. 2000. World Histories in the twentieth century and beyond. *Storia della Storiografia* 38: 129–137.

Townsend, C. 2003. Burying the white gods: New perspectives on the conquest of Mexico. *American Historical Review* 108 (3): 659–687.

Townsend, R.B. 2005. Job market report 2004. *Perspectives on History: The News Magazine of the American Historical Association* (Jan.). At http://www.historians.org/perspectives/issues/2005/0501/0501new1.cfm (accessed Mar. 2012).

Townsend, R.B. 2007. What's in a label? Changing patterns of faculty specialization since 1975. *Perspectives* 45 (1): 12–14.

Townsend, R.B. 2010. A grim year on the academic job market for historians. *Perspectives on History: The News Magazine of the American Historical Association* (Jan.). At http://www.historians.org/Perspectives/issues/2010/1001/1001new1.cfm (accessed Mar. 2012).

Toynbee, A.J. 1974. *Toynbee on Toynbee: A Conversation between Arnold J. Toynbee and G.R. Urban.* Oxford: Oxford University Press.

Toynbee, A. and Royal Institute of International Affairs. 1947. *A Study of History.* New York: Oxford University Press.

Trautmann, T. 1997. *Aryans and British India.* Berkeley: University of California Press.

Trentmann, F. 2007. Citizenship and consumption. *Journal of Material Culture* 7 (2): 147–158.

Trentmann, F. 2008. *Free Trade Nation: Consumption, Civil Society, and Commerce in Modern Britain.* Oxford: Oxford University Press.

Trentmann, F. 2009. Crossing divides: Consumption and globalization in history. *Journal of Material Culture* 9 (2): 187–220.

Trentmann, F. 2010. The long history of contemporary consumer society: Chronologies, practices, and politics in modern Europe. In Alan Warde, ed., *Consumption*. London: Sage, vol. 2, chap. 20.

Trivellato, F. 2009. *The Familiarity of Strangers: The Sephardic Diaspora, Livorno, and Cross-Cultural Trade in the Early Modern Period*. New Haven: Yale University Press.

Trouillot, M.-R. 2002. The perspective of the world: Globalization then and now. In E. Mudimbe-Boyi, ed., *Beyond Dichotomies: Histories, Identities, Cultures, and the Challenge of Globalization*, pp. 3–20. Albany: State University of New York Press.

Tsing, A.L. 1993. *In the Realm of the Diamond Queen*. Princeton: Princeton University Press.

Tsing, A.L. 2005. *Friction: An Ethnography of Global Connection*. Princeton: Princeton University Press.

Tsing, A.L. and C. Gluck. 2009. *Words in Motion: Toward a Global Lexicon*. Durham: Duke University Press.

Turchin, P. 2003. *Historical Dynamics*. Princeton: Princeton University Press.

Turchin, P., J.M. Adams, and T.D. Hall. 2006. East–West orientation of historical empires and modern states. *Journal of World-Systems Research* 12 (2) (Dec.): 218–229.

Turner, B.S. 1994. *Orientalism, Postmodernism and Globalism*. London: Routledge.

Tymowski, M. 2003–2004. Use of the term "empire" in historical research in Africa: A comparative approach. *Afrika Zamani* 11 and 12: 18–26.

Tyrrell, I.R. 1991. *Woman's World/Woman's Empire: The Woman's Christian Temperance Movement in International Perspective, 1880–1930*. Chapel Hill: University of North Carolina Press.

Tzonis, A. and P. Giannisi. 2004. *Classical Greek Architecture: The Construction of the Modern*. Paris: Flammarion.

UNEP (United Nations Environment Programme). 2010. 2010: International year of biodiversity. At http://www.unep.org/iyb (accessed Mar. 2012).

Vaissière, É. 2005. *Sogdian Traders: A History*, trans. J. Ward. Leiden: Brill.

Valdés, M. and L. Hutcheon. 1994. Rethinking literary history – comparatively. Occasional Paper 27. American Council of Learned Societies, New York.

Valencius, C.B. 2002. *The Health of the Country: How American Settlers Understood Themselves and Their Land*. New York: Basic Books.

van Binsbergen, W. 2000. Le point de vue de Wim van Binsbergen. *Politique Africaine* 79 (Oct.): 175–180.

van Creveld, M. 1977. *Supplying War: Logistics from Wallenstein to Patton*. Cambridge: Cambridge University Press.

Van De Mieroop, M. 2007. *A History of the Ancient Near East, ca. 3000–323 BC*. 2nd edn. Oxford: Wiley-Blackwell.

van der Linden, M. 2002. Globalizing labour historiography: The IISH approach. Position paper, International Institute of Social History, Amsterdam.

van der Linden, M. 2008. *Workers of the World: Essays toward a Global Labor History*. Boston: Brill.

van der Vleuten, E. and A. Kaijser, eds. 2006. *Networking Europe: Transnational Infrastructures and the Shaping of Europe 1850–2000*. Sagamore Beach, MA: Science History.

Van Schendel, W. and I. Abraham, eds. 2005. *Illicit Flows and Criminal Things: States, Borders, and the Other Side of Globalization*. Bloomington: Indiana University Press.

Van Wees, H. 2004. *Greek Warfare: Myths and Realities*. London: Duckworth.

Van Young, E. 1990. To see someone not seeing: Historical studies of peasants and politics in Mexico. *Mexican Studies/Estudios Mexicanos* 6 (1): 133–159.

Van Young, E. 2001. *The Other Rebellion: Popular Violence, Ideology, and the Mexican Struggle for Independence*. Stanford: Stanford University Press.

van Zanden, J.L. n.d. On global economic history: A personal view on an agenda for future research. Paper. At http://socialhistory.org/sites/default/files/docs/jvz-research_1.pdf (accessed Feb. 2012).

Vanhaute, E. 2008. The end of peasantries? Rethinking the role of peasantries in a world-historical view. *Review* (Fernand Braudel Center) 31 (1): 39–59.

Vanhaute, E. 2009. Who is afraid of global history? Ambitions, pitfalls and limits of learning global history. In P. Vries, ed., *Global History*. Issue of *Österreichische Zeitschrift für Geschichtswissenschaften* 20 (2): 22–39.

Vansina, J. 1961. *Oral Tradition: A Study in Historical Methodology*. Chicago: Aldine.

Vansina, J. 1990. *Paths in the Rainforests: Toward a History of Political Tradition in Equatorial Africa*. Madison: University of Wisconsin Press.

Vásquez, M.A. 2008. Studying religion in motion: A networks approach. *Method and Theory in the Study of Religion* 20 (2): 151–184.

Vaughan, M. 1991. *Curing Their Ills: Colonial Power and African Illness*. Cambridge: Polity.

Veenhof, K.R. 2008. The Old Assyrian period. In K.R. Veenhof and J. Eidem, *Mesopotamia: The Old Assyrian Period*, ed. M. Wäfler, pp. 13–263. Fribourg: Academic Press.

Veenhof, K.R. 2010. Ancient Assur: The city, its traders, and its commercial network. In J. Gommans, ed., *Empires and Emporia: The Orient in World Historical Space and Time*. Jubilee issue of *Journal of the Economic and Social History of the Orient* 53 (1–2): 39–82.

Vélez, A. 1998. *Del big bang al Homo sapiens*. Medellín: Universidad de Antioquia.

Vélez, K. 2011. "A sign that we are related to you": The transatlantic gifts of the Hurons of the Jesuit Mission of Lorette, 1650–1750. *French Colonial History* 12: 31–44.

Venuti, L. 2004. *The Translation Studies Reader*. New York: Routledge.

Veyne, P. 1984. *Writing History: Essay on Epistemology*. Manchester: University of Manchester Press.

von Glahn, R. 2003. Towns and temples: Urban growth and decline in the Yangzi Delta, 1100–1400. In P.J. Smith and R. von Glahn, eds, *The Song-Yuan-Ming Transition in Chinese History*, pp. 176–211. Cambridge, MA: Harvard University Asia Center.

von Hirschhausen, U. and K.K. Patel. 2010. Europeanization in history: An introduction. In M. Conway and K.K. Patel, eds, *Europeanization in the Twentieth Century: Historical Approaches*, pp. 1–18. Basingstoke: Palgrave Macmillan.

Voros, J. 2007. Macro-perspectives beyond the world system. *Journal of Futures Studies* 11 (3): 1–28.

Vosniadou, S. and W. Brewer. 1992. Mental models of the Earth: A study of conceptual change in childhood. *Cognitive Psychology* 24: 535–585.

Voyages. 2009. The Trans-Atlantic Slave Trade Database. At http://www.slavevoyages.org (accessed Mar. 2012).

Vries, P. 1998. Should we really ReORIENT? *Itinerario* 22 (3): 19–38.

Vries, P. 2003. *Via Peking Back to Manchester: Britain, the Industrial Revolution, and China*. Leiden: Leiden University.

Waghorne, J.P. 2004. *Diaspora of the Gods: Modern Hindu Temples in an Urban Middle-Class World*. New York: Oxford University Press.

Wald, P. 2008. *Contagious: Cultures, Carriers, and the Outbreak Narrative*. Durham: Duke University Press.

Walker, J. 1994. Reading genres across cultures: The example of autobiography. In S. Lawall, ed., *Reading World Literature: Theory, History, Practice*, pp. 203–235. Austin: University of Texas Press.

Walkowitz, D.J. and L.M. Knauer, eds. 2009. *Contested Histories in Public Space: Memory, Race, and Nation*. Durham: Duke University Press.

Walkowitz, R. 2009. Comparison literature. *New Literary History* 40: 567–582.

Wallerstein, I. 1974–2011. *The Modern World-System*. 4 vols. Berkeley: University of California Press.

Wallerstein, I. 1991. *Unthinking Social Science: The Limits of Nineteenth-Century Paradigms*. Cambridge: Polity.

Wallerstein, I. 1998. The unintended consequences of Cold War area studies. In Noam Chomsky et al., eds, *The Cold War and the University: Toward an Intellectual History of the Postwar Years*, pp. 195–231. New York: New Press.

Wallerstein, I. 1999. *The End of the World As We Know It: Social Science for the Twenty-First Century.* Minneapolis: University of Minnesota Press.

Wallerstein, I. 2000. *The Essential Wallerstein.* New York: New Press.

Wallerstein, I. 2004. *World-Systems Analysis: An Introduction.* Durham: Duke University Press.

Wallerstein, I., H. Decdeliand, and R. Kasaba. 1987. Incorporation of the Ottoman Empire into the world-economy. In H. Islamoğlu, ed., *The Ottoman Empire and the World-Economy,* pp. 88–97. Cambridge: Cambridge University Press.

Wallerstein, I. *et al.* 1996. *Open the Social Sciences: Report of the Gulbenkian Commission on the Restructuring of the Social Sciences.* Stanford: Stanford University Press.

Ward, H.N. 2009. *Women Religious Leaders in Japan's Christian Century, 1549–1650.* Burlington, VT: Ashgate.

Ward, K. 2009. *Networks of Empire: Forced Migration and the Dutch East India Company.* Cambridge: Cambridge University Press.

Warf, B. 2009. From surface to networks. In B. Warf and S. Arias, eds, *The Spatial Turn: Interdisciplinary Perspectives,* pp. 59–76. London: Routledge.

Warner, M. 2002. *Publics and Counterpublics.* New York: Zone Books.

Watts, D. 1987. *The West Indies: Patterns of Development, Culture and Environmental Change since 1492.* Cambridge: Cambridge University Press.

Watts, S. 1997. *Epidemics and History: Disease, Power, and Imperialism.* New Haven: Yale University Press.

Weaver, J.C. 2003. *The Great Land Rush and the Making of the Modern World, 1650–1900.* Montreal: McGill-Queen's University Press.

Webb, J.L.A. 2009. *Humanity's Burden: A Global History of Malaria.* Cambridge: Cambridge University Press.

Webster, D. 2002. *The Fall of the Ancient Maya: Solving the Mystery of the Maya Collapse.* London: Thames & Hudson.

Weible, R. 2006. The blind man and his dog: The public and its historians. *Public Historian* 28 (4): 9–17.

Weidman, S. 1898. *A Contribution to the Geology of the Pre-Cambrian Igneous Rocks of the Fox River Valley, Wisconsin.* Madison: Wisconsin Geological and Natural History Survey, no. 3.

Weinbaum, A.E., L.M. Thomas, P. Ramamurthy, U.G. Poiger, M.Y. Dong, and T.E. Barlow. 2008. *The Modern Girl around the World: Consumption, Modernity, and Globalization.* Durham: Duke University Press.

Weinstein, B. 2005. History without a cause? Grand narratives, world history, and the postcolonial dilemma. *International Review of Social History* 50: 71–93.

Wellman, J.K., Jr, ed. 2007. *Belief and Bloodshed: Religion and Violence across Time and Tradition.* New York: Rowman & Littlefield.

Wells, H.G. 1930. *The Outline of History: Being a Plain History of Life and Mankind.* New York: Garden City. First published in 1920.

Wells, P. 1999. *Barbarians Speak.* Princeton: Princeton University Press.

Wendt, A. 1976. Towards a New Oceania. *Mana Review* 1: 49–60.

Wengrow, D. 2006. *The Archaeology of Early Egypt: Social Transformations in North-East Africa, 10,000–2650 BC.* Cambridge: Cambridge University Press.

Wengrow, D. 2010. *What Makes a Civilization? The Ancient Near East and the Future of the West.* Oxford: Oxford University Press.

Werbner, P. 2003. *Pilgrims of Love: The Anthropology of a Global Sufi Cult.* Bloomington: Indiana University Press.

Werner, M. and B. Zimmermann, eds. 2004. *De la comparaison à l'histoire croisée.* Paris: Seuil.

Werner, M. and B. Zimmermann. 2006. Beyond comparison: Histoire croisée and the challenge of reflexivity. *History and Theory* 45 (1): 30–50.

Wesch, M. 2009. YouTube and you: Experiences of self-awareness in the context collapse of the recording webcam. *Explorations in Media Ecology* 8 (2): 19–34.

West, M.O., W. G. Martin, and F. C. Wilkins, eds. 2009. *From Toussaint to Tupac*. Chapel Hill: University of North Carolina Press.

Westad, O.A. 2005. *The Global Cold War: Third World Interventions and the Making of Our Times*. Cambridge: Cambridge University Press.

Wheeler, M. 1968. *The Indus Civilization*. 3rd edn. Cambridge: Cambridge University Press. First published in 1953.

WHFUA (World History for Us All). 2011. *History of the World in Seven Minutes*. Video for the Classroom, WHFUA project, San Diego State University and National Center for History in the Schools, University of California at Los Angeles.

White, A.D. 1886. On studies in general history and the history of civilizations. *Papers of the American Historical Association* 1: 49–72. At http://www.historians.org/info/AHA_History/adwhite.htm (accessed Feb. 2012).

White, R. 1983. *The Roots of Dependency: Subsistence, Environment, and Social Change among the Choctaws, Pawnees, and Navajos*. Lincoln: University of Nebraska Press.

White, R. 1991. *The Middle Ground: Indians, Empires, and Republics in the Great Lakes Region, 1650–1815*. Cambridge: Cambridge University Press.

Whitehouse, H. 2000. *Arguments and Icons: Divergent Modes of Religiosity*. New York: Oxford University Press.

Whitehouse, H. and L.H. Martin, eds. 2004. *Theorizing Religions Past: Archaeology, History, and Cognition*. New York: Altamira Press.

Whitfield, S. 2001. *Life along the Silk Road*. Berkeley: University of California Press.

Wiesner-Hanks, M. 2007. World history and the history of women, gender, and sexuality. *Journal of World History* 18 (1): 53–67.

Wilder, G. 2005. *The French Imperial Nation-State: Negritude and Colonial Humanism between the Two World Wars*. Chicago: University of Chicago Press.

Williams, E. 1944. *Capitalism and Slavery*. Chapel Hill: University of North Carolina Press.

Williams, M., ed. 1990. *Wetlands: A Threatened Landscape*. Oxford: Blackwell.

Williams, M. 2003. *Deforesting the Earth: From Prehistory to Global Crisis*. Chicago: University of Chicago Press.

Williams, P. 2007. *Memorial Museums: The Global Rush to Commemorate Atrocities*. Oxford: Berg.

Wills, J.E. 1993. Maritime Asia, 1500–1800: The interactive emergence of European dominance. *American Historical Review* 98 (1) (Feb.): 83–105.

Wilson, E.O. 2003. *Consilience: The Unity of Knowledge*. New York: Knopf.

Wilson, R. and C. Connery, eds. 2007. *The Worlding Project: Doing Cultural Studies in the Era of Globalization*. Berkeley: New Pacific Press.

Wineburg, S. 2001. *Historical Thinking and Other Unnatural Acts: Charting the Future of Teaching the Past*. Philadelphia: Temple University Press.

Witz, L. and C. Rassool. 2008. Making histories. *Kronos: Southern African Histories* 34: 6–15.

Wolf, E. 1969. *Peasant Wars of the Twentieth Century*. New York: Harper & Row.

Wolf, E. 1982. *Europe and the People without History*. Berkeley: University of California Press.

Wolmar, C. 2009. *Blood, Iron and Gold: How the Railways Transformed the World*. London: Atlantic.

Wong, R.B. 1997. *China Transformed: Historical Change and the Limits of European Experience*. Ithaca, NY: Cornell University Press.

Wong, R.B. 2002. The search for European difference and domination in the early modern world: A view from Asia. *American Historical Review* 107: 447–469.

Woo-Cumings, M., ed. 1999. *The Developmental State*. Ithaca, NY: Cornell University Press.

Wood, F. 2002. *The Silk Road: Two Thousand Years in the Heart of Asia*. Berkeley: University of California Press.

Woodside, A. 2006. *Lost Modernities: China, Vietnam, Korea, and the Hazards of World History*. Cambridge, MA: Harvard University Press.

Woodward, C.V. ed. 1968. *The Comparative Approach to American History*. New York: Basic Books.

Worsley, P. 1968. *The Trumpet Shall Sound: A Study of "Cargo" Cults in Melanesia*. New York: Harper.

Wrangham, R. 2009. *Catching Fire*. New York: Basic Books.

Wreschner, E.E. 1976. The red hunters: Further thoughts on the evolution of speech. *Current Anthropology* 17 (4) (Dec.): 717–719.

Wreschner, E.E. 1980. Red ochre and human evolution: A case for discussion. *Current Anthropology* 21 (5) (Oct.): 631–644.

Wreschner, E.E. 1981. More on Palaeolithic ochre. *Current Anthropology* 22 (6) (Dec.): 705–706.

Wright, D. 2004. *The World and a Very Small Place in Africa: A History of Globalization in Niumi, the Gambia*. 2nd edn. Armonk, NY: M.E. Sharpe.

Wright, R. 2010. *The Ancient Indus: Urbanism, Economy, and Society*. Cambridge: Cambridge University Press.

Yang, B. 2008. *Between Winds and Clouds: The Making of Yunnan (Second Century BCE to Twentieth Century CE)*. New York: Columbia University Press; through Gutenberg-e, at http://www.gutenberg-e.org/yang/index.html (accessed Feb. 2012).

Yanni, C. 2005. *Nature's Museums: Victorian Science and the Architecture of Display*. Princeton: Princeton Architectural Press.

Yiqiang, C. 2008. World art studies and the historiography of Chinese art. In K. Zijlmans and W. van Damme, eds, *World Art Studies: Exploring Concepts and Approaches*, pp. 119–133. Amsterdam: Valiz.

Yiqiang, C. and F. Jingzhong. 1997. Ershi shiji Zhongguohua: Chuantong de yanxu yu yanjin [Chinese painting and the twentieth century: creativity in the aftermath of tradition]. Hangzhou: Zhejiang Renmin Meishu Chubanshe.

Yoffee, N. 2005. *Myths of the Archaic State: Evolution of the Earliest Cities, States, and Civilizations*. Cambridge: Cambridge University Press.

Yoffee, N. 2009. Collapse in ancient Mesopotamia: What happened, what didn't. In P. McAnany and N. Yoffee, eds, *Questioning Collapse: Human Resilience, Ecological Vulnerability, and the Aftermath of Empire*, pp. 176–206. Cambridge: Cambridge University Press.

Yook, Y. 2009. Kukga/gŭndaehwa gihoekurosŏui sŏyangsa [Western history as a national modernization project]. In *Yŏksahakui Segi*. Seoul: Humanist.

Zea, L. 1976. *El pensamiento Latinoamericano*. Barcelona: Ariel.

Zhou Y. and Wu Y., eds. 1962. *Shi jie tong shi* [A general history of the world]. 4 vols. Beijing: People's Publishing House.

Zhuangzi [Chuang Tsu]. 1974. *Inner Chapters*, trans. G.-F. Feng and J. English. New York: Vintage.

Zijlmans, K. and W. van Damme, eds. 2008. *World Art Studies: Exploring Concepts and Approaches*. Amsterdam: Valiz.

Zong Y., Z. Chen, J.B. Innes, C. Chen, Z. Wang, and H. Wang. 2007. Fire and flood management of coastal swamp enabled first rice paddy cultivation in east China. *Nature* 449: 459–462.

Index

Note: page numbers in italics denote tables or figures

A Companion to World History, First Edition. Edited by Douglas Northrop.
© 2012 Blackwell Publishing Ltd. Published 2012 by Blackwell Publishing Ltd.